The

MC Press
Desktop Encyclopedia

of

Tips, Techniques, and Programming Practices

for

iSeries and AS/400®

Developed by Merrikay Lee, the MC Press line of professional books emphasizes practical solutions, application-based examples, tips, and techniques for the IBM midrange community of IT professionals.

Merrikay Lee is series editor for the MC Press line of professional books, which comprises more than 75 titles. She has spent more than 20 years as a technical professional in the IBM midrange industry and 15 years in the publishing field. She is the author of four books and has worked with numerous IT technical professionals to develop titles for the IBM midrange community of IT professionals. She is president of Lee Publishing Services Inc. in Dallas, Texas, and can be reached at mlee@leepublishing.com.

The

MC Press
Desktop Encyclopedia

of

Tips, Techniques, and Programming Practices

for

iSeries and AS/400®

Edited by Ted Holt and Shannon O'Donnell

PRESS

First Edition
First Printing—May 2001

©1989 through 2001 Midrange Computing
ISBN: 1-58347-026-3

Midrange Computing
5650 El Camino Real, Suite 225
Carlsbad, CA 92008–7147 USA
www.midrangecomputing.com

For information on translations or book distribution outside the USA or to arrange bulk-purchase discounts for sales promotions, premiums, or fund-raisers, please contact Midrange Computing at the above address.

I gratefully acknowledge the many midrange programmers who have freely shared their knowledge with others. It is because of them that this book is possible, and to them this book is dedicated.

—Ted Holt

I want to acknowledge and thank all the readers who submitted the tips you are about to read and all the great folks at *Midrange Computing* who have worked hard over the years to publish these tips. And special thanks to my wife, Diane, who perservered through the trials and tribulations of compiling this book.

—Shannon O'Donnell

Contents

Introduction

*H*ow much is a programmer's time worth? To answer that question, begin with a typical programmer's monthly salary. Add to the base salary additional payroll expenses such as Social Security, unemployment, workers' compensation taxes, and medical coverage. Add to that subtotal the typical office expenses (office space, furniture, supplies, long distance telephone calls, travel expenses, etc.). Add the employer's contribution to vacation pay, pension plans, and perhaps employee stock-purchase plans. Sum up all of this for a month, divide by 160 hours, and you'll see that each hour a programmer is on the job is an expensive proposition. Productivity thus becomes essential.

Now think about what might make employees less productive than they should be. Beyond common interruptions, which for programmers as well as other professionals are a part of life, what issues are within the employer's control? This book addresses two of the most important issues—a need for education and resources.

Lack of education in the world of programming is death to productivity. The world of computing changes rapidly and programmers must keep up to date. If a problem with an unfamiliar topic slows a programmer down for a day or two, the employer has lost valuable company resources. The *MC Press Desktop Encyclopedia of Tips, Techniques, and Programming Practices for iSeries and AS/400* is a practical educational tool offering programmers techniques they can use—today—on their iSeries and AS/400 computers.

Another productivity killer is a lack of resources for problem resolution. When programmers come across seemingly unsolvable problems, whom or what do they consult for ideas or resolutions? They can begin by consulting *The MC Press Desktop Encyclopedia*. Programmers who use the same operating system and programming language face similar challenges. This volume contains expert solutions to common (and many uncommon) iSeries and AS/400 challenges.

This book is a collection of nearly a thousand tips, written by hundreds of AS/400 professionals, categorized into chapters by broad categories, and further categorized within each chapter by topic—it is truly encyclopedic in scope. Whether you're programming the "old stuff" (System/36, RPG III, etc.), the current native standard (ILE, RPG IV), or the "new stuff" (Java, Domino), you'll find tips, techniques, and programming practices that will make you more productive.

Some tips and techniques are written in a question/answer format. You'll soon discover that many of your questions already have been asked and answered. Most techniques include illustrative snippets of code, and you'll also find printed versions of practical utilities that are also stored on the companion CD-ROM.

In short, this is a desktop encyclopedia of proven solutions. *Desktop* means you can keep it close at hand. *Encyclopedia* means a wide assortment of pertinent information. *Proven solutions* means people have used these tips and techniques to solve problems in IT shops around the world.

Now, think again of the worth of a programmer's time. It is our hope that any iSeries or AS/400 IT professional who keeps a copy of this encyclopedia at hand will find time-saving answers that will be repaid many, many times over.

—Ted Holt
—Shannon O'Donnell

CL

*E*very computer system has some form of an operating control language that lets you control such things as external flags, file overrides, and other common maintenance tasks. On the mainframe, one such language is JCL (Job Control Language), a rather difficult language to learn with a somewhat limited set of instructions. On the System/36, the operating control language was called, appropriately enough, OCL (Operation Control Language). The AS/400, with its operating system OS/400, provides a powerful native operating control language known as CL (control language).

The name may not be very original, but don't let that fool you. CL goes beyond a simple operating control language. In a CL program you can do such things as:

- Open and display a user interface screen.
- Perform error checking on that screen.
- Retrieve the user input and use that input for preprocessing record selection (such as running an OPNQRYF command).
- Send a message to the user or another program, create and destroy objects used by the job, and much, much more.

CL truly gives the programmer the power to control every aspect of a job's operating environment. Because CL is such a rich and complex control language, learning all the ins and outs on your own environment can be very difficult. That's why this chapter on CL tips and techniques will be so valuable to you. You'll learn how to:

- Alter the run priority of a submitted job.
- Use the ILE Date APIs to work with dates.
- Check for open files in a CL program.
- Find out if your Submit Job (SBMJOB) command was successful, and many other tips and techniques—all of which will give you an in-depth understanding of CL.

—*Shannon O'Donnell*

✦ ✦ ✦ Active Jobs

Active Job Test in CL

Q: Can you tell me how to test for an active job in CL? On the S/36 it was simple:

```
// IF ACTIVE-OTHERJOB MYJOB
```

I tried using the CHGJOB command but I got the same results whether or not the job was active. The CL statement I used was CHGJOB (OTHERJOB) JOBQ(QBATCH) followed by a few MONMSG statements. Keep in mind that I do not know the job number of OTHERJOB, nor do I want to use data areas to alleviate the situation. I would appreciate any answers to my dilemma.

A: In your startup CL, you can submit to batch a CL program to monitor your UPS. Sometimes, throughout the day, we rerun the startup program to generate reports, etc. Here's how to find out if the job was already running:

1. Create a message queue with the name OTHERJOBQ, or whatever, and have OTHERJOB allocate it when it starts with exclusive use (ALCOBJ).

2. When you need to know IF ACTIVE, have the program also try to ALCOBJ. Then, you can monitor message CPF1002, to check for the message queue not being available.

If you wanted to check IF ACTIVE on more than one CL program, you just have each one create a MSGQ. The method is similar to data areas, but you don't need to write data. You just need one statement in each program to allocate.

—Art Tostaine

✦ ✦ ✦ APIs

Converting Case in CL

Converting the case of character data when you're writing RPG code is a pretty simple task. Just use the XLATE op code to convert uppercase to lowercase and vice versa. But what if you're coding a CL program and you need to convert the case of character data? One option would be to call an RPG program, pass it the data to be converted, and let it use the XLATE function to convert the data for you. However, that method adds an unnecessary step. Another option is to call API QDCXLATE, but the use of that API requires the existence of a table object (*TBL) describing the conversion to be performed; if you're converting to uppercase, you can use IBM-supplied table QSYSTRNTBL, but there's no IBM-supplied table for converting to lowercase.

Instead of using either of those problematic methods, use the Convert Case (QLGCNVCS) API to convert the case data from within your CL program, or, better yet, use our Convert Case (CVTCASE) utility command (see Figure 1.1), whose CPP (Figure 1.2) invokes the API. Using the command is easy, because you don't have to remember the API's parameters.

```
/*================================================================*/
/* To compile:                                                    */
/*                                                                */
/*        CRTCMD      CMD(XXX/CVTCASE) PGM(XXX/CAS001CL) +         */
/*                    SRCFILE(XXX/QCMDSRC) TEXT('Convert Case') +*/
/*                    ALLOW(*IPGM *BPGM *IMOD *BMOD)              */
/*                                                                */
/*================================================================*/
         CMD        PROMPT('Convert Case')

         PARM       KWD(INPUT) TYPE(*CHAR) LEN(2000) MIN(1) +
                    EXPR(*YES) PROMPT('Input string')
         PARM       KWD(CONVERT) TYPE(*CHAR) LEN(6) RSTD(*YES) +
                    DFT(*UPPER) VALUES(*UPPER *LOWER) +
                    PROMPT('Conversion option')
         PARM       KWD(OUTPUT) TYPE(*CHAR) LEN(2000) +
                    RTNVAL(*YES) PROMPT('Output string (2000A)')
```

Figure 1.1: Command CVTCASE is an example of using the Convert Case API.

```
/*================================================================*/
/* To compile:                                                    */
/*                                                                */
/*        CRTCLPGM    PGM(XXX/CAS001CL) SRCFILE(XXX/QCLSRC) +      */
/*                    TEXT('CPP for CVTCASE command')             */
/*                                                                */
/* Prerequisite:                                                  */
/*    FWDPGMMSG utility command (see Chapter 21).       */
/*                                                                */
/*================================================================*/
PGM        PARM(&INPUT &CONVERT &OUTPUT)

  DCL      VAR(&CONVERT) TYPE(*CHAR) LEN(6)
```

Figure 1.2: The CPP for the CVTCASE command is shown here (part 1 of 2).

```
DCL         VAR(&CTLBLK) TYPE(*CHAR) LEN(22)
DCL         VAR(&ERRPARM) TYPE(*CHAR) LEN(8) +
              VALUE(X'0000000000000000')
DCL         VAR(&INPUT) TYPE(*CHAR) LEN(2000)
DCL         VAR(&INPUTLEN) TYPE(*CHAR) LEN(4)
DCL         VAR(&OUTPUT) TYPE(*CHAR) LEN(2000)

MONMSG      MSGID(CPF0000 MCH0000) EXEC(GOTO CMDLBL(ERROR))

/* Build options control block */
CHGVAR      VAR(%SST(&CTLBLK 1 4)) VALUE(X'00000001')
CHGVAR      VAR(%SST(&CTLBLK 5 4)) VALUE(X'00000000')
IF          COND(&CONVERT *EQ '*UPPER') THEN(DO)
  CHGVAR      VAR(%SST(&CTLBLK 9 4)) VALUE(X'00000000')
ENDDO
ELSE        CMD(DO)
  CHGVAR      VAR(%SST(&CTLBLK 9 4)) VALUE(X'00000001')
ENDDO
CHGVAR      VAR(%SST(&CTLBLK 13 10)) +
              VALUE(X'00000000000000000000')

/* Convert string */
CHGVAR      VAR(%BIN(&INPUTLEN)) VALUE(2000)

CALL        PGM(QLGCNVCS) PARM(&CTLBLK &INPUT &OUTPUT +
              &INPUTLEN &ERRPARM)

RETURN

ERROR:
  FWDPGMMSG
  MONMSG      MSGID(CPF0000)

ENDPGM
```

Figure 1.2: The CPP for the CVTCASE command is shown here (part 2 of 2).

The API uses five parameters:
- CONTROL BLOCK.
- INPUT DATA.
- OUTPUT DATA.
- DATA LENGTH.
- ERROR PARAMETER.

The CONTROL BLOCK parameter consists of the following:

TYPE OF REQUEST—The TYPE OF REQUEST is a 1-byte character field that specifies the input format of the data to be converted. A value of 1 tells the API to use the CCSID as the data format, 2 tells the API to use a Table Object as the data format, and 3 tells the API to use a user-defined format for the data. The value you place in this field controls what you put in the rest of the CONTROL BLOCK. This example uses the CCSID, or value 1.

To see how the other types of data formatting work (i.e., Table Data and User Defined) in the CONTROL BLOCK parameter, see chapter 13, section 1 of the *System API Reference Manual* (SC41-5801-03, QB3AMA03).

CCSID—CCSID is a 4-byte binary field that specifies which CCSID to use. A value of 0 here tells the API to use the CCSID of the job running this command. You may also enter any valid CCSID in this field.

CASE REQUEST—CASE REQUEST is a 4-byte binary field that tells the API in which direction to convert the data, either lowercase to uppercase or uppercase to lowercase. A value of 0 tells the API to convert lowercase data to uppercase, while a value of 1 tells the API to convert the uppercase data to lowercase.

RESERVED—The last field you'll need is a 10-byte character RESERVED field that you must set to hexadecimal zeros.

INPUT DATA—The INPUT DATA parameter is the data you want converted, and you can pass it a length of up to 16,773,104 bytes.

OUTPUT DATA—The OUTPUT DATA parameter will contain the converted data when the API finishes. Make sure you define this as long enough to hold the data returned from the INPUT DATA parameter. Otherwise, your data will be truncated when returned.

LENGTH OF INPUT DATA—The LENGTH OF INPUT DATA parameter is a 4-byte binary field that tells the API how long the INPUT DATA parameter is. Don't confuse this with the actual number of characters to be converted. You can pass embedded blanks to the API and it will ignore them. For example, you might have only 50 characters to convert, but your input string might be 69 characters long because of the embedded blanks.

ERROR—The ERROR parameter is the standard API ERROR parameter. You must initialize the bytes provided (&BYTE_PRV) field with a value that specifies how many bytes you are passing in this ERROR parameter. If the API returns an error, the bytes-available (&BYTE_AVL) field will contain something other than zero. For more information on the standard API ERROR parameter, check out the *System API Reference Manual*, chapter 1, section 2.1 (SC41-5801-03, QB3AMA03).

All binary variables are coded in the CL program as character variables. The decimal representation of the number is then passed in its hexadecimal format. This format is required for passing binary data as a parameter. This process requires that you create your character variable with a length of twice the size required for the binary field. For example, if you need to pass a field that has a length of binary four, you would define a character variable with a length of eight. You then place the hexadecimal representation of the decimal value into this field, left padded with zeros. In this example, the &BYTE_PRV field needs to pass a value of decimal 272, which translates to hexadecimal 110 (1 x 256 + 1 x 16 + 0 = 272).

To use the CVTCASE command, you need to have utility command FWDPGM-MSG already installed (see "How to Forward Messages in CL," in chapter 21, "Utilities"). In your CL program, you could code the following:

```
CVTCASE INPUT(&NAME) CONVERT(*UPPER) OUTPUT(&NEWNAME)
```

After the above statement, variable &NEWNAME contains the same value as &NAME, but in uppercase. You have to declare &NEWNAME as a character variable of 2,000 bytes. The prompter will remind you of this fact.

—*Shannon O'Donnell*
—*Ernie Malaga*

Determining the Size of a Variable at Runtime

There might be times when you have to specify the size of a variable in a command or call to another program. This is especially true of many APIs. If you're sure the size of the variable will never change, you can hard code the length. If you'd like to allow for the possibility that the length might change someday, you can have the program determine the variable's length at runtime. The advantage of this setup is that you eliminate the possibility of changing the variable's length but not the hardcoded references.

To illustrate this, let's consider one API, Convert Edit Code (QECCVTEC). The seventh and eighth parameters of this API are the length and decimal positions of the decimal value being edited. Consider the program fragment shown in Figure 1.3.

```
PGM        PARM(&CUTOFF)
DCL        VAR(&CUTOFF) TYPE(*DEC) LEN(7 2)
DCL        VAR(&SRCVARPRC) TYPE(*CHAR) LEN(4) /* BINARY */
DCL        VAR(&SRCVARDEC) TYPE(*CHAR) LEN(4) /* BINARY */
/* ... more variables ... */
CHGVAR     VAR(%BIN(&SRCVARPRC)) VALUE(7)
CHGVAR     VAR(%BIN(&SRCVARDEC)) VALUE(2)

/* Build the edit mask for variable &CUTOFF */
CALL       PGM(QECCVTEC) PARM(&EDITMASK &EDITMASKLN +
               &RCVVARLN &ZEROBAL &EDITCODE &CURRENCY +
               &SRCVARPRC &SRCVARDEC &ERROR)
```

Figure 1.3: Using hardcoded parameters is not always a good idea.

While the code shown in Figure 1.3 will run fine, there is a danger that someday you might change the size of &CUTOFF, but fail to change the value parameter of the CHGVAR commands to reflect the new size. If you want to avoid that possibility, you can use code (as shown in Figure 1.4) to determine the precision and number of decimal positions of &CUTOFF each time the program runs. Note: The example uses the variable &DECVAR rather than &CUTOFF.

```
          DCL        VAR(&DECVAR) TYPE(*DEC) LEN(9 9)
          DCL        VAR(&WORK) TYPE(*CHAR) LEN(17)
          DCL        VAR(&DECPOSCT) TYPE(*DEC) LEN(1 0)
          DCL        VAR(&DECVARLEN) TYPE(*DEC) LEN(2 0)
          DCL        VAR(&IX) TYPE(*DEC) LEN(3 0)

          /* Find declared size of variable &DECVAR */
          /* Note: the value of &DECVAR will be destroyed */
          CHGVAR     VAR(&DECVAR) VALUE(999999999999999)
          MONMSG     MSGID(MCH1210)
          CHGVAR     VAR(&WORK) VALUE(&DECVAR)

          /* Count trailing zeros to find */
          /* number of decimal positions */
          CHGVAR     VAR(&IX) VALUE(17)
          CHGVAR     VAR(&DECPOSCT) VALUE(0)
COUNT_DEC: IF        COND(%SST(&WORK &IX 1) *EQ '0') THEN(DO)
          CHGVAR     VAR(&DECPOSCT) VALUE(&DECPOSCT + 1)
          CHGVAR     VAR(&IX) VALUE(&IX - 1)
          GOTO       CMDLBL(COUNT_DEC)
          ENDDO

          /* Skip decimal point if necessary */
          IF         COND(%SST(&WORK &IX 1) *EQ '.') THEN(DO)
```

Figure 1.4: Determine the declared size of a decimal variable by using soft-coded parameters as shown in this code fragment (part 1 of 2).

```
               CHGVAR      VAR(&IX) VALUE(&IX - 1)
               ENDDO

               /* Count number of 9's, then add number of */
               /* decimal positions to get overall length */
               CHGVAR      VAR(&DECVARLEN) VALUE(0)
COUNT_LEN:     IF          COND(%SST(&WORK &IX 1) *EQ '9') THEN(DO)
               CHGVAR      VAR(&DECVARLEN) VALUE(&DECVARLEN + 1)
               CHGVAR      VAR(&IX) VALUE(&IX - 1)
               GOTO        CMDLBL(COUNT_LEN)
               ENDDO
               CHGVAR      VAR(&DECVARLEN) VALUE(&DECVARLEN + &DECPOSCT)

               /* End routine to find size of &DECVAR */
               /* The size of the variable is in &DECVARLEN */
               /* The number of decimal positions is in &DECPOSCT *
```

Figure 1.4: Determine the declared size of a decimal variable by using soft-coded parameters as shown in this code fragment (part 2 of 2).

You might also need to allow for a change in the size of a character variable. If so, you can use the routine shown in Figure 1.5.

```
               DCL         VAR(&CHARVAR) TYPE(*CHAR) LEN(1024)
               DCL         VAR(&WORK) TYPE(*CHAR) LEN(9999)
               DCL         VAR(&VARLEN) TYPE(*DEC) LEN(5 0)
               DCL         VAR(&IX) TYPE(*DEC) LEN(5 0)

               /* Find declared size of variable &CHARVAR       */
               /* Note: the value of &CHARVAR will be destroyed */

               CHGVAR      VAR(&CHARVAR) VALUE(' ')
               CHGVAR      VAR(&WORK) VALUE(&CHARVAR *CAT 'X')
               CHGVAR      VAR(&VARLEN) VALUE(0)
               CHGVAR      VAR(&IX) VALUE(1)
SCAN:          IF          COND(%SST(&WORK &IX 1) *NE 'X') THEN(DO)
               CHGVAR      VAR(&VARLEN) VALUE(&VARLEN + 1)
               IF          COND(&IX *LT 9999) THEN(DO)
               CHGVAR      VAR(&IX) VALUE(&IX + 1)
               GOTO        CMDLBL(SCAN)
               ENDDO
               ENDDO

               /* End routine to find size of &CHARVAR */
               /* The size of the variable is in &VARLEN *
```

Figure 1.5: You might need to allow for changing size in the program variables. Use this sample code as your guide.

—Ted Holt

Retrieving Commands

Q: When I press F9 from a menu, OS/400 retrieves previously executed commands. How can I make my programs retrieve previously executed commands?

A: Your program needs to call the QMHRTVRQ API, which retrieves the request messages for the job. The code in Figure 1.6 illustrates how to do this.

```
PGM
  DCL VAR(&APIDTAFMT) TYPE(*CHAR) LEN(8) VALUE('RTVQ0100') +
    /* API data formt */
  DCL VAR(&APIDTALEN) TYPE(*CHAR) LEN(4) VALUE(X'000007D0') +
    /* API data length: 2000 */

  DCL VAR(&APIDTARTV) TYPE(*CHAR) LEN(2000) /*Retrieved API data */
  DCL VAR(&APIERRCD) TYPE(*CHAR) LEN(4) VALUE(X'00000000') +
    /* API error code (no data returned) */

  DCL VAR(&APIMSGKEY) TYPE(*CHAR) LEN(4) /* No message key */
  DCL VAR(&APIMSGTYP) TYPE(*CHAR) LEN(10) /* Request message type */
  DCL VAR(&BYTESAVL) TYPE(*DEC) LEN(5)
  DCL VAR(&BYTESRTN) TYPE(*DEC) LEN(5)
  DCL VAR(&CMD) TYPE(*CHAR) LEN(256)
  DCL VAR(&CMDLEN) TYPE(*DEC) LEN(5) +
    /* Set to retrieve info on last request message ***/

  CHGVAR VAR(&APIMSGTYP) VALUE('*LAST')
  CHGVAR VAR(&APIMSGKEY) VALUE(' ')

NEXT:
  CALL PGM(QMHRTVRQ) PARM(&APIDTARTV &APIDTALEN &APIDTAFMT +
                           &APIMSGTYP &APIMSGKEY        &APIERRCD)
  CHGVAR VAR(&BYTESAVL) VALUE(%BIN(&APIDTARTV 1 4))
  CHGVAR VAR(&BYTESRTN) VALUE(%BIN(&APIDTARTV 5 4))
  IF COND((&BYTESAVL *EQ 8) *AND (&BYTESRTN *EQ 0)) THEN(GOTO
CMDLBL(END))
  IF COND(&BYTESRTN *GT 0) THEN(DO)
    CHGVAR VAR(&CMDLEN) VALUE(&BYTESRTN - 40)
    CHGVAR VAR(&CMD) VALUE(%SST(&APIDTARTV 41 &CMDLEN))
  ENDDO
  ELSE CMD(CHGVAR VAR(&CMD) VALUE(' '))
/* Variable &CMD now contains a command or blanks */
/* set to get previous messages */
  CHGVAR VAR(&APIMSGTYP) VALUE('*PRV')
  CHGVAR VAR(&APIMSGKEY) VALUE(%SST(&APIDTARTV 9 4))
  GOTO CMDLBL(NEXT)
  END:
  ENDPGM
```

Figure 1.6: The QMHRTVRQ API can retrieve commands previously executed during a job.

—*Jerry Jewel and Ted Holt*

Retrieving Journal Entries

Q: I would like to retrieve journal information programmatically. Ideally, I'd like to have the functionality of the Work with Journal Attributes (WRKJRNA) command or the Display Journal Attribution (DSPJRNRCVA) command in a program. I can't find any Retrieve (RTV) journal commands or, even better, journal APIs that will give me this information.

A: V4R2 introduced several new journaling APIs. Two that will be of interest to you are QjoRetrieveJournalInformation() and QjoRtvJrnReceiverInformation(). These are documented in the "Journal and Commit APIs" chapter of the *System API Reference* manual (SC41-5801-00). For earlier releases, the information also was available through the MI instructions MATJPAT and MATJSAT; and for systems at security level 40 and above, the systems MI were handled by APIs like QusMaterializeJournalPortAttr and QusMaterializeJournalSpaceAttr. The APIs were provided to get around the domain failures seen in the direct MI usage at higher security levels. These APIs are also in the *System API Reference and Journal and Commit APIs* (SC41-5882-02) manuals.

—Bruce Vining

✦ ✦ ✦ Attention Key

AS/400 Attention Key Tip

One of the many parameters in the Change User Profile (CHGUSRPRF) command is one to set and enable an Attention key program. An Attention key program is one that runs when the Attention key has been pressed. This should be a CLP or RPG program. It can be any type of program that can be called using the CALL command.

For the Attention key program parameter, I use QCMD in library QSYS, which is the AS/400 command entry display. Thus, whatever program I am in, I can interrupt it and get a command display by a single press of the Attention key. This sure beats having to do the Shift-SysReq-1 sequence to get an alternate session.

As with any changes to a user profile, the user must sign off and then sign back on for the change to take effect.

—Midrange Computing Staff

✦ ✦ ✦ Batch and Interactive

Forcing an Interactive Job to Batch

Q: Do you know how to intercept an interactive job and force it into batch mode?

A: Let's say you have a CL program called MYCLPROG. Suppose the user keys in CALL
MYCLPROG at a command line. The program starts running interactively. Because the job
is running interactively, the Retrieve Job Attribute (RTVJOBA) command puts a '1' in
&JOBTYPE. The IF statement evaluates as true, MYCLPROG gets submitted to batch, and
the interactive invocation of MYCLPROG ends. Another copy of MYCLPROG starts up in
batch. RTVJOBA returns a value of '0,' the IF statement evaluates as false, and the program continues after the comment.

If your problem is with commands that you don't want run interactively, the ALLOW parameter on the Create Command (CRTCMD) and Change Command (CHGCMD) commands prevents commands from running interactively. For example, if you have
programmers who constantly compile RPG programs interactively with the Create RPG
Program (CRTRPGPGM) command, you can change the CRTRPGPGM command to run only
in batch mode with this command.

```
CHGCMD CMD(CRTRPGPGM) ALLOW(*BATCH *BPGM *BREXX)
```

—Ted Holt

✦ ✦ ✦ CL Programming Practices

Some CL Oddities

There are some very strange things that CL allows you do and some crystal-clear ones
that it doesn't. In the first category, I have found a couple of oddballs:

1. You can code a DO command all by itself—that is, not as part of an IF or
   MONMSG statement. For instance, the following code is perfectly valid:

```
DO
CHGVAR   &A   &B
ENDDO
```

Both the DO and the ENDDO are ignored; the CHGVAR runs without trouble.

2. To describe the condition, the IF command has only one required parameter: COND. The THEN parameter is optional. This means that you can code the following with impunity:

```
IF COND(&A *EQ &B)
```

This line of code does nothing. It checks if &A and &B have the same value, but it does nothing with the outcome of the test. I've always felt that the THEN parameter should have been mandatory.

As for those things it doesn't let you do, again I have two examples:

1. You cannot nest any number of DO/ENDDO groups. Actually, the maximum is 10. If you attempt an 11th nested group, the compiler chokes and aborts the compilation.

2. You cannot code more than 10 ELSE statements after an IF. I suspect the rationale (or lack thereof) is the same as for #1 above, but it creates lots of problems. You see, you could have written a CL program to drive a menu with more than 11 options, requiring more than 10 ELSEs to compare the user's input against option numbers.

Of course, there are other "fun" oddities, such as coding a Send Program Message (SNDPGMMSG) command with no parameters at all. SEU accepts it, but the compiler complains that either MSG or MSGID must be specified.

Go figure.

—Ernie Malaga

✦ ✦ ✦ Command Processing

Changing Command Defaults

Annoyed with having to override the same command parameter defaults over and over again? The command CHGCMDDFT will let you change the system defaults for any

OS/400 command. For example, you could change the WRKSPLF command to default to your main printer, rather than *ALL. The command to do this would look like this:

```
CHGCMDDFT CMD(WRKSPLF) NEWDFT('SELECT(*CURRENT P1)')
```

(*CURRENT is placed before P1 because it is the first default parameter in the SELECT list.)

—Midrange Computing Staff

Commands with Optional Return Parameter

A very useful aspect of the iSeries and AS/400 computers is that they enable you to write your own CL commands. Unfortunately, the documentation is not always clear in explaining the parameters and values of the command definition statements. An example is the RETURN VALUE parameter of the Parameter (PARM) command. This parameter allows a command to return a value to the program using it through a CL variable.

The shop where I work keeps a separate database for each location. Normally we use the library list from the user's job description to control which database is accessed; however, programs used by Operations must have the ability to access more than one database. It seemed that we could write a command to retrieve information about a database from a file. That would make it easier to write other programs.

With this approach, there would be no need for the programmer to know how the underlying programs worked, and, in most cases, they could be changed without changing the programs that used the command. In addition, a CL program can only read one file, and the command would save this resource for some other use (such as a display file).

A problem arises when using return values in a command: They are allowed to be optional parameters. This is great if you need only one or two values to be returned—why clutter the program with variables that will not be used? But in the command processing program (CPP), unpassed parameters cause escape message MCH3601 to be issued. The AS/400 text for this message is, "Referenced location in a space that does not contain a pointer." That's it! No suggestions on how to fix it or what it really means. An ancient S/38 user dubbed this the "confuse programmer" message. I take it to mean that, because parameters are passed by reference instead of by value, what is passed is a pointer to the data. Because nothing has been passed, no pointer has been created. Thus the message.

The good news is that it can be handled by a MONMSG command. What might not be obvious is that when you call a secondary program from your CPP, you will have the same problem unless you create a duplicate set of variables to handle any parameters that might not have been specified in the command. By using this technique, you can use CHGVAR to change the duplicate variable to the value of the parameter. You can see this technique at work in Figures 1.7 through 1.10.

A simplified version of our Retrieve Database Attributes (RTVDBATTR) command is shown in Figure 1.7. It has one required parameter, ACTION, and four optional parameters that return values—that is, they have RTNVAL (*YES).

```
RTVDBATTR:  CMD        PROMPT( Retrieve Data Base Attributes )
            PARM       KWD(ACTION) TYPE(*CHAR) LEN(6) RSTD(*YES) +
                       DFT(*FIRST) VALUES(*FIRST *NEXT *PREV +
                       *FIND *CLOSE) PROMPT( Attribute file +
                       action: )
            /* The following parameters are optional */
            PARM       KWD(DATABASE) TYPE(*CHAR) LEN(8) +
                       RTNVAL(*YES) PROMPT( CL var for +
                       database:        (8) )
            PARM       KWD(JOBD) TYPE(*CHAR) LEN(10) RTNVAL(*YES) +
                       PROMPT( CL var for job descript:  (10) )
            PARM       KWD(JOBDLIB) TYPE(*CHAR) LEN(10) +
                       RTNVAL(*YES) PROMPT( CL var for jobd +
                       library:    (10) )
            PARM       KWD(STATUS) TYPE(*CHAR) LEN(9) RTNVAL(*YES) +
                       PROMPT( CL var for command status: (9) )
```

Figure 1.7: Command RTVDBATTR allows you to easily retrieve database attributes.

Figure 1.8 lists the CPP, which is CL program DB001CL. Notice that parameters DATABASE, JOBD, JOBDLIB, and STATUS have two CL variables each. For instance, parameter JOBD has &PJOBD (both matching the type and length).

```
DB001CL:    PGM        PARM(&PACTION &PDATABASE &PJOBD &PJOBDLIB +
                       &PSTATUS)
            /* Parameters */
            DCL        VAR(&PACTION) TYPE(*CHAR) LEN(6) /* for +
                       file: *FIRST *NEXT *PREV *FIND *CLOSE */
            DCL        VAR(&PDATABASE) TYPE(*CHAR) LEN(8) /* +
                       Database to perform action on or returned */
            DCL        VAR(&PJOBD) TYPE(*CHAR) LEN(10) /* Job +
                       description returned */
```

Figure 1.8: CL program DB001CL is the CPP for the Retrieve Database Attributes command (part 1 of 2).

```
            DCL         VAR(&PJOBDLIB) TYPE(*CHAR) LEN(10) /* Job +
                          description library returned*/
            DCL         VAR(&PSTATUS) TYPE(*CHAR) LEN(9) /* Return +
                          status: *BOF *EOF *FOUND *NOTFOUND */
/* Program variables */
/* Duplicates of return parms above */
            DCL         VAR(&DATABASE) TYPE(*CHAR) LEN(8)
            DCL         VAR(&JOBD) TYPE(*CHAR) LEN(10)
            DCL         VAR(&JOBDLIB) TYPE(*CHAR) LEN(10)
            DCL         VAR(&STATUS) TYPE(*CHAR) LEN(9)
            DCL         VAR(&MSGID) TYPE(*CHAR) LEN(7)
            DCL         VAR(&MSGDATA) TYPE(*CHAR) LEN(512)
            MONMSG      MSGID(CPF0000 MCH0000) EXEC(GOTO +
                          CMDLBL(ERRORTRAP)) /* Global monitor */
/* With the exception of &PACTION and &PDATABASE, all other +
   parameters are strictly return variables.  &PACTION is +
   always passed.  &PDATABASE may or may not be passed and returned */
            CHGVAR      VAR(&DATABASE) VALUE(&PDATABASE)
            MONMSG      MSGID(MCH3601) EXEC(CHGVAR VAR(&DATABASE) +
                          VALUE(   )) /* Parameter not passed but +
                          needed by the secondary command +
                          processor.              */
/* Secondary command processor */
            CALL        PGM(DB001RG) PARM(&PACTION &DATABASE +
                          &JOBD &JOBDLIB &STATUS)
/* Attempt to pass back all return values, but ignore any +
   parameters that were not specified.                    */
            CHGVAR      VAR(&PDATABASE) VALUE(&DATABASE)
            MONMSG      MSGID(MCH3601)
            CHGVAR      VAR(&PJOBD) VALUE(&JOBD)
            MONMSG      MSGID(MCH3601)
            CHGVAR      VAR(&PJOBDLIB) VALUE(&JOBDLIB)
            MONMSG      MSGID(MCH3601)
            CHGVAR      VAR(&PSTATUS) VALUE(&STATUS)
            MONMSG      MSGID(MCH3601)
            RETURN
ERRORTRAP:  RCVMSG      MSGTYPE(*EXCP) MSGDTA(&MSGDATA) MSGID(&MSGID)
            SNDPGMMSG   MSGID(&MSGID) MSGF(QCPFMSG) MSGDTA(&MSGDATA) +
                          MSGTYPE(*ESCAPE)
            ENDPGM
```

Figure 1.8: CL program DB001CL is the CPP for the Retrieve Database Attributes command (part 2 of 2).

First, issue a CHGVAR to copy &PDATABASE into &DATABASE. Because the DATABASE parameter is optional, however, the statement might receive an MCH3601 message. You can recover by using CHGVAR within a MONMSG, in order to initialize the duplicate variable to some default value before calling the second program, DB001RG (see in Figure 1.9).

```
FDBATTR  IF  E          K        DISK
 * PARMs 2 - 4 are filled from this file and are the field names
 *==================================================================*
C              *ENTRY    PLIST
C                        PARM              ACTION  6
C                        PARM              DBASE
C                        PARM              JOBD
C                        PARM              JOBDLB
C                        PARM              STATUS  9
 *----------------------------------------------------------------*
C                        MOVEL  *          STATUS
C                        MOVE   FOUND      STATUS
 *
C              ACTION    CASEQ  *FIRST     FIRST      Get first DB rec
C              ACTION    CASEQ  *NEXT      NEXT       Get next DB rec
C              ACTION    CASEQ  *PREV      PREV       Get previous DB
C              ACTION    CASEQ  *FIND      FIND       Find a DB rec
C              ACTION    CASEQ  *CLOSE     CLOSE      Close the file
C                        END
C                        RETRN
 *==================================================================*
C              FIRST     BEGSR
C              *LOVAL    SETLLDBATTRIB
C                        READ DBATTRIB                    LR
C    LR                  MOVE   EOF        STATUS
C                        ENDSR
 *----------------------------------------------------------------*
C              NEXT      BEGSR
C                        READ DBATTRIB                    99
C    99                  MOVE   EOF        STATUS
C                        ENDSR
 *----------------------------------------------------------------*
C              PREV      BEGSR
C                        READPDBATTRIB                    99
C    99                  MOVE   BOF        STATUS
C                        ENDSR
 *----------------------------------------------------------------*
C              FIND      BEGSR
C              PLT       CHAINDBATTRIB              99
C    99                  MOVE   NOTFOUND STATUS
C                        ENDSR
 *----------------------------------------------------------------*
C              CLOSE     BEGSR
C                        MOVE   EOF        STATUS
C                        MOVE   1          *INLR
C                        ENDSR
```

Figure 1.9: RPG program DB001RG is the workhorse behind the Retrieve Database Attributes command.

Before returning from the CPP, each parameter variable is changed to the value of its corresponding duplicate and monitored again for MCH3601. Only those passed will be returned and those not passed will have been gracefully ignored.

Program DB002CL (Figure 1.10) shows an example of using the RTVDBATTR command.

```
DB002CL:    PGM

            DCL       VAR(&JOBD) TYPE(*CHAR) LEN(10)
            DCL       VAR(&STATUS) TYPE(*CHAR) LEN(9)
NEXTDB:     RTVDBATTR ACTION(*NEXT) JOBD(&JOBD) STATUS(&STATUS)
            IF        COND(&STATUS = *EOF) THEN(RETURN)
            SBMJOB    JOB(REPORTS) JOBD(&JOBD) RQSDTA( CALL +
                         DBREPORTS )
            GOTO      CMDLBL(NEXTDB)
            ENDPGM
```

Figure 1.10: CL program DB002CL demonstrates how you might use the RTVDBATTR command.

—Joseph Cattano

Logging Commands

Q: Commands entered into a command line of an IBM display are logged and can be retrieved with the F9 key. However, commands entered into a command line in a display file and executed by QCMDEXC in one of my programs are not logged. How can I make the system log commands executed within my program?

A: You need to send the command to the job as a request message. To add a command that is not executed from a command line to the job's request messages, send the command as a request message and immediately receive it. You must receive it or QCMD will consider it an "active" request message and try to execute it. Figure 1.11 shows an example of how to send a command as a request message. Each time your application issues a command, call this program—passing it the command string and a blank message key.

```
PGM PARM(&CMD)
DCL VAR(&CMD) TYPE(*CHAR) LEN(2000)
DCL VAR(&MSGKEY) TYPE(*CHAR) LEN(4)
SNDPGMMSG MSG(&CMD) TOPGMQ(*EXT) MSGTYPE(*RQS) +
KEYVAR(&MSGKEY)
RCVMSG PGMQ(*EXT) MSGTYPE(*RQS) MSGKEY(&MSGKEY) +
RMV(*NO) MSG(&CMD)
ENDPGM
```

Figure 1.11: This code can be used to send commands as request messages.

—Jerry Jewel and Ted Holt

Outfile Creation Even When a Command Doesn't Support It

You know how it is: You're counting on a crucial command to have outfile support, only to discover that it doesn't—the OUTPUT parameter offers a choice between * and *PRINT only. How do you get the command's output to a database file? There are two ways, both of which require you to select OUTPUT(*PRINT).

The first (traditional) method is to override the printer file with HOLD(*YES), run the command that produces the output, and then copy the spooled file to a database file using the Copy Spooled File (CPYSPLF) command. Of course, you still have to delete the spooled file (which would otherwise remain on the system) and delete the printer file override.

But there's a better way. You can perform file redirection using the Override with Database File (OVRDBF) command. For example, let's say you wish to capture the output of the Display Log (DSPLOG) command on a database file. Here's what you would do:

```
OVRDBF FILE(QPDSPLOG) TOFILE(MYLIB/OUTF133)
DSPLOG OUTPUT(*PRINT)
DLTOVR FILE(QPDSPLOG)
```

The first command, OVRDBF, overrides QPDSPLOG (the printer file used by the DSPLOG command) so that output is redirected to database file OUTF133 in library MYLIB. The DSPLOG command is then carried out with OUTPUT(*PRINT), and then DLTOVR deletes the override for QPDSPLOG.

Of course, you must have OUTF133 in library MYLIB already. The easiest way to ensure it exists is as follows:

```
CRTPF FILE(MYLIB/OUTF133) RCDLEN(133) LVLCHK(*NO)
```

The reason for the odd record length is that the first byte of each record will be reserved for forms control—for example, 1 means "new page." You must ignore the first byte. The Level Check (LVLCHK) parameter is set to *NO because, more often than not, this technique produces level checks if the system tries to write to a database file when a printer file was expected. Because you already know about this problem, it's okay to prevent level checks.

By the way, file redirection works both ways (from database file to printer file) and even between other types of files. For instance, by using the Override with Tape File

(OVRTAPF) command, you can redirect output that normally goes to a database file, making it write to tape instead. The tape file must already exist, of course.

—Ernie Malaga

Prompting in CL

When using CL programs there is often a need to supply input to a CL command within the program. This is often accomplished by using a display prompt or by passing parameters to the program. You can have the system prompt a system-supplied CL command or a user-defined command by placing a ? before the CL command. For example, ?DLTF will prompt the DLTF command.

But this only scratches the surface of what you can do. You can assign values to parameters and them prompt the command using a ?. The values you assigned cannot be changed by the user. This example will prompt the command INZTAP and not allow the user to change the DENSITY parameter value, as shown in Figure 1.12.

```
PGM
.
?INZTAP DENSITY(3200)
.
ENDPGM
```

Figure 1.12: Here's how you initialize a tape in a CL program.

If you choose, you can supply a command with default parameters and allow the user to either accept the defaults or supply their own values. You also can select which parameters you want to prompt. IBM calls this *selective prompting*. In the following example, only the three defined parameters are displayed (see Figure 1.13).

```
PGM
.
OVRPRTF ??FILE(REPORT) +
        ?*TOFILE(QPRINT) +
        ??COPIES(3)
.
ENDPGM
```

Figure 1.13: As has been done here, you can easily override a command's parameters.

A double question mark (??) indicates the parameter can be changed, while a single question mark followed by an asterisk (?*) does not allow modification. In the preceding example, the operator can change the default values on the FILE and COPIES parameters, but not the TOFILE parameter. If the operator presses F3 or F12 while a command is prompted, they will receive an escape message (CPF6801), which could be monitored.

You can use this technique in menus. A user-defined command is prompted using a ?. The operator enters the necessary values for the selected parameters. The parameters are then passed to an RPG program.

A question mark followed by a hyphen (?-) allows selective display omissions. A question mark followed by the less than character (?<) is used for IBM-supplied commands. It causes a parameter to be displayed and is input-capable, but the command default is sent to the CPP unless the value displayed is changed.

As with most things in programming, there are some restrictions when prompting. For an in-depth discussion, check out the *Control Language Programmer's Guide* (SC21-8077) for the restrictions and the valid selective prompting characters.

—Blake Messenbrink

✦ ✦ ✦ Comments

Universal CL Comment Delimeter

The string /*/ can begin and end CL comments. It's useful for commenting out lots of CL code. It can be assigned to a single key combo for quick pasting.

For commenting an entire line at a time, I created a Client Access macro called COMMENT.MAC and assigned it to Ctrl-Shift-C. On an 80-column screen, it puts /*/ at the beginning of a line (assuming you start there) and also in the last three positions; then it goes to the start of the next line. The macro's source code is shown in Figure 1.14.

```
Description =Comment CL source
[wait app]
"/*/
[backtab]
[backtab]
[backtab word]
[fast left]
[fast left]
[fast left]
[right]
[down]
"/*/
[tab field]
```

Figure 1.14: The COMMENT.MAC macro comments out entire lines of CL.

—Ken Rokos

✦ ✦ ✦ Data Areas

Accessing the LDA in CL

Often you need to retrieve or change the contents of the local data area (LDA) in a CL program. The most widely known method uses the Retrieve Data Area (RTVDTAARA) command and the Change Data Area (CHGTDTAARA) command. For example, let's say the LDA contains a library name in bytes 101–110. A CL program needs to change the name to QTEMP if the LDA contains QGPL. The code shown in Figure 1.15 is an example of what you might do.

```
DCL        VAR(&LIB) TYPE(*CHAR) LEN(10)
RTVDTAARA DTAARA(*LDA (101 10)) RTNVAR(&LIB)
IF         COND(&LIB *EQ 'QGPL') THEN(DO)
CHGDTAARA DTAARA(*LDA (101 10)) VALUE('QTEMP')
ENDDO
```

Figure 1.15: Accessing the LDA through xxxDTARA commands is very easy.

There's another method, however, that uses the Change Variable (CHGVAR) command exclusively (see Figure 1.16).

```
IF        COND(%SST(*LDA 101 10) *EQ 'QGPL') THEN(DO)
CHGVAR    VAR(%SST(*LDA 101 10)) VALUE('QTEMP')
ENDDO
```

Figure 1.16: Accessing the LDA through the CHGVAR command lets you manipulate the LDA's contents.

Because there's no need to store the retrieved value, this method eliminates the need for variable &LIB. The trick is to use the substring (%SST) built-in function and to code special value *LDA instead of a variable name.

—Ernie Malaga

Determining If a Program Is in Use

I have worked on many applications that use a value in a data area to determine whether or not an application is running. The problem I have with this technique is that, if an application that checks/updates this data area ends abnormally, the value in the data area may be incorrect. In other words, the next time a program runs and checks that data area, perhaps to see whether it is busy, it might get bad data because the previous program didn't get a chance to update the data area's contents.

Rather than use a value within the contents of the data area, use the data area itself. Have your application allocate (*EXCL) the data area when it starts. If you do that, any other application that attempts to allocate that data area with an *EXCL lock will be unable to. In addition, the program can take some appropriate action to end its process or perhaps even wait until the data area's lock is released by the first program.

What's nice about this technique is that, if the first program terminates abnormally, the *EXCL lock will be released and the data area will no longer be allocated. Other programs can allocate the data area and put their own locks on it—thereby preventing programs from executing after they finish—but they will also prevent programs from attempting to get a lock on the data area.

—Greg Leister

✦ ✦ ✦ Data Handling

String Manipulations Made Easy

Here's a basic CL string manipulation tip: CL documentation shows that, when changing a variable, it is possible to use a portion of another variable to change your target. So, if the value of &TARGET is ABCDEFGH and the value of &SUBJECT is 12345, the following command string would result in a value of 2345BBBB for &TARGET, where *b*=blank:

```
CHGVAR VAR(&TARGET) VALUE(%SST(&SUBJECT 2 5)
```

What is not so well known is that you could change a portion of the target, as opposed to changing the entire variable, by using the same technique reversed:

```
CHGVAR VAR(%SST(&TARGET 2 5)) VALUE(&SUBJECT)
```

In this case, the resulting value would be A12345GH.

This technique isparticularly useful in setting up OPNQRYF shells where the number of variables to be used is unknown.

—David G. Abramowitz

◆ ◆ ◆ Database Files

Chaining in a CL Program

Most AS/400 programmers are familiar with the Override Database File (OVRDBF) command for substituting one file for another, changing a file to share an open data path (ODP), and other common uses. But many users might not be aware that it also can be used with the Receive File (RCVF) command to perform random record access, similar to CHAIN or SETLL operation codes in RPG.

The way to do this is to use the POSITION parameter of the OVRDBF command to get a record with a certain key value. To do this, you must specify the name of a field and one of the following search values:

> KEY (Key Equal)—The record with the given key value will be retrieved.
>
> KEYA (Key After)—The record following the record with the given key value will be retrieved.
>
> KEYAE (Key After or Equal)—If a record with the given key value exists, it will be retrieved. If not, the record with the next higher value will be retrieved.
>
> KEYB (Key Before)—The record preceding the record with the given key value will be retrieved.
>
> KEYBE (Key Before or Equal)—If a record with the given key value exists, it will be retrieved. If not, the record with the next lower value will be retrieved.

The following code fragment demonstrates the use of the POSITION parameter of the OVRDBF command:

```
DCLF FILE(MYFILE)
OVRDBF FILE(MYFILE) +
  POSITION(*KEY 1 MYFMT KEYFLD)
RCVF
```

This example will retrieve a record from file MYFILE (format MYFMT), which has a key value matching the value in the field KEYFLD. The other key search values work similarly.

—Sharon Cannon

Checking for Open Files in CL

Q: Do you know if it's possible to check for an open database file in CL? For example, I want to execute the Close File (CLOF) command only if the file is open.

A: The most straightforward way to do this is to execute the CLOF command for the file unconditionally and monitor for message CPF4520-No file open with identifier [file]. Don't take any action if the error message is received; simply ignore it and continue.

—Midrange Computing Staff

CL Can Read, but It Can't Write

IBM could have given CL more I/O capabilities, but the company chose not to. Maybe IBM was afraid CL would replace RPG as the AS/400 programming language of choice. In any event, I've found it helpful to stretch CL's file-processing abilities through the years. Figure 1.17 contains the source code for the Write File (WRTF) command. Its command processing program (CPP) is WRT001CL (Figure 1.18), which calls RPG program WRT001RG (Figure 1.19). This program writes up to 12 records to a physical file.

```
/*===================================================================*/
/* To compile:                                                       */
/*                                                                   */
/*          CRTCMD     CMD(XXX/WRTF) PGM(XXX/WRT001CL) +             */
/*                     SRCFILE(XXX/QCMDSRC)                          */
/*                                                                   */
/*===================================================================*/
             CMD        PROMPT('Write to a file')

             PARM       KWD(TEXT) TYPE(*CHAR) LEN(96) MIN(1) MAX(12) +
                        EXPR(*YES) PROMPT('Text to be written')
             PARM       KWD(FILE) TYPE(QUAL1) MIN(1) PROMPT('File')
             PARM       KWD(FILETYPE) TYPE(*CHAR) LEN(6) RSTD(*YES) +
                        DFT(SOURCE) VALUES(SOURCE DATA) +
                        PROMPT('Source or data file?')
             PARM       KWD(MEMBER) TYPE(*NAME) DFT(*FIRST) +
                        SPCVAL((*FIRST)) EXPR(*YES) PROMPT('Member')

QUAL1:       QUAL       TYPE(*NAME) MIN(1) EXPR(*YES)
             QUAL       TYPE(*NAME) DFT(*LIBL) SPCVAL((*CURLIB) +
                        (*LIBL)) EXPR(*YES) PROMPT('Library')
```

Figure 1.17: The WRTF command lets CL append records to disk files.

```
/*==================================================================*/
/* To compile:                                                      */
/*                                                                  */
/*            CRTCLPGM    PGM(XXX/WRT001CL) SRCFILE(XXX/QCLSRC)      */
/*                                                                  */
/*==================================================================*/
PGM         PARM(&TEXT &FILE &FILETYPE &MEMBER)
   DCL         VAR(&TEXT) TYPE(*CHAR) LEN(1154)
   DCL         VAR(&FILE) TYPE(*CHAR) LEN(20)
   DCL         VAR(&FILETYPE) TYPE(*CHAR) LEN(6)
   DCL         VAR(&MEMBER) TYPE(*CHAR) LEN(10)

   /*  Declare error processing variables */
   DCL         VAR(&ERRBYTES) TYPE(*CHAR) LEN(4) +
                 VALUE(X'00000000')
   DCL         VAR(&ERROR) TYPE(*LGL) VALUE('0')
   DCL         VAR(&MSGKEY) TYPE(*CHAR) LEN(4)
   DCL         VAR(&MSGTYP) TYPE(*CHAR) LEN(10) VALUE('*DIAG')
   DCL         VAR(&MSGTYPCTR) TYPE(*CHAR) LEN(4) +
                 VALUE(X'00000001')
   DCL         VAR(&PGMMSGQ) TYPE(*CHAR) LEN(10) VALUE('*')
   DCL         VAR(&STKCTR) TYPE(*CHAR) LEN(4) +
                 VALUE(X'00000001')

   MONMSG      MSGID(CPF0000) EXEC(GOTO CMDLBL(ERRPROC))

   CHKOBJ      OBJ(%SST(&FILE 11 10)/%SST(&FILE 1 10)) +
                 OBJTYPE(*FILE) MBR(&MEMBER) AUT(*ADD)
   OVRDBF      FILE(FILEOUT) TOFILE(%SST(&FILE 11 +
                 10)/%SST(&FILE 1 10)) MBR(&MEMBER)
   CALL        PGM(WRT001RG) PARM(&TEXT &FILETYPE)
   DLTOVR      FILE(FILEOUT)

   RETURN


   /*==============================================================*/
   /* Error processing routine                                     */
   /*==============================================================*/
ERRPROC:
   IF          COND(&ERROR) THEN(GOTO CMDLBL(ERRDONE))
   ELSE        CMD(CHGVAR VAR(&ERROR) VALUE('1'))

   /* Move all *DIAG messages to previous program queue */
   CALL        PGM(QMHMOVPM) PARM(&MSGKEY &MSGTYP +
                 &MSGTYPCTR &PGMMSGQ &STKCTR &ERRBYTES)

   /* Resend last *ESCAPE message */
ERRDONE:
   CALL        PGM(QMHRSNEM) PARM(&MSGKEY &ERRBYTES)
   MONMSG      MSGID(CPF0000) EXEC(DO)
     SNDPGMMSG  MSGID(CPF3CF2) MSGF(QCPFMSG) +
                 MSGDTA('QMHRSNEM') MSGTYPE(*ESCAPE)
     MONMSG      MSGID(CPF0000)
   ENDDO
ENDPGM
```

Figure 1.18: WRT001CL is the CPP for the WRTF command.

```
 *=================================================================
 * To compile:
 *
 *      CRTRPGPGM  PGM(XXX/WRT001RG) SRCFILE(XXX/QRPGSRC)
 *
 *=================================================================
FFILEOUT O   F    108           DISK
E                 DTA        12 96
IDATA        DS                           1154
I                               B   1   20DCT
I                                   31154 DTA
C            *ENTRY   PLIST
C                     PARM          DATA
C                     PARM          FILTYP  1        SOURCE, DATA
C*
C            FILTYP   IFEQ 'D'
C                     MOVE *ON      *IN21
C                     ENDIF
C*
C            X        DOWLTDCT
C            X        ANDLT12
C                     ADD  1        X        30
C                     EXCPTDLINE
C                     ENDDO
C*
C                     MOVE *ON      *INLR
OFILEOUT E            DLINE
O                 N21 DTA,X     108
O                 21  DTA,X     96
```

Figure 1.19: WRT001RG is the brawn behind WRTF.

Once you grant CL the ability to write to disk files, you won't have any trouble coming up with useful things to do with it. The following is a list of just a few things you can do:

- Log the contents of CL variables to a disk file to aid in debugging.

- Record each time a CL program runs, with full information about it (e.g., user profile, date, and time).

- Build a source member from user input or other disk files and immediately compile it.

- Load a single-record data member with record-selection values or general information to be passed into a query, and then join that member to a query with a Cartesian product.

If you implement this command in your shop, you might want to change the limiting numbers. Because I usually use this command to write a single record to a source file, allowing 12 records of 96 bytes is more than adequate for my purposes. By the way, you might already have a utility like this on your system. If you have QUSRTOOL or the TAA Productivity Tools, look for Write Source File (WRTSRCF).

—Ted Holt

Copying a File Member in a CL Program

If you want to make a backup copy of a file member, you might include a Copy File (CPYF) command like this one in a CL program:

```
CPYF  FROMFILE(FILE1) TOFILE(FILE2) MBROPT(*REPLACE)
```

However, there is a problem with this command. If FILE1 is empty, the program receives diagnostic message CPF2869 (Empty member FILE1 in file FILE1 in library QTEMP is not copied), followed by escape message CPF2817 (Copy command ended because of error).

Here's a better way to make the backup copy:

```
CLRPFM  FILE(FILE2)
CPYF    FROMFILE(FILE1) TOFILE(FILE2) MBROPT(*ADD)
```

Clearing the member yourself lets you use MBROPT(*ADD) on the copy. This does not cancel when copying an empty file member.

—Ted Holt

Create Physical Files from Logical View

The other day we needed to ship a customer name and address file to a client in ZIP code sequence. The file wasn't indexed by ZIP code. However, a logical view by ZIP code did exist. Our first thought was to write a simple RPG program to read the file through the logical view and output to a new physical file. But before we did, we tried using the Copy File (CPYF) command using the logical file name in the FROMFILE parameter and the physical file name in the TOFILE parameter, as follows:

```
CPYF FROMFILE(logical_file) TOFILE(physical_file) CRTFILE(*YES)
```

It worked! We had a physical copy of the file in the sequence we needed—with no programming.

Note: The TOFILE will always be a sequential file unless you create it with DDS describing a key. In this case, however, the CRTFILE parameter must be *NO and the MBROPT parameter must be *ADD.

—Midrange Computing Staff

Direct Files on the AS/400

Q: Does the AS/400 allow direct files? If so, how does processing of these files compare to a S/36?

A: These commands will create the AS/400 equivalent of a direct file. The file APTRANS will have 1,000 records of 80 bytes, initialized to blanks.

```
CRTPF FILE(TESTLIB/APTRANS) RCDLEN(80)SIZE(1000 0 0) +
      ALLOCATE(*YES) TEXT('A/P + Transaction File')
INZPFM FILE(APTRANS)
```

Any physical file on the AS/400 can be accessed as a direct file if it is program-described like APTRANS. Be very careful not to have any overrides to APTRANS in effect when you run this program.

—Jonathan Yergin

Faster CPYF File Copies

When you are copying one indexed file to another file and the physical record sequence of the resulting file does not matter, key a '1' in the FROMRCD parameter of the CPYF command. This will cause the copy to read the FROM file in arrival sequence, which is much faster than reading the file in keyed sequence. Here is an example of the command:

```
CPYF FROMFILE(LIB1/AAA) TOFILE(LIB2/BBB) MBROPT(*REPLACE) +
     CRTFILE(*YES) FROMRCD(1)
```

—Midrange Computing Staff

Files in CL

Q: I want to be able to reference a temporary file in a CL program. However, I run into a problem when I try to compile my CL program because the file does not yet exist. Is there any easy way around this problem?

A: To solve your problem, do the following:

1. Manually create the file your CL program is going to use. You can use DDS if you want to refer to fields within your program. In your case, I suspect that you won't want to because you'll use it for a spool file. Use the CRTPF command as follows:

```
CRTPF FILE(lib/file) RCDLEN(132) TEXT('text-description')
```

   The record length of 132 assures that every column of the spooled report will be included in the file.

2. Compile your program. Because the file exists now, the compile will be successful. If you created the file in QTEMP (you probably should), the compile should be performed interactively. This is because a compile submitted to batch processing won't be able to reference your interactive job's QTEMP.

3. Delete the file you created in step 1 once the compile is done.

On a different note...

If you use outfiles, the process is different because IBM already provides the model outfiles in QSYS. You shouldn't use the files in QSYS in your programs, but you can reference them to create your own. For example, suppose you've coded a CL program that performs a DSPOBJD to an outfile. Rather than coming up with your own outfile, use IBM's: QADSPOBJ. Automatically, you gain complete field descriptions for the file (IBM created it with DDS). Then simply compile the program. You don't have to do anything special.

—Ernie Malaga

One Open, One Close

If you will be sharing a file among programs of a job, you should consider keeping the file open between programs. This will eliminate the time it takes to re-open the file for each program. The OPNDBF command, with TYPE(*PERM), will open the file—and keep it open—until you explicitly close it with the CLOF command. You must also be sure to specify a high enough level of usage in the OPTION parameter of OPNDBF. For example, if one of your programs updates the file, you must open it as an update file. If you opened it as input, no program could update it.

For further information, see pages 8–7 through 8–13 of *Programming: Database Guide* (SC21-9659), and pages 1–20 through 1–22 of *Programming: Data Management Guide* (SC21-9658).

—Midrange Computing Staff

Opening/Closing Files in CL

Q: I am developing a CL program that retrieves information about certain files. In order to get this information, I use the Display File Description (DSPFD) command to send the information to an outfile. I then use the Receive File (RCVF) command to read the outfile and access the appropriate field.

The problem is that when I try to use the DSPFD command and send the information to the same outfile, I get message CPF3084 (Error clearing member...) indicating that the system cannot clear the file. I close the file before executing the second DSFPD and then open the file before I read it with RCVF. The program is shown in Figure 1.20.

```
/*TRANSFER INVOICES TRANSACTIONS FROM CURRENT FILES TO HISTORY*/
   PGM

   DCLF        FILE(SMRCHIST/TRFLIBNAM)

   DCL         VAR(&RBFILEP) TYPE(*CHAR) LEN(10)
   DCL         VAR(&RIFILEP) TYPE(*CHAR) LEN(10)


      /*RBFILEP*/
   CLOF        OPNID(TRFLIBNAM)
   MONMSG      MSGID(CPF4520)
   DSPFD       FILE(RBFILEP) TYPE(*RCDFMT) OUTPUT(*OUTFILE) +
```

Figure 1.20: You cannot clear a file in a CL program that already has a lock on the file (part 1 of 2).

```
                    FILEATR(*PF) OUTFILE(SMRCHIST/TRFLIBNAM)
       OPNDBF       FILE(SMRCHIST/TRFLIBNAM) OPTION(*ALL)
       RCVF
       CHGVAR       VAR(&RBFILEP) VALUE(&RFLIB)

        /*RIFILEP*/
       CLOF         OPNID(TRFLIBNAM)
       MONMSG       MSGID(CPF4520)
       DSPFD        FILE(RIFILEP) TYPE(*RCDFMT) OUTPUT(*OUTFILE) +
                    FILEATR(*PF) OUTFILE(SMRCHIST/TRFLIBNAM)
       OPNDBF       FILE(SMRCHIST/TRFLIBNAM) OPTION(*ALL)
       RCVF
       CHGVAR       VAR(&RIFILEP) VALUE(&RFLIB)

       ENDPGM
```

Figure 1.20: You cannot clear a file in a CL program that already has a lock on the file (part 2 of 2).

When I look at program status, the system says that the file member (TRFLIBNAM) is locked. I've tried working with the Override Database File (OVRDBF) command using SHARE(*YES) and the Deallocate Object (DLCOBJ) command, but I can't get the program to work.

A: Put the DCLF and RCVF commands in a subprogram, and have the subprogram pass back the &RFLIB value in a parameter. Each time the subprogram returns, the file will be closed. CL is very limited when it comes to manipulating database records. Solving this problem requires either two programs or a different language.

—Pete Hall

A: You can't do it using your method. The system ignores the opens and closes in a CL program—the file is locked from the first time it's referenced in the program until the program ends.

The only solution I've found (ugly, but it works) is to put the reads in a separate CL (or RPG) program and then call it from the main program. If you do that, you can eliminate the open and close (because they're done implicitly).

You'll also have a problem like this if you try to execute a Clear Physical File Member (CLRPFM) command, a Remove Member (RMVM) command, or other file operations to a file that's in use in a CL program.

—Matt Fulton

A: As previously mentioned, the close and open statements won't work using the method you've specified. CL automatically opens the file when you do the first read, and the file remains open until an end-of-file condition is reached or the program terminates. Once it's closed, you can't open it again within that program.

But I bet you could use other methods to get the information you want. It looks like the information you need is always in the first record. Give this a try:

1. Use the DSPFD command on RBFILEP and send the information to an outfile in QTEMP.

2. Run CPYF against the file you created in step one and select the first record. The output from CPYF should be directed to TRFLIBNAM, specifying REPLACE(*YES).

3. Use the DSPFD command on RIFILEP and send the information to the same QTEMP outfile.

4. Run CPYF again, selecting the first record from the outfile in QTEMP. This time, the output to TRFLIBNAM should specify REPLACE(*NO).

This process loads file TRFLIBNAM with the two records you need before the file is even opened. With two RCVFs, you've got your data.

If your objective is to find what library these files are in, you could use the Retrieve Object Description (RTVOBJD) command and not have to worry about reading outfiles.

—Matt Seargent

Reading a File Twice with CL

Have you ever wished you could read a file more than once within a CL program? Writing two programs to accomplish multiple passes of a file is unnecessary. The key to the solution is to use the Transfer Control (TFRCTL) command.

The TFRCTL and CALL commands are similar. If you execute a CALL command in a CL program, control returns to the command following the CALL after the called program completes. TFRCTL is the same as CALL, except that the invoking program does not regain control after the called program completes. A CL program may use TFRCTL to invoke itself without a recursion error. Figure 1.21 contains an example of a CL program that uses TFRCTL to read through a data file twice: once to accumulate a total cost and once to calculate the percent of total cost for each record in the file.

```
THISCLPGM:  PGM         PARM(&PASS &TOTAL)

            DCL         VAR(&PASS) TYPE(*CHAR) LEN(1)
            DCL         VAR(&TOTAL) TYPE(*DEC) LEN(15 5)
            DCL         VAR(&PERCENT) TYPE(*DEC) LEN(5 2)
            DCLF        FILE(SALES)

            IF          COND(&PASS *EQ '1') THEN(DO)

            CHGVAR      VAR(&PASS) VALUE('2')
            CHGVAR      VAR(&TOTAL) VALUE(0)

    LOOP1:  RCVF
            MONMSG      MSGID(CPF0864) EXEC(TFRCTL PGM(THISCLPGM) +
                          PARM(&PASS &TOTAL))
            CHGVAR      VAR(&TOTAL) VALUE(&TOTAL + &COST)
            GOTO        CMDLBL(LOOP1)
            ENDDO

    LOOP2:  RCVF
            MONMSG      MSGID(CPF0864) EXEC(GOTO CMDLBL(ENDPGM))
            CHGVAR      VAR(&PERCENT) VALUE((&COST /&TOTAL) * 100)
            CALL        PGM(UPDSUMRY) PARM(&ITEMID &PERCENT)
            GOTO        CMDLBL(LOOP2)

    ENDPGM:  ENDPGM
```

Figure 1.21: Reading a file twice with a CL program can only be accomplished by using the TFRCTL command.

You can invoke the program in Figure 1.21, THISCLPGM, from any AS/400 command line by entering the CALL THISCLPGM PARM('1' 0) command. The second parameter in the program, *DEC (15 5), is the only type of numeric parameter that you can pass from the command line. Because THISCLPGM receives a value of '1' in the first parameter (&PASS) on the first pass, it executes the code starting at tag LOOP1. The program reads through the file to produce the portfolio total. It uses the variable &TOTAL to accumulate this amount. When the program reaches end of file, it invokes itself through the TFRCTL command. See the first Monitor Message (MONMSG) statement. This time, the &PASS parameter contains the value '2' to signify the second pass. It also passes the total sales (&TOTAL) as the second parameter.

Because the value in &PASS is '2', the program executes the code starting at tag LOOP2. This time, while reading through the SALES file, it calculates a percentage of sales amount using the &TOTAL accumulated in the original call of the program. This calculation, done with the Change Variable (CHGVAR) command, is necessary because the program that this program calls (UPDSUMRY) requires this percentage value as a passed parameter.

—Mike Cravitz

Redefining Records Without Changing

I recently had to read a file in a CL program that wasn't defined in a very user-friendly manner. It was a packaged software file that was converted to the AS/400 from a S/36. Therefore, the file's DDS described the file as follows:

```
A         KEYDTA        8A
A         CNTDTA       54A
```

The packaged software used a data structure to redefine the CNTDTA field. This data contained character, zoned, and packed data. I couldn't figure out how to read the file using the CNTDTA field because it contained hexadecimal data (my CL program kept giving various error messages). So, this is the solution that I arrived at, and it worked! I created a physical file format for use in my CL program. I gave it a unique name (different from the file's name) and defined the data that I needed as follows:

```
A         KEYDTA        8A
A         DTEDTA        4P 0
A         JNKDTA       50A
```

In my CL program, I used the following commands:

```
DCLF  FILE(my_new_file_name)
OVRDBF FILE(my_new_field_name) TOFILE(existing_file_name) LVLCHK(*NO)
RCVF
```

I had a numeric CL variable declared for the DTEDTA field. I was then able to manipulate the packed data as I needed. It worked great!

—Ted Holt

Rereading Files in CL

As a rule, a CL program can read a database file only once. After the Receive File (RCVF) command finds the end of the file, there is no way to reset the file pointer and read the file again. There is a way to reread a database file in a CL program, however. Here is what you must do:

1. Use the Number of Current Records (NBRCURRCD) parameter of the Retrieve Member Description (RTVMBRDR) command to determine the number of active records in the member.

2. Override the database file to SHARE(*YES). This establishes an open data path (ODP) and allows the Position Database File (POSDBF) command to function properly.

3. Use the Open Database File (OPNDBF) to establish a file ID link that can be referenced by POSDBF.

4. Count the records as you process them.

5. When the record counter matches the number of active records, you have processed the last record. Use the POSDBF command to reset the file pointer to the first record.

The short CL program in Figure 1.22 illustrates this technique.

```
PGM
DCL VAR(&COUNT) TYPE(*DEC) LEN(10)
DCL VAR(&NBRCURRCD) TYPE(*DEC) LEN(10)
DCLF FILE(MYFILE)
RTVMBRD FILE(MYFILE) NBRCURRCD(&NBRCURRCD)
OVRDBF FILE(MYFILE) SHARE(*YES)
OPNDBF FILE(MYFILE) OPTION(*INP)
LOOP:
RCVF
MONMSG MSGID(CPF0864) EXEC(GOTO CMDLBL(END_LOOP))
/* Process record here */
SNDUSRMSG MSG(&MYFILE) MSGTYPE(*INFO) TOUSR(*REQUESTER)
CHGVAR VAR(&COUNT) VALUE(&COUNT + 1)
IF COND(&COUNT *EQ &NBRCURRCD) THEN(DO)
/* End of File has been reached for the first time */
POSDBF OPNID(MYFILE) POSITION(*START)
ENDDO
GOTO LOOP
END_LOOP:
CLOF OPNID(MYFILE)
DLTOVR FILE(MYFILE)
ENDPGM
```

Figure 1.22: This CL program reads a database file twice.

Be aware that this technique won't work correctly if other jobs are adding records to the file, or deleting records from the file, at the same time.

—Tom Conover

✦ ✦ ✦ Date and Time

CEELOCT + CEEDATM = Qdate + Pizzazz!

The easy way to retrieve the current date and time in a CL program is with the Retrieve System Value (RTVSYSVAL) command, specifying the QDATE and QTIME system values as arguments. Time and date are returned as 6-byte values. If you need something with more pizzazz, use the Get Current Local Time (CEELOCT) and Convert Seconds to Character Timestamp (CEEDATM) APIs, as in Figure 1.23.

```
/**************************************************************/
/*                                                          */
/* To compile:                                              */
/*                                                          */
/*    CRTBNDCL PGM(xxx/AN0C1)    SRCFILE(xxx/QCLSRC) +      */
/*             SRCMBR(AN01C1)                               */
/*                                                          */
/**************************************************************/
PGM


    /*-------------------------------------------------------*/
    /*  declaration                                          */
    /*-------------------------------------------------------*/
             dcl      &Lilian     *dec   (9 0)
             dcl      &Second     *char   8
             dcl      &GregDt     *char  17
             dcl      &Picture    *char  50
             dcl      &Message    *char  78  'Today is '
             dcl      &CurrTs      *char  50

             dcl      &error      *lgl                        /* std err */
             dcl      &msgkey     *char   4                   /* std err */
             dcl      &msgtyp     *char  10  '*DIAG'          /* std err */
             dcl      &msgtypctr *char   4 X'00000001' /* std err */
             dcl      &pgmmsgq    *char  10  '*'              /* std err */
             dcl      &stkctr     *char   4 X'00000001' /* std err */
             dcl      &errbytes   *char   4 X'00000000' /* std err */

             monmsg   msgid(cpf0000) exec(goto error)
```

Figure 1.24: Use the CEELOCT API to retrieve the system date in a CL program (part 1 of 2).

```
/*----------------------------------------------------------*/
/*  Get the current timestamp & convert to output format    */
/*----------------------------------------------------------*/
                callprc    CEELOCT    (&Lilian    +
                                       &Second    +
                                       &GregDt )
                chgvar     &Picture   'Wwwwwwwwwwz, Mmmmmmmmmmz ZD, YYYY
ZH:MI AP'
                chgvar     &CurrTs    '
'
                callprc    CEEDATM    (&Second    +
                                       &Picture   +
                                       &CurrTs    +
                                       *OMIT )
                chgvar     %sst(&Message 10 50)   &CurrTs
                chgvar     &Message   (&Message |< '. Have a nice day')

                sndpgmmsg  msgid(cpf9898)         +
                             msgf(qcpfmsg)        +
                             msgdta(&Message)
                Goto       End

/*----------------------------------------------------------*/
/*  error routine:                                          */
/*----------------------------------------------------------*/
 error:
                if         &error     (goto errordone)
                   else    chgvar     &error '1'
        /*------------------------------------------------*/
        /*  move all *DIAG message to *PRV program queue*/
        /*------------------------------------------------*/
                call       QMHMOVPM   (&msgkey    +
                                       &msgtyp     +
                                       &msgtypctr  +
                                       &pgmmsgq    +
                                       &stkctr     +
                                       &errbytes)
        /*------------------------------------------------*/
        /*  resend the last *ESCAPE message              */
        /*------------------------------------------------*/
 errordone:
                call       QMHRSNEM   (&msgkey    +
                                       &errbytes)
                monmsg     cpf0000    exec(do)
                  sndpgmmsg  msgid(cpf3cf2) msgf(QCFPMSG) +
                                msgdta('QMHRSNEM') msgtype(*escape)
                    monmsg   cpf0000
                enddo
 end:           endpgm
```

Figure 1.24: Use the CEELOCT API to retrieve the system date in a CL program (part 2 of 2).

When you run this example, you'll get a message sent to the program message queue saying something like:

> "Today is Sunday, November 29, 1998, 5:57 p.m. Have a nice day."

—Alex Nubla

Date Validation of CL

The easiest way to validate dates in CL is to use the Convert Date (CVTDAT) command. If the command fails, it's because the date is invalid. For example, the following code fragment shows how you can easily validate a date in a CL program:

```
CVTDAT DATE(&DATE) TOVAR(&DATE) FROMFMT(*MDY) TOFMT(*MDY) TOSEP(*NONE)
MONMSG MSGID(CPF0000) EXEC(DO)
CHGVAR VAR(&IN70) VALUE('1') /* Error indicator */
GOTO CMDLBL(ERROR) /* Redisplay */
ENDDO
```

In this case, no conversion takes place because the from-format and to-format are the same. However, an exception message will be sent if the variable &DATE does not contain a valid date.

—Midrange Computing Staff

Day of Week Calculation

In our shop, we run a nightly cycle to manipulate our data. We have added many new jobs to the nightly job stream; however, not all the jobs are run every night. In an effort to have one main CL program drive all the programs that need to be submitted each night of the week, we have developed the CL program DOW001CL, shown in Figure 1.25, to allow us to determine what day of the week it is on a given day.

```
/*================================================================*/
/* To compile:                                                    */
/*                                                                */
/*          CRTCLPGM    PGM(XXX/DOW001CL) SRCFILE(XXX/QCLSRC)      */
/*                                                                */
/*================================================================*/

          PGM
```

Figure 1.25: CL Program DOW001CL demonstrates how to perform a "day of week" calculation (part 1 of 3).

```
DCL          VAR(&JULDAYC) TYPE(*CHAR) LEN(5)
DCL          VAR(&SYSDATE) TYPE(*CHAR) LEN(6)
DCL          VAR(&SYSJULDATE) TYPE(*CHAR) LEN(5)
DCL          VAR(&SYSJULDATC) TYPE(*DEC) LEN(5 0)
DCL          VAR(&CALCDATE) TYPE(*DEC) LEN(2 0)
DCL          VAR(&DAYCALCC) TYPE(*CHAR) LEN(1)
DCL          VAR(&DAYCALC) TYPE(*DEC) LEN(1 0)
DCL          VAR(&JULDATE) TYPE(*DEC) LEN(5 0)

RTVDTAARA    DTAARA(DAYOFWEEK (11 5)) RTNVAR(&JULDAYC)
RTVSYSVAL    SYSVAL(QDATE) RTNVAR(&SYSDATE)
RTVDTAARA    DTAARA(DAYOFWEEK (20 1)) RTNVAR(&DAYCALCC)

CHGVAR       VAR(&DAYCALC) VALUE(&DAYCALCC)
CHGVAR       VAR(&JULDATE) VALUE(&JULDAYC)

CVTDAT       DATE(&SYSDATE) TOVAR(&SYSJULDATE) +
               FROMFMT(*MDY) TOFMT(*JUL) TOSEP(*NONE)

CHGDTAARA    DTAARA(DAYOFWEEK (11 5)) VALUE(&SYSJULDATE)

CHGVAR       VAR(&SYSJULDATC) VALUE(&SYSJULDATE)
CHGVAR       VAR(&CALCDATE) VALUE(&SYSJULDATC - &JULDATE)
MONMSG       MSGID(CPF0000)

IF           COND(&CALCDATE *EQ 0) THEN(GOTO CMDLBL(ENDPGM))

IF           COND(&CALCDATE *NE 0) THEN(DO)
CHGVAR       VAR(&DAYCALC) VALUE(&CALCDATE + &DAYCALC)
MONMSG       MSGID(CPF0000)
ENDDO

IF           COND(&DAYCALC *GT 7) THEN(DO)
CHGVAR       VAR(&DAYCALC) VALUE(&DAYCALC - 7)
ENDDO

IF           COND(&DAYCALC *EQ 1) THEN(DO)
CHGDTAARA    DTAARA(DAYOFWEEK (1 10)) VALUE('MONDAY')
ENDDO

IF           COND(&DAYCALC *EQ 2) THEN(DO)
CHGDTAARA    DTAARA(DAYOFWEEK (1 10)) VALUE('TUESDAY')
ENDDO

IF           COND(&DAYCALC *EQ 3) THEN(DO)
CHGDTAARA    DTAARA(DAYOFWEEK (1 10)) VALUE('WEDNESDAY')
ENDDO
```

Figure 1.25: CL Program DOW001CL demonstrates how to perform a "day of week" calculation (part 2 of 3).

```
        IF          COND(&DAYCALC *EQ 4) THEN(DO)
        CHGDTAARA   DTAARA(DAYOFWEEK (1 10)) VALUE('THURSDAY')
        ENDDO


        IF          COND(&DAYCALC *EQ 5) THEN(DO)
        CHGDTAARA   DTAARA(DAYOFWEEK (1 10)) VALUE('FRIDAY')
        ENDDO


        IF          COND(&DAYCALC *EQ 6) THEN(DO)
        CHGDTAARA   DTAARA(DAYOFWEEK (1 10)) VALUE('SATURDAY')
        ENDDO


        IF          COND(&DAYCALC *EQ 7) THEN(DO)
        CHGDTAARA   DTAARA(DAYOFWEEK (1 10)) VALUE('SUNDAY')
        ENDDO


        CHGVAR      VAR(&DAYCALCC) VALUE(&DAYCALC)
        CHGDTAARA   DTAARA(DAYOFWEEK (20 1)) VALUE(&DAYCALCC)

ENDPGM:     ENDPGM
```

Figure 1.25: CL Program DOW001CL demonstrates how to perform a "day of week" calculation (part 3 of 3).

Before you run this program for the first time, you'll need to create a 20-byte character data area called DAYOFWEEK. When you create this data area, load it with the day of the week in positions 1–10, the Julian date in positions 11–15, and the relative day of the week in position 20. For example, you could use the following command:

```
CRTDTAARA DTAARA(xxx/DAYOFWEEK) TYPE(*CHAR) LEN(20) +
  VALUE('MONDAY       95212     1')
```

In this case, we're using Monday, July 31, 1995, as the starting date. Any past date will do as long as the day of the week you pick occurred on the Julian date specified and the relative day of the week (position 20) coincides with the other fields. After you create this data area, you can call the DOW001CL program at the beginning of your nightly job. Then you can retrieve the data from the data area into a variable in your program and use it to determine the day of the week as shown in the example in Figure 1.26.

```
PGM

        DCL       VAR(&DAYOFWEEK) TYPE(*CHAR) LEN(10)

        CALL      PGM(DOW001CL)
        RTVDTAARA DTAARA(DAYOFWEEK (1 10)) RTNVAR(&DAYOFWEEK)

        IF        COND(&DAYOFWEEK *EQ 'MONDAY') THEN(DO)
        .
        .
        .
        ENDDO

        IF        COND(&DAYOFWEEK *EQ 'TUESDAY') THEN(DO)
        .
        .
        .
        ENDDO

        ENDPGM
```

Figure 1.26: Use this sample program as your guide to calling the day-of-week calculation program.

—Neely Loring

Precision System Time

Q: I am searching for a way to access subsecond time on the AS/400, but I'm coming up empty. The application is trying to use sub- or millisecond time slicing. Can anybody offer a suggestion?

A: CL and PL/I let you retrieve the system time with accuracy up to milliseconds. In CL, you do it by retrieving system value QTIME into a 9-character variable, as follows:

```
RTVSYSVAL SYSVAL(QTIME) RTNVAL(&SYSTIME)
```

Variable &SYSTIME will be in the HHMMSSTTT format.

—Ernie Malaga

Retrieve the System Date in any Date Format

One problem you might have faced is that of how to retrieve the current system date in a specific format from within a CL program. If you retrieve the QDATE system value, it might be in any of several formats, depending on the value of the QDATFMT system value. QDATFMT can be set to YMD, MDY, DMY, or JUL.

Here's a way to retrieve the system date in a CL program and always be sure it's in the format you want. First, retrieve the QDATE system value into a CL variable. Next, use the Convert Date (CVTDAT) command to convert the date. You can convert it from whatever format it's in by specifying FROMFMT(*SYSVAL). This converts it from the date format specified in the QDATFMT system value.

For example, suppose you want to write a CL program and, in that program, you want to retrieve the current system date in YMD format. The CL program shown in Figure 1.27 will accomplish this task. It will work no matter what format the QDATFMT system value is set to.

```
PGM

DCL        VAR(&QDATE) TYPE(*CHAR) LEN(6)
DCL        VAR(&YMD) TYPE(*CHAR) LEN(6)

/* Retrieve the current date */
RTVSYSVAL  SYSVAL(QDATE) RTNVAR(&QDATE)

/* Convert the date from whatever format it's in to YMD */
CVTDAT     DATE(&QDATE) TOVAR(&YMD) FROMFMT(*SYSVAL) +
             TOFMT(*YMD) TOSEP(*NONE)

ENDPGM
```

Figure 1.27: You can use a CL program to retrieve the current date.

—Robin Klima

Retrieving the Century in CL

There's a potential "gotcha" when you use the special value *YEAR to return a four-digit year and expect the first two digits to determine the current century.

The trouble is that *YEAR returns not the current year, but the year in which the job started. Therefore, if at 23:00 on December 31, 1999, you submitted a batch job to update a transaction file and the job ended at 02:00 on January 1, 2000, all transactions would reflect the year 1999 and, therefore, the 20th century.

Because of this limitation, I don't recommend using *YEAR to retrieve the current year or the current century. The solution is to retrieve the system date from system values.

To get the current century, retrieve QCENTURY (a system value that showed up in V3R2). If you have a version earlier than V3R2, you can retrieve QYEAR and assume 20th century if QYEAR returns 40 to 00, or 21st century if QYEAR returns 01 to 39.

—Mike Grant

Search by Using a Text Month Name in a Numeric Date

Q: I have an interactive program that allows the user to search through the database. I would like to give the user the capability to search on a date field. The field is stored in the database as YYMMDD, but I need to provide search capabilities in the format DD month abbreviation YY (e.g., 04JUN96). For example, the user may search on *JU* and I need to return records for the months of June and July.

I'm using Open Query File (OPNQRYF) to query the database inside an RPG III program. I would like to avoid creating another file with the appropriately formatted date because this is an interactive program.

A: You have to convert the date field in the database to DD month abbreviation YY format to compare it to the wildcard search value. In Figure 1.28, you can see how to accomplished this feat.

```
PGM         PARM(&SEARCH)
DCL         VAR(&SEARCH) TYPE(*CHAR) LEN(7)
DCL         VAR(&QRYSLT) TYPE(*CHAR) LEN(256)

CHGVAR      VAR(&QRYSLT) VALUE('SLTDATE *EQ %WLDCRD("' +
              *CAT &SEARCH *TCAT '")')

OVRDBF      FILE(TESTPF2) SHARE(*YES)
OPNQRYF     FILE((TESTPF2)) QRYSLT(&QRYSLT) +
              MAPFLD((MONTHLIST '"    +
              JANFEBMARAPRMAYJUNJULAUGSEPOCTNOVDEC"') +
              (CHARDATE '%DIGITS(SDTRDJ)' *CHAR 6) +
              (MONTH '%SST(CHARDATE 3 2)' *ZONED 2 0) +
              (OFFSET 'MONTH * 3 + 1') (SLTDATE +
              '%SST(CHARDATE 5 2) *CAT %SST(MONTHLIST +
              OFFSET 3) *CAT %SST(CHARDATE 1 2)'))
CALL        PGM(LISTPGM)
CLOF        OPNID(TESTPF2)

ENDPGM
```

Figure 1.28: Use this code fragment as your guide to search a database based on month names.

The passed-in value (&SEARCH) is what you're searching for, such as *JU*. The power is in the MAPFLD parameter. Here's what each mapped field does.

MONTHLIST is a list of three character abbreviations. Notice that the value in this variable begins with three blank spaces.

CHARDATE is the database date field (SDTRDJ) converted to character. If the database date is in character format, skip this step and use the database field name instead of CHARDATE in the mapped field definitions that follow:

- MONTH—The month portion of the database date as a zoned decimal number.

- OFFSET—The position in the MONTH.

- LIST—Where the abbreviation for the month starts. January starts at position 4, February at position 7, and so on.

- SLTDATE—The database date reformatted as DD month abbreviation YY. It gets compared to the search string in the QRYSLT parameter.

—Ted Holt

The Trick to DATE(*CURRENT)

Q: I need to define a parameter with the type of *DATE in a command definition. This data type will edit for valid dates. I want the parameter value to default to *CURRENT for processing purposes. When I compile the command, however, I get errors as follows:

```
CPD0271: Special value *CURRENT not valid.
CPD0265: Default value *CURRENT ignored because not valid.
```

I am putting *CURRENT in the default parameter and in the special values parameter. Any help on this one will be greatly appreciated.

A: You just need to give *CURRENT a numeric replacement value that won't correspond to a valid date. I generally use 999999. The code should look something like the following:

```
PARM KWD(DATE) TYPE(*DATE) DFT(*CURRENT)
           SPCVAL((*CURRENT 999999)) PROMPT('DATE')
```

In your program, you'll want to check for a value of 0999999 because the system will automatically append the century digit. Be sure to define your receiver variable in your CPP as TYPE(*CHAR) LEN(7). If your program receives 0999999, it means that *CURRENT was selected and you should replace this value with today's date; otherwise, the date will be passed in CYYMMDD format.

—Matt Seargent

Working with Date Fields in CL

I have found an effective method of manipulating date fields (data type L) in a CL program that must use Open Query File (OPNQRYF) to select records based on such database fields. The program in Figure 1.29 shows how.

```
PGM         PARM(&DATE1 &DATE2)

DCL         VAR(&DATE1) TYPE(*CHAR) LEN(6)
DCL         VAR(&DATE2) TYPE(*CHAR) LEN(6)
DCL         VAR(&FROM) TYPE(*CHAR) LEN(10)
DCL         VAR(&INVALID1) TYPE(*LGL) LEN(1)
DCL         VAR(&INVALID2) TYPE(*LGL) LEN(1)
DCL         VAR(&TO) TYPE(*CHAR) LEN(10)
DCL         VAR(&TRUE) TYPE(*LGL) LEN(1) VALUE('1')

CVTDAT      DATE(&DATE1) TOVAR(&FROM) FROMFMT(*MDY) +
              TOFMT(*ISO)
MONMSG      MSGID(CPF0000) EXEC(DO)
  CHGVAR      VAR(&INVALID1) VALUE(&TRUE)
  SNDPGMMSG   MSGID(CPF9898) MSGF(QCPFMSG) MSGDTA('Invalid +
                beginning date') MSGTYPE(*DIAG)
ENDDO

CVTDAT      DATE(&DATE2) TOVAR(&TO) FROMFMT(*MDY) +
              TOFMT(*ISO)
MONMSG      MSGID(CPF0000) EXEC(DO)
  CHGVAR      VAR(&INVALID2) VALUE(&TRUE)
  SNDPGMMSG   MSGID(CPF9898) MSGF(QCPFMSG) MSGDTA('Invalid +
                ending date') MSGTYPE(*DIAG)
ENDDO

IF          COND(&INVALID1 *OR &INVALID2) THEN(DO)
  SNDPGMMSG   MSGID(CPF9898) MSGF(QCPFMSG) MSGDTA('Invalid +
                date entered') MSGTYPE(*ESCAPE)
ENDDO

/* Select records between dates */
OVRDBF      FILE(X) SHARE(*YES)

OPNQRYF     FILE((X)) QRYSLT('SVCDAT = %RANGE("' *CAT '" +
              "' *CAT &TO *CAT '")') KEYFLD(*FILE)

/* Continue processing */
ENDPGM
```

Figure 1.29: This program demonstrates how to manipulate dates in CL.

First, the program runs the Convert Date (CVTDAT) command to convert the input dates (which arrive as 6-byte parameters) from the *MDY format to *ISO (which requires a 10-byte variable). The source format must match the format you use for your dates; if you use a format other than *MDY, you must make the appropriate modifications to both CVTDAT commands—in the FROMFMT parameter. Also, the target format must match the format used in the database fields; for this example, I picked *ISO, because that's what I use in my date fields.

CVTDAT issues an error message if the date it's trying to convert is invalid, and this error is trapped by the Monitor Message (MONMSG) command that follows each CVTDAT. Consequently, the program sets a logical value (&INVALID1 or &INVALID2) to signal the invalidity of either input date, and it sends a diagnostic message to the caller. After both input dates are checked and converted, the program sends an escape message if one or both input dates were invalid (thus terminating the program).

Finally, the OPNQRYF command is executed, with a Query Select (QRYSLT) parameter value build on the spot. In the example, the database date field is named SVCDAT, but it could be any field name you use in your own files. The QRYSLT expression examines SVCDAT to see if it falls within a range of values, which is delimited by the two input dates converted to *ISO.

—Keith Green

✦ ✦ ✦ Debugging

Encoding Job to Abend

Q: I was wondering if there is a way that a flag can be set in a CL program so that, when it ends, the system sends an "Ended Abnormally" message. I'd like a nighttime batch job that doesn't meet certain criteria (that I can trap for) to end without blowing up, but I still want the operator notified that something went wrong.

A: You can send an escape message to any program higher up in your program stack if you want to short-circuit the processing at intermediate levels. It's a handy trick once in a while. For example:

```
SNDPGMMSG MSGID(CPF9897) MSGF(QCPFMSG) MSGTYPE(*ESCAPE)
```

—Pete Hall

Two Easy Ways to Debug CL Programs

When I need to debug a CL program, I don't use the Start Debug (STRDBG) command. Instead, I enter the following command to force the commands in the program to be recorded in the job log:

```
CHGJOB LOGCLPGM(*YES)
```

After executing the program, I use the Display Job Log (DSPJOBLOG) command to check each command and parameter.

If this technique doesn't provide enough information, I insert the Dump CL Program (DMPCLPGM) command into the program. I recompile and run the program again; then I display the QPPGMDMP spooled file so that I can see all the variables used in the program.

—Jean-Jacques Risch

✦ ✦ ✦ Decompiling

Decompiling CL Programs

If you inadvertently delete the source code of a compiled CL program, you can retrieve the source (minus comments) with the Retrieve CL Source (RTVCLSRC) command. (Of course, if you had a good backup of the source, you would most likely want to restore the source from the backup copy.) The command's format is:

```
RTVCLSRC PGM(library/compiled_program_name) SRCFILE(library/QCLSRC) +
         SRCMBR(source_program_name)
```

This process will work only if the Allowed Retrieve Source (ALWRTVSRC) parameter of the original CL program has a value of *YES, which is the default value for the Create CL Program (CRTCLPGM) command.

—Midrange Computing Staff

✦ ✦ ✦ Display Files

Creating an Autorefresh Screen in CL

I wanted to monitor my network information and display it on a screen that would update itself automatically without any user intervention. I was able to accomplish this by employing the following technique.

1. Use the Override Display File (OVRDSPF) command to assign a maximum Wait Record (WAITRCD) time. Normally, this value is *NOMAX, which makes the file wait until a user presses Enter.

2. Write and read the display file record with the Send Receive File (SNDRCVF) command and specify WAIT(*NO). This causes the system to not wait for input from the user. Instead, the program continues to process the commands that follow the SNDRCVF command.

3. Code a WAIT command to cause the program to wait the number of seconds specified by the WAITRCD keyword of the OVRDSPF command executed previously. The WAIT command issues message CPF0889 when the WAITRCD time of the display file expires. Monitor for this message and, when it is detected, redisplay the record. The partial CL code shown in Figure 1.30 illustrates this technique:

```
OVRDSPF FILE(SCREENFM) WAITRCD(30)
.
.
.
LOOP: SNDRCVF RCDFMT(DELAY) WAIT(*NO)
IF COND(&IN12) THEN(GOTO +
CMDLBL(ENDPGM))
WAIT
MONMSG MSGID(CPF0889) EXEC(GOTO +
CMDLBL(LOOP))
.
.
.
ENDPGM: ENDPGM
```

Figure 1.30: Coding a combination of the WAIT and MONMSG commands makes the screen perform a refresh.

—*Ted Holt*

Creating CL Menus

Q: I wrote a CL program that acts like a menu when called, using a display file with the Send Receive File (SNDRCVF) command. It works great. I decided that I would like to be able to use the GO command so that it could be used like a normal menu such as GO MYMENU. I ran the Create Menu (CRTMNU) command and specified TYPE(*PGM). It created successfully. When I typed in GO MYMENU, I received an error message: "Total parameters passed does not match number required." I know what that normally means, but my CL program does not require any parameters. What's up?

A: The GO command passes parameters to the program that displays the menu. I have written entire articles on the subject, but to save you from having to research the article, the parameters needed are:

- CHAR(10). Name of the menu.
- CHAR(10). Library that contains the menu.
- BIN(2). Return code. If you're using CL, you can use CHAR(2).

The return code is an output parameter. Your program must set it to -1 if the user pressed F3 (use x'FFFF' in CL). If the user pressed F12, the program must set this parameter to -2 (x'FFFE' in CL). If the user pressed the Home key, set it to -4 (x'FFFC' in CL).

—Ernie Malaga

A: Use the User Interface Manager (UIM) menus. They are documented in the *Programming for Displays* manual (SC41-5715-00, QB3AUK00). You will be very pleasantly surprised with the ease and functionality you get. And you only need one object.

—Wayne James

How to Display Info Messages on Line 24

Q: I'm trying to duplicate IBM's method of displaying informational messages on line 24 of our AS/400 displays while processing an AS/400 command/program. I don't want to clear the display first—just display a short informational message on line 24 every few seconds as a CL program is running. How do I do this?

A: You need to use the Send Program Message (SNDPGMMSG) command, specifying MSGTYPE(*STATUS) TOPGMQ(*EXT). *STATUS messages require you to use the MSGID/MSGF/MSGDTA parameter trio instead of the MSG parameter; but you can use

MSGID(CPF9898) or MSGID(CPF9897) in QCPFMSG, specifying the text of your message in the MSGDTA parameter. The only difference between CPF9898 and CPF9897 is that CPF9898 adds a period after whatever you type in MSGDTA.

For example, suppose you want to send the following message while the CL program is running: "Now reorganizing Customer Master file. Please wait." You'd code the CL program as follows:

```
SNDPGMMSG MSGID(CPF9898) MSGF(QCPFMSG) MSGDTA('Now reorganizing +
    Customer Master file.  Please wait') +
    TOPGMQ(*EXT) MSGTYPE(*STATUS)
RGZPFM FILE(CUSTMAST)
```

Notice that the message text is in the MSGDTA parameter, minus the ending period; that's because CPF9898 automatically adds a final period.

The message will stay in line 24 until another status message is issued either by you or by IBM-supplied commands. (OPNQRYF, for example, sends status messages of its own.)

If you want to remove a message without sending another, send a blank status message using CPF9897:

```
SNDPGMMSG MSGID(CPF9897) MSGF(QCPFMSG) MSGDTA(' ') TOPGMQ(*EXT) +
          MSGTYPE(*STATUS)
```

This allows you to remove a message some time after sending it, when it is no longer relevant.

One final note. Both the user profile and the job have attributes to display or omit status messages. For example, you can use CHGJOB STSMSG(*NONE) to change your job so that no *STATUS messages are ever displayed.

—Ernie Malaga

Want to Timeout a Display?

My company's system has the system value Inactive Job Timeout (QINACTITV) set to 30 minutes. If a user walks away from the desk, we can automatically sign that user off. This works great except for those few terminals or user profiles we don't want to log off automatically. To get around this problem, we developed a little routine to monitor for a specific message ID (CPI1126) to be placed on a message queue (see Figure 1.31). Message CPI1126 indicates that a job has not been active for a given amount of time.

```
/*****************************************************************/
/* To Compile                                                   */
/* CRTCLPGM PGM(xxx/DEVTIMMON) +                                */
/* SRCFILE(xxx/QCLSRC) MBR(DEVTIMMON)                           */
/*                                                              */
/*****************************************************************/
PGM
DCL &JOB *CHAR 10 /* Job(WSID) Name */
DCL &JOBNO *CHAR 6 /* Job Number */
DCL &KEYVAR *CHAR 4 /* Key Var for retrieving response*/
DCL &MSG *CHAR 132 /* Message */
DCL &MSGDTA *CHAR 100 /* Message Data */
DCL &MSGDTALEN *DEC (5 0) +
     /* Message Data Length */ DCL &MSGID *CHAR 7 /* Message ID */
DCL &RTNTYPE *CHAR 2 /* Returned Message Type */
DCL &TYPE *CHAR 1 /* Job Type (0=Batch, 1=OnLine) */
DCL &USER *CHAR 10 /* User ID */
/* Retreive and assemble Required Job Attributes */
/* Also assure this job * HAS * been submitted to batch. */
RTVJOBA TYPE(&TYPE)
IF (&TYPE *EQ '1') (GOTO END) /* Not a Batch Process */
/* Put a low level lock on the message Q so no other copies of */
/* This job will be started. */
ALCOBJ OBJ((INACTIVE *MSGQ *EXCL)) WAIT(30)
MONMSG CPF1002 EXEC(GOTO END) /* Already Active */
ALCOBJ OBJ((INACTIVE *MSGQ *SHRRD)) WAIT(30)
DLCOBJ OBJ((INACTIVE *MSGQ *EXCL))
/* Change Inactive Message Handling to correct Message Queue */
CHGSYSVAL SYSVAL(QINACTMSGQ) VALUE('INACTIVE QGPL ')
/* Sit here until a message is recieved. */
MAINLOOP: RCVMSG MSGQ(INACTIVE) MSGTYPE(*ANY) WAIT(900) +
RMV(*YES) KEYVAR(&KEYVAR) MSG(&MSG) +
MSGDTA(&MSGDTA) MSGDTALEN(&MSGDTALEN) +
MSGID(&MSGID) +
RTNTYPE(&RTNTYPE)
/* Check to see what type of message was received from the Q */
IF (&MSGID *EQ 'CPI1126') THEN(GOTO INACTJOB)
GOTO MAINLOOP
/* An Inactive Job was Detected. */
/* Retreive and extract attributes of timed out job. */
INACTJOB: CHGVAR VAR(&JOB) VALUE(%SST(&MSGDTA 1 10))
CHGVAR VAR(&USER) VALUE(%SST(&MSGDTA 11 10))
CHGVAR VAR(&JOBNO) VALUE(%SST(&MSGDTA 21 6))
DMPCLPGM
/* DON'T CANCEL VRU JOBS */
IF COND(%SST(&JOB 1 3) *EQ 'VRU') THEN(DO)
```

Figure 1.31: While the system automatically ends some jobs, this routine allows you keep specific jobs or specific users active (part 1 of 2).

```
GOTO MAINLOOP
ENDDO
/* DON'T CANCEL CERTAIN USER JOBS */
/* ADD ALL USERS NECESSARY IN A SIMILAR IF LOOP BEFORE THE ENDJOB COMMAND
*/
IF COND(&USER *EQ 'TIM') THEN(DO)
GOTO MAINLOOP
ENDDO
/* If this is not a job we want to keep active, end it. */
ENDJOB JOB(&JOBNO/&USER/&JOB) OPTION(*IMMED) +
LOGLMT(0)
MONMSG CPF0000 GOTO MAINLOOP
END: DLCOBJ OBJ((INACTIVE *MSGQ *SHRRD))
CHGSYSVAL SYSVAL(QINACTMSGQ) VALUE('*ENDJOB')
CHGSYSVAL SYSVAL(QINACTITV) VALUE('120')
ENDPGM
```

Figure 1.31: While the system automatically ends some jobs, this routine allows you keep specific jobs or specific users active (part 2 of 2).

Buried within the text of the message is the name of the job that has exceeded the time limit specified in system value QINACTITV. The utility checks the job name and, if it matches a predetermined job (one we don't want to log off automatically), logoff is by-passed. We also can exempt certain users from being caught by this system value. Otherwise, if it is any other interactive job, we issue the ENDJOB command for that terminal to log it off. You need to create a new message queue named INACTIVE and point the Inactive Message Queue (QINACTMSGQ) system value to use the new message queue rather than the default message queue, QSYSOPR. This cuts down on the number of messages you need to read because the only messages going into this queue are about jobs that are timing out.

—Larry Bolhuis

✦ ✦ ✦ Editing Data

Editing Numbers in CL

Q: I have retrieved the number of records in a file and want to use that number in a message. Is there a way to move a number to text in CL?

A: If you want an edited number, there is an easy way to handle it. You can define a message in a message file and specify a message data field with a type of binary and a length of 2 or 4 bytes. (The maximum value of 2-byte binary numbers is 32,767; 4-byte binary numbers go up to 2,147,483,647.) In your CL program, define a 2- or 4-byte character value to contain the binary numeric value. Convert your decimal value to binary by using %BIN. To test this, try the program shown in Figure 1.32.

```
/*================================================================*/
/* To compile: */
/* */
/* CRTCLPGM PGM(XXX/EDTV00CL) SRCFILE(XXX/QCLSRC) */
/* */
/*================================================================*/
PGM
DCL VAR(&BIN) TYPE(*CHAR) LEN(4)
DCL VAR(&DEC) TYPE(*DEC) LEN(9 0)
CRTMSGF MSGF(QTEMP/TESTMSG)
ADDMSGD MSGID(TST0000) MSGF(TESTMSG) MSG('Number is &1') FMT((*BIN 4))
CHGVAR VAR(&DEC) VALUE(100)
CHGVAR VAR(%BIN(&BIN)) VALUE(&DEC)
SNDPGMMSG MSGID(TST0000) MSGF(TESTMSG) MSGDTA(&BIN)
ENDPGM
```

Figure 1.32: Here's a handy way to edit variables in CL.

—*David Morris*

Significant Trailing Blanks

To copy selected records that include trailing blanks into selection criteria, you need to use single quotes in the Copy File (CPYF) command's records by character test option. For example, if you need to copy all records from position one through four that contain the characters ABC followed by a blank, you must enter the value in single quotes ('ABC '). Otherwise, the system will consider only the leading, nonblank characters, and you will also get records that contain values like ABCD. Your CPYF command must look as follows:

```
CPYF FROMFILE(OLDFILE) TOFILE(NEWFILE) MBROPT(*ADD) +
     INCCHAR(*RCD 1 *EQ 'ABC ')
```

However, what if this CPYF command is in a CL program and record selection depends on a variable passed to the program? You might think you could replace the fourth value in the INCCHAR parameter with a variable, like this:

```
CPYF FROMFILE(OLDFILE) TOFILE(NEWFILE) MBROPT(*ADD) +
     INCCHAR(*RCD 1 *EQ &PATTERN)
```

If you do replace the fourth value, the CPYF command will ignore the trailing blanks on the &PATTERN and will match only the leading, nonblank characters. To make this work correctly, build the CPYF command in a CL variable to include single quotes in the command string, and call QCMDEXC to execute the command, as in Figure 1.33.

```
DCL VAR(&PATTERN) TYPE(*CHAR) LEN(4)
DCL VAR(&CMD) TYPE(*CHAR) LEN(512)
CHGVAR VAR(&CMD) VALUE('CPYF FROMFILE(QTEMP/ONE)TOFILE(QTEMP/TWO) MBROPT(*ADD) +
INCCHAR(*RCD 1 *EQ ''' *CAT &PATTERN *CAT ''') FMTOPT(*NOCHK)')
CALL PGM(QCMDEXC) PARM(&CMD 512)
```

Figure 1.33: Executing CPYF through QCMDEXC embeds needed single quotes in the INCCHAR parameter

—Ronald Katz

✦ ✦ ✦ Error Handling

Detect Diagnostic Messages

The Monitor Message (MONMSG) command can monitor only for escape, notify, and status messages. Diagnostic messages cannot be monitored. Here is a technique I use for detecting diagnostic messages using the Receive Message (RCVMSG) command.

The idea is to send a dummy message to the program message queue. Then, you can issue the command you want to monitor. Finally, you receive the messages in the program message queue starting from the last message and reading backward until you reach the dummy message that serves as an "end of messages" marker. Here's an example of how it works:

Suppose you want to know if one of two conditions occurred following the running of a Copy File (CPYF) command.

1. Was a FROMFILE member empty? (CPF2869)

2. Did we exceed the maximum allowable members in the file specified as TOFILE? (CPF3213)

Both of these messages are sent as diagnostic messages and cannot be monitored using the MONMSG command. See Figure 1.34 for an example of how this can be done.

```
              PGM

              DCL        VAR(&MSG) TYPE(*CHAR) LEN(7)
              DCL        VAR(&MSGID) TYPE(*CHAR) LEN(7)
              DCL        VAR(&MSGKEY) TYPE(*CHAR) LEN(4)

/* Put a dummy message in the program message queue               */
              SNDPGMMSG  MSG('@#@@##%') TOPGMQ(*SAME)

/* Do the CPYF                                                    */
              CPYF       FROMFILE(TESTPF) TOFILE(TEST2PF) +
                         FROMMBR(*ALL) TOMBR(*FROMMBR) +
                         MBROPT(*REPLACE) FMTOPT(*NOCHK)
              MONMSG     MSGID(CPF0000)

/* Get the last message                                           */
              RCVMSG     MSGTYPE(*LAST) RMV(*NO) KEYVAR(&MSGKEY) +
                         MSG(&MSG) MSGID(&MSGID)

/* Check to see if this is the dummy message. If so, quit         */
  LOOP:       IF         COND(&MSG *EQ '@#@@##%') THEN(GOTO +
                         CMDLBL(NEXT))

/* See if this is the "empty member in from file" message.        */
              IF         COND(&MSGID *EQ 'CPF2869') THEN(DO)
  /*         ...insert code to process this error...               */
              ENDDO

/* See if this is the "more members than allowed" message         */
              IF         COND(&MSGID *EQ 'CPF3213') THEN(DO)
  /*         ...insert code to process this error...               */
              ENDDO

/* Receive the next message.                                      */
              RCVMSG     MSGTYPE(*PRV) MSGKEY(&MSGKEY) RMV(*NO) +
                         KEYVAR(&MSGKEY) MSG(&MSG) MSGID(&MSGID)

              GOTO       CMDLBL(LOOP)

NEXT:
/* Rest of program...                                             */

              ENDPGM
```

Figure 1.34: Checking for unmonitorable messages can be handled as shown in this code sample.

Another way to accomplish this would be to use the command RMVMSG CLEAR(*ALL) to remove all messages from the program message queue before doing the CPYF. Then you would simply start from the last message and read backward until there were no more messages. However, the RMVMSG command also removes messages from your job log.

By sending a message as a "marker" and reading back to it, the messages in your job log are preserved.

—Mike Cravitz

✦ ✦ ✦ File Processing

Be Careful When Using the INCREL Parameter of the CPYF Command

Be careful how you use the Copy File (CPYF) command with the Include Relationships (INCREL) parameter. The CL program shown in Figure 1.35 demonstrates one problem you might run into.

```
PGM
DCL VAR(&NAME) TYPE(*CHAR) LEN(10) +
VALUE('Rob ')
/* Copy file using a literal in the INCREL parameter */
CPYF FROMFILE(MYLIB/CUSTOMER) +
TOFILE(QTEMP/CUSTOMER) MBROPT(*REPLACE) +
CRTFILE(*YES) INCREL((*IF FIRSTNAME *EQ +
'Rob '))
/* Copy file using a variable in the INCREL parameter */
CPYF FROMFILE(MYLIB/CUSTOMER) +
TOFILE(QTEMP/CUSTOMER) MBROPT(*REPLACE) +
CRTFILE(*YES) INCREL((*IF FIRSTNAME *EQ +
&NAME))
ENDPGM
```

Figure 1.35: An example program demonstrates the kinds of problems you might encounter using the CPYF command with the INCREL parameter.

While both CPYF commands are the same, with the exception of the literal 'Rob' in the first CPYF and the field containing 'Rob' in the second CPYF, the results of the two commands might surprise you. The first CPYF command with the literal will select only records in which the first name is Rob. The second CPYF command, however, will select any name that begins with Rob (e.g., Rob, Robert, Robin, Robinson).

This happens because all trailing blanks are ignored when using a CL variable in the INCREL parameter on the CPYF command. Then, a left-to-right comparison is performed with the database field for only the length of the truncated CL variable.

—David Wilson

✦ ✦ ✦ Formatting Data

Creating Comma-delimited Text Files

Do you need to create a comma-delimited text file on your PC but don't want to spend a lot of time doing it? Check out the code shown in Figure 1.36. This is a very quick way to create your comma-delimited text file and send it to the PC.

```
/*****************************************************************************/
/* To Create:                                                             */
/* Crtclpgm Pgm(xxx/DM01) Srcfil(xxx/Qclsrc) MBR(DM01)                    */
/*****************************************************************************/
PGM
CPYTOIMPF FROMFILE(DAVID/CFM10P) +
TOSTMF('QDLS/DAVID/CFM10P.TXT') +
RCDDLM(*CRLF) STRDLM('"')
CHGDOCD DOC(CFM10P.TXT) FLR('DAVID') +
DOCD('Comma Delimited Text Fie')
SNDDST TYPE(*DOC) TOINTNET((USER@DOMAIN.COM)) +
DSTD('Recipient Distribution Directory') +
MSG('Message Text') DOC(CFM10P.TXT) +
FLR(DAVID)
ENDPGM
```

Figure 1.36: Here's a quick way to create a comma-delimited text file on your PC.

—David Morris

Professional Format

A problem with using numbers in messages in CL is that, when you convert them to text for displaying in the message description, you're stuck with leading zeros. This looks pretty amateurish, but there is a better way that will give your messages a "professional" look. What you need to do is edit the numbers in the CL program before you convert them to text. Here's how.

Define a message in a message file by using the Add Message Description (ADDMSGD) command, and specify a message variable with a type of binary and a length of 2 or 4 bytes. In your CL program, define a 2- or 4-byte character value to contain the binary numeric value. Convert your decimal value to binary by using the %BIN function. Next, use the converted variable in the Send Program Message (SNDPGMMSG) command. Figure 1.37 shows an example of how to do this.

```
/**************************************************************************/
/* To Create:                                                           */
/* CRTCLPGM PGM(XXXLIB/DM001C) SRCFIL(XXXLIB/QCLSRC)                     */
/**************************************************************************/
PGM
DCL VAR(&BIN) TYPE(*CHAR) LEN(4)
DCL VAR(&DEC) TYPE(*DEC) LEN(9 0)
/* Create a temporary message file */
CRTMSGF MSGF(QTEMP/TESTMSGF)
/* Add a message to the message file */
ADDMSGD MSGID(TST0000) MSGF(QTEMP/TESTMSGF) +
MSG('Number is &1') FMT((*BIN 4))
/* Set the variable to a number */
CHGVAR VAR(&DEC) VALUE(100)
/* Change the variable to a binary value using %BIN */
CHGVAR VAR(%BIN(&BIN)) VALUE(&DEC)
/* Send the message using the SNDPGMMSG command */
SNDPGMMSG MSGID(TST0000) MSGF(QTEMP/TESTMSGF) +
MSGDTA(&BIN)
ENDPGM
```

Figure 1.37: Here's a way to add edited numbers to messages in CL.

—*David Morris*

Variable-length Edit Words?

Q: We want to pass an edit word and nine-digit decimal value with two decimal places to a program and receive back an edited string. The called program uses the QECCVTEW and QECEDT APIs to carry out the editing.

We would like the capability of choosing whether or not the edited string includes a floating dollar sign. Here's our problem: Edit words that include a floating dollar sign have to be one character larger than those that do not include the dollar sign. Passing an edit word that is too long or too short generates a CPF27AF error.

Is it possible to include a dollar sign sometimes and omit it other times?

A: An edit word has to have a blank for each digit. Because you're passing in a nine-digit number, you'll need nine blanks. A zero (to end zero suppression) can count for one of the digits. Therefore, the edit word must be 12 characters long (nine for the digits, one for the decimal point, and two for the commas.)

If you want a floating dollar sign, you'll have to make the edit word one character larger. Otherwise, one of the digits won't fit when the first digit is not zero. If you want to be able to pass in a dollar sign sometimes and not pass one in at other times, use two different edit words. One will have the dollar sign, and the other will have a leading or trailing ampersand (&), which forces a blank. Your two 13-byte edit words would be as shown below:

```
'bb,bbb,b$0.bb'
```

and

```
'b,bbb,bbb.bb&'
```

So, you don't need two different-sized edit words.

—Ted Holt

✦ ✦ ✦ Integrated File System

What Page Are You On?

Converting the code page (i.e., translating EBCDIC to ASCII) of a file on the AS/400 Integrated File System (AS/400 IFS) is much simpler than you might think. You can simply run the Copy to Import File (CPYTOIMPF) command and then use the Move (MOV) command, specifying the OBJ and TOOBJ parameters with the TOCODEPAGE(*PCASCII) and DTAFMT(*TEXT) parameter values. Doing this will convert the file "in place." Here is an example:

```
MOV OBJ('\mydir\test.ebc') +
TOOBJ('\mydir\test.txt') +
TOCODEPAGE(*PCASCII) DTAFMT(*TEXT)
```

I have written a utility that addresses this EBCDIC-to-ASCII conversion issue as well as the issue of using the AS/400 IFS directory structure in development, test, and production environments. Figure 1.38 shows the Copy to (AS/400) IFS (CPYTOIFS) command. The command processing program (CPP) CPYTOIFSC and the help panel group for the command are on the companion CD-ROM. To execute the command, enter CPYTOIFSC on a command line and press Enter. This utility will handle all of your AS/400 IFS copying needs.

```
/*==============================================================*/
/* To compile:                                                  */
/*                                                              */
/* CRTCMD CMD(XXX/CPYTOIFS) PGM(XXX/CPYTOIFSC) +                */
/* SRCFILE(XXX/QCMDSRC) HLPPNLGRP(XXX/CPYTOIFSH)                */
/*                                                              */
/*==============================================================*/
CMD PROMPT('Copy To Standard IFS File')
PARM KWD(FROMFILE) TYPE(QUAL1) MIN(1) +
PROMPT('From file' 1)
QUAL1: QUAL TYPE(*NAME) LEN(10) MIN(1) EXPR(*YES)
QUAL TYPE(*NAME) LEN(10) DFT(*LIBL) +
SPCVAL((*LIBL) (*CURLIB)) PROMPT('Library')
PARM KWD(TOSTMD) TYPE(*PNAME) LEN(50) MIN(1) +
PROMPT('To stream directory')
PARM KWD(TOSTMF) TYPE(*CHAR) LEN(8) MIN(1) +
PROMPT('To stream file')
PARM KWD(MBROPT) TYPE(*CHAR) LEN(8) RSTD(*YES) +
DFT(*ADD) VALUES(*ADD *REPLACE) +
PROMPT('Replace to add records')
PARM KWD(CVTOPT) TYPE(*CHAR) LEN(4) RSTD(*YES) +
DFT(*CSV) VALUES(*CSV) PROMPT('Conversion +
option')
PARM KWD(FILESYS) TYPE(*CHAR) LEN(5) RSTD(*YES) +
DFT(*ROOT) VALUES(*ROOT *QDLS) +
PROMPT('File system')
/* FROMMBR placed here but is prompted after FROMFILE */
/* This is so &FROMMBR can have a default before required &TOSTMD */
PARM KWD(FROMMBR) TYPE(*NAME) LEN(10) DFT(*FIRST) +
SPCVAL((*FIRST)) PROMPT('From member' 2)
```

Figure 1.38: CPYTOIFS is used to copy AS/400 IFS files and perform EBCDIC-to-ASCII conversions.

Here are some things to keep in mind when using this utility:

- The command includes the "Order prompt is displayed" value for the PROMPT keyword of the last PARM statement (FROMMBR). This allows the FROMMBR keyword, which is a default value, to be listed before the other parameters that have required fields when the command is prompted. Note, too, that CL lists parameters in the same order as the command source.

- The MOV statement handles the conversion of EBCDIC to ASCII on the AS/400 IFS.

- QDLS is allowed, because the SNDDST TYPE(*DOC) command can be used to send an email with an AS/400 IFS file as an attachment only if it is in the QDLS file system.

- The first seven characters of the group profile are used as the "Environment" directory (that is a standard in our shop). The directory could be changed to use all 10 characters of the group profile or even to use the special value "~" with the group profile appended as the first characters of the path to use the group profile's "Home" directory as specified in the Create User Profile (CRTUSRPRF) command.

While I was working on this code, I made a few hard-won discoveries that I'll share with you here so that you won't have to attend the School of Hard Knocks as I did. When a CLP is written to copy an AS/400 file to an ASCII-delimited file on the AS/400 IFS, it is usual for the programmer to hardcode the directory to which the file is being copied. This is a problem in structured environments where a given program uses the library list to access files based on the current environment (test versus production, for example). At my company, I have created a set of rules that define specific AS/400 IFS directories to use based on the environment. The environment is defined using the current user's group profile. This provides a separate "environment" for AS/400 IFS directories when in test versus production. See the structure shown in Figure 1.39.

```
MYAS400
PRODGRP
Application1
Application2
Application3
TESTGRP
Application1
Application2
Application3
PGMRGRP
Application1
Application2
Application3
```

Figure 1.39: This figure demonstrates the possible environment structure you might have on your system.

When you develop a new application that requires an AS/400 IFS directory, that directory is created under each environment directory. Using the CPYTOIFS utility, included here, you can easily copy files and objects from one environment to another without the need for hard coding paths.

—Michael Hagey

✦ ✦ ✦ IPL

A Onetime Startup Program Can Save You Work During an IPL

Some system maintenance can be done only when the machine has no users. Examples are changes to subsystem descriptions, deleting or moving files that are normally open, and applying PTFs to Licensed Program Products (LPP). If you IPL the system during off-hours, you normally have to change your startup program to do these things for you, each time they need to be done, or do them manually.

If you add the following lines to your system startup program before it starts any subsystems, you can create programs on the fly to take care of these tasks:

```
CALL PGM(IPLPGMCL)
MONMSG MSGID(CPF0000)
DLTPGM PGM(IPLPGMCL)
MONMSG MSGID(CPF0000)
```

An example of a program to call is shown in Figure 1.40. Just add what needs to be done and compile the program. The next time the system is IPLed, your program object will be called, your tasks will be run, and the program object will be deleted. Deleting the program will keep it from being called twice.

```
PGM
            MONMSG      MSGID(CPF0000)

/* Insert onetime code here */

            DSPJOBLOG   OUTPUT(*PRINT)
            HLDSPLF     FILE(QPJOBLOG) SPLNBR(*LAST)

/* If you have more than one AS/400, send the joblog */
            SNDNETSPLF FILE(QPJOBLOG) TOUSRID((PLUTH MCEDIT)) +
                        SPLNBR(*LAST)
            DLTSPLF     FILE(QPJOBLOG) SPLNBR(*LAST)

            ENDPGM
```

Figure 1.40: Use this program as an example of what you might call in your own one-time startup program.

You should take some safety measures when using this technique. First, because the system will need user intervention to answer error messages if your program fails, you should include a global Monitor Message (MONMSG) command in IPLPGMCL. To see if everything was successful, force the creation of a job log. You can even have the program send the job log to your central AS/400 if you have more than one system.

If your startup program adopts authority, this technique will create a security exposure. To eliminate it, create a library that can be accessed only by the profile that owns the startup program. Place the onetime program in this library. You can then hardcode the CALL in the startup program, preventing anyone from creating a onetime program in another library in the library list that will inherit the caller's authority.

—Martin Pluth

✦ ✦ ✦ Library Lists

Changing a Command

Q: I want to restrict users from running queries interactively. I used the Change Command (CHGCMD) command as outlined in the *Query* manual. Then I wanted to grant DP personnel the authority to run queries interactively, so I created a duplicate object of the command and placed it in another library, as discussed in the book *Query/400 Use* (SC41-5210-00, QB3AGG00). Then the book says to place that library in front of QSYS in my *LIBL. Is there an easy way to do that? QSYS is the first library in my system library list.

A: The way to change the system portion of the library list depends on the scope you want for this change.

If you want all users to share the same system portion of the library list, change system value QSYSLIBL; the easiest way to do this is from the WRKSYSVAL command, selecting option 2. In this way you get a convenient data entry panel.

If you want some users to have a different system portion of the library list, you'll have to change their initial (sign-on) program, including one or more Change System Library List (CHGSYSLIBL) commands. The CHGSYSLIBL command changes the current job's copy of the system portion of the library list, without affecting other jobs on the system. With CHGSYSLIBL, you can add a library at the top or remove a library.

Because you want some users to run your changed command and your programmers to run the original command, you'll have to use the second method with CHGSYSLIBL. Otherwise, all users would use the duplicate command you created.

Let's assume you've changed QSYS/RUNQRY to remove *INTERACT from the ALLOW parameter (thereby not allowing it to run interactively), and have created an ALTQSYS/RUNQRY command that does include *INTERACT, for your programmers. ALTQSYS is the name of the library where you've created the duplicate RUNQRY command.

Your regular users should not run any CHGSYSLIBL commands, in order to use the system portion of the library list as QSYSLIBL dictates with QSYS on top. Your programmers need to run the following command in their initial program:

```
CHGSYSLIBL LIB(ALTQSYS) OPTION(*ADD)
```

In this way, ALTQSYS is placed ahead of QSYS in the system portion of the library list (for that job only). As a consequence, the duplicate command would be found (allowing *INTERACT) instead of the changed QSYS command.

By the way, I'd recommend you proceed the other way around. First, create a copy in ALTQSYS, then change the ALTQSYS copy—not the original. As much as possible, it's better to leave QSYS objects alone.

—Ernie Malaga

A: Do a CHGCMD to RUNQRY with ALLOW(*IPGM) but no ALLOW (*INTERACT). This allows a CL program that is run interactively to use the command, but does not allow anyone to just do RUNQRY from a command line. Without this change, any compiled program can use the command regardless of whether it was submitted to batch or run interactively.

—David Wallen

Flexible Library References

Some commands such as Create Duplicate Object (CRTDUPOBJ) require a library name, but hard coding a library name in a CL program is something you should try to avoid. A better method is to use the RTNLIB parameter of the Retrieve Object Description (RTVOBJD) command to retrieve the library name. For example, to retrieve the library where WKFILE resides, use the RTVOBJD command as follows:

```
RTVOBJD OBJ(WKFILE) OBJTYPE(*FILE) RTNLIB(&LIB)
```

The value in the RTNLIB parameter could then be used in any command, including those that require a library name to specify the library. The WKFILE file could be moved to any library in your library list and any program that uses the above command would still work. No program changes would be required. The library where the file exists could even be renamed without affecting the programs.

—Midrange Computing Staff

So You Thought You Knew the *LIBL

If you have the same file name in two different libraries in your library list and you reference the file with *LIBL and a specific member, the system searches the first library looking for the file and member. If the file is found in the first library but it doesn't contain the requested member, the search continues without notification.

We were expecting to get a "Member not found" error when the system found the file without the correct member in the first library. It didn't, but rather continued the search, finding the file and member in the second library and using that occurrence.

—Gary M. Mayfield

✦ ✦ ✦ Locks

Are You Busy?

Even though the Allocate Object (ALCOBJ) command is normally used in a routing step to reserve an object for later use, it also can be used to determine if an object is in use. This could be helpful in any job that requires an exclusive use of an object.

Running ALCOBJ with a lock-state parameter value of *EXCL (Exclusive, no read) against the object in question and subsequently monitoring message (MONMSG) CPF1002, you can determine if the object is busy.

—Midrange Computing Staff

Running Only One Copy of a Program

Sometimes, you must ensure that only one occurrence of a program is running at a time. On the S/36, the operation control language (OCL) allowed you to test whether a program was running with the statement IF ACTIVE-*procname*. This statement could be executed from an OCL procedure that had the name being tested, but the test would yield a true value only if another copy of the same procedure was already running. Strangely enough, even though this statement functioned properly on an AS/400 in a S/36 environment (which meant the system was capable of doing that), the same ability does not exist in native CL programming.

IBM offered a solution to this by using a data area to set a flag (thus indicating that the program was running). The flag is then cleared when the program finishes. The problem with this solution is that the flag is not reset if the program fails for any reason.

A simple, self-cleaning solution to this test is the Allocate Object (ALCOBJ) command, shown in Figure 1.41. By allocating an exclusive lock on the program object, you force any other occurrence of the program to receive error CPF1002 (Cannot allocate object *xxx*). That error message can be handled with a wait loop, a wait loop with a counter, or an immediate end. In the event the program terminates abnormally, the lock is automatically released.

```
PGM

    /* Allocate the program to indicate the job has begun */
    /* and runs exclusively */

ALLOCATE:
    ALCOBJ      OBJ((library/program *PGM *EXCL)) WAIT(0)
    MONMSG      MSGID(CPF1002) EXEC(DO)
      DLYJOB      DLY(60)
      GOTO        CMDLBL(ALLOCATE)
    ENDDO

    /* The above loop could have a counter, which when */
    /* exceeded would send a message and exit the loop */
    /* or it could end immediately.                    */
    CALL        PGM(library/program)

    /* Continue with batch process */

    /* Deallocate the program to indicate the job has finished */
    DLCOBJ      OBJ((library/program *PGM *EXCL))

ENDPGM
```

Figure 1.41: You can use the ALCOBJ command to determine if a job is currently active.

—Gary C. Mulock

✦ ✦ ✦ Message Processing

Automatically Replying to Inquiry Messages

Programs send escape messages when something goes wrong. The CL Monitor Message (MONMSG) command lets you trap these error messages so that you don't have to handle them manually. However, MONMSG does not work for inquiry messages. Suppose you try to delete a journal receiver that has not been saved to disk. As your AS/400 is shipped, you'll receive inquiry message CPA7025 [Receiver &1 in &2 never fully saved. (I C)]. You can use the Inquiry Message Reply (INQMSGRPY) parameter of the Change Job (CHGJOB) command to answer these messages automatically.

The default reply to CPA7025 is "I" (meaning the system should delete the journal receiver, even though it has not been saved). In that case, you could use code like this in a CL program:

```
CHGJOB INQMSGRPY(*DFT)
DLTJRNRCV JRNRCV(&RCV)
```

Another possible setting of INQMSGRPY is *SYSRPYL, which makes the job use the system reply list. Add reply list entries for the messages you want answered automatically, like this:

```
ADDRPYLE SEQNBR(80)MSGID(CPA7025) RPY('I')
```

Then, make your program use the system reply list like this:

```
CHGJOB INQMSGRPY(*SYSRPYL)
DLTJRNRCV JRNRCV(&RCV)
```

Of course, this changes the way the job handles inquiry messages from this point. If you'd like to use the default reply for only one command, save the current setting and restore it after deleting the journal receiver, like this:

```
DCL &INQMSGRPY *CHAR 10
RTVJOBA INQMSGRPY(&INQMSGRPY)
CHGJOB INQMSGRPY(*DFT)
DLTJRNRCV JRNRCV(&RCV)
CHGJOB INQMSGRPY(&INQMSGRPY)
```

—Ted Holt

Display Status Messages in Reverse Image

To display status messages in reverse image, define two single-character fields to hold the hex code for display attributes: one to contain the reverse-image attribute byte and one to contain the normal attribute byte. Then, concatenate these fields with your message field, as the partial program in Figure 1.42 illustrates.

```
DCL VAR(&REVERSE) TYPE(*CHAR) LEN(1) VALUE(X'21')
DCL VAR(&NORMAL) TYPE(*CHAR) LEN(1) VALUE(X'20')
SNDPGMMSG MSGID(CPF9898) MSGF(QCPFMSG) +
MSGDTA(&REVERSE *CAT &MSG *CAT &NORMAL) + TOPGMQ(*EXT) +
MSGTYPE(*STATUS)
```

Figure 1.42: Use variables to hold the display attributes to display messages in reverse image.

Get Rid of Status Messages

When you run a CL program that performs a Copy File (CPYF) or Open Query File (OPNQRYF) command, you usually see a status message such as "Copying member or label..."or "Query running..." at the bottom of the screen. Sometimes, you don't want the user to see these messages or you want to show your own message. Placing the following command into your CL program easily does the trick:

```
CHGJOB STSMSG(*NONE)
```

—*Jean-Jacques Risch*

IBM-supplied Completion Message

For interactive jobs, I like to give the users IBM-supplied messages whenever possible (such as the completion message after a Submit Job (SBMJOB) command). This can be accomplished by adding a few extra lines within a CL program. See Figure 1.43 for an example.

```
          PGM
          DCL       VAR(&MSG) TYPE(*CHAR) LEN(512)
          SBMJOB    CMD(CALL PGM(pgm-name)) JOB(job-name)
          RCVMSG    MSGTYPE(*COMP) MSG(&MSG)
          MONMSG    MSGID(CPF0000) EXEC(GOTO CMDLBL(EXIT))
          SNDPGMMSG MSG(&MSG) MSGTYPE(*COMP)
EXIT:     ENDPGM
```

Figure 1.43: Sending a completion message in your CL program is easy. Use the code shown here as your guide.

The IBM-supplied completion message for SBMJOB is sent to the previous program queue.

—Rick Brandl

Message ID CPF9898

Q: In many CL programs, I keep noticing SNDPGMMSG MSGID(CPF9898). Then the message goes on to be unique by having different stuff in the MSGDTA parameter. I think I've missed something along the way. What's so special about using CPF9898?

A: What is so special about CPF9898 is that it's a general-purpose message description that, except a period at the end, has no constant portions. Instead of being something like:

```
File &1 in &2 not found.
```

(where you can replace only &1 and &2 for the name of a file and its library, but the rest of the message remains constant), CPF9898 is just this:

```
&1.
```

When you feed the text you want to display through MSGDTA, it is displayed with a period at the end. If you don't want the period, use CPF9897 instead. In real-life applications, you should always create your own message descriptions instead of using CPF9898. By creating them, you can include many things (such as numeric variables) that CPF9898 cannot accommodate. Besides, the MSGDTA parameter won't have to include the entire text of the message.

—Midrange Computing Staff

Monitoring Job Completion Messages

If you would like to access your completed job messages without having to look for them with a Display Message (DSPMSG) command and you do not want the annoyance of break messages interrupting your current work, try the Monitor Message (MONMSG) message handling program shown in Figure 1.44.

```
/*================================================================*/
/* To compile:                                                    */
/*                                                                */
/*          CRTCLPGM   PGM(XXX/MONMSG) SRCFILE(XXX/QCLSRC) +      */
/*                     TEXT('Display completed job messages')     */
/*                                                                */
/*================================================================*/
PGM         PARM(&MSGQ &MSGQLIB &MSGK)

   DCL      VAR(&MSGDTA) TYPE(*CHAR) LEN(132)
   DCL      VAR(&MSGK) TYPE(*CHAR) LEN(4)
   DCL      VAR(&MSGQ) TYPE(*CHAR) LEN(10)
   DCL      VAR(&MSGQLIB) TYPE(*CHAR) LEN(10)

   RCVMSG   MSGQ(&MSGQLIB/&MSGQ) MSGKEY(&MSGK) RMV(*NO) +
              MSG(&MSGDTA)
   SNDPGMMSG MSGID(CPF9897) MSGF(QCPFMSG) MSGDTA(&MSGDTA) +
              TOPGMQ(*EXT) MSGTYPE(*STATUS)

   ENDPGM
```

Figure 1.44: Use the MONMSG CL program to access completed job messages.

After compiling program MONMSG, execute the following command to cause your completion messages to appear unobtrusively as status messages at the bottom of your screen. You might add this command to your initial program or setup routine:

```
CHGMSGQ MSGQ(current_message_queue) DLVRY(*BREAK) PGM(MONMSG)
```

It works by changing a message queue to *BREAK delivery mode and specifying a message-handling program. This will cause OS/400 to call the MONMSG program each time a message arrives at the message queue. MONMSG will then send the message to the external program message queue.

—*Bill O'Toole*

Mysterious Message IDs

Q: I have to work on a CL program and it has the following MONMSGs: TKM0075 and CPF9841. Not knowing what command uses them makes it hard to look up something in the CL book. I would appreciate any help. Thanks.

A: If you don't know what a MONMSG is monitoring for, you could use something like DSPMSGD CPF9841 to display the message text and details. If the message is not in QCPFMSG, as in the case of TKM0075, you must supply the MSGF name.

If you want to find out which IBM commands might issue a given CPF message, the easiest way is to use the CD-ROM and do a search for the message ID in book SYSSUM.BOO, which is *Programming: Reference Summary*, SX41-0028-00, Chapter 7, CD topic section number 2.3. Then use Ctrl-F4 to move to each occurrence. For message CPF9841, it is only listed in DLTOVR and DLTOVRDEVE for V2R1M0.

The TKM0075 message must be from a program product or user application I'm not familiar with. Try QUSERMSG or see if the CL references any other message files in the MSGF parameter.

Also, when looking at MONMSG statements, don't forget that entries ending with *xx*00 or 0000 are generic entries, not specific messages.

—Douglas Handy

Using Predefined Messages

Q: If you have messages defined with multiple parameters—such as FILE, LIB, and MEMBER parameters—how do you actually pass the variable data into those parameters from a CL program? Those parameters aren't really defined variables within your CL program. I can see how having just the &1 variable would work with the MSGDTA parameter, but how would it handle multiple variables?

A: Every time you have predefined substitution variables in a message description, the message description knows the format and length of each variable. Suppose you want to create a message description in MYLIB/MYMSGF, which goes like this:

```
Program &1 in &2 not found.
```

This message description is to have an ID of PGM0001. This is the command you use to create the message description:

```
ADDMSGD MSGID(PGM0001) MSGF(MYLIB/MYMSGF) +
    MSG('Program &1 in &2 not found.') FMT((*CHAR 10) (*CHAR 10))
```

This means that, when you send PGM0001 with the Send Program Message (SNDPGMMSG) command, the MSGDTA parameter's value will be assigned as follows: the first 10 characters to &1, the next 10 characters to &2. Therefore:

```
SNDPGMMSG MSGID(PGM0001) MSGF(MYLIB/MYMSGF) +
          MSGDTA('PGM1      PRODLIB') +
          MSGTYPE(*DIAG)
```

sends PGM0001 as a diagnostic message, and will read: Program PGM1 in PRODLIB not found.

Optionally, you can use a CL variable in the MSGDTA parameter and set its value before running SNDPGMMSG. See Figure 1.45. The &PGM and &LIB objects are both TYPE (*CHAR) LEN(10).

```
DCL VAR(&MSGDTA) TYPE(*CHAR) LEN(80)    /* LEN(80) as example */
  :
  CHKOBJ OBJ(&LIB/&PGM) OBJTYPE(*PGM)
  MONMSG MSGID(CPF9801) EXEC(DO)
     CHGVAR VAR(&MSGDTA) VALUE(&PGM *CAT &LIB)
     SNDPGMMSG MSGID(PGM0001) MSGF(MYLIB/MYMSGF) MSGDTA(&MSGDTA) +
        MSGTYPE(*ESCAPE)
     RETURN
  ENDDO
```

Figure 1.45: Using predefined messages in a CL program is easy.

———*Midrange Computing Staff*

✦ ✦ ✦ OPNQRYF

Let the Query Optimizer Do the Work for You

Recently, we had a situation where a job began taking 10 times longer to run than it ever had before. Upon further analysis, it turned out that most of the extra time was spent in the IDX-filename (index build) step associated with an Open Query File (OPNQRYF) command. As far as we knew, the program containing the OPNQRYF command had not changed in months. So, what had happened?

We called IBM, and one of its database experts asked me to start Debug with the Update Production Files (UPDPROD) set to *YES. After doing that, we ran the OPNQRYF interactively. When it was finished, we displayed the job log and found a message generated by the Query Optimizer. This message suggested a permanent index be built via a logical file (or even a keyed physical file). It also identified the field names and the order in which they should appear in the index! In this particular application, the field names that the Optimizer chose didn't appear to make sense because they weren't part of the sort fields in the query. Thinking it was worth a shot anyway, I created the new logical, using the fields defined by the Optimizer, and re-ran the query. Amazingly, the query runtime went from 20 minutes to five seconds!

—Van C. Baker

✦ ✦ ✦ OS/400

Determining the Version and Release Level of OS/400

If you are writing software for multiple AS/400s, or if your job requires you to program on more than one AS/400, you've probably worked on more than one release of OS/400 at the same time. Sometimes, the ability of your software to function correctly is dependent upon a particular release level of the operating system. For example, you might need to call a certain program or command if your software is running on a CISC machine and call a different program or command if it is running on a RISC machine. So, how can you programmatically check the OS/400 level? Simply insert the code fragment, shown in Figure 1.46, in your CL program, and then execute the appropriate commands (depending on the release of the operating system). The OS level will be returned as a 9-byte character variable of the format V*xx*R*xx*M*xx*, where *xx* indicates version, release, and modification level numbers in two-digit format.

```
DCL VAR(&VRM) TYPE(*CHAR) LEN(9)
RTVOBJD OBJ(QSYS) OBJTYPE(*LIB) SYSLVL(&VRM)
```

Figure 1.46: Determining the version and release level of OS/400 can be accomplished using a CL program.

—T. V. S. Murthy

Retrieve the OS Level in CL

Q: How can I retrieve the system operating level from within a CLP? I need to put it into a variable to test against.

A: Although there are many indirect ways to find the operating system level of an AS/400, the supported approach is to use the Retrieve Product Information (QSZRTVPR) API documented in the "Software Products" chapter of the *System API Reference* manual (SC41-4800, CD-ROM QBJAVC00). By using special values of *OPSYS for Product ID and *CUR for Release Level, you need to know only that you are running on an AS/400 at V2R3 or later. Figure 1.47 illustrates how to use this API.

```
DCL VAR(&RCVVAR) TYPE(*CHAR) LEN(256)
DCL VAR(&RELEASE) TYPE(*CHAR) LEN(6)
CALL PGM(QSZRTVPR) PARM(&RCVVAR X'00000100' 'PRDR0100' +
'*OPSYS *CUR 0000*CODE ' X'00000000')
CHGVAR VAR(&RELEASE) VALUE(%SST(&RCVVAR 20 6))
```

Figure 1.47: Another way to determine the system release level is demonstrated here.

—Bruce Vining

✦ ✦ ✦ Parameters

On CALLing and PARMing

Q: I have a program I'd like to be able to CALL but also run from a menu. When I run it from the menu, I receive an error that says that I didn't pass the parameter. Is there a way to override this message?

A: You can do two things:

1. Change your menu so that the program is called passing dummy parameters such as blanks or zeros. The called program will have to be modified, of course, to recognize this situation as valid.

2. If the called program is an RPG program, you can use the program-status data structure to retrieve the number of parameters that were received by the program. I don't have the manuals with me here, so I can't tell you where in the data structure you'll find this information. As long as your program does-n't attempt to use the parameters it didn't receive, it should run okay. CL doesn't have this capability—you must always supply all parameters when you call the program.

—Ernie Malaga

A: In RPG, you can call the program without passing any parameters to it, provided you never use the PARM field in the called program if it was not passed. To find out if any pa-rameters were passed to the called program, you can check the *PARMS subfield in the program status data structure.

—Tibor Reich

A: In CL, the program status data structure contains predefined subfields that provide information about the program and the exception/error conditions that occur. It is defined by using an S in position 18 of the data structure statement. Look in the *RPG/400 Reference Guide* for more information and subfield sizes and contents.

—*Greg Leister*

Passing CL Parameters

Q: I'm trying to submit a report job from within a CL program, and I get a decimal data error in the called program. (Figure 1.48 shows the CL source for submitting the job.) The subprogram (written in CL) overrides some print file settings and then calls an RPG program to print the report.

```
PGM PARM(&PG &JB &FR &TO)

    DCL VAR(&PG) TYPE(*CHAR) LEN(10)
    DCL VAR(&JB) TYPE(*CHAR) LEN(10)
    DCL VAR(&FR) TYPE(*DEC) LEN(8)
    DCL VAR(&TO) TYPE(*DEC) LEN(8)

    /* The following statement causes decimal data error */
    SBMJOB CMD(CALL PGM(&PG) PARM(&FR &TO)) JOB(&JB)

    /* The following call statement works without error */
    CALL PGM(&PG) PARM(&FR &TO)

ENDPGM
```

Figure 1.48: Decimal data errors can crop up when using the SBMJOB command.

The DUMP received on the RPG program shows that the sign bit has been dropped from the DATE parameters passed to it. For example, if the packed start date should be X'19970507F', the DUMP shows X'019970507'.

I know I can convert the packed numeric to character and then convert it back to numeric in my RPG program. I also know I can use a data area to hold my parameters. I'll pick one of those solutions if I can't solve the problem.

A: You don't need such subterfuge to make this work. The difference between the Submit Job (SBMJOB) and CALL commands is that CALL uses variables as is (because both called and caller use the same storage for the variables), but SBMJOB pretends you have manually typed the command at the command line. The command interpreter comes into the picture then.

One quirk of the command interpreter is that numeric values are assumed to be in the format DEC(15,5), indicating 15 digits, of which 5 are decimal positions. Anything else corrupts the numeric value. Knowing this, you have two alternatives (in addition to those two you mentioned).

First, you can simply change your programs so they use DEC(15,5) for all numeric parameters. This guarantees that the program will run correctly whether it's invoked by CALL or SBMJOB. Of course, this requires heavy maintenance programming. Therefore, it might not be a correct solution for you. I should point out, however, that you would have to change only those programs you expect to run via SBMJOB and CALL.

The second alternative is to create a custom command for those programs you expect to run via SBMJOB and then submit that command instead of submitting a CALL. When the command interpreter examines the command you created, it will automatically format all numeric values to the correct hexadecimal representation, resulting in freedom from decimal data error messages.

—Ernie Malaga

Passing Parameters to a Batch Job

Look at the two programs shown in Figures 1.49 and 1.50. At first glance, you would think that PGM2 would have the following two parameter values: &X (containing the value 'FIRST' followed by trailing blanks) and &Y (containing the value 'SECOND' followed by trailing blanks). Wrong! &X and &Y will contain a mess!

```
PGM

    DCL         VAR(&A) TYPE(*CHAR) LEN(500)
    DCL         VAR(&B) TYPE(*CHAR) LEN(500)

    CHGVAR      VAR(&A) VALUE('FIRST')
    CHGVAR      VAR(&B) VALUE('SECOND')

    SBMJOB      CMD(CALL PGM(PGM1) PARM(&A &B))

    ENDPGM
```

Figure 1.49: Program PGM1 demonstrates the SBMJOB command passing two parameters.

```
PGM         PARM(&X &Y)

DCL         VAR(&X) TYPE(*CHAR) LEN(500)
DCL         VAR(&Y) TYPE(*CHAR) LEN(500)
 .
 .
 .
ENDPGM
```

Figure 1.50: Program PGM2 shows how the parameters being passed to it are defined.

Usually, when a program calls another program directly, the system passes character parameters by address. This allows the called program to access the same data passed by the calling program. However, when a program submits another one to batch, the system makes a copy of the parameters. Unfortunately, this copy contains only the used part of the parameters or the first 33 bytes—whichever is less. Past that point, the results are very unpredictable. This area usually contains hexadecimal garbage.

To avoid this problem, I usually declare the parameter variables in the calling program one character longer than in the called program and put a nonblank character in the last position. For example, in PGM1, this is what I would code:

```
DCL VAR(&A) TYPE(*CHAR) LEN(501)
CHGVAR VAR(%SST(&A 501 1)) VALUE('.')
```

As a result, the system is forced to make a copy of the whole variable. There is no problem if a character parameter is defined longer in the calling program than in the called program. This solves the problem by ensuring that the correct data is passed between the two programs.

—Sorin Caraiani

✦ ✦ ✦ Performance

Increasing Perceived Speed

I would like to address the operating speed of the AS/400. Actually, I am referring to the perceived operating speed. A job seems to run faster when messages are displayed notifying the workstation operator of the current processing. An example for the S/36 would be:

```
// * 'Sorting Customer File'
  ...
// * 'Printing Customer Master List'
```

The AS/400 command SNDPGMMSG can be used for this purpose. However, the command parameters must be correct for a neat status message at the bottom of the screen. Otherwise, you will get a display of the PROGRAM MESSAGES queue. The old S/34-to-S/38 conversion aid produced such messages and they are out of the question for a user interface.

The IBM message identifier CPF9898 can be used for application messages and displays the message data followed by a period. Be sure to send the message to the external program queue (TOPGMQ(*EXT)) and use MSGTYPE(*STATUS).

—Jonathan E. Yergin

Reclaim Resource

You probably know that you can use the Reclaim Resource (RCLRSC) command to clean up open files and reclaim program storage. The default value for the Program Level (LVL) parameter is an asterisk (*), which says to close all open files and programs—including the calling program—once the called programs have finished running.

Did you know that you can also specify *CALLER in this parameter? Use this parameter value when you want to leave programs and files open in the calling program while still closing programs and files that were called by the original program. Let's see what this means by way of an example.

PGMSTART (Figure 1.51) opens FILE1 and calls PGMA (Figure 1.52), which opens FILE2. The program then exits with the file still open, using the RETRN op code. PGMSTART then calls PGMB (Figure 1.53), which opens FILE3 and then exits with the file still open, using the RETRN op code. PGMSTART then calls RCLPGMC (Figure 1.54), a CL program that executes the RCLRSC command, using *CALLER in the LVL parameter. When control returns to PGMSTART, it stops execution, ending with the RETRN op code. When PGMSTART finishes, only FILE1 is left open. The files in PGMA and PGMB are closed, and all storage allocated for them is reclaimed. Another operation could execute PGMSTART again and would be able to use the open access path to FILE1, and all variables would still be in their previous state.

```
FFILE1 IF E  K       DISK
 *
C          READ  FILE1        99
C  *IN99   IFEQ  *OFF
C          CALL  'PGMA'
C          CALL  'PGMB'
C          CALL  'RCLPGMC'
C          ENDIF
C          RETRN
```

Figure 1.51: RPG III program PGMSTART opens a file, and then calls PGMA, PGMB, and the CL program RCLPGMC.

```
FFILE2 IF E  K        DISK
 *
C          READ  FILE2         99
C          RETRN
```

Figure 1.52: RPG III program PGMA is called by PGMSTART.

```
FFILE3 IF  E  K     DISK
 *
C          READ   FILE3           99
C          RETRN
```

Figure 1.53: RPG III program PGMB is also called by PGMSTART.

```
PGM
RCLRSC LVL(*CALLER)
ENDPGM
```

Figure 1.54: CL program RCLPGMC is called by PGMSTART to reclaim resources used.

—*Shannon O'Donnell*

Editor's Note: *The help text for the RCLRSC command provides additional information you should know. For instance, RCLRSC is not needed to reclaim the resources of all CL programs that end (return) normally, of RPG programs that have the last record (LR) indicator set on, or of any COBOL programs. RCLRSC should not be used if it might be processed while any COBOL program is still active in the application; instead, use the COBOL CANCEL statement.*

Other important facts: RCLRSC should not specify LVL(*CALLER) if it is used in a CL program that also uses the Send File (SNDF), Receive File (RCVF), or Send Receive File (SNDRCVF) commands; using *CALLER in such a program causes unpredictable results when the other commands are used after the program runs. Unpredictable results can also occur if RCLRSC is executed from a command line with the LVL(*CALLER) parameter.

✦ ✦ ✦ Printing

Direct Printing on the AS/400

Q: We are trying to use direct printing on the AS/400. In all the manuals all they talk about is spooling. I've heard it can be done but can't find any information about it. We use direct printing for all check printing and for check and forms alignment. I've heard it has something to do with routing entries.

A: If you have the source for the CL programs that control the printing, you can add an OVRPRTF (Override with Printer File) command, with an option of SPOOL(*NO).

—Midrange Computing Staff

Global Printer File Override

Some AS/400 printers require special print file characteristics in order to print correctly. Print file characteristics such as page size, lines per inch, and characters per inch can be changed using the Override Printer File (OVRPRTF) command. But what if you don't know the name of the printer file you want to override?

No problem. Just use the special value *PRTF for the printer file name in the OVRPRTF command. This method overrides all printer files used by a job. For example, I happen to quite often use an HP LaserJet printer that is attached to our AS/400. When I do, I first issue the following command:

```
OVRPRTF FILE(*PRTF) PAGESIZE(88 132) LPI(8) CPI(16.7) +
        OVRFLW(80) PAGRTT(0)
```

This forces all spool files that I create interactively to automatically print in compressed mode. This way, I am able to print a 132-column report on an 8 ½-x-11 sheet of paper. Even the printer files used by OS/400 commands that allow OUTPUT(*PRINT) are overridden, including the output created by pressing the Print key. This technique also could be used to create spool files already on hold or save mode, or directed to a particular output queue or device.

—Robin Klima

Printer File Names

Q: I am trying to write an RPG program that will create print files with varying spool file names. The input file I am reading will contain the name of the print file to be created. I have tried using OVRPRTF, but the spool file name that is created is the same as the file name in the RPG program. I have tried to change the name using CHGSPLFA but this command does not allow you to change the file name.

A: On the OVRPRTF command, there is a parameter called SPLFNAME that you can use to make the spooled file any name you want.

If you want to do it all in RPG, code UC in columns 71–72 of the F-spec for the PRINTER file. Then run the OVRPRTF command using QCMDEXC before you OPEN the printer file manually in the RPG program.

—Midrange Computing Staff

Using OUTPUT(*PRINT)

Many CL commands produce some kind of information output that can often be routed to the display or to the printer by choosing between OUTPUT(*) or OUTPUT(*PRINT). Comparatively few commands offer a third option, OUTPUT(*OUTFILE), to send the output to a database file directly.

If the command you want to run doesn't offer outfile support, such as the Display Library (DSPLIB) command, there's a rather clumsy way to circumvent it and obtain the output in a database file. It involves the following steps:

1. Override the printer file used by the command with HOLD(*YES).
2. Run the command, specifying OUTPUT(*PRINT).
3. Copy the spool file to the database file.
4. Delete the spool file from the output queue.
5. Delete the override to the printer file.

For example, to capture the printed output of DSPLIB to database file SPLF132, you would code your CL program as shown in Figure 1.55. It requires five commands. Omit one of them and your CL program might blow up.

```
OVRPRTF    FILE(QPDSPLIB) HOLD(*YES)
DSPLIB     LIB(QGPL) OUTPUT(*PRINT)
CPYSPLF    FILE(QPDSPLIB) TOFILE(SPLF132) JOB(*) +
             SPLNBR(*LAST) TOMBR(*FIRST) MBROPT(*REPLACE)
DLTSPLF    FILE(QPDSPLIB) JOB(*) SPLNBR(*LAST) +
             SELECT(*CURRENT)
DLTOVR     FILE(QPDSPLIB)
```

Figure 1.55: Capturing output from a command is easy using the *PRINT option of a command.

I created the Convert Print to Physical File (CVTPRTPF) command to simplify this kind of process. Compare Figure 1.55 with Figure 1.56, which makes use of the CVTPRTPF command. One command takes care of everything. See also Figure 1.57.

```
CVTPRTPF   CMD(DSPLIB LIB(QGPL) OUTPUT(*PRINT)) +
           PRTF(QPDSPLIB) TOFILE(SPLF132) +
           MBROPT(*FIRST *REPLACE)
```

Figure 1.56: Use the CVTPRTPF command to simplify capturing command output as shown here.

```
CVTPRTPF:  CMD      PROMPT('Convert Print to Physical File')

           PARM     KWD(CMD) TYPE(*CMDSTR) LEN(3000) MIN(1) +
                      PROMPT('Command to produce output')
           PARM     KWD(PRTF) TYPE(*NAME) LEN(10) MIN(1) +
                      PROMPT('Printer file name')
           PARM     KWD(TOFILE) TYPE(Q1) MIN(1) PROMPT('To +
                      physical file')
           PARM     KWD(MBROPT) TYPE(E1) PROMPT('Member options')

Q1:        QUAL     TYPE(*NAME) LEN(10) MIN(1)
           QUAL     TYPE(*NAME) LEN(10) DFT(*CURLIB) +
                      SPCVAL((*CURLIB)) PROMPT('Library')

E1:        ELEM     TYPE(*NAME) LEN(10) DFT(*FIRST) +
                      SPCVAL((*FIRST)) PROMPT('Member to +
                      receive output')
           ELEM     TYPE(*CHAR) LEN(8) RSTD(*YES) DFT(*REPLACE) +
                      VALUES(*REPLACE *ADD) PROMPT('Replace or +
                      add records')
```

Figure 1.57: Command CVTPRTPF is simple to create and use.

The CVTPRTPF command (Figure 1.58) has four parameters. The first parameter, CMD, lets you enter the command you want to execute (the command that produces the output, like DSPLIB in this example). Parameter PRTF requires the name of the printer file used by the command. Parameter TOFILE lets you enter the qualified name of the physical file to receive the converted information. Parameter MBROPT allows you enter the name of the member to receive the data (defaults to *FIRST) and whether to add or replace records within the member (the default is *REPLACE).

```
PRT004CL: +
    PGM PARM(&CMD &PRTF &QF &MEMBER)

    DCL VAR(&CMD)        TYPE(*CHAR) LEN(3000)
    DCL VAR(&FILE)       TYPE(*CHAR) LEN(10)
    DCL VAR(&LIB)        TYPE(*CHAR) LEN(10)
    DCL VAR(&MBR)        TYPE(*CHAR) LEN(10)
    DCL VAR(&MBROPT)     TYPE(*CHAR) LEN(8)
    DCL VAR(&MEMBER)     TYPE(*CHAR) LEN(20)
    DCL VAR(&PRTF)       TYPE(*CHAR) LEN(10)
    DCL VAR(&QF)         TYPE(*CHAR) LEN(20)

    CHGVAR VAR(&FILE) VALUE(%SST(&QF 1 10))
    CHGVAR VAR(&LIB) VALUE(%SST(&QF 11 10))
    CHGVAR VAR(&MBR) VALUE(%SST(&MEMBER 3 10))
    CHGVAR VAR(&MBROPT) VALUE(%SST(&MEMBER 13 8))

    CHKOBJ OBJ(&LIB/&FILE) OBJTYPE(*FILE)
    MONMSG MSGID(CPF9810) EXEC(DO)
        SNDPGMMSG MSGID(CPF9898) MSGF(QCPFMSG) MSGDTA('Library' *BCAT +
            'not found') MSGTYPE(*ESCAPE)
        RETURN
    ENDDO
    MONMSG MSGID(CPF9801) EXEC(DO)
        CRTPF FILE(&LIB/&FILE) RCDLEN(512)
    ENDDO

    CHKOBJ OBJ(&LIB/&FILE) OBJTYPE(*FILE) MBR(&MBR)
    MONMSG MSGID(CPF9815) EXEC(DO)
        ADDPFM FILE(&LIB/&FILE) MBR(&MBR)
    ENDDO

    OVRPRTF FILE(&PRTF) HOLD(*YES)
    CALL PGM(QCMDEXC) PARM(&CMD 3000)
    MONMSG MSGID(CPF0000) EXEC(DO)
        FWDPGMMSG FROMPGMQ(PRT004CL)
        RETURN
    ENDDO
```

Figure 1.58: CL program PRT004CL is used by the CVTPRTPF command to retrieve the output of a file (part 1 of 2).

```
CPYSPLF FILE(&PRTF) TOFILE(&LIB/&FILE) JOB(*) SPLNBR(*LAST) +
    TOMBR(&MBR) MBROPT(&MBROPT)
DLTSPLF FILE(&PRTF) JOB(*) SPLNBR(*LAST) SELECT(*CURRENT)
DLTOVR FILE(&PRTF)

ENDPGM
```

Figure 1.58: CL program PRT004CL is used by the CVTPRTPF command to retrieve the output of a file (part 2 of 2).

CVTPRTPF uses the CL program PRT004CL (Figure 1.57) to reproduce the manual steps. CVTPRTPF takes the pain out of retrieving printed information. I'm sure that you'll begin using OUTPUT(*PRINT) more when you realize its potential.

—*Ernie Malaga*

✦ ✦ ✦ Program Name

Retrieving the Name of a Calling Program

When your telephone rings and someone at the other end starts talking without providing identification, you have every bit of right to feel annoyed. It's only common courtesy to at least say, "My name is so-and-so." After the formalities have been complied with, the caller can start with the business at hand.

AS/400 programs aren't so polite. When program A calls program B, program A is ordering program B to run; yet program B has no direct way of knowing who called it. Sometimes this information would be useful. The Retrieve Previous Program (RTVPRVPGM) command (shown in Figures 1.59 and 1.60) satisfies this need.

```
RTVPRVPGM:   CMD          PROMPT('Retrieve Previous Program')

             PARM         KWD(LEVELS) TYPE(*DEC) LEN(3 0) DFT(1) +
                          RANGE(1 100) PROMPT('Number of levels to +
                          backtrack')
             PARM         KWD(RTNPGM) TYPE(*CHAR) LEN(10) RTNVAL(*YES) +
                          PROMPT('Program name (10)')
```

Figure 1.59: Command RTVPRVPGM is the command you'll execute to get the caller's name.

```
PRV001CL: +
    PGM PARM(&LEVELS &RTNPGM)

    DCL VAR(&CALLER)    TYPE(*CHAR) LEN(10)
    DCL VAR(&COUNTER)   TYPE(*DEC)  LEN(3 0)
    DCL VAR(&LEVELS)    TYPE(*DEC)  LEN(3 0)
    DCL VAR(&MSGDTA)    TYPE(*CHAR) LEN(132)
    DCL VAR(&MSGF)      TYPE(*CHAR) LEN(10)
    DCL VAR(&MSGFLIB)   TYPE(*CHAR) LEN(10)
    DCL VAR(&MSGID)     TYPE(*CHAR) LEN(7)
    DCL VAR(&MSGKEY)    TYPE(*CHAR) LEN(4)
    DCL VAR(&RTNPGM)    TYPE(*CHAR) LEN(10)
    DCL VAR(&SENDER)    TYPE(*CHAR) LEN(80)

    MONMSG MSGID(CPF0000) EXEC(GOTO CMDLBL(ERROR))

    SNDPGMMSG MSG(X) TOPGMQ(*PRV *) MSGTYPE(*INFO) KEYVAR(&MSGKEY)
    RCVMSG PGMQ(*PRV *) MSGKEY(&MSGKEY) RMV(*YES) SENDER(&SENDER)
    CHGVAR VAR(&CALLER) VALUE(%SST(&SENDER 56 10))

LOOP: +
    SNDPGMMSG MSG(X) TOPGMQ(*PRV &CALLER) MSGTYPE(*INFO) +
        KEYVAR(&MSGKEY)
    RCVMSG PGMQ(*PRV &CALLER) MSGKEY(&MSGKEY) RMV(*YES) SENDER(&SENDER)
    CHGVAR VAR(&COUNTER) VALUE(&COUNTER + 1)
    IF COND(&COUNTER *EQ &LEVELS) THEN(DO)
        CHGVAR VAR(&RTNPGM) VALUE(%SST(&SENDER 56 10))
        RETURN
    ENDDO
    ELSE CMD(DO)
        CHGVAR VAR(&CALLER) VALUE(%SST(&SENDER 56 10))
        GOTO CMDLBL(LOOP)
    ENDDO

ERROR: +
    RCVMSG MSGTYPE(*EXCP) MSGDTA(&MSGDTA) MSGID(&MSGID) MSGF(&MSGF) +
        MSGFLIB(&MSGFLIB)
    SNDPGMMSG MSGID(&MSGID) MSGF(&MSGFLIB/&MSGF) MSGDTA(&MSGDTA) +
        MSGTYPE(*ESCAPE)
    ENDPGM
```

Figure 1.60: CL program PRV001CL is the power behind the RTVPRVPGM command.

To give you an idea of its usefulness, you might have created a single program that performs one function nine times out of ten. The remaining time the program performs—with a slight alteration to accommodate different requirements—the same function. Granted, you probably should have created two different programs (according to the basic tenets of modular programming), but in real life this is not always practical.

If your CL program needs to know what program called it, include the RTVPRVPGM command in the CL program, as follows:

```
RTVPRVPGM LEVELS(1) RTNPGM(&CALLER)
```

Variable &CALLER must be declared as a 10-character string. The LEVELS parameter indicates how many levels to go back in the program stack. You can put LEVELS(2) if you want to know the caller's caller's name, for instance.

If the program that needs the caller's name is written in RPG/400, you can call the program activated by the RTVPRVPGM command directly. Just include the code from Figure 1.61 in your program.

```
... 1 ...+... 2 ...+... 3 ...+... 4 ...+... 5 ...+... 6
C                    CALL 'PRV001CL'
C                    PARM 1          LEVELS  30
C                    PARM            RTNPGM  10
```

Figure 1.61: This code fragment demonstrates how to call the RTVPRVPGM to determine which program called it.

This utility does its work by sending an *INFO message to *PRV (the caller of PRV001CL) and obtaining the key of this message. Then the message is received by key and erased, obtaining the sender information structure in &SENDER. Part of the information structure is the name of the program that actually received the message (which will be the name of the program from which you used this utility command).

Next, repeat the cycle. Use the program name retrieved in the first cycle as the basis for another SNDPGMMSG to *PRV and RCVMSG, with the &SENDER option (which obtains the name of your program's caller). The process is repeated the number of times indicated by the LEVELS parameter. It's pretty simple and very efficient.

Now, if only we could do the same on the telephone, perhaps those pesky, malicious callers (who love to call at 3 A.M. just to hang up on you) would think twice about it!

—*Ernie Malaga*

Retrieving the Name of the Current Program

Don't hard-code program names. A CL program can obtain its own name via the code fragment shown in Figure 1.62.

```
DCL VAR(&SENDER) TYPE(*CHAR) LEN(80)
DCL VAR(&PGM) TYPE(*CHAR) LEN(10)
DCL VAR(&MSGKEY) TYPE(*CHAR) LEN(4)
SNDPGMMSG MSG(' ') TOPGMQ(*SAME) MSGTYPE(*INFO) KEYVAR(&MSGKEY)
RCVMSG PGMQ(*SAME) MSGTYPE(*INFO) SENDER(&SENDER) RMV(*YES)
MSGKEY(&MSGKEY)
CHGVAR VAR(&PGM) VALUE(%SST(&SENDER 56 10))
```

Figure 1.62: This code fragment demonstrates how to determine a program's name in CL.

RPG programs can obtain their names from the program status data structure, as shown in Figure 1.63.

```
... 1 ...+... 2 ...+... 3 ...+... 4 ...+... 5 ...+... 6
I SDS
I *PROGRAM PGM
```

Figure 1.63: Retrieving the program name in RPG is easy using the program data structure.

—Midrange Computing Staff

✦ ✦ ✦ Security

Improve Security Control

To access the command Entry Display while a CL program is running, use the following command:

```
RCVMSG PGMQ(*EXT) MSGTYPE(*RQS)
```

It looks as if you have called QCMD, but there is a big difference; the commands are neither executed nor prompted. Key a command and press Enter to execute, F4 to prompt it, or F3 or F12 to exit. The CL program goes to the command after the Receive Messages (RCVMSG) command in the original CL program. If you need to improve the security on your system, put some users on with Limit Capabilities (LMTCPB *YES) and write a small program as illustrated in Figure 1.64. This program will accept or reject each command they type, process the commands, and log them so you know what they are doing.

```
PGM

              DCL       VAR(&MSG) TYPE(*CHAR) LEN(512)
              DCL       VAR(&KEYVAR) TYPE(*CHAR) LEN(4)
              DCL       VAR(&RTNTYPE) TYPE(*CHAR) LEN(2)
              DCL       VAR(&REJECT) TYPE(*LGL)

  /* Display QCMD */
    RECEIVE:  RCVMSG    PGMQ(*EXT) MSGTYPE(*RQS) RMV(*NO) +
                        KEYVAR(&KEYVAR) MSG(&MSG) RTNTYPE(&RTNTYPE)

  /* F3 or F12 requested from QCMD */
              MONMSG    MSGID(CPF2415) EXEC(RETURN)

  /* F4 prompt requested from QCMD */
              IF        COND(&RTNTYPE *EQ '10') THEN(CHGVAR +
                        VAR(&MSG) VALUE('?' *CAT &MSG))

  /* Check command, and if F4 prompt it */
              CALL      PGM(QCMDCHK) PARM(&MSG 512)
              MONMSG    MSGID(CPF0000) EXEC(GOTO CMDLBL(RECEIVE))

  /* Replace typed command with prompted command with all parameters */
              RMVMSG    PGMQ(*EXT) MSGKEY(&KEYVAR) CLEAR(*BYKEY)
              SNDPGMMSG MSG(&MSG) TOPGMQ(*EXT) MSGTYPE(*RQS)
              RCVMSG    PGMQ(*EXT) MSGTYPE(*RQS) RMV(*NO)

  /* Here, call your own PGM to accept/reject, and log the command */
  /*          CALL      PGM(XXX) PARM(&MSG &REJECT)                 */
  /*          IF        COND(&REJECT) THEN(GOTO CMDLBL(RECEIVE))    */

  /* Process the command */
              CALL      PGM(QCMDEXC) PARM(&MSG 512)
              GOTO      CMDLBL(RECEIVE)

    ENDPGM:   ENDPGM
```

Figure 1.64: You can restrict command usage by using the techniques shown here.

—Jean-Jacques Risch

✦ ✦ ✦ SEU

CL Source Comments Made Easy

When testing or debugging my CL programs, I often need to inactivate certain command statements within the program. I usually do this by converting the statements to comments (in the statement, insert /* at the beginning and */ at the end). This can be cumbersome when I need to convert more than a few statements.

Fortunately, you can use the SEU Copy (C) and Overlay (O) line commands to make this easier. Create a blank comment line in your CL program (place /* in the first two positions of the statement and */ in positions 79–80). To convert a statement to a comment, place a C on the blank comment line and an O on the statement you want to convert. SEU will overlay the source statement with the blank comment line. If you want to convert a block of statements to comments, use the block overlay line command (OO) on the first and last statements of the block. This technique assumes that positions 1–2 and 79–80 of the statement you want to convert are not used.

—Jim Schecklman

Setting Uppercase / Lowercase in SEU

Q: Because CL programs may be coded in either uppercase or lowercase, why does SEU force uppercase-only entry with CL program members?

A: I don't know why the default is set this way, but it's easy to change. You can simply type 'S CAPS OFF' on the SEU command line and then code in lowercase. An alternate solution can eliminate the need to key the command every time you edit a CL program. Go into the session defaults for SEU (F13) and page down one page. There you'll find a setting, "Default to uppercase input for this source type," which accepts a value of Yes (Y) or No (N). Set the value to (N). Next, from the SEU command line, key the CAPS setting you prefer (OFF or ON). From that point on, you never have to type S CAPS OFF again for that member type.

—Ted Holt

✦ ✦ ✦ Source Members

Reading All Source Members

Q: Is there a way to process a source physical file with an RPG program processing all members (like a S/36 FROMLIBR procedure with *ALL)? If not, do I need a CL program to Override Database File (OVRDBF) and loop through the members?

A: The OVRDBF command accepts MBR(*ALL) to do precisely that. When you use MBR(*ALL), LR won't turn on until all records in all members have been processed. The INFDS for the file includes a field that contains the name of the member currently being processed. This field is in bytes 129–138 of the INFDS. Other than that, there's no separator between members (no record with blanks, nulls, X'FF', or whatever). Because this member identifier is in a data structure, you cannot determine when it changes using a control level indicator such as L1. You'll have to code your own.

—Ernie Malaga

✦ ✦ ✦ Subfiles

CL Subfiles

Try this method to simulate a load-all display subfile with file positioning in CL. The example is a simple Territory Inquiry program. Figures 1.65 and 1.66 show the DDS for the physical file and the display file. Figure 1.67 shows the CL program, TERRCL1, that declares the subfile and then displays it. CL program TERRCL2 (shown in Figure 1.68) is used to process the display file defined in Figure. 1.67

```
     A                                          UNIQUE
     A           R TERRFLR                      TEXT('Territory File')
     A             ITERNM         25A           TEXT('Territory Name')
     A             ITERCD          3A           TEXT('Territory Code')
     A           K ITERNM
```

Figure 1.65: Physical file TERRFL will hold the data you'll display in your subfile.

```
A                                        DSPSIZ(24 80 *DS3)
A                                        CA03(03 'Exit')
A                                        PRINT
A                                        ERRSFL
A           R TERDSP
A                                      1 29'Territory File Inquiry'
A                                      3  2'Territory:'
A             TERDSC       25A  B  3 13
A 20                                     ERRMSG('No records to display.' 20)
A                                      5  2'Territory Name'
A                                      5 32'Code'
A           R MSGSFL                    SFL
A                                        SFLMSGRCD(06)
A             MSGKEY                     SFLMSGKEY
A             PGMQ                       SFLPGMQ
A           R MSGCTL                    SFLCTL(MSGSFL)
A                                        OVERLAY
A                                        SFLDSP
A                                        SFLDSPCTL
A N40                                     SFLEND
A                                        SFLINZ
A                                        SFLSIZ(0018)
A                                        SFLPAG(0017)
A             PGMQ                       SFLPGMQ
A           R FKEYS                     OVERLAY
A                                     24  2'F3=Exit'
```

Figure 1.66: Display file TERRD will be the DDS you'll use for the CL-driven subfile.

```
PGM
            DCLF      FILE(TERRDF)
            CHGVAR    VAR(&PGMQ) VALUE(TERRCL1)
  LOOP:     SNDF      RCDFMT(TERDSP)
            SNDF      RCDFMT(MSGCTL)
            SNDF      RCDFMT(FKEYS)
            RCVF      RCDFMT(TERDSP)
            IF        COND(&IN03) THEN(GOTO CMDLBL(END))
            RMVMSG    CLEAR(*ALL)
            CALL      PGM(TERRCL2) PARM(&TERDSC &IN20)
            GOTO      CMDLBL(LOOP)
  END:      RMVMSG    CLEAR(*ALL)
            ENDPG
```

Figure 1.67: CL Program TERRCL1 is used to declare the subfile and then display it.

```
PGM         PARM(&TERDSC &IN20)
            DCL       VAR(&TERDSC) TYPE(*CHAR) LEN(25)
            DCL       VAR(&IN20) TYPE(*CHAR) LEN(1)
            DCLF      FILE(TERRFL)
            OVRDBF    FILE(TERRFL) POSITION(*KEYAE 1 *N &TERDSC)
LOOP:       RCVF
            MONMSG    MSGID(CPF0864) EXEC(RETURN)
            MONMSG    MSGID(CPF4167) EXEC(DO)
            CHGVAR    VAR(&IN20) VALUE('1')
            RETURN
            ENDDO
            SNDPGMMSG MSGID(CPF9897) MSGF(QCPFMSG) MSGDTA(&ITERNM +
                        *CAT '        ' *CAT &ITERCD)
            GOTO      CMDLBL(LOOP)
            ENDPGM
```

Figure 1.68: CL Program TERRCL2 is used to process the display file defined in the previous figure.

The program TERRCL1 displays multiple lines of a message subfile that contains file data instead of error messages. The file is positioned through an Override Database File (OVRDBF) command and the data is read, formatted, and sent as a program message to the program message queue that is displayed by the message subfile.

If the file is positioned beyond the last record, an error message will be displayed. By using the ERRSFL keyword in the display file, the keyboard remains unlocked and multiple error messages can be displayed!

—Tom Conover

✦ ✦ ✦ Submitted Jobs

Altering Run Priority of Submitted Jobs

Not all jobs are created equal. And there are cases when you'd like to force a job you just submitted to batch to run at a different priority or time slice than the default values. Unfortunately, the SBMJOB command cannot accept override values for either the priority or the time slice. You could start the WRKSBSJOB SBS(QBATCH) command at a terminal and have a humanoid, in the sitting position, repeatedly press F5 all day long to catch newly submitted jobs, and change them with the Change Job (CHGJOB) command to RUNPTY(60). However, this avenue is too expensive (it requires three full-time employees to cover around-the-clock operations). Fortunately, there's a better way.

1. Create a new class object (type *CLS), QBATCH60, that assigns a priority of 60 and a time slice of 4000 (for example):

```
CRTDUPOBJ  OBJ(QBATCH) FROMLIB(QGPL) OBJTYPE(*CLS) +
           TOLIB(QGPL) NEWOBJ(QBATCH60)
CHGCLS     CLS(QGPL/QBATCH60) RUNPTY(60) TIMESLICE(4000)
```

2. Add a routing entry to subsystem QBATCH that forces the system to use the new class object when the appropriate routing data is submitted with the new job:

```
ADDRTGE  SBSD(QGPL/QBATCH)  SEQNBR(9000) CMPVAL(RUNPTY60) +
         PGM(QSYS/QCMD) CLS(QGPL/QBATCH60)
```

From now on, all you need to do is include RTGDTA(RUNPTY60) in the SBMJOB command whenever you submit a job to a job queue that is attached to subsystem QBATCH. If you need to use the new class code when submitting jobs to job queues that are attached to other subsystems, repeat step 2 for each subsystem.

For example, suppose you want to run DSPLIB LIB(QSYS) OUTPUT(*PRINT). Because QSYS contains so many objects, DSPLIB will probably take a long time and consume many system resources. Then you decide to use priority 60 and a time slice of 4000 milliseconds:

```
SBMJOB CMD(DSPLIB LIB(QSYS))  JOB(DSPQSYS) JOBQ(QBATCH) +
       RTGDTA(RUNPTY60)
```

When the system picks up this job from the job queue, it goes through the routing entries and realizes that there's an entry with a matching compare value of "RUNPTY60." The routing entry references a class object, so it is used to set the runtime attributes for the job (priority 60 and time slice 4000).

—*Ernie Malaga*

Giving CL Programs Option to Be Sent To

If you have ever been frustrated with the need to write two programs in order to JOBQ a program (one to perform the task, another to do a SBMJOB), take heart. The program shown in Figure 1.69 submits itself to the JOBQ or runs interactively (depending on the response by the operator).

```
PROG01CL:    PGM
             DCL         VAR(&DSP) TYPE(*CHAR) LEN(10)
             DCL         VAR(&JOBQ) TYPE(*CHAR) LEN(1)
             DCLF        FILE(PROMPT)
   /* Retrieve job type.  If '0', it is running in BATCH */
             RTVJOBA     TYPE(&JOBQ)
             IF          COND(&JOBQ *EQ '0') THEN(GOTO CMDLBL(CALL))
   /* If not, find out if the user wants to JOBQ it */
             SNDRCVF
             IF          COND(&ANSWER *EQ 'N') THEN(GOTO CMDLBL(CALL))
             SBMJOB      CMD(CALL PGM(PROG01CL)) JOB(PROG01) +
                           JOBPTY(5) OUTPTY(5) LOGCLPGM(*NO)
             RETURN
   CALL:     OVRDBF      FILE(FILEA) TOFILE(PAYROLL)
             CALL        PGM(PROG01)
             ENDPGM
```

Figure 1.69: CL program PROG01CL submits itself to the job queue.

The display file declared in PROG01CL is shown in Figure 1.70.

```
A                                   DSPSIZ(24 80 *DS3)
A           R JOBQ
A                                   BLINK
A                              6 12'Do you wish to submit this job to -
A                                   the JobQ?'
A                             13 12'Y=Yes, N=No:'
A                             16 12'Press Enter to continue'
A           ANSWER       1    B 13 36VALUES('Y' 'N')
```

Figure 1.70: This display file is used by program PROG01CL to prompt the user to run this program in batch or interactively.

When the job is called initially, it is running interactively. If the operator types a Y option to the question, then the program submits this same job to the JOBQ and returns. Now the job is running in BATCH and the TYPE attribute is 0. When tested, the program knows it is running in batch and doesn't present the prompt screen to the operator. Instead, it branches over this and calls program PROG01.

—Ted May

Nasty Errors Can Occur When Using SBMJOB

If you use the Submit Job (SBMJOB) command in a CL program to submit to batch a CALL to another CL program, be aware that the SBMJOB command can corrupt the parameter data if:

- The parameter data being passed is in a character variable.
- The character variable is longer than 32 characters.
- And the character variable ends in one or more blanks.

To try one case on for size, see Figures 1.71 and 1.72 (which list programs X and Y).

```
X:          PGM

            DCL         VAR(&STRING) TYPE(*CHAR) LEN(90)
            DCL         VAR(&PART1)  TYPE(*CHAR) LEN(30)
            DCL         VAR(&PART2)  TYPE(*CHAR) LEN(30)
            DCL         VAR(&PART3)  TYPE(*CHAR) LEN(30)

            CHGVAR      VAR(&PART1) +
                        VALUE('A                               ')
            CHGVAR      VAR(&PART2) +
                        VALUE('B                               ')
            CHGVAR      VAR(&PART3) +
                        VALUE('C                               ')

            CHGVAR      VAR(&STRING) VALUE(&PART1 *CAT &PART2 *CAT +
                        &PART3)
            SBMJOB      CMD(CALL PGM(Y) PARM(&STRING))

            ENDPGM
```

Figure 1.71: Program X will call program Y, passing it a string of data as a parameter.

```
Y:          PGM         PARM(&STRING)

            DCL         VAR(&STRING) TYPE(*CHAR) LEN(90)
            DCL         VAR(&PART1)  TYPE(*CHAR) LEN(30)
            DCL         VAR(&PART2)  TYPE(*CHAR) LEN(30)
            DCL         VAR(&PART3)  TYPE(*CHAR) LEN(30)

            CHGVAR      VAR(&PART1) VALUE(%SST(&STRING 1 30))
            CHGVAR      VAR(&PART2) VALUE(%SST(&STRING 31 30))
            CHGVAR      VAR(&PART3) VALUE(%SST(&STRING 61 30))

            SNDMSG      MSG(&PART1) TOUSR(QSYSOPR)
            SNDMSG      MSG(&PART2) TOUSR(QSYSOPR)
            SNDMSG      MSG(&PART3) TOUSR(QSYSOPR)

            ENDPGM
```

Figure 1.72: Program Y will return errors to the calling program when it is submitted to run in batch, but not if it runs interactively.

When you call program X from the keyboard, program Y runs in batch and sends three messages to QSYSOPR. The first one contains the letter A (plus 29 blanks) and the second message contains the letter B (plus 29 blanks). The third message contains the letter C (plus a lot of garbage). The funny thing is that, if you change program X so that it calls program Y (instead of submitting to batch), all three messages arrive clean and proper into QSYSOPR.

—Gail Lorsing

Editor's Note: We believe that operating systems should work in a sensible manner, without requiring the user (or programmer) to remember exceptions to the rules or strange behavior patterns that violate common sense. Therefore, we reported this as a bug to IBM Level 2 and were told, in a nutshell, that this is the way OS/400 works. They faxed us a printout of the closure of APAR SA05183, dated July 31, 1989 (someone else was bitten by the same bug, apparently). The document includes the following text:

"When the CALL command is being used as the argument for the SBMJOB command, it operates as a noncompiled CALL command (interactive CALL). Therefore, the rules for passing parameters in the embedded CALL code are the same as if the CALL command is run from the Command Entry screen or the command line. These rules apply whether or not the SBMJOB command is being invoked inside the CL program, any other High Level Language program, or from the command line.

"The following rules apply to passing parameters if the CALL command is invoked via the SBMJOB command issued by a CL program:

- *"Character string constants of 32 bytes or less are always passed with a length of 32 bytes (padded on the right with blanks).*

- *"Constants longer than 32 characters are not padded to the length expected by the receiving program. In this case the calling program passes the exact number of bytes.*

- *"Character strings, resulting from variables substitutions, of 32 bytes or less, are passed with a length of 32 bytes (padded on the right with blanks).*

- *"If the resulting string is longer than 32 bytes, the exact number of bytes up to the last nonblank character is passed to the receiving program, not padded to the length expected by the receiving program.*

- *"Neither the variable's length defined in the calling program nor the receiving program have any effect on how the parameters are passed.*

- *"Numeric variables (whether passed as constants or passed as variables declared as numerics in the calling program) are passed in packed form and with a length of (15 5). Thus, the receiving program must declare the decimal field with a length of (15 5)."*

These limitations are unreasonable and should be eliminated. The SBMJOB command is old and probably has undergone very little change since Release 1 of CPF, the System/38's operating system, circa 1980. We think it's time IBM made a complete overhaul of some of this ancient code.

In the meantime, to circumvent the problems see Figures 1.73 and 1.74. They implement a character string 1 byte longer than necessary, which we set to a nonblank character in order to force the parameter data to end in a nonblank character.

```
X:          PGM

            DCL          VAR(&STRING) TYPE(*CHAR) LEN(91)
            DCL          VAR(&PART1)  TYPE(*CHAR) LEN(30)
            DCL          VAR(&PART2)  TYPE(*CHAR) LEN(30)
            DCL          VAR(&PART3)  TYPE(*CHAR) LEN(30)

            CHGVAR       VAR(&PART1) +
                         VALUE('A                                    ')
            CHGVAR       VAR(&PART2) +
                         VALUE('B                                    ')
            CHGVAR       VAR(&PART3) +
                         VALUE('C                                    ')

            CHGVAR       VAR(&STRING) VALUE(&PART1 *CAT &PART2 *CAT +
                         &PART3 *CAT '*')
            SBMJOB       CMD(CALL PGM(Y) PARM(&STRING))

            ENDPGM
```

Figure 1.73: Program X has been revised to allow it to contain a "forced" blank.

```
Y:          PGM          PARM(&STRING)

            DCL          VAR(&STRING) TYPE(*CHAR) LEN(91)
            DCL          VAR(&PART1)  TYPE(*CHAR) LEN(30)
            DCL          VAR(&PART2)  TYPE(*CHAR) LEN(30)
            DCL          VAR(&PART3)  TYPE(*CHAR) LEN(30)

            CHGVAR       VAR(&PART1) VALUE(%SST(&STRING 1 30))
            CHGVAR       VAR(&PART2) VALUE(%SST(&STRING 31 30))
            CHGVAR       VAR(&PART3) VALUE(%SST(&STRING 61 30))

            SNDMSG       MSG(&PART1) TOUSR(QSYSOPR)
            SNDMSG       MSG(&PART2) TOUSR(QSYSOPR)
            SNDMSG       MSG(&PART3) TOUSR(QSYSOPR)

            ENDPGM
```

Figure 1.74: Program Y now works correctly in both interactive and batch environments.

Alas, there's no circumvention for numeric parameters other than passing them as character and converting them to decimal inside the submitted program. Didn't we say it stinks?

—Midrange Computing Staff

97

SBMJOB Command Successful

I was working on a batch process for one of our clients, which is initiated by a single command from any command line, and I wanted to devise some method of reporting back to the user that the request had been submitted for processing. The best way to accomplish this was to send the user a message from the command screen much like you receive when a program is submitted to batch for compilation.

After some research, I discovered that the message I needed is CPC1221 in message file QCPFMSG. Using this information, I added the following section to the program that submits the job to batch (as shown in Figure 1.75).

```
DCL        VAR(&MSGDTA) +
             TYPE(*CHAR) +
             LEN(46)
SBMJOB     CMD(...) JOB(...)
RCVMSG     MSGDTA(&MSGDTA)
SNDPGMMSG  MSGID(CPC1221) +
             MSGF(QCPFMSG) +
             MSGDTA(&MSGDTA) +
             TOPGMQ(*PRV) +
             MSGTYPE(*INFO)
```

Figure 1.75: You can send relevant information about a job based on the message information it returns.

The pertinent operations are the DCL, RCVMSG, and SNDPGMMSG commands.

The declaration of correct length and type for the &MSGDTA variable was ascertained by performing the DSPMSGD command for CPC1221 in QCPFMSG and then taking option 2 to display field data. This option shows all of the variables used in a message and their respective data type, length, decimal positions, varying length, and dump status as applicable.

The command RCVMSG acts much like the MONMSG command (although it doesn't substitute) in that you can place the command immediately after an operation to capture any message generated. In this case, I wanted to capture the job submission message. Therefore, I placed the command right after the SBMJOB command. There are several items of information available through the RCVMSG command. However, in this case, all I wanted to capture was the variable message data.

Once I had captured the message data from the submit, it was turned around and sent to the requesting user through the SNDPGMMSG command. Using this command, you can format messages either free form or use messages already defined in message files such as QCPFMSG (as I did in this case).

When you use a predefined message, there can be variable data that needs to be passed. In this case, the &MSGDTA held the five variables: job number, user ID, job name, job queue, and job queue library. By placing this variable in the MSGDTA parameter of the SNDPGMMSG, the appropriate information is sent. An additional key point here is the designation of TOPGMQ. By using the *PRV designation for this parameter, the message is sent to the calling program in the invocation stack (in this case, the program, menu, or other object on which the command was entered). Finally, it is important to note the use of the *INFO value for the MSGTYPE parameter. This designates the message as informational only and thus requires no user action.

—Jim Johnson

Self-submitting CL Programs

Q: I am designing a cost accounting application for the furniture manufacturing firm where I work. The Finance department staff wants me to design many different reports, and each report should be available by taking an option from a menu. My problem is that I end up writing two CL programs: one to prompt for the report options and the other to actually generate the report. The first CL program runs the Submit Job (SBMJOB) command to place the second program in a job queue. I remember doing this hundreds of times on the S/36 with the // IF JOBQ statement. Is there a simple way to do the same on the AS/400?

A: Yes, there is a way. Your CL program needs a 1-byte character variable and the Retrieve Job Attributes (RTVJOBA) command, which can determine if the program is running interactively or in batch. See Figure 1.76 for a self-submitting CL program named PGM1.

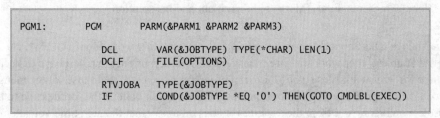

```
PGM1:      PGM        PARM(&PARM1 &PARM2 &PARM3)

           DCL        VAR(&JOBTYPE) TYPE(*CHAR) LEN(1)
           DCLF       FILE(OPTIONS)

           RTVJOBA    TYPE(&JOBTYPE)
           IF         COND(&JOBTYPE *EQ '0') THEN(GOTO CMDLBL(EXEC))
```

Figure 1.76: Here's a sample of a self-submitting CL program (part 1 of 2).

```
/* Present options display */
            SNDRCVF

            SBMJOB      CMD(CALL PGM(PGM1) PARM(&PARM1 &PARM2 &PARM3)) +
                        JOB(REPORT) JOBQ(QBATCH)
            RETURN

/* Generate report */
  EXEC:         (etc.)

            ENDPGM
```

Figure 1.76: Here's a sample of a self-submitting CL program (part 2 of 2).

When this program is called by taking an option from a menu, it runs interactively. The RTVJOBA command assigns &JOBTYPE a value of 1, which makes the IF command fail. So the program displays the options panel with the SNDRCVF command. When the user presses Enter, the CL program runs SBMJOB to submit itself to the job queue.

When the program begins running from the job queue, the RTVJOBA command assigns '0' to variable &JOBTYPE; the IF command then transfers control to tag EXEC, bypassing the SNDRCVF and SBMJOB commands and going directly to the portion that generates the report.

—Elsie Novodny

✦ ✦ ✦ Work Files

A Permanent Solution to Work Files

I once read a tip by Ernie Malaga regarding using permanent work files. (See "Using Permanent Work Files" later in this section.) I'd like to offer an alternate solution to the problem he presents. First, I'll recap the problem and his solution.

Mr. Malaga talks about the problem associated with creating work files in QTEMP. He says that unless your work files are flat (without field definitions) that you have to keep source for your work files somewhere. If a programmer realizes that those source members have no corresponding objects, the programmer might believe the source code to be obsolete and remove it from the system. He goes on to say that the next time you attempt to create the work file in QTEMP, the program fails.

Mr. Malaga offers the following solution: He suggests that you create your work files in one of your production libraries and leave them there permanently. When a job needs to write to a work file, use the Add Physical File Member (ADDPFM) command to add a uniquely named member. Then, when the job is near completion, use the Remove Member (RMVM) command to remove the member.

The reason that I don't feel that this is the best solution is that if the job ever gets cancelled or terminates abnormally, the RMVM command might never be executed. The member would then be left there and it might have many records in it. It also can happen more than once, and leave multiple unnecessary members in the file. In my opinion, this is an accident waiting to happen and has the potential to use up a substantial amount of wasted disk space. I believe I have a better solution.

My solution is to first use the Retrieve Object Description (RTVOBJD) command to retrieve the name of the library where the work file exists. Then, use the Create Duplicate Object (CRTDUPOBJ) command to create a duplicate object of the work file into QTEMP. In this way, the permanent work file on disk never actually gets written to. If the job ever gets cancelled or terminates abnormally, the work file goes away because it is in QTEMP. By using this method, you also have not run the risk of using obsolete or missing source code to create the work file.

—*Robin Klima*

Editors' Note: *We liked this solution so much that we wrote a command for easy inclusion in CL programs and called it Create Work File (CRTWRKF) command. See Figures 1.77 and 1.78.*

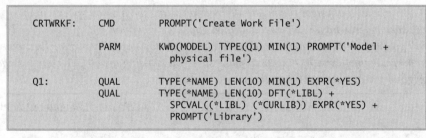

```
CRTWRKF:    CMD        PROMPT('Create Work File')

            PARM       KWD(MODEL) TYPE(Q1) MIN(1) PROMPT('Model +
                         physical file')

Q1:         QUAL       TYPE(*NAME) LEN(10) MIN(1) EXPR(*YES)
            QUAL       TYPE(*NAME) LEN(10) DFT(*LIBL) +
                         SPCVAL((*LIBL) (*CURLIB)) EXPR(*YES) +
                         PROMPT('Library')
```

Figure 1.77: Command CRTWRKF calls CPP program WRKF002CL to process work files.

```
wrkf002cl: +
    pgm parm(&qmodel)

    dcl var(&model)      type(*char) len(10)
    dcl var(&modellib)   type(*char) len(10)
    dcl var(&msgdta)     type(*char) len(80)
    dcl var(&msgf)       type(*char) len(10)
    dcl var(&msgflib)    type(*char) len(10)
    dcl var(&msgid)      type(*char) len(7)
    dcl var(&qmodel)     type(*char) len(20)
    dcl var(&rtnlib)     type(*char) len(10)

    monmsg msgid(cpf0000) exec(goto cmdlbl(error))

    /* Break qualified name */
    chgvar var(&model) value(%sst(&qmodel 1 10))
    chgvar var(&modellib) value(%sst(&qmodel 11 10))

    /* Create work file */
    dltf file(qtemp/&model)
    monmsg msgid(cpf0000)
    rtvobjd obj(&modellib/&model) objtype(*file) rtnlib(&rtnlib)
    crtdupobj obj(&model) fromlib(&rtnlib) objtype(*file) +
        tolib(qtemp) newobj(*obj) data(*no)
    return

    /* Send error message */
  error: +
    rcvmsg msgtype(*excp) msgdta(&msgdta) msgid(&msgid) msgf(&msgf) +
        msgflib(&msgflib)
    sndpgmmsg msgid(&msgid) msgf(&msgflib/&msgf) msgdta(&msgdta) +
        msgtype(*escape)
    endpgm
```

Figure 1.78: The command processor for command CRTWRKF lets you very easily process work files.

CRTWRKF creates a physical file in QTEMP by duplicating the file you specify in the MODEL parameter, which receives a qualified name. As you point out, quite correctly, the file will go away at the end of the job—whether this occurs normally or not. Just remember to override the file with OVRDBF to make sure you're using the QTEMP copy instead of the original file in the production library.

—Ted Holt and Shannon O'Donnell

Self-destructing AS/400 Files

You've probably seen the QTEMP library on the AS/400. But do you know why it is there? The QTEMP library is designed to specifically contain objects that are only necessary for the duration of a job. In other words, if you have a job that creates a file that is deleted before the job terminates, it can be changed to create the file in QTEMP. The specific deletion of the file is no longer required. At the end of the job, the file is scratched.

In addition to automatic deletion, any files in QTEMP only exist for their creating job. When using QTEMP, you don't need to worry about file name uniqueness among jobs.

If you plan on using the QTEMP library, there is one thing to keep in mind: The time between sign-on and sign-off is considered one job. If you run an interactive job that creates a file in QTEMP, it will be there until you sign off the session. While the "quasi-temporary" nature of QTEMP files in interactive jobs can sometimes be a limiting factor, the invisibility of the files to other jobs is still a great benefit.

—Midrange Computing Staff

Using Permanent Work Files

Most programmers I've spoken with use QTEMP whenever they need a temporary work file in an application. Why not, after all? QTEMP is meant to be used for temporary stuff anyway. The big advantage of using QTEMP is that it's unique to each job and it's gone as soon as the job ends.

Using QTEMP has one slight disadvantage, however. It requires you to create the file each time you need it. If your work files are flat (without field definitions) and intended to be used as program-described files, that's no hardship. In the AS/400 world, however, most programmers would rather work with externally described files.

This means that you'd have to keep the source DDS for your work files somewhere (and it can't be QTEMP!). If a programmer realizes that those source members have no corresponding objects, the programmer might believe the source code to be obsolete and remove it from the system. Next time you attempt to create the work file in QTEMP, the program fails.

A good alternative is to create your work files in one of your production libraries (preferably the same library you use for the programs and actual database files), and leave them there—permanently. The work file can have a rich field definition provided by complicated DDS (including references to permanent database files, edit codes, the works). You can even create logical files (even join files) on top of your work files!

This can be called a permanent work file. Because they're not in QTEMP, any job can access them. This does present a problem because two or more jobs could have a legitimate need to write records to the same work file. How do you tell apart the data from the two jobs? The answer is, fortunately, quite simple: Use a different member for each job's data.

It's not hard to do. Your permanent work file must be created with MAXMBRS(*NOMAX) to allow multiple members. Then each time a job needs to write to the file, add a member with the ADDPFM command. When the job is near completion, remove the member with the RMVM command.

Because each member must have a different name, you can name the member as 'JOB*nnnnn*' where nnnnn is the six-character job number—which you can retrieve with the RTVJOBA command, specifying NBR(&JOBNBR). Last, but not least, you must remember to override the permanent work file with the OVRDBF command so that all programs that follow reference the member just added.

It sounds complicated—and it is—but it works more efficiently than using QTEMP. To simplify the task, you can use the Add Work File Member (ADDWRKFMBR) command and the Remove Work File Member (RMVWRKFMBR) command (shown in Figures 1.79 and 1.80). Figure 1.81 shows CL program WRKF001CL and Figure 1.82 shows CL program WRKF002CL.

```
ADDWRKFMBR: CMD           PROMPT('Add Work File Member')

            PARM          KWD(FILE) TYPE(Q1) MIN(1) PROMPT('Work file +
                            name')
            PARM          KWD(OVERRIDE) TYPE(*CHAR) LEN(4) RSTD(*YES) +
                            DFT(*YES) VALUES(*YES *NO) +
                            PROMPT('Override to new member')
            PARM          KWD(RTNMBR) TYPE(*CHAR) LEN(10) RTNVAL(*YES) +
                            PMTCTL(*PMTRQS) PROMPT('CL var for new +
                            member (10)')
            PARM          KWD(ACTION) TYPE(*CHAR) LEN(4) CONSTANT(*ADD)

Q1:         QUAL          TYPE(*NAME) LEN(10) MIN(1)
            QUAL          TYPE(*NAME) LEN(10) DFT(*LIBL) +
                            SPCVAL((*LIBL) (*CURLIB)) PROMPT('Library')
```

Figure 1.79: Command ADDWRKFMBR makes it easier to process work file members.

```
RMVWRKFMBR: CMD        PROMPT('Remove Work File Member')

           PARM        KWD(FILE) TYPE(Q1) MIN(1) PROMPT('Work file +
                         name')
           PARM        KWD(OVERRIDE) TYPE(*ZEROELEM)
           PARM        KWD(RTNMBR) TYPE(*ZEROELEM)
           PARM        KWD(ACTION) TYPE(*CHAR) LEN(4) CONSTANT(*RMV)

Q1:        QUAL        TYPE(*NAME) LEN(10) MIN(1)
           QUAL        TYPE(*NAME) LEN(10) DFT(*LIBL) +
                         SPCVAL((*LIBL) (*CURLIB)) PROMPT('Library')
```

Figure 1.80: Command RMVWRKFMBR will be used to remove the temporary work file member.

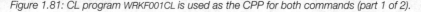

```
WRKF001CL: +
    PGM PARM(&QFILE &OVERRIDE &RTNMBR &ACTION)

    DCL VAR(&ACTION)    TYPE(*CHAR) LEN(4)
    DCL VAR(&FILE)      TYPE(*CHAR) LEN(10)
    DCL VAR(&JOBNBR)    TYPE(*CHAR) LEN(6)
    DCL VAR(&LIB)       TYPE(*CHAR) LEN(10)
    DCL VAR(&MBRNAME)   TYPE(*CHAR) LEN(10)
    DCL VAR(&MSGDTA)    TYPE(*CHAR) LEN(80)
    DCL VAR(&MSGF)      TYPE(*CHAR) LEN(10)
    DCL VAR(&MSGFLIB)   TYPE(*CHAR) LEN(10)
    DCL VAR(&MSGID)     TYPE(*CHAR) LEN(7)
    DCL VAR(&OVERRIDE)  TYPE(*CHAR) LEN(4)
    DCL VAR(&QFILE)     TYPE(*CHAR) LEN(20)
    DCL VAR(&RTNMBR)    TYPE(*CHAR) LEN(10)

    MONMSG MSGID(CPF0000) EXEC(GOTO CMDLBL(SNDERRMSG))

    /* Determine name of member */
    CHGVAR VAR(&FILE) VALUE(%SST(&QFILE 1 10))
    CHGVAR VAR(&LIB) VALUE(%SST(&QFILE 11 10))
    RTVJOBA NBR(&JOBNBR)
    CHGVAR VAR(&MBRNAME) VALUE('JOB' *CAT &JOBNBR)
    CHGVAR VAR(&RTNMBR) VALUE(&MBRNAME)
    MONMSG MSGID(MCH3601)

    /* Add or remove member as needed */
    IF COND(&ACTION *EQ '*ADD') THEN(ADDPFM FILE(&LIB/&FILE) +
        MBR(&MBRNAME))
    ELSE CMD(RMVM FILE(&LIB/&FILE) MBR(&MBRNAME))

    /* Override if necessary */
    IF COND(&OVERRIDE *EQ '*YES') THEN(OVRDBF FILE(&FILE) +
        TOFILE(&LIB/&FILE) MBR(&MBRNAME))
    GOTO CMDLBL(ENDPGM)
```

Figure 1.81: CL program WRKF001CL is used as the CPP for both commands (part 1 of 2).

```
    /* Send error message */
SNDERRMSG: +
    RCVMSG MSGTYPE(*EXCP) MSGDTA(&MSGDTA) MSGID(&MSGID) MSGF(&MSGF) +
        MSGFLIB(&MSGFLIB)
    SNDPGMMSG MSGID(&MSGID) MSGF(&MSGFLIB/&MSGF) MSGDTA(&MSGDTA) +
        MSGTYPE(*ESCAPE)

    /* End program */
  ENDPGM: +
ENDPGM
```

Figure 1.81: CL program WRKF001CL is used as the CPP for both commands (part 2 of 2).

```
wrkf002cl: +
    pgm parm(&qmodel)

    dcl var(&model)        type(*char) len(10)
    dcl var(&modellib)     type(*char) len(10)
    dcl var(&msgdta)       type(*char) len(80)
    dcl var(&msgf)         type(*char) len(10)
    dcl var(&msgflib)      type(*char) len(10)
    dcl var(&msgid)        type(*char) len(7)
    dcl var(&qmodel)       type(*char) len(20)
    dcl var(&rtnlib)       type(*char) len(10)


    monmsg msgid(cpf0000) exec(goto cmdlbl(error))

    /* Break qualified name */
    chgvar var(&model) value(%sst(&qmodel 1 10))
    chgvar var(&modellib) value(%sst(&qmodel 11 10))

    /* Create work file */
    dltf file(qtemp/&model)
    monmsg msgid(cpf0000)
    rtvobjd obj(&modellib/&model) objtype(*file) rtnlib(&rtnlib)
    crtdupobj obj(&model) fromlib(&rtnlib) objtype(*file) +
        tolib(qtemp) newobj(*obj) data(*no)
    return

    /* Send error message */
  error: +
    rcvmsg msgtype(*excp) msgdta(&msgdta) msgid(&msgid) msgf(&msgf) +
        msgflib(&msgflib)
    sndpgmmsg msgid(&msgid) msgf(&msgflib/&msgf) msgdta(&msgdta) +
        msgtype(*escape)
    endpgm
```

Figure 1.82: CL program WRKF002CL shows how work files may have been created in the past.

Figure 1.83 provides an example of how to use the ADDWRKFMBR command.

```
ADDWRKFMBR FILE(workfile) OVERRIDE(*YES)
CALL       PGM(PGM1)
CALL       PGM(PGM2)
RMVWRKFMBR FILE(workfile)
```

Figure 1.83: Using the ADDWRKFMBR command is easy, as shown here.

The ADDWRKFMBR command has an optional parameter, RTNMBR, in which you can enter a 10-character CL variable. If used, ADDWRKFMBR returns to the CL variable the name of the member it just added.

—*Ernie Malaga*

COBOL

◆   ◆   ◆   ◆

In This Chapter

Data Conversion

Data Definition

Data Integrity

Data Manipulation

OS/400 Specific

◆   ◆   ◆   ◆

CHAPTER 2

COBOL

*C*ommon business-oriented language (COBOL) has lived up to its name. One of the most widely used languages ever developed, COBOL is available for microcomputers to mainframes. Its death has been falsely predicted time and time again, and its supposed replacements didn't survive in the marketplace.

COBOL achieved its prominence because it was good for business data processing. Before COBOL was available, many shops used FORTRAN (short for *for*mula *tran*slator). In its earliest incarnations, FORTRAN had no character data type. Characters were supported with integer variables. Because FORTRAN did not support decimal arithmetic, column totals on reports sometimes would be off a few cents here or there.

COBOL has suffered the same fate as other languages as manufacturers have added extensions to the language to take advantage of hardware or operating-system features. This means that programmers who move from one platform to another already know the basic language, but must learn new features.

The iSeries, like its predecessors, the System/38 and AS/400, has a COBOL compiler that doesn't conform 100 percent to the standards. The iSeries COBOL reference manual explains all of the machine-specific features. This chapter mentions a few of them. But mostly this chapter provides some tips that COBOL programmers have already found to be useful.

—Ted Holt

✦ ✦ ✦ Data Conversion

Converting Hexadecimal to Decimal in COBOL

If you've ever had to migrate data from a mainframe or a UNIX box, you've probably been exposed to data that was stored as hexadecimal. Generally, when you migrate it to the AS/400, you might find that you have a problem showing that data on a display screen or report. Here's an easy solution.

With a simple MOVE statement, a character field containing a hex value can be converted to a decimal number for display purposes (see Figure 2.1). The hex value is moved to the low-order byte of a 2-byte binary field (which, in COBOL, is created by defining a 4-decimal digit binary field). Because the field has been redefined as alpha, the MOVE statement is legal, and the decimal equivalent can now be displayed.

```
*****************************************************************
*
* To Create: CRTCBLPGM PGM(xxx/CVTHEXDEC) SRCFILE(xxx/QLBLSRC) +
*                      SRCMBR(CVTHEXDEC)
*
*****************************************************************
  IDENTIFICATION DIVISION.
  PROGRAM-ID. CVTHEXDEC.
  DATA DIVISION.
  WORKING-STORAGE SECTION.
* CHARACTER FIELD HEX-CHAR-INPUT CONTAINS THE LETTER "A"
  01  HEX-CHAR-INPUT PIC X VALUE X"C1".
  01  BINARY-VALUE PIC S9(4) BINARY VALUE 0.
  01  BINARY-VALUE-CHAR REDEFINES BINARY-VALUE.
      05  HIGH-ORDER-BYTE PIC X.
      05  LOW-ORDER-BYTE PIC X.
*
  PROCEDURE DIVISION.
  MAINLINE.
* ===> CONVERT HEX TO DECIMAL FOR DISPLAY
      MOVE HEX-CHAR-INPUT TO LOW-ORDER-BYTE.
      DISPLAY BINARY-VALUE.
* BINARY-VALUE WILL = 193
```

Figure 2.1: With a MOVE statement, you can convert a hex value to a decimal for a display in COBOL.

If, for some reason, you want to display a decimal number as a hexadecimal number on a screen, use the "remainder method" (Figure 2.2). To use this method, first divide the decimal number by 16 (Hex is in base 16); place the quotient in byte 1 and the remainder in byte 2. Next, check the numeric value of each byte. Values less than 10 can be moved.

On the other hand, values 10 through 16 must be first evaluated as characters A through F and then moved accordingly. The converted hex value can now be displayed.

```
************************************************************************
*
* To Create: CRTCBLPGM PGM(xxx/CVTDECHEX) SRCFILE(xxx/QLBLSRC) +
*            SRCMBR(CVTDECHEX)
*
************************************************************************
 IDENTIFICATION DIVISION.
 PROGRAM-ID. CVTDECHEX.

DATA DIVISION.
 WORKING-STORAGE SECTION.
 01  BINARY-VALUE PIC S9(4) BINARY VALUE 193.
 01  BINARY-VALUE-CHAR REDEFINES BINARY-VALUE.
     05 HIGH-ORDER-BYTE PIC X.
     05 LOW-ORDER-BYTE PIC X.
*
 01  BYTE-1 PIC S9(3) COMP-3 VALUE 0.
 01  BYTE-2 PIC S9(3) COMP-3 VALUE 0.
 01  BYTE-HOLD PIC S9(3) COMP-3 VALUE 0.
 01  SINGLE-DIGIT PIC S9 COMP-3 VALUE 0.
 01  START-POS PIC S9 COMP-3 VALUE 0.
 01  HEX-CHAR-DISPLAY PIC X(2) VALUE SPACES.

 PROCEDURE DIVISION.
 MAINLINE.
* ===> CONVERT DECIMAL TO HEX FOR DISPLAY
      DIVIDE 16 INTO BINARY-VALUE
         GIVING BYTE-1
         REMAINDER BYTE-2.
     IF BYTE-1 < 10
         MOVE BYTE-1 TO SINGLE-DIGIT
         MOVE SINGLE-DIGIT TO HEX-CHAR-DISPLAY(1:1)
     ELSE
         MOVE 1 TO START-POS
         MOVE BYTE-1 TO BYTE-HOLD
         PERFORM CONVERT-BYTE-HOLD
     END-IF.
     IF BYTE-2 < 10
         MOVE BYTE-2 TO SINGLE-DIGIT
         MOVE SINGLE-DIGIT TO HEX-CHAR-DISPLAY(2:1)
     ELSE
         MOVE 2 TO START-POS
         MOVE BYTE-2 TO BYTE-HOLD
         PERFORM CONVERT-BYTE-HOLD
     END-IF.
```

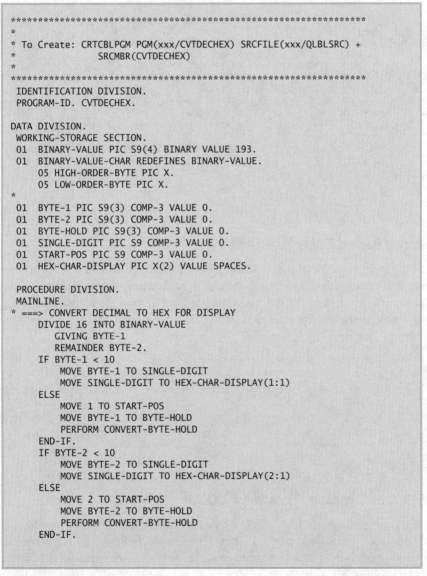

Figure 2.2: Use the remainder method to convert a decimal to hexadecimal for a display in COBOL (part 1 of 2).

```
      DISPLAY HEX-CHAR-DISPLAY.
 * HEX-CHAR-DISPLAY WILL = C1
      GOBACK.

 CONVERT-BYTE-HOLD.
     EVALUATE BYTE-HOLD
         WHEN 10 MOVE "A" TO HEX-CHAR-DISPLAY(START-POS:1)
         WHEN 11 MOVE "B" TO HEX-CHAR-DISPLAY(START-POS:1)
         WHEN 12 MOVE "C" TO HEX-CHAR-DISPLAY(START-POS:1)
         WHEN 13 MOVE "D" TO HEX-CHAR-DISPLAY(START-POS:1)
         WHEN 14 MOVE "E" TO HEX-CHAR-DISPLAY(START-POS:1)
         WHEN 15 MOVE "F" TO HEX-CHAR-DISPLAY(START-POS:1)
     END-EVALUATE.
```

Figure 2.2: Use the remainder method to convert a decimal to hexadecimal for a display in COBOL (part 2 of 2).

—Tom Conover

Selecting Packed Fields from Tables

COBOL programs with embedded SQL statements present a wrinkle you might not be aware of. If you are selecting a group of fields in packed format from tables and you try to use those fields in your COBOL program, you have to fetch the fields into working storage variables (which are defined as packed). Then you must unpack them before using them in the COBOL program.

Suppose a field is packed (numeric) in a table. You have to define that field in working storage as S9(n) COMP-3 and then unpack this field before you can use it in your program.

— Douglas Holleman

✦ ✦ ✦ Data Definition

Define Your Own Data Types in ILE COBOL

It's fairly common to want to duplicate all the elementary and group items below a base item and place them under a new base item. For example, in Figure 2.3, I have duplicated elem1 and elem2. Now, I have to remember to change both copies of elem1 if I change elem1 (and similarly for elem2). Of course, some people use COPY libraries to get around this problem, but, in complicated scenarios, you could end up with many COPY statements.

```
01  mygroup1.
     05 elem1 PIC X .
     05 elem2 PIC s9.

01  mygroup2.
     05 elem1 PIC X .
     05 elem2 PIC s9.
```

Figure 2.3: These two group items are defined with the same elementary items.

The TYPEDEF reserved word in V4R2 ILE COBOL allows you to define templates that can be used by both **mygroup1** and **mygroup2**. In Figure 2.4, both **mygroup1** and **mygroup2** end up with the exact same definition as before. However, if I want to change the way **elem1** is defined, I have to do it only once.

```
DATA DIVISION.
WORKING-STORAGE SECTION.

01  mytemplate IS TYPEDEF.
     05   elem1 PIC X.
     05   elem2 PIC S9.

01  mygroup1    TYPE mytemplate.
01  mygroup2    TYPE mytemplate.
77  mygroup3    TYPE mytemplate.

PROCEDURE DIVISION.
MAIN-LOGIC.
     MOVE "B" TO elem1 OF mygroup1.
     MOVE "C" TO elem1 OF mygroup2.
     MOVE "D" TO elem1 OF mygroup3.
     COMPUTE elem2 OF mygroup1 = 7.
     COMPUTE elem2 OF mygroup2 = 8.
     COMPUTE elem2 OF mygroup3 = 9.
     DISPLAY mygroup1.
     DISPLAY mygroup2.
     DISPLAY mygroup3.
     GOBACK.
```

Figure 2.4: The TYPEDEF keyword allows group items to share common definitions.

TYPEDEF can even be used with data defined with the level number 77, which normally are not divided into subordinate elementary items. Variable **mygroup3**, like **mygroup1** and **mygroup2**, also has data elements **elem1** and **elem2**.

— Chris Tandy

Easy and Meaningful COBOL Indicators

COBOL programmers can take advantage of the language's ability to define level-88 conditions to make indicators more self-documenting. Doing so, however, requires fore-thought and strict compliance with coding standards.

First, devise your indicator standards. For example, always condition the Subfile Clear (SFLCLR) keyword with indicator 80, and Subfile End (SFLEND) with indicator 81. Second, create a separate source member, STDINDIC, as shown in Figure 2.5.

```
01 standard-indicators.
*        Indicator 50 controlled by CHANGE keyword.
    02 data-changed-indic        PIC 1        INDIC 50.
       88 data-changed           VALUE B"1".
       88 data-not-changed       VALUE B"0".

*        Indicator 80 controls SFLCLR.
    02 subfile-clear-indic       PIC 1        INDIC 80.
       88 subfile-clear-active   VALUE B"1".
       88 subfile-clear-inactive VALUE B"0".

*        Indicator N81 controls SFLEND.
    02 subfile-end-indic         PIC 1        INDIC 81.
       88 subfile-end-active     VALUE B"0".
       88 subfile-end-inactive   VALUE B"1".

*        Indicator 99 controls ALARM.
    02 sound-alarm-indic         PIC 1        INDIC 99.
       88 sound-alarm-active     VALUE B"1".
       88 sound-alarm-inactive   VALUE B"0".
```

Figure 2.5: Standard indicator assignments are defined in the STDINDIC copy member.

Notice that every indicator you use must be defined in a level-02 entry, using PIC 1 and the INDIC clause to specify which actual, numbered indicator is mapped. Below each level-02 entry, code two level-88 conditions with meaningful names and give them values of 1 and 0 (bit) for the ON and OFF conditions, respectively.

Every interactive program you write should follow these steps.

1. Be sure to use a separate indicator area for all of your display files. This involves using the INDARA keyword in the DDS and the -SI attribute in the
   SELECT statement of the COBOL program.

2. Don't code a COPY DD-ALL-FORMATS-INDIC for the display file. It is unnecessary.

3. Somewhere in the WORKING-STORAGE section in Area A, code a COPY for your STDINDIC member. This declares your version of the indicators as a data structure that has meaningful subfield names, each one with level-88 conditions.

4. Use INDICATORS ARE STANDARD-INDICATORS in any display file I/O that uses indicators. This forces the program to use your version of the indicators.

You can now employ the level-88 condition names as you see fit. To test an indicator, use an IF statement with the level-88 condition name. To set an indicator, use a SET statement. An example is shown in Figure 2.6.

```
* The following code tests indicator 50.  Indicator 50 is the response
* indicator for the CHANGE keyword in the display file DDS.

    READ display-file
       INTO detail-i
       FORMAT IS "DETAIL"
       INDICATORS ARE standard-indicators
    END-READ.

    IF data-changed THEN
       PERFORM check-input
    END-IF.

* The following code initializes a subfile.  Indicator 80 controls
* SFLCLR, indicator 81 controls SFLEND.

    SET subfile-clear-active TO TRUE.
    SET subfile-end-active   TO TRUE.

    WRITE display-record
       FROM detail-o
       FORMAT IS "DETAIL"
       INDICATORS ARE standard-indicators
    END-WRITE.
```

Figure 2.6: COBOL programs can use STDINDIC to set indicators.

If the previous technique for easy and meaningful indicators is not satisfactory for you (for example, you find the requirement of strict adherence to coding standards too limiting), you can use this technique to give indicators meaningful names. However, because they will no longer be level-88 conditions, you'll have to test them with an IF that has an equal (=) sign, and you'll have to set your indicators with a MOVE instead of a SET.

For example, suppose you have created a display file that uses indicator 61 to condition the DSPATR(HI) keyword (thereby allowing you to display a field in high intensity by turning on indicator 61). Figure 2.7 shows how to code your COBOL program.

```
WORKING-STORAGE SECTION.
01 display-file-indicators.
   COPY DD-ALL-FORMATS-INDIC OF dspfnam
        REPLACING in61 BY high-intensity.

01 program-literals.
   02 false-value      PIC 1 VALUE B"0".
   02 true-value       PIC 1 VALUE B"1".

PROCEDURE DIVISION.
   MOVE true-value TO high-intensity.

   WRITE display-record
      FROM panel-o
      FORMAT IS "PANEL"
      INDICATORS ARE display-file-indicators
   END-WRITE.
```

Figure 2.7: This COBOL program uses meaningful indicator names.

The key to this technique is making sure you use the REPLACING phrase of the COPY statement. In the preceding example, I took advantage of REPLACING to rename IN61 as HIGH-INTENSITY. Also, I have to declare two literals, FALSE-VALUE and TRUE-VALUE, with PIC 1 and values of 0 and 1 (bit) respectively.

As you can see, this method is easier to set up initially (it doesn't require any code standards), but is harder to code because it requires you to code the REPLACING phrase listing all indicators in every program that uses them.

—*Ernie Malaga*

✦ ✦ ✦ Data Integrity

Avoiding MCH1202 Errors

One of COBOL's limitations is that it doesn't automatically initialize numeric fields to zeros when writing data to a file (something that RPG does very well). Instead, by default, it places blanks in numeric fields. When another program tries to read a numeric field containing invalid data, it receives the infamous MCH1202 error.

You can make sure that you move zero values to empty numeric fields when writing data to a file in programs that you are working on, but how can you avoid getting the MCH1202 error when working with data written by other COBOL programs? As more and more mainframe shops migrate to the AS/400, the occurrence of this error message has become more prevalent.

Using the IF NUMERIC command phrase in COBOL (see the code fragment shown in Figure 2.8), you can perform a simple test to determine if a field contains numeric data. IF NUMERIC is similar to the TESTN operation code in RPG. If the test fails, perform the appropriate routine to take corrective action.

```
IF NUMERIC-VARIABLE NOT NUMERIC
    MOVE ZEROS TO NUMERIC-VARIABLE.
```

Figure 2.8: Use the NUMERIC test to avoid COBOL decimal data errors.

—Jeff Mileham

Compute Is Imprecise

Suppose you were asked to write a simple COBOL program to calculate Joe Montana's pass completion percentage. You calculate it by dividing pass completions by pass attempts. See Figure 2.9.

```
        IDENTIFICATION DIVISION.
        PROGRAM-ID. CMP001CB.
        AUTHOR. TOM CONOVER
        DATE-WRITTEN. OCTOBER 27, 1994.
        *
        *    JOE MONTANA'S STATS THRU WEEK EIGHT OF 1994-95 NFL SEASON
        *
        ENVIRONMENT DIVISION.
        CONFIGURATION SECTION.
        SOURCE-COMPUTER. IBM-AS400.
        OBJECT-COMPUTER. IBM-AS400.
        DATA DIVISION.
        WORKING-STORAGE SECTION.
        *
```

Figure 2.9: The COBOL compiler generates intermediate result variables that are too small (part 1 of 2).

```
01  WS-PASS-COMPLETIONS        PIC 9(3) VALUE 181.
01  WS-PASS-ATTEMPTS           PIC 9(3) VALUE 280.
01  WS-COMPLETION-PERCENTAGE   PIC 9(3)V9.
01  DETAIL-LINE.
    05  DL-PASS-COMPLETIONS    PIC 999.
    05  FILLER                 PIC X(6) VALUE SPACES.
    05  DL-PASS-ATTEMPTS       PIC 999.
    05  FILLER                 PIC X(9) VALUE SPACES.
    05  DL-COMPLETION-PERCENTAGE PIC ZZ9.9.
/
PROCEDURE DIVISION.
000-MAINLINE.
    DISPLAY "COMP      ATTEMPTS     AVERAGE".
*
    COMPUTE WS-COMPLETION-PERCENTAGE =
        (WS-PASS-COMPLETIONS / WS-PASS-ATTEMPTS) * 100
*
    MOVE WS-PASS-COMPLETIONS    TO DL-PASS-COMPLETIONS.
    MOVE WS-PASS-ATTEMPTS       TO DL-PASS-ATTEMPTS.
    MOVE WS-COMPLETION-PERCENTAGE TO DL-COMPLETION-PERCENTAGE.
*
    DISPLAY DETAIL-LINE.
    GOBACK.
*-----------------------------------------------------------------
* RESULTS:
* >CALL CMP001CB
*  COMP     ATTEMPTS    AVERAGE
*  181      280         60.0
```

Figure 2.9: The COBOL compiler generates intermediate result variables that are too small (part 2 of 2).

A yellow flag is thrown for roughing the passer when you run this program using COBOL/400. The answer should be 64.6, not 60.0. The problem is that the IBM COBOL/400 compiler generates intermediate field sizes that are too small when used with the COMPUTE verb.

You'll encounter another problem when using the ROUNDED option. This option causes rounding at all intermediate stages of computation. Rounding should be done, in this case, once—at the end of the calculation.

Figure 2.10 shows the corrected program. It resolves the problem by creating a higher precision work field to receive the result (thereby causing the compiler to create more precise work fields). Then it rounds the result into the receiving field at the precision desired. Be aware that this method will not work for fields that approach the COBOL limit of 18 digits. Unless you are trying to calculate Joe Montana's salary, that shouldn't be a problem.

```
           IDENTIFICATION DIVISION.
           PROGRAM-ID. CMP001CB.
           AUTHOR. TOM CONOVER
           DATE-WRITTEN. OCTOBER 27, 1994.
          *
          *    JOE MONTANA'S STATS THRU WEEK EIGHT OF 1994-95 NFL SEASON
          *
           ENVIRONMENT DIVISION.
           CONFIGURATION SECTION.
           SOURCE-COMPUTER. IBM-AS400.
           OBJECT-COMPUTER. IBM-AS400.
           DATA DIVISION.
           WORKING-STORAGE SECTION.
          *
           01  WS-PASS-COMPLETIONS        PIC 9(3) VALUE 181.
           01  WS-PASS-ATTEMPTS           PIC 9(3) VALUE 280.
           01  WS-COMPLETION-PERCENTAGE   PIC 9(3)V9.
           01  WS-HIGH-PRECISION-RESULT   PIC 9(3)V9999.
           01  DETAIL-LINE.
               05  DL-PASS-COMPLETIONS    PIC 999.
               05  FILLER                 PIC X(6) VALUE SPACES.
               05  DL-PASS-ATTEMPTS       PIC 999.
               05  FILLER                 PIC X(9) VALUE SPACES.
               05  DL-COMPLETION-PERCENTAGE PIC ZZ9.9.
          /
           PROCEDURE DIVISION.
           000-MAINLINE.
               DISPLAY "COMP    ATTEMPTS     AVERAGE".
          *
               COMPUTE WS-HIGH-PRECISION-RESULT =
                   (WS-PASS-COMPLETIONS / WS-PASS-ATTEMPTS) * 100
          *
               COMPUTE WS-COMPLETION-PERCENTAGE ROUNDED =
                   WS-HIGH-PRECISION-RESULT
          *
               MOVE WS-PASS-COMPLETIONS        TO DL-PASS-COMPLETIONS.
               MOVE WS-PASS-ATTEMPTS           TO DL-PASS-ATTEMPTS.
               MOVE WS-COMPLETION-PERCENTAGE TO DL-COMPLETION-PERCENTAGE.
          *
               DISPLAY DETAIL-LINE.
               GOBACK.
          *-------------------------------------------------------------
          * RESULTS:
          * >CALL CMP002CB
          *  COMP    ATTEMPTS    AVERAGE
          *  181     280         64.6
```

Figure 2.10: To make the calculations accurate, define your own working variable.

—Tom Conover

✦ ✦ ✦ Data Manipulation

Built-in Functions for COBOL

IBM added a lot of new functions to ILE COBOL with V3R7. Generally, you can use these functions in the PROCEDURE DIVISION wherever you would normally code a data item name. However, there are a few places you can't use functions:

- At the receiving end of an assignment statement, such as MOVE or COMPUTE.

- Where specifically forbidden in the manual, for every statement in the PROCEDURE DIVISION.

- Where a data item requires special usage, size, or other characteristics, and the function would yield different characteristics.

Table 2.1 shows the list of functions. Figure 2.11 shows a few examples of use.

Table 2.1: COBOL Built-in Functions

ACOS	DAY-TO-YYYYDDD	NUMVAL-C
ASIN	INTEGER-OF-DATE	ORD
ATAN	INTEGER-OF-DAY	REVERSE
CHAR	LENGTH	SIN
COS	LOG	SQRT
CURRENT-DATE	LOG10	TAN
DATE-OF-INTEGER	LOWERCASE	UPPERCASE
DAY-OF-INTEGER	MEAN	WHEN-COMPILED
DATE-TO-YYYYMMDD	NUMVAL	YEAR-TO-YYYY

```
PROCEDURE DIVISION.
retrieve-system-date.
    MOVE FUNCTION CURRENT-DATE(1:8) TO system-date.

* The following paragraph takes a numeric date in YYYYMMDD
* and adds DELTA-DAYS to obtain a NEW-DATE.
add-to-date-yyyymmdd.
    COMPUTE new-date =
        FUNCTION DATE-OF-INTEGER(
            FUNCTION INTEGER-OF-DATE(numeric-date) + delta-days).

compare-ignoring-case.
    IF FUNCTION UPPER-CASE(string-1) =
        FUNCTION UPPER-CASE(string-2) THEN
        PERFORM strings-are-equal
    END-IF.
strings-are-equal.

calculate-average-of-numbers.
    COMPUTE average = FUNCTION MEAN(num-1 num-2 num-3).

* The following paragraph calculates the average of all
* elements in a one-dimensional table.
calculate-average-of-table.
    COMPUTE average = FUNCTION MEAN(table-name(ALL)).

* Perform a simple ROT-3 cryptography (i.e., rotate all characters
* three positions forward).
rot-3-cryptography.
    PERFORM VARYING i FROM1 BY 1
        UNTIL i =FUNCTION LENGTH(xxx)
        COMPUTE character-number = FUNCTION ORD(xxx(i:1)) + 3
        IF character-number 256 THEN
            SUBTRACT 256 FROM character-number
        END-IF
        MOVE FUNCTION CHAR(character-number) TO xxx(i:1)
    END-PERFORM
```

Figure 2.11: COBOL functions can generally be used wherever data items are used.

—*Ernie Malaga*

Reference Modification

RPG IV programmers are understandably excited about the %SUBST (substring) function. Recently, I have met many veteran COBOL programmers who didn't know that COBOL has had this powerful substringing capability, called *reference modification*, since the early '80s.

To reference modify a variable, follow the variable name with a parenthesized expression consisting of a starting position, a colon, and, optionally, a length. As with %SUBST, if the length is omitted, the rest of the string is assumed.

One advantage of reference modification over %SUBST is that reference modification may be used on zoned decimal data as well as character data. In contrast, %SUBST cannot access any type of numeric data. Figure 2.12 contains some examples of reference modification.

```
* Reference modifying a scalar variable
     MOVE file-date(5:2) TO screen-year.

* Reference modifying a table element
     MOVE table-file-date(1)(5:2) TO screen-year.

* Reference modifying zoned decimal data
     IF screen-date(5:2) < 50 THEN
         MOVE 20 TO file-date(1:2)
     ELSE
         MOVE 19 to file-date(1:2)
     END-IF.
```

Figure 2.12: COBOL's reference modification reduces the need for substring variables.

—Anthony P. Gerasch

Sorting Tables in COBOL

Q: I have a table in COBOL that has 100 occurrences in it. I would like a way to "order" these occurrences based on the values of the elements in the table. Can anyone help me?

A: Here are several methods:

1. Save the records to a temporary keyed database file and read them back in keyed order.

2. Use a bubble sort. It is one of the easiest sort algorithms to understand and is practically as efficient as other sort algorithms if you're sorting a small set of data. An added advantage of the bubble sort is that the only additional storage required is equal in length to one element of the set and is used for the swapping operation.

3. If you want to get adventurous, check out the new sorting APIs, QLGSORT and QLGSRTIO.

4. Pass the table to an RPG program. After entry, the RPG program will have just two lines of executable calculations: a SORTA table name and a RETURN. When your COBOL program gets the table back, all the entries should be sorted.

5. I had to do this once. I wrote my table entries to a user index. Check the API reference for creating, filling, and retrieving user indexes.

6. The COBOL sort is very efficient on the AS/400. Therefore, the SORT verb should do a good job. In the input procedure, RELEASE the table elements into the sort file. In the output procedure, RETURN the sort file records into the table.

—David Abramowitz
—Tom Conover
—Ted Holt
—Mario Martinez
—Martin Neugebauer

✦ ✦ ✦ OS/400 Specific

Data Area Support in COBOL

Q: Is it possible for a COBOL program to read a data area? I've asked many people but, so far, no one knows. Of course, I could just create a CL program and pass the data to the COBOL program (which I did), but I would just like to know if it can be done the other way. I'm not talking about a local data area (LDA).

A: IBM added support for data areas to COBOL with V3R7. To read from a data area, use the ACCEPT statement; to write to a data area, use the DISPLAY statement. Figure 2.13 shows the correct syntax.

```
WORKING-STORAGE SECTION.
01 alex-data.
    02 stored-data PIC X(5).

PROCEDURE DIVISION.
write-data-area.
    MOVE "hello" TO stored-data.
    DISPLAY alex-data UPON data-area
        FOR "ALXDTAARA" LIBRARY "MYLIB"
    END-DISPLAY.

get-data-area.
    ACCEPT alex-data FROM data-area
        FOR "ALXDTAARA" LIBRARY "MYLIB"
    END-ACCEPT.
```

Figure 2.13: COBOL supports data areas.

First, you must define a data structure containing the data from the data area. In Figure 2.13, I assume the data area is of type *CHAR, 5 bytes long; this makes PIC X(5) the correct definition for the variable.

Next, use the DISPLAY or ACCEPT statement, as required. Notice the syntax of DISPLAY; the UPON clause references a mnemonic that must have been defined earlier, in the SPECIAL-NAMES paragraph. ACCEPT needs the same mnemonic in the FROM clause. In addition, you can include any of the following:

- An AT clause to indicate where within the data area to read or write.

- A WITH LOCK clause if you want to lock the data area after the read or write operation.

- An ON EXCEPTION or a NOT ON EXCEPTION clause with imperative statements.

Finally, you can use explicit END-ACCEPT and END-DISPLAY delimiters.

—Alex Nubla

Dealing with Record Locks in COBOL

Q: I need help understanding the finer points of record locking management in COBOL on the AS/400. If I read a record from a file opened in I/O mode, does OS/400 lock this record for me? How do I read a record without locking it? Can COBOL programs determine which job has a record locked?

A: In COBOL, as in RPG, reading a record from a database file opened as I/O places a lock on the record. Check the file status code to see if the record is locked. Locked records are indicated by status code 9D.

The READ statement accepts a WITH NO LOCK clause that does for COBOL what (N) does for RPG IV. For example, consider the code shown in Figure 2.14.

```
READ customer-master-file WITH NO LOCK
    INVALID KEY
        SET customer-not-found TO TRUE
    NOT INVALID KEY
        SET customer-found TO TRUE
        PERFORM get-customer-info\
```

Figure 2.14: Read a record from a database file with NO LOCK specified.

—Midrange Computing Staff

Commands

Commands

✦ ✦ ✦ ✦

In This Chapter

Alternate Command Access

Command Logging

Cross Reference

Error Messages

Interactive Command Processing

Menus

Parameters

Prompting

Shortcut Commands

UIM

Working with Commands

✦ ✦ ✦ ✦

*T*he AS/400 is famous for its intuitive command interface. If you know what a command is supposed to do, such as configure TCP/IP services, then you can guess the actual command name (CFGTCP in this case). Intuitive command names are just one of the many things that make the AS/400 an easy-to-use system. In addition, built into the AS/400 is the capability for you to create your own intuitive commands to perform your unique functions. You have a system that can't be beat for its ease of use and developer-friendly interface.

However, actually creating commands—like anything else that you can do on the AS/400—can range from very easy to extremely difficult. Much depends upon the level of complexity you are after. Because of this, working with OS/400 commands, and creating your own user-defined commands, can sometimes be quite a challenge. That's when you'll benefit from the assistance of folks who have been there before you and have already worked through some of that complexity. And that's why this chapter on commands is so important.

Within this chapter you'll find some of the very best command tips and tricks published over the years in the pages of *Midrange Computing* magazine. Find out how to create your own shortcuts for AS/400 commands, how to create ad hoc commands, how to work with command parameters, and so much more.

—Shannon O'Donnell

✦ ✦ ✦ Alternate Command Access

Using System Request to Execute a Command

The AS/400 allows you to send a message to a message queue by using the System Request key with option 5 (Send a message). This can be done even while your workstation is input inhibited (unlike the Attention key program). By using the program shown in Figure 3.1, the "Send a message" option can be used to send a command that gets executed by the operating system.

The program EXCMD (Figure 3.1) executes a command that is sent to it from a message queue. After creating the program, enter the commands in Figure 3.2 or add them to your initial program.

```
/* The following command must be executed before EXCMD can be +
       used: +
       ADDLIBLE  LIB(QTEMP) +
       CRTMSGQ   MSGQ(QTEMP/Q) +
       CHGMSGQ   MSGQ(QTEMP/Q) DLVRY(*BREAK) PGM(EXCMD) */

   EXCMD: +
     PGM PARM(&QUE &LIB &KEY)

     DCL VAR(&QUE)        TYPE(*CHAR) LEN(10)
     DCL VAR(&LIB)        TYPE(*CHAR) LEN(10)
     DCL VAR(&KEY)        TYPE(*CHAR) LEN(4)
     DCL VAR(&CMD)        TYPE(*CHAR) LEN(132)

     MONMSG MSGID(CPF0000)
     RCVMSG MSGQ(&LIB/&QUE) KEYVAR(&KEY) MSG(&CMD)
     CALL PGM(QCMDEXC) PARM(&CMD 132)

     ENDPGM
```

Figure 3.1: The EXCMD command can make sending commands, even with an inhibited workstation, easy.

```
ADDLIBLE   LIB(QTEMP)
CRTMSGQ    MSGQ(QTEMP/Q)
CHGMSGQ    MSGQ(QTEMP/Q) DLVRY(*BREAK) PGM(EXCMD)
```

Figure 3.2: Here's how to work with the EXCMD command.

To enter a command at any time, press the System Request key and enter a "5" followed by a command in single quotes and the parameter TOMSGQ(Q). For example:

```
5 'wrksbmjob *job' tomsgq(q)
```

If you want to prompt the command, put a question mark in front of the command (i.e. ?WRKSBMJOB). You might also want to use this technique to CALL QCMD to see any error messages that might be generated.

—Robin Klima

✦ ✦ ✦ Command Logging

Logging All CL Commands

Q: Do you know of a tool that can save, display, or print the actions of each signed-on user throughout the day? I know the history log shows the date and time the user signed on to the AS/400 and whether there were any messages. However, I would also like to see the different jobs they ran (interactive and batch).

A: In V2R3 and later, you can activate user-profile auditing, which causes the system to create a journal entry for each command entered by specified users. You can then display these journal entries to find out which commands a user has executed. Perform the following steps to activate this feature:

1. Check to see if library QSYS contains a journal called QAUDJRN. If so, skip to step 4.

   ```
   CHKOBJ OBJ(QSYS/QAUDJRN) OBJTYPE(*JRN)
   ```

2. Create a journal receiver. Give it any valid name and place it in any library.

   ```
   CRTJRNRCV JRNRCV(xxx/journal-receiver)
   ```

3. Create the system-auditing journal. The journal must be called QAUDJRN and must be placed in library QSYS. Specify the journal receiver you created in step 2 in the JRNRCV parameter.

   ```
   CRTJRN JRN(QSYS/QAUDJRN) JRNRCV(xxx/journal-receiver)
   ```

129

4. Change the auditing control-system value to activate auditing.

```
CHGSYSVAL SYSVAL(QAUDCTL) VALUE(*AUDLVL)
```

5. Change user auditing to log CL commands for the users whom you want to audit.

```
CHGUSRAUD USRPRF(user-profile) AUDLVL(*CMD)
```

Now, when you want to know which commands a user has executed, use the Display Journal (DSPJRN) command.

```
DSPJRN JRN(QSYS/QAUDJRN) OUTPUT(*OUTFILE) OUTFILE(xxx/file-name)
```

The *OUTFILE option creates a file that contains the entries. You can query this file to retrieve the records for a particular user and time period.

—Midrange Computing Staff

✦ ✦ ✦ Cross Reference

Where Did I Use That Command?

When you modify a command, by adding or deleting a parameter or changing a parameter's attributes, you might need to change some or all of the CL programs that call the command. But what if you don't recall the names of all these CL programs? The PRTCMDUSG command comes to the rescue by spooling a list of all CL programs that use the command in question. Actually, you can specify up to 50 commands on which to search.

Note: Any HLL programs that executes a command by calling QCMDEXC *will not be listed.*

—Midrange Computing Staff

✦ ✦ ✦ Error Messages

Cleaning Up the Job Log

Q: I have a CL program that calls QCMDEXC to execute a command built as a string. If that command has an error, I get the CPF0001 from QCMDEXC, but the original CPF0001 sent by the command to QCMDEXC is still in the job log. I'd really like the job log to be clean because I'm handling the error. How can I receive or remove that message sent to QCMDEXC (which is, of course, no longer on the call stack) when I don't have the message key and don't want to use RMVMSG CLEAR(*ALL) or *ALLINACT?

A: Use QCAPCMD instead of QCMDEXC. It returns the actual exception rather than the silly "command failed" exception that QCMDEXC returns.

—Derek Butland

✦ ✦ ✦ Interactive Command Processing

Commands to Avoid Running in QINTER

Some commands should never be run interactively. But no matter how often people hear this, someone always thinks "one time won't hurt anything." To prevent people from executing commands interactively, the following command should be executed from each command to inhibit:

```
CHGCMD CMD(xxx) ALLOW(*BATCH *BPGM)
```

When someone attempts to run the command interactively, an error message, CPD0031 - "Command *xxx* not allowed in this setting", is issued.

Here are a few notes on using this technique. The CHGCMD should be coded in a CL program so that the same commands can be issued when a new release of the operating system is installed. Also, you should *EXCLUDE the public from using the CHGCMD; they could change it right back!

—Louise Best

Editor's Note:
The preceding technique will work provided that there are no interactive programs that legitimately run the commands being blocked. In order for this technique to work better, each command should be changed by issuing:

```
CHGCMD CMD(xxx) ALLOW(*BATCH *BPGM *IPGM *EXEC)
```

*If you use REXX, add *BREXX and *IREXX to the ALLOW parameter.*

✦ ✦ ✦ Menus

Execute Multiple Commands
from an SDA Menu Without Writing a CL Program

I like building AS/400 menus with SDA. I can create or change a menu quickly and easily and move on to other things. One thing I dislike about SDA menus is that I can put only one command behind an option. I often have to write a CL program just to run two CL commands behind a menu option, and I dislike cluttering up my libraries with tiny CL programs that are used on only one menu.

The Execute Command (XC) command (shown in Figures 3.3 and 3.4) provides a way to execute more than one command when choosing a menu option.

```
/*================================================================*/
/* To compile:                                                    */
/*                                                                */
/* CRTCLPGM PGM(XXX/XC) SRCFILE(XXX/QCLSRC)                        */
/*                                                                */
/*================================================================*/
CMD PROMPT('Execute commands')

PARM KWD(C) TYPE(*CHAR) LEN(110) MIN(1) +
PROMPT('Commands')

PARM KWD(D) TYPE(*CHAR) LEN(1) DFT('\') +
PROMPT('Command delimiter')

PARM KWD(F) TYPE(*CHAR) LEN(1) RSTD(*YES) DFT(C) +
VALUES(C I) CHOICE('C=cancel, I=ignore') +
PROMPT('Command failure option')
```

Figure 3.3: The XC command provides a very easy to use command interface.

```
/*================================================================*/
/* To compile:                                                    */
/*                                                                */
/* CRTCLPGM PGM(XXX/XCL) SRCFILE(XXX/QCLSRC)                       */
/*                                                                */
/*================================================================*/
PGM PARM(&CMDSTRING &DELIMITER &FAILOPTION)
DCL VAR(&CMDSTRING) TYPE(*CHAR) LEN(110)
DCL VAR(&DELIMITER) TYPE(*CHAR) LEN(1)
DCL VAR(&FAILOPTION) TYPE(*CHAR) LEN(1)
DCL VAR(&CMDS) TYPE(*CHAR) LEN(111)
DCL VAR(&COMMAND) TYPE(*CHAR) LEN(110)
DCL VAR(&FX) TYPE(*DEC) LEN(3)
DCL VAR(&TX) TYPE(*DEC) LEN(3)
DCL VAR(&MSGDTA) TYPE(*CHAR) LEN(132)
DCL VAR(&MSGF) TYPE(*CHAR) LEN(10)
DCL VAR(&MSGFLIB) TYPE(*CHAR) LEN(10)
DCL VAR(&MSGID) TYPE(*CHAR) LEN(7)
CHGVAR VAR(&CMDS) VALUE(&CMDSTRING *CAT &DELIMITER)
/* Begin extraction of next command in series */
NEXTCMD: CHGVAR VAR(&COMMAND) VALUE(' ')
CHGVAR VAR(&TX) VALUE(0)
/* Build a command 1 character at a time */
BLDCMD: CHGVAR VAR(&FX) VALUE(&FX + 1)
IF COND(%SST(&CMDS &FX 1) *EQ &DELIMITER) +
THEN(GOTO CMDLBL(RUNCMD))
CHGVAR VAR(&TX) VALUE(&TX + 1)
CHGVAR VAR(%SST(&COMMAND &TX 1)) VALUE(%SST(&CMDS +
&FX 1))
GOTO CMDLBL(BLDCMD)
/* Command has been extracted - execute it */
RUNCMD: IF COND(&COMMAND *NE ' ') THEN(DO)
CALL PGM(QCMDEXC) PARM(&COMMAND 110)
MONMSG MSGID(CPF0000) EXEC(DO)
FWDMSG: RCVMSG MSGDTA(&MSGDTA) MSGID(&MSGID) MSGF(&MSGF) +
SNDMSGFLIB(&MSGFLIB)
IF COND(&MSGID *NE ' ') THEN(DO)
SNDPGMMSG MSGID(&MSGID) MSGF(&MSGFLIB/&MSGF) +
MSGDTA(&MSGDTA)
GOTO CMDLBL(FWDMSG)
ENDDO
IF COND(&FAILOPTION *EQ C) THEN(GOTO +
CMDLBL(ENDPGM))
ENDDO
ENDDO
IF COND(&FX *LT 110) THEN(GOTO CMDLBL(NEXTCMD))
ENDPGM: ENDPGM
```

Figure 3.4: CL program XCL provides the processing power behind the XC command.

The first parameter is a series of CL commands separated by some delimiter. The system executes each command in order. All commands in the command string must be executable by the QCMDEXC program. To check whether QCMDEXC will execute a command, use the Display Command (DSPCMD) command. If the "Where allowed to run" parameter includes *EXEC, you can use the command within an XC command string. The second parameter is the delimiter. It defaults to a backslash (\), but any character that isn't used in the command's command string will do. The third parameter tells the job what to do if a command terminates abnormally. You can ignore the error and continue with the next command or cancel processing the command string.

—Ted Holt

✦ ✦ ✦ Parameters

Expanding Command Parameter Length

Here is a bit of well-hidden midrange folklore that has been handed down from programmer to programmer. This feature was documented in some obscure place in the S/38 manuals, and I'm not sure that the AS/400 manuals document it at all.

You can enter an ampersand (&) followed by one or more spaces starting in the first position of an input field on any command prompt to expand its length. The maximum length is 80 for qualifier and 512 for all the other parameters.

To enter a value even longer than the maximum prompt length, press F3 to return to the Command Entry display and enter the value in the command string without using command prompting. This can be very helpful when you're entering an expression through the prompter while editing a CL program.

—Midrange Computing Staff

Placing Required Parameters After Optional

If you've ever written command definitions, you might have discovered that creating a parameter with a default value forces that parameter to be optional. Once a parameter is defined as optional (MIN value of 0), no parameter defined after it can be made mandatory (MIN value greater than 0). This requirement often causes programmers to make a parameter optional when it should be mandatory. There is a workaround for this problem that you might want to consider.

Here's an example to illustrate this technique: Let's say you want to create a command with two parameters. The first parameter is FROMDATE, for which you want to supply a default value of *CURRENT. The second parameter is TODATE, which must be entered.

Because FROMDATE is optional (because it has a default value), you can't make TODATE mandatory.

To get around this problem, you can specify a display position relative to the other parameters in the PROMPT parameter of the PARM statement. The display position is specified as the second element of the PROMPT parameter, immediately after the prompt text. For an example of how this is done, see the command definition shown in Figure 3.5.

```
CMD PROMPT('Example Command')
  PARM KWD(TODATE) TYPE(*DATE) MIN(1) PROMPT('To Date' 2)
  PARM KWD(FROMDATE) TYPE(*DATE) DFT(*CURRENT) SPCVAL((*CURRENT 000000)) +
  PROMPT('From date' 1)
```

Figure 3.5: Use this example command source as a guideline for learning to use parameters.

In this example, you can define TODATE first as a mandatory parameter with a relative display position value of 2. You can then define FROMDATE second with a relative display position value of 1. In this way, you're satisfying the command compiler's requirement of a mandatory parameter definition ahead of an optional parameter definition. At the same time, you're causing the parameters to appear in the order you want.

—Robin Klima

✦ ✦ ✦ Prompting

Colorized Commands

Virtually everyone knows how to add hex codes in their source code to add color to their source. Examples of hex characters that can be used are x'22' for white or high intensity and x'38' for pink. This same technique works to add color to command prompts.

While creating the source for your command, place a hex character such as x'38' as the first byte of the PROMPT parameter. After compiling the command, you will have a colored prompt within your command. The sample code shown in Figure 3.6 specifies where to place the hex code (indicated by an *x*) to colorize your command.

```
CMD PROMPT('Command Title')
PARM KWD(FLD) TYPE(*CHAR) LEN(10) +
    PROMPT(x'38')
```

Figure 3.6: Use this command to color your source files!

—Todd Fisher

✦ ✦ ✦ Shortcut Commands

Abbreviated OS/400 Commands

One quality of OS/400 that makes it nicer than other operating systems is that the commands are logically named. You can often guess the name of a command. The drawback, however, is that command names are often long.

You can save yourself hundreds of keystrokes a day by creating abbreviated versions of OS/400 commands you use often. I'm going to show you two of my favorites: SJ and WJ4.

The SJ command is an abbreviated form of the Work with Submitted Jobs (WRKSBMJOB) command using the SBMFROM(*JOB) parameter. I like SJ because it lets me see only the jobs that are submitted from the current job, and it's at least 12 keystrokes shorter than its native counterpart. The SJ command source is shown in Figure 3.7.

```
/*===============================================================*/
/* To compile:                                                   */
/*                                                               */
/* CRTCMD CMD(XXX/SJ) PGM(XXX/QCMDEXC) +                         */
/* SRCFILE(XXX/QCMDSRC)                                          */
/*                                                               */
/*===============================================================*/
CMD PROMPT('WRKSBMJOB *JOB')
PARM KWD(CMD) TYPE(*CHAR) LEN(23) +
CONSTANT('WRKSBMJOB SBMFROM(*JOB)')
PARM KWD(LEN) TYPE(*DEC) LEN(15 5) CONSTANT(23)
```

Figure 3.7: The abbreviated WRKSBMJOB command SJ makes working with submitted jobs easy.

The WJ4 command lets you see only the spool files created by the current job. WJ4 is similar to keying the Work with Job (WRKJOB) command and taking option 4. You won't have to wade through page after page of spool files as you would have to do with WRKOUTQ or WRKSPLF. The WJ4 command source is shown in Figure 3.8.

```
/*==============================================================*/
/* To compile:                                                  */
/*                                                              */
/* CRTCMD CMD(XXX/WJ4) PGM(XXX/QCMDEXC) +                       */
/* SRCFILE(XXX/QCMDSRC)                                          */
/*                                                              */
/*==============================================================*/
CMD PROMPT('WRKJOB Option 4')
PARM KWD(CMD) TYPE(*CHAR) LEN(20) +
CONSTANT('WRKJOB OPTION(*SPLF)')
PARM KWD(LEN) TYPE(*DEC) LEN(15 5) CONSTANT(20)
```

Figure 3.8: The abbreviated WRKJOB command WJ4 makes working with a job's spooled files easy.

In both of these examples, I've specified QCMDEXC as the command-processing program, which eliminated the need for me to write a CPP. I'll bet there are many other AS/400 commands you use often that could be condensed and thereby save you significant key strokes throughout your day.

—Ted Holt

AS/400 Shorthand Commands

One of the nice things on the System/36 is the capability to enter abbreviations for commonly used commands: D U to display users, D P to display spool files, D W to display workstations, and so on.

On the AS/400 (running System/36 Environment) these commands function much the same way they did on the S/36. In native mode, no such shorthand commands are available. However, the AS/400 gives us the tools to create our own abbreviated commands. The command and program (Figures 3.9 and 3.10) shows how some of the commonly used "work with" commands can be shortened.

```
CMD         PROMPT('Work With Selected Jobs')

PARM        KWD(JOB) TYPE(*CHAR) LEN(2) RSTD(*YES) +
              VALUES('A' 'C' 'D' 'JL' 'JQ' 'P' 'P2' 'Q' +
              'QP' 'S' 'SJ' 'U' 'W') +
              CHOICE(*VALUES) +
              PROMPT('Select job to work with')
```

Figure 3.9: Work With Selected Jobs can be accomplished very easily by using this command.

```
PGM PARM(&OPT)

DCL VAR(&OPT)       TYPE(*CHAR) LEN(2)

IF COND(&OPT *EQ 'A') THEN(WRKACTJOB)
IF COND(&OPT *EQ 'C') THEN(WRKCFGSTS CFGTYPE(*DEV))
IF COND(&OPT *EQ 'D') THEN(WRKDOC)
IF COND(&OPT *EQ 'JL') THEN(WRKOUTQ OUTQ(JOBLOGS))
IF COND(&OPT *EQ 'JQ') THEN(WRKJOBQ JOBQ(QBATCH))
IF COND(&OPT *EQ 'P') THEN(WRKOUTQ OUTQ(PRT01))
IF COND(&OPT *EQ 'P2') THEN(WRKOUTQ OUTQ(PRT02))
IF COND(&OPT *EQ 'Q') THEN(WRKOUTQ)
IF COND(&OPT *EQ 'QP') THEN(WRKOUTQ OUTQ(QPRINT))
IF COND(&OPT *EQ 'S') THEN(WRKSPLF)
IF COND(&OPT *EQ 'SJ') THEN(WRKSBMJOB)
IF COND(&OPT *EQ 'U') THEN(WRKUSRJOB)
IF COND(&OPT *EQ 'W') THEN(WRKWTR)
IF COND(&OPT *EQ ' ') THEN(WRKJOB)

ENDPGM: +
ENDPGM
```

Figure 3.10: The CL driver for the Work With Selected Jobs command provides the power behind the command.

The command is simply called "W" and, by itself, it will execute the Work with Job (WRKJOB) command. Add your own shorthand command to the program shown in Figures 3.9 and 3.10. Create an entirely new command, such as "C" command for some of the commonly used AS/400 "Change" commands. Maybe you will want to retain the System/36-style short commands in native mode. Any way you go, you will save quite a bit of typing.

—*Steven Kontos*

Generic Commands and CPPs

Many times, you need to write an ad hoc command, without parameters, to perform a very specific task you perform time after time. For example, suppose you often need to know which users are signed on in all display stations. You know that the Work with User Jobs (WRKUSRJOB) command gives that information to you, but you must type a very long command string to do so:

```
WRKUSRJOB USER(*ALL)  STATUS(*ACTIVE)  JOBTYPE(*INTERACT)
```

If you're a lightning-fast typist (say, 120 words per minute), you might not mind typing all that a dozen or more times a day. But we simple folk prefer a simpler approach—such as typing DSPSGNUSR (which stands for Display Signed-on Users, a command name I just made up) and pressing Enter. Of course, the DSPSGNUSR command is going to need a command processing program (CPP), which in most cases means writing CL source code and compiling it. As you can imagine, not only the commands but also the CPPs proliferate.

Thinking along these lines, I decided to create a generic CPP (named, simply enough, GENCPP) for use in these cases. The central idea is that the command passes only one parameter to the CPP: a message ID. When the CPP receives it, the CPP retrieves the corresponding message text from a designated message file and uses the message text as a command string, running it with QCMDEXC. Figure 3.11shows the command source for DSPSGNUSR. As you can see, its lone parameter, MSGID, shows a constant value of CMD0001. Because the parameter is a constant, it never shows up when the user prompts DSPSGNUSR and, what's more, the user cannot override its value in any way.

When the CPP starts running (Figure 3.12), it receives the message ID and uses the Retrieve Message (RTVMSG) command to get the text from the message description in message file GENCPPMSGF, which you must create and maintain yourself. Then, the CPP sends an *INFO message to itself before executing the command string. The reason for the *INFO message is to have something in the job log that identifies the command to be carried out. If you didn't send that message, the job log would record a CALL to QCMDEXC, but it would give you no clues about what was executed.

```
/*================================================================*/
/* To compile:                                                    */
/*                                                                */
/* CRTCMD CMD(XXX/DSPSGNUSR) PGM(XXX/GENCPP) +                    */
/* SRCFILE(XXX/QCMDSRC) TEXT('Display +                          */
/* Signed-On Users')                                              */
/*                                                                */
/*================================================================*/
CMD PROMPT('Display Signed-On Users')
PARM KWD(MSGID) TYPE(*NAME) LEN(7) CONSTANT(CMD0001)
```

Figure 3.11: The DSPSGNUSR command lets you know which users are signed on where.

```
/*================================================================*/
/* To compile:                                                    */
/*                                                                */
/* CRTCLPGM PGM(XXX/GENCPP) SRCFILE(XXX/QCLSRC) +                */
/* TEXT('Generic command CPP')                                    */
/*                                                                */
/*================================================================*/
PGM PARM(&IN_MSGID)
DCL VAR(&CMDSTR) TYPE(*CHAR) LEN(256)
DCL VAR(&CMDSTRLEN) TYPE(*DEC) LEN(15 5)
DCL VAR(&IN_MSGID) TYPE(*CHAR) LEN(7)
DCL VAR(&MSGDTA) TYPE(*CHAR) LEN(256)
DCL VAR(&MSGF) TYPE(*CHAR) LEN(10)
DCL VAR(&MSGFLIB) TYPE(*CHAR) LEN(10)
DCL VAR(&MSGID) TYPE(*CHAR) LEN(7)
DCL VAR(&MSGTXT) TYPE(*CHAR) LEN(256)
DCL VAR(&MSGTXTLEN) TYPE(*DEC) LEN(5)
MONMSG MSGID(CPF0000 MCH0000) EXEC(GOTO CMDLBL(ERROR))
/* Retrieve message text and use it as command string */
RTVMSG MSGID(&IN_MSGID) MSGF(GENCPPMSGF) +
MSG(&MSGTXT) MSGLEN(&MSGTXTLEN)
CHGVAR VAR(&CMDSTR) VALUE(%SST(&MSGTXT 1 &MSGTXTLEN))
CHGVAR VAR(&CMDSTRLEN) VALUE(&MSGTXTLEN)
/* Execute command */
SNDPGMMSG MSG('Executing command' *BCAT &CMDSTR) +
TOPGMQ(*SAME (*)) MSGTYPE(*INFO)
CALL PGM(QCMDEXC) PARM(&CMDSTR &CMDSTRLEN)
RETURN
/* Forward any error messages to caller */
ERROR:
RCVMSG MSGTYPE(*EXCP) MSGDTA(&MSGDTA) MSGID(&MSGID) +
MSGF(&MSGF) SNDMSGFLIB(&MSGFLIB)
MONMSG MSGID(CPF0000)
SNDPGMMSG MSGID(&MSGID) MSGF(&MSGFLIB/&MSGF) +
MSGDTA(&MSGDTA) MSGTYPE(*ESCAPE)
MONMSG MSGID(CPF0000)
ENDPGM
```

Figure 3.12: This generic CPP receives a message ID.

To implement this technique, you'll need a message file named GENCPPMSGF somewhere in your library list. If you prefer to use a different message file name, by all means do so; however, be sure to change the referenced message file name in the CPP's RTVMSG statement. You must also have message descriptions (one per generic command). For example, I coded DSPSGNUSR so that it uses a message description identified as CMD0001. It's my responsibility, then, to run the Add Message Description (ADDMSGD) command to create that message ID in the selected message file. Your code should look like this:

```
CRTMSGF xxx/GENCPPMSGF ADDMSGD CMD0001 xxx/GENCPPMSGF +
        MSG('WRKUSRJOB USER(*ALL) STATUS(*ACTIVE) +
        JOBTYPE(*INTERACT)') SECLVL('Display all signed-on users')
```

When you create another generic command, use DSPSGNUSR as a model, changing the text in the CMD statement and the message ID in the MSGID parameter. Then, run ADDMSGD to create the new message description, and—voilà!—the new command is ready for use.

—Ernie Malaga

✦ ✦ ✦ UIM

Help with Help Panels

Q: I am trying to reference an existing IBM panel group help text in my new commands. Instead of retyping the User Interface Manager (UIM) for the help screen, I want to include a link to an existing IBM help panel. How do I find the names of existing panel groups so that I can reuse them?

A: Try using the Display Command (DSPCMD) command to locate the information you're looking for. For example, you can use DSPCMD and give it a parameter value of WRKUSRJOB to display command information for the Work with User Jobs (WRKUSRJOB) command. Once the information is displayed, scroll to the second page. In the middle of the screen, you'll find the help panel name.

—Vadim Rozen

✦ ✦ ✦ Working with Commands

Use Generic Commands at the Command Line

Did you know that if you type (for example) WRK* at a command line and press Enter, you get all commands that start with WRK and the capability to select the one you want to use? Or you can type WRKU* or WRKUSR* if you know how it starts but can't remember the rest. These lists come to you courtesy of the Select Command (SLTCMD) command, which is invoked automatically.

Because I can usually remember enough of the first part of a command to narrow down the possibilities quite a bit, I much prefer this approach to using the F4 or GO CMD*xxx* menus. This method saves me from having to plow through all the menus.

I learned this accidentally one day while working on a terrifically slow emulation package. I got keyed ahead, miskeyed, and accidentally issued a command that ended with an asterisk.

—Rebecca Whittemore

Editor's Note: *Using the* SLTCMD *command directly is risky. On the regular* QWERTY *keyboards, the S and D keys are next to each other. You might accidentally type* DLTCMD *when you intend to type* SLTCMD. *Because the Delete Command (*DLTCMD*) accepts a generic command name, you could accidentally delete a number of IBM-supplied commands. For this reason, using* SLTCMD *should be discouraged.*

CHAPTER 4

Communications

*C*ommunications is the backbone of any network and under-standing communications is integral to keeping your AS/400s, PCs, and other peripherals talking to one another. The AS/400 has come a long ways since the days of twinaxial connectivity. Now, you have many connectivity options such as TCP/IP. You also have a lot more hardware and software options—such as the Integrated Netfinity Server and Frame Relay networks—to worry about. Understanding everything that's going on can be a real chore!

This chapter on communications tips and tricks will help you to gain a better understanding of many aspects of OS/400 communications. In it, you'll find real-world advice from some of the industry's leading experts in AS/400 communications and connectivity. Everything from how to connect an AS/400 to an RS/6000 to how to test a SNADS pass-through session on a single AS/400 is included here, and it's all just waiting for you to learn about it.

—Shannon O'Donnell

✦ ✦ ✦ Connectivity

AS/400-to-RS/6000 Connectivity

Q: I have heard of connecting the AS/400 to an RS/6000 through an Ethernet or token-ring network. I assume that this connection allows data transfer between the two machines. What I want to know is whether the network connection will allow the CRTs on the AS/400 to act as CRTs on the RS/6000. Any caveats or information regarding this connection and how you did it would be greatly appreciated.

A: The physical network connection does not determine the available access between the two systems. Access is determined by what you're running on the network and how well what you're running is supported on both systems. For example, if you are running TCP/IP on an Ethernet link, you should be able to Telnet from the AS/400 to the RS/6000 and vice versa. You should also be able to perform operations such as file transfers. The TCP/IP utilities provide this functionality.

On the other hand, if you were running LAN Manager or another network package, you would have less functionality. One of the reasons for the popularity of TCP/IP is that it provides a lot of real-world usability on supported platforms.

—Matt Fulton

✦ ✦ ✦ Device Configuration

Creating a Communications Configuration Backup

The demand for computer networking and connectivity is increasing at an astonishing rate. The bottom line is that most of us are dealing with more communications configurations on our AS/400s than ever before. In a typical AS/400 installation, it would be difficult to recreate those communications configurations because they are too numerous and complex. Fortunately, IBM supplies a method to deal with this problem.

The Retrieve Configuration Source (RTVCFGSRC) command can create a source member (type CL) with all the necessary CL commands to recreate all communications objects on your system. By compiling this source member and running the resultant program, you can easily recreate your entire communications configuration.

To create the source member for all of your communications configurations, you could execute RTVCFGSRC as follows:

```
RTVCFGSRC CFGD(*ALL)  CFGTYPE(*ALL)  SRCFILE(xxx/QCLSRC)
         SRCMBR(COMCFG)
```

This would create a source member in library *xxx* named COMCFG. Once the source member is created, change the source member type from CL to CLP, and compile it. Ideally, you should run the RTVCFGSRC command every time your communications configuration changes, and you should save the resultant source member as part of your daily backup.

—Richard Shaler

✦ ✦ ✦ Diagnostics

Port Diagnostics

Q: Is there an AS/400 utility or third-party package that allows diagnostic testing on individual ports for I/O cards? I am mainly interested in testing my synchronous ports. Unfortunately, it's just isn't enough to use breakout boxes and to vary configuration objects on and off. Any suggestions will help!

A: When a working communication link fails, or when a newly configured link just will not function (even when you swear it should), it is a relatively easy task to check your cables and the communications I/O card itself. The Verify Communications (VFYCMN) command allows a simple wrap test of the cable and I/O card, allowing you to eliminate two possible causes for problems.

To use this command, enter VFYCMN. You are asked to enter the name of the line to test and the type of test to run. By selecting the cable wrap test first, the card and cable are both tested. If this test fails, you should run the communications I/O adapter wrap test to isolate the problem to either the card or the cable.

For the cable wrap test, you specify how many test runs you want to perform. The tests take about 15 seconds each. If your cable goes through a traffic area where it might be kicked or bumped, you should request enough tests to give you time to wiggle or kick the cable in that area. The screens guide you through the test, prompting you to plug the cable into the wrap plug (a female plug usually mounted on the cable itself). Upon completion, you are instructed to reconnect the modem. Then the display informs you whether the cable passed the test.

If the test fails, you should run the card test, which is the same as the cable test, except without the cable involved. Your system should have a free wrap plug to use with this test, but the plug attached to the cable will work if you cannot find the separate plug. Assuming that your system passes both tests, there are now two fewer possibilities to investigate. If your modems support LPDA1 and LPDA2, the VFYCMN command also includes local and remote modem tests. Several other link tests are also supported. For more information on the testing procedures, see *Volume I* of the *Diagnostic Aids Manual* (LY44-0597).

—Midrange Computing Staff

✦ ✦ ✦ Integrated Netfinity Server

Adding Another Integrated Netfinity Server to a Network

Q: We want to add another Integrated Netfinity Server (INS) to our network. However, we want to put it in a different AS/400 system and have it participate in the same domain. Is this possible?

A: Yes. On the AS/400 with the new INS, be sure to change the domain name to match that specified on the AS/400 with the original INS (use the Change Network Attributes—CHGNETA—command). Put the new INS on the same physical LAN. Then, use the Domain role (DMNROLE) parameter of the Create Network Server Description (CRTNWSD) command to specify the INS as backup domain controller (*BKUCTL) or additional server (*SERVER). Create the appropriate line descriptions and network server storage spaces and link the storage spaces to the network server description. Finally, vary on the network server descriptions.

—Jan Glowacki

✦ ✦ ✦ LANs

Bridging the Ethernet LAN

Q: Our installation is running a 10-megabits per second (Mbps) Ethernet LAN. We're using bridges to segment our network. It seems as if we're experiencing a slowdown when data packets cross the bridge. Is there a simple solution to this problem?

A: Based on the information provided, I'd have to say yes, there is a simple solution: a switching hub. Switching hubs reduce contention on shared network topologies (such as

Ethernet) via microsegmentation. In a microsegmented network, a LAN segment may contain as little as one node. The switching hub is charged with connecting the different segments without the delays typically associated with bridges. Traffic is handled through an internal matrix switch, with all switching being performed at the medium access control (MAC) layer. A packet's origination and destination addresses are quickly determined by the switching hub, and a connection is rapidly established with the appropriate end segment. Because no other stations share the communications port, no contention arises, and full bandwidth is available for transmission.

—Kris Neely

LAN Bridged Frames

Q: We're having trouble configuring the connection between our two LANs. We're using a bridge to connect them. IBM has told us that we have "bridged framing size conflicts." What does this mean?

A: If a data frame is being transmitted to a station that resides on a different LAN, the frame is copied and retransmitted by a bridge/router. If the bridge/router isn't set up to support a frame size as large as that configured on the AS/400's communication line description, the frame will be discarded. The frame may also be discarded if the network does not support the frame size specified on the AS/400 communication line description used for a bridged frame relay configuration.

When running SNA in a token-ring environment, the system that originated the connection is informed of the frame size supported by the bridge/router and will automatically retry with that frame size. The CPF5908 message "Controller contacted..." sent to the QSYSOPR message queue informs you of the effective maximum frame size for that connection. If you are unable to configure the bridge/router to support larger frame sizes, you might need to adjust one of the following parameters to a value acceptable to the bridge/router in question:

- MAXFRAME—controller description parameter.
- *SSAP—line description parameter.
- *MAXFRAME—line description parameter (except Ethernet lines).

Keep in mind that larger values for these parameters might yield better performance.

—Kris Neely

✦ ✦ ✦ Line Descriptions

Communication Line Descriptions

When creating a line description, do you know what to type each time the system asks you to specify the resource name? Do you know what to do when your attempt to vary on a line fails because another line on the same resource is already varied on (and you have so many communication lines that you don't know which one it is)?

If this sounds familiar to you, you need the Display Hardware Resource (DSPHDWRSC) command. Execute the command by entering the following:

```
DSPHDWRSC TYPE(*CMN)
```

*CMN indicates you want the communications resource information. This will display each resource name available, with all the communications lines attached to it. The default output is to the display, but through the OUTPUT parameter you can specify *PRINT for printer output or *OUTFILE for file output.

—Jean-Jacques Risch

Network Line Description Addresses

Q: Why do I need to specify an X in the address for the line descriptions of my network server?

A: Line descriptions to be used with network servers use a local adapter address that you specify when you create the line description. This address must contain an X in the last position for a token-ring adapter or an X in the second to last position for an Ethernet adapter. For example, a valid token-ring address would be 40001234567X. Any system identifying the address, such as PCs using the INS as a communications adapter, should consider the X to be a zero. The X reserves the other 15 addresses (400012345671–40001234567F) for internal AS/400 and INS functions.

Because the AS/400 has only one domain name, all INSs residing in the same AS/400 participate in the same domain (even if the INSs do not exist on the same LAN). This allows you to have and manage several LANs as if they were physically connected. LAN Server/400 provides an interconnection between the AS/400 system's INSs that reside on different physical LANs. This is possible because of the 15 reserved addresses created by the X in the locally administered address. The interconnection allows for users of any of these disjointed LANs to access data managed by any of the INSs residing in the AS/400.

While this capability is provided, it is not tuned for performance. Therefore, when superior performance is crucial and you have disjointed LANs, you should install one or more bridges to connect the LANs.

—Jan Glowacki

Retrieve Line Description API

Q: I have a program I'm trying to write and I've hit a snag. I need to get a list of controllers attached to a line description. Is there a way within a program to provide the line description name and get a list of the controllers attached?

A: The Retrieve Line Description (QDCRLIND) API that is described in the *System Programmer's Interface Reference* (SC41-8223, CD-ROM QBKA8402) provides that type of information.

Using the WRKHDWRSC Command

You can configure multiple line descriptions for a single communication line resource. However, you cannot use more than one of those line descriptions at a time. For example, most systems have a communication resource called LIN011. IBM provides two communication line descriptions that use this resource: QTILINE and QESLINE. Whenever you configure a new line description, you must know the name of the communication resource you intend to use. Whenever you intend to use a line description, you must make sure that no other line is varied on that uses the same communication resource.

The Work with Hardware Resource (WRKHDWRSC) command is very useful for configuring new line descriptions or determining which lines use a particular communication resource. Invoke the command by entering the following:

```
WRKHDWRSC TYPE(*CMN)
```

If you use option 5 on the line description on the resulting display, you get to a screen that allows you to work with the configuration descriptions for that resource.

—Steve Bisel

✦ ✦ ✦ Modems

Automatic Answer and Dial

Q: Our company wants to change our AS/400 communications lines from manual answer/dial to automatic answer/dial. Can you tell me what we need to do and where I can find more information?

A: From a hardware standpoint, your modems must have automatic answer/dial capability. From a software standpoint, an automatic answer/dial connection can be accomplished if the modem attached to the AS/400 communication line has an automatic answer feature and if the line description is created with the following parameters: AUTOANS(*YES), SWTCNN(*BOTH or *ANS), and AUTODIAL(*YES).

Keep in mind, however, that if the controller description is created with the INLCNN(*ANS) parameter, the controller cannot make contact by dialing. If the controller description is created with INLCNN(*DIAL), then dialing occurs when an application program opens a file. The INLCNN parameter does not prevent a controller from being contacted by a call, though, if AUTOANS is *YES. Only an automatic answer is possible. There's more information on automatic answer/dial in the *AS/400 Communication Configuration* manual (SC41-3401, CD-ROM QBKANB00).

—Kris Neely

Modem Problems Checklist

Over the past several years, I've used the following checklist as a "try-this-first" approach to determining modem problems. I've used this list on every type of computer, from PCs to AS/400s to Cray supercomputers.

1. Verify the modem is plugged in (you'd be surprised how often this is the problem).
2. Plug a lamp or other electrical device into the power outlet to make sure electricity is flowing.
3. Check to ensure that the modem is turned on (again, you'd be amazed).
4. Make sure the modem is plugged into the phone outlet.
5. Check the COM port setting against your communications software.
6. Reduce the speed of your modem and attempt the connection again.
7. Call the number you're trying to connect with. If you hear a high-pitched tone, you at least know you're dialing somebody's modem or fax machine.

8. Double-check your bit and parity settings.

9. Reinstall or reconfigure your communications software.

10. Now panic.

—Kris Neely

Resolving Modem-sharing Conflicts

Often, a modem on the AS/400 is shared by several uses. You might use your Electronic Customer Support (ECS) modem for ECS, dial up to IBMLink, and dial in to another AS/400. Each of these usually uses a different line description. However, if one of the other lines is varied on, you won't be able to start the application you want. There needs to be an easy way to review which lines are attached to a given hardware resource.

Fortunately, there is. Use the Work with Hardware Resources (WRKHDWRSC) command and, in the TYPE parameter, use *CMN WRKHDWRSC TYPE(*CMN). You'll see a screen similar to the one shown in Figure 4.1. The screen shows each hardware resource and port. By placing a 5 next to one of the ports, you'll see all of the lines that use that port. You can review the status of the lines and see if any of them are varied on. It's the fastest way I know of to resolve modem-sharing conflicts.

```
                    Work with Communication Resources
                                                  System:    MC170
 Type options, press Enter.
   5=Work with configuration descriptions    7=Display resource detail

 Opt  Resource     Type  Status        Text
   ▮  CMB01        6757  Operational   Combined function IOP
   _    LIN01      2721  Operational   Comm Adapter
   _      CMN01    2721  Operational   V.24 Port
   _      CMN02    2721  Operational   Comm Port
   _    LIN02      2850  Operational   File Server IOA
   _      CMN05    2838  Not detected  LAN Port
   _      CMN06    2838  Operational   Ethernet Port
   _      CMN03    6B00  Operational   Virtual Port
   _    LIN03      285A  Operational   LAN Adapter
   _  CMB02        2809  Operational   Combined function IOP
   _    LIN04      2723  Operational   LAN Adapter
   _      CMN04    2723  Operational   Ethernet Port

                                                          Bottom
 F3=Exit   F5=Refresh   F6=Print   F12=Cancel
```

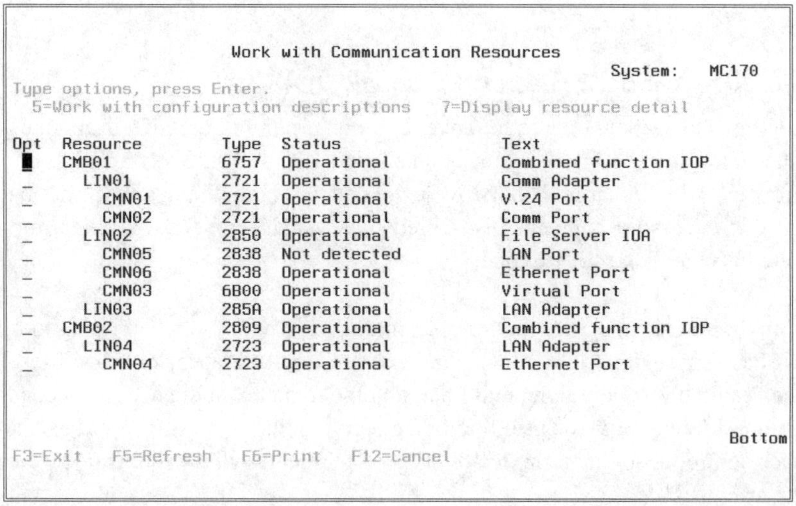

Figure 4.1: The Work with Communication Resources Screen is used to display the resources used by your communication lines.

—Jim Hoopes

✦ ✦ ✦ Pass-through

ENDPASTHR or SIGNOFF

If you deal with communications often and use the Start Pass-Through (STRPASTHR) command to sign on to a remote system, you probably use the End Pass-Through (ENDPASTHR) command when you are done working on the remote system and want to go back to the local one. If you use the SIGNOFF command, you could go back to the sign-on screen of the target system without stopping the communication. Especially if you don't know which system you're on, this might be confusing.

The SIGNOFF command has a parameter (V2R3 and higher), End Connection (ENDCNN), that solves this problem. It defaults to *NO. To make it *YES, key the following:

```
CHGCMDDFT CMD(QSYS/SIGNOFF)   NEWDFT('ENDCNN(*YES)')
```

This will end pass-through when signing off from a remote system. If you change the command directly in QSYS, keep track of it because this change will be lost when you install a new release.

—Jean-Jacques Risch

Pass-through and DDM Files on a Standalone AS/400

A recent project I worked on was to move all users, programs, and data from one AS/400 to another. The client had recently installed a new RISC model. She wanted to migrate users from an old F20 that was badly overextended. Users on the two machines had communicated with pass-through and Distributed Data Management (DDM) files, and now they were to share the same machine.

It was, on the surface, a simple matter of changing programs and recompiling to remove the Start Pass Through (STRPASTHR) commands and the references to DDM files. However, the deadline was very tight, and I had no time to make all the necessary changes. The solution I found might be useful to other people in the same situation. I used a loop-back controller so that a single AS/400 communicates with itself as if it were two separate machines!

Start with two AS/400s. The first AS/400 has a local location name AS400A. The second AS/400 has a local location name AS400B. After you have moved everything from AS400B to AS400A, take the following steps to create a loop-back controller:

1. Use the Create APPC Controller (CRTCTLAPPC) command to create a controller of type *LOCAL. Note that no line description is needed for this type of controller:

```
CRTCTLAPPC CTLD(LOOPBACK)LINKTYPE(*LOCAL)
```

2. Create a pair of APPC devices that mirror each other's local and remote location names:

```
CRTDEVAPPC DEVD(AS400A) RMTLOCNAME(AS400B)
           LCLLOCNAME(AS400A) APPN(*NO)
CRTDEVAPPC DEVD(AS400B) RMTLOCNAME(AS400A)
           LCLLOCNAME(AS400B) APPN(*NO)
```

3. Vary on the devices and the controller and execute the following command to pass through to the same AS/400:

```
STRPASTHR RMTLOCNAME(AS400B) LCLLOCNAME(AS400A)
```

or (going in the other direction) execute this command:

```
STRPASTHR RMTLOCNAME(AS400A) LCLLOCNAME(AS400B)
```

DDM files will work in the same way, as long as the loop-back devices are created with the correct local and remote location names. Once the loop-back controller is up and running, the pass-through programs and DDM files can be removed at a more leisurely pace.

—*David Rowswell*

Simplified Pass-through

The Start Pass-Through (STRPASTHR) command is a useful tool for accessing alternate AS/400s on your network. But trying to remember the correct parameters to get to the system you want can be frustrating. I have developed a technique that makes the STRPASTHR command very easy to use, even for the nontechnical users in your company. Implementing this technique allows you to pass through to a secondary system simply by signing on to the first system with a user profile that's specifically designed for this purpose.

Here's an example of how this technique can work. (Shortly, I'll explain how to implement the technique.) Suppose you're at a sign-on screen for a system called ALPHA, but you really want to access another AS/400 on your network called BRAVO. All you have to do is sign on to ALPHA with the user profile BRAVO. The next thing you see is the intermediate pass-through screen followed by the sign-on screen for system BRAVO. Once you're finished using system BRAVO, you can just run the End Pass-Through (ENDPASTHR) command, and you're back to a sign-on screen at system ALPHA.

This technique can be used to gain access to multiple AS/400s on your network. In this case, you would have a separate user profile for each remote system you want to access. Here's how to implement this technique. On the originating system, create a user profile for each remote AS/400 you want to access. You can give the user profile the same name as the remote system name to make it easy to remember. When you create the user profile, specify the program PASSCL as the initial program, as illustrated in the following example:

```
CRTUSRPRF USRPRF(BRAVO) INLPGM(xxx/PASSCL) TEXT('Pass-through
            to BRAVO')
```

Next, create the PASSCL program. An example of this program is shown in Figure 4.2. You need to modify the highlighted section of this program for your particular environment. Just change the STRPASTHR commands to access the systems for which you created the user profiles. Depending on how many systems you need to access, you also might need to add or remove some commands.

```
/*================================================================*/
/* To compile:                                                    */
/*                                                                */
/* CRTCLPGM PGM(XXX/PASSCL) SRCFILE(XXX/QCLSRC)                   */
/*                                                                */
/*================================================================*/
PGM
DCL VAR(&USER) TYPE(*CHAR) LEN(10)
DCL VAR(&MSGID) TYPE(*CHAR) LEN(7)
DCL VAR(&MSGF) TYPE(*CHAR) LEN(10)
DCL VAR(&MSGFLIB) TYPE(*CHAR) LEN(10)
DCL VAR(&MSGDTA) TYPE(*CHAR) LEN(80)
MONMSG MSGID(CPF0000) EXEC(GOTO CMDLBL(ERROR))
RTVJOBA USER(&USER)
IF COND(&USER *EQ 'BRAVO') +
THEN(STRPASTHR RMTLOCNAME(S1011652))
ELSE CMD(IF COND(&USER *EQ 'CHARLIE') +
```

Figure 4.2: Use this CL program, named PASSCL, to provide pass-through to an alternate system (part 1 of 2).

```
THEN(STRPASTHR RMTLOCNAME(S1034786)))
ELSE CMD(IF COND(&USER *EQ 'DELTA') +
THEN(STRPASTHR RMTLOCNAME(S1014011)))
GOTO CMDLBL(ENDPGM)
ERROR: RCVMSG MSGTYPE(*EXCP) MSGDTA(&MSGDTA) MSGID(&MSGID) +
MSGF(&MSGF) MSGFLIB(&MSGFLIB)
MONMSG MSGID(CPF0000)
SNDPGMMSG MSGID(&MSGID) MSGF(&MSGFLIB/&MSGF) +
MSGDTA(&MSGDTA) MSGTYPE(*ESCAPE)
MONMSG MSGID(CPF0000)
ENDPGM: SIGNOFF
ENDPGM
```

Figure 4.2: Use this CL program, named PASSCL, to provide pass-through to an alternate system (part 2 of 2).

This program works by retrieving the name of the current user profile (e.g., BRAVO) and issuing the appropriate STRPASTHR command, depending on the profile name. Once the user enters the ENDPASTHR command on the secondary system, control returns to PASSCL and the program issues the SIGNOFF command. This brings the user back to a sign-on screen on the original system.

—Robin Klima

✦ ✦ ✦ Workstations

Local vs. Remote Workstation Performance

Q: We're currently running local and remote workstations in the same AS/400 subsystem. We seem to be getting uneven local and remote communications performance with this configuration. Any suggestions?

A: Separate the local and remote devices into different subsystems. Because of the typically slow response times associated with remote devices, the subsystem may be delayed from promptly servicing requests for locally attached devices. To separate your remote devices from your local ones, create a new subsystem for your remote devices and use your existing subsystem for your local devices. You'll then need to use the Add Work Station Entry (ADDWSE) command to identify the remote devices in the remote subsystem description and the local devices in the local subsystem description. You can use the WRKSTN parameter to identify the workstations by name or the WRKSTNTYPE parameter to identify them by type.

—Kris Neely

CHAPTER 5

Database

*T*he AS/400 database is one of the easiest to use and easiest to understand of any computer system in the world. The AS/400 database is one of the most complex and hardest to understand of any computer system in the world. Does it sound like I'm contradicting myself? Actually, I'm not. Both of those statements are true. It is the very complexity of the DB2/400 (DB2 for OS/400) database that makes it both easy and hard to use and understand, all at the same time.

It's easy to use because you won't find another database that does so much for you, right out of the box. For example, you don't need to understand how records are stored internally. You just need to know that you can very easily access them through a variety of means (i.e., a high-level language, ODBC, OS/400 command interfaces, etc.). You also do not need to know how OS/400 security is integrated into the DB2/400 database. You just need to know that, when you write data to a file, your data is protected from unauthorized access without your having to do anything special.

But it's also a very complex database because you can configure it to hold a variety of objects, join records using a variety of methods, subset data within individual fields, retrieve data using numerous data-access methods, and on and on and on. You'll find more complexity and features built into this "simple" database than you will in any other database on any other computer system.

Ub this chapter, you'll find everything from how to use record blocking and ODBC to gain the best database access, to how to reorganize physical files when using journal receivers, and to how to display your DASD utilization. The tips and techniques in this chapter will have you fine tuning your DB2/400 database and with a better understanding of this complex (and simple) system.

—*Shannon O'Donnell*

✦ ✦ ✦ Access Paths

Proper Order Promotes Sharing

Not every keyed file you create has its own access path. The system will try to share access paths among keyed files (physical file or logical file) whenever it can. This is called *implicit access path sharing*. When you ask the system to add a new member to a keyed file, it checks to see if there already is an access path it can share before it creates its own. By adding the members in the correct order, you can make sure the system will find an access path it can borrow if one is available. Figures 5.1 and 5.2 show two logical files over the same physical file.

```
A            R KEYSREC              PFILE(KEYSPF)
A            K KEY1
A            K KEY2
```

Figure 5.1: A logical file with longer keys is shown here.

```
A            R KEYSREC              PFILE(KEYSPF)
A            K KEY1
```

Figure 5.2: A logical file with shorter keys is shown here.

Both examples start with field KEY1 as the first key, but only the code shown in Figure 5.1 has the field KEY2. If an access path is created for the file with the longer keys first, it can be shared when the second file's member is created. Because the file with the shorter key is missing sorting information that the file with the longer key needs, the reverse isn't true.

Access path sharing is done at the member level because that's where access paths are made. If you want to see if your files are implicitly sharing access paths, use the Display File Description (DSPFD) command and specify TYPE(*MBR). The line "Implicit access path sharing" will tell you if the access paths are shared.

Because access paths are shared at the member level, you don't need to delete and re-create logical files to correct improper creation order. You can remove the members from the logicals and add them back in the correct order.

—Martin Pluth

Shared Data Paths May Cause You Problems

Q: I have two programs that use the same file, and one program calls the other. The second (called) program does some work on the file and then returns to the first program. When it returns, the keys for the file point to the next record, but the field data is from the original record. What is going on?

A: It sounds like you are having trouble with shared open data paths (ODPs). When you tell DB2/400 (also known as DB2 for OS/400) to share ODPs, it will open a file once; then, any programs in the call stack that refer to the file will use the same data path. This means that, when a called program changes the current record, the record pointer will point to the new current record when it returns.

ODPs are often shared for performance and memory reasons. Reducing the number of files that your application opens and sharing these open files can have a significant effect on performance.

You can overcome this by using many different techniques. If you don't want to share ODPs, change the file or override it to SHARE(*NO). If you do want to share data paths, you can save any key values before you call a program that uses the file and reposition the file when the program returns. An alternative technique is to just be sure your key values can't be changed by another program, and then reread the file with these values before you use any data from the file.

—Brian Singleton

✦ ✦ ✦ Code Pages

How to Use CCSID

Q: We have software to be distributed on an AS/400 in the United Kingdom. When distributing files created on our U.S. machine, such as physical files and logical files, the coded character set ID (CCSID) and language ID (LANGID) parameters are 37 and ENU, respectively. However, they're 285 and ENG on the U.K. machine. What are the implications or problems, if any, that we risk running into if the files were distributed with U.S. defaults for CCSID and LANGID parameters?

A: It is impossible to predict what may happen in a mixed CCSID environment such as you describe without in-depth knowledge of the application you are porting. That is why it is crucial that the developers of the application have access to and understanding of the

AS/400 National Language Support V4R2 (SC41-5101-01, CD-ROM QB3AWC01) and *AS/400 International Application Development* V4R2 (SC41-5603-01, CD-ROM QB3AQ501) manuals for the AS/400.

Having said that, I will go through one scenario that might or might not be relevant to your application. Assume that you have a control file for field names and that this file is CCSID tagged with 37. Also assume that one of the valid characters used in field names is the dollar ($) sign (or X'5B' in CCSID 37) and that you have a field called $Y2KA, which you generate into target RPG application source. Now assume that your application program runs on the customer systems under job CCSID 285 and modifies RPG source in customer CCSID 285 tagged files. Data management causes your control file dollar sign (X'5B') to become a 285 dollar sign (X'4A') when read into the application. If your application then outputs the dollar sign to the customer file, the dollar sign is written as X'4A'. If the Original Program Model (OPM) compiler attempts to compile the RPG source containing a field name, the compile fails. The key to making this type of scenario work, then, is proper planning and a good understanding of *National Language Support*.

—Bruce Vining

✦ ✦ ✦ Copying Files

MBROPT(*UPDADD)

As of V3R6, the value *UPDADD is acceptable for the MBROPT (member option) parameter of the CPYF (Copy File) command.

To review, *ADD means that the records of the "from" files (the files being copied) are added to the end of the "to" file (the file to which records are being copied). *REPLACE means that the "to" file is cleared, and the records of the "from" files replace the records of the "to" file.

You may use *UPDADD if the "to" file is uniquely keyed. When a record of a "from" file has the same key field values as a record of the "to" file, the "to" file record is updated. If a "from" file record does not match any record in the "to" file, the record is added to the end of the "to" file.

To illustrate, assume there are two copies of customer master file CUSTMAS in two libraries: A and B. The CUSTMAS files are uniquely keyed on CUSNO (customer number). The files and their contents are shown in Figure 5.3. After running the following CPYF command, B/CUSTMAS will look like the file shown in Figure 5.4

```
CPYF FROMFILE(A/CUSTMAS)   TOFILE(B/CUSTMAS)   MBROPT(*UPDADD)
```

```
A/CUSTMAS:

CUSNO   CUSNM      CUSTYP
  1     ONE          A
  2     TWO          A
  3     THREE        C

B/CUSTMAS:

CUSNO   CUSNM      CUSTYP
  3     TRES         Z
  4     CUATRO       K
```

*Figure 5.3: Customer Master Files Before CPYF MBROPT(*UPDADD) are shown here.*

```
CUSNO   CUSNM      CUSTYP
  3     THREE        C
  4     CUATRO       K
  1     ONE          A
  2     TWO          A
```

*Figure 5.4: B/CUSTMAS after CPYF MBROPT(*UPDADD) are shown here.*

—Ted Holt

Copy Logical to Physical

If you need a logical file for testing purposes, but you don't want to update the physical file, you can create a copy of the logical file to be in a physical file. Your program won't know the difference between accessing the test physical file directly or accessing the production physical file via the logical file. Just use the Copy File (CPYF) command to make a physical file copy of the logical file like this:

```
CPYF FROMFILE(production/logical_file) TOFILE(testlib/physical_file)
     CRTFILE(*YES)
```

Before you run your test, make sure the test library is ahead of the production library in your library list or perform an override against the file.

—Midrange Computing Staff

Copying a Group of Files

CPYGRPF was originally designed to allow a quick copy of one or more files into library QTEMP. This allowed a quick program-testing area. Command CPYF didn't have the right defaults for my needs, so I wrote my own command.

The command Copy a Group of Files (CPYGRPF) allows entry of 1 to 50 file names to be copied. These file names are qualified and defined at the QFILE label. The library to copy from is defaulted as the Library List. The TO library defaults to the current library. If the file already exists in the destination library, you can enter an appropriate action, just as CPYF allows. See the command definition shown in Figure 5.5 and the CPP shown in Figure 5.6.

```
CPYGRPF:    CMD         PROMPT('Copy a Group of Files')

            PARM        KWD(FILE) TYPE(QFILE) MIN(1) MAX(50) +
                          PROMPT('File to copy')
            PARM        KWD(TOLIB) TYPE(*SNAME) LEN(10) DFT(*CURLIB) +
                          SPCVAL((*CURLIB)) PROMPT('To library')
            PARM        KWD(MBROPT) TYPE(*CHAR) LEN(8) RSTD(*YES) +
                          DFT(*NONE) VALUES(*NONE *ADD *REPLACE) +
                          PROMPT('Replace or add records')

QFILE:      QUAL        TYPE(*SNAME) LEN(10) MIN(1)
            QUAL        TYPE(*SNAME) LEN(10) DFT(*LIBL) +
                          SPCVAL((*LIBL)) PROMPT('Library')
```

Figure 5.5: The CPYGRPF command makes it easy to copy a group of files all at once.

```
GRP001CL: +
    PGM PARM(&FILE &TOLIB &MBROPT)

    DCL VAR(&BINCNT)    TYPE(*CHAR) LEN(2)
    DCL VAR(&CNTR)      TYPE(*DEC)  LEN(5 0)
    DCL VAR(&CPYA)      TYPE(*CHAR) LEN(2)
    DCL VAR(&CPYD)      TYPE(*DEC)  LEN(2 0)
    DCL VAR(&ERRORS)    TYPE(*DEC)  LEN(3 0)
    DCL VAR(&FILE)      TYPE(*CHAR) LEN(1002)
    DCL VAR(&FNMS)      TYPE(*CHAR) LEN(1000)
    DCL VAR(&FROMFILE)  TYPE(*CHAR) LEN(10)
    DCL VAR(&FROMLIB)   TYPE(*CHAR) LEN(10)
    DCL VAR(&MBROPT)    TYPE(*CHAR) LEN(8)
    DCL VAR(&NCPYA)     TYPE(*CHAR) LEN(2)
```

Figure 5.6: CL program GRP001CL provides the power behind the CPYGRPF command (part 1 of 3).

```
     DCL  VAR(&NCPYD)      TYPE(*DEC)  LEN(2 0)
     DCL  VAR(&PNTR)       TYPE(*DEC)  LEN(5 0)
     DCL  VAR(&TODO)       TYPE(*DEC)  LEN(5 0)
     DCL  VAR(&TOLIB)      TYPE(*CHAR) LEN(10)

     /* Find the number of files to be copied */
     CHGVAR VAR(&BINCNT) VALUE(%SST(&FILE 1 2))
     CVTBINDEC FROMBIN(&BINCNT) TODEC(&TODO)

     /* Validate file names */
     CHGVAR VAR(&FNMS) VALUE(%SST(&FILE 3 1000))
     CHGVAR VAR(&CNTR) VALUE(1)

LOOP_CHK: +
     IF COND(&CNTR *GT &TODO) THEN(GOTO CMDLBL(END_CHK))
     CHGVAR VAR(&PNTR) VALUE((&CNTR * 20) - 19)
     CHGVAR VAR(&FROMFILE) VALUE(%SST(&FNMS &PNTR 10))
     CHGVAR VAR(&PNTR) VALUE(&PNTR + 10)
     CHGVAR VAR(&FROMLIB) VALUE(%SST(&FNMS &PNTR 10))

     CHKOBJ OBJ(&FROMLIB/&FROMFILE) OBJTYPE(*FILE)
     MONMSG MSGID(CPF9801) EXEC(DO)
        CHGVAR VAR(&ERRORS) VALUE(&ERRORS + 1)
        SNDPGMMSG MSG('File' *BCAT &FROMFILE *BCAT 'not found.') +
           MSGTYPE(*DIAG)
     ENDDO
     MONMSG MSGID(CPF9810) EXEC(DO)
        CHGVAR VAR(&ERRORS) VALUE(&ERRORS + 1)
        SNDPGMMSG MSG('Library' *BCAT &FROMLIB *BCAT 'not found.') +
           MSGTYPE(*DIAG)
     ENDDO
     CHGVAR VAR(&CNTR) VALUE(&CNTR + 1)
     GOTO CMDLBL(LOOP_CHK)

     /* Validate destination library */
END_CHK: +
     IF COND(&TOLIB *NE '*CURLIB') THEN(DO)
        CHKOBJ OBJ(&TOLIB) OBJTYPE(*LIB)
        MONMSG MSGID(CPF9801) EXEC(DO)
           CHGVAR VAR(&ERRORS) VALUE(&ERRORS + 1)
           SNDPGMMSG MSG('Destination library' *BCAT &TOLIB *BCAT +
              'not found.') MSGTYPE(*DIAG)
        ENDDO
     ENDDO

     /* If any errors were found, stop processing */
     IF COND(&ERRORS *GT 0) THEN(DO)
        SNDPGMMSG MSGID(CPF0002) MSGF(QCPFMSG) MSGTYPE(*ESCAPE)
        GOTO CMDLBL(ENDPGM)
     ENDDO
```

Figure 5.6: CL program GRP001CL provides the power behind the CPYGRPF command (part 2 of 3).

```
        /* Copy each of the files */
        CHGVAR VAR(&CNTR) VALUE(1)

LOOP_CPY: +
    IF COND(&CNTR *GT &TODO) THEN(GOTO CMDLBL(END_CPY))
    CHGVAR VAR(&PNTR) VALUE((&CNTR * 20) - 19)
    CHGVAR VAR(&FROMFILE) VALUE(%SST(&FNMS &PNTR 10))
    CHGVAR VAR(&PNTR) VALUE(&PNTR + 10)
    CHGVAR VAR(&FROMLIB) VALUE(%SST(&FNMS &PNTR 10))

        /* Determine whether the destination file exists */
    CHKOBJ OBJ(&TOLIB/&FROMFILE) OBJTYPE(*FILE)
    MONMSG MSGID(CPF9801) EXEC(GOTO CMDLBL(NEW_FILE))

        /* Destination file already exists */
    IF COND(&MBROPT *EQ '*NONE') THEN(DO)
        SNDPGMMSG MSG('File' *BCAT &FROMFILE *BCAT 'already exists +
            in' *BCAT &TOLIB *TCAT '. File not copied.') MSGTYPE(*INFO)
        CHGVAR VAR(&NCPYD) VALUE(&NCPYD + 1)
        GOTO CMDLBL(NXT_CPY)
    ENDDO

    CPYF FROMFILE(&FROMLIB/&FROMFILE) TOFILE(&TOLIB/&FROMFILE) +
        FROMMBR(*ALL) TOMBR(*FROMMBR) MBROPT(&MBROPT)
    CHGVAR VAR(&CPYD) VALUE(&CPYD + 1)
    GOTO CMDLBL(NXT_CPY)

NEW_FILE: +
    CPYF FROMFILE(&FROMLIB/&FROMFILE) TOFILE(&TOLIB/&FROMFILE) +
        FROMMBR(*ALL) TOMBR(*FROMMBR) CRTFILE(*YES)
    CHGVAR VAR(&CPYD) VALUE(&CPYD + 1)

NXT_CPY: +
    CHGVAR VAR(&CNTR) VALUE(&CNTR + 1)
    GOTO CMDLBL(LOOP_CPY)

END_CPY: +
    CHGVAR VAR(&CPYA) VALUE(&CPYD)
    CHGVAR VAR(&NCPYA) VALUE(&NCPYD)
    SNDPGMMSG MSG('Files copied =' *BCAT &CPYA *CAT '. Files not +
        copied =' *BCAT &NCPYA *CAT '.') MSGTYPE(*COMP)

ENDPGM: +
    ENDPGM
```

Figure 5.6: CL program GRP001CL provides the power behind the CPYGRPF command (part 3 of 3).

The first task is to find out the number of files the user has entered. This information is contained in the first 2 bytes of parameter &FILE. Remember, when a list is fed to a program from a command, the number of elements to be processed are in binary in the first 2 bytes of the list. Command CVTBINDEC from QUSRTOOLS is borrowed to convert this binary number to a decimal number you can work with. If you don't have access to the CVTBINDEC tool from QUSRTOOL, you can remove the line that used the CVTBINDEC tool and replace it with the following:

```
CHGVAR VAR(&TODO) VALUE(%BIN(&BINCNT 1 2))
```

After you know the number of files to process, check to make sure each one exists in the library specified. This is handled in the loop LOOP_CHK. &TODO contains the number of files to process, &PNTR is the index to the file names. &FROMFILE and &FROMLIBR are loaded with the appropriate information and a CHKOBJ is used to validate the file. If the file or library is not found, a diagnostic message is sent and the error counter is incremented. If it exists, the next file is validated. The destination library is validated at label END_CHK.

If any errors were found, escape message CPF0002 is sent. This will cause the command to return to the screen and allow the user to list all of the errors it found.

If all is okay, do another loop (LOOP_CPY) to proecess each file. If the destination file already exists, &MBROPT is checked for the appropriate action. If the action was *NONE, then an informational message will be sent to the user at the completion of the procedure saying the file was not copied. Keep track of the number of files copied and not copied to tell the user at job completion.

This command does make testing easier. Perhaps more importantly, it also gives you experience programming commands using lists.

—Bill Robins

✦ ✦ ✦ Database Tools

V4R4 Offers New EDTF Tool

V4R4 introduced a new Edit File (EDTF) command that allows you to edit a stream file (something I'm finding more useful all the time) or database file member. In earlier releases, you could find an EDTF tool in the QUSRTOOL library. The EDTF tool is also available as a PTF. If you use EDTF from the QUSRTOOL library, you should start using the EDTF command found in QSYS beginning with V4R4. (There's no guarantee that IBM will continue to ship the source for the EDTF tool in QUSRTOOL library.)

—Richard Shaler

✦ ✦ ✦ Date and Time

Copying Zoned Decimal Dates

Q: I have heard of an AS/400 function that converts zoned decimal fields to date fields. Can you tell me what function this is and where to find it?

A: The Change Physical File (CHGPF) and Copy File (CPYF) commands will make certain data type conversions when fields of the same name are defined differently in a file from which data is being copied (a "from" file) and the one to which data is being copied (the "to" file). One of those conversions is from zoned decimal to date.

For example, assume a file has a six-digit zoned decimal field that stores dates in MMDDYY format.

```
A            R JNLREC
A              ACCT          10
A              JEDATE        6S 0
A              AMOUNT        9P 2
```

To convert the zoned field to a date field, build another file like this one, but change the zoned decimal date field to date data type. The format of the date field doesn't matter.

```
A            R JNLREC
A              ACCT          10
A              JEDATE         L
A              AMOUNT        9P 2
```

Copy the old file to the new file with CPYF, specifying FMTOPT(*MAP).

```
CPYF FROMFILE(JNL)  TOFILE(JNLNEW)  MBROPT(*REPLACE) FMTOPT(*MAP)
```

CPYF will convert the zoned data to date data type.

CPYF assumes the dates in the zoned field are in the job's date format. If they're different, you'll have to issue a Change Job (CHGJOB) command first to make the job's date format match the file being copied. For example, if the data is in YYMMDD format, use this command:

```
CHGJOB DATFMT(*YMD)
```

As I said, CPYF supports only certain types of conversions. If you try to copy a packed decimal date, for example, you'll get message CPF2960 (Field JEDATE will not map from file JNL in MYLIB). However, you can get around this limitation by building a logical file in which the packed field is redefined as zoned decimal and then by copying the logical file instead of the physical file.

You also have to be sure that the dates stored in the zoned decimal field are valid dates. If there is an invalid date value (such as zeros), you'll receive message CPF2958 (Conversion error occurred copying from-file field value). The records will still be copied, but CPYF will replace the invalid date values with the current date.

For more information, see the *Data Management* manual (SC41-4710, CD-ROM QBJAUG00).

—Ted Holt

Creating a Logical File over a Packed MMDDYY Field

If you are stuck with a packed MMDDYY date field, and need to create a logical access path by date over the file, you can break it down using the substring feature in DDS (see Figures 5.7 and 5.8). To do this, you must first override its definition to zoned because, technically, you cannot substring a packed numeric field. The SST keyword uses three parameters: the field name, the starting position, and the result length. The result must be defined as input-only and is always character. Note also that because a record format containing an input only field cannot be shared with the physical file, you must list all of the other fields from the physical if you wish to use them.

```
A           R RECORD
A             FLD1            3  0      COLHDG('FIELD #1')
A             FLD2            1         COLHDG('FIELD #2')
A             MMDDYY          6  0      COLHDG('DATE' 'FIELD')
A           K FLD1
```

Figure 5.7: The physical file definition shown here can be parsed. See Figure 5.8.

```
A              R RECORD                    PFILE(FILENAME)
A                FLD1
A                FLD2
A                MMDDYY          S
A                FLDYY           I         SST(MMDDYY 5 2)
A                FLDMM           I         SST(MMDDYY 1 2)
A                FLDDD           I         SST(MMDDYY 3 2)
A              K FLDYY
A              K FLDMM
A              K FLDDD
```

Figure 5.8: Parsing the individual fields from a physical file can be accomplished in a logical file.

—Kathleen Kostuck

Partial Numeric Date Selection with SQL

Recently, I needed to select records using the year portion of a six-digit numeric date field for the selection criteria. I discovered two ways to construct an SQL statement to accomplish this. The key to both methods is the DIGITS function. The DIGITS function returns a character representation of a numeric column. Because a numeric column can then be treated as a character column, the column can be used with the LIKE predicate and with the SUBSTR function.

—Mary Ann Warren

✦ ✦ ✦ DB2/400

Data Loader Commands Enhancements

PTFs have enhanced the functionality of the Copy from Import File (CPYFRMIMPF) and Copy to Import File (CPYTOIMPF) commands.

One of the enhancements is the Remove blank (RMVBLANK) parameter for CPYFRMIMPF. The values available for the RMVBLANK parameter are *LEADING and *NONE. If *LEADING is specified, DB2 UDB strips leading blanks from a character string before placing the resulting string in the specified target character column. With *NONE, all leading blanks are included in the result string that is copied into the specified target character column.

Another enhancement is a new Allow null values (ALWNULLVAL) parameter for CPYFRMIMPF. The values available for ALWNULLVAL are *NO and *FLDDFT. When *FLDDFT is specified, DB2 UDB assigns the default value to the target column if the data being imported (e.g., blanks in a numeric field) would cause DB2 UDB to try to place a null value in a target column that doesn't allow nulls.

There is also a new Stream file code page (STMFCODPAG) parameter for CPYTOIMPF that allows you to specify the code page of the target stream file. In the past, you would have used another tool or command to first create the stream file with the desired code page to override the default behavior of the command.

Finally, there is a new behavior for the CPYTOIMPF MBROPT(*REPLACE) option. Now, when MBROPT(*REPLACE) is specified, DB2 UDB clears the target stream file if CPYTOIMPF is given an empty database table to copy.

The PTF numbers for V4R4 are SF61859 and SF61937. This functionality is part of the base operating system for subsequent releases.

—Kent Milligan

Displaying DASD Utilization

Q: I'm trying to call the Retrieve System Status (QWCRSSTS) API in a CL program to display the percentage of DASD utilization used. The problem is that every time I run the program, I get the error message, "Receiver variable too small to hold result" (MCH1210 message identifier).

A: I had the same problem trying to access the percentage of Auxiliary Storage Pool (ASP) utilized. This problem occurred because I used a field defined as packed 3,0. What I should have done was use a field defined as packed 7,0 because the data from the API is returned in a field defined as binary 4 and the value returned is 10,000 times the actual percentage. For example, a value of 850883 means 85.0883 percent. A field defined less than packed 7,0 just won't hold the result (hence the error message). Try using the CL example shown in Figure 5.9

```
DCL VAR(&RCVDTA) TYPE(*CHAR) LEN(067) /* +
Receiver var for API */
DCL VAR(&RCVLEN) TYPE(*CHAR) LEN(4) +
VALUE(X'00000043') /* &rcvdta is 067 +
bytes */
DCL VAR(&RESETO) TYPE(*CHAR) LEN(10) +
VALUE('*YES ') /* Reset Statistics +
Opt */
DCL VAR(&FMTNAM) TYPE(*CHAR) LEN(08) +
VALUE('SSTS0200') /* Fmt name for API rqs */
DCL VAR(&ERRSTS) TYPE(*CHAR) LEN(08) +
VALUE(X'0000000800000000') /* Err code +
struc */
DCL VAR(&PCTASP) TYPE(*DEC) LEN(7) VALUE(0) /* % +
System ASP used */
/* get system status : DASD percentage */
CALL PGM(QWCRSSTS) PARM(&RCVDTA &RCVLEN &FMTNAM +
&RESETO &ERRSTS)
CHGVAR VAR(&PCTASP) VALUE(%BIN(&RCVDTA 53 4))
```

Figure 5.9: Use the QWCRSSTS API to retrieve DASD utilization.

—Chuck Pence

Forcing Records to Disk

Recently, I spent an hour or more debugging a new program that didn't have a bug. The program is a never-ending program that runs in a batch subsystem and spends most of its time waiting to read data from a data queue. When a user presses a certain function key, the interactive program writes information to the data queue with a call to QSNDDTAQ. The never-ending program then reads the data queue, performs some processing, and writes information to a file. During the unit-testing stage, I discovered that the program didn't appear to write to the file. Or so I thought. After I ended the program, the records were there!

A colleague and I discovered that this strange behavior was due to the default value of the "Records to force a write" or FRCRATIO parameter of the Create Physical File (CRTPF) and Create Logical File (CRTLF) commands. The default is *NONE; when I changed it to 1, the program worked as I thought it should.

Here's why. When OS/400 writes records to DASD, it does not always write them immediately. Instead, the operating system writes the records to a buffer area in memory. Records are written to DASD when the buffer is full or when the file is closed. Assuming that the memory buffer is a fixed size, records for files with large record sizes will be written to DASD sooner than records for files with small record sizes.

When you set the FRCRATIO parameter to *NONE, you have no control over when the operating system writes the records to DASD. OS/400 determines when it is appropriate to write them. The AS/400 can operate more efficiently this way. If your program ends after writing to the file, then you should let this parameter default to *NONE because OS/400 writes the records then anyway. A program that writes several records before it closes the file will operate more efficiently if it can write all the records in one burst.

If you set this parameter to a number, you control when the records are written. The number represents how many records you want OS/400 to buffer before it will write them to DASD. In my situation, I wanted the record to be written immediately so I set FRCRATIO to 1.

Proper use of this parameter could save considerable time when you write or debug programs. It also could make your system more efficient once your program enters the production environment.

—Kenneth Fordham

Here is an alternative to the suggestion in the preceding section, "Forcing Records to Disk." Instead of changing the FRCRATIO keyword for a file, the Override Database File (OVRDBF) command can be used. It also has a FRCRATIO keyword that would accomplish the same task within the current job stream, leaving the file's force ratio set to *NONE so the system can retain its default blocking function for all other programs and queries.

And, as yet a third alternative, instead of using the FRCRATIO parameter of the Create Physical File (CRTPF), Change Physical File (CHGPF), or Override Database File (OVRDBF) commands to force records to disk, use the RPG force-end-of-data (FEOD) operation as shown in Figure 5.10.

```
*. 1 ...+... 2 ...+... 3 ...+... 4 ...+... 5 ...+... 6 ...+... 7
C                          WRITERECORD
C                          FEOD FILEX
```

Figure 5.10: You can force records to disk with the FEOD operation.

The FEOD operation allows you to force to disk all changes your program makes to a file. Normally, the system determines when to force changes to disk; use the FEOD operation in an RPG program to ensure that changes are forced to disk.

—Midrange Computing Staff

✦ ✦ ✦ DDS

Solution for Fields with No Column Headings

Sometimes, you run a query on a file and it turns out that the columns have no headings. Instead of meaningful headings, there are only cryptic field names of no more than 10 characters. What can you do to stop this problem from occurring again? On newer releases of OS/400, you can modify the DDS and run the Change Physical File (CHGPF) command. But what if you're on an older release? It's unlikely that you'll want to change the DDS for the file (adding suitable COLHDG keywords to all fields) and recreate the file. Such recreation of the file means potentially losing all data in the file. You can do it by cloning the file, recreating the original, and moving all the data back, but you still have logical files to worry about.

There's a better solution: SQL's LABEL ON statement, simply put, adds either column headings or text description (TEXT keyword) to database fields. You can execute the LABEL ON statement either from an interactive SQL session, started with the Start SQL command (STRSQL), or from a Query Management Query, started with the Start Query Management Query (STRQMQRY) command. The key is in knowing how LABEL ON's syntax goes. Two examples follow.

Suppose file CONTACTS has a field named FAXNBR—but no column headings—and a field named TELNBR, but no text description. The SQL statement shown in Figure 5.11 fixes the first problem.

```
LABEL ON contacts (faxnbr IS 'Fax Number',
faxnbr TEXT IS 'Work fax number',
telnbr IS 'Telephone Number',
telnbr TEXT IS 'Work telephone number')
```

Figure 5.11: This SQL statement fixes the problem with no text or column headings.

As you can see, you have to list in parentheses the fields that are to be labeled, separating them by commas. For each field, use the TEXT reserved word to add text description; for column headings, simply omit it. In the case of column headings, bear in mind that whatever character string you supply will be processed as follows:

- The first 20 characters represent the first line of column headings.
- The second 20 characters represent the second line of column headings.
- The last 20 characters represent the third line of column headings.

Changes made by the LABEL ON statement are permanent. Even so, just in case you ever recompile, it is a good idea to go back to the DDS of the file and add appropriate COLHDG and/or TEXT keywords.

—Allan Telford

✦ ✦ ✦ Dependency

And Now a Word on Dependency

Q: Would you explain functional dependency as it pertains to database design?

A: Functional dependency means that the value of one field can be determined from the value of another. For example, suppose a customer master file has the following fields:

- Customer number (key)
- Customer name
- Street address
- City
- State abbreviation
- State name

This file has an undesirable functional dependency. State name is functionally dependent on state abbreviation. For example, any record with state abbreviation TX must have the state name Texas. All other fields are functionally dependent on customer number, but that's okay and desirable because customer number is the key. A file is normalized when all fields are functionally dependent only on the key. To normalize this file, you should divide it into two files:

File 1: Customer master file

- Customer number (key)
- Customer name
- Street address
- City
- State abbreviation

File 2: State master file

- State abbreviation (key)
- State name

The state name is no longer stored in the customer master file but is stored in a state master file. Now, if you want to know the name of the state in which a customer lives, take the state abbreviation in the customer master file and find the matching state abbreviation in the state master file. This process is called *joining*. I have given you only a brief explanation. You can use a search engine on the Web to find more information.

—Ted Holt

Using File Dependency Information

The AS/400 maintains a system file, QADBFDEP, which contains file dependency information. Each record contains the following fields:

- DBFFIL File name
- DBFLIB Library name
- DBFFDP Dependent file name
- DBFLDP Dependent file library
- DBFTDP Dependency type (Data, View, Indirect)

The key to the file is DBFLIB, DBFFIL, DBFLDP, DBFFDP. The CL program shown in Figure 5.12 is an example of how you can use this file to delete all dependent logical files belonging to a specified file.

```
            PGM       PARM(&LIBRARY &FILE)
            DCL       VAR(&LIBRARY) TYPE(*CHAR) LEN(10)
            DCL       VAR(&FILE) TYPE(*CHAR) LEN(10)
            DCL       VAR(&KEY) TYPE(*CHAR) LEN(20)
            DCLF      FILE(QADBFDEP)
            CHGVAR    %SST(&KEY 1 10) &LIBRARY
            CHGVAR    %SST(&KEY 11 10) &FILE
            OVRDBF    FILE(QADBFDEP) MBR(*FIRST) POSITION(*KEYAE 2 +
                        *N &KEY) LVLCHK(*NO) SEQONLY(*YES)

LOOP:       RCVF
            MONMSG    MSGID(CPF0864) EXEC(GOTO CMDLBL(END))
            IF (&DBFLIB *NE &LIBRARY) GOTO END
            IF (&DBFFIL *NE &FILE) GOTO END
             ?DLTF FILE(&DBFLIB/&DBFFDP)
            MONMSG CPF0000
            GOTO LOOP
END:        ENDPGM
```

Figure 5.12: Use this CL program to delete dependent logical files.

The program is called using a library name and a file name. The database dependency file is positioned to the requested file and is read until the file or library name is changed or until the end of file is reached. The dependent file is deleted with a prompt. You can call this program from any other program.

—*Alon Fluxman*

Editor's Note: *Notice the* POSITION *parameter in the* OVRDBF *command. This essentially lets you position a file in a CL program. This program uses* *KEYAE *(key-after or equal). The record identified by the search values (in this case the search value is the variable* &KEY*) is the first record received. There are five position types related to keyed files:*

*KEYB (key-before)
*KEYBE (key-before or equal)
*KEY (key-equal)
*KEYA (key-after)
*KEYAE (key-after or equal)

You can also retrieve the first record of the file with *START*, the last record in the file with* *END*, or a specific relative record number with* *RRN*. See the* CL Reference, *Volume 4 manual (SC21-9778).*

The "2" after *KEYAE *is the number-of-fields value. This value specifies that only the first two fields of the key are being used as the key (file* QADBFDEP *has a four-field key). By displaying the file description for file* QADBFDEP*, you can determine the characteristics of the key. The* *N *specifies that all record formats in this file are to be read.* &KEY *is the variable whose value is compared to the partial composite key specified in the* OVRDBF *command.*

—*Shannon O'Donnell*

✦ ✦ ✦ DFU

Instant File Updating

The AS/400 has a terrific utility that hasn't received much press. With it you can quickly update any field of any file without having to first write a custom program or manually create a DFU. The Update Data (UPDDTA) command will automatically create and begin a DFU update program that will include all the fields in the file. It takes just a moment for UPDDTA to build the program from the DDS specifications. No matter if the field is alpha, packed, binary, or zoned-decimal, any field defined in the DDS will be displayed.

Only use UPDDTA if the file is defined by DDS. If it is not, it will still compile an update program for you, but there will be one large alphanumeric field for the entire record. This, of course, spells trouble if you have any packed or binary data in the record.

UPDDTA also can be called with option 18 in PDM's "Work With Objects" display.

—Midrange Computing Staff

✦ ✦ ✦ Direct Files

Direct Files in Native?

Q: Is there a way to create direct files using CL commands? I'm used to creating RETAIN-J direct files in the S/36 environment but I can't seem to "nativize" it.

A: It takes two commands: Create Physical File (CRTPF) and Initialize Physical File Member (INZPFM). You run the CRTPF command as usual (supplying either the record length in the RCDLEN parameter or by using DDS). Then you run the Initialize Physical File Member (INZPFM) command to initialize a certain number of records, as in:

```
INZPFM FILE(lib/file)  RECORDS(*DFT)  TOTRCDS(1000)
```

This command creates 1000 records in the "direct" file, initializing them to their default values (blanks for alphanumeric fields, zeros for numeric fields). RECORDS(*DLT) initializes all 1000 records to deleted records.

—Ernie Malaga

✦ ✦ ✦ Field Names

For Longer Field and File Names, Use SQL

One benefit of using SQL is that it allows you to create database column (field) and table (file) names longer than 10 characters. Of course, not all AS/400 interfaces support these longer names. The FOR COLUMN clause on the CREATE TABLE statement allows you to specify a short name for your long column names. This short name can be used on the interfaces that can't support field names longer than 10 characters (if a short name is not specified, the system will automatically generate one). The CREATE TABLE statement, however, does not allow you to specify a short name for the table name. Again, the system does generate a short name automatically, but the short name is not user friendly (e.g., the system short name for CUSTOMER_MASTER is CUSTO00001) and is not guaranteed to have the same short name if you recreate the database file object multiple times.

You need to use the RENAME TABLE SQL statement in conjunction with the SQL CREATE TABLE statement to control the long and short file names for your database files.

—Kent Milligan

✦ ✦ ✦ Field Reference Files

File Reference File

The AS/400 keeps a reference file with an entry for each file on the system. The file can be queried to list the files in file name order or library order. The file is called QADBXREF and is found in QSYS. Each record contains the fields shown in Figure 5.13.

```
DBXFIL          File name
DBXLIB          Library name
DBXDIC          Dictionary name
DBXOWN          Owner Name
DBXTXT          Text
DBXATR          Attribute (PF, LF, TB, VW, IX)
DBXLNK          "E" if externally described
                "P" if program described
DBXSQL          "I" if IDDU
                "S" if SQL
                "C" if CRTDTTADCT
                "X" if Migrated
                Blank = no link
DBXTYP          "D" of Data, "S" if Source
DBXNFL          Number of fields
DBXNKF          Number of key fields
DBXRDL          Maximum record length
DBXIDV          Internal file definition for dictionary
```

Figure 5.13: Here's a useful list of AS/400 reference file field names.

As you can see, this file can be useful in locating information by file, library, or owner. There is a multitude of useful reports that you can create from this file.

—Alon Fluxman

Save Space in Field Reference Files

When creating field reference files, specify the parameter MBR(*NONE) on the Create Physical File (CRTPF) command to prevent a member from being added to the file. This will save disk space by eliminating unnecessary members.

By their nature, field reference files have no use for the data space (member) portion of the object. The only part that is required is the file description. This is the part that is looked at when a FLDREF or other keyword is used to refer to the field reference file.

Existing field reference files can be trimmed down by using the following command:

```
RMVM xxxxx MBR(*ALL)
```

—Paul Jackson

✦ ✦ ✦ Indexing

Indexing Mixed-case Fields

When a logical file is keyed on a field that contains mixed-case text, it doesn't always sort the way you might want it to. The reason is that lowercase letters always come before uppercase letters in the EBCDIC collating sequence. So what you end up with is *a* through *z* (lowercase), followed by *A* through *Z* (uppercase).

To correct this problem, translate the field to uppercase, before indexing, by using the logical file DDS keywords RENAME and TRNTBL. See Figure 5.14.

```
... 1 ...+... 2 ...+... 3 ...+... 4 ...+... 5 ...+... 6 ...+
A          R CTREC                          PFILE(CATGRY)
A            CTDESC
A            CTCAPS              I           RENAME(CTDESC)
A                                            TRNTBL(QSYSTRNTBL)
A          K CTCAPS
... 1 ...+... 2 ...+... 3 ...+... 4 ...+... 5 ...+... 6 ...+
```

Figure 5.14: Use DDS keywords RENAME and TRNTBL to translate a field to uppercase.

Field CTDESC contains a mixed case text. Field CTCAPS contains a capitalized version of CTDESC. Notice that the file is keyed on CTCAPS. When the file is read in keyed sequence and field CTDESC is presented, the data appears to be more naturally sorted. All records starting with *a* or *A* will be together, followed by all records starting with *b* or *B*, and so on. There is a slight variation of the code that will also work, as shown in Figure 5.15.

```
....1.... ....2.... ....3.... ....4.... ....5.... ....6.... ....7....
A          R CTREC                      PFILE(CATGRY)
A            CTDESC
A            CTCAPS              I       RENAME(CTDESC)
A                                        TRNTBL(QSYSTRNTBL)
A          K CTCAPS
....1.... ....2.... ....3.... ....4.... ....5.... ....6.... ....7....
```

Figure 5.15: You can try an alternate method of using RENAME and TRNTBL in DDS.

Field CTDESC contains mixed-case text. Field CTCAPS contains a capitalized version of CTDESC. Notice that the field is keyed on CTCAPS. When the file is read in keyed sequence and field CTDESC is presented, the data appears to be more naturally sorted. All records starting with uppercase or lowercase *A* will be together, followed by all records starting with *B*, and so on.

—Robin Klima

✦ ✦ ✦ Joined Files

Join Me in Updating this File

OS/400 V4R3 introduced a feature many had been requesting for a long time. With V4R3 and higher, it is possible to update data in one file with field-level data from another file. In other words, you can now update through a join. Figure 5.16 illustrates how it's done.

```
UPDATE DABLIB/MYRECON2 SET (SMIFLG, SEDFLG, ASSSMI, ASSSED) = (SELECT
SMIFLG, SEDFLG, ASSSMI, ASSSED FROM MHSFLA/CISINT WHERE CISINT.CLIENT =
MYRECON2.CLIENT AND CISINT.INTDAT = MYRECON2.INT
```

Figure 5.16: Updates through a join are possible.

—David Babashanian

✦ ✦ ✦ Journaling

Error-free Deletion of Journal Receivers

Q: I am journaling changes to a particular file and, each night, displaying those journaled records to an outfile for some reports. After I extract that data, I retrieve the name of the journal receiver and change the journal to a new receiver using the Change Journal (CHGJRN) command with parameter JRNRCV(*GEN). Then, I delete the detached journal receiver. The problem I am running into is that, when I try to delete the journal receiver, I get error message CPA7025, "Receiver never fully saved." How can I avoid this error message?

A: Message CPA7025 has a default reply of "I," for ignore. If that is the reply given, the journal receiver will be deleted, even though it isn't saved. If the job that deletes the receiver is changed to have the attribute INQMSGRPY(*DFT), all messages will be answered with their default reply. You probably don't want all messages answered with their default. Figure 5.17 shows what I normally do.

```
DCL VAR(&INQMSGRPY) +
  TYPE(*CHAR) LEN(10)
...
RTVJOBA INQMSGRPY(&INQMSGRPY)
CHGJOB INQMSGRPY(*DFT)
DLTJRNRCV JRNRCV(RECEIVER)
CHGJOB INQMSGRPY(&INQMSGRPY)
```

Figure 5.17: This code fragment demonstrates how to answer messages with a default reply.

This way, you're affecting only the Delete Journal Receiver (DLTJRNRCV) command.

—Martin Pluth

Journaling and RGZPFM

Q: If I want to reorganize a physical file to remove the deleted records, what do I need to do if the file is journaled? I believe that journaling keeps track of records by relative record number. Reorganize means moving records to different relative positions in the file. What should I do in case I ever need to recover the file? Do I save the file or the journal receiver before using Reorganize Physical File Member (RGZPFM) or save both? Is there anything else I need to do?

A: There is no journal entry for each changed record when you reorganize, remove, or clear a member. Instead, one entry for the whole command is written to the journal. The Apply Journal Changes (APYJRNCHG) and Remove Journal Changes (RMVJRNCHG) commands will produce an error when they hit one of those entries. You then have to handle the error yourself.

If you're doing a RMVJRNCHG, you're stuck; there is no data in the journal about the state of the file before the event. If you restore the file and use APYJRNCHG to bring the file up to date, you can just perform the action that caused the entry. In the case of a reorganization, the entries in the journal are in the same relative-record number (RRN) order as they were before the recovery, and all the journal entries after the reorganization will be correct.

—Martin Pluth

Journals Made Easy

Journaling used to require a lot of management. New receivers had to be created, attached, detached, and deleted regularly. Otherwise, they could use all available disk space.

You can let the system handle journaling management for you. There are two parameters on the Create Journal (CRTJRN) and Change Journal (CHGJRN) commands that tell the system how much of the journal's maintenance it should do. These parameters are MNGRCV and DLTRCV.

Here's how to use these parameters. If you have existing journal receivers that aren't using the Journal Receiver Threshold (THRESHOLD) parameter of the Create Journal Receiver (CRTJRNRCV) command, or if you are creating a new journal, create a new journal receiver. The THRESHOLD parameter of the journal receiver needs to be set to the maximum receiver size you want. The THRESHOLD value must be at least 5,000 kilobytes for the system to manage the receivers. Create or change the journal, specifying the new receiver and MNGRCV(*SYSTEM).

If you also want the system to delete receivers when they aren't needed, use DLTRCV(*YES) on the CHGJRN command. If you are changing an existing journal and there are previously attached journal receivers, delete these receivers before using DLTRCV(*YES). Only use this option if you aren't using journaling for data recovery because the system might delete receivers before they are saved.

—Martin Pluth

Specify Only One File per STRJRNPF Command

You can specify more than one file name in a single Start Journal Physical File (STRJRNPF) command, but you might not want to. Here's why.

I recently had to fix a job that had ended abnormally. The problem turned out to be a STRJRNPF command that had 11 files in the FILE parameter. Under normal circumstances, none of the 11 files was being journaled when this job would run. However, when the job began to run on this day, one of the files was already being journaled. The STRJRNPF command failed and the other 10 files did not start journaling.

The job didn't cancel at this point because CPF7030 (File or access paths for file &1 being journaled) was being trapped by a global Monitor Message (MONMSG) command. The job finally stopped when an RPG program tried to open a file with commitment control.

From a command line, I ran an End Journal Physical File (ENDJRNPF) command to stop journaling the one file. I restarted the job and it ran fine. When the job finished, I replaced the one STRJRNPF command with 11 commands.

This change means that if one or more files are already journaling, for whatever reason, the others will begin journaling, and the job should work correctly.

—Ted Holt

✦ ✦ ✦ Level Checks

Adding a Field to a Database File

If a field is added to the end of a database file record format, compiling the new file definition with LVLCHK(*NO) does not always save you the effort of recompiling all the programs that use the file. If the new field is numeric, any programs that add records to the file should be recompiled anyway.

You might not be aware of the disadvantages of the following steps, which programmers have been known to use to add a new field to an AS/400 database file:

- Delete any logical files that are built over the file to be changed.
- Rename the existing file to save the current data.
- Modify the DDS for the file by adding the new field to the end of the existing record format.
- Compile the new file definition with LVLCHK(*NO).
- Copy the data back from the renamed file using the Copy File (CPYF) command with FMTOPT (*MAP *DROP).
- Recreate the logical files using LVLCHK(*NO).

Because the new file is compiled with LVLCHK(*NO), all existing programs that don't refer to the new field will work normally with the new version of the file—with one exception. The initialization of the new field when new records are written. When a program that was compiled with the old version of the file writes new records to the file, the new field will be properly initialized to blanks if it is alphanumeric. However, if the new field is numeric, it will not be initialized to zero and will contain invalid data.

—Midrange Computing Staff

Editors' Note: *Instead of recompiling the physical file when you add a new field, you may instead want to use the CHGPF command. The CHGPF command will automatically update the logical file(s) and properly format the data for you—all this without requiring you to delete logical files and copy data. You may not even need to recompile the programs that use the file(s). However, you should test the latter on each program as individual programs may have unique requirements.*

Database File Level Checking

If you make a change to a physical or logical file definition, you must either recompile the file using LVLCHK(*NO) or you must recompile all the programs that use the file in order to avoid getting a level check when attempting to open the file. In other words, programs must always be compiled after files. This is a common misconception. If you enter the Display File Description (DSPFD) command, you will see a file level identifier that consists of the creation date and time for the file. Further down, you will also see a member level identifier that consists of the creation date and time for the file member.

From the member level identifier, you might expect that the file creation date and time were being used to verify that the current definition of the file is the same as the definition that the program was compiled with. However, the file level identifier and the member level identifier are not used in level checking.

Even further down on the file description display, you will find a record format level identifier. This is the level identifier that is used for level checking. This record format level identifier is determined only by the:

- Total length of the record format.
- Record format name.
- Number and order of the fields in the record format.
- Data type and size of the fields.
- Field names.
- Number of decimal positions in the fields.

Changes to any other DDS information have no effect on the record format level identifier and can be changed without having to specify LVLCHK(*NO) or recompiling the programs that use the file. For example, the following DDS keywords can be changed without causing a level check:

TEXT, COLHDG, CHECK, EDTCDE, EDTWRD, REF, REFFLD, CMP, RANGE, VALUES, TRNTBL, REFSHIFT, and DFT.

Join specifications, join keywords, and access path keywords can be changed. You can even change the key fields and select/omit fields without causing a level check.

—Midrange Computing Staff

Finding Level Check Conflicts

Here is a program that uses SQL to produce a report showing level check conflicts. The system stamps every file created with a format level identifier. This identifier changes when major attributes (such as field attributes, number of fields, or order of fields) of the file change. The format level is not affected by the creation date or edit codes. When a program is compiled, the format level identifier becomes a part of the program. When the program executes, the system checks the format level identifier in the program against the one in the file. If they don't match, a MCH3601 error will be generated. (The format check is ignored if LVLCHK(*NO) is specified for the file when it is created.)

CL program LEVELCK (Figure 5.18), along with RPG program LEVELCKR (Figure 5.19) will produce a list of all programs in which the format level identifier does not agree with the one in the file.

```
LEVELCK: +
    PGM PARM(&LIBRARY1 &LIBRARY2)

    DCL VAR(&LIBRARY1)    TYPE(*CHAR) LEN(10)
    DCL VAR(&LIBRARY2)    TYPE(*CHAR) LEN(10)

    DSPFD FILE(&LIBRARY1/*ALL) TYPE(*RCDFMT) OUTPUT(*OUTFILE) +
        OUTFILE(QTEMP/FILEFILE)
    DSPPGMREF PGM(&LIBRARY2/*ALL) OUTPUT(*OUTFILE) +
        OUTFILE(QTEMP/PROGFILE)

    CALL PGM(LEVELCKR)

    ENDPGM
```

Figure 5.18: CL program LEVELCK produces a list of level -heck problems with files.

```
    FQSYSPRT O   F      132      OF      PRINTER
    IF1         DS
    I                                     1  10 WHPNAM
    I                                    11  20 WHLIB
    I                                    21  30 WHOTYP
    I                                    31  41 WHFNAM
    I                                    42  42 WHOBJT
    I                                    43  53 WHLNAM
    I                                    54  63 WHRFNM
    I                                    64  76 WHRFSN
    I                                    77  86 RFFILE
    I                                    87  96 RFLIBM
    I                                    97  97 RFFTYP
    I                                    98 107 RFNAME
    I                                   108 120 RFID
    C                    EXCPT#HEAD
    C/EXEC SQL WHENEVER SQLERROR GOTO ERROR
    C/END-EXEC
    C/EXEC SQL DECLARE R1 CURSOR FOR SELECT
    C+        WHPNAM, WHLIB, WHOTYP, WHFNAM,
    C+        WHOBJT, WHLNAM, WHRFNM, WHRFSN, RFFILE, RFLIB, RFFTYP,
    C+        RFNAME, RFID    FROM PROGFILE, FILEFILE
    C+        WHERE WHFNAM = RFFILE AND WHRFNM = RFNAME
    C+        AND                       WHOBJT = 'F' AND WHRFSN > ' '
    C+        AND WHRFSN <> RFID
    C/END-EXEC
    C/EXEC SQL
    C+ OPEN R1
    C/END-EXEC
    C            SQLCOD    DOUNE0
    C/EXEC SQL
    C+   FETCH R1 INTO :F1
    C/END-EXEC
```

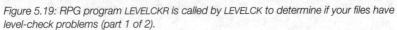

Figure 5.19: RPG program LEVELCKR is called by LEVELCK to determine if your files have level-check problems (part 1 of 2).

```
C                          EXCPT#PRT
C      OF                  EXCPT#HEAD
C      OF                  SETOF                         OF
C                          END
C              ERROR       TAG
C                          SETON                         LR
OQSYSPRT E    203              #HEAD
O                                          06 'OBJECT'
O                                          20 'LIBRARY'
O                                          30 'TYPE'
O                                          45 'FILE NAME'
O                                          49 'TP'
O                                          56 'FORMAT'
O                                          70 'LEVEL'
O                                          90 'FORMAT LEVEL'
OQSYSPRT E                     #PRT
O                          WHPNAM         10
O                          WHLIB          22
O                          WHOTYP         34
O                          WHFNAM         47
O                          WHOBJT         49
O                          WHRFNM         60
O                          WHRFSN         76
O                          RFID           90
```

Figure 5.19: RPG program LEVELCKR is called by LEVELCK to determine if your files have
level-check problems (part 2 of 2).

The CL program LEVELCK is called with two parameters. The first parameter is the name
of the library for the files and the second parameter is the name of the library for the programs. The program uses the DSPFD command to create a file with all the format descriptions (TYPE(*RCDFMT)). The Display Program Reference (DSPPGMREF) command is used
to create a file with all the programs and the objects that they reference, including the format level of each referenced object. The program LVL uses SQL to produce a list of the
unmatched format levels.

F1 is a data structure with the necessary field names from both files. The first SQL statement will handle all errors by ending the program. The second statement identifies the selection and joining of the two files. If the following conditions are met, the files will be
joined and data will be returned to the program:

- The file name and format name match.
- The referenced object is a file.
- The record format identification is not SPACES.
- Neither the ID in the record format nor the ID in the program match the ID in the
  file.

The main processing loop is simple. The program reads the joined file (FETCH R1 INTO :F1) until the SQL return code (SQLCOD) is not zero. You can see how easy programming can be if you let SQL do the work for you.

—Alon Fluxman

Using Level Check *NO with Database Files

When in a hurry to add a field to a database file, you might have considered telling the system to ignore level checking by using the LVLCHK value of *NO. This way you won't have to recompile all the programs that use the file to avoid getting level check errors on those programs. You think, "Why recompile them anyway, when they don't even reference the new fields that I've added?"

Beware! Unless you recompile it, a program that adds or updates records on the changed file will not initialize the new fields. The chances of having decimal data errors will be high.

Ideally you should recompile all programs that use the file. You must, at least, compile all programs that update or add to the file.

— Richard Shaler

✦ ✦ ✦ Logical Files

Beware of Logical Files That Are Too Large!

Recently, a problem occurred with a minor change to our vendor's software package. A change was made to a logical file that increased the processing time from 2 to 4 hours for a nightly batch job. Our vendor could see no reason for this to occur. Also, when the program was running, the response time was incredibly slow, and the amount of CPU used was at 100 percent, or ++++.

On analysis of the program, I found that the vendor had built the logical file over three of our largest physical files using three different record formats. The total number of records in this multiformat logical exceeded 10 million. I also found out that the program was using only one of the record formats.

I split the logical into three separate logicals using the same exact keys and selection criteria. Then I changed the program to use the logical I had just built that contains the record format the program needed. The total runtime was cut down to 12 minutes. Also, I received no complaints about the system being slow. CPU usage was at normal levels.

I placed a call to IBM and explained the problem to them. IBM said that the AS/400 suffers from a condition called *fan-out*. On a logical built over the large physical files, the system spends a lot of time trying to keep the records in a particular order even though they are in three separate formats. The solution is to split the single logical into three separate logicals. IBM explained that it is easier on the system to have one logical keep track of one large physical file rather than have one logical keep track of several large physical files.

—Marvin Mooney

Creating Logical Files

DB2/400 helps you keep information well organized by allowing physical files to have multiple members. This support is great, but creating a logical file over each and every member of the physical file can be a chore. Specifying DTAMBRS(*ALL) in the CRTLF command causes an access path to be built over all members. But there is no easy way to create a multimember logical file with one-to-one correspondence to each member of the physical file. If you ever have to create a logical file over a multimember physical file you have two options:

1. Specify each member on the DTAMBRS parameter, which is a tedious task.

2. Perform a CRTLF with no members and run the ADDLFM command for each member, which again is a tedious task.

Therefore, the solution was to create the command ADDLFMALL (Figure 5.20) and its processing program LFM002CL (Figure 5.21) for the programmers. The only requirement is that the logical file must be created with MBR(*NONE) and MAXMBRS(*NOMAX) for this to operate correctly. If a member already exists, it just proceeds to the next one. In addition, RCVMSGS are used to send the user every message that is encountered.

```
ADDLFMALL:  CMD         PROMPT('Add All Logical File Members')

            PARM        KWD(LF) TYPE(Q1) MIN(1) PROMPT('Logical file')
            PARM        KWD(PF) TYPE(Q1) MIN(1) PROMPT('Physical file')

Q1:         QUAL        TYPE(*SNAME) LEN(10) MIN(1)
            QUAL        TYPE(*SNAME) LEN(10) DFT(*LIBL) +
                          SPCVAL((*LIBL)) PROMPT('Library')
```

Figure 5.20: Command ADDLFMALL makes adding data members easy.

```
LFM002CL: +
   PGM PARM(&QUALLF &QUALPF)

   DCL VAR(&LF)       TYPE(*CHAR) LEN(10)
   DCL VAR(&LFLIB)    TYPE(*CHAR) LEN(10)
   DCL VAR(&MSG)      TYPE(*CHAR) LEN(132)
   DCL VAR(&MSGID)    TYPE(*CHAR) LEN(7)
   DCL VAR(&OK)       TYPE(*LGL)  LEN(1)      VALUE('0')
   DCL VAR(&PF)       TYPE(*CHAR) LEN(10)
   DCL VAR(&PFLIB)    TYPE(*CHAR) LEN(10)
   DCL VAR(&QUALLF)   TYPE(*CHAR) LEN(20)
   DCL VAR(&QUALPF)   TYPE(*CHAR) LEN(20)

   DCLF FILE(QAFDMBRL)

   CHGVAR VAR(&PF) VALUE(%SST(&QUALPF 1 10))
   CHGVAR VAR(&PFLIB) VALUE(%SST(&QUALPF 11 10))
   CHGVAR VAR(&LF) VALUE(%SST(&QUALLF 1 10))
   CHGVAR VAR(&LFLIB) VALUE(%SST(&QUALLF 11 10))

   DSPFD FILE(&PFLIB/&PF) TYPE(*MBRLIST) OUTPUT(*OUTFILE) +
      OUTFILE(QTEMP/MBRS)
   MONMSG MSGID(CPF0000) EXEC(GOTO CMDLBL(SNDMSG))

   OVRDBF FILE(QAFDMBRL) TOFILE(QTEMP/MBRS)
   CHGVAR VAR(&OK) VALUE('1')

READ: +
   RCVF
   MONMSG MSGID(CPF0864) EXEC(GOTO CMDLBL(END))

   ADDLFM FILE(&LFLIB/&LF) MBR(&MLNAME) DTAMBRS((&PFLIB/&PF +
      (&MLNAME))) TEXT('Logical - ' *CAT &MLMTXT)
   MONMSG MSGID(CPF0000)

SNDMSG: +
   RCVMSG MSG(&MSG) MSGID(&MSGID)
   IF COND(&MSGID *NE ' ') THEN(DO)
      SNDPGMMSG MSG(&MSG) TOPGMQ(*PRV) MSGTYPE(*INFO)
      GOTO CMDLBL(SNDMSG)
   ENDDO

   IF COND(&OK) THEN(GOTO CMDLBL(READ))

END: +
   ENDPGM
```

Figure 5.21: CL program LFM002CL is the power behind adding data members to a multiformat logical file.

—Midrange Computing Staff

Logical over Flat S/36E File

Q: How do you create a native AS/400 logical file (with noncontiguous keys) over a S/36 Environment file?

A: The code shown in Figure 5.22 creates a native logical file with noncontiguous keys over a S/36 Environment file.

```
BLDFILE TESTPHY,I,RECORDS,1,80,,T,1,5,DFILE,NODUPKEY


 ... 1 ...+... 2 ...+... 3 ...+... 4 ...+... 5 ...+... 6 ...+... 7
 A          R TESTLOGR                   PFILE(TESTPHY)
 A            K00001
 A            F00001
 A            VNDR              I        SST(F00001 40 3)
 A            SEQN              I        SST(F00001 20 4)
 A          K VNDR
 A          K SEQN
 ... 1 ...+... 2 ...+... 3 ...+... 4 ...+... 5 ...+... 6 ...+... 7
```

Figure 5.22: You can create a logical file with noncontiguous keys.

—Midrange Computing Staff

Non-keyed Physical Files

When you need a primary access path over a physical file, do not key the physical file. Create a logical access path over the physical instead. This gives you more flexibility. If the access path becomes damaged, you lessen the risk of the actual data being damaged. Also, if you need to bypass rebuilding the access path, you can remove the logical file member (it's a little hard to do with a physical if you need to keep the data).

—William MacKenzie Picou

✦ ✦ ✦ Object Locks

Accessory to WRKOBJLCK

Here is a useful utility I wrote to have the system let me know when a file is not being used by anyone. It comes in handy when you have to replace a physical or logical file that's in production with one that's been in testing. Because recompiling the file entails actually deleting the existing one, this cannot be done while someone is using it.

The Work With Object Locks (WRKOBJLCK) command will tell you who is using the file. My utility, Wait for File (WAITF) will run in the background and check every 30 seconds for you. WAITF will notify you with a break message when the file is available.

The utility ensures that the object exists and, if it does, attempts to allocate the object with a lock of *EXCL. Using the Monitor Message (MONMSG) command to determine if the allocation was successful is the key to how this utility works. (Figure 5.23 contains the WAITF command source code and Figure 5.24 contains the source code for the CPP, F003CL.)

```
/*================================================================*/
/* To compile:                                                    */
/*                                                                */
/*         CRTCMD    CMD(XXX/WAITF) PGM(XXX/F003CL) +             */
/*                   SRCFILE(XXX/QCMDSRC)                          */
/*                                                                */
/*================================================================*/
 WAITF:     CMD         PROMPT('Wait for File')

            PARM        KWD(FILE) TYPE(QUAL) PROMPT('File')
 QUAL:      QUAL        TYPE(*NAME) LEN(10) MIN(1)
            QUAL        TYPE(*NAME) LEN(10) DFT(*LIBL) +
                        SPCVAL((*LIBL)) PROMPT('Library')
```

Figure 5.23: The WAITF command is used to determine if a file is in use and to alert you when it's not.

```
/*================================================================*/
/* To compile:                                                    */
/*                                                                */
/*         CRTCLPGM   PGM(XXX/F003CL) SRCFILE(XXX/QCLSRC)         */
/*                                                                */
/*================================================================*/
 F003CL:    PGM         PARM(&QUALFILE)
            DCL         VAR(&QUALFILE) TYPE(*CHAR) LEN(20)
            DCL         VAR(&FILE) TYPE(*CHAR) LEN(10)
            DCL         VAR(&LIB) TYPE(*CHAR) LEN(10)
            DCL         VAR(&TYPE) TYPE(*CHAR) LEN(1)
            DCL         VAR(&MSGQ) TYPE(*CHAR) LEN(10)
            DCL         VAR(&MSGQLIB) TYPE(*CHAR) LEN(10)
            DCL         VAR(&MSG) TYPE(*CHAR) LEN(40)

            RTVJOBA     JOB(&MSGQ) TYPE(&TYPE)
```

Figure 5.24: CPP F003CL is the workhorse behind the WAITF command (part 1 of 2).

```
                IF (&TYPE *EQ '1') THEN(DO)
                SBMJOB     CMD(CALL PGM(F003CL) PARM(&QUALFILE)) +
                             MSGQ(&MSGQ)
                GOTO       CMDLBL(ENDPGM)
                ENDDO

                RTVJOBA    SBMMSGQ(&MSGQ) SBMMSGQLIB(&MSGQLIB)
                CHGVAR     VAR(&FILE) VALUE(%SST(&QUALFILE 1 10))
                CHGVAR     VAR(&LIB) VALUE(%SST(&QUALFILE 11 10))

                CHKOBJ     OBJ(&LIB/&FILE) OBJTYPE(*FILE)
                MONMSG     MSGID(CPF9801) EXEC(DO)
                CHGVAR     VAR(&MSG) VALUE('File' *BCAT &LIB *TCAT +
                             '/' *CAT &FILE *BCAT 'was not found.')
                SNDBRKMSG  MSG(&MSG) TOMSGQ(&MSGQLIB/&MSGQ)
                             GOTO CMDLBL(ENDPGM)
                ENDDO
TOP:            ALCOBJ     OBJ((&LIB/&FILE *FILE *EXCL)) WAIT(0)
                MONMSG     MSGID(CPF1085 CPF1002) EXEC(DO)
                DLYJOB DLY(30)
                GOTO CMDLBL(TOP)
                ENDDO

                DLCOBJ     OBJ((&LIB/&FILE *FILE *EXCL))
                CHGVAR     VAR(&MSG) VALUE('File' *BCAT &LIB *TCAT '/' +
                             *CAT &FILE *BCAT 'is now available.')
                SNDBRKMSG  MSG(&MSG) TOMSGQ(&MSGQLIB/&MSGQ)

ENDPGM:         ENDPGM
```

Figure 5.24: CPP F003CL is the workhorse behind the WAITF command (part 2 of 2).

If the allocation is successful, a break message is sent to the message queue from which the job was submitted. It is important to deallocate any object allocated. I do so as part of the utility, although you might want to deallocate the object from the command line after you are done replacing or reorganizing the object.

—Andrew Longo

✦ ✦ ✦ ODBC

Accessing a Specific Member of a Multiple Member File Through ODBC

Q: We have a DB2/400 physical file with multiple members. We are creating a client/server program that needs to be able to access specific members in that file. Is there a way to do this using ODBC?

A: If you're at least at V3R1 of OS/400, you can execute the OVRDBF command as a stored procedure. To execute a command using ODBC, call QCMDEXC in QSYS with two parameters: the command text and the length of the command text. For example, the SQL command might look like this:

```
CALL QSYS.QCMDEXC('OVRDBF  FILE(TEST1) TOFILE(LIB/TEST)
     MBR(TESTMBR) OVRSCOPE(*JOB)',   0000000063.00000)
```

In this statement, 63 is the command length. Note that you have to put the leading and trailing zeros on the command length to make sure the command receives the correct data type. Once the override is done, you can refer to the file in SQL statements just as you would any other file, and the action will take place on the member you are overriding to. You can even join different members of the same file using this method.

—Brian Singleton

Allow for Plenty of Users in Prestart Jobs

AS/400 ODBC and Java Database Connectivity (JDBC) toolbox users can encounter slow database connect times. Often, this is because of the low number of default prestart job entries for the QZDASOINIT (TCP/IP) and QZDAINIT (SNA) jobs. When the initial number of prestart active jobs reaches a threshold, additional jobs are started. But the ODBC user who trips the threshold pays the response-time price of waiting for the additional number of jobs to start. To avoid this, set the initial number of prestart jobs to a higher number (such as some number greater than the number of users), and then restart the prestart jobs as in Figure 5.25.

```
CHGPJE SBSD(QSYS/QSERVER) PGM(QIWS/QZDASOINIT) INLJOBS(50)
CHGPJE SBSD(QSYS/QSERVER) PGM(QIWS/QZDAINIT) INLJOBS(50)
ENDPJ SBS(QSERVER) PGM(QIWS/QZDASOINIT) OPTION(*IMMED)
ENDPJ SBS(QSERVER) PGM(QIWS/QZDAINIT) OPTION(*IMMED)
STRPJ SBS(QSERVER) PGM(QIWS/QZDASOINIT)
STRPJ SBS(QSERVER) PGM(QIWS/QZDAINIT)
```

Figure 5.25: Increasing the initial number of users in prestart jobs can improve performance.

—Lance A. Amundsen

Blocking Data Transfer Can Improve ODBC

Q: I wrote a program that downloads a large number of records from our AS/400 to a client PC. The program is written in Visual Basic and uses the Client Access ODBC driver. It works correctly but is a bit slow. Is there anything I can do that might improve the performance?

A: When data is transferred between the AS/400 and an ODBC client, it is moved in blocks. Some communications overhead is associated with each block transmitted to the client PC. Fortunately, you can control the block size on the client to optimize it for your particular environment. The Client Access ODBC driver's default block size of 32KB is optimized for general use and should work for most installations. However, if you are transferring a large amount of data to the PC, you might want to increase this value to decrease the number of blocks transmitted (thereby reducing communications overhead).

To change the size of the blocks transmitted with the Client Access ODBC driver, you need to edit the ODBC.INI file in the Windows directory. Using NOTEPAD.EXE or some other text editor, locate the section for your data source name and add or change the **BlockSizeKB** entry to a value between 1 and 512. This is the size in KB of the transfer block. Experiment with different values to see what works best in your environment. Also, for this setting to have an effect, be sure the **RecordBlocking** entry is set to the default value of "2."

—Brian Singleton

Creating an Index with ODBC

Q: I know I need a unique index to update files with ODBC, but how do I create that index?

A: You can create the index as a logical file over the physical file using DDS, but a quicker way is to use SQL. You can use SQL either from OS/400 (STRSQL or a Query Management Query) or from your ODBC client program. From a place where you can enter SQL commands (i.e., RUMBA for Database Access for example, or MS Access), type the following code:

```
CREATE UNIQUE INDEX idxlib/idxnam ON fillib/filnam (fldnam ASC)
```

In this statement, substitute the library you want the index to go to for idxlib and the name of the index you want to create for idxnam. Also, substitute the library and file names of the file you want to update for fillib and filnam, respectively. Fldnam represents the field that you want to use to create the index, and ASC stands for ascending sort (you can put DESC for descending sort).

You can specify more than one field to create the index. Just be sure the combination of fields is unique for each record. Once the index is created, the index will automatically be picked up the next time you connect to your data source, and you can then update your data.

—Brian Singleton

Creating an OS/400 Library Using ODBC

Q: How can I create a library using ODBC? I will be using Visual Basic (VB). I can use SQL pass-through to issue OS/400 SQL commands directly, but I don't know the SQL command to create a library.

A: The SQL command to create a library is CREATE COLLECTION. The command will also create a journal, journal receiver, and catalog views for the collection. Any subsequent CREATE TABLEs added into the collection will automatically be journaled.

—Brian Singleton

ODBC Job Number Tracking

One of the hardest things about client/server programming on the AS/400 is finding your ODBC job. The Work with Active Jobs (WRKACTJOB) command will list all of the jobs running in the QSERVER subsystem, which is where all ODBC prestart jobs run. If your shop is like mine, you have many ODBC users cluttering up the screen, and the user is always displayed as QUSER! To find the logged-in user profile, you have to display the job log of each QSERVER job until you see the user profile you want to debug. This is a time-wasting pain in the posterior, to say the least.

Enter the most useful stored procedure in the world! Stored procedure RETJOBI eliminates the need to search for a particular ODBC job! As shown in Figure 5.26, the code for this procedure is only four lines long.

```
/*================================================================*/
/* TO COMPILE:                                                    */
/*                                                                */
/* CRTBNDCL PGM(xxx/RETJOBI) SRCFILE(xxx/QCLSRC)                  */
/*                                                                */
/*================================================================*/
PGM PARM(&NBR)
DCL VAR(&NBR) TYPE(*CHAR) LEN(6)
RTVJOBA NBR(&NBR)
ENDPGM
```

Figure 5.26: This CL code for the RETJOBI procedure retrieves your ODBC job attributes.

The procedure begins with the declaration of a CL variable to hold the job number, and then it executes a call to the Retrieve Job Attributes (RTVJOBA) command to return the number of the job currently running. Once you wrap this command by issuing a CREATE PROCEDURE statement in your ODBC program, you will be able to call it as a stored procedure and see your job number. I have found this technique so useful that this procedure is called from every program in my shop, and the job number is then posted on each screen in the application.

This way, my operators can tell me their job number when they have a problem, and I can use the Display Job Log (DSPJOBLOG) or the Work with Jobs (WRKJOB) command to see why they are having problems. You'll need to know how jobs are named under the version of Windows you are using. For example, the job name might be QZDASOINIT, QZADAINIT, or some similar value. To display the job log of a Windows 95/NT ODBC job, you would type DSPJOBLOG *xxxxxx*/ QUSER/QZDASOINIT, where *xxxxxx* is the job number returned by the stored procedure.

To prepare the RETJOBI command for execution, use the Create Bound CL Program (CRTBNDCL) command to create an executable version of the RETJOBI program in your QSYS library. However, be aware that, when you upgrade to the next release of OS/400, you might lose what you had in QSYS. Perhaps a better approach might be to put the object in QGPL. Next, execute the following statement from an interactive SQL session:

```
CREATE PROCEDURE QSYS/RETJOBI (INOUT :job CHAR(6)) EXTERNAL NAME
        QSYS/RETJOBI SIMPLE CALL;
```

Once the create-procedure statement has been executed, DB2 knows what arguments the procedure will accept and their data type. You are now ready to execute code, as shown in Figure 5.27, to find your job number.

```
Dim Con1 As New Connection
Dim Cmd1 As New Command
Dim Prm1 As Parameter
'Activate the connection with the AS/400
Con1.Open "AS400", "HOWARD", "HOWARD"
'Associate the connection with the command object
Cmd1.ActiveConnection = Con1
'set the command into commandtext property
Cmd1.CommandText = "CALL QSYS.RETJOBI(?)"
'Create a parameter object to hold job number
Set Prm1 = Cmd1.CreateParameter("job", adChar, adParamInputOutput, 6, "")

'append parameter object into command object Cmd1.Parameters.Append Prm1
'execute the command
Cmd1.Execute
'show user the job number
MsgBox "Your job number is: " & Cmd1.Parameters("job").Value
'Release the command and the connection
Set Cmd1 = Nothing
Set Con1 = Nothing
```

Figure 5.27: This VB code connects to an AS/400 and executes the RETJOBI procedure.

The code shown in Figure 5.27 was written using VB 5.0. For the code to work, create a VB form inside the program with a command button labeled Command_1. When the user clicks Command_1, the VB code executes and displays the user's AS/400 job number. When you enter this code into VB, be sure to do the following:

1. Activate the following VB Project References in the program: the Microsoft ActiveX Data Objects 2.0 library and the Microsoft ActiveX Data Objects Recordset 2.0 library. Project references are activated in VB 5.0 by clicking Project from the VB dropdown menu and then clicking References. Find these entries and place a check mark next to them. If they are missing from your VB references, download and install the Microsoft Data Access Software Development Kit (SDK) and the Microsoft Data Access Components Version 2.0 from the Microsoft Universal Data Access Web site at *www.microsoft.com/data/download.htm*. This download fixes problems with the earlier releases, adds connection pooling, and provides better parameter object support. I don't recommend running this code without the new components.

2. Replace the "AS/400" literal in the CON1.OPEN line with the name of your ODBC data source name. Also in that line, replace the "HOWARD" literal

with a valid AS/400 user name for your system, and replace the "PASSWORD" literal with the password for that user.

Once these changes are in place, you can retrieve your AS/400 job number at will.

—Howard F. Arner, Jr.

Why Does ODBC Return a "Column *N" Not Found

Q: I've configured my ODBC data source, and I am trying to use it to retrieve data. However, when I try to run an SQL statement, I receive an error saying "column *N not found." I'm not requesting this *N column. What's going on?

A: You need to make sure there's a *LOCAL relational database entry on the system you want to connect to. Do this by running the Work with Relational Database Directory Entries (WRKRDBDIRE) command. If there is no entry with *LOCAL, select option 1 to add a new entry. Make an entry that is the same name as your AS/400 system name. Then, for the remote location, enter *LOCAL. You might also have to restart the server support job to make sure it picks up the new entry. End the job by issuing the following command:

```
ENDPJ QSERVER QIWS/QZDAINIT
```

Start it again by entering this command:

```
STRPJ QSERVER QIWS/QZDAINIT
```

This should pick up the new database entry.

—Brian Singleton

✦ ✦ ✦ Performance

Aborting a RGZPFM

Q: What happens if a job ends during a Reorganize Physical File Member (RGZPFM)? Is the file corrupted, or does the system recover?

A: The RGZPFM sequence occurs as follows:

1. Create a new data space.

2. Copy nondeleted records from old data space using the specified access path.

3. Change member header to point to new data space.

4. Mark old data space addresses as available.

5. Rebuild all indexes over member.

If the job ends prior to step 3, you might need to use the Reclaim Storage (RCLSTG) command to take care of a disconnected data space. Step 3 is probably not interruptible and might have fail-safes anyway. If the job ends before step 4 completes, you need to clean up with RCLSTG again. Each keyed access path will be rebuilt the first time it's used. Rebuilding of keyed access paths also happens if the job ends at step 5.

The short answer is: The file's okay, regardless.

Choose the Right File Sequencing Path

Here is a way to make certain types of programs run more efficiently. If a program reading a file does not need the records in any particular order, then sequential processing will be much more efficient than reading by an access path. To do this in RPG, leave position 31 of the "F" specification for the file blank. This will cause the program to read the file sequentially.

When reading files sequentially, you can improve performance even more by overriding the file prior to calling the program. There are two parameters on the OVRDBF command, which can improve the performance of sequential processing.

- The NBRRCDS parameter specifies the number of records moved as a unit from auxiliary storage to main storage.
- The SEQONLY parameter specifies whether sequential processing is to be used and, if so, the number of records moved as a unit from the database to the internal data management buffer.

To calculate the values for these parameters, use the following calculation: 4096 / record length. Round the answer to the nearest integer. This will cause the file to be blocked by a factor of 4K (which is what IBM recommends).

For example, if the file CUSTMAST has a record length of 68 bytes, the command would be:

```
OVRDBF FILE(CUSTMAST) NBRRCDS(60) SEQONLY(*YES 60)
```

Using this technique causes double buffering to occur, which results in very efficient processing.

—*Robin Klima*

Efficient File Conversion

We recently made some enhancements to a purchased package, including adding a single field to a large file. Converting the production file to the new layout caused some pain that we could have avoided.

The traditional approach, which we used, is to:

- Remove the logicals.
- Rename the existing file.
- Create the new file.
- Use CPYF *MAP *DROP to copy in the data.
- Then recreate the logicals.

We had an 8-hour install window and didn't give this file conversion a second thought. Six hours into the install, the only thing still running was the copy. An analysis of the I/O counts indicated that it would run for another 12 to13 hours and we would still have to re-build the logicals after the copy finished. The installation had to be aborted so production wouldn't be impacted.

The boss wasn't happy. On Monday, my assignment (and I had to accept it) was to shoe-horn a 15-hour-plus file copy into 8 hours.

There turned out to be several approaches and permutations in this file conversion. The shortest technique took just over an hour and the longest (also the traditional approach) took well over 15 hours. Paying attention up front can save some embarrassment if you are working with large files.

Obviously "large" is a relative term. Your perceptions can be influenced by your proces-sor speed, memory, disk configuration, etc. And you'll have to decide for yourself when to be concerned about conversion times. In our case, the file had nearly 8 million records, 473 fields, and a record length of just over 2,000 bytes. The physical file was unkeyed and had 4 logicals.

The first thing I tried was blocking the CPYF because blocking can often improve runtimes if you are not memory constrained. Because we were on V4R3, I divided 128K by the record size and came up with a blocking factor of 58. I started a blocked CPYF, but just watching the I/O counts quickly made it obvious that blocking wasn't going to be the solution and this was going to be more complicated than I had thought.

In a test library, I created a scaled-down version of the file and logicals (consisting of 10% of the records) and started testing. All of my tests, except for the CHGPF, included deleting and recreating the logicals; this was an essential part of the conversion process. I figured there were three things to try:

- CPYF with blocking.
- Custom RPG with blocking.
- CHGPF.

It turned out that there was another significant variable: the *position* of the new field in the record. We had inserted the new field at a logical position close to the beginning of the record, but the conversion always went faster if the new field was added at the end.

If we put the new field at the end of the record, CHGPF was by far the best way to convert the file, especially because in this case no logicals needed rebuilding.

For an inserted field, it turned out that a custom RPG cycle program was most efficient and CPYF was by far the worst.

Given our available install window, we chose to insert the field in a logical position and use an RPG program. Figure 5.28 shows the program. The actual install time was almost exactly the 3.2 hours my tests had predicted.

```
Foldfile          ip        e                   disk      rename(newfilef:old)
Fnewfile          o         e                   disk
C                 write           newfilef
```

Figure 5.28: You can use a custom RPG copy program for inserting fields in a logical order.

You can review the results of my tests as listed in Table 5.1.

Table 5.1: Results Sorted by Elapsed Time

Method	New Field Location	Minutes for 10%	Extrapolated Hours
CHGPF	End	7	1.2 hours
CPYF *MAP Block-58	End	29	4.8 hours
CPYF *MAP *DROP Block-58	End	30	5.0 hours
CPYF *NOCHK Block-58	End	43	7.1 hours
RPV IV, cycle, Block-58	Inserted	19	3.2 hours
CHGPF	Inserted	72	12.0 hours
CPYF *MAP Block-58	Inserted	91	15.1 hours

Notes:

- Results with a keyed physical will probably be different.
- The testing was done on a 4-way 530 with other users on the machine.
- Test results are not scientific but are intended to show trends. Most tests were run only once.
- There might be other techniques not tested.

When changing a large file:

- Add new fields at the end of the record if possible.
- Convert using CHGPF when fields are added at the end.
- If you are inserting a field, convert using a custom RPG program with blocking.
- CPYF is usually the most inefficient conversion method.
- If in doubt, test.

—Sam Lennon

Improving Performance by Deleting Logicals

Q: We're doing a project in which we need to read through records and change the product number field. The problem is that we have 64 logicals attached to the physical file, which will hurt the program's performance. We thought about deleting the logicals and recreating them when done. Does anyone have a quick way to accomplish this?

A: It's easier to remove the logical file members with the Remove Member (RMVM) command and create them again with the Add Logical File Member (ADDLFM) command when you're done. You don't have to worry about finding the source and, unless you have multiple-member physical files, you can do the whole thing with PDM user options.

—Pete Hall

Speed Up Month-end File Purge Jobs

There's an easy way to speed up certain types of purge programs. You can use this technique if the file you're purging records from has any dependent logical files attached to it. If so, you should consider using the Remove Member (RMVM) command to remove the logical file members before running the purge job and then adding them back in afterward with the Add Logical File Member (ADDLFM) command.

This can improve the performance of purge jobs because, every time a record is deleted, access paths for dependent logical files are also updated. So, if you're deleting a large number of records, you would want to remove any dependent logical file members, run the purge program, reorganize the physical file to drop the deleted records, and then "re-add" the logical file members. If the purge program accesses the file through a logical file, don't remove the member for that specific logical file.

It is not necessary to delete the logical files; just remove the members. The object definition will remain on disk. When you add the logical file member back in, the access path will be recreated. I sped up a month-end transaction file purge from 12 hours to 7.5 hours with this technique.

—Andre Nortje

Speeding Record Access

Before you reorganize a physical file, consider which access path is most important to you. Taking the default of reorganizing by the key specified in the physical file DDS might not always produce the best performance for your particular applications. Let's use the example of a customer master file that is indexed by customer number, but must be scanned quickly by your phone order-entry users in company name order. The reorganization default is to physically order the records by customer number. The best performance can be achieved by sequencing the file in the same order as the customer name access path used by the order-entry program. This is easy to do with the RGZPFM command. The following command will reorganize file CUSTMAST by customer name by using the existing logical file member CUSTMAST01 in the logical file.

```
CUSTMAST01:
RGZPFM FILE(CUSTLIB/CUSTMAST)  MBR(*FIRST) +
       KEYFILE(CUSTLIB/CUSTMAST01 CUSTMAST01)
```

—Midrange Computing Staff

✦ ✦ ✦ Query

Getting Around the Rounding Problem

Q: I have an end-of-day report I created in Query/400 that summarizes inventory adjustments by type. The problem is that the adjustments are accurate to the penny, but the report displays only whole dollars. I'm afraid the numbers are inaccurate because the cents aren't being accumulated. Figure 5.29 shows how I defined the fields in Query/400 on the Define Result Fields screen.

Field	Expression	Column Heading	Len	Dec
CSTDLR	INCST	Dollar Amount	7	0
CSTCNT	INCST - CSTDLR	Adjustment Amount	7	2

Figure 5.29: Note that cents are not accumulated on this Define Results Fields screen.

The problem is that the first result field, CSTDLR, does not truncate the cost field but rounds it up when the cents are greater than or equal to 50. Can you show me how to write this result field definition so that the cost number is truncated instead of rounded?

A: Define your field as 9.2 instead of 7.0. Then, go to field formatting and make it 7.0. That should take care of the rounding problem for you.

—Bill Robins

Quantifiably Quicker Queries

We've all experienced a system that has ground to a halt from an out-of-control query. Usually, this happens because a poorly designed query was created and run. Sometimes, though, a long-running query can simply be due to a large number of records in a database. Whatever the reason, it would be nice to know ahead of time how long a query will take to run, as well as to receive suggestions on how to speed it up.

Relax! There is a method you can use to determine how long a query will run, as well as to get suggestions on how to speed up the query processing.

Although it is little known, and even less used since the days of the S/38, there has existed a means to predict the amount of processing cycles a query will use. This is what's known as the *Query Predictive Governor*. IBM didn't make this feature available to the general AS/400 population at first, supposedly because it wasn't 100 percent accurate. Having used it myself many times, however, I can tell you that its accuracy is close enough for the purpose of this tip. The Predictive Query Governor measures, or "predicts," the number of CPU cycles a given query will take to process, and this tool can be used to fine-tune your queries.

If the number of CPU cycles used exceeds the limit set in the system value Query Processing Time Limit (QQRYTIMLMT) or at the job level set by the Change Query Attributes (CHGQRYA) command, the query will halt. You can use the query's failure to find out how to improve performance. To do so, you need to ensure that the query fails. The easiest way to do this is to set the query processing time limit to 0 in either the system value QQRYTIMLMT or in the job. Now, run your query interactively. When you attempt to run the query after setting this value to 0, it will immediately timeout and fail with error message CPF427F:

```
"Estimated query processing time xx exceeds limit 0," in which xx
    is the actual number of CPU cycle seconds used by the query.
```

Answer this message with a "C" to cancel it, and then display the job log. The job log will tell you how many CPU cycles were used by the query.

To potentially improve the performance of the query, you must do one more thing. In the job log, you might also see a message that says something like "Access path built for file FILENAME," in which FILENAME is the name of the primary file used by the query. Position your cursor over this message and press the F1 key to display the second-level help. As you read through the message, you will see, beginning at the bottom of the page, a message telling you which fields from the primary file were used to build the new access path. This information is your key to improving the query's performance. Create a permanent index of this access path either by creating a logical file or by using the SQL command CREATE VIEW, and run your query again. Make sure you again set the query time limit to 0 before you run the query. You should now see a message showing you that the number of CPU cycles used by the query is significantly less than the number used on the first go-around. You now have a fine-tuned query!

—*Shannon O'Donnell*

Use Debug Mode to Optimize Queries

If you want to find out what decisions the query optimizer is making for your SQL, Open Query File (OPNQRYF) or other database queries, and turn on the debug mode with the Start Debug (STRDBG) command.

—*Martin Pluth*

✦ ✦ ✦ Remote Databases

Your AS/400's Database Needs a Name

When you are first installing an AS/400, one of the first actions that you should perform is to add a Relational Database (RDB) directory entry. Without this entry, you will notice messages that contain a value of "*N" where there should be a database, system, or device name. Not having a RDB directory entry also can cause referential integrity errors, requiring you to perform a reclaim storage procedure. If you are an AS/400 systems administrator, you already know that this can take a long time. I have also seen the omission of a RDB directory entry cause ODBC errors.

To work with your existing (if any) RDB directory entries, issue the Work with Relational Database Directory Entries (WRKRDBDIRE) command from an AS/400 command line. If your system doesn't have a directory entry, enter a 1 in the leftmost column and press the Enter key to add it. Specify "*LOCAL" for the remote location name.

—*Chris Green*

✦ ✦ ✦ Security

Securing Individual Database Fields

The AS/400 database doesn't directly support field-level security for a file under native interfaces ; that is, there's no direct way to protect an individual field from unauthorized access while leaving all others unprotected. At most, you can give users *READ authority (to read records), *ADD (to add records), *UPD (to update records) or *DLT (to delete records), but this is a blanket authority that covers the entire record (not a specific field).

However, there's a circumvention to protect a particular field in a physical file: Create a logical file that contains a subset of the fields in the physical file. For example, picture an Employee Master file. You want anyone to be able to read the nonsensitive part of the record (such as employee number, name, and the department number). You don't want anyone outside of Human Resources to be able to read the rest of the fields, such as hourly pay rate and deductions. Figure 5.30 shows the physical file and Figure 5.31 shows the logical file. The logical file only "sees" the employee number, name, and department number, but not the rest of the confidential information.

```
... 1 ...+... 2 ...+... 3 ...+... 4 ...+... 5 ...+... 6 ...+... 7
A          R EMREC
A            EMEMPL       5P 0      TEXT('Employee number')
A            EMNAME       30A       TEXT('Employee name')
A            EMADR1       30A       TEXT('Address line 1')
A            EMADR2       30A       TEXT('Address line 2')
A            EMCITY       25A       TEXT('City')
A            EMSTAT       2A        TEXT('State')
A            EMZIP        9P 0      TEXT('Zip code')
A            EMDEPT       4P 0      TEXT('Department number')
A            EMHIRE       8P 0      TEXT('Hire date, YYYYMMDD')
A            EMHPAY       5P 2      TEXT('Hourly pay rate')
A          K EMEMPL
... 1 ...+... 2 ...+... 3 ...+... 4 ...+... 5 ...+... 6 ...+... 7
```

Figure 5.30: Here's an example of a typical employee master physical file.

```
... 1 ...+... 2 ...+... 3 ...+... 4 ...+... 5 ...+... 6 ...+... 7
A          R EMREC          PFILE(EMPMST)
A            EMEMPL
A            EMNAME
A            EMDEPT
A          K EMEMPL
... 1 ...+... 2 ...+... 3 ...+... 4 ...+... 5 ...+... 6 ...+... 7
```

Figure 5.31: Here's how you'd subset the Employee Master Logical File for restricted access.

Now consider which users would be given access to the limited information. Give them all *OBJOPR authority to the logical file. This gives the users the authority to open the logical file and use the data authorities of the physical file on which the logical is based (the Employee Master).

Then give the users the desired data rights to the physical file. If you only want them to be capable of reading the data, give them *READ authority to the physical file. Don't, however, give them *OBJOPR authority to the physical file. Because they don't have *OBJOPR authority, they cannot open the physical file itself (thus protecting the confidential fields).

You can use the same technique to allow some users to change certain fields but not others. Again, create a logical file with *OBJOPR authority to the users, and give *CHANGE authority (but not *OBJOPR) to the physical file.

—Christopher Andrle

✦ ✦ ✦ SQL

Another Way to Sort Mixed-case Data

I have read various ways to translate and sort mixed-case data. There is another solution to the problem of mixed uppercase and lowercase key fields.

First, you create an alternate sequence table, using the Create Table (CRTTBL) command. For example, to create a table called ULCSQ, you would enter the following command:

```
CRTTBL TBL(ULCSQ) SRCFILE(*PROMPT) TBLTYPE(*SRTSEQ) +
       TEXT('Upper/lower case table')
```

When the next screen appears, use F17 to position to character A. The sequence numbers for A–I are 1290-1370. Now position the display to character A. The sequence numbers for A–I are 0650–0730. Now change the sequence numbers for A–I to sequence numbers 1290–1370. Position the display to character A, and you see that both uppercase and lowercase characters A–I have the same sequence numbers. Repeat the same for the remaining characters (J–Z). After all characters are done, press F20 to renumber, and then press F6 to create the table.

You can now use the table to create a logical file whenever you have a mixed uppercase and lowercase key field, as shown in Figure 5.32.

```
A                                    ALTSEQ(ULCSQ)
A         R MXREC                    PFILE(MIXEDPF)
A         K MIXED
```

Figure 5.32: Creating a logical file using a sort sequence table can help with mixed-case data.

For the Open Query File (OPNQRYF) command, use the SRTSEQ keyword, as shown in the following example:

```
OPNQRYF FILE((MIXEDPF))  KEYFLD((MIXED))  SRTSEQ(ULCSQ)
```

This is a much easier and cleaner solution to the problem. You only have to specify the sort sequence table name and, no matter how many uppercase and lowercase key fields you have in your DDS or Query, the data will be sorted correctly.

—Ingwald Rickers

Finding Duplicates in a File

Here's an easy way to find out if a file contains duplicate records for a given field. Use an SQL statement like this, substituting your file and field names for ORDLINE and ITEMNO:

```
SELECT itemno, COUNT(*)
   FROM ordline
   GROUP BY itemno
   HAVING COUNT(*) > 1
```

The system will return a list of all values of ITEMNO in the ORDLINE file that occur more than once. It will also list the number of occurrences.

—Anup Mayekar

In That CASE

SQL-based conditional processing was added to DB2 UDB for AS/400 in V4R2 with the SQL CASE expression. However, Query/400 can use the SQL CASE expression indirectly to perform conditional processing in a Query/400 report. The idea is to create an SQL view that uses CASE to perform the necessary conditional processing. The SQL CREATE VIEW statement creates a logical file that can then be referenced in your Query/400 definition.

Figure 5.33 shows how to use CASE to determine different vehicle license fees condition-ally. The SQL Create View statement can be executed in any SQL interface, such as an AS/400 or PC client communicating with the AS/400. Once you've created the new view, start a Query/400 session, create a new query, and specify the name of the new view as the file to be queried (in this case, "**Licview**," which was created in library "**mylib**").

```
CREATE VIEW mylib/licview (license,licfee) AS
SELECT license,
CASE type WHEN 'Car' THEN 0.05 * weight
WHEN 'Truck' THEN 75 * nbr_wheels
WHEN 'Motorcyle' THEN 35.00 END
FROM vehicles
```

Figure 5.33: Use SQL to create a view that can be then queried by Query/400.

—Kent Milligan

When UPDATE Doesn't Work with SQL on a DB2 Database

Q: I have an UPDATE statement that works in SQLServer. Do you know how it could be made to work on a DB2 database? I tried running it in DB2 as is, but it gives me a syntax error with the period (.). When I remove the period and reference to the STGMFRMST ta-ble in the SET statement, it gives me a syntax error on the word FROM. According to the error message, it's not a valid token for the UPDATE statement; valid tokens are the comma (,), WITH, and WHERE. Figure 5.34 shows a simplified version of the SQLServer UPDATE statement.

```
SET CbcMfrMst.MfrName = StgMfrMst.MfrName
FROM StgMfrMst
WHERE CbcMfrMst.AcctNbr = 10
AND CbcMfrMst.MfrNbr = StgMfrMst.MfrNbr
```

Figure 5.34: This SQL statement works great on an SQLServer, but not so well in DB2/400.

My goal is to update table A with data from table B all in one SQL statement without having to loop through each record in table B programmatically. When I use this (and the full-blown) statement in SQLServer 7.0, I get remarkable performance. I'd like to see whether the same could be accomplished in DB2.

A: Yes, it is possible. Look at the code shown in Figure 5.38.

```
UPDATE CbcMfrMst as A SET MfrName = ( SELECT B.MfrName
FROM StgMfrMst as B
WHERE a.MfrNbr = B.MfrNbr)
WHERE A.AcctNbr = 10
```

Figure 5.35: This SQL code updates one table with values from another table.

Figure 5.35 demonstrates the syntax to make SQL work the way you want it to. Here's an example we ran on our own system. You're given tables **A** and **B** with columns **Adesc** and **Acode** (primary key). In each table, update all rows in **A** that have **Adesc** starting with **L** with values from **B** where primary keys match:

```
UPDATE A
SET Adesc =
(SELECT B.Adesc FROM B
WHERE A.Acode = B.Acode)
WHERE A.Adesc LIKE 'L%';
```

Note that the SELECT cannot return more than one row; otherwise, the query would end in error. If the column (field) updated does not allow null values, use the COALESCE function to assign a default value:

```
UPDATE A
SET Adesc =
(SELECT COALESCE(B.Adesc, ' ') FROM
...
```

Also be aware that all the rows that match the last WHERE are updated, even if no matching record is in the other file. In your example, all rows that have account number 10 are updated, even if the manufacturer number in **A** does not exist in **B**. To make sure the statement does not update rows that do not exist in **B**, use the following form:

```
UPDATE A
SET Adesc =
(SELECT B.Adesc FROM B
WHERE A.Acode = B.Acode)
WHERE A.Adesc LIKE 'L%' and a.acode in (select acode from b);
```

—Howard F. Arner, Jr.
—Ted Holt

✦ ✦ ✦ SQL Column Formatting

Generate Horizontal Summary Figures from Relational Database

Relational databases are structured to make it easy to summarize data and display it verti-cally. Figure 5.36 contains an SQL statement and the data that it retrieves. This SQL command summarizes goods returned to a chain of stores by store code and reason code.

```
select store#, reason, sum(qty * price) from rtn group by store#, reason

    Store   Reason   Dollars returned
    ------  ------   ----------------
    BAT     A              100.00
    BAT     B              750.00
    NAT     B              131.25
    NAT     C              375.00
    OXF     B              762.50
    VIC     A               20.00
```

Figure 5.36: Displaying summary figures vertically isn't as hard as it looks.

The information is there, but it's not very pretty. Because there are only three reason codes, it would be nice to generate one line of output for each store—with each reason in its own column. Relational databases don't usually have tools to do that sort of thing.

One way to transform vertical figures into horizontal ones is through the use of a binary matrix table. The first field in the binary matrix file is the field by which you want to summarize (in this case, the reason code). The other fields are all one-digit numbers, and there is a field for each value of the summary field. In this case, there are three possible values for the reason code—*A*, *B*, and *C*—so there are three one-digit fields that I call RSNA, RSNB, and RSNC.

There is one record in the matrix file for each possible value of the summary field. In this case, there are three records:

- one with reason code of *A*.
- one with a reason code of *B*.
- one with a reason code of *C*.

In each of the one-digit fields, put a value of either 0 or 1. You put a 1 in the one-digit field corresponding to the value in the code field and a 0 in the other one-digit fields. In

212

other words, the record with a reason code of "A" gets a 1 in RSNA, and 0 goes in RSNB and RSNC.

In Figure 5.37, you can see the complete matrix file contents. Figure 5.38 contains the revised SQL query and shows how the data is presented horizontally.

```
    REASON              RSNA            RSNB            RSNC
    -------             -----           ----            ----
       A                  1               0               0
       B                  0               1               0
       C                  0               0               1
```

Figure 5.37: Data is stored in the Reason Matrix File (RSNMTX).

```
Select store#, sum(rsna * qty * price),
            sum(rsnb * qty * price)
            sum(rsnc * qty * price)
 from rtn, rsnmtx
 where rtn.reason=rsnmtx.reason
 group by store#')


Store    Reason A         Reason B        Reason C
BAT       100.00           750.00            .00
NAT          .00           131.25         375.00
OXF          .00           762.50            .00
VIC        20.00              .00            .00
```

Figure 5.38: Displaying summary figures horizontally is accomplished using an SQL statement.

I have used SQL to illustrate this technique because of its conciseness, but this technique works with other relation tools, such as Query and Open Query File (OPNQRYF).

—Ted Holt

✦ ✦ ✦ Testing

Easier Program Testing

There are times when you may want to run a program that writes records to a file, but for test purposes, you want to prevent this from happening. You could recompile your test program, commenting out the write or update operations, and changing the file specs so the compiler doesn't give you an error message. However, a much better and easier approach is to use the INHWRT(*YES) parameter on the OVRDBF command. You should execute this command for each file you want to inhibit at the beginning of your job stream. Be careful not to misspell the file name. You will not get an error message if you do, but the file will not be overridden. (To check that the override has occurred, use the DSPOVR command.) After the override command is executed successfully, the program will act just as before, but no data will be written.

—Jon Vote

✦ ✦ ✦ Triggers

Beware of Triggers When Testing

Anyone testing and implementing trigger programs should watch out for the following scenario. We are currently writing and testing trigger programs to attach to our production files. We test these trigger programs by adding the triggers to files in our test library. We typically copy some key files from our production libraries into our test library during the night in order to have current data available for testing. We have a physical file in the test library that has Insert, Delete, and Update triggers attached to it. The library list in effect does not have the test library in it, as we use the Copy File (CPYF) command with *REPLACE to copy the production data to the test library.

The first problem occurred when the *REPLACE parameter of the CPYF command attempted to clear our test library's physical file prior to copying the production data to it. The system will not allow you to clear a physical file if you have a Delete trigger attached to the file. This problem simply meant that for one day we did not have current test data. To solve this problem, we issued a Remove Physical File Trigger (RMVPFTRG) for the Delete trigger on the file in the test library. CPYF proceeded the following night without a hitch (or so we thought).

The second problem (and the more insidious one, I might admit) occurred because there was an Insert trigger attached to the file in the test library. The trigger was fired every time a record was copied from the production database to the test database. Guess what? Because the library list, in effect, did not include the test library, the insert trigger was updating a production database file when it fired. This resulted in our production inventory file appearing with double the inventory we actually had. (It's hard enough selling what you do have, but making customers angry by selling them merchandise you don't really have could set you up for a trip to the unemployment office.) We solved this problem by removing all the triggers from the test database file prior to executing the CPYF command and then putting them back after CPYF completes.

I should have seen this coming. The fact that I didn't points to an important fact. Although the new capabilities of DB2/400 and ILE RPG are well worth learning and implementing, the value of caution, research, and shared experiences cannot be overemphasized.

—Kim Williams

Can a Trigger Program Update the Record That Causes the Trigger Condition?

Q: I have a question regarding an insert/update *BEFORE trigger program written in ILE C. If I modify the value of a field in the current record in a trigger program, will the modification be written to the database? From what I've read in the manuals, the trigger program can change the value but cannot issue an update.

A: You're correct. The OS/400 DB2/400 *Database Programming V3R1* manual (SC41-3701, CD-ROM QBKAUC00) says the following:

"A trigger program can call other programs or can be nested (that is, a statement in a trigger program causes the calling of another trigger program). In addition, a trigger program may be called recursively by itself. The maximum trigger nested level for insert and update is 200. The trigger program must not cause the following situations. These situations result in an error if programs run under commitment control.

- "Update the same record of the same file that has already been changed by the change operation or by an operation in the trigger program.

- "Produce conflicting operations on the same record within one change operation. For example, a record is inserted by the change operation and then deleted by the trigger program."

Note: If the change operation is not running under commitment control, the change operation is always protected. However, updating the same record within the trigger program will not be monitored.

The update to the record cannot be done by the trigger program. It can update or write to other files (for example, audit logs) but not the record the program is being triggered by.

—Peter Rowley

Trigger Tips Learned the Hard Way

Here are a few points I've learned about triggers in my experience.

1. Never reference the BEFORE portion of the trigger buffer on an insert. You might get a data decimal error.

2. Never reference the AFTER portion of the trigger buffer on a delete. You might get a data decimal error.

3. You cannot recompile a trigger program while the file to which the trigger program is attached is open. Even though the compilation listing will show no errors, the program will refuse to compile

   *(**Editor's Note:** This could be caused by declaring the file in the trigger program and not setting on the LR indicator. The other issue, not mentioned here, is that all the jobs that have fired the trigger hold a lock on the trigger program. You need to end all those jobs to get a clean recompilation.)*

4. Always test your trigger program. Insert a record, delete it, and check the trigger program's response.

—Kim Williams

Use Triggers to Execute Commands

When writing client/server applications, you sometimes need to execute commands to set up the execution environment on the AS/400. Examples are overriding files to the correct member, clearing work files, and changing execution priority. There are APIs to execute commands, but the fewer interfaces you have to use, the better. When the program shown in Figure 5.39 is made a trigger program for a simple file, you can execute commands using the same interfaces (such as ODBC) used to read and write data to DB2/400 databases. Here are the steps you need to take:

1. Create the program TRG004RG, shown in Figure 5.39.

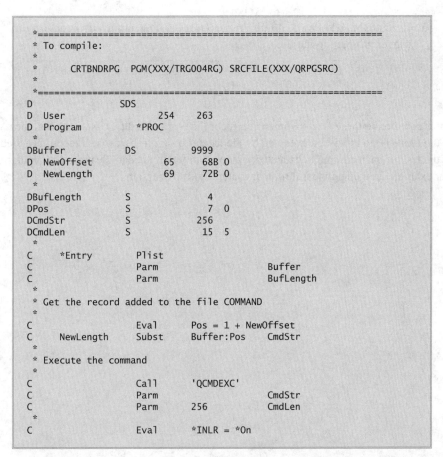

```
*==============================================================
* To compile:
*
*        CRTBNDRPG  PGM(XXX/TRG004RG) SRCFILE(XXX/QRPGSRC)
*
*==============================================================
D                 SDS
D  User                      254     263
D  Program               *PROC
*
DBuffer           DS                9999
D  NewOffset                  65      68B 0
D  NewLength                  69      72B 0
*
DBufLength        S                   4
DPos              S                   7 0
DCmdStr           S                 256
DCmdLen           S                  15 5
*
C     *Entry      Plist
C                 Parm                        Buffer
C                 Parm                        BufLength
*
* Get the record added to the file COMMAND
*
C                 Eval       Pos = 1 + NewOffset
C     NewLength   Subst      Buffer:Pos      CmdStr
*
* Execute the command
*
C                 Call       'QCMDEXC'
C                 Parm                        CmdStr
C                 Parm       256              CmdLen
*
C                 Eval       *INLR = *On
```

Figure 5.39: Step one in executing trigger commands is accomplished by creating this RPG IV program.

2. Create the physical file COMMAND, shown in Figure 5.40.

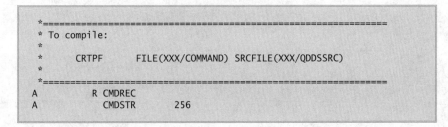

```
*==============================================================
* To compile:
*
*        CRTPF      FILE(XXX/COMMAND) SRCFILE(XXX/QDDSSRC)
*
*==============================================================
A          R CMDREC
A            CMDSTR       256
```

Figure 5.40: Physical file COMMAND is step two in executing trigger commands.

3. Execute the Add Physical File Trigger (ADDPFTRG) command to connect the trigger program to the file.

```
ADDPFTRG FILE(COMMAND) TRGTIME(*BEFORE) TRGEVENT(*INSERT)
         PGM(TRG004RG)
```

After completing these steps, whenever a record is written to the COMMAND file, the data in the CMDSTR field will be executed by the trigger program. Because a record is added to the file for each command executed, you probably will need to clear the file regularly. For example, you could clear it in your system startup program.

—Nghi Le

Display Files

*A*ccording to some people who write magazine articles for a living, nobody, but nobody still uses "green screens." To which it is possible to reply, "Ha! That's what you think." While graphical user interfaces (GUIs) have become more widespread and common, even in businesses (due to the success of the Apple Macintosh computer and the Windows operating system for IBM-compatible PCs), text-based data entry and access is still the method of choice for many applications. It's especially effective for heads-down data entry.

While the iSeries can act as a Web server or a host to many other client applications, it is still one of the best computers (if not the best computer) for text-based (also known as "green-screen") applications. Other systems don't support subfiles. Other systems don't have an easy language like DDS for defining displays. Other systems don't treat a terminal as if it were an externally described database file, but require the programmer to embed presentation logic and processing logic in the same program. Other systems—including graphical user interfaces—don't make heads-down data entry so easy with features like automatic right-adjust and automatic record advance.

This chapter contains a good variety of tips for working with display files. Here you'll find tips for subfiles, cursor positioning, using the Screen Design Aid, data entry, and how to format displayed data. Where program code is included for completeness, it is usually written in RPG III, but most tips are applicable to any programming language. You will find more than one way to do several things.

—Ted Holt

✦ ✦ ✦ Cursor Location

Cursor in Protected Area

There probably isn't an AS/400 user who hasn't gotten that annoying, blinking 0005 at the bottom of the screen. This message (which you can read if you press Help) means that you attempted to enter information in an area of the screen that is not input capable. Often, the cursor moves to a protected area when you use the arrow keys incorrectly or accidentally.

The CSRINPONLY keyword in the DDS for the display file can eliminate the annoyance. Place it at the file level, and your arrow keys won't be able to move the cursor to protected areas. Actually, the cursor will go only to input fields. It will also go to message subfiles and to choice fields. In order to work, the display station must be attached to a workstation controller that supports enhanced interface for "dumb" terminals.

Take care when using this keyword on panels that have help areas defined. If a help area is defined outside of an input-capable field, CSRINPONLY won't let the user move the cursor there to read the help text.

—Ernie Malaga

Cursor-sensitive Searches

Q: I have started programming my interactive programs with cursor-sensitive searches. If the user presses a function key to perform a search, I calculate the location of the cursor. If it falls within a hard-coded range, I present the user with the requested search. I want to soft-code that range from the display file. I should be able to match the cursor position to the field location and present the user with the desired search. Is there a way to retrieve the location of a field within a display file (other than reading the display file source)?

A: There's an easy way to accomplish this. Use the DDS Return Cursor Location (RTNCSRLOC) record-level keyword in your display file. It returns the name of the field that the cursor is on. This method has some advantages over using hard-coded screen coordinates. It means that if you move a field in a display file from one location on the screen to another, you don't have to worry about changing the program that uses that display file.

The Return Cursor Location keyword has two required parameters as well as an optional third parameter. For an example of how to use this keyword look at the four lines of code shown in Figure 6.1. The two required parameters, (CURSOR-RECORD and CURSOR-FIELD), must be defined as 10-character hidden fields. The CURSOR-RECORD variable returns the name of the record format and the CURSOR-FIELD variable returns the name of the field where the cursor is located. The third parameter (CURSOR-POSITION) is optional and, if used, must be defined as a four-position, signed-numeric, hidden field. This field returns the relative position within the field where the cursor is located.

```
 *. 1 ...+... 2 ...+... 3 ...+... 4 ...+... 5 ...+... 6 ...+... 7
 A                                      RTNCSRLOC(&RCD &FLD &POS)
 A          RCD           10A  H
 A          FLD           10A  H
 A          POS            4S  0H
```

Figure 6.1: The RTNCSRLOC keyword makes cursor-sensitive searches possible.

In your program, just test the value of the cursor-field variable. If it matches a field for which the user can perform a search, then present the search results. If it doesn't, you might want to display a message that says something like, "Search not valid for cursor location." Using this technique, you can code cursor-sensitive searches within your programs without hard-coding screen coordinates.

—*Midrange Computing Staff*

Keep the Cursor Position

When a user presses the Enter key, the cursor normally moves to the first unprotected input field on the display. In some interactive programs, I want the cursor to remain where it was when the user pressed Enter. To do this, I retrieve the cursor location from positions 370 and 371 of the file's information data structure (INFDS), and then I transfer the value from the INFDS fields to the fields listed in the cursor location (CSRLOC) parameter of the display file's DDS. The DDS and RPG IV fragments, shown in Figure 6.2, illustrate how this is done.

```
A              R SCREEN
A                                      CSRLOC(ROW COLUMN)
A                ROW            3S 0H
A                COLUMN         3S 0H
A                A              1  B  5  6
A                B              1  B  6  6
A                C              1  B  7  6

Falber1df cf    e                     workstn infds(WSFeedback)
D WSFeedback        ds
D  CursorLoc           370    371b 0
C                      dou    a = '*'
C                      exsr   pos
C                      exfmt  screen
C                      enddo
C                      move   *on             *inlr
C*****
C        pos          begsr
C*
C        CursorLoc    div    256              Row
C                      mvr                    Column
C*
C                      endsr
```

Figure 6.2: Making the cursor return to its position on the previous display is easy.

—John Albert

✦ ✦ ✦ Data Entry

CNTFLD in DDS

Q: I am trying to use the Continuation Field (CNTFLD) keyword in DDS to break a comment field into two rows on the screen. It looks fine in SDA, but when I run the program and it EXFMTs the screen with the CNTFLD field, it will not display the field. The display file acts as if the field doesn't even exist. Could this behavior be the result of having an old workstation controller?

A: The field should appear in all cases (I've confirmed that in the manuals). But, without an ENPTUI workstation controller, the input fields will act independently when editing is performed on the field. For example, deleting on the first entry field won't pull in text from the second entry field. So, even when you get the field to display, it might not behave the way you want.

You need to be careful with CNTFLD; it requires two spaces on either side of it, not just one like most other fields. You might have overlapped the field, causing it to not show up.

—Edmund Reinhardt

Date Entry Fields

Entry screens that allow the user to enter or modify a date can sometimes cause confusion when the field has the date edit code (Y) on it. The user might not know whether to enter the date with or without the separator characters. Actually, you can enter it either way; but if you key the separator characters, you are wasting keystrokes.

You can prevent this type of confusion in two ways. If your workstation is attached to a controller that supports an enhanced data stream, you can use the DDS Edit Mask (EDTMSK) keyword (see Figure 6.3). This keyword allows you to protect specific areas (positions) within a field. If you don't have one of these controllers, I have developed a technique that offers the same functionality as the EDTMSK keyword.

```
A*==============================================================
A* To compile:
A*
A*      CRTDSPF    FILE(XXX/XMS003DF) SRCFILE(XXX/QDDSSRC)
A*
A*==============================================================
A*. 1 ...+... 2 ...+... 3 ...+... 4 ...+... 5 ...+... 6 ...+... 7
A                                          DSPSIZ(24 80 *DS3)
A                                          CA03(03)
A          R DSP01
A            MM             2Y 0B  4 10
A            DD             2Y 0B  4 13
A            YY             2Y 0B  4 16
A          R DSP02
A                                          CLRL(*NO)
A            MMDDYY         6Y 00  4 10EDTCDE(Y)
A                                          DSPATR(UL)
```

Figure 6.3: The key to skipping edit characters in input fields is CLRL.

My technique allows you to create a field that displays the date separator characters and skips over them as the user enters the date. The user can only enter values into positions 1, 2, 4, 5, 7, and 8. Positions 3 and 6 contain a slash (/) separator character as output only. If you want to see this technique in action, try running the sample program shown in Figure 6.4.

```
*===================================================================
* To compile:
*
*          CRTRPGPGM  PGM(XXX/XMS003RG)  SRCFILE(XXX/QRPGSRC)
*
*===================================================================
*. 1 ...+... 2 ...+... 3 ...+... 4 ...+... 5 ...+... 6 ...+... 7
FXMS003DFCF  E                     WORKSTN
I            IDS
I                                      1   60MMDDYY
I                                      1   20MM
I                                      3   40DD
I                                      5   60YY
C            *INKC      DOUEQ*ON
C                       WRITEDSP01
C                       WRITEDSP02
C                       READ DSP01                            99
C                       ENDDO
C                       MOVE *ON       *INLR
```

Figure 6.4: RPG program XMS003RG illustrates how to write both input and edited fields to the same line.

This technique works by exploiting a quirk in the way the Clear Line (CLRL) record-level keyword works. CLRL lets you write more than one record format on the same line. The input-capable fields in all formats remain input-capable.

—*Matt Seargent*

Distinguishing Between Zeros and Blanks

Q: We allow users to enter a temperature into a numeric field in a display file. How can a program determine whether a user keyed a zero or left the field blank?

A: Use the BLANKS keyword with a response indicator in the display file DDS (Figure 6.5). The COBOL or RPG program will interpret the keyed value as zero either way, but the indicator will indicate whether the user keyed zero or left it blank.

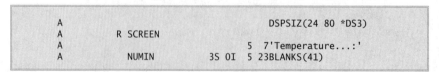

```
A                                         DSPSIZ(24 80 *DS3)
A            R SCREEN
A                                     5  7'Temperature...:'
A            NUMIN          3S OI     5 23BLANKS(41)
```

Figure 6.5: The BLANKS keyword enables a program to distinguish between zeros and missing values.

—*Hin Chui*

DUP Key Processing

Q: How can I allow field duplication for input-capable fields? I want a data-entry operator to have the option of duplicating information keyed from the previous input operation.

A: Use the duplication (DUP) field-level keyword in your display file DDS for any field
you want duplication-enabled. Pressing the DUP key initiates the duplication process by
allowing your application program to become aware that the DUP key was pressed. Your
application program must perform the actual duplication. There are two ways you can duplicate fields: duplicate the entire field or duplicate the field one character at a time. The
easiest method is to duplicate the entire field, which can be done with the following
procedure.

Specify two fields in your DDS for each input-capable field you want to allow duplication for. Create one field as input-capable and specify the DUP keyword with a response
indicator. Condition the DUP keyword with an indicator. Create another field as a hidden
field. Figure 6.6 illustrates the DDS.

```
     *.. 1 ...+... 2 ...+... 3 ...+... 4 ...+... 5 ...+... 6 ...+... 7
     A           R INFMT
     A             INDTE          5  I  3  2
     A  20                                    DUP(30)
     A             INDTEH         5     2
```

Figure 6.6: With a few lines of DDS, DUP key activation is easily handled.

On the first output operation, make sure the conditioning indicator for the DUP keyword
is off. After the first input operation, move the input-capable field to the hidden field. Set
the conditioning indicator for the DUP keyword on for the remaining output operations.

For the remaining input operations, test the DUP keyword response indicator. If it's on,
the value of the hidden field should be moved to the input-capable field. If the response
indicator is off, just move the input-capable field to the hidden field.

The procedure for duplicating a field one character at a time is a little more complicated.
You can find out how to perform this procedure in the *DDS Reference* manual.

—*Matt Kofsky*

Edited Data Entry

You have probably upgraded your hardware over the past few years, but did you upgrade your programming accordingly? If you have one of the newer workstation controllers that supports the enhanced data stream, you can use some nice data-entry features you might not be in the habit of using because your old controllers didn't support them.

The Edit Mask (EDTMSK) keyword can help a data entry operator. It's designed to make entering dates, Social Security numbers, and other numeric fields easy for the user. Figure 6.7 shows EDTMSK used with a date and a Social Security number. It works with both edit words (EDTWRD) and edit codes (EDTCDE) to protect editing characters without interrupting data flow.

```
A          R RECORD1
A                                       PUTOVR
A                                     1 22'Test for Screen Design'
A            DATE1      6  0B   4   3EDTWRD('  /  /  ')
A                                     EDTMSK('  &  &  ')
A            DATE2      6  0B   7   3EDTCDE(Y)
A                                     EDTMSK('  &  &  ')
A            SSN        9  0B  10   3EDTWRD('   -    -     ')
A                                     EDTMSK('    &  &     ')
```

Figure 6.7: Edit masks are helpful for data entry.

The ampersand character (&) represents a protected part of the field. A blank represents unprotected characters. The total length of the field must be represented by blank characters. Because data is not returned, if the field is changed, only nonnumeric characters should be protected.

The Field Cursor Progression (FLDCSRPRG) keyword lets you move the cursor to the field that you specify. Figure 6.8 shows how this keyword can be used in a display file. In this case, when the user field exits from Item, the cursor jumps to Quantity, even though Description is the field immediately following Item.

The Subfile Cursor Progression (SFLCSRPRG) keyword helps control proper cursor positioning when the user scrolls through a subfile. By specifying it as shown in Figure 6.9, the cursor moves from a field in one subfile record to the same field in the next subfile record, rather than to the next field in the same subfile record.

```
A                                   DSPSIZ(24 80 *DS3)
A                                   PRINT
A                                   CA03(03)
A          R REC01
A                                1  2TIME
A                                1 68DATE
A                                   EDTCDE(Y)
A                                1 32'Item Inquiry'
A                                5  2'Item Number:'
A            ITEM          6A  B  5 16FLDCSRPRG(PRC)
A                                9  2'Item Description:'
A            DESC         30A  B  9 21FLDCSRPRG(QTY)
A                               11  2'Price:'
A            PRC          7S 2B 11 10FLDCSRPRG(DESC)
A  30                               DSPATR(RI)
A                               13  2'Quantity:'
A            QTY          5S 0B 13 13FLDCSRPRG(ITEM)
A  31                               DSPATR(RI)
A                               15  2'Location:'
A            LOC           3A  B 15 13CHANGE(33)
A  32                               DSPATR(RI)
A                               23  2'F3 to Exit'
```

Figure 6.8: Cursor progression overrides the normal cursor movement from field to field.

```
A          R SFLRCD                 SFL
A            SFLRRN        4S 0H
A            ITEM         10A  B  7  6SFLCSRPRG
A            DESC         20A  B  7 27
A            PRICE         9Y 2B  7 41EDTCDE(3)
A            QTY           5Y 0B  7 51
A          R SFLCTL                 SFLCTL(SFLRCD)
A                                   SFLSIZ(0008)
A                                   SFLPAG(0007)
A  21                               SFLDSP
A                                   SFLDSPCTL
A                                   OVERLAY
A  25                               SFLCLR
A  41                               SFLEND(*MORE)
A N41                               ROLLUP(27)
A                                   ROLLDOWN(28)
```

Figure 6.9: Subfile cursor progression moves the cursor from record to record.

—D. Ellis Green

Entry Field Attributes

Does this sound familiar? One of your users complains that the screen you designed is too busy and, because of that, it's hard to tell where the cursor is. You suggest that you could remove half of the fields and put them on a second screen. The user rejects your idea because the system is no good unless all of the fields are on one screen.

Here's another solution you might try. If the workstation is attached to a controller that supports an enhanced interface, you can add the following keyword to the record format and recompile the display file:

```
ENTFLDATR((*DSPATR RI))
```

Now, every time the cursor is in an input field, that field is displayed in reverse image. As it moves out of the field, the field returns to normal. Voilà, you are an instant hero!

The ENTRY FIELD ATTRIBUTE keyword also lets you define the color for the field and whether or not the cursor is visible when it enters the field. Valid values for the *DSPATR parameter are BL, CS, HI, ND, RI, and UL. Valid values for the *COLOR parameter are BLU, GRN, PNK, RED, TRQ, YLW, and WHT. So go on, be a hero. You deserve it.

—Ron Hawkins

The DDS Change Keyword

CHANGE is a very useful DDS keyword that can be a great help when you need to know if any of the input fields of a display record have been changed. If CHANGE is used at the record level, the response indicator will turn on if any field in the record has changed. If specified at the field level, the response indicator will turn on if that particular field is changed. There are a few things you should remember:

- The response indicator will turn on any time data is entered into the field, even when the resultant value is exactly the same as the previous value.

- The response indicator is not set on when a command attention key (CA*nn*, Help, Print, Home, or Clear) is used.

- Option indicators are not allowed.

- You can force your program to read a field conditioned by the CHANGE keyword, even when the data has not changed, by using the display attribute keyword (DSPATR) value of Set Changed Data Tag (MDT), like this: DSPATR(MDT).

Condition the DSPATR keyword with an indicator whenever you want to force a read.

The format is:

```
CHANGE(response-indicator ['text'])
```

Instead of saving previous values of fields and comparing them to current values to determine if anything has changed, use the CHANGE keyword. It sure is a lot easier.

—*Richard Shaler*

Use MAPVAL to Eliminate Date Confusion

The V4R2 Mapped Value (MAPVAL) keyword in DDS allows you to map a given value to another for display purposes. You could, for instance, specify that 01/01/0001 should display as *BLANK. Upon input to the program, workstation data management would convert the blank field back to 01/01/0001. Figure 6.10 illustrates how to use MAPVAL.

```
A           R FMT01
A                               6  5'DATE:'
A             ADATE      L  B   +  1DATFMT(*USA)
A                                  MAPVAL(('01/01/0001' *BLANK))
```

Figure 6.10: MAPVAL converts dates, times, and time stamps from one value to another.

—*Bruce Vining*

Using Word-wrap in Data Entry

Display files are the primary means by which users and the CPU communicate. Therefore, it's important to make your display files as user-friendly as possible. Your user's trust of his machine may be marred by seeing words improperly broken in the middle. After all, users are accustomed to word processors, which break words only into syllables and only when the hyphenation feature is on.

Unfortunately, display files don't support hyphenation. However, they do provide for whole-word separation in long sentences. Suppose you enter comments about a vendor or a sales order, and the comments span more than 80 characters. When the vendor information is displayed, the comments will have to appear in two or more lines. To avoid the system default of chopping off the comments wherever each line ends, simply place the Block Fold (BLKFOLD) DDS keyword at the field level. (BLKFOLD is usable only in output fields and only if the field is not of type floating point.)

The catch is that the field must be longer than necessary. For example, if the original comments field is 100 characters long, you're advised to use BLKFOLD on a field that has a length of some 110 characters. The reason is that BLKFOLD forces the system to insert enough blank spaces to guarantee that words are not interrupted in the middle. And these blanks increase the length of the output field. Fortunately, you can define the longer field by referencing another file's field and supplying something like +10 as the length; doing so increases the length by 10 bytes. Your mileage may vary; perhaps you'll have to increase the length by 20 characters (or more), depending on how many blank spaces the system is likely to insert.

Of course, what works in output fields should also work in input or I/O fields. Unfortunately, that's not the case. But there's a different DDS keyword for input or I/O fields: Word Wrap (WRDWRAP). Unlike BLKFOLD, WRDWRAP can be placed at the file, record, or field level.

It also has a number of exclusions. You cannot use it on fields of type S, Y, D, M, F, J, O, E, or G. You cannot use it conjunction with AUTO(RAZ or RAB), CHECK(MF, M10F, M11F, RB, RZ, RL, RLTB), CHGINPDFT(MF), DSPATR(OID, SP), DUP, FLTFIXDEC, or IGCALTTYP. You may not use option indicators.

As with BLKFOLD, you're advised to use WRDWRAP in a field that is longer than necessary so that the extra blanks have room to be placed. Your program should then move the data from the longer field to the actual database field. Be warned, however, that updating a database field using WRDWRAP in the corresponding input field will result in the extra blank spaces inserted in the database as well. Also, WRDWRAP works only if your display station is connected to a controller that supports an enhanced interface.

—*Ernie Malaga*

✦ ✦ ✦ Formatting Data

Display Attributes Without Indicators

You can use DDS to control lots of special display attributes in a display file (such as underline, high intensity, or color) without using indicators. By employing this trick, you can reduce the number of indicators used in your programs, thereby increasing program readability and ease of maintenance.

Figure 6.11 shows a sample display file, DSPATRDSPF, that uses the technique. You simply use a 1-byte, program-to-system variable (named ATTRIB in the example) to control the display attribute for a field or constant. Notice the use of the DSPATR keyword—it names ATTRIB instead of an indicator, but it uses an ampersand (&) before ATTRIB.

```
     A                                        DSPSIZ(24 80 *DS3)
     A           R PANEL
     A             ATTRIB          1  P
     A                                     13 30'This is a data field.'
     A                                        DSPATR(&ATTRIB)
```

Figure 6.11: Use program-to-system fields to condition fields and constants.

Next, your program (which can be written in any language) must give ATTRIB a 1-byte hexadecimal value, such as X'20' for green (or normal display) and X'28' for red (or blink, on a monochrome display station). As you can see in Figure 6.12, the RPG IV program DSPATRRPG4 first gives ATTRIB a value equal to named constant DA_GRN (which stands for "display attribute, green"), then puts the panel on the screen, and then assigns ATTRIB another value and repeats the process.

```
     FdspatrdspfCF   E           WORKSTN

      /COPY @dspatrrg4

     C                 EVAL      attrib = da_grn
     C                 EXFMT     panel
     C                 EVAL      attrib = da_red
     C                 EXFMT     panel

     C                 EVAL      *INLR = *ON
```

Figure 6.12: Use this RPG code to test the display file.

Figure 6.13 contains a /COPY member, @DSPATRRG4, which will simplify the implementation of this technique in your RPG IV programs.

```
           * COLOR(BLU):  normal, RI, UL.
          D da_blu           C                    X'3A'
          D da_blu_r         C                    X'3B'
          D da_blu_u         C                    X'3E'

           * COLOR(GRN):  normal, RI, UL, UL+RI.
          D da_grn           C                    X'20'
          D da_grn_r         C                    X'21'
          D da_grn_u         C                    X'24'
          D da_grn_ur        C                    X'25'

           * DSPATR(ND)
          D da_nondsp        C                    X'27'

           * COLOR(PNK):  normal, RI, UL, UL+RI.
          D da_pnk           C                    X'38'
          D da_pnk_r         C                    X'39'
          D da_pnk_u         C                    X'3C'
          D da_pnk_ur        C                    X'3D'

           * COLOR(RED):  normal, BL, BL+RI, BL+UL, RI, UL, UL+RI.
          D da_red           C                    X'28'
          D da_red_b         C                    X'2A'
          D da_red_br        C                    X'2B'
          D da_red_bu        C                    X'2E'
          D da_red_r         C                    X'29'
          D da_red_u         C                    X'2C'
          D da_red_ur        C                    X'2D'

           * COLOR(TRQ):  normal, RI, UL, UL+RI.
          D da_trq           C                    X'30'
          D da_trq_r         C                    X'31'
          D da_trq_u         C                    X'34'
          D da_trq_ur        C                    X'35'

           * COLOR(WHT):  normal, RI, UL.
          D da_wht           C                    X'22'
          D da_wht_r         C                    X'23'
          D da_wht_u         C                    X'26'

           * COLOR(YLW):  normal, RI, UL.
          D da_ylw           C                    X'32'
          D da_ylw_r         C                    X'33'
          D da_ylw_u         C                    X'36'
```

Figure 6.13: This /COPY member, named @DSPATRRG4, defines display attributes.

—Ernie Malaga

Embed Display Attributes in Text Fields

The display attribute (DSPATR) keyword is used in DDS to make a field appear in reverse image, in high intensity, underlined, blinking, or some combination of these. IBM doesn't tell you in its manuals that you can change the appearance of only a part of a field.

The trick is to embed display attribute control characters within a text field. IBM calls these control characters P-fields, and you can find a list of them in chapter 3 of the *DDS Reference* manual.

For example, assume a display file defines a 60-byte character field called MSG (see Figure 6.14). If MSG contains control characters, portions of MSG will appear with other attributes. Figure 6.15 shows one method of accomplishing this. Most of the MSG field appears in normal text, but the contents of the TRANSACTION variable are displayed in high intensity.

```
A          R SCRN1
A            MSG           60   0  6 8
```

Figure 6.14: MSG is defined as a 60-byte text field in a display file.

```
Fmydspf    cf   e                workstn
D Transaction   s                20
D HI            c                        const(x'22')
D NORMAL        c                        const(x'20')
C                    eval        Transaction = 'loan'
C                    eval        Msg = 'The' + HI +
C                                %trim(Transaction) + NORMAL +
C                                'has not been approved.'
C                    exfmt       scrn1
```

Figure 6.15: The word in the TRANSACTION variable appears in high intensity.

—Anthony P. Gerasch

String Highlights

Q: I want to highlight certain characters in a string of data. Has anyone done this? I would like to display selected characters within a string in high intensity.

A: This might or might not be possible, depending on your requirements and terminal types. A crucial factor is whether or not you are highlighting complete words (that is, if there is a space on either side of the characters to be highlighted).

Text-mode PC display buffers have an attribute byte for each display position. (The buffer is twice the length of the screen, using alternating pairs of a display character and an attribute.) This enables them to change the color or display attribute of each byte without regard to adjacent positions.

However, the original 5250 data stream design uses a buffer the same length as the screen. Screen attributes are interspersed with the characters to be displayed and affect all characters up to the next display attribute character. It is impossible for a display attribute and a displayable character to occupy the same screen position. (The display attributes are nothing more than the characters in the range of hex "20" through hex "3F." Normally, they only exist at boundaries of fields; but wherever they appear, they have the same effect.)

If you are doing something like text searches where you can highlight complete words, it is quite simple to accomplish what you want. In your output field, you just have to replace the blank preceding the word(s) with the desired display attribute (e.g., hex "21") for high intensity or white, and replace the blank following the word(s) with the display attribute to return to normal (hex "20").

This works regardless of terminal type and even with PCs emulating terminals. If you're working with an input-capable field, you need to translate the attributes back to blanks (hex "40") using XLATE or a similar operation.

—*Douglas Handy*

✦ ✦ ✦ Menus

UIM Menus

Q: I'm converting a menu to UIM, and I'm stumped. I have a menu item entry that looks similar to the one shown in Figure 6.16. The problem is that there are about six parameters where the three dots are. Therefore, the CPYF command won't fit on one line. How do I continue the action parameter across lines of UIM source code?

```
:MENUI help=G1 option=3
        action='cmd ?cpyf ...'
        .Load data
```

Figure 6.16: UIM tag keywords are typically not repeated.

A: Not all UIM attributes can be continued, but **action** is one that can. All you need to do is close the command string with a quote, repeat the **action** attribute on the next statement, and continue with your command string. (A blank will automatically be inserted between continued attribute values.) Figure 6.17 illustrates what the statements might look like:

```
:MENUI help=G1 option=3
       action='cmd ?cpyf fromfile(from_file) tofile(to_file)'
       action='mbropt(*add) fmtopt(*nochk)'
       .Load data
```

Figure 6.17: The UIM action attribute can be continued across two or more lines.

—Midrange Computing Staff

Using F9 to Retrieve Commands

One nice feature of OS/400 is the ability to use the F9 key to recall commands that were previously keyed from the command line. If I'm going to run the same command several times, with different parameter values each time, I can recall the command by pressing F9, modify the necessary parameters, and press Enter to rerun it.

Menu-bound users don't usually get to take advantage of this feature. They have to take the same menu option over and over, filling in the same parameters and making changes as needed.

If you're willing to do a little extra work, you can make it possible for users to recall a command they chose as a menu option.

Suppose you have a command called SOMECMD (see Figure 6.18) that runs a CL program called SOMEPGM (see Figure 6.19).

```
CMD   PROMPT('Some command')
PARM  KWD(THINGTYPE) TYPE(*CHAR) LEN(1) RSTD(*YES) +
        DFT(A) VALUES(A B C) PROMPT('Type of thing')
PARM  KWD(THINGSIZE) TYPE(*DEC) LEN(3) +
        PROMPT('Size of thing')
```

Figure 6.18: A sample command that allows for F9 retrieval.

SOMECLP has two parameters—type and size. Suppose a user sometimes runs four or five of these back-to-back, changing one or both parameters each time. You put the command

? SOMECMD

behind an option of a menu (a menu object, not a CL program menu) so that the user can run the SOMECMD command and be prompted for parameters.

A user who wants to run three versions of this job has to select the menu option three times. Wouldn't it be more convenient to be able to select the menu option once, change the necessary parameters, and rerun the job?

To make it possible to use the F9 key to retrieve the SOMECMD command, make the command-processing program, SOMEPGM, send the command back to the caller (the menu) in a request message. As shown in Figure 6.19, SOMEPGM builds a character string containing the SOMECMD command along with the parameter values supplied to the program. The Send Program Message (SNDPGMMSG) command sends this command string back to the caller as a request message, and the Receive Message (RCVMSG) makes the caller receive the command string and add it to the list of commands that have already been executed.

```
PGM   PARM(&TYPE &SIZE)

DCL   VAR(&CMD)       TYPE(*CHAR)  LEN(80)
DCL   VAR(&SIZE)      TYPE(*DEC)   LEN( 3)
DCL   VAR(&MRK)       TYPE(*CHAR)  LEN( 4)
DCL   VAR(&TYPE)      TYPE(*CHAR)  LEN( 1)
DCL   VAR(&WORKFIELD) TYPE(*CHAR)  LEN( 3)

/* send command back to requestor */

CHGVAR    VAR(&WORKFIELD) VALUE(&SIZE)
CHGVAR    VAR(&CMD) VALUE('SOMECMD THINGTYPE(' *CAT +
            &TYPE *CAT ') THINGSIZE(' *CAT &WORKFIELD +
            *CAT ')')
SNDPGMMSG MSG(&CMD) TOPGMQ(*PRV) MSGTYPE(*RQS) +
            KEYVAR(&MRK)
RCVMSG    PGMQ(*PRV) MSGKEY(&MRK) RMV(*NO)

/* do calcs to run the job here */

ENDPGM
```

Figure 6.19: This program sends the executed command string back to the requesting program.

Be sure to compile the command to allow users with limited command line access to run it. That is, specify ALWLMTUSR(*YES) on the Create Command (CRTCMD) command.

—Ted Holt

✦ ✦ ✦ OS/400

DDS Keyword for System Name and User Profile

The DDS keyword SYSNAME automatically incorporates the system name into your display files. It works much like the two other DDS keywords, DATE and TIME, which have been in existence for years.

By the same token, there's a DDS keyword, USER, that brings the user profile name to your display files. Both SYSNAME and USER can be easily added to your display files while in SDA by using the *SYSNAME and *USER commands; again, this works like *DATE and *TIME.

It's too bad IBM didn't take this a bit further and make SYSNAME and USER available to printer files as well as display files. After all, DATE and TIME can be included in printer files.

—Midrange Computing Staff

✦ ✦ ✦ Performance

Shared ODPs for Display Files

If you are designing or recoding a system that has many interactive programs, and many of the programs call each other, you should check to see if you can use the shared ODP for the WORKSTN (in RPG terms). The advantage of using the shared ODP is that—because they are able to make use of the ODP created by the first program in the series—every called program will initiate faster. To do this, though, you have to include all of the record formats used in the different programs in the same display file.

This is probably a foreign concept to many programmers. The usual technique seems to be coding a separate display file for each program. But apart from the shared ODP advantage, you also can reuse formats in different programs, rather than having duplicate formats in different files. I know that most display formats are completely different and can't be reused in any event, but you might find that perhaps 10 percent of formats within an application could be reused or made common.

Now, the big disadvantage of this is in the compiling of the RPG program. The problem is, if you have defined a display file with 40 different formats, all 40 of those will be compiled into the program. This, most assuredly, is not desirable. Actually, it can cause the compile to fail if you have used a field with the same name but different attributes in different formats. The solution to this problem is to use the IGNORE F-spec continuation, in which you tell the compiler, literally, to ignore the record formats that you name. Record formats that are not IGNOREd are included in the compile. Therefore, you get the same effect as compiling with a display file that includes only the formats that you want.

So, why go through all this bother? I have found that the appearance of response time is noticeably improved with the shared display file ODP. There is a difference in going from program to program with the shared ODP. Also, I tend to think that the fewer objects the better. All of the formats are in one file rather than in 24 different display files.

Like everything else about this machine, there are tradeoffs either way. But don't nix the idea until you've tried it. If you do decide to try it, you can specify the SHARE(*YES) parameter on the Create Display File (CRTDSPF) or the Override Display File (OVRDSPF) command.

—Craig Pelkie

Workstation Data Management Tips

Everybody likes using the DDS keywords that support the programming of windows. However, if you're running the job across a communications line, you should be aware that windows programming has some drawbacks. Displaying a window requires workstation data management to read the current 5250 screen, to save the state of that screen, and to be prepared to restore the screen at a moment's notice. The more windows you build on the display, the harder the system has to work to manage this emulated desktop. If you have a user on a communications line, the response time can lag. So, how can you minimize the impact?

Use the User Restore Display (USRRSTDSP) DDS keyword in your display files. This keyword places the function of saving and restoring the display under program control, allowing you to tailor the effects of the windowing without punishing the system. Programming with USRRSTDSP requires a bit more attention on your part, but ultimately provides a windowing screen that is maximized for your real environment. Here are some other tips:

- Use the Display Size (DSPSIZ) DDS keyword consistently on your screen formats. Every time the system has to reformat the screen size for the remote workstation, the system takes a hit.

- Use the Erase Input (ERASEINP) keyword when the user is doing lots of heads-down keying. The 5250 data-stream actually has an "erase all input fields" control code it can send to the display to zap the fields on the workstation. This is less overhead than sending back a data stream of blanks or zeros to the remote workstation.

- Keep the number of display formats that you overlay onto the workstation to a minimum. When the user presses Enter, each one of them has to tunnel back to the system. Nevertheless, if your application requires you to splatter multiple formats on the screen, here's something else to think about: The 5250 hardware always processes input in a top-to-bottom, left-to-right manner. If you send Format A to the bottom of the screen and follow it by sending Format B to the top of the screen, you've created a knot for the 5250 hardware to unravel. It's best to send the screens out and position them on the display in the same order in which your program expects them back.

- Use the Clear Line Number (CLRL) DDS keyword instead of sending back an entire updated format. The CLRL keyword allows you to zap a particular line on the screen. For instance, if the user presses Enter and the program sends back the same format with a single line of data updated, the CLRL keyword can greatly reduce the turnaround time.

- Check out the real functionality of the override trio of record-level and field-level keywords (PUTOVR, OVRATR, and OVRDTA). If you're repeatedly sending the same format back to the display, these override functions can individually control the fields and their attributes.

- Whenever possible, use DDS keywords for validity checking of input fields. The 5250 hardware has been optimized so that all of these validity-checking functions actually occur in the workstation. That means you don't have to send the entire screen down the communications line, chew up a couple of CPU cycles, and spit it back all the way to the remote display just to inform a user that they keyed in a bad field.

- Don't use the 5250 Numeric Only field types. The Numeric Only function allows the user to enter decimal points and commas on numeric fields. Unfortunately, workstation data management has to parse through these input fields to perform decimal alignment before it passes the fields to the program. If you have a lot of people using this function, performance can be impacted.

- Break the Write/Read habit of sending and receiving display formats. It takes two line turnarounds using Write/Read when—in the majority of cases—a single

EXFMT operation code would suffice. EXFMT will only create a single line turnaround.

- If you're outputting only to a display station, be sure to use the Defer Write—DFRWRT(*YES)—keyword. An RPG WRITE operation forces a line turnaround unless DFRWRT is also issued.

—Thomas M. Stockwell

✦ ✦ ✦ Programming Practice

Avoid Program Recompilation

Normally, if you change a display file field from input/output to output only, your input buffer will change and you will need to recompile your program.

A quick way to change fields to disallow input is to add the attribute DSPATR(PR) to the input/output field. This attribute prohibits users from keying into the field, but it does not change the input buffer; therefore the program does not have to be recompiled.

—Lee Marcus

Cancel with CA12 Instead of CF12

While testing one of my RPG/400 programs, I typed invalid data into several fields that were coded with validity-checking keywords such as RANGE and VALUES. As I expected, after pressing the Enter key, the system locked the keyboard and issued error messages. When I tried to cancel by pressing the F12 key, the system would not allow me to leave the record format until the data was valid; I had to correct all of the offending fields before I could cancel.

I needed to be able to cancel because I knew that my users would not appreciate having to correct data that they did not even want to save. My solution is to code the display file DDS with CA12 instead of CF12. Because no input data is transmitted to the workstation when a Command Attention (CA) key is pressed, no validation occurs. Hence, I am able to cancel as intended and remain on good terms with the users.

—Andy Stubbs

RTNDTA Keyword Trick

The DDS keyword Return Data (RTNDTA) can eliminate the need to create separate variable names in display files used for database file updates. The display file can reference the database fields instead. No need to worry about field attributes matching between the database file and the display file. I don't have to code any MOVEs or Z-ADDs, and my program size is smaller as there are not as many variables. Here's how it's done:

Place the RTNDTA keyword at the record level on the appropriate record of the display file. Use the database field names and reference the database file. This will bring the database fields into the display file automatically when you retrieve the database record.

1. CHAIN and release the database record.

2. Display the screen.

3. Read the screen looking for changes and, if changes have been made, CHAIN again to the database record.

4. Reread the display format, using the READ operation.

   This is what makes this technique work. Because I CHAINED again to the database record, the internal representation of the display file record is overlaid, and any changes to the display record are lost. But, by reading the display record again (with the RTNDTA keyword), you can retrieve the original values of the screen.

5. Update the database record.

—Andrew Krueger

✦ ✦ ✦ Screen Refresh

Displaying Self-updating Data

A question often asked in technical forums is, "How do I code a program to update displayed data without requiring a user to press Enter?" For example, you might want the screen to automatically update and display the current time.

First, you design your display file using SDA or a similar tool. As shown in Figure 6.20, the DDS illustrates one such file, which I've called CLOCKDF. Then, you have to code a loop in your program, as shown in CL program CLOCK (Figure 6.21).

```
A                                           DSPSIZ(24 80 *DS3)
  *
A            R PANEL
A              HOURS          2    O 12 35COLOR(RED)
A                                  12 38':'
A                                        COLOR(RED)
A              MINUTES        2    O 12 40COLOR(RED)
A                                  12 43':'
A                                        COLOR(RED)
A              SECONDS        2    O 12 45COLOR(RED)
```

Figure 6.20: Display file CLOCKDF is an example of a display that must be updated from a program.

```
PGM

    DCLF        FILE(CLOCKDF)

LOOP:
    RTVSYSVAL   SYSVAL(QHOUR) RTNVAR(&HOURS)
    RTVSYSVAL   SYSVAL(QMINUTE) RTNVAR(&MINUTES)
    RTVSYSVAL   SYSVAL(QSECOND) RTNVAR(&SECONDS)

    SNDF        RCDFMT(PANEL)
    DLYJOB      DLY(1)
    GOTO        CMDLBL(LOOP)

ENDPGM
```

Figure 6.21: CL Program CLOCK updates the display without operator intervention.

The trick is to make the thing work. If you compile the display file and the CL program, and then you execute the program, the time won't be updated. Actually, nothing at all will appear on the screen because of the way the AS/400 treats display files by default.

To optimize operations, the AS/400 doesn't update the screen until (or unless) you request a READ operation from the display file. Program CLOCK contains no READ operations—either Receive File (RCVF) or Send Receive File (SNDRCVF)—so the AS/400 never updates the screen. In most cases, this is desirable behavior. If you "paint" the screen by writing several pieces one after another, the AS/400's default treatment makes the result appear all at once.

You need to defeat this feature with the DFRWRT parameter of either the Create Display File (CRTDSPF) command or the Change Display File (CHGDSPF) command. If you haven't already compiled the display file, run CRTDSPF with DFRWRT(*NO). If the display file already exists, use CHGDSPF DFRWRT(*NO).

—Ernie Malaga

✦ ✦ ✦ Screen Timeout

Timing Out AS/400 Workstations

To timeout workstations from an RPG program on the AS/400, do this:

1. When you create your DDS specs for the workstation use the INVITE keyword at the file level.

2. When you compile the workstation DDS specs, specify a number of seconds to wait on the WAITRCD (Wait Record) parameter. This can be changed later using CHGDSPF if you want. Specify a number of devices (1) on the file continuation spec for the workstation file in the RPG program using the NUM keyword on the K spec.

3. Specify a file information data structure for the workstation file using the INFDS keyword on the K spec.

4. Define the file information data structure you specified for the file using the *STATUS keyword to define a field to contain the status code for the workstation.

5. When you want to display the file, WRITE the format name and READ the file name. You may not use EXFMT. Use an error indicator on the READ (the "lo" resulting indicator). If the READ fails, check the status code for the file. If it is 1331, the display timed out. From there you can have the program do whatever you want.

—Midrange Computing Staff

✦ ✦ ✦ SDA

Entering Constants in SDA

An easy way to tell where a constant begins and ends in SDA is to press F20 on the Design Image Work Screen. Pressing F20 displays all constants on the screen in reverse image. Pressing F20 again returns the screen to normal. The reverse image is only temporary and is not saved as part of the display file. By using this feature, you might discover that some of your constants have been defined incorrectly. Fortunately, SDA gives us a way to combine multiple constants together, and to split constants apart.

To combine constants, place one pair of single quotes around the outside of the constants you want to combine. For example, 'Customer number:' becomes one constant. To split a single constant apart, place one pair of single quotes around the outside of the constant, and place one or more double quotes where you wish to split it apart. For example, 'Customer"number:' becomes two constants.

—Midrange Computing Staff

How to Key Quotation Marks Within Strings

If you have ever tried to enter quotes, apostrophes or other special characters onto a display screen using SDA, you might have run into some problems. If you just type them in, SDA will interpret them as SDA commands and get confused. This led me to many frustrating moments until I discovered an easy way to solve this problem.

The trick is to enter the special character as a normal character initially, and then change it to what you want afterward. For example, to enter the line:

```
Enter the customer's number, then "M" to modify
```

First type it in like this:

```
'Enter the customerxs number, then xMx to modify'
```

Press the enter key, then go back and type over the *x*s like this:

```
Enter the customer's number, then "M" to modify
```

—Jonathan M. Vote

Quick Cursor in SDA

When you are in the SDA Work Screen and have several fields, you can use F18 and F19 to move the cursor to the next or previous field in SDA. It sure beats using the arrow keys!

—Midrange Computing Staff

✦ ✦ ✦ Sign-on Display

Add a News Line to the Sign-on Display

One advantage of a customized sign-on display is the ability to add a single line of site news. This could advise users of scheduled system downtime or other information that changes frequently enough so that you don't want to change the sign-on display DDS. This feature is implemented by adding a MSGID entry to the DDS, which can appear anywhere on the screen. The same position (line 24) as the IBM field QSNERROR can be used. The two lines of code shown in Figure 6.22 were added at the end of the DDS.

```
 *. 1 ...+... 2 ...+... 3 ...+... 4 ...+... 5 ...+... 6 ...+... 7
 A N02        MSGLINE       80A  O 24  1MSGID(USR0001 QGPL/USRMSGF)
 A                                      DSPATR(HI)
```

Figure 6.22: Add a message line to the sign-on display file.

Caution: Do not change the original IBM source code. Work with a copy of the original source code.

Because the QSNERROR field is conditioned by indicator 02, the MSGID keyword uses the opposite (N02) to allow the two fields to use the same screen location. This entry causes the first-level text of message USR0001 from message file USRMSGF in library QGPL to display on line 24, starting at column 1, unless indicator 02 is on. The DSPATR(HI) keyword highlights the line.

To create the message file and message text, the commands shown in Figure 6.23 are used.

```
CRTMSGF MSGF(QGPL/USRMSGF) +
  TEXT('Test message file for +
  signon screen')

ADDMSGD MSGID(USR0001) +
  MSGF(QGPL/USRMSGF) +
  TEXT('This line of text will +
  appear on the signon screens')

CRTDSPF FILE(QGPL/SIGNON) +
  SRCFILE(QGPL/QDDSSRC) +
  MAXDEV(256)
```

Figure 6.23: These commands create the objects needed for a newsline on the sign-on display.

In this example, the sign-on display DDS source member is named SIGNON. The next step is to change the sign-on display file for QINTER:

```
CHGSBSD SBSD(QSYS/QINTER) +
  SGNDSPF(QGPL/SIGNON)
```

This change takes effect when QINTER is restarted. To change the one-line message, all that is required is to use the CHGMSGD command:

```
CHGMSGD MSGID(USR0001) +
  MSGF(QGPL/USRMSGF) +
  TEXT('Here is some new text')
```

Note that this does not change the screens already showing the sign-on display, but the new message is picked up when the sign-on display is next shown. Also note that the sign-on display does not allow users to display the second-level text of the message description.

This method could be used to provide a number of different messages on the sign-on display. Different fields, each with a different message ID, could be used for different categories of messages, such as operating hours or coming events.

Depending on local requirements, the news message could be placed anywhere on the screen. If you don't use line 24, there is no need to qualify the field with the N02 indicator as in the preceding example.

—*Steve Bisel*

Add a Newsletter to the Sign-on Screen

IBM gave us two ways to send a message to all users: SNDMSG to *ALLWS, and
SNDBRKMSG to *ALLACT. These methods, however, leave it to the receiving user to remove the messages from their message queues after reading them. Most users, though,
forget to do so. The result is that message queues steadily increase in size unless periodically cleaned up.

Using the sign-on display is a better way to distribute a "newsletter." After all, every user
must see the sign-on display. The technique presented here discusses that approach.

First, customize your sign-on display in such a way that messages are shown on it. Execute the commands shown in Figure 6.24.

```
CRTMSGF MSGF(lib_name/SGN001MF) +
        TEXT('Message file for +
        Sign-On Newsletter')

ADDMSGD MSGID(SGN0001) +
        MSGF(lib_name/SGN001MF) +
        MSG(' ')
```

Figure 6.24: Store news in a message file.

Notice that the message file was created in library **lib_name**. This must be the name of a
library that is part of the system portion of the library list. Repeat the last command 15
more times, using MSGIDS SGN0002 to SGN0016. Now copy the IBM-supplied sign-on display source code to a member of your own, as shown in Figure 6.25.

```
CPYSRCF FROMFILE(QGPL/QDDSSRC) +
        TOFILE(lib_name/QDDSSRC) +
        FROMMBR(QDSIGNON) +
        TOMBR(SGN001DF) +
        MBROPT(*ADD)
```

Figure 6.25: Work with a copy of IBM's display file.

Start SEU to edit member SGN001DF in source file **lib_name**/QDDSSRC, changing it to
match Figure 6.26. Please notice that the last field, MSG16, is only 78 characters long
(while MSG1 to MSG15 are 79 characters long). This is needed to allow the system to display the error messages on the sign-on display; if MSG16 were enlarged to 79 characters,
the last byte would "eat" the attribute byte of the error message.

```
A                                       DSPSIZ(24 80 *DS3)
A          R SIGNON
A                                       CLEAR
A                                       BLINK
A                                  1 23'              Sign On        '
A                                       DSPATR(HI)
A                                  2  2'System . . . . . :'
A          SYSNAME      8A  O  2 23
A                                  3  2'Subsystem . . . . :'
A          SBSNAME     10A  O  3 23
A                                  4  2'Display . . . . . :'
A          DEVNAME     10A  O  4 23
A                                  2 36'User . . . . . . . . . . .'
A          USERID      10A  B  2 71
A    01                           3 36'Password . . . . . . . . .'
A    01    PASSWRD     10A  I  3 71DSPATR(ND)
A                                  4 36'Program/procedure . . . . .'
A          PROGRAM     10A  B  4 71CHECK(LC)
A                                  5 36'Menu . . . . . . . . . . .'
A          MENU        10A  B  5 71CHECK(LC)
A                                  6 36'Current library . . . . . .'
A          CURLIB      10A  B  6 71CHECK(LC)
A    02    QSNERROR    80A  O 24  1DSPATR(HI RI)
A          COPYRIGHT   40A  O 24 40DSPATR(HI)
A          UBUFFER    128A  H
A          MSG1        79A  O  8  2MSGID(SGN 0001 SGN001MF)
A                                       DSPATR(HI)
A          MSG2        79A  O  9  2MSGID(SGN 0002 SGN001MF)
A                                       DSPATR(HI)
A          MSG3        79A  O 10  2MSGID(SGN 0003 SGN001MF)
A                                       DSPATR(HI)
A          MSG4        79A  O 11  2MSGID(SGN 0004 SGN001MF)
A                                       DSPATR(HI)
A          MSG5        79A  O 12  2MSGID(SGN 0005 SGN001MF)
A                                       DSPATR(HI)
A          MSG6        79A  O 13  2MSGID(SGN 0006 SGN001MF)
A                                       DSPATR(HI)
A          MSG7        79A  O 14  2MSGID(SGN 0007 SGN001MF)
A                                       DSPATR(HI)
A          MSG8        79A  O 15  2MSGID(SGN 0008 SGN001MF)
A                                       DSPATR(HI)
A          MSG9        79A  O 16  2MSGID(SGN 0009 SGN001MF)
A                                       DSPATR(HI)
A          MSG10       79A  O 17  2MSGID(SGN 0010 SGN001MF)
A                                       DSPATR(HI)
A          MSG11       79A  O 18  2MSGID(SGN 0011 SGN001MF)
A                                       DSPATR(HI)
A          MSG12       79A  O 19  2MSGID(SGN 0012 SGN001MF)
```

Figure 6.26: The customized sign-on display file, SGN001DF, allows for a newsletter to be loaded from messages (part 1 of 2).

```
A                                    DSPATR(HI)
A            MSG13     79A  O 20  2MSGID(SGN 0013 SGN001MF)
A                                    DSPATR(HI)
A            MSG14     79A  O 21  2MSGID(SGN 0014 SGN001MF)
A                                    DSPATR(HI)
A            MSG15     79A  O 22  2MSGID(SGN 0015 SGN001MF)
A                                    DSPATR(HI)
A            MSG16     78A  O 23  2MSGID(SGN 0016 SGN001MF)
A                                    DSPATR(HI)
```

Figure 6.26: The customized sign-on display file, SGN001DF, allows for a newsletter to be loaded from messages (part 2 of 2).

When you're done with this change, create the display file and make it the sign-on display file for subsystem QINTER, as shown in Figure 6.27.

```
CRTDSPF FILE(lib_name/SGN001DF) +
        SRCFILE(lib_name/QDDSSRC) +
        MAXDEV(256)

CHGSBSD SBSD(QINTER) +
        SGNDSPF(lib_name/SGN001DF)
```

Figure 6.27: Create the modified display file and assign it to a subsystem.

QINTER will show the new sign-on display the next time it is started.

You can now create display file NWS001DF, CL program NWS001CL, and command CHGNWSLTR (Figures 6.28, 6.29, and 6.30, respectively), which are used to change the newsletter area of QINTER's sign-on display. As in the modified sign-on display, display file NWS001DF has a MSG16 field, which must be only 78 characters long in order to match the last message line of the sign-on newsletter.

Simply execute command CHGNWSLTR (no parameters), which displays a facsimile of QINTER's sign-on display, presenting the current newsletter text. Type over it (or blank it out, as you wish), and press Enter. Your users will see the newsletter as soon as the sign-on display is redisplayed (such as when a user signs off, or when QINTER is started).

```
A                                          DSPSIZ(24 80 *DS3)
A                                          PRINT
A                                          INDARA
A                                          CHECK(AB)
A            R ENTER
A                                          CF03(03 'EXIT')
A                                          CF12(12 'CANCEL')
A                                          CF21(21 'Command line')
A                                          BLINK
A                                    1  2'UPDNWSBLT'
A                                          COLOR(BLU)
A                                    1 31'Update News Bulletin'
A                                          COLOR(WHT)
A                                    3  2'Type text of this news bulletin:'
A                                          COLOR(BLU)
A                                    4  2'Use'
A                                          COLOR(BLU)
A                                    4  6'*'
A                                          COLOR(WHT)
A                                    4  8'on left margin to highlight the
A                                          line in'
A                                          COLOR(BLU)
A                                    4 48'white.'
A                                          COLOR(WHT)
A            LINE01       75A  B  5  2CHECK(LC)
A            LINE02       75A  B  6  2CHECK(LC)
A            LINE03       75A  B  7  2CHECK(LC)
A            LINE04       75A  B  8  2CHECK(LC)
A            LINE05       75A  B  9  2CHECK(LC)
A            LINE06       75A  B 10  2CHECK(LC)
A            LINE07       75A  B 11  2CHECK(LC)
A            LINE08       75A  B 12  2CHECK(LC)
A            LINE09       75A  B 13  2CHECK(LC)
A            LINE10       75A  B 14  2CHECK(LC)
A            LINE11       75A  B 15  2CHECK(LC)
A            LINE12       75A  B 16  2CHECK(LC)
A            LINE13       75A  B 17  2CHECK(LC)
A            LINE14       75A  B 18  2CHECK(LC)
A            LINE15       75A  B 19  2CHECK(LC)
A            LINE16       75A  B 20  2CHECK(LC)
A            LINE17       75A  B 21  2CHECK(LC)
A            LINE18       75A  B 22  2CHECK(LC)
A                                   23  2'F3=Exit   F12=Cancel
A                                          Enter=Store-
A                                            F21=Cmd line'
A                                          COLOR(BLU)
```

Figure 6.28: The display file NWS001DF is used for entering the newsletter.

```
nws001cl: +
  pgm

  dclf file(nws001df)
  dcl var(&dtaara)    type(*char) len(10)

  /* If data area does not exist, create it. */
  chgvar var(&dtaara) value($nwsblt)
  chkobj obj(nwsbltlib/$nwsblt) objtype(*dtaara)
  monmsg msgid(cpf9801) exec(do)
    chgvar var(&dtaara) value($$nwsblt)
    crtdtaara dtaara(nwsbltlib/$$nwsblt) type(*char) len(1350) +
      text('News Bulletin data area') aut(*all)
  enddo

  /* Retrieve current text of news bulletin before displaying */
  rtvdtaara dtaara(nwsbltlib/&dtaara (0001 75)) rtnvar(&line01)
  rtvdtaara dtaara(nwsbltlib/&dtaara (0076 75)) rtnvar(&line02)
  rtvdtaara dtaara(nwsbltlib/&dtaara (0151 75)) rtnvar(&line03)
  rtvdtaara dtaara(nwsbltlib/&dtaara (0226 75)) rtnvar(&line04)
  rtvdtaara dtaara(nwsbltlib/&dtaara (0301 75)) rtnvar(&line05)
  rtvdtaara dtaara(nwsbltlib/&dtaara (0376 75)) rtnvar(&line06)
  rtvdtaara dtaara(nwsbltlib/&dtaara (0451 75)) rtnvar(&line07)
  rtvdtaara dtaara(nwsbltlib/&dtaara (0526 75)) rtnvar(&line08)
  rtvdtaara dtaara(nwsbltlib/&dtaara (0601 75)) rtnvar(&line09)
  rtvdtaara dtaara(nwsbltlib/&dtaara (0676 75)) rtnvar(&line10)
  rtvdtaara dtaara(nwsbltlib/&dtaara (0751 75)) rtnvar(&line11)
  rtvdtaara dtaara(nwsbltlib/&dtaara (0826 75)) rtnvar(&line12)
  rtvdtaara dtaara(nwsbltlib/&dtaara (0901 75)) rtnvar(&line13)
  rtvdtaara dtaara(nwsbltlib/&dtaara (0976 75)) rtnvar(&line14)
  rtvdtaara dtaara(nwsbltlib/&dtaara (1051 75)) rtnvar(&line15)
  rtvdtaara dtaara(nwsbltlib/&dtaara (1126 75)) rtnvar(&line16)
  rtvdtaara dtaara(nwsbltlib/&dtaara (1201 75)) rtnvar(&line17)
  rtvdtaara dtaara(nwsbltlib/&dtaara (1276 75)) rtnvar(&line18)

again: +
  sndrcvf

  if cond(&in21) then(do)
    call pgm(quscmdln)
    goto cmdlbl(again)
  enddo

  if cond(&in03 *or &in12) then(do)
    if cond(&dtaara *eq '$$NWSBLT') then(do)
      dltdtaara dtaara(nwsbltlib/$$nwsblt)
    enddo
    goto cmdlbl(endpgm)
  enddo

  /* Update data area */
  chgdtaara dtaara(nwsbltlib/&dtaara (0001 75)) value(&line01)
```

Figure 6.29: CL program NWS001CL stores the newsletter in messages (part 1 of 2).

```
chgdtaara dtaara(nwsbltlib/&dtaara (0076 75)) value(&line02)
chgdtaara dtaara(nwsbltlib/&dtaara (0151 75)) value(&line03)
chgdtaara dtaara(nwsbltlib/&dtaara (0226 75)) value(&line04)
chgdtaara dtaara(nwsbltlib/&dtaara (0301 75)) value(&line05)
chgdtaara dtaara(nwsbltlib/&dtaara (0376 75)) value(&line06)
chgdtaara dtaara(nwsbltlib/&dtaara (0451 75)) value(&line07)
chgdtaara dtaara(nwsbltlib/&dtaara (0526 75)) value(&line08)
chgdtaara dtaara(nwsbltlib/&dtaara (0601 75)) value(&line09)
chgdtaara dtaara(nwsbltlib/&dtaara (0676 75)) value(&line10)
chgdtaara dtaara(nwsbltlib/&dtaara (0751 75)) value(&line11)
chgdtaara dtaara(nwsbltlib/&dtaara (0826 75)) value(&line12)
chgdtaara dtaara(nwsbltlib/&dtaara (0901 75)) value(&line13)
chgdtaara dtaara(nwsbltlib/&dtaara (0976 75)) value(&line14)
chgdtaara dtaara(nwsbltlib/&dtaara (1051 75)) value(&line15)
chgdtaara dtaara(nwsbltlib/&dtaara (1126 75)) value(&line16)
chgdtaara dtaara(nwsbltlib/&dtaara (1201 75)) value(&line17)
chgdtaara dtaara(nwsbltlib/&dtaara (1276 75)) value(&line18)

if cond(&dtaara *eq '$$NWSBLT') then(do)
   rnmobj obj(nwsbltlib/$$nwsblt) objtype(*dtaara) newobj($nwsblt)
   enddo

/* End program */
endpgm: +
   endpgm
```

Figure 6.29: CL program NWS001CL stores the newsletter in messages (part 2 of 2).

```
CHGNWSLTR:   CMD        PROMPT('Change Sign-On Newsletter')
```

Figure 6.30: Command CHGNWSLTR drives CL program NWS001CL.

—Charlie McLean

Changing the AS/400 Sign-on Display

Initially, all subsystems use QDSIGNON as their sign-on display file. You can easily modify its appearance, and each subsystem can have a different sign-on display file. The default display file for the AS/400 sign-on screen is stored in library QSYS under the name of QDSIGNON. The source code (DDS specs) for this file is stored in source physical file QDDSSRC in the QGPL library by the same name.

Change the sign-on display by performing the following steps:

1. Copy source member QDSIGNON from QDDSSRC in QGPL library to a new member with a different name.

2. Make desired changes to the new member, remembering two things: First, the order in which the fields are declared must not be changed. Second, do not change the total size of the input or output buffers. For example, you could move all sign-on information to the first five lines of the display file. If you use only the profile and password entries, you can assign non-display and protect attributes to the other input fields and move them out of the way (keeping the order the same).

3. Create the new sign-on display file with the CRTDSPF command, placing the file in library of your choice.

4. After you compile your display file, you can test it by assigning it to a subsystem that you don't use for interactive jobs. To do this, use the Change Subsystem Description (CHGSBSD) command and specify the name of your new display file in the SGNDSPF parameter. End and restart the subsystem, then transfer your job from QINTER to that subsystem using the Transfer Job (TFRJOB) command. Then sign off and you should see the new sign-on screen.

5. When you are ready to put the new display into production, change the subsystem description (CHGSBSD) sign-on display parameter (SGNDSPF) to the new sign-on display file.

6. Either end and restart the subsystem or wait until the next IPL to activate the new sign-on display.

One additional note: There is a 128-byte hidden field that can be changed to an input/output buffer, which could be made available to application programs when the interactive job is started. See the *Work Management Guide* for more information.

—Midrange Computing Staff

✦ ✦ ✦ Subfiles

An Easy Way to Handle the SFLEND Indicator

If you've ever used the SFLEND keyword in your subfiles, you know that this keyword requires an indicator. There is an easy way to handle this requirement. Assign your response indicator (F3, F12, etc.) to your SFLEND statement and use its negative condition
as illustrated below.

```
 ... 1 ...+... 2 ...+... 3 ...+... 4 ...+... 5 ...+... 6
 A                                  CA03(03)
   *
 A N03                              SFLEND(*MORE)
```

With this method, you don't have to search for an unused indicator and your RPG program doesn't have to set the indicator on. The F3 response indicator will never be on
while the record is displayed; therefore, the SFLEND keyword will always be active.

—Midrange Computing Staff

Clear Message Subfiles by Request

The typical way to display only current messages in a message subfile is to first clear the
program message queue after every operation. This is done by specifying the command
RMVMSG CLEAR(*ALL).

This drastic solution clobbers every message sent to your program's message queue and
obliterates part of your job log. By using this technique, you are forced to resend those
messages to the program's caller if you want to see them in the job log.

An alternative is shown in Figures 6.31 and 6.32. Figure 6.31 contains the DDS needed to
define a message subfile. The code shown in Figure 6.32 sets a request boundary by
sending and receiving a request message after each display of the subfile. As a result, the
subfile will be initialized with all of the messages on the program message queue for the
current request. In other words, the subfile will be cleared, and it will display only the
current messages. Because no messages will have been removed from the program message queue, the messages will remain in the job log.

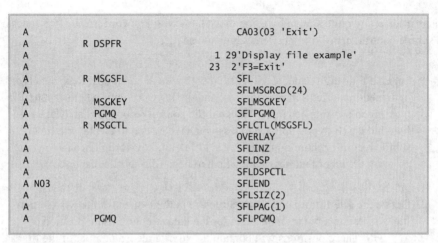

```
A                                    CA03(03 'Exit')
A         R DSPFR
A                                  1 29'Display file example'
A                                 23  2'F3=Exit'
A         R MSGSFL                    SFL
A                                     SFLMSGRCD(24)
A           MSGKEY                    SFLMSGKEY
A           PGMQ                      SFLPGMQ
A         R MSGCTL                    SFLCTL(MSGSFL)
A                                     OVERLAY
A                                     SFLINZ
A                                     SFLDSP
A                                     SFLDSPCTL
A  N03                                SFLEND
A                                     SFLSIZ(2)
A                                     SFLPAG(1)
A           PGMQ                      SFLPGMQ
```

Figure 6.31: Define a message subfile in order to display messages at the bottom of the display.

```
          PGM
          DCLF      FILE(MSGDSPF)
          CHGVAR    VAR(&PGMQ) VALUE(MSGCL)
SNDF:     SNDF      RCDFMT(DSPFR)
          SNDF      RCDFMT(MSGCTL)
          RCVF      RCDFMT(DSPFR)
          IF        COND(&IN03) THEN(GOTO CMDLBL(ENDPGM))
          SNDPGMMSG MSG(' ') TOPGMQ(*SAME) MSGTYPE(*RQS)
          RCVMSG    MSGTYPE(*RQS) RMV(*NO)
          SNDPGMMSG MSG('Test message for display') TOPGMQ(*SAME)
          GOTO      CMDLBL(SNDF)
ENDPGM:   ENDPGM
```

Figure 6.32: Sending a request message causes the system to display only current messages.

—*Tom Conover*

Don't Lose Your Place in a Subfile Display

One of the common uses for subfiles is to display fields from multiple records, and then allow selection on any of the records for a complete display of the selected record's information. After viewing the detail information, a return to the multiple record display is usually desirable. However, how do you get the subfile display to begin with the same page of records that was displayed before?

This is made really quite simple by using the SFLRCDNBR keyword in the DDS specs of the subfile control record format. Here's how to use it:

1. Set up a four-digit zoned decimal field with zero decimal positions, data type of signed-numeric (S in position 35), and the keyword entry SFLRCDNBR (starting in position 45) in the DDS subfile control record format. Make the field hidden (H in position 38) unless you have a need to display the first subfile record's record number. The SFLRCDNBR keyword indicates to your program the record number with which to begin the subfile display.

2. Define the File Information Data Structure in the F-spec for the workstation file, and define a binary input field for the data structure using positions 378–379. These positions will contain the subfile record number of the first subfile record displayed on the current page.

3. Before overlaying the subfile display with another display, save the value of the field you defined in step 2. When it is time to redisplay the subfile, just move the saved value into the DDS field you defined in step 1. The same subfile page that was displayed before will appear when you write the subfile control record.

—Midrange Computing Staff

Easy Access to Message Subfile Messages

Q: My application uses a display record format with I/O fields in which errors could occur, based on the data entered in those fields. When one or more errors occurs, the message subfile displays the errors on line 24. When there is more than one message in the subfile, the user can only scroll through messages in the subfile if the cursor is on line 24. How can I cause the cursor to automatically be positioned on line 24 when an error occurs?

A: Use the Cursor Location (CSRLOC) display-file keyword to force the cursor to line 24 anytime an error occurs. Condition the CSRLOC keyword with an indicator that your program sets on when an error occurs.

—Midrange Computing Staff

Retain the Drop or Fold Setting

Most of the time, the operating system does a great job of handling drop or fold for subfiles. However, when control returns to the program and the screen is redisplayed, the drop or fold is lost.

The solution is to use the SFLMODE and SFLCSRRRN keywords in conjunction with the SFLFOLD and SFLDROP keywords. When these keywords are used, a value is returned in the variable associated with SFLMODE. The variable contains 0 (or *OFF) for folded mode or 1 (*ON) for dropped mode.

Before initially displaying the screen, move *ON or *OFF to the SFLMODE variable (depending on which mode you want to display first). Then move the variable to the controlling indicator for the SFLFOLD/SFLDROP keywords before displaying the screen. When you need to redisplay the screen, the last status of drop or fold will be in the SFLMODE variable, which can be used to reset the indicator. To see the keywords in action, refer to the partial display file shown in Figure 6.33 and the partial RPG program shown in Figure 6.34.

```
 *. 1 ...+... 2 ...+... 3 ...+... 4 ...+... 5 ...+... 6 ...+... 7
A           R CONTROL                     SFLCTL(SUBFILE)
A                                         SFLSIZ(0011)
A                                         SFLPAG(0010)
A                                         SFLMODE(&SFLMOD)
A                                         SFLCSRRRN(&RELRCD)
A                                         SFLDSP
A                                         SFLDSPCTL
A  60                                     SFLDROP(CF11)
A N60                                     SFLFOLD(CF11)
A             SFLMOD        1A  H
A             RELRCD        5S  OH
 *. 1 ...+... 2 ...+... 3 ...+... 4 ...+... 5 ...+... 6 ...+... 7
```

Figure 6.33: Use SFLMODE in a display file to specify folded or dropped subfile records.

```
 *. 1 ...+... 2 ...+... 3 ...+... 4 ...+... 5 ...+... 6 ...+... 7
C                    MOVE *ON      SFLMOD              Start with drop
C                    MOVE *OFF     SFLMOD              or fold
C*
C          *IN03     DOUEQ*ON
C                    MOVE SFLMOD   *IN60               Reset drop/fold
C                    EXFMTCONTROL
C                    ENDDO
 *. 1 ...+... 2 ...+... 3 ...+... 4 ...+... 5 ...+... 6 ...+... 7
```

Figure 6.34: You can retain fold or drop in RPG.

—Rick Brandl

Roll Keys with Subfiles

Q: I want to use the roll keys to perform the natural roll up/roll down function. The subfile is a schedule grid with multiple horizontal window views and up to 999 vertical lines. The subfile is loaded at program initiation with all of the elements needed for the chosen display.

The window left and right function keys work normally; but if the user rolls up or down and then chooses to window sideways, the index places the display on the last value referenced by an Enter or Cmd function instead of the line displayed. If I'm positioned at line 1 and I roll down to view line 500, windowing sends me right back to line 1 because the roll keys currently do not affect the subfile record index.

I have also used the ROLLUP and ROLLDOWN keywords with indicators in the DDS, but this did not work for me.

How can I use the roll keys within this subfile to position the display at a chosen line, and then remain at that line as I window sideways?

A: You need to use the SFLRCDNBR keyword on your DDS specs (see Figure 6.35). This displays the page containing the number in the variable associated with the SFLRCDNBR keyword. Always make it a hidden field. The CURSOR parameter will place the cursor by the subfile entry that contains the value in RCDNBR.

```
   ... 1 ...+... 2 ...+... 3 ...+... 4 ...+... 5 ...+... 6 ...+... 7
   A            RCDNBR          3S 0H        SFLRCDNBR(CURSOR)
```

Figure 6.35: The SFLRCDNBR keyword with the CURSOR option positions not only to a specific page of a subfile, but also places the cursor at a particular record.

—*Eric Hill*

A: When I need to preserve the subfile position, I generally code something like the example shown in Figure 6.36.

```
A           R S1CTL                      SFLCTL(S1SFL)
A                                        TEXT('Subfile control')
A* . . .
A             SFLCSR         4S 0H       SFLRCDNBR

FPRGOBJFMCF  E                    WORKSTN
F                                        SFLCSRKSFILE S1SFL
F                                              KINFDS WSINF
 * . . .
IWSINF       DS
I                                   B 378 3790D@LSFR
 * . . .
C                        EXFMTS1CTL
C                        Z-ADDD@LSFR    SRCSFR         LOWEST SFL REC
 *
C            SRCSFR      IFLT 1                         FORCE 1 IF INVALID
C                        Z-ADD1         SRCSFR
C                        ENDIF                          >SRCSFR IFLT ONE
 *
 *  . . .
 *
C            LODDSP      BEGSR
 *
 * . . . LOAD THE SUBFILE
C            SFLCSR      IFLT SRCSFR
C                        Z-ADDSFLCSR    SRCSFR
C                        ENDIF                          >SFLCSR IFLT SRCSFR
 *
C                        ENDSR
```

Figure 6.36: Here's a tried-and-true method of preserving the subfile position.

The SFLCSR field is used on the SFILE line for the F-spec, as well as on the SFLRCDNBR keyword in the DDS. That way I have only one value to worry about when I want to position the subfile. The INFDS returns the lowest subfile record on the display the last time it was read. By storing the lowest subfile record immediately after the Execute Format (EXFMT) operation, I avoid problems that occur when other I/O to the display corrupts the value before I get around to using it.

After reloading the display, which positions SFLCSR to the last record in the subfile, I restore the value from SRCSFR only if there are currently enough records in the subfile to display the page that contains that record. (There might be fewer records now than there were when Enter or a function key was last hit.) The net result is that the display is always positioned, as closely as possible, to the same page that it was on before. If you need to, you can take it one step further and save the actual display cursor position and restore that to the same coordinates, too.

—*Pete Hall*

Side-by-Side Display Technique

Here is a technique that works similarly to side-by-side subfiles, but it's easier for the user and easier to program.

Define a subfile with the fields you need to see, keeping fields from one file in one half and fields from the other file in the other half. Load the subfile a page at a time. Initially, load the subfile from both files. Use the cursor position returned through the file information data structure (INFDS) to detect which half of the screen the user is in. Update only the fields for the file belonging to the half of the screen where the cursor is located. (Use the CHAIN and UPDAT operation on the subfile because you will be changing the records already in the subfile.)

The page-at-a-time technique I used allowed me to save the key from the first record on each page in an array and use that key to reset the file pointer for each roll-up or roll-down request.

This technique works great. Use it any time you need to present two lists side by side without using two subfiles.

—Michael Veit

Stay Put in Subfiles

When a subfile supports multiple pages (SFLSIZ greater than SFLPAG), you might lose your place if you roll to a page somewhere in the middle of the subfile and press Enter. It's not uncommon for the program to take you back to the first page of the subfile. This behavior can become irritating if you have to roll many times to reach the record you are after.

You can use a combination of SFLRCDNBR (in the DDS of the display file) and the INFDS (in your RPG program) to overcome this problem. In the display file, code the SFLRCDNBR keyword in a hidden field that has four digits and no decimal places. In the RPG program, use the INFDS positions 378–379 (which contain a binary number). Then Z-ADD this value into the SFLRCDNBR hidden field every time you press Enter, and you'll be all set. Your subfiles will stay put, as they should.

—Wayne Johnson

Editor's Note: *You can code the display file DDS with SFLRCDNBR(CURSOR) if you want the subfile to place the cursor at the subfile record where it was when you pressed Enter; otherwise, it will be placed into the first input-capable field by default.*

Subfile Paging

I like to use the *MORE value on the SFLEND keyword, but I ran into a problem when building a subfile one page at a time. When I roll up and a new page is built, the screen always says **Bottom**. To prevent this, you can use a resulting indicator from the READ statement to condition both the SFLEND and ROLLUP keywords (see Figure 6.37). When the indicator is OFF, it will say **More**, and when it's ON, it will say **Bottom**.

```
Display file:
  *. 1 ...+... 2 ...+... 3 ...+... 4 ...+... 5 ...+... 6 ...+... 7
A N99                                ROLLUP(66)
A  99                                SFLEND(*MORE)

RPG program:
  *. 1 ...+... 2 ...+... 3 ...+... 4 ...+... 5 ...+... 6 ...+... 7
C                    READ QDBXREF                    99
```

Figure 6.37: Simplify subfile paging by conditioning SFLEND to the end-of-file indicator.

You can get a false **More** when you reach the end of file at the same time you reach the last record in a subfile page, however. Avoid this by reading (but not writing to the subfile) the next database record for your roll-up routine. This will serve as a look ahead, and your user will not get a false **More**.

—Todd Fisher

Subfile Sharing

Q: Is it possible to read a subfile that resides in program A from another program that is called from program A?

A: Yes, it is. Here's the technique I use. It works with separate programs or procedures. I'll illustrate using procedures.

You'll need to make the display file share an open data path. To do that, use the Override with Printer File (OVRPRTF) command, specifying SHARE(*YES) before calling the first bound RPG module.

I use a CLLE module to perform the override and issue a call procedure (CALLPRC) to the first RPG module. This RPG module fills the subfile and displays it. I then select a record in the subfile to display. The first module then does a Call Bound (CALLB) procedure to the second RPG module. The second RPG module then does a Read Changed Record (READC) operation and reads the selected record.

—Mark McCall

Subfile Synchronization

Do you have a program that uses multiple subfiles? Do you want to keep the records in all of the subfiles synchronized? I have a simple technique to solve the problem.

Suppose you have a program that presents three views of a list of customer records: phone number, billing address, and shipping address. Each view is displayed through a different subfile. The program allows the user to rotate through the three different views by pressing a function key. If the user pages forward on the phone numbers view and then requests the billing address view, you want the program to display the same group of records that were displayed on the phone number view. If the user requests the shipping address view, you also want the same group of records to appear.

My technique uses the relative-record number (RRN) of the last subfile displayed. This RRN can be obtained through the File Information Data Structure (INFDS) in positions 378–379. In the example, whenever F11 is pressed, a counter called SCREEN increments. By placing the last RRN of the last display in the Subfile Record Number (SFLRCDNBR) field, the subfile records stay synchronized. (Make sure that the SFLRCDNBR field has a value when the subfile is first displayed. Otherwise, the program will issue a device error for trying to write a record with an RRN value of 0.) The last subfile displayed moves its value into the first subfile (so the view starts from the beginning again). The SCREEN field is also reset to 0. Figures 6.38 and 6.39 contain DDS and RPG code segments for this technique.

```
*. 1 ...+... 2 ...+... 3 ...+... 4 ...+... 5 ...+... 6 ...+... 7
*
* Subfile A's hidden field for subfile record positioning
*
A             RECO1          4S 0H      SFLRCDNBR(CURSOR)
*
* Subfile B's hidden field for subfile record positioning
*
A             RECO2          4S 0H      SFLRCDNBR(CURSOR)
*
* Subfile C's hidden field for subfile record positioning
*
A             RECO3          4S 0H      SFLRCDNBR(CURSOR)
```

Figure 6.38: Use the SFLRCDNBR keyword to synchronize subfiles.

```
    * Relative record number of the lowest subfile record number
    * displayed on page
    *
    *. 1 ...+... 2 ...+... 3 ...+... 4 ...+... 5 ...+... 6 ...+... 7
    IWSDS      DS
    I                                      B 378 3790RTNRRN
    *
    * F11 changes view (controls which subfile is displayed)
    C          *IN11    IFEQ *ON
    C                   ADD  1            SCREEN
    C                   ENDIF
    *
    C                   SELEC
    *
    C          SCREEN   WHEQ 1
    C                   EXFMTSUBFA
    C                   Z-ADDRTNRRN       REC02
    *
    C          SCREEN   WHEQ 2
    C                   EXFMTSUBFB
    C                   Z-ADDRTNRRN       REC03
    *
    C          SCREEN   WHEQ 3
    C                   EXFMTSUBFC
    C                   Z-ADDRTNRRN       REC01
    C                   Z-ADD0            SCREEN
    *
    C                   ENDSL
```

Figure 6.39: Subfile synchronization takes only a few extra lines of RPG code.

—Michael Veit

Subfiles with Pizzazz

While subfiles can be very powerful in how they handle information, in some circumstances they are very limiting. For example, consider a screen design that would display multiple customers and their invoices. This could possibly be done with a fold, but the information would be redundant from line to line for a single customer.

The trick that I use is to make a subfile with one field that is as long as is necessary. I format this field in an RPG program before writing it to the subfile. This way I have one line with all the pertinent customer information and underneath it one line for every invoice. But there is one trick that will make this screen look even better.

When I am formatting the subfile line in the RPG program I stick hexadecimal bytes in between the fields depending on what screen attribute, such as color, underline, or reverse image, would be best.

This method allows you to use the power of a subfile with the enhancements of selected screen attributes to create a first-class screen presentation.

—Rick Romanek

✦ ✦ ✦ Windows

Automatic Window Placement

Do you ever tire of having to determine and specify the start row and column of your DDS windows? If so, here's some good news. You can specify a special value of *DFT in place of the start-line and start-position parameters of the WINDOW keyword.

The old method required that you indicate the specific window location coordinates with literals like this:

```
WINDOW(5 10 8 20)
```

or with variables like this:

```
WINDOW(&ROW &COL 8 20)
```

With V2R3, IBM introduced a simpler specification like this:

```
WINDOW(*DFT 8 20)
```

The *DFT value causes the system to automatically determine a start line and start position relative to the cursor location so as not to overlay the cursor.

For more information about the rules the system uses to position the window, see the *Guide to Programming Displays*.

—Richard Shaler

Color My World with Windows

We write all of our maintenance programs as DDS windows. While in an application, the user can call up a maintenance program window or several windows. The DDS keyword allows you to dynamically control the position of the window on your screen, but the color is hardwired. A way around this is to code seven WDWBORDER keywords in your DDS, each conditioned by a different indicator and each with a separate color.

To give each window displayed a different border color, when the window program is called, pass it a 1-byte decimal field initialized to zero. The window program receives this window color parameter, adds 1 to it, and then sets the indicator for that particular color. On subsequent program calls, it passes the same parameter and adds 1 to get a different color. If the color exceeds 7 (the limit), the program resets it to 1. This gives each window a different color. (Because the programs could be called in any order, you would not be able to hardwire the different colors in.)

You can dynamically position a window displayed by program X by passing a 1-byte code to X instead of the actual coordinates. This simplifies coding and eliminates having to change the programs that call X should you change the size of the window. For example, you could use the table shown in Table 6.1. The numbers have been selected to match the positions of the keys in the numeric keypad of your display station.

Table 6.1: Window Positioning Codes		
7 = Upper-left corner	8 = Upper edge, centered	9 = Upper-right corner
4 = Left edge, centered	5 = Center of screen	6 = Right edge, centered
1 = Lower-left corner	2 = Lower edge, centered	3 = Lower-right corner

Using this approach, program X could position the window by setting values for the variables coded in the WINDOW DDS keyword for the display file. For instance, if WINDOW(&LIN &COL 6 20) is coded, program X could set LIN to 1 and COL to 2 when it receives 'UL', thereby positioning the window at line 1, column 2 (upper-left corner).

—James Droke

Doing Windows

Q: I am trying to display a window showing the status of the program like the "Printing..." window on the ResourceLibrary. The window should show while I am building a subfile. I think I have the window coded correctly because if I do an EXFMT to the window, it works; but if I do a WRITE to the window format, it never displays.

A: You must do either one of two things to make a WRITE put a screen out:

1. Change the display file to be DFRWRT(*NO).

2. Put the FRCDTA keyword on the format.

Formats are not displayed until the program performes a READ operation. This is the default for the AS/400. The two preceding methods are how you change this.

—James Coolbaugh

Program Messages and DDS Windows

Q: I have written a couple of programs using the DDS WINDOW keyword. I enjoy its ease of use and flexibility; however, I can't get my program-controlled messages to appear in the last line of the window. Is this even possible?

A: The sample display file source member, shown in Figure 6.40, illustrates how to place subfile messages in your windows. Be sure your program moves an asterisk (*) to the first position of the PGMQ field in its initialization subroutine. The special asterisk value causes OS/400 to automatically supply the name of the program message queue used by the program to build the message subfile. This eliminates the need to hard-code a message queue name.

```
A*==============================================================
A* To compile:
A*
A*      CRTDSPF    FILE(XXX/XES001DF) SRCFILE(XXX/QDDSSRC)
A*
A*==============================================================
A*. 1 ...+... 2 ...+... 3 ...+... 4 ...+... 5 ...+... 6 ...+... 7
A                                    DSPSIZ(24 80 *DS3)
A                                    PRINT
A                                    CA03(03)
```

Figure 6.40: This display file includes a message subfile line (part 1 of 2).

```
A            R WIND1
A                                      WINDOW(4 6 8 50)
A                                      OVERLAY
A                                    1 18'CONFIRM'
A            TXT         11A  O  1 26DSPATR(HI)
A                                    3  4'TYPE "Y" TO CONTINUE'
A                                    4  4'TYPE "N" TO CANCEL'
A            YESNO        1A  B  6 29
A                                    6 32'Y/N'
A*================================================================
A            R MSGSFL                  SFL
A                                      SFLMSGRCD(07)
A            MSGKEY                    SFLMSGKEY
A            PGMQ                      SFLPGMQ(10)
A*================================================================
A            R MSGCTL                  SFLCTL(MSGSFL)
A                                      OVERLAY
A                                      SFLDSP
A                                      SFLDSPCTL
A                                      SFLINZ
A  N03                                 SFLEND
A                                      SFLSIZ(0002)
A                                      SFLPAG(0001)
A                                      WINDOW(WIND1)
A            PGMQ                      SFLPGMQ(10)
A*================================================================
A            R DUMMY
A                                      ASSUME
A                                    1  2' '
```

Figure 6.40: This display file includes a message subfile line (part 2 of 2).

—*Midrange Computing Staff*

Spice Up Your Windows!

Pop-up windows are great things in applications, but sometimes they need to be spiced up. One way of doing this is to place headings and comments in the border of the window rather than within it (see Figure 6.41). Additionally, headings and comments can have different color and display attributes from the border that contains them. DDS has special keywords to allow you to do this. The DDS that causes the window heading to be displayed within the Window surround is as follows: WDWTITLE((*TEXT 'Put your Title Here') *CENTER *TOP (*COLOR RED)).

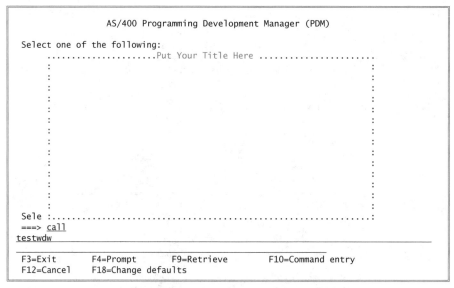

```
                    AS/400 Programming Development Manager (PDM)

    Select one of the following:
            .....................Put Your Title Here .....................
           :                                                          :
           :                                                          :
           :                                                          :
           :                                                          :
           :                                                          :
           :                                                          :
           :                                                          :
           :                                                          :
           :                                                          :
           :                                                          :
           :                                                          :
    Sele :..........................................................:
    ===> call
    testwdw
    _____

    F3=Exit        F4=Prompt      F9=Retrieve       F10=Command entry
    F12=Cancel     F18=Change defaults
```

Figure 6.41: Spice up window titles by placing them in the border in color.

Notice the use of the COLOR parameter. This lets you add colors to the title. Titles can be positioned at the top or bottom of the window as well as left or right justified. You can even use the reverse image and blink attributes! Go for it! Make your windows a little more exciting!

—Allan M. Telford

Why a DDS Window Clears the Screen

Q: I am trying to use the DDS window keywords. The program works—it displays the window okay—but clears the screen before displaying the window. As there is no documentation provided for these keywords, I am asking for some help.

A: If this window is in another program, then you need to have another format in the display used by the called program that contains the ASSUME keyword. This tells the system to assume that this display file is already there, even though it isn't. You need this because the default for the AS/400 is to clear the screen when you open a new display file. The format that contains this keyword does not have to be used in your program; you just need it in the display file. Also consider using the KEEP keyword in the record that is displayed by the called program. This will prevent the screen from flickering when the called program is ended and the underlying panel is redisplayed.

—James Coolbaugh

CHAPTER 7

General Programming Tasks

*N*o matter which programming languages a shop uses, there are certain tasks of a general nature that are not language specific, such as source editors, edit codes, testing, debugging, and more. This chapter contains tips that programmers can put to work, regardless of which programming language they use.

OS/400 includes an interactive debugger that, ideally, programmers should never have to use. But, realistically, it's a practical tool that should be mastered. Several of the tips in this chapter will help you with the debugging process. You'll also find some tips to help you use PDM and SEU, two of the iSeries programmer's most important tools, as well as some tips for the compilation process.

Business computing differs from scientific computing in that business computing centers on the manipulation of a database. This is true regardless of which application programming language a programmer uses. For that reason, this chapter has some tips dealing with the storage of data in files and data areas.

Other areas for which you'll find support are processing dates and sequencing data. Included are a good number of tips dealing with the practice of programming—that is, the methodology used in developing programs—and also quite a few support tips (i.e., information that might come in handy as you develop applications).

There's a lot of general programming information in this chapter, perhaps more than you'll ever need. I hope that you'll find answers to the programming challenges you face.

—*Ted Holt*

✦ ✦ ✦ Commands

Ampersand to Extend Prompted Fields' Lengths

If you are filling out a command prompt screen and need more room in an input field, try putting an ampersand (&) in the first position followed by one or more blanks. This will expand the field to its next size increment. The increments are 25, 80, 132, 256, and 512 characters. This is handy when working with CL programs that have expressions longer than the standard-length input field.

—Greg Doyle

Finding Command Names

Ever want to enter a command name but can't remember the proper spelling? The most common way to solve this problem is to press F4 on a blank command line. This presents you with the Major Command Groups menu, where you can select either option 1 (Select command by name), 2 (Verb commands), or 3 (Subject commands). Another way is to use the Select Command (SLTCMD) command with a partial command name followed by an asterisk. Here's an even simpler method: By entering a partial name on a command line followed by an asterisk, and then pressing Enter, the system will provide a list of commands from which you can make a selection. Because this involves even fewer keystrokes, it's easier to use. Although this is a simple technique, it's very useful.

—Jim Walker
—Clint Haley

✦ ✦ ✦ Compiling

Compiling Service Programs That Reference Each Other

We have a number of service programs that correspond to business "classes." They have names like CUSTOMER, PART, and ORDER. If programmers want a procedure that returns a fully formatted customer name—with title, initials, and full name—they expect to find it in service program CUSTOMER.

We are constantly adding new procedures to these service programs. Over time, many of these programs have come to reference each other. Two examples of this might be (1) a procedure named RtvPartName that resides in PART and is called by service program ORDER and (2) a procedure in ORDER named IsPartOrdered that is called by PART.

An outcome of this is that recreating these service programs from source (i.e., no existing service program objects exist) is not as straightforward as you would think. We can create the modules without any difficulty, but as soon as we try to create service program ORDER, it fails because it needs PART. Likewise, PART can't be created because it needs ORDER.

We found the solution to our problem in the OPTION(*UNRSLVREF) parameter in the Create Service Program (CRTSRVPGM) command. If you specify it, the service program will be created even if procedures and field names that are imported from other service programs can't be located. In our example, ORDER could be created without the need for PART. The procedure **RtvPartName** would be an unresolved reference as far as ORDER is concerned, but the ORDER service program object would be created nonetheless.

Of course, ORDER couldn't be expected to work at runtime if any attempt to call **RtvPartName** was made. However, you can create PART in the normal way because ORDER now exists. And once you've done that, you can return to ORDER and recreate it without the OPTION(*UNRSLVREF) parameter.

If you want to create an entire ILE environment from source, first create all service programs with the OPTION(*UNRSLVREF) parameter, and then recreate them without it.

—John V. Thompson
—Derek Butland

Don't Lose an Object's Authority When It's Recreated

If you compile a program using REPLACE(*YES), be aware that the values for the USRPRF and AUT parameters on the create commands are ignored and the values from the object being replaced are used. If you want to change the authority parameters, you must either delete the object before recompiling or use the Change Program (CHGPGM) command.

—Christopher Andrle

Getting a Quick Compile Listing

How many times have you compiled a program into QTEMP because you needed an up-to-date compile listing? Well, here's an easy and fast way to accomplish that.

When you take the defaults for the CRTxxxPGM commands, the compiler will generate an executable object. This process takes extra time and resources. If you compile the program with the parameter OPTION(*NOGEN), no program object will be created, but you will still get the full compile listing and cross-reference. This is faster because the system doesn't have to create an object.

Rather than prompt the CRTxxxPGM command to fill in the OPTION parameter, I've set up a user-defined PDM option for the different types of programs. Two examples are listed in Table 7.1.

Table 7.1: User-Defined PDM Options

Function	PDM Option	Command
RPG Listing	RL	SBMJOB CMD(CRTRPGPGM PGM(QTEMP/&N) SRCFILE(&L/&F) OPTION(*NOGEN) JOB(&N) JOBD(&G/&H)
CL Listing	CL	SBMJOB CMD(CRTCLPGM PGM(QTEMP/&N) SRCFILE(&L/&F) OPTION(*NOGEN) JOB(&N) JOBD(&G/&H)

When I need a compile listing of an RPG program, for example, I just use the RL option.

—Paul Jackson

More Detail on Compile Errors

Normally, when you compile an RPG program (CRTRPGPGM) on the AS/400, only the first-level message text (messages on the AS/400 can have first- and second-level text) is printed at the end of the compile listing. Often, this is not enough to let the programmer know what the real problem is. Additionally, you can print the second-level text by specifying *SECLVL in the OPTION parameter of the CRTRPGPGM command.

However, if you don't realize you need the second-level text until after your compile, and you don't feel like resubmitting the compile, you can view it on your CRT instead. Just use the Display Message Description (DSPMSGD) command. Use the message number (e.g. QRG5199) in the RANGE parameter and QRPG/QRPGMSG in the MSGF parameter. You will be able to display the first- and second-level text to the screen.

—Midrange Computing Staff

Overriding Compile Listing Attributes

Both the Create RPG/400 Program (CRTRPGPGM) and the Create COBOL Program (CRTCBLPGM) commands have a PRTFILE parameter. This parameter allows you to specify the name of the printer file you want the compiler to use when it creates the compile listing. The default print file is QSYSPRT. If you want your compile listings to have different attributes (e.g., page size, lines per inch) from those that are defined in QSYSPRT, here's a technique you can use.

Use the Create Duplicate Object (CRTDUPOBJ) command to make copies of the QSYSPRT printer file. Call the new printer files RPGSRCPRTF and CBLSRCPRTF. Then change the attributes of the new printer files to whatever you prefer by using the Change Printer File (CHGPRTF) command. For example, I used the following command for my RPG compiler listings:

```
CHGPRTF FILE(RPGSRCPRTF) +
    PAGESIZE(88 132) LPI(8) +
    CPI(15) OVRFLW(83) HOLD(*YES)
```

Once you have the attributes you want for your compiler list, you can use the Change Command Default (CHGCMDDFT) command to make the CRTRPGPGM and CRTCBLPGM commands default to your new printer files.

—*Tom Liotta*

✦ ✦ ✦ Data Areas

Accessing Remote Data Areas Through DDM

The AS/400 has always had the ability to let you access remote files through Distributed Data Management (DDM). In versions V3R2 and V3R7 and later, you can use DDM to access remote data areas as well. Here's a quick overview of how this capability works.

When you prompt the Create Data Area (CRTDTAARA) command, you'll find a new option for the TYPE parameter. You can now enter a value of *DDM to tell the system that the data area being created is a DDM data area. When you create a DDM data area, you don't specify the length or initial value as you would for a regular data area. Instead, you enter the name and location of the remote data area. For example, you might enter the following command:

```
CRTDTAARA DTAARA(QGPL/RMT1MRI) TYPE(*DDM) +
    RMTDTAARA(QGPL/QSS1MRI) +
    RMTLOCNAME(S1034786)
```

This example creates, on the local system, a DDM data area called RMT1MRI, which points to an existing data area called QSS1MRI on the remote system. The CRTDTAARA command stores the name of the remote data area and remote location name in the DDM data area on the local system. You can view this information by using the Display Data Area (DSPDTAARA) command:

```
DSPDTAARA DTAARA(QGPL/RMT1MRI)
```

To view the contents of the data area on the remote system, just add the SYSTEM(*RMT) parameter to the DSPDTAARA command:

```
DSPDTAARA DTAARA(QGPL/RMT1MRI) SYSTEM(*RMT)
```

Other data area commands, such as Change Data Area (CHGDTAARA) and Retrieve Data Area (RTVDTAARA), work transparently. You don't need to code any special parameters. They automatically access remote data areas when the data area on the local system is a DDM data area. Access to data areas through RPG programs is also transparent.

—Robin Klima

Handling File and Data Area Record Locks

I'd like to propose solutions to two problems I've experienced with file record locks and data area locks. The first problem involves how users typically respond to file record locks.

After the record wait time has expired on a file record lock, the user must answer a message. IBM has set the default reply to "C" or Cancel. If the user has not already keyed ahead (through buffering), just pressing Enter (the typical user idea) cancels the job. Instead of changing the maximum record wait time on all files, why not change the default reply from Cancel to Retry?

```
CHGMSGD MSGID(RPG1218) MSGF(QRPGMSGE) DFT('R')
```

On data area locks, the wait time comes from the default wait time for the job. Because data areas give you no retry option, try the following solution:

```
CHGJOB DFTWAIT(*NOMAX)
```

Preferably, this statement would be a part of the initial program specified in the user profile. Only users with *JOBCTL authority may run this command.

—Steve Cherkas

✦ ✦ ✦ Dates

QDAYOFWEEK and QCENTURY System Values

With V3R7, IBM added two date-related system values. First, there's QDAYOFWEEK, which tells you the day of the week for the system date (which is stored in system value QDATE). QDAYOFWEEK holds a 4-byte character string, which can have one of the following values: *SUN, *MON, *TUE, *WED, *THU, *FRI, or *SAT. You cannot change this system value.

Then, there's QCENTURY, which complements QDATE to provide a complete date, including the century. In a strange bending of the rules, IBM decided to expand the meaning of century 0 and century 1. You'll remember that any year between 1940 and 1999 has been considered as century 0, while years between 2000 and 2039 are century 1. Not so with QCENTURY; so be careful. QCENTURY considers century 0 to be any year (system value QYEAR) between 1928 and 1999, while century 1 is between 2000 and 2053.

—Ernie Malaga

QEZDATVL and Security Level 40

If you use program QSYS/QEZDATVL to convert, edit, and verify dates, you shouldn't. This program will not run under security level 40 because it resides in the system domain. If you move to security level 40, as IBM recommends, your programs will fail when they call QEZDATVL. One alternative is to write a CL program (Figure 7.1).

```
PGM PARM(&DATEIN &DATEOUT)

   DCL VAR(&DATEIN) TYPE(*CHAR) LEN(6)
   DCL VAR(&DATEOUT) TYPE(*CHAR) LEN(8)
   DCL VAR(&MSGID) TYPE(*CHAR) LEN(7)
   DCL VAR(&MSGF) TYPE(*CHAR) LEN(10) VALUE('QCPFMSG')
   DCL VAR(&MSGFLIB) TYPE(*CHAR) LEN(10) VALUE('*LIBL')
   DCL VAR(&MSGDTA) TYPE(*CHAR) LEN(256)

   MONMSG MSGID(CPF0000) EXEC(GOTO CMDLBL(ERROR_MSG))

   QSYS/CVTDAT DATE(&DATEIN) TOVAR(&DATEOUT) FROMFMT(*JOB) +
      TOFMT(*JOB) TOSEP(*JOB)
   RETURN

ERROR_MSG:
   QSYS/RCVMSG MSGTYPE(*EXCP) MSGDTA(&MSGDTA) MSGID(&MSGID) +
      MSGF(&MSGF) SNDMSGFLIB(&MSGFLIB)
   MONMSG MSGID(CPF0000)
   QSYS/SNDPGMMSG MSGID(&MSGID) MSGF(&MSGFLIB/&MSGF) +
      MSGDTA(&MSGDTA)
   MONMSG MSGID(CPF0000)

ENDPGM
```

Figure 7.1: Use this CL code instead of QEZDATVL.

—Bruce Vining

✦ ✦ ✦ Debugging

Breaking an Active Program Out of a Loop

If a program is caught in an infinite loop and observability has not been removed, it might be possible to break the loop without canceling the program. Use DSPJOB OPTION(*PGMSTK) to determine the program, its library, and a statement within the loop that is being executed. Use Start Service Job (STRSRVJOB), then Start Debug (STRDBG) and Add Breakpoint (ADDBKP) to set a breakpoint within the loop. When the breakpoint is displayed, press F10 to go to a command entry screen and use the Change Program Variable (CHGPGMVAR) command to set the conditions necessary for the loop to end.

—Midrange Computing Staff

Ending Debugging Sessions

If you run the Start Debug (STRDBG) command with option UPDPROD (*NO) and forget to issue End Debug (ENDDBG) after debugging, you could create problems for yourself.

If you start an SEU session for a source member in a production library, you cannot save your changes when you exit the SEU session. To get around this problem and avoid losing your changes, press F21 for a command line, type ENDDBG, and press Enter. This ends the debugger, and you can now save your changes.

—Jan Jorgensen

How to Force Jobs to Run in Debug Mode

In our shop, programmers are restricted from updating production data by staying in debug mode. However, when a job in debug mode submits another job to run in batch, the new job does not run in debug mode. We needed a way for programmers' batch jobs to run in debug mode also.

We accomplished this by using a customized routing entry program for our batch subsystem. We created a CL routing program that tests the current user profile for that of a programmer. If the user is a programmer, the program does a Start Debug (STRDBG) command and transfers control to the system program QCMD to continue execution. Our program, ROUTINGCL, is shown in Figure 7.2.

```
/* BATCH SUBSYSTEM DEFAULT ROUTING */
PGM
DCL VAR(&USERID) TYPE(*CHAR) LEN(10)
RTVJOBA USER(&USERID)
/*-----------------------------------*/
/* My naming convention has all Programmer user profiles begin with */
/* PGMR, you will change this to match your naming convention. */
/*-----------------------------------*/
IF COND(%SST(&USERID 1 4) *EQ 'PGMR') THEN(STRDBG UPDPROD(*NO))
TFRCTL PGM(QSYS/QCMD)
ENDPGM
```

Figure 7.2: Program ROUTINGCL forces programmers' jobs to run in debug mode.

We changed the default routing entry attached to the batch subsystem to use our new CL program. This is done using the Change Routing Entry (CHGRTGE) command.

```
CHGRTGE SBSD(QBATCH) SEQNBR(9999) PGM(ROUTINGCL)
```

—Mark McCall

Is My Program Caught in a Loop?

One day I was testing a piece of code that I suspected was stuck in a loop. I was about to take the time to stop the program and set up a debug when I realized I could get this information from the DSPJOB command. When you run DSPJOB (from WRKUSRJOB, WRKSBSJOB, or other means) you are provided with a list of options, which include "Display program stack, if active." This display includes a column that shows the line of code the program is on. This display can be updated with the F5 key. While the program executes too fast to let F5 give you a step-by-step display, repeated F5s will show you approximately where the program is. It definitely showed me where my loop was happening.

After I knew the code was looping, I could use the "Display open files, if active" option to find out which records were up at the time of the loop. Just this information let me look at my code and figure out what the problem was.

—Kathreen Kruse

Quick Job Log Display

When testing CL programs, if the job attribute LOGCLPGM is set to *YES, then CL commands are visible from Command Entry. If you press F10 for low-level messages, these can be displayed and retrieved. This is very useful when debugging an OPNQRY string that builds at runtime. The actual substituted string is shown, and by placing the cursor on the displayed string and pressing F9 to retrieve, the command can be tested with different variables in place.

—Kevin Heiman

Understanding the INST Column of a Job Log

Q: How do you map to a source line number from a job log's INST column? I know the INST number is hexadecimal. However, I think the hexadecimal number is not a source line number but a compile listing STMT number. I used the Win95 calculator (in Scientific view) to enter the hexadecimal number to convert it to decimal. I then compiled the source to get the STMT numbers, making sure the source change date and time agreed with the program object. I knew I was looking for some kind of I/O function, because the job log message I was trying to track down was about a record lock, but the steps I took did not get me to an I/O source line. The program was not ILE, and the default GENOPT option *NOOPTIMIZE was used.

A: Here's one method you can use. The INST column in the job log shows MI statement numbers. Follow these steps to determine the SEU line number:

1. Recompile the program and specify GENOPT(*LIST).

2. Look near the end of the compiler listing for a section of MI code. Look for the INST column (the second column from the left). Find the number in this column that appears in your job log.

3. Look in the far-left column on the line matching your instruction number. This is the SEU line number (e.g., 12300).

—Gene Gaunt

Universal Graphical Debugger

Confused by the difference in function keys between the Start Debug (STRDBG) command for ILE programs and the Start Interactive Source Debugger (STRISDB) command for Original Program Model (OPM) programs? Frustrated because you need to debug a combination of OPM and ILE programs? Relax. IBM has rationalized its graphical debugger offerings.

STRDBG is the survivor and, if you set everything up correctly, it will debug a program that is OPM, ILE, or mixed-program model.

To use STRDBG as your universal debugger, you must compile your program correctly and start STRDBG correctly. To compile correctly, do the following:

- For RPG OPM programs, specify either OPTION(*SRCDBG) or OPTION(*LSTDBG) on the Create RPG Program (CRTRPGPGM) command.

- For CLP programs, specify OPTION(*SRCDBG) on the Create CL Program (CRTCLPGM) command.

- For RPGLE, CLLE, or CBLLE programs, specify either DBGVIEW(*SOURCE) or DBGVIEW(*LIST), or DBGVIEW(*ALL) on the Create Bound *xxx* Program (CRTBND*XXX*) or Create xxx Module (CRT*XXX*MOD) commands (*xxx* is the language abbreviation).

To start STRDBG correctly, include OPMSRC(*YES) on the STRDBG command if you are debugging an OPM program.

—Sam Lennon

Use DSPMODSRC to Redisplay Source Code in Debugger

You've loaded four programs, you've set seven breakpoints, you've pressed F12, and you're about to invoke your program—when you pound your forehead in frustration. You should have set eight breakpoints and, without the eighth, the whole debugging session will be a waste of time. With no way to get back into the debugger setup, you simply ENDDBG and start all over....

No! Wait! Just issue the Display Module Source (DSPMODSRC) command. No parameters are required. DSPMODSRC will take you right back into the debugger, and you can set that one essential breakpoint and continue.

—Sam Lennon

✦ ✦ ✦ Edit Codes

Create Your Own Edit Codes

One of the better features of OS/400 is the ability to create your own edit codes. Three of the ones that I use are one for a modified "Y" edit code, a Social Security edit code, and a telephone number edit code. The three edit code commands are Create Edit Description (CRTEDTD), Delete Edit Description (DLTEDTD), and Display Edit Description (DSPEDTD). There is no command to change an edit code description.

To create an edit code of your own, you must first delete one of the edit codes, numbered 5–9, that IBM provides as samples (DLTEDTD 5). Then you can replace that code with one of your own. Figure 7.3 shows the three that I use, but I use a lowercase 'x' for the edit code. You can choose your own. The character '**b**' represents a blank. Figure 7.3 shows these three new edit codes.

```
CRTEDTD EDTD(x) INTMASK('b0/bb/bb') DECPNT(N) ZEROBAL(*NO) +
        TEXT('Similar to Y, but no print if date = 000000')
CRTEDTD EDTD(x) INTMASK(' - - ') DECPNT(N) +
        FILLCHAR(0) +
        ZEROBAL(*YES) TEXT('Social Security Edit Code')
CRTEDTD EDTD(x) INTMASK('bbb)&bbb-bbbb') DECPNT(N) +
        ZEROBAL(*NO) LFTCNS('(') TEXT('Telephone edit code')
```

Figure 7.3: User-defined edit codes simplify programming.

—Tim Johnston

Handy Date Edit Code

When you edit a date using the standard IBM-supplied 'Y' edit code, the date will have format *xx/xx/xx*. If the date is zero, it will print as 00/00/00.

Our problem was that we had standard forms on which we did not want 00/00/00 to print if the date was zero. One solution to this would be to compare each date to zero and set on an indicator, and then use this to condition the output. An easier method would be to create a new edit code description. You are allowed to define your own edit codes 5, 6, 7, 8, and 9. IBM supplies a definition for each of these codes, which must be deleted (DLTEDTD) before you are allowed to create a new one.

The following Create Edit Description command will create a new edit code description, "5" that will zero suppress the left-most digit and insert the "/"s. All blanks will print instead if the date is zero:

```
CRTEDTD EDTD(5) INTMASK(' / / ') DECPNT(*NONE) +
        FILLCHAR(*BLANK) ZEROBAL(*NO)
```

—Monica Zeno

Phone Number Edit Code

I have developed an edit code for phone numbers that displays, in this order, the area code in parentheses, a space, and the phone number with a hyphen in the middle: (123) 456-7890. The good thing about it is that missing phone numbers are displayed as blanks, not as (000) 000-0000. I assigned it to edit description 5 by using the Create Edit Description (CRTEDTD) command.

```
CRTEDTD EDTD(5) INTMASK('0  )   0    ') ZEROBAL(*NO) LFTCNS('(') +
        TEXT('''Phone number (area code in parentheses)')
```

Now, when you create a new display file field or printer file field and assign it to edit code 5, you'll get a perfectly edited telephone number.

—Michael Daly

✦ ✦ ✦ Files

Browse Source Command

Sometimes, I need to quickly browse a source member for a program, but I'm unable to recall the source file name that contains the source member. I solved this problem by creating the Display Source Member (DSPSRCMBR) command. DSPSRCMBR uses the Display Object Description (DSPOBJD) command to retrieve the source member's location from information found in the program object. The program then uses the browse mode in SEU to display the source member.

The source code for DSPSRCMBR is shown in Figure 7.4. The source code for the CPP, SRC013CL, is shown in Figure 7.5.

```
/*================================================================*/
/* To compile:                                                    */
/*                                                                */
/*          CRTCMD      CMD(XXX/DSPSRCMBR) PGM(XXX/SRC013CL) +     */
/*                      SRCFILE(XXX/QCMDSRC)                       */
/*                                                                */
/*================================================================*/
 DSPSRCMBR:  CMD         PROMPT('Display Source through SEU')

             PARM        KWD(PROGRAM) TYPE(PROGRAM) MIN(1) +
                         PROMPT('Program name')

 PROGRAM:    QUAL        TYPE(*NAME) LEN(10)
             QUAL        TYPE(*NAME) LEN(10) DFT(*LIBL) +
                         SPCVAL((*LIBL) (*CURLIB)) PROMPT('Library')
```

Figure 7.4: DSPSRCMBR finds a compiled program's source and displays it.

```
/*================================================================*/
/* To compile:                                                    */
/*                                                                */
/*           CRTCLPGM   PGM(XXX/SRC013CL) SRCFILE(XXX/QCLSRC)      */
/*                                                                */
/*================================================================*/
PGM          PARM(&QUALOBJ)

   DCL       VAR(&QUALOBJ) TYPE(*CHAR) LEN(20)
   DCL       VAR(&OBJ) TYPE(*CHAR) LEN(10)
   DCL       VAR(&OBJLIB) TYPE(*CHAR) LEN(10)
   DCL       VAR(&MSG) TYPE(*CHAR) LEN(80)
   DCLF      FILE(QADSPOBJ)

   MONMSG    MSGID(CPF0000)
   CHGVAR    VAR(&OBJ) VALUE(%SST(&QUALOBJ 1 10))
   CHGVAR    VAR(&OBJLIB) VALUE(%SST(&QUALOBJ 11 10))

   DSPOBJD   OBJ(&OBJLIB/&OBJ) OBJTYPE(*PGM) +
               DETAIL(*SERVICE) OUTPUT(*OUTFILE) +
               OUTFILE(QTEMP/QADSPOBJ)
   MONMSG    MSGID(CPF2105) EXEC(DO)
      CHGVAR    VAR(&MSG) VALUE('Object' *BCAT &OBJ *BCAT +
                  'in library' *BCAT &OBJLIB *BCAT 'not +
                  found or is not a program.')
      SNDPGMMSG  MSG(&MSG)
      RETURN
   ENDDO
   MONMSG    MSGID(CPF2110) EXEC(DO)
      CHGVAR    VAR(&MSG) VALUE('Library' *BCAT &OBJLIB +
                  *BCAT 'not found or invalid')
      SNDPGMMSG  MSG(&MSG)
      RETURN
   ENDDO
   MONMSG    MSGID(CPF9860) EXEC(DO)
      CHGVAR    VAR(&MSG) VALUE('Object' *BCAT &OBJ *BCAT +
                  'in library' *BCAT &OBJLIB *BCAT 'is in +
                  use at the moment - cannot retrieve.')
      SNDPGMMSG  MSG(&MSG)
      RETURN
   ENDDO

   OVRDBF    FILE(QADSPOBJ) TOFILE(QTEMP/QADSPOBJ)
   RCVF
   STRSEU    SRCFILE(&ODSRCL/&ODSRCF) SRCMBR(&ODSRCM) +
               OPTION(5)
   MONMSG    MSGID(EDT0000) EXEC(DO)
      CHGVAR    VAR(&MSG) VALUE('Source for' *BCAT &OBJLIB +
                  *TCAT '/' *CAT &OBJ *BCAT 'not found.')
   ENDDO
   DLTOVR    FILE(*ALL)
   CLOF      OPNID(QADSPOBJ)
ENDPGM:      ENDPGM
```

Figure 7.5: SRC013CL is the command-processing program for DSPSRCMBR.

— Midrange Computing Staff

Decimal Data Errors

To fix decimal data errors in a file (e.g., when migrating a S/36 file to native), use a simple program like the one shown in Figure 7.6. You'll need one such program for each physical file. *Note:* Compile this program with the IGNDECERR parameter set to *YES.

```
... 1 ...+... 2 ...+... 3 ...+... 4 ...+... 5 ...+
FFILE    UPE E                    DISK
C                     UPDATFILE
```

Figure 7.6: Using a short program like this one is an effective way to fix decimal data errors.

—*Eric Hill*

Faster Processing by Sequential Read

When processing a file in an RPG (or COBOL) program, it is more efficient to process it sequentially. So, if you don't need to process by keys, leave the 'K' out of column 31 in the F Specs. The first time I tried this, I saved 20 minutes off a 2-hour batch job.

—*Kristen Ball*

Finding a Record's Relative Record Number

I sometimes find that DFU is helpful when working with test data. If the file I want to modify is indexed and I know the key value, it is easy to retrieve the record for updating. With nonindexed files, however, DFU requires the record's relative record number to retrieve the record for updating.

The solution is to use the Display Physical File Member (DSPPFM) command to determine a record's relative record number. Here's how it works.

Use DSPPFM to display the file you're working with. Search for the record you want to modify with some kind of search criteria—such as a character string, a number, or even a hexadecimal value. When the record has been found, a message will appear at the bottom of the screen showing the relative record number. Use that number to retrieve the record with DFU.

—*Eugene Knight*

Finding Programs That Use a Specific File

Here's the method I use to locate the programs that use a specific file. About once a week, I run this command:

```
DSPPGMREF PGM(*ALLUSR/*ALL) +
    OUTPUT(*OUTFILE) OBJTYPE(*ALL) +
    OUTFILE(TESTLIBR/PGMFLXREF)
```

I keep the resulting cross-reference file in my testing library. When I need to know what programs use a file, I run Query/400 or SQL/400 queries against the cross-reference file, selecting for the file names I want. You can run the Display File Field Description (DSPFFD) command on the cross-reference file to find out the field names in the record.

—Sharon Cannon

Formatted Record Dumps

Here's a way to get a formatted dump of records in a physical or logical file. On any command line type the following:

```
CPYF LIBNAME/FILENAME TOFILE(*PRINT)
```

All records in the PF or LF are printed in CHAR format.

```
CPYF LIBNAME/FILENAME TOFILE(*PRINT) OUTFMT(*HEX)
```

All records in the PF or LF are printed in CHAR and HEX.

But wait....there's more! If you specify a LOGICAL file name, the records are printed in their logical access path order. I use this to help check for duplicate keys. Because all the select/option parameters of CPYF apply, you don't have to print all records if the file is very large.

—Cynthy Johnson

Refreshing Test Data

In the course of running stress tests on an application, I found it useful to create a PDM user-defined option to repopulate my database. The user option allows you to restore the records in a database without having to rewind a tape, restore objects, or be concerned with database authority differences from one system to another. This technique assumes that you have one library containing production data and another containing test data, and that these libraries contain the same files.

By using the Copy File (CPYF) command in a PDM user-defined option, you can type the user option next to each file in the production library you wish to copy on the Work with Objects using the PDM (WRKOBJPDM) screen. Once you press Enter, the CPYF command copies all of the selected files to the destination you specify in the CPYF command. If there is a lock on a file or there aren't any records to copy, a message appears at the bottom of the screen. Once you've resolved any problems, you can press Enter again to resume the process.

Creating the PDM user-defined option is simple. At a command line, type WRKOBJPDM. Press F16 to get the Work with User-Defined Options menu. Press F6 to create a user-defined option.

On the Create User-Defined Option screen, type CF for the option name and the following for the command parameter:

```
CPYF FROMFILE(&L/&N) TOFILE(to-library/&N) MBROPT(*REPLACE)
```

Replace the name of your test library in the TOFILE parameter and press Enter. Then run the WRKOBJPDM command against your production library and use option CF to copy the data to the files in the hard-coded to-library.

—*Eugene Knight*

Some Changes Don't Require a Recompile

You've just made a minor change to your display file. Now you must recompile all the programs that use it to avoid getting level-check errors. Right? Or do you?

The system assigns a unique level identifier to each record format when the display file is created. When you compile a program that uses the file, the compiler includes the format-level identifiers in the compiled program.

Use the Display File Description (DSPFD) command to display the record format-level identifiers for the file. Use the Display Program References (DSPPGMREF) command to display the record format level identifiers that were used when the program was created.

If they are the same, you do not need to recompile the program to avoid a level-check error. Only changes to the following will affect the record format-level identifier:

- Record format name.
- Field names.
- Length of the record format.
- Number of fields in the record format.
- Field attributes such as length and decimal positions.
- The order of the fields in the record format.

You can change field attributes such as highlight, underline, reverse image, and colors without recompiling programs. Constants such as headings or labels can be added, changed, or deleted.

The screen locations of fields and constants can be changed as long as the order of the fields or length of the record format is not changed. This means that you can change the location and order of fields on the screen as long as you don't change their order in the DDS source member for the display file.

—Christopher Andrle

Use UPDDTA to Create Permanent DFU Programs

You can use the Update Data (UPDDTA) command to quickly generate DFU programs for files. You can bypass the start-up time involved with each use by saving and reusing the generated program.

1. Use the SETATNPGM command to set the Attention Key program to QCMD.

2. Run UPDDTA for the file.

3. As soon as you get into DFU, press the ATTN key.

4. Display QTEMP library. There will be a program and display file with names beginning with a 'Q' (like QDZTD00001). Do a Create Duplicate Objects (CRTDUPOBJ) command for the file and the program, duplicating and renaming them into a library of your choice. The name of the program and the display file must be the same.

5. In the future, use the Change Data (CHGDTA) command, substituting the name of the program from step 4.

—Craig Pelkie

What Programs Use a File?

The following procedure provides a cross-reference of all programs that use certain file(s). Initially, perform the following two steps:

1. Create a CL program that contains the following command:

```
DSPPGMREF PGM(Yourlib/*ALL) OUTPUT(*OUTFILE) +
          OUTFILE(Yourlib/Youroutfile)
```

(After initially running this program, add a statement to clear your outfile immediately before the DSPPGMREF command.)

2. Create a query over your outfile.

Each time you need a cross-reference listing, perform the following three steps:

1. Call the CL program.

2. Run the DSPDBR command on the physical file(s) you are interested in to determine the names of all dependent logical files.

3. Modify the query to select records for the physical as well as the logical files and then run the query.

—Lois Reed

✦ ✦ ✦ PDM

How to Avoid Losing Overrides in PDM

Q: A colleague of mine complained that he loses his overrides during a PDM session if he accidentally presses Enter at the Work with Members screen in a source physical file such as QRPGSRC.

A: I understand his frustration, but this is a simple problem to solve. You simply press F18 in the Work with Members screen to change your options. If you roll to the next screen, you will find the option "Exit Lists on ENTER." This defaults to "Y."

If you change this to "N," the Work with Members screen will not terminate when you press Enter. To exit the Work with Members screen, you have to press F3 or F12.

—Bret Myrick, Sr.

Making OS/400 Commands Work Generically

Some OS/400 commands will process only one object at a time. For example, Change Object Owner (CHGOBJOWN) and Change Physical File (CHGPF) are examples of commands that accept the name of only a single object. You can't specify *ALL or even a generic value. However, when you want to process a generic list of values using one of these commands, you can—easily. Just use PDM to create a user-defined option. You can get to PDM's user-defined options by running the Start PDM (STRPDM) command and selecting option 9 (Work with user-defined options).

For example, suppose you want to change the owner of every program in a library. You could start by creating a PDM user-defined option called CO (for Change Owner) that looks like this:

```
CHGOBJOWN OBJ(&L/&N) OBJTYPE(&T)
```

In this case, **&L**, **&N**, and **&T** are substitution parameters that are replaced when the option is used against an entry in a PDM list. When working with objects, **&L** is replaced by the name of the library that contains the object, **&N** is replaced by the name of the object, and **&T** is replaced by the object type.

This allows you to change all of the programs in a library by running the Work with Objects Using PDM (WRKOBJPDM) command, as shown:

```
WRKOBJPDM LIB(MYLIB) OBJ(*ALL) OBJTYPE(*PGM)
```

This command displays a list of all programs in library MYLIB. Now, all you have to do is type CO next to the first program and press F13 to repeat the option to the end of the list. Then, on the command line at the bottom of the screen, enter the NEWOWN keyword followed by the name of the owner in parentheses. For example, you could specify NEWOWN(QPGMR) to change the owner to QPGMR. When you press Enter, all of the programs are changed at once.

This technique allows you to make OS/400 commands run against a generic list of libraries, objects, or members—even if they weren't specifically designed to do so.

—Robin Klima

Run Confirmation Window in PDM

In my shop, many people—operators as well as programmers—have access to PDM. I wanted to have a warning come up any time someone tried to use the user-defined option 'C' to call a program from PDM. I came up with a pop-up window that overlays the PDM screen and asks the users to confirm that they want to run the program.

I replaced the user-defined option 'C', which resides in the QAUOOPT file, with a call to my command, CALLPGM (see Figure 7.7). I passed the library (&L) and object name (&N) supplied by PDM. The Command Processing Program (CPP) for the command is PGM006CL (see Figure 7.8).

Display file PGM006DF (see Figure 7.9) uses the ASSUME and PUTOVR keywords and is compiled with the USRDSP option set to *YES. The window overlays the screen without erasing it. The option defaults to 'N' so that accidentally hitting the Enter key won't start the program. I display the library and the object name in the window so that the users know exactly what program they are trying to run.

While this program doesn't prevent someone from accidentally running a dangerous program, it helps to confirm choices and slows down the user .

```
/*===============================================================*/
/* To compile:                                                   */
/*                                                               */
/*          CRTCMD     CMD(XXX/CALLPGM) PGM(XXX/PGM006CL) +       */
/*                     SRCFILE(XXX/QCMDSRC)                       */
/*                                                               */
/*===============================================================*/
 CALLPGM:   CMD        PROMPT('Call Program')

            PARM       KWD(PGMNAME) TYPE(QUAL) PROMPT('Program name')
 QUAL:      QUAL       TYPE(*NAME) LEN(10) MIN(1)
            QUAL       TYPE(*NAME) LEN(10) DFT(*LIBL) +
                       SPCVAL((*LIBL)) PROMPT('Library')
```

Figure 7.7: The CALLPGM command prevents accidental program activation.

```
/*================================================================*/
/* To compile:                                                    */
/*                                                                */
/*          CRTCLPGM    PGM(XXX/PGM006CL) SRCFILE(XXX/QCLSRC)      */
/*                                                                */
/*================================================================*/
PGM005CL:   PGM         PARM(&QNAME)

            DCL         VAR(&QNAME) TYPE(*CHAR) LEN(20)
            DCL         VAR(&LIB) TYPE(*CHAR) LEN(10)
            DCL         VAR(&NAME) TYPE(*CHAR) LEN(10)
            DCL         VAR(&DEV) TYPE(*CHAR) LEN(10)
            DCLF        FILE(PGM006DF)

            CHGVAR      VAR(&NAME) VALUE(%SST(&QNAME 1 10))
            CHGVAR      VAR(&LIB)  VALUE(%SST(&QNAME 11 10))
            RTVJOBA     JOB(&DEV)
            CHGVAR      VAR(&DRSPNC) VALUE('N')

            SNDRCVF     DEV(&DEV) RCDFMT(SCRWIN) WAIT(*YES)

            IF          COND(&IN12 *EQ '1') THEN(GOTO CMDLBL(ENDPGM))
            IF          COND(&DRSPNC *EQ 'Y') THEN(DO)
            CALL        PGM(&LIB/&NAME)
            MONMSG      MSGID(CPF0000) EXEC(DO)
            SNDBRKMSG   MSG('Program could not execute properly') +
                          TOMSGQ(&DEV)

            ENDDO
            ENDDO

ENDPGM:     ENDPGM
```

Figure 7.8: CPP CL Program PGM006CL is CALLPGM's command processing program.

```
 *================================================================
 * To compile:
 *
 *          CRTDSPF    FILE(XXX/PGM006DF) SRCFILE(XXX/QDDSSRC)
 *
 *================================================================
 *. 1 ...+... 2 ...+... 3 ...+... 4 ...+... 5 ...+... 6 ...+... 7
 A                                         DSPSIZ(24 80 *DS3)
 A                                         CA12(12)
 A          R DUMMY
 A                                         PUTOVR
 A                                         ASSUME
 A                                1 2' '
 A          R SCRWIN
 A                                         WINDOW(7 40 7 20)
 A                                         OVERLAY
 A                                         WDWBORDER((*COLOR WHT))
 A                                         WDWBORDER((*DSPATR RI))
```

Figure 7.9: Display file PGM006DF prompts the user for confirmation (part 1 of 2).

```
A                                         WDWBORDER((*CHAR '         '))
A                                   2  3'Confirm you want'
A                                   3  8'to run:'
A             NAME        10A  O    4  6COLOR(WHT)
A                                   5  3'(Y = Yes, N = No)'
A             DRSPNC       1A  B    6 11
```

Figure 7.9: Display file PGM006DF prompts the user for confirmation (part 2 of 2).

—Michael Veit

Scanning with PDM

Perhaps you have discovered PDM option 25, which lets you find a string in a file. Have you wondered if you can perform the scanning process without having to go through the PDM displays?

There is a way. Simply run the Find String with PDM (FNDSTRPDM) command. When you prompt this command, you will see that you have much more flexibility than you get when you use option 25. For instance, you can indicate that all members be scanned or provide generic member names (having the asterisk at either or both ends, or in the middle).

For instance, suppose you have just inserted a field in database file FILEA and consequently need to change all the RPG programs that use that file. As the command in Figure 7.10 shows, nothing could be simpler.

```
FNDSTRPDM STRING('FILEA') FILE(MYLIB/QRPGSRC) +
    MBR(*ALL) OPTION(*CMPL) COL(7 11) +
    PRTMBRLIST(*YES) PARM('REPLACE(*YES)')
```

Figure 7.10: FNDSTRPDM searches for strings in source members.

This command will scan for string 'FILEA' in file MYLIB/QRPGSRC in all members. The search is to be made between columns 7 and 11. When found, the system will automatically compile it with REPLACE(*YES), and at the same time will print a list of all the members where 'FILEA' was found.

Now get this. You can submit this command to batch processing by simply including that command string in the SBMJOB command! While the SBMJOB command is a powerful command that will no doubt make your programmers' lives easier, there is a little problem in the documentation. Although the help text and the PDM manual claim that the MBR parameter can have all sorts of wonderful generic names (X*, *X, *X*, X*Y), only the "X*" format actually works; the others require you to enclose the generic name in single quotes.

—Midrange Computing Staff

✦ ✦ ✦ Performance

Evaluating Sluggish Program with the PAG

If your programs seem to be either running poorly or hurting general system performance, consider using the Display Access Group (DSPACCGRP) command to take a quick look at the program's Process Access Group (PAG). The size of the PAG affects memory utilization, which in turn affects program and system performance.

DSPACCGRP shows the size of the PAG, the names and I/O counts for all open files, and the program data storage used. This information can be shown on the screen for an individual job. It can be printed to printer file QPPTPAGD or output to a database file for one or more selected jobs. Jobs can be selected for analysis using job type, job name, user name, and job number.

You can either type in the command or use option 5 from the IBM Performance Tools/400 menu to access the Performance Utilities menu. From this menu, option 3 brings you to the Select File and Access Group Utilities menu, where option 4 brings up the DSPACCGRP command.

If you display more than one job, it will be printed, not displayed on the screen. This command gives you a quick synopsis of the job statistics. You can specify *PRINT, *FILE, or *BOTH on the Output Type parameter. *BOTH will write the data to a file as well as display or print the data, depending on how many jobs are being analyzed.

I've found that this is a nice command to quickly take a look at programs that are having performance problems. After you trace a problem to a specific program, you can use the other performance tools to drill down to find the exact cause of the problem. The DSPACCGRP command takes few resources to run, yet it can quickly let you see the vitally important PAG size, open files, and I/O performance—all of which could be adversely affecting job performance.

—D. Ellis Green

✦ ✦ ✦ Programming Practices

Activate the Attn Key in Attention Programs

If you configure a program such as the Command Entry screen (QCMD) or the Command Line window (QUSCMDLN) as your attention program, you're able to enter a command when you press the Attn key. When you return from having entered a command and exit the command line, you end up right back where you were before you pressed the Attn key.

The only problem with using an attention program such as QCMD or QUSCMDLN is that, once you press the Attn key, it's deactivated until you return to where you were before you pressed it. For example, consider the following sequence of events:

1. You press the Attn key, which takes you to a command line.

2. At the command line, you enter a command that takes you to some other screen.

3. At that point, you press the Attn key, but nothing happens.

This situation might seem frustrating, but there is a solution. Compile the program shown in Figure 7.11 and set it as your attention program with the Set Attention Program (SETATNPGM) command.

```
/*=============================================*/
/* TO COMPILE:                                 */
/*                                             */
/* CRTCLPGM PGM(XXX/CMDLINE) SRCFILE(XXX/QCLSRC) */
/*                                             */
/*=============================================*/
PGM
    SETATNPGM PGM(CMDLINE)
    CALL PGM(QUSCMDLN)
ENDPGM
```

Figure 7.11: CL Program CMDLINE activates the attention key within an attention key program.

This program works by setting the attention program to itself and then calling the Command Line window (QUSCMDLN) API. (You can change this CALL statement with whatever program you want your attention key to call.) Using this technique, you can repeatedly use your Attn key (even when your attention program is already active).

—Robin Klima

Automatic Current Library

The library list can hold a maximum of 42 library names. Of these, 15 reside in the system portion of the library list and 25 in the user portion. The remaining two are the current library and the product library. Programmers often attempt to cram into the library list the name of every library that could possibly be used, resulting in a lot of unnecessary clutter. Fortunately, that's rarely necessary.

If you develop your applications with a menu or command interface, you can take advantage of OS/400's support for automatic current libraries. You simply specify a library name in the CURLIB parameter when creating or changing the menu or command. For instance, suppose you create a menu for accounts receivable (AR) tasks, and all your programming support for AR is in library ARLIB. The main menu for your AR application could be created as follows:

```
CRTMNU MNU(ARLIB/ARMAIN) CURLIB(ARLIB)
```

Every time a user invokes the menu (typically, with the GO command), OS/400 automatically changes the current library to ARLIB. So, ARLIB becomes available through the library list, even if it wasn't there before. It's a trick worth remembering.

—Ernie Malaga

CHGPGM Ignores Authority Parameters

Be careful when you use the Change Program (CHGPGM) command. A client of mine has used it extensively to set the adopted authority to *OWNER. Using CHGPGM to change the characteristics of a program when that program is executing can lead to undesirable results. CHGPGM apparently recreates an internal pointer to the program, effectively removing it from the stack of any executing jobs and leading to a crash.

—Van C. Baker

Determining When to Update a File

Programmers often need to determine when a user has made a change to a screen so that the data in a file can be updated. A commonly used technique is to create two data structures. One structure contains all the screen fields and the other contains all the file fields. If the two data structures differ, then the file needs to be updated. However, if you have a complex screen, it is cumbersome to keep track of the start and stop positions on the I-specs and to describe so many fields. There's an easier way to accomplish the same task. An example of this technique is shown in Figure 7.12.

```
FFILE    UF  E              K        DISK
FSCREEN  CF  E                       WORKSTN
 * Externally described data structure will be the entire record.
IRECORD     E DSFILE
 * Internal data structure to save the incoming data.
IREC        DS                       299
 * Display the screen
C                       EXFMTSCREENFM
 * Retrieve a record from the file
C           SCCUST      CHAINFILE                90
C           *IN90       IFEQ *OFF
 * The successful chain fills the external data structure with
 * a copy of the file data. Copy this to the internal data
 * structure.
C                       MOVELRECORD    REC
 * At this point both data structures are identical.
 * Move file data to screen fields.
C                       MOVE MCCUST    SCCUST
C                       MOVE MCADDR    SCADDR
 * Display the screen
C                       EXFMTSCREENFM
 *Move screen fields back to file fields.
 * This will update the externally described data structure.
C                       MOVE SCCUST    MCCUST
C                       MOVE SCADDR    MCADDR
 * Compare the two data structures. If not equal then something
 * has changed on the screen and you need to update the file.
C           RECORD      IFNE REC
C                       UPDATFILEREC
C                       ELSE
C                       UNLCKFILE
C                       ENDIF
C                       ENDIF
 *
C                       MOVE *ON       *INLR
```

Figure 7.12: You might improve performance by not updating records if data has not changed.

Here's how it works.

1. Create an externally described data structure that refers to your physical file.

2. Create an internal data structure in which to move a copy of the first data structure but, instead of describing each field in the file, describe only one dummy field that is as long as the whole file record.

3. Retrieve your file information. When you retrieve it, the external data structure automatically becomes filled with the file data. Move that data structure to the internal one and save it.

4. Move the file data to the screen fields and display the screen. When the Enter key is pressed, move the screen fields back to the file fields. This updates the external data structure.

5. Compare the two data structures. If they differ, the user made a change and you need to update the file. If they are the same, then unlock the record.

The beauty of this method is that there are so few lines of code to deal with.

—Lee Marcus

Hard-coded Library Names Are Bad News

Some commands such as Create Duplicate Object (CRTDUPOBJ) require a library name, but hard-coding a library name in a CL program is not a good practice. A better method is to use the RTNLIB parameter of the RTVOBJD command to retrieve the library name. For example, suppose you want to create a duplicate object of a file called WKFILE into QTEMP, then call an RPG program. You could use the program shown in Figure 7.13.

```
PGM

    DCL VAR(&LIB) TYPE(*CHAR) LEN(10)

    RTVOBJD OBJ(WKFILE) OBJTYPE(*FILE) RTNLIB(&LIB)
    CRTDUPOBJ OBJ(WKFILE) FROMLIB(&LIB) +
               OBJTYPE(*FILE) TOLIB(QTEMP)
    OVRDBF FILE(WKFILE) TOFILE(QTEMP/WKFILE)
    CALL PGM(RPG001)

ENDPGM
```

Figure 7.13: Using RTVOBJD and RTNLIB to avoid a hard-coded library name.

This program could be run in a test library. Then the program and file could be moved to a production library without any changes. The library where the file exists could even be renamed without affecting the program.

—Robin Klima

How Y2K Made Me a Better Programmer

Having written a tool that analyzes and modifies RPG code, I have learned some valuable lessons from the Y2K challenge:

- "Sneaky" code is bad. The less intuitive a piece of code is the more likely someone or something else is to break it.

- Hard-coded library names are absolutely horrible, and any program that plays with the library list had better have a darn good reason to do so. If you need to test a job stream and some part of the stream does library-list manipulation, you are in serious trouble.

- Cross-library logicals are the single most difficult thing to manage on the AS/400. When a logical and its physical reside in the same library, there is magic that is not present when the two reside in different libraries, and this shows up in save/restore and duplication. Trust me; this is seriously bad mojo.

- "Special values" in fields are bad. If a field is a date field and you need to specify "no date," you should try to have a second field specify whether or not the first field contains a date. While not always practical, it should be a goal.

- Never, ever trust that the source matches the object. When in doubt, recompile.

—Joe Pluta

One Source File Only

Use a single source file for all the source code for a library or a development project, rather than separate source files for each member type. This keeps you from needing to jump around in different files with PDM.

—Greg Prior

Optimize Your Programs

After developing and testing your new or updated programs, make it a habit to optimize them before putting them into the production environment. The optimization process will usually result in a leaner and more efficient program. Some programs can be created with optimization with the option GENOPT(*OPTIMIZE) but, because it takes longer to compile optimized programs, it is usually best to wait until the program is ready for production.

To change existing programs, use the Change Program (CHGPGM) command with the OPTIMIZE(*YES) parameter. If you specify the program name and prompt the CHGPGM command, you can see if the program is already optimized. The Display Program (DSPPGM) command will also show if the program is optimized. Note that the program will need to be recreated before being optimized if observability has been removed.

There are special considerations when using the option on ILE programs. *BASIC can be specified instead of *YES on the OPTIMIZE parameter, and it will perform some optimizations.

If any optimization level other than *NO or *NONE is specified for ILE programs, program variables might not be current when displayed during debug sessions.

I have set up a user-defined option in PDM to do the optimization so that I can put OP next to the program to be optimized. Just add the following command for the option OP:

```
CHGPGM &L/&N OPTIMIZE(*YES)
```

—Paul Jackson

Packed Data Tip

The AS/400 works internally with numbers in packed-numeric format. This is the opposite of the System/36, where numbers are handled internally in zoned-decimal format. Consequently, it is much more efficient to define your file's fields in the AS/400 default format, packed numeric data. If you do not, extra instructions must be processed whenever a zoned-decimal field is encountered by a program. The zoned-decimal field must be internally converted to a packed-numeric format before the system can do anything with it.

But there is another consideration aside from the definition of fields in your in your files. This relates to fields that are defined in a program, such as calculation work fields, arrays, and the like. Because only numbers with an odd number of digits fit neatly into a packed-numeric field, a numeric field that is defined with an even number of digits will result in extra instructions being generated to keep track of the unused high-order digit.

—Mark Grant

Product Library Cuts Code

There are times when you need your library to be first in the library list when a command runs.

You can write some code that removes your library from the library list. (Monitor for an error if it's not already in there.) Then add your library to the top of the library list. At the end of the program, reset the library list to the order it had when the program started.

Or you can write no code. The Product Library (PRDLIB) parameter on the Create Command (CRTCMD) or Change Command (CHGCMD) commands allows you to specify a single library that goes at the top of the library list. The only libraries that will end up higher on the list are the libraries in system value QSYSLIBL. When the command is complete, the library is automatically removed, even if the user does an end request from the system request menu. For example:

```
CHGCMD(MYLIB/MYCMD) PRDLIB(MYLIB)
```

—Jim Hoopes

Reducing Disk Access

Often, it is possible to substantially decrease the amount of disk access in a program (and hence speed it up) by storing information from records that have already been read. For example, a program might need to access item-type information for each product when processing the item master file. Instead of chaining to the item-type file for each record in the master file (as shown in Figure 7.14), use arrays to store the information already obtained. See Figure 7.15. The next time item-type details are required, a check is made to see whether the information has already been read. If the information has not been read, it is then read from disk and added to the arrays.

This technique is only suitable when obtaining details from files that are modified infrequently. It should not be used if the information that is being retrieved is being updated regularly and the program requires the latest information.

```
C              ITTYPE     CHAINITEMTYPE          50
```

Figure 7.14: Chaining for each record could cause unnecessary I/O.

```
*. 1 .. + .. 2 .. + .. 3 .. + .. 4 .. + .. 5 .. + .. 6
E                   ITKY      20 2   ITDT     30
C         GETTYP    BEGSR
 *                                             HiLoEq
C                   Z-ADD1         X        50
C         ITTYPE    LOKUPITKY,X                    50
C         *IN50     IFEQ *ON
C                   MOVELITDT,X    TYDATA
C                   ELSE
C         ITTYPE    CHAINITEMTYPE            50
C         *IN50     IFEQ *OFF
C         *BLANKS   LOKUPITKY,X                    50
C         *IN50     IFEQ *ON
C                   MOVE ITTYPE    ITKY,X
C                   MOVE TYDATA    ITDT,X
C                   ENDIF
C                   ENDIF
C                   ENDIF
 *
C                   ENDSR
```

Figure 7.15: Using arrays to reduce chains could improve execution speed.

—Stephen J. Corbett

Retrieve ILE Source Code

If you're used to using Retrieve CL Source (RTVCLSRC) to retrieve the source for Original Program Model (OPM) CL programs and you've tried it on ILE CL modules, you've found that it doesn't work for this new object type. It's true that RTVCLSRC works only with OPM CL programs. However, you can get the source for ILE CL modules. If you have created the module with the DBGVIEW parameter value of *ALL or *LIST, you can retrieve the source by starting a debug and manually copying the lines.

—David Morris

Editor's Note: *This technique works for all ILE languages, not just CL.*

Terminating Called Programs

It is extremely important to terminate called programs properly. Failure to terminate a called program properly can cause damage to production data if you think you're using test data to test program modifications.

Suppose your production library list consists of production data files (PRODF) and production programs (PRODP). Now, suppose your test library list consists of test data files (TESTF), programs in testing (TESTP), and production programs (PRODP). PRODP contains only executable programs, print files, and display files. This way, duplicates of these objects do not need to be kept in the test libraries.

TESTP contains only programs that are actually in testing. Many shops use similar library list structures. Here's how damage can occur:

- You execute PRODP/PGMA. This program calls PRODP/PGMB, which opens PRODF/FILE1. Then, PGMB terminates with a RETRN statement. Control is returned to PGMA, but PGMB remains resident and PRODF/FILE1 remains open.

- You terminate PRODP/PGMA and set up your test library list to test modifications to PGMA. PGMB has not been modified.

- You call TESTP/PGMA, which calls PGMB. Because PGMB is not in testing, PRODP/PGMB is called. But PRODP/PGMB is already resident, and its files are open. Therefore, your test affects PRODF/FILE1. You've compromised your production data, thinking you were in your test environment.

To prevent this problem, make PGMA pass a parameter telling PGMB to set on its LR indicator. This method might not be practical if this error is widespread throughout your software (as is the case with some commercially available software packages).

Another solution is to execute the Reclaim Resource (RCLRSC) command in the CL program that calls PGMA. This technique disposes of stray resident programs and closes the files associated with them.

If you use CL programs to set up your library list, a simple solution is to put the RCLRSC command at the beginning of those programs. Any stray programs left over from production processing will be cleaned up before you start testing and vice versa.

—Sam Stafford

✦ ✦ ✦ Programming Support

Checking the Program Stack

Program A can call program B and at the same time pass data as parameters. While program B is running, it can call program C. At this point, there are three programs in your program stack: A, B, and C. This process can continue indefinitely, calling program after program and never returning to the caller.

There is a problem, however. In some HLLs such as RPG, program C cannot call program B or A (which is already in the program stack) because doing so would create an infinite loop of programs calling one another. Adding insult to injury, OS/400 has no built-in function that will let you determine, before calling program *X*, whether program *X* is already in the stack. You must call the program and hope for the best.

Enter the Check Program Stack (CHKPGMSTK) command . This command (Figures 7.16 and 7.17) accepts a program name as a parameter and returns a character value '**Y**' if the program is in your program stack, or '**N**' if it isn't.

```
CHKPGMSTK: CMD PROMPT('Check Program Stack')
PARM KWD(PGM) TYPE(*SNAME) LEN(10) MIN(1) +
      PROMPT('Program name')
PARM KWD(RTNCDE) TYPE(*CHAR) LEN(1) RTNVAL(*YES) +
      CHOICE('''Y'' or ''N''') PROMPT('Return +
      code (CHAR(1))')
```

Figure 7.16: Command CHKPGMSTK looks for a certain program in the call stack.

```
PGM001CL: +
  PGM PARM(&PGM &RTNCDE)

  DCL VAR(&PGM) TYPE(*CHAR) LEN(10)
  DCL VAR(&RTNCDE) TYPE(*CHAR) LEN(1)
  DCL VAR(&MSGKEY) TYPE(*CHAR) LEN(4)
  CHGVAR VAR(&RTNCDE) VALUE('Y')
  SNDPGMMSG MSG(TEST) TOPGMQ(*SAME &PGM) +
     MSGTYPE(*INFO) KEYVAR(&MSGKEY)
  MONMSG MSGID(CPF2479 CPF2469) EXEC(DO)
     CHGVAR VAR(&RTNCDE) VALUE('N')
  ENDDO
  IF COND(&RTNCDE *EQ 'Y') THEN(DO)
     RMVMSG PGMQ(*SAME &PGM) MSGKEY(&MSGKEY) +
        CLEAR(*BYKEY)
  ENDDO

ENDPGM
```

Figure 7.17: CL program PGM001CL is the command-processing program for CHKPGMSTK.

This is accomplished with the SNDPGMMSG command. Because the SNDPGMMSG command attempts to send a message to the program that you named, SNDPGMMSG will fail if the program is not in your program stack. If SNDPGMMSG is successful, the message just sent is removed, "just in case."

To solve your problem, therefore, you could call the processing program for CHKPGMSTK (program PGM001CL) from your RPG program. See Figure 7.18.

```
CALL 'PGM001CL'
PARM 'PGMX'    PGMNAM 10
PARM           RTNCDE  1
```

Figure 7.18: Checking for a program already in the stack requires only a simple CALL.

If RTNCDE has 'Y' you can't call program PGMX from your RPG program.

—*Ernie Malaga*

Comparing Objects Against Source

This utility produces a report about the objects in a library. It checks all commands, programs, and files. It looks at the date/time of the source used to create the object, and then checks if the source member has been changed since then. A report is printed, showing the results.

This helps to identify which objects do not have source or have source with a different date/time. Both situations are a problem. The utility consists of command Compare Objects and Source (CMPOBJSRC) in Figure 7.19, two CL programs (OBJ006CL and OBJ006CLA, in Figures 7.20 and 7.21), and an RPG program (OBJ006RG, Figure 7.22).

```
CMPOBJSRC:  CMD     PROMPT('Compare Object and Source')
            PARM    KWD(OBJ) TYPE(NAME1) MIN(1) PROMPT('Objects')
            PARM    KWD(ERRONLY) TYPE(*CHAR) LEN(4) RSTD(*YES) +
                      DFT(*YES) VALUES(*YES *NO) PROMPT('Print +
                      errors only')
NAME1:      QUAL    TYPE(*GENERIC) LEN(10) SPCVAL((*ALL)) MIN(1)
            QUAL    TYPE(*NAME) LEN(10) SPCVAL((*LIBL) +
                      (*USRLIBL) (*CURLIB) (*ALL) (*ALLUSR)) +
                      MIN(1) PROMPT('Library')
```

Figure 7.19: Command CMPOBJSRC looks for source-object mismatches.

```
PGM          PARM(&OBJ &ERRONLY)
  DCL        VAR(&OBJ) TYPE(*CHAR) LEN(20)
  DCL        VAR(&LIBRARY) TYPE(*CHAR) LEN(10)
  DCL        VAR(&SCANOBJ) TYPE(*CHAR) LEN(10)
  DCL        VAR(&ERRONLY) TYPE(*CHAR) LEN(4)
  /* Split qualified name */
  CHGVAR     VAR(&SCANOBJ) VALUE(%SST(&OBJ 1 10))
  CHGVAR     VAR(&LIBRARY) VALUE(%SST(&OBJ 11 10))
  /* Run DSPOBJD for requested objects */
  DSPOBJD    OBJ(&LIBRARY/&SCANOBJ) OBJTYPE(*PGM *FILE +
               *CMD) OUTPUT(*OUTFILE) OUTFILE(QTEMP/DSPOBJD)
  MONMSG     MSGID(CPF2123) EXEC(DO)
    SNDPGMMSG  MSG('No objects were selected. Report not +
               executed.') MSGTYPE(*DIAG)
    SNDPGMMSG  MSGID(CPF0002) MSGF(QCPFMSG) MSGTYPE(*ESCAPE)
    GOTO       CMDLBL(ENDPGM)
  ENDDO
  /* Read object description and produce report */
  OVRDBF     FILE(QADSPOBJ) TOFILE(QTEMP/DSPOBJD)
  CALL       PGM(OBJ006RG) PARM(&ERRONLY)
  DLTOVR     FILE(*ALL)
  /* Delete work file */
  DLTF       FILE(QTEMP/DSPOBJD)
  /* End program */
ENDPGM:
ENDPGM
```

Figure 7.20: CL program OBJ006CL is the command-processing program for CMPOBJSRC.

```
PGM          PARM(&LIBRARY &FILE &MEMBER &SRCCHGDATE)
  DCL        VAR(&LIBRARY) TYPE(*CHAR) LEN(10)
  DCL        VAR(&FILE) TYPE(*CHAR) LEN(10)
  DCL        VAR(&MEMBER) TYPE(*CHAR) LEN(10)
  DCL        VAR(&SRCCHGDATE) TYPE(*CHAR) LEN(13)
  RTVMBRD    FILE(&LIBRARY/&FILE) MBR(&MEMBER) +
               SRCCHGDATE(&SRCCHGDATE)
  MONMSG     MSGID(CPF9810 CPF9812 CPF9815) EXEC(CHGVAR +
               VAR(&SRCCHGDATE) VALUE(' '))
ENDPGM
```

Figure 7.21: CL program OBJ006CLA retrieves the timestamp of a source member.

```
FQADSPOBJIP  E                   DISK
FQPRINT  O   F      132    OA    PRINTER
*
I                  'OBJ006CLA'            C         PGM1
I                  'Missing source'       C         MSG1
I                  'Different date/time'  C         MSG2
*
I            DS
I                                         1  13 MBRCHG
I                                         2   7 MBRDAT
I                                         8  13 MBRTIM
I            DS
I                                         1  13 OBJCHG
I                                         1   1 ODSRCC
I                                         2   7 ODSRCD
I                                         8  13 ODSRCT
*
* Parameter is whether to print errors only (*YES, *NO)
C            *ENTRY    PLIST
C                      PARM           OPTION  4
*
C            ODSRCM    IFNE *BLANK
* Format object name for printing
C                      CLEAROBJECT
C            ODLBNM    CAT  '/':0     OBJECT 21
C            OBJECT    CAT  ODOBNM:0  OBJECT
* Format source member name for printing
C                      CLEARSRCMBR
C            ODSRCL    CAT  '/':0     SRCMBR 32
C            SRCMBR    CAT  ODSRCF:0  SRCMBR
C            SRCMBR    CAT  '/':0     SRCMBR
C            SRCMBR    CAT  ODSRCM:0  SRCMBR
* Get last date/time changed for source used to create object
C                      CALL PGM1
C                      PARM           ODSRCL
C                      PARM           ODSRCF
C                      PARM           ODSRCM
C                      PARM           MBRCHG
* Check for errors
C                      CLEARMESSAG
C            MBRCHG    IFEQ *BLANK
C                      MOVELMSG1      MESSAG 24
C                      ELSE
C            MBRCHG    IFNE OBJCHG
C                      MOVELMSG2      MESSAG
C                      END
C                      END
* Print
C            OPTION    IFEQ '*NO'
C            MESSAG    ORNE *BLANK
C                      EXCPTPRINT
C                      END
C                      END
* Before first cycle: get system date and time
```

Figure 7.22: RPG program OBJ006RG builds a report of compiled objects and source-code information (part 1 of 2).

```
C              *INZSR    BEGSR
C                        TIME           SYS    120
C                        MOVELSYS       SYSTIM  60
C                        MOVE SYS       SYSDAT  60
C                        ENDSR
    *
OQPRINT  H  202   OA
O           OR         1P
O                        SYSDATY    8
O                        SYSTIM    18 '0  :  :  '
O                                  69 'INTEGRITY OF SOURCE USED'
O                                  87 'TO CREATE OBJECTS'
O                                 127 'CMPOBJSRC - Page'
O                        PAGE   3 132
O        H  0    OA
O           OR         1P
O                                   6 'Object'
O                                  55 'Source Member'
O                                  84 'Comments'
O        H  2    OA
O           OR         1P
O                                   6 '_____'
O                                  55 '_____'
O                                  84 '_____'
O        EF 1          PRINT
O                        OBJECT    21
O                        ODOBTP    30
O                        ODOBAT    41
O                        SRCMBR    74
O                        MESSAG   100
O        TF 1    LR
O                                + 10 '** END OF REPORT **'
```

Figure 7.22: RPG program OBJ006RG builds a report of compiled objects and source-code information (part 2 of 2).

—*Rex M. Oliva*

Find the Hex Representation of a Character

Here are a couple of ways you can find the hex value of a character:

1. From a sign-on screen of a dumb terminal, press Alt Test. Choose option 1 (Display verification), and then option 2 (Displayable characters). This shows a table of all displayable characters.

2. Create a 1-byte character data area in QTEMP, specifying the character whose hex value you want to know as the initial value. Then display the data area in hex. For example, if you want to know the hex value of an apostrophe, use code like that shown in Figure 7.23.

```
CRTDTAARA DTAARA(QTEMP/XYZ) TYPE(*CHAR) +
          LEN(1) VALUE('''')
DSPDTAARA DTAARA(QTEMP/XYZ) OUTFMT(*HEX)
```

Figure 7.23: Load and display a data area to find the hex value of a character.

—Midrange Computing Staff

Find the Source Code to Change the Program

I am often handed a printout from a screen and asked to change the corresponding program. Many of our interactive programs do not have the name of the display file or program on the screen. I have developed a quick workaround to find the source code. As with any sophisticated system, there are many different ways to access the same information. I will describe the method that I have found to be the fastest for me.

First, I display the job. Then, I press the System Request key and choose option 3 (Display current job). Because I'm looking for the program that is running, I select option 11 (Display call stack, if active). The call stack lists all the active programs and shows the last statement executed. (The current program might not show at the bottom of the list.) Option 11 runs the Display Job (DSPJOB) command, which provides a wealth of information. To see the open files and their libraries, try option 14 (Display open files, if active). Press F11 to look for the display file; it should have DSP in the File Type column.

Using this technique gives me half of the information I need. I still need to find the source used to compile the program. The Display Program (DSPPGM) command provides all the pertinent source information: the program creation date and time; the source file, library, and member; and the source file change date and time.

—Novella Peters
—Michael Kaplan

The QSYSINC Library

With V3R1, IBM released a new library called QSYSINC. It comes with files containing source members that define many of the structures used by OS/400 application program interfaces (APIs). For example, you can find data structures and variables defined for many of the list-and-retrieve APIs. Instead of keying tedious formats into numerous programs, you can simply include these source members in your program (e.g., use preprocessor compile directives /COPY for RPG or #INCLUDE for C). You'll find source physical file QRPGSRC for OPM RPG; QRPGLESRC for ILE RPG; QLBLSRC for COBOL; and H, SYS, NET, and NETINET for the C language.

In the past, many of these formats were found in the QUSRTOOL library. QSYSINC is now the source for accessing include files. If you were using the include members from the QUSRTOOL library, be aware that the member names in the QSYSINC library are different.

Before you start defining variables and data structures for an API, check this library out; you might find just what you need.

—Richard Shaler

V4R2 File Layout Gotcha!

V4R2 introduced a couple of changes to the system database that could cause problems. IBM changed the record formats of files QADBIFLD and QADBKFLD. QADBIFLD contains the field definitions for all of the files on your AS/400, while file QADBKFLD contains all of the key fields for all of the files on your system. If you use these files in your own applications (as I do), you might need to modify your code to handle these changes.

—David Mayle

You Can Personalize Messages

The Override with Message File (OVRMSGF) command can be used to customize the messages you and your users see. OVRMSGF works differently from other types of file overrides. Other override commands, such as Override with Database File (OVRDBF), tell the system to use one file instead of another. OVRMSGF tells the system to give precedence to the overriding message file, but to resort to the overridden file if necessary. If a message ID is found in a message file I have created, the system will use that message. Otherwise, it will look for the message ID in IBM's message file. To use your own custom messages, do the following:

1. Create a message file in your test library.

2. Use the Merge Message File (MRGMSGF) command to duplicate the messages you wish to customize.

3. Use the Work with Message File (WRKMSGF) command to modify the message file in your test library. Do not modify IBM's message files.

   You need to run OVRMSGF in any job you want to customize. My initial program includes the code shown in Figure 7.24. The overrides remain in effect for the duration of the job because my initial program stays in the call stack until I sign off.

```
CHKOBJ OBJ(JEWEL/JEWEL) OBJTYPE(*MSGF)
MONMSG MSGID(CPF9801) EXEC(GOTO CMDLBL(SKIP1))
OVRMSGF MSGF(QCPFMSG) TOMSGF(JEWEL/JEWEL)
OVRMSGF MSGF(QEDTMSG) TOMSGF(JEWEL/JEWEL)
OVRMSGF MSGF(QUOMSGF) TOMSGF(JEWEL/JEWEL)
SKIP1:
```

Figure 7.24: Override message files to make your own custom messages display.

4. Table 7.2 contains a list of some of my custom message texts. Most of them are humorous changes I have made to lighten my day. Others, like CPD8061, give me more information than, or different information from, the versions IBM supplies.

Table 7.2: Use Your Imagination When Customizing Messages

Message ID	Severity	MSG
CPC8061	0	File &1 member &2 rec'd into &7/&6. Thanks!
CPF9897	40	Jerry ... &1
CPF9898	40	Jerry ... &1.
EDT0229	0	Mbr &1 in &2/&3 changed with &4 recs. More fine code!
EDT0601	0	Member is being saved. Well done!
EDT1513	0	All dates changed to &1. Glad to be of service!
EDT1619	0	String &1 found. Good eye!
PDM0018	30	&1 submitted. Better living through fine code and hot coffee!

The second-level message text of CPX2423 contains the heading seen on the command entry display. I changed this to my personal slogan, "Better living through fine code and hot coffee!"

The message text for CPX2313 should look familiar to you. These are the commands executed from the system request menu. I usually modify the DSPJOB to WRKJOB—which gives me a command line from almost anywhere. You might prefer to change DSPJOB to WRKJOB instead. Figure 7.25 contains one-time sample code you can use to build your custom message file from frequently used original messages.

```
PGM PARM(&MSGF)

   DCL VAR(&MSGF) TYPE(*CHAR) LEN(10)
/* Create message file in *CURRENT library */
   CRTMSGF MSGF(*CURLIB/&MSGF) TEXT('Custom messages')
/* Copy the original messages */
/* In the SELECT parameter, list the IDs */
/* of the messages you want to modify */
   MRGMSGF FROMMSGF(QSYS/QCPFMSG) TOMSGF(&MSGF) +
       SELECT(CPC8061 CPF9897 CPF9898 CPI3405 +
       CPX2313 CPX2423)
   MRGMSGF FROMMSGF(QPDA/QEDTMSG) TOMSGF(&MSGF) +
       SELECT(EDT0229 EDT0601 EDT1513 EDT1618 +
       EDT1619)
   MRGMSGF FROMMSGF(QPDA/QUOMSGF) TOMSGF(&MSGF) +
       SELECT(PDM0018)
   WRKMSGF MSGF(*CURLIB/&MSGF)

ENDPGM
```

Figure 7.25: Use this one-time CL program to build a custom message file.

—Jerry Jewel

Mod 10 Check Digit

Q: I would like to know more about the use of check digits and how to code them (RPG) into strings of data. We are printing account numbers and amounts due on a continuous line of output on our bill, and the bank has requested that we place an "IBM Mod 10 Check Digit" between the two fields. I've quickly looked through my manuals to no avail and would greatly appreciate a suggestion.

A: Starting from the right-most digit of number, give a weight of 2 then 1 then 2 then 1 until you run out of numbers. For example, if you need a check digit for 9876543, the weight is 2121212.

Multiply each digit by its weight, then add up each digit. You get as the result:

```
1+8+8+1+4+6+1+0+4+6 = 39
```

Subtract this number from next higher number ending in 0. So, 40-39=1, the modulus 10 check digit.

—Chris Ringer

A: We have used Modulus 10 check digits for years to verify data entry without operators knowing we were checking them. They think we have a 6-digit item number. What
we have is really a 5-digit number with a check digit at the end. The RPG routine,
Mod10Chk, shown in Figure 7.26 is the one we use to verify and also create check
digits.

```
E                       M10         14  1 0
E                       MWO         14  2 0
E                       MXO          6  1 0
*
I            DS
I                                        1   14 0UNCHEK
I                                        1   14 M10
I                                        1   15 0CHEKED
I                                       15   15 0CHECKD
I                                       16   21 MXO
I                                       16   21 0MXORES
*
C           MOD10C      BEGSR
* SUBMITTED : *
* THE BASIC NUMBER IN UNCHEK IF THE *
* CHECK DIGIT IS TO BE APPENDED, OR *
* THE NUMBER IN CHECKED IF THE CHECK *
* DIGIT IS ALREADY PROVIDED FOR *
**
* RETURNED : *
* CHEKED = MODULO 10 NUMBER *
C           2           DO    14      MO         20
C           M10,MO      MULT  2       MWO,MO
C                       END   2
C           1           DO    13      MO
C                       Z-ADDM10,MO   MWO,MO
C                       END   2
C                       Z-ADD0        WK0010    10
C           1           DO    14      MO
C                       Z-ADDMWO,MO   MXORES
C                       XFOOTMXO      WK0020    20
C                       ADD   WK0020  WK0010
C                       END
C           10          SUB   WK0010  WK0010
C                       Z-ADDWK0010   CHECKD
C                       ENDSR
```

Figure 7.26: This short RPG program illustrates how to calculate a Mod10 check digit.

If you place the number in UNCHEK, and EXSR MOD10C, the number returned in CHEKED
is the original number with the check digit appended. If you want to test a number that
supposedly has a check digit attached, place it in CHEKED, EXSR MOD10C, and compare
your original number with the value that is returned in CHEKED.

—*Iceman Batten*

✦ ✦ ✦ SEU

Command Line Window in SEU

One of the nice things about SEU is the F21 option for the command line window. You can invoke this same command-line window in your user applications as well, by calling program QUSCMDLN, as follows:

```
CALL QUSCMDLN
```

—Steven Kontos

Don't Lose Your SEU Changes

Have you ever been in the middle of modifying an existing AS/400 source file, such as an RPG IV program, and deleted or changed lines of code that you didn't really want to by using SEU? This is a frustrating and common occurrence, but there are a few things you can do to remedy the situation.

You could just press the F3 key to exit and not save any of your changes. At least your original source will remain unchanged. This option will work fine, but it might not be the most desirable. You will lose all the changes that you made. We all have enough to do without having to redo our own work.

You could exit, save your changes to another member name, edit the new member, and copy the source code you deleted or changed from the original member. This option will also work fine (with the exception of being a minor pain). Of course, you have to remember what you named the new member and then copy the changes back into the original source member. That could turn into a pretty big nightmare in a hurry.

The method that I have found that works best for me is to use the Browse/Copy Options (F15) in SEU to display a copy of the same source member I'm currently editing. Now all I have to do is position the copy to the lines that I accidentally deleted, copy them, and paste them into the current source. You also can use this method to browse the original code to see what it looked like before you made your changes.

—Greg Leister

Ejecting to a New Page in SEU

An undocumented feature of SEU that we have used since our S/38 days and which is still in AS/400 SEU, allows you to skip to a new page when you print out a TXT member upon exiting SEU.

If you place a "%" (percent sign) in column 1 of a line and then exit SEU and choose Print=Y on the exit screen, the line with the "%" will start on a new page and the "%" will not print. Note, however, that this does not work when you use STRSEU with PDM OPTION(6). You must go into the member and print it from the exit screen.

—Blair Hamren

Finding Changed Lines in SEU

Here is a quick and easy solution for isolating changed lines in your source file, particularly if someone else made the program changes. Given any specific date, you can determine the lines entered on that date, prior to that date, or after that date. Here's how:

1. While in edit mode or browse mode, use the exclude line command "X999999" at the first line of the program and exclude all of the lines in the source file.

2. Press F14 (Find Options). Change the Occurrences to Process parameter to ALL, and enter your search date and compare parameter.

3. Press F16 (Repeat Find) and presto...SEU will list all of the lines that meet your search criteria while all other lines in the source file remain excluded.

4. To return to the entire program, press F5 (Refresh).

—Midrange Computing Staff

Print Parts of a Source Member

When debugging, you might need to print parts of a source member rather than the entire source member. To print a range of source statements from within SEU, key LLP over the sequence numbers of the first and last lines to print and press Enter.

—Harry Morris

Editor's Note: If you use the X or XX commands to exclude lines from view on the display, the lines also will be excluded when printed.

Quick Removal of RPG Serialization Numbers

To remove obsolete serialization from columns 1–5 in RPG source members, key LLT5 in the line command area of the top line in SEU. On the last statement prior to compile timetables or arrays, enter a matching LLT. This will shift the entire block left 5 bytes while allowing truncation. The screen will light up like a Christmas tree with syntax errors. Repeat the process with RR5 and RR to restore the proper column positions. The 5 may be specified at either the top or bottom of the blocks.

—Douglas Handy

Repeat Last Search Field in SEU

If you do a FIND or CHANGE command at the "SEU==>" line, then run another command, you can repeat the FIND or CHANGE by using * after the FIND command instead of retyping the search argument or pressing F9 multiple times.

—Greg Prior

SEU Find/Change Improvement

Here is an AS/400 tip that I have found very useful. When I am using SEU, I often like to have only what I am finding or changing on the screen. To do this:

1. At the first line of the program, enter line command "X9999" to exclude all lines of program. "X99" or "X999" can be used depending on size of program.

2. Run F xxx ALL or C xxx xxx ALL.

3. The screen returns with only your finds or changes.

4. To return to the entire program, press F5 (Refresh).

—Don DeChamps

Undo Changes in SEU

Press the Clear key in SEU to undo any changes since the last Enter or function key. This tip is especially great for when you hit the Field Exit key accidentally.

—Greg Prior

User-defined Prompt Screens in SEU

One little-known feature of the AS/400 SEU product is the ability to design custom prompt screens. For example, you could create a prompt for project information to be included in every source member in a standard format. This example is illustrated with a simple prompt for project name.

1. While on the SEU edit display, press F23. This brings up the Select Prompt display. Press F23 again for the User-defined Prompt display.

2. Type Project Name (PN) in the "Create a prompt..." field. Press Enter.

3. On the User-defined Prompt Definition display, enter "PROJNAME" for New field... and enter "Project Name" for Prompt text.

   The next two steps require you to complete the information to define the Project Name heading and then the attributes of the field itself (its length, where it appears on the screen, highlighting, and so on).

4. Press Enter. On the Field Description display, enter "Project Name" for the field text. This will become the heading. Put the heading on line 17 starting in column 1. Select "Y" for highlighting. After pressing Enter, you will see the User Prompt Field Attribute screen. Place the PROJECT field on line 18, column 1 and make it 10 alphanumeric characters long. For "Column in the source record..." start the project number in position 1. Specify a 'Y' in the "Underline..." prompt and press Enter to complete the definition of the Project Name field.

Repeat the above steps for additional fields. Press F10 to save your work before exiting the Work with User-defined Prompt Definition screen. Press F11 to get a preview of what the PN prompt looks like. To test your newly defined prompt, use the SEU line command IPPN (which stands for Insert Prompt Project Name). Key in some data and press Enter.

There is no interface to syntax-check your user-defined fields and there isn't Help-key support for user prompts. Prompts can only appear from line 6 to line 20 on a standard display. Field headings must be on a single line and cannot be stacked.

I believe the intent of user-defined prompts is to help programmers maintain tabular data in source members. Whether it is programmer log notes or program source code indented just the way the programmer wants, a user prompt can help extend the power of SEU.

—Midrange Computing Staff

Using *ERR in SEU

We've all been there. We're in SEU, editing our favorite source member. We've made the changes and pressed F3 to exit. Suddenly the impossible happens. The dreaded "Member contains syntax errors" pops up and we're right back in the source with the challenging task of finding the error in all those source lines. Well, SEU has a neat little feature that addresses this problem. Type *ERR on the search line, press F16, and up pops the line with the error.

—Joe Starr

Windowing with F11 in SEU

In SEU, you can window left and right with F19 and F20, but try F11 instead. F11 makes windowing left and right easier by toggling between the left side and the right side of the source member; you need only to use one function key, and the key doesn't require you to use the Shift key.

If you browse a spool file and press F11, the browser folds the lines in the spool file.

—Jan Jorgensen

✦ ✦ ✦ Sorting and Sequencing

Alternating Sequences in Logical Files

When I have to read the keys of an AS/400 file in R-O-Y-G-B-I-V order (the order of the colors of the spectrum) instead of the normal alphabetical order, FMTDTA is not appropriate because the file needs to be used in both CHAIN and SETLL operations.

The DDS Reference manual mentions the ALTSEQ keyword for both physical and logical files, but is very vague as to how to create the source for a table containing the alternative sequence.

The section in the *CL Reference* manual on the Create Table (CRTTBL) command is not very helpful, either. Asking some of my peers didn't yield anything I didn't know already. So, I had to reinvent the wheel myself. Here it is:

Create source physical file QTBLSRC, with a record length of 76, in whatever library you're working:

```
CRTSRCPF FILE(xxx/QTBLSRC) +
         RCDLEN(72) TEXT('Table source')
```

Use SEU to create a source member of type TBL in the file you created in the previous step. The source member must contain eight records having the hexadecimal gibberish listed in Figure 7.27.

```
000102030405060708090A0B0C0D0E0F101112131415161718191A1B1C1D1E1F
202122232425262728292A2B2C2D2E2F303132333435363738393A3B3C3D3E3F
404142434445464748494A4B4C4D4E4F505152535455565758595A5B5C5D5E5F
606162636465666768696A6B6C6D6E6F707172737475767778797A7B7C7D7E7F
808182838485868788898A8B8C8D8E8F909192939495969798999A9B9C9D9E9F
A0A1A2A3A4A5A6A7A8A9AAABACADAEAFB0B1B2B3B4B5B6B7B8B9BABBBCBDBEBF
C0C1C2C3C4C5C6C7C8C9CACBCCCDCECFD0D1D2D3D4D5D6D7D8D9DADBDCDDDEDF
E0E1E2E3E4E5E6E7E8E9EAEBECEDEEEFF0F1F2F3F4F5F6F7F8F9FAFBFCFDFEFF
```

Figure 7.27: To develop a new translation table, start from the normal EBCDIC collating sequence.

Using a standard EBCDIC collating sequence chart of hexadecimal values, place a new hexadecimal value in the position normally occupied by each character whose sequence you want to change. For example, the source member shown in Figure 7.28 resequences the letters W, R, O, Y, G, B, I, V, M and N by giving their normal positions the hexadecimal values of R, \, S, T, U, V, W, X, Y and Z.

```
000102030405060708090A0B0C0D0E0F101112131415161718191A1B1C1D1E1F
202122232425262728292A2B2C2D2E2F303132333435363738393A3B3C3D3E3F
404142434445464748494A4B4C4D4E4F505152535455565758595A5B5C5D5E5F
606162636465666768696A6B6C6D6E6F707172737475767778797A7B7C7D7E7F
808182838485868788898A8B8C8D8E8F909192939495969798999A9B9C9D9E9F
A0A1A2A3A4A5A6A7A8A9AAABACADAEAFB0B1B2B3B4B5B6B7B8B9BABBBCBDBEBF
C0C1E5C3C4C5C6E4C8E6CACBCCCDCECFD0D1D2D3E8E9E2D7D8E0DADBDCDDDEDF
D6E1C7C2C9E7D9D4E3D5EAEBECEDEEEFF0F1F2F3F4F5F6F7F8F9FAFBFCFDFEFF
```

Figure 7.28: Modify the hex codes to create the proper character sequence.

Compile the table source member using the CRTTBL command as shown in Figure 7.29.

```
CRTTBL TBL(xxx/MYTABLE) SRCFILE(xxx/QTBLSRC)
```

Figure 7.29: Use CRTTBL to build the translation table object.

In the DDS for the file, use the file-level keyword ALTSEQ. The format for this keyword is:

```
ALTSEQ(library/table)
```

Create the file as usual.

—*Sharon Cannon*

Sorting Based on LANGID

Throughout OS/400, the capability exists to sort either in the "normal" sequence or by using a special sort table. The keyword you'll find on the various commands that let you specify sorting is named SRTSEQ, and the default setting is *HEX, which sorts in sequence based on the hexadecimal values of characters in the field. You also can enter your own table name to perform the equivalent of ALTSEQ sorting.

There is, however, a special value, *LANGIDSHR, that provides some interesting features of its own. *LANGIDSHR sorts by the shared weight table that corresponds to the LANGID specified. What does the shared weight table do? Well, it basically sorts in a more user-friendly manner. Among other things, the shared weight table sorts fields in true alphabetical order regardless of case. Table 7.3 shows how a few things would be sorted using *HEX. Because the hexadecimal representation of lowercase is lower than uppercase, letters are lower than numbers and blanks are lower than punctuation.

On the other hand, *LANGIDSHR sorts data as listed in Table 7.4 because uppercase and lowercase letters have the same weight (hence, the weight is "shared") as do blanks

Table 7.3: You Can Sort Data Using the *HEX Sequence
AbACUS
ABsolutely
ABEND
30 cents
30 days
30 zebras
30 DAYS
30 MINUTES
30-days

and punctuation, allowing a sort by actual text without regard to case. This method is useful when sorting things such as field descriptions. You will also notice that numbers are sorted before letters. This might be to conform with ASCII, in which digits have lower hexadecimal representations than characters. Be careful with this; it means the high–low range of "printable" alphanumeric characters is blank to Z rather than blank to 9, as with normal EBCDIC.

For other languages, *LANGIDSHR might act slightly differently. For instance, it might group accented letters with their unaccented equivalents. In addition, equivalently weighted values, such as uppercase and lowercase versions of the same word, are sorted in arrival sequence. Therefore, you might see the data sorted as it is in Table 7.5. In Table 7.5, "30 DAYS," "30 days," and "30-days" could appear in any order, depending on their arrival sequence. If your sorting must be case-sensitive, don't use the *LANGIDSHR value!

Table 7.4: *LANGIDSHR Also Can Be Used to Sort Data
30 cents
30 DAYS
30 days
30-days
30 MINUTES
30 zebras
AbACUS
ABEND
About
ABsolutely

To use the *LANGIDSHR option in interactive SQL, press F13 to go to the SESSION attributes panel and change the Sort sequence parameter to *LANGIDSHR. For OPNQRYF, you can specify the SRTSEQ(* LANGIDSHR) keyword. This parameter is available on CRTLF, CRTPF, and other file creation commands to specify the handling of key fields and to select or omit criteria and field editing. It is also available with Create RPG Program (CRTRPGPGM) and other program compilation commands to specify internal table, compare, and sort sequencing. There are additional considerations; review the help text for the SRTSEQ keyword for the specific command you want to use. *LANGIDSHR also can be defined or changed at the system, user profile, and job levels. The system value is QSRTSEQ; for user profiles and jobs, the keyword is SRTSEQ.

Table 7.5: Equally Weighted Values Are Sorted in Arrival Sequence
Case
cAse
CASE
case
CASE
casE

—*Joe Pluta*

Sorting Data Queues in Descending Order

Q: Is it possible to read a keyed data queue in descending order? We've read everything we can find about data queues and tried everything we can think of, but the messages always come out in ascending order.

A: When you issue a QRCVDTAQ to a keyed data queue, and two or more messages on the data queue match the search criteria you specify, the one with the lowest key value is retrieved. In other words, messages come off the queue in ascending order by key. If you want them to come out in descending order, you can use a complementary key.

I can illustrate using nonnegative numbers. Suppose you want to put three messages on a data queue, with key values of 254, 973, and 806. Instead of using the actual key values, subtract each one from all 9s (in this case, 999) and use the results as the key values.

- 254 becomes 745

- 973 becomes 026

- 806 becomes 193

Now the entries come out in ascending order by the modified keys. Therefore, you get them in the order you really wanted. This is commonly known as 9's complement.

Figure 7.30 illustrates this technique using three-digit customer account numbers. Figure 7.31 shows how to retrieve the queued messages.

```
C              999       SUB  CUSTNO   MODKEY  30
C                        MOVELMODKEY   KEY
C                        CALL 'QSNDDTAQ'
C                        PARM 'SOMEDTAQ'DQNAME  10       Data queue name
C                        PARM 'QTEMP'   DQLIB   10       Data queue library
C                        PARM 1024      DQLEN   50       Data queue length
C                        PARM           DQDTA            Queued data
C                        PARM 3         KEYLEN  30       Key length
C                        PARM           KEY     3        Key value
```

Figure 7.30: Use 9's complement to modify a nonnegative numeric key.

```
C                        CALL 'QRCVDTAQ'
C                        PARM 'SOMEDTAQ'DQNAME  10       Data queue name
C                        PARM 'QTEMP'   DQLIB   10       Data queue library
C                        PARM 1024      DQLEN   50       Data queue length
C                        PARM           DQDTA            Queued data
C                        PARM -1        WAIT    50       Seconds to wait
C                        PARM 'LE'      KEYSLT  2        Key selection
C                        PARM 3         KEYLEN  30       Key length
C                        PARM *HIVAL    KEY     3        Key value
C                        PARM 0         SNDLEN  30       Sender info length
C                        PARM           SND     8        Sender info
```

Figure 7.31: Use this pattern for retrieving a message from a keyed data queue.

If you want to use alpha keys, you can reverse all the bits in the key before putting it on the data queue. But that's a lot of trouble because RPG doesn't have a logical NOT operation.

Figure 7.32 shows an alternate method. You'll need a list of all possible characters that can be in the key value, in order by their position in the EBCDIC collating sequence. As shown in Figure 7.32, this list is in the named constant C1. The possible characters are blanks, uppercase letters, and digits. Next, you'll need the same list in reverse order. This is constant C2. To get the complementary key, use the XLATE (translate) op code to convert each character to its opposite in the lists. All blanks become 9s, and vice versa. All As become 8s, and so on.

```
I                ' ABCDEFGHIJKLMNOPQRS-C        C1
I                'TUVWXYZ0123456789'
I                '9876543210ZYXWVUTSRQ-C        C2
I                'PONMLKJIHGFEDCBA '
 *... (more code)
C          C1:C2    XLATEITEMNO    KEY
C                   CALL 'QSNDDTAQ'
C                   PARM 'MYDTAQ'   DQNAME 10       Data queue name
C                   PARM 'QTEMP'    DQLIB  10       Data queue library
C                   PARM 1024       DQLEN  50       Data queue length
C                   PARM            DQDTA           Queued data
C                   PARM 8          KEYLEN 30       Key length
C                   PARM            KEY    8        Key value
```

Figure 7.32: Translate an alpha key to make it sort in descending order.

It's unlikely you'll need to sort data queue messages on signed numbers. Even when you want the entries to come out in ascending order, working with signed numbers is a headache because the way the system stores signs in negative numbers doesn't match the collating sequence. If you sort signed numbers based on their character values, they won't come out in numeric order.

For completeness, however, here's a way to retrieve signed numbers in descending order from a keyed data queue (see Figure 7.33). For unsigned numbers, you'll have to slightly modify this technique. The key has to be separated into two parts: a sign and a numeric value. For nonnegative numbers, set the sign to 0 and subtract the value from all 9s, as in the first example.

For negative numbers, set the sign to some value greater than a blank (I've used a hyphen in this example) and leave the number portion as is.

```
IKEY          DS                            8
I                                   1    1 KEYSGN
I                                   2   80KEYVAL
*... (more code)
* AMOUNT is defined as 7 digits with zero decimal positions
C             AMOUNT    IFGE *ZERO
C                       MOVE *BLANK  KEYSGN
C             9999999   SUB  AMOUNT  KEYVAL
C                       ELSE
C                       MOVE '-'     KEYSGN
C                       MOVE AMOUNT  KEYVAL
C                       ENDIF
C                       CALL 'QSNDDTAQ'
C                       PARM 'MYDTAQ'  DQNAME 10    Data queue name
C                       PARM 'QTEMP'   DQLIB  10    Data queue library
C                       PARM 1024      DQLEN  50    Data queue length
C                       PARM           DQDTA        Queued data
C                       PARM 8         KEYLEN 30    Key length
C                       PARM           KEY          Key value
```

Figure 7.33: Modifying keys of signed numbers is slightly more involved than modifying keys of unsigned numbers.

—*Ted Holt*

✦ ✦ ✦ Source Files

Easy Program Access to Source Members

Unlike the System/36, source members are very easy to process within programs on the AS/400. Source physical files are automatically externally described with three field names. For example, the external field names for file QRPGSRC (source file containing RPG source members) are SRCSEQ, SRCDAT, and SRCDTA. To find out the external field names and their attributes for a file, use the Display File Field Description command (DSPFFD) against the file.

To access a source member, define the source physical file in your program as an external file with a continuation spec that uses the RENAME keyword to rename the record format to something different from the file name. (The record format name in a source physical file is the same as the file name, which RPG will not accept.)

This type of processing is well suited for writing documentation systems, such as cross-reference programs.

—*Midrange Computing Staff*

Lost Members

Q: Once in a while, I accidentally delete a source member, or make modifications to a member and then discover that I should have left the source as it was. If I haven't modified the source since the last backup, I'm okay because I can restore it. But what if I have made changes that I need to retain?

A: This doesn't happen very often, fortunately. But more than once I've been spared the trouble of rewriting source because I had a compilation listing with the desired source still in an output queue. To retrieve source from a spooled file, follow these steps:

1. Create a new source member with SEU.

2. Press F15 to get the copy service.

3. Use option 2 and fill in the name, job, and spool file number of the spooled file.

4. Press Enter, and the compiler listing will fill the bottom window of the screen.

5. Use the copy (C) and/or block copy (CC) commands to copy the desired lines into the source member.

6. Use left-shift-with-truncate (LLT) instructions to align the source in the proper columns.

The moral of the story is that if you've lost a source member, don't despair until you've made sure it's not in a spool file.

—Ted Holt

✦ ✦ ✦ Spool Files

Shared Spool Files

If you need to run several programs—each of which creates a report—and you want them all in a single print file, you need to override or change your printer file to use a shared access path. If you are using the default printer file QSYSPRT, you could do this with:

```
OVRPRTF FILE(QSYSPRT) SHARE(*YES)
```

Then you must open the printer file and keep it open. This can be done with a very small RPG program like the one in Figure 7.34.

```
FQSYSPRT O   F    132    OF    PRINTER
C                      RETRN
C                      EXCPTDUMMY
C                      MOVE *ON      *INLR
```

Figure 7.34: Use a short RPG program to open a file for shared access.

—*Midrange Computing Staff*

✦ ✦ ✦ **Work Management**

Creating Never-ending Jobs

Often, you'll have to create a job that runs in the background all the time. For example, you might need a job that monitors a data queue for new entries or monitors QSYSOPR for new messages. These jobs are easy to create, but they require prior setup.

First, create a multithreaded job queue for these never-ending jobs. Call it something meaningful (such as BACKGROUND), and place it in a library where any job can find it (such as library QGPL).

```
CRTJOBQ JOBQ(QGPL/BACKGROUND)
```

Then attach the job queue to a subsystem. Any batch subsystem will do (e.g., QBATCH). To attach the job queue to a subsystem, use the Add Job Queue Entry (ADDJOBQE) command:

```
ADDJOBQE SBSD(QBATCH) JOBQ(QGPL/BACKGROUND) +
           MAXACT(*NOMAX) SEQNBR(200)
```

I've assigned a sequence number of 200 for this job queue entry, but you might have to use a different number if 200 is already in use for another job queue. The MAXACT(*NOMAX) setting makes BACKGROUND a multithreaded job queue.

That's all there is to it! You can now submit any number of never-ending jobs to job queue BACKGROUND. The following command, for instance, submits job MONSYSOPR to BACKGROUND:

```
SBMJOB JOB(MONSYSOPR) +
     JOBQ(BACKGROUND) CMD(...)
```

If you need to submit this job every time you IPL, change the start-up program. The start-up program's name can be retrieved from system value QSTRUPPGM. To end the job, use the End Job (ENDJOB) command. You also can end the job by running an End Subsystem (ENDSBS) command. However, ENDSBS also will end all other jobs currently running in the affected subsystem.

—Ernie Malaga

Monitor Start, Stop, and Queuing Status of a Job

Looking for a way to know when a particular job starts, ends, or is placed on a job queue? You can get all this information by using the Job Notification Exit Point described in the "Work Management Exit Programs" chapter of the *System API Reference*. This exit program notifies you by subsystem whenever a job starts, ends, or is placed on a job queue. It's also flexible enough for you to ask for only starts or only ends if that better meets your needs.

Based on the criteria you specify, when the job starts, ends, or is placed on a job queue, a notification is sent to a data queue. The information sent to this data queue includes both the internal job identifier (an internal handle used by most APIs to locate a specific object) and the name of the job itself. To know programmatically when a job starts, ends, or is placed on a job queue, create a monitoring program that receives entries from the data queue. Once you have the job in formation, you can call other APIs to do whatever you need to do in response to this action.

—Bruce Vining

CHAPTER 8

Miscellaneous Programming Languages

Miscellaneous Programming Languages

◆   ◆   ◆   ◆

In This Chapter

C

Domino

Java

OfficeVision

OS/400

REXX

◆   ◆   ◆   ◆

A computer programmer must know a little about a lot of things. A computer programmer has to understand, at least superficially, what buyers and sales reps and shipping clerks and customer service people do. IT personnel have to know what other people do in order to provide the computer services they need.

So, one of the things a programmer should understand is that there is more to being a computer programmer than computer programming. A programmer must take the initiative to develop new skills as needed. In the world of computers, the only constant is change. The programmer who says, "This is what I learned in trade school, so this is what I do" is preparing for unemployment. Programmers have no choice but to be retrained. Often that means retraining themselves as technology and the working environment change.

The tips offered in this chapter are of two basic types. Some, such as REXX, deal with programming languages that are available to iSeries programmers, but are not in widespread use. It's good for programmers to learn about other languages, instead of resting on their RPG and CL skills, because other languages feature capabilities that can help solve problems more widely used languages can't handle or can't handle as easily.

The other tips in this chapter don't fit easily within other broad categories. I hope you find something useful here.

—Ted Holt

✦ ✦ ✦ C

Don't Call the main( ) Function of a C Module

Some posts to the *Midrange Computing* Web Forums mention calling the "main" function of a C module directly. That might work as long as you have only one C module in a program, but I don't think the C folks would recommend it.

Let me review a bit about ILE. A module can either have a program entry procedure (PEP) or not. A C module with a procedure called "main" has a PEP. An RPG module that doesn't have NOMAIN in the H-spec has a PEP. A program with several modules has one that is designated the "PEP module." This is the one that is called when you first call the program.

C and RPG both have a concept of a main procedure, but they are slightly different. C allows only one main( ) function in a program, and it's expected to be in the PEP module. RPG allows one main procedure per module. Because they have different names (the name given to the main procedure is the name of the module when it was created), you can freely call between the main procedures.

C programs are intednded to be broken up into logical units (modules), and any procedures within the modules that were useful outside the module were exported. The rest were kept private to the module. No C programmer would ever code with only one procedure per module.

The classic RPG way was one procedure per module (because a module was equivalent to a program). When you first migrated from OPM, it was convenient to continue this, just using CALLB instead of CALL, and basically calling your source-member name.

You can still do that, but you also can group your procedures together. While this can be awkward at first, because you don't know where your procedures are, this isn't hard to get used to.

—Barbara Morris

✦ ✦ ✦ Domino

Create and Access Hidden Views

Hidden views are a must in Notes/Domino applications. I use them to perform view lookups within keyword fields and back-end LotusScript routines. Creating a hidden view is easy; just wrap the view name with parentheses. As long as the view name is enclosed in parentheses, it won't display on the navigation pane. For example, a hidden view I recently created looks up all policies that have been approved (vwlookupPolicyApproved).

It is a good idea to use hidden views whenever you're relying on a view for LotusScript processing or looking up information using a keyword list because views can get changed and you risk the chance that an agent or keyword list won't work.

So, how do you see a hidden view without changing the view name? To open a database from the Notes Desktop, select a database so it has focus, hold down the Ctrl and Shift keys, and then double-click on the database. When it opens, all of your hidden views are presented just like the other views are. I use this feature a lot when testing an application.

—*Matt L. Vredenburg*

Directory Links Provide Quick Access to Notes Databases

When developing in Notes, I find that my \notes\data (standard Notes/ Domino directory configuration) directory gets filled with lots of templates and Notes databases because of client projects. Once in a while, I clean out my \notes\data directory by moving related templates and databases into a new directory tree, such as \datafiles\notesfiles.

Within that directory tree, I create specific directories for each project. But, once I have these directories created, getting to the directories' databases using the Notes Open Database dialog/browser can be frustrating because the browser initially displays databases in the \notes\data directory. I find that traversing up and down my directory tree to find my databases can take a lot of time.

Instead of going through that effort each time I want to open a database, I now create directory links instead. There are two ways to create directory links. One way is to use the Notes/Domino Server Administration panel. By using this panel, you also can restrict who can access (from the Name and Address Book) the directory link.

I prefer the other way: Create a text file with the extension of .DIR (.dir for UNIX). Name it something that describes the information in the linking directory. Then, add the directory path in the text file. Make sure the .DIR file is in the \notes\data directory. For example, I create a separate .DIR file for each of my client projects. When I browse databases on my local hard drive or server, I can see each of the .DIR files as directories within the \notes\data directory. When I select the project directory, Notes directs the Open Database dialog/browser to the path defined in the .DIR file.

—Matt L. Vredenburg

✦ ✦ ✦ Java

Give the Java Class Path Plenty of Environment Space

Some Java applications require rather lengthy additions to the CLASSPATH environment variable when executing those applications from a DOS window. For instance, if you are using IBM's Java Toolbox for the AS/400, you have to add your PC's location of the jt400.jar or jt400.zip files to your CLASSPATH, and, if you start to use Java's JFC Swing library, you'll have to add the path for the swingall.jar file. You can make these additions easily with the following DOS batch commands:

```
SET CLASSPATH=%classpath%;C:\jt400\lib\jt400.jar
SET CLASSPATH=%classpath%;C:\swing\swingall.jar
```

But when you start to add more and more Java ZIP and JAR files to your CLASSPATH environment variable, you might experience the DOS "Out of environment space" error. So, how do you increase your PC's environment space?

To permanently increase environment space, add a SHELL command to your CONFIG.SYS file, as below, and restart your system.

```
shell=command.com /e:8192 /p
```

—Don Denoncourt

Improve the Performance of Stream I/O

The AS/400 Toolbox for Java provides classes for accessing files in the integrated file system of the AS/400. IFSFileInputStream reads data from a file, and IFSFileOutputStream writes data to a file. These files do not buffer or cache data; they access the AS/400 when they receive a request to read or write data. If your application does file I/O many times or in small chunks, performance will suffer.

Fortunately, the following Toolbox classes were designed to improve performance via the Java buffering technology. **IFSFileInputStream** extends **java.io.InputStream**. **IFSFileOutput-Stream** extends **java.io.OutputStream**. Java classes that improve the performance of **java.io.InputStream** and **java.io.OutputStream** can also be used with **IFSFileInputStream** and **IFSFileOutputStream**.

For example, the program shown in Figure 8.1 accesses data in a file on the AS/400 via the **IFSFileInputStream** and **IFSFileOutputStream** classes of the Toolbox. In the first case, it uses a **BufferedInputStream** class to cache data. In the second case, it accesses data directly via a call to the Toolbox class. Performance is greatly improved when reading and writing data through buffers.

```
import java.io.*;
import java.util.*;
import java.math.*;
import com.ibm.as400.access.*;

public class readfile2 extends Object
{
    public static void main(String[] args)
    {
    System.out.println(" ");
    System.out.println("Starting application");
    System.out.println(" ");

    try
    {
        AS400 system = new AS400();
        int loopCount = 5000;
        System.out.println("writing to file - cached");
        IFSFileOutputStream outFileIFS = new
            IFSFileOutputStream(system,"/daw/a.a");
        BufferedOutputStream outputFile = new BufferedOutputStream(outFileIFS,
            1024);
        byte data = 0;
        long timeStart = System.currentTimeMillis();
        for (int i = 0; i < loopCount; i++)
        {
            outputFile.write(data);
        }
        outputFile.flush();
        System.out.println(" Write time: " + (System.currentTimeMillis() -
            timeStart));
```

Figure 8.1: Access data in a file on the AS/400 via IFSFileInputStream and IFSFileOutputStream (part 1 of 2).

```
        System.out.println("reading from file - cached");
        timeStart = System.currentTimeMillis();
        IFSFileInputStream inFileIFS = new IFSFileInputStream(system, "/daw/a.a");
        BufferedInputStream inputFile = new BufferedInputStream(inFileIFS, 1024);
        for (int i = 0; i < loopCount; i++)
        {
           data = (byte) inputFile.read();
        }
        System.out.println(" Read time: " + (System.currentTimeMillis() -
                            timeStart));
        System.out.println("");
        System.out.println("writing to file - no cache");
        IFSFileOutputStream outFileIFS2 = new IFSFileOutputStream(system,
                    "/daw/a.a2");
        timeStart = System.currentTimeMillis();
        for (int i=0; i < loopCount; i++)
        {
           outFileIFS2.write(data);
        }
        outFileIFS2.flush();
        System.out.println(" Write time: " + (System.currentTimeMillis() -
                            timeStart));
        System.out.println("reading from file - no cache");
        timeStart = System.currentTimeMillis();
        IFSFileInputStream inFileIFS2 = new IFSFileInputStream(system,
                    "/daw/a.a2");
        for (int i = 0; i < loopCount; i++)
        {
           data = (byte) inFileIFS2.read();
        }
        System.out.println(" Read time: " + ( System.currentTimeMillis() -
             timeStart));
        }
     catch (Exception e) { System.out.println(e);}

     System.exit(0);
     }
}
```

Figure 8.1: Access data in a file on the AS/400 via IFSFileInputStream and IFSFileOutputStream (part 2 of 2).

—David Wall

JDBC Error Information

By default, the AS/400 Toolbox for Java JDBC driver returns only first-level text for error messages. If you want more information about errors, add *;errors=full* to the URL you use for connecting to the database. This addition tells the driver to return both first- and second-level text for error messages.

—Clifton M. Nock

Resolve Java Class Attribute Ambiguity

The concept of scope is important in Java. Midrange programmers are typically familiar only with global scope, which means that variables defined anywhere in a program are accessible throughout the program. RPG IV programs have local as well as global scope. Variables defined within an RPG IV subprocedure have local scope (they're accessible only within that subprocedure), whereas variables defined in the mainline code are still globally accessible.

With Java, a class has attributes that have global scope—that is, the attributes (essentially variables) are accessible to all functions of that class. But a variable defined within a function of that class is accessible only within that function. This goes the same for the function parameters.

Class attributes are usually declared private so that nothing outside the class can modify them. The functions that modify class attributes are usually named "**setxxx**," where **xxx** is the attribute. The obvious name for the parameter to a set function would be the attribute name.

The Order class, shown in Figure 8.2, has an **orderDate** attribute and a **setOrderDate** function to modify the **orderDate** attribute. The parameter to **setOrderDate** is also called **orderDate**, the same name as the class attribute. Within the **setOrderDate** function, any references to **orderDate** would refer to the parameter (local), not to the class attribute (global).

The Java keyword **this** can be used to resolve the ambiguity between the **orderDate** parameter and the **orderDate** class attribute. The Java reserved word **this** refers to is the object itself. The class example, shown in Figure 8.12, sets the class's **orderDate** attribute to the passed parameter of the same name.

```
class Order {
    private int orderNumber;
    private int orderDate;

    void setOrderDate(int orderDate)
    {
        this.orderDate = orderDate;
    }
}
```

*Figure 8.2: Using the Java reserved word **this** eliminates ambiguity between variables of the same name.*

Some publications suggest using a naming convention to resolve ambiguity of passed parameter variable names. One suggestion is to prefix an "a" to the beginning of parameter names. I find the prefix makes the code harder to read. I think use of the **this** qualifier is clearer.

—Don Denoncourt

Trace a JDBC Program

When debugging a Java application or applet that uses JDBC, it can be helpful to examine a trace of what the JDBC driver is doing. With the AS/400 Toolbox for Java JDBC driver, the trace will show a lot of information, including full-stack traces for any errors that occur and summaries of which SQL statements are prepared and executed, what results are returned, and when various resources are opened and closed.

There are two ways to turn on tracing. In the Java program itself, the following code will tell the JDBC driver manager to dump trace information to the standard output device. If you do not have access to the source code of the JDBC application or applet, add *;trace=true* to the URL that you use for connecting to the database.

```
DriverManager.setLogStream ( System.out);
```

—Clifton M. Nock

Use the main( ) Function Properly

When you first start to program in Java, you learn to code a function called **main( )**. The **main( )** function of a class is automatically invoked by the Java runtime environment. Most RPG programmers who learn Java use the **main( )** function like the main routine of an RPG program. But the **main( )** function is not the best place to put your driver code. Consider the Java application shown in Figure 8.3.

```
public class JavaApplication {
    int field;
    public static void main(String argv[]) {
        field = 1;
        doStuff();
    }
    private void doStuff() {
        field++;
    }
}
```

Figure 8.3: The main( ) function drives the program

This class seems to make sense, but you get the following compile errors:

- Cannot make a static reference to a nonstatic field in class JavaApplication.
- Cannot make a static reference to the instance method named doStuff for class JavaApplication.

The reason for these errors is that object fields and functions are different from class fields and functions. A class field or function is qualified with the Java keyword static. The main( ) function is a good example. It's static, which means it can only operate on fields declared as static and invoke functions declared as static. Static fields are considered class fields because there is never more than one instance of those variables for a class, no matter how many objects of that class type are instantiated (created).

Nonstatic fields are considered object fields because there are separate instances of those fields for every object instantiated from that class. Static class functions can be invoked without having an object instance of that class. The only restriction on static functions is that they can operate only on static fields—hence the term *class function*.

Nonstatic fields and functions are considered object fields and functions because there is a unique instance of them for every object created of that class type. Using main( ) as a driver function works fine if you make all of your other functions static and use local variables or static class fields, but that is not object-oriented programming. You'd be better off using Visual Basic.

The main( ) function should be used only to bootstrap or jumpstart a class by having it instantiate itself. Then, whatever driver code the application requires goes in the class's constructor function. I've illustrated this in Figure 8.4.

```java
public class JavaApplication {
    int field;
    public static void main(String argv[]) {
        new JavaApplication ();
    }
    public JavaApplication() {
        field = 1;
        doStuff();
    }
    private void doStuff() {
        field++;
    }
}
```

Figure 8.4: The main( ) function jumpstarts the class, which in turn drives the program.

—*Don Denoncourt*

What Are JAR Files?

If you're new to Java programming, and most of us are, then some of the concepts and terms may be unfamiliar to you. One of those terms you may not be familiar with is the *Java ARchive* (JAR) file, which is nothing more than a repository of compressed (or optionally, uncompressed) Java classes (programs and objects) that make up a particular "toolbox." For example, the AS/400 Toolbox for Java has many JAR files, such as JT400.jar and UTIL400.jar. These JAR files contain classes that have already been created by other Java programmers, IBM programmers in this case, to provide you with prewritten objects, or tools, you can use to help build your own Java programs. For example, the Java class AS400 is in the JT400.jar file. This is the class you would use in your own Java program to create a logon to the AS/400.

Because it's hard to see what is inside them, JAR files can seem ominous. But don't despair; there are a couple of ways to open a JAR file and peek inside. The first is to change the file type of the JAR file from JAR to ZIP. Now, by using a utility, such as WinZip or PKZIP, you can open that ZIP file and look inside. The second method is to use an updated version of WinZip or PKZIP. Both these tools will authomatically open *.jar files.

I've found that this makes programming in Java easier for me. I can visually scan for a class, which, based on its name, appears to perform the function that I need. Then it's a simple matter to read the Java documentation about that particular class to verify that it actually does what you think it should. The alternative is to manually dig through IBM's AS/400 Toolbox for Java documentation, searching for classes that do what I need. That's a process that is made unnecessarily difficult because the online HTML documentation lacks a SEARCH feature.

—Shannon O'Donnell

What's in a Java Class?

To be a power Java programmer, you need to become familiar with the wide variety of classes delivered with standard Java. Not only that, but you also need to be able to quickly pick up and understand a variety of third-party classes.

Java's standard documentation facility, Javadoc, helps, but I find the HTML help files too wordy and difficult to follow. What I use to quickly understand a class is Sun's javap utility. This utility lists the public functions of a class. I don't need the verbose comments. If the function name and its parameters do not define the use of the function, then the class itself is not well designed.

The following code illustrates how to use **javap** to list the public API of the **Integer** class. Note that you must fully qualify the package of the class.

```
javap.exe java.lang.Integer
```

The result of executing this instruction is shown in Figure 8.5.

```
Compiled from Integer.java
public final synchronized class java.lang.Integer extends
java.lang.Number
    /* ACC_SUPER bit set */
{
    public static final int MIN_VALUE;
    public static final int MAX_VALUE;
    public static final java.lang.Class TYPE;
    public static java.lang.String toString( int, int);
    public static java.lang.String toHexString( int);
    public static java.lang.String toOctalString(int);
    public static java.lang.String toBinaryString(int);
    public static java.lang.String toString( int);
    public static int parseInt( java.lang.String, int);
    public static int parseInt( java.lang.String);
    public static java.lang.Integer valueOf(java.lang.String, int);
    public static java.lang.Integer valueOf(java.lang.String);
    public java.lang.Integer( int);
    public java.lang.Integer( java.lang.String);
    public byte byteValue();
    public short shortValue();
    public int intValue();
    public long longValue();
    public float floatValue();
    public double doubleValue();
    public java.lang.String toString();
    public int hashCode();
    public boolean equals(java.lang.Object);
    public static java.lang.Integer getInteger( java.lang.String);
    public static java.lang.Integer getInteger( java.lang.String, int);
    public static java.lang.Integer getInteger( java.lang.String,
java.lang.Integer);
    public static java.lang.Integer decode(java.lang.String);
    static static {};
}
```

Figure 8.5: JAVAP reveals the public contents of the Integer class.

I find this concise listing is all I need to understand a class and its public API.

—Don Denoncourt

✦ ✦ ✦ OfficeVision

Convert OV/400 Documents to Microsoft Word

Q: Do you know of any conversion software I can purchase to enable me to convert OfficeVision/400 documents to Microsoft Word?

A: You probably don't need to buy any conversion software to do this. OfficeVision already gives you the capability to convert documents into other formats. The trick is to convert the document into a format that both OfficeVision and Microsoft Word can understand. One type of document that works with both word processors is Revisable Form Text Document Content Architecture (RFTDCA). To convert an OfficeVision document to RFTDCA format, you can use the Convert Document (CVTDOC) command and specify RFTDCA in the TYPE parameter. For example, to convert a document called MYDOC in a folder called MYFLR, you would enter the command as below:

```
CVTDOC DOC(MYDOC) FLR(MYFLR) TYPE(RFTDCA)
```

Next, you would need to copy the document from your AS/400 to your PC. One way you can do this is to use the shared folders function of Client Access. Once the document is on your PC, you can open it with Word. If for some reason Word is unable to open the document, it could be because you didn't install the RFTDCA conversion option when you originally installed Word. If so, you can just rerun Word's Setup to install the RFTDCA conversion option.

—Robin Klima

✦ ✦ ✦ OS/400

Command Entry Panel

If you're new to the AS/400, you might have been using menus exclusively. Menus are nice and handy, and they sport a command line from which you can type commands. But there's something better out there: the Command Entry panel. The command line takes up the entire screen, and you get a running history of the commands you've executed, along with whatever messages they've produced.

To invoke the Command Entry panel, call program QCMD, as follows:

```
CALL QCMD
```

From that point on, any command you type won't simply go away (the way it does in a menu); it will scroll up. You can then move the cursor up as far as you want (you can even roll up to see even older commands), press F9 once, and retrieve a command you executed two hours ago. Or you can press F4 and have it prompted, without having to press F9 first.

If your system has a library named QSYS38 installed, you can even work with commands using S/38 syntax. To do so, call program QCL, rather than QCMD, to invoke the S/38 environment's Command Entry panel. Not all S/38 commands are supported, but most of those used every day are available. For instance, you can run the Browse Physical File Member (BRWPFM) command there, instead of having to remember that the AS/400 names it Display Physical File Member (DSPPFM). And, of course, qualified names go in the old *object.library* format.

—Ernie Malaga

Modify ENDJOB to End Group Jobs

Q: I have written a CL program that runs Work with Active Jobs (WRKACTJOB), sends the output to a spooled file, and then uses the job name, user name, and job number in the output to perform an End Job (ENDJOB). The problem is that some of the jobs have a plus sign to the left of their names, and ENDJOB does not end them, even with the *IMMED option.

A: If a job has a plus sign to the left of its name in WRKACTJOB, it is a group job. You have to use ADLINTJOBS(*GRPJOB) on the ENDJOB command to end all the jobs in the group. This option can be used for any interactive job, even if the job is not a group job.

—Martin Pluth

✦ ✦ ✦ REXX

AS/400 Adding Machine

I've created what I call a "tally calculator," which gives an AS/400 user the ability to tally a batch of numbers. Using the REXX language built into OS/400, I was able to create the program (called a "procedure," in REXX terms) with very little effort.

Figure 8.6 contains the source code. When you create the source member, specify REXX as the source member type. No compiling is necessary because REXX interprets the language statements as it executes.

```
/* REXX Adding Machine */
tally = 0
numb = 0
say
say date('w')center("System Adding machine", 60) date()
say
say "Enter + or - number, RESET, or press Enter to end"
do n = 1 to 400
   tally = tally + numb
   do until datatype(numb,num)
      pull numb
      if length(numb) < 1 then exit
      if numb = "RESET" | numb = "R" | numb = "r" then tally = 0
   end
   say tally " + " numb " = " tally+numb
end
```

Figure 8.6: Thanks to REXX, a dumb terminal can be an adding machine.

To run the procedure, use the Start REXX Procedure (STRREXPRC) command and specify the source file and library that contains the REXX source member. This REXX procedure illustrates how useful the REXX language can be.

—Jim Stephenson

Base 36 Algorithm

Q: I need a program (or at least directions) on taking a number from base 10 and changing it to base 36. I know that, in base 36, A=10, B=11...Z=35. I have no idea how to do this. If anybody can help me out, I would appreciate it.

A: I don't know if this is something you need to do interactively on an impromptu basis or if you need to incorporate this into an HLL program. If it's the former, Figure 8.7 shows a little REXX procedure that will do what you're looking for.

```
say 'Enter a base 10 value'
pull base10
base = 36
base36 = ''
b36digits = '0123456789ABCDEFGHIJKLMNOPQRSTUVWXYZ'
do until base10 = 0
   modulo = base10 // base
   base36 = substr(b36digits,modulo+1,1)base36
   base10 = base10 % base
end
say 'Base 36 value is' base36
```

Figure 8.7: REXX easily converts numbers to base 36 (or any other base).

Figure 8.8 shows essentially the same routine in RPG. Pass the number you want to convert in the BASE10 parameter. The converted base 36 value will be passed back left-adjusted in the BASE36 parameter. Note that these routines are designed to handle positive integer values only.

```
I              36                    C         BASE
I              '0123456789ABCDEFGHIJ-C         DIGITS
I              'KLMNOPQRSTUVWXYZ'
*
C        *ENTRY     PLIST
C                   PARM              BASE10  90
C                   PARM              BASE36  10
*
C        BASE10     DOUEQ*ZERO
C        BASE10     DIV   BASE        MODULO  90
C                   MVR               MODULO
C        MODULO     ADD   1           X       30
C        1          SUBSTDIGITS:X     CHAR1   1
C        CHAR1      CAT   BASE36:0     BASE36
C                   DIV   BASE         BASE10
C                   ENDDO
*
C                   MOVE *ON          *INLR
```

Figure 8.8: The RPG Base 36 Conversion routine works, but is cumbersome.

Also, in both routines, you can convert to any base lower than 36 by changing the value in the field BASE.

—*Matt Sargent*

Embed SQL in a REXX Procedure

When I use SQL in a REXX procedure, I code the REXX command ADDRESS followed by the command environment that will execute the passed expression. In Figure 8.9, you can see a segment of a procedure that I use to list a file.

```
ARG Wave
RC =0
ADDRESS COMMAND 'OVRDBF FILE(STDOUT) TOFILE(QSYSPRT)'
ADDRESS EXECSQL EXECSQL 'SET OPTION COMMIT = *NONE'
IF SQLCODE
SELECT_STMT = 'SELECT lane, type, length ',
'FROM wbpwawrk ',
'WHERE wave = ? ',
'ORDER BY lane'
...
ERROR: SAY 'Error occurred.'
```

Figure 8.9: The ADDRESS command lets you use multiple command environments within REXX.

This REXX procedure goes on to use the SQL PREPARE, DECLARE, OPEN CURSOR, and FETCH statements to print a report using the REXX SAY command. Using the ADDRESS command allows multiple command environments to be used from within REXX. It's also nice for those of us who tend to forget to change the parameter before pressing Enter on the STRREXPRC command.

—Frank Hill

Prompt CL Commands in REXX

When working in SEU with REXX, CL commands cannot be prompted. To use commands in these members, you have to either find the manual or a command line and prompt the command, remember or write the keywords down, then return to SEU and type the command. This is not only time-consuming, but also error-prone.

There is a simple way to prompt the command in SEU. While editing, press F13 to change defaults, tab down to "Source Type," change it to CL or CLP, and press Enter. When you return to SEU, you're working on a CL program. Now you can prompt the command, fill in the blanks, and let the system generate the keywords and do syntax checking for you.

When the CL command is displayed in the source member, it will be indented and line wrapping might occur. CL commands will need to be placed inside single quotes.

To change back, press F13, and change the "Source Type" back to its original value. The REXX statements will generate syntax errors if edited before switching back to the original source type.

Now you have a good CL command in your procedure in a lot less time and without having to worry about syntax errors.

—Brad Hooley

REXXTRY Procedure

A good way to introduce yourself to REXX is by running the REXXTRY procedure. REXXTRY runs an interactive terminal session that allows you to key in REXX statements and see them executed immediately. You can find the REXXTRY procedure in appendix E of the *REXX/400 Programmer's Guide*. If you have OS/2, you can find a more sophisticated version in file REXXTRY.CMD in the OS/2 subdirectory. I have run both versions successfully under both OS/400 V3R1 and OS/2 Warp.

Put REXXTRY into a source file called QREXSRC, with a member type of REXX, and execute it from PDM with option 16.

—Ted Holt

Use REXX to Retrieve the Day of the Week

Figure 8.10 shows how to use REXX to determine the day of the week. The first statement retrieves the current day of the week. The second statement uses the **parse** instruction to convert the day of the week to uppercase. The last statement executes a CL command to place the day of the week value into a data area called DAYOFWEEK.

```
wd = date('W')
parse upper var wd wd
'CHGDTAARA DTAARA(DAYOFWEEK) VALUE(&wd)'
```

Figure 8.10: A few lines of REXX easily retrieve the day of the week.

Be sure you create this data area before running the procedure. After you create the data area, you can run the REXX procedure from within a CL program and retrieve the day of the week from the data area. An example of this technique is shown in Figure 8.11.

```
PGM
DCL VAR(&DAYOFWEEK) TYPE(*CHAR) LEN(10)
STRREXPRC SRCMBR(DOW001RX)
RTVDTAARA DTAARA(DAYOFWEEK) RTNVAR(&DAYOFWEEK)
IF (&DAYOFWEEK *EQ 'MONDAY') THEN(DO)
...
ENDDO
IF (&DAYOFWEEK *EQ 'TUESDAY') THEN(DO)
...
ENDDO
```

Figure 8.11: Write a short CL driver to execute a REXX procedure.

—Darren Molitor

Using REXX to Increase Precision

Q: I have a calculation that requires field lengths of more than 30 digits. Unfortunately, RPG IV allows up to only 30 digits for a numeric field definition. Is there any way to get around this?

A: If you need more than 30 digits of precision, try using REXX instead of RPG IV. REXX allows you to set the precision for numeric calculation via the NUMERIC DIGITS command. Using this command, you can make the size of the numeric field as large as you need. If you need to handle only very large or very small numbers, and 17 or so digits of precision is enough, define your RPG IV numeric field as a floating point field on the D-spec:

```
D Numeric_Fld  S  8f
```

Note: Floating point fields are supported only on V3R7 and above.

—*Barbara Morris*

CHAPTER 9

Operations

*T*he heart of any successful IT undertaking is the operations that provide support for both the human and computer infrastructure. While it is hard to quantify a set of tips and tricks that can be used to improve human operations, doing the same thing for a computer's operations is much easier. Easy, that is, until you get to the complex system known as the AS/400.

The AS/400 provides so many easy-to-use and simple interfaces for you that its very simplicity causes it to become one of the most complex operational systems in the world. Think about it for a moment. Someone with little or no AS/400 experience can very quickly figure out how to display an output queue, or start a system save, by simply navigating through the AS/400's very intuitive menu interface. That same inexperienced person—with the right authority and, again using the AS/400's menu system—can change the amount of memory used in interactive subsystems and change it so much that they bring a user's display screen to its knees. In this example, the implementation was simple, but the results lead to extremely complex problems that only an experienced AS/400 person will be able to resolve.

OS/400 operations go beyond simply setting a system value and forgetting about it. To be a successful operator of the AS/400, you have to understand work management, system values, user profiles, and so much more. That's where this chapter on OS/400 operations tips and tricks comes in handy. You'll learn to perform operational duties in such a way as to make your system sing! You'll learn how to automatically remove unwanted spooled files, set IPL values, work with tape systems and labels, work with submitted jobs, and lots more. This chapter is chock full of the kinds of behind-the-scene information you need to make your job as an AS/400 IT professional both easier and more exciting to perform.

—Shannon O'Donnell

✦ ✦ ✦ Access Paths

Save the Access Path

Did you know that your access paths are being journaled? Unless you've turned it off, System Managed Access Path Protection (SMAPP) is working on your system. SMAPP is a valuable addition to IBM's suite of AS/400 recovery tools. It requires no setup. If you're at release V3R1 or later, the system-wide recovery time is set to 150 minutes unless you've changed it.

SMAPP was developed to reduce the amount of time required for an initial program load (IPL) after an abnormal system end. The time required to rebuild open access paths can be quite substantial. Until the release of SMAPP, only explicit access path journaling reduced the time required to rebuild access paths after an abnormal system end. This method requires journaling all underlying physical files before using the Start Journaling Access Path (STRJRNAP) command to start access-path journaling. Because SMAPP creates and manages its own internal journals and journal receivers, this chore is no longer required. All you do is specify the target recovery time either for the entire system or for individual auxiliary storage pools (ASPs) if you have any user ASPs defined. Don't specify both because the system will do extra work trying to balance them.

The Edit Recovery for Access Paths (EDTRCYAP) display is all you'll need if you want to work with SMAPP. You can use the *SYSDFT value (which is 150 minutes for V3R1), *MIN (which will set the value to the minimum recovery time for your system), *OFF, *NONE, or a specific value. SMAPP looks at all access paths to determine how it can meet the specified rebuild target time. It determines which access paths to protect based solely on the recovery time for all access paths. It also constantly evaluates which access paths to protect, automatically responding to any system changes.

You might want to experiment with different target recovery times to achieve the correct balance for your system. SMAPP uses a small amount of processor time and causes increased disk activity. The internal journal receivers take additional storage space, but the system manages this to minimize system impact. If you shorten the target recovery time, the system will use more resources for SMAPP. If your system cannot dedicate any resources to SMAPP, specify *OFF for the system target recovery time to stop SMAPP completely. You might also consider specifying *NONE, which stops the journaling of access paths but allows you to see estimated recovery times and to decide whether those times are acceptable. If the time is too long, you need to dedicate some resources to SMAPP.

You can't control which access paths the system will choose to protect. If too short a time is specified, SMAPP might choose to bypass an access path. For this reason, you should consider explicit journaling if some access paths are crucial to your operation. If you do journal some access paths, the system can use those journal entries to recover, instead of rebuild, the access paths.

Unless you turn it off, SMAPP is working for you. If you want to play with it, you can maximize its use. If you don't want to be bothered, you still have some access path protection. Either way, IBM has come up with an effective method of reducing the time required to recover your system after an abnormal end. Just don't forget that this tool exists.

—D. Ellis Green

✦ ✦ ✦ Active Jobs

Check for Active Jobs from a Batch Program

Do you have jobs that need to run continuously but sometimes terminate for whatever reason? You can easily set up a CL program to check for active jobs in a specific job queue, and start jobs that should be active but are not. This program will check all of the jobs in a subsystem. If the job you specify is found, the CL program will terminate. If the job that you specify is not found, the CL program will submit a job to start it.

You will need to declare variables for job, user, and job number, and retrieve these variables with the Retrieve Job Attributes (RTVJOBA) command. You also will need to declare a file that contains one text field of 132 characters. This file will need to be created before the CL program is compiled. Because it requires no cleanup after the job ends, I have chosen QTEMP for the file's library.

First, trap all of the jobs currently running in the specified subsystem. Do this by using the Work with Subsystem Jobs (WRKSBSJOB) command, with the output going to *PRINT. Override the printer file QPDSPSBJ to hold on the output queue. Next, copy the spooled file to the work file created in QTEMP, using the Copy Spooled File (CPYSPLF) command. This is where you will need the variables for job, user, and job number. Delete the spooled file after it is copied. Finally, read the work file. Positions 4 through 13 contain the name of the job. Use the substring function to extract this field and compare it to the name of the job you are looking for. If you find the job, leave the program. If you do not find the job, read the next record. If EOF is encountered and you have not found your job, submit it and exit the program.

The complete program is shown in Figure 9.1. You can put this program in your job scheduler to run at whatever frequency you desire, eliminating the need for an operator to check for these jobs on a regular basis.

```
/*================================================================*/
/* To compile:                                                    */
/*                                                                */
/* CRTPF FILE(QTEMP/TEST132) RCDLEN(132)                          */
/* CRTCLPGM PGM(XXX/CHKACTJOB) SRCFILE(XXX/QCLSRC)                */
/*                                                                */
/*================================================================*/
PGM
DCL VAR(&CURUSER) TYPE(*CHAR) LEN(10)
DCL VAR(&CURJOB) TYPE(*CHAR) LEN(10)
DCL VAR(&CURJOBNBR) TYPE(*CHAR) LEN(6)
DCL VAR(&JOBTOCHECK) TYPE(*CHAR) LEN(10) +
VALUE(TESTROUT)
DCL VAR(&SBS) TYPE(*CHAR) LEN(10) VALUE(QBATCH)
DCLF FILE(QTEMP/TEXT132)
MONMSG MSGID(CPF0000) EXEC(GOTO CMDLBL(ENDPGM))
CHGJOB LOGCLPGM(*YES)
RTVJOBA JOB(&CURJOB) USER(&CURUSER) NBR(&CURJOBNBR)
/* Output all active jobs in the subsystem to a spool file. */
/* If the subsystem is not active, return */
OVRPRTF FILE(QPDSPSBJ) PRTTXT(*BLANK) HOLD(*YES)
WRKSBSJOB SBS(&SBS) OUTPUT(*PRINT)
MONMSG MSGID(CPF1003) EXEC(GOTO CMDLBL(ENDPGM))
/* Clear or create a work file to hold active job information */
CLRPFM FILE(QTEMP/TEXT132)
MONMSG MSGID(CPF3132) EXEC(CRTPF +
FILE(QTEMP/TEXT132) RCDLEN(132))
/* Copy the spool file to the work file, then delete the spool file */
CPYSPLF FILE(QPDSPSBJ) TOFILE(QTEMP/TEXT132) +
JOB(&CURJOBNBR/&CURUSER/&CURJOB)
MONMSG MSGID(CPF3309) EXEC(GOTO CMDLBL(ENDPGM))
DLTSPLF FILE(QPDSPSBJ) JOB(&CURJOBNBR/&CURUSER/&CURJOB)
MONMSG MSGID(CPF0000)
/* Read a record from the work file. If the job name is not the */
/* one you're looking for, read the next record. If end of file, */
/* drop to EOF label and submit the job to batch. If the job is */
/* found, exit the program. */
READ:
RCVF
MONMSG MSGID(CPF0864) EXEC(GOTO CMDLBL(EOF))
IF COND(%SST(&TEXT132 4 13) *NE &JOBTOCHECK) +
THEN(GOTO CMDLBL(READ))
GOTO CMDLBL(ENDPGM)
EOF:
SBMJOB CMD(CALL PGM(HOLT/TESTROUT)) JOB(&JOBTOCHECK) +
JOBQ(QBATCH)
ENDPGM:
ENDPGM
```

Figure 9.1: This program monitors for jobs that should be active.

—*Lisa Patterson*

Editor's Note: *This is a simple and easily implemented solution to a problem, but don't forget that IBM has been known to change the format of reports. You might have to modify this program when upgrading to a new version or release, or installing PTFs.*

✦ ✦ ✦ Attn Key

Activate Attn Key Program

Q: I would like to change the processing of the Attention key. If an operator hits it, I want the Attention key to bring up a program instead of the Operational Assistant screen. Can you supply any ideas or pointers on how to do this?

A: Right now, you get the Operational Assistant screen because the Attention program (ATNPGM) parameter of your user profile is set to a value of *ASSIST or *SYSVAL (and the system value QATNPGM is set to *ASSIST). Use the Change User Profile (CHGUSRPRF) command and specify the program and the library in which the program resides in the ATNPGM parameter. Have the user sign off and sign on again, and you should be in business. It's as simple as keying the following command:

```
CHGUSRPRF USRPRF(user-profile) ATNPGM(library/program)
```

—Midrange Computing Staff

Are Your Users SysRq-2 Happy?

Many tasks require normal completion and can be adversely affected when your users select option 2 of the System Request (SysRq) menu. This option cancels a request, and is used by many to regain control of their keyboards when a task takes too long. Option 2 runs the End Request (ENDRQS) command.

To show you how detrimental ENDRQS can be, imagine you're running a typical order-entry program without commitment control. You're entering the fifth line item when—oh, my—your keyboard remains locked. If you now run ENDRQS (using the SysRq option 2), the data in the order you were entering can be inconsistent. To prevent users from selecting option 2, remove their authority to the ENDRQS command as follows:

```
GRTOBJAUT OBJ(QSYS/ENDRQS) OBJTYPE(*CMD) USER(usrprf1 usrprf2 ...)
          AUT(*EXCLUDE)
```

The next time they select option 2, a message will inform the user that they are not authorized to use this option.

—Ernie Malaga

Getting Back to an Alternate Job

Have you ever mistakenly called the System Request Menu Option 1 (Display sign-on for alternative job)? Here's a way to get back to your original job quickly. First, create a CL program called DFTSIGNOFF, which looks like this:

```
PGM
SIGNOFF
ENDPGM
```

Next, create a dummy user profile called "X" with a password of "X" with an initial program of DFTSIGNOFF. Now, if you accidentally do a System Request 1, just sign on with User X, Password X. You'll end up right back where you started.

—*Midrange Computing Staff*

Keep Your Attn Key Active

Like most programmers, I have my interactive job set up so that when I press the Attention key, a program is called. I generally use a program that has a command line (e.g., the command entry screen [QCMD] or the command line window [QUSCMDLN]). That way, when I press the Attention key, I am able to enter a command. When I return from having entered the command and exit the command line, I end up right back where I was before I pressed the Attention key. The problem I found is that, once I press my Attention key, it is deactivated until I return to where I was before I pressed it. For example, consider the following typical sequence of events:

- You press the Attention key, which takes you to a command line.

- At the command line, you enter a command, which takes you to some screen.

- At that point, you press the Attention key, but nothing happens.

If you find this situation as frustrating as I do, you will be glad to know that I have found a solution to this problem. Write the CL program CMDLINE, as shown in Figure 9.2, and make it your Attention key program.

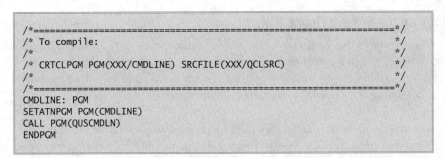

```
/*===============================================================*/
/* To compile:                                                   */
/*                                                               */
/* CRTCLPGM PGM(XXX/CMDLINE) SRCFILE(XXX/QCLSRC)                  */
/*                                                               */
/*===============================================================*/
CMDLINE: PGM
SETATNPGM PGM(CMDLINE)
CALL PGM(QUSCMDLN)
ENDPGM
```

Figure 9.2: Set this program as your Attention key program.

Here's how the program works. The first thing it does is to set the Attention program to it-self. It then calls the command line window. You can replace the line that says CALL PGM(QUSCMDLN) with whatever program you would like to have your Attention key call. After you have compiled this program, use the Set Attention Program (SETATNPGM) com-mand to set your Attention key to it. At this point, you can press the Attention key repeat-edly; each time, it will give you a new command line. Now the sequence of events might look something like this:

- You press the Attention key, which takes you to a command line.

- At the command line, you enter a command, which takes you to some screen.

- At that point, you press the Attention key, which takes you to another command line.

- At that command line, you enter a command, which takes you to some other screen.

- Etc., etc., etc.

This sequence of events can continue as long as you want. Each time, it will take you deeper into your invocation stack. Using this technique allows you to repeatedly use your Attention key even when your Attention program is already active. The only drawback is that eventually you will want to go back to where you started. To do this, you will have to back out of every one of the command lines, and any programs you have called from those command lines, until you get back to where you were before you pressed the Atten-tion key for the first time.

—Robin Klima

Modifying the System Request Menu

When a user presses the SysRq key at the display station, the AS/400 presents a very special menu, the System Request menu. From this menu, the user can select a number of options, such as option 1 to go to a secondary session, option 2 to cancel the command currently running, or option 90 to sign off from the system.

Although this functionality can be very useful, the possibility exists for the user to do more harm than good from the System Request menu, possibly even compromising security and data integrity. For example, what if a user interrupts a complicated database update by selecting option 2 while the system is halfway through the process? Although there are other ways to remove these dangers, the approach I like best is to modify the commands the system runs when a particular option is selected. The names of the commands are stored in a message description, CPX2313, in message file QSYS/QCPFMSG. You could use either the Change Message Description (CHGMSGD) or Work with Message Descriptions (WRKMSGD) command to make these modifications, but doing that changes the System Request menu for everyone, and the change is permanent (or, at least, until you upgrade to a new release).

Here's a much safer and much more flexible approach. First, create your own message file. It doesn't have to be called QCPFMSG, and it can reside in any library you want—even if it's not in the library list of your users. For example, you could call it SYSRQMSGF and place it in QGPL:

```
CRTMSGF MSGF(QGPL/SYSRQMSGF) TEXT('Alter SysRq menu options')
```

Then, copy message description CPX2313 from QCPFMSG to SYSRQMSGF:

```
MRGMSGF FROMMSGF(QSYS/QCPFMSG) TOMSGF(QGPL/SYSRQMSGF) SELECT(CPX2313)
```

Now, you can edit this copy of CPX2313 the way you see fit. For example, you can replace the End Request (ENDRQS) command with a RETURN command. Usually, the system runs ENDRQS when the user selects option 2 from the System Request menu. But, if you make this change, option 2 won't do anything at all. Always ensure that you don't alter the relative starting positions of each command name. The names occupy 11 characters each and are left-adjusted within each 11-byte bucket. Keep it that way.

Once you're done, you can place your new message file into production. For each user whose System Request menu you want to change, insert the following command in the initial program (the program assigned to his user profile to run immediately after the user signs on):

```
OVRMSGF MSGF(QCPFMSG) TOMSGF(QGPL/SYSRQMSGF) SECURE(*YES)
```

There! Only CPX2313 is affected. If the job needs to issue any other message, it will find that message in the original QCPFMSG. But when the user selects option 2 from the System Request menu, nothing will happen, and your database integrity will be saved.

—Ernie Malaga

More Ways to Use the Attn Key

Need a program quick? Don't want to go through a menu and option scheme? Do you say, "I call this program 50 times a day; I wish there were an easier and quicker way." Do I have a technique for you!

The ATNPGM parameter of the CRTUSRPRF and CHGUSRPRF commands, and the Set Attention Program (SETATNPGM) command provide ways for a user to call a program by pressing the Attn key. Because I like to make the Attn key give me a command line in a pop-up window, I included the following command in the initial program (INLPGM) assigned to my user profile:

```
SETATNPGM PGM(QSYS/QCMD)
```

QCMD is a good attention key program for system administrators, but not for end users. Instead, I recommend that users call a menu that holds some common options for them. Figures 9.3 and 9.4 show the source members for menu ATN007, created with SDA. Figure 9.5 has the source of a small CL program to display the menu.

```
A                              CHGINPDFT
A                              INDARA
A                              PRINT(QSYSPRT)
  *================================================================
A          R ATN007
A                              LOCK
A                              SLNO(01)
A                              CLRL(*ALL)
A                              CF03
A                              HELP
A                              HOME
```

Figure 9.3: This display file is used as the menu for the attention key program (part 1 of 2).

```
A                                  HLPRTN
A                             1  2'ATN007'
A                                  COLOR(BLU)
A                             1 33'ATN007 Menu'
A                                  DSPATR(HI)
A                             3  2'Select one of the following:'
A                                  COLOR(BLU)
A                             5  7'1. Work with my spooled output'
A                             6  7'2. Work with output queue PRT01'
A                             7  7'3. Start printer PRT01'
A                             8  7'4. Display messages'
A* CMDPROMPT  Do not delete this DDS spec.
A                             019 2'Selection or command'
```

Figure 9.3: This display file is used as the menu for the attention key program (part 2 of 2).

```
ATN007QQ,1
0001 WRKSPLF
0002 WRKOUTQ OUTQ(PRT01)
0003 STRPRTWTR DEV(PRT01)
0004 DSPMSG
```

Figure 9.4: Member ATN007QQ defines the commands for menu ATN007.

```
/*==============================================================*/
/* To compile:                                                  */
/*                                                              */
/* CRTCLPGM PGM(XXX/ATN007CL) SRCFILE(XXX/QCLSRC)               */
/*                                                              */
/*==============================================================*/
PGM
GO MENU(ATN007)
ENDPGM
```

Figure 9.5: CL program ATN007CL becomes the user's Attn key program.

Run the following command for any user who should see this menu when the user presses the Attn key:

```
CHGUSRPRF USRPRF(XXX) ATNPGM PGM(XXX/ATN007CL)
```

You can specify any program on your system to be an Attn key handling program, and different users can benefit from different Attn key handling programs. Actually, a user can have different Attn key handling programs in different sessions. It's just a matter of running SETATNPGM.

—Tim Johnston

Pressed Sysreq 1 by Mistake?

The AS/400 presents a sign-on display when you run the Transfer to Secondary Job (TFRSECJOB) command or select option 1 of the SysReq menu. If you get to this sign-on display by accident, you can cancel it instead of doing the sign-on shuffle (sign on, sign off). Hit the Test key on your keyboard (Alt+Test or Cmd+Backspace). When the Prime Options Menu appears, type a "C" and press Enter. You will save a lot of time not having to sign on and will be right back at your previous session.

—Steve Sampson

Quick Return from Interrupted Session

If you ever select option 1 from the System Request menu to start a secondary job and then you change your mind, you can return to your primary session without signing on and off. All you need to do is use the Alt + Test key combination (in PC Support, this defaults to Alt + Pause) to get the Prime Option Menu and then select option C to end. On older keyboards, you need to use the Cmd + Backspace key combination.

—Midrange Computing Staff

System Request Function

Q: One of our users has found out about the system request function and has started to abuse it. What can we do to prevent him from using this while retaining DP staff access?

A: Perform the following command:

```
GRTOBJAUT OBJ(QSYS/QGMNSYSR) OBJTYPE(*PNLGRP) USER(username)
AUT(*EXCLUDE)
```

—Midrange Computing Staff

The AS/400 Attn Key

The Attention key on the AS/400 does not function the same as it does on the System/36. Instead of presenting an Inquiry Options menu, it simply interrupts the current program and loads a user-specified Attention key handling program. (The closest thing to the System/36 Inquiry Options menu on the AS/400 is the System Request menu presented when the System Request key is used.)

Many new AS/400 users have probably noticed that the Attention key doesn't do anything when it is pressed. This is because no Attention key handling program has been specified. You can use the Set Attention Program (SETATNPGM) command with the SET(*ON) parameter specified to identify a program as the Attention key handling program. Generally, if the Attention key is pressed and the keyboard is unlocked for input (input inhibited light is off), the current job is interrupted, the display is saved, and the Attention key handling program is immediately loaded. (See the *Work Management Guide* and the *Control Language Reference* manuals for exceptions to this general rule.) No parameters are passed to the Attention key handling program when it is called.

—Midrange Computing Staff

✦ ✦ ✦ Command Processing

DSPOBJD Outfile Fix

If you use the Display Object Description (DSPOBJD) command to create an outfile, be warned that field ODOBSZ (Database Size) within the outfile has a maximum capacity of 10 digits. Because ODOBSZ reports the size of the object in bytes (not kilobytes or megabytes), this field cannot correctly describe the size of objects of 10 gigabytes or larger. Fortunately, there is an alternate method that works in all cases.

Multiply field ODBPUN (bytes per unit of measure) by ODSIZU (object size in units of measure), making sure to store the result in a field of at least 11 digits. For convenience, use a 15-digit field so that you can correctly describe the size of objects of up to 1 petabyte (1 million gigabytes). The AS/400 is not likely to soon exceed this capacity.

—Chris Fuller

Editor's Note: *For your convenience, here are the prefixes used to indicate multiples of a byte: kilo (one thousand), mega (one million), giga (one thousand million), tera (one million million), peta (one thousand million million), and exa (one million million million). To avoid confusion, don't use terms like billion and trillion; these terms describe different quantities around the world.*

✦ ✦ ✦ Commitment Control

No More Fear of Commitment Control

If you are running an interactive session on the AS/400 and are desperate to get to a command line, here's one method. Press and hold the Shift key and then press the SysRq key. (This is the sequence of keystrokes for terminals; you might have to use another sequence from a PC.) When the Display Job (DSPJOB) screen appears, select option 16 (Display Commitment Control Status) and press Enter. Surprise! You are now on a screen that has access to the command line via the F9 key. Because I rarely use commitment control or option 16 on the DSPJOB screen, I was surprised to find this.

—*Chris Ringer*

✦ ✦ ✦ Copy File

Reorganizing Large Files

Even if you don't have much DASD, you can still reorganize a large file. Our AS/400 has a work order file with over 1.4 million records consuming over 1.3GB of disk space. This file has numerous deleted records, and we need to reorganize it. Unfortunately, we do not have sufficient unused disk space to allow us to do a Reorganize Physical File Member (RGZPFM) on a file of that size.

I have discovered that if you use the Copy File (CPYF) command to copy the file to tape and then use the Copy from Tape (CPYFRMTAP) command to copy the file back from tape, you can successfully remove the deleted records without needing all that disk space. The TOFILE parameter of the CPYF command should contain the name of a tape file you create. The tape file should specify a label as well as record and block length of the data file. If you want your records to be in the same sequence as the original file, specify 1 in the FROMRCD parameter. This way, only the deleted records get left out.

The Copy to Tape (CPYTOTAP) command will do the same thing as the CPYF command, but it does not give you the option of changing the processing sequence. It will sort the records using the access path (if one exists) as it does the copy.

—*Adrian Ramotar*

✦ ✦ ✦ Cross Reference

File/Program Cross Reference

You can create your own cross-reference list to view file usage. The report will list each file and all the programs that call each file. It will work for both native and S36EE files and programs.

- Run the DSPPGMREF command for all programs in a library. Specify output to go to *OUTFILE.

- Create a query using the output file and include the following fields: WHFNAM, WHOBJT, WHPNAM, WHLIB, WHTEXT, WHLNAM, WHSNAM, WHFUSG. Sort the file by WHFNAM, WHPNAM.

—Alon Fluxman

What Programs Use a File

IBM gave us the Display Program References (DSPPGMREF) command as a way to list the files used by a given program, or by all programs in a library. This command could be used more effectively if it worked the other way around (listing the programs that use a specific file). Turning DSPPGMREF around would make life so much easier. You would be able to tell which programs to recompile after you change a file.

Fortunately, you can run DSPPGMREF to an outfile and use the outfile to print a report that contains only the information you need. I created the List File Programs (LSTFPGM) command (Figure 9.6) and its associated programs, F001CL (Figure 9.7) and F001RG (Figure 9.8) to solve this common problem. The utility uses an externally described printer file, F001P1 (Figure 9.9).

```
LSTFPGM:    CMD         PROMPT('List File Programs')

            PARM        KWD(PGMLIB) TYPE(*NAME) LEN(10) +
                        SPCVAL((*ALL) (*ALLUSR) (*CURLIB) (*LIBL) +
                        (*USRLIBL)) MIN(1) EXPR(*YES) +
                        PROMPT('Program library')
            PARM        KWD(FILE) TYPE(*NAME) LEN(10) MIN(1) +
                        EXPR(*YES) PROMPT('File name')
```

Figure 9.6: The LSTFPGM command can be used to list files used by a program.

```
F001CL: +
    PGM PARM(&PGMLIB &FILE)

    DCL VAR(&PGMLIB)      TYPE(*CHAR) LEN(10)
    DCL VAR(&FILE)        TYPE(*CHAR) LEN(10)
    DCL VAR(&MSGDTA)      TYPE(*CHAR) LEN(132)
    DCL VAR(&MSGF)        TYPE(*CHAR) LEN(10)
    DCL VAR(&MSGFLIB)     TYPE(*CHAR) LEN(10)
    DCL VAR(&MSGID)       TYPE(*CHAR) LEN(7)

    DCLF FILE(QADSPOBJ)

    MONMSG MSGID(CPF0000) EXEC(GOTO CMDLBL(ERROR))

    DSPOBJD OBJ(&PGMLIB/*ALL) OBJTYPE(*PGM) OUTPUT(*OUTFILE) +
        OUTFILE(QTEMP/QADSPOBJ)
    OVRDBF FILE(QADSPOBJ) TOFILE(QTEMP/QADSPOBJ)

READ: +
    RCVF
    MONMSG MSGID(CPF0864) EXEC(GOTO CMDLBL(ENDLOOP))

    DSPPGMREF PGM(&ODLBNM/&ODOBNM) OUTPUT(*OUTFILE) +
        OUTFILE(QTEMP/QADSPPGM) OUTMBR(*FIRST *ADD)
    GOTO CMDLBL(READ)

ENDLOOP: +
    OVRDBF FILE(QADSPPGM) TOFILE(QTEMP/QADSPPGM)
    CALL PGM(F001RG) PARM(&FILE)
    DLTOVR FILE(*ALL)
    RETURN

ERROR: +
    RCVMSG MSGTYPE(*EXCP) MSGDTA(&MSGDTA) MSGID(&MSGID) MSGF(&MSGF) +
        MSGFLIB(&MSGFLIB)
    SNDPGMMSG MSGID(&MSGID) MSGF(&MSGFLIB/&MSGF) MSGDTA(&MSGDTA) +
        MSGTYPE(*ESCAPE)

    ENDPGM
```

Figure 9.7: The F001CL command processor is the power behind the LSTFFPGM command.

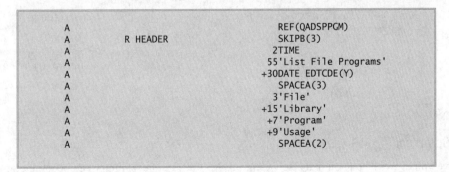

```
A                                      REF(QADSPPGM)
A            R HEADER                   SKIPB(3)
A                                       2TIME
A                                       55'List File Programs'
A                                      +30DATE EDTCDE(Y)
A                                       SPACEA(3)
A                                       3'File'
A                                      +15'Library'
A                                      +7'Program'
A                                      +9'Usage'
A                                       SPACEA(2)
```

Figure 9.8: Printer file F001P1 is used to print the files used by a program (part 1 of 2).

```
        *
        A         R DETAIL                              SPACEA(1)
        A           WHFNAM    R                3
        A           WHLIB     R                +8
        A           WHPNAM    R                +4
        A           USAGE           12A        +6
```

Figure 9.8: Printer file F001P1 is used to print the files used by a program (part 2 of 2).

```
        FQADSPPGMIP  E                      DISK
        FF001P1  O   E              99      PRINTER
        *
        C          WHFNAM     IFEQ FILE
        C                     SELEC
        C          WHFUSG     WHEQ 1
        C                     MOVEL'Input'    USAGE
        C          WHFUSG     WHEQ 2
        C                     MOVEL'Output'   USAGE
        C          WHFUSG     WHEQ 3
        C          WHFUSG     OREQ 4
        C                     MOVEL'Update'   USAGE
        C                     OTHER
        C                     MOVE *BLANK     USAGE
        C                     ENDSL
        C          *IN99      IFEQ *ON
        C                     WRITEHEADER
        C                     MOVE *OFF       *IN99
        C                     ENDIF
        C                     WRITEDETAIL
        C                     ENDIF
        *
        C          *INZSR     BEGSR
        C          *ENTRY     PLIST
        C                     PARM            FILE   10
        C                     WRITEHEADER
        C                     ENDSR
```

Figure 9.9: RPG program F001RG provides the processing power for listing the files used by a program.

—*Eugene Arencibia*

✦ ✦ ✦ DASD

A Self-cleaning AS/400

Have you ever wished you had a self-cleaning AS/400? A query library can become cluttered with physical files and one-time queries if users build database files with Query/400 so that they can subsequently query them or join them to other files. Most users cannot delete their own physical files, and it's too much work for you to constantly delete them yourself. Placing these files in QTEMP is not effective because QTEMP is deleted when the job ends, and thus your files will disappear. To solve the problem, build a library called QRYTMP or TMPLIB, and instruct your Query/400 users to build temporary database files there. They can even use the library for one-time queries that they do not want to save. Configure the OS/400 job scheduler to automatically run the CLRLIB command on that new library each night.

—Dave Jackson

Checking for Disk Errors

Q: Is there a way that I can automatically scan the error log for disk errors and notify the operators when one is found?

A: As shown in Figures 9.10 and 9.11 you can see the source for the Check Disk Error (CHKDSKERR) command that I use to do what you described. The program prints the error log and then copies it to a physical file. It then uses QCLSCAN to check for certain error codes. In the sample program, it is looking for error code 6109. You might need to modify the program to look for error codes that pertain to your site. If it finds the specified code in the listing, the program sends a message to the system operator message queue. Then the operator can review the error log using the Print Error Log (PRTERRLOG) command.

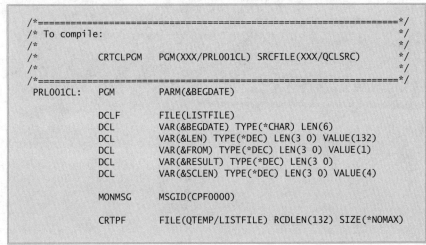

```
/*================================================================*/
/* To compile:                                                    */
/*                                                                */
/*            CRTCLPGM   PGM(XXX/PRL001CL) SRCFILE(XXX/QCLSRC)     */
/*                                                                */
/*================================================================*/
 PRL001CL:  PGM        PARM(&BEGDATE)

            DCLF       FILE(LISTFILE)
            DCL        VAR(&BEGDATE) TYPE(*CHAR) LEN(6)
            DCL        VAR(&LEN) TYPE(*DEC) LEN(3 0) VALUE(132)
            DCL        VAR(&FROM) TYPE(*DEC) LEN(3 0) VALUE(1)
            DCL        VAR(&RESULT) TYPE(*DEC) LEN(3 0)
            DCL        VAR(&SCLEN) TYPE(*DEC) LEN(3 0) VALUE(4)

            MONMSG     MSGID(CPF0000)

            CRTPF      FILE(QTEMP/LISTFILE) RCDLEN(132) SIZE(*NOMAX)
```

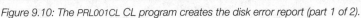

Figure 9.10: The PRL001CL CL program creates the disk error report (part 1 of 2).

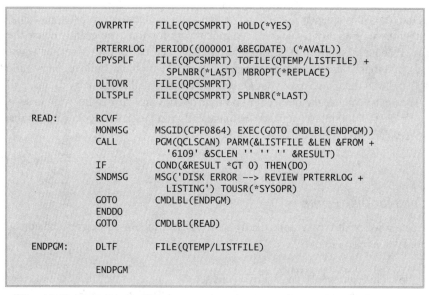

```
                OVRPRTF      FILE(QPCSMPRT) HOLD(*YES)

                PRTERRLOG    PERIOD((000001 &BEGDATE) (*AVAIL))
                CPYSPLF      FILE(QPCSMPRT) TOFILE(QTEMP/LISTFILE) +
                               SPLNBR(*LAST) MBROPT(*REPLACE)
                DLTOVR       FILE(QPCSMPRT)
                DLTSPLF      FILE(QPCSMPRT) SPLNBR(*LAST)

READ:           RCVF
                MONMSG       MSGID(CPF0864) EXEC(GOTO CMDLBL(ENDPGM))
                CALL         PGM(QCLSCAN) PARM(&LISTFILE &LEN &FROM +
                               '6109' &SCLEN '' '' '' &RESULT)
                IF           COND(&RESULT *GT 0) THEN(DO)
                SNDMSG       MSG('DISK ERROR --> REVIEW PRTERRLOG +
                               LISTING') TOUSR(*SYSOPR)
                GOTO         CMDLBL(ENDPGM)
                ENDDO
                GOTO         CMDLBL(READ)

ENDPGM:         DLTF         FILE(QTEMP/LISTFILE)

                ENDPGM
```

Figure 9.10: The PRL001CL CL program creates the disk error report (part 2 of 2).

```
/*================================================================*/
   /* To compile:                                              */
   /*                                                          */
   /*          CRTCMD    CMD(XXX/CHKDSKERR) PGM(XXX/PRL001CL)   +  */
   /*                      SRCFILE(XXX/QCMDSRC)                 */
   /*                                                          */
   /*================================================================*/
CHKDSKERR:  CMD         PROMPT('Check For Disk Errors')
            PARM        KWD(DATE) TYPE(*CHAR) LEN(6) RANGE('000000' +
                          '999999') MIN(1) PROMPT('Date To Look For +
                          Disk Error')
```

Figure 9.11: The CHKDSKERR command makes finding disk errors a snap.

—Midrange Computing Staff

362

Cleaning Up AS/400 Libraries

Utility CLEANLIBS (see Figure 9.12) will "clean up" all user libraries on an AS/400. In this case, cleanup means:

- Reorganize all files that have more than 10 percent of their records marked as deleted.
- Remove observability from programs that have observability information.
- Optimize unoptimized programs.

The benefits are improved performance and less wasted disk space. It is a perfect job to run during any idle period such as nights or weekends.

```
CLEANLIBS: +
    PGM

    DCLF FILE(QADSPOBJ)
    MONMSG MSGID(CPF0000)

    DSPOBJD OBJ(QSYS/*ALL) OBJTYPE(*LIB) OUTPUT(*OUTFILE) +
        OUTFILE(QTEMP/LIBLIST)

    OVRDBF FILE(QADSPOBJ) TOFILE(LIBLIST)
    OPNDBF FILE(QTEMP/LIBLIST) OPTION(*INP)

READ: +
    RCVF RCDFMT(QLIDOBJD)
    MONMSG MSGID(CPF0864) EXEC(GOTO CMDLBL(EOF))
    IF COND(%SST(&ODOBNM 1 1) *EQ 'Q') THEN(GOTO CMDLBL(READ))
    IF COND(%SST(&ODOBNM 1 1) *EQ '#') THEN(GOTO CMDLBL(READ))
    IF COND(%SST(&ODOBNM 1 1) *EQ '$') THEN(GOTO CMDLBL(READ))
    IF COND(%SST(&ODOBNM 1 1) *EQ '%') THEN(GOTO CMDLBL(READ))
    IF COND(%SST(&ODOBNM 1 1) *EQ '&') THEN(GOTO CMDLBL(READ))

REORGF: +
    CALL PGM(REORGPF) PARM(&ODOBNM)
RMVOBS: +
    CHGPGM PGM(&ODOBNM/*ALL) RMVOBS(*ALL)
OPTIMIZE: +
    CHGPGM PGM(&ODOBNM/*ALL) OPTIMIZE(*YES)

    GOTO CMDLBL(READ)

EOF: +
    CLOF OPNID(LIBLIST)

    ENDPGM
```

Figure 9.12: Use this CL program, CLEANLIBS, to reorganize your system.

We all know what file reorganization is, but what is observability and optimization? Observability is data, required for online debugging, which is automatically inserted into a program when you compile it. Unless you are still in the process of debugging the program, the observability information is just using precious disk space. Because optimization deals mainly with register usage optimization, a program would benefit in path lengths, and possibly instruction paging. There is an OPTIMIZE keyword on the compiler commands, but the default is set to *NO to save compile time (the compiler has to go through another phase to optimize the code). There is no negative side effect to optimization. CLEANLIBS will remove observability and optimize every program that needs it by use of the CHGPGM command.

The reorganization takes place if the number of deleted records is greater than 10 percent of the entire file. You can easily change this to any number that you want.

It is interesting how CLEANLIBS accesses information from the DSPOBJD output file. Each CL command that gives you the option of outputting to a file also has a model file on the system, which identifies the record format. This format contains a field name for each field in the output file. You can find the formats for these output files under "Writing the Output from a Command Directly to a Database File" in the *Database Guide* (SC21-9659). The model files cannot be used as the actual output file for the command. You must create your own file, and then override the model file with the name of your output file. Because the default for these CL commands is to replace the first member of a file, you don't need to delete the file first.

The format for the DSPOBJD output file is QLIDOBJD in model file QADSPOBJ of library QSYS. The field name &ODOBNM is the object name of the objects listed (in this case, libraries only). To find variable names of the model files, use the Display File Field Description (DSPFFD) command. The CLEANLIBS program checks &ODOBDM and omits system libraries (those starting with Q, #, $, %, and &) from being processed. You might want to omit development libraries and any other nonproduction type libraries.

Another program, CLEANLIBSF (see Figure 9.13), has to be created to perform the file reorganization. This is because a CL program only allows you to declare one file. CLEANLIBSF also uses the same technique as CLEANLIBS to obtain the information from the output file created by the DSPFD command.

```
CLEANLIBSF: +
    PGM PARM(&LIB)

    DCL VAR(&LIB)        TYPE(*CHAR) LEN(10)
    DCL VAR(&PERC)       TYPE(*DEC)  LEN(5 2)
    DCLF FILE(QAFDMBRL)

    MONMSG MSGID(CPF0000)

    DSPFD FILE(&LIB/*ALL) TYPE(*MBRLIST) OUTPUT(*OUTFILE) +
        FILEATR(*PF) OUTFILE(QTEMP/FILELIST)
    MONMSG MSGID(CPF0000) EXEC(GOTO CMDLBL(ENDPGM))

    OVRDBF FILE(QAFDMBRL) TOFILE(FILELIST)
    OPNDBF FILE(QTEMP/FILELIST) OPTION(*INP)

READ: +
    RCVF RCDFMT(QWHFDML)
    MONMSG MSGID(CPF0864) EXEC(GOTO CMDLBL(EOF))

    CHGVAR VAR(&PERC) VALUE(000.00)

    IF COND(&MLNRCD *GT 0) THEN(DO)
        CHGVAR VAR(&PERC) VALUE(&MLNDTR / &MLNRCD)
    ENDDO

    IF COND(&PERC *EQ 00.10) THEN(DO)
        RGZPFM FILE(&LIB/&MLFILE) MBR(&MLNAME)
    ENDDO

    GOTO CMDLBL(READ)

EOF: +
    CLOF OPNID(FILELIST)

ENDPGM: +
    ENDPGM
```

Figure 9.13: Here's the command processor for the CLEANLIBS CL command.

—Midrange Computing Staff

Clearing/Reorganizing All Members

OS/400 provides two commands you can use to reduce the amount of DASD used by your application programs: Reorganize Physical File Member (RGZPFM) and Clear Physical File Member (CLRPFM).

Both commands accept a specific member name, *FIRST or *LAST. Because neither command accepts *ALL, your "house-cleaning" can become more difficult than it has to be. This is especially true if you keep multimember physical files.

Weep no more! Commands Clear Physical File, All Members (CLRPFMALL) and Reorganize Physical File, All Members (RGZPFMALL) process all members of a database file.

Figures 9.14 and 9.15 show the command definition for CLRPFMALL and RGZPFMALL, respectively. Notice that the second parameter has been defined as a constant.

```
CLRPFMALL:  CMD        PROMPT('Clear all File Members')

            PARM       KWD(FILE) TYPE(Q1) MIN(1) PROMPT('File name')

            PARM       KWD(ACTION) TYPE(*CHAR) LEN(4) CONSTANT(*CLR)

Q1:         QUAL       TYPE(*SNAME) LEN(10) MIN(1)
            QUAL       TYPE(*SNAME) LEN(10) DFT(*LIBL) +
                         SPCVAL((*LIBL)) PROMPT('Library')
```

Figure 9.14: Here's the CLRPFMALL command.

```
RGZPFMALL:  CMD        PROMPT('Reorganize All Members')

            PARM       KWD(FILE) TYPE(Q1) MIN(1) PROMPT('File name')

            PARM       KWD(ACTION) TYPE(*CHAR) LEN(4) CONSTANT(*RGZ)

Q1:         QUAL       TYPE(*SNAME) LEN(10) MIN(1)
            QUAL       TYPE(*SNAME) LEN(10) DFT(*LIBL) +
                         SPCVAL((*LIBL)) PROMPT('Library
```

Figure 9.15: This is the RGZPFMALL command.

Both commands share the same command-processing program (PFM001CL, as shown in Figure 9.16). This second parameter tells the CPP whether to clear all members or reorganize all members. This second parameter is invisible to the user (the command prompter will not display it).

```
PFM001CL: +
    PGM PARM(&QF &ACTION)

    DCL VAR(&ACTION)     TYPE(*CHAR) LEN(4)
    DCL VAR(&FILE)       TYPE(*CHAR) LEN(10)
    DCL VAR(&LIB)        TYPE(*CHAR) LEN(10)
    DCL VAR(&MSGDTA)     TYPE(*CHAR) LEN(80)
    DCL VAR(&MSGID)      TYPE(*CHAR) LEN(7)
    DCL VAR(&MSGF)       TYPE(*CHAR) LEN(10)
    DCL VAR(&MSGFLIB)    TYPE(*CHAR) LEN(10)
    DCL VAR(&QF)         TYPE(*CHAR) LEN(20)
    DCL VAR(&RTNMBR)     TYPE(*CHAR) LEN(10)

    MONMSG MSGID(CPF0000) EXEC(GOTO CMDLBL(SNDERRMSG))

    CHGVAR VAR(&FILE) VALUE(%SST(&QF 1 10))
    CHGVAR VAR(&LIB) VALUE(%SST(&QF 11 10))
    CHKOBJ OBJ(&LIB/&FILE) OBJTYPE(*FILE) AUT(*OBJMGT)

    RTVMBRD FILE(&LIB/&FILE) MBR(*FIRST) RTNMBR(&RTNMBR)
    MONMSG MSGID(CPF0000) EXEC(DO)
       SNDPGMMSG MSG('File' *BCAT &FILE *BCAT 'has no members.') +
          MSGTYPE(*INFO)
       GOTO CMDLBL(ENDPGM)
    ENDDO

LOOP: +
    IF COND(&ACTION *EQ '*CLR') THEN(DO)
       SNDPGMMSG MSGID(CPF9898) MSGF(QCPFMSG) MSGDTA('Clearing +
          member' *BCAT &RTNMBR *BCAT 'from file' *BCAT &FILE) +
          TOPGMQ(*EXT) MSGTYPE(*STATUS)
       CLRPFM FILE(&LIB/&FILE) MBR(&RTNMBR)
       MONMSG MSGID(CPF0000)
    ENDDO
    ELSE CMD(DO)
       SNDPGMMSG MSGID(CPF9898) MSGF(QCPFMSG) MSGDTA('Reorganizing +
          member' *BCAT &RTNMBR *BCAT 'from file' *BCAT &FILE) +
          TOPGMQ(*EXT) MSGTYPE(*STATUS)
       RGZPFM FILE(&LIB/&FILE) MBR(&RTNMBR)
       MONMSG MSGID(CPF0000)
    ENDDO

    RTVMBRD FILE(&LIB/&FILE) MBR(&RTNMBR *NEXT) RTNMBR(&RTNMBR)
    MONMSG MSGID(CPF0000) EXEC(DO)
       SNDPGMMSG MSG('All members of file' *BCAT &FILE *BCAT +
          'processed successfully.') MSGTYPE(*INFO)
       GOTO CMDLBL(ENDPGM)
    ENDDO
    GOTO CMDLBL(LOOP)

SNDERRMSG: +
    RCVMSG MSGTYPE(*LAST) MSGDTA(&MSGDTA) MSGID(&MSGID) MSGF(&MSGF) +
```

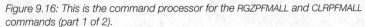

Figure 9.16: This is the command processor for the RGZPFMALL and CLRPFMALL commands (part 1 of 2).

```
      MSGFLIB(&MSGFLIB)
      SNDPGMMSG MSGID(&MSGID) MSGF(&MSGFLIB/&MSGF) MSGDTA(&MSGDTA) +
        MSGTYPE(*DIAG)
      SNDPGMMSG MSGID(CPF0002) MSGF(QCPFMSG) MSGTYPE(*ESCAPE)

   ENDPGM: +
     ENDPGM
```

Figure 9.16: This is the command processor for the RGZPFMALL and CLRPFMALL commands (part 2 of 2).

The logic of program PFM001CL is actually quite simple. Retrieve the name of the first member with RTVMBRD MBR(*FIRST) RTNMBR(&RTNMBR). Now, variable &RTNMBR contains the name of the first member. The program goes into a loop that runs either CLRPFM or RGZPFM on this member. This is followed by another RTVMBRD to retrieve the name of the next member using MBR(&RTNMBR *NEXT), meaning the member that follows &RTNMBR. The name of this member is placed, again, in &RTNMBR, and the loop continues until all members have been processed.

—*Midrange Computing Staff*

Create Your Own QTEMP

Create a library (SCRATCH) for submitting queries to batch. Users can create queries in this library and then submit them for batch processing. This library is cleared using a nightly/weekly processing routine. Queries can now be submitted instead of running in QTEMP interactively.

Temporary queries can be cleaned up automatically. Use this library for all temporary objects, such as DFUs, and as a work area for restores.

—*Kevin Heiman*

Deleting Spool Files to Reclaim Disk Space

Spool files can really waste space on your disk. The AS/400 stores spooled file data in physical file members in the QSPL library. The members remain on the system even after printing and are removed only if they are not used after *seven* IPLs. Only up to 200 members are removed during an IPL. It is easy to see how keeping spool files on the OUTQ, and infrequent IPLs will make the QSPL library grow in size. You can use the following command to get the name and size of the spool database file:

```
   DSPOBJD QSPL/*ALL *ALL
```

The next command will display the number of members in the file:

```
DSPFD FILE(QSPL/filename) TYPE(*ATR)
```

For additional information, refer to the section "OS/400 IPL" in appendix B of the *Backup and Recovery Guide* (SC21-8079), and the "Spooling Subsystem and Spooling Library" sections in chapter 6 of the *Data Management Guide* (SC21-9658).

—Alon Fluxman

Disk Space Available for Save Operations

Q: How much DASD do I need in the system auxiliary storage pool (ASP) to perform save and restore procedures for network server storage spaces?

A: A save operation for an entire network server storage space is done by using the SAV command and specifying the OBJ parameter as **'/qfpnwsstg/stg_name'**. For example, to save the storage space named NETSRV to tape, you could use this command:

```
SAV DEV('/qsys.lib/tap01.devd') OBJ(('/qfpnwsstg/netsrv'))
```

The save operation does not require additional space in the system ASP (unless you are saving to a save file, in which case you need at most the size of the network server storage space, but generally less because of the compression algorithms). However, the restore operation (using the RST command) always requires free space equal to the size of the network server storage space being restored (and this is true whether or not the storage space already exists).

For example, if NETSRV is a 500MB network-server storage space being restored, at least 500MB of free disk space must be in the system ASP. If a network server storage space named NETSRV already exists on the system, data will be restored into NETSRV through a temporary object. The space taken by this temporary object will be freed when the restore completes.

On the other hand, if a network server storage space named NETSRV does not exist, the data will be restored to a temporary object that will be named NETSRV upon completion of the restore. In other words, when the network server storage space does not exist, it will be created by the restore command.

As you would suspect, the RST command is very similar to the SAV command. For example, to restore NETSRV from tape, you can use this command:

```
RST DEV('/qsys.lib/tap01.devd') OBJ(('/qfpnwsstg/netsrv'))
```

Or, to restore this network server storage space to one named NETSRV2, you would use this command:

```
RST DEV('/qsys.lib/tap01.devd') OBJ(('/qfpnwsstg/netsrv' *INCLUDE
'/qfpnwsstg/netsrv2'))
```

When restoring a network server storage space that doesn't exist on the AS/400 system, don't create it first. The restore command will create it for you.

—*Russ Bruhnke*

✦ ✦ ✦ Debugging

Dumping an Object's Contents

Want a quick way to find out what's inside an object? Use the Dump Object (DMPOBJ) command. This command dumps the contents or the attributes of most AS/400 objects to a spooled file named QPSRVDMP. You can display the spooled file to see the object's contents. This command is especially useful for dumping the contents of objects that have no display command (like data queues). DMPOBJ is much easier to use than the Retrieve Data Queue Message (QMHRDQM) API, and is not destructive like the Receive Data Queue (QRCVDTAQ) API. Whether it's the contents or the attributes of the object that get dumped depends on the object type. You might use this command to dump other objects, such as directories, modules, user spaces, journal receivers, and even entire libraries, as well.

—*Brian O'Gara*

✦ ✦ ✦ Devices

Allocating Devices to Subsystems

By default, the subsystem QINTER allocates all devices by workstation type—not by name. The purpose of this is to capture and allocate all devices regardless of the naming convention used. As you go about configuring your system, you might want to allocate workstations by subsystems other than QINTER. The following information can be found in the manual *OS/400 Work Management V3R1* (SC41-3306, CD-ROM QBKLAG00):

- When a subsystem starts, it attempts to allocate all workstation devices in the subsystem description. There is no hierarchy regarding device names versus device types.

- If the device is varied off, the subsystem cannot allocate it. The system arbiter (QSYSARB) holds a lock on all devices that are varied off.

- If the device is varied on and is not allocated by another subsystem, then the subsystem can allocate it and display the sign-on display.

- If the device is allocated by another subsystem and is at the sign-on display (i.e., no active job), the second subsystem can allocate the device from the first subsystem.

- If the device is varied off and all subsystems have started before you vary on the device, and if more than one subsystem could potentially allocate the device, it is unpredictable which subsystem will actually allocate it.

To avoid the situation of unpredictability, you can do one of the following things:

- Do not use workstation type entries in any subsystem—use only workstation name entries. This means removing the workstation type entries from the IBM-supplied subsystem descriptions. Use the Remove Workstation Entry (RMVWSE) command. You can enter workstation name entries using generic prefixes (e.g., DSP*).

- Vary the workstation on when the system is started by specifying ONLINE(*YES) in the device description for the workstation. The subsystem that allocates the device is determined by the order in which the subsystems start.

- You can add workstation entries to a subsystem description, which causes the subsystem to allocate the device or not allocate the device.

To include the device, use this command:

```
ADDWSE SBSD(xxx/sbsd) WRKSTN(dev) AT(*SIGNON)
```

To exclude the device, use this command:

```
ADDWSE SBSD(xxx/sbsd) WRKSTN(dev) AT(*ENTER)
```

The AT(*ENTER) parameter keeps the subsystem from allocating the device at subsystem startup, but allows you to use the Transfer Job (TRFJOB) command to transfer the job after subsystem startup.

—Steve Bisel

AS/400 Printer Alignment Messages

Q: After an IPL on our AS/400 model 40, the QSYSOPR is prompted to verify alignment on device PRT9999 and all other printers attached to the system. Is there a way to auto-answer these messages or not receive them and have the printers start printing automatically?

A: Take a look at the CL Change Reply List Entry (CHGRPYLE) command. You'll need the system error message and then you can get the system to automatically answer the message. It works like a charm. Good luck.

—Kim Beattie

A: In my experience, changing the system reply list entry can get you in trouble if you use your printer for different forms. If you don't want to have your printers start at IPL, just change the system value (this can only be done from an attended IPL). Then attach a CL program to your system operator's user profile that will start all the writers. We use this method at our client sites because some of our code prints directly to the writer without spooling. This necessitates a printer that is not active in the QSPL subsystem.

—Keith Biggs

AS/400 Tape Cartridge Tip

Whenever a cartridge tape is loaded, the first thing the AS/400 does is make what is referred to as a *tensioning run*. The tape winds to the end from where it was positioned at the time it was loaded, and then rewinds to the beginning of the tape. This ensures that the entire length of the tape has equal and correct tension. So, if a tape is positioned at the very beginning of the tape, it must be wound from beginning to end, and then rewound. If the tape is at the halfway point, it must be wound forward the remaining 50 percent, and then rewound.

You can help minimize the amount of tape that has to be wound by always specifying *LEAVE on any operation that reads or writes to tape. *LEAVE will leave the tape at the position it was last at when the operation is completed.

On the other hand, *REWIND will always rewind the tape back to the start. By leaving the tape in a more forward position, there will be less tape to read during the forward winding of the tensioning run.

Also, *LEAVE saves time when you perform multiple sequential writes to the tape by leaving the tape in the proper position for the next write. *REWIND would perform unneccessary rewinding steps.

—Jay Ramboldini

Automatic Tape Label Type Processing

Let's say you are receiving a variety of tapes, all of which must be loaded to your AS/400 using the Copy from Tape (CPYFRMTAP) command. Some of the tapes are nonlabeled, some use labels, still others use nonstandard labels. The CPYFRMTAP command requires that you supply the correct value for the label processing type as part of the Copy from Reels (FROMREELS) parameter—*NL for nonlabeled tapes, *SL for standard labels, or *BLP (bypass label processing) for nonstandard labels.

If you specify an incorrect value in the FROMREELS parameter, the system issues message CPA4158. You can manually determine the correct value by repeatedly running either the CPYFRMTAP command—using different values in the FROMREELS parameter each time or the Dump Tape (DMPTAP) command. Both processes are trial and error.

You might think that all you need to do is to try each of the FROMREELS values in turn, monitoring for CPA4158 until you get it right. That method won't work because CPA4158 goes to the system operator message queue (QSYSOPR) and it cannot be monitored by the Monitor Message (MONMSG) command. However, replying to CPA4158 with a C (cancel) results in message CPF2952, which can be monitored. Of course, you don't want to confuse your operator with C responses that don't cancel jobs. Therefore, you need to make this reply automatic. Because the default message reply to CPA4158 is C, use the Change Job (CHGJOB) command to change the inquiry message reply value to *DFT (default).

```
CHGJOB INQMSGRPY(*DFT)
```

This technique creates a problem. The job will automatically respond to other messages with their default replies. The solution is to temporarily add CPA4158 to the system reply list from within the CL program. By finding the first available entry on the system reply list (the system issues CPF2555 if a system reply list sequence number is in use), the program can add the reply list entry and then remove it once it is no longer needed. Figure 9.17 shows all the code.

```
PGM
DCL VAR(&INQMSGRPY) TYPE(*CHAR) LEN(10)
DCL VAR(&SEQNBR) TYPE(*DEC) LEN(4 0) VALUE(0)
RTVJOBA INQMSGRPY(&INQMSGRPY)
CHGJOB INQMSGRPY(*SYSRPYL)
TRYSEQ: CHGVAR VAR(&SEQNBR) VALUE(&SEQNBR + 1)
ADDRPYLE SEQNBR(&SEQNBR) MSGID(CPA4158) RPY('C')
MONMSG MSGID(CPF2555) EXEC(GOTO CMDLBL(TRYSEQ))
TRYSL: CPYFRMTAP FROMFILE(QTAPE) TOFILE(XXX/tgt_file) +
FROMREELS(*SL) MBROPT(*REPLACE)
MONMSG MSGID(CPF2952) EXEC(GOTO CMDLBL(TRYNL))
GOTO CMDLBL(DONE)
TRYNL: CPYFRMTAP FROMFILE(QTAPE) TOFILE(XXX/tgt_file) +
FROMREELS(*NL) MBROPT(*REPLACE)
MONMSG MSGID(CPF2952) EXEC(GOTO CMDLBL(TRYBLP))
GOTO CMDLBL(DONE)
TRYBLP: CPYFRMTAP FROMFILE(QTAPE) TOFILE(XXX/tgt_file) +
FROMREELS(*BLP) MBROPT(*REPLACE)
DONE: RMVRPYLE SEQNBR(&SEQNBR)
CHGJOB INQMSGRPY(&INQMSGRPY)
ENDPGM: ENDPGM
```

Figure 9.17: Automatic tape label type processing can be accomplished.

—J.D. Hunt

Avoid Tape Drive Conflicts

Q: Because our data center runs a weekly process that's dependent on an outside tape, it can't be scheduled. However, the operators at the data center forget that Operational Assistant runs the daily backup automatically at 4:30 A.M. Each week, they start their job and it runs a while. Then the backup starts and eventually locks a file that the program tries to access. Of course, the CL program then blows up. I want to add an exit program to the Operational Assistant backup to see if the data center's CL program is running. If it is not running, the backup should start; otherwise, the exit program needs to delay the backup and recheck periodically. The Check Active Program (CHKACTPGM) QUSRTOOL works great to check itself, but not another program—unless I'm doing it all wrong. Does someone have a better idea?

A: You can find out if a specific job is running by building logic into the job to let you know that it's there. If the problem is contention for the tape drive, you could put something like the code shown in Figure 9.18 in the front end of all your jobs that might need to use the tape drive in question. Once past this bit of code, you are assured that the job containing it has control of the data area and, as a result, the tape drive. Other jobs containing this code will go into a 5-minute wait state before retrying.

```
ALCTAPE: CHKOBJ OBJ(QGPL/TAPEINUSE) OBJTYPE(*DTAARA) AUT(*OBJEXIST)
MONMSG MSGID(CPF9801) EXEC(DO)
CRTDTAARA DTAARA(QGPL/TAPEINUSE) TYPE(*LGL)
ENDDO
ALCOBJ OBJ((QGPL/TAPEINUSE *DTAARA *EXCL)) WAIT(0)
MONMSG MSGID(CPF1002) EXEC(DO)
DLYJOB DLY(10)
GOTO CMDLBL(ALCTAPE)
ENDDO
```

Figure 9.18: Use this CL code to avoid tape drive conflicts.

—*John Wagner*

A: I suggest you create a data area. In the CL, change the data area to a known value CHGDTAARA DTAARA(XXX) VALUE('ACTIVE'). As the last step in the CL, change the data area back to blanks:

```
CHGDTAARA DTAARA(XXX) VALUE('')
```

In the backup job, test the data area to determine if the CL program is running. This method has two advantages:

1. If the CL program terminates abnormally and you need to rerun it before the backup starts, the data area will still be "set" and the backup won't start. You can manually clear the data area or rerun the CL program.

2. The same data area can be used for all jobs that need to lock out the backup.

—*Matt Fulton*

Beware of Autoconfiguration

Q: Every once in a while our device descriptions on the AS/400 are erased and recreated. How can this happen?

A: Well, we don't use autoconfiguration, but we periodically activate it in order to configure a Client Access 5250 emulation session. As it turns out, if someone powers their display station or printer off and then back on while autoconfiguration is active, the system might delete the device description and recreate it.

Whether the device description is deleted and recreated depends on the accuracy of the device type and model number. If either is incorrect, the operating system will "fix" it for you. For example, if you have a 5292 that was configured as a 5291, OS/400 will delete the old device description and create a new one—which, of course, will have a different name in the format DSP*nn* and PRT*nn*. Gotcha!

Beware. If you must activate autoconfiguration, even for a short period of time, do so at a time when you are confident that no one will be powering on any devices.

—Don Schenck

Editor's Note:

1. *To activate or deactivate autoconfiguration, change system value* QAUTOCFG *using the Change System Value (*CHGSYSVAL*) command. A value of '0' turns it off, while '1' turns it on.*

2. *We recommend keeping autoconfiguration off at all times. This gives the system administrator the capability to name the devices as he or she sees fit. The system-generated name DSP29, for instance, is less meaningful than PURDSP05, which includes PUR (Purchasing) as an indication of its location.*

Determining the Device Name of a Tape Drive

Have you ever put a tape in your AS/400's tape drive and then prompted a command like Display Tape (DSPTAP) or Initialize Tape (INZTAP), only to realize that you don't know the device name of the tape drive? That can be frustrating because there's no way to look it up from the prompt screen.

Fortunately, there's an easy way to find out the names of all tape devices on an AS/400. Just run this Work with Configuration Status (WRKCFGSTS) command:

```
WRKCFGSTS CFGTYPE(*DEV) CFGD(*TAP)
```

The parameters on the WRKCFGSTS command allow you to filter the resulting display to see just what you want. In the example, the parameters limit the display to tape devices. From there, you can make a quick mental note of the device name and get back to the real work of running the tape command you wanted to run originally.

This same technique can be used to determine the name of other types of devices, such as display stations, printers, and diskette drives. The only difference is in the value you supply for the CFGD parameter (i.e., *DSP, *PRT, or *DKT).

—Robin Klima

Device Error Recovery

Have you ever had someone accidentally trip over a display station power cord and wish you could just pick up where you left off without any hassle? Or more likely, have you had your UPS keep the system and controlling console running while dozens of users despair over not having their display on a UPS circuit during a 2-second outage?

Left to its own devices—so to speak—a message will be issued to QSYSOPR and you'll be left with a device that must be manually brought back up to the point of failure. But system value QDEVRCYACN determines the default device recovery action that is to be taken when an error occurs. And with it comes the capability to recover almost completely.

Beginning with V1R3, there are several alternatives, but my favorite is *DSCMSG. This causes the job to be disconnected, much like issuing the DSCJOB command. Unlike DSCJOB, however, when you sign back on you will be presented with an error recovery screen.

From here you may choose to have the previous job ended or to attempt recovery. If you attempt recovery, the job is resumed and the program is returned with an error status. For RPG programs, this means the indicator in columns 56–57 comes on or the *INFSR routine gains control, if specified. The *STATUS code in INFDS will have the value 01255, which indicates that a session error occurred, and the major return code will be 83. All that is necessary is to redisplay the screen or repeat the EXFMT instruction. Any data the operator had already keyed on the format will be lost, but otherwise the program can continue as if nothing had happened.

If you don't normally include *INFSR or error indicators in your programs, consider the use of *DSCENDRQS instead of *DSCMSG. This also disconnects the job, but upon sign-on will issue an ENDRQS for the current request level. While not as full a recovery as *DSCMSG, it does keep the rest of the job intact and can still allow operators to resume operations more quickly.

If you only have full error handling in selected mission-crucial programs or applications, you can use CHGJOB DEVRCYACN(*DSCMSG) in the CL prior to loading the programs and CHGJOB DEVRCYACN(XXX) upon completion. Individual job descriptions also may have a device recovery action other than the default *SYSVAL by using CHGJOBD DEVRCYACN(XXX).

—Douglas Handy

Retrieve Configuration Source

A good change log for system work should include a CL program containing all the changes you have made to your system. But somehow you don't always remember to put all those changes into the CL program right away. When the system modifications involve configuration changes, RTVCFGSRC can be used to "decompile" a line/controller/device configuration into CL source code. Don't worry if you lost all those little scraps of paper on your desk describing controllers, lines, and so on. Just run this command and send the CL to your source file.

If you have not been recording your configuration changes, you might want to specify all configurations and all configuration types the first time you use the command, like this:

```
RTVCFGSRC CFGD(*ALL) CFGTYPE(*ALL) SRCFILE(SYSMOD/QCLSRC) +
          SRCMBR(CFGMOD)
```

In this example, configuration modifications are kept in library SYSMOD under the name CFGMOD.

—Doug Talley

Rewind or Unload Tapes from the Command Line

You can use the Check Tape (CHKTAP) command using the ENDOPT parameter to rewind or unload tapes without leaving your desk. There are three options: *LEAVE, *REWIND, and *UNLOAD. Besides performing the ENDOPT action, the command will tell you the volume name of the mounted tape.

Having the tape already unloaded when you get to the tape drive is not the only benefit this offers. When analyzing data on a tape, I usually use the default of *REWIND for the ENDOPT parameter on the Display Tape (DSPTAP) command. This lets me make multiple tries at getting the data I want. When I'm done, I run this command:

```
CHKTAP DEV(TAP01) ENDOPT(*UNLOAD)
```

If many people use the same tape drive, you should unload the tape when you are done so that others can't accidentally destroy your data.

—Martin Pluth

Your Tape Density Might Not Be What You Expect

I used the Initialize Tape (INZTAP) command to initialize a tape to 1600bpi and then used the Copy to Tape (CPYTOTAP) command to put data on the tape. Much to my surprise, when I dumped the tape, I found that the tape was initialized to 6250bpi instead of 1600bpi.

The CPYTOTAP command doesn't allow you to specify the density; it uses the density of the tape file you specify in the TOFILE parameter (QTAPE in my case). QTAPE is a default tape data device file found in QGPL library with the density set to *DEVTYPE, which in our case is 6250.

To get around the problem, I created a new tape file and specifically set the density to 1600bpi. I then referenced the new tape file in the TOFILE parameter of the CPYTOTAP command.

—Sharla Tolleson

✦ ✦ ✦ Disk Storage

AS/400 Space Saving Tips

I have a couple of tips for those concerned with saving space on the AS/400.

First, if a program does not need to be debugged in the near future, you can "Remove Observability" information to drastically reduce the size of the program. You do this with the Change Program (CHGPGM) command, using *YES for the Remove Observable info

(RMVOBS) keyword. You can remove observability for one program, several programs, or all programs in a library.

Second, whenever you compile a program, the system automatically places the old version of the program into QRPLOBJ library. These old objects are saved in case a user is attached to the object. QRPLOBJ is cleared at each IPL, but if you do not perform IPLs very often, QRPLOBJ can get very large. A shop that doesn't IPL often and does a lot of programming should occasionally clear (CLRLIB) or delete (DLTLIB) QRPLOBJ. If you delete it, it will automatically rebuild during the next IPL.

—Phil H. Kestenbaum

✦ ✦ ✦ Documentation

Copy AS/400 Screens to a File

The STRCPYSCN command's main function is to monitor a remote workstation, but you can also use it to document step-by-step processing. By issuing the following command, every screen will be copied to the output file CPYS in QGPL without the use of the print key.:

```
STRCPYSCN SRCDEV(*REQUESTER) OUTDEV(*NONE) OUTFILE(QGPL/CPYS)
```

You will be prompted with a message telling you that a copy screen request has been issued. You can use "C" to cancel or "G" to continue. Every screen you see will be copied to the output file as soon as you press the Enter key. Use the ENDCPYSCN command to end the function. The created file can now be converted to a source file and any necessary editing can be done. To convert the file to a source file use the following:

```
CPYF FROMFILE(QGPL/CPYS) TOFILE(QGPL/QRPGSRC) TOMBR(MBRNAME) +
     REPLACE(*YES) FMTOPT(*CVTSRC)
```

This is useful in documenting operational procedures for your users.

—Alon Fluxman

Removing Control Characters

A technique I recently saw explained how the STRCPYSCN command allows you to capture each new screen and place it into one large file for documentation.

What wasn't mentioned was what you have in this file. By using the DSPPFM command, you will notice that your file contains all the funny characters that delimit the fields. If you create a PC file on the AS/400 from your file and then download it to the PC, you are stuck with trying to get rid of these creatures so that you can print your documentation.

Even though I'm sure there are plenty of PC programmers who could write a program to eradicate these creatures, there is no need to even attempt it.

The AS/400 will automatically do this for you. Just take your original copy screen file and use CPYF to copy this file to a spool file. This will strip all the funny characters away. Then use command CPYSPLF to copy your new good file back into a database file. You can then proceed to take the good database file and create your PC file to download.

Before running the CPYSPLF command, use CRTDUPOBJ with no data on file CPYS to create file GOODFILE. When done, file GOODFILE will contain the edited file ready for documentation.

—Greg Alvey

✦ ✦ ✦ File Commands

Peek into Logical Files

I was wondering why IBM did not provide a command to display logical files similar to the one for physical files. Sometimes there is the need to actually see your data in its arrival sequence and, optionally, to include or omit the data that you have described for the logical file. Therefore, I have written Display Logical File Member (DSPLFM).

The command structure (Figure 9.19) requires three parameters: the file name, the library in which the file resides, and the member of that file. Usually, when I use this command, the file is somewhere in my library list. Therefore, I have caused the default library name to be *LIBL, substituting the library list. Also, I have caused the default for the member to be *ALL. Later, I will explain why.

```
DSPLFM:    CMD         PROMPT('Display Logical File Member')

           PARM        KWD(FILE) TYPE(Q1) MIN(1) PROMPT('Logical +
                         file name')

           PARM        KWD(MBR) TYPE(*NAME) LEN(10) DFT(*ALL) +
                         SPCVAL((*ALL)) PROMPT('Member')

  Q1:      QUAL        TYPE(*NAME) LEN(10) MIN(1)
           QUAL        TYPE(*NAME) LEN(10) DFT(*LIBL) +
                         SPCVAL((*LIBL)) PROMPT('Library'
```

Figure 9.19: The DSPLFM command will display a logical file member.

The CPP (LFM001CL, Figure 9.20) describes five input variables; &QUALFILE, &FILE, &LIB, &MBR, and &MSG. &QUALFILE contains the file and library names. &FILE and &LIB are broken out of the &QUALFILE variable by the substring function. &MBR will be the member of that file. The last, &MSG, is for sending error messages in the event of file not found, library not found, or member not found.

```
LFM001CL: +
    PGM PARM(&QUALFILE &MBR)

    DCL VAR(&QUALFILE)    TYPE(*CHAR) LEN(20)
    DCL VAR(&MBR)         TYPE(*CHAR) LEN(10)
    DCL VAR(&FILE)        TYPE(*CHAR) LEN(10)
    DCL VAR(&LIB)         TYPE(*CHAR) LEN(10)
    DCL VAR(&MSG)         TYPE(*CHAR) LEN(60)

    /* Break qualified name */
    CHGVAR VAR(&FILE) VALUE(%SST(&QUALFILE 1 10))
    CHGVAR VAR(&LIB) VALUE(%SST(&QUALFILE 11 10))

    /* Check for existence of logical file */
    CHKOBJ OBJ(&LIB/&FILE) OBJTYPE(*FILE)
    MONMSG MSGID(CPF9801) EXEC(DO)
       CHGVAR VAR(&MSG) VALUE('File' *BCAT &LIB *TCAT '/' *CAT &FILE +
          *BCAT 'not found')
       GOTO CMDLBL(ERRMSG)
    ENDDO
    MONMSG MSGID(CPF9810) EXEC(DO)
       CHGVAR VAR(&MSG) VALUE('Library' *BCAT &LIB *BCAT 'not found')
       GOTO CMDLBL(ERRMSG)
    ENDDO

    /* Validate member name if not *ALL */
    IF COND(&MBR *NE '*ALL') THEN(DO)
       CHKOBJ OBJ(&LIB/&FILE) OBJTYPE(*FILE) MBR(&MBR)
```

Figure 9.20: LFM001CL is the command processor for DSPLFM (part 1 of 2).

```
        MONMSG MSGID(CPF9815) EXEC(DO)
            CHGVAR VAR(&MSG) VALUE('Member' *BCAT &MBR *BCAT 'in' +
                *BCAT &LIB *TCAT '/' *CAT &FILE *BCAT 'not found')
            GOTO CMDLBL(ERRMSG)
        ENDDO
    ENDDO

    /* Copy logical file to QTEMP/DSPLFMPF */
    CHKOBJ OBJ(QTEMP/DSPLFMPF) OBJTYPE(*FILE)
    MONMSG MSGID(CPF9801) EXEC(DO)
        CPYF FROMFILE(&LIB/&FILE) TOFILE(QTEMP/DSPLFMPF) +
            FROMMBR(&MBR) TOMBR(*FROMMBR) MBROPT(*ADD) CRTFILE(*YES)
        GOTO CMDLBL(DSPFILE)
    ENDDO
    CPYF FROMFILE(&LIB/&FILE) TOFILE(QTEMP/DSPLFMPF) FROMMBR(&MBR) +
        TOMBR(*FROMMBR) MBROPT(*REPLACE) CRTFILE(*NO)

    /* Display logical file member */
DSPFILE: +
    IF COND(&MBR *EQ '*ALL') THEN(DO)
        DSPPFM FILE(QTEMP/DSPLFMPF)
    ENDDO
    ELSE CMD(DO)
        DSPPFM FILE(QTEMP/DSPLFMPF) MBR(&MBR)
    ENDDO
    GOTO CMDLBL(ENDPGM)

    /* Send error messages */
ERRMSG: +
    SNDPGMMSG MSGID(CPF9898) MSGF(QCPFMSG) MSGDTA(&MSG) MSGTYPE(*DIAG)
    SNDPGMMSG MSGID(CPF0002) MSGF(QCPFMSG) MSGTYPE(*ESCAPE)

ENDPGM: +
    ENDPGM
```

Figure 9.20: LFM001CL is the command processor for DSPLFM (part 2 of 2).

The CPP first checks for the existence of the object. Message CPF9801 is given if the file itself is not found, and CPF9810 for a library not found. Then, if the file member parameter is not *ALL, the CPP checks for the existence for the actual member by monitoring for CPF9815. If any error situation is reached, a message is sent, and the CL program is exited.

I decided that it would be best for my own use to use one file name in QTEMP. That way, if I wanted to look at it again, all I had to do was remember one file name. Anyone who wants to change that logic need only replace the file name DSPLFMPF (DSPLFM physical file) with &FILE. The physical file DSPLFMPF (or &FILE, if you choose) is deleted each time the command is executed, and message ID CPF2105 is checked in case the file to be deleted does not exist.

The reasoning behind this is as follows: If a file has record format "A," and we try to copy record format "B," the vast majority of the time, the formats are incompatible. Also, by copying the file to QTEMP, we don't have to do our own housekeeping. When a user signs off, all objects for that user in QTEMP will automatically be deleted. Lastly, it uses the Display Physical File Member (DSPPFM) command. Because DSPPFM defaults to *FIRST for the member, if the member selected is *ALL, DSPPFM will only show the first member. If a particular file member is selected, that member will be displayed.

As stated before, the member parameter of the command defaults to *ALL. Because the member will reside in QTEMP until changed or until the user signs off, the user can use the DSPPFM command to display the particular member if it isn't the *FIRST one.

—Tim Johnston

✦ ✦ ✦ File Processing

Alternative to DSPPFM

The next time you want to view data in a file, get a view with field names and selection capabilities as well. Instead of using command DSPPFM, which displays only the data, try the RUNQRY command with prompting.

You can create an interactive display online by placing your file name in the file-name field. Because you don't have an existing query set up, skip the top parameters. To just display, that's it; press Enter. The data comes up with field separation and headings. If you say *YES to the record selection parameter, you will receive another screen that displays field names for additional selection. A neat selection keyword, called "LIKE," allows for a pretty powerful selection capability.

—Greg Alvey

*Editor's Note: We ran a couple of tests of RUNQRY against SQL and the results were incredible indeed. RUNQRY always beat SQL, delivering the output before SQL had even begun reading the file. There's also another feature Greg Alvey didn't mention. The OUTTYPE parameter defaults to *RUNOPT, which ends up being the same as *DISPLAY because you have not created the Query program; however, you can change this to *PRINTER or *OUTFILE so that you can get a hard copy of the information.*

Update on UPDDTA

A recent tip suggested using the UPDDTA command to quickly generate DFU programs for files. You can bypass the start-up time involved with each use by saving and reusing the generated program:

1. Use the SETATNPGM command to set the attention key program to QCMD.

2. Run UPDDTA for the file.

3. As soon as you get into the DFU, press the Attn key.

4. Display QTEMP library. There will be a program and display file with names beginning with a "Q" (like QDZTD00001). Do a CRTDUPOBJ for the file and the program, duplicating and renaming them into a library of your choice. The name of the program and the display file must be the same.

5. In the future, use the CHGDTA command, substituting the name of the program from step 4.

—Craig Pelkie

✦ ✦ ✦ Integrated File System

Changing the Code Page of AS/400 IFS Files

For those who have used a PC-based tool such as Microsoft Word or Excel or Lotus 1-2-3 to view the contents of an AS/400 Integrated File System (AS/400 IFS) file created using Copy to Import File (CPYTOIMPF), the file probably appeared to contain gibberish. This was probably because the PC-based program expected the file to be ASCII and the file contained EBCDIC characters. One way to remedy this is to set the code page of the AS/400 IFS files to ASCII before using CPYTOIMPF to load the file with data. This translates the data being placed in the file to ASCII. Follow these six steps to create an ASCII code page AS/400 IFS file that can be used as a base to set the code page of new AS/400 IFS files:

1. CRTPF lib/temp rcdlen(1) (Add a record to this file by using a utility program such as DFU.)

2. CD DIR('/qdls/foldername')

3. CPYTOIMPF FILE(LIB/TEMP) TOSTMF('temp') RCDDLM(*CRLF)

4. MOV OBJ('temp') TOOBJ('CCSID00367') TOCODEPAGE(00367)

5. Copy the ASCII code page file to create the output AS/400 IFS file for your CPYTOIMPF command when you first use an output AS/400 IFS file. Issue the following command to replace **myASCIIfile.csv** with the name of the file you are specifying on the CPYTOIMPF command:

```
CPY OBJ('CCSID00367') TOOBJ('myASCIIfile.csv')
```

When you specify your new AS/400 IFS file on the CPYTOIMPF command, the data is translated to ASCII as it is copied to the output AS/400 IFS file.

6. CPYTOIMPF FILE(LIB/FILE) TOSTMF ('myASCIIfile.csv') RCDDLM(*CRLF) REPLACE(*YES)

—David Morris

◆ ◆ ◆ **IPL**

AS/400 IPL

Q: I want to perform some special routines at IPL time. I seem to remember something about an object that could be translated into CL source—along the lines of "startup." Is there actually a command that will perform the translation from object form? I called IBM reps, but they said that they were unaware of any such routine. If I am losing my mind, hey, that's no big deal; but if not, I would really appreciate any help I could get. Thanks a bunch.

A: Yes, there is a way to accomplish what you are trying to do. There is a system value QSTRUPPGM that references the CL program that runs during an IPL. The default is QSYS/QSTRUP. You can change this value to reference any program name or *NONE. If you would like to pattern your changes after the default program, you can run the Retrieve CL Source (RTVCLSRC) command on QSYS/QSTRUP to convert the object into source code.

—Midrange Computing Staff

Auto Subsystem Startup

Q: I am powering my system down every seven days through the auto power-down function of Operational Assistant. QSNADS subsystem does not start at IPL time; I have to start it after the IPL. Is there a way to start it, and, if so, how? If the solution is changing the subsystem description, which parameter gets changed?

A: During the system start, a CL (usually) program is called that starts all of the subsystems, writers, etc. The name of this program is contained in the system value, QSTRUPPGM. By examining this system value with WRKSYSVAL, you can determine the name of your startup program and modify it to start QSNADS. If you cannot find the source for the program, you can use the RTVCLSRC command to place the source into one of your source files. When I did ours, I retrieved the source into QCLSRC in QGPL. I made the changes to the source file, and recompiled the program into QGPL. I then changed the system value to call the startup program from QGPL, rather than QSYS, where it originally was.

—Midrange Computing Staff

Editor's Note: Be sure you make a copy of the original startup program and/or its source code in case you need it.

IPL Options

V4R2 of OS/400 introduced many enhancements in the area of IPLs, one of which was a new attribute table for IPLs. You can view this table with the Display IPL Attributes (DSPIPLA) command, which works much like the Display Net Attributes (DSPNETA) command. You can change the values in this table using the Work IPL Attributes (WRKIPLA) command to specify where certain IPLs are to begin—e.g., Power Down System (PWRDWNSYS) with RESTART. Using this new table, you can eliminate some of the early IPL steps, like the one that checks resources three times during IPL. Depending on the machine size, this can save up to 10 or 15 minutes off the IPL.

—Jack McGuigan

Startup Program Customization

Coming into a new AS/400 shop as System Administrator, the first thing I had to do was change the system startup program. The startup program is like the AUTOEXEC.BAT file on a DOS-based PC (the first job that runs when the system is powered up). On the AS/400, it starts all the important subsystems such as QINTER, QBATCH, and QSPL, and it also starts up some jobs that need to be run at IPL time, such as the automatic cleanup.

Like us, you might need to modify the startup program to add programs or start subsystems at IPL. Here's how we did it.

In our case, we had to alter the program to start the RBTSLEEPER subsystem that runs Help Systems' Robot program. Because our startup program is the IBM-supplied program, QSTRUP—and they don't supply the source code for it—we had to:

- Retrieve the source code.

- Alter it to start RBTSLEEPER.

- Recompile the program to a different library and indicate to the AS/400 that it should now run the modified code instead of the IBM-supplied program.

In order to retrieve the name of your startup program, run the Display System Value (DSPSYSVAL) command, specifying system value QSTRUPPGM. The system presents a panel that shows the name of the startup program.

If your startup program is QSTRUP in library QSYS, retrieve the source code for it with the Retrieve CL Source (RTVCLSRC) command, as follows:

```
RTVCLSRC PGM(QSYS/QSTRUP) SRCFILE(QGPL/QCLSRC)    SRCMBR(*PGM)
```

This command places the source code in source file QGPL/QCLSRC, member QSTRUP. PDM then allows you to change the code. (You may, of course, use a different source file and library.) We compiled ours to QGPL (instead of QSYS) because we preferred to keep the original version of the program intact. That meant that we needed to change system value QSTRUPPGM to point to the new, updated program in QGPL rather than the original, IBM-supplied program in QSYS.

To change QSTRUPPGM, run the Work with System Values (WRKSYSVAL) command, position the system value list to QSTRUPPGM and place an option 2 next to it. Then type in the new name of the program and its library. In our case, the program name was the same (QSTRUP), but the library was QGPL.

At the next IPL, the operating system looked into system value QSTRUPPGM to determine what program to run at startup, and consequently ran QGPL/QSTRUP. This procedure enabled us to start subsystem RBTSLEEPER at IPL and retrieve the CL code of the startup program for future modifications.

—*Joe Hertvik*

✦ ✦ ✦ Job Termination

Ending a Job Abnormally

A bad job dies a thousand deaths; a good job dies but once. Some jobs are difficult to end. Communication jobs that have gone awry are particularly prone to not ending, even when you've executed an End Job (ENDJOB) command with *IMMED specified for the OPTION parameter. The End Job Abnormal (ENDJOBABN) command can help kill those cowardly jobs.

ENDJOBABN is used to end a job that will not end through normal means. The parameters on this command are job name, user, and job number. The ENDJOBABN command requires that an ENDJOB OPTION(*IMMED) has already been run against the job you are trying to end. It also requires a lapse of 10 minutes for the ENDJOB command to have effect. Once those conditions are met, you can then run ENDJOBABN.

The only consideration for the ENDJOBABN command is that it makes your next IPL abnormal. So, if you are testing the system value QABNORMSW in your IPL start-up program, it will be set to '1' at the next IPL. That isn't a problem; it just lets you know that clean-up processing was done during the IPL.

—*Jim Hoopes*

Ending Jobs Without a Job Log

Q: I ended a job recently and it took almost 15 minutes for the job to finally end. I later found out that the job was producing a job log that was several thousand pages long. I often don't care what's in the job log; I already know what's wrong. Is there a way to end a job without having it produce a job log?

A: On the End Job (ENDJOB) command there is a parameter, Maximum Log Entries (LOGLMT), that lets you limit the number of entries written to the job log. If you don't want a job log at all, set this parameter to zero. If you want a small job log, set it to a small value such as 100.

—*Jim Hoopes*

✦ ✦ ✦ Jobs

Breaking an Active Program out of a Loop

If a program is caught in an infinite loop and observability has not been removed, it might be possible to break the loop without canceling the program. Use DSPJOB OPTION(*PGMSTK) to determine the program, its library, and a statement within the loop that is being executed. Use Start Service Job (STRSRVJOB), then Start Debug (STRDBG) and Add Breakpoint (ADDBKP) to set a breakpoint within the loop. When the breakpoint is displayed, press F10 to go to a command entry screen, and use the Change Program Variable (CHGPGMVAR) command to set the conditions necessary for the loop to end.

—Midrange Computing Staff

How to Control CHGJOB and ENDJOB

People have been doing all sorts of things to control the use of two important OS/400 commands: Change Job (CHGJOB) and End Job (ENDJOB). Both commands are readily available for general use in helpful list panels presented by other commands, such as Work with User Jobs (WRKUSRJOB) and Work with Submitted Jobs (WRKSBMJOB).

This means trouble. Big trouble. If any menus available to the user bring up any WRKxxxJOB commands, the user can run them and thus gain access to CHGJOB or ENDJOB. There are other ways to get to either of these commands, too. Both are dangerous. CHGJOB is dangerous because it allows the user to change the job's run priority to something like 01 (so it receives top priority and dominates the system). ENDJOB is dangerous because it allows the user to terminate running jobs, perhaps corrupting database files. The easiest way to control both commands is as follows:

1. Make a copy of both commands in a library that is higher than QSYS in the system portion of the library list (I call mine ALTQSYS):

```
CRTDUPOBJ OBJ(CHGJOB) OBJTYPE(*CMD) FROMLIB(QSYS) TOLIB(ALTQSYS)
CRTDUPOBJ OBJ(ENDJOB) OBJTYPE(*CMD) FROMLIB(QSYS) TOLIB(ALTQSYS)
```

    (If you don't have an ALTQSYS library, create it and then change system value QSYSLIBL, inserting the name of your new library before QSYS.)

2. Change both copies in ALTQSYS so that the commands can be run only from within CL programs or program modules:

```
CHGCMD CMD(ALTQSYS/CHGJOB) ALLOW(*IPGM *IMOD *BPGM *BMOD)
CHGCMD CMD(ALTQSYS/ENDJOB) ALLOW(*IPGM *IMOD *BPGM *BMOD)
```

3. Give the public *EXCLUDE authority to the original commands and give *USE authority to a few trustworthy users:

```
GRTOBJAUT OBJ(QSYS/CHGJOB) OBJTYPE(*CMD) USER(*PUBLIC)
AUT(*EXCLUDE)GRTOBJAUT OBJ(QSYS/ENDJOB) OBJTYPE(*CMD)
USER(*PUBLIC) AUT(*EXCLUDE)
```

From then on, no one (not even QSECOFR) will be able to run CHGJOB or ENDJOB by selecting option 2=Change or 4=End from a WRKxxxJOB panel. The reason is that the list panels provided by WRKxxxJOB invoke CHGJOB and ENDJOB without a library qualifier, thereby picking up the duplicates in ALTQSYS. And those duplicates can be run only from within a program or program module, not from the command line. When you need to run either CHGJOB or ENDJOB from a WRKxxxJOB panel, you can select option 5=Work with, which provides the fully qualified name of the job and a command line. At the command line, type the following:

```
QSYS/CHGJOB JOB(jobnbr/jobuser/jobname)
```

Then, press the F4 key to prompt. You'll be running the original CHGJOB command, which doesn't have restrictions. If a user sees you do this and tries it, the user won't be authorized; remember, you gave the user *EXCLUDE authority by giving such authority to the public. This method has advantages over others I've seen recommended over the years:.

One popular method is to first give the public *EXCLUDE authority to the original commands and then compile programs that need to use either command as adopting authorities from its owner (and the owner must be a user who has specific authorities to the commands in question). This method requires adopting authorities, which has side effects that could create security risks and breaches.

Another method is to create a validity-checking program (VCP) for the original commands and have this program control what the user can and cannot do. The problem with this method is that IBM might change the parameter structure of the commands at any time, rendering your VCP useless and, what's worse, preventing the commands from being run at all.

If you implement the trick I'm describing here, remember to redo it after each release upgrade to ensure that both versions (QSYS and ALTQSYS) of the commands have the same parameter structure.

—Ernie Malaga

Printing Job Descriptions

Q: Is there a command to print all job descriptions from *LIBL?

A: You'd think you could use the Display Job Description (DSPJOBD) command with a wild card as follows:

```
DSPJOBD JOBD(QSYS/*ALL)
```

But the wild card is invalid, so you would get this error: **Value "*ALL ' for parameter JOBD not a valid name**. To get around this, use the Display Object Description (DSPJOBD) command qualifying the object type as job description (*JOBD):

```
DSPJOBD OBJ(QSYS/*ALL) OBJTYPE(*JOBD)
```

This command displays a screen with all the job descriptions. If you want to automate this process, use the OUTFILE parameter of the DSPJOBD command and use Query/400 or whatever to list the outfile.

—Don Denoncourt

Realistic Job Logging

Each job you run has the potential to create a job log. Job logs have the potential to eat up disk space that you might need for more important things. How many job logs are produced and how large they are made is something you have to decide.

Job or message logging is defined by the three elements of the LOG parameter in the Create Job Description (CRTJOBD) and Change Job Description (CHGJOBD) commands. The first refers to the logging level, which can be a value from 0 to 4. If you specify 0 for this value, no messages will be logged. Levels 1 through 3 log progressively more messages. Level 4 logs all requests and commands being logged from a CL program, as well as any messages with a severity greater than or equal to the logging severity specified for the job. The second element, a value from 0 to 99, indicates the minimum severity of messages to be logged. If you set this value to 0, all error messages will be logged. The third element indicates which error text should be shown. *NOLIST will not produce a job log unless the job ends abnormally, in which case both first- and second-level message texts are written to the log. *MSG shows only the first-level message text, and *SECLVL shows first- and second-level message text.

You can eliminate job logging entirely by setting each job description with message logging to LOG(0 0 *NOLIST), but this method leaves you no way to trace errors that occur during a job's execution. If you want this setting, I suggest specifying it on the Submit Job (SBMJOB) command, but beware: This method could waste system resources. The system must remove all messages as it receives them. Intermittent errors are particularly troublesome, and eliminating job logging gives you no way to trace them.

Another important parameter for logging messages is the log CL program (LOGCLPGM) attribute of the job, which controls the logging of CL commands. This can be:

- *SAME, which leaves the logging attribute unchanged.

- *NO, which logs no CL commands.

- *YES, which logs all CL commands if *JOB was specified in the LOG parameter of the Create CL Program (CRTCLPGM) command.

IBM default job descriptions are set to LOG(4 0 *NOLIST) and LOGCLPGM(*NO). Many programmers suggest changing this to LOG(4 0 *NOLIST) LOGCLPGM(*YES). Again, this will produce a job log only if errors occur. I prefer to specify LOG(3 30 *SECLVL) LOGCLPGM(*YES). This specification screens out inconsequential messages, but gives detailed information on errors of severity level 30 or greater, which are errors that I definitely want to track.

Unfortunately, job logs add to the number of jobs shown on the Work with System Status (WRKSYSSTS) display, and they require some storage area. You have to judge your own needs and determine how much overhead your system can handle when setting the logging parameters. Be aware of how often the job logs are cleared (either by an operator or by the Operational Assistant). Most operators or administrators set the Operational Assistant to clear job logs at least every seven days to avoid overburdening the system. Consider saving the job logs by using the Copy Spooled File (CPYSPLF) command or by printing them before they are deleted. Sometimes the only way to see a pattern in an error condition is to view job logs over a period of time. Therefore, I like to keep job logs for as long as possible. Setting a reasonable logging level is essential to keeping your system resources from being overused while still logging important errors. For more information on logging messages, see *OS/400 Work Management* (SC41-3306, CD-ROM QBKALG00).

—*D. Ellis Green*

Run Batch Jobs at Different Priorities

Q: I am having trouble with two subsystems. I want programmers to use QBATCH and run jobs at run priority 30. I want user batch jobs to go through subsystem QUSERS at priority 50. I set up two job queues and two subsytems, but jobs in both subsystems run at priority 30. How do I get QUSERS to use the new class?

A: Provided you simply used the Create Duplicate Object (CRTDUPOBJ) command from QBATCH to set up your QUSERS subsystem, the following commands should do the trick:

```
CRTCLS CLS(QGPL/QUSERS) RUNPTY(50) PURGE(*NO) DFTWAIT(120) +
    TEXT('User Batch Jobs')+ CHGRTGE SBSD(QUSERS) SEQNBR(9999) +
    CLS(QGPL/QUSERS)
```

The first creates a new class with priority 50 and typical batch attributes. Set your PURGE and DFTWAIT parameters however you wish. The second changes the default routing entry (normally at sequence number 9999) for subsystem QUSERS to use that class. Use this code only if you already have a routing entry 9999 with compare value *ANY. (I'm pretty sure this is how QBATCH is shipped.) Use DSPSBSD QUSERS to make sure. You should see a line like this:

```
9999 QCMD QSYS *ANY
```

—Joe Pluta

Running from What JOBQ?

I've often wanted to find out which job is holding up a single-threaded job queue. The Work with Active Jobs (WRKACTJOB) command shows which jobs are running in a subsystem, but it doesn't identify the job queue name. If you have more than one single-threaded job queue assigned to the subsystem, you can't determine which job queue originated a job.

After a little research, I was surprised to find a command that does list all job queues and their associated active jobs. It is the Work with User Jobs (WRKUSRJOB) command executed in the following form:

```
WRKUSRJOB USER(*ALL) STATUS(*ACTIVE) JOBTYPE(*BATCH) ASTLVL(*BASIC)
```

The trick to making this work is to use the basic assistance level. In this case, the Work with Jobs panel lists each job queue; and below the job queue name, is a list of the jobs running from the queue.

—Tim Greenan

Schedule Submitted Jobs

If you would like a submitted job to begin at a particular time on a particular day, instead of immediately, consider using the schedule date and time parameters of the Submit Job (SBMJOB) and Change Job (CHGJOB) commands. The Schedule date (SCDDATE) parameter can be any valid date in the job date format or one of the following special values:

- *CURRENT—Job will run on the current date.
- *MONTHSTR—Job will start on the first day of the month.
- *MONTHEND—Job will start on the last day of the month.
- *MON–*SUN—Job will start on the next day of the week specified.

The Schedule time (SCDTIME) parameter specifies the time on the scheduled date that the job will be released in the job queue. The time can be entered in 24-hour format with or without separators, in HHMMSS or HHMM format, or the special value *CURRENT.

For example, to submit a job next Saturday at 10:30 P.M., you might use the following command:

```
SBMJOB CMD(CALL DLTRCDPRG) JOB(DLT_PURG) SCDDATE(*SAT) SCDTIME(2230)
```

The job will be shown with a status of Scheduled (SCD) until the time specified. At that time, it will be changed to Released (RLS) status and will run when there is an available subsystem slot. After a job has been submitted but has not yet started, it is possible to change the scheduled date and time with the CHGJOB command. The Display Job (DSPJOB) command can be used to see what date and time the job is scheduled to start.

—Paul Jackson

Should Missed Jobs Run or Not?

When you add entries to the AS/400 Job Scheduler, the default recovery action (parameter RCYACN) is *SBMRLS, which means that if the job can't run because the machine is off (power outage, maintenance, etc.), the job will be submitted as soon as possible after the machine is restarted. Sometimes that's fine, but sometimes it can be disastrous.

The company I work for had to backdate our machine after one of our rare "snow days" down here (northeast Alabama) so that we could "recover" December 29, 1997, as a 1997 date for accounting purposes. We ran one whole day with the system backdated, and everything worked fine that day.

The next day, however, when we reset the system date value, we had major problems. Job scheduler jobs that should have run on 1/1/98, but didn't because of the backdating, fired up immediately and simultaneously!

Needless to say, system response went to zilch, and conflicting jobs were at cross purposes right and left until we could safely shut them down. To save ourselves future grief, we set recovery action to *NOSBM on all job scheduler jobs. In the future, we will manually submit any missed jobs that need rerunning after restart. This might be appropriate for some or all scheduled jobs in your shop, but, if you use it, be sure you have a way to know if a job was not submitted.

—Barry Jones

Tracking Multiple Active Sessions

My job as a consultant sometimes finds me logged onto more than one AS/400 at a time for more than one client. It's easy to get confused in this kind of environment and forget which session is which. To keep things straight, I use the Display Workstation User (DSPWSUSR) command. This command displays such relevant information as the display station ID, the number of interactive jobs in this session, and the current interactive job. The command even works for group jobs! Because DSPWSUSR is one of those commands that is easy to misspell, and to make things easier for those times when I'm in a hurry, I used the Create Duplicate Object (CRTDUPOBJ) command to create a copy of the DSPWSUSR command and named the new command WHO. Now, when I get confused as to which session is which, I simply type WHO on any command line and press Enter—and I instantly know where I am.

—Bob Gillespie

Use SBMJOB to Schedule Jobs

If you use "canned" software packages, you know that functions sometimes need to be performed during off-peak hours. Unfortunately, some of these packages do not provide the means for scheduling the work. Either a job is submitted immediately via a menu option or you must sign on at some bizarre hour to run the job. Taking full advantage of the

Submit Job (SBMJOB) command, however, can make your life much easier. SBMJOB has two parameters, Schedule date (SCDDATE) and Schedule time (SCDTIME), that allow you to control when a batch job runs. Here is an example of how I use the parameters to save time for more important things—like golf.

On the last day of the month, one of our canned systems needs a month-end close. I go to the menu and make the selection, and the job is submitted to batch. Unfortunately, because this job takes several hours and requires a dedicated system, I have to sign on at 1:00 A.M. to run it. Using SBMJOB, I simply put the appropriate job queue on hold before taking the menu option. Next, I use Work with Job Queue (WRKJOBQ) to display all pending jobs and find the one I have submitted. Using option 2 (Change Job), I then change the Schedule date and time parameters to 1:00 A.M. the following day. The job now sits in the job queue until the specified time it is to be submitted. This is a great technique for submitting batch jobs at your leisure and having them run at the optimal time.

—David Mayle

What Happens When the System Job Counter Goes Past 999999?

Q: A counter is used on the AS/400 to create a unique number for every job started on the system. It's a six-digit number, and our AS/400 is approaching 999999. What will happen when the first job after 999999 is submitted?

A: When that first job after number 999999 is submitted, the counter will wrap around to 000000. Nothing bad happens, and you don't have to do anything special.

—Mark Russo

✦ ✦ ✦ Journals

Journaling Specific Types of Transactions

Q: I want to be able to journal files to find out which program deleted the records in my shop's order note file. I've created a journal receiver and journal, but can I restrict the system so that it audits only deleted transactions and ignores transactions such as update and read?

A: A trigger program added to the file for delete operations can log to a journal by using the send journal entry function. You can format the order number or any other data you desire, making a query of the Display Journal (DSPJRN) output much simpler to do.

—*Chuck Pence*

Receiver Not Saved Error

Q: When changing receivers attached to my journal and then trying to delete the old journal receiver, I keep getting message CPA7025: "Receiver never fully saved (I C)." I'd like to ignore this error or answer it with the default IGNORE. Sounds simple, eh? The system ignores a MONMSG CPA7025 command; a SNDRPY or RCVMSG does nothing at all. I added the commands to the save CL in order to know the library that contains the receiver is saved before the deleted receiver is run. This was to no avail. Did IBM actually decide that this one message requires human intervention no matter what? Is there really no way to ignore this error message?

A: You could use the system reply list to take care of this annoying message. For example:

```
ADDRPYLE SEQNBR(500) MSGID(CPA7025) RPY(I)
```

This adds an automatic reply of "I" (ignore) to message CPA7025, in sequence 500 of the system reply list. If sequence 500 is already used, use another number. To view your system reply list, user the Work with Reply List Entry (WRKRPYLE) command. Now all you need to do is make your job pay attention to the system reply list. You do that with the CHGJOB command, specifying INQMSGRPY(*SYSRPYL). You can specify this in the job description, which would save you from having to repeat the CHGJOB command for every job, every time.

—*Midrange Computing Staff*

✦ ✦ ✦ Library List Processing

Update Production Systems Fearlessly

Updating a production system can often be a harrowing experience. If the system is one that is in use 24 hours a day, or even during normal work hours, it is essential that the downtime be kept to a minimum. You can make things a little easier by using library lists to your advantage.

First of all, you should place a temporary library at the beginning of the production system's library list. This will become a permanent addition to the library list and serve as a temporary holding place for objects that are to be updated. Be sure to treat this as any other production library (as for security and so on).

When you want to make an update, first move the old objects into the temporary library. If it is a program you are updating, you can do this while it is being executed. As long as the temporary library is in the user's library list, the users will not be affected. If it is a file you want to update, you will need to do this while it is not in use. In any case, it takes only a second to move an object.

Now you can compile the new objects into the production library, at your leisure, without worrying that something terrible will go wrong (as users are standing around waiting for the update to take place). After you are sure that the update has gone successfully, you simply rename the object in the temporary library, and then the users will be using the updated version. Again, if it is a program you are updating, you can do this as the users are executing it. Anyone using the program at the time of the rename will be unaffected. When the program is called again, the new version will be used.

You need to use this method only a few times to realize the value of doing it this way. For crucial applications, program changes can be made while the system is still up and running. For changes to files, downtime is kept to an absolute minimum, and there are never any surprises.

—Jon Vote

Editor's Note: *Keep in mind that if you use this technique, all versions of library lists referenced by the production library programs must have the temporary library added to them. For example, a library list that is referenced through a job description must include the temporary library.*

✦ ✦ ✦ Licensed Software

List Installed IBM Software

You know you can display all IBM software installed on your system through option 10 of GO LICPGM, but what if you want this printed? You can press the Print Screen key, but there is a better solution. Use the Display Software Resources (DSPSFWRSC) command and use the *PRINT value for the OUTPUT parameter. This command will do the job and even give you a bonus. For each licensed program, the library name in which it is located will be listed.

—Jean-Jacques Risch

✦ ✦ ✦ Menus

Reveal Menu Options

There are times when you need to know what command is executed when you select an option from a menu generated by SDA. Consider the following scenario:

A user comes to you complaining, "The report you wrote for me is giving incorrect totals." To clarify this vague statement, you ask a few questions, finally getting the user to tell you that taking Option 7 from menu OERPT1 in OELIB produces the misbehaving report.

The next step is to figure out what the system does when that option is selected. The easiest way to find out is by using the Work with Message Descriptions (WRKMSGD) command, as follows:

```
WRKMSGD MSGID(*FIRST) MSGF(OELIB/OERPT1)
```

In other words, you enter the name of the menu where WRKMSGD expects the name of the message file. This works because menus created by SDA contain the commands in the message descriptions of a message file, which is given the same name as the menu.

WRKMSGD presents a typical "work with" panel. Option numbers are listed in the format USR00NN, so Option 7 is USR0007. The text of the message is the command string; it might look something like this:

```
CALL PGM(OELIB/OE507)
```

Now you know where to begin! Look up program OE507 in library OELIB.

—Ernie Malaga

Rolling Menus

Q: I have a suggestion for SDA. I would like to be able to create rolling menus. The only way I know to do that is to use the UIM tag language. Would it be feasible to have SDA generate rolling menus?

A: SDA option 2 is basically a front-end to the Create Menu (CRTMNU) command. The three kinds of input CRTMNU command will take are a:

1. Display file with one record and a message file full of commands.

2. UIM panel group.

3. Program name.

The first option is fully covered already by SDA option 2. Because there can be only one record in the display file, these menus can't roll. Using the UIM tag language is the second option. This language is flexible, powerful, and not too difficult to use. We could have SDA generate the UIM panel group, but, after giving the matter some consideration, this method didn't look so attractive.

Because UIM is a tag-based language, you tell it the essentials (menu item names, associated commands, and associated help) and it figures out the rest for you—including the layout. On the other hand, SDA is a layout tool. Its strength is a WYSIWYG way of specifying how you want the elements of the menu to appear. In UIM, you have no choice where things will appear; SDA and UIM do not get along.

As a result, programmers are better off using UIM directly. Just take a boilerplate menu (see Figures 9.21 and 9.22) and change the values to what you need. You can add as many options as you want (up to 999) to the menu, and UIM will take care of creating the necessary additional pages.

```
.*===============================================================*
.* To compile:                                                  *
.*                                                              *
.* CRTMNU MENU(XXX/MENUSHELL) TYPE(*UIM) +                       *
.* SRCFILE(XXX/QMNUSRC)                                          *
.*                                                              *
.*===============================================================*
:pnlgrp.
:keyl name=small help=FKHLP.
:keyi key=f1 help=FKHLP action='HELP'.
:keyi key=f3 help=FKHLP action='EXIT' varupd=no .F3=Exit
:keyi key=f4 help=FKHLP action='PROMPT' .F4=Prompt
```

Figure 9.21: Use this UIM source to create your own rolling menu (part 1 of 2).

```
:keyi key=f9 help=FKHLP action='RETRIEVE' .F9=Retrieve
:keyi key=f12 help=FKHLP action='CANCEL' varupd=no .F12=Cancel
:keyi key=enter help=FKHLP action='ENTER'.
:keyi key=help help=FKHLP action='HELP'.
:keyi key=pageup help=FKHLP action='PAGEUP'.
:keyi key=pagedown help=FKHLP action='PAGEDOWN'.
:ekeyl.
:panel name=main help=MAINHLP keyl=small .Menu Shell
:menu depth='*' scroll=yes.
:topinst .Select one of the following:
:menugrp .ADT Utilities
:menui help=OP1HLP option=1 action='CMD strpdm' .Start PDM
:menui help=OP2HLP option=2 action='CMD strsda' .Start SDA
:menui help=OP3HLP option=3 action='CMD strdfu' .Start DFU
:emenugrp.
:menugrp .Others
:menui help=OP90HLP option=90 action='CMD signoff' .Sign off
:emenugrp.
:emenu.
:cmdline size=long .Selection or command
:epanel.
:help name=FKHLP .Function key help
:ehelp.
:help name=MAINHLP .Main help
:ehelp.
:help name=OP1HLP .Option 1 help
:ehelp.
:help name=OP2HLP .Option 2 help
:ehelp.
:help name=OP3HLP .Option 3 help
:ehelp.
:help name=OP90HLP .Option 90 help
:ehelp.
:epnlgrp.
```

Figure 9.21: Use this UIM source to create your own rolling menu (part 2 of 2).

```
                          Menu Shell
                                                    System: MC
PGMR
Select one of the following:
  ADT Utilities
    1. Start PDM
    2. Start SDA
    3. Start DFU
  Others
    90.Sign off


Bottom
Selection or command
===
F3=Exit F4=Prompt F9=Retrieve F12=Cancel
```

Figure 9.22 Here's what the UIM Menu Shell screen will look like.

The third option is completely up to you. Write a program to do whatever you want and CRTMNU will generate a menu object. Total flexibility and total responsibility are yours.

—Edmund Reinhardt

Editor's Note: *For more information about UIM menus, refer to IBM's* Guide to Programming and Application and Help Displays *(SC41-0011, CD-ROM QBKA7902).*

Using a Generic Value with GO

Many of us use the GO command to access AS/400 menus. What you might not know is that the GO command permits you to enter a generic value in the menu-name parameter. For example, if you key GO US*, your library list is searched for menus that start with the letters US. You are then presented with a list of menus from which you can make a selection. Use option 1 to select one of the menus for display.

—Ted Holt

Using the GO Command to Find a Menu

Have you ever needed to run a command from a GO menu, but you couldn't remember the name of the menu or the library it's located in? Rather than wracking your brain trying to figure it out, why don't you try using the GO command's wildcard search facility to find the menu? It's incredibly easy to use and quick. Let's look at an example.

Suppose you want to run the TCP/IP administrator menu but can't remember its name and library location. All you know is that it starts with a T. You can still use the GO command to find the menu and run it. Like many other OS/400 commands—such as Work with Objects (WRKOBJ) or Work with Subsystem Description (WRKSBSD)—GO allows you to place generic and wildcard parameters in the object name fields. So, if you want to search all libraries for menus that begin with T, you type in the GO command with the following parameters:

```
GO MENU(*ALL/T*)
```

This tells GO to show you a list of all menus that start with the letter T—in all libraries. When you find the menu you want to run, simply put a 1 in front of it, and away you go. You can also specify GO to search for menus in a specific library, your library list, the current library, the user portion of the library list, or all user libraries. On the prompt screen, simply enter F1 (Help) on the library portion of the menu location to get a list of your possible choices.

Alternatively, you can use the Work with Menus (WRKMNU) command to do the same thing: WRKMNU *ALL/T*. When the list shows up, use option 5 to display the selected menu. Don't rely on your memory when running menus. Use the power of OS/400 to get the right menu at the right time.

—Joe Hertvik

✦ ✦ ✦ Messages

Avoiding the "Member Is Full" Message

Suppose you are running a job that outputs to a file, and suddenly you get the dreaded CPA5305 "Record not added. Member is full." message. You have added 13,000 of 50,000 records. Your choices are to cancel the job, to change the member size and restart it, or to answer the message 37 times with an I to ignore. An easier way to solve the problem is to temporarily add a system reply list entry with a value of I for message CPA5305.

```
ADDRPYLE SEQNBR(sequence_number) MSGID(CPA5305) RPY(I)
```

Use a sequence number not already used in your reply list. You can use the Work with System Reply List Entry (WRKRPYLE) command to find an available number. Change the job to use the system reply list for messages:

```
CHGJOB JOB(jobnbr/user/jobname) INQMSGRPY(*SYSRPYL)
```

Then answer the original message with an I. Any time the system sends the CPA5305 message, the job will automatically answer with an I and will continue running. When the job completes, remove the reply list entry.

```
RMVRPYLE SEQNBR(sequence_number)
```

Never again will you have to cancel and restart a job because you forgot to change the maximum file size.

—Fred Gamache

Filtering Operator Messages

Q: Does anyone know how to filter messages going to the QSYSOPR message queue? Every day at 5 P.M. we receive a message for every terminal that is turned off. The operators have missed important messages because of all the "Device no longer communicating..." messages.

A: By default, the QSYSOPR message queue automatically filters any message sent to QSYSOPR with a severity less than 40. Therefore, any message with a severity of 40 or higher in its description will break to the screen.

The message you're referring to is CPF2677, and I believe it ships with a severity of 40. So that particular message will not break to the workstation, we've changed the severity of this message to 39 using the Change Message Description (CHGMSGD) command. If you do this, you will probably have to redo it after every release upgrade you install.

—Dave Shaw

Get the Messages You Need

When users tell me they have submitted a job that is hung up in the job queue, the first thing I do is look at the message that the job sent to QSYSOPR to determine the facts of the matter. Because QSYSOPR usually has a lot of messages, I want to quickly weed through the informational messages to get to the ones that need replies (the inquiry messages). To get to those messages, I key the following command:

```
DSPMSG QSYSOPR MSGTYPE(*INQ)
```

All inquiry messages will be displayed, whether they have been answered or not. I often use this display as my starting point for finding and fixing problems. To further filter out the routine messages, I sometimes indicate a minimum severity level:

```
DSPMSG QSYSOPR MSGTYPE(*INQ) SEV(70)
```

All inquiry messages with a severity level of 70 or above will be displayed. From there, I can easily find the message that was sent by my user's job.

—Lisa Patterson

Editor's Note: This is a good way to quickly find a message needing a reply, especially if you don't know the name of the user profile under which the job is running, or the name of the subsystem in which it is running. Other good commands for locating unanswered batch job messages are Work with User Jobs (WRKUSRJOB) and Work with Subsystem Jobs (WRKSBSJOB).

Help for Those Who Want to Monitor for Escape Messages

To write functional, well-behaved CL programs, it is necessary to monitor for escape messages sent to CL commands. But trying to remember the message IDs of all those escape messages is impossible. Tell me again: What is the CPF message for end-of-file with Receive File (RCVF)? What is the message for an object not found with Check Object (CHKOBJ)?

With Version 4 Release 1 of OS/400, you don't need to consult hopelessly obsolete manuals or plagiarize other programs or run the command from a command line to determine which escape messages need to be monitored. Simply prompt a command, move the cursor to the top line (where the command name is), and press F1. Roll through the help text, and you will find every escape message that applies to that command.

—Mark Strong

Monitor Messages More Efficiently

When you display the QSYSOPR message queue, you probably spend a lot of time trying to locate important messages. This is because everything is sent to this queue. You should consider creating an alternate message queue—QSYSMSG. Key in the following:

```
CRTMSGQ MSGQ(QSYS/QSYSMSG) +
    TEXT('Optional MSGQ to receive specific system messages')
```

When this queue exists (in QSYS only), certain messages are directed to it instead of, or in addition to, the QSYSOPR message queue. You can then run DSPMSG QSYSMSG to view the messages. You can also write a break-handling program to receive messages for which you can perform special actions. The program can send messages to the QSYSOPR message queue or another message queue. Disk unit failure messages, for instance, are sent to QSYSMSG. For a complete list of all the messages directed to QSYSMSG, and for an example of a break-handling program, see the *AS/400 CL Programmer's Guide* (SC41-8077, CD-ROM QBKA7102).

—Jean-Jacques Risch

Reduce the Number of Messages System Operators Review

Q: I'm having a problem with our operations staff not being aware of error messages in the QSYSOPR message queue. I've asked the operators to review the message queue periodically, but there are so many messages in there because of communications and other issues that they often miss an important message. Is there anything I can do to make it easier for my operators to find the messages that are most important?

A: You have several options to make it easier to find important system-operations messages. One of my favorites is to use the following command:

```
DSPMSG MSGQ(QSYSOPR) MSGTYPE(*INQ)
```

That shows you only the inquiry messages in QSYSOPR, which is a much shorter list of messages to review. Another option is to create a message queue called QSYSMSG in the library QSYS. When you do this, the system starts storing specific operations messages in this message queue. Many of the messages that go into the QSYSMSG message queue deal with hardware problems and, specifically, disk drive failures. You can find a list of messages that the system places in QSYSMSG in the *OS/400 CL Programming V3R1* manual (SC41-3721, CD-ROM QBKAUO00).

The final option is to create a message-monitoring program. You could, for example, create a file of the message IDs that are especially important and send a break message to one or more workstations. The trick is to narrow down the amount of data that your operators need to go through. Otherwise, finding the important messages is a bit like finding a needle in a haystack.

—*Jim Hoopes*

The QSYSMSG Message Queue

Creating a message queue called QSYSMSG in library QSYS will cause OS/400 to automatically send certain crucial messages to this message queue. This will allow you to respond quickly to what could be a serious condition. Figure 9.23 shows a sampling of some of the messages that will be routed to SYSMSG.

```
CPF0907 SERIOUS STORAGE CONDITION MAY EXIST
CPF1269 PROGRAM START REQUEST RECEIVED ON COMMUNICATIONS
DEVICE WAS REJECTED WITH REASON CODES
CPF1397 SUBSYSTEM VARIED OFF WORK STATION
CPI0920 ERROR OCCURRED ON DISK UNIT
CPI0950 STORAGE UNIT NOW AVAILABLE
CPI0953 ASP STORAGE THRESHOLD REACHED
CPI0954 ASP STORAGE LIMIT EXCEEDED
CPI0955 SYSTEM ASP UNPROTECTED STORAGE LIMIT EXCEEDED
CPI0964 WEAK BATTERY CONDITION EXISTS
CPI0965 FAILURE OF BATTERY POWER UNIT FEATURE IN SYSTEM UNIT
CPI0966 FAILURE OF BATTERY POWER UNIT FEATURE IN EXPANSION UNIT
CPI0970 DISK UNIT NOT OPERATING
CPI0988 MIRRORED PROTECTION IS RESUMING ON DISK UNIT
```

Figure 9.23: Here's just a sampling of messages sent to the QSYSMSG message queue.

Simply create the message queue with the following command:

```
CRTMSGQ MSGQ(QSYS/QSYSMSG)
```

Why create a special queue for this purpose? First, you might want to isolate the most important messages into this message queue. OS/400 does this automatically for you as soon as you create the queue. Second, you can put your interactive session into *BREAK delivery mode on the QSYSMSG message queue and be interrupted with a break message only if a serious problem arises. There is a discussion of QSYSMSG in the *AS/400 CL Programmer's Guide*, which has a sample program and a list of messages sent to QSYSMSG.

You might want to write a program to process these very serious messages. Why would you want to write a program instead of just putting your interactive job into *BREAK delivery mode on QSYSMSG? Probably the best reason is to ensure that these essential messages are sent to interested parties as early as possible. Let's say that the system operator, who normally comes to work at 8 A.M., won't arrive until 10 A.M. Your program should have a list of user profiles and should try to send break messages (perhaps using the SHOUT command from QUSRTOOL) to someone on the list. If no one is available, the program should put itself to sleep and wake up every so often (perhaps once every 30 seconds) to try sending break messages again to interested parties.

The other reason for the program is to route these messages to QSYSOPR. When you create QSYSMSG, these essential messages are sent only to QSYSMSG. A program also could send these messages to QSYSOPR. That's a good idea because the message is then logged in the history file, which can be used for future reference. Finally, maintaining messages of this magnitude in two different message queues provides additional insurance that the problem will be noticed as early as possible.

IBM has provided the QSYSMSG mechanism to help isolate problems on our machines. When you create the QSYSMSG message queue, you can help to ensure that your system operator's interactive session is interrupted with break messages primarily when crucial problems surface, and not every time a new message arrives in QSYSOPR. If you do decide to create the QSYSMSG message queue, you should consider writing a message-handling program to help ensure that interested parties are informed of potential problems as early as possible.

—Mike Cravitz

Use System Request to Send EZ Messages

Option 5 on the System Request menu executes the Send Message (SNDMSG) command and it provides a convenient way to send a message to another user. However, the problem with this method is that it requires you to know the user profile of the person you want to send a message to.

An answer to this problem comes in the form of one of the Operational Assistant APIs called QEZSNDMG. This API allows you to press F4 to obtain a list from which you can select one or more user profiles. To see this capability in action, enter the following command:

```
CALL QEZSNDMG
```

Tab down to the "Send to" field and press the F4 key. From there, you can use option 1 to select user profiles, using the roll keys if necessary.

To take this one step further, you can execute this API from option 5 on the System Request menu in place of the default SNDMSG command. This change would affect everyone on your system. Implementing this on your system involves two steps.

This first step is to key in the command shown in Figure 9.24 and compile it. Be sure to put this command in a library that is in everyone's library list. We put the command in QGPL.

```
/*===============================================================*/
 /* To compile:                                                   */
 /*                                                               */
 /*          CRTCMD      CMD(XXX/QEZSNDMG) PGM(QSYS/QEZSNDMG)  +  */
 /*                      SRCFILE(XXX/QCMDSRC)                     */
 /*                                                               */
 /*===============================================================*/

            CMD         PROMPT('Send Message')
```

Figure 9.24: Use this front end to the QEZSNDMG command.

The second step involves changing a message description. All of the commands that execute from the System Request menu are stored in the message CPX2313 in message file QCPFMSG in QSYS. Each command has a fixed starting position within the message text. To make this work, you need to modify one of the commands without changing the starting positions of any of the other commands. To accomplish this, enter the following command:

```
WRKMSGD MSGID(CPX2313) MSGF(QSYS/QCPFMSG)
```

When the list of messages appears, take option 2 (change) for message CPX2313 and you will see what the message currently looks like. Move the cursor over to the first letter of the SNDMSG command using your arrow keys, and type QEZSNDMG over it.

Be careful not to change anything else. Also, be sure your Insert key is not on. If you make a mistake, do not use your Delete key, as this would change the starting position of other commands in the message.

After you make the change, press Enter. The message CPX2313 is now changed. Press F3 to exit the Work with Message Descriptions (WRKMSGD) command. From this point on, System Request 5 will present you with the Operational Assistant "Send a Message" screen.

—Roy Morita

Editor's Note: *You should make a copy of the QCPFMSG message file before you modify it. Just use the Create Duplicate Object (CRTDUPOBJ) command to accomplish this.*

Using ADDRPYLE for Automatic Replies

In our company, we have several programs that generate printer output containing barcodes. Unfortunately, we also have some old printers that are not able to print barcodes (i.e., old matrix printers). In this case, the AS/400 displays message CPA3388, which the system operator can answer with C, G, T, or H. You don't have to manually answer this message every time the output comes through an old printer. The operating system provides the capability to answer these types of questions automatically. With the Add Reply List Entry (ADDRPYLE) command, you can add the number of this message and the appropriate answer (for example, G for go). The next time the output comes on an old printer, the message will be answered automatically, and the printer will print the output automatically without any user intervention.

—Walter Butikofer-Spuhler

✦ ✦ ✦ Object Commands

Library Sizes

A neat trap everyone seems to fall into is one provided by the Display Object Description (DSPOBJD) command. DSPOBJD shows the size of an object right on the screen, and it does so accurately, unless the object being displayed is a library. Libraries are different beasts. The *LIB object (which is what you display with DSPOBJD) doesn't represent the entire library, but only its directory. None of the objects inside the library are accounted for in the library size reported by DSPOBJD.

To get the accurate size of a library, use the Display Library (DSPLIB) command instead, making sure you specify OUTPUT(*PRINT). Right at the bottom of the screen, you'll have a total size for all objects in the library. Therefore, DSPOBJD reports my library QRPG as having 86,016 bytes, but DSPLIB reports a size of 4,841,472, which is some 50 times greater.

—Ernie Malaga

What Does It Mean to Search *ALLUSR Libraries?

On many OS/400 commands—such as Work with Object Descriptions (WRKOBJD), Work with Subsystem Descriptions (WRKSBSD), and even the GO command for running menus—you have the option to specify which specific library or groups of libraries you want the command to search for objects in. For the library on the Object (*OBJ) parameter of these commands, you can usually specify one of the following:

- A specific library name.
- *LIBL—Search for the objects in the user's library list.
- *CURLIB—Search for the objects in the user's current library.

- *ALL—Search for the object in all libraries on your AS/400 (user and system).

- *ALLUSR—Search for the object in all user libraries on your AS/400.

For example, if I wanted to run WRKOBJ on all objects that started with MID* in all my user libraries, I would type in the following command:

```
WRKOBJ OBJ(*ALLUSR/MID*)
```

Now, this is all fairly straightforward, but there is one trick to using this parameter: Specifying *ALLUSR as the library name doesn't mean that all system libraries will be skipped in the search. System libraries are usually defined as any library that starts with a Q, and *ALLUSR is supposed to tell OS/400 not to search any of these libraries. However, IBM states in its documentation that—because certain system libraries contain user data that changes often—these libraries also will be searched when you specify *ALLUSR as the library portion of your object name. In essence, IBM considers certain system libraries also to be user libraries, and they will be searched in commands in which *ALLUSR is specified. So, in addition to searching your user libraries when *ALLUSR is specified, OS/400 will display any objects that meet the search criteria in the following system libraries:

```
QDSNX
QGPL
QRCL
QS36F
QUSRINFSKR
QUSRBRM
QUSRIJS
QUSRSYS
QUSRVxRxMx
QGPL38
QPFRDATA
QUSER38
QUSRADSM
QUSRRDARS
```

The point to remember is that IBM gives you additional search capability when you specify *ALLUSR as your object library. You get more mileage out of an *ALLUSR search than you might think, and that can make your processing run more effectively.

—Joe Hertvik

✦ ✦ ✦ OfficeVision

OV/400 Is More Useful Than You Might Think!

Office Vision/400, IBM's host word processing software, has lots of neat features (such as a floating cursor point) that are not available in DDS. It's hard to try to replicate this type of functionality with the standard block-mode data transfer capability available to you with standard DDS.

There is a way to put a dumb terminal into OV/400-like mode. Use the User Defined (USRDFN) keyword in your DDS display file to send the Write Structured Field (X'F3') command along with Text Support commands. When you use the USRDFN keyword in your display file, you are telling OS/400 that your program will handle all formatting, reading, and writing of the 5250 data stream to the display. The IBM *5494 Remote Control Unit: Functions Reference* manual contains all the specifications you will need to make this work.

Some of the more interesting Work Station Function (WSF) commands available to you on dumb terminals using the USRDFN keyword are as follows:

- Define Audit Window—activates pop-up balloon help as the cursor moves over a field.

- Define Command Key—allows you to program the DEL or other keys to perform textprompt/locate/copy/move/delete/hyphenate.

- Read Text Screen—allows you to capture every keystroke.

- Define Special Characters—allows you to display required carriage return symbols.

- Define Fake DP Command Key—allows you to respond to combinations, such as CMD/U (underline), CMD/B (bold), CMD/J (normal).

With IBM's eventual end of support for OV/400, maybe some creative individual will find a new use for the WSF APIs.

—Joe Pluta

✦ ✦ ✦ OS/400

What Model Is This?

Q: I see that the AS/400 model can be retrieved by viewing the system value QMODEL. Is there a way to find out the processor feature for the machine?

A: System value QPRCFEAT will give you the processor feature.

—Chris Scholbe

A: You can also use the command WRKHDWRSC TYPE(*PRC). Your system's hardware feature options will appear in the resulting list.

—Shannon O'Donnell

✦ ✦ ✦ OS/400 Commands

Quickly Locating AS/400 Objects

Sometimes on the AS/400 you have to locate an object and you have no idea in which library it resides. There is a command on the AS/400 that will help you to locate any object on the system. Not only will it find the object for you, but it will show you every occurrence of that object. This makes it also useful for finding duplicate named objects (something you must be aware of when setting up library lists).

The command is DSPOBJD. You just use *ALL for the library name to search and *ALL for the object type. Each occurrence of the object will be displayed one at a time for every library in which it is found.

—Midrange Computing Staff

✦ ✦ ✦ PDM

Define Your Own PDM Options

If you're not defining your own Programming Development Manager (PDM) options, you're overlooking a great productivity aid.

PDM reserves numeric options for its own use. You can define options AA through Z9 as anything you want. This opens up an enormous number of possibilities.

To explore these options, type in the Start PDM (STRPDM) command and take option 9. (Or, press F16 from a Work with Members Using PDM [WRKMBRPDM] display.) You will see the user-defined options that have already been defined. Let's define option SO to sign off.

Press F6 to create an option. You will see the Create User-Defined Option display. In the Option field, type **SO**. In the Command field, type **signoff**. Press Enter, and the user defined option SO for signing off will now be available.

Press F3 from the Work with User-Defined Options display, and make sure you have a source or other file with the members displaying on your screen. Now, key in **SO** in the PDM options. Behold, you will shortly be signed off. Table 9.1 lists some of the other shortcuts to commands I frequently use.

Table 9.1: Sample PDM Options

Option	Command	Description
CR	? CRTRPGPGM pgm(&l/&n) srcfile(&l/&f) option(*optimize)	Optimized RPG compilation
DJ	DSCJOB	Disconnect job
DM	DSPMSG	Display messages
DR	DSPRCDFMT	MC's Display Record Format utility
PR	? STRRLU srcfile(&l/&f) srcmbr(&n) option(6)	Prototype a report
RL	? STRRLU srcfile(&l/&f) srcmbr(&n) option(2)	Edit report with RLU
SA	WRKSPLF *ALL	Work with all spooled files
SP	WRKSPLF	Work with spooled files by the signed-on user
WA	WRKACTJOB	Work with active job
WS	WRKSBMJOB	Work with submitted jobs

Some of the commands include two-character substitution variables. PDM will substitute values into these variables when the command runs. I've listed the substitution variables in Figure 9.25.

```
&A      object attribute
&B      list type
&C      user-defined option code
&D      member/part change date
&E      run in batch option
&F      file name
&G      job description library
&H      job description name
&J      job description
&L      library
&N      item name
&O      object library
&P      compile in batch option
&R      replace object option
&S      item type without leading asterisk (*)
&T      item type with leading asterisk (*)
&U      user-defined option file name
&V      user-defined option file library
&W      user-defined option file member
&X      item text
&Zx     ADM/400 options
```

Figure 9.25: Here are the command abbreviations for User Defined Options in SEU.

You can find out more about them by pressing the F1 key while the cursor is in the Command field in the Create User-Defined Option display.

—Tim Johnston

✦ ✦ ✦ Performance

Cataloging Troubles?

Q: My system's database cross-reference file, QSYS/QADBIFLD, appears to be damaged. It doesn't return field names to ODBC when I execute an SQL call from a PC. What's really strange is that, when I use Query/400, I can see all of my files in the cross-reference physical file, QSYS/QADBXREF, but very few of those files exist in QSYS/QADBIFLD. How can I get the system to rebuild the catalog files? This problem started when the system suddenly increased from 85 percent DASD to 96 percent and suddenly dropped to 66 percent 16 hours later. After that, my ODBC application started failing because it couldn't find the files it needed. Any suggestions?

A: The Reclaim Storage (RCLSTG) command has an option to rebuild database cross-reference files. Run this command to clean up auxiliary storage when you have an unexpected system failure.

—David Morris

Find Hidden CPU with WRKSYSACT

What do you do if the system is running at 99.9 percent CPU utilization and the Work with Active Jobs (WRKACTJOB) command shows your jobs taking only 5 percent of the total? What is using the remaining 94.9 percent? It's probably being used by hidden system tasks. Two types of processes run on the AS/400: jobs and tasks. Of course, users and the system both initiate jobs. Jobs can be displayed with the job commands, such as Work with Jobs (WRKJOB), End Job (ENDJOB), and WRKACTJOB. Tasks are created only by the system and are normally invisible to users.

The Performance Tools licensed program includes a command called Work with System Activity (WRKSYSACT). It gives you a list of the jobs and tasks using more than .1 percent CPU, with the highest percentage users listed first. There is also an automatic refresh option, and you can set the interval between updates. Keep a couple of things in mind about tasks. First, because they are all started by the system, they don't have a user name or job number. Second, you have to do some detective work to be able to determine what the task is doing. For example, tasks that start with "SM" are storage management tasks, which manage virtual memory and disk drives.

—Martin Pluth

Locating Resource-intensive Jobs

Does your system occasionally slow down to a snail's pace? This problem is usually the result of one job taking up an inordinate amount of system resources. The first step in solving this problem is to locate the offending job. Once found, you can do a number of things such as holding or ending the job or changing the job's priority and time slice. But how do you find out which job is slowing down the system? Fortunately, the system provides a way to do this.

The Work with Active Jobs (WRKACTJOB) command contains a sequence (SEQ) parameter that sorts the active jobs on the display. One of the values for this parameter is *CPUPCT. This sorts the display by the percent of processing resource used by each job during the elapsed time. For example:

```
WRKACTJOB SEQ(*CPUPCT)
```

This command produces a Work with Active Jobs screen. Notice that the display is sorted in descending order on the column labeled "CPU %." This means the job taking up the most resources will be at the top of the list. From there, you can use menu options such as 2 (change), 3 (hold), or 4 (end) to alleviate the problem.

Another way to use this feature is to enter the WRKACTJOB command without any parameters. In this case, the command defaults to sorting the list by subsystem and job name. However, you can still resequence the list by any column you want. Just place the cursor on the column you want to sequence (in this case CPU%) and press F16.

One thing to keep in mind when using this technique is that the elapsed time has an effect on the CPU percent. (The elapsed time is shown at the top of the WRKACTJOB screen.) The system keeps track of the amount of time that has elapsed since the statistics were reset. The elapsed time starts the first time you use WRKACTJOB and continues until you reset it, until you cancel WRKACTJOB (using System Request 2), or until you sign off. You can reset the statistics by using the RESET(*YES) parameter on the WRKACTJOB command or by pressing F10 or F13 on the WRKACTJOB screen. If the elapsed time is too high, you might want to reset it to get current CPU percentages.

—Robin Klima

Restricting Job Priorities

Q: We have a software package that submits jobs to QBATCH to run. The users have discovered that they can use Work with Active Jobs (WRKACTJOB), which is an option on their menu, to view their jobs and also to change the run priority to a small number. The problem is they cause performance problems for the rest of the system. I have tried to restrict authority to the Change Job (CHGJOB) command but the software package uses it. I can't restrict the use of WRKACTJOB because the users need to be able to view their submitted jobs. How can I prevent users from changing priority limits without restricting the use of the CHGJOB command?

A: The problem really isn't what command they use but the amount of authority given them on their user profiles. If a user has job control (*JOBCTL) special authority on his or her user profile, he or she can change the run priority from commands such as Work with Submitted Jobs (WRKSBMJOB), Work with Active Jobs (WRKACTJOB), and Work with User Jobs (WRKUSRJOB). Use the Change User Profile (CHGUSRPRF) command to remove the *JOBCTL special authority from the SPCAUT parameter. You might need separate profiles for the "package" and the users.

—Ray Vaughn

Q: I can't remove *JOBCTL from their user profiles because one of the first things the software package does is use the CHGJOB command. For the same reason, I can't restrict access to the CHGJOB command. I'm still at a loss. There should be a parameter in the subsystem description, user profile, or system value to restrict the run priority. You can control most of the other parameters, but not that one.

A: You can remove *JOBCTL authority from your users and still allow them to successfully execute the program. First, change the CL program that runs the CHGJOB command to run under the authority of the program's owner. Then grant the profile that owns the program *JOBCTL authority. That's it!

—Pete Hall

✦ ✦ ✦ Print Screen

Print Key's Changed Behavior

Q: We recently upgraded to a newer version of OS/400. Since the upgrade, all my printers (4028s) now print (from the Print key) in landscape with a small font. They printed in portrait before. All other printing is normal. Where do I correct this annoying problem?

A: When you press the Print key, the system uses a printer file to generate the screen image. This printer file is QSYS/QSYSPRT by default, but it can be customized. There are two solutions to your problem.

First, you could alter QSYSPRT so that it prints the way you like it. Although this seems like the easiest solution, it can actually cause you even more grief because QSYSPRT is used by many other system programs (and even user-written programs). So, any change you make to QSYSPRT to accommodate the Print key will affect those other programs as well.

Second, you can customize the behavior of your Print key by creating your own printer file, using whatever formatting you like, and then tell the system to use your own printer file instead of QSYSPRT. Although it requires more work, this is the better method. Here's what you need to do.

Create the printer file using the Create Printer File (CRTPRTF) command, specifying all the parameter values you want. Do not specify a source file, library, or member in the

SRCFILE parameter. Place the printer file in a library to which all jobs have access. Typically, this would be a system-supplied library such as QGPL.

Change the device description for all your display devices so that they "point" to the file you just created. You need to use the Change Device Description for Display (CHGDEVDSP) command, making sure you specify the printer file name in the PRTFILE parameter. You must run this command repeatedly for all existing display stations. Don't forget "virtual" display stations, such as those created by Client Access/400.

Change the default value for the PRTFILE parameter in the Create Device Description for Display (CRTDEVDSP) command so that it too points to the printer file you created. To change the default value, use the Change Command Default (CHGCMDDFT) command.

For instance, if I want to change the Print key in display stations DSP01 and DSP02 so that they use 66 x132 common stock paper, I do the following:

```
CRTPRTF FILE(QGPL/PRINTKEY) PAGESIZE(66 132) FORMTYPE(*STD)
CHGDEVDSP  DEVD(DSP01) PRTFILE(QGPL/PRINTKEY)
CHGDEVDSP DEVD(DSP02) PRTFILE(QGPL/PRINTKEY)
CHGCMDDFT  CMD(CRTDEVDSP) NEWDFT('PRTFILE(QGPL/PRINTKEY)')
```

—Ernie Malaga

Print Screen Options

There are several options for the way the output is created when the Print key is pressed. When the system is shipped, the default value for the QPRTKEYFMT system value is *PRTHDR, which specifies that header information is provided when the Print key is pressed. By changing this system value to *PRTBDR, you can request that border information be printed instead. If you specify *PRTALL, then both header and border information are included with the output from the Print key. The QPRTKEYFMT system value affects the print key output for all jobs on the system. If you want to change the Print key output for your job only, then use the Change Job (CHGJOB) command and specify an option on the PRTKEYFMT parameter. This parameter has all of the same options as the system value.

—Midrange Computing Staff

✦ ✦ ✦ **Printing**

Archive Reports by Copying Them into a Database File

I have found that many of the reports I run are needed for archival purposes. Rather than leave them on an output queue, where they can be accidentally erased or lost if the system needs to be restored, I copy them into a database file. You first need to create a file to hold the spooled files with a command such as the following:

```
CRTPF FILE(Library/File)   RCDLEN(133)  MAXMBRS(*NOMAX)
```

The record length needs to be one more than the maximum line length of the spooled files that will be archived. The extra byte is used to store forms control data.

The Copy Spooled File (CPYSPLF) command is used to copy the spooled files to the database file. The information you will need to use this command can be found by using the Work with Spooled Files (WRKSPLF) command.

```
CPYSPLF FILE(File) TOFILE(Library/File) JOB(Job#/User/Job)   +
SPLNBR(Spool#) TOMBR(Member) CTLCHAR(*FCFC)
```

CTLCHAR(*FCFC) tells the command to put the First Character Forms Control characters (such as new page or skip a line) in the first byte of each record.

For some important reports, you might want to add the CPYSPLF to the CL program that runs the report. There could be a member in the database file for each report you want to save.

When you need to print the stored report, you just need to override a printer file to correctly interpret the forms control character and use the Copy File (CPYF) command to put the report back into a spooled file.

```
OVRDBF FILE(QSYSPRT) CTLCHAR(*FCFC)
CPYF FROMFILE(Library/File)  TOFILE(QSYSPRT) FROMMBR(Member)
```

—Mike Kaplan

Change the Default Output Queue

Our shop is configured with multiple printers attached to PCs via a network. We have a requirement for users to direct output to various printers on demand. CHGDFTOUTQ command (Figure 9.26) and CL program DFT001CL (Figure 9.27) were created to change the user's Default Output Queue.

```
CMD          PROMPT('Change Default OUTQ')
PARM         KWD(OUTQ) TYPE(*CNAME) LEN(10) PROMPT('Outq +
               Name') DFT(*USRPRF) SPCVAL((*USRPRF))
```

Figure 9.26: The CHGDFTOUTQ command can be used to change which output queue spool files go to.

```
/* This program must be compiled with the parameter USRPRF set +
      to '*OWNER' so users can execute the program. */
  DFT001CL: +
    PGM PARM(&OUTQ)

    DCL VAR(&OUTQ)      TYPE(*CHAR) LEN(10)
    DCL VAR(&PRTR)      TYPE(*CHAR) LEN(10)
    DCL VAR(&MSGID)     TYPE(*CHAR) LEN(7)
    DCL VAR(&MSGDTA)    TYPE(*CHAR) LEN(100)

    MONMSG MSGID(CPF0000) EXEC(GOTO CMDLBL(ERROR))

    IF COND(&OUTQ *EQ '*USRPRF') THEN(DO)
       RTVUSRPRF OUTQ(&OUTQ) PRTDEV(&PRTR)
    ENDDO
    IF COND(&OUTQ *EQ '*DEV') THEN(DO)
       CHGVAR VAR(&OUTQ) VALUE(&PRTR)
    ENDDO
    IF COND(&OUTQ *EQ '*SYSVAL') THEN(DO)
       RTVSYSVAL SYSVAL(QPRTDEV) RTNVAR(&OUTQ)
    ENDDO

    CHGOUTQ OUTQ(&OUTQ)
    CHGJOB OUTQ(&OUTQ)
    CHGVAR VAR(&MSGDTA) VALUE('Output queue changed to')
    CHGVAR VAR(%SST(&MSGDTA 26 10)) VALUE(&OUTQ)
    SNDPGMMSG MSG(&MSGDTA)
    RETURN

  ERROR: +
    RCVMSG MSGDTA(&MSGDTA) MSGID(&MSGID)
    SNDPGMMSG MSGID(&MSGID) MSGF(QCPFMSG) MSGDTA(&MSGDTA) +
       MSGTYPE(*COMP)

    ENDPGM
```

Figure 9.27: The DFT001CL command processor is the power behind the CHGDFTOUTQ command.

The CL program defaults to resetting the queue to the one specified in the user's profile. It also edits the input to ensure a valid OUTQ is entered and returns a verification message upon completion. The user must have special authority of *SPLCTL (spool control) to change the OUTQ; therefore the CL program was compiled with the user profile set to *OWNER so that anyone could execute it.

—Brooks Stephan

Changing Spool File Attributes

There is a way to change the attributes, such as the characters-per-inch (cpi) value, of a spool file that is already on the output queue. Here is an example of how you would change from 10 cpi to 15.

1. Create a physical file to receive a copy of the spool file:

```
CRTPF FILE(*curlib/spl001) RCDLEN(133)
```

2. Copy the spool file to the created physical file using the First Character Form Control (***fcfc**) value in the CTLCHAR parameter:

```
CPYSPLF FILE(spool file) TOFILE(*curlib/spl001)
        JOB(number/userid/job) CTLCHAR(*fcfc)
```

3. Override QSYSPRT to the new cpi and specify control character ***fcfc**:

```
OVRPRTF FILE(qsysprt)  CPI(15)  CTLCHAR(*fcfc)
```

4. Copy the saved spool file to QSYSPRT:

```
CPYF FROMFILE(spl001)  TOFILE(qsysprt)
```

—Alon Fluxman

Keep Spool File Storage from Cluttering Your System

Prior to V2R3, IBM recommended frequent IPLs to recover unused spool storage. With V2R3, IBM introduced the command Reclaim Spool Storage (RCLSPLSTG), which can be run anytime. It's also incorporated in the cleanup routines associated with ASSIST.

—Jack McGuigan

Editor's Note: Spool files are stored as members in database files. When a spool file is deleted, the system clears the member and makes it available for reuse. RCLSPLSTG removes empty members.

✦ ✦ ✦ PTFs

Displaying the Cumulative PTF Level on Your System

To display the cumulative PTF level on your system, enter the following command:

```
DSPPTF LICPGM(5769SS1)
```

The cumulative PTFs appear at the beginning of the list and are identified as T*cyyddd* (where *yy* is the year and *ddd* is the Julian date). The cumulative PTFs are listed in reverse chronological order.

—Steve Bisel

Download PTFs in Batch

Like many of you, I download the complete list of PTFs from time to time to look for hidden new functionality and fixes to bugs that are causing me problems. To download the complete list of PTFs for V3R1, you run the following command:

```
SNDPTFORD PTFID((SF97310))
```

After you press Enter, you're prompted with a screen to verify some contact information. After you complete that screen and press Enter, you get a screen asking you to select a reporting option. Selecting 1 sends the service request now, selection 2 says, "Do not send service request," and selection 3 lets you send the service request by voice. The problem is, if you take option 1, you find your PC locked up for quite a while as the PTF information is downloaded.

You can submit PTF requests in batch. To do so, take option 2, which has that seemingly odd label of "Do not send service request." That logs your request into the system problem file with a status of Prepared. You can request multiple PTFs this way, and each of them will end up in the file. I recommend reviewing the problems that are prepared using the following command:

```
WRKPRB STATUS(*PREPARED)
```

You'll see a list of all problems with a status of Prepared. If there are any you don't want sent, use option 8 on the Work with Problems screen and change the status to Closed. You're then ready to send the PTF request to IBM. Here's the command you might use to get the PTFs from a batch job:

```
SBMJOB CMD(SNDSRVRQS  ACTION(*PREPARED))
```

Embedded in the Submit Job (SBMJOB) command is the Send Service Request (SNDSRVRQS) command. The SNDSRVRQS command uses the ECS modem to send all problems that have a status of Prepared. So you can send that long-running PTF request to IBM and not tie up your terminal for hours on end.

—*Jim Hoopes*

Installing PTFs

You might encounter a problem if you attempt to install a PTF for a licensed program that is at a different release level than OS/400. Fortunately, there's a solution to such a problem. Let me explain.

IBM occasionally creates a substantial update to a licensed program that can cause it to end up at a different release level than OS/400. This update is often referred to as a "refresh." For example, IBM created a refreshed Client Access for Windows program (5763XC1) that put that product at release V3R1M1 while OS/400 was still at V3R1M0.

After downloading a PTF for the refreshed Client Access for Windows product, I tried to load the PTF with the Load PTF (LODPTF) command. However, the command failed with message CPF3586, "List of PTFs not correct." I was planning to use the Apply PTF (APYPTF) command after I loaded the PTF, but how could I apply the PTF when I couldn't load it?

I found out from IBM Support that the solution is relatively simple—use a different method to load and apply the PTF. Specifically, use option 8 (Install program temporary fix package) from the PTF menu instead of using the LODPTF and APYPTF commands. Option 8 of the PTF menu will load and apply any uninstalled PTFs that you have downloaded through ECS. For ECS-downloaded PTFs, specify:

- *SERVICE for the DEVICE parameter.

- N for the Automatic IPL option, unless you want to cause an IPL after the install.

- 1 (all PTFs) for the PTF type parameter.

- N for the Other options parameter, unless you want to omit some PTFs or you don't want to delay applying the PTFs.

—Richard Shaler

Manually Delete PTF Save Files to Free Additional Disk Space

The PTF application process could produce save files on disk, depending on how you acquire the PTFs. After the PTFs are loaded, there is no need to keep these save files. The Operation Assistant automatically cleans PTF save files from previous releases. However, you might be able to free up additional disk space by manually deleting PTF save files for your current release.

The Delete Program Temporary Fix (DLTPTF) command can be used to delete PTF save files, their associated cover letters, and the records of PTFs that have been ordered. The syntax for the command is this:

```
DLTPTF PTF(ptf_number) LICPGM(program_number)
```

One way to access these save files is to use the following command:

```
WRKF FILE(QGPL/Q*) FILEATR(SAVF)
```

Use option 4 to delete the files you no longer need. The PTF names follow the convention of Q*aannnnn* where *aannnnn* is the PTF designation (that is, SF04718).

—Steve Bisel

Using the Web to Find the Latest PTF

Want a quick way to find out if your AS/400 has the most current PTFs? Here's how: From an AS/400 command line, type in the following Display PTF (DSPPTF) command and press Enter.

```
DSPPTF LICPGM(*ALL) SELECT(*ALL)
```

You'll be presented with a screen showing all PTFs on your system. Now, get on the Internet, and point your browser to:

http://as400service.rochester.ibm.com/

You'll find yourself on IBM's AS/400 Technical Support Web page. From there, you can find a link to the Preventive Service Planning (PSP) documents for the release of the operating system you are on. IBM uses PSPs to let you, the AS/400 operator and user, know what PTFs are currently available. This site will also inform you of any last-minute changes or modifications that might affect system upgrades. In fact, in the Power PC Upgrade Roadmap (used as the checklist for doing a CISC-to-RISC migration), you are strongly encouraged to check this Web site before starting the upgrade. This information is the most up-to-date information available regarding AS/400 changes and fixes.

If you find you need to download a PTF, use the Send PTF Order (SNDPTFORD) command from your AS/400 to download or order that PTF.

—Shannon O'Donnell

✦ ✦ ✦ Query

Files Used by Queries

When you change the definition of a file on the AS/400, you'll often have to recompile all objects that access that file. For example, if you add a century flag to a date field of a certain file, you need to change the DDS for the file and recompile it. Now all objects accessing that file will need to be recompiled if you recreate the file with LVLCHK(*YES), which is the default setting.

You can determine what programs to recompile by running the Display Program References (DSPPGMREF) command to an outfile. This prints the list of programs that you have to recompile. The problem comes with Query/400 programs that might use the changed file (the DSPPGMREF command does not cross-reference Query programs). If a Query uses the changed file for input or output, the Query will then display the message, "Level for file does not match query."

To solve this problem, always code the file name into the Run Query (RUNQRY) command that runs your Query programs, so that the value of the QRYFILE parameter matches the name of the file that you defined in the Query. For example, instead of the line:

```
RUNQRY QRY(TRY)
```

code the following:

```
RUNQRY QRY(TRY) QRYFILE((SRS/SRSD110A)) OUTTYPE(*OUTFILE) +
    OUTFILE(TEMP/WORKING)
```

Sure, you have to type more into the CL program, but now you can use the Scan All Source (SCNALLSRC) command, which is part of QUSRTOOL, to search for the file name and obtain a complete picture instead of a partial one.

—Donna Gateley

Editor's Note: You can also use the Find String with PDM (FNDSTRPDM) command instead of SCNALLSRC.

♦ ♦ ♦ Recovery

Include IFS Files in Your Nightly Backup

If you are running the AS/400's HTTP server for serving Web pages, you are probably storing HTML and other files on the AS/400's Integrated File System (IFS). You might be storing other "PC-style" files in IFS directories on your AS/400. Are you backing up this data regularly?

Our Web materials are stored in a directory named /WEBSAMP. We back up all the files and subdirectories it contains by using the following command, which is included in our nightly backup process:

```
SAV DEV('/QSYSLIB/TAP02.DEVD') OBJ(('/WEBSAMP/*'))
```

Even though the Save Entire System command, run from option 21 of the SAV menu, does save them, you might be executing that command only on a monthly basis.

—Steve Swett

Monthly Backup Procedures

Before you do a monthly backup, it's a good idea to first do a Reclaim Storage (RCLSTG). This is because the AS/400 backup commands will back up damaged objects, but the restore commands will not restore them. If you run RCLSTG before doing a monthly backup, the command will clean up your libraries before committing them to tape. Although it's not a guarantee, this could make it easier to restore those libraries and objects later on.

—*Joe Hertvik*

Reload

Q: We have to do a complete reload of our system in the very near future. I'm interested in hearing people's experiences. Any advice would be appreciated.

A: I have had to do numerous reloads, usually at the most inconvenient of times. If it is an option, look at the SAVSTG command. It will back up and reload your system faster than anything else. There are limitations on using this command (you cannot restore individual objects, just the entire system). Refer to the *Backup and Recovery Guide*.

If the SAVSTG command isn't an option, I would recommend saving the access paths for your logical files. This doesn't cause much increase in time for the backup, but can drastically reduce the reload time. This is done in the SAVLIB *NONSYS section of your total system backup.

—*Michael Catalani*

Restoring File to a New Name

Q: Am I missing something, or is there no easy way to restore an individual file from tape with a new name? I don't want to have to delete or rename the current version of the file on disk just to use data from the tape backup. Something like RSTFRMTAP FROMFILE(filename) TOFILE(newname) would be nice. Is there a way to do this?

A: You cannot rename a file when you restore. However, you can restore that file to another library and then rename it. If you wanted to automate the step, you could restore the file to QTEMP, rename the object, and then move it to the library you want. See Figure 9.28. Obviously, you would have to work on this shell. I just threw this together.

```
PGM PARM(&FILENAME &LIBRARY &NEWFILE)
DCL VAR(&FILENAME) TYPE(*CHAR) LEN(10)
DCL VAR(&LIBRARY) TYPE(*CHAR) LEN(10)
DCL VAR(&NEWFILE) TYPE(*CHAR) LEN(10)
RSTOBJ OBJ(&FILENAME) LIB(&LIBRARY) DEV(QTAPE) +
RSTLIB(QTEMP) ... (whatever else you need)
RNMOBJ OBJ(QTEMP/&FILENAME) OBJTYPE(*FILE) +
NEWOBJ(&NEWFILE)
MOVEOBJ OBJ(QTEMP/&NEWFILE) OBJTYPE(*FILE) +
TOLIB(&LIBRARY)
```

Figure 9.28: Use this program for restoring a file to a different name.

Transferring Objects with SAVRST

OS/400 includes a set of commands to save an object from one AS/400 and restore it automatically on another AS/400. Table 9.2 shows a list of the commands. The only requisite is that you have a configured and active SNA connection between the two AS/400s.

Table 9.2: Commands to Transfer Source Code

Command	Object
Save Restore (SAVRST)	All Objects
Save Restore Object (SAVRSTOBJ)	QSYS.LIB Objects
Save Restore Change (SAVRSTCHG)	Changed Objects in QSYS.LIB
Save Restore Library (SAVRSTLIB)	Entire Libraries
Save Restore Document folders and documents (SAVRSTDLO)	Library Object
Save Restore Configuration (SAVRSTCFG)	Configuration

—*Diego Santini*

✦ ✦ ✦ Security

Beware of AS/400 Hackers

If you haven't changed the default passwords to the IBM-supplied user profiles, here's a word of warning: The news is out and in the hands of 2,600 magazine readers. The magazine bills itself as *The Hacker Quarterly* and gives details on how to gain unauthorized use of phone systems and computers.

While browsing computer magazines at a bookstore, I spotted an issue of *The Hacker Quarterly*. It contains a letter detailing the requirements for a PC to dial into an AS/400 and log on with the QSECOFR or QSRV user profiles. It also discussed the ECS modem models. This is the second such letter sent to *The Hacker Quarterly* from a reader. Actually, it was encouraged by the earlier letter. The letter says, "KR is absolutely correct. AS/400 security is very lax." (KR is the author of the first letter.)

I posted information about the first letter on *Midrange Computing*'s bulletin board and asked if this seemed like a serious concern. The slight response indicated that it wasn't. It shouldn't be, if you've changed the default passwords and know who your PC users are. And the default settings of an ECS modem never permit dial-ins.

The users of the AS/400 and its predecessors have led a sheltered life. More and more PCs are finding new ways to get connected to the AS/400, and the AS/400's contact with the non-AS/400 world is certainly increasing. So, let's be careful out there!

—Ed Smith

Could You Please Sign Off?

How many times have you asked your AS/400 users to please sign off the system when they leave for a lunch break or for the day? If you have a security problem or your night processing aborts because there is a workstation left signed on somewhere, you can use the following method to solve your troubles.

System value QINACTITV contains the number of minutes an inactive job is allowed to remain on the system before automatic action is taken. Perhaps 30 minutes is generous enough. Run the following command:

```
CHGSYSVAL SYSVAL(QINACTITV) VALUE('30')
```

What action is taken depends on system value QINACTMSGQ. This system value contains either the qualified name of a message queue, where a message is sent, the value '*ENDJOB' if the job is to be ended, or '*DSCJOB' if it is to be disconnected. To solve your problem, you could set it to '*DSCJOB', as follows:

```
CHGSYSVAL SYSVAL(QINACTMSGQ) VALUE('*DSCJOB')
```

Because the job is simply disconnected, the user can return to his or her job and resume it at the exact point where he or she left by simply signing on to the same workstation (using the same user profile name).

But wait. If the job is only disconnected, the night processing might still abort if there is a conflict of object allocations, for example. You need to end these jobs. Try the following:

```
CHGSYSVAL SYSVAL(QDSCJOBITV) VALUE('60')
```

Now all interactive jobs will end automatically 60 minutes after being disconnected—whether this disconnection was manual (DSCJOB command) or automatic.

—Midrange Computing Staff

Device Security

Q: Is there any reason why a user with *ALLOBJ special authority is not authorized to sign on to a specific device? Shouldn't *ALLOBJ special authority override the authority for a device description (*DEVD)?

A: Your system value to limit security officer device access (QLMTSECOFR) is probably set to '1' (explicit device access required). It limits users with *ALLOBJ or *SERVICE special authority to only those devices for which they have specific authority. It's the one exception to authority checking I know of that is bypassed when a user has the *ALLOBJ special authority value.

You must either change system value QLMTSECOFR to '0' (explicit device access not needed) or grant the users in question the device authority needed. (A user needs *CHANGE authority to sign on.)

Group Profiles Make Object Security Easy

A user in the accounting department has quit and is being replaced. You must now set up a new user profile with the same characteristics and object authority as the previous user. Unless you are using group profiles, you might be in for more work than you bargained for. The AS/400 provides a list of object authorizations by user that can be printed and used to grant authority for each object. However, this process could be very time consuming and tedious.

The solution to this headache is to use group profiles. Group profiles are used to give the identical authority to each of a group of users. Instead of assigning the same objects over and over again to each user in a group, you can assign the objects to a group profile once, and then just assign the group profile to each user.

There is nothing mysterious about a group profile. It is really just another user profile for which you will grant object authority once for a number of other user profiles logically grouped together. In the accounting department example, you would use Create User Profile (CRTUSRPRF) to create a "group" profile named something like GRPACCTNG.

(The GRP prefix makes identifying group profiles easier.) Use Grant Object Authority (GRTOBJAUT) to assign authority for all authorized objects to the group profile GRPACCTNG. Now, you can create the user profile for the new user, keying GRPACCTNG in the GRPPRF keyword. This will assign the object authority given to GRPACCTNG to the new user. Any new users can just as simply be added.

If you want to add or delete an object for the entire group of accounting users, you only need to change the group profile with GRTOBJAUT or Revoke Object Authority (RVKOBJAUT). If a user is transferred to another department, just change his or her GRPPRF keyword. Even if you only have one user in a department, you should consider always using group profiles. While it might take you a couple extra minutes up front, it will provide you with more future flexibility.

—Midrange Computing Staff

Triggers Can Cause New Problems

Many AS/400 programmers have taken advantage of database triggers to let OS/400 protect their data integrity. For example, they use triggers to validate data when a record is added and to ensure that, if a record is deleted, any other business rules that should be in effect for related records are also enforced. For the most part, this technique works great. However, there is at least one instance when database triggers cannot protect your data.

If someone runs Clear Physical File Member (CLRPFM) over a database file being protected by a trigger, that trigger is not fired. Triggers act at the row level not the file level. In other words, the trigger is not activated unless the deletion is performed one row at a time (for example, using the DELETE operation in RPG or pressing F23, the Delete function key, while in the DFU).

—Chuck Pence

✦ ✦ ✦ Sign-on

Add a News Line to the Sign-on Display

One advantage of a customized sign-on display is the capability to add a single line of site news. This could advise users of scheduled system downtime or other information that changes frequently enough that you don't want to change the sign-on display DDS. This feature is implemented by adding a MSGID entry to the DDS used by OS/400, which can appear anywhere on the screen. The same position (line 24) as the IBM field QSNERROR can be used. The two lines of code in Figure 9.29 were added at the end of the sign-on DDS. *Caution:* Do not change the original IBM source code. Instead, you should be working with a copy of the original source code.

```
A  N02       MSGLINE     80A  O 24  1MSGID(USR0001 QGPL/USRMSGF)
A                                    DSPATR(HI)
```

Figure 9.29: Add this code to the sign-on display to display a message line.

Because the QSNERROR field is conditioned by indicator 02, the MSGID keyword uses the opposite (N02) to allow the two fields to use the same screen location. This entry causes the first-level text of message USR0001 from message file USRMSGF in library QGPL to display on line 24, starting at column 1, unless indicator 02 is on. The DSPATR(HI) keyword highlights the line. To create the message file and message text, use the commands shown in Figure 9.30.

```
CRTMSGF MSGF(QGPL/USRMSGF) +
  TEXT('Test message file for +
  signon screen')

ADDMSGD MSGID(USR0001) +
  MSGF(QGPL/USRMSGF) +
  TEXT('This line of text will +
  appear on the signon screens')

CRTDSPF FILE(QGPL/SIGNON) +
  SRCFILE(QGPL/QDDSSRC) +
  MAXDEV(256)
```

Figure 9.30: Here are the commands you need to run to create a message line on the sign-on display.

For this example, the sign-on display DDS source member is named SIGNON. The next step is to change the sign-on display file for QINTER:

```
CHGSBSD SBSD(QSYS/QINTER) SGNDSPF(QGPL/SIGNON)
```

This change takes effect when QINTER is restarted. To change the one-line message, all that is required is to use the CHGMSGD command:

```
CHGMSGD MSGID(USR0001) MSGF(QGPL/USRMSGF) +
        TEXT('Here is some new text')
```

Note that this does not change the screens already showing the sign-on display, but the new message is picked up when the sign-on display is next shown. Also, note that the sign-on display does not allow users to display the second-level text of the message description.

This method could be used to provide a number of different messages on the sign-on display. Different fields, each with a different message ID, could be used for different categories of messages—such as operating hours or coming events.

Depending on local requirements, the news message could be placed anywhere on the screen. If you don't use line 24, there is no need to qualify the field with the N02 indicator as in the preceding example.

—Steve Bisel

Messages on the Sign-on Display

You are planning to shut down the system tomorrow at 3:00 P.M. because your CE is coming in to install the new disk drive you have been eagerly awaiting. How can you remind your users of this event?

There are several ways, but the one I like best is to do a quick change to the sign-on display. It is not as difficult as it sounds, especially if you include messages from a message file. Simply follow these steps:

1. Copy the source code for the IBM-supplied sign-on display. You will find it in member QDSIGNON in file QGPL/QDDSSRC. Do not, under any circumstances, change the original source. Your copy should have a different name and should be in a different library (preferably a library you created yourself). Let's pretend that you have called your source member MODSIGNON and have placed it in file YOURLIB/QDDSSRC.

2. Create a message file in YOURLIB. For example, we can call it SGNONDMSGF. This message file will contain all the messages that are to be displayed on the sign-on display.

3. Run SDA on your copy and change it as you see fit. Do not alter the length and order of the fields; do not delete them either. If you do not want to have a field displayed, put a DSPATR(ND) on it.

4. Add as many output fields as you need for the message that is to appear on the sign-on display. You can put these messages anywhere, and they can be as long or short as you prefer. They can also have whatever display attributes you want: high intensity, underline, color, and so on.

5. Each message field must have the MSGID keyword indicating which message is to be displayed on that field. Suppose you defined three 79-character message fields on the sign-on display, named MSG1, MSG2, and MSG3. Your DDS should look like Figure 9.31.

```
A     MSG1                    79A  O nn nnDSPATR(HI)
A                                      MSGID(SGN0001 SGNONDMSGF)
A     MSG2                    79A  O nn nnDSPATR(HI)
A                                      MSGID(SGN0002 SGNONDMSGF)
A     MSG3                    79A  O nn nnDSPATR(HI)
```

Figure 9.31: Here is the sample Message Display File to use for the sign-on display.

6. Compile your DDS. It does not matter if the message file exists or not, or whether it has the messages being referenced. The CRTDSPF command merrily does its work without a problem.

7. Now add messages SGN0001, SGN0002, and SGN0003 to file YOURLIB /SGNONDMSGF using the ADDMSGD command. Feel free to type whatever text you feel is appropriate for these message fields. If you do not want to display any messages, add blank messages; the messages being referenced by the sign-on display must exist in the message file.

8. Now change your subsystem description to start using your sign-on display instead of IBM's. To do so, you have to end the subsystem, change it with SGNDSPF (YOURLIB/MODSIGNON), and start the subsystem again.

—Midrange Computing Staff

Monitoring Your AS/400 Users

I have a tip for anyone who needs to see exactly what a particular user or operator has typed in from the command line. I have created a command called SIGNOFF (see Figure 9.32), which I place in a library that precedes QSYS in my system library list. When anyone on the system issues the SIGNOFF command, the system automatically uses my SIGNOFF command.

```
/*==============================================================*/
/* To compile:                                                  */
/*                                                              */
/* CRTCMD CMD(XXX/SIGNOFF) PGM(XXX/SIGNOFFCL) +                 */
/* SRCFILE(XXX/QCMDSRC)                                         */
/*                                                              */
/*==============================================================*/
SIGNOFF: CMD PROMPT('Sign Off')
```

Figure 9.32: Command SIGNOFF can be used to log user's activity.

The CL program that does all the work is very short. It retrieves the user name with the Retrieve Job Attributes (RTVJOBA) command and compares it to the list of names I want to track. If the user's name matches my list, then I call the SIGNOFF command from QSYS library and put *LIST in the LOG parameter. This creates a job log for the user's workstation. This program is shown in Figure 9.33.

```
/*==============================================================*/
/* To compile:                                                  */
/*                                                              */
/* CRTCLPGM PGM(XXX/SIGNOFFCL) SRCFILE(XXX/QCLSRC)             */
/*                                                              */
/*==============================================================*/
SIGNOFF: +
PGM


DCL VAR(&USER) TYPE(*CHAR) LEN(10)
RTVJOBA USER(&USER)
IF COND(&USER *EQ 'xxxxxxxxxx') THEN(QSYS/SIGNOFF LOG(*LIST))
ELSE CMD(QSYS/SIGNOFF)
ENDPGM
```

Figure 9.33: CL Program SIGNOFFCL dumps the user job log to a spool file.

The job log will show every command that the user typed in from the command line. If the user doesn't match my list, I simply use the SIGNOFF command in QSYS with the default parameters, which doesn't produce the job log.

In the CL where you see **COND (&USER *EQ 'xxxxxxx')**, plug in the user profile you want to track where I have the **X**'s. If you want to track more than one user, simply add *OR conditions based on the additional user names. For this to work, the command must be named SIGNOFF and must be placed in a library before QSYS in the system library list.

—Jamie Barnes

✦ ✦ ✦ Subsystems

Closing Down an Interactive Subsystem

If you have multiple interactive subsystems on your AS/400, you can allow or restrict entry to each subsystem by workstation name or workstation type. This feature can be used for:

- Security (you specify which workstation names or types can use each interactive subsystem).

- Performance (you give certain crucial workstations—such as those used for order entry—access to an interactive subsystem that runs jobs at a higher priority).

- Scheduling (you deny access to certain workstations at specific times of the day, while allowing other workstations to sign on).

Implementation is easy and, once you know the ropes, you can restrict or allow subsystem access in a few minutes. To present an example, suppose that, in addition to QINTER, you have a second interactive subsystem called QINTER2. Over the weekend, your company shuts down the QINTER subsystem—disabling interactive jobs for most of the organization—and leaves QINTER2 up for designated interactive users. You want to give all your accounting users (whose machines have device names starting with ACCT) access to QINTER2. Here's a quick way to do it.

1. Subsystem access for interactive workstations is controlled through workstation entries contained within the subsystem description. Workstation entries tell a subsystem which specific types of workstations (5250, VT100, 3270, etc.) or specific workstation names (e.g., workstations that have OS/400 device names starting with ACCT) can start interactive jobs in a subsystem. You can view the workstation entries for a subsystem by choosing option 4 (Workstation name entries) or option 5 (Workstation type entries) from the Work with Subsystem Description (WRKSBSD) menu for a subsystem.

2. If a subsystem has a workstation type entry of *ALL, it allows any workstation type to process jobs. To restrict access only to specific users, that entry
   must be removed from the subsystem to cut off universal access. To remove
   the *ALL entry from the QINTER2 example, run the following command:

   ```
   RMVWSE SBSD(QINTER2) WRKSTNTYPE(*ALL)
   ```

3. To add a generic entry for all accounting users to tell QINTER2 it's okay to
   enter the subsystem, run the following generic Add Workstation Entry
   (ADDWSE) command:

   ```
   ADDWSE  SBSD(QINTER2)   WRKSTN(ACCT*)   AT(*SIGNON)
   ```

   This tells QINTER2 that any workstation with a name that starts with ACCT
   (e.g., ACCT01, ACCT02, etc.) can enter the subsystem through a Transfer Job
   (TFRJOB) command or by having QINTER2 allocate the workstation when it
   starts up.

   Add a generic entry in your other interactive subsystems, for generic workstation name ACCT*, but this time using AT(*ENTER). For example, to add
   such a workstation entry in QINTER, do the following:

   ```
   ADDWSE SBSD(QINTER)   WRKSTN(ACCT*)   AT(*ENTER)
   ```

   This workstation entry prevents the other interactive systems (which still
   have a workstation entry for type *ALL) from "grabbing" the ACCT* display
   stations when the subsystems are restarted. AT(*ENTER) means that QINTER
   could allocate the display station, but only when the user specifically requests that through the Transfer Job (TFRJOB) command.

4. Next time QINTER2 is started, it will allocate all display stations having names
   beginning with ACCT, presenting the sign-on display on all of them, even if
   QINTER is ended. You can use this technique on any interactive subsystem.

   —Joe Hertvik

Interactive Subsystems

Q: I recently added a new remote location to our AS/400, and I want to have the new users run in their own interactive subsystem. I created a new subsystem QINTERT, and I created additional generic workstation name entries in both QINTER and QINTERT.

Even though QINTER's generic workstation entry is DSP0*, and all of the remote location's workstations are named DSPTxxxxx, if QINTERT is not active, they will come up under QINTER.

A: Both QINTER and QINTERT need to have two workstation entries. When you do this, DSPT* display stations will not come up under QINTER, even if QINTERT is down, because of the AT(*ENTER) parameter. AT(*SIGNON) means that the subsystem should grab the display station and present the sign-on display when you start up the system; AT(*ENTER) means that the subsystem should grab the display station only when the user presses the Enter key after typing in TFRJOB JOBQ(QINTER).

—Ernie Malaga

A: One problem that I had when setting up dual interactive subsystems was that QINTER had a workstation entry of *ALL plus the WSE of DSP*. I removed the *ALL WSE from QINTER. Everything comes up okay now. If you use this method, you need to make sure that every device name (i.e., DSP* or DSPT*) is associated with a specific subsystem.

—John Brown

Is the Subsystem Active?

There is a standard technique that determines if a subsystem is inactive: If the subsystem is inactive when the Work Subsystem Job (WRKSBSJOB) command is executed against it, a certain CPF message is returned. I found this technique to be inefficient. If the subsystem is active, this method takes too long to complete, and it creates a useless spool file that has to be manually deleted.

I found a faster, more efficient way to determine the status of a subsystem. I created a command called Check Subsystem Status (CHKSBSSTS) that uses an IBM-supplied API, QWDRSBSD, to retrieve the status of a subsystem. The command input is the qualified name of the subsystem description for which you want the status. The command output is the STATUS parameter. The STATUS parameter returns one of three values: Y if the subsystem is active, N if the subsystem is inactive, and ? if the subsystem description isn't found.

Because the command returns a value, it can only be allowed to run in a CL program or
*REXX procedure. Figure 9.34 shows the compile instructions and the CHKSBSSTS com-
mand source code. The command-processing program (CPP) for CHKSBSSTS is RPG program SBS001RG (see Figure 9.35).

```
/*================================================================*/
/* To compile:                                                    */
/*                                                                */
/* CRTCMD CMD(XXX/CHKSBSSTS) PGM(XXX/SBS001CL) +                  */
/* SRCFILE(XXX/QCMDSRC) ALLOW(*IPGM *BPGM +                       */
/* *IREXX *BREXX *IMOD *BMOD)                                     */
/*                                                                */
/* Returns a value in STATUS parameter:                          */
/* 'Y' = Subsystem active                                        */
/* 'N' = Subsystem inactive                                      */
/* '?' = Subsyste description not found                          */
/*                                                                */
/*================================================================*/
CHKSBSSTS: CMD PROMPT('Check Subsystem Status')
PARM KWD(SBSD) TYPE(QUAL1) MIN(1) +
PROMPT('Subsystem description')
QUAL1: QUAL TYPE(*NAME) LEN(10)
QUAL TYPE(*NAME) LEN(10) DFT(*LIBL) SPCVAL(*LIBL) +
PROMPT('Library name')
PARM KWD(STATUS) TYPE(*CHAR) LEN(1) RTNVAL(*YES) +
PROMPT('Subsystem status (A, I, ?)')
```

Figure 9.34: The CHKSBSSTS command can determine if a subsystem is active.

```
*================================================================
* To compile:
*
*       CRTRPGPGM  PGM(XXX/SBS001RG) SRCFILE(XXX/QRPGSRC)
I          IDS
I                                   B  1    40LEN
I                                   B  5    80ERRCOD
I          DS
I@SBSI      DS
I                                      29  38 STATUS
I            '*ACTIVE'              C         $ACT
```

*Figure 9.35: Command Processing Program SBS001RG is the power behind determining if
a subsystem is active (part 1 of 2).*

```
I                   '*INACTIVE'              C           $INACT
    *
C          *ENTRY    PLIST
C                    PARM              @SBSD  20
C                    PARM              ACT    1
    *
C                    MOVE @SBSD        LIB    10
    *
C          LIB       IFEQ *BLANKS
C                    MOVEL'*LIBL'      LIB         P
C                    ENDIF
    *
C                    CALL 'QWDRSBSD'                      99
C                    PARM              @SBSI
C                    PARM 38           LEN
C                    PARM 'SBSI0100'FORMAT  8
C                    PARM              @SBSD
C                    PARM              ERRCOD
    *
C          STATUS    IFEQ $ACT
C                    MOVE 'Y'          ACT
C                    ELSE
C          STATUS    IFEQ $INACT
C                    MOVE 'N'          ACT
C                    ELSE
C                    MOVE '?'          ACT
C                    ENDIF
C                    ENDIF
C                    MOVE *ON          *INLR
```

Figure 9.35: Command Processing Program SBS001RG is the power behind determining if a subsystem is active (part 2 of 2).

In the command-processing program, I'm using the QWDRSBSD API to retrieve the status of the subsystem. However, you can retrieve much more information about subsystem descriptions through this API. See the *OS/400 System API Reference V3R1* manual (SC41-3801, CD-ROM QBKAVD00) for more information.

—Robert T. Fisher

✦ ✦ ✦ System Values

There's a Way to Find Out Who Changed System Values

Q: Does the AS/400 log changes to systems values, perhaps in a system journal? Recently, someone on our system changed the system value for the startup program (system value QSTRTUPGM). As you might imagine, this change had undesirable effects on our system. Specifically, it failed to start correctly after an IPL.

A: The AS/400 does log changes to system values in the history log. To locate the correct error message showing who made certain changes, use the Display Log (DSPLOG) command and search for message ID CPF1815 (DSPLOG MSGID (CPF1815)). Both the original system value and the new value will appear in the message text, along with the date, time, and user ID of the person who changed it. To see the all the details, press F9 to display message details.

—Bob Crothers

A: Sure, you can track this information. Use the Change System Value (CHGSYSVAL) command for system value QAUDLVL (security auditing level). Enter *SECURITY for this system value and press Enter to log a wide variety of security-related activities, including changes to system values and to system journal QAUDJRN. After that, it's a simple matter of displaying the system audit journal, perhaps by using a query so that you can subset only changes to system values.

—Kenneth E. Graap

✦ ✦ ✦ Upgrading

Don't Lose Subsystem Modifications When Installing a New Release

Once upon a time, when OS/400 was very young (not higher than Version 2), the typical subsystem descriptions used by most installations were defined in library QGPL. During the teenage years (Version 3), IBM moved some of these objects to library QSYS.

What a great idea this was, and is—except when user modifications to the subsystem description, particularly for tuning and work management, get wiped out. During a new release installation, all objects in QSYS get replaced. (I've seen people bitten by this beast more than once!)

One thing you can do is copy the appropriate subsystem descriptions to another library, such as QGPL:

```
CRTDUPOBJ OBJ(sbsd_name) FROMLIB(QSYS) OBJTYPE(*SBSD) TOLIB(QGPL)
```

Then, change your startup program to start the subsystems from the copied descriptions:

```
STRSBS QGPL/sbsd_name
```

Now, installing new releases will not replace your tuned subsystem description. Consider subsystems with names that begin with Q (e.g., QCTL, QBATCH, QPGMR, and QINTER) as candidates for this protective change. You might have changed the pools, the routing entries, or the like. on any or all of these subsystems.

This tip is, of course, true for any user objects in QSYS that you might have changed. I have observed changed commands, command options, tuned subsystem descriptions, and queues of all kinds. Think about the idea, and fix it so that you won't be bothered by release installations causing operational problems.

—Dan Herron

Editor's Note: It is a good idea to rename the subsystem descriptions when you copy them. OS/400 does not require them to start with the letter Q. Giving them other names distinguishes them from the IBM-supplied objects. If you do not rename IBM-supplied objects, you should put your versions in a library that precedes QSYS in the system library list (in case programs scan the library list for those objects).

✦ ✦ ✦ Users

Checking to See If a User Is Signed On

Q: I would like to be able to test from within a CL program whether or not a particular user is signed onto our AS/400. Any ideas?

A: Until someone suggests a better way, see Figure 9.36 for how it could be done.

```
RTVUSRPRF USRPRF(xxx) MSGQ(&MSGQ) MSGQLIB(&MSGQLIB) +
   ALCOBJ OBJ(&MSGQLIB/&MSGQ *MSGQ *EXCL) WAIT(0)
MONMSG MSGID(CPF1002 CPF1085) +
      EXEC(DO)
 .
 .
 .
ENDDO
```

Figure 9.36: Here's how you can tell if a user is signed on.

Whatever you include in the DO group is executed if the user is signed on. This method takes advantage of the fact that when a user is signed on, his or her message queue is allocated exclusively to his or her job. Therefore, the ALCOBJ command in the above CL program will fail, issuing an escape message. If you implement this method, it won't matter if users don't have their message queues named after themselves, provided that there are no two users who share the same message queue. That's why I included the RTVUSRPRF command with MSGQ(&MSGQ) MSGQLIB(&MSGQLIB); it will get the user profile's message queue name and library name no matter what they're called. In other words, user profile FRED could have MSGQ(MYLIB/MARY) and the method would still work, provided that there isn't another user who has MSGQ(MYLIB/MARY) in the user profile.

—Ernie Malaga

Customize Your Interactive Session with User Profile User Options

User profiles have an attribute that you can set to customize certain behaviors of your interactive session. To modify this attribute, use the Change User Profile (CHGUSRPRF) command and enter one or more of the following values into the USROPT parameter:

- *CLKWD—CL keywords are shown instead of the possible values when a command is prompted.

- *EXPERT—More detailed information is shown on certain operations, such as when editing or displaying object authority.

- *ROLLKEY—The opposite action is taken when the Roll keys are pressed (i.e., Rollup becomes Rolldown and vice versa).

- *NOSTSMSG—Status messages are not shown.

- *STSMSG—Status messages are shown.

- *HLPFULL—Online help is displayed full-screen rather than in a window.

- *PRTMSG—A message is sent when a spooled file owned by the user is printed or held by a writer.

—Robin Klima

Who's Signed On Here?

I've heard this question asked dozens of times: "How can I find out who is signed on at this display station?" Users often forget to sign off, leaving an active display station ready for anyone's use (creating a security risk). In other cases, you might need to know the name of the display station or the system to which it is currently attached (it could be one of many, if you have several AS/400s in a network).

Instead of writing a command and a CL program, you can retrieve all the pertinent information with the Display Workstation User (DSPWSUSR) command. DSPWSUSR presents a panel showing the following:

- System name.

- Date and time.

- User profile name and its text description.

- Display station name and its text description.

- Number of interactive jobs in session.

- Interactive job currently active (A or B).

- Qualified job name for jobs A and B.

The last three items are meaningful (and useful) when you have selected option 1 from the SysRq menu, thereby running a secondary interactive job from the same display station.

—Ernie Malaga

✦ ✦ ✦ WRKACTJOB

Alternatives to WRKACTJOB

Get your operators in the habit of using Work with User Jobs (WRKUSRJOB) instead of Work with Active Jobs (WRKACTJOB) on the AS/400. Because WRKACTJOB also displays system and subsystem information and statistics, it is much more resource intensive than WRKUSRJOB.

The command WRKUSRJOB *ALL *ACTIVE will display all active jobs on the system.

You can also narrow down the display to a single user.

The command WRKUSRJOB QSYSOPR will display all system operator jobs on the system (active jobs, job queue jobs, and jobs that have finished running but have output on a queue). Another alternative to WRKACTJOB is Work with Subsystem Jobs (WRKSBSJOB).

The command WRKSBSJOB QINTER displays all jobs in the IBM-supplied interactive subsystem. The display is very similar, if not identical to WRKUSRJOB. The difference is that you are only looking at jobs running in QINTER.

The command WRKSBSJOB QBATCH shows all jobs currently running in the batch subsystem.

The command WRKSBSJOB with no parameters takes you through all active jobs in all subsystems, one subsystem at a time.

—Steven Kontos

Automatically Refreshing Your WRKACTJOB Screen

You can set your Work with Active Jobs (WRKACTJOB) screen to automatically refresh itself after a set period of time. Here's how you do it:

1. When you start WRKACTJOB, press F4 for a command prompt. On the Command Prompt screen, press F10 for additional parameters. This displays the Additional Parameters screen.

2. On the Additional Parameters screen, there is a parameter called INTERVAL (Automatic Refresh Interval) that specifies the number of seconds WRKACTJOB will wait before it refreshes itself while in refresh mode. The factory default is 300 seconds (5 minutes). If the INTERVAL value is set to *PRV, that means the value has been previously changed and WRKACTJOB is using the last changed value. To set your own value, change INTERVAL to any number between 5 seconds and 999 seconds. This will become your new default INTERVAL refresh rate and will be used whenever someone executes WRKACTJOB and puts the screen into refresh mode.

3. Press Enter to start WRKACTJOB.

4. To put WRKACTJOB into refresh mode, press F19 on your keyboard.

WRKACTJOB will now refresh its data according to the schedule you established in the INTERVAL parameter. If you specified 30 seconds, for example, it will refresh the screen every 30 seconds. To exit from refresh mode, press F19 a second time and it will stop refreshing.

Be aware, however, that refresh mode is a restricted mode for WRKACTJOB. You cannot display information about running jobs while in refresh mode, and you are limited to using the following function keys:

```
F3: Exit
F10: Restart Statistics
F11: Display Elapsed Data
F12: Previous
F19: End Automatic Refresh
```

If you want to reconfigure WRKACTJOB using its other function key features (such as Include, Exclude, Sort, etc.), you must configure WRKACTJOB using these keys before you go into refresh mode. Refresh mode will redisplay current information based on how the WRKACTJOB screen was configured before refresh mode was started.

One last point: If you use WRKACTJOB in refresh mode, be careful that you don't bog down your AS/400 by using inappropriate parameters. You can refresh your screen every 5 seconds if you want to, but the constant polling and refreshing of activity data will choke off your other jobs and negatively affect response time. Even the rate of 30 seconds discussed here will somewhat affect performance. The key to using WRKACTJOB in refresh mode is to use it to gather data at whatever reasonable interval you want and then end it as quickly as possible so that it doesn't degrade your system performance.

—Joe Hertvik

OPNQRYF

OPNQRYF

◆ ◆ ◆ ◆

In This Chapter

Data Handling

Date and Time

File Handling

ILE

Multiple Files and
Formats

Selection

Sorting and
Sequencing

◆ ◆ ◆ ◆

*O*pen Query File (OPNQRYF) is possibly the most powerful
command in the CL language. A person could certainly make
a strong case for the idea. OPNQRYF is to a program what a query
tool (like Query/400) is to a programmer. It presents data to a program in a way that might be inconsistent with reality, but meaningful to the program. That is, rather than present an entire database
file to a program for processing, it might present only selected records. OPNQRYF can make data fields from two or more files appear as if they're all in a single record format for one file.
OPNQRYF sorts, it groups, and it calculates wild things like logarithms and trig functions.

This chapter, of course, is not an exhaustive treatment of OPNQRYF.
That requires an entire book. But it does include a collection of
useful tips and answers to problems to help you better use this powerful CL command. For example, do you know how to negate the
%VALUES function? A lot of programmers don't. The answer is in
this chapter. Did you know the wildcard function, %WLDCRD, can
be used to search for numeric data? Believe it or not, it's true, and
the technique is in these pages. Have you tried making OPNQRYF
work with ILE programs and did you give up in frustration? Many
AS/400 programmers have banged their heads against that wall.
This chapter tells you how to avoid such frustration.

Maybe someday iSeries shops will use only SQL for data access. If
so, that day is still far in the future. In the meantime, take advantage of the tips in this chapter to make more powerful use of
OPNQRYF.

—Ted Holt

✦ ✦ ✦ Data Handling

ALWCPYDTA(*OPTIMIZE) Doesn't Like Invalid Decimal Data

Most of us in the AS/400 community are fortunate enough to work on data that has integrity. In other words, we expect the data in a field to be in the format that has been defined for it.

This is not always the case. If you are using data that originated on another system, such as a mainframe or a S/36, you could be in for a surprise. Many old COBOL programs define numeric fields as alpha so that they can be tested for valid numeric data. As long as the file is internally defined, this poses no problem.

Fast-forward now to the AS/400. A file is defined with DDS, and data could be copied to the new definition with a Copy File (CPYF) command using the FMTOPT(*NOCHK) parameter. While a numeric field might have invalid decimal data in it, that doesn't cause a problem. Programs using this file with invalid decimal data are written. They work well provided they never refer to the field with invalid decimal data.

Then, one day, you try to improve the performance of a program that uses this file by specifying ALWCPYDTA(*OPTIMIZE) in an Open Query File (OPNQRYF) command. ALWCPYDTA(*OPTIMIZE) allows the query engine to use a sort routine if that appears to be the fastest way to access the data. However, in the process of sorting, it also performs integrity checking on the data fields—even on those that are not key fields, mapped fields, or selection fields!

The OPNQRYF command completes normally, but the program that uses the opened file will fail with a CPF5029 error.

The solution is to fix the data, of course. In the meantime, changing ALWCPYDTA (*OPTIMIZE) to ALWCPYDTA(*YES) allows the program to run.

—David Abramowitz

Copying an Open Query File Data Path

Q: Can I use the Copy File (CPYF) or Open Query File (OPNQRYF) command to update the value of a field when copying data into a file? I want to add records from multiple files into one history file. The history file has the same format as the other files except that it has one additional field to contain a value that describes where the data came from.

The only other way I can think of is to write a generic program and fill the field based on a data structure and recompile it each time I change the file.

A: You can use the OPNQRYF command for this. Just specify the name of your input file in the FILE parameter and put the name of your output file in the FORMAT parameter. Then use the MAPFLD parameter to define a constant (or a variable in CL) for the extra field you want to update. Finally, use the Copy from Query File (CPYFRMQRYF) command to copy the records. A CL program to execute these commands would look like the example shown in Figure 10.1.

```
PGM PARM(&FILE &ORIGIN)

 DCL VAR(&FILE) TYPE(*CHAR) LEN(10)
 DCL VAR(&ORIGIN) TYPE(*CHAR) LEN(10)

 OVRDBF FILE(&FILE) SHARE(*YES)
 OPNQRYF FILE((&FILE)) +
   FORMAT(HISTFILE) +
   MAPFLD((NEWFLD ('''' *CAT &ORIGIN *CAT '''')))
 CPYFRMQRYF FROMOPNID(&FILE) TOFILE(HISTFILE) MBROPT(*ADD)
 CLOF OPNID(&FILE)
 DLTOVR FILE(&FILE)
 ENDPGM
```

Figure 10.1: CPYFRMQRYF reduces the need to write simple programs to copy data.

You would execute this program for each file to be added to the history file, specifying a different file name and origin for each.

—*Jim Schecklman*

Did OPNQRYF Select Any Records?

In various situations, it is important to know if at least one record was selected after running the OPNQRYF command. If no records were selected, you would want to take an appropriate action. I have created a technique that allows you to determine if any records were selected by an OPNQRYF command. Figure 10.2 presents a sample usage of the technique. I use the Copy from Query File (CPYFRMQRYF) command to determine whether or not at least one record was selected. I skip execution of the program and issue a meaningful message to an external message queue when no records are selected.

```
DCL        VAR(&QRYSLT) TYPE(*CHAR) LEN(128)
DCL        VAR(&NBRCURRCD) TYPE(*DEC) LEN(10)
CHGVAR     VAR(&QRYSLT) VALUE('LSSTE *EQ "PA"')

OVRDBF     FILE(LIST) SHARE(*YES)
OPNQRYF    FILE((LIST LIST)) QRYSLT(&QRYSLT) +
             KEYFLD((LSSUB) (LSTITL))

CRTPF      FILE(QTEMP/TEMPFILE) RCDLEN(1)
MONMSG     MSGID(CPF7302)
CPYFRMQRYF FROMOPNID(LIST) TOFILE(QTEMP/TEMPFILE) +
             MBROPT(*REPLACE) NBRRCDS(1) FMTOPT(*NOCHK)
POSDBF OPNID(LIST) POSITION(*START)
RTVMBRD    FILE(TEMPFILE) NBRCURRCD(&NBRCURRCD)

IF         COND(&NBRCURRCD > 0) THEN(DO)
   SNDPGMMSG  MSG('Records exist in file.') TOPGMQ(*EXT)
ENDDO
ELSE CMD(DO)
   SNDPGMMSG  MSG('No records were selected from file by +
               QRYSLT(' *BCAT &QRYSLT *BCAT ')') +
               TOPGMQ(*EXT)

ENDDO

CLOF       OPNID(LIST)
DLTOVR     FILE(LIST)
```

Figure 10.2: Here's how to determine whether OPNQRYF selected any records.

—Ira Shapiro

Eliminate OPNQRYF Divide-by-Zero Errors

When using the MAPFLD parameter in the OPNQRYF command to assign the result of a division to a field, a "division by zero" error can occur. This will happen whenever the field or expression used as a divisor has a value of zero for the record being processed. You cannot test for this condition within OPNQRYF, but you can handle it by rearranging the expression in such a way that, if the divisor is zero, the value yielded by the expression also will be zero.

Suppose you are calculating the number of phone calls per sale for each of the products offered by a telemarketing firm. You could code this as:

```
MAPFLD((CALSAL 'NCALLS/UNSOLD'))
```

In this code, CALSAL is the calls per sale, NCALLS is the number of calls, and UNSOLD is the units sold. If no units had been sold for a given product, a "division by zero" error message would be issued. To avoid this, rearrange the expression as:

```
MAPFLD((CALSAL 'NCALLS * UNSOLD/ +
    %MAX((UNSOLD * UNSOLD) 0.1)'))
```

This evaluates to 0, and the divisor evaluates to 0.1, resulting in a quotient with a value of 0. The number to be used along with the divisor as arguments for the %MAX function (e.g., 0.1) should be equal to 10–(2d+1), with *d* representing the number of decimal places in the divisor. In the example above, UNSOLD had no decimal places; therefore, 10–(2*0+1)=0.1.

—Rafael Valenzuela

✦ ✦ ✦ Date and Time

OPNQRYF and MDY Dates

By using mapped fields on an OPNQRYF command, you can use date selection in reports even when the dates are in *MDY format in the database. For example, the command shown in Figure 10.3 selects only records whose LRDAT field (which is a packed date in *MDY format) falls within 1992.

```
OPNQRYF FILE(lrds) +
    QRYSLT('yymmdd = %RANGE(''920101'' ''921231'')') +
    MAPFLD((date1 lrdat *ZONED 6 0) +
        (date2 date1 *CHAR 6 ) +
        (yymmdd '(%SST(date2 5 2) *CAT %SST(date2 1 4)' +
            *CHAR 6))
```

Figure 10.3: You can perform MDY date selection with OPNQRYF.

Note that if the date is already in zoned or character format, the first or first and second mapped field specifications can be eliminated. This still allows the data to be updated or deleted.

You can sort by date this way by adding a mapped field specification to map the new date back to another field in the file that you specify on the KEYFLD parameter. The field must be one that you don't need for that application. Data will not be affected; however, you cannot update the file when this map is added.

—Bryan Leaman

Referencing Date Fields in OPNQRYF

Q: How would you code a date comparison in OPNQRYF, using a date data type in a data-base file and a CL variable?

A: There are multiple ways to do it. We like to stick the dates in the local data area (LDA). The LDA looks like Figure 10.4. Notice that the quotes surround the dates. Then, we compare within the OPNQRYF statement as in Figure 10.5. We use the MAPFLD to pull the 12-character dates (including separator characters and surrounding quotes) and then use them in the OPNQRYF.

```
*...+....1....+....2....+....3....+....4....+....5
'8801019710220099                          Y11NO'
'PRINT   01QPADEV0005           99999     '1988-'
'01-01''1997-10-22'                        '
 '                                         '
 '                                         '
```

Figure 10.4: Use the LDA to code a date comparison in OPNQRYF.

```
RTVDTAARA    DTAARA(*LDA (1 118))    RTNVAR(&PMLIST)
OVRDBF       FILE(APAPT)   SHARE(*YES)
CHGVAR       VAR(&FORMAT) VALUE(%SST(&PMLIST 48 1))

IF COND(&FORMAT *EQ '1') THEN(DO)
   OPNQRYF FILE((APAPT)) QRYSLT('RAADAT=%RANGE(FRDT TODT)') +
      KEYFLD((RAALOC) (RAADAT *ASCEND)) +
      MAPFLD((FRDT %SST(&PMLIST 95 12) *CHAR 12) +
          (TODT %SST(&PMLIST 107 12) *CHAR 12))
ENDDO
```

Figure 10.5: Perform record selection against the date data type.

—Doug Pence and Ron Hawkins

Revise QRYSLT Expressions to Subtract Two Date Fields

Q: I am trying to use OPNQRYF to subtract two date fields to determine if they are more than one year apart. The runtime error I get is that the operand for the *GT is not valid. Here's the OPNQRYF statement I'm using:

```
OPNQRYF FILE((xxxxxxx)) +
   QRYSLT('%CURDATE - CDATE +
   *GT %DURDAY(365)')
```

A: When you subtract one date from another, the difference is an eight-digit decimal called a date duration. It is in the format yyyymmdd. What you're trying to do in the QRYSLT is very logical, but OPNQRYF will not accept the %DURDAY function. Revise the QRYSLT expressions as follows:

```
OPNQRYF FILE((xxxxxxxx)) +
    QRYSLT('%CURDATE - CDATE +
    *GT 00010000')
```

The literal 00010000 means one year, no months, and no days.

Another way is like this:

```
OPNQRYF FILE((xxxxxxxx)) +
    QRYSLT('CDATE *LT +
    %CURDATE - %DURDAY(365)')
```

Because 365 days is not the same as one year, you will probably get different results with the two expressions. Pick the one that gets the results you want, if it matters.

—Ted Holt

Select Records Across the Centuries

Suppose you have a program that selects purchase orders created over a range of dates, as shown in Figure 10.6. This program selects the correct records if &FROMDT and &THRUDT are both from the 1900s, but it doesn't work when &FROMDT is from the 1900s and &THRUDT is in the year 2000 or after.

```
DCL &FROMDT *CHAR 6 /* YYMMDD FORMAT */
DCL &THRUDT *CHAR 6 /* YYMMDD FORMAT */

OVRDBF   FILE(PURCHORD) SHARE(*YES)
OPNQRYF  FILE((PURCHORD)) +
            QRYSLT('PODATE = %RANGE(' *CAT +
                &FROMDT *BCAT &THRUDT *CAT ')') +
            KEYFLD((VENDOR))
CALL PGM(PUR0110RG)
CLOF OPNID(PURCHORD)
DLTOVR FILE(PURCHORD)
```

Figure 10.6: This record selection logic works if the first two digits of two dates are the same.

An easy way to solve this problem is to use different record selection logic in different circumstances, as demonstrate in Figure 10.7. If &FROMDT is less than or equal to &THRUDT, the record selection logic is unchanged. But if &FROMDT is greater than &THRUDT, the program gets all records with creation dates greater than or equal to &FROMDT and records with creation dates less than or equal to &THRUDT.

```
DCL &QRYSLT *CHAR 256 /* YYMMDD FORMAT */

IF (&FROMDT *LE &THRUDT) DO
   CHGVAR &QRYSLT ('PODATE = %RANGE(' *CAT +
             &FROMDT *BCAT &THRUDT *CAT ')')
ENDDO
ELSE DO
   CHGVAR &QRYSLT ('(PODATE *GE ' *CAT &FROMDT *BCAT ' *OR +
                 PODATE *LE ' *CAT &THRUDT *CAT ')')
ENDDO
OVRDBF FILE(PURCHORD) SHARE(*YES)
OPNQRYF FILE((PURCHORD)) QRYSLT(&QRYSLT) KEYFLD((VENDOR))
(etc.)
```

Figure 10.7: This program considers that an ending date may be less than a beginning date.

—Ted Holt

Sort on a Calculated Date Field with OPNQRYF

Q: I'm trying to sort by a calculated date defined as a mapped field. The OPNQRYF command I'm using looks like this:

```
OPNQRYF FILE((MYFILE)) +
   FORMAT(DUMMY) KEYFLD((SDATE)) +
   MAPFLD((SDATE '%DATE(DXNDTE) +
   %DURDAY(GRPRDN)' *DATE))
```

DXNDTE and GRPRDN are fields from MYFILE. DXNDTE is a six-digit numeric field containing a date in month-day-year format, and GRPRDN is a numeric field with a number of days to be added to the date. The DUMMY file has all the fields I need from MYFILE, as well as SDATE, which is defined as an L data type in the DDS with no length specified.

When I attempt to run the CL, I get the runtime error that the field SDATE is not the same length as the MAPFLD length. What's wrong? Don't the two fields default to a length of 14?

A: The system is trying to build the mapped field in the date format used by the job, which is probably *MDY on your system. *MDY is eight characters long (you have to count the separators). In the DDS, the default is *ISO, which is 10 characters long. The field lengths aren't the same.

Here's how you fix it. First, let the mapped field default to *CALC rather than defining it as *DATE. That will make OPNQRYF use the definition from the format file. Second, reformat DXNDTE to be a character field with separators before you use it with the %DATE function. When you use %DATE with a numeric field, OPNQRYF treats it as the number of elapsed days since January 1, 1 A.D. Your OPNQRYF should look like the example shown in Figure 10.8.

```
OPNQRYF FILE((MYFILE)) +
   FORMAT(DUMMY) KEYFLD((SDATE)) +
   MAPFLD((WKDT1 '%DIGITS(DXNDTE)') +
         (WKDT2 '%SST(WKDT1 1 2) *CAT "/" *CAT +
                %SST(WKDT1 3 2) *CAT "/" *CAT +
                %SST(WKDT1 5 2)') +
         (SDATE '%DATE(WKDT2) + %DURDAY(GRPRDN)'))
```

Figure 10.8: Reformat numeric dates to character format before passing them to %DATE.

—*Ted Holt*

Sorting Six-digit Dates Correctly

Here is a way to make six-digit dates sort correctly.

Assume that file XACTS has a six-digit date field, XDATE, in YYMMDD format. Assume also that years 40–99 are understood to be 1940-1999, while years 00–39 are 2000–2039.

The trick is to use the OPNQRYF command to modify the date by adding 60 to the year and dropping any overflow into the hundreds column. Years 40–99 become 00–59, and 00–39 become 60–99.

Figure 10.9 illustrates how to do this. The MAPFLD (Mapped field) parameter redefines XDATE. Adding 600,000 to the XDATE value from XACTS modifies the year but might cause the date to overflow into the millions. The // operator returns the remainder of division. In this case, // removes the millions, leaving a six-digit date with the modified year.

```
OPNQRYF    FILE((XACTS)) KEYFLD((XDATE) (XSEQ)) +
              MAPFLD((XDATE '(1/XDATE + 600000) // 1000000'))
```

Figure 10.9: Modify a six-digit date to make it sort correctly.

The program that reads the XACTS file under the control of OPNQRYF will see the modified date, not the real one. Figure 10.6 shows some ways an RPG III program can convert the modified date back to something usable.

```
      * convert to correct year in yyyy-mm-dd format
      C           XDATE     ADD  19400000 DATE2     80
      * convert to correct year in yy-mm-dd format
      C                     ADD  400000   XDATE
```

Figure 10.10: Convert the modified date back to its original form.

This technique also can be used if the date is in MMDDYY format, as shown in Figure 10.11.

```
OPNQRYF    FILE((XACTS)) KEYFLD((XDATE) (XSEQ)) +
              MAPFLD((YEAR1      '1/XDATE // 100' *DEC 2 0) +
                 (MONTHDAY1 '(1/XDATE - YEAR1) * 0.01' *DEC 4 0) +
                 (YEAR2     '(YEAR1 + 60) // 100' *DEC 2 0) +
                 (XDATE     '(YEAR2 * 10000) + MONTHDAY1'))
```

Figure 10.11: Modify a date in MMDDYY format to make it sort correctly.

—Ted Holt

✦ ✦ ✦ File Handling

A Few Ways to Use the Powerful CPYFRMQRYF Command

When I test, I like to copy production data into the test environment. If possible, I'll take the whole file. If it's too big, I'll subset it by selecting on various criteria. I also prefer to copy the data using CL commands, rather than writing a high-level language (HLL). Once I get my test data, I make a copy of it, out of the way, and keep refreshing my test file from that until I'm done. So, most of the time, I need to use the production files only once—when I start testing.

The Copy File (CPYF) command is the most obvious choice for pulling these records, especially if there are no complex selection criteria. However, as the selection criteria become more complex, it gets less and less useful.

I discovered that I could get everything done with two commands: Open Query File (OPNQRYF) and Copy from Query File (CPYFRMQRYF). You can do some pretty fancy stuff to set up your selection criteria using OPNQRYF. And then CPYFRMQRYF can turn the open data path created by OPNQRYF into an actual physical file with test data.

For example, I can create a control file containing the keys of specific records I want from production. If I join a specified production file to that file on those keys with the OPNQRYF, CPYFRMQRYF copies only those records defined in the control file. I can even join the production file I'm extracting to other production files if the criteria include information in other files. And these commands can be run interactively from the command line or in a simple "down and dirty" CL program—if you think you'll want to reuse the logic.

I'm not spelling anything out in detail here. And there are some tricks to getting this to work, especially for the more complex selection scenarios, such as joining files. But, once I learned the tricks, I found this approach to be the very simplest and quickest.

One hint if you're doing this interactively: As soon as you're done, if you're not going to be signing right off, be sure to run the Close File (CLOF) command to close the access path that OPNQRYF leaves open.

— Rebecca Whittemore

Properly Closing OPNQRYF

Q: I have inherited a CL program that uses OPNQRYF to join two files. The author of the program included two Close File (CLOF) commands, one for each file listed in the Open Query File (OPNQRYF) command. When the program runs, the second CLOF ends in error. Does the second CLOF serve a purpose? If so, how can we fix it?

A: You need only one CLOF command to close the open data path created by OPNQRYF. Its OPNID parameter must match the OPNID parameter of the OPNQRYF, which defaults to the name of the first file listed in the OPNQRYF FILE parameter.

—Ted Holt

Reusing an OPNQRYF Data Path

Q: We have a recurring OPNQRYF problem. After running the OPNQRYF command, we run a program and it runs perfectly. The second program can't get the OPNQRYF—it seems that the file closes. We have tried several changes to get the file to stay open, i.e., *PERM, but that hasn't worked. We don't want to run the OPNQRYF twice and we don't want a logical file. Anybody have the answer?

A: There are two ways to reuse an OPNQRYF command. The easy way is to use a POSDBF command between the two calls.

```
OVRDBF FILE(...) SHARE(*YES) ...
OPNQRYF ...
CALL  PGMA
POSDBF OPNID(XYZ) POSITION(*START)
CALL  PGMB
```

The other way is to have the second program reposition the file pointer, using a command such as RPG's SETLL or COBOL's START verb.

This is a good technique to use when you want to view the records/sequence that OPNQRYF is producing. Issue the OPNQRYF command, then do a CPYFRMQRYF to a test file, then issue the POSDBF command, and then call your program. It's a nice feature.

—Cynthy Johnson
—Ted Holt

✦ ✦ ✦ Functions

Include Nongrouped Fields in Grouped Queries

The Open Query File (OPNQRYF) command allows you to summarize groups of records by specifying one or more fields in the GRPFLD parameter. Using this technique, you can create one query record for each group of records. Normally, you can only include fields other than the ones you're grouping by in the query record if they are summarized with the %SUM function. However, by using the %MAX function on fields that are not going to be grouped or summarized (e.g., description and date fields), you can include all of the fields in the original record format and actually summarize a database file using its own format. This method provides a number of benefits:

460

- Eliminates the usual requirement to create an additional record format.

- Eliminates the need to override to another file.

- Allows the HLL program to view the same file and format.

- Makes the fields not grouped or summed available.

- Provides an alternative to Format Data (FMTDTA) summarizing.

Figures 10.12 and 10.13 provide an example of this technique. Figure 10.12 shows the description of the SALESPF file. Figure 10.13 shows a CL program that uses OPNQRYF to summarize the Sales Amount (SALAMT) by the Product Number (PRDNO). Note that you must qualify all mapped field names with the file name. In that way, you avoid the OPNQRYF error of referencing a field to itself, which in this case is exactly what is being done. Also, be sure that any fields you summarize (in this case SALAMT) are large enough to contain the total value for a group.

```
A           R SALESR                    TEXT('Sales Record')
A             PRDNO      12A             TEXT('Product Number')
A             PRDDSC     50A             TEXT('Description')
A             SALAMT     7P 2            TEXT('Sales Amount')
A             INVYR      4S 0            TEXT('Invoice Year')
A             INVMM      2S 0            TEXT('Invoice Month')
A             INVDD      2S 0            TEXT('Invoice Day')
```

Figure 10.12: A powerful feature of OPNQRYF is the capability to summarize data in an externally described file.

```
OVRDBF      FILE(SALESPF) SHARE(*YES)
OPNQRYF     FILE((SALESPF)) KEYFLD((PRDNO)) +
              GRPFLD(PRDNO) +
              MAPFLD((PRDDSC '%MAX(SALESPF/PRDDSC)') +
                     (SALAMT '%SUM(SALESPF/SALAMT)') +
                     (INVYR  '%MAX(SALESPF/INVYR)') +
                     (INVMM  '%MAX(SALESPF/INVMM)') +
                     (INVDD  '%MAX(SALESPF/INVDD)'))
CALL        PGM(HLLPGM)
CLOF        OPNID(SALESPF)
DLTOVR      FILE(SALESPF)
```

Figure 10.13: OPNQRYF can use a file's own format when summarizing data.

—*Tom Conover*

Negating the %VALUES Function

Q: Can anyone think of a simple equivalent for the following QRYSLT theoretical parameter of the Open Query File (OPNQRYF) command?

```
FLD_A *NE %VALUES("x" "y" "z")
```

This parameter is invalid because the %VALUES function must be used with an equal operation. I'd like to use OPNQRYF to do something similar to the Query/400 NLIST test.

A: Use *NOT in front of the comparison, and then test for an equal condition.

```
*NOT (FLD_A *EQ  %VALUES("x" "y" "z"))
```

—Sharon Cannon

Use %WLDCRD to Match the End of a Field

The OPNQRYF command's wildcard (%WLDCRD) function is great for selecting records based on the contents of character fields, but sometimes you have to go to extra lengths to make it do what you want. For example, suppose you have an inventory file with item numbers of one to six characters. If you want to select all items that start with 1T, you can use the following OPNQRYF command:

```
OPNQRYF FILE((ITEMPF)) QRYSLT('ITEM = %WLDCRD("1T*")')
```

If you want the items that have 1T anywhere in the item number, you would change the QRYSLT parameter to this:

```
QRYSLT('ITEM = %WLDCRD("*1T*")')
```

Or

```
QRYSLT('ITEM *CT "1T"')
```

What if you want the items whose item numbers end in 1T? You might think this would do it:

```
QRYSLT('ITEM = %WLDCRD("*1T")')
```

This will work if all item numbers use the full 6 bytes. But if there are shorter item numbers, such as 4X1T, this query selection expression won't work. To retrieve shorter item numbers is a little messy but not difficult. The trick is to add some blanks to both parts of the expression. The minimum number of blanks is the length of the field minus the number of matching characters in the wildcard. In this case, the minimum number of blanks is four, because the item number is six characters long and 1T is two characters long. The safe way to figure out how many characters to add is to just use the length of the field. There is one additional requirement. You have to add an extra "match-all" character (usually an asterisk) to the end of the wildcard. The query select parameter looks like this:

```
QRYSLT('ITEM *CAT "       " = %WLDCRD("*1T       *")')
```

This expression will select items such as 1T, 4X1T, and 53351T. To see how it works, consider the case in which ITEM has the value 4X1T. The left side of the expression is 4X1T followed by eight trailing blanks. The characters 4X match the first asterisk in the wildcard. The characters 1T and the following six blanks match exactly. The remaining two blanks match the last * in the wildcard.

—Ted Holt

Wildcard Searches over Numeric Fields

You might know that the DB2 UDB query engine can perform a wildcard search over character fields, but did you know that it can do the same for numeric fields? The trick is to convert the numeric field to a character field and strip out the leading zeros.

For example, users tend to remember pieces of a dollar amount, especially the cents. Figure 10.14 shows the OPNQRYF and SQL/400 commands that retrieve records with dollar amounts and with a cents portion of 95. The query engine retrieves amounts like $.95, $149.95, and $10.95.

```
OPNQRYF FILE((GLJRNL)) +
   QRYSLT('%STRIP(%DIGITS(GJAMT) "0" *LEAD) *EQ %WLDCRD("*95")')

select * from gljrnl
   where strip(digits(gjamt), leading, '0' ) like '%95'
```

Figure 10.14: OPNQRYF and SQL can use wildcard functions when searching numeric fields.

Suppose users know that a payment was received in the amount of $11,793.00. They also know that a fee was probably deducted from this amount and the rest credited to a customer. They can pass to OPNQRYF a wildcard value of 117??00*.

—Alan A. Urtubia

◆ ◆ ◆ ILE

OPNQRYF and Activation Groups

Be careful when converting to RPG IV any RPG III programs that run in conjunction with OPNQRYF. Your new RPG IV program may ignore the data path opened by OPNQRYF, depending on how you compiled the program.

I discovered that a converted application worked correctly when I compiled the RPG IV program with the Create Bound RPG Program (CRTBNDRPG) command. But, when I used Create RPG Module (CRTRPGMOD) followed by Create Program (CRTPGM) with the default ACTGRP(*NEW), the program ignored the OPNQRYF. I had to specify ACTGRP(*CALLER) on the CRTPGM command to make the RPG IV program use the OPNQRYF.

To experiment further with this, I wrote an ILE CL program that runs OPNQRYF to select records and then calls an ILE RPG program that simply reads the file and prints each record processed. The problem boils down to this: The OPNQRYF and the RPG program must run in the same activation group. Here are three approaches that I have found to work:

1. Specify *JOB on the open scope (OPNSCOPE) parameter of either the Override Database File (OVRDBF) or the OPNQRYF command. It does not have to be specified on both.

2. Create CL and RPG programs, specifying the same named activation group for both.

3. Create modules from the CL and RPG source members. Combine them into one program with CRTPGM.

The first of these, scoping to the job, is the easiest way to go in jobs that use only one activation group. It could cause problems in a job with more than one activation group, because a program that should not run under OPNQRYF might do so.

The second option, using a named activation group, has the disadvantage that it might quit working correctly if one of the programs is recompiled. It is possible that the programmer recompiling the program might accept the default rather than use the correct activation group name.

The last option, combining two modules into one program, might be best for interactive jobs. The disadvantage of this approach is that the program will have to be recreated or updated each time one of the modules is changed.

—*Jim Michie*

✦ ✦ ✦ Multiple Files and Formats

Joining the Same File Twice with OPNQRYF

Q: I seem to come across a most unusual way of processing files. I need to know if someone has ever joined two of the same file to a third file. For example, I have a customer representative file and an employee master file. I want to join the employee master file to the rep file twice to get the rep's name and the rep's supervisor's name. The error I get tells me that the LAST NAME field is found in more than one record format. My OPNQRYF statement is shown in Figure 10.15.

```
OVRDBF FILE(KRM105W2) TOFILE(EMPREPPF) SHARE(*YES)
OPNQRYF FILE((EMPREPPF) (LOSRTOPF) (KRMEMPPF) (KRMEMPPF)) +
    FORMAT(KRM105W2) +
    QRYSLT(&QRYSLT2) +
    KEYFLD((ERSUPV) (ERAGNT)) +
    JFLD((ERFND# LOFND#) (ERMEMB LOMEMB) (ERMSUB LOMSUB) +
        (ERAGNT 3/KREMP#) (ERSUPV 4/KREMP#)) +
    JDFTVAL(*YES) +
    MAPFLD((SPLNAM '4/KRLNAM') (SPFNAM '4/KRFNAM')) +
    SEQONLY(*NO)
```

Figure 10.15: Joining a file to itself introduces ambiguities that must be resolved.

A: You can join the same file more than once in the same query. In the example you gave, you need to define two last name fields and two first name fields—one for the rep and one for the supervisor—in the KRM105W2 file. I'm assuming you've already done that, and the supervisor fields are SPLNAM and SLFNAM, and the rep fields are KRLNAM and KRFNAM. If so, you only need to add two more mapped fields for the rep:

```
MAPFLD((KRLNAM '3/KRLNAM') +
        (KRFNAM '3/KRFNAM'))
```

—*Ted Holt*

Running OPNQRYF over a Multiformat Logical File

Q: I need a little help with OPNQRYF. I have a multiformat logical file built over two physical files: the invoice header and detail files. I want to select certain invoices to print. I am having no problem building the correct string for the QRYSLT parameter. My problem is in using the multiformat logical file. I get record format errors. I want to use this file because it will plug right into the current invoice run program. What do I need in the FILE parameter? What about the FORMAT parameter?

A: OPNQRYF will run over a multiformat logical file, but you have to choose one of the formats in the third part of the FILE parameter. One OPNQRYF command won't return records from different formats. These are your options:

1. Run two OPNQRYF commands: one over the header file and one over the detail file. They can reference the physical files or the correct formats of the logical file.

2. Run one OPNQRYF command over the header to select the invoices you want. In your RPG program, read the detail records for each header record with random processing (SETLL, READE). This is assuming that the detail file is keyed on field(s) from the header file, which is usually the case.

3. Join the two files with a join logical. Run the OPNQRYF command over the join logical.

4. Join the two files with one OPNQRYF command.

In my opinion, option 1 is the worst. Option 2 is okay if you don't have to sort on fields from both files. I would use option 3 only if I had an existing join logical. That is, I wouldn't create a join logical just for this. Option 4 is good, but if the files are big, performance can get pretty bad. Keep in mind that options 3 and 4 won't work if you're updating the files. In your case, because you're reprinting invoices, I'd say option 2 is probably the way to go.

—*Ted Holt*

✦ ✦ ✦ Selection

OPNQRYF Templates

As an OPNQRYF beginner, I stumbled along making the usual mistakes, getting acquainted with error message CPD3129 ("Missing operand on expression...") and often getting lost in quotes and *BCATS. However, I have since written a number of CL programs that use the OPNQRYF command and now use the following technique:

1. I declare a &QRYSLT variable, giving it an initial value that exactly matches what I'll need in the QRYSLT parameter of the OPNQRYF command. In this initial value, I use Xs to substitute any character values and 9s to substitute any numeric values.

2. Then I use %SST in a CHGVAR command to replace the X's and 9's with the actual values I require in my QRYSLT expression. In the example shown in Figure 10.16, the user is expected to give &STATE a two-character value and &ZIP a five-digit value, which the program receives as parameters. When the CHGVAR commands are executed, the computer "sees" the &QRYSLT variable as shown in Figure 10.17.

```
PGM         PARM(&STATE &ZIP)
DCL         VAR(&STATE) TYPE(*CHAR) LEN(2)
DCL         VAR(&ZIP) TYPE(*DEC) LEN(5 0)
DCL         VAR(&QRYSLT) TYPE(*CHAR) LEN(512) +
    /* ....+... 1 ...+... 2 ...+... 3 ...+ */ +
  VALUE('STATE *EQ "XX" *OR ZIP *EQ 99999')
CHGVAR      VAR(%SST(&QRYSLT 12 2)) VALUE(&STATE)
CHGVAR      VAR(%SST(&QRYSLT 28 5)) VALUE(&ZIP)
OPNQRYF     FILE((CUSTOMER)) QRYSLT(&QRYSLT)
ENDPGM
```

Figure 10.16: Use template code to make record selection easier.

```
    /* ....+... 1 ...+... 2 ...+... 3 ...+ */
QRYSLT('STATE *EQ "CA" *OR ZIP *EQ 92008')
```

Figure 10.17: After the substitutions are made, the query selection expression is easy to understand.

Notice the placement of the comment containing a scale in Figure 10.16. This eliminates the tedious counting of characters to determine where, along &QRYSLT, to substitute the actual values. This method also eliminates the need to use concatenation operators and significantly reduces the number and placement of quotes. The important thing to remember is that if the variable part of the string is alphanumeric, enclose it in double quotes. It's easier to use one double-quote character (") than to use the single quote (') twice. If you do use the single-quote characters, the start position of the substitution variable will actually be one less than indicated for every pair of quotes encountered reading the template statement from left to right. In my example, I kept things simple and used the one double quote around my character literal.

—*Susan Berrey*

QRYSLT with Binary Fields

Q: I need to preselect records out of a physical file through either a logical or OPNQRYF file. My problem is that the field I need to select on is a character field with one position that contains a binary switch. I need only records with certain bits "on." I have created a logical file and attempted to convert the field into a hexadecimal field by using the data type. Yet, when I use DFU to view the data through the logical, the data looks binary to me.

Has anyone done anything similar? Can anyone help? The program is currently reading 1.2 million records each night, but only needs to process a handful of those. If I could get the select to work in some way, it would greatly improve our nightly processing.

A: What you want to do is not impossible, just a little unusual.

File BINDATA contains a field FLAGS, which is a character, 10 bytes long. To select records where the fifth byte of FLAGS is as follows: (1) The first bit (bit 0) is on and (2) either the fourth or fifth bit (bits 3 and 4) is on. See Figure 10.18.

```
DCL        VAR(&QRYSLT) TYPE(*CHAR) LEN(256)

CHGVAR     VAR(&QRYSLT) VALUE('TEST0 *NE X''00'' *AND +
           TEST3 *NE X''00'' *OR TEST4 *NE X''00''')
OVRDBF     FILE(BINDATA) SHARE(*YES)
OPNQRYF    FILE((BINDATA)) QRYSLT(&QRYSLT) +
           MAPFLD((TESTBYTE '%SST(FLAGS 5 1)') +
           (TEST0 '%AND(TESTBYTE X''80'')') +
           (TEST3 '%AND(TESTBYTE X''10'')') +
           (TEST4 '%AND(TESTBYTE X''08'')'))
CALL       PGM(BINRPG)
CLOF       OPNID(BINDATA)
DLTOVR     FILE(BINDATA)
```

Figure 10.18: OPNQRYF can work with individual bits in a character field.

The three %AND functions isolate the three different bits we're testing. The %AND function does a logical AND operation. It compares two strings, bit by bit. If the same bit is on in both strings, it turns on the corresponding bit in the result string. Figure 10.19 shows a couple of examples of how the first %AND would work with different values of TESTBYTE.

```
TESTBYTE    10100010    00001111
X'80'       10000000    10000000
            _____    _____
TEST0       10000000    00000000
```

Figure 10.19: The logical %AND can determine whether bits are on or off.

TEST0 will come back as all zeros if bit 0 is not on. The same is true for the other two TESTx fields. You can use these fields to see if they are equal to hex 00 or not. If they are not equal, the bit is on.

By the way, if the flag field is only 1 byte long, you don't have to use the first mapped field; you can just use the flag field in the other three mapped fields instead of TESTBYTE. The QRYSLT doesn't change.

—Ted Holt

Runtime Record Selection for a Batch Query

Q: Is there a way to prompt the record selection screen in Query/400 that will allow the user to key in selection criteria and then submit the job to batch? The RCDSLT parameter of the Run Query (RUNQRY) command lets me select records at runtime, but I have to run the command interactively for it to work.

A: We use OPNQRYF to perform the record selection that the query used to perform. In the query, locate the names of the files you are selecting data from in the Specify File Selections prompt and the way you're selecting data in the Select Records prompt (Figure 10.20). You will need to decide whether to let OPNQRYF select all the data or to let Query/400 select some data and let OPNQRYF select the rest. Modify the Select Records prompt appropriately.

```
                              Select Records

  Type comparisons, press Enter.  Specify OR to start each new group.
    Tests:  EQ, NE, LE, GE, LT, GT, RANGE, LIST, LIKE, IS, ISNOT...

  AND/OR  Field            Test   Value (Field, Number, 'Characters', or ...)
          STATE            LIST   'IL' 'MO' 'IA'
   ___    _____        ____   _____
   ___    _____        ____   _____
   ___    _____        ____   _____
   ___    _____        ____   _____
                                                                     Bottom
 _____
  Field
  CUSTNO
  CITY
  STATE
  ZIP
                                                                     Bottom
  F3=Exit         F5=Report        F9=Insert         F11=Display text
  F12=Cancel      F13=Layout       F20=Reorganize    F24=More keys
```

Figure 10.20: Determine the criteria Query uses to select records.

In library QTEMP, create duplicates of the files you will be using OPNQRYF to select the data from. You need to change the name of the file to avoid getting an error on the copy you will be doing later. I usually just add a Q to the end of the file name. Change the library parameter on the file selection prompt in Query/400 to point to the files in QTEMP. Save the query definition, and delete the QTEMP files you just created.

Create a prompt screen that will allow the users to enter their selections (Figure 10.21). The DDS for this screen is shown in Figure 10.22. This prompt will run from a CL program (like the one in Figure 10.23) that uses the OPNQRYF to select the records from the file based on the user input. In your CL program, right after the OPNQRYF, add the Copy from Query File (CPYFRMQRYF) command to copy the selected data to a duplicate of the queried files in library QTEMP. CPYFRMQRYF will create the file for you in QTEMP if you want it to.

```
                         Customer Master Report              2/12/98
20:57:51


                 Select customer number range for report

                       From:  ____180   To:  254








F3=Exit
```

Figure 10.21: Create a prompt screen for entering record selection criteria.

```
*===============================================================
* To compile:
*
* CRTDSPF FILE(XXX/QRY001DF) SRCFILE(XXX/QDDSSRC)
*
*===============================================================
A                                      DSPSIZ(24 80 *DS3)
A                                      CA03(03 'Exit')
A                                      PRINT
A          R QRY00001
A                                  1  3USER
A                                  1 26'Customer Master Report'
A                                      DSPATR(HI)
A                                      DSPATR(UL)
A                                  1 57DATE
A                                      EDTCDE(Y)
A                                  1 68TIME
A                                  6 17'Select customer number range-
A                                      for report'
A                                  8 21'From:'
A            FCUST      8   B  8 27CHECK(FE RB)
A                                  8 39'To:'
A            TCUST      8   B  8 27CHECK(FE RB)
A                                      'F3=Exit'
```

Figure 10.22: This DDS creates the prompt screen.

471

```
/*================================================================*/
/* To compile:                                                    */
/*                                                                */
/* CRTCLPGM PGM(XXX/QRY001CL) SRCFILE(XXX/QCLSRC)                 */
/*                                                                */
/*================================================================*/

PGM

    DCLF FILE(QRY001DF)
    DCL VAR(&QRYSLT) TYPE(*CHAR) LEN(2000)

    /* Display Prompt Screen */
PROMPT:
    SNDRCVF
    /* User Requests Exit */
    IF COND(&IN03 *EQ '1') THEN(GOTO CMDLBL(ENDPGM))
    /* Edit Check Input Fields */
    IF COND(&FCUST *EQ *BLANKS *OR &TCUST *EQ +
                *BLANKS) THEN(GOTO CMDLBL(PROMPT))
    /* Build Query Select Variable */
    CHGVAR VAR(&QRYSLT) VALUE(&QRYSLT *BCAT 'CMNBR +
                *GE ' || &FCUST || ' *AND CMNBR *LE +
                ' || &TCUST)

    /* Override File To Query and Run Open Query Command */
    OVRDBF FILE(CSTMST) TOFILE(*LIBL/CSTMST) SHARE(*YES)
    OPNQRYF FILE((*LIBL/CSTMST)) QRYSLT(&QRYSLT)
    /* Copy Records Selected In Open Query To Temporary Member */
    CPYFRMQRYF FROMOPNID(CSTMST) TOFILE(QTEMP/CSTMSTQ) +
                MBROPT(*ADD) CRTFILE(*YES)
    /* Run OS/400 Query Program Using Copied Data As Input */
    RUNQRY QRY(*LIBL/CUSTQRY) QRYFILE((QTEMP/CSTMSTQ +
                *FIRST))
    /* Close Files and Delete Temporary File */
    DLTOVR FILE(CSTMST)
    CLOF OPNID(CSTMST)
    DLTF FILE(QTEMP/CSTMSTQ)

ENDPGM:
ENDPGM
```

Figure 10.23: Use a CL program to drive the prompt screen, OPNQRYF, and Query.

Finally, use the RUNQRY to run the original query. You will need to pass the temporary files to the query in the QRYFILE parameter on the RUNQRY command. Now, the original query will run, using the data extracted with the OPNQRYF and any additional selections you might have defined in the Query/400 definition.

This technique has the advantage of reusing the existing report the user is familiar with, without requiring a programmer to rewrite it in RPG, and it's a very quick way to create a user-selectable report that can be easily added to a menu.

—Shannon O'Donnell

✦ ✦ ✦ Sorting and Sequencing

Dynamic Sorting with OPNQRYF

Am I the only one who missed this OPNQRYF trick? I needed to sort nine fields in any order requested by the user. The file being sorted has the potential to be large, and I wanted to use OPNQRYF with a real sort. I always use a variable with QRYSLT, but I never thought of trying the same thing with the KEYFLD parameter. I came up with a statement like this:

```
OPNQRYF FILE((TSTQRYF)) +
    QRYSLT(&QRYSLT) +
    KEYFLD((&KEY1) (&KEY2) +
        (&KEY3) (&KEY4) (&KEY5) +
        (&KEY6) (&KEY7) (&KEY8) +
        (&KEY9)) ALWCPYDTA(*OPTIMIZE)
```

My program inserts the proper field names in the &KEYX variables. The result is one OPNQRYF statement that handles all of my users' sort selections.

—Brian Kautz

Mixed Case Sequencing with OPNQRYF

Q: Is there anything we can do to change the collating sequence used by OPNQRYF to allow true sequencing regardless of records with mixed case?

A: I handle sorting by mixed case as follows: Assuming a field name of ENAME in mixed case, specify ENAME (or whatever) in the KEYFLD parameter, then on a MAPFLD parameter, MAP ENAME to:

```
'%XLATE(ENAME QSYSTRNTBL)'
```

QSYSTRNTBL is the IBM lower-to-uppercase translation table. This will put your data in uppercase before it is keyed.

—David Knittle

Sorting on a Contrived Field with OPNQRYF

Q: I am trying to write a CL program that will sort a file on the sum of two fields in the same file. For example, I want to add total price and shipping price together and sort on the sum of the two fields. I have tried using MAPFLD, but I keep getting an error on QRYSLT.

A: You need to define a dummy physical file to serve as a record format. Your total field doesn't exist in your database file. This dummy file must contain any fields from your database file that your program requires, plus any contrived fields (in your case, the total field). You'll end up with something similar to the example shown in Figure 10.24.

```
 *. 1 ...+... 2 ...+... 3 ...+... 4 ...+... 5 ...+... 6 ...+... 7
 A                                        REF(DICTIONARY)
 A          R DUMREC
 A            ITEM#      R
 A            PRICE      R
 A            SHIPNG     R
 A            SUM        R            REFFLD(PRICE)
```

Figure 10.24: Use a dummy physical file to define virtual fields.

Write your HLL program just as though it were using the dummy file. Then, in your CL program, override the dummy file to the real file before executing the OPNQRYF command. See Figure 10.25 for a sample CL program.

```
 PGM
 OVRDBF     FILE(DUMMY) TOFILE(YOURFILE) SHARE(*YES)
 OPNQRYF    FILE((DUMMY)) +
              FORMAT(DUMMY) +
              KEYFLD((SUM)) MAPFLD((SUM 'PRICE + SHIPNG'))
 CALL       PGM(PROGRAM)
 CLOF       OPNID(DUMMY)
 DLTOVR     FILE(*ALL)
 ENDPGM
```

Figure 10.25: OPNQRYF sorts on the sum of two fields.

—Midrange Computing Staff

Sorting with OPNQRYF on Incomplete Fields

Q: How can I sort a file by part of a field? I have the field put together on the MAPFLD parameter (concatenating a few substrings) and then it's specified in the KEYFLD parameter as *MAPFLD/name, but OPNQRYF won't accept it.

A: All key fields in OPNQRYF must exist in the record format specified in the FORMAT parameter, which defaults to the value in the FILE parameter. You'll have to create a dummy physical file which has all the fields you need from the database file(s) listed in the FILE parameter, plus the fields you want to sort on.

Let's say you're reading a file called FILEA, which has fields FLD1, FLD2, and FLD3. You want to sort on a substring of FLD2.

First, create a dummy physical file (let's call it WORKFILE) with fields FLD1, FLD2, FLD3, and SORT. Compile your high-level language program to read WORKFILE. By the way, WORKFILE doesn't even need to have a member.

The process shown in Figure 10.26 should get you headed in the right direction.

```
OVRDBF  FILE(WORKFILE) TOFILE(FILEA) SHARE(*YES)
OPNQRYF FILE((FILEA)) FORMAT(WORKFILE) +
          MAPFLD((SORT '%SST(FLD2 2 2)')) +
          KEYFLD((SORT))
CALL    your program
CLOF    OPNID(FILEA)
DLTOVR  FILE(WORKFILE)
```

Figure 10.26: OPNQRYF can sort on a portion of a field or concatenated portions of one or more fields.

—Midrange Computing Staff

OPNQRYF MAPFLD and KEYFLD

Q: The AS/400 manuals say that I can use a mapped field as the key field when using OPNQRYF. Every time I try, however, I get an error message stating that the field used for KEYFLD must exist in the physical file.

With some files, I can create a mapped field using the same name as another field that exists in the physical file (as long as that field is not referenced by any program that reads the open data path (ODP) created by the OPNQRYF). However, when a program needs to use all of the fields in the physical file, I have to create a logical file (Yuck!).

A: Create another physical file that contains no data. This dummy file doesn't even have to have a member. It needs all the fields from the real file (or at least the ones your RPG program is using), plus the mapped field.

Write your RPG program to read the dummy file. In your CL program, override the dummy file to the real file. Be sure to tell it to share the open data path: SHARE(*YES).

In the OPNQRYF command, put the real file name in the FILE parameter and the dummy file name in the FORMAT parameter. Be sure to include the mapped field definition, just as you're already doing. Figure 10.27 shows an example of the CL program:

```
OVRDBF FILE(DUMMY) TOFILE(REALFILE) SHARE(*YES)
OPNQRYF FILE((REALFILE)) FORMAT(DUMMY) +
  KEYFLD((MF1)) MAPFLD((MF1 '%SST( etc. ...
CALL PGM(RPGPGM)
CLOF OPNID(REALFILE)
DLTOVR FILE(DUMMY)
```

Figure 10.27: Sorting on a mapped field usually requires a dummy format file.

The RPG program (RPGPGM) file specification references file DUMMY.

—Ted Holt
—Ken Stratton

Unique Key Processing with OPNQRYF

Q: I have multiple records with the same key values and different dates. For each unique key value, I need to select the record with the most current date. How would I use OPNQRYF to do this?

A: Use the UNIQUEKEY keyword, like this:

```
OPNQRYF FILE((MYFILE)) +
  KEYFLD((FIELDA) (DATE *DESCEND)) +
  UNIQUEKEY(1)
```

The UNIQUEKEY keyword value needs to be the number of key fields before the date.

—Ted Holt

Q: Recently, I had to convert a file with a duplicate key field to one with a unique key field. My first thought was to use the Copy File (CPYF) command (with the target file having a unique key), but this does not work. So, I wrote a small RPG III program to do the job. My RPG III program reads the original file from beginning to end (about 45,000 records), attempting to WRITE each record to the new file (about 6,000 records). I put an error indicator in positions 56 and 57 to keep the program from canceling when I try to write a duplicate record.

This program takes a very long time to finish. Can you tell me why it takes so long and suggest either another coding improvement or a completely different way to do this?

A: Trying to write a record with a duplicate key value to a uniquely keyed file puts a lot of strain on the system. Instead, use the Open Query File (OPNQRYF) command to pull out the records you want. Then, write only the selected records into the uniquely keyed file. (See Figure 10.28.)

```
OPNQRYF FILE((OLD)) +
    KEYFLD((KEY1) (KEY2)) +
    UNIQUEKEY(1) +
    ALWCPYDTA(*OPTIMIZE)

CPYFRMQRYF FROMOPNID(OLD) +
    TOFILE(NEW) +
    MBROPT(*REPLACE)

CLOF OPNID(OLD)
```

Figure 10.28: OPNQRYF provides a quick method for selecting unique key fields.

I'm assuming you have only one key field (KEY1). The second key field is another sort field, so you can pick the record you want from each key group. UNIQUEKEY(1) tells the system to get only one record from each group that shares a common value for the first key field. I did a quick test of this, using a file of 45,000 records with 6,000 unique key values. The RPG III method you're using took 26 times as long to run as the OPNQRYF method.

—Ted Holt

CHAPTER 11

PCs

*I*n the old days, the only access you had to your AS/400 was by way of a dumb terminal connected to your AS/400 through twinax. Today, you have so many access methods it would take a book to describe them all. Everything from RF terminals riding around on forklifts to hand-held devices to cell phones can now interact with your AS/400. But by far, the ubiquitous personal computer is the most common means of providing user access to your AS/400 today.

As an AS/400 professional, you've had to continually learn new technologies and build up your PC skills just to stay current with your user's demands. And as we all know, supporting PCs is a full time job in itself! Never mind also being required to support your AS/400! There is just so much information out there you're expected to learn that it's hard to imagine how you'd ever have time to keep up with it all.

This chapter of tips and techniques, focusing on maintaining your PC and its connection to your AS/400, is just what the doctor ordered! In it, you'll find tips on how to:

- Assign a unique workstation ID to a TCP/IP 5250 Session.
- Update ODBC tables.
- Capture an AS/400 5250 screen and paste it into a PC document.
- Use Windows 95/98 to copy from one AS/400 to another.
- Change the limit on the number of transfer sections.
- And much, much more!

—Shannon O'Donnell

✦ ✦ ✦ Client Access Errors

Some Client Access Errors

I've discovered a few quirks about Client Access (CA/400) that some users might not be aware of. For example, if you're trying to connect to an AS/400 using CA/400 and you get security error message CWBSY1000 (Communication error while validating security information on system XXXXXX) when trying to sign on, it could mean that the host server isn't started on the target AS/400.

If you receive this error, you should run the Start Host Server (STRHOSTSVR) command with SERVER (*ALL) on the AS/400. You can substitute a server name for *ALL if you want to start only one server. Let the command run, and then try to sign on again. You should be able to connect. If this is happening often, possibly because someone forgets to start the server, I suggest automating this command by including a CL program that's an Autostart Job Entry in the communications subsystem. This way, you'll always have access to the AS/400.

Another error I've discovered happens when I try to send a text file from my PC to the AS/400. This error, CWBTF0023 (PC file description file was not specified or is empty), occurs because the transfer request is trying to use the PC file description. To avoid this error, click on Details on the main Data Transfer to AS/400 screen. This brings up the AS/400 File Details screen (shown in Figure 11.1), which defaults to Use PC file description. Remove the check mark in this dialog box, and make sure the File type box has ASCII Text in it, as shown in Figure 11.1. Try the transfer again; it should work now. Just make sure the file you're transferring the data to exists on the AS/400. If it doesn't, you'll get another error: CWBDB0036 (Server returned SQL error). Creating the file you're sending the ASCII text to can eliminate this error.

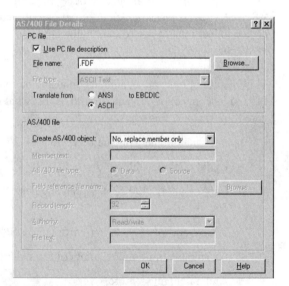

Figure 11.1: You'll set the AS/400 File Details on a CA/400 File Transfer from this screen.

—D. Ellis Green

✦ ✦ ✦ Client Access License

Valid Client Access/400 License Required

Want to find out who's currently using one of your Client Access/400 licenses? Type in the Work with License Information (WRKLICINF) command on an AS/400 command line and press the Enter key. Page down until you see the entry for Client Access/400 Windows Family Base (or its equivalent). Enter option 8 next to this entry, and you are presented with a list of job information for all current users of the product. This tip works for any AS/400 licensed program.

—Shannon O'Donnell

✦ ✦ ✦ Client Access Macros

Put Client Access Macros to Work for You

The PC5250 emulator that comes with the Client Access/400 for Windows 95/NT client has the capability to record and play macros. Macros can be created with limited prompting by using the Assist menu in PC5250 or they can be created manually by using the Windows Notepad program. PC5250 requires you to save macros to the **\program files\ ibm\client access\emulator\private** folder, and they must be saved with the .MAC file type.

The macro script shown in Figure 11.2 can be run inside the SEU while you are working on an RPG or RPGLE program. It excludes the C-specs within subroutines, resulting in a cleaner display when doing maintenance on a complex program.

```
[home]
[home]
[home]
; replace the following two lines with [tab field] to have
  body excluded as well
"f begsr
[enter]
[tab field]
"x999999
[enter]
[home]
"t
[enter]
[home]
```

Figure 11.2: This Client Access macro, Shrink.mac, hides the details of RPG subroutines and excludes all C-specs except for BEGSR, ENDSR, and EXSR tags (part 1 of 2).

```
[wait inp inh]
"f begsr
[enter]
:top1
[pf16]
wait 1 second until "String begsr found"
goto continue1 on timeout
goto top1
:continue1
[home]
"t
[enter]
"f endsr
[enter]
:top2
[pf16]
wait 1 second until "String endsr found"
goto continue2 on timeout
goto top2
:continue2
[home]
"t
[enter]
"f exsr
[enter]
:top3
[pf16]
wait 1 second until "String exsr found"
goto continue3 on timeout
goto top3
:continue3
[home]
[home]
"t
[enter]
:alldone
```

Figure 11.2: This Client Access macro, Shrink.mac, hides the details of RPG subroutines and excludes all C-specs except for BEGSR, ENDSR, and EXSR tags (part 2 of 2).

To run a macro, click on Assist from the PC5250 menu bar and select Keyboard/macro function from the dropdown menu.

—Drew Dekreon, CCP

✦ ✦ ✦ Client Access Security

Lock Down Client Access Security Holes

If you have smart PC users at your office or users who think they're smart, you might have come across folks who have discovered how to get to your AS/400 files and programs in the QSYS.LIB file system by using Windows Explorer. It's actually very easy to do. With Client Access/400 installed on a user's PC, you simply map a network drive to the AS/400, and you're in. With Client Access Express, you also have easy access to the library file system if the user is set up to use file and print sharing via NetSever on the AS/400. A user can even click the Windows Start button, click Find, click Computer, and type in the name of your AS/400. Windows will return a link to your system, and the user can easily navigate to QSYS.LIB.

Now, if you follow good security practices, your users probably can't get into anything they are not specifically authorized to anyway. However, if you use the old "menu-level security" method, which has been so prevalent in the past (especially with vendor-packaged software), you could have a serious security hole.

The best thing to do to protect yourself in this situation is to create a security policy that defines what objects and levels of authority a given user has to a given object. If that doesn't work, you should, at the very minimum, plug the hole in security that gives Client Access users access to QSYS.LIB from Windows Explorer. To do this, change the AS/400 authorization list from QPWFSERVER authority to *PUBLIC *EXCLUDE. This prevents all users from getting to QSYS.LIB from a PC. If you need to grant this type of access to specific users, add them to the authorization list authority for this object on a case-by-case basis.

—*Shannon O'Donnell*

✦ ✦ ✦ Client Access Taskbar

Naming Your PC5250 Session in the Windows 95/NT Taskbar

Q: How can I change the name of a PC5250 Client Access/400 for Windows 95/NT session in the Windows taskbar so that it comes up with something more descriptive for my users than "Session A - [24x80]"?

A: Inside your PC5250 session, click on the Appearance option from the PC5250 menu. On the drop-down menu that appears, click on Window Setup to bring up the Window Setup screen shown in Figure 11.3.

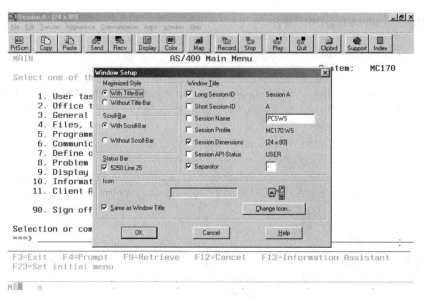

Figure 11.3: The Window Setup screen lets you change the name of your PC5250 window.

In the Windows Title area, there are a number of options for changing the window title of your session. To remove the "Session A" literal from your title, remove the checkmark from the Long Session-ID check box. To remove the "[24x80]" window size literal, turn off the checkmark in the Sessions Dimensions check box. To type in your own text so that something more descriptive comes up in your window title, click the Session Name check box so that it contains a check mark. Then, in the adjoining text box, type in any character string (17 characters or fewer) that you want to appear. When you click on OK to return to your PC5250 session, this new title will appear in the following places on your PC:

- The window title of your PC5250 session.

- The taskbar button for your program on the Windows 95/NT taskbar.

- The icon description that appears when you use the Alt-Tab key combination to choose a program to transfer to.

There are other options as well, but these settings will solve your problem and make your sessions more descriptive for your users.

—Joe Hertvik

Removing the Client Access Tray Icon

By default, Client Access for Windows 95 puts an icon in the Windows 95 Taskbar Notification Area (sometimes called the Taskbar Tray) whenever you start an AS/400 connection. Right-clicking your mouse on this icon brings up a menu that lets you open the Client Access Connections window, the Client Access User's Guide, or the About Client Access window.

Sometimes the Taskbar Tray becomes crowded with icons from various applications, and you might want to eliminate one or more of them. Fortunately, the Client Access icon is one that you can get rid of if you don't want it. To do that, open the Windows 95 control panel. Then, open the Client Access properties applet and select the Other tab. There, you'll find a check box labeled Show Indicator in Taskbar Notification Area. By deselecting this check box, you can prevent Client Access from putting the icon in the Taskbar Tray.

—Robin Klima

✦ ✦ ✦ Client Access TCP/IP

Assigning a Unique Workstation ID to a TCP/IP PC5250 Session

Until release V3R7 of OS/400, running a PC5250 session over TCP/IP has been problematic because you were unable to specify a static and unique workstation ID for your display session. This was because AS/400 TCP/IP uses a dynamic device name assignment algorithm that automatically assigns any one of a number of virtual devices (beginning with the literal 'QPADEV') to your PC5250 session. Dynamic assignment causes problems for application programmers and AS/400 administrators because there is no easy way to identify that a specific device belongs to a specific user or location. This hampers application development and system troubleshooting.

With the V3R1M3 release of Client Access for Windows 95/NT, this problem was solved. On the Configure PC5250 screen, you can now specify a unique workstation ID name for your TCP/IP sessions. When you enter a workstation ID, OS/400 bypasses dynamic device-name assignment and creates a new device with that name for your PC5250 TCP/IP session to use. This new feature can be used for both PC5250 display and printer sessions. This field is optional, and—if you leave it blank—OS/400 will return to using dynamic assignment for your sessions. PC5250 TCP/IP Workstation ID assignment is available only in Client Access for Windows 95/NT V3R1M3 running Service Pack SF46891 and above. According to IBM, it is compatible only with OS/400 V3R2, V3R7,

V4R1, V4R2, and above with the appropriate PTFs installed. For a list of AS/400 PTFs that need to be installed and other considerations in using this feature, consult APAR II10918 from the Client Access Web page at:

http://www-1.ibm.com/servers/eserver/iseries/

and search for "Client Access."

—Joe Hertvik

✦ ✦ ✦ Client Access Toolbox

Enable the Ruler Function of Client Access

The Client Access/400 for Windows 95/NT client's PC5250 emulation program comes with a ruler function that provides horizontal and vertical guide lines to help you align columns in RPG. You also can use the ruler to select records. The problem with this feature is that it's annoying to keep the ruler visible all the time when you need it only for certain functions. However, an easy fix will allow you to toggle the ruler on and off during your emulation session. Here's the procedure:

1. Pull down the Assist menu in a session.

2. Choose Keyboard Setup... from the dropdown menu.

3. Click the Customize button on the Keyboard Setup window.

4. On the Customize Keyboard Setup window, click on the picture of the F12 key.

5. On the lower right corner of the Customize Keyboard Setup screen, you will now see a box labeled Change Current Actions for Selected Key. In that box, find the line labeled Alt. To the right of that line is a box that says [dead]. Click on that box, and replace [dead] with [rule].

6. Click on the Change Key button.

   Editor's Note*: In the PC5250 emulator with the Client Access V3R2 client, there is no Change Key button. Changes are posted to the key and file when you save the keyboard file in the next step.*

7. Pull down the File menu and choose Exit. When asked if you want to save changes, choose the Yes button. The system will ask you to provide a name for the keyboard map. Enter a name of your choice.

8. You will be returned to the Keyboard Setup window. Change Current Keyboard to User-defined and fill in the name of the keyboard map you just saved.

9. Press the OK button on the Keyboard Setup window.

Ta-da! Pressing Alt-F12 will toggle the ruler line on your PC5250 screen on and off.

—Drew Dekreon

Use the Client Access for Windows 95/98/Me System List Box Control

Client Access for Windows 95/98/Me includes a set of custom controls called the Client Access Toolkit. One of the controls, the System List Box, allows you to easily present a user with a list of AS/400 connections. You might need to do this if you have multiple AS/400s and want to allow the user to select one of them.

To install the controls, you need to perform a "custom" installation of Client Access for Windows 95/98/Me and select Toolkit from the list of optional components. You can then access the controls from a development environment such as Microsoft Visual Basic (VB). To access the controls in VB, select the Tools menu and then Custom Controls. Next, select Client Access Control Library from the list of available controls. This adds the controls to your VB Toolbox. Figure 11.4 shows some sample code you can use to experiment with the System List Box control.

```
Private Sub cwbSystemListBox1_Click()
Dim I As Long
For I =0 To cwbSystemListBox1.NumberOfItems -1
If cwbSystemListBox1.GetItemSelectStatus(I) = True Then
MsgBox ("You selected " & cwbSystemListBox1.GetItemText(I))
End If
Next I
End Sub
```

Figure 11.4: Use this VB code to enable the System List Box in PC 5250.

To run this example, place a System List Box on a form and leave the name of the control at its default value. Enter the code shown in Figure 11.4 into the Declaration section of the form and press F5. You'll see a list of configured Client Access connections. Select one of them, and a message box appears telling you which one you selected.

The way this sample program works is by performing a loop for the number of systems in the list. It determines this value by accessing the **NumberOfItems** property of the System List Box control. Within this loop, the program determines if the system is selected by testing the **GetItemSelectStatus** property of the current system. If the property is True, the program uses the **MsgBox** function to display the name of the selected system.

This example will help you get started using the System List Box control. After that, you may want to try experimenting with the other controls included in Client Access for Windows 95/98/Me.

—Robin Klima

✦ ✦ ✦ Client Access Version Check

Remove the Check Service Pack Function in CA/400

Q: Since I installed the Client Access for Windows 95/NT client on my PC, a "Check Version" program runs every time I boot up. How do I keep it from running?

A: The Client Access/400 Windows 95/NT client automatically installs a shortcut in your startup folder that points to the Client Access Check Service Pack Level program. This program checks the Service Pack Level of your Client Access installation against the managing system (usually your main AS/400) to see if they are the same. If they match, nothing happens. If they don't match, you will see a prompt that allows you to install the newest Service Pack Level from the managing system to your Windows 95/NT client.

This is IBM's attempt to allow your users to automatically update their Client Access/400 PC configurations when an upgrade is installed.

However, many people dislike the additional time it takes to perform the service pack check. In addition, because many companies don't install service packs that often and they like to control when a service pack is loaded on a user's PC (for compatibility and debugging purposes), a lot of companies like to remove this program from their user's Windows 95/NT startup folders. If you want to remove the service program from your Windows startup folder, here's how to do it:

1. Click on the Win95 Start button.

2. Click Settings.

3. Click Taskbar.

4. Click the Start Menu Programs.

5. Click Remove.

6. Scroll down until you see StartUp on the Remove Shortcuts/Folders panel.

7. Double-click StartUp.

8. You'll see the Check Version Program icon.

9. Click this once to highlight it, then click the Remove button.

10. Answer "Yes" to the message "Are You Sure You Want to Send This Icon to the Recycle Bin?"

If you want, you can empty your recycle bin to permanently remove the shortcut from your system. The check version executable will still be on your system. Emptying the recycle bin will just permanently remove the shortcut that was in Startup.

In the Client Access Express product, click Start/Settings/Control Panel, Client Access and change the Service Check settings there.

—Shannon O'Donnell
—Joe Hertvik

✦ ✦ ✦ Copying Files

Use Windows 95 to Copy from One AS/400 to Another

Q: Can I use Client Access/400 for Windows to copy a file from a folder in one AS/400 to a folder in another AS/400?

A: Yes. Here are two simple methods:

1. Use Windows Network Neighborhood to navigate down to your first folder. Do the same for the second folder. Then, drag and drop.

2. Use Explorer to map two network drives, one for each AS/400. Drag and drop.

✦ ✦ ✦ Data Transfer

Browsing Libraries with the Client Access/400 File Transfer

Q: When I use the Windows 95/NT Client Access/400 data transfer programs to browse available libraries on the AS/400, only the QGPL and QIWS libraries appear in the Browse Files and Members window. How can I access other libraries through file transfer?

A: By default, Client Access' file transfer program uses the QUSRLIBL system value—which determines the user part of the library list—to determine what libraries to make available in the Browse Files and Members window. Your default user library list probably consists of the QGPL and QIWS libraries. To allow your users to perform file transfers from the libraries they want, you have the following options:

- Specify the explicit AS/400 library and file name you want to transfer to or from by typing that name in the data transfer file name field (as shown in Figure 11.5). The field must be in the format *lib/file*. In this example, we are transferring the Test file from library **MyOwnLib**.

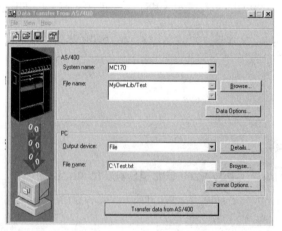

Figure 11.5: If all else fails, you can type in the explicit AS/400 path name to the file you want to download or upload.

- Use the Change System Value (CHGSYSVAL) command to change your user library list to include any library your user wants to perform a file transfer to or from. Be aware, however, that this is a global change that will modify the user library list for every AS/400 user on your system. Every user will now have access to these libraries.

- Change the individual user's user library list by creating a unique job description that contains its own user library list and then assigning it to that individual's user profile. First, create a unique job description with its own user library list by using the Create Job Description (CRTJOBD) command:

```
CRTJOBD JOBD(job-description-name) INLLIBL(QGPL SHARELIB)
```

- Now attach this job description to the user's profile by using the Change User Profile (CHGUSRPRF) command:

```
CHGUSRPRF USRPRF(profile-name)JOBD(job-description-name)
```

Now, whenever the user signs on, the user library list in the job description will override the user library list specified in QUSRLIBL. The library list will be customized according to the individual's needs, and it can be modified without affecting other users. An additional benefit is that this job description can be assigned to as many users as you want, giving groups of users access to the same libraries from a central location.

—Joe Hertvik

Changing the Limit on the Number of Transfer Sessions

I am currently involved in a project using Visual FoxPro (VFP) to both send and retrieve data between the PC and the AS/400, and I ran into a problem in which VFP would "choke" when trying to open more than two remote files on the AS/400. After a lot of searching, I found a parameter under the Common tab in the NetSoft (NS) Router Administration panel. When I clicked on the Advanced Properties button of the Common tab, I found an entry for subsystem QSERVER and a category called Session Limit. The number shown was 2, which was the same number of successful connections I could make. I wanted to change it to a much higher number, but the window stated that this parameter could not be changed.

I decided to look in the Windows NT Registry to see what I could find there. Using the REGEDIT command (which you can reach by clicking on Start/Run, typing REGEDIT, and clicking OK), I opened the Registry and searched for the string QSERVER. Surprise! I found it. I displayed the value of the key and behold! It had a binary value of 2! I changed this to a binary value of 8 and was able to run my program successfully.

—Bill Robins

Commands Missing on Upgrade

We had a client who had migrated from a CISC AS/400 to a RISC AS/400 running V4R4. This client also had an electronic data interchange (EDI) application running on an old DOS machine, and the EDI application required a file transfer from the AS/400 to process EDI data. In the past, we accomplished this by using the Copy to PC Document (CPYTOPCD) command. The strange thing was that, on the new RISC system, the CPYTOPCD and Copy from PC Document (CPYFRMPCD) commands weren't there! After much searching, we finally learned that these commands are available only if you install the OS/400 Licensed Program OS/400—Host Servers. This licensed program comes standard, as part of OS/400, and it was simple to load it from CD-ROM. As soon as we did that, we were back in business.

—Pete Sultatos

Excel Add-ins Are Easy!

Client Access provides a Microsoft Excel add-in for data transfer from the AS/400. I use Office 97 on NT workstations in my office and find this a very useful tool for putting AS/400 data into a spreadsheet. Once it's there, this data is available to all of the Office 97 products, such as Word.

Installing the add-in couldn't be easier, either. The Client Access online Users Guide provides very good instructions on installing and using this add-in. Simply open the Client Access Express User Guide and type **Excel Add-in** in the Index search box. You'll be presented some very short and easy instructions to follow on how to plug this add-in into your Excel spreadsheet.

—Jim Dole

Editor's Note: If you already had Excel installed on your PC when you installed Client Access Express (Express client) and performed a Full or Typical install of Express client, the Data Transfer add-in was automatically installed for you. If you performed a Custom install, you would need to select the Data Transfer Excel Add-in Support option manually.

Perform File Transfers with Client Access

Q: I read an *Midrange Computing* magazine article about Client Access file transfer, and I have a question. I have been working with the Client Access for Windows 95 file transfer product. I cannot find a way to do a transfer from the AS/400 to a PC file in an append mode. The only options here seem to be Overwrite or New file. In most of our file transfers, we need to do a transfer every day from an AS/400 query to the same Excel worksheet, adding to the daily query until the end of the month. Then we start a new worksheet. Any suggestions?

A: When you select the name of the file to which you want to write the data, you'll find a button beside the output device called details. Pressing this button reveals some information about the transfer and offers a check box to overwrite an existing file. You would think IBM would have placed an Append option here as well, but, as you discovered, it did not.

To perform this transfer daily to accumulate information, I suggest one of the following workaround methods. However, there are a couple of provisos.

Method 1: Transfer the file as a strict ASCII text or comma-delimited file.

This method is a two-step process. First, build the transfer request with the transfer request wizard (as you no doubt already have). Save the transfer query in a file named with the PC download file name followed by .TTO. Be sure you save the request, and run the program from the Client Access directory.

Next, build a batch file that looks something like the one shown in Figure 11.6. This DOS window batch program uses the unattended version of the transfer facility RTOPCB.EXE. The unattended version exists in the Client Access/400 subdirectory and is normally installed with the file transfer facility.

```
Transfer Program
 @echo off
 cls
 echo Downloading [pc download file name] and appending to [accumulated file
name]

 rtopcb.exe [pc download file name].TTO
 if exist [pc download file name] goto accumulate
 goto nodownload

 :accumulate
 copy [accumulated file name]+[pc download file name] [accumulated file name]
 echo [accumulated file name] was updated successfully
 del [pc download file name]
 goto exit

 :nodownload
 echo [pc download file name] was not downloaded or accumulated
 pause

 :exit
```

Figure 11.6: Use this PC batch file to transfer files.

If the file successfully downloads, the program then appends the newly downloaded file to the previously downloaded file. The program then deletes the new file so that it won't be appended twice. If no file was successfully downloaded, the program displays a message telling the user that nothing happened.

This append method works with ASCII text or comma-delimited files. It might not work on other specially formatted files that were designed for direct import into your spreadsheet.

Method 2: Transfer the file as a spreadsheet file.

Your best option is to transfer the new additions, import them into your spreadsheet, and cut and paste the cells into your accumulated data. Although this isn't very flashy, it'll do the trick. As your user gains proficiency, you can use spreadsheet macros to automate the process.

The best solution for this type of routine spreadsheet update is to bypass the file transfer facility altogether. Instead, use the Client Access/400 ODBC driver. Using the ODBC driver provides you with the most transparent means of maintaining the spreadsheet (the ODBC driver then becomes an integral part of the spreadsheet program itself). The query resides with the spreadsheet, instead of as a separate process.

—Thomas M. Stockwell

♦ ♦ ♦ DOS

Don't Let Zip Files Halt DOS Processing

Q: I have an application that reads from a PC diskette every month and retrieves some files to be loaded onto the AS/400. The problem is that the files are all text files (*.TXT) some times and all zip files (*.ZIP) at other times. To confuse the issue further, a mixture of *.TXT and *.ZIP files might even be on the same diskette! Is there any way to determine the file type programmatically so that I can use the appropriate technique to load it on my AS/400?

A: A DOS batch file could be the answer to your problem. Figure 11.7 shows a DOS batch file I wrote to extract data files. It reads the files on the diskette and appends the data in them to a new file using the DOS COPY operation. This new file is then uploaded to the AS/400. It also unzips any zip files before starting the append operation.

```
@Echo Off
Cls
:: variables: TempDir is a PC Work directory/folder to process files in
:: : DataFile is data file name(s) to be processed from A:
:: : Sendfile is PC file name to be sent to AS/400
Set TempDir=Qtemp1
Set DataFile=*.txt
Set SendFile=PCto400a.dta
Echo PC Batch Program %0 is running:
Echo.
Echo Processing PC file(s) received on Diskette...
Echo.
:AGAIN
:: errorlevels: 1=Yes, 2=No, 3=Cancel
Choice /C:YNC /N /T:C,60 Is Diskette in Drive A:? [Y-es,N-o,C-ancel]
If ErrorLevel 3 Goto :TheEnd
If ErrorLevel 2 Goto :AGAIN
:CLEARING
Echo Clearing Transfer work folder on PC...
C:
If not Exist \%TempDir%\nul Md \%TempDir%
Cd \%TempDir%
If Exist %DataFile% Del %DataFile%
If Exist %SendFile% Del %SendFile%
If Exist *.zip Del *.zip
Echo Copying %DataFile% PC files from A: to C:...
If Exist A:\%DataFile% Copy A:\%DataFile% C:
If Exist A:\*.Zip Copy A:\*.Zip C:
Echo Checking newly copied files on C:...
If Exist *.zip Goto :ZIPFILE
If Exist %DataFile% Goto :DATAFILES
Goto :ERROR1
:ZIPFILE
Echo Testing PC Zip file(s) for integrity...
PkUnZip -t *.zip
If ErrorLevel 1 Goto :ERROR2 Echo Unzipping PC file(s) with overwrite...
PkUnZip -o *.zip
Del *.Zip
:DATAFILES
Echo Appending PC %DataFile% data files together into one file...
Copy %DataFile% %SendFile%
If Not Exist %SendFile% Goto :ERROR3
:UPLOAD
Echo Uploading %SendFile% file to AS/400...
:: (put your FTP or RFROMPCB in here to upload PCto400a.dta)
Goto :TheEnd
:ERROR1
Echo ERROR: PC File(s) to be processed NOT found!
Pause
Goto :TheEnd
:ERROR2
```

Figure 11.7: This DOS batch file determines a file type before uploading it to your AS/400 (part 1 of 2).

```
Echo ERROR: PC Zip File could not be unzipped...
Pause
Goto :TheEnd
:ERROR3
Echo ERROR: PC Data file(s) could not be appended together...
Pause
Goto :TheEnd
:TheEnd
Echo PC Batch Program %0 is ending...
:: delete environment variables
Set TempDir=
Set DataFile=
Set SendFile=
Exit
```

Figure 11.7: This DOS batch file determines a file type before uploading it to your AS/400 (part 2 of 2).

For this technique to work, you must fill several requirements:

1. Process only files containing data. You should not process files such as a README.TXT file. If a file like this exists, delete it before the append operation in the example (DEL README*.*). Other "common" files might be relevant to your installation. If so, you need to add a line of text to the batch program to delete those files as well.

2. The *.TXT files sent to you must contain nonbinary data. The example batch program has no provisions for converting binary data.

3. The *.ZIP files must have a .ZIP extension, and text files within the zip file must have a *.TXT extension.

4. This example uses PKUNZIP, which is a data compression tool you can download from *www.pkunzip.com*, to unzip zip files. You might need to change this to use the zip utility on your system. If you do, make sure you also change the command line parameters required by that utility.

In this example, I've uploaded a file named **Pcto400a.Dta** to the AS/400. (You can change this file name to anything you like.) If you want this operation to run in "silent" mode (that is, without user input), remove the CHOICE and PAUSE keywords contained in the example batch program. Because DOS might be a bit foreign to many folks nowadays, I'll briefly review a few of the DOS commands used in the example.

- CLS clears the screen.

- SET sets a global DOS variable, which exists until the PC shuts down or the DOS window is closed or the variable is explicitly deleted. To learn more about this command, type SET /? at the DOS prompt.

- ECHO displays text on the screen.

- CHOICE lets the user input a character to the batch file. To learn more about this command, type CHOICE /? at the DOS prompt.

- ERRORLEVEL is a number set by certain DOS commands, such as MONMSG. "If errorlevel 3" actually means "If errorlevel >= 3."

- PAUSE makes the application wait until the user presses a key.

- %0 is the name of the PC .BAT file running. The parameter strings after %0 are %1, %2, etc.

To demonstrate this, create a one-line .BAT with "ECHO %0 %1 %2 %3 %4 %5" and run it with "YOURBAT.BAT THIS IS A PARM LIST."

Put the example in a file called something like BATXFER1.BAT, and you should be able to run it from Windows or DOS.

—Chris Ringer

✦ ✦ ✦ ODBC

Can't Update ODBC Table

Q: I am connecting to an AS/400 database using Visual Basic (VB) and the Open Database Connectivity (ODBC) driver from Client Access. I can't write to a table I need to update. Has anyone else had a similar problem?

A: In order for a table to be updatable using ODBC, it must have a unique key. If the table you are trying to update is attached to an Access database, you can determine if Access is recognizing the unique key by going into design mode on the table and looking at the primary key or the indexes. If there is no unique key, create one on the AS/400 table through normal means and then reattach the table to your database. You should then be able to update it from either VB or Access.

—Brian Singleton

✦ ✦ ✦ OV/400

MS Word Does OV/400

Did you know that Microsoft Word can read OfficeVision/400 documents directly? Just open Word and click on File/Open. If you have QDLS mapped to a drive letter, select that drive. Otherwise, look for your computer name by using the Windows Find command, which is available on the Windows Start menu.

Note: You'll need to search for Computer, not Files or Folders, on the Find command. Once you've located the QDLS folder, click on it to open it. Drill down until you find the document you want to use in Word, and open it. You might get a screen asking whether you want to translate. If you do, select Rich Text Format (RTF) as the document type to convert from.

That's all there is to it! One other thing to keep in mind is that most word processors will be able to translate these documents, too. For example, Corel WordPerfect also has a translator to convert your OV/400 documents.

—David Abramowitz

✦ ✦ ✦ Printing

Enhance PC5250 Visibility

Many times after you configure a Client Access/400 PC5250 session and begin using it, you need to print whatever is on the screen to your local printer. If you are using the default printer settings, you might find that the printed output is so small that you can't read it. There's an easy way to fix this; just change the font used by PC5250 for printing to use Courier New. You can do this by following these steps:

1. Bring up the PC5250 display session.

2. Select File/Printer Control/Text on the PC5250 menu bar.

3. Click on the down arrow next to Font and select Courier New out of the list; then, click on the OK button to close the Printer Control dialog box.

Now, your screen prints should print in a readable size.

—Shannon O'Donnell

Temporary Files Can Cause Permanent Printing Problems

General protection faults (GPFs), page faults, and stack faults that occur when printing are often caused by garbage on the hard drive. Problems include leftover temp files, lost allocation units, cross-linked files, and defragmentation. Therefore, before pursuing a defect in one of the Client Access/400 printer emulators, it is best to clean up the hard drive. This up-front work could resolve the problem and relieve you from having to deal with PTFs, Service Packs, printer drivers, traces, and so on. Following are the steps to take to clean up your hard drive.

When Using Windows 95/98 or Windows NT

1. Close all applications.

2. Click on the Windows Start button, select Programs and MS-DOS Prompt.

3. At the DOS prompt, type SET to find out the name of the TEMP directory. For example, it might say TEMP=C:\WINDOWS\ TEMP or TEMP=C:\DOS.

4. Bring up the Windows Explorer, and check the TEMP directory for any leftover temp files or temp folders. Anything in the TEMP folder is, by default, a temporary file. If you find any, delete them by selecting all of them and then selecting File/Delete on the menu bar (or by pressing the Delete key on your keyboard).

5. From inside Windows Explorer, right-click on the hard drive and select Properties from the pop-up menu.

6. From the Properties dialog box for the hard drive, click on the Tools tab and then click on the Check Now button. This process brings up the ScanDisk utility, which scans the hard drive for lost allocation units and cross-linked files. Select which hard drives you wish to scan, select the type of test you wish to run (usually, a standard test is sufficient), make sure that Automatically fix errors is checked, and click on the Start button. Go back to your hard drive properties again when the program finishes.

7. From the Properties dialog box for the hard drive, click on the Tools tab and then click on the Defragment Now button. This process brings up the Disk Defragmenter utility, which improves the performance of your hard drive. You can use the Select Drive button to choose which hard drive to defragment (it is recommended that you defragment all of your hard drives at this point).

Once a hard drive has been selected, click on the Start button to defragment that hard drive.

8. If running the ScanDisk utility reveals any problems, reinstall Client Access/400 for Windows 95/NT (including PC5250) and the Windows 95 or Windows NT printer driver.

When Using Windows 3.1 or Windows for Workgroups 3.11

1. Exit Windows 3.1 or Windows for Workgroups 3.11.

2. At the DOS prompt, type **SET** to find out the name of the TEMP directory. For example, it might say TEMP=C:\WINDOWS\TEMP or TEMP=C:\DOS.

3. Type **CD** followed by the temp directory name (for example, **CD C:\WINDOWS\TEMP** or **CD C:\DOS**).

4. Go to the temp directory and type **DIR*.TMP** to check for any leftover temp files. If you find any, type **DEL *.TMP**.

5. Type either **SCANDISK** or **CHKDSK /F** to scan the hard drive for lost allocation units and cross-linked files.

6. Type **DEFRAG C: /F /R /H /SE /B** to defragment the hard drive. *Note:* This command automatically reboots the PC when finished.

7. If you do not have SCANDISK, CHKDSK, or DEFRAG, obtain a third-party utility such as Norton Disk Doctor to ensure that the hard drive is cleaned up.

8. If running SCANDISK, CHKDSK, or a third-party utility reveals any problems, reinstall Client Access for Windows 3.1 (including RUMBA/400 or PC5250) and the Windows printer driver.

Note: *In either case, you may need to reinstall the operating system to replace important modules that might have been damaged.*

—*Shannon O'Donnell*

✦ ✦ ✦ Screen Capture

Capturing the Elusive AS/400 Screen

Designing or documenting a system often requires that word-processing documents contain AS/400 screen captures, but have you tried to do this? Before I learned the following trick to handle this problem, I would create a box or some other word-processing structure and fill it with the contents of the screen. I had to concern myself with fonts and font sizes to ensure that everything lined up as it would on an AS/400 screen.

If you use a Windows workstation with emulation, however, there is an easier way. Hold down the Alt key and press Print Screen, and the current window is placed onto the Windows clipboard. If the current window is an AS/400 session, for example, that screen is placed on the clipboard. This is always the case even if Alt+Print Screen is defined as System Request. If the System Request line appears at the bottom of your window, press Reset. You may then go to your word-processing program (or spreadsheet or presentation program) and paste the contents.

Because the clipboard pastes in the same fashion for Windows paint or imaging programs, the technique works for any active window you might want to place onto another document. I even use it to save the last screen of a game after I've reached my personal high!

—William W. Smyth

Screen Printing Uses Less Paper

I have a tip for how to capture a PC screen by using the Print key. In my Client Access color mapping, I set the screen color to white and change the field colors to black (or any dark color). When I print these screens, they are easier to read, and I use less ink.

—Tim Cortez

Taking a Snapshot Without Pasting

I read an article in *Midrange Computing* magazine that noted how to copy the entire Windows desktop image into the clipboard by pressing Print Screen and then pasting into another application such as Paint. You should also note that, to copy an image of just the active window, you can simply press the key combination Alt+Print Screen. For instructional purposes, it is advantageous to include screens of your AS/400 interactive programs as part of your user documentation. However, in 5250 sessions, Alt+Print Screen maps to System Request and therefore prevents you from capturing the active 5250 window. To overcome this, start a temporary 5250 session and delete the keyboard mapping for Alt+Print Screen inside your new 5250 session.

—Chris Ringer

Printing

Printing

In This Chapter

Date and Time

Graphics

Overflow

PC Printers

Performance

Print Key

Printer Messages

Remote Printing

RLU

Routing Spool Files

Security

Spool File Attributes

Spool File Contents

Spool File
    Management

*I*f you want to enjoy an exciting or stimulating conversation with someone, you might talk about art or literature or politics or religion or sports, but you most likely will not talk about printing. Printing is something every information-processing shop must do, but about which no one gives more thought than is necessary. Yet, printing is one of the most important tasks that takes place in businesses, and therefore deserves more attention and better treatment than what it gets. Information professionals should strive to excel at printing.

The "paperless office" was predicted years ago, but the truth is that businesses generate more paper than ever before. Paperless technologies such as electronic data interchange (EDI) and email have served only to curb the rate of growth in paper.

For these reasons, IT shops should concern themselves less with buying the latest and greatest hardware or "killer app" software and concentrate more on the basics—beginning with printing.

To print, somebody must generate a report. Of course, every iSeries programmer knows how to write programs that build reports, but you'll find a few topics here for enhancing the appearance and contents of spool files. Once the spool file is produced, it must be routed to the appropriate destination. Some topics included here address that challenge. Then there's the matter—which is no small matter—of managing the printers. That chore eats up a lot of valuable time in many iSeries shops. Maybe one or more of the tips in this chapter will help you get a better grip on the printing problems you face.

—*Ted Holt*

✦ ✦ ✦ Date and Time

Printer File Dates

Q: In printer file DDS, the DATE and TIME keywords are used to print the date and time of the spool file. When a job is submitted and run on the same day, the date and time match the spool file date and time. When a job is submitted before midnight, and the spool file is created after midnight, the date printed is the job date (before midnight), but the time printed is the actual time. The date and time the spool file is created is displayed on the WRKSPLF screen. The date printed should be the spool file creation date, and not the job date. Is this possible?

A: The printer file DATE keyword has two possible parameters: *JOB (the default) or *SYS. So simply specify DATE(*SYS) and you are done!

—Edmund Reinhardt

✦ ✦ ✦ Graphics

Print Graphics on iSeries Printers

Q: IBM says you can print images and graphics on the AS/400 using an intelligent printer data stream (IPDS) printer, but no documentation tells you how to put the images onto the machine. Do I need a special software package? Isn't there a quick and inexpensive means of putting images on the AS/400?

A: Two types of image files can reside on the AS/400: Page Segments and Overlays. Both are raster image file formats—files that are composed of pixel representations. The import support to convert images to these native AS/400 formats was primarily designed for S/370 IOCA and GOCA file formats. Consequently, IBM's solutions to place image files on the AS/400 have a particular S/370 flavor about them.

Fortunately, a freethinking programmer in Rochester sneaked a nifty conversion trick into PC Support (now known as Client Access). This trick allows you to "print" any Windows image into an AFPDS file and then convert it to a page segment or overlay on the AS/400. This means that any image you can create in Windows can be used as an image on the AS/400. Briefly, here are the steps.

Install the Client Access AFPDS printer driver onto Windows. This printer driver is a standard option with the Client Access Windows installation program PCSETUPW.EXE.

In the Windows Control Panel, open the Printers icon and find the new IBM AFPDS printer. Use the Connect button to connect this driver to FILE. This will redirect the AFPDS output to a file of your choosing when the driver is activated.

Create your images using any Windows tool at your disposal. Don't forget that handheld scanners are a quick way to capture real-life product images. When the image is ready, print it to the AFPDS driver. Windows will redirect the driver to output the AFPDS image to a file. It will prompt you for the file name.

Using a file transfer program, like Client Access's file transfer facility, copy this new image file to the AS/400. Put it into an empty physical file with a record length of 1024 bytes.

Use the Create Page Segment (CRTPAGSEG) or Create Overlay (CRTOVL) command to convert the AFPDS file to the appropriate Page Segment (*PAGSEG) or Overlay (*OVL) object. Place the newly created object in an appropriate library. You can then clear or delete the physical file that held the AFPDS output.

Your image is now on the AS/400, ready for use by RPG, DDS, or the OVRPRTF command.

—*Thomas M. Stockwell*

Print in Black-and-White to Save Ink

I have a tip for capturing and printing green screen displays. In my Client Access color mapping, I set the screen color to white and change the field colors to black (or any dark color). When I print these screens, they are easier to read, and I use less ink.

—*Tim Cortez*

✦ ✦ ✦ Overflow

How Do You Spell Overflow?

RPG programmers are well accustomed to checking for printer overflow in RPG programs. Perhaps the most common method is by coding an indicator in the file description specification of a printer file. Another method, one that works for externally described printer files, is to code an indicator in the "Lo" resulting indicator position of a C-spec, using the WRITE operation.

There's another way that gives more flexibility than either of those methods. Use the printer information data structure (INFDS). When coding the file specification, specify a file INFDS. In the following F-spec, the RPG III program defines printer file PRINT with a file information data structure called PINFDS.

```
     FPRINT   O   E                01     PRINTER       KINFDS PINFDS
```

The data structure needs two subfields, one for overflow line and one for current line, as follows.

```
     IPINFDS       DS
     I                                           B 188 1890CURLIN
     I                                           B 347 3680OFLINE
```

This comes in handy with multiple line printing. Suppose you have a group of lines, each one defined as a separate record, which should print together on the same page. If you use either the indicator on the WRITE op code or the indicator on the file specification, you will not know you hit overflow until you hit it. Part of the group might print at the bottom of one page while the rest of the group prints on the top of the next page. Using the printer INFDS lets you determine how many lines remain until page overflow. If you determine that there is not enough room left on the page to accommodate the entire group, you can print them at the top of the next page instead.

Even when I use this method, I still code an indicator in each printer file specification I use. RPG will hard halt if you reach overflow and do not have an indicator specified either in the file definition spec or on the WRITE op code. Because there is only one file definition spec and there are many WRITES, I opt for the easier of the two.

—Tim Johnston

✦ ✦ ✦ PC Printers

OpsNav Prints Spool Files

If you have Client Access/400 V2R3 or above and CA/400 Operations Navigator (OpsNav) loaded on your PC, there's a handy way to transfer a spool file from your AS/400 to your PC. Open OpsNav and double-click on the Basic Operations icon. Then, double-click on the Printer Output icon.

The PC client queries your AS/400 and returns a list of AS/400 spooled files owned by your user profile. To move one or all of these spooled files to the PC, click on it and drag it to the desktop. You now have a text file (**.txt**) of the same name as the spool file on your PC. To print it, double-click on the document to open the word processor registered to handle ***.txt** file types and select Print from within. That's all there is to it!

—Shannon O'Donnell

Printing AS/400 Spool Files on a PC

Most software that connects a PC to an AS/400 provides a way to treat the PC printer as an AS/400 printer. However, printing an AS/400 report on your PC printer can be slow and can get expensive when you're running a dial-up connection.

To keep my long-distance bill from getting out of hand, I wrote a PC application to print AS/400 spool files to my PC without being connected to an AS/400. I dial up the AS/400, save the spool file to a database file, and transfer the database file to my PC. Only after hanging up the phone do I print the spool file to my PC printer.

This application consists of a DOS batch file called PRT400.BAT (see Figure 12.1) and a QBASIC program, PRT400.BAS (see Figure 12.2). To run this application, do the following:

1. Build the report on the AS/400.

2. Create a database file with a record length that is 4 bytes longer than the report's record length. For example,

```
CRTPF QGPL/REPORT RCDLEN(136)
```

3. Copy the spool file into the database file, specifying CTLCHAR(*PRTCTL).

```
CPYSPLF FILE(QPRINT) +
   TOFILE(QTEMP/REPORT) +
   CTLCHAR(*PRTCTL)
```

4. Transfer the database file to the PC.

5. Run batch file PRT400 (Figure 12.1), which calls the QBASIC program (Figure 12.2) on the PC.

```
@rem . Print an AS/400 report stored in a disk file
@rem . The report must have been built with CPYSPLF, specifying CTLCHR(*PRTCTL)
@if not "%1"=="" set prtin=%1
@if not "%2"=="" set prtout=%2
@qbasic /run prt400.bas
```

Figure 12.1: Use DOS batch file PRT400.BAT to print a spool file.

```
' Print an AS/400 report built by CPYSPLF CTLCHR(*PRTCTL)

GOSUB OpenFiles
CurLine% = 1

DO WHILE EOF(1) <> -1
   LINE INPUT #1, PrtLine$
   IF MID$(PrtLine$, 1, 3) > "   " THEN
      SkipBefore% = VAL(MID$(PrtLine$, 1, 3))
      IF SkipBefore% < CurLine% THEN
         PRINT #2, CHR$(12)
         CurLine% = 1
      END IF
      DO WHILE CurLine% < SkipBefore%
         PRINT #2, ""
         CurLine% = CurLine% + 1
      LOOP
   END IF
   IF MID$(PrtLine$, 4, 1) > " " THEN
      SpaceBefore% = VAL(MID$(PrtLine$, 4, 1))
      FOR i% = 1 TO SpaceBefore%
         PRINT #2, ""
         CurLine% = CurLine% + 1
      NEXT i%
   END IF
   PRINT #2, MID$(PrtLine$, 5);
LOOP

CLOSE #1
CLOSE #2
SYSTEM

OpenFiles:

RptIn$ = ENVIRON$("PRTIN")
IF RptIn$ = "" THEN
   INPUT "Enter the name of the file containing the report. ", RptIn$
   IF RptIn$ = "" THEN
      PRINT "No input file specified, job is canceled."
      SYSTEM
   END IF
END IF
```

Figure 12.2: The input file to QBASIC program PRT400.BAS must be built by CPYSPLF (part 1 of 2).

```
RptOut$ = ENVIRON$("PRTOUT")
IF RptOut$ = "" THEN
    INPUT "Enter the name of the printer file. ", RptOut$
    IF RptOut$ = "" THEN
        RptOut$ = "LPT1"
    END IF
END IF

ON ERROR GOTO BadFileName
FileName$ = RptIn$
FileMode$ = "input"
OPEN RptIn$ FOR INPUT AS #1
FileName$ = RptOut$
FileMode$ = "output"
OPEN RptOut$ FOR OUTPUT AS #2
ON ERROR GOTO 0

' Include printer setup commands here, if desired
IF RptOut$ = "LPT1" THEN
    PRINT #2, CHR$(15);
END IF

RETURN

BadFileName:
PRINT "File "; FileName$; " could not be opened for ";
PRINT FileMode$; ". Job is canceled."
SYSTEM
```

Figure 12.2: The input file to QBASIC program PRT400.BAS must be built by CPYSPLF (part 2 of 2).

The batch file accepts two parameters: the name of the PC file containing the AS/400 spool file and the name of the file to print to. If you don't enter a parameter, the QBASIC program will prompt for it. If you don't specify a printer file name in the second parameter, the QBASIC program defaults to LPT1.

To print the report, then, you would enter a command like this:

```
C:\>prt400 \temp\report1.txt lpt1
```

If you use this utility, you might need to modify it for your printer. There is a place at the end of the OpenFiles subroutine to put printer setup commands. In this version, I print an ASCII 15, which sets an Epson printer to condensed mode. I also have used this application in situations in which I had no printer connection. For instance, I can print a spool file sent to me by Internet email. Information on QBASIC can be found at: *http://www.qbasic.com/*.

—Ted Holt

✦ ✦ ✦ Performance

Duplication of Spool Files

Sometimes we want to split a big spool file between two or more printers to speed up a printing process. To do that, we must duplicate the spool file and then, using the Change Spooled File Attributes (CHGSPLFA) command, we specify the PAGERANGE parameter for each spool file.

I found that the Send TCP/IP Spooled File (SNDTCPSPLF) command could do the job. To use this feature, you need V3R1 or higher of OS/400. Spool files can be duplicated to any output queue entered at the PRTQ keyword. The command creates a duplicate spool file in the job named QPRTJOB as shown in Figure 12.3.

```
SNDTCPSPLF RMTSYS(*INTNETADR) +
   PRTQ('QGPL/QPRINT') +
   FILE(QSYSPRT) +
   JOB(012345/USER/JOBNAME) +
   SPLNBR(1) DESTTYP(*AS400) +
   TRANSFORM(*NO) +
   INTNETADR('127.0.0.1') +
   DLTSPLF(*NO)
```

Figure 12.3: SNDTCPSPLF provides one way to duplicate a spool file.

IP address 127.0.0.1 is a reserved address for any local machine.

—Ira Shapiro

Split Consecutive Processing Jobs

You can speed up the processing of certain types of jobs that perform consecutive processing by splitting them into separate jobs that perform smaller tasks. For example, suppose you run a monthly statement program that prints statements in customer number order. You could change the program to print only statements for a range of customer numbers. Then you could submit a statement run for the first half of the customers by specifying customers 0 through 499999 and one for 500000 through 999999. By running these two jobs at the same time, the overall process should run more quickly. All you have to do is split up the process into logical sections and run these jobs simultaneously.

—Andre Nortje

✦ ✦ ✦ Print Key

Modifying Print Screen Output

There are several options for the way output is created when you press the Print key. When the system is shipped, the default value for the QPRTKEYFMT system value is *PRTHDR, which specifies that header information is provided in the output. If you change this system value to *PRTBDR, border information is printed instead. If you specify *PRTALL, then header and border information are included with the output.

The QPRTKEYFMT system value affects the Print Key output for all jobs on the system. If you want to change the Print key output for your job only, use the Change Job (CHGJOB) command and specify an option on the PRTKEYFMT parameter. This parameter has all of the same options as the system value.

—Midrange Computing Staff

✦ ✦ ✦ Printer Messages

Automatically Reply to Printer Messages

In our data center, we print hundreds of spool files with thousands of pages each day. Our operators rely on messages CPA3394 (load a certain form) and CPA4002 (verify alignment).

Our users, however, use virtual printers. These messages don't apply to them and only confuse them.

We use the system reply list to automatically answer inquiry messages when they are sent from virtual printers. Entries in the system reply list are easily added using the Add Reply List Entry (ADDRPYLE) command. Required parameters for this command are sequence number, message ID, and reply.

The sequence number is a unique reply list number between 1 and 9999. Message ID is the inquiry message that we want the system to intercept. The reply parameter is how the system will reply to the intercepted inquiry message.

ADDRPYLE also has an optional Compare data (CMPDTA) parameter, which has two fields. In the first field, you may enter up to 32 characters of message text. In the second field, you can specify at what starting position within the message to look for the compare data text. When you use this parameter, each message is searched for the compare data text at the designated starting point. Figure 12.4 shows the commands to add system reply list entries for one of our virtual printers.

```
ADDRPYLE SEQNBR(3001) MSGID(CPA3394) CMPDTA(ACCT_HP5SI 41) RPY(I)
ADDRPYLE SEQNBR(3002) MSGID(CPA4002) CMPDTA(ACCT_HP5SI 41) RPY(G)
```

Figure 12.4: These commands eliminate unneeded operator messages for a virtual printer.

We wrote a CL program (Figure 12.5) to add all virtual printers (about 150 of them) to the system reply list. We run this program through the job scheduler. It updates our reply list for all added and deleted printers since the last time it was run. We randomly selected the 3*xxx* series of sequence numbers in the system reply list to be used only for virtual printers, and we will not manually add any entries within the range we wouldn't want the CL program to remove.

```
/*===============================================================*/
/* To compile:                                                   */
/*                                                               */
/*           CRTCLPGM    PGM(XXX/RPY001CL) SRCFILE(XXX/QCLSRC)   */
/*                                                               */
/*===============================================================*/
PGM

    DCLF       FILE(QADSPOBJ)
    DCL        VAR(&SEQNBR) TYPE(*DEC) LEN(4 0)
    DCL        VAR(&BGNSEQNBR) TYPE(*DEC) LEN(4 0) VALUE(3000)
    DCL        VAR(&ENDSEQNBR) TYPE(*DEC) LEN(4 0)

    CHGVAR     VAR(&ENDSEQNBR) VALUE(&BGNSEQNBR + 999)

    /* Clear existing reply list entries for virtual printers */
    CHGVAR     VAR(&SEQNBR) VALUE(&BGNSEQNBR)
LOOP1:
    IF         COND(&SEQNBR *GT &ENDSEQNBR) THEN(DO)
        GOTO       CMDLBL(MAKEDEVLST)
    ENDDO

    RMVRPYLE   SEQNBR(&SEQNBR)
    MONMSG     MSGID(CPF2556)
    CHGVAR     VAR(&SEQNBR) VALUE(&SEQNBR + 1)
    GOTO       CMDLBL(LOOP1)

    /* Create file of all device descriptions */
MAKEDEVLST:
    DSPOBJD    OBJ(*ALL) OBJTYPE(*DEVD) OUTPUT(*OUTFILE) +
```

Figure 12.5: RPY001CL creates system reply list entries for all virtual printers (part 1 of 2).

```
                 OUTFILE(QTEMP/QADSPOBJ)

   /* Reset reply list sequence number */
   CHGVAR      VAR(&SEQNBR) VALUE(&BGNSEQNBR)

   /* Receive list of virtual printers & add each to system reply list */
   OVRDBF      FILE(QADSPOBJ) TOFILE(QTEMP/QADSPOBJ)
LOOP2:
   RCVF
   MONMSG      MSGID(CPF0864) EXEC(DO) /* End of file */
      GOTO        CMDLBL(FINISH)
   ENDDO

   IF          COND(&ODOBAT *EQ PRTVRT) THEN(DO) /* Virtual +
                  printer */
      CHGVAR      VAR(&SEQNBR) VALUE(&SEQNBR + 1)
      ADDRPYLE    SEQNBR(&SEQNBR) MSGID(CPA3394) +
                    CMPDTA(&ODOBNM 41) RPY(I) /* Ignore load +
                    forms messages */
      CHGVAR      VAR(&SEQNBR) VALUE(&SEQNBR + 1)
      ADDRPYLE    SEQNBR(&SEQNBR) MSGID(CPA4002) +
                    CMPDTA(&ODOBNM 41) RPY(G) /* Take GO to +
                    verify alignment messages */
   ENDDO
   GOTO        CMDLBL(LOOP2)

FINISH:
   DLTOVR      FILE(QADSPOBJ)
ENDPGM
```

Figure 12.5: RPY001CL creates system reply list entries for all virtual printers (part 2 of 2).

It's not enough to create these reply list entries. Users' jobs must be instructed to use the system reply list. One way to do this is with the Change Job (CHGJOB) command:

```
CHGJOB INQMSGRPY(*SYSRPYL)
```

Another way is to change the job descriptions that the users use:

```
CHGJOBD JOBD(USRJOBD) INQMSGRPY(*SYSPLYL)
```

One note of caution: Before changing users' jobs or job descriptions, make sure there are no reply list entries you wouldn't want them to have. We had an entry of MSGID(RPG0000) RPY(D) in our reply list. This caused all RPG messages, even those the calling program was monitoring for, to be dumped.

Try using the system reply list to intercept printer messages. It might just intercept messages that are headed for your help desk as well!

—Gordon Brucks

Eliminate Undesired Alignment Messages

Are you tired of answering all those messages in order to get your AS/400 printer started? Are you a user experienced in loading a new form type and aligning it at the same time? If so, this solution is for you.

If you don't want any "load form type" messages for a particular printer, you can specify *NOMSG in the Message option element of the FORMTYPE parameter of the Start Printer Writer (STRPRTWTR) command. You can also use the Change Writer (CHGWTR) command or change the command default value to affect all printers on the system. See the *CL Reference* manual for more information.

Another way to reduce the number of messages that require a reply is to specify *INFO for the printer error message in the printer device description. See the Create Device Description Printer (CRTDEVPRT) and Change Device Description Printer (CHGDEVPRT) commands in the *CL Reference* manual for information about setting the PRTERRMSG parameter.

If the printer error message is *INFO, the printer writer automatically rechecks the printer after issuing message CPA3387 ("device not available"). For example, if a writer is started to printer PRT01, but PRT01 is not ready, message CPA3387 is sent to the message queue. If PRT01 has *INFO specified for PRTERRMSG, the writer retries PRT01 after 30 seconds. If PRT01 is ready, the writer starts printing files. If PRT01 is still not ready, the writer keeps checking PRT01 every 30 seconds.

—Janine Fix

✦ ✦ ✦ Remote Printing

Eliminate an LPD Timing Problem

I recently had a problem when sending a large spool file to a printer via an LPD output queue. The report wasn't printing. The problem was that the AS/400 would contact the printer and then begin to convert the file for transmission. By the time the AS/400 finished converting the file, the session had timed out on the printer (LaserJet 5SI), so the file wouldn't get sent.

I solved the problem by creating two output queues, as in Figure 12.6. The first, CONVERT, specifies TRANSFORM(*YES), to cause the system to convert an SNA Character Stream (SCS) printer stream to ASCII. CONVERT is directed to the Internet address *LOOPBACK and the remote printer name of the second output queue, TRANSMIT. The second output queue was directed to the printer's address. This setup enabled the AS/400 to have the spool file already converted before attempting to send it.

```
CRTOUTQ OUTQ(QGPL/CONVERT) RMTSYS(*INTNETADR) RMTPRTQ(TRANSMIT) +
    CNNTYPE(*IP) DESTTYPE(*OTHER) TRANSFORM(*YES) +
    MFRTYPMDL(*HP4) INTNETADR(*LOOPBACK) +
    TEXT('outq to convert spool files and return them to400')

CRTOUTQ OUTQ(QGPL/TRANSMIT) RMTSYS(*INTNETADR) RMTPRTQ(PR1) +
    CNNTYPE(*IP) DESTTYPE(*OTHER) TRANSFORM(*NO) +
    INTNETADR('170.21.200.31') +
    TEXT('outq to transmit converted spool files')
```

Figure 12.6: Using two output queues eliminated an LPD timing problem.

—*Monty Green*

✦ ✦ ✦ RLU

Conversion from Display File to Printer File

Recently, I had the need to create a history report, and I wanted it to have the same look and feel as the display used by the history inquiry program. I used Report Layout Utility (RLU) to work with the display file source. Upon saving the member, RLU converts the display file source to printer file source, commenting out the display-specific DDS. The member type will still be DSPF, but you can change this to PRTF.

—*Steve Kontos*

Renaming PRTF Source and RLU

If an RLU-created printer file source member is renamed or if it is copied to another member, the resulting member will contain the old default printer device file and library names as maintained by RLU. Because RLU uses these default names for creating the printer file, the printer file could be inadvertently created using the wrong printer file or library name. The default values in the DDS for creating the printer file can be changed by using SEU or by selecting 'Y' for the Create printer file and Change defaults parameters on the Exit RLU panel.

—*Andy Stubbs*

✦ ✦ ✦ Routing Spool Files

Help Users Find Their Output

Banner pages are a great way to help you identify who owns printer output. But if the banner page is separated from the rest of the report, or if you turn off banner pages to save paper, you're stuck. There is a job attribute, Print Text (PRTTXT) that you can use to solve this problem. The text in PRTTXT will be at the bottom of every printed page.

Figure 12.7 shows a program that changes the print text to indicate the owner of the output. It can be called from your initial program and, because the default PRTTXT parameter on the Submit Job (SBMJOB) command is *CURRENT, even output from batch jobs will be easy to recognize.

```
PGM
  DCL       VAR(&USER) TYPE(*CHAR) LEN(10)
  DCL       VAR(&FOOTER) TYPE(*CHAR) LEN(32)

  RTVJOBA   USER(&USER)
  CHGVAR    VAR(&FOOTER) VALUE('This page belongs to ' +
              *CAT &USER *TCAT '.')
  CHGJOB    PRTTXT(&FOOTER)
ENDPGM
```

Figure 12.7: Make a user's initial program call this program in order to identify printer output.

—Jim Stephenson

Print a Spooled File to More Than One Printer

You can speed up printing of large reports by using two or more printers at the same time. Use the SNADS Send Network Spooled File (SNDNETSPLF) command on the command line or as option 1 on the Work with Spooled Files (WRKSPLF) command; instead of sending the spooled file to another system, send it to a user on the same system. Make sure to specify DTAFMT(*ALLDATA) on the SNDNETSPLF command to preserve all the spooled file's attributes on the copy.

After the spooled file has been duplicated, use the Change Spooled File Attributes (CHGSPLFA) command to change the output queue to the proper printer and the PAGERANGE parameter to get each printer to print a different range of pages.

—Adrian Ramotar

Printing Anywhere on Demand

Our users can send reports to any printer on the system on demand. Pressing the attention key from any program or menu displays our office productivity menu, which has an Attn to select printers. When the user selects this option, program CHGPRTRCL (Figure 12.8) is called to retrieve the printers from the system and put the list in a file with the DSPOBJD command. The nice thing about this is that the object text is also put in the file. Therefore, the description of the printer is available to be displayed and the users can then identify where the printer is.

```
CHGPRTRCL: +
  PGM

  DCL VAR(&OUTQ)        TYPE(*CHAR) LEN(10)

  DSPOBJD OBJ(QUSRSYS/*ALL) OBJTYPE(*OUTQ) OUTPUT(*OUTFILE) +
    OUTFILE(TEMPOUTQ) OUTMBR(*FIRST *REPLACE)
  MONMSG MSGID(CPF9860)

  RTVJOBA OUTQ(&OUTQ)
  OVRDSPF FILE(CHGPRTR) TOFILE(CHGPRTRDF)
  CALL PGM(CHGPRTRPG) PARM(&OUTQ)
  DLTOVR FILE(CHGPRTR)
  CHGJOB JOB(*) OUTQ(&OUTQ)

  ENDPGM
```

Figure 12.8: The CL program CHGPRTRCL retrieves the list of available printers.

Program CHGPRTRRG (Figure 12.9) is then called, which displays the printers (based on our naming conventions) in a subfile display, CHGPRTRDF (Figure 12.10). The users can place an 'X' beside the printer they want to use. When the user exits the program, the CHGJOB command is executed using the selected printer name as the new OUTQ.

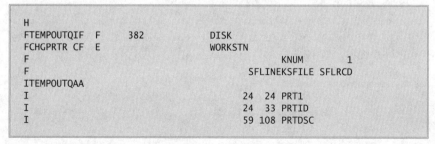

Figure 12.9: The RPG program CHGPRTRRG allows a user to select a printer from a subfile (part 1 of 2).

```
C            *ENTRY    PLIST
C                      PARM             PRINT  10
C*
C                      MOVE PRINT       SCPRT
C                      EXSR SUB1
C                      WRITEFKEYS
C                      EXFMTSFLCTL
C*
C            *INKC     DOWEQ'0'
C            *IN98     DOUEQ'1'
C                      READCSFLRCD                        98
C            *IN98     IFEQ '0'
C                      MOVE *BLANK      SFSEL
C                      UPDATSFLRCD
C                      MOVE SFPRT       SCPRT
C                      SETON                        98
C                      MOVE SCPRT       PRINT
C                      END
C                      END
C                      WRITEFKEYS
C                      EXFMTSFLCTL
C                      END
C                      SETON                             LR
C*
C            SUB1      BEGSR
C                      Z-ADD1           SFLINE  30
C                      READ TEMPOUTQ                      99
C            *IN99     DOWEQ'0'
C            PRT1      IFEQ 'P'
C            PRT1      OREQ 'Q'
C                      MOVE PRTID       SFPRT
C                      MOVE PRTDSC      SFDSC
C                      WRITESFLRCD
C                      ADD  1           SFLINE
C                      END
C                      READ TEMPOUTQ                      99
C                      END
C                      ENDSR
```

Figure 12.9: The RPG program CHGPRTRRG allows a user to select a printer from a subfile (part 2 of 2).

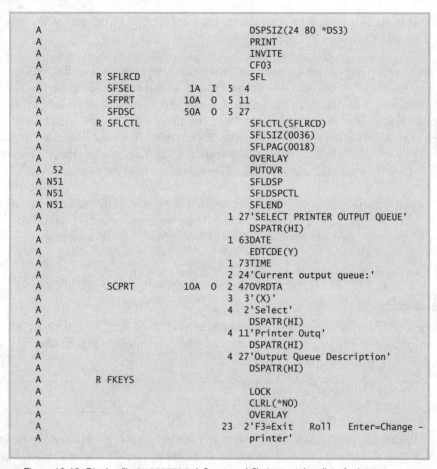

```
A                                           DSPSIZ(24 80 *DS3)
A                                           PRINT
A                                           INVITE
A                                           CF03
A           R SFLRCD                        SFL
A             SFSEL      1A  I  5  4
A             SFPRT     10A  O  5 11
A             SFDSC     50A  O  5 27
A           R SFLCTL                        SFLCTL(SFLRCD)
A                                           SFLSIZ(0036)
A                                           SFLPAG(0018)
A                                           OVERLAY
A    52                                     PUTOVR
A   N51                                     SFLDSP
A   N51                                     SFLDSPCTL
A   N51                                     SFLEND
A                                        1 27'SELECT PRINTER OUTPUT QUEUE'
A                                           DSPATR(HI)
A                                        1 63DATE
A                                           EDTCDE(Y)
A                                        1 73TIME
A                                        2 24'Current output queue:'
A             SCPRT     10A  O           2 47OVRDTA
A                                        3  3'(X)'
A                                        4  2'Select'
A                                           DSPATR(HI)
A                                        4 11'Printer Outq'
A                                           DSPATR(HI)
A                                        4 27'Output Queue Description'
A                                           DSPATR(HI)
A           R FKEYS
A                                           LOCK
A                                           CLRL(*NO)
A                                           OVERLAY
A                                       23  2'F3=Exit   Roll   Enter=Change -
A                                           printer'
```

Figure 12.10: Display file CHGPRTRDF defines a subfile to contain a list of printers.

Note: *This program gives you the capability to change your output only to an OUTQ with a corresponding printer of the same name.*

—*Bruce Knoll*

Route Printer Output by User Profile

As with most AS/400 shops, my company needed to direct certain printed output to specific printers. After trying several methods to accomplish this, we decided on the following technique: We created a database that contains user ID/document/printer combinations. This method required the least amount of effort on our part while remaining accurate and effective.

When users initiate print jobs, we present them with a screen that displays the possible printers to which they can send their documents and suggests the "best" printer for the specific document. For example, if certain users should be printing only on printers defined with 8-x-15-inch continuous feed forms, we accommodate them by presenting a list of printers as defined in our user ID/document/printer database. Once they select a printer, we use the values defined in our database for that printer, apply them to the Override Printer File (OVRPRTF) command, and voilà! The document is routed to the correct printer!

When you initialize a program, this same method can be used so that screen prints are routed to the correct printer and output queue. In such a case, apply the values from your user ID/program combination database to the Change Job (CHGJOB) command.

—Matti Kujala

Routing Reports

Using the Change User Print Information (CHGUSRPRTI) and Retrieve User Print Information (RTVUSRPRTI) commands, you can add routing instructions to your reports. Use CHGUSRPRTI to maintain your routing text information.

```
CHGUSRPRTI USER(JONES) +
    TEXT('Deliver to Mr. Jones')
```

Once you've done that, you can use RTVUSRPRTI to retrieve this information for use in your programs. Figure 12.11 illustrates how to add the text from the user's print information to the bottom of every page of the report.

```
PGM

DCL        VAR(&USERINF) TYPE(*CHAR) LEN(100)

RTVUSRPRTI USER(*CURRENT) RTNTEXT(&USERINF)
OVRPRTF    FILE(QSYSPRT) PRTTXT(&USERINF)
CALL       PGM(PGM0001)

ENDPGM
```

Figure 12.11: Retrieve routing instructions from the user print information.

The text entered with CHGUSRPRTI (and retrieved with RTVUSRPRTI) can have a length of up to 100 characters, while the PRTTXT attribute of printer files used by the Override Printer File (OVRPRTF) command can only have 30.

If you're afraid you might forget to code the RTVUSRPRTI and OVRPRTF command combo, a safer approach might be to store the text in the job description assigned to each user profile. In this way, the print text is automatically placed by the system when the job starts. This alternative method requires creating job descriptions for each individual user, but you might prefer doing that to having a single job description that services more than one user.

—Mike Hockley

Store Text for a User Profile

In V3R1, IBM added a place to store up to 100 bytes of text for each user profile. This text gets assigned to an attribute of each spooled file that the user creates.

To set the text for a user, run the Change User Print Information (CHGUSRPRTI) command. This command has two parameters. The first parameter, USER, allows you to specify the name of a user profile (the default is *CURRENT). The second parameter, TEXT, lets you enter up to 100 bytes of information. For example, you might enter a command such as the following:

```
CHGUSRPRTI USER(JOHNSON) +
    TEXT('Accounting Dept, Bldg 310')
```

In this case, whenever user JOHNSON creates a spooled file, this text appears as one of the spooled file's attributes. You can view this text for a spooled file by running the Work with Spooled File Attributes (WRKSPLFA) command. An easy way to do that is to select option 8 off the Work with Spooled Files (WRKSPLF) display. You'll find the text on the last page of that display. You can use this text to help identify how to locate the owner of a spooled file.

—Robin Klima

✦ ✦ ✦ Security

Allowing a User to Create but Not View Spool Files

Q: Is there a way I can allow a user to create spool files in an output queue and not allow the user to view or change these spool files? Only a certain user should be able to change or view these spool files.

A: If the program that creates the report adopts authority, it can write the report to an output queue to which the user who ran the report is not authorized. The user wouldn't be able to look at or change the report after the program ends.

—Matt Fulton

✦ ✦ ✦ Spool File Attributes

Controlling Spool File Names

Suppose you want to write an RPG program that will create print files with varying spool file names. Normally, the spool file name that is created is the same as the file name in the RPG program. You can give the spooled file any name you want by specifying the spooled file name in the SPLFNAME parameter of the Override Print File (OVRPRTF) command. If you want to do it all in RPG, code UC in columns 71-72 of the F-spec for the printer file. Then run the OVRPRTF command using QCMDEXC before you open the printer file manually in the RPG program. The code is shown in Figure 12.12.

```
... 1 ...+... 2 ...+... 3 ...+... 4 ...+... 5 ...+... 6 ...+... 7 .
FQPRINT  O   F    132      OF    PRINTER                             UC
I                'OVRPRTF QPRINT -    C         CMD
I                'SPLFNAME(INVOICE)'
C                     CALL 'QCMDEXC'
C                     PARM CMD        COMAND 50
C                     PARM 32         LENGTH 155
C                     OPEN QPRINT
```

Figure 12.12: Give a spool file any name you want it to have.

—Midrange Computing Staff

How Many Copies Do You Need?

Q: The number-of-copies option on my remote output queue doesn't work. How do I fix this?

A: First, end the writer associated with the remote output queue. Then, use the Change Output Queue (CHGOUTQ) command and enter **XAIX XAUTOQ** on the Destinations option (DESTOPT) parameter. Finally, restart the writer.

—Bradley V. Stone

✦ ✦ ✦ Spool File Contents

Literals in Message Files

A message file is a useful place to store short, descriptive information that can be used in an application. One of the handiest things about a message file is that a message can be changed to reflect some new function or instruction, but the program does not have to be recompiled. Most of us use messages to a greater or lesser extent by sending them to an interactive program message queue and then displaying them in a message subfile.

Another use for messages that you might not have considered is that you can use them on reports. You can list the text of an error that has occurred in the job or you can retrieve literals, such as report headings and column headings, from a message file.

The bad thing about using message files, though, is that the messages and their associated text are not easily retrieved. However, that's all changed now by using the example I've provided in Figure 12.13.

```
****************************************************************
*Program Information Summary
****************************************************************
*
* Program ID     -   EXAMP01
* Program Name   -   How to retrieve messages from message file.
* Programmer     -   Vadim Rozen
*
* Description
****************************************************************
* This program allows printing messages from message file
****************************************************************
```

Figure 12.13: Use program EXAMP01 as a skeleton for using the recursive message text retrieval technique of the service program CCRTVM (part 1 of 3).

```
 * Program creation:
 * 1. CRTRPGMOD MODULE(xxx/EXAMP01) SRCFILE(xxx/SrcFile) +
 *    SRCMBR(EXAMP01)
 * 2. CRTBNDDIR BNDDIR(xxx/EXAMP01)
 * 3. ADDBNDDIRE BNDDIR(xxx/EXAMP01) OBJ((EXAMP01 *MODULE))
 * 4. ADDBNDDIRE BNDDIR(xxx/EXAMP01) OBJ((CCRTVM *SRVPGM))
 * 5. CRTPGM PGM(xxx/EXAMP01) BNDDIR(xxx/EXAMP01) +
 *    ACTGRP(*CALLER)
 ***********************************************************************
H  Debug
 ***********************************************************************
 * Files
 ***********************************************************************
 * Print file
FQSysPrt   o   f 132         Printer
F                                        infds(@FP1)
 ***********************************************************************
 * Printer information data structure
D @FP1            DS
 * Overflow line number
D   p1@OL                188     189b 0
 * Current Line Number
D   p1@CL                367     368b 0
 ***********************************************************************
 * Work variable definitions
D #MsgFile        s             10    inz('QCPFMSG')
D #MsgLib         s             10    inz('QSYS')
D #MsgId          s              7
D #RtnMsg         s             80
D #RplData        s            128
D #RError         s              1
 ***********************************************************************
 * Procedure prototypes
 ***********************************************************************
 * Retrieve Message
D RtvMsgTxt       pr           256
D  MsgId                         7    Value
D  RplData                     128    Value
D  MsgF                         10    Value
D  MsgL                         10    Value
D  Error                         1
 ***********************************************************************
 * Main Line
 ***********************************************************************
C                   ExSr      Sb1000
 *
C                   Eval      *InLR = *On
 ***********************************************************************
 * Print message
 ***********************************************************************
C     Sb1000        BegSr
 *
```

Figure 12.13: Use program EXAMP01 as a skeleton for using the recursive message text retrieval technique of the service program CCRTVM (part 2 of 3).

```
    * Print Report Header
c                    Except    Header
*
    * Retrieve existing message
C                    Eval      #MsgId = 'CPF4131'
C                    Eval      #RplData = 'FILE01    ' +
C                                          'FILE01    ' +
C                                          'MYLIBRARY ' +
C                                          'MEMBR01   '
C                    Eval      #RtnMsg = RtvMsgTxt(#MsgId:#RplData:
C                                        #MsgFile:#MsgLib:#RError)
*
    * Print result on report
C                    Except    Detail
*
    * Retrieve unexisting message
C                    Eval      #MsgId = 'CPFXXXX'
C                    Eval      #RtnMsg = RtvMsgTxt(#MsgId:#RplData:
C                                        #MsgFile:#MsgLib:#RError)
*
    * Print result on report
C                    Except    Detail
*
C                    EndSr
    ****************************************************************
    * Report
    ****************************************************************
OQSysPrt   e            Header       2  1
O                       UDate        Y     8
O                                          80 'Demonstrate Retrieve -
O                                             Message Service Program'
O                                         126 'Page:'
O                       Page         z   132
O          e            Header       2
O                                          10 'Message Id'
O                                          24 'Message Text'
O          e            Detail       2
O                       #MsgId             7
O                       #RtnMsg          + 5
```

Figure 12.13: Use program EXAMP01 as a skeleton for using the recursive message text retrieval technique of the service program CCRTVM (part 3 of 3).

In this example, I use the Retrieve Message (QMHRTVM) API to print message text on a report. I also use the message ID CPF4131 (Level Check on File) from message file QCPFMSG. This particular message has four substitute variables, which must be removed from the message text and replaced with real data. I accomplish this using the **RtvMsgTxt** procedure on the EVAL statement.

The second message, CPFXXXX, is invalid. That is, it does not exist in the QCPFMSG message file. When this message is passed to the service program CCRTVM, the **RtvMsgTxt** procedure receives error CPF2499. This message ID is loaded in the error parameter data structure. In this case, the **RtvMsgTxt** procedure calls itself and returns the error text, which will also be printed on the report.

Figure 12.13 is an example of how to use the service program CCRTVM, which appears in Figure 12.14. You can use this as the skeleton for implementing this technique in your own applications.

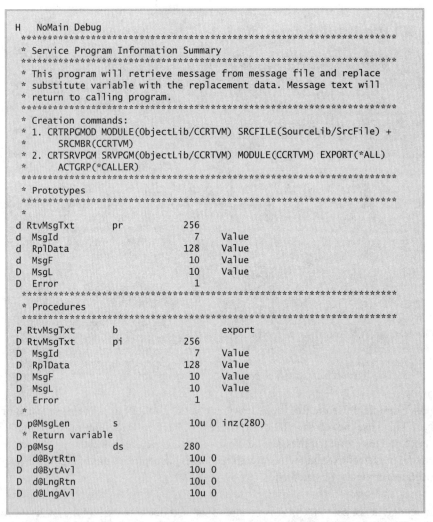

```
H   NoMain Debug
*****************************************************************
* Service Program Information Summary
*****************************************************************
* This program will retrieve message from message file and replace
* substitute variable with the replacement data. Message text will
* return to calling program.
*****************************************************************
* Creation commands:
* 1. CRTRPGMOD MODULE(ObjectLib/CCRTVM) SRCFILE(SourceLib/SrcFile) +
*      SRCMBR(CCRTVM)
* 2. CRTSRVPGM SRVPGM(ObjectLib/CCRTVM) MODULE(CCRTVM) EXPORT(*ALL)
*      ACTGRP(*CALLER)
*****************************************************************
* Prototypes
*****************************************************************
*
d RtvMsgTxt       pr           256
d   MsgId                        7     Value
d   RplData                    128     Value
d   MsgF                        10     Value
D   MsgL                        10     Value
D   Error                        1
*****************************************************************
* Procedures
*****************************************************************
P RtvMsgTxt       b                    export
D RtvMsgTxt       pi           256
D   MsgId                        7     Value
D   RplData                    128     Value
D   MsgF                        10     Value
D   MsgL                        10     Value
D   Error                        1
 *
D p@MsgLen        s            10u 0 inz(280)
 * Return variable
D p@Msg           ds           280
D   d@BytRtn                   10u 0
D   d@BytAvl                   10u 0
D   d@LngRtn                   10u 0
D   d@LngAvl                   10u 0
```

Figure 12.14: Service program CCRTVM retrieves literals from message files (part 1 of 3).

```
D   d@LngRtnH                      10u 0
D   d@LngAvlH                      10u 0
D   d@Msg                          256
    *
D p@Format          s               8    inz('RTVM0100')
D p@MsgID           s               7
D p@MsgFL           ds
D   p@MsgF                         10
D   p@MsgL                         10
D p@RplData         s             128    inz
D p@RDLeng          s              10u 0 inz
D p@RplFlg          s              10    inz('*YES')
D p@RtnFCC          s              10    inz('*NO')
    *
D p@Error           DS
D   BYTPRV                         10U 0 inz(116)
D   BYTAVA                         10U 0
D   ERRMID                          7
D   ERR##                           1
D   ERRDTA                        100
D #sError           s               1    inz(*Off)
D #ErrMsg           s             256
    *****************************************************************
    * Main Line
    *****************************************************************
    *
C                   Eval      p@MsgID = MsgId
C                   Eval      p@MsgF  = MsgF
C                   Eval      p@MsgL  = MsgL
C                   Eval      p@RplData = RplData
C                   If        p@RplData <> *Blank
C         ' '       CheckR    p@RplData       p@RDLeng
C                   EndIf
    * Save Error
C                   Eval      #sError = Error
C                   Eval      Error = *Off
    *
    * Call API pgm
C                   ExSr      Sb1000
    *
    * Retreive error message
C                   If        ErrMId <> *Blank and #sError <> *On
C                   Clear                     p@Msg
C                   Eval      #ErrMsg = RtvMsgTxt(ErrMId:ErrDta:
C                                       'QCPFMSG':'QSYS':#sError)
C                   Eval      d@Msg = #ErrMsg
C                   Eval      Error = *On
C                   EndIf
    *
C                   Return    d@Msg
    *****************************************************************
    * Call API pgm
```

Figure 12.14: Service program CCRTVM retrieves literals from message files (part 2 of 3).

```
****************************************************************
C     Sb1000      BegSr
*
C                 Call      'QMHRTVM'
C                 Parm                  p@Msg
C                 Parm                  p@MsgLen
C                 Parm                  p@Format
C                 Parm                  p@MsgID
C                 Parm                  p@MsgFL
C                 Parm                  p@RplData
C                 Parm                  p@RDLeng
C                 Parm                  p@RplFlg
C                 Parm                  p@RtnFCC
C                 Parm                  p@Error
*
C                 If        ErrMId = *Blank
C                 Eval      d@Msg = %SubSt(d@Msg:1:d@LngRtn)
C                 EndIf
*
C                 EndSr
****************************************************************
* Error handling subroutine
****************************************************************
C     *PSSR       BegSr
C                 Dump
C                 Return    'Error occured in subprocedure'
C                 EndSr
****************************************************************
P RtvMsgTxt        e
```

Figure 12.14: Sevice program CCRTVM retrieves literals from message files (part 3 of 3).

—Vadim Rozen

Put the Qualified Program Name in Report Headings

As a rule, you probably include report date and page numbers in report headings. Several years ago, I added the qualified program name to that list. Printing the qualified program name in page headings is helpful because:

- I can determine at a glance exactly which program created a report. This is handy when a user shows me a report and asks me to modify it.

- I can tell at a glance whether a report was built by a program in production or by an experimental version in a test library. This is especially handy when I have both production and experimental versions lying side by side on my desk for comparison.

Thanks to two copybook members I created, including the qualified program name on a
report is easy. The first example, shown in Figure 12.15, defines the RPG program status
data structure. I named the member PSDS.

```
I* Program Status Data Structure
ISDS          SDS
I*                      Program name
I                                        1  10 S#PGM
I*                      Status code
I                                       11  150S#STAT
I*                      Previous status code
I                                       16  200S#PSTA
I*                      Source statement sequence number
I                                       21  28 S#SEQ#
I*                      Routine
I                                       29  36 S#RTN
I*                      Number of parameters
I                                       37  390S#PARM
I*                      Exception type
I                                       40  42 S#EXCT
I*                      Exception number
I                                       43  46 S#EXC#
I*                      HI/ODT number
I                                       47  50 S#ODT#
I*                      Message work area
I                                       51  80 S#MWA
I*                      Library in which program is located
I                                       81  90 S#LIB
I*                      Exception data
I                                       91 170 S#EXCD
I*                      Exception ID
I                                      171 174 S#EXCI
I*                      First 2 digits of *YEAR
I                                      199 200 S#YEAR
I*                      Last file on which operation was performed
I                                      201 208 S#FILE
I*                      File status
I                                      209 243 S#FLST
I*                      Job name
I                                      244 253 S#JOB
I*                      User profile
I                                      254 263 S#USER
I*                      Job number
I                                      264 2690S#JOB#
I*                      Date job entered system
I                                      270 2750S#EDAT
I*                      System date
I                                      276 2810S#SDAT
I*                      System time
```

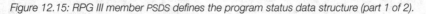

Figure 12.15: RPG III member PSDS defines the program status data structure (part 1 of 2).

```
I                                    282 2870S#STIM
I*               Compile date
I                                    288 293 S#CDAT
I*               Compile time
I                                    294 299 S#CTIM
I*               Compiler level
I                                    300 303 S#LEVL
I*               Source file name
I                                    304 313 S#SRCF
I*               Source file library
I                                    314 323 S#SRCL
I*               Source file member
I                                    324 333 S#SRCM
```

Figure 12.15: RPG III member PSDS defines the program status data structure (part 2 of 2).

Copybook member PGMNAME, shown in Figure 12.16, builds the qualified program name.

```
C         S#LIB    CAT  '/':0    PGMNAM 21
C         PGMNAM   CAT  S#PGM:0  PGMNAM
```

Figure 12.16: Member PGMNAME consists of two simple lines of RPG III that build the qualified program name.

Figure 12.17 illustrates how I typically include these copy members in an RPG III program. The only other requirement is to include field PGMNAM in the printer file DDS or output specs.

```
FSOMERPT O   E          88      PRINTER
I/COPY XXX/QRPGSRC,PSDS
C                  WRITEPAGEHDR
 *** record format PAGEHDR has 21-byte variable PGMNAM
C         *INZSR    BEGSR
C*
C/COPY XXX/QRPGSRC,PGMNAME
C*
C                  ENDSR
```

Figure 12.17: The qualified report name will appear on printed output.

—*Ted Holt*

Resetting DDS PAGNBR

We've all had the opportunity to write a report that required resetting the page number to page 1. For example, a sales report gets separated and distributed to district managers, and each section should begin with page 1.

It's easy when using a program-described print file; we have direct access to the PAGE field and can reset it to zero before printing the next page. But what about externally defined printer files?

Use a controlling indicator with the PAGNBR keyword in the external print file (see Figure 12.18). Whenever the record is written with the indicator on, the page counter will be set back to 1. Write the record format with the indicator off, and the page counter will increment normally.

```
A                                    120'PAGE:'
A                                    +1
A   80                               PAGNBR
A                                    EDTCDE(Z)
```

Figure 12.18: An indicator controls page number reset.

The important trick is to place the PAGNBR keyword on a source line separate from the starting position so that the indicator will only control the keyword. Placing them on the same line would cause the indicator to control whether the page number printed at all.

—Chris Denman

Underline Printing Technique

Our users frequently ask to have certain items underlined in their printed output and, indeed, like to have the report headings underlined for all reports. Depending on your underlining technique, your report will look either very nice or quite nasty when viewed in the output queue.

When you have two characters printed in the same position, IBM decided to display the last character printed (not the combination of characters or the first character printed). I always print the underlines first. Then, using overstrike, I print the actual data on the same line. This produces a spooled file that is very close to the printed result and provides a way to view underlined material without sending it to the printer.

There's also an UNDERLINE keyword available to externally described printer files. You won't see the output underlined when viewing the report from WRKSPLF's panel, but you don't have to worry about programming underlines yourself, either.

—Dirk Shelley

✦ ✦ ✦ Spool File Management

Job Accounting Tracks Spool Files

How many times a week do users complain because they've run a program that produces a report, but they can't find the listing? Maybe they think that somebody has deleted the spooled file or that the program doesn't work. Anyway, after investigating a bit and using a lot of your time (which is already in short supply), you find out that the program ran just fine and someone else took the report off the printer by accident.

I have something that can help. You can use the AS/400's job accounting capabilities to track completed printing. You first need to turn on the storage of completed printout information, which you can get to using the command GO SETUP.

Once in the menu that lets you customize the system, users, and devices, take option 1 to bring up the Change System Options screen. Roll down until you see Save job accounting information about completed printer output. Change the option to a Y and exit the screen. This will change the system value QACGLVL to *PRINT and create the necessary system accounting journals (QSYS/QACGJRN).

Once you make this change, the system will start tracking completed printouts for new jobs. You can see completed printouts by using the WRKSPLF command at the *BASIC assistance level. When you do, you'll see a new command key (F6) that will display completed printing. This saves a lot of time tracking down whether a report really printed or not.

—Jean-Jacques Risch

Monitoring Spool Files

Q: How can I monitor spooled files (unattended) and convert them to a physical file? I know there is a way to get the spooled list through an API function, but this method seems too slow to intercept a ready-to-print spooled file before it begins to print. I need to find a better way to intercept every spooled file before it prints and convert it to a physical file. Maybe this monitoring job has to run repeatedly in a separate subsystem?

A: On the Create Output Queue (CRTOUTQ) command, you can specify a data queue in the Data queue (DTAQ) parameter to receive a message whenever a spool file on that queue goes to a ready (RDY) status. Each time a spooled file on the output queue reaches RDY status, an entry is sent to the data queue.

You could have your spool files go to an output queue with no active printer writer running. When a spool file gets to a RDY status, your job would detect it through the data queue and copy the spool file to a database file. Then you could move the spool file to an output queue attached to a writer. This would ensure that the capture is done before the file prints.

—Midrange Computing Staff

User Options

When creating or changing your user profiles, look closely at the User Options (USROPT) parameter. This parameter has several values. An interesting one, *PRTMSG, sends a message to the owner of a spooled file indicating that printing of the file has either been completed or held by the printer writer.

—Jean-Jacques Risch

Query

Query

♦   ♦   ♦   ♦

In This Chapter

Administration

Data Manipulation

Date and Time

Formatting Output

Record Selection

♦   ♦   ♦   ♦

*I*n the early days of information processing, professionals did everything. If you were a humble clerk or measly accountant, you were at
the mercy of the computer people. If you needed the computer to store
a certain piece of information (a "datum," but nobody uses that word),
you had to ask the Data Processing department to set that up for you.
The keypunch operators typed the data onto paper cards. The computer
operators fed the cards to the computer. If you wanted to see that data,
you asked the operators to do their magic, and the computer responded
by spitting out a report on a line printer.

Someone started wondering why users couldn't do more for themselves.
This wasn't just users demanding a greater degree of autonomy. Computer professionals wanted it even more. The backlog of needed programs was growing, not shrinking, and industry analysts were saying
that something had to be done.

Query packages were developed as a partial answer. The idea behind
query packages is that a user with little or no training should be able to
extract data from a database. The ideal has never been achieved. Users
still must know something about databases and their structure. But
query packages have helped ease the burden on programmers.

AS/400 Query was introduced in 1988, when the AS/400 itself was announced. There's nothing flashy about AS/400 Query, but that's okay.
Users don't need "bells and whistles" to get their jobs done; they need
dependable software. Query's text-based interface is easy to use.

As dependable and effective as Query is, it has its shortcomings. Lack
of conditional calculations and the capability to summarize data horizontally are two glaring problems. You'll find these two, and other
shortcomings, addressed in this chapter.

—Ted Holt

✦ ✦ ✦ **Administration**

A Better DSPPFM

Here's a way that you can view data in a physical file instantly. The Run Query (RUNQRY) command is a good alternative to Display Physical File Member (DSPPFM). On any command line, type the following:

```
RUNQRY *NONE libname/filename
```

A formatted display of the file contents appears. If you prompt RUNQRY, other parameters allow for record selection and spooling to *PRINT.

—Cynthy Johnson

Controlling Query/400 Runtime and Output Options

When Query/400 was opened up to users throughout our organization, we experienced problems with large files being created. I searched for a way to control the size of query output files (the default is *NOMAX). Thanks to our IBM Business Partner and a contact at IBM, I received the following information about controlling Query/400 queries.

Query/400 scans the library list for a data area named QQUPRFOPTS. If this data area exists, Query/400 retrieves runtime options from positions 2–75, as described in Table 13.1. If this data area is not found, or if any parameter values are left blank in the data area, the default values are used. The SBMJOB parameters in the Purpose column refer to the 8=Batch option from the Work with Queries display.

If you want to use this data area, you'll have to create it yourself. Use the CL command below as a guide, replacing *xxx* with the name of the library to contain the data area.

```
CRTDTAARA  DTAARA(xxx/QQUPRFOPTS) TYPE(*CHAR) LEN(80) +
    AUT(*USE) TEXT('Query/400 user profile options')
```

The following code illustrates how you might use this command to change the default size of a Query/400 output file. The file will be created with 50,000 initial records, with an increment of 5,000 records, and allow up to 10 increments.

```
CHGDTAARA DTAATA(xxx/QQUPRFOPTS (56 20)) +
    VALUE('00000500000500000010')
```

—Bruce Nyberg

Table 13.1: Subfields of the Query Options Data Area Control File Creation in Query

Position	Purpose	Options
1	Future use	
2	RTGDTA for SBMJOB	'B' = QCMDB (QBATCH)
		' ' = *JOBD
3	OUTQ for SBMJOB	'J': *JOBD (default)
		'C': *CURRENT
		'U': *USRPRF
		'D': *DEV
4	PRTDEV for SBMJOB	'J': *JOBD (default)
		'C': *CURRENT
		'U': *USRPRF
		'S': *SYSVAL
5	INQMSGRPY for SBMJOB	'J': *JOBD (default)
		'R': *RQD
		'D': *DFT
		'S': *SYSRPYL
6 - 15	JOB for SBMJOB	10-character name associated with the batch job
		*JOBD: Use the job description
		*QRY: Use the query definition
16 - 35	JOBD for SBMJOB	10 character job description
		+ 10 character library
		*USRPRF – Use the job description from the user profile
36 - 55	JOBQ for SBMJOB	10 character job queue name + 10 character library
		*JOBD – Use the job description from the user profile
56 - 65	Initial number of records for the output file	10,0 zoned decimal number from 1 through 2,147,483,646
66 - 70	Increment number of records for the output file	5,0 zoned decimal number from 0 through 32,767
71 - 75	Maximum number of increments for the output file	5,0 zoned decimal number from 0 through 32,767

Forcing a Query to Use the Library List

One of the problems with running a query from within a CL program is that, by default, queries don't use the library list to find the file they were designed to access. When the query is defined, the name of the library for the file is essentially hard coded into the query. One way to get around this problem is to use the QRYFILE parameter of the RUNQRY command. Here, you can specify the name of the original file and *LIBL for the library name.

For example, suppose you have a query called HISTQRY that was designed to read file ITEMHIST in library PRODLIB. You can force the query to read the first occurrence of the ITEMHIST file in your library list by placing this command into your CL program:

```
RUNQRY QRY(HISTQRY) QRYFILE((*LIBL/ITEMHIST))
```

In this example, if another copy of the ITEMHIST file was in a library called TESTLIB that was higher in the library list than PRODLIB, then the query would read the file from TESTLIB. If you then removed TESTLIB from your library list, the query would read the file in PRODLIB. This technique gives your queries more flexibility by forcing them to use the library list to locate the files they were designed to read.

—Blair Hamren

Limit How Long Queries Run

The system value QQRYTIMLMT establishes an upper limit for the estimated number of seconds that a query will run. If the estimated time lapse is greater than what you specify in QQRYTIMLMT, the query simply doesn't run.

By default, QQRYTIMLMT contains *NOMAX, which means that there's no time limit. If you have "query-happy" users, however, you might want to make a change. Valid values are 0 to 2,147,352,578 seconds. By the way, the maximum value is roughly equal to 68 years, which ought to be enough.

—Ernie Malaga

Preventing Interactive Query

You can prevent the interactive execution of query requests by changing the Run Query (RUNQRY) command. To do so, change the command so that RUNQRY is not allowed from an interactive session.

First, use the Display Command (DSPCMD) command to display the RUNQRY command. RUNQRY, as shipped by IBM, is allowed during an interactive session.

Next, make a copy of the RUNQRY command in case the changes do not work correctly. Users (such as yourself) who are allowed to run interactive queries can access this copy of the command. Use the Create Duplicate Object (CRTDUPOBJ) command to copy the RUNQRY command, as follows:

```
CRTDUPOBJ OBJ(RUNQRY) FROMLIB(QSYS) +
    OBJTYPE(*CMD) TOLIB(SAVQSYS)
```

Using the Change System Library List (CHGSYSLIBL) command, place the library that contains the unchanged RUNQRY command below QSYS on the system portion of the library list. Change the RUNQRY command in QSYS to remove *INTERACT from the allowed environment (as shown in the example that follows). This prevents the command from being used in interactive sessions, which prohibits users from running interactive queries.

```
CHGCMD CMD(QSYS/RUNQRY) +
    ALLOW(*IREXX *BREXX *BPGM *IPGM *EXEC *BATCH)
```

Record these changes in a source file. When you install a new release, the changes to commands are lost.

—Wayne O. Evans

Two Queries Are Better Than One

To improve performance of Query/400 where large files (over 100,000 records) are joined, use paired queries. The first query selects records and uses a database file for output (the choice of "data in file" option is important here). The second query uses the file created by the first query and sorts it, using either a printer or another database file for output. Our query performance improved three to one using this method.

—Debbie DeDuck

Two Ways to Comment Result Fields in Query/400

I often take advantage of the capability to create new result fields in Query/400. However, many times, the calculations being performed are rather complex, and I'd like to add comments to each calculation, explaining what is being done and why. Other times, I want to comment on the calculation, not because it's overly complex, but because the field names being used aren't descriptive all by themselves. Our shop, like others, uses field names made up of standard prefixes and sequential numbers (e.g., ITM001 and ITM002). Although this naming convention helps with consistency, query calculations such as "(SOD004 – SOD005)/RTG009" don't easily lend themselves to self-documenting. Fortunately, I've found two simple methods for adding documentation comments to Query/400 result-field calculations.

The simplest way to add documentation comments is to put all the necessary comments into the three Column Heading lines that are available for each result field being created. In an RPG III program, this would be similar to placing comments in columns 60–74 of the C-spec line.

The advantage to this method is that the comments are directly tied to the calculated field. Even if the field is selected as part of the query output, you can always use the option to Specify report column formatting to override the "comment heading" you assigned to the field. This ensures that the query is output with the desired heading.

A disadvantage to this method is that the amount of space available in the three Column Heading lines is very limited and might not be enough to adequately document the calculation.

Another (and still simple) way to add comments to a calculated field is to create "comment" result fields that serve no other purpose except to document the calculations that follow them.

Again referring to an RPG program, using this method would be similar to using the entire line that precedes a section of logic to document what's being done.

Using this method, you can load up all three of the Expression and Column Heading lines with comments. If necessary, you can create an almost unlimited number of "comment" result fields until you have properly documented the calculations being performed.

An additional benefit to this method is that, if the calculated result field is to be output and does need a Column Heading, the desired heading can be assigned along with the calculated field (no separate heading override is needed). If you choose to use this method, remember these two things:

1. The comment result fields you create must all have unique names. I suggest using "COMMENT*xxxx*" names (in which *xxxx* is a sequential number).

2. The comment text you place in the Expression area must start and end with a single quote (the starting and ending quotes will not necessarily be on the same line).

An example of these commenting methods is shown in Figure 13.1.

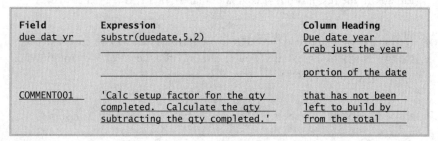

Field	Expression	Column Heading
due dat yr	substr(duedate,5,2)	Due date year
		Grab just the year
		portion of the date
COMMENT001	'Calc setup factor for the qty completed. Calculate the qty subtracting the qty completed.'	that has not been left to build by from the total

Figure 13.1: *Here are two ways to create result field comments in Query/400.*

—*Jack Dalglish*

✦ ✦ ✦ Data Manipulation

Query/400 Finds the Larger of Two Numbers

We had a request from a user who wanted a Query/400 report that showed the greater of average monthly usage and minimum order quantity. Query/400 does not include conditional (if-then-else) statements, but you can make it work through simple mathematical functions. Here's how:

1. Under Specify processing options, set the Use Rounding option to N.

2. Define a result field that finds the difference between the two numbers, which I'll refer to as A and B. See the calculation for field DIFF in Table 13.2. If A is greater than B, DIFF is positive; otherwise, DIFF is negative.

Table 13.2: Query/400 Can Determine the Larger of Two Numbers

Field	Expression
DIFF	A - B
FACTOR	((DIFF - 0.001) * (DIFF - 0.001)) / ((DIFF * DIFF) + 0.0001)
LARGER	(A * (-1)) * (FACTOR - 1)) + (B * FACTOR)

3. Define a one-digit field with zero decimal positions. In Table 13.2, this is the FACTOR field. If DIFF is negative, the numerator is greater than the denominator, and the result is more than 1. If DIFF is positive, the numerator is less than the denominator, and the result is less than 1. The 0.0001 ensures that there's no divide-by-zero if A is equal to B. Because the rounding has been turned off, the result is 0 if A is greater than B, or 1 if B is greater than A.

4. Define a final result field (LARGER in Table 13.2) that will be the greater of the two numbers. Essentially, you're turning off either A or B by multiplying the lower number by zero.

To find the smaller of two numbers, just switch A with B and B with A in step 4.

—Bob Ellsworth

Using Character Functions with Numeric Fields

I'd like to illustrate the method I use to have the substring functions in Query/400 and SQL work on a numeric field. My example operates on an order file, and what I'm going to demonstrate is how to extract the year out of a numeric date. To accomplish this, I use a combination of the DIGITS function and the SUBSTR function in Query/400.

In my example order file, I have a field called FDATE. Because FDATE is numeric, Query (and SQL) cannot use SUBSTR to extract the year. Fortunately, with the help of the DIGITS keyword, my query is able to convert FDATE to an alphanumeric value, which then allows the query to perform a substring. Figure 13.2 shows how to combine the two keywords. The result of the expression is placed in a field I defined in Query/400 and called YEAR.

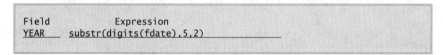

```
Field          Expression
YEAR    substr(digits(fdate),5,2)
```

Figure 13.2: Use built-in functions to extract the year from a numeric date.

Now I can simply use the YEAR variable I just created to select records from the file for the year 95. You can see an example of the selection process shown in Figure 13.3. The method I've come up with is simple, and it also works in SQL.

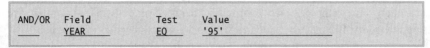

AND/OR	Field	Test	Value
	YEAR	EQ	'95'

Figure 13.3: Once the year is extracted, you can use it like any database field.

—*Jean-Jacques Risch*

✦ ✦ ✦ Date and Time

Converting Dates in Query/400

I have seen numerous articles and tips on how to manipulate dates in Query/400. There is always a need to break out month, day, or year or to convert the format—such as MMDDYY to YYMMDD. All of the suggested methods seem to use complex mathematical calculations that are difficult to remember.

An easier way, I believe, is to use the DIGITS operator in the Define Result Fields option. This allows you to convert numeric fields to alpha, giving you the capability to use the substring operation. Table 13.3 illustrates how to do this.

This same technique, using the concatenation operation, can convert dates to other formats. This seems much easier to me than the other methods!

Table 13.3: Extracting the Month Portion of a Date in Query/400	
Field	**Expression**
ALPHADATA	digits(NUMERICDATE)
MONTH	substr(alphadate,1,2)

—*Kris Hudnut*

Converting Julian Dates in Query/400

I work as a consultant, and most of my clients have software in which dates are stored in the Julian format (0YYDDD).

If any of these dates need to be displayed in a report, an RPG program would have to be written instead of using a simpler tool, such as Query/400. Nobody could tell me how to convert Julian dates to the DD/MM/YY format, which is common here in Australia. After perusing the Query/400 manual, I found a way to do this conversion in one line.

In my example, I'll use a field called SDTRDJ, which stores a Julian format date. Using the Work with Query (WRKQRY) command or some similar command, I select the Define Result Fields screen (see Table 13.4). Define the PRINTDATE field and use the functions shown in Table 13.4 to reformat the date. PRINTDATE prints in the format defined by your system value for the date format. This has been a great help to me.

Table 13.4: You Can Reformat a Julian Date in Query/400	
Field	Expression
PRINTDATE	date(substr((digits(SDTRDJ+1900000)),2,7))

—Selwyn M. Abrahams

✦ ✦ ✦ Formatting Output

Create Comma-delimited Files

When I have to export data from the AS/400 to a PC, I use Query to create a comma-separated values (CSV) text file. I concatenate double quotes to each end of character fields, and a comma to the end of all but the last field. I use the DIGITS function to convert numeric fields to character format. As an example, suppose I want to download three fields:

- A character field called NAME.

- An eight-digit numeric field with two decimal positions called AMOUNT.

- A numeric field with no decimal positions called DATE.

I would define fields in Query as illustrated in Table 13.5.

I select only one field, DTAOUT, for output to a database file. Then, I use FTP to transfer the file to the PC.

This method is handy, but it won't work in all cases. For instance, if there is a quotation mark in a character field, it needs to be doubled, but Query will not do that. Another problem is negative values in numeric fields. Numeric fields are always transferred as positive values.

Table 13.5: Query Can Create a CSV File

Field	Expression
XNAM	'"' || NAME || '",'
DA	DIGITS(AMOUNT)
XAMT	SUBSTR(DA,1,6) || '.' || SUBSTR(DA,7,2) || ','
XDAT	DIGITS(DATE)
DTAOUT	XNAM || XAMT || XDAT

—Carl Seeger

Print Labels with Query

Query/400 can produce mailing labels. Take the following into account for designing the query.

Choose Select and sequence fields. Order the selected fields in ascending order based on where they should appear on the form in a left-to-right, from-the-top-down fashion.

Select Specify report column formatting. Set all column headings to *NONE. (The value *NONE must be in all caps.) Adjust column spacing to move a field within a line or to force it to the next line.

Choose Select output type and output form. Set line wrapping to Y and choose a wrap length based on the width of your form. Press Enter.

Set the Form size to the length and width of your form. Specify start and end lines such that the end line minus the start line, plus one, is equal to the number of lines required to produce one page of output. Specify that you do not want to print the query definition.

Press Enter twice more.

On the following screens, specify that you do not want to print a cover page, standard page headings, specified page headings, or specified page footers.

Also, make sure that your job is not producing print text (PRTTXT).

—Chuck Pence

Spreadsheet Format with Query/400

Here is a tip for Query/400 users. Suppose you want to write a report that looks like a typical spreadsheet in which each column represents a month.

The problem is that your sales history database contains one record for each transaction. Query won't let you conditionally determine which column to place a transaction in based on the transaction date in the record.

The solution involves the Kronecker Delta function: an integer function of two discrete valued variables.

$$K(i,j)$$

The function evaluates to one if i is equal to j, otherwise it evaluates to zero.

The Kronecker Delta function works as an "if equal" test on two variables. You can use it to cause each sales transaction to be included in the appropriate monthly column.

Here's how you do it in Query/400. Define a result field containing the transaction month (the way you do this will depend on the date format used in your database).

Suppose that field is TMONTH. Define a series of result fields as shown in Figure 13.4. Notice that on the first set of expressions, subtracting 0.5 defeats rounding.

Field	Expression	Len	Dec
F1A	tmonth/1 - 0.5	2	0
F1B	1/tmonth - 0.5	2	0
F2A	tmonth / 2 - 0.5	2	0
F2B	2 / tmonth - 0.5	2	0
F3A	tmonth / 3 - 0.5	2	0
F3B	3 / tmonth - 0.5	2	0
... through F12A and F12B			
K1	f1a * f1b	1	0
K2	f2a * f2b	1	0
K3	f3a * f3b	1	0
... through K12			

Figure 13.4: Define the necessary Kronecker Delta functions in Query/400.

K1 through K12 are the Kronecker Delta functions. For instance, if the transaction month is 5, then F5A and F5B are both 1, and K5=1. But if the transaction month isn't 5, then either F5A or F5B will be zero, thus K5=0.

Suppose your transaction amount field is called TAMNT. Define the result fields to be used as report columns as shown in Figure 13.5. Because variables K1 through K12 are zero, except for the variable corresponding to the transaction month, your sales data will be placed in the correct column.

```
Field          Expression
SALES1         k1 * tamnt
SALES2         k2 * tamnt
SALES3         k3 * tamnt
 ... through SALES12
```

Figure 13.5: Apply the Kronecker Delta Function in Query/400 to force data into columns.

Print SALES1 through SALES12 as report columns, as shown in Figure 13.6.

```
              Select and Sequence Fields

    Type sequence number (0-9999) for the names of up to 500 fields to
       appear in the report, press Enter.

    Seq   Field          Text                            Len   Dec
    _10_  TYEAR                                            4     0
    _20_  SALES1         k1 * tamnt                       12     2
    _30_  SALES2         k2 * tamnt                       12     2
    _40_  SALES3         k3 * tamnt                       12     2
    _50_  SALES4         k4 * tamnt                       12     2
          ... select SALES5 through SALES11 in the same way
    _130_ SALES12        k12 * tamnt                      12     2
    ____  F1A            tmonth/1 - 0.5                    2     0
    ____  F1B            1/tmonth - 0.5                    2     0
    ____  K1             f1a * f1b                         1     0
    ____  F2A            tmonth / 2 - 0.5                  2     0
    ____  F2B            2 / tmonth - 0.5                  2     0
```

Figure 13.6: Select only the control fields and the fields that were calculated with the Kronecker Delta function.

The report will make a lot more sense if you summarize the amount columns, rather than printing a detail report. The following figures show how to summarize a report.

First, choose an appropriate sort sequence, as shown in Figure 13.7.

```
                        Select Sort Fields

        Type sort priority (0-999) and A (Ascending) or D (Descending) for
          the names of up to 32 fields, press Enter.

        Sort
        Prty A/D  Field            Text                         Len  Dec
         10   A   TYEAR                                          4    0
        ____  _   SALES1           k1 * tamnt                    12   2
        ____  _   SALES2           k2 * tamnt                    12   2
        ____  _   SALES3           k3 * tamnt                    12   2
        ____  _   SALES4           k4 * tamnt                    12   2
        ... define SALES5 through SALES11 in the same way
        ____  _   SALES12          k12 * tamnt                   12   2
```

Figure 13.7: Sort on the fields by which data is to be summarized.

Next, tell Query that you want to summarize the calculated sales columns, which were built with the Kronecker Delta functions. See Figure 13.8.

```
                    Select Report Summary Functions

        Type options, press Enter.
          1=Total   2=Average   3=Minimum    4=Maximum    5=Count

        --Options--   Field           Text                      Len  Dec
        _ _ _ _ _     TYEAR                                      4    0
        1 _ _ _ _     SALES1          k1 * tamnt                 12   2
        1 _ _ _ _     SALES2          k2 * tamnt                 12   2
        1 _ _ _ _     SALES3          k3 * tamnt                 12   2
        1 _ _ _ _     SALES4          k4 * tamnt                 12   2
        ... summarize SALES5 through SALES11 in the same way
        1 _ _ _ _     SALES12         k12 * tamnt                12   2
```

Figure 13.8: Total the fields that were built from the Kronecker Delta function.

You will probably need a report break on some or all of the sort fields, as Figure 13.9 shows.

```
                    Define Report Breaks

Type break level (1-6) for up to 9 field names, press Enter.
(Use as many fields as needed for each break level.)

Break    Sort
Level    Prty   Field        Text                    Len  Dec
  1       10    TYEAR                                  4   0
 __       ___   SALES1       k1 * tamnt              12   2
 __       ___   SALES2       k2 * tamnt              12   2
 __       ___   SALES3       k3 * tamnt              12   2
 __       ___   SALES4       k4 * tamnt              12   2
 ... SALES5 through SALES12 not shown
 __             SALES12      k12 * tamnt             12   2
```

Figure 13.9: The report should break on control fields.

Change the "Form of output" option to 2. See Figure 13.10.

```
             Select Output Type and Output Form

    Type choices, press Enter.

       Output type  . . . . . . . . . .    1      1=Display
                                                  2=Printer
                                                  3=Database file

       Form of output . . . . . . . . . .   2      1=Detail
                                                  2=Summary only

       Line wrapping  . . . . . . . . . .   N      Y=Yes, N=No
       Wrapping width . . . . . . . . .    ___    Blank, 1-378
       Record on one page . . . . . . .     N      Y=Yes, N=No
```

Figure 13.10: Choosing "Summary only" omits detail lines.

Figure 13.11 shows the left-hand portion of the summary report.

TYEAR	SALES1	SALES2	SALES3
1999			
TOTAL	1.00	200.00	.00
2000			
TOTAL	.00	2.00	.00
FINAL TOTALS			
TOTAL	1.00	202.00	.00

Figure 13.11: Vertical data has been changed to horizontal data.

Obviously, this function isn't restricted to reporting sales in columns by month. It can be used anytime you want to use a field value as a report column number.

—*Sam Stafford*

✦ ✦ ✦ Record Selection

Passing Parameters to a Query

Everybody knows that you can pass parameters to a Query Management query. Not everybody knows that you can do the same with a Query/400 query (object type *QRYDFN). It is very easy to set up. Figure 13.12 shows you an example of the Select Records panel in which variables are used to receive parameters. (The colon is very important. It indicates a dependent value. The variable name following the colon can be any name you want.)

```
AND/OR  Field       Test   Value (Field, Number, 'Characters', or ...)
        GLCOMP      EQ     :company
AND     GLBRAN      EQ     :branch
AND     GLACC       EQ     :account
```

Figure 13.12: Code dependent values in the Select Records panel.

After setting up the parameters, press Enter to obtain a screen similar to the example shown in Figure 13.13. Just supply a name for a "dummy" query or file; it doesn't have to exist and is not used in this example.

```
                    Specify Dependent Value Qualifiers

    Type choices, press Enter.

        Qualifier type . . . .   1           1=Query, 2=File

        Query or file  . . . .   DUMMY       Name, F4 for list of files
          Library  . . . . . .   *LIBL       Name, *LIBL, F4 for list

        For choice 2=File:
          File member  . . . .               Name, *FIRST, F4 for list




    F3=Exit              F4=Prompt       F10=Process/previous     F12=Cancel
    F13=Layout           F18=Files
```

Figure 13.13: Specify a Dummy Dependent Value Qualifier.

To run the query, you can't use the Run Query (RUNQRY) command. You must use the Start Query Management Query (STRQMQRY) command as in the example in Figure 13.14.

```
STRQMQRY QMQRY(QGPL/TEST) +
    ALWQRYDFN(*YES) +
    SETVAR((COMPANY 1) +
    (BRANCH 1) +
    (ACCOUNT 12000))
```

Figure 13.14: Use STRQMQRY to run a Query with substitution variables.

The trick to making this work is to specify *YES for the ALWQRYDFN parameter. A value of *YES allows Query Management to run a query definition (*QRYDFN) object instead of a query management (*QMQRY) object. You can either specify values for the parameters on the STRQMQRY command or let Query Management prompt you for them.

Character fields require some additional considerations. When specifying the value to be used by a dependent character field, you must enclose the value in single or triple quotes. If you let STRQMQRY prompt you for the value, you must enclose the character value in single quotes. If you specify the value through the SETVAR parameter of the STRQMQRY command, you must enclose the value in triple quotes.

—Jean-Jacques Risch

Query/400 Runtime Record Selection

You can specify record selection at runtime for existing Query/400 program by specifying the RCDSLT parameter on the RUNQRY command, as follows:

```
RUNQRY QRY(query name) RCDSLT(*YES)
```

When executed, this command presents the Query/400 record selection panel with the previously defined criteria, allowing you to modify or add selection criteria. After the desired changes are made, press Enter to run the query program.

—Eugene Arencibia

RUNQRY with Record Selection

To create an ad hoc report for any database file—physical or logical—without creating a DFU or Query object, use the QRYFILE parameter of the Run Query (RUNQRY) command. This will display the file in columns, with the column headings defined for the fields in DDS. The file also can be printed or output to an outfile by changing the OUTTYPE parameter to either *PRINTER or *OUTFILE. Using RCDSLT(*YES) will permit record selection based upon field contents. Use RUNQRY as follows:

```
   RUNQRY QRYFILE(file_name)
or RUNQRY QRYFILE(file_name) OUTTYPE(*PRINTER) RCDSLT(*YES)
```

—Midrange Computing Staff

Editor's Note: *The RCDSLT(*YES) parameter can only be used if Query/400 is installed on your system.*

CHAPTER 14

RPG — All

*W*ant to know which computer language is used in more businesses worldwide than all other languages combined? If you guessed RPG, you'd be correct. It has been estimated that there are over 100 million lines of RPG code out there serving as the backbone of business systems. And with that many lines of code, you can bet that RPG programmers have discovered at least 100 different ways to accomplish any given task. Sometimes the methods used are so poor you wonder how the program ever compiled. At other times, the solutions border on genius. If you're learning RPG from other people's examples, or even if you're just trying to improve your own RPG skills, how do you know which of these multitudinous methods are the best ones to use? It can be nearly impossible!

Midrange Computing magazine has been bringing you RPG techniques and advice for over 15 years, separating the wheat from the chaff, to give you the best information available. This book brings you the best of the best. If you need to know how to do something in RPG, chances are very good that you'll find it somewhere in this volume.

But RPG is a huge topic. There are things that you'd do in RPG III, but not do in RPG IV and visa versa. And then there are those RPG techniques that transcend a language subtype (i.e., RPG III or RPG IV). This chapter contains those RPG tips that are relevant over the entire RPG language spectrum. Within this chapter, you'll find RPG techniques that show you how to:

- Use a Key List (KLIST) when chaining to a file for Reading and Deleting.
- Use array names as DDS field names.
- Perform faster array lookups.
- Efficiently use Multiple Occurrence Data Structures.
- Create floating brackets in your RPG program.

This chapter might just help you become the best RPG programmer in your shop!

—*Shannon O'Donnell*

✦ ✦ ✦ Arrays

Counting Compile-time Array Source Statements

Do you need an easy way to count the number of lines in a compile-time table or array? You can do it with the Exclude Lines command in SEU. Just key XX over the first and last lines of the compile-time data and press Enter. SEU will tell you how many lines it excluded. You can press F5 to get the statements back. This really helped me when I had to build a compile-time array with almost 250 entries.

—Ted Holt

Faster LOKUP

As RPG III and RPG/400 programmers, have you wondered why IBM cannot give us an operation that would search an array starting from any array index and backwards to element 1? This would reduce processing time drastically when there is an application that requires storing unique data values in an array.

Sometimes, you have a maximum array size of 999 (or even 9,999) and need to scan through the entire array using LOKUP, in order to find out if the new element to be added already exists in the array, even though you know that most of the array is empty.

One technique you can use in such cases is to fill the array backwards. With a maximum array size of 9,999, the first element is stored at index 9,999, the second at 9,998, the third at 9,997, and so on.

In this way, the LOKUP operation can start from the index that is filled and go to the maximum. It certainly makes a lot of difference in the response time when you do this in an interactive program, such as to stop the user from entering a duplicate item number in order entry.

Of course (tongue in cheek) IBM could make our lives much easier by providing a new op code (LOKDN maybe?) and do this elegantly.

—Midrange Computing Staff

Implementing Stacks in RPG

A stack is a sequence in which all insert and remove operations occur at one end. The classic analogy is the spring-loaded plate dispenser found in cafeterias. When clean plates are added to the stack, the other plates are pushed down. When a plate is removed, the next plate pops up.

A good use of stack operations on the AS/400 is to implement **F9=Retrieve** to recall recently executed commands. This function can be included in any program that provides a command line for user execution of commands. Figure 14.1 shows how to use an array to implement a stack.

```
   ... 1 ... ... 2 ... ... 3 ... ... 4 ... ... 5 ... ... 6 ... ... 7 ...
E                   CMD          100100                    Previous CMD s
C                   Z-ADD1         X          20           Cmd Stack Indx
 /SPACE 1
C          SCNCMD   IFNE *BLANKS
C                   MOVELSCNCMD   CMD,X
C          X        IFLT 99
C                   ADD  1         X
C                   END
C                   END
 /SPACE 1
C          *INKI    IFEQ 1                                 F9=Retrieve
C                   MOVELCMD,X    SCNCMD
C          X        IFGT 1
C                   SUB  1         X
C                   END
C                   END
 ... 1 ... ... 2 ... ... 3 ... ... 4 ... ... 5 ... ... 6 ... ... 7 ...
```

Figure 14.1: Here's how to use an array to implement a stack in RPG.

One example is an order-entry program used by a data-entry operator who takes orders over the telephone. A command line is provided so that the operator can execute common commands (such as WRKSPLF) without exiting the program.

Another example is a menu program for the system operator, which retrieves menu option text and the program to be called from a database file. Figures 14.2 and 14.3 show how to achieve this technique.

The program also provides a command line. In both cases, when a command is executed, it is pushed onto the stack. When the **F9=Retrieve** key is pressed, the most recently executed command is popped off of the stack and displayed on the command line.

```
CRTDTAQ    DTAQ(QTEMP/STAKDTAQ) MAXLEN(155) SEQ(*LIFO) +
               TEXT( Data Queue for Stack Operations )
   CALL        PGM(STACKR2)
   DLTDTAQ    DTAQ(QTEMP/STAKDTAQ)
```

Figure 14.2: This CL program creates a data queue and then calls an RPG program to add a value to the data queue stack.

```
C*  Initialize fields.
C                     MOVEL STAKDTAQ DATAQ@ 10        Data Queue
C                     MOVEL *LIBL    DQLIB@ 10        DTAQ Library
C                     MOVE 155       FLDLN@  50       Field Length
C                     MOVE *ZEROS    WAITS@  50       WAIT Seconds
C                     MOVE *BLANKS   FIELD@155        Data Field
C                     MOVE *BLANKS   DQOPCD  4        OP Code
 /SPACE 1
C*  PUSH commands onto the DTAQ stack.
C          SCNCMD     IFNE *BLANKS
C                     MOVE  PUSH     DQOPCD
C                     MOVELSCNCMD    FIELD@
C                     EXSR XPRCDQ
C                     END
 /SPACE 1
C*  POP commands off the DTAQ stack.
C          *INKI      IFEQ  1                         F9=Retrieve
C                     MOVE  POP      DQOPCD
C                     EXSR XPRCDQ
C*   If field length is not zero, an entry was retrieved.
C          FLDLN@     IFNE *ZEROS
C                     MOVELFIELD@    SCNCMD
C                     ELSE
C*    Else, no more entries.  Reinitialize field length.
C                     MOVE 155       FLDLN@
C                     END
C                     END
 /SPACE 3
C*_____-*
C*  Process data queue PUSH/POP request.
C*_____-*
C          XPRCDQ     BEGSR
 /SPACE 1
C          DQOPCD     IFEQ  PUSH
C                     CALL  QSNDDTAQ
C                     PARM           DATAQ@
C                     PARM           DQLIB@
C                     PARM           FLDLN@
C                     PARM           FIELD@
C                     ELSE
```

Figure 14.3: Here's an RPG program that uses a data queue to implement a stack (part 1 of 2).

```
/SPACE 1
C            DQOPCD    IFEQ  POP
C                      CALL  QRCVDTAQ
C                      PARM        DATAQ@
C                      PARM        DQLIB@
C                      PARM        FLDLN@
C                      PARM        FIELD@
C                      PARM        WAITS@
C                      END
C                      END
/SPACE 1
C                      ENDSR
```

Figure 14.3: Here's an RPG program that uses a data queue to implement a stack (part 2 of 2).

—Jonathan Yergin

Multidimensional Array Conversions

RPG lacks one feature that other languages have had for a long time—multidimensional arrays. If you need arrays, you can use single-dimensional arrays instead. The trick is to convert the multidimensional subscripts to single subscripts.

Let's say you need a two-dimensional array that has three rows and five columns. You can use a 15-element, one-dimensional array instead. Row 1 goes in elements 1–5, row 2 in 6–10, and row 3 in 11–15.

To access element (R,C) use the calculation **(R-1) * row length + C** to find the subscript to the one-dimensional array. In this example, row length is 5 because there are five elements per row. So, element (2,4) would be found at **(2 - 1) * 5 + 4**, or element 9 of the one-dimensional array.

—Ted Holt

Screen Fields

Q: I have a display screen that consists of input/output fields for 18 part numbers and quantities, a single field for a warehouse number, and a function key. I defined a portion of the screen input/output buffer as an array of quantities in the RPG program that controls the display file. The code I'm using looks similar to the code shown in Figure 14.4.

```
*. 1 ...+... 2 ...+... 3 ...+... 4 ...+... 5 ...+... 6 ...+... 7
FSFC351DFCF  E                    WORKSTN
E                    QTY          18   3 0
IEXTDS1     E DSSFC351DF
I                                        2  55  QTY
```

Figure 14.4: Defining the I/O buffer as an array is the first step in using array elements as screen fields.

When I compile the RPG program, I get a compile-time error that says the field *IN03 is not valid for a data structure because the compiler repeats the "fields" from the file the data structure is referring to. For screens, the indicators are part of the I/O buffer and are therefore being included. I'd like to be able to manipulate my screen input to the program using array logic, if there is a means of doing so. Is there a way I can accomplish this?

A: There is a way to do what you want, but you can't use an external data structure. You have to rename the fields from the display file to array elements. For example, look at the RPG code shown in Figure 14.5. In this example, the quantity fields in the display file are named QTY01, QTY02, QTY03, and so on. The RPG program first defines an array called QTY. It then renames each of the quantity fields in the display file to a corresponding element of the QTY array. From that point on, the program can perform calculations or output by specifying the QTY array instead of the individual screen field names.

```
*. 1 ...+... 2 ...+... 3 ...+... 4 ...+... 5 ...+... 6 ...+... 7
FSFC351DFCF  E                    WORKSTN
E                    QTY          18   3 0
ISFC351FM
I             QTY01                       QTY,01
I             QTY02                       QTY,02
I             QTY03                       QTY,03
.
.
.
I             QTY16                       QTY,16
I             QTY17                       QTY,17
I             QTY18                       QTY,18
```

Figure 14.5: Here's how to use array elements as screen fields.

—*Midrange Computing Staff*

✦ ✦ ✦ Calling Programs

AS/400 Called Programs

Q: On the AS/400, is there a way to terminate called programs from the calling program? I have an interactive program that calls another program. If the called program uses F12 to return to the caller and then F3 is used from the caller, the called program remains active. I would like to keep the called program active until F3 is used from the called program or the calling program.

A: Assuming the language you're using is RPG III, the way to end the called program is with the FREE operation in the C-specs of the caller, or simply SETON LR within the called program. The FREE operation has the following format:

1. You may condition it with indicators.

2. Factor 1 is not used.

3. The op code is FREE.

4. Factor 2 must have a literal with the name of the program, or an alphanumeric field containing the name of the program and library name (or library list). Ex.: The field could have 'PRGM1.*LIBL' (System/38 or S/36 with RPG III) or '*LIBL/PRGM1' on AS/400.

5. The LOW resulting indicator can have an optional indicator that will turn ON if there is an error returned from the called program.

Because you want to stop the subprogram if F3 is pressed, I guess you could condition the FREE statement with KC.

On the other hand, the called program will stop itself automatically if you SETON LR in the called program prior to RETRN. There is one additional consideration. The FREE operation doesn't close files or unlock data areas. Therefore, you need to close the files opened by the called program. Simply use '*library/program*' or just plain '*program*' in Factor 2.

—*Ernie Malaga*

Calling with Fewer Parameters

RPG programs don't bomb when parameters defined in their *ENTRY parameter list are not passed; they only bomb when the unpassed parameters are referenced. This doesn't mean you have to always pass every parameter. There is a way to determine how many parameters have been passed. Set up a Program Status Data Structure (PSDS) and define a field for the special keyword *PARMS. You can code the PSDS as follows:

```
IPSDS        SDS
I                                    *PARMS    PARMS
```

Access the PARMS field to determine the number of parameters passed. Now your program can avoid referencing unpassed parameters.

—Midrange Computing Staff

On CALLing and PARMing

Q: I have a program I'd like to be able to CALL but also run from a menu. When I run it from the menu, I receive an error that says that I didn't pass the parameter. Is there a way to override this message?

A: You can do two things:

1. Change your menu so that the program is called passing dummy parameters such as blanks or zeros. The called program will have to be modified, of course, to recognize this situation as valid.

2. If the called program is an RPG program, you can use the program-status data structure to retrieve the number of parameters that were received by the program, as shown:

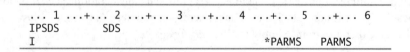

```
... 1 ...+... 2 ...+... 3 ...+... 4 ...+... 5 ...+... 6
IPSDS         SDS
I                                    *PARMS    PARMS
```

—Ernie Malaga

✦ ✦ ✦ Data Formatting

Case Conversion

With more and more computers talking to each other and exchanging data, the situation of having to convert uppercase characters to upper lowercase characters, and visa versa arises occasionally. Converting lowercase to uppercase is very easy. Just set on the second bit of each alphabetic character with the following operation:

```
BITON'1'    CHAR    1
```

Converting from upper to lowercase uses the BITOF command:

```
BITOF'1'    CHAR    1
```

Don't try to convert anything other than alphabetic characters. If you do, you could change a character to something completely different. Converting from uppercase to upper-lowercase adds more to think about—you must not change the first character of a word to lowercase if the word is in a name or address field.

Figure 14.6 shows a sample program that will convert uppercase to uppercase-lowercase for an alphanumeric field within a length of 100. All words or abbreviations will retain an uppercase first character. This program assumes that the input field has been loaded into array F (100 x 1). The code was created for the S/36 but will work on the S/38 or AS/400. However, S/38 and AS/400 programmers would probably want to make the three IFXX operations into an explicit AND group, which would eliminate levels 3 and 4 of the logic.

```
C*
C* Converts all upper case character string to upper-lower case
C*
C*  Input is array F (100 x 1) which is loaded with field to be converted
C*
C           2         DO   100      A       30
C           A         SUB  1        B       30
C*
C*  If previous character was not blank and this character is uppercase
C*  A-Z, then make it lowercase
C*
```

Figure 14.6: The uppercase-to-lowercase conversion process is demonstrated here using the BITOF keyword (part 1 of 2).

```
C            F,B      IFNE ' '
C            F,A      IFGE 'A'
C            F,A      IFLE 'Z'
C                     BITOF'1'        F,A
C                     END
C                     END
C                     END
C                     END
```

Figure 14.6: The uppercase-to-lowercase conversion process is demonstrated here using the BITOF keyword (part 2 of 2).

If you want to convert your own files, assess your requirements carefully for any changes or additions to the very basic logic of the sample program.

—Midrange Computing Staff

Floating Brackets for Negative Numbers

I recently had a fun problem. One of our accountants wanted to put brackets around negative numbers. I quickly added a compare-to-zero setting on an indicator and hard-coded brackets when the indicator was on. The output looked like this:

```
<      1.00>
<    315.00>
<  1,412.00>
```

The accountant said that it was not what he wanted. He wanted output that looked like this:

```
        <1.00>
      <315.00>
    <1,412.00>
```

He wanted floating brackets. I know how to do a floating $ sign:

```
O            SALES J   25 '$'
```

But how do you do floating brackets? The solution uses the foreign currency symbol capability. You put the symbol that you want to float in position 18 of the H-spec. Then you use that symbol just like the floating $ sign:

```
H        <
...
O        SALES J   25 '<'
O                  26 '>'
```

—Matt Kofsky

Watch for Default H-specs

When compiling working programs from our European offices on our U.S. system, we were getting errors QRG5150 (Literal factor 1 entry invalid) and QRG5167 (Factor 2 literal entry invalid). The lines with the errors had literal values such as 5,2 and 10000,01. We found out the problem was caused by having different default H-specs on each system.

Most AS/400 RPG programmers ignore the H-spec because they almost always want the default values. If no H-spec is declared, the RPG III compiler looks for data area RPGHSPEC in the library list and RPG IV looks for data area RPGLEHSPEC. If there is no data area in the library list, data area QRPG/DFTHSPEC is used for RPG III and QRPGLE/DFTLEHSPEC for RPG IV.

Our European programmers had created an RPGHSPEC data area with a J in column 21. This allows them to use the period for a thousands separator and the comma as the decimal separator. On their system, 5,2 is interpreted as five and two-tenths. However, on our system, it's a character string causing the errors.

—Kevin R. Cathey

String Manipulation with CAT

The expanded use of electronic date interchange (EDI) using ANSI X12 and other standards has created a greater demand for building delimited messages, but before you start putting messages together with your favorite operation, consider the performance implications. Let's say you are building a message with a maximum size of about 2 KB. The message consists of 40 data elements with a maximum size of 50 bytes each. Assume that each of the 40 data elements contains an average of 25 bytes of data and that the delimiter is already included in the individual data element.

Using CAT

The CAT operation is the simplest way to construct delimited messages. It requires only repeated use of the following operation:

```
C                        CAT   Source:0  Target
```

The CAT operation concatenates a source string to the end of a target string, meaning it must scan from the end of the target string back to the last nonblank character in the target string. Given the parameters described above, each CAT operation would scan through an average of 1.5 KB (longest scan = 2 KB; shortest scan = 1 KB). Building the message requires 40 CAT operations, meaning that the job would have to scan through 60 KB of data (40 * 1.5 KB) to build a single message. This might not sound like much overhead, but the processor must test each byte as it scans. When building a delimited message using the CAT operation, it is important to keep the size of the target string to a minimum.

Using %TRIMR

%TRIMR works the same way as CAT and is almost as simple. See the following code:

```
C                    EVAL    Target = %TRIMR(Target) + Source
```

The %TRIMR function scans the target string from the end to the last nonblank character and then adds the source string. This results in the same number of bytes being scanned as with the CAT operation.

Using CHECKR and %SUBST

This method requires a bit more effort on the programmer's part but drastically improves performance. In this scenario, you must manually keep track of the end of the target string, but you need to calculate only the length of the source string, as shown in Figure 14.7.

```
C        ' '    CHECKR    Source Length
C               EVAL      %SUBST(Target:Position:Length) =
C                             Source
C               EVAL      Position = Position + Length
```

Figure 14.7: Here's the best way to concatenate strings when you don't know their size.

Working with the original scenario of 40 data elements of length 50 containing 25 bytes of data each, the CHECKR operations used to build one message would require scanning a total of only 1KB (25 * 40) as compared to the 60 KB required by the CAT operation. The Position and Length variables could be defined as length-5 integer fields for maximum performance.

Another option would be to use the SCAN operation in combination with the %SUBST function, assuming there is a specific character to scan for at the end of each data element. Try setting up some tests with multiple- or different-sized messages, and compare the different methods yourself. You'll notice a difference, especially if you are still developing on a CISC box.

—*Lloyd Deviney*

✦ ✦ ✦ Data Structures

Multiple Occurrence External Data Structure

How many times have you had a program that had already retrieved a record and temporarily needed to get another record from the same file without overlaying the original field values? The most widely used method of performing this task is to define identical fields and move the data back and forth. This technique performs the task intended, but it requires the fields to be hard-coded in the program. This effectively circumvents the database concept of dynamic fields and field definitions.

A multiple-occurrence external data structure will perform the same task without requiring the fields or their definitions to be coded into the program. Additionally, this technique only requires a few lines of code, regardless of the number of fields in the file. In the example shown in Figure 14.8, a data structure is defined with two occurrences that reference the file name for the subfield definitions. An OCUR (OCCUR in RPG IV) statement is placed to access the first occurrence immediately before the initial read. Another OCUR statement is placed to access the second occurrence immediately before the "temporary" read.

```
... 1 ...+... 2 ...+... 3 ...+... 4 ...+... 5 ...+... 6
FCUSTMASTIF E           K        DISK
ICUSTDS    E DSCUSTMAST                    2
C          1           OCUR CUSTDS
C          KLIST       CHAINCUSTMAST                99
C          2           OCUR CUSTDS
C          KLIST       CHAINCUSTMAST                99
... 1 ...+... 2 ...+... 3 ...+... 4 ...+... 5 ...+... 6
```

Figure 14.8: This data structure, with two occurrences, references the file name for the subfield definitions.

Now the field values are safely stored away in the first occurrence of the data structure. After processing the "temporary" record, when you are ready to restore the field values, simply perform an OCUR operation to the first occurrence and the fields return to the values that they had before the "temporary" read was performed.

—*Midrange Computing Staff*

565

No More Tedious MOVE Statements

If you are like me and are tired of coding pages and pages of MOVE statements in your RPG programs, take note. The next time a vendor requires you to send them one file with two or more different record layouts, do not fear. Go ahead and populate those two or three files and then combine them into one using data structures with the keyword EXTNAME. Just give the data structures a name and key in the file name in parentheses after the keyword. Note: There are no date structure variables to follow the data structure name.

Then, read through each of the files, moving the data structure name to the target flat file field name. You've just moved the entire record to a flat file. You didn't have to predefine data structure variables for each field of each file, and you didn't have to MOVE every record field to them. Depending on the number of fields involved, you can save 50 to 1,000 lines of code with this technique.

—Steven W. McConnell

Retrieving an RPG Program Name

Occasionally, users bring me an old report in need of modification. After a little research, I sometimes find that the hard-coded RPG program name on the report is incorrect. Does the situation sound familiar?

Using the program status data structure, you can retrieve the RPG program name and place it in a 10-byte alphanumeric field (see Figure 14.9).

```
*. 1 ...+... 2 ...+... 3 ...+... 4 ...+... 5 ...+... 6 ...+... 7
I          SDS
I                                      *PROGRAM PRGNAM
```

Figure 14.9: You can retrieve the name of the RPG program that is executing via the Program Status Data Structure.

This field can then be placed in your output specs, alleviating the need to hard-code the program name.

—Aaron Barnes

What's This Program's Name?

Don't hard-code program names. A CL program can obtain its own name using the code fragment shown in Figure 14.10.

```
DCL VAR(&SENDER) TYPE(*CHAR) LEN(80)
DCL VAR(&PGM) TYPE(*CHAR) LEN(10)
DCL VAR(&MSGKEY) TYPE(*CHAR) LEN(4)
SNDPGMMSG MSG(' ') TOPGMQ(*SAME) MSGTYPE(*INFO) +
KEYVAR(&MSGKEY)
RCVMSG PGMQ(*SAME) MSGTYPE(*INFO) SENDER(&SENDER) +
RMV(*YES) MSGKEY(&MSGKEY)
CHGVAR VAR(&PGM) VALUE(%SST(&SENDER 56 10))
```

Figure 14.10: Don't hard-code program names.

RPG programs can obtain their names from the program status data structure. See Figure 14.11.

```
ISDS            DS
I                                        *PROGRAM PRGNAM


ISDS            DS
I                                            110     PGM
```

Figure 14.11: Use the program status data structure to obtain the program name.

—Midrange Computing Staff

✦ ✦ ✦ Database Files

Accessing an Externally Defined Record in RPG

Q: Something that really bugs me from time to time is that I can't access (in RPG) the entire record of an externally described file without having to put all the fields in the I-specs. Am I missing something? Is there a way to do this? One of the great benefits of having files externally described in RPG is that it pulls all the field definitions into the program for you. But what about the record? Is there a way to access the record format name?

A: As shown in Figure 14.12, you can use an externally defined data structure in conjunction with an externally defined file.

```
FMYFILE  IF  E          K        DISK
IMYREC      E DSMYFILE
C                    MOVE MYREC    THERE
```

Figure 14.12: The externally defined data structure in RPG can be accessed very easily.

The disadvantage is that a field cannot appear in more than one data structure. Therefore, you would have conflicts if you used this technique with two files with a common field name. Also, this won't work with a multiformat file; the data structure will be defined with the first record format. To access the name of the record format, use positions 261–270 of the INFDS File Information Data Structure.

—Midrange Computing Staff

Keep SETLL in Auxiliary Programs

When creating RPG programs that need only a SET*xx* op code to position a pointer in the file(s), you can first use a CL program to:

- Override the database file with SHARE(*YES)
- Call your RPG program from the CL
- Create a second RPG program, which is called from the first RPG passing the key values as parameters (which will position the pointer in the file, then return).

By eliminating any op code that changes the position of the pointer (other than a READ or READP) from within the main program, the RPG program will be able to block records during input and, therefore, reduce I/O count on the input files. This can reduce time and overhead considerably.

—Greg Leister

Noncontiguous Keys

Q: I've encountered a big problem. My shop is currently on an AS/400 and most of the software is still in the S/36 Environment. Any new development must be in RPG III.

There is one S/36 file on the system that is the core of the entire operation. This file contains multiple-record formats and each record contains repeating groups of data. Needless to say, this file would be difficult to convert to native without disrupting the current programs that use it.

I tried to write an RPG III program to utilize a logical file built over this physical file. The original file had a record key in positions 1 through 10. The alternate index file had a noncontiguous key, and thus EXTK had to be specified on the S/36 file-description specification to indicate this.

Using RPG III, I could not specify EXTK in the key starting location columns on the file-description specification. It demanded BLANKS or numeric data. Does this mean I will not be able to use any of my S/36 logical files with noncontiguous keys in RPG III?

A: RPG III doesn't distinguish between contiguous and noncontiguous keys. Code your F-spec as if the key begins in position 1 of the record. RPG won't know the difference, and your program will work just fine.

—Pete Hall

Retrieving a Relative Record Number

Q: In an RPG program, how do I retrieve the relative record number (RRN) of a record read using a keyed file? The file being read is a logical with duplicate keys allowed. After loading the records into a subfile in key sequence, I want to select a record for update. In order to grab the correct record, I thought I would write out the RRN to the subfile in a hidden field. Where can I find the RRN?

A: The relative record number of a database record in an RPG program is in binary form in positions 397 to 400 of the INFDS. If the RPG compiler requests blocking, the INFDS will be updated only when a block of records is read. You might need to prevent your program from reading blocks of records in order to get the RRN for each read. You can do this by specifying SEQONLY(*YES 1) on the Override Database File (OVRDBF) command.

—Midrange Computing Staff

✦ ✦ ✦ Display Files

Positioning the Cursor in a Window

The following is a typical scenario in one of our maintenance programs. A user displays a maintenance screen. The user then presses a command key to display additional information. Upon exiting, the user is returned to the maintenance screen and the cursor is positioned at the same screen location as it was prior to the press of the command key. This function is accomplished through the File Information Data Structure (INFDS in RPG) for the display file. The INFDS contains the current cursor location in positions 370–371. This information can then be used with the Cursor Location (CSRLOC) DDS keyword to position the cursor at its previous location.

A problem arises, however, when the first screen is a window. Positions 370–371 of the INFDS contain the cursor location relative to the full screen, but the CSRLOC keyword needs the cursor location relative to the starting position of the window.

The first time I tried the DDS window keywords, the cursor jumped around the screen every time I returned to it. My original solution to this problem was to calculate offset values based on the starting row and column of the window and adjust the values before redisplaying the screen. However, this can be a cumbersome solution if you design a window with variable starting locations. I have found a better, more generic solution.

In V2R2, IBM changed the File Information Data Structure for display files to include a field for the cursor position within the window (positions 382–383 of the INFDS). This binary field contains zeros if the screen being processed is not a window and contains the cursor position when processing a window format. The partial DDS and RPG code shown in Figures 14.13 and 14.14 illustrate the use of this technique.

```
*. 1 ...+... 2 ...+... 3 ...+... 4 ...+... 5 ...+... 6 ...+... 7
A                                          CSRLOC(ROW COL)
A           ROW            3  OH
A           COL            3  OH
```

Figure 14.13: Here's the partial display file for the cursor-positioning example.

```
*. 1 ...+... 2 ...+... 3 ...+... 4 ...+... 5 ...+... 6 ...+... 7
FDSPF    CF  E                     WORKSTN
F                                           KINFDS CSRPOS
 *
 * File Information Data Structure to determine cursor position
ICSRPOS      DS
I                                  B 370 3710SCR
I                                  B 382 3830WDW
 * If not a window, position cursor based on screen location
C           WDW     IFEQ *ZEROS
C           SCR     DIV  256       ROW
C                   MVR            COL
C                   ELSE
 *
 * Else (a window), position cursor based on window location
C           WDW     DIV  256       ROW
C                   MVR            COL
C                   ENDIF
```

Figure 14.14: Here's the RPG code segment for the cursor-positioning example.

—*Bruce Guetzkow*

RTNDTA Keyword Technique

The DDS keyword Return Data (RTNDTA) can eliminate the need to create separate variable names in display files used for database file updates. The display file can reference the database fields instead. There is no need to worry about field attributes matching between the database file and the display file. I don't have to code any MOVEs or Z-ADDs. In addition, my program size is smaller because there aren't as many variables. Here's how it's done.

DDS Coding

Place the RTNDTA keyword at the record level on the appropriate record of the display file. Use the database field names and reference the database file. This will bring the database fields into the display file automatically when you retrieve the database record.

RPG Coding

1. CHAIN and release the database record.

2. Display the screen.

3. Read the screen looking for changes and, if changes have been made, CHAIN again to the database record.

4. Reread the display format, using the READ operation.

   This is what makes this technique work. Because I chained again to the database record, the internal representation of the display file record is overlaid, and any changes to the display record are lost. But, by reading the display record again (with the RTNDTA keyword), you can retrieve the original values of the screen.

5. Update the database record.

—Andrew Krueger

✦ ✦ ✦ Error Handling

Taking Care of Decimal Data Errors

If you are plagued with decimal data errors (especially if you have migrated from a S/36) and you need a quick fix, try out this technique. You can compile your program with the compiler option, Ignore Decimal Data Error (IGNDECERR), set to *YES. Not only will it ignore the error, but—if you are updating files—it will initialize the numeric fields to 0. If you do have a file with decimal data errors that you would like to clean up quickly, a program to do this follows:

```
... 1 ...+... 2 ...+... 3 ...+... 4 ...+
FFILENAMEUP   E                     DISK
C                       UPDATRCDFMT
```

Make sure to compile with IGNDECERR(*YES).

—Midrange Computing Staff

✦ ✦ ✦ Indicators

Add Meaning to Your Display File Indicators

A good way to make your programs more readable and easier to maintain is to use the simple technique of renaming display-file response indicators. Response indicators are those indicators that are assigned to keywords (e.g., ROLLUP, ROLLDOWN, CFxx, CAxx). By using an RPG "I" specification with the applicable display-file record format name, you can rename any *IN response indicator to a descriptive name such as ROLLUP, EXIT, or PROMPT (see Figure 14.15).

```
6..10....+...20....+...30....+...40....+...50....+...60....+
IDSPFL01
I              *IN03                      EXIT
I              *IN05                      PROMPT
I              *IN61                      ROLLUP
```

Figure 14.15: Renaming display-file response indicators is a good way to avoid indicator errors.

Not only will your programs be more readable but, by looking at your "I" specifications, you can instantly cross reference all of your command keys. Unfortunately, option indicators (the indicators that condition display file fields) cannot be renamed.

—John Rittenhouse

Saving and Restoring Indicators

By making use of the RPG/400 predefined *IN array, you can save up to 99 indicators for those times when you don't have any indicators left or you don't want to be bothered finding an unused indicator. Here's an example of saving selected contiguous indicators 61–68.

```
... 1 ...+... 2 ...+... 3 ...+... 4 ...+... 5 ...+... 6
C                    MOVEA*IN,61     SAV8      8
C                    EXSRSUB1
C                    MOVEASAV8       *IN,61
```

The idea here is that all of the numeric indicators, 01–99, are mapped into the *IN array. The settings of a contiguous group of indicators can be saved by moving the *IN array to a save field, then restoring the save field into the *IN array. Using the same technique, you can also save all 99 indicators. Simply use a larger save field and apply the MOVEA to the entire *IN array, as illustrated here.

```
... 1 ...+... 2 ...+... 3 ...+... 4 ...+... 5 ...+... 6
C                    MOVEA*IN        SAV99    99
C                    EXSRSUB1
C                    MOVEASAV99      *IN
```

If you use a separate save field for each subroutine, this technique also can be used for nested subroutines.

—Midrange Computing Staff

✦ ✦ ✦ Key Fields

Always Use a Key List When Chaining

Factor 1 of an RPG CHAIN operation to an indexed file may contain either a variable name or a key list. For program-described files, factor 1 must contain a variable name. If the file is externally described and there are two or more key fields, factor 1 must contain a key list name. If the file is externally described and there is only one key field, factor 1 may contain cithcr. It is always good practice to use a key list for externally described files, even when only one key field is used in the CHAIN.

Look at the code shown in Figure 14.16. The employee master file, EMPMAS, is keyed on a single field, EMPNO. If EMPMAS has 500 records, one of which is for employee 9295, the CHAIN fails to find the record because it is looking for relative record number 9,295, not employee number 9295. The programmer has forgotten to include a K in the record address type field of the F-spec to indicate keyed access. This is an easy error to make and can result in debugging. If the programmer used a key list, as in Figure 14.17, the compiler would catch the error.

```
Fempmas   if      e        disk
C                 eval      empno = 9295
C         empno   chain     empmasr                99
C                 eval      *inlr = *on
```

Figure 14.16: The compiler doesn't catch the programmer's error in this example.

```
Fempmas   if      e        disk
C                 eval      empno = 9295
C         empkey  chain     empmasr                99
C                 eval      *inlr = *on
C
C         empkey  klist
C                 kfld      empno
```

Figure 14.17: Using a key list enables the compiler to catch the programmer's error.

—*Trent Holt*

Partial Key Lists

Q: Can someone point me to the reference manual explaining partial KLISTS? I am referring to a situation we all have where we need to read all of the detail records for a certain header file record. For example:

File	Key field	Positions	Decimals
HDR	HDORD#	1 – 6	
DTL	DTORD#	1 – 6	
	DTLNE#	7 – 8	0

I have seen KLISTs for file DTL where the only KFLD is HDORD#. The program is then coded to READE the detail file using the partial KLIST. I love the flexibility, but don't know where it is explained.

A: Actually, partial KLISTS can be used for any of the RPG record retrieval op codes. They work not only for SET*xx*, READE, REDPE, READ, and READP, but also for CHAIN, which can occasionally be very helpful if you need to validate something like a product category or region code, which might not be formally defined in a valid codes file. You could also use SETLL with a result indicator if you didn't actually need to retrieve the data.

The only requirement for a partial KLIST is that the KFLD definitions must exactly match the data definitions of the first *n* key fields in the access path. For a file with four key fields, see Figure 14.18.

```
DIVISION     2    *CHAR
CUSTOMER     9.0  *ZONED
ORDER        7.0  *DEC
LINE         3.0  *DEC

Any of the following would be valid key lists:

ORDKY1       KLIST
             KFLD         DIV     2
*
ORDKY2       KLIST
             KFLD         DIV     2
             KFLD         CUST    90
*
ORDKY3       KLIST
             KFLD         DIV     2
             KFLD         CUST    90
             KFLD         ORD#    70
*
ORDKY4       KLIST
             KFLD         DIV     2
             KFLD         CUST    90
             KFLD         ORD#    70
             KFLD         LINE#   30
```

Figure 14.18: Using partial key lists is a good way to read records.

If you want to retrieve records by order number, regardless of division and customer however, you would need to define a different access path.

As an aside, database management actually will let you retrieve records based on any substring of the entire key, regardless of key field boundaries. This is an unpublished feature, which IBM doesn't exactly say won't work. It actually does work. If you used a program-described file, you could use SETLL and READE to retrieve records based on the division and the first 2 bytes of the customer number, for instance. You could not chain directly to a record in the file using this type of a partial key, however. For a program-described file, the CHAIN op code requires a key field for factor 1, which matches the length of the entire key. KLISTS can't be used for program-described files.

—Pete Hall

Search Deletions

You're probably familiar with the DELET op code in RPG, but you might not know that you can place a key or relative record number in factor 1, the search argument. If the system finds duplicate records, the first record is removed. Figure 14.19 illustrates a technique I use to delete all records that match a key list value.

```
    *. 1 ...+... 2 ...+... 3 ...+... 4 ...+... 5 ...+... 6 ...+... 7
    C           *IN99     DOUEQ*OFF
    C           KEYLST    DELETERECORD                 99
    C                     ENDDO
```

Figure 14.19: Use a key list to accurately delete records.

—Aaron Barnes

Using Delete with a Key Value

I have seen many programs coded to use SETLL/READE or CHAIN and then DELETE when deleting records by a certain key value. You can use a key value with DELETE. Using DELETE with a key value deletes the first record found containing the specified key value; you do not need to use SETLL/READE, READ, or CHAIN before executing the delete. To delete multiple records with the same key value, use the following code:

```
*in99   doueq '1'
  key   delete  file    99 (=)
        endif
```

Doing this deletes all records containing the specified key value. You can use a field, data structure name, key list, or constant in factor 1.

—Greg Leister

✦ ✦ ✦ Level Breaks

Level Breaks on Partial Fields

Q: I'm new to RPG and I am having a problem with level breaks. I need to create a report that breaks on a 12-byte character field, but I want to break on only the first two positions of the field. Is this possible? How? The field is from an externally defined file. Thank you for your help.

A: Are you using the cycle for the level breaks or are you doing this yourself in the program? If you are using the cycle, you might be able to create a field definition in the I-specs for the external file and then put your level indicator on that. It would look something like the I-specs shown in Figure 14.20.

```
 ... 1 ...+... 2 ...+... 3 ...+... 4 ...+... 5 ...+... 6 ...+... 7
IFORMAT   NS
I                                         10  11 BREAK L1
```

Figure 14.20: Defining control breaks is as simple as providing the field name and level indicator.

This would create a field over positions 10 and 11 within the database record. Your program will still pull in every field available. If you are performing the tests within your program yourself, you can just move the first two characters to a work field, as shown in Figure 14.21.

```
 ... 1 ...+... 2 ...+... 3 ...+... 4 ...+... 5 ...+... 6 ...+... 7
C                        MOVELFIELD    BREAK   2
```

Figure 14.21: Program-defined breaks are automatically handled by the RPG cycle.

You can then perform your tests on this. You would just use NEWFLD as your level break. Another alternative would be to create a logical view of the data, containing a field that is a substring of the physical file field. Then you may use this derived field for your level break, as Figure 14.22 illustrates. Note that you would still use the data in FIELD2.

```
Physical file DDS
... 1 ...+... 2 ...+... 3 ...+... 4 ...+... 5 ...+... 6 ...+... 7
A          R PFREC
A            FIELD1         5
A            FIELD2        12
A            FIELD3         7  0

Logical file DDS
... 1 ...+... 2 ...+... 3 ...+... 4 ...+... 5 ...+... 6 ...+... 7
A          R LFREC                      PFILE(PFNAME)
A            FIELD1
A            FIELD2
A            FIELD3
A            NEWFLD               I      SST(FIELD2 1 2)
```

Figure 14.22: Creating a subset of a field is easy using DDS.

—James Coolbaugh
—Pete Hall

✦ ✦ ✦ Message Handling

Retrieving User Messages from an RPG Program

While searching the Resource Library topics list for message handling ideas for the AS/400, I came across several conversations on this subject that had been taken from the BBS. Someone was trying to figure out how to display a message on the screen in an interactive program in a way similar to the method of using message members on the S/36. Of the many suggestions offered, none of them included the use of the IBM-supplied subroutine SUBR23R3—Message Retrieval Subroutine. This routine is used in conjunction with message files. First you create the message file (CRTMSGF); then create your messages (ADDMSGD); then on an error in your RPG/400 program you simply tell SUBR23R3 which message to retrieve by calling the subroutine with the required parameters.

After creating your message file using USR9999 (9999 = any 4-digit ID number) for your MSGID codes, use OVRMSGF in your CL to use your own message file instead of the default QUSERMSG. (You could also add your message to QUSERMSG and eliminate this step, but I prefer to keep my messages separate.)

```
OVRMSGF MSGF(QUSERMSG)  TOMSGF(library/msgfile name)
```

There are five parameters that you must pass to the subroutine from your RPG/400 program. For more information on these parameters, see the section on "Calling Special Subroutines" in chapter 10 of the *RPG/400 User's Guide* (SC09-2074-01; QBJAQD01).

MSGID: A four-digit numeric field that will be prefixed with 'USR' and used to retrieve your message (similar to MIC).

Text Area: The name of the alpha field where the message text will be placed (I used the same name as an output-only field on the screen conditioned by my error indicator).

Level: A 1-byte numeric field that designates message level. Level 1 for this example is message text that is less than 132 characters.

Return Code: A 1-byte number field that will contain the return code from the call to SUBR23R3.

Text Length: A 4-byte number field that contains the length of the message text.

RPG/400 Example: In the first cycle routine in your program, initialize the parameter values as shown in Figure 14.23.

```
Z-ADD0       MSG#   40
MOVE *BLANKS MSGTXT 75
Z-ADD1       LVL    10
Z-ADD0       RTNCD  10
Z-ADD75      TXTLEN 40
```

Figure 14.23: To initialize the parameter values, use this code in the first cycle routine in your program.

When an error is encountered on the screen, just load MSG# with the MIC you want to retrieve from the message file and call the subroutine, as shown in Figure 14.24.

```
ERROR     IFEQ 'Y'
          Z-ADD0001    MSG#
          CALL 'SUBR23R3'
          PARM         MSG#
          PARM         MSGTXT
          PARM         LVL
          PARM         RTNCD
          PARM         TXTLEN
          END
```

Figure 14.24: This routine loads the message text to the field MSGTXT.

MSGTXT now contains the message text retrieved from message USR0001 in the specified message file.

—*Laura Collin*

Sending Messages from an RPG Program

Sending messages (even those that require a response) to a message queue from an RPG/400 program is simple with the DSPLY operation. Information messages, field values, and reply messages can be sent to the message queue with this operation.

For example, a batch job extracts certain records from a file based on a selection criteria. If a certain number of records is not extracted, the job is aborted. By using the DSPLY operation, one simple statement can notify the user through the user's message queue that the job has been aborted.

Here is the basic format of the statement (the compile time array ARM is used to accomplish easy message text set-up):

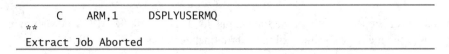

```
     C     ARM,1      DSPLYUSERMQ
  **
  Extract Job Aborted
```

Factor 1 contains the field name, literal, table name, or array element whose value is to be displayed.

Factor 2 contains the name of the message queue to which the message will be sent. If the job is batch and factor 2 is not specified, QSYSOPR becomes the default queue. If the job is interactive and factor 2 is not specified, *EXT becomes the default queue.

Result field contains the field that is to accept the response (see in the second example that follows).

You can display messages from a message file. This statement will display user message USR0001 from message file QUSERMSG:

```
C       *MUSR0001 DSPLY
```

The message identifier must be preceded by *M to indicate that this is a message.

The most powerful way in which to use the operation is to display a message and request a response. For example, you might want to give the operator the option to continue a batch job. The following statement will send the question, "Do you want to continue? (Y/N)" to the QSYSOPR message queue and the program will wait until a response is given.

```
C       ARM,1      DSPLY          RESP
```

There are some restrictions:

- You can DSPLY to any message queue except a program message queue.

- The maximum length of information that can be displayed is 52.

For more information about the DSPLY operation refer to the *RPG/400 Reference* manual (SC09-1089).

—Midrange Computing Staff

✦ ✦ ✦ Op Codes

RPG CLEAR Operation

The RPG CLEAR operation is a handy way to initialize all the elements in a structure or variable. It sets numeric fields to zero, character fields to blanks, and indicator fields to '0'. By specifying *NOKEY in factor 1, you can clear all fields in a DISK record format except key fields.

However, there is a catch. When the CLEAR operation is applied to a record format name, only output fields are affected. For file record formats with WORKSTN specified as the device in the file specification, only fields with a usage of output or both are affected by the CLEAR. Fields in DISK, SEQ, or PRINTER file record formats are cleared only if those record formats are output in the program. Input-only fields are not affected.

This means that if you define a file for input-only in the file specification record, any attempt to CLEAR its record format will have no effect at all.

—Midrange Computing Staff

Use the CLEAR Operation to Reduce Program Statements

The CLEAR op code can save a lot of time and headaches. For example, when writing a program that adds records to a file, don't code a series of MOVE, *BLANK, or *ZERO statements; instead, code a single CLEAR operation with record name in factor 2. The CLEAR op code automatically sets fields to their default value based on their field type. The CLEAR operation works against record formats, data structures, tables, arrays, and variables.

—Michael Catalani

✦ ✦ ✦ Parameters

Make Your RPG Programs More Flexible

You can call any RPG program that receives parameters, with or without actually passing parameters to the program, by using the program status data structure and the *PARMS keyword within your I-specs. The program status data structure is set up like any other data structure except you specify an 'S' in column 18. The subfields of the data structure are defined by special keywords. In this case, we use the keyword *PARMS (see Figure 14.25). We assign field name INPARM to contain the value that is returned through the *PARM keyword. Whatever the field name assigned to the *PARM keyword, it will be a three-digit numeric field. It will contain the number of parameters that are passed to your RPG program from the calling program. If the value is zero (no parameters passed), you cannot access the name of the field that is in your *ENTRY PLIST.

To get around this, you can simply check whether the value is zero or not, then take the proper action (such as MOVE *BLANKS) to another field to use in your program. This will bypass the error message "Reference to unpassed parameter." This message is saying that you are trying to use a field that you did not receive any data for (and you should have). So you are bypassing the use of the field, but you are taking the appropriate action if no parameters were passed. See the example shown in Figure 14.25.

```
.... ....1.... ....2.... ....3.... ....4.... ....5.... ....6.... ....7
1000 ISDS      SDS
1100 I                                      244 253 WSID
1200 I                                      254 263 USER
1300 I                                      *PARMS   INPARM
1400 C         *ENTRY    PLIST
1500 C                   PARM           PARTNO  5
1600 C*
1700 C         INPARM    IFEQ 0
1800 C                   MOVE *BLANKS    SCPART  5
1900 C                   ELSE
2000 C                   MOVE PARTNO     SCPART
2100 C                   END
2200 C*
.... ....1.... ....2.... ....3.... ....4.... ....5.... ....6.... ....7
```

Figure 14.25: Use this RPG code fragment as an example of how to count input parameters.

On line 1000, the program status data structure is defined. On line 1300, the field INPARM for the keyword *PARMS is defined. On line 1500, the field PARTNO (in which you should receive a value from the calling program) is defined. On line 1700, INPARM is checked to see if a parameter was passed. If so, move it into SCPART to be used in the program. If a parameter was not passed, INPARM will have a value of zero. Therefore, move blanks into SCPART.

If INPARM is zero, the program will never execute statement 2000 and we will not receive the message "Reference to unpassed parameter." This way the program will run perfectly.

You can use this for programs that are looking for any number of parameters to be passed. Or you can do any processing that you want based on the value of INPARM (as long as you do not use the field name of the variable for which you did not receive data).

We have used this technique for all of our inquiry programs. They can be called from a menu (without parameters), from another RPG program (to select and return parameters), or from a CL program. You can use this technique to eliminate the need for many three-line CL programs that do nothing more than CALL the RPG program and pass a blank parameter to it. Therefore, you can cut down on the number of CL programs and make your RPG programs more flexible at the same time. Plus, you can have one RPG program handle both your viewing data function and selecting data function.

—*Bruce Knoll*

✦ ✦ ✦ Performance

I/O Speed Demons

Because disk drives are not nearly as fast as memory, I/O operations are the slowest part of a program. You can speed up a program by replacing disk operations with operations to memory or by eliminating unnecessary disk operations. Suppose you have an employee master file that has:

- A department number field identifying which department an employee works in.

- A department master file keyed on department number, which also identifies the department.

- A payroll program that reads the employee master file sequentially and chains to the department master file to get the department description (Figure 14.26).

```
   *. 1 ...+... 2 ...+... 3 ...+... 4 ...+... 5 ...+... 6 ...+... 7
   FEMPMAST IF  E          K         DISK
   FDPTMAST IF  E          K         DISK
   *
   C                       READ EMPREC                        LR
   C           *INLR       DOWEQ*OFF
   *
   C           EM#DPT      CHAINDPTREC                    99
   C           *IN99       IFEQ *OFF
                            .
                            .
                            .
   C                       ENDIF
   *
   C                       READ EMPREC                        LR
   C                       ENDDO
```

Figure 14.26: Use this sample application as a guide to creating speedy program I/O.

To speed up this application, use a memory operation instead of a disk operation. Replace the random reads (RPG CHAIN) with array lookups. Read the entire department master file into an array at program initialization. Then, instead of chaining to the department master file to determine the department, look up the department in the array as shown in Figure 14.27.

```
*. 1 ...+... 2 ...+... 3 ...+... 4 ...+... 5 ...+... 6 ...+... 7
C           EM#DPT      LOKUPDPT,X                    99
C           *IN99       IFEQ *OFF
                           .
                           .
                           .
C                       ENDIF
```

Figure 14.27: You can reduce record I/O by using an array.

Another technique is to eliminate any unnecessary file I/O. If your file is too big to fit in a table or array, or you usually access only a few records, chain only if necessary. Save the department number in a variable, and chain only if the department number in an employee master record is different from the one saved in the variable, as shown in Figure 14.28.

```
*. 1 ...+... 2 ...+... 3 ...+... 4 ...+... 5 ...+... 6 ...+... 7
C           EM#DPT      IFNE SAVDPT
C           EM#DPT      CHAINDPTREC                   99
C           *IN99       IFEQ *OFF
                           .
                           .
                           .
C                       ENDIF
C                       MOVE EM#DPT   SAVDPT
C                       ENDIF
```

Figure 14.28: Reduce I/O by using a save field instead of another record chain.

—Ted Holt

✦ ✦ ✦ Printing

Large Page Numbers

A few years ago, while employed by a furniture manufacturer, I was asked to develop a report program to print a detailed list of inventory transactions. Contrary to most inventory transaction reports, this one would be costed, breaking down each transaction into its material, labor, and overhead costs for each work center—and sometimes there were eight work centers. This report never ran for less than 1,500 pages, and was usually much longer.

This company was relatively small. It occurred to me that, in a much larger organization (with a correspondingly larger volume of transactions), the report might exceed 9,999 pages. I wondered what would happen—after all, the PAGE field in RPG is implicitly defined as holding a maximum of four digits. So, I wrote the program shown in Figure 14.29.

```
FQSYSPRT O   F     132     OA      PRINTER
  *
C                         DO   10010
C                         EXCPTHEADER
C                         ENDDO
C                         MOVE *ON        *INLR
  *
OQSYSPRT E   306               HEADER
O                                      4 'PAGE'
O                              PAGE  1 +  1
```

Figure 14.29: RPG program XEM004RG demonstrates how page numbers are reused.

Then I ran it as follows:

```
SBMJOB CMD(CALL XEM004RG) JOB(TEST-PAGE) PRTTXT(*BLANK) OUTQ(QPRINT)
```

It quickly produced 10,009 pages in QPRINT. I selected the QPRINT output queue because it wasn't attached to any printers (so this huge report wouldn't kill any trees). Using option 5 of the Work with Spool Files (WRKSPLF) command, I displayed the report and went to the bottom (using "B" in the control field). Not good! The page number was reset to 0 after reaching 9,999, and kept increasing as 1, 2, and so on.

The trick here is that RPG allows you to define the PAGE field (including PAGE1 to PAGE7) with the width you want. In the *INZSR, simply Z-ADD *ZERO to PAGE, specifying the number of digits you want in columns 49–51, making sure the number of decimal places is zero (0 in column 52). Figure 14.30 shows a similar program using this technique.

```
FQSYSPRT O   F     132     OA      PRINTER
  *
C            COUNT        DOUEQ10010
C                         EXCPTHEADER
C                         ADD   1        COUNT
C                         Z-ADDCOUNT     PAGE
C                         ENDDO
C                         MOVE *ON        *INLR
  *
C            *INZSR       BEGSR
C                         Z-ADD1         COUNT    50
C                         ENDSR
  *
OQSYSPRT E   306               HEADER
O                                      4 'PAGE'
O                              PAGE  1 +  1
```

Figure 14.30: RPG program XEM005R shows how to recycle page numbers with *INZSR .

I ran this program with the following command:

```
SBMJOB CMD(CALL XEM005RG)   JOB(PAGE-OK)   PRTTXT(*BLANK)   OUTQ(QPRINT)
```

This produced the result that I wanted: I got page number 10,000 and higher. This technique can be used on a S/36, too. Now, if I could only find a way to redefine the PAGNBR DDS keyword....

—Midrange Computing Staff

More Than Eight Printer Files in RPG

Did you ever have the need for more than eight printer files in an RPG program? If so, you probably learned that you are limited to a maximum of eight. So, what to do?

Here is a solution. Create a disk file of a length equal to the maximum required printer output line length, plus 6 (e.g., a 132-column printer file will have a disk file length of 138 bytes).

Code your program to output your formatted print data to this disk file instead of a printer file. For each line, place the printer control values for space before, space after, skip before, and skip after in the extra 6 bytes of this disk file. Simply code these as literals in the output specs.

For example, if your printer file statements are as shown in Figure 14.31, then your disk file statements will be as shown in Figure 14.32.

```
OQSYSPRT E 1201           PRINT
O                         FIELD1    12
O                         FIELD2    37
O                         FIELD3    59
O                                   110 'Literal 1'
```

Figure 14.31: Here's what your original output file might look like in your RPG program.

```
ODISKFILEE                PRINT
O                         FIELD1    12
O                         FIELD2    37
O                         FIELD3    59
O                                   110 'Literal 1'
O                                   138 '1201'
```

Figure 14.32: Add the output specs to define the disk file, which you'll write to instead.

If the printer file in this example had a skip after value, then that value would have replaced the two blank bytes in positions 137–138 in the disk file.

Your next step is to write a short RPG program (like the example shown in Figure 14.33) to read this disk file and print each line. But how can you control the line spacing? Easily. Just use the PRTCTL option by specifying it as a continuation line on the printer file F-spec and include the LINE data structure as shown in Figure 14.33.

```
FDISKFILEIF F    138              DISK
FQSYSPRT O  F    132              PRINTER      KPRTCTLLINE
 *
IDISKFILENS
I                                   1 132 DATA
I                                 133 133 SBF
I                                 134 134 SAF
I                                 135 136 SKBF
I                                 137 138 SKAF
 *
ILINE       DS
I                                   1   1 SPBEFR
I                                   2   2 SPAFTR
I                                   3   4 SKBEFR
I                                   5   6 SKAFTR
I                                   7  90CURLIN
 *
C           *INLR     DOUEQ '1'
C                     READ DISKFILE                  LR
C           *INLR     IFEQ '0'
C                     MOVE SBF    SPBEFR
C                     MOVE SAF    SPAFTR
C                     MOVE SKBF   SKBEFR
C                     MOVE SKAF   SKAFTR
C                     EXCPTPRINT
C                     END
C                     END
 *
OQSYSPRT E            PRINT
O                     DATA    132
```

Figure 14.33: Now read the disk file you wrote to (Figure 14.32) and print the line, using the PRTCTL option.

Each time you read a record of your disk file, move the spacing and skipping control values from the last 6 bytes of the record into the data structure fields. Use one output line with no spacing or skipping control values. The PRTCTL option will take care of this for you. There you have it. Your printed output should look exactly as it would have printed in the original program.

—Lee Marcus

Editor's Note: When you write any numeric variables to DISKFILE, be sure not to pack them (leave column 44 blank). You should act as though you're writing directly to the PRINTER file. This means that you should also use edit codes or edit words if appropriate.

✦ ✦ ✦ Record Locking

Avoid Record Lock Errors

To prevent RPG programs running in batch from blowing up on a record lock, use the error indicator on the CHAIN operation (pos. 56–57) as follows:

```
 ... 1 ...+... 2 ...+... 3 ...+... 4 ...+... 5 ...+... 6 ...+
 C           *IN59        DOUEQ'0'
 C           Key          CHAINFormat                   5059
 C                        ENDDO
```

Indicator 59 will be set on only if there is an error with retrieving the format—it does not replace or interfere with the no-record-found indicator (50). In interactive programs you would not want to use the do-until loop; however, using the error indicator is a good way to let a user know that someone else is using the record. The error indicator is also available with any of the read operations, but the file has to be repositioned if it is set on.

—William MacKenzie Picou

Record Locking with READE/READPE

Recently, a record-lock error popped up randomly, and the only thing we could figure was that it was on a READE or READPE statement. After referencing the *ILE RPG/400 Reference* manual and performing some serious debugging, we identified the problem.

If the file you are performing the READE or READPE on is defined as update, a temporary lock is placed on the next record and compared to the search argument in factor 1. This happens even if the next record does not meet the search criteria. If the record is found not to match the key value, the record-not-found indicator is turned on and the lock is removed.

A simple example shows how this could cause problems. Suppose you have a file that is used to receive items into the warehouse. These items are spread out among different users so that everyone with an RF terminal can share the work. The key to the file is user ID. A user selects the menu option, and the program begins processing READE operations on the file, using the current user ID as the search argument. Figure 14.34 shows a simple example of what this data might look like in the file.

User	Item	Quantity ordered	Quantity Rcvd
BVSTONE	AB-109	10	10
BVSTONE	KT-44	19	42
BVSTONE	LL-009	19	18
CHWELLS	BT-873	5	
CHWELLS	BU-909	1	
RJLARSON	FY-310	2	
RJLARSON	GR-250	25	

Figure 14.34: Example data keyed on user ID.

Users Brad Stone (BVSTONE), Chad Wells (CHWELLS), and Rod Larson (RJLARSON) receive items. Suppose Brad Stone begins receiving items a few minutes before Chad. By the time Chad gets to work, Brad is almost done. He is entering in the amount received on his last item (LL-009). Chad begins to receive items and has just read his first record. Before Chad enters the amount received for his first item (BT-873), Brad completes his last transaction and presses Enter. He gets an error saying that the requested record is in use.

In this case, Chad has a record lock on his first item, and Brad's job tried to check that record to see if the key matched the search criteria (in this case, his user ID, BVSTONE). Before the program can check the value, it must obtain a temporary lock, but it couldn't because of Chad's record lock. So the program crashed.

An easy solution to this problem is to put an error indicator in the low-resulting indicator of the READE statement, as in Figure 14.35. I use the same indicator that I use to detect EOF so that, if this problem arises, the program treats the error the same as EOF.

```
C**                                        HiLoEq
C              READEFMT01                   5151
```

Figure 14.35: An error indicator prevents record lock.

Another solution is to use the No-Lock option on the READE operation. When you are ready to update, simply chain to the file using the unique key, and process the update. This technique eliminates the need for the temporary lock that the system will try to place on the next record.

—Bradley V. Stone

✦ ✦ ✦ Source Editing Tips

A Quick and Easy Way to Find a Subroutine in an RPG Program

Very often, when coding RPG programs, a programmer needs to jump to the beginning of a subroutine. When writing or modifying very large programs, finding a specific subroutine can be a very time-consuming process. However, there's a way to quickly and easily accomplish this. On the SEU command line, at the top of the screen, simply type the following command: **F <subroutine name> 18 F**. This will cause SEU to scan forward through the source code for the first occurrence of <subroutine name> starting in column 18. For RPG IV source, change the number 18 to 12.

—Reynaldo G. Cabanban Jr.

✦ ✦ ✦ Subfiles

How to Display an Empty Subfile

I've recently discovered a solution to the problem of not being able to display an empty subfile. For the most part, you would not want to display a subfile without records. However, there are occasions when this concept would be very useful. For example, suppose you are displaying a search screen that contains a subfile. Then a user enters a value that is past the end of the file you are reading. It would be nice to display an empty subfile and a message specifying that the parameters entered are out of the limits of the file. However, if you try this, you receive the IBM message "Session or device error occurred" stating that it cannot process the subfile request.

All that is needed to correct this problem on the AS/400 is to successfully load the subfile one time in the program. After that, it can be displayed even when it is empty. I achieve this by adding a few lines of code in my INIT subroutine (see Figure 14.36), which is executed only once during the program.

```
   ...1.... ....2.... ....3.... ....4.... ....5.... ....6.... ....7....
   ************************************************************************
   * INIT - Housekeeping subroutine only executed once
   ************************************************************************
               INIT      BEGSR
   * Clear and activate subfile
                         MOVEA'01'      *IN,95
                         WRITESFLCTL
                         MOVEA'00'      *IN,95
```

Figures 14.36: Displaying an empty subfile is not hard. Here's how to do it (part 1 of 2).

```
* Write one record to subfile
                    ADD  1        SFLRRN
                    WRITESFLREC
* Clear subfile again
                    MOVEA'01'     *IN,95
                    WRITECTL
                    MOVEA'00'     *IN,95
*
                    ENDSR
  *IN95 - SFLDSPCTL
  *IN95 - SFLDSP
  *IN96 - SFLCLR
...1.... ....2.... ....3.... ....4.... ....5.... ....6.... ....7....
```

Figures 14.36: Displaying an empty subfile is not hard. Here's how to do it (part 2 of 2).

First, I clear the subfile to activate it; then, I write just one record to it. After that, I clear the subfile again and the system still thinks it is successfully loaded. When this routine is complete, the subfile can be displayed at any point in the program—even when it is empty.

—*Donald McGrath*

Multiple Error Message Processing

Perhaps the best example of how RPG programming methods vary is the variety of ways to handle screen error messages. In many programs when a user fills a screen with data and presses Enter, he or she is presented with a single error message, only to find that when the user presses Enter again, another message is displayed about the data in some other field. This error checking process is fairly common, but is not always the most efficient way to display multiple errors.

Using a subfile for the display of error messages lets you present a one-line-at-a-time subfile display that allows you to roll through multiple error messages. When looking at the first message, you know there are other messages to look at if you see a plus sign at the right of the message.

The following code samples illustrate how to code for multiple error messages by using a subfile. They are simple enough for you to integrate them easily into your coding style. Before long, the use of those one-at-a-time methods will become less common.

Figure 14.37 contains the record formats that must exist in the display file in order to display the errors. These record formats can be added "as is" to any DDS and require no changes to work in most situations. The only limits they place on your screens are that line 24 must be reserved for use by the error subfile, and indicator 99 must not be used elsewhere in your program or DDS.

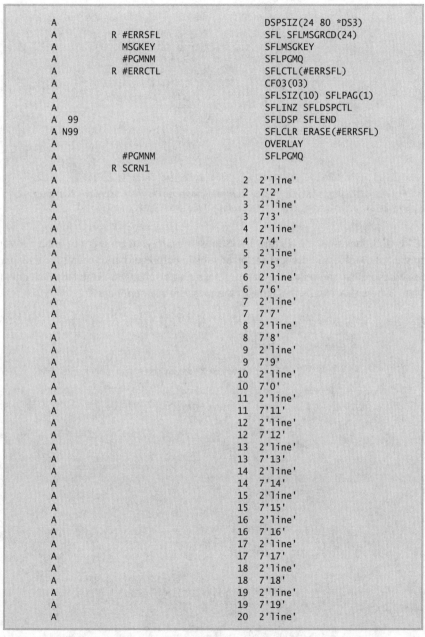

```
A                                        DSPSIZ(24 80 *DS3)
A           R #ERRSFL                    SFL SFLMSGRCD(24)
A             MSGKEY                      SFLMSGKEY
A             #PGMNM                      SFLPGMQ
A           R #ERRCTL                    SFLCTL(#ERRSFL)
A                                        CF03(03)
A                                        SFLSIZ(10) SFLPAG(1)
A                                        SFLINZ SFLDSPCTL
A  99                                     SFLDSP SFLEND
A N99                                     SFLCLR ERASE(#ERRSFL)
A                                        OVERLAY
A             #PGMNM                      SFLPGMQ
A           R SCRN1
A                                     2  2'line'
A                                     2  7'2'
A                                     3  2'line'
A                                     3  7'3'
A                                     4  2'line'
A                                     4  7'4'
A                                     5  2'line'
A                                     5  7'5'
A                                     6  2'line'
A                                     6  7'6'
A                                     7  2'line'
A                                     7  7'7'
A                                     8  2'line'
A                                     8  7'8'
A                                     9  2'line'
A                                     9  7'9'
A                                    10  2'line'
A                                    10  7'0'
A                                    11  2'line'
A                                    11  7'11'
A                                    12  2'line'
A                                    12  7'12'
A                                    13  2'line'
A                                    13  7'13'
A                                    14  2'line'
A                                    14  7'14'
A                                    15  2'line'
A                                    15  7'15'
A                                    16  2'line'
A                                    16  7'16'
A                                    17  2'line'
A                                    17  7'17'
A                                    18  2'line'
A                                    18  7'18'
A                                    19  2'line'
A                                    19  7'19'
A                                    20  2'line'
```

Figure 14.37: Display file SFLMSGDF contains the record formats and fields that must exist in your own display files to use a message subfile (part 1 of 2).

```
A                                    20  7'20'
A                                    20 60'Enter'
A                                    20 66'an'
A                                    20 70'A'
A          FLD001      1   B 20 76
A                                    22 11'F3=Exit'
A                                    23  2'Line'
A                                    23  7'23'
A                                    21  2'line'
A                                    21  7'21'
A                                     1  2'line'
A                                     1  7'1'
```

Figure 14.37: Display file SFLMSGDF contains the record formats and fields that must exist in your own display files to use a message subfile (part 2 of 2).

The RPG/400 lines shown in Figure 14.38 must exist in your program in order for you to set up the #MSG table and process the error subfile before and after each time a display is processed. Note that the only line that might need to be changed is the MOVE 'SAMPMF' #MSGFIL, where SAMPMF is the name of the message file being used.

```
**********************************************************************
*     PROGRAM NAME:  SFLMSGRPG
*           AUTHOR:  Bernal Schooley
*          PURPOSE:  Example of processing multiple error messages
*                    through the use of a subfile.
**********************************************************************
FSFLMSG  CF  E                     WORKSTN
E                   ARM      1   7   7
E                   #MSG        25   7
I* Get this program name
I          SDS
I                                      *PROGRAM #PGMNM
C                   DO   7       I      10
C                   MOVE ARM,I      #MSG,I
C                   END
 *
C          *INKC    DOWNE'1'
C                   EXFMTSCRN1
C          FLD001   IFEQ 'A'
C                   Z-ADD7          E      20
C* SAMPMF is the name of the message file containing user messages
C                   MOVEL'SAMPMF'   #MSGFL 10
C                   EXSR #ERDSP
C                   EXSR #ERCLR
```

Figure 14.38: RPG program SFLMSGRPG demonstrates how to write to the message subfile (part 1 of 2).

```
C                     END
C                     END
 *
C                     SETON                        LR
C          #ERDSP     BEGSR
C          E          IFNE 0
C* Call generic CL program to send message to program message
C* queue.
C                     CALL 'SFLMSGCL'
C                     PARM           #MSGFL
C                     PARM           #MSG
C                     PARM           #PGMNM
C                     PARM           E
C                     MOVE '1'       *IN99
C                     EXFMT#ERRCTL
C                     END
C                     ENDSR
C          #ERCLR     BEGSR
C          E          IFNE 0
C                     MOVE *BLANKS   #MSG
C                     Z-ADD*ZERO     E
C                     MOVE '0'       *IN99
C                     WRITE#ERRCTL
C                     END
C                     ENDSR
** User defined message numbers stored in message file SAMPMF
USR0001
USR0002
USR0003
USR0004
USR0005
USR0006
USR0007
```

Figure 14.38: RPG program SFLMSGRPG demonstrates how to write to the message subfile (part 2 of 2).

The library in which the CL program resides (see Figure 14.39) must exist in the library list of the person who will be executing your program. The ERRCTL25 program is used to clear any accumulated messages in the program message queue, and send any new error messages.

```
SFLMSGCL: +
    PGM PARM(&MSGFL &MSGTBL &PGMNM &E)

    DCL VAR(&MSGFL)      TYPE(*CHAR) LEN(10)
    DCL VAR(&MSGTBL)     TYPE(*CHAR) LEN(175)
    DCL VAR(&PGMNM)      TYPE(*CHAR) LEN(10)
    DCL VAR(&E)          TYPE(*DEC)  LEN(2 0)
    DCL VAR(&MSG)        TYPE(*CHAR) LEN(7)
    DCL VAR(&X7)         TYPE(*DEC)  LEN(3 0)    VALUE(1)
    DCL VAR(&X)          TYPE(*DEC)  LEN(2 0)    VALUE(1)


    RMVMSG PGMQ(*SAME &PGMNM) CLEAR(*ALL)

  LOOP: +
    CHGVAR VAR(&MSG) VALUE(%SST(&MSGTBL &X7 7))
    SNDPGMMSG MSGID(&MSG) MSGF(*LIBL/&MSGFL) TOPGMQ(*SAME &PGMNM)
    CHGVAR VAR(&X) VALUE(&X + 1)
    CHGVAR VAR(&X7) VALUE(&X7 + 7)
    IF COND(&X *LE &E) THEN(GOTO CMDLBL(LOOP))

    ENDPGM
```

Figure 14.39: CL program SFLMSGCL demonstrates how to use a load and clear the message subfile.

In order to send the appropriate messages, add the following code for each error that you are processing.

```
C           ADD   1          E
C           MOVE  'AAA0001'  #MSG,E
```

where AAA0001 is the message number of the error. Then, just before you redisplay the screen which is in error, the following subroutine should be called to display the error subfile:

```
C           EXSR  #ERDSP
```

After the screen is displayed and control has returned to the program, the following subroutine should be called to clear the subfile for the next set of field-checking routines:

```
C           EXSR  #ERCLR
```

An additional consideration is that your screen has the OVERLAY keyword so that the subfile is not erased when your screen is written to the display.

—Bernal Schooley

596

Reading from Subfiles

Q: I am in the middle of creating an interactive program that uses a subfile. The subfile provides input-capable fields on the left-most column so that the user can enter option numbers (such as IBM's WRKSPLF command). In addition, I would like to provide several other input fields. Circumstances have forced me to include some of the additional input fields into a separate record format that is not the subfile control record. How can I code my RPG program so that it receives all input: the option numbers and the additional input fields?

A: All you need to do is code several READ operations one after the other. For example, let's suppose your subfile control record is called CTL1 and the other input-capable panel is called INPUT1. Code the following:

```
C          WRITEINPUT1
C          EXFMTCTL1
C          READ INPUT1        99
```

The EXFMT operation on the subfile control record (CTL1) reads the subfile control record (if any input fields are present) and the option fields from the subfile records. The READ operation that follows processes the additional panel you have.

—Midrange Computing Staff

Reading Multiple Subfile Records

Q: Is there a way to allow entry above, in, and below a subfile at the same time? I can do above and in, but there are problems when I try to add below. Any suggestions?

A: One little-known fact about RPG is that it can process several READ op codes simultaneously. You can take advantage of this feature in your situation. Suppose you name your subfile control record SFLCTL. Above it, there's an input-capable record named ABOVE, and below it is another called BELOW. Code your RPG program as shown in Figure 14.40. You can do this in any order that makes sense to you and be sure that all input-capable fields in all three records (SFLCTL, ABOVE, and BELOW) will be processed by the program.

```
....!... 1 ...+... 2 ...+... 3 ...+... 4 ...+... 5 ...+... 6 ...+... 7
          C                    WRITEABOVE
          C                    WRITEBELOW
          C                    EXFMTSFLCTL
          C                    READ ABOVE                   90
          C                    READ BELOW                   91
```

Figure 14.40: Reading multiple subfile records is easy when you know how!

—*Midrange Computing Staff*

Subfiles, Rolling, and Enter

Q: I'm having trouble with subfiles. I have set subfile size one greater than subfile page and then loaded the subfile. The problem occurs if I press Roll Up several times and then press Roll Down to the top (which is handled by OS/400), and then press Enter. OS/400 jumps back to the last record in the subfile. I would rather have the subfile not roll when I press the Enter key. Is this possible? I have tried experimenting with the RRN, but have had no success.

A: Yes, you can control which page is displayed at any given time. In the information data structure for a display file, there are three values available to give you information about the subfile that is currently being displayed. These are as follows:

```
IINFDS     DS
I               B 376 3770SFLRR#
I               B 378 3790SFLPG#
I               B 380 3810SFLREC
```

The one you are interested in is SFLPG#. This value will give you the relative record number of the first subfile record currently being displayed. In other words, the current page you are on. The information data structure is updated by OS/400 when the subfile page changes. So, all you need to do is take this value and load it into the variable you have specified on the SFLRCDNBR keyword on your subfile. This will then position you to the page that contains that record.

—*James Coolbaugh*

RPG III

*A*lthough IBM no longer enhances RPG III, the language is still very much in use. Also frequently called "RPG/400," many shops still use it as their primary development language and others still maintain code written in it.

It's undeniable that RPG III has been tremendously successful since its introduction with the System/38. And that is no wonder. RPG III is not a "sexy" language, but it's easy to learn and is well suited to typical business-programming tasks such as report generation, interactive processing, and file processing.

This chapter will give the RPG III programmer a full toolbox of powerful techniques as well as methods to circumvent some of RPG III's inherent weaknesses. Here are some of them:

- RPG III cannot do date arithmetic. Actually, it can't even recognize a date of the date data type. Instead, the compiler generates instructions to convert the date to an alphameric string.

- RPG III has only rudimentary string-handling capabilities, implemented in the SUBST, CAT, and SCAN operations.

- Although most business information processing requires only basic math operations, RPG III has no operation codes for the occasional higher math functions required of business programmers.

- RPG III's fixed format calculations do not allow programmers to indent source code to show levels of nesting.

- RPG III does not support local variables. All identifiers are global in scope.

While IBM has addressed many of these shortcomings in the RPG IV language, that's no help to programmers who must still write, maintain, and modify RPG III programs. Most of the techniques in this chapter were developed to address such shortcomings.

—Ted Holt

✦ ✦ ✦ Arrays and Tables

Commands in Compile-time Arrays

When calling QCMDEXC in an RPG program to execute a command, you might sometimes find it useful to define that command as a compile-time entry. An easy way to get the syntax of the command correct the first time in SEU is to use F13 to change the session defaults. Move down to the source type line, change it to CLP, and press Enter. Type the CL command and press F4 to prompt. When done, be sure to use F13 again to change the source type back to RPG.

—Midrange Computing Staff

External Fields to Array Elements

Here is an example of renaming fields from an external file to array elements so that they can be referenced by an index. Figure 15.1 shows a series of identical fields defined in DDS. Figure 15.2 shows how they are renamed as an array in RPG input specifications. Refer to Input Specifications, Externally Described Files in the *RPG Reference Manual and Programmer's Guide* for more information. Note that the display file fields must be defined as B, both input and output. To prevent input, you may specify DSPATR(PR).

```
A          R FM01
A            SLN01        65A  B   3  8DSPATR(PR)
A            SLN02        65A  B   4  8DSPATR(PR)
A            SLN03        65A  B   5  8DSPATR(PR)
A            ...          ...  ...  ...
A            SLN20        65A  B  22  8DSPATR(PR)
```

Figure 15.1: DDS does not support arrays.

```
FARRAY1FMCF  E                      WORKSTN
E                  LIN        20 65               DISPLAY LINES
I*  The following external                will be renamed to the
I*  fields from format FM01 ...           following RPG fields.
IFM01
I             SLN01                        LIN,01
I             SLN02                        LIN,02
I             SLN03                        LIN,03
I             ...                          ...
I             SLN20                        LIN,20
```

Figure 15.2: Rename external fields as array elements in input specs.

—Jonathan E. Yergin

✦ ✦ ✦ Data Handling

Decimal-to-Binary Conversion

Q: Is there a way to convert decimal data to binary in "character" form using RPG or CL on an AS/400? Figure 15.3 illustrates the type of conversion I need.

Decimal number	Binary representation in character format
1	"00000001"
2	"00000010"
255	"11111111"

Figure 15.3: Decimal numbers need to be converted to binary literals.

A: Yes, there is an easy way to perform this conversion. The code shown in Figure 15.4 will do the job.

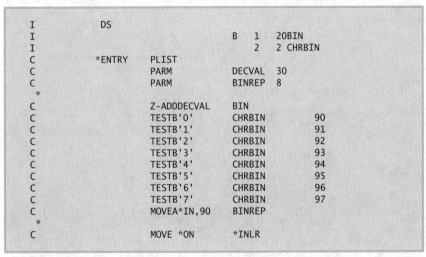

```
I            DS
I                              B   1   20BIN
I                                  2   2 CHRBIN
C       *ENTRY   PLIST
C                PARM          DECVAL 30
C                PARM          BINREP  8
 *
C                Z-ADDDECVAL   BIN
C                TESTB'0'      CHRBIN         90
C                TESTB'1'      CHRBIN         91
C                TESTB'2'      CHRBIN         92
C                TESTB'3'      CHRBIN         93
C                TESTB'4'      CHRBIN         94
C                TESTB'5'      CHRBIN         95
C                TESTB'6'      CHRBIN         96
C                TESTB'7'      CHRBIN         97
C                MOVEA*IN,90    BINREP
 *
C                MOVE *ON       *INLR
```

Figure 15.4: This short routine converts a decimal number to an 8-byte character string representing the binary equivalent.

Just pass in a decimal value between 0 and 255 that you want to convert and this program will pass back the binary representation in an 8-byte character field.

—Midrange Computing Staff

Decimal-to-Hex Conversion

When communicating with ASCII computers through the async workstation controller of our AS/400, I sometimes need to convert a decimal number to its equivalent hexadecimal value. I wrote a short RPG program (HEX001RG) to handle the conversion. See Figure 15.5.

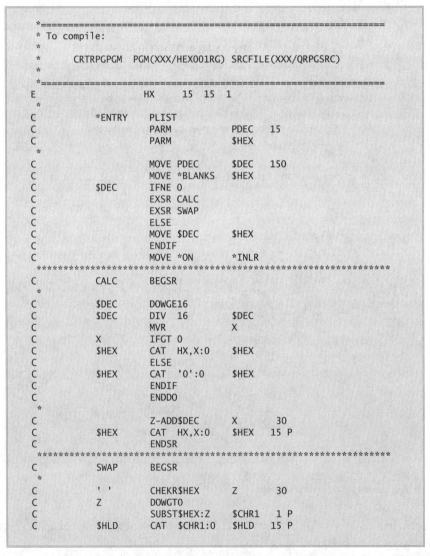

```
*=================================================================
* To compile:
*
*     CRTRPGPGM  PGM(XXX/HEX001RG) SRCFILE(XXX/QRPGSRC)
*
*=================================================================
E                 HX     15  15  1
 *
C        *ENTRY   PLIST
C                 PARM            PDEC   15
C                 PARM            $HEX
 *
C                 MOVE PDEC       $DEC   150
C                 MOVE *BLANKS    $HEX
C        $DEC     IFNE 0
C                 EXSR CALC
C                 EXSR SWAP
C                 ELSE
C                 MOVE $DEC       $HEX
C                 ENDIF
C                 MOVE *ON        *INLR
 ***************************************************************
C        CALC     BEGSR
 *
C        $DEC     DOWGE16
C        $DEC     DIV  16         $DEC
C                 MVR             X
C        X        IFGT 0
C        $HEX     CAT  HX,X:0     $HEX
C                 ELSE
C        $HEX     CAT  '0':0      $HEX
C                 ENDIF
C                 ENDDO
 *
C                 Z-ADD$DEC       X      30
C        $HEX     CAT  HX,X:0     $HEX   15 P
C                 ENDSR
 ***************************************************************
C        SWAP     BEGSR
 *
C        ' '      CHEKR$HEX       Z      30
C        Z        DOWGT0
C                 SUBST$HEX:Z     $CHR1  1 P
C        $HLD     CAT  $CHR1:0    $HLD   15 P
```

Figure 15.5 This RPG routine converts decimal values to hexadecimal literals (part 1 of 2).

```
C                     SUB  1          Z
C                     ENDDO
  *
C                     MOVE *BLANKS    $HEX
C             ' '     CHEKR$HLD        Z
C             15      SUB  Z           Z
  *
C             Z       DOWGT0
C             $HEX    CAT  '0':0      $HEX
C                     SUB  1           Z
C                     ENDDO
  *
C             $HEX    CAT  $HLD:0     $HEX
C                     ENDSR
** HX
123456789ABCDEF
```

Figure 15.5 This RPG routine converts decimal values to hexadecimal literals (part 2 of 2).

The program accepts a 15-digit, right-justified decimal integer through a character variable. It returns the equivalent hexadecimal value in another 15-character variable. This program is meant to be called from another program that requires the conversion. For example, you could write a display file and program to accept a decimal integer and display the converted value.

—*Dave Richards*

Numbers-to-Words Conversion Program

Program CVT001RG, shown in Figure 15.6, converts a numeric value to words for check-printing purposes. It's a separate callable program that requires two parameters: an 8-digit, 2-decimal position, input parameter used to accept the numeric value to be converted; and an 80-character output parameter used to pass back the converted value.

```
*================================================================
* To compile:
*
*       CRTRPGPGM  PGM(XXX/CVT001RG) SRCFILE(XXX/QRPGSRC)
*
*================================================================
*. 1 ...+... 2 ...+... 3 ...+... 4 ...+... 5 ...+... 6 ...+... 7
E                   A       6 102 13
IAMT        DS
I                                        1    10HTHO
I                                        2    30TTHO
```

Figure 15.6: The CVT001RG program converts numbers to words (part 1 of 2).

```
I                                         4   40HUN
I                                         5   60TEN
I                                         1   60DOL
I                                         7   8 CEN
C           *ENTRY    PLIST
C                     PARM            AMTIN   82
C                     PARM            WRDS    80
C                     MOVELAMTIN      AMT
C           HTHO      IFGT *ZEROS
C                     CAT  A,HTHO:1   WRDSWK 80
C                     CAT  A,100:1    WRDSWK
C                     ENDIF
C           HTHO      IFGT *ZEROS
C           TTHO      ANDEQ*ZEROS
C                     CAT  A,101:1    WRDSWK
C                     ENDIF
C           TTHO      IFGT *ZEROS
C                     CAT  A,TTHO:1   WRDSWK
C                     CAT  A,101:1    WRDSWK
C                     ENDIF
C           HUN       IFGT *ZEROS
C                     CAT  A,HUN:1    WRDSWK
C                     CAT  A,100:1    WRDSWK
C                     ENDIF
C           TEN       IFGT *ZEROS
C                     CAT  A,TEN:1    WRDSWK
C                     ENDIF
C           DOL       IFGT *ZEROS
C                     CAT  'AND':1    WRDSWK
C                     ENDIF
C                     CAT  CEN:1      WRDSWK
C                     CAT  A,102:0    WRDSWK
C           79        SUBSTWRDSWK:2   WRDS    80 P
C                     MOVE *ALL'*'    ASTER   80
C                     CAT  ASTER:1    WRDS       P
C                     MOVEL*ON        *INLR
  *. 1 ...+... 2 ...+... 3 ...+... 4 ...+... 5 ...+... 6 ...+... 7
**
ONE           TWO           THREE         FOUR          FIVE          SIX
SEVEN         EIGHT         NINE          TEN           ELEVEN        TWELVE
THIRTEEN      FOURTEEN      FIFTEEN       SIXTEEN       SEVENTEEN     EIGHTEEN
NINETEEN      TWENTY        TWENTY-ON     TWENTY-TWO    TWENTY-THREE  TWENTY-FOUR
TWENTY-FIVE   TWENTY-SIX    TWENTY-SEVEN  TWENTY-EIGHT  TWENTY-NINE   THIRTY
THIRTY-ONE    THIRTY-TWO    THIRTY-THREE  THIRTY-FOUR   THIRTY-FIVE   THIRTY-SIX
THIRTY-SEVEN  THIRTY-EIGHT  THIRTY-NINE   FORTY         FORTY-ONE     FORTY-TWO
FORTY-THREE   FORTY-FOUR    FORTY-FIVE    FORTY-SIX     FORTY-SEVEN   FORTY-EIGHT
FORTY-NINE    FIFTY         FIFTY-ONE     FIFTY-TWO     FIFTY-THREE   FIFTY-FOUR
FIFTY-FIVE    FIFTY-SIX     FIGTY-SEVEN   FIGTY-EIGHT   FIFTY-NINE    SIXTY
SIXTY-ONE     SIXTY-TWO     SIXTY-THREE   SIXTY-FOUR    SIXTY-FIVE    SIXTY-SIX
SIXTY-SEVEN   SIXTY-EIGHT   SIXTY-NINE    SEVENTY       SEVENTY-ONE   SEVENTY-TWO
SEVENTY-THREESEVENTY-FOUR  SEVENTY-FIVE  SEVENTY-SIX   SEVENTY-SEVENSEVENTY-EIGHT
SEVENTY-NINE  EIGHTY        EIGHTY-ONE    EIGHTY-TWO    EIGHTY-THREE  EIGHTY-FOUR
EIGHTY-FIVE   EIGHTY-SIX    EIGHTY-SEVEN  EIGHTY-EIGHT  EIGHTY-NINE   NINETY
NINETY-ONE    NINETY-TWO    NINETY-THREE  NINETY-FOUR   NINETY-FIVE   NINETY-SIX
NINETY-SEVEN  NINETY-EIGHT  NINETY-NINE   HUNDRED       THOUSAND      /100
```

Figure 15.6: The CVT001RG program converts numbers to words (part 2 of 2).

The maximum value of 999,999.99 should be large enough for most shops. However, modifying it for a larger value should be easy for an RPG programmer because the logic is so simple.

—Midrange Computing Staff

Simulating Local Indicators

By making use of the RPG/400 predefined *IN array, you can save the current settings of selected or all indicators when calling subroutines that might alter the indicators, as shown below.

```
C                     MOVEA*IN,61       SAVE8   8
C                     EXSR SUB1
C                     MOVEASAVE8        *IN,61
```

The idea here is that all of the numeric indicators, 01–99, are mapped into the *IN array. The settings of a contiguous group of indicators can be saved by moving the *IN array to a save field, then restoring the save field into the *IN array. Using the same technique, you also can save all 99 indicators simply by using a larger save field and applying the MOVEA to the entire *IN array, as follows.

```
C                     MOVEA*IN          SAV99   99
C                     EXSR SUB1
C                     MOVEASAV99        *IN
```

If you use a separate save field for each subroutine, this technique also can be used for nested subroutines.

—Craig Pelkie

Simulating Local Variables

One of RPG's greatest faults, in my opinion, is the lack of local variables in subroutines. You can treat a variable (or indicator) as local to a subroutine by saving the variable's value upon entry to the subroutine, and restoring it when exiting. The code shown in Figure 15.7 illustrates this. (Three dots indicate source code that would be needed for a complete program.)

```
C       ...
C                       EXSR SUB001
C       ...
C       SUB001          BEGSR
C                       MOVE *IN31       SAV31    1
C                       MOVE NDX         SAVNDX
C       *LIKE           DEFN NDX         SAVNDX
C       ...
C                       Z-ADD1           NDX
C       FLD             LOKUP ARR,NDX                   31
C       *IN31           IFEQ *ON
C       ...
C                       MOVE SAV31       *IN31
C                       MOVE SAVNDX      NDX
C                       ENDSR
```

Figure 15.7: Use work fields to simulate a local variable in an RPG program.

Advantages of this technique are:
- Fewer chances for a subroutine to undesirably change a variable or indicator
- Fewer variables needed by the program
- Easier copies of blocks of source from one program to another.

—Ted Holt

Editor's Note: *RPG IV permits local variables in subprocedures, but predefined indicators remain global.*

Use the CLEAR Operation to Reduce Program Statements

The CLEAR op code (as shown in Figure 15.8) can save a lot of time and headaches. For example, when writing a program that adds records to a file, don't code a series of MOVE *BLANK or *ZERO statements; instead, code a single CLEAR operation with the record name in factor 2. The CLEAR op code automatically sets fields to their default value based on their field type. The CLEAR operation works against record formats, data structures, tables, arrays, and variables.

```
Old Method:
C       @INIT           BEGSR
C                       Z-ADDO CUCST#
C                       MOVEL*BLANKS     CUNAME
C                       MOVEL*BLANKS     CUADR1
C                       MOVEL*BLANKS     CUADR2
C                       MOVEL*BLANKS     CUCITY
C                       MOVEL*BLANKS     CUSTTE
C                       MOVEL*BLANKS     CUZIP
```

Figure 15.8: The CLEAR operation is superior to clearing all fields of a record format to default values by hand (part 1 of 2).

```
C                    ENDSR
New Method:
C          @INIT     BEGSR
C                    CLEARCMCUST10
C                    ENDSR
```

Figure 15.8: The CLEAR operation is superior to clearing all fields of a record format to default values by hand (part 2 of 2).

—Michael Catalani

Using the CLEAR Op Code on Input-only Fields

When the RPG CLEAR operation is applied to a record-format name, only output fields in the record format are cleared; input-only fields are not affected by the CLEAR operation. If you need to use the CLEAR operation on input-only fields, try this simple technique.

- Define a data structure with an external description. Use the name of the input file as the external file.

- Give the data structure a name (positions 7–12).

- Use the CLEAR operation code with the data structure name in factor 2.

All numeric fields will be set to zero, and all character fields will be set to blanks. For an example of this technique, see Figure 15.9. If you are currently using a series of statements to move blanks or zeros to each field in the file, this technique can ensure that all the fields will be clear should the record format change.

```
FCUSTMASTIF  E            K        DISK
ICSTDTA      E DSCUSTMAST
 *
C          CUSTNO     CHAINCUSTMAST                  99
C          *IN99      IFEQ *OFF
 *                       .
 *                       .
 *                       .
C                     ELSE
C                     CLEARCSTDTA
C                     ENDIF
 *
C                     MOVE *ON      *INLR
```

Figure 15.9: Use a data structure if you want CLEAR to work with input-only fields.

—Paul Jackson

✦ ✦ ✦ Date and Math Functions

Calculating the Day of the Week

Figure 15.10 contains a little routine that converts a date to the day of the week.

```
*=========================================================
* To compile:
*
*        CRTRPGPGM  PGM(XXX/XMS001RG) SRCFILE(XXX/QRPGSRC)
*
*=========================================================
*. 1 ...+... 2 ...+... 3 ...+... 4 ...+... 5 ...+... 6 ...+... 7
I           DS
I                                           1   7 DATE$
I I                                         1  70DATE
I           DS
I                                           1   6 JULDT$
I I                                         1  60JULDAT
I                                           1  30JULCYY
I                                           4  60JULDDD
IAPIERR     DS
I I            15                       B   1  40APIE01
I                                       B   5  80APIE02
I                                           9  15 APIE03
*
C           *ENTRY    PLIST
C           DATE      PARM                   PARM01 155
*
C                     CALL 'QWCCVTDT'
C                     PARM '*YMD'     APIP01 10
C                     PARM DATE$      APIP02  7
C                     PARM '*JUL'     APIP03 10
C           JULDT$    PARM            APIP04  7
C           APIERR    PARM APIERR     APIP05 16
*
C           JULCYY    SUB  1          @DTWRK  50
C                     MULT 365.25     @DTWRK
C                     ADD  365        @DTWRK
C                     ADD  JULDDD     @DTWRK
C           @DTWRK    DIV  7          DOTW    10
C                     MVR             DOTW
C                     ADD  1          DOTW
*
* Display day-of-week value to the screen. (FOR EXAMPLE USE)
C           DOTW      DSPLY
*
C                     MOVE *ON        *INLR
```

Figure 15.10: This RPG routine calculates the day of the week.

The routine itself is short, but it requires some data structures and a parameter list to work. It uses a call to the IBM Convert Date (QWCCVTDT) application program interface (API). This gives it several advantages over routines I've used in the past:

- No array look-ups to get lengths of the months.

- No need for leap-year calculations.

- Allows any input date format that the QWCCVTDT API can handle.

- Performs validation on the input date.

To run it, just call the program interactively and pass a date in CYYMMDD format. The program expects decimal input (so don't put quotes around the date). The RPG DSPLY function is used to display the resulting day-of-the-week code to your terminal (1=Sunday, 2=Monday, ... 7=Saturday). Of course, the *ENTRY parameter list and DSPLY are included for demonstration purposes only.

If it's possible that the date being used isn't valid, check field APIE03 immediately after the call to the API. If the date was okay, this field will contain blanks. Otherwise, it will contain the appropriate CPF error code. If you know the dates will be valid, you can skip this.

This example is set up to receive dates in the CYYMMDD format. The API doesn't follow the old standard of assuming that the years between 00 and 39 are of the next century. You must use the correct century number. For example, to convert the date 5/27/2003, use the value 1030527.

—Jeff Griffith
—Matt Sargent

RPG III Random Number Generator

One easy way to generate a random number between .000 and .999 is to use the thousandths position of system value QTIME. Although quick and easy, there are better ways to generate an evenly distributed sampling of random numbers. One such random number generator passes the spectral test used by statisticians in determining how good a random number generator is.

I have re-coded this random number generator in RPG/400 for the benefit of our AS/400 users. The program GENRNDNBR (Figure 15.11) is an independent callable program you can use anytime you need a good random number. It uses three input parameters: seed (SEED), beginning number (BEGNBR), and ending number (ENDNBR). The output parameter of the program is a generated random number that will be a number between the range specified by BEGNBR and ENDNBR. If no seed is provided, a seed is generated from the system time.

A beginning and ending number can be specified between the range of 1 and 999,999. If no beginning or ending numbers are specified or the beginning number is larger than the ending number, 1 and 999,999 will be the default values respectively. Once a seed is provided, the random number generated (prior to the range qualification) becomes the seed for the next number, unless you provide another seed. This allows you to obtain many random numbers in successive calls to the program without worrying about the first three parameters.

```
C          *ENTRY     PLIST
C                     PARM                    SEED      99
C                     PARM                    BGNNBR    60
C                     PARM                    ENDNBR    60
C                     PARM                    RNDNBR    60
C          SEED       IFEQ *ZERO
C                     TIME                    TIME      120
C          TIME       MULT .000000001SEED
C                     ENDIF
C          BGNNBR     IFEQ 0
C          ENDNBR     ANDEQ0
C          ENDNBR     ORLT BGNNBR
C                     Z-ADD1          BGNNBR
C                     Z-ADD999999     ENDNBR
C                     ENDIF
C          ENDNBR     SUB  BGNNBR     RANGE     60
C                     ADD  1          RANGE
C                     MULT 9821       SEED
C                     ADD  .211327    SEED
C          SEED       MULT RANGE      RNDNBR
C                     ADD  BGNNBR     RNDNBR
C                     RETRN
```

Figure 15.11: RPG III can generate random numbers.

—*Richard Shaler*

RPG Logarithm Calculation

While RPG contains some basic mathematical functions, it is missing some important, advanced functions. For example, we needed a logarithmic function to calculate bond yield. Because RPG does not supply a logarithmic function, I wrote my own program called LOG001RG. See Figure 15.12.

```
*==============================================================
* To compile:
*
*       CRTRPGPGM  PGM(XXX/LOG001RG) SRCFILE(XXX/QRPGSRC)
*
*==============================================================
*. 1 ...+... 2 ...+... 3 ...+... 4 ...+... 5 ...+... 6 ...+... 7
* Square root of natural log base e: 2.718281828
I            1.648721271              C          ESQRT
* Common log base 10
I            2.302585093              C          COMLOG
*
C          *ENTRY    PLIST
C                    PARM              LOGTYP  1
C                    PARM              PARMI   159
C                    PARM              PARMO   159
*
C                    Z-ADD0            PARMO
C                    Z-ADDPARMI   X         159
* Input parm if < 0 or = 1, then the output is 0
C          X         IFGT 0
C          X         ANDNE1
* If 1 > X > 0, then result is negative, LOG(X)=-LOG(1/X)
C          X         IFLT 1
C                    Z-ADD-1           SIGN    10
C          1         DIV  X            X         H
C                    ELSE
C                    Z-ADD1            SIGN
C                    ENDIF
* Divide X by ESQRT until 1 < X <= ESQRT, each time add .5
C          X         DOWGTESQRT
C                    DIV  ESQRT        X         H
C                    ADD  0.5          PARMO
C                    ENDDO
* Use the Taylor Series to calculate the output:
*    LOG(1 + X) = X - X ** 2/2 + X ** 3/3 - X ** 4/4 ...
*    and add the result to the final result
C                    SUB  1            X
C                    Z-ADDX            TERM    159
C                    Z-ADD1            N        50
C          TERM1     DOUEQ0
C          TERM      DIV  N            TERM1   159H
C                    ADD  TERM1        PARMO
C                    ADD  1            N
C                    MULT X            TERM      H
C                    MULT -1           TERM
C                    ENDDO
* Multiply the sign
C                    MULT SIGN         PARMO
* Calculate common logarithm if necessary
C          LOGTYP    IFEQ 'C'
C                    DIV  COMLOG       PARMO     H
C                    ENDIF
C                    ENDIF
*
C                    MOVE *ON          *INLR
```

Figure 15.12: RPG III can calculate logarithms.

To understand how to use this program, let me explain a little bit about how logarithms work. The definition of a logarithm is as follows: The logarithm of a number is the exponential power to which a number must be raised to produce a given number. The calculation of a logarithm is expressed as $y = \log_b x$, which is stated "y equals log to the base b of x."

Two bases are commonly used when calculating logarithms. Log to the base 10 is called the *common logarithm*. The other base is a special number often referred to as "e" (with a value of 2.718281828...). This type of logarithm is called the *natural logarithm*. Most scientific calculators have two buttons for calculating logarithms. The button for calculating common logarithms is normally labeled "log" while the one for calculating natural logarithms is usually labeled "ln."

The LOG001RG program calculates both common and natural logarithms. Use the first parameter to specify which type of logarithm you want to calculate. Pass the parameter a 'C' to calculate the common logarithm or an 'N' to calculate the natural logarithm. Use the second parameter to pass your input number. The program passes back your answer in the third parameter.

—*Xue Zhong Li*

✦ ✦ ✦ Error Processing

Defining the API Error Parameter

Q: I am trying to create a program that will run in the background to monitor QBATCH job queue. I want to send a break message alerting someone to the bottleneck when the job queue has more than 10 jobs. I'm using the QSPRJOBQ API to retrieve information on the number of jobs in the job queue.

My problem is that I'm getting an error message saying "Error code parameter not valid." It seems that the API doesn't like my error parameter. I have consulted the API reference but have been unable to determine what to do.

A: With some APIs, the error code parameter is optional, but for the one you're using it is required. You don't say how you've defined the parameter, but the easiest way is to pass a 4-byte binary field that contains the value of 0. This value essentially tells the API to ignore the error code parameter. In this case, the error will be handled by the system. Ideally, you want your program to trap for and handle any potential errors.

Take a look at Figure 15.13, which contains part of an RPG program I wrote to use the QSPRJOBQ API. As you can see, I've initialized the subfield of the ERROR data structure to 0. I could have simply referenced the subfield BYTPRV for the error parameter, but defining the ERROR data structure sets the stage for defining additional subfields if I ever decide to let the program trap and handle errors from the API.

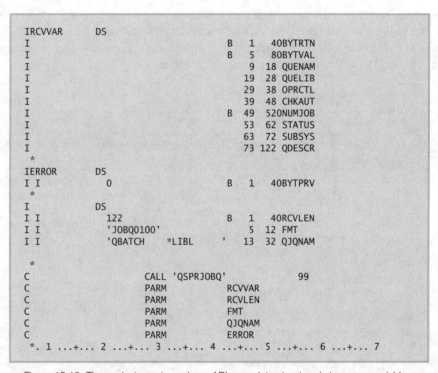

```
IRCVVAR      DS
I                                   B   1    40BYTRTN
I                                   B   5    80BYTVAL
I                                       9   18 QUENAM
I                                      19   28 QUELIB
I                                      29   38 OPRCTL
I                                      39   48 CHKAUT
I                                   B  49   520NUMJOB
I                                      53   62 STATUS
I                                      63   72 SUBSYS
I                                      73  122 QDESCR
 *
IERROR       DS
I I           0                     B   1    40BYTPRV
 *
I            DS
I I          122                    B   1    40RCVLEN
I I          'JOBQ0100'                 5   12 FMT
I I          'QBATCH    *LIBL    '     13   32 QJQNAM

 *
C                    CALL 'QSPRJOBQ'                99
C                    PARM           RCVVAR
C                    PARM           RCVLEN
C                    PARM           FMT
C                    PARM           QJQNAM
C                    PARM           ERROR
 *. 1 ...+... 2 ...+... 3 ...+... 4 ...+... 5 ...+... 6 ...+... 7
```

Figure 15.13: The easiest way to code an API error data structure is to pass a variable indicating zero bytes available.

—*Richard Shaler*

Save Contents of a Data Area on Abend

The data areas used in an RPG program are not normally written out if the program ends abnormally. So, the UDS style of defining data areas is not suitable when you need a data area written out—even if the program crashes. I've come up with a way to solve this problem.

You might use my technique in an error recovery situation. For example, you might keep track of the last record number processed in a data area. If the program ends abnormally, the program can look at the data area to tell which record to begin with the next time it's run. If you try to lock and update the data area on every record read, you'll use a lot of system resource.

My method works by locking the data area at the beginning of the program. It then increments a counter to reflect every record read and codes an update to the data area (once for a normal end of the program and once for an abnormal end). You can see an example of this in Figure 15.14. I've found this technique to be quite useful.

```
*================================================================
* To compile:
*
*       CRTRPGPGM  PGM(XXX/ABD001RG)  SRCFILE(XXX/QRPGSRC)
*
*================================================================
*. 1 ...+... 2 ...+... 3 ...+... 4 ...+... 5 ...+... 6 ...+... 7
C           *ENTRY    PLIST
C                     PARM           TYPE    1
C*
C                     MOVE 'N'       ENPSSR  1
C           *NAMVAR   DEFN DTAARA    DTAVAR 10
C           *LOCK     IN   DTAVAR
C*
C                     Z-ADD*ZERO     ZERO    30
C           TYPE      IFEQ 'A'
C                     DIV  ZERO      ZERO
C                     ENDIF
C*
C                     MOVEL'NORMAL'  DTAVAR
C                     OUT  DTAVAR
C                     MOVE *ON       *INLR
C*
C           *PSSR     BEGSR
C*
C           ENPSSR    IFEQ 'N'
C                     MOVE 'Y'       ENPSSR
C                     MOVEL'ABEND '  DTAVAR
C                     OUT  DTAVAR
C                     ENDIF
C                     MOVE *BLANKS   RTNPNT  6
C*
C                     ENDSRRTNPNT
```

Figure 15.14: Updating a data area after an abnormal program end can be a lifesaver.

—*T. V. S. Murthy*

✦ ✦ ✦ File Handling

Build Comma-delimited Files

Midrange programmers are so used to writing files with fixed-length fields in fixed-length records that they might forget there are other file structures to use. If there are users of your system who download data from the AS/400 into a PC program, you might want to build the data in some other format.

One type of file that many PC packages can read is the BASIC sequential file, so named because it's the type of sequential file built and read by the BASIC programming language. BASIC sequential files are also known as comma-delimited (or comma-separated values) files. Comma-delimited files have the following characteristics:

- Fields and records are of variable length.

- Fields are separated by commas. Records are separated by a pair of characters—carriage return and line feed—commonly referred to as "end of line."

- The end of file marker is ASCII 26 (control-Z).

- Character fields are surrounded by quotation marks and must not contain quotation marks. Numeric fields have no delimiters.

- Negative numbers have a leading minus sign.

- Leading zeros on numbers are suppressed up to, but not including, the zero immediately to the left of the decimal point.

- Trailing zeros after the decimal point are suppressed.

- The decimal point is included only if there are digits after the decimal point.

- There is no separator for thousands or millions.

Figure 15.15 shows an example of a comma-delimited file.

```
1,"Jacob C.",500
99,"Nathan T.",-12
36,"Amy R.",2.48
2,"Caleb Z.",-3.17
0,"Anna K.",0
100,"Tabitha K.",0.31
101,"Kyle C.",1200
```

Figure 15.15: Many PC-based programs can import comma-delimited files.

It's not difficult to build a comma-delimited file in RPG. Figure 15.16 contains an RPG program that reads a file and writes three fields to a comma-delimited file. The important parts of the program are the two subroutines that build the fields—CHAR and NUM. If you decide to build comma-delimited files this way, you might want to put these subroutines into separate members and /COPY them into your programs. The subroutines have both calculations and variable declarations, which makes them easier to plug into a program. The only variable used by these subroutines but defined outside of them is CSVREC, the comma-delimited record.

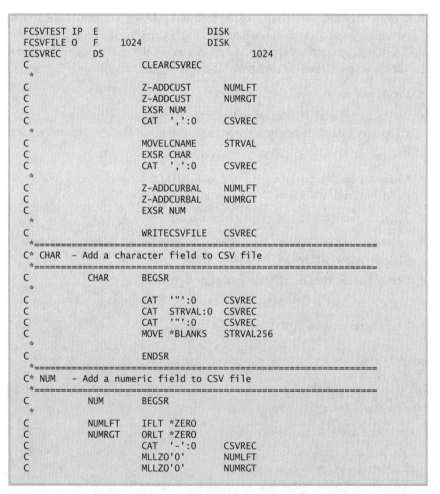

```
FCSVTEST IP  E                        DISK
FCSVFILE O   F    1024                DISK
ICSVREC     DS                             1024
C                    CLEARCSVREC
 *
C                    Z-ADDCUST      NUMLFT
C                    Z-ADDCUST      NUMRGT
C                    EXSR NUM
C                    CAT  ',':0     CSVREC
 *
C                    MOVELCNAME     STRVAL
C                    EXSR CHAR
C                    CAT  ',':0     CSVREC
 *
C                    Z-ADDCURBAL    NUMLFT
C                    Z-ADDCURBAL    NUMRGT
C                    EXSR NUM
 *
C                    WRITECSVFILE   CSVREC
 *===============================================================
C* CHAR  - Add a character field to CSV file
 *===============================================================
C           CHAR     BEGSR
 *
C                    CAT  '"':0     CSVREC
C                    CAT  STRVAL:0  CSVREC
C                    CAT  '"':0     CSVREC
C                    MOVE *BLANKS   STRVAL256
 *
C                    ENDSR
 *===============================================================
C* NUM   - Add a numeric field to CSV file
 *===============================================================
C           NUM      BEGSR
 *
C           NUMLFT   IFLT *ZERO
C           NUMRGT   ORLT *ZERO
C                    CAT  '-':0     CSVREC
C                    MLLZO'0'       NUMLFT
C                    MLLZO'0'       NUMRGT
```

Figure 15.16: You can use a simple RPG program like this one to build a comma-delimited file (part 1 of 2).

```
C                  ENDIF
*
C        NUMLFT    IFNE *ZERO
C                  MOVE NUMLFT    NUML   30
C        '0'       CHECKNUML      XX        30
C                  SUBSTNUML:XX   NUML        P
C                  CAT  NUML:0    CSVREC
C                  ELSE
C                  CAT  '0':0     CSVREC
C                  ENDIF
*
C        NUMRGT    IFNE *ZERO
C                  CAT  '.':0     CSVREC
C                  MOVE NUMRGT    NUMR   9
C        '0'       CHEKRNUMR      XX        30
C        XX        SUBSTNUMR:1    NUMR        P
C                  CAT  NUMR:0    CSVREC
C                  ENDIF
*
C                  MOVE *ZERO     NUMLFT 300
C                  MOVE *ZERO     NUMRGT 99
*
C                  ENDSR
```

Figure 15.16: You can use a simple RPG program like this one to build a comma-delimited file (part 2 of 2).

To load character data into the comma-delimited file, copy it left-justified into the work variable STRVAL and execute the CHAR subroutine. It's not necessary to blank out the rest of STRVAL because the CHAR subroutine already does that. To load numeric data, Z-ADD the number into both NUMLFT (left of decimal point) and NUMRGT (right of decimal point) and execute the NUM subroutine.

If you have a TCP/IP connection to your AS/400, you can use FTP to transfer the file. FTP doesn't normally allow you to create a comma-delimited file, but by using this routine, you can. You might also want to use the Copy to PC Document (CPYTOPCD) command to make the file available to PCs through shared folders. Both CPYTOPCD and FTP handle the EBCDIC-to-ASCII translation.

So, now you have two ways to build a comma-delimited file: You can use the Client Access transfer function or you can use this method. The advantage to this method is that you can use other file transfer facilities besides Client Access and still create comma-delimited files.

—*Ted Holt*

Editor's Note: *You also can use the Copy to Import File (CPYTOIMPF) command.*

Finding the Relative Record Number

There is an RPG extension to the File Description Specification, called RECNO, that will return the relative record number to the program. But, as ridiculous as it might sound, this keyword is valid only if you are processing the file sequentially. To retrieve the relative record number in a randomly processed file, you have to define a field in the file information data structure.

An example of the need for this technique is a subfile maintenance program over a file that does not have a unique key. Depending upon the data, it can be impossible to differentiate the various records on the screen to tell which record to update.

A solution to this problem would be to store the relative record number in the subfile as a hidden field to be used later when you want to update a record. You could then chain to the record using the relative record number and perform the update operation. To do this, you would need to define the file twice in the file description specifications as shown in Figure 15.17. In this case, TRANS is a physical file and TRNDATE is a logical file built over TRANS. If the two files have the same record format name, you'll need to use the RENAME extension specification to change one of the record format names.

In this example, TRNDATE is processed randomly and used to create a subfile. TRANS is processed by relative record number and is only used for update operations. The TRNINF file information data structure is used to tell the program the relative record number of each randomly processed record in the TRNDATE file. The relative record number is moved to a hidden field called HDNRRN and written to the subfile.

When a record is selected on the screen to be updated, the program chains to the correct record of the TRANS file using the hidden field (HDNRRN). It then performs the update on the desired record.

You really have to search through the manuals to find this solution. Here's how I did it. I looked in the *RPG/400 Reference* manual (SC09-1817, CD-ROM QBKAQV00) under "File Information Data Structure." In the area labeled "File Dependent Feedback Information," I found the formula used to calculate the From and To positions within the file information data structure for the relative record number. The formula is as follows:

```
From = 367 + Offset
To = (From - 1) + Character_Length
```

Next I looked in the *Data Management* guide under "I/O Feedback Area for Database Files" to determine the length and offset used. To compute the location of the relative record number, I performed the following calculations:

```
From = 367 + 30 = 397
To = (397 - 1) + 4 =  400
```

```
FTRNDATE IF  E           K         DISK
F                                            KINFDS TRNINF
FTRANS   UF  E                     DISK
F            TRNREC                           KRENAMEBYRRN
 *
ITRNINF      DS
I                                  B 397 4000RRN
 *                      .
 *                      .
 *                      .
C                       MOVE RRN     HDNRRN
C                       WRITESFLRCD
 *                      .
 *                      .
 *                      .
C            HDNRRN     CHAINBYRRN                68
C            *IN68      IFEQ *OFF
C                       MOVE NEWDAT  TRNDAT
C                       UPDATBYRRN
C                       ENDIF
```

Figure 15.17: Use the file information feedback data area to access the relative record number when processing a file randomly.

—*Doug Pence*

Select Ranges of Numbers

A common process in business computing is to key data into batches, print a report of the data for editing and audit purposes, and post the data when it is determined to be correct. One of my clients needed to be able to select lists and ranges of batch numbers to be printed and posted as a whole. For instance, he wanted to be able to select batches 9 through 18, batches 22 and 27, and batches 34 through 39 for one run. So I needed an easy way for him to indicate which batches he needed.

I decided to use a syntax that is common in PC software. I let him specify ranges of batch numbers by using a hyphen between the two batch numbers, and I let him separate individual batch numbers and ranges with commas. (I decided to let him key spaces as separators, too.) To select the preceding batches, he would key 9-18,22,27,34-39.

Figure 15.18 shows the program I wrote called RNG001RG. Given a field name and string of numbers and ranges, it builds a record selection expression that can be used with the QRYSLT parameter of the Open Query File (OPNQRYF) command. If the string is valid, RNG001RG returns a value of 0 in the return code parameter. Otherwise, the return code indicates the position where the invalid data (e.g., a letter) is found.

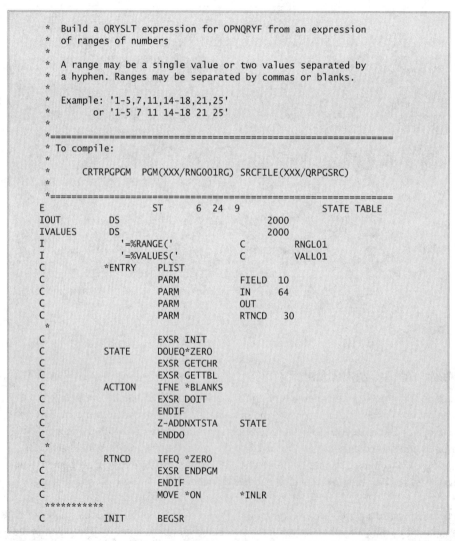

```
    *  Build a QRYSLT expression for OPNQRYF from an expression
    *  of ranges of numbers
    *
    *  A range may be a single value or two values separated by
    *  a hyphen. Ranges may be separated by commas or blanks.
    *
    *  Example: '1-5,7,11,14-18,21,25'
    *       or '1-5 7 11 14-18 21 25'
    *
    *==============================================================
    * To compile:
    *
    *      CRTRPGPGM  PGM(XXX/RNG001RG) SRCFILE(XXX/QRPGSRC)
    *
    *==============================================================
    E                   ST      6  24  9              STATE TABLE
    IOUT        DS                          2000
    IVALUES     DS                          2000
    I              '=%RANGE('           C       RNGL01
    I              '=%VALUES('          C       VALL01
    C          *ENTRY   PLIST
    C                   PARM            FIELD  10
    C                   PARM            IN     64
    C                   PARM            OUT
    C                   PARM            RTNCD  30
    *
    C                   EXSR INIT
    C          STATE    DOUEQ*ZERO
    C                   EXSR GETCHR
    C                   EXSR GETTBL
    C          ACTION   IFNE *BLANKS
    C                   EXSR DOIT
    C                   ENDIF
    C                   Z-ADDNXTSTA     STATE
    C                   ENDDO
    *
    C          RTNCD    IFEQ *ZERO
    C                   EXSR ENDPGM
    C                   ENDIF
    C                   MOVE *ON         *INLR
    ***********
    C          INIT     BEGSR
```

Figure 15.18: The RNG001RG program builds a record selection string that OPNQRYF can use (part 1 of 4).

```
     *
     C                        MOVE *BLANKS   OUT
     C                        MOVE *ZERO     RTNCD
     C                        Z-ADD01        STATE    30
     C            ' '         CHEKRIN        LINLEN   30
     C                        MOVE *ZERO     LX       30
     C                        MOVE *BLANKS   FROM      5
     C                        MOVE *BLANKS   TO        5
     C                        MOVE *BLANKS   VALUES
     C                        MOVE *BLANKS   RNGEXP   48
     *
     C                        ENDSR
     ***********
     C          GETCHR        BEGSR                             GET NEXT CHAR
     *
     C                        ADD  1         LX
     C          LX            IFLE LINLEN
     C                        SUBSTIN:LX     CURCHR    1
     C                        ELSE
     C                        MOVE *LOVAL    CURCHR            END OF LINE
     C                        ENDIF
     *
     C                        ENDSR
     *
     ***********
     C          GETTBL        BEGSR                             GET TABLE ENTRY
     *
     C                        SELEC
     C          CURCHR        WHEQ *BLANK
     C                        Z-ADD1         COL      10
     C          CURCHR        WHEQ *LOVAL
     C                        Z-ADD2         COL
     C          CURCHR        WHEQ '-'
     C                        Z-ADD3         COL
     C          CURCHR        WHEQ ','
     C                        Z-ADD4         COL
     C          CURCHR        WHGE '0'
     C          CURCHR        ANDLE'9'
     C                        Z-ADD5         COL
     C                        OTHER
     C                        Z-ADD6         COL
     C                        ENDSL
     *
     C          STATE         SUB  1         ROW      30
     C          ROW           MULT 6         TX       30
     C                        ADD  COL       TX
     *
     C                        SUBSTST,TX:1   ACTION    5
     C                        SUBSTST,TX:7   NXTAAA    2
     C                        MOVELNXTAAA    NXTSTA   20
```

Figure 15.18: The RNG001RG program builds a record selection string that OPNQRYF can use (part 2 of 4).

```
      *
      C                     ENDSR
      ***********
      C           DOIT      BEGSR                              DO ACTION
      *
      C                     SELEC
      C           ACTION    WHEQ 'BLDFM'
      C                     CAT  CURCHR:0 FROM
      C           ACTION    WHEQ 'BLDTO'
      C                     CAT  CURCHR:0 TO
      C           ACTION    WHEQ 'ENDFM'
      C                     CAT  FROM:1   VALUES
      C                     MOVE *BLANKS  FROM
      C           ACTION    WHEQ 'ENDTO'
      C                     EXSR ENDTO
      C           ACTION    WHEQ 'ERROR'
      C                     Z-ADDLX       RTNCD
      C                     ENDSL
      *
      C                     ENDSR
      ***********
      C           ENDTO     BEGSR                              END RANGE
      *
      C           '('       CAT  FIELD:0  RNGEXP    P
      C                     CAT  RNGL01:0 RNGEXP
      C                     CAT  FROM:0   RNGEXP
      C                     CAT  TO:1     RNGEXP
      C                     CAT  '))':0   RNGEXP
      *
      C           OUT       IFEQ *BLANKS
      C                     MOVELRNGEXP   OUT
      C                     ELSE
      C                     CAT  '|':0    OUT
      C                     CAT  RNGEXP:0 OUT
      C                     ENDIF
      *
      C                     MOVE *BLANKS  RNGEXP
      C                     MOVE *BLANKS  FROM
      C                     MOVE *BLANKS  TO
      *
      C                     ENDSR
      ***********
      C           ENDPGM    BEGSR
      *
      C           VALUES    IFNE *BLANKS
      C           OUT       IFNE *BLANKS
      C                     CAT  '|':0    OUT
      C                     ENDIF
      C                     CAT  '(':0    OUT
      C                     CAT  FIELD:0  OUT
```

Figure 15.18: The RNG001RG program builds a record selection string that OPNQRYF can use (part 3 of 4).

```
C                        CAT  VALL01:0  OUT
C                        CAT  VALUES:0  OUT
C                        CAT  '))':0    OUT
C                        ENDIF
 *
C            OUT         IFNE *BLANKS
C            '('         CAT  OUT:0     OUT
C                        CAT  ')':0     OUT
C                        ENDIF
 *
C                        ENDSR
 * ===========================================
 *          State table
 *
Blank *    EOL   Hyphen    Comma    Digit     Other
**
     :01       :00 ERROR:00 ERROR:00 BLDFM:02 ERROR:00
ENDFM:01 ENDFM:00      :03 ENDFM:01 BLDFM:02 ERROR:00
ERROR:00 ERROR:00 ERROR:00 ERROR:00 BLDTO:04 ERROR:00
ENDTO:01 ENDTO:00 ERROR:00 ENDTO:01 BLDTO:04 ERROR:00
```

Figure 15.18: The RNG001RG program builds a record selection string that OPNQRYF can use (part 4 of 4).

I've used batches to illustrate this tool, because that's what I've used it for so far. However, it works for any type of nonnegative numeric value such as customer numbers, vendor numbers, and inventory item numbers. This program uses a finite state machine to extract the numbers.

—Ted Holt

Use SETLL to Search Mixed-case Strings

Q: I have an RPG program in which I use a key as my search argument to set lower limits (SETLL) to a file based on user input. I then do a read to load my records into a subfile. How can I make the SETLL case insensitive? For example, a user might key in the word "LAB," but this word exists as "Lab" or "lab" in my file. I want to be able to get a hit on the word, regardless of whether it's uppercase or lowercase. Can you help me?

A: One way to resolve this problem is to create a logical file that translates a mixed-case field to uppercase. You can accomplish this by using the rename (RENAME) and translation table (TRNTBL) keywords. Figure 15.19 shows the DDS code for physical file CASEPF.

```
*=================================================================
* To compile:
*
*       CRTPF       FILE(XXX/CASEPF) SRCFILE(XXX/QDDSSRC)
*
*=================================================================
*. 1 ...+... 2 ...+... 3 ...+... 4 ...+... 5 ...+... 6 ...+... 7
A           R CASEPFR
A             MIXED           10
A           K MIXED
```

Figure 15.19: Physical file CASEPF is an example of a database file with mixed-case data.

This file contains a single field called MIXED, which is used to store mixed-case data. Figure 15.20 shows the code for logical file CASELF. This file contains the same MIXED field from the physical file, plus a translated uppercase version called UPPER.

```
*=================================================================
* To compile:
*
*       CRTLF       FILE(XXX/CASEPF) SRCFILE(XXX/QDDSSRC)
*
*=================================================================
*. 1 ...+... 2 ...+... 3 ...+... 4 ...+... 5 ...+... 6 ...+... 7
A           R CASELFR                     PFILE(CASEPF)
A             MIXED
A             UPPER           I           RENAME(MIXED)
A                                         TRNTBL(QSYSTRNTBL)
A           K UPPER
```

Figure 15.20: Logical file CASELF translates mixed-case to uppercase, which permits case-insensitive searches.

The RENAME keyword allows you to map one physical file field to two or more logical file fields. In this case the physical file field, MIXED, is mapped to both MIXED and UPPER in the logical file. The TRNTBL keyword lets you specify the name of a translation table used by the logical file when accessing data in the physical file.

The translation table QSYSTRNTBL translates the mixed-case data in the field MIXED to uppercase data in the field UPPER. Because the logical file is indexed on the UPPER field, your RPG program can set lower limits with the value "LAB" and begin reading records where the MIXED field contains values such as "Lab" or "lab." Using this technique, you can load your subfile with mixed data requested by the user, while internally taking advantage of the index built over the uppercase version of the data.

—Midrange Computing Staff

✦ ✦ ✦ Formatting Print and Display Output

Centering Text with a Subprogram

Designing displays and reports often involves placing text at the center of a field. For example, most reports need a title centered at the top. Subfiles display columns of data; the heading for such columns could be centered, too.

Program CTRTXT (Figure 15.21) centers a text string of up to 256 characters within a field that can have a maximum width of 256 bytes. Figure 15.22 shows an RPG program calling CTRTXT to get a string centered.

```
E                   STR        256 1
 *
C        *ENTRY     PLIST
C                   PARM            INSTR 256
C                   PARM            WIDTH   30
C                   PARM            OUTSTR256
 *
C                   MOVEAINSTR      STR
C                   MOVE *BLANK     OUTSTR
 *
C        1          DO   WIDTH      X        30
C        STR,X      IFNE *BLANK
C                   Z-ADDX          LSTNBL  30
C                   END
C                   END
 *
C        WIDTH      SUB  LSTNBL     TRLBLK  30
C        TRLBLK     DIV  2          Y        30
C        OUTSTR     CAT  INSTR:Y    OUTSTR
 *
C                   RETRN
```

Figure 15.21: RPG program CTRTXT centers a text string within a character field.

```
FQSYSPRT O   F    132              PRINTER
  .
  .
  .
C                       CALL 'CTRTXT'
C                       PARM TEXT      INSTR 256
C                       PARM 132       WIDTH   30
C                       PARM           OUTSTR256
  *
C                       MOVELOUTSTR    PRTLIN132
C                       EXCPTPRINT
  .
  .
  .
OQSYSPRT E  1                  PRINT
```

Figure 15.22: This code fragment illustrates how to use the CTRTXT routine.

You can call this program from other programs. Simply supply the text string to be centered as first parameter, the width of the receiving field as second parameter, and expect to receive the centered string in the third parameter. Some common widths are:

- Display file at size *DS3: 80 characters.

- Display file at size *DS4: 132 characters.

- Printer file, standard stock paper: 132 characters (10 cpi) or 198 characters (15 cpi).

- Printer file, standard letter size (8 x 11): 85 characters (10 cpi) or 127 characters (15 cpi).

—Eduardo Cardenas

Centering Text with a Subroutine

Sometimes it's necessary to center text within a field on a display or a report. To accomplish this task, I have written the CENTER subroutine shown in Figure 15.23. To implement this subroutine, you'll need to define two character fields in your program: INPUT and OUTPUT. These fields can be defined with any valid RPG character field length. Before your program executes the CENTER subroutine, place the text you want to center in the INPUT field. After your program executes the subroutine, the centered text will be contained in the OUTPUT field.

```
C           CENTER    BEGSR
C                     MOVE *BLANKS    OUTPUT
C           'X'       CHEKROUTPUT     LEN     30
C           ' '       CHEKRINPUT      POS     30
C           POS       IFLT LEN
C           LEN       SUB  POS        BLKS    30
C           BLKS      DIV  2          HAF     30
C                     CAT  INPUT:HAF OUTPUT
C                     ELSE
C                     MOVE INPUT      OUTPUT
C                     ENDIF
C                     ENDSR
```

Figure 15.23: This handy RPG subroutine centers text.

Here's how the subroutine works. First, it clears the OUTPUT field in which the centered text will be placed. The next line of code determines the length of the OUTPUT field. The length of the text in the INPUT field is calculated by determining the position of the last nonblank character. If the length of the text in the INPUT field is less than the length of the OUTPUT field, blanks are added to the beginning of the text in the INPUT field and placed in the OUTPUT field. Otherwise, the original text in the INPUT field is placed in the OUTPUT field without being centered.

—Gary Whitten

Lining Up Proportional Spacing

To line up columns of output with variable fonts, put an ending position for one character at the beginning position and leave off the ending position for the rest of the text. Using an ending position on a string with a variable font causes the left side to not line up. Figure 15.24 illustrates this technique.

```
Correct:

OFILE   E  1           PRINT1
O                              15 'M'
O                                 'IDRANGE'
O       E  1           PRINT1
O                              15 C'
O                                 'OMPUTING'

  Incorrect:

OFILE   E  1           PRINT1
O                              22 'MIDRANGE'
O       E  1           PRINT1
O                              23 'COMPUTING'
```

Figure 15.24: On proportional printers, align the first character of each column.

The catch to this is that each line without an ending position generates a warning message during compilation. The RPG compiler halts a compile when too many error messages are generated, and issues a message about a message file being full. In our case, it was about 400 errors, and IBM support could not tell us how to expand the error-file size. On this one, we broke our output into two separate programs.

Not using ending positions is a great time saver and is sometimes essential. But, as usual, IBM stuck us with some limitations.

—Russell Mierta

Right-adjust and Zero-fill

Q: How can I right-adjust and zero-fill a 4-byte character field containing digits?

A: The following code will take care of what you need. It works regardless of whether the data is left-adjusted, right-adjusted, or even stuck in the middle with leading and trailing blanks. It also works if the field is all blanks or has no blanks.

```
C           ' '         CHEKRFIELD    POS    30
C           4           SUB  POS      POS
C           ' '         CAT  FIELD:POS FIELD  4
C           ' ':'0'     XLATEFIELD    FIELD
```

Be sure to set the value for factor 1 (4, in this example) in the second line equal to the length of the field you are processing (FIELD).

The first line determines the position of the last non-blank byte in the field. The second line calculates the number of leading blanks that need to be added in order to right-justify the data. The third line actually inserts the leading blanks. And the last line translates all blanks to zeros.

—Matt Sargent

Right-adjust or Left-adjust Subroutine

Once upon a time, it was a rather tedious task to left-adjust decimal values and right-adjust character values with RPG. Nowadays, some of the more modern operation codes make the adjustments easy. Figure 15.25 contains the source code for RPG subroutine ADJUST, which will left- or right-adjust the contents of a 30-byte variable. All you need

to do is load the receiver variable field (RCVVAR) with the value you want to adjust and
load the adjustment type field (ADJTYP) with an '**L**' to left adjust or '**R**' to right-adjust.

```
 *===============================================================
 C                       Z-ADD1234567    FLDDEC 120
 C                       MOVEL'ABCDEFGH'FLDALF 12
 C                       MOVE FLDDEC     RCVVAR 30 P
 C                       MOVEL'L'        ADJTYP  1
 C                       EXSR LRADJ
 C          RCVVAR       DSPLY
 C                       MOVE FLDALF     RCVVAR    P
 C                       MOVEL'R'        ADJTYP
 C                       EXSR LRADJ
 C          RCVVAR       DSPLY
 C                       MOVEL*ON        *INLR
 *===============================================================
 C          LRADJ        BEGSR
 * Load RCVVAR with value to be left or right adjusted
 * Load ADJTYP with 'L' to left adjust; 'R' to right adjust
 C                       MOVE ' 0'       BLKZRO  2
 C                       MOVE *BLANK     BLANK   1
 C          *LIKE        DEFN RCVVAR     STRING+ 1
 * Left adjust
 C          ADJTYP       IFEQ 'L'
 C          31           ADD  1          FACTOR  30
 C                       MOVE RCVVAR     STRING    P
 C          BLKZRO       CHECKSTRING     POS     30
 C          FACTOR       SUB  POS        STRLGT  30
 C          STRLGT       SUBSTSTRING:POSSTRING    P
 C                       MOVELSTRING     RCVVAR
 C                       ELSE
 * Right adjust
 C                       Z-ADD31         FACTOR
 C                       MOVELRCVVAR     STRING    P
 C          BLANK        CHEKRSTRING     POS
 C          FACTOR       SUB  POS        BLK     30
 C          BLANK        CAT  STRING:BLKSTRING    P
 C                       MOVE STRING     RCVVAR
 C                       ENDIF
 C                       ENDSR
```

Figure 15.25: This RPG subroutine can left- or right-adjust a value.

—*Carsten Flensburg*

Trimming Leading Zeros

Here's one method for trimming leading zeros from a character field in RPG. Let's say a
character field with a length of 10, named CHRNUM, contains the value '**002300450**'. The
TRMZRO subroutine, shown in Figure 15.26, will remove all leading zeros and return a
value of '**2300450**'.

```
C                   CLEARWRK30
C                   MOVE  CHRNUM      WRK30  30
C                   EXSR  TRMZRO
C                   MOVE  WRK30       CHRNUM
C                   MOVEL *ON         *INLR
 *=====================================================================
C         TRMZRO    BEGSR
 *=====================================================================
C         WRK30     IFNE  *ALL'0'
C         WRK30     ANDNE *BLANKS
C         ' ':'0'   XLATEWRK30        WRK30
C         '0'       CHECKWRK30        Y      30
C         '0':' '   XLATEWRK30        WRK30
C         ' ':'0'   XLATEWRK30:Y      WRK30
C                   ELSE
C                   MOVE  *BLANKS     WRK30
C                   ENDIF
C                   ENDSR
```

Figure15.26: TRMZRO removes leading zeros from a character field.

This technique eliminates the need for array processing and therefore is very efficient. If you want to remove leading zeros from a character field that was originally a negative number, you will have to append a negative sign. This can be done easily by using the CAT operation

—*Ira Shapiro*

Figure 15.27 (subroutine STRIPZ) contains another technique for stripping the leading zeros from a character field. This routine works regardless of the size of the fields I work with.

```
C                   MOVE  NUMFLD      NUMBER
C                   EXSR  STRIPZ
C                   MOVE  NUMBER      CHRFLD  7
 *=====================================================================
 * Strip leading zeros from alpha-numeric integer
 *=====================================================================
C         STRIPZ    BEGSR
C                   MOVE  *BLANKS     BLANKS 15
C         ' 0'      CHECKNUMBER       C      20
C                   SELEC
C         C         WHEQ  *ZERO
C                   MOVE  '0'         NUMBER 15 P
C         C         WHGT  1
C                   SUB   1           C
C         C         SUBSTBLANKS       NUMBER
C                   ENDSL
C                   ENDSR
```

Figure 15.27: Subroutine STRIPZ provides a second method for removing leading zeros from a character field.

—*Marc Salvatori*

And yet another routine that works well is shown in Figure 15.28. It's very compact and requires only one work field (@ZS). CFIELD is the character field containing the numeric data to be processed. I translate all the zeros to blanks; then I translate all the blanks past the first nonblank character back to zeros. The XLATE operations make this very easy.

```
C              '0':' '   XLATECFIELD    CFIELD
C              ' '       CHECKCFIELD    @ZS      30
C              @ZS       IFNE *ZERO
C              ' ':'0'   XLATECFIELD:@ZSCFIELD
C                        ENDIF
```

Figure 15.28: This code fragment provides a third method for removing leading zeros from a character field.

—Matt Sargent

Use XLATE to Apply Edit Masks to Character Strings

It's commonly known that RPG's XLATE operation code will translate character data from one set of characters to another. A good example of this is converting lowercase to uppercase. But XLATE has another good use: applying edit masks to character strings.

To apply an edit mask to a character string, you'll need:

- Data to edit.
- A mask to define the format of the unedited data.
- A mask to define the format of the edited data.
- A variable to hold the edited result.

In the unedited mask, use a different character for each byte of the unedited data. For a 10-digit telephone number, for example, you could use the first 10 letters of the alphabet (ABCDEFGHIJ).

The edited mask uses the same characters to show where the data is to go, plus any characters to be inserted into the string. For an edited phone number, the mask could be (ABC) DEF-GHIJ.

Put the unedited data mask in the first half of factor 1, the unedited string in the second half of factor 1, the edited data mask in factor 2, and the edited variable in the result. The phone number example would look like the code below. If PHONE has the value 6015551212, EPHONE would be (601) 555-1212.

```
I                'ABCDEFGHIJ'         C        PH1
I                '(ABC) DEF-GHIJ'     C        PH2
  *
C          PH1:PHONE XLATEPH2         EPHONE 14
```

In this case, all the characters in the input mask were used in the output mask, and in the same order. However, that's unnecessary. The code below shows an example that converts an eight-digit date from year-month-day format to a six-digit month-day-year format. If DATE is 19961021, DTOUT will be 10/21/96.

```
I                'ABCDEFGH'           C        DT1
I                'EF/GH/CD'           C        DT2
     *
C          DT1:DATE   XLATEDT2        DTOUT  8
```

—Matt Sargent

✦ ✦ ✦ Interactive Processing

Make Inactive Interactive Programs Timeout

Users tend to leave interactive programs running unnecessarily, sometimes causing problems. Another user might need a record that's locked or other people might obtain access to information to which they're not authorized.

You can easily make interactive programs timeout. The technique shown here works with both RPG III and RPG IV. I will illustrate with RPG III.

In your display file, code the INVITE keyword at the record level. See Figure 15.29.

```
A                                    DSPSIZ(24 80 *DS3)
A                                    INVITE
A          R SCRN01
A                                 5  5'ENTER A LETTER:'
A            LETTER       1   B   + 1
```

Figure 15.29: The INVITE keyword is necessary for interactive programs that check for timeout.

Then create the display file, specifying WAITRCD(x), where *x* is the number of seconds you want to allow the display to remain untouched before timing out. In your RPG program, add two file continuation lines. One should have the NUM keyword, with a value of 1. (This causes RPG to treat the program as a multiple device file, which is necessary for this technique to work.) The other should have the information data structure (INFDS) keyword and the name of a file information data structure. See Figure 15.30 for an example.

```
FTIMOUTDFCF  E                    WORKSTN
F                                         KNUM         1
F                                         KINFDS INFDS
IINFDS       DS
I                                   *STATUS  STATUS
C          LETTER    DOUEQ*BLANK
C                    MOVE *BLANK    LETTER
C                    WRITESCRN01
C                    READ TIMOUTDF              2021
C          *IN20     IFEQ *ON
C          STATUS    IFEQ 1331
C                    MOVE *BLANK    LETTER
C                    ENDIF
C                    ENDIF
C                    ENDDO
C                    MOVE *ON       *INLR
```

Figure 15.30: This RPG program allows a display to timeout.

The file INFDS can have as many subfields as you like, but one of them should be the *STATUS subfield so that you can test whether the display file timed out or had some other problem.

Instead of EXFMT, use WRITE to a record format name followed by READ to a file name. In the "Lo" resulting indicator position, specify an indicator that you want to turn on when the display times out.

Follow the READ with a test of the indicator and the *STATUS code. If the display times out, the indicator will turn on and the status code will be set to 1331.

—Ted Holt

Use the AID Byte to Handle Function Keys

In your RPG program, there is a method to check which function key was used on a screen—without using any indicators.

The usual method is to code your DDS including keywords, such as CF03(03) and ROLLUP(15), and have your RPG program check the status of indicators 03 and 15. Another method (at least for F1–F24) is to use the KA–KY indicators. There is a different technique that requires no indicators at all and can positively check for the Enter key being pressed (instead of assuming that it was pressed because none of the indicators associated with function keys were on). With this technique, you code your DDS for the display file without response indicators: CF03, ROLLUP, and so on.

A workstation file can have an information data structure associated with it (coded with a K-continuation on the F-spec). This data structure contains a byte in position 369 called the Attention Indicator (AID) Byte. After a screen is read, it tells which function key was pressed, including F1–F24, Roll keys, Clear, Help, Home, or Enter key. This is in chapter 2 of the *RPG/400 Reference* manual and the *Data Management Guide* (appendix A).

Using the AID byte is great because it eliminates the need for any indicators, and the Enter key itself can be checked for. The RPG program logic can be set up in a nice CASE structure (or SELECT/WHEN/OTHER). An additional benefit is being able to check for an invalid function key being pressed. That might happen if your DDS accidentally allows a function key, which your RPG program does not expect (maybe you copied DDS source and erroneously included an extra function key).

See Figure 15.31. You need to code a K-continuation line on your workstation F-spec: KINFDS DSPDS. INFDS is the keyword for information data structure, and DSPDS is the name I chose for my data structure. Create a data structure with that name, and define subfield AID as 1 byte long, at position 369.

After you have read a screen, call the external program AID2FKEY, shown in Figure 15.32. The first parameter is the AID byte and the second parameter is an 8-character field that contains the name of the function key. The possible values returned are: F1, F2, ..., F24, ENTER, CLEAR, HELP, ROLLDOWN, ROLLUP, PRINT, HOME, AUTOENT and INVALID.

```
    FDSPFILE CF   E                    WORKSTN
    F                                              KINFDS DSPDS
     *
    IDSPDS       DS
    I                                        369 369 AID
     *
    C                      EXFMTRECORD
     *
    C                      CALL 'AID2FKEY'
    C                      PARM           AID
    C                      PARM           FKEY    8
     *
    C            FKEY      CASEQ'ENTER'   ENTER
    C            FKEY      CASEQ'F3'      EXIT
    C            FKEY      CASEQ'F4'      LIST
    C            FKEY      CASEQ'F12'     CANCEL
    C            FKEY      CASEQ'F24'     MOREKY
    C            FKEY      CASEQ'HELP'    HELP
    C            FKEY      CASEQ'ROLLUP'  ROLLUP
    C            FKEY      CASEQ'ROLLDOWN'ROLLDN
    C                      CAS            INVALD
    C                      END
```

Figure 15.31: This sample RPG program uses meaningful names for controlling keys.

```
    E                      TABKEY  1 32  4 0 TABDSC  8
     *
    IBINARY      DS
    I                                      B  1  20BIN4
    I                                         1   1 BYTE1
    I                                         2   2 BYTE2
     *
    C            *ENTRY    PLIST
    C                      PARM           AID     1
    C                      PARM           FKEY    8
     *
    C                      CLEARBIN4
    C                      MOVE AID       BYTE2
     *
    C            BIN4      LOKUPTABKEY    TABDSC          31
    C                      CLEARFKEY
    C            *IN31     IFEQ '1'
    C                      MOVELTABDSC    FKEY
    C                      ELSE
    C                      MOVEL'INVALID' FKEY
    C                      END
     *
    C                      RETRN
    ** Table of Function Key Values
```

Figure 15.32: RPG program AID2FKEY converts the AID-byte value to a meaningful name (part 1 of 2).

```
0049F1
0050F2
0051F3
0052F4
0053F5
0054F6
0055F7
0056F8
0057F9
0058F10
0059F11
0060F12
0063AUTOENT
0177F13
0178F14
0179F15
0180F16
0181F17
0182F18
0183F19
0184F20
0185F21
0186F22
0187F23
0188F24
0189CLEAR
0241ENTER
0243HELP
0244ROLLDOWN
0245ROLLUP
0246PRINT
0248HOME
```

Figure 15.32: RPG program AID2FKEY converts the AID-byte value to a meaningful name (part 2 of 2).

I suggest using a nice CASE structure (or SELECT/WHEN/OTHERWISE) that includes all allowable function keys, the Enter key, and a catch-all for any invalid keys. If that doesn't fit in well with your existing program structure, just change from testing indicators to testing the return parameter (for example, FKEY IFEQ 'F3').

—Rex M. Oliva

Editor's Note: *Notice how the binary AID byte is converted to decimal in program AID2FKEY. AID is passed as a character parameter, moved to the low order byte (BYTE2) of the two-byte data structure, BINARY. BIN4 now contains the decimal equivalent of the binary byte AID. The key to the technique is the 2-byte binary field (BIN4) defined over the two character fields, BYTE1 and BYTE2.*

Using Data Queues for Automatic Screen Painting

We have radio frequency (RF) units scanning trailers and tractors into the yard, and we want to have an airport-type arrivals screen constantly refreshing. We could have up to five dispatch screens around the building. The technique really isn't that difficult. However, none of it is written down in any one place. What follows is an explanation of how I currently have it working with automatic update.

Figure 15.33 contains the RPG code that sends the data to a data queue. Each truck we dispatch to has its own frequency, and each dispatcher watches two to three frequencies. When dispatchers log in, I write their device names and what frequencies they have to a file (more on this later). The code shown in Figure 15.33 reads the Emergency Road Service Frequency (ERSFREQ) and sends just the frequency to all dispatchers in the file who match that frequency.

```
I           DS
I                               1   7 DQDATA
I                               1   5 DQRQST
I                               6  70DQFRQ


C*=============================================================
C*    Write records to data queues
C           CLRAFQ    SETLLERSFREQ
C           CLRAFQ    READEERSFREQ                      61
C           *IN61     DOWEQ*OFF
C                     CALL 'QSNDDTAQ'
C                     PARM          DEVNAM
C                     PARM          DQLIB
C                     PARM          LEN
C                     PARM          DQDATA
C           CLRAFQ    READEERSFREQ                      61
C                     ENDDO
```

Figure 15.33: An RPG programs sends data to a data queue.

Next, I use a CL program (see Figure 15.34) to call the dispatcher's program. I create a non-keyed data queue (keyed data queues are not supported) using the name of the device. The program does some error checking to see if the data queue already exists. Then the program overrides the display file to associate the data queue with it. Using this method, dispatchers get their own data queues!

```
PGM
 /* */
                DCL       VAR(&USRDEV) TYPE(*CHAR) LEN(10)
                RTVJOBA   JOB(&USRDEV)
                CRTDTAQ   DTAQ(AAAPROD/&USRDEV) MAXLEN(100) TEXT('ERS +
                            Data Queue') AUT(*ALL)
                MONMSG    MSGID(CPF9870) EXEC(GOTO CMDLBL(CLRQUE))
                GOTO SKPCLR
 /* */
 CLRQUE:        DLTDTAQ   DTAQ(AAAPROD/&USRDEV)
                CRTDTAQ   DTAQ(AAAPROD/&USRDEV) MAXLEN(100) TEXT('ERS +
                            Data Queue') AUT(*ALL)
 /* */
 SKPCLR:        OVRDSPF   FILE(SERS998) TOFILE(AAAPROD/SERS998) +
                            DTAQ(AAAPROD/&USRDEV)
                CALL      PGM(AAAPROD/ERS998)
                DLTDTAQ   DTAQ(AAAPROD/&USRDEV)
 ENDPGM
```

Figure 15.34: A CL program creates a data queue named the same as the device name.

Figure 15.35 shows a segment of the RPG code for the program used by the dispatchers. The first three statements clear the data queue because I just updated the screens. I then wrote the subfile that displays the outstanding calls. Setting on indicator 89 activates the INVITE keyword in the display file.

Next, I wrote the KEYS1 record. By calling the QRCVDTAQ program, the RPG program waits (WAIT = -1) until it receives input from the screen or the data queue. (If you receive something from the data queue, write KEYS1 again with indicator 89 off to turn off the INVITE keyword, and then update the subfile. Otherwise, read KEYS1 and proceed as normal.)

```
C                          CALL  'QCLRDTAQ'
C                          PARM           STJOB
C                          PARM           DQLIB
C                          WRITESFLCTL1
C             BADRID       TAG
C                          SETON                      89
C                          WRITEKEYS1
C*=================================================================
C                          CALL  'QRCVDTAQ'
C                          PARM           STJOB
C                          PARM           DQLIB
C                          PARM  7        LEN
C                          PARM           DQDATA
C                          PARM  -1       WAIT    50
```

Figure 15.35: This partial RPG code receives input from a data queue and automatically refreshes a display (part 1 of 2).

```
C*=======================================================
C                   SETOF                           89
C          DQRQST   IFEQ '*UPDT'
C                   WRITEKEYS1
C                   GOTO UPDSTS
C                   ENDIF
C                   READ KEYS1                        99
C*=======================================================
```

Figure 15.35: This partial RPG code receives input from a data queue and automatically refreshes a display (part 2 of 2).

This is my first attempt with data queues. No "real" data is being sent from one program to another. It's just a message saying, "Hey, I wrote a record to the file. Update your screen."

—*Art Tostaine*

✦ ✦ ✦ Nesting and Looping

Help with RPG Nesting Levels

Here is a useful technique that helps me work with nested levels of IF/DO/CAS structures in RPG programs. It adds nesting level information (like what is found on a compiled print-out) to columns 1–5 of the source. For example: "B001," "B002", "E002", and "E001." I find this helpful when I go into SEU because that information is online for me to look at.

Command Write RPG Levels (WRTRPGLVL, Figure 15.36) asks for library, RPG source file and member, and an option. The option lets you clear out positions 1–5 only, without adding the nesting information. The command calls CL program RPG001CL (Figure 15.37), which validates the names of the library, source file, and member, and then calls RPG program RPG001CL (Figure 15.38), which adds the nesting level information in columns 1–5 or clears the same columns.

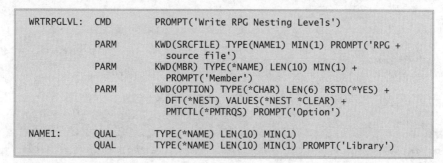

```
WRTRPGLVL:  CMD        PROMPT('Write RPG Nesting Levels')

            PARM       KWD(SRCFILE) TYPE(NAME1) MIN(1) PROMPT('RPG +
                         source file')
            PARM       KWD(MBR) TYPE(*NAME) LEN(10) MIN(1) +
                         PROMPT('Member')
            PARM       KWD(OPTION) TYPE(*CHAR) LEN(6) RSTD(*YES) +
                         DFT(*NEST) VALUES(*NEST *CLEAR) +
                         PMTCTL(*PMTRQS) PROMPT('Option')

NAME1:      QUAL       TYPE(*NAME) LEN(10) MIN(1)
            QUAL       TYPE(*NAME) LEN(10) MIN(1) PROMPT('Library')
```

Figure 15.36: Command WRTRPGLVL adds nesting information to columns 1–5 of an RPG source member.

```
RPG001CL: +
   PGM PARM(&SRCFILE &MBR &OPTION)

   DCL VAR(&LIB)       TYPE(*CHAR) LEN(10)
   DCL VAR(&MBR)       TYPE(*CHAR) LEN(10)
   DCL VAR(&MSG)       TYPE(*CHAR) LEN(80)
   DCL VAR(&OPTION)    TYPE(*CHAR) LEN(6)
   DCL VAR(&SRCF)      TYPE(*CHAR) LEN(10)
   DCL VAR(&SRCFILE)   TYPE(*CHAR) LEN(20)

   /* Break qualified name */
   CHGVAR VAR(&SRCF) VALUE(%SST(&SRCFILE 1 10))
   CHGVAR VAR(&LIB) VALUE(%SST(&SRCFILE 11 10))

   /* Validate input */
   CHKOBJ OBJ(&LIB/&SRCF) OBJTYPE(*FILE) MBR(&MBR)
   MONMSG MSGID(CPF9810) EXEC(DO)
      CHGVAR VAR(&MSG) VALUE('Library' *BCAT &LIB *BCAT 'not found.')
      GOTO CMDLBL(SNDERRMSG)
   ENDDO
   MONMSG MSGID(CPF9801) EXEC(DO)
      CHGVAR VAR(&MSG) VALUE('Source file' *BCAT &SRCF *BCAT 'not +
         found.')
      GOTO CMDLBL(SNDERRMSG)
   ENDDO
   MONMSG MSGID(CPF9815) EXEC(DO)
      CHGVAR VAR(&MSG) VALUE('Member' *BCAT &MBR *BCAT 'not found.')
      GOTO CMDLBL(SNDERRMSG)
   ENDDO

   /* Process source member */
   IF COND(&OPTION *EQ '*NEST') THEN(CHGVAR VAR(&MSG) +
      VALUE('Writing nesting levels.  Please wait'))
   ELSE CMD(CHGVAR VAR(&MSG) VALUE('Clearing columns 1-5.  Please +
      wait'))
   SNDPGMMSG MSGID(CPF9898) MSGF(QCPFMSG) MSGDTA(&MSG) TOPGMQ(*EXT) +
      MSGTYPE(*STATUS)
   OVRDBF FILE(QRPGSRC) TOFILE(&LIB/&SRCF) MBR(&MBR)
   CALL PGM(RPG001RG) PARM(&OPTION)
   DLTOVR FILE(*ALL)
   GOTO CMDLBL(ENDPGM)

   /* Send error messages */
SNDERRMSG: +
   SNDPGMMSG MSG(&MSG) MSGTYPE(*DIAG)
   SNDPGMMSG MSGID(CPF0002) MSGF(QCPFMSG) MSGTYPE(*ESCAPE)

   /* End program */
ENDPGM: +
   ENDPGM
```

Figure 15.37: CL program RPG001CL is the command-processing program for WRTRPGLVL.

```
FQRPGSRC UP  F      92          DISK
   *
E               D       80  1
   *
IQRPGSRC NS  01
I                                        13  92 SRCDTA
I          DS
I                                         1  80 SRCDTA
I                                         1  80 D
I                                         1   2 LDTABL
I                                         1   5 NEST
I                                        28  32 OPCODE
I                                        28  29 OP2
I                                        28  30 OP3
   *
C          *ENTRY      PLIST
C                      PARM           OPTION  6
   *
 * PROCESS RECORDS
C          LDTABL     CASEQ'**'      ENDPGM
C          OPTION     CASEQ'*CLEAR'  CLEAR
C          D,6        CASNE'C'       CLEAR
C          D,7        CASEQ'*'       CLEAR
C          D,7        CASEQ'/'       CLEAR
C          OP2        CASEQ'DO'      INDENT
C          OP2        CASEQ'IF'      INDENT
C          OP3        CASEQ'CAS'     CASE
C          OPCODE     CASEQ'END'     END
C          OPCODE     CASEQ'ELSE'    ELSE
C                     CAS            LEVEL
C                     END
   *
 * SAVE OPCODE, CASXX OPCODES NEED THIS
C          D,6        IFEQ 'C'
C          D,7        ANDNE'*'
C          D,7        ANDNE'/'
C                     MOVE OP3       SVOP3   3
C                     ELSE
C                     CLEARSVOP3
C                     END
   *
 * END THE PROGRAM EARLY
C          ENDPGM     BEGSR
C                     MOVE '1'       *INLR
C                     ENDSR
   *
 * CLEAR COLUMNS 1-5
C          CLEAR      BEGSR
C                     CLEARNEST
C                     ENDSR
   *
 * INDENT A LEVEL
```

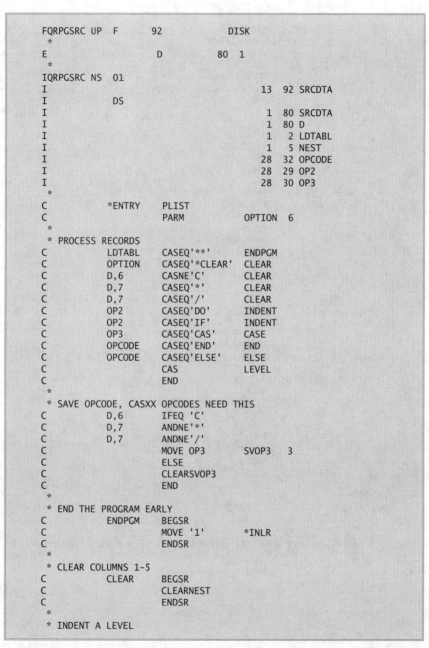

Figure 15.38: RPG program RPG001RG updates columns 1–5 of an RPG source member (part 1 of 2).

```
C           INDENT    BEGSR
C                     EXSR CLEAR
C                     MOVEL'B'      D,1
C                     ADD  1        NSTLVL   30
C                     MOVE NSTLVL   ALPHA3    3
C                     MOVEAALPHA3   D,2
C                     ENDSR
 *
 * CASXX OPCODES
C           CASE      BEGSR
C           SVOP3     CASNE'CAS'    INDENT
C                     END
C                     ENDSR
 *
 * GO BACK A LEVEL (UNINDENT)
C           END       BEGSR
C                     EXSR CLEAR
C                     MOVEL'E'      D,1
C                     MOVE NSTLVL   ALPHA3
C                     MOVEAALPHA3   D,2
C                     SUB  1        NSTLVL
C                     ENDSR
 *
 * ELSE OPCODE
C           ELSE      BEGSR
C                     MOVEL'*'      D,1
C                     MOVE NSTLVL   ALPHA3
C                     MOVEAALPHA3   D,2
C                     ENDSR
 *
 * PUT NESTING LEVEL ON C-SPEC
C           LEVEL     BEGSR
C                     CLEARNEST
C           NSTLVL    IFNE *ZERO
C                     MOVEL' '      D,1
C                     MOVE NSTLVL   ALPHA3
C                     MOVEAALPHA3   D,2
C                     END
C                     ENDSR
 *
OQRPGSRC D         01
O                        SRCDTA    92
```

Figure 15.38: RPG program RPG001RG updates columns 1–5 of an RPG source member (part 2 of 2).

—Rex M. Oliva

Keeping Iterations in a DO Loop Equal to the Subfile Size

When loading page-at-a-time subfiles, programmers often create DO loops in which the iteration count is equal to the subfile size. For example, if the subfile size is 10, you might see code like the example shown in Figure 15.39.

```
C                         DO   10
    .
    .
    load subfile fields and write a subfile record
    .
    .
C                         ENDDO
```

Figure 15.39: Some programmers use a DO loop with a hard-coded subfile page size in a subfile load routine.

However, this approach has a weakness. If the subfile size changes, the programmer must change the DO statement in the program to agree with the subfile size. Fortunately, there is a method you can employ that will eliminate this weakness. Refer to the Load Subfile (LOADSF) subroutine, as shown in Figure 15.40, as I describe how the technique works.

```
C           LOADSF    BEGSR
C                     Z-ADD0         RRN
C                     MOVE *OFF      *IN21
C                     READ CUSTOMER                  23
    *
C           *IN23     DOWEQ*OFF
C                     MOVE *ON       *IN21
C                     MOVELNAME      SFNAME
C                     MOVE CUST#     SFACCT
C                     ADD  1         RRN
C                     WRITESFLRCD                    23
C           *IN23     IFEQ *OFF
C                     READ CUSTOMER                  23
C                     ENDIF
C                     ENDDO
C                     ENDSR
```

Figure 15.40: When loading a subfile, assign the end-of-file indicator to the write operation.

Before the program enters the DO loop, an initial read of the database file is performed. by The last record indicator of the database READ operation conditions the DO loop. Once in the loop, the program moves the database fields to the subfile fields, adds one to the subfile relative-record number (RRN) field, and writes to the subfile.

Here's the key to the technique. The resulting error indicator of the WRITE operation is the same indicator as the database READ operation. If the program encounters the end of the subfile, this indicator will be set on. This prevents the next READ of the database and terminates the DO loop.

With this method, there's no need to be concerned about changing your program when you change your subfile size.

—Richard Shaler

Limitation of RPG DO Loop

When using DO loops in RPG/400 with an increment value specified in factor 2 of the ENDDO statement, make sure the increment value is always positive. The *RPG/400 Reference* manual description of the ENDDO op code increment simply says:

"It can be positive or negative, requires no decimal positions, and can be one of the following: an array element, table name, data structure, field, named constant, or numeric literal. If factor 2 is not specified on the ENDDO, then by default, the increment increases by 1."

While that is true, it is misleading at best. Most languages would let you code the following to decrement through an array:

```
C           100        DO   1       X
C                       [code]
C                       END  -1
```

But RPG would simply set X to 100, decide 100 is greater than the limit value, 1, and never execute the loop even once.

—Douglas Handy

✦ ✦ ✦ Performance

Be Careful Using the FREE Op Code

I had several users whose jobs would end abnormally after about three hours of work because the Process Access Group (PAG) would grow too large. I was finally able to track down the problem.

A programmer used the FREE op code to close down an RPG program, removing the program from memory but not closing the open data paths (ODPs) for the files. The program with the FREE op code was called many times; each time it opened new ODPs over the same files. After about three hours, the PAG was so full of ODPs that the job ended abnormally. Taking FREE out and setting on *INLR solved the problem.

—*Stephen Villanueva*

Performance Tips

Recently, our company started implementing a software package written by another company. This package allows us to receive and put away goods using online Radio Frequency (RF) technology. It is replacing batch processing.

We are taking great pains to identify inefficiencies in the application to improve performance. Here are a few tips I have found that will improve the response time of interactive programs. Many of these tips might not seem important, but I have noticed a big difference. Because of the online nature of the programs, any improvement helps.

- When calculating a percentage, use the MULT op code instead of DIV whenever possible. We have a field in a file that is a percentage. Multiplying by .01 instead of dividing by 100 has noticeably improved the performance of our applications.

- Our programs are using large element arrays (999 to 9,999 elements). Many times, they are being initialized back to zero or blanks. We slightly changed the code to only initialize those elements populated. This helped improve the response time.

  Figure 15.41 shows an example of the type of change we made. X1 is a numeric field that contains the last element used. ARR is an array with 999 elements. With this slight change, the programs ran more efficiently and the same amount of work was done.

```
Instead of coding this:
*. 1 ...+... 2 ...+... 3 ...+... 4 ...+... 5 ...+... 6 ...+... 7
C                      Z-ADD*ZEROS    ARR

Code this:
*. 1 ...+... 2 ...+... 3 ...+... 4 ...+... 5 ...+... 6 ...+... 7
C           X1         DOWGT*ZERO
C                      Z-ADD*ZEROS    ARR,X1
C                      SUB  1         X1
C                      ENDDO
```

Figure 15.41: Initializing only the used elements of an array will improve performance.

- While performing a lookup on an array of more than 200 elements, it might be quicker to eliminate the array by placing the data in a file and accessing it with a CHAIN operation. In our code, we have arrays with as many as 9,999 elements. The lookups were killing the system. Eliminate the array if you populate most of the elements or backward fill the array if very few elements are populated.

- Another consideration is the sheer amount of memory being consumed by extremely large arrays or data structures. Your system will do much more paging of memory if you have large arrays.

- When doing nested IF processing or SELEC processing, place the IF/SELEC that is most likely to succeed first. This will reduce the number of tests the system is required to do. This is a fairly trivial thing, but when running a program that could be run thousands of times per day online, any savings in processing should be done. With good technique, programmers might avoid buying a processor upgrade.

- Pay close attention to execution of code that does not have to take place. You have a report that reads a transaction file by part number and the file has many transactions per part number. The report has a description for each part number. CHAINing to the description file for each record is a waste of resources. Many extra lines of code are executed and many extra I/O operations take place. CHAIN to the description file only when a change in part number takes place.

The last item might seem trivial, but I have seen many programmers do this. This does not always take place in report programs, but in any program that is processing many similar items at a time.

—Bill Cressy

✦ ✦ ✦ String Handling

Scanning a String for Multiple Occurrences

When using the SCAN operation code in an RPG program, you normally define the result field as numeric with no decimals. Then you scan a string for a certain occurrence and, if the scan is successful, the position of the first occurrence is placed in the result field.

But if you define the result field as a numeric array with no decimals, you get a totally different scan. The scan operation will place all the occurrences in the array, starting with element 1 and continuing until the end of the string is reached or there are no more array elements. This is very useful if you want to scan a string for more than one occurrence.

Figure 15.42 shows an example of how this scan might work. This program splits up the words in field STRNG and puts them in array WRK.

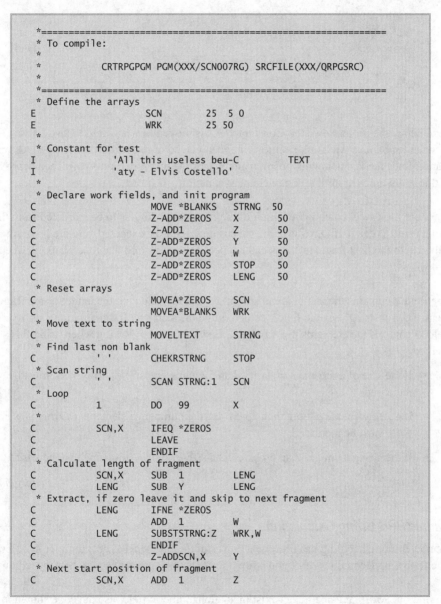

```
 *================================================================
 * To compile:
 *
 *             CRTRPGPGM PGM(XXX/SCN007RG) SRCFILE(XXX/QRPGSRC)
 *
 *================================================================
 * Define the arrays
E                       SCN        25  5 0
E                       WRK        25 50
 *
 * Constant for test
I               'All this useless beu-C           TEXT
I               'aty - Elvis Costello'
 *
 * Declare work fields, and init program
C                       MOVE *BLANKS   STRNG 50
C                       Z-ADD*ZEROS    X        50
C                       Z-ADD1         Z        50
C                       Z-ADD*ZEROS    Y        50
C                       Z-ADD*ZEROS    W        50
C                       Z-ADD*ZEROS    STOP     50
C                       Z-ADD*ZEROS    LENG     50
 * Reset arrays
C                       MOVEA*ZEROS    SCN
C                       MOVEA*BLANKS   WRK
 * Move text to string
C                       MOVELTEXT      STRNG
 * Find last non blank
C               ' '     CHEKRSTRNG     STOP
 * Scan string
C               ' '     SCAN STRNG:1   SCN
 * Loop
C               1       DO   99        X
 *
C       SCN,X           IFEQ *ZEROS
C                       LEAVE
C                       ENDIF
 * Calculate length of fragment
C       SCN,X           SUB  1         LENG
C       LENG            SUB  Y         LENG
 * Extract, if zero leave it and skip to next fragment
C       LENG            IFNE *ZEROS
C                       ADD  1         W
C       LENG            SUBSTSTRNG:Z   WRK,W
C                       ENDIF
C                       Z-ADDSCN,X     Y
 * Next start position of fragment
C       SCN,X           ADD  1         Z
```

Figure 15.42: RPG program SCN007RG scans for all occurrences of a blank (part 1 of 2).

```
* If next start pos greater than last non blank, stop program
C              Z         IFGT STOP
C                        LEAVE
C                        ENDIF
 *
C                        ENDDO
 *
C                        MOVE *ON       *INLR
```

Figure 15.42: RPG program SCN007RG scans for all occurrences of a blank (part 2 of 2).

Here's how the program works: Constant TEXT is moved to work field STRNG, which is scanned for blanks. All blank positions are then placed in the SCN array. The CHEKR operation finds the last nonblank position and places the result in field STOP. Then the DO will loop 99 times or until an array element containing 0 is met.

The field LENG will contain the length of the fragment, which is to be extracted from the string (field STRNG). If LENG is 0, the substring will not be executed, and the program will skip to the next fragment. This can happen if there is more than one blank between two words.

The field Y contains the last blank position; it's used to calculate the length of the fragment. The substring uses the field Z to determine the start of a fragment in the string. The field W controls the elements in array WRK. Beware of the following when using this method:

- If the size of a fragment is larger than 50 bytes, the size of array WRK must be increased.

- If a string contains more than 25 words, the number of elements in array SCN and WRK must be increased.

- If the string is longer than 50 bytes, the size of field STRNG must be increased.

—Jan Jorgensen

Simple RPG String Calculations

Character string handling has become a powerful tool in the RPG programmer's toolbox. The following techniques offer you a few shortcuts for jobs that used to be very tedious.

To find out how many characters exist in an alphanumeric field, use the code shown in the first example in Figure 15.43. The Check Reverse (CHEKR) operation will look for the last nonblank character in the input field (INPFLD) and return its position in the variable X. The result of this operation is that the value in field X will be the length of the data in the field INPFLD.

```
    * Example 1 - Calculate data length
    C            ' '         CHEKRINPFLD    X         20
    *
    * Example 2 - Left justify data
    C            ' '         CHECKINPFLD    X         20
    C                        SUBSTINPFLD:X  INPFLD    P
    *
    * Example 3 - Right justify data
    C            ' '         CHEKRINPFLD    X         20
    C                        MOVELINPFLD    WRKFLD 20 P
    C            FLDLEN      SUB  X         X
    C                        MOVE *BLANKS   INPFLD 20
    C                        CAT  WRKFLD:X  INPFLD
```

Figure 15.43: Here are some handy RPG III string calculations.

To left-justify data in an alphanumeric field, remove leading blanks using the code in the second example shown in Figure 15.43. The CHECK operation will locate the first nonblank character in INPFLD and put its position into variable X. The subsequent Substring (SUBST) operation will move the INPFLD data back into itself beginning at the first nonblank character address. The P extender is specified so that all characters beyond those that were moved will be replaced with blanks.

To right-adjust data in an alphanumeric field, remove trailing blanks using the code in the third example shown in Figure 15.43. Use the CHEKR operation to find the last nonblank character. The result in variable X represents the length of the field. The contents of INPFLD are then saved in a work field (WRKFLD).

Subtract the length of the data (currently stored in variable X) from the field length (stored in FLDLEN) and return the results back to variable X. The result in variable X is now the number of trailing blanks that exist in the input field.

Clear the original input field (INPFLD) and then perform a concatenation (CAT) operation from WRKFLD back into INPFLD using the number of trailing blanks as the new number of leading blanks. Swapping the number of trailing blanks for the number of leading blanks right adjusts INPFLD.

—Doug Pence

Use CAT Instead of MOVEL

The RPG operation code MOVEL is restricted to moving eight characters in factor 2 to the Result field. Use the CAT operation code to move left up to 16 characters in one operation, as in:

```
C               '12345678'CAT    '90ABCDEF'RESULT  16
```

—Midrange Computing Staff

CHAPTER 16

RPG IV

*W*hen introduced, RPG IV (also known as ILE RPG), was a radical departure from the RPG II and RPG III midrange programmers had known for so long. For one thing, it did not use the same specification layouts. Another big difference was the elimination of extension and line counter specifications. The former was replaced with a definition spec, indicated by a D in column 6. The new D-spec, however, is more powerful than the old E-spec. The introduction of RPG IV also saw the beginning of free-format calculations, which many RPG programmers had wanted for a long time.

But these are cosmetic changes, merely new syntax conventions to master. The greatest change is not in syntax, but in program construction. RPG IV is part of the ILE family of languages, which permits new types of binding. Perhaps finally midrange programmers can quit writing large programs that do everything, instead of building programs from debugged components and snapping pieces together as needed.

Whatever your feelings, RPG IV is now the standard for iSeries programming. IBM will continue to enhance RPG IV; it will not update RPG III. This chapter contains some tips that RPG programmers will find useful, and plenty of advice on how to develop more techniques. If you find a tip that's not quite to your liking, continue to look. A few tips (e.g., centering a text field) come in more than one version.

—Ted Holt

RPG IV

♦ ♦ ♦ ♦

In This Chapter

APIs
Arrays and Tables
Calculations
Compiling
Copyrights
Data Handling
Data Structures
Date and Time
Debug
File Handling
File Processing
Formatting Print and
  Display Output
Interactive Processing
Nesting and Looping
Parameter Passing
Performance
Pointers
Service Programs
SEU
Source Members
String Handling
Subprocedures
Triggers and
  Referential Integrity

♦ ♦ ♦ ♦

✦ ✦ ✦ APIs

Prototype Type Conversion

You can ensure that the parameters passed to a system API match what the API expects by defining a prototype for the API. Both C and RPG IV permit prototyping.

To create a prototype for an API, first determine the format of the API's parameters from the manual. If the manual specifies that a parameter is for input only, then pass the parameter as a constant or by value. Doing so causes the system to convert the value passed to the format specified on the prototype. In RPG IV, specify the CONST or VALUE keyword on the prototype.

Refer to Figure 16.1 for an RPG IV prototype of the Test Argument (CEETSTA) API. Notice the CONST keyword on the second parameter argument number. You might pass a constant or a variable of any numeric format for this parameter. The system will convert whatever numeric value you pass to a 4-byte integer.

```
DCEETSTA             PR                    EXTPROC('CEETSTA')
D PR_ArgPas                        10I 0
D PR_ArgNum                        10I 0  CONST
D PR_FBCod                         12A    OPTIONS(*OMIT)
```

Figure 16.1: Using an RPG IV prototype ensures that parameters are properly passed to an API.

See Figure 16.2 for an example of how to call a prototyped API. Notice that you must use the CALLP op code (not CALL).

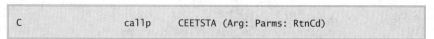

```
C                    callp     CEETSTA (Arg: Parms: RtnCd)
```

Figure 16.2: Use CALLP to call a prototyped API.

—David Morris

Retrieving Commands

Q: When I press F9 from a menu, OS/400 retrieves previously executed commands. How can I make my programs retrieve previously executed commands?

A: Your program needs to call the QMHRTVRQ API, which retrieves the request messages for the job. The code shown in Figure 16.3 illustrates how to do this.

```
D ApiDtaFmt       s              8a   inz('RTVQ0100')
D ApiDtaLen       s             10i 0 inz(2000)
D ApiDtaRtv       ds           2000
D   BytesAvl                    10i 0
D   BytesRtn                    10i 0
D ApiErrCd        s             10i 0 inz(*zero)
D ApiMsgKey       s             10a
D ApiMsgTyp       s             10a
D Cmd             s            256a


 * Set to retrieve info about last request message
C                   eval      ApiMsgTyp = '*LAST'
C                   eval      ApiMsgKey = *blanks

C                   dow       (0  1)
C                   call      'QMHRTVRQ'
C                   parm                    ApiDtaRtv
C                   parm                    ApiDtaLen
C                   parm                    ApiDtaFmt
C                   parm                    ApiMsgTyp
C                   parm                    ApiMsgKey
C                   parm                    ApiErrCd
C                   if        (BytesAvl = 8) and
C                             (BytesRtn = *zero)
C                   leave
C                   endif
C                   if        (BytesRtn > *zero)
C                   eval      Cmd = %subst(ApiDtaRtv: 41:
C                                      (BytesRtn - 40))
C                   else
C                   eval      Cmd = *blanks
C                   endif
 * Variable &CMD now contains a command or blanks
 *
 * set to get previous messages
C                   eval      ApiMsgTyp = '*PRV'
C                   eval      ApiMsgKey = %subst(ApiDtaRtv:9:4)
C                   enddo

C                   eval      *inLR = *on
```

Figure 16.3: The QMHRTVRQ API can retrieve commands previously executed during a job.

—Jerry Jewel

Retrieving Journal Entries

Q: I would like to retrieve journal information programmatically. Ideally, I'd like to have the functionality of the Work with Journal Attributes (WRKJRNA) command or the Display Journal Receiver Attributes (DSPJRNRCVA) command in a program. I can't find any Retrieve (RTV) journal commands or, even better, journal APIs that will give me this information.

A: In V4R2, there are several new journaling APIs. Two that will be of interest to you are QjoRetrieveJournalInformation( ) and QjoRtvJrnReceiverInformation( ). These are documented in the "Journal and Commit APIs" chapter of the *System API Reference* manual.

For earlier releases, the information was also available through the MI instructions MATJPAT and MATJSAT; and, for systems at security level 40 and above, the systems MI were handled by APIs like QusMaterializeJournalPortAttr and QusMaterializeJournal-SpaceAttr. The APIs were provided to get around the domain failures seen in the direct MI usage at higher security levels. These APIs are also in the *System API Reference and Journal* and *Commit APIs* manuals.

—Bruce Vining

Trapping the Error Code in UNIX APIs

Q: How does a program determine errors after calling a UNIX-type API?

A: The code in Figure 16.4 shows how to retrieve the error value when calling UNIX-type APIs.

```
H debug
D errno           Pr              10i 0
D strerror        Pr             128A
**
D fclose          Pr                     extproc('fclose')
D   parm                           *     value
D errnbr          s               10i 0
D errtxt          s               46A    noopt
**
C                     callp     fclose (*NULL)
C                     eval      errnbr = errno
C         errnbr      dsply
C                     eval      errtxt = strerror
C         errtxt      dsply
```

Figure 16.4: This code fragment finds the error value when you call UNIX-type APIs (part 1 of 2).

```
C                     dump
**
C                     seton                                            1r
**
P errno           B
D errno           Pi              10I 0
D sys_errno       Pr                 *    ExtProc('__errno')
D errnbr          S               10I 0 Based(errptr)
D errptr          S                  *
**
C                     Eval        errptr = sys_errno
C                     Return      errnbr
**
P                 E
**
P strerror       B
D strerror       Pi              128A
D sys_strerror   Pr                 *    ExtProc('strerror')
D                                 10I 0 Value
D errtxt         S               128A   Based(txtptr) Noopt
D txtptr           S                *

**
C                     Eval        txtptr = sys_strerror(errno)
C                     dump
C                     Return      %Str(txtptr)
**
P                 E
```

Figure 16.4: This code fragment finds the error value when you call UNIX-type APIs (part 2 of 2).

—Carsten Flensburg

✦ ✦ ✦ Arrays and Tables

Array Techniques Using %ELEM

I try to write code that won't get messed up when I modify it. Here are two techniques I use to avoid changing code when working with arrays. (These techniques also apply to tables, which I rarely use.)

The first technique is to define array dimensions with named constants rather than with numeric literals. Suppose I write a program that accumulates numbers in an array of six elements. I might use code like that shown in Figure 16.5. Suppose that I later have to increase the number of elements from six to eight. I have to change four lines of code (not counting the compile-time array data). If I miss one, the program won't work correctly.

```
         D RegX              s               10i 0
         D SalesRegion       s                3     dim(6)
         D                                          ctdata
         D RegionName        s               12     dim(6)
         D                                          alt(SalesRegion)
         D TotalSales        s               11  2 dim(6)
         C    1              do              6            RegX
         ... do something for each element of the arrays
         C                   enddo
    **
    N  North
    S  South
    E  East
    MW Midwest
    W  West
    PACPacific
```

Figure 16.5: This code is not easily changed.

If, instead, I code it as shown in Figure 16.6, I'll make only one change. I'll change the value of NbrOfRegions from 6 to 8.

```
         D RegX              s               10i 0
         D NbrOfRegions      c                      const(6)
         D SalesRegion       s                3     dim(NbrOfRegions)
         D                                          ctdata
         D RegionName        s               12     dim(NbrOfRegions)
         D                                          alt(SalesRegion)
         D TotalSales        s               11  2 dim(NbrOfRegions)
         C    1              do              NbrOfRegions  RegX
         ... do something for each element of the arrays
         C                   enddo
    **
    N  North
    S  South
    E  East
    MW Midwest
    W  West
    PACPacific
```

Figure 16.6: This code needs only one change if the number of Sales Regions changes.

There might be other modifications, of course. I might have to add a couple of new fields to a screen or a report line, for instance. I'll need to add more regions to the compile-time arrays. Those are changes I am not likely to overlook. At least my DO loops will continue to loop through all the elements, and the **RegionName** array will continue to have the same number of elements as **SalesRegion**.

The second technique is to use the %ELEM function to avoid using literals. %ELEM returns the number of elements in an array. As shown in Figure 16.7, using %ELEM ensures that alternating tables have the same number of elements.

```
     D TabSalesRegion  s              3    dim(6)
     D                                      ctdata
     D TabRegionName   s             12    dim(%elem(TabSalesRegion))
     D                                      alt(TabSalesRegion)
         ... more code
**
N  North
S  South
E  East
MW Midwest
W  West
PACPacific
```

Figure 16.7: The %ELEM function ensures that these alternating tables have the same number of elements.

—Ted Holt

Linking Arrays to Compile-time Data in RPG IV

RPG II and RPG III require data for compile-time arrays to be in the same order as the corresponding definitions of the arrays in the Extension specifications. In RPG IV, that's not a requirement. You have the option of linking array definitions with their corresponding compile-time data so that the compile-time data can be in any order. The way you do this is by coding the name of the array on the statement that identifies the beginning of the compile-time data. The format of the statement is as follows:

```
**CTDATA arrayname
```

In this case, **arrayname** is the name of the array that the data belongs to. By using this technique, you don't have to be sure that the data for the compile time arrays is presented in the same order as the corresponding definitions of the arrays in the Definition specifications. Figure 16.8 shows an example of how this works.

```
        FQPRINT    O   F  132          Printer OFLIND(*InOf)
        D NumArray         S                  1  0 Dim(3) Ctdata PerRcd(3)
        D TxtArray         S                  5    Dim(3) Ctdata PerRcd(3)
        D X                S                  3  0
        C                     Do        3                    X
        C                     Except
        C                     Enddo
        C                     Eval      *InLr = *On
        OQPRINT    E                                  1
        O                               NumArray(X)           3
        O                               TxtArray(X)          10
    **CTDATA TxtArray
    ONE  TWO  THREE
    **CTDATA NumArray
    123
```

Figure 16.8: Compile-time table and array data does not have to appear in the order in which it is declared.

In this example, there are definitions for two arrays. **NumArray** is defined first, followed by **TxtArray**. The bottom of the program contains the data for the arrays. In this case, the data for the arrays is presented in the opposite order as the array definitions. The data for **TxtArray** is first followed by the data for **NumArray**. Even though this is true, the program still works as it should. While you might not want to change the order, it's nice to know that, if you do, it won't cause problems.

—Robin Klima

Redefine a Database Field as an Array in RPG IV

Have you ever needed to redefine a database field as an array? RPG IV contains some useful keywords and built-in functions that let you do this rather easily without even having to hard-code the array size. To see how this can be done, refer to the sample program shown in Figure 16.9. This program reads a control file called CTRLPF, which contains a 25-byte character field called CTDATA. The program is able to access the contents of CTDATA 1 byte at a time by redefining it as an array.

```
FCTRLPF     IF   E             Disk

D                E DS                       EXTNAME(CTRLPF)
D CTARRAY                         1         OVERLAY(CTDATA) DIM(%SIZE(CTDATA))

D CTCOUNT         C                         CONST(%ELEM(CTARRAY))

C                     Read      CTRLPF                            99
C                     Dow       *In99 = *Off

C                     Do        CTCOUNT       X              3 0
 *                        .
 * Process each byte of CTDATA by accessing CTARRAY(X)
 *                        .
C                     Enddo

C                     Read      CTRLPF                            99
C                     Enddo

C                     Eval      *InLr = *On
```

Figure 16.9: *You can easily redefine a database field as an array.*

Here's how the program works. In the F-specs, the CTRLPF file is defined as an input file. Then, in the D-specs, the EXTNAME keyword is used to also define the CTRLPF file as an externally described data structure. Next, an array called CTARRAY is added to the end of the externally described data structure. On the array definition, the OVERLAY keyword is used to overlay CTARRAY over the CTDATA field. The DIM keyword is also used, along with the %SIZE built-in function, to define CTARRAY as having the same number of elements as the size of CTDATA. Next, a constant called CTCOUNT is defined. The CONST keyword is used along with the %ELEM built-in function to set the value of CTCOUNT to count the number of elements in CTARRAY.

In the C-specs, the program reads through the CTRLPF file. For each record read, the program performs a loop. The loop repeats for the number of elements in CTARRAY. (This value is stored in the CTCOUNT constant.) For each iteration, an index called X is incremented. The first time through the loop, the first byte of CTDATA is available to the program by accessing CTARRAY(X). The second time, the second byte is available, and so on. This continues until all bytes have been processed.

This is just one example of how RPG IV's keywords and built-in functions can be combined in various ways to produce some very useful results. In this case, it's easy to redefine a database field as an array without even having to hard-code the array size.

—*Robin Klima*

Using Alternate Tables and Arrays in RPG IV

Programmers are often required to use the alternate tables' feature in RPG programs. In previous versions of RPG (RPG III and lower), only one alternate table could be defined at a time (via the E-specs). However, RPG IV's OVERLAY keyword, in the D-specs, provides practically unlimited power to handle alternate tables. You can define as many alternate tables as you want. For example, assume that an employee record is defined as listed in Table 16.1.

You can load these records into an array and further define alternate arrays. See Figure 16.10.

Table 16.1: Employee Record	
Positions	Field
1–2	Region code
3–5	District code
6–25	Employee name

```
D                   DS
D code              S         25A   DIM(5)
D   reg             S          2A   OVERLAY(code:1)
D   dst             S          3A   OVERLAY(code:3)
D   name            S         20A   OVERLAY(code:6)

C             EVAL     code(1) = '02005Robert Smith'
C             EVAL     code(2) = '01005Ken Pepsico'
C             EVAL     code(3) = '02001John Ramsey'
C             EVAL     code(4) = '01002Kim Nordeen'
C             EVAL     code(5) = '02003Faz Quereshi'

 * Sort the entire code (i.e., sort by reg/dst/name).
C             SORTA    code

 * Sort by region.
C             SORTA    region

 * Sort by district.
C             SORTA    dst

 * Sort by name.
C             SORTA    name

C             EVAL     *INLR = *ON
```

Figure 16.10: RPG IV makes it easy to sort related arrays.

The most amazing benefit derived from this technique is that you can sort on any of the component arrays and have all others sorted as well. To achieve the same goal in older versions of RPG, programmers had to create temporary work files, thus having extra objects to handle.

—*Vijay Yadav*

✦ ✦ ✦ **Calculations**

Binary OR Operation in RPG IV

Q: What is the equivalent of a binary OR in RPG? What is the result of ORing **X'00000F'** with another variable? What is the result of ORing **X'F0F0'** with another variable?

A: RPG does not have a binary OR operator or function. Binary OR compares corresponding bits of two character strings from left to right. If a bit is on in either string, the corresponding bit is turned on in the resulting string. If both bits are off, the corresponding bit is turned off in the resulting string.

ORing **X'00000F'** with a five-digit packed decimal number ensures that that variable is positive. ORing **X'F0F0'** with a two-digit alpha field or zoned decimal number ensures that the zone portion of each byte of the field is **X'F'**. This not only prevents a decimal data error in the field but also makes it a positive number.

—Ted Holt

A: Use the code shown in Figure 16.11 to get the RPG equivalent of **X=A OR B** for 1-byte fields.

```
C* X = A OR B
C                    MOVE A        X        1
C                    BITONB        X
```

Figure 16.11: RPG III easily ORs a 1-byte field.

—Douglas Handy

A: To perform a bitwise inclusive OR of two strings, use the MI _ORSTR function, as shown in Figure 16.12. This function, along with other bitwise functions, logarithms, copy and compare null-terminated strings, and translation functions, is documented in chapter 3 of the *Machine Interface Functional Reference* manual.

```
*=================================================================
* Demonstrate use of bitwise inclusive OR in RPG program
*=================================================================
* To compile:
*
*      CRTRPGMOD  MODULE(XXX/ORTEST) SRCFILE(XXX/QRPGLESRC) +
*                 DBGVIEW(*SOURCE)
*      CRTPGM     PGM(XXX/ORTEST) BNDDIR(QC2LE)
*
*=================================================================
D OR              PR                  extproc('_ORSTR')
D   Receiver                        * value
D   Source_1                        * value
D   Source_2                        * value
D   Length                     10I 0 value

D A              s              4
D B              s              4    inz(x'00F00F11')
D C              s              4    inz(x'0001F044')
D

C* A = B OR C
C                   callp     OR(%addr(A) : %addr(B) :
C                             %addr(C) : %size(A))

 * Using the debugger, view variable A in hex: (eval a :x).
 * A has the value X'00F1FF55'

C                   eval      *inLR = *on
```

Figure 16.12: RPG IV programs can easily bind to the MI _ORSTR function.

—Gene Gaunt

RPG Programs Can Calculate Logarithms

Q: Is there some way of calculating the natural logarithm of a number using RPG IV functions?

A: Yes, you can easily get a natural logarithm in an RPG IV program. The C language functions library (included with OS/400 even if you don't have a C compiler) has a log function. This function is available to RPG ILE programs through procedure prototyping. Look at the code in Figure 16.13 for an example of how to do this.

When this little program runs, x gets the value 6.907755. For your own real-world situation, you want to pass your own variable to log. I just used a literal of 1,000 as an example.

The log function is prototyped in the D-specs. To properly create the program, you must use the QC2LE binding directory when compiling.

```
*=============================================================
* To compile:
*
*        CRTBNDRPG PGM(XXX/YYY) SRCFILE(ZZZ/QRPGLESRC) +
*                  DFTACTGRP(*NO) BNDDIR(QC2LE)
* *=============================================================

D Log            pr           8f    extproc('log')
D   Arg                       8f    value
D
D X              s            8f

C              eval      x = log(1000.0)
C              eval      *inlr = *on
```

Figure 16.13: Here's a handy little routine to calculate logarithms in RPG IV.

—Ted Holt

The CLEAR and RESET Op Codes

The RPG op code CLEAR resets a variable or record format to zero and blank values. Another op code, RESET, performs a similar function. Like CLEAR, RESET may appear anywhere in the calc specs except for the *INZSR subroutine. Like CLEAR, the result field for this op code will be a variable (standalone field, single, or multiple-occurrence data structure, table name, array name, or array element) or record format name. Unlike CLEAR, which sets the result field to zeros or blanks, RESET sets to the value that it had at the end of the *INIT portion of the RPG program cycle.

This value is defined as either the values that the variable or record format items had at the completion of the INZSR subroutine, or—if no *INZSR subroutine exists—the value as specified on the INZ parameter, if one is defined. If neither of these conditions is true, then the default values of zeros and blanks are used.

This op code is particularly useful when you want to continually reset a field or structure to a value or set of values that is predefined. Here are a couple of notes on CLEAR and RESET:

1. For a multiple-occurrence data structure or a table, only the current element is cleared or reset, unless *ALL is specified in factor 2, in which case all elements are cleared or reset.

2. For an array, the entire array is cleared or reset unless a single element is specified, in which case only that element is cleared or reset.

—William W. Smyth

✦ ✦ ✦ Compiling

Conditional Compilation Directives

Conditional compilation directives were added to RPG IV in V3R7. These directives allow you to conditionally include or exclude sections of source code from the compiler. There are a couple of ways you can use this feature. One way to use them is in conjunction with the /COPY directive, which was also enhanced in V3R7 to allow nested copies. Because /COPY now supports nested /COPY members, there's a good chance that a single block of code could get into your program more than once. To avoid this situation, you should code all of your /COPY members as shown in Figure 16.14.

```
/IF NOT DEFINED(CPYMBR1)
/DEFINE CPYMBR1
          .
          .
          .
(your code goes here)
          .
          .
          .
/ENDIF
```

Figure 16.14: Use conditional compiler directives to avoid copying the same source member twice during a compilation.

By using this technique, you ensure that any program that uses this /COPY member will bring in the code in CPYMBR1 only once. When you implement this code, you should replace CPYMBR1 with a more meaningful name.

The other way to use the conditional compilation directive is in conjunction with the Create RPG Module (CRTRPGMOD) and Create Bound RPG Program (CRTBNDRPG) commands. These commands now have a new parameter called DEFINE. Specifying a value for the DEFINE parameter is equivalent to coding a /DEFINE statement on the first line of the source file. So, for example, if you write an update program that optionally produces a report, you can compile it two ways:

```
CRTBNDRPG PGM(PGM1) +
   DEFINE(REPORT)
CRTBNDRPG PGM(PGM1) +
   DEFINE(NO_REPORT)
```

Your program might then contain code that looks like this:

```
/IF DEFINED(REPORT)
C                         Except
/ENDIF
```

In this case, the first compiled object will produce a report when it runs, and the second won't.

—Robin Klima

No-cost RPG Indenter

One of RPG's features that I see as a shortcoming is its fixed columnar nature. If you have a series of nested structures (such as an IF/ELSE/ENDIF block nested within a DOW/ENDDO block), RPG's fixed columns make it difficult to make sure which statements fall within the IF group, which fall within the DO group, and which fall outside both. Things get worse as the number of nested structures increases.

Fortunately, RPG has a solution: the INDENT parameter of the compiler commands Create RPG Program (CRTRPGPGM), Create RPG Module (CRTRPGMOD), and Create Bound RPG (CRTBNDRPG).

INDENT lets you specify one or two characters to be used for indentation purposes—on the printed compiler listing only. I've found that specifying a period, or a vertical line and a space, does the trick pretty well. Next time you compile an RPG program or module, specify INDENT('.') and look at the compiler listing. You'll see a world of difference.

If you like INDENT and want to always use it, you should change the default value for this parameter in all three compiler commands. To make sure you don't alter IBM-supplied commands, however, you should clone all three commands into a library that is higher than QSYS in the system portion of the library list (create one if you don't have it). Then change the default parameter values of the clones, using the Change Command Default (CHGCMDDFT) command. For instance, I have a library named ALTQSYS for that very purpose. Here's what I'd do to change the default for the CRTRPGPGM command:

```
CHGCMDDFT CMD(ALTQSYS/CRTRPGPGM) NEWDFT('INDENT(''.'')')
```

—Ernie Malaga

The DFTACTGRP Factor

Q: Is an RPG IV program compiled with DFTACTGRP(*YES) an OPM or ILE program?

A: It's an ILE program but has some OPM characteristics. If it ends with the LR indicator on, its static storage is freed. An RPG IV program compiled to run in the caller's activation group is marked to be reinitialized the next time it is called. In addition, an RPG IV program running in the default activation group is always a control boundary. To illustrate, suppose program A calls program B with an error indicator or other monitor on the CALL. If B gets an exception (e.g., division by zero), the behavior depends on the activation group being used. If both programs are in the default activation group, an inquiry message appears for B. If both are *CALLER, the error indicator on A's CALL handles the divide-by-zero exception.

—Barbara Morris

✦ ✦ ✦ Copyrights

Copyrighting ILE Objects

ILE modules, programs, and service programs contain an attribute to store copyright information. You can display this copyright information by using the following commands:

```
DSPMOD MODULE(xxx) +
    DETAIL(*COPYRIGHT)
DSPPGM PGM(xxx) +
    DETAIL(*COPYRIGHT)
DSPSRVPGM SRVPGM(xxx) +
    DETAIL(*COPYRIGHT)
```

By default, ILE objects you create from source code contain blank copyright attributes. In V3R2 and V3R7, you can now add up to 256 characters of your own copyright information by placing a copyright statement in your source code.

For ILE CL objects, use the COPYRIGHT command as shown in Figure 16.15. The COPYRIGHT command must follow the PGM command and must precede any other commands except for Declare (DCL) and Declare File (DCLF). Only one COPYRIGHT command is allowed per object. For ILE RPG objects, use the COPYRIGHT keyword on the Control Specification (H-spec) as shown in Figure 16.16.

```
COPYRIGHT TEXT('Copyright My Company Inc. 1997. All rights reserved.')
```

Figure 16.15: ILE CL includes a COPYRIGHT command.

```
H COPYRIGHT('Copyright My Company Inc. 1997. All rights reserved.')
```

Figure 16.16: ILE RPG allows copyright information in the control specifications.

—Robin Klima

✦ ✦ ✦ Data Handling

Don't Compare to Floating Point Variables

Midrange programmers are spoiled. We've been using decimal numbers, and everything has always come out nice and precise. Beware of floating point numbers. You can almost bet they won't be exact. A variable you expect to have the value 5 might be something like 4.99998 or 5.001338 instead.

Convert floating-point values to decimal values before comparison. An easy way to convert is with the Convert to Packed Decimal Format with Half Adjust (%DECH) built-in function, as shown in Figure 16.17.

```
D floatvar        s              8f

  ... assume floatvar = 1.0000011

  ... this test will prove false
C                 if            floatvar = 1.0
  ... this test will prove true
C                 if            %dech(floatvar:6:2) = 1.0
```

Figure 16.17: Compare decimal values instead of floating-point values

%DECH requires three arguments: the numeric value to be converted to decimal, the number of digits of the resulting decimal value, and the number of decimal positions in the decimal value.

—Ted Holt

EVAL Is Not Always Accurate

EVAL makes free-form math possible, but it doesn't always provide the accuracy we midrange programmers are accustomed to, especially when it carries out division. Look at the third EVAL statement shown in Figure 16.18.

```
D a               s              7p 4
D b               s              7p 4
D rslt            s              7p 4
C                 eval          a = 7
C                 eval          b = 50
C                 eval          rslt = a / (b / 7)
```

Figure 16.18: EVAL gives the wrong answer.

What will the value of RSLT be? If you guessed 000.0000, you're right! The reason for this is that EVAL doesn't maintain enough decimal precision when calculating intermediate results. Here are some ways to get better results from EVAL:

- Specify EXPROPTS(*RESDECPOS) in the control (H) specification.

- Change division to multiplication. For example, instead of dividing by 8, multiply by 0.125.

- Break one EVAL into a series of EVALs, each one with only one arithmetic operation, or use ADD, SUB, MULT, and DIV. Make sure intermediate result fields have plenty of decimal positions.

In this case, adding EXPROPTS(*RESDECPOS), as shown in Figure 16.19, gives the correct answer: 000.9800.

```
H expropts(*resdecpos)
D a               s            7p 4
D b               s            7p 4
D rslt            s            7p 4
C                 eval         a = 7
C                 eval         b = 50
C                 eval         rslt = a / (b / 7)
```

Figure 16.19: EVAL gives the correct answer.

Even this doesn't always work. For example, 7 * (50 / 7) always yields 49.9999 because the AS/400 cannot accurately represent 50 divided by 7. To allow for situations like this, a good rule of thumb is to specify half-adjust when dividing.

With V3R7, RPG IV gained a new control specification option, FLTDIV(*YES), that causes the AS/400 to carry out division with floating point numbers. Adding FLTDIV(*YES) to the control specification, as in Figure 16.20, yields 50.0000.

```
H fltdiv(*yes)
D a               s            7p 4
D b               s            7p 4
D rslt            s            7p 4
C                 eval         a = 7
C                 eval         b = 50
C                 eval         rslt = a / (b / 7)
```

Figure 16.20: EVAL gives the correct answer.

—*Rick Crowe*
—*Ted Holt*

Finding Numeric Values in Packed Fields

Q: I have a program that writes to and updates packed decimal fields. Because of the way the program is structured, I'm not always sure that the data going into that field is valid for the data type. When invalid data goes into the field, it causes problems, such as decimal data errors if other programs try to access the data in that field. Is there a method I can use to test for valid data in packed decimal fields before I write it to a file?

A: TESTN tests only zoned fields. To test a packed field, you could use Check/Check Right (CHECK/CHECKR) to test a character view of the field. Figure 16.21 shows a program I wrote that checks whether the program parameter contains a valid packed number. Call the program and pass it a packed field, the number of bytes in the packed field, and an OK field.

```
 *  ===============================================================  *
 *  To compile:                                                     *
 *                                                                  *
 *     CRTBNDRPG  PGM(xxx/BM000R1) SRCFILE(xxx/QRPGLESRC) +         *
 *                SRCMBR(BM000R1)                                   *
 *                                                                  *
 *  ===============================================================  *
d valBegin        c                   X'+
d                                     000102030405060708 09+
d                                     10111213141516171819+
d                                     20212223242526272829+
d                                     30313233343536373839+
d                                     40414243444546474849+
d                                     50515253545556575859+
d                                     60616263646566676869+
d                                     70717273747576777879+
d                                     80818283848586878889+
d                                     90919293949596979899'
d valLast         c                   x'+
d                                     0A0B0C0D0E0F+
d                                     1A1B1C1D1E1F+
d                                     2A2B2C2D2E2F+
d                                     3A3B3C3D3E3F+
d                                     4A4B4C4D4E4F+
d                                     5A5B5C5D5E5F+
d                                     6A6B6C6D6E6F+
d                                     7A7B7C7D7E7F+
d                                     8A8B8C8D8E8F+
d                                     9A9B9C9D9E9F'
d lastByte        s              1a
c     *ENTRY      PLIST
c                 PARM                     charView         16
c                 PARM                     len               5 0
```

Figure 16.21: Use this program to test for numeric values in packed variables (part 1 of 2).

```
C                   PARM                    ok              1
 * Check the last byte for digit (0-9) + sign (A-F)
C      1            SUBST      charView:len  lastByte
C      valLast      CHECK      lastByte                         11=FD
 * Check the first n-1 bytes for digits (0-9) in both nibbles
C                   EVAL       len = len - 1
C      valBegin     CHECKR     charView:len                     10=FD
 *
C                   EVAL       ok = NOT (*IN10 OR *IN11)
C                   IF         ok = '0'
C      'invalid'    DSPLY
C                   ELSE
C      'ok'         DSPLY
C                   ENDIF
 *
C                   RETURN
```

Figure 16.21: Use this program to test for numeric values in packed variables (part 2 of 2).

If the OK field returns a value of 1, the field contains valid packed data. You can easily modify this little program and include it as either a subroutine or a subprocedure in your programs.

—Barbara Morris

Pass Data Through Imports and Exports in RPG IV

Imports and exports can be used to pass fields or data structures between one RPG IV module and another. The use of imports and exports is similar in concept to passing parameters. One module defines the storage for a data item and exports it to another module. The second module then imports the data item and can access the same storage variable.

The EXPORT keyword on the D-spec allows a data item defined within a module to be used by another module in the program. Storage for the data item is allocated in the module containing the EXPORT definition. The IMPORT keyword specifies that storage for the data item being defined is allocated in another module, but may be accessed in the module containing the IMPORT keyword.

See Figure 16.22 for an example of how the IMPORT and EXPORT keywords can be used. Figure 16.22 shows an example of a module called MOD1 that uses the EXPORT keyword to export a field called Counter.

```
D Counter           S              7P 0 Export
  *
C                   Dou            Counter = 100
C                   Callb          'MOD2'
C                   Enddo
  *
C                   Eval           *InLR = *On
```

Figure 16.22: Exporting makes a data item available to other modules.

This module performs a loop that repeats until the **Counter** field reaches 100. Within this loop, the CALLB operation is used to call a second module, MOD2, as shown in Figure 16.23.

```
D Counter           S              7P 0 Import
  *
C                   Eval           Counter = Counter + 1
  *
C                   Eval           *InLR = *On
```

Figure 16.23: Importing makes a module use another module's data.

In MOD2, the IMPORT keyword is used to import the **Counter** field. This module incre-ments the **Counter** field by a value of 1 and passes control back to the first module. After the CALLB to MOD2 in the first module, the value **Counter** is one greater than before the CALLB instruction. When **Counter** reaches 100, the program ends. This example shows you how the IMPORT and EXPORT keywords can be used to share data between RPG IV modules instead of having to pass parameters.

—Robin Klima

STATIC Storage Is Not Reinitialized

Recently, we discovered an "undiscovered feature" in RPG IV and STATIC variables. When a STATIC variable is used in a procedure, its value is not reinitialized, even if the program ends with *INLR=*ON and is called again later. So, even though module-level data variables are reinitialized each time the program ends with *INLR=*ON and is called again, STATIC procedure variables are never reinitialized (at least not as long as the vari-ables continue in memory for that job). If you use STATIC variables, take note of this tip; it could save you some headaches later on!

—Bob Bordeaux

TESTN Negative

If you use the test numeric (TESTN) operation in your RPG programs, you should be aware of how negative numbers are tested. To review, TESTN determines whether a character field contains all numeric data, numeric data with leading spaces, all spaces, or none of the above. When stored in a character field, negative numbers encode the sign into the right-most character.

Uppercase letters J through R represent -1 through -9, respectively (hexadecimals D1 through D9), and the right brace (}) represents zero in a negative number (hexadecimal D0). Consequently, a field defined as 5a with a value of 1234} becomes -12340 when moved to a numeric field defined as 5.0. This means that your character field turns on the HIGH indicator in a TESTN operation, indicating all numeric data. Furthermore, if the right-most character is an uppercase letter from A through I (hexadecimals C1 through C9) or the left brace ({) (hexadecimal C0) and all other characters are numeric, this field also tests as all numeric data. Try it yourself. Uppercase letters A through I translate to positive 1 through 9, respectively, and the left brace ({) becomes zero when moved to a numeric field.

Suppose your system receives an electronic data interchange (EDI) purchase order from your trading partner and one of the fields received is an order quantity sent to you in a mutually agreed upon character field. In addition, suppose your batch RPG program always edits this field for actual numeric data before moving the character field to a numeric field, subsequently creating a sales order. Would receiving a value of 1000A cause a problem? A TESTN on this field passes, and congratulations! You've just ordered 10,000 widgets for your trading partner when they wanted only 1,000. Imagine the surprise if a shipment actually hits their receiving dock.

Fortunately, the workaround for this particular situation is simple, as shown by the code fragment in Figure 16.24. Just move your character field left into a bigger character field before the TESTN statement. Make certain that the rightmost character of the bigger field is a number from 0 through 9, and TESTN will work as you expect. Another solution would be to use the CHECK operation to scan explicitly for just the numbers 0 through 9.

```
*  =========================================================  *
*  To compile:                                                *
*                                                             *
*     CRTBNDRPG  PGM(xxx/CR000R1) SRCFILE(xxx/QRPGLESRC) +    *
*                SRCMBR(CR000R1)                              *
*                                                             *
*  =========================================================  *
D CharQty         s               5a    Inz('1000A')
D IntQty          s               5s 0
D Char30          s              30a
D Wk0to9          c                     Const('0123456789')

   * Using TESTN                                                      HiLoEq
C                   move      *ZEROS          Char30
C                   movel     CharQty         Char30
C                   testn                     Char30              50
C                   If        (*IN50 = *On)
C                   move      CharQty         IntQty
C                   else
   * ..not numeric
C                   endif

   * Using CHECK
C     Wk0to9        Check     CharQty                             51
C                   If        (*IN51 = *Off)
C                   move      CharQty         IntQty
C                   else
   * ..not numeric
C                   endif
C                   eval      *Inlr = *On
```

Figure 16.24: This code fragment tests for numeric values in negative numbers.

—*Chris Ringer*

Use EVAL to Set Adjacent Indicators

Q: In RPG III, I can use MOVEA to set a string of adjacent indicators, as shown in the following example. Is there a way to do this using EVAL in RPG IV?

```
C                           MOVEA'001'      *IN,01
```

A: If the indicators are contiguous, you can use code like that in Figure 16.25; as a by-product, you get named indicators without waiting for V4R2.

```
D Indicators       DS                    BASED(IndPtr)
D  iAllowF1                  1    1A
D  iAllowF2                  2    2A
D  iAllowF3                  3    3A
D  iOptionalKey              1    3A
D IndPtr           S              *      INZ(%ADDR(*IN))

C                  EVAL      iOptionalKeys = *ALL'1'
C                  EVAL      iOptionalKeys = *ALL'0'
C                  EVAL      iOptionalKeys = '110'
```

Figure 16.25: Use a data structure based on a pointer to set a group of indicators in RPG IV.

—Derek Butland

A: You don't have to name the individual indicators if you don't want to. The code in Figure 16.26 shows how to access all 99 general indicators or some portion thereof.

```
D Indicators       S              99     BASED(IndPtr)
D IndPtr           S              *      INZ(%ADDR(*IN))

C                  EVAL      Indicators = *ALL'1'
C                  EVAL      %subst(Indicators:11:9) = '111000010'
```

Figure 16.26: The substring function aids in accessing all general indicators through EVAL in RPG IV.

—Ted Holt

What Causes a "Receiver Too Small" Error?

Q: No matter how large I define result, the RPG IV code shown in Figure 16.27 produces error MCH1210 ("Receiver value too small to hold result"), followed by RNQ0103 ("The target for a numeric operation is too small to hold the result"). However, if I replace the EVAL with a MULT operation, as in Figure 16.28, it works fine. What gives?

```
D a                s             10I 0 inz(2255288)
D b                s             10I 0 inz(1024)
D result           s             17S 0 inz(0)
C                  eval      result = a * b
```

Figure 16.27: Using EVAL produces MCH1210 and RNQ0103 errors.

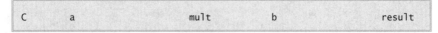

```
C           a              mult         b              result
```

Figure 16.28: Using MULT does not produce an error.

A: Because both operands are integers, the result of **a** * **b** is put into a temporary integer variable. Because **2255288** * **1024** doesn't fit in an integer, an overflow error occurs on the assignment to the temporary variable. You can avoid the error by forcing the compiler to use a temporary packed decimal variable. Figure 16.29 shows a couple of ways. The first method introduces a packed value (0.0) into the expression; therefore, a packed temporary must be used. The second method uses the %DEC built-in function (available with V3R7 and above) to explicitly "declare" a packed temporary.

```
CLON01Factor1+++++++Opcode&ExtExtended-factor2++++++++++++++++++++++++++
C                   eval      result = (a + 0.0) * b
C                   eval      result = %dec(a * b)
```

Figure 16.29: Here are two ways to force a temporary packed decimal variable.

—Barbara Morris

✦ ✦ ✦ Data Structures

Save All Fields with Externally Defined Data Structures

If an application calls for you to save all of the field values from a particular record format, you could either MOVE the values one by one into their respective "save" fields or move them in a single operation by using data structures. As shown in Figure 16.30, each record in record format RECFMT from file INPUTFILE contains five fields.

```
FINPUTFILE IF    E        K DISK

DREC_FORMAT    E DS            EXTNAME(INPUTFILE)
DSAV_FORMAT    E DS            EXTNAME(INPUTFILE) PREFIX(SAV_)

C                READ    RECFMT                              99

C                EVAL    SAV_FORMAT = REC_FORMAT

C                EVAL    *INLR = *ON
```

Figure 16.30: This RPG IV code shows how to save all fields in a record format.

By defining two externally defined data structures (each referring to file INPUTFILE), all of the fields in the record format can be saved in one operation by assigning the value of one data structure to the other. The "save" data structure makes use of the PREFIX keyword to give all of the subfields unique names. Displaying the data structure values in DEBUG mode after the EVAL operation shows the values of the "save" fields (see Figure 16.31).

```
> EVAL REC_FORMAT
    FIELD1 OF REC_FORMAT = 'A'
    FIELD2 OF REC_FORMAT = 'B'
    FIELD3 OF REC_FORMAT = 'C'
    FIELD4 OF REC_FORMAT = 'D'
    FIELD5 OF REC_FORMAT = 'E'
> EVAL SAV_FORMAT
    SAV_FIELD1 OF SAV_FORMAT = 'A'
    SAV_FIELD2 OF SAV_FORMAT = 'B'
    SAV_FIELD3 OF SAV_FORMAT = 'C'
    SAV_FIELD4 OF SAV_FORMAT = 'D'
    SAV_FIELD5 OF SAV_FORMAT = 'E'
```

Figure 16.31: These are the values in the data structures after the EVAL operation.

The same concept is available in RPG III; however, the "save" data structure could not be defined externally because, without a PREFIX keyword, the subfields would not have unique names.

—Paul Espinosa

The LIKE Keyword Creates Packed Fields

Be aware of an important issue when using the D-spec LIKE keyword for a data structure subfield in RPG IV and then subsequently using an OVERLAY keyword. The LIKE keyword is supposed to result in a field that has the same attributes of the reference field. While this is true of the field length, number of decimal positions, and for whether the field is character, numeric, or binary, it isn't true with respect to whether a numeric field is packed or zoned. Regardless of whether the field referenced by the LIKE keyword is packed or zoned, the new field will be created as packed (the default for numeric fields). See the example shown in Figure 16.32.

```
 * Example 1: Will not compile
D                   DS
D NEW_NUMBER                        LIKE(NUMBER)
D CHAR_NBR                    6     OVERLAY(NEW_NUMBER)

 * Example 2: Will compile; however, the functionality of
 * the LIKE keyword is lost
D                   DS
D NEW_NUMBER                  6S 0
D CHAR_NBR                    6     OVERLAY(NEW_NUMBER)
```

Figure 16.32: Beware of the idiosyncrasies of the LIKE keyword.

For example, assume the field NUMBER is externally defined in a database record as 6,0 zoned. The first data structure shown in Figure 16.33 wouldn't compile because the field referenced on the OVERLAY keyword is determined to be too large for the overlay (because field NEW_NUMBER is a packed field). The second data structure shown in Figure 16.33 would compile because NEW_NUMBER is specified as zoned.

—Paul Espinosa

Using LIKE to Define Return Values

Q: I am writing procedures to look up and return names and so forth, based on a customer number that is passed in. Here's my problem: When I define the procedure interface, I want to define the return value with LIKE so that if the field definition changes all I have to do is recompile the programs. Otherwise, I have to go in and change the hard-coded return lengths. Can I use LIKE or something similar so that I don't have to modify the code for file changes?

I've tried LIKE and the compiler says "not expecting a return value for procedure." I copied a working procedure and prototype and then changed to LIKE. Therefore, I'm pretty sure I have everything—besides the LIKE part—defined correctly.

A: If I understand your problem, you have a procedure called, for example, **RtvName** defined as in Figure 16.33, and you would like to use it as shown in Figure 16.34. To replace the **50A** definition with **like(CustName)**, an alternative approach is to define **RtvName** as shown in Figure 16.35. Then, use **RtvName** as shown in Figure 16.36.

```
D RtvName          PI              50A
D  Cust#                           7P 0 value
```

Figure 16.33: Procedure RtvName shows how parameter definitions must be hard-coded.

```
C                  eval       CustName = RtvName(Cust#)
```

Figure 16.34: This way of retrieving a field would be ideal.

```
D RtvName          PI
D  CustName@                       *   value
D  Cust#                           7P 0 value
 *
 * Local variables
D  Name            S               like(CustName) based(CustName@)
```

Figure 16.35: An alternative method of defining RtvName avoids the hard-coding problem.

```
C                 callp    RtvName(%addr(CustName):Cust#)
```

Figure 16.36: Passing an address allows you to use RtvName as you want to.

—John V. Thompson

✦ ✦ ✦ Date and Time

Add Hours to a Date

I use the module shown in Figure 16.37 to calculate the estimated completion date of customer jobs.

```
****************************************************************
*   This module receives a YYYYMMDD starting date, and the
*   number of hours.  The program then computes the ending
*   business date based on the hours and return it as
*   YYYYMMDD to caller.
*
****************************************************************
D               DS
D   date$                      1      7
D   date                       1      7 0 INZ(*ZEROS)

D               DS
D   juldt$                     1      6
D   juldat                     1      6 0 INZ(*ZEROS)
D   julcyy                     1      3 0
D   julddd                     4      6 0

D apierr       DS
D   apie01                     1      4B 0 INZ(15)
D   apie02                     5      8B 0
D   apie03                     9     15

D               DS
D   pyyyymmdd                  1      8A
D   pyyyy                      1      4A
D   pmm                        5      6A
D   pdd                        7      8A

D               DS
D   startdate                  1     10A
D   syyyy                      1      4A
D   syy1                       1      2A
D   syy2                       3      4A
D   sds1                       5      6A   INZ('-')
```

Figure 16.37: Use the power of ILE to generate powerful generic date routines (part 1 of 4).

```
D   smm                      6       7A
D   sds2                     8       8A   INZ('-')
D   sdd                      9      10A

D                  DS
D   enddate                  1      10A
D   eyyyy                    1       4A
D   eyy1                     1       2A
D   eyy2                     3       4A
D   eds1                     5       6A   INZ('-')
D   emm                      6       7A
D   eds2                     8       8A   INZ('-')
D   edd                      9      10A

D                  DS
D   date7                    1       7
D   dct                      1       1
D   dyy                      2       3
D   dmm                      4       5
D   ddd                      6       7

D   @hours         S                 7S 2 INZ(*ZEROS)
D   @days          S                 5P 0 INZ(*ZEROS)
D   @dow           S                 1A   INZ(*BLANKS)
D   apip01         S                10A   INZ(*BLANKS)
D   apip02         S                 7A   INZ(*BLANKS)
D   apip03         S                10A   INZ(*BLANKS)
D   apip04         S                 7A   INZ(*BLANKS)
D   apip05         S                16A   INZ(*BLANKS)
D   @dtwrk         S                 5P 0 INZ(*ZEROS)
D   dotw           S                 1S 0 INZ(*ZEROS)
D   @enddate       S                 D

 *******************************************************************
 * Mainline.
 *******************************************************************

C                  EXSR      $hours_day
C                  EXSR      $add_days
C                  EXSR      $chk_wkend
C                  EXSR      $adj_date

C                  EVAL      *INLR = *ON

 *******************************************************************
C   $hours_day     BEGSR
 *******************************************************************
 * Compute the number of days(based on an 8-hour work-day)

C                  CLEAR               @hours
C                  CLEAR               @days

C                  MOVE      phours    @hours
```

Figure 16.37: Use the power of ILE to generate powerful generic date routines (part 2 of 4).

```
C                      EVAL(H)   @days = @hours / 8

C                      ENDSR

      ****************************************************************
C     $add_days        BEGSR
      ****************************************************************
*     Add the number of days computed to the starting date
*         to  calculate the ending date...

C                      MOVE      pyyyy          eyyyy
C                      MOVE      pmm            emm
C                      MOVE      pdd            edd
C                      MOVE      enddate        @enddate

C                      ADDDUR    @days:*days    @enddate
C                      MOVE      @enddate       enddate

C                      ENDSR


      ****************************************************************
C     $chk_wkend       BEGSR
      ****************************************************************
*         Compute the day-of-the-week for completion date...

C                      CLEAR                    date7
C                      MOVE      '0'            dct
C                      MOVE      eyy2           dyy
C                      MOVE      emm            dmm
C                      MOVE      edd            ddd
C                      IF        eyy1 = '20'
C                      MOVE      '1'            dct
C                      ENDIF
C                      MOVE      date7          date$

C                      CALL      'QWCCVTDT'
C                      PARM      '*YMD'         apip01
C                      PARM      date$          apip02
C                      PARM      '*JUL'         apip03
C           juldt$     PARM                     apip04
C           apierr     PARM      apierr         apip05

C           julcyy     SUB       1              @dtwrk
C                      MULT      365.25         @dtwrk
C                      ADD       365            @dtwrk
C                      ADD       julddd         @dtwrk
C           @dtwrk     DIV       7              dotw
C                      MVR                      dotw
C                      ADD       1              dotw

C                      MOVE      dotw           @dow
```

Figure 16.37: Use the power of ILE to generate powerful generic date routines (part 3 of 4).

```
C                      ENDSR

      ***********************************************************
C       $adj_date      BEGSR
      ***********************************************************
*       If the ending date is a '7'(Saturday)
*           then you'll want it to end on a Monday...
*       If the ending date is a '1'(Sunday)
*           then you'll want it to end on a Tuesday...
*       So, just add 2 days to either date...

C                      MOVE      enddate       @enddate

C                      SELECT

C                      WHEN          @dow = '7'
C                                 OR @dow = '1'

C                      ADDDUR    2:*DAYS       @enddate

C                      ENDSL

C                      MOVE      @enddate      enddate

C                      CLEAR                   pyyyymmdd
C                      MOVE      eyyyy         pyyyy
C                      MOVE      emm           pmm
C                      MOVE      edd           pdd

C                      MOVE      pyyyymmdd     penddate

C                      ENDSR

      ***********************************************************
C       *INZSR         BEGSR
      ***********************************************************
C       *ENTRY         PLIST
C                      PARM                    pstartdate     8
C                      PARM                    phours         7
C                      PARM                    penddate       8

C                      MOVE      pstartdate    pyyyymmdd

C                      ENDSR
```

Figure 16.37: Use the power of ILE to generate powerful generic date routines (part 4 of 4).

Given a starting date in the YYYYMMDD format (8 bytes alphanumeric) and a number of hours (7 digits, packed decimal, 2 decimal places), the module returns the completion date in the YYYYMMDD format.

—Paul J. Sgroi

An RPG IV Date Calculation Routine

One of the long-awaited features of RPG IV is the capability to do date math. With date math capability, there are many ways to take advantage of it, even if your date fields aren't date data types. One way is by writing a generic date calculation routine, such as the one shown in Figure 16.38.

```
D WorkDate        S             10D    DATFMT(*ISO)
D InputDate       S              8S 0
D Duration        S              5  0
D DurCode         S              1A
D ReturnDate      DS             8
D  Year                          4
D  Month                         2
D  Day                           2
 *
C     *Entry        PLIST
C                   PARM                      InputDate
C                   PARM                      Duration
C                   PARM                      DurCode
C                   PARM                      ReturnDate
 *
C     *ISO          TEST(D)                   InputDate              99
 *
C                   IF          *IN99 = *OFF
C     *ISO          MOVE        InputDate     WorkDate
 *
C                   SELECT
C                   WHEN        DurCode = 'D'
C                   ADDDUR      Duration:*D   WorkDate
C                   WHEN        DurCode = 'M'
C                   ADDDUR      Duration:*M   WorkDate
C                   WHEN        DurCode = 'Y'
C                   ADDDUR      Duration:*Y   WorkDate
C                   OTHER
C                   ADDDUR      Duration:*D   WorkDate
C                   ENDSL
 *
C                   EXTRCT      WorkDate:*Y   Year
C                   EXTRCT      WorkDate:*M   Month
C                   EXTRCT      WorkDate:*D   Day
 *
C                   ELSE
 *
C                   MOVE        *ALL'9'       ReturnDate
C                   ENDIF
 *
C                   EVAL        *INLR = *ON
```

Figure 16.38: Use RPG IV for date arithmetic, even if your dates are not stored in the date data type.

683

This routine will return a calculated date based on the values passed into it. The four parameters to this routine are a:

1. Starting date

2. Duration value

3. Duration code

4. Return date

The first parameter (starting date) should be passed as an 8-byte character field in the format YYYYMMDD. The second parameter is the duration value that you want to use to increment the date. This routine supports both calculating dates later than the start date and calculating dates earlier than the start date. To calculate a date later than the start date, pass a positive value in the second parameter. To calculate a date earlier than the start date, pass in a negative value in the second parameter. The third parameter is a duration code. Pass a value of D to increment by days, M to increment by months, or Y to increment by years. The calculated date is returned through the fourth parameter as an 8-byte character field in YYYYMMDD format. If the routine determines that an invalid date has been passed in through the first parameter, it will pass back a date of all 9s through the fourth parameter.

As with most ILE routines, there are several ways to implement this code. You could compile it as a standalone program with the Create Bound RPG Program (CRTBNDRPG) command. This would allow you to make external calls to it from your own programs, whether they're ILE programs or not.

Alternatively, you could compile this routine using the Create RPG Module (CRTRPGMOD) command, followed by either the Create Service Program (CRTSRVPGM) or the Create Program (CRTPGM) command. This would give you better performance by allowing you to bind the executable code into your own programs.

—Izzy Munoz
—T.V.S. Murphy

Date Arithmetic Templates

Recently, I was asked how to use the RPG IV date addition and subtraction op codes to determine a date one month from the current date. Not being the type of person who likes to use five words when 105 will do, I wrote a little demo program to show how to perform a variety of date calculations. Figure 16.39 shows how to:

- Retrieve the current date.

- Add one month to the current date.

- Subtract one month from the current date.

- Add 30 days to the current date.

- Subtract 30 days from the current date.

```
*******************************************************************
* TO COMPILE:
*
*   CRTBNDRPG PGM(xxx/ADDSUBR1) SRCFILE(xxx/QRPGLESRC)
*
*
*******************************************************************
*   This program demonstrates how to retrieve the current date,
*   how to add one month to the current date, how to subtract
*   one month from the current date, how to add 30 days to the
*   current date, and how to subtract 30 days from the current date.
*
*
*
*******************************************************************
HDATEDIT(*YMD)
D Current_Date   S              8  0
D WorkDate       S                D   DATFMT(*YMD)
 * Retrieve current date
C                   Eval      Current_Date  = *Date
 * Move Current Date to WorkDate
C                   Move      Current_Date  WorkDate
 * Add 1 Month to WorkDate
C                   Adddur    1:*Months     WorkDate
 * Subtract 1 Month from WorkDate
C                   Subdur    1:*Months     WorkDate
 * Add 30 Days to WorkDate
C                   Adddur    30:*D         WorkDate
 * Subtract 30 days from WorkDate
C                   Subdur    30:*D         WorkDate
C                   Eval      *Inlr = *On
```

Figure 16.39: Use this RPG IV date arithmetic blueprint to make sure your dates come out like they're supposed to.

The reason I show not only how to add an entire month but also how to add 30 days is to demonstrate the difference between how the ADDUR and SUBDUR op codes work. When you run the program, you'll notice that adding an entire month might not necessarily return the same value as adding 30 days would, even if the month has only 30 days. This is because of the way RPG IV handles the addition and subtraction of dates. It does this to prevent invalid dates. Consider this example: Add one month to January 31, and you get February 28 (or February 29 if it's a leap year). However, if you add 30 days to January 31, you end up with a date of March 2.

Use this little program as a guideline the next time you need to perform date arithmetic.

—Shannon O'Donnell

Last Day of Month in RPG IV

Q: Is there a way to get an end-of-month date from a date data type in RPG IV?

A: The RPG IV date fields and data operators give you an easy way to calculate the last day of a month. Figure 16.40 shows a callable program that returns the last day of the month for the month and year passed in as parameters.

```
DDate            S          D
DMonth           S          2S 0
DYear            S          2S 0
DLastDay         S          2S 0
   *
D                DS
D   DateDS           1       6S 0
D   MonthDS          1       2S 0
D   DayDS            3       4S 0
D   YearDS           5       6S 0
   *
C       *Entry    Plist
C                 Parm                    Month
C                 Parm                    Year
C                 Parm                    LastDay
C                 Z-Add   Month           MonthDS
C                 Z-Add   Year            YearDS
   *
C                 Eval    MonthDS = MonthDS + 1
   *
C                 If      (MonthDS > 12)
C                 Eval    MonthDS = 1
C                 EndIf
   *
C                 Eval    DayDS = 1
C       *MDY      Move    DateDS          Date
C       Date      SubDur  1:*D            Date
C                 Extrct  Date:*D         LastDay
   *
C                 Eval    *INLR = *On
```

Figure 16.40: Use this RPG IV program to calculate the last day of the month.

The program works by converting the requested date to the first day of the next month and then subtracting one day to make it the last day of the requested date. You can use the sample program as it is or use the same technique in your own programs.

—Mike Hockley

A: Here's a three-line solution (Figure 16.41) that ought to do the trick. This code will add a month, then subtract the *DAYS part, giving you the end-of-month date.

```
C       d1          addur     1:*m        tempd
C                   extrct    tempd:*days days
C       tempd       subdur    days:*days  tempd
```

Figure 16.41: Here's a handy method to determine the date of the last day of the month.

—Barbara Morris

Nice Date, Wrong Century!

Does the code shown in Figure 16.42 look familiar by now? If so, maybe you have the same exposure to an inaccurate date that we had.

```
C*                                                        HiLoEq
C       *ISO        TEST(D)               DATE80          30
C       *IN30       IFEQ      *ON
```

Figure 16.42: This code tests for valid dates but isn't adequate for robust applications

This code does a great job of checking for month 13, day 32, etc., but the year range might be a bit larger than most of our applications are expecting. For example, 1066-10-14 (Battle of Hastings) and 1492-10-12 (Columbus' arrival to America) also pass the edit check of TEST(D).

IBM does draw the line at year 0001. But, for most of us, something like the code shown in Figure 16.43 might be a better test when validating eight-digit dates.

```
C*                                                          HiLoEq
C      *ISO        TEST(D)                  DATE80              30
C      *IN30       IFEQ        *ON
C      DATE80      ORLT        18000000
```

Figure 16.43: This code tests for valid dates and restricts the range of permitted dates.

—*Skip Forster*

Potential Snag with Time Fields

I've noticed a potential "gotcha" with using time fields and how 12:00 A.M. is represented. Depending on how a time field is used (stored, sorted, compared, displayed, etc.) various companies will choose to represent 12:00 A.M. as either '00.00.00' or '24.00.00'. Actually, both of these values are valid for a time field. If you move *LOVAL to a time field, the result is '00.00.00'. If you move *HIVAL, the result is '24.00.00'.

Things work a little differently when computing durations involving a time field. If you add or subtract a duration to a time field that results in precisely 12:00 A.M., it is always represented as '00.00.00'. Thus, for example, if you compute a duration and write the result to a file expecting 12:00 A.M. to be '24:00:00', you would be in for a surprise.

—*Mason Eckley*

Removing Separator Characters from a Date Field

Here is a simple technique for removing editing characters from a date field. Use the CHECK op code to find the delimiters, and use the EVAL op code and %SUBST built-in function to take them out.

Figures 16.44 and 16.45 contain the prototype and the subprocedure Remove Date Separators (RMVDTSEP) for this technique.

```
DRMVDTSEP       PR          10
DVAR1                       10
```

Figure 16.44: Member RMVDTSEPPR is the prototype for the RMVDTSEP subprocedure.

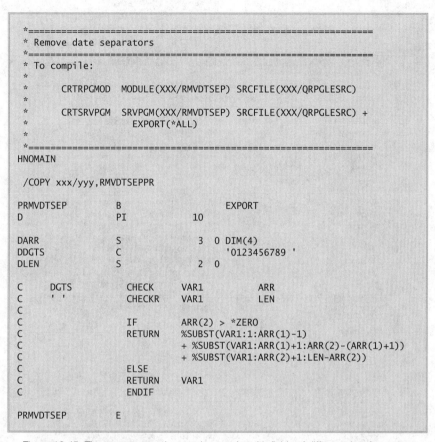

```
*===============================================================
* Remove date separators
*===============================================================
* To compile:
*
*        CRTRPGMOD  MODULE(XXX/RMVDTSEP) SRCFILE(XXX/QRPGLESRC)
*
*        CRTSRVPGM  SRVPGM(XXX/RMVDTSEP) SRCFILE(XXX/QRPGLESRC) +
*                   EXPORT(*ALL)
*
*===============================================================
HNOMAIN

 /COPY xxx/yyy,RMVDTSEPPR

PRMVDTSEP          B                   EXPORT
D                  PI           10

DARR               S            3  0 DIM(4)
DDGTS              C                  '0123456789 '
DLEN               S            2  0

C     DGTS         CHECK     VAR1            ARR
C     ' '          CHECKR    VAR1            LEN
C
C                  IF        ARR(2) > *ZERO
C                  RETURN    %SUBST(VAR1:1:ARR(1)-1)
C                            + %SUBST(VAR1:ARR(1)+1:ARR(2)-(ARR(1)+1))
C                            + %SUBST(VAR1:ARR(2)+1:LEN-ARR(2))
C                  ELSE
C                  RETURN    VAR1
C                  ENDIF

PRMVDTSEP          E
```

Figure 16.45: The RMVDTSEP subprocedure works with fields of different date formats.

This method can be used with dates in formats MM/DD/YY, YY/MM/DD, CCYY/MM/DD, or MM/DD/CCYY, and it works with any nonblank separator character.

—*Shashi K. Narasimhan*

Retrieving Time Stamps with Milliseconds

Q: Does RPG IV provide a way to retrieve a time stamp that includes milliseconds?

A: There's no direct way, but you can use the RTVTIMSTP module (Figure 16.46). You should note that RTVTIMSTP takes some time to execute. Even if you cannot measure that time, it is enough to render inaccurate the milliseconds portion of the time stamp. You'll have to decide whether this inaccuracy is significant or not.

```
     *==============================================================
     * To compile:
     *
     *       CRTRPGMOD  MODULE(XXX/RTVTIMSTP) SRCFILE(XXX/QRPGLESRC)
     *
     *==============================================================
     * Retrieve System Value (QWCRSVAL) API.
D RtnSysVal       DS
D   NbrRtnVal                     9B 0 Inz(%Elem(NamSysVal))
D   OffSysVal                     9B 0 Dim(4)
D   SysValTbl                    100A
     *==============================================================
     * Timestamp Data Structure.
D                 DS
D TimeStamp                       Z  Inz
D   Century                       2A  Overlay(TimeStamp:  1)
D   Year                          2A  Overlay(TimeStamp:  3)
D   Month                         2A  Overlay(TimeStamp:  6)
D   Day                           2A  Overlay(TimeStamp:  9)
D   Hour                          2A  Overlay(TimeStamp: 12)
D   Minute                        2A  Overlay(TimeStamp: 15)
D   Second                        2A  Overlay(TimeStamp: 18)
D   Millisec                      3A  Overlay(TimeStamp: 21)
     *==============================================================
     * Record structure for error code parameter.
D ErrData         DS
D   BytesProv                     9B 0 Inz(100)
D   BytesAval                     9B 0
D   ExcpId                        7A
D   Reserved1                     1A
D   ExcpData                    184A
     *==============================================================
     * Stand-alonefields.
D LenSysVal       S               9B 0 Inz(%Size(RtnsysVal))
D NamSysVal       S              10A  Dim(4) PerRcd(4) CtData
D NbrSysVal       S               9B 0 Inz(%Elem(NamSysVal))
D Offset          S               9B 0
D OutTimStp       S                    Like(TimeStamp)
     ***************************************************************
C     *Entry         PList
C                    Parm                           OutTimStp

     * Retrieve the time from the system values.
C                    Call      'QWCRSVAL'
C                    Parm                           RtnSysVal
C                    Parm                           LenSysVal
C                    Parm                           NbrSysVal
C                    Parm                           NamSysVal
C                    Parm                           ErrData
     * Retrieve QMONTH (first offset).
C                    Eval      Offset   = OffSysVal(1) - 3
C                    Eval      Month    = %Subst(SysValTbl: Offset: 2)
```

Figure 16.46: RPG IV Module RTVTIMSTP retrieves a time stamp with milliseconds (part 1 of 2).

```
 * Retrieve QDAY (second offset).
C                    Eval      Offset  = OffSysVal(2) - 3
C                    Eval      Day     = %Subst(SysValTbl: Offset: 2)
 * Retrieve QYEAR (third offset).
C                    Eval      Offset  = OffSysVal(3) - 3
C                    Eval      Year    = %Subst(SysValTbl: Offset: 2)
 * Retrieve QTIME (fourth offset).
C                    Eval      Offset  = OffSysVal(4) - 3
C                    Eval      Hour    = %Subst(SysValTbl: Offset: 2)
C                    Eval      Offset  = Offset + 2
C                    Eval      Minute  = %Subst(SysValTbl: Offset: 2)
C                    Eval      Offset  = Offset + 2
C                    Eval      Second  = %Subst(SysValTbl: Offset: 2)
C                    Eval      Offset  = Offset + 2
C                    Eval      Millisec = %Subst(SysValTbl: Offset: 3)
 * Determine Century.
C                    If        Year < '40'
C                    Eval      Century = '20'
C                    Else
C                    Eval      Century = '19'
C                    EndIf

C                    Eval      OutTimStp = TimeStamp
C                    Return

**CTDATA NamSysVal
QMONTH     QDAY       QYEAR      QTIME
```

Figure 16.46: RPG IV Module RTVTIMSTP retrieves a time stamp with milliseconds (part 2 of 2).

To use the program, call it with a single parameter, which must be of data type Z (time stamp). RTVTIMSTP returns the time stamp in that parameter.

—Alex Nubla

What Day of the Week Is It?

Q: Does RPG IV have a way to determine the day of the week?

A: Here's an easy way. Subtract from some known Saturday (e.g., May 1, 1999) any date in a date-type data field and divide the resulting number of days by 7. The remainder gives you the day of the week as a one-digit number, where 0 = Saturday, 1 = Sunday, 2 =Monday, etc. See Figure 16.47 for an example.

```
****************************************************************
* determine the day of week of date_char
* date_char is in MMDDYY format
****************************************************************
D date_char       s              6
D date_work       s               d
D saturday        s               d
D weeks           s             15  0
D dayofweek       s              1  0
D elapsed         s             15  0

C     *mdy          movel     '05/02/99'    saturday
C     *mdy0         move      date_char     date_work
C     date_work     subdur    saturday      elapsed:*D
C     elapsed       div       7             weeks
C                   mvr                     dayofweek
C                   if        dayofweek < *zero
C                   eval      dayofweek = dayofweek + 7
C                   endif
```

Figure 16.47: RPG IV can determine the day of the week.

—Michael Daly

You Can Validate Any Date

Figure 16.48 contains a short data validation routine that I wrote. It's written in RPG IV and is very versatile.

```
*==============================================================
* To compile:
*
*        CRTBNDRPG  PGM(XXX/DAT004RG)  SRCFILE(XXX/QRPGLESRC)
*
*==============================================================
*. 1 ...+... 2 ...+... 3 ...+... 4 ...+... 5 ...+... 6 ...+... 7
* Incoming numeric date
D Date_Parm       DS
D Date_Fmts                      8
D Date@5                         5  0 OVERLAY(Date_Fmts)
D Date@6                         6  0 OVERLAY(Date_Fmts)
D Date@8                         8  0 OVERLAY(Date_Fmts)

* Work field for date
D Date_In         DS
```

Figure 16.48: DAT004RG is a generic date-validation routine that can be called from OPM and ILE programs (part 1 of 2).

```
D Date_In@                              LIKE(Date_Fmts)
D Date_In@5                             LIKE(Date@5) OVERLAY(Date_In@)
D Date_In@6                             LIKE(Date@6) OVERLAY(Date_In@)
D Date_In@8                             LIKE(Date@8) OVERLAY(Date_In@)

 * Position: 1=MDY, 2=DMY, 3=YMD, 4=JUL, 5=ISO, 6=USA, 7=EUR, 8=JIS
D Fmt_Parm        S               8
D Fmt_Ind         S                     LIKE(Fmt_Parm)
D InLR            S               1

 * Entry/Exit parms
C     *Entry        Plist
C     Date_In       Parm                    Date_Parm
C                   Parm        Fmt_Ind     Fmt_Parm
C                   Parm                    InLR

 * Vaidation tests
C     *MDY          Test(D)                 Date_In@6              01
C     *DMY          Test(D)                 Date_In@6              02
C     *YMD          Test(D)                 Date_In@6              03
C     *JUL          Test(D)                 Date_In@5              04
C     *ISO          Test(D)                 Date_In@8              05
C     *USA          Test(D)                 Date_In@8              06
C     *EUR          Test(D)                 Date_In@8              07
C     *JIS          Test(D)                 Date_In@8              08

C                   Movea       *In(01)     Fmt_Ind
C                   Eval        *InLR = InLR
C                   Return
```

Figure 16.48: DAT004RG is a generic date-validation routine that can be called from OPM and ILE programs (part 2 of 2).

Here's how it works. Pass it any date (left-justified in a 10-byte character field without separators) and a TSR switch, and it will return to you an array of eight indicators. The position of the resulting indicator determines whether or not the date is valid for a particular format. The positions are 1=MDY, 2=DMY, 3=YMD, 4=JUL, 5=ISO, 6=USA, 7=EUR, and 8=JIS. A return value of *OFF indicates a valid date.

This routine can be used in an Original Program Model (OPM) environment as a statically called program or as an ILE bound service program module. It will replace many archaic, cumbersome lines of code that have probably been replicated hundreds of times throughout many systems in the mainline of a program or as separate subroutines.

—*Claude Osgood*

Date Field Mysteries

Here are some quirks I've discovered with the way RPG IV works with fields of the date data type:

- The date data type fields can never be left blank or zeroed. The easiest way to set an acceptable value is to 'Clear' the date field. This cannot be done if the %NullInd = *ON.

- The %NullInd built-in function (BIF) can be used only with database fields. Program-defined fields may contain cleared data, but the %NullInd cannot be used to condition the contents of the data.

- The %NullInd BIF is similar to the modified data tag (MDT) that is associated with display fields. The indicator cannot be seen along with the data. You must do special testing to determine the condition of the data element.

- The data in the field cannot be used in any way when a data field has the null attribute set in the *ON condition. It is always best to test the condition of the null indicator prior to attempting to use the data. If the contents of a known "allow nulls" field is to be changed unconditionally, always set the null indicator to the *OFF condition first.

—Bill Green

✦ ✦ ✦ Debug

Debugging an ILE Module in Statement View

Q: How can I add a breakpoint when debugging an ILE program compiled with DBGVIEW(*STMT)?

A: On the Display Module Source (DSPMODSRC) command line, enter BREAK PROCNAME/STMT. For the main procedure, PROCNAME is the same as the name of the module; otherwise, it's the name of the subprocedure. STMT is the number on the left side of the compiler listing. If you specify OPTION(*SRCSTMT) in the control specification, STMT is also the SEU sequence number.

—Barbara Morris

Help with RPG IV Debugging

Early versions of the full-screen debugger have problems with RPG IV programs. The first problem is that runtime error messages indicate compiler listing line numbers, rather than the source member sequence numbers. This requires programmers to recompile a program to find out what line of code was failing. To overcome this, you can specify OPTION(*SRCSTMT) on the control (H) spec if you want the object to contain source sequence numbers.

The second problem is that input and output specs generate debugging breakpoints. IBM added another permissible OPTION keyword—*NODEBUGIO—in this same fix. OPTION(*NODEBUGIO) prevents the generation of breakpoints on input and output specifications. If you want to specify both values, separate them with a colon.

```
OPTION(*SRCSTMT : *NODEBUGIO)
```

There are also opposite values of *NOSRCSTMT and *DEBUGIO, but you probably won't need them because they are the default values.

—Doug Pence
—Ron Hawkins
—Jon Paris

The Built-in Functions of the Full-screen System Debugger

The full-screen system debugger that became available in V3R1 is great! Finally, AS/400 programmers can view a program's source statements while the program is running in debug mode. Viewing the value of a variable in an ILE program running in debug mode can be as simple as placing the cursor on the field name and pressing F11 (Display Variable).

Unfortunately, using this method to display data contained in a particular occurrence of a multiple-occurrence data structure has a limitation. If you use the F11 key, the debugger displays only the value of the current occurrence. Fortunately, the debugger's built-in %INDEX function solves this problem by letting you set the current index of a multiple-occurrence data structure.

You use the %INDEX function through the EVAL statement. For example, if you want to look at the thirteenth occurrence of data structure **MODS**, you key the following debug command in the debugger command line:

```
EVAL MODS = %INDEX(13)
```

Now you can display the value of the thirteenth occurrence by either placing the cursor in the **MODS** variable and pressing F11 or using EVAL. You also can display any of the subfields of the data structure with the F11 technique or with the EVAL command.

There are two other built-in debug functions to assist you in displaying variables: %SUBSTR and %ADDR. The %SUBSTR function allows you to substring a character string variable. Similar to the RPG IV %SUBSTR operator, the first parameter is the variable name, the second parameter is the starting position, and the third parameter is the number of bytes to display. For example, to display 25 bytes of a variable named **LONGSTR** beginning with position 1001, you would enter the following debug command:

```
EVAL %SUBSTR(LONGSTR 1001 25)
```

The %ADDR function displays the memory address of a variable. To display the address of example variable **LONGSTR**, you would enter the following debug command:

```
EVAL %ADDR(LONGSTR)
```

For more information about the system debugger, see *The RPG Programmer's Guide to ILE and RPG IV*.

—Richard Shaler

✦ ✦ ✦ File Handling

Random Access to an IFS File

Q: Is there a POSIX API that can CHAIN (i.e., perform a random access) or use SQL from an RPG program to position the file pointer at a specific spot in a file in the AS/400 Integrated File System (AS/400 IFS)?

A: You can use the Lseek( ) external procedure to position the file pointer at any point in a file stored in the AS/400 IFS. This is more like the RPG op code Set Greater Than (SETGT) or Set Lower Limit (SETLL) than it is like CHAIN, but it's as close as you can get with flat files. Lseek( ) is part of the UNIX-type APIs and follows the POSIX standard. Using Lseek( ), you can position the file pointer in a number of ways. For example, if you have a flat file in the AS/400 IFS that has records that are 189 characters long and you want to start reading the file from the second record, you can use Lseek( ) to accomplish this. You can also read the file from the end or read it backwards, which is much like the ReadP op code in RPG. It works like this:

You open the AS/400 IFS file with the **Open( )** external procedure call and then use the **Lseek( )** external procedure call to position the file pointer. You must specify the OFFSET (i.e., where the next read will begin) and whether to read from the beginning of the file, the current file pointer position, or the end of the file. If the OFFSET contains a positive number when the **Lseek( )** procedure is called, the next file access (e.g., a READ) will move forward through the file. However, if the OFFSET field contains a negative number, the next file access will move backward through the file.

You control whether the pointer is positioned from the beginning, the current position, or the end of the file by the value you place in the WHENCE parameter. A value of 0 indicates that the OFFSET is relative to the beginning of the file; a value of 1 indicates that the OFFSET is relative to the current file pointer; and a value of 2 indicates that the OFFSET is relative to the end of the file.

Look at the code shown in Figure 16.49. I've included an **Lseek()** prototype near the beginning of the program and an **SkFile** procedure, which uses the **Lseek()** external procedure call, at the bottom. In this example, I have a comma-separated file stored in a directory named Shannon in the AS/400 IFS. Each record in this file is 189 characters long, and I want to start reading from the second record. I accomplish this by setting the file pointer OFFSET to 190 (i.e., record length + 1) and setting the WHENCE parameter to 0 to indicate that the OFFSET should start from the beginning of the file. After calling the **Lseek()** procedure, I set WHENCE to 1 so, the next time through this procedure, the OFFSET will start relative to the current file position.

```
 *==================================================================
 * To Compile:
 *
 *    CRTBNDRPG  PGM(XXX/QSEEKOR1) DFTACTGRP(*NO) BNDDIR(QC2LE)
 *==================================================================
 *
FRcfile2    O    E           K Disk
 *
 * open  - open an IFS file
D open            pr              10i 0    ExtProc('open')
D   Filepath                        *      value
D   openflags                     10i 0    value
D   mode                          10u 0    value options(*nopass)
D   codepage                      10u 0    value options(*nopass)
 * = = = = = = = = = = = = = = = = = = = = = = = = = = = = = = =
 * read - read a QNTC file
```

Figure 16.49: This SkFile procedure uses the Lseek() external procedure call (part 1 of 4).

```
  *
D read            pr           10i 0   ExtProc('read')
D   filehandle                 10i 0   value
D   datareceived                 *     value
D   nbytes                     10u 0   value
  * = = = = = = = = = = = = = = = = = = = = = = = = = = = = =
  * write - write file
  *
D write           pr           10i 0   ExtProc('write')
D   filehandle                 10i 0   value
D   datatowrite                  *     value
D   nbytes                     10u 0   value
  * = = = = = = = = = = = = = = = = = = = = = = = = = = = = =
  * close- close file
  *
D close           pr           10i 0   ExtProc('close')
D   filehandle                 10i 0   value
  * = = = = = = = = = = = = = = = = = = = = = = = = = = = = =
  * lseek - position file pointer
  *
D lseek           pr           10i 0   ExtProc('lseek')
D   filehandle                 10i 0   value
D   Offset                      4b 0   value
D   Whence                     10i 0   value
  * = = = = = = = = = = = = = = = = = = = = = = = = = = = = =
  * values for oflag parameter, used by open()
  * from QSYSINC/H, member FCNTL
D O_Rdonly        s            10i 0   inz(1)
D O_Textdata      s            10i 0   inz(16777216)

  * Prototype for reading from the IFS file
D RdFile          PR          100A
D   Filepath                  100A     CONST

  * Prototype for Seeking from the IFS file
D SkFile          PR          100A
D   Filepath                  100A     CONST

D CodePage        S            10u 0 inz(819)
D Cr              C                  const(x'0D')
D Data_Rec        S           190A
D Eol             C                  Const(x'0D25')
D Error_Flag      S             1A   INZ('0')
D File            S           100A
D Filepath        S           100A   INZ('/shannon/NEWCUST.CSV')
D Fp              S            10i 0
D I_Net_Adr       S            20A   Inz
D Lf              C                  const(x'25')
D N               S             5  0
D Oflag           S            10i 0
D Omode           S            10u 0
D R               S             5  0
D Rc              S            10i 0
D Rec_Pos         S            10  0
```

Figure 16.49: This SkFile procedure uses the Lseek() external procedure call (part 2 of 4).

```
*_____
* MAIN
*_____
C                   Eval      Error_Flag = RdFile(Filepath)
C                   Eval      *Inlr = *On
*_____
*    RdFile   - Subprocedure To Read a file
*_____
P RdFile        B                         Export
D RdFile        PI            100A
D  Filepath                   100A    Const
D CharsRead     S              10i 0
D CurChar       S               1
D Eof           C                         const(x'00')
C                   Eval      Oflag = O_Rdonly + O_Textdata
C                   Eval      File = %trim(Filepath) + x'00'
C                   Eval      Fp = open(%addr(File): Oflag)
C                   If        Fp < 0
C                   Eval      Error_Flag = *On
C                   Return    Error_Flag
C                   Endif

C                   Eval      R = 0
C                   Eval      N = 0
 *
 * Use LSeek to position to first desired record
C                   Eval      Error_Flag = SkFile(Filepath)
 *
C                   Eval      Data_Rec = *Blanks
C                   Exsr      GetChar
 *
 * Loop until End of File
C                   Dow       CurChar <> Eof
C                   Select
 * Carriage Return
C                   When      CurChar = Cr
C                   Exsr      Write_Rec
C                   Eval      R = *zero
C                   Eval      Text = *blanks
 *
 * Seek next record
C                   Eval      Error_Flag = SkFile(Filepath)
 *
C                   Other
C                   Eval      R = R + 1
C                   Eval      %Subst(Text: R: 1) = CurChar
C                   Endsl
C                   Exsr      GetChar
C                   Enddo

 * Close the File
C                   CallP     Close(Fp)

C                   Return    Error_Flag
```

Figure 16.49: This SkFile procedure uses the Lseek() external procedure call (part 3 of 4).

```
     *_____
     *     GetChar - Process Record, One Character At A Time
     *_____
C        GetChar      begsr
     *        If input buffer is empty, or all characters have been
     *        processed, refill the input buffer.
C                     If        N = CharsRead
C                     Eval      Data_Rec = *Blanks
C                     Eval      CharsRead  = Read(Fp: %Addr(Data_Rec): 189)
C                     Eval      N = *Zero
C                     Endif
     *        Get the next character in the input buffer.
c                     If        CharsRead <= 0
C                     Eval      CurChar = Eof
C                     Else
C                     Eval      N = N + 1
C                     Eval      CurChar = %Subst(Data_Rec: N: 1)
C                     Endif
C                     Endsr
     *_____
     *     Write_Rec  - Write Data from QNTC file to database
     *_____
C        Write_Rec    Begsr
C                     Write     Rcrec
C                     Endsr
P RdFile         E
     *_____
     *     SkFile    - Subprocedure To Position to record in file
     *_____
P SkFile         B                     Export
D SkFile         PI            100A
D  Filepath                    100A    Const
D Offset         S              4b 0
D Fil_Pos        S             10i 0
D Whence         S             10i 0 inz(0)

     * Use LSeek to position to Next record (Offset + (record length)) in file)
     * The record length is 189. By setting the seek pointer to 190, the seek
     * will begin at the second record on first pass, and then it is positioned
     * to the begining of next record(s) on each successive pass.

C                     Eval      Offset = Rec_Pos + 190

C                     Eval      Fil_Pos = Lseek(Fp: Offset: Whence  )

     * Set "Whence" to SEEK_CUR (Seek from current file position)
     * After first read of file
C                     Eval      Whence = 1
C                     Eval      Rec_Pos = Offset

C                     Return    Error_Flag

P SkFile         E
```

Figure 16.49: This SkFile procedure uses the Lseek() external procedure call (part 4 of 4).

Now all I do in the rest of the program is read the record (beginning at the OFFSET located by Lseek()) and then loop until a carriage return is found. At that point, I write the data to a physical file and execute the SkFile procedure call again, positioning the file at the next record. Once I hit the end of the file, I exit the loop, close the AS/400 IFS file, and end the program.

—Shannon O'Donnell

Searching by a Partial Key

The code fragment shown in Figure 16.50 is an RPG IV example of a DOW loop that executes while part of a field is equal to a "key" or predetermined literal. I use it to load to a subfile part numbers or customer numbers that begin with a specific character sequence. The comparison can be made to a variable that a user enters.

```
CLON01Factor1+++++++Opcode&ExtFactor2+++++++Result++++++++Len++D+HiLoEq

C       'RBC '       SetLL     FILE
C                     Read      FILE
C                     DoW       Not %EOF(FILE) And
C                               %subst(FIELD:1:4) =
C                               'RBC '
C                     eval      sc1rrn = sc1rrn + 1
C                     Write     scrn01sf
C                     Read      FILE
C                     EndDo
```

Figure 16.50: Use this technique to perform a read equal on a partial key value.

—Jeff Kinzer

✦ ✦ ✦ File Processing

%FOUND vs. %EOF

Here's a "gotcha!" with the %FOUND and %EOF built-in functions that has bitten a couple of people in our shop. The program compiles correctly but produces incorrect results or loops. The original code (like that in Figure 16.51) used resulting indicators and worked fine. The problem came about when we tried to replace indicators with built-in functions, as in Figure 16.52. The problem is that CHAIN sets the %FOUND condition, but READE sets the %EOF condition instead.

```
*                                                          HiLoEq
C      Key           chain     MYFILE                      90
C                    dow       not *in90
  *             some processing
C      Key           reade     MYFILE                           90
C                    enddo
```

Figure 16.51: Here is an example of indicator-laden code that works fine.

```
C      Key           chain     MYFILE
C                    dow       %found
  *             some processing
C      Key           reade     MYFILE
C                    enddo
```

Figure 16.52: Replacing resulting indicators with the %FOUND function introduces an error.

For your future reference, Table 16.2 lists which I/O operations set %EOF and which set %FOUND. Are you surprised to see that WRITE can set %EOF? This case only applies to subfiles and means the subfile is full.

To fix the problem, we had to replace the CHAIN with SETLL and READE, as shown in Figure 16.53. Notice that the file is specified on the %EOF function. Specifying the filename results in more bulletproof code for two reasons:

1. If you use %FOUND or %EOF without specifying a file, you are checking a global condition that can be set by I/O operations on other files and by the LOOKUP, SCAN, CHECK, and CHECKR op codes. If you specify a file, you are checking a condition that is unique to that file.

2. The code is easier to understand with the filename specified and doesn't require significant effort to maintain.

Table 16.2: I/O Operations for Setting the %EOF and %FOUND

%EOF	%FOUND
READ	CHAIN
READC	DELETE
READE	SETGT
READP	SETLL
READPE	
WRITE	

```
C      Key            setll    MYFILE
C      Key            reade    MYFILE
C                     dow      not %eof(MYFILE)
 *           some processing
C      Key            reade    MYFILE
C                     enddo
```

Figure 16.53: This is the proper way to replace the resulting indicator with a BIF.

—*Sam Lennon*

Record Locking with READE/READPE

Recently, we had a record lock error pop up randomly, and the only thing we could figure was that it was on a READE or READPE statement. After referencing the *ILE RPG/400 Reference* manual and performing some serious debugging, we discovered the problem.

If the file you are performing the READE or READPE on is defined as update, a temporary lock is placed on the next record and compared to the search argument in factor 1. This happens even if the next record does not meet the search criteria. If the record is found not to match the key value, the record-not-found indicator is turned on and the lock is removed.

A simple example shows how this could cause problems. Suppose you have a file that is used to receive items into the warehouse. These items are spread out among different users so that everyone with an RF terminal can share the work. The key to the file is user ID. A user selects the menu option, and the program begins processing READEs on the file, using the current user ID as the search argument. Table 16.3 shows a simple example of what this data might look like in the file.

Table 16.3: Data Keyed on User ID

User	Item	Quantity Ordered	Quantity Received
BVSTONE	AB-109	10	10
BVSTONE	KT-449	4	2
BVSTONE	LL-009	19	18
CHWELLS	BT-873	5	
CHWELLS	BU-909	1	
RJLARSON	FY-310	2	
RJLARSON	GR-250	25	

Users Brad Stone (BVSTONE), Chad Wells (CHWELLS), and Rod Larson (RJLARSON) receive items. Suppose Brad Stone begins receiving items a few minutes before Chad. By the time Chad gets to work, Brad is almost done. He is entering in the amount received on his last item (LL-009). Chad begins to receive items and has just read his first record. Before Chad enters the amount received for his first item (BT-873), Brad completes his last transaction and presses Enter. He gets an error saying that the requested record is in use.

In this case, Chad has a record lock on his first item, and Brad's job tried to check that record to see if the key matched the search criteria (in this case, his user ID, BVSTONE). Before the program can check the value, it must obtain a temporary lock, but it couldn't because of Chad's record lock. So the program crashed.

An easy solution to this problem is to put an error indicator in the "Lo" resulting indicator of the READE statement, as shown in Figure 16.54. I use the same indicator that I use to detect EOF so that, if this problem arises, the program treats the error the same as EOF.

```
C**                                                            HiLoEq
C                    READE     FMT01                              5151
```

Figure 16.54: An error indicator prevents record lock.

Another solution is to use the No-Lock option on the READE operation. When you are ready to update, simply chain to the file using the unique key, and process the update. This technique eliminates the need for the temporary lock that the system will try to place on the next record.

—Bradley V. Stone

Reread a Sequential File

Q: I have a nonindexed file that is read sequentially. Is it possible to get to the top of this file again after I hit the last record on a read?

A: In RPG IV, you can use the keyword *START to get to the top of any file:

```
     C     *START          SETLL     FILE
```

In RPG III and RPG IV, to reposition the nonindexed file to the first record, try this:

```
     C     1               SETLL     FILE
```

—Barbara Morris

♦ ♦ ♦ Formating Print and Display Output

Natural Partners: %EDITC & %DEC

The %DEC and %DECH built-in-functions (BIFs) have been around for a while, but, until recently, I had never put them to any use. As it turns out, this was my loss. I've come to realize that the %DEC and %DECH BIFs, in partnership with the %EDITC and %EDITW BIFs, are very effective.

In the past, whenever I wanted to use an edit code on a number, but the number was too big or had too many decimal places, I moved it to a field of the correct size; then, I did the %EDITC on the correctly sized field. I hated having to do this—it made a simple operation span three separate lines of code: a D-spec for the temporary field, and two EVALs.

The %DEC function allows you to adjust a numeric field's size without using a temporary field. (The %DECH function is similar; the difference is that it half-adjusts.) For example, suppose you had a field called BigField that was defined as being 13-packed with three decimal places, but you wanted to print it on a report as a rounded 6-packed with one decimal place. In Figure 16.55, the code fragments demonstrate how you can easily do this using the %DECH and %EDITC BIFs.

```
C                     eval      PrintString=%editc(%dech(BigField:6:1)
C                               :'4')
C                     eval
PrintString=%editc(%dech((BigField*TaxRate):6:1)
C                               :'4')
```

Figure 16.55: Use %DECH and %EDITC to edit non-like fields.

—*John V. Thompson*

Editor's Note: *If significant digits get truncated when copying a larger variable to a smaller one, you'll get an error. Be sure the values in the large variable are no bigger than the size parameter of %DEC and %DECH.*

Three Ways to Center Text

Looking for a quick way to center text in RPG IV? Try the technique I put together in Figure 16.56. It's fast, simple, and, best of all, doesn't take a lot of lines of code!

```
 * Field to contain centered data (pick one definition)
 *
D target_field   S                 LIKE(source_field)
C     *LIKE       DEFINE    target_field  source_field
 *
 * Center field
 *
C                 EVAL      %SUBST(target_field:
C                           %INTH((%SIZE(source_field) -
C                           %LEN(%TRIM(source_field))) / 2 + 1):
C                           %LEN(%TRIM(source_field))) =
C                           %TRIM(source_field)
```

Figure 16.56: Here's a quick way to center text in RPG IV.

—*Michael C. Schlemme*

Everyone looks for an easy way to solve a problem. If you can do something in fewer steps, so much the better. The capability to center text in RPG IV is a task programmers frequently perform and one that we constantly rewrite every time we need it, usually trying to improve on our technique. Here's a method for centering text that uses a minimal amount of statements and that you can include in a copybook or create as a service program for all your RPG IV centering needs. This algorithm has only four executable statements and a couple of declarative lines:

- Declare an array with each element containing a single character and the number of elements equal to the size of the variable containing the text to be centered.

- Trim the leading and trailing blanks.

- Compute the starting position of the centered text as [(*declared size of the variable-length of text with leading and trailing blanks trimmed*) / 2] + 1.

- Move the trimmed text from the variable into the array with the starting position computed above.

- Move the centered array elements back to the original variable.

In Figure 16.57, the example code shows how to center text using a minimal number of statements. By changing the length of the TEXT parameter, this technique can be easily modified to handle character strings of any size.

```
*==============================================================
* To Compile:
*
*    CRTBNDRPG  PGM(XXX/CenterTxt) SRCFILE(xxx/QRPGLESRC) +
*                   MBR(CenterTxt)
*
*==============================================================
DArrDArr        S              1    DIM(45)
DI              S              2 0
DReply          S              1a
DText           S             45a   Inz('My Very Special Data')
C               Eval      Text = %Trim(Text)
C               Eval      I = ((%Len(Text) - %Len(%Trim(Text))) / 2 )+1
C               MoveA     Text          Arr(I)
C               MoveA     Arr           Text
C      Text     Dsply                   Reply
C               Eval      *INLR = *ON
```

Figure 16.57: Here's a great way to center text with RPG IV.

—Mahendra Reddy

Mahendra Reddy's text-centering routine, which uses array techniques, is fine but not very flexible. I've created a function called CENTER (see Figure 16.58) that uses the OPDESC keyword and variable-size parameters to provide a bit more flexibility that readers might find more useful.

```
****** Function Prototypes *********************************************
   * Center Function
D  Center        PR          32767     Opdesc
D  Instring                  32767     Const Options(*Varsize)
D  OutLength                 10I 0


   * Retrieve Operational Descriptors API
D CEEDOD        PR
D ParmNum                    10I 0 Const
D                            10I 0
D                            10I 0
D                            10I 0
D                            10I 0
D                            10I 0
D                            12A    Options(*Omit)
```

Figure 16.58: Here's a method of centering text that uses the OPDESC keyword on the D-Spec (part 1 of 2).

```
P Center            B                   Export

 * Procedure Interface
D Center            PI          32767   Opdesc
D InString                      32767   Const Options(*Varsize)
D OutLength                     10I 0

 * Center Local Variables
D Offset            s            5  0 Inz(*Zero)
D WrkString         s          32767   Inz(*Blanks)
D OutString         s          32767   Inz(*Blanks)
 ********************************************************************
 * Retrieve the true length of the *VARSIZE input string using
 *   the retrieve operational desriptors API.
C                   Callp       CEEDOD(1:DescType  : DataType : DescInfo1
C                                      :DescInfo2 : DataLen  : *OMIT)

 * Extract the actual input string
C                   Eval        WrkString = %Subst(InString:1:DataLen)

 * If the Output length is smaller the the Input String length
 *   change the output length to the input length.
 *   ( The string will be truncated. )
C                   If          OutLength < %Len(%Trim(WrkString))
C                   Eval        OutLength = %Len(%Trim(WrkString))
C                   Endif

 * Calculate the number of blanks needed on each side of the string
C                   Eval        Offset = ( OutLength -
C                                   %Len(%Trim(WrkString))) / 2

 * Substring the input string to the center of the output string
C                   Eval        %Subst(OutString:Offset + 1:
C                                   %Len(%Trim(WrkString))) = %Trim(WrkString)

 * Return the centered string
C                   Return      OutString

P Center            E
```

Figure 16.58: Here's a method of centering text that uses the OPDESC keyword on the D-Spec (part 2 of 2).

The OPDESC keyword indicates to the RPG IV program that operation descriptors are to be passed with the parameters that are defined within a prototype. Add this function to your service program so that you're all set the next time you need to center text.

—Ken Dalton

✦ ✦ ✦ Interactive Processing

A Hidden Link to the Command Line

Don't you sometimes wish that you could get to a command line while in an application that doesn't allow it? I do.

I have an attention program that transfers me between group jobs automatically when I press the Attn key. If one of my jobs is showing me an order-entry screen and I want to see the local data area (LDA) without exiting the program, what can I do? If I press the Attn key, I will be flipped over to another group job that uses a completely different LDA.

A solution I have come up with is to define a specific location on the screen. When the cursor is in that position and the Attn key is pressed, a command line is presented. Think of it as a hidden command hot spot.

In my case, whenever I place the cursor on line 24, column 80, and press the Attn key, my attention program calls the QUSCMDLN API. Now I can look at the LDA and check file contents, all while still in an active application.

The technique relies on creating a command I called Retrieve Cursor Location (RTVCSRLOC). You can see the source in Figure 16.59. The command calls the RPG IV program CSR001RG, which you can see in Figure 16.60.

```
/*================================================================*/
/* To compile:                                                    */
/*                                                                */
/*         CRTCMD      CMD(XXX/RTVCSRLOC) PGM(XXX/CSR001RG) +      */
/*                       SRCFILE(XXX/QCMDSRC) ALLOW(*IPGM)         */
/*                                                                */
/*================================================================*/
            CMD         PROMPT('Retrieve Cursor Location')
            PARM        KWD(ROW) TYPE(*DEC) LEN(3 0) RTNVAL(*YES) +
                          MIN(1) PROMPT('Row (3,0)')
            PARM        KWD(COL) TYPE(*DEC) LEN(3 0) RTNVAL(*YES) +
```

Figure 16.59: The RTVCSRLOC command returns the cursor location.

```
*================================================================
* To compile:                                                   *
*       CRTBNDRPG  PGM(XXX/CSR001RG) SRCFILE(XXX/QRPGLESRC) +    *
*                  DFTACTGRP(*NO) ACTGRP(*CALLER)               *
*================================================================
*. 1 ...+... 2 ...+... 3 ...+... 4 ...+... 5 ...+... 6 ...+... 7
DRow              s              9B 0
DCol              s              9B 0
DEnv              s              9B 0
DRtnCode          s              9B 0
DErrorDS          DS
DBytesProv                       9B 0 INZ(0)
C     *entry      plist
C                 parm      Row            RtnRow          3 0
C                 parm      Col            RtnCol          3 0
C                 callb     æQsnGetCsrAdr£
C                 parm                     Row
C                 parm                     Col
C                 parm                     Env
C                 parm                     ErrorDS
C                 parm                     RtnCode
C                 return
```

Figure 16.60: CSR001RG is the command-processing program for RTVCSRLOC.

The RPG IV program uses the **QsnGetCsrAdr** API, which returns the cursor location without requiring a user input operation. Figure 16.61 shows an example of how I implemented this in my attention program.

```
DCL &ROW *DEC (3 0)
DCL &COL *DEC (3 0)

RTVCSRLOC ROW(&ROW) COL(&COL)

IF (&ROW *EQ 24 +
   *AND &COL *EQ 80) DO
   CALL QUSCMDLN
   RETURN
ENDDO
```

Figure 16.61: This code illustrates how to use RTVCSRLOC in a CL program.

—Paul Jackson

Prompt for Confirmation

For many interactive programs, pressing the Enter key means, "Edit the values I've entered, and if OK, proceed with the transaction." Often, though, I want the screen format to redisplay the current values and issue a message like "Press Enter to confirm" before proceeding. An example of this would be a transaction that accepts a company code, and when Enter is pressed, the full company name is displayed so that I can be sure the code I entered matches the company I intended. If I press the Enter key again, then I want the program to proceed with the transaction. However, if I change the company code, I want the screen to redisplay with the new company name. In other words, I want the format to redisplay whenever some field values change.

A technique I use to keep this simple is to define a data structure consisting of the display fields I want to test for change, and a character field to record the most recent value of this data structure. Assume I have a display format with the fields **X_Coy#**, **X_Area**, and **X_Amt**. I want the format to redisplay if either **X_Coy#** or **X_Area** change. I code the data structure as shown in Figure 16.62.

```
D X_DS              DS
D X_Coy#
D X_Area
D X_DS_Cpy          S                 Like(X_DS)
```

Figure 16.62: List the fields that will cause screen redisplay if changed.

I don't have to define **X_Coy#** and **X_Area** in the data structure because they are already defined in the DDS of the display format. Similarly, the data structure **X_DS** needs no further definition as it consists of two subfields that are already defined. Finally, **X_DS_Cpy** needs no specific definition as it is defined like **X_DS**.

In the body of the display program, I set **X_DS_Cpy** to the value of **X_DS** immediately before I display the screen format, creating a snapshot of the screen fields prior to any changes the user might make (see Figure 16.63).

```
C                   Eval      X_DS_Cpy = X_DS
C                   Exfmt     Scrfmt
```

Figure 16.63: Save the screen field value.

Finally, as part of my "Enter pressed" logic, I compare the "snapshot" **X_DS_Cpy** with the current display field values in **X_DS** (see Figure 16.64).

```
C                    Callp     Edit
C                    If        ErrorCount>0
C                    Return
C                    Endif
C                    If        X_DS_Cpy <> X_DS
C* ...Display "Press Enter To Confirm" message
C                    Return
C                    Endif
```

Figure 16.64: Test for changed screen fields.

The simplicity of this technique becomes apparent when I add new fields to the format. Say I want the format to redisplay if the field **X_Amt** changed. I just add it to the data structure **X_DS**, and no other logic change is necessary.

—*John V. Thompson*

Screen Timeout

Q: I would like my RPG IV interactive program to timeout if there's no response from the workstation after *x* number of seconds. I have several CL programs that do this very thing. I've even done it in RPG III on the System/38, but, for the life of me, I can't seem to get it to work in my RPG IV program.

A: In order to make a display file timeout after a given number of seconds, there's a couple of things you need to do. I've included a working example.

The display file shown in Figure 16.65 is pretty generic except for the use of the INVITE keyword. Use this keyword in your display file so that you can read from the display device. When you compile display file DSP00D1, place a value on the Wait record (WAITRCD) parameter of the Create Display File (CRTDSPF) command. The value you put here is the number of seconds the program will wait for input from the user before it times out.

When I created the file, I put a value of 10 seconds in this parameter so I could very quickly make sure this technique worked. When you use this technique in the real world, you should make this value high enough so that the user has at least a fighting chance to get to the keyboard before the program times out.

```
A*****************************************************************
A*
A*  CRTDSPF FILE(XXX/DSP00D1) SRCFILE(XXX/QDDSSRC) +
A*          MBR(DSP00D1) WAITRCD(10)
A*
A*****************************************************************
A                                     DSPSIZ(24 80 *DS3)
A                                     CA03(03 'EXIT')
A                                     INVITE
A          R SCREEN1
A                                   1 19'Test Waitrcd Paramter To Timeout D-
A                                     isplay'
A                                     DSPATR(HI)
A                                     DSPATR(UL)
A                                   9 28'Input:'
A          INPUT         1A  B      9 35
A                                  22  7'F3=Exit'
```

Figure 16.65: Display file DSP00D1 demonstrates use of the INVITE keyword.

The RPG IV program DSP00R1, shown in Figure 16.66, has a couple of lines that you
need to add to your program to make this all work. In order to get the program to timeout,
you need to code an INFDS keyword on the F-spec as well as code the MAXDEV keyword
with a value of 1. This tells the program that there is only one device to read from. On the
D-spec, INFDS should be coded to use the *STATUS keyword. The program will read the
values placed in *STATUS by the display file and perform some appropriate action based
on their content.

```
      ******************************************************************
      *
      *  CRTBNDRPG PGM(xxx/Dsp00r1) SRCFILE(xxx/QRPGLESRC) +
      *            MBR(Dsp00r1)
      *
      *
      ******************************************************************
FDsp00d1   CF   E             Workstn Infds(Infds)
F                                     Maxdev(*File)
D Infds           DS
D  Status             *Status
C                 Dow       *IN03 = *OFf
C                 Write     Screen1
C                 Read      Dsp00d1                              99LR
C                 If        *In99 = *On And Status = 1331
C                 Eval      *IN03 = *On
C                 Endif
C                 Enddo
C                 Eval      *Inlr = *On
```

Figure 16.66: Use the MAXDEV keyword in your RPG IV program to cause it to timeout.

When you read the display file (with INVITE active), make sure that you WRITE to the record format but READ from the file name itself. This is different from the normal EXFMT op code you'd normally use when working with display files. After the READ, check to see that the STATUS field contains a value of 1331; this status code indicates that the display file has timed out. If it does, you can either end the program or perform some other logic.

—*Shannon O'Donnell*

The ILE Dynamic Screen Manager APIs

In V2R3, a set of bindable OS/400 APIs called Dynamic Screen Manager (DSM) APIs became available, giving programmers a higher-level interface to the previously tedious method of 5250 data-stream programming. Like 5250 data-stream programming, DSM APIs provide the capability to dynamically read and write screens without the use of DDS display files or User Interface Manager (UIM) panel groups. The main advantage of this type of programming is that it allows you to dynamically build screens at runtime rather than statically build screens at design time. However, because these APIs are bindable, they can only be used by ILE languages.

In V2R3, the only language that could be used with the DSM APIs was ILE C/400. In V3R1, with the release of RPG IV (which operates in the ILE environment), these APIs became accessible to RPG programmers. To demonstrate how these APIs can be used in an RPG program, I wrote the example shown in Figure 16.67. The purpose of this program is to display the message "Hello World!" in the center of the screen. While it's not a particularly useful program, it does provide you with a starting point to build your own programs using these APIs.

```
*=================================================================
* To compile:
*
*       CRTBNDRPG  PGM(XXX/DSM001RG)  SRCFILE(XXX/QRPGLESRC) +
*                  DFTACTGRP(*NO)
*
*=================================================================
*. 1 ...+... 2 ...+... 3 ...+... 4 ...+... 5 ...+... 6 ...+... 7
D Size             S              9B 0 INZ(4500)
D Increment        S              9B 0 INZ(50)
D BufHandle        S              9B 0
D Mode             S              1A   INZ('0')
D Data             S             12A   INZ('Hello World!')
D DataLength       S              9B 0 INZ(12)
D Row              S              9B 0 INZ(13)
```

Figure 16.67: Use the DSM APIs to achieve powerful interactive programs (part 1 of 2).

```
D Column            S            9B 0 INZ(35)

 * Create command buffer
C                   CALLB     'QsnCrtCmdBuf'
C                   PARM                     Size
C                   PARM                     Increment
C                   PARM                     *OMIT
C                   PARM                     BufHandle
C                   PARM                     *OMIT

 * Clear screen
C                   CALLB     'QsnClrScr'
C                   PARM                     Mode
C                   PARM                     BufHandle
C                   PARM                     *OMIT
C                   PARM                     *OMIT

 * Write data
C                   CALLB     'QsnWrtDta'
C                   PARM                     Data
C                   PARM                     DataLength
C                   PARM                     *OMIT
C                   PARM                     Row
C                   PARM                     Column
C                   PARM                     *OMIT
C                   PARM                     *OMIT
C                   PARM                     *OMIT
C                   PARM                     *OMIT
C                   PARM                     BufHandle
C                   PARM                     *OMIT
C                   PARM                     *OMIT

 * Put buffer
C                   CALLB     'QsnPutBuf'
C                   PARM                     BufHandle
C                   PARM                     *OMIT
C                   PARM                     *OMIT

 * Get AID key
C                   CALLB     'QsnGetAID'
C                   PARM                     *OMIT
C                   PARM                     *OMIT
C                   PARM                     *OMIT

C                   EVAL      *INLR = *ON
```

Figure 16.67: Use the DSM APIs to achieve powerful interactive programs (part 2 of 2).

To give you a better understanding of how this program works, I'll briefly explain the purpose of the various API calls. The program starts by calling the Create Command Buffer (**QsnCrtCmdBuf**) API. A command buffer is simply an area in memory where subsequent DSM API calls will place instructions until the API that "puts" the command buffer is called to execute those instructions. The Create Command Buffer API returns a handle that is used by the subsequent DSM API calls to locate the address of the buffer.

Next, the program calls the Clear Screen (QsnClrScr) API to place instructions into the command buffer that will clear the screen. The third call is to the Write Data (QsnWrtDta) API, which puts instructions into the command buffer to write data to the display. The data to display, as well as the row and column to display it at, are passed as parameters to this API. The next API call is to the Put Command Buffer (QsnPutBuf) API to execute the instructions that reside in the command buffer. At this point, the data is written to the screen. However, the program doesn't stop to wait for user input. Instead, it continues to execute. That's the reason for the last API call, which is to the Get AID (QsnGetAID) API. This API stops the program and waits for user input before continuing.

That's a quick overview of a sample program that uses the DSM APIs. Many more DSM APIs are available for you to try writing this type of code yourself. You'll find them documented in *OS/400 System API Reference*.

—Robin Klima

✦ ✦ ✦ Nesting and Looping

An Easy Way to Exit a Subroutine

In V4R4, an op code called LEAVESR was added to RPG IV. LEAVESR lets you "manually" control program flow by specifying the point at which logic jumps out of a given subroutine. Pretty handy, but I have been using a technique that gives me the same capability without having to write a whole lot more code. I use it most often in edit subroutines for situations where an error is found and I want to exit the subroutine.

To perform this functionality, which is equivalent to that of LEAVESR, I use a single DO statement at the top of a subroutine and place the ENDDO statement at the bottom of the subroutine. Now, when I want to exit the subroutine, I simply use the LEAVE op code to leave that DO loop. When program flow reaches LEAVE, control is passed outside to the next statement past the ENDDO statement, which, in this case, is the ENDSR op code. This causes the program to exit the subroutine. Of course, once I move to V4R4, I'll start using LEAVESR.

—Greg Leister

◆ ◆ ◆ Parameter Passing

Avoid Passing Garbage Data Between Modules in ILE

When passing parameters from a CL module to an RPG module, both of which are part of a single bound program, the length of alpha variables must be the same. For example, the receiving module needs 10 alpha characters if the sending module uses 10. If my sending module passes only eight characters, the program fills the last two characters with garbage.

This is different from the way we used to call Original Program Model (OPM) programs; we never had to worry about this. Now we must pad our sending parameter with the correct number of blanks so that the receiving module gets the correct data.

—*William W. Smyth*

What's NOOPT About?

Q: I've read what the manual has to say about the NOOPT keyword in RPG IV, but it's still not clear to me why or when you would use it. Can you shed some light on this?

A: Optimization by the compiler may mean that, at runtime, some values are stored in registers and restored to your program storage only at predefined points during normal program execution. Exception handling may break this normal execution sequence, and, consequently, program variables contained in registers may not be returned to their assigned storage locations. NOOPT ensures that the content of the associated data item always contains the latest value.

The *ILE RPG Reference* (SC09-2508, CD-ROM QB3AGZ00, section 3.4.2.22) states, "Any data item defined in an OPM RPG/400 program is implicitly defined with NOOPT. So, if you are creating a prototype for an OPM program, you should specify NOOPT for all parameters defined within the prototype. This will avoid errors for any users of the prototype."

From this, I take it that, unless the called program expects the "optimized" behavior, there may be circumstances in which you have problems. Unless you can be sure of the implementation details of both called and caller programs and are prepared to delve into the intricacies of code optimization, it seems to me that the only way you can be sure the interface is bulletproof is to specify NOOPT. Because you usually put prototype definitions in copybooks, you want only one version of a prototype anyway—presumably the version that will work in all circumstances.

I don't have any information about QMHSNDPM other than the published interface and the fact that it is an OPM program. I sleep better at night knowing that the interface definition I'm using will continue to work no matter what clever optimization is used or how QMHSNDPM does or does not behave.

I don't usually use NOOPT on bound calls to the ILE APIs (like CEE*). These ILE APIs presumably have been designed for an ILE environment, so I don't usually bother. I'm not sure if this is sensible or not, but I haven't had any problems so far.

The other place you need to specify NOOPT is on fields referenced in any exception handling code (like PSSR and condition handlers).

—Derek Butland

A: Say you have a NOOPT variable that you want to pass by address to an OPM program. The compiler won't allow it if the parameter isn't defined as NOOPT. Therefore, by coding NOOPT on all OPM program calls, you avoid this potential problem. The code shown in Figure 16.68 illustrates the problem.

```
D fld            s              10a  noopt
D proc           pr
D   parm                        10a

C               callp    proc(fld)
```

Figure 16.68: This incorrect use of NOOPT generates a compiler error.

The RPG IV compiler will generate error *RNF5423 (the NOOPT variable cannot be passed by reference to a parameter that did not specify NOOPT). Coding NOOPT on the prototype doesn't actually cause any different code to be generated for calls.

—Barbara Morris

◆ ◆ ◆ Performance

Argument Optimization in Service Programs

Q: When I display a service program, the exported procedures have a column for Argument Optimization (ARGOPT). All of ours are listed as *NO.

I looked through the manuals and found ARGOPT mentioned in the ILE C manual. It states that if you pass space pointer parameters, you can specify ARGOPT rather than ARGUMENT to tell the compiler to pass the PARM in the register. Are we missing out on anything or is this just some obscure feature? Back in the CISC days when we were using MI programs, register-based variables were many times faster to process. Is this the case here? When would you use the ARGOPT parameter?

A: ARGOPT improves the performance of call-intensive ILE applications by providing the following capabilities. It allows:

- Space pointer procedure parameters to be passed in a machine register.

- A space pointer function result to be returned in a machine register.

- The translator to determine if a parameter list is needed to pass parameters to a procedure. If it's not needed, the storage is not allocated and a parameter list is not passed.

Both bound *PGMs and *SRVPGMs can take advantage of these capabilities. ARGOPT improves the performance of bound calls only, including the following:

- Calls to and from procedures within the bound program.

- Calls to and from procedures in a service program.

- Calls made through procedure pointers.

Note that both the caller and the recipient of the call must agree in terms of their optimization setting.

—Bruce Vining

PSDS Affects ILE RPG Program Initialization

ILE RPG programs with either no Program Status Data Structure (PSDS) or a very short PSDS go through the initialization (*INIT) part of the cycle very quickly, compared to OPM RPG. Some of the fields in the PSDS—for example, the program, module, library, job name, and number—are expensive to fill in. If the PSDS isn't long enough to contain these fields, ILE RPG doesn't bother to fill them in during initialization, but OPM RPG does.

—Barbara Morris

Editor's Note: *The moral of the story seems to be, don't code any more of the PSDS than you have to in RPG IV.*

✦ ✦ ✦ Pointers

ILE RPG Pointer Arithmetic

With the release of V3R1, IBM made pointers available to ILE RPG programmers. Pointers are useful when writing calls to APIs; they can make programs faster, and they allow greater flexibility. IBM has failed, however, to fully implement pointer arithmetic. The only method available is to define an array based on a pointer. With an upper limit of 32767 for array sizes, though, this technique limits the maximum offset possible. The program shown in Figure 16.69 allows pointer offset calculations greater than 32767.

```
D WrkPtr          S               *
D Arr             S              1      BASED(WrkPtr) DIM(32767)
D SpcPtr          S               *
D NewPtr          S               *
D OffSet          S             15  0
D WrkOffSet       S             15  0
 *
C     *ENTRY      PLIST
C                 PARM                        SpcPtr
C                 PARM                        OffSet
C                 PARM                        NewPtr
 *
 * Set work variables
C                 EVAL      WrkPtr = SpcPtr
C                 EVAL      WrkOffSet = OffSet
 *
 * While the offset is greater than the size of the array,
 *   set the based on array pointer to the end of the array
 *   and decrement the offset by the same amount
C                 DOW       WrkOffSet > 32760
```

Figure 16.69: Use an array to implement pointer arithmetic (part 1 of 2).

```
C                EVAL      WrkPtr = %ADDR(Arr(32761))
C                EVAL      WrkOffSet = WrkOffSet - 32760
C                ENDDO
 *
 * When the new pointer is somewhere within the array, set
 *   the new pointer to the address of the calculated offset
C                EVAL      NewPtr = %ADDR(Arr(WrkOffSet +1))
 *
C                EVAL      *INLR = *ON
```

Figure 16.69: Use an array to implement pointer arithmetic (part 2 of 2).

This program assumes that the calling program has already allocated a block of memory. These are the incoming parameters:

- **SpcPtr:** A pointer to the beginning of the block of memory.

- **OffSet:** A zoned decimal number containing the offset from **SpcPtr**. The offset must be positive; the program will only perform pointer addition.

- **NewPtr:** A pointer returned to the caller. It contains the result of adding **OffSet** to **SpcPtr**.

The program works by defining an array (**Arr**) of size 32767 based on the pointer **WrkPtr**. If the offset is greater than 32760, the program sets **WrkPtr** to the address of element 32761 of the array and decrements the temporary offset by 32760. The program does this until the temporary offset is less than 32760. (I use 32760 rather than 32766 to ensure that I don't run off the end of the array.) The variable **NewPtr** is set to the address of the array element subscripted by the temporary offset plus one. This technique effectively leapfrogs through the array until the offset address is located.

You can incorporate this program in a larger program or compile it separately as a module and bind it into other ILE programs.

—Simon Ritchie

✦ ✦ ✦ Service Programs

Keeping ILE Service Programs Compatible

ILE service programs can be used by other ILE programs, including other service programs. You can change a service program, but how you do it determines whether the service program will still be compatible with programs already calling it.

When a service program is compiled, the binder (part of the compile function) generates a 16-byte signature from the list of exportable procedures and data items. When an ILE program runs, it checks the signature of any service program it uses to verify that the service program's signature hasn't changed. If the signature has changed, there's a level check, and the call to the service program fails. You must recompile the calling program to make it accept the new signature.

It doesn't have to be this way, however. To maintain compatibility, add another export list, specifying PGMLVL(*PRV), as shown in the binding source in Figure 16.70.

```
STRPGMEXP PGMLVL(*CURRENT)
  EXPORT SYMBOL('NUM002RG')
  EXPORT SYMBOL('TST001RG')    <- new export
  EXPORT SYMBOL('GAR001RG')    <- new export
  ENDPGMEXP
STRPGMEXP PGMLVL(*PRV)
  EXPORT SYMBOL('NUM002RG')
  ENDPGMEXP
```

Figure 16.70: The ILE binder language allows multiple export lists.

In this export list, list the same exports in exactly the same sequence as they were before you made the change. Add the new exports to the current export list only. The binder will generate a signature for each export list. A program that uses the service program will still accept the service program if one of the export lists generates the signature it's expecting. You can have more than one *PRV export list, but only one *CURRENT export list.

An alternate, but inferior, method is to not check the signature. You do this by compiling the service program with LVLCHK(*NO) in the binding source (see Figure 16.71).

```
STRPGMEXP PGMLVL(*CURRENT) LVLCHK(*NO)
  EXPORT SYMBOL('NUM002RG')
  EXPORT SYMBOL('TST001RG')    <- new export
  EXPORT SYMBOL('GAR001RG')    <- new export
  ENDPGMEXP
```

Figure 16.71: Adding exports when bypassing level checking is not usually a good idea.

When bypassing the level check, you must add new exports to the end of the export list for the service program to remain compatible.

—Ted Holt

Qualified Service Program Names

Q: I created a service program (Program A) in one library and bound it with another program (Program B) in a different library. When I use the CALLP op code in a program to call Program A and the library in which Program B resides is not in my library list, CALLP fails. Is there any way to get around this problem without adding a library to my library list?

A: The CALLP op code should work if you qualify the name on the Create Program (CRTPGM) command. You can see what service program is used by displaying the program. If the names are qualified there, they will be qualified when the program is called.

—David Morris

✦ ✦ ✦ SEU

RPG IV Source Editing

I would like to point out a problem you might encounter when editing an RPG IV source member. SEU defaults to windowing the source statements of an RPGLE member to column 6. Columns 1 through 5 are preserved in the statements, but they aren't initially visible. If you want to see the left-most five columns, you have to window to the first column. This normally isn't a problem, because most RPG IV source statements don't use columns 1 through 5.

However, the data for compile-time arrays does use those columns. Because the data for compile-time arrays starts in column 1, the first five characters are not visible unless you window the source statements to column 1. If a programmer doesn't realize this and edits the compile-time array data without windowing to column 1 or prompting the data line, the program may not run correctly.

—Vincent Van Steen

✦ ✦ ✦ Source Members

Duplicate RPG Members Utility

A programmer from our shop wanted to modify an RPG III program. Because he wanted to use some new ILE functions, he converted it from Original Program Model (OPM) RPG to RPG IV with the Convert RPG Source (CVTRPGSRC) command. Then he modified the new source in QRPGLESRC and compiled it. However, he made a big mistake: He didn't delete the old RPG source from QRPGSRC!

A few weeks later, another programmer needed to modify the same program. He looked in QRPGSRC and found the source. (He didn't know that the latest version was in QRPGLESRC.) He modified the RPG source and compiled it. As a result, we ended up with two different versions of the same program.

To avoid this situation, I wrote a utility called the Display Duplicate RPG Members (DSPDUPRPGM) command (see Figures 16.72 and 16.73). This utility checks a single library or all user libraries for QRPGLESRC files and looks for corresponding member names in QRPGSRC within the same library. If it finds any members with the same name in both source files, it displays them in a list.

```
/*==============================================================*/
/* To compile:                                                  */
/*                                                              */
/*          CRTCMD     CMD(XXX/DSPDUPRPGM) PGM(XXX/DUP001CL) +   */
/*                     SRCFILE(XXX/QCMDSRC)                      */
/*                                                              */
/*==============================================================*/
            CMD        PROMPT('Display Duplicate RPG Members')
            PARM       KWD(LIB) TYPE(*NAME) DFT(*ALLUSR) +
                       SPCVAL((*ALLUSR)) PROMPT('Library')
```

Figure 16.72: The DSPDUPRPGM command helps find extra RPG source members.

```
/*==============================================================*/
/* To compile:                                                  */
/*                                                              */
/*          CRTCLPGM   PGM(XXX/DUP001CL) SRCFILE(XXX/QCLSRC)     */
/*                                                              */
/*==============================================================*/
            PGM        PARM(&LIB)
            DCL        VAR(&LIB) TYPE(*CHAR) LEN(10)
            DCL        VAR(&DUPS) TYPE(*LGL)
            DCLF       FILE(QAFDMBRL)
            RMVMSG     PGMQ(*EXT) CLEAR(*ALL)
            DSPFD      FILE(&LIB/QRPGLESRC) TYPE(*MBRLIST) +
                       OUTPUT(*OUTFILE) OUTFILE(QTEMP/DSPRPGLE)
            MONMSG     MSGID(CPF0000) EXEC(GOTO CMDLBL(DONE))
            OVRDBF     FILE(QAFDMBRL) TOFILE(QTEMP/DSPRPGLE)
```

Figure 16.73: CL Program DUP001CL is the command-processing program for the DSPDUPRPGM command (part 1 of 2).

```
READ:       RCVF
            MONMSG      MSGID(CPF0000) EXEC(GOTO CMDLBL(DONE))
            CHKOBJ      OBJ(&MLLIB/QRPGSRC) OBJTYPE(*FILE) +
                          MBR(&MLNAME)
            MONMSG      MSGID(CPF0000) EXEC(GOTO CMDLBL(READ))
            SNDPGMMSG   MSGID(CPF9898) MSGF(QCPFMSG) +
                          MSGDTA('Duplicate RPG member' *BCAT +
                          &MLNAME *BCAT 'found in library' *BCAT +
                          &MLLIB) TOPGMQ(*EXT) MSGTYPE(*DIAG)
            CHGVAR      VAR(&DUPS) VALUE('1')
            GOTO        CMDLBL(READ)
DONE:       IF          COND(&DUPS) THEN(SNDUSRMSG MSGID(CPF9897) +
                          MSGF(QCPFMSG) MSGTYPE(*INFO) TOMSGQ(*EXT))
            ELSE        CMD(SNDPGMMSG MSGID(CPF9898) MSGF(QCPFMSG) +
                          MSGDTA('No duplicate RPG members found in +
                          library' *BCAT &LIB))

            ENDPGM
```

Figure 16.73: CL Program DUP001CL is the command-processing program for the DSPDUPRPGM command (part 2 of 2).

—Helmut Salzer

✦ ✦ ✦ String Handling

Find the Last Word in a String

Q: I need to extract the last word of a string that is 30 characters long. Take this string, for example:

```
STRING = Leather Calf White
```

I want to be able to extract the word **White** into another field. I have an old routine that does this by using the Check Right (CHECKR) op code in RPG to search for the last nonblank character. It then performs a second CHECKR from the position of the last nonblank character and searches for the first blank character from right to left in the string. From this, I can calculate the length of the word and substring it out of the longer field and into another field. Does anyone have an idea about how to accomplish this using a better and/or newer technique?

A: One thing you could immediately do to make the code more readable and easier to re-use is to put the logic that you currently have into an ILE service program:

```
eval string = LastWordOf( 'Leather Calf White' )
```

Another alternative to the technique you're currently using is to write an RPG IV program that calls the C library function **strtok( )** (String Token), but I don't know whether or not this method would necessarily be more efficient than the one you're using now. Another thing to consider is that fewer people would be able to understand it—because C library functions aren't so widely known among RPG programmers—if they had to go back and maintain that code.

—Douglas Handy

A: You can use REXX to parse the last word from the character string. Consider the code shown in Figure 16.74:

```
/*******************************************************************/
/* To Execute:                                                   */
/*             STRREXPRC SRCMBR(LASTWORDR) SRCFILE(QREXSRC) */
/*******************************************************************/
    NbrWords = Words(Record)
    Last = Word(Record, NbrWords)
```

Figure 16.74: Use REXX to parse the last word from the character string.

In this example, **Record** contains the character string to be parsed, and **NbrWords** is a variable that contains the number of words in that string. The second line retrieves the last word into the variable **Last** by using the REXX function **Word** over the character string **Record**. Alternatively, for a more direct method that uses a single statement, try the code shown in Figure 16.75 instead.

```
/*******************************************************************/
/* To Execute:                                                   */
/*             STRREXPRC SRCMBR(LASTWORDR) SRCFILE(QREXSRC) */
/*******************************************************************/
Last = Word("Leather Calf White", Words("Leather Calf White"))
Say "The last word is" Last
```

Figure 16.75: This is a more direct method to parse the last word from a character string with REXX.

—Bob Hamilton

A: If you're looking for an RPG IV solution, you could try the code shown in Figure 16.76. I'm not sure whether or not this is any better than what you are currently using, but it is a newer technique. You can place it in a service program for reuse in all programs that need the last-word function.

```
******************************************************************
* TO COMPILE:
*
*   CRTBNDRPG PGM(xxx/LASTWORD) SRCFILE(xxx/QRPGLESRC)
*
*
******************************************************************
D w_String        S             30     inz('Leather Calf White')
D w_Word          S             30
D w_Pos           S              6 0

 * Find the last non-blank position
C                   eval      w_Pos = %len(%trim(w_String))

 * Find the beginning of the last word by searching backwards for
 * a blank character

C                   Dow       w_Pos >= 1
C                             and %subst(w_String:w_Pos:1) <>   *BLANK
C                   eval      w_Pos = w_Pos - 1
C                   enddo

 * Position to the beginning of the last word and place in w_Word

C                   eval      w_Word = %subst(w_String:(w_Pos +1))
C       w_Word      dsply

C                   eval      *INLR = *ON
```

Figure 16.76: You also can use RPG IV to parse the last word from a string.

—Jerry Hensley

Retrieve the Next Character in a Series

Everyone knows how to use RPG to add two numbers together to get the next number in a sequence. Piece of cake, right? But what if you had to add two letters together to get the next letter in a sequence? That's a bit tougher. But not to worry! There is a way to accomplish this.

Adding one to B to get C, for example, is achieved through the XLATE op code, which enables the (surprise!) translation of a character string on a byte-by-byte basis from one value to another. Laying out the numbering sequence in the "from" argument and offsetting it by one in the "to" argument turns one into two and A into B. Just as in addition done by hand, the procedure increments from right to left, controlling any carriers that might result.

727

For this to work, every byte in the source string must be processed individually. Unfortunately, the XLATE op code does not yet have a %XLATE built-in function counterpart that allows translation to take place as part of an expression. To bypass this limitation and avoid the necessity of array processing, I've wrapped the XLATE op code in a subprocedure (see Figure 16.77).

```
**********************************************************************
** To Create:
**
**    CrtRpgMod   Module(FNC001MR)
**    CrtSrvPgm   Srvpgm(FNC001S)   Module(FNC001MR)   Export(*ALL)
**
**    CrtBndDir   BndDir(FNC001B)   Text('General Functions Directory')
**    AddBndDirE  BndDir(FNC001B)   Obj((FNC001S *SRVPGM))
**
**********************************************************************
H NoMain Option( *SrcStmt )
**- Alfa indexer: ------------------------------------------------**
D AlfIdx          Pr             64a   Varying
D  String                        64a   Varying Value
**- Translate: ---------------------------------------------------**
D Xlate           Pr             64a   Varying
D  String                        64a   Varying Value
D  Xfrom                         64a   Varying Const
D  Xto                           64a   Varying Const
**- Alfa indexer: ------------------------------------------------**
P AlfIdx          B                    Export
D                 Pi             64a   Varying
D  String                        64a   Varying Value
**
D Len             S              5u 0
D Ofs             S              5u 0
**
D Cur             C                    ' 0123456789ABCDEFGHIJKLMNOPQR-
D                                      STUVWXYZ'
D Nxt             C                    '0123456789ABCDEFGHIJKLMNOPQRS-
D                                      TUVWXYZ0'
**
C                 Eval      Len       = %Len( String )
C                 Eval      Ofs       = Len
**
C                 Do        Len
C                 Eval      %Subst( String: Ofs : 1 ) =
C                           Xlate( %Subst( String: Ofs: 1 ): Cur: Nxt )
**
C                 If        %Subst( String: Ofs: 1 ) <>   '0'
C                 Leave
C                 EndIf
**
C                 Eval      Ofs       = Ofs - 1
C                 EndDo
**
```

Figure 16.77: This RPG IV module automatically indexes alpha characters (part 1 of 2).

```
C                    Return    String
**
P AlfIdx            E
**- Translate:  ------------------------------------------------**
P Xlate             B
D                   Pi              64a     Varying
D  Xstring                          64a     Varying Value
D  Xfrom                            64a     Varying Const
D  Xto                              64a     Varying Const
**
C     Xfrom:Xto     Xlate     Xstring         Xstring
**
C                    Return    Xstring
**
P Xlate             E
```

Figure 16.77: This RPG IV module automatically indexes alpha characters (part 2 of 2).

All parameters are declared using the VARYING keyword to make the compiler keep track of the actual length and reduce the number of bytes passed through the parameter stack. The VALUE keyword indicates that the actual parameter value, not its pointer, is passed to the procedure, protecting the source value from possibly unwanted modification.

If overflow occurs, the result is all zeros. Using the source debugger on the sample program shown in Figure 16.78, you can see the effect of various source strings.

```
**************************************************************
** To Create:
**
**
**    CrtRpgMod Module(FNC002MR) DbgView(*LIST)
**    CrtPgm    Pgm(FNC002I)      Module(FNC002MR)  ActGrp(QILE)
**
**************************************************************
H BndDir( 'FNC001B' )  Option( *SrcStmt )
**- Global variables:  --------------------------------------**
D Field          S           7a    Inz
**- Functions:  ----------------------------------------------**
D AlfIdx         Pr          64a   Varying
D  String                    64a   Varying Value
**- Main routine:  ------------------------------------------**
**
C                    Do        100
C                    Eval      Field    = AlfIdx( Field )
C                    EndDo
**
C                    Return
```

Figure 16.78: This program shows you how to use the Alpha Indexer shown in Figure 16.77.

—*Carsten Flensberg*

✦ ✦ ✦ Subprocedures

Common Calculations Make Good Subprocedures

If you still haven't started writing RPG IV subprocedures, you're missing a great feature of RPG IV. Perhaps you're just not sure where to begin.

I began by looking for common business processes. Every organization has them. They're calculations that you find over and over in programs. When you modify one of these routines, you end up having to change 50 programs.

For example, suppose several programs calculate a gross profit margin. You could start your adventure into subprocedures by creating a service program with one subprocedure. You'll need a function prototype (see Figure 16.79) that can be copied into both the service program source and into the source of the programs that use the function.

```
PGROSSMARGN         PR          5P 2
D MARGNSLS                      9P 2 VALUE
D MARGNCST                      9P 2 VALUE
```

Figure 16.79: Member FINCALXCPY illustrates how to define a prototype for the financial calculation procedure.

You'll also need to write the subprocedure, as in Figure 16.80. To use the subprocedure, use code like that in Figure 16.81. As you identify more common routines, add them to the service program.

```
 *=========================================================
 * To compile:
 *
 *    CRTRPGMOD  MODULE(XXX/FINCALX) SRCFILE(XXX/QRPGLESRC)
 *    CRTSRVPGM  SRVPGM(XXX/FINCALX) EXPORT(*ALL)
 *
 *=========================================================

H NOMAIN FLTDIV(*YES) EXPROPTS(*RESDECPOS)
 *
 /COPY XXX/QRPGLESRC,FINCALXCPY
 *
PGROSSMARGN        B                    EXPORT
D                  PI          5P 2
```

Figure 16.80: Member FINCALX implements the financial calculations service program (part 1 of 2).

```
 D MARGNSLS                          9P 2 VALUE
 D MARGNCST                          9P 2 VALUE
  * GET THE GROSS PROFIT MARGIN...
 C                   IF         MARGNSLS > *ZERO
 C                   RETURN     %DECH(
 C                              (((MARGNSLS - MARGNCST)/MARGNSLS)*100)
 C                              : 5 : 2)
 C                   ELSE
 C                   RETURN     *ZERO
 C                   ENDIF
 PGROSSMARGN        E
```

Figure 16.80: Member FINCALX implements the financial calculations service program (part 2 of 2).

```
 *===========================================================
 * To compile:
 *
 *    CRTRPGMOD  MODULE(XXX/FINCALXTST) SRCFILE(XXX/QRPGLESRC)
 *    CRTPGM     PGM(XXX/FINCALXTST) BNDSRVPGM(XXX/FINCALX)
 *
 *===========================================================
 *
 /COPY XXX/QRPGLESRC,FINCALXCPY
 *
 D SALES           S            9P 2 INZ(10.00)
 D COST            S            9P 2 INZ( 5.00)
 D MARGIN          S            5P 2 INZ(*ZEROS)
 *
 C                   EVAL       MARGIN   = GROSSMARGN(SALES:COST)
 *
 C                   EVAL       *INLR = *ON
```

Figure 16.81: Once the subprocedure is compiled and working, begin to retrofit it into your programs.

If you've put off using subprocedures, now you know where to begin. Get out those back issues of *Midrange Computing* magazine, read about subprocedures, and have at it!

—*Paul Sgroi*

Naming RPG IV Procedures

Here is a little tip I wish someone had given me when I first started on our RPG IV effort. A lot of procedures take only one parameter and return a value. An example of this might be a procedure that takes a date in *YMD format and returns the *ISO data type equivalent. You might be tempted to call this procedure **YMDtoISO** (I did!). I wish now I had called it **ISOfromYMD**.

The reason can best be explained with an example. Suppose you have a number of date conversion procedures, all using the **FMTfromFMT** naming convention. The following code takes a date called **MDYDate** and assigns the **CYMD** equivalent to field **CYMDDate**.

```
eval CYMDDate = CYMDfromISO(ISOfromYMD(YMDfromMDY(MDYDate)))
```

The point is not that there are far better ways of achieving this conversion, but that it's easy to figure out what's going on with this one. Because the return value of a procedure is to its left and the parameter is to the right, the **FMTfromFMT** naming convention naturally matches this in use (notice how the **ISO** butts up to **ISO** and **YMD** with **YMD**).

The equivalent using **FMTtoFMT** would be far more complicated to figure out, as you can see here.

```
eval CYMDDate = ISOtoCYMD(YMDtoISO(MDYtoYMD(MDYDate)))
```

I keyed in the first example without hesitation, but the second one made me stop and think for a while!

—*John V. Thompson*

✦ ✦ ✦ Triggers and Referential Integrity

Determine Which Program Fired a Trigger

Q: Is it possible for a trigger program to determine what program caused it to fire?

A: The ILE procedure **RtvTgrCaller** shown in Figure 16.82 will do the trick. This module can be bound into your trigger program or, much better, added to a service program—which must be compiled with ACTGRP(*CALLER).

```
*  ================================================================  *
*  Return Name of Trigger Program                                    *
*  ================================================================  *
*  To compile:                                                       *
*                                                                    *
*     CRTRPGMOD  MODULE(xxx/RTVTGRCALR)                              *
*                                                                    *
*  ================================================================  *
H NOMAIN

/COPY QRPGLESRC,PROTOTYPES


 *_____
P RtvTrgCaller    B                        EXPORT
D                 PI          277A

D sysSndPgmMsg    PR                       EXTPGM('QMHSNDPM')
D  Msgid                        7A    CONST
D  Msgf                        20A    CONST
D  Msgdta                   32767A    CONST OPTIONS(*VARSIZE)
D  MsgdtaLen                  10I 0  CONST
D  Msgtype                    10A    CONST
D  CallStk                  4096A    CONST OPTIONS(*VARSIZE)
D  CallStkOffset              10I 0  CONST
D  Msgkey                       4A
D  ErrorDS                  32767A          OPTIONS(*VARSIZE)
D  CallStkLen                 10I 0  CONST OPTIONS(*NOPASS)
D  CallStkQual                20A    CONST OPTIONS(*NOPASS)
D  WaitTime                   10I 0  CONST OPTIONS(*NOPASS)
D  CallStkType                10A    CONST OPTIONS(*NOPASS)
D  CCSID                      10I 0  CONST OPTIONS(*NOPASS)

D sysRcvPgmMsg    PR                       EXTPGM('QMHRCVPM')
D  RtnData                  32767A          OPTIONS(*VARSIZE)
D  RtnDataLen                 10I 0  CONST
D  RtnDataFmt                   8A    CONST
D  CallStk                  4096A    CONST OPTIONS(*VARSIZE)
D  CallStkOffset              10I 0  CONST
D  MsgType                    10A    CONST
D  Msgkey                       4A    CONST
D  WaitTime                   10I 0  CONST
D  Action                     10A    CONST
D  ErrorDS                  32767A          OPTIONS(*VARSIZE)
D  CallStkLen                 10I 0  CONST OPTIONS(*NOPASS)
D  CallStkQual                20A    CONST OPTIONS(*NOPASS)
D  CallStkType                10A    CONST OPTIONS(*NOPASS)
D  CCSID                      10I 0  CONST OPTIONS(*NOPASS)

D MsgKey          S            4A

D ApiErrorDS      DS
D                             10I 0  INZ(0)
```

Figure 16.82: The RtvTrgCaller procedure determines which program caused a trigger to fire (part 1 of 2).

```
D RCVM0300       DS
D                            113A
D  rcvSenderInfo             630A
D   rcvPgmType                 1A    OVERLAY(rcvSenderInfo: 41)
D   rcvPgmName                10A    OVERLAY(rcvSenderInfo:355)
D   rcvModName                10A    OVERLAY(rcvSenderInfo:365)
D   rcvPrcName               256A    OVERLAY(rcvSenderInfo:375)

C              CALLP      sysSndPgmMsg( *BLANK
C                                     : *BLANK
C                                     : '?'
C                                     : 1
C                                     : '*INFO'
C                                     : '*CTLBDY   '
C                                     : 2
C                                     : MsgKey
C                                     : ApiErrorDS )
C
C              CALLP      sysRcvPgmMsg( RCVM0300
C                                     : %SIZE(RCVM0300)
C                                     : 'RCVM0300'
C                                     : '*        '
C                                     : *ZERO
C                                     : '*INFO'
C                                     : MsgKey
C                                     : *ZERO
C                                     : '*REMOVE'
C                                     : ApiErrorDS )
C
C              RETURN       rcvPgmName
C                         + rcvPgmType
C                         + rcvModName
C                         + rcvPrcName

P RtvTrgCaller    E
```

Figure 16.82: The RtvTrgCaller procedure determines which program caused a trigger to fire (part 2 of 2).

Procedure **RtvPgmCaller** returns a 277-byte character variable (Table 16.4) containing four pieces of information. The four are the:

1. Name of the program that fired the trigger.

2. Type of program.

3. Name of the module.

4. Name of the procedure.

Table 16.4: The RtvPgmCaller Procedure Returns Information about the Caller in a 277-Byte Data Structure

Positions	Length	Description
1–10	10	Program name
11–11	1	Program type
12–21	10	Module name
22–277	256	Procedure name

Look at the code fragment shown in Figure 16.83 for an example of how to call this procedure.

```
    /COPY QRPGLESRC,PROTOTYPES

    D PgmName         S               10A

    D dsTrgCaller     DS
    D  dsPgmName                      10A
    D  dsPgmType                       1A
    D  dsModName                      10A
    D  dsPrcName                     256A

     *              To just get program name...
    C              EVAL      PgmName = RtvTrgCaller
    C
     *              OR, to get all the information...
    C              EVAL      dsTrgCaller = RtvTrgCaller
```

Figure 16.83: The program example uses RtvTrgCaller to find the name of a trigger program.

You'll need a procedure prototype for the procedure member itself, as well as the source code for any callers. See Figure 16.84 for the prototype.

```
    D RtvTrgCaller    PR              277A
```

Figure 16.84: RtvTrgCaller requires this prototype declaration.

This procedure relies on some convenient OS/400 and DB2 behavior, which makes it vulnerable to any changes IBM makes in DB2/400 (DB2 for OS/400). However, short of IBM supplying an API or adding the name of the trigger program to the trigger buffer, in my opinion, this is about as good as it's going to get.

—*Derek Butland*

CHAPTER 17

S/36

S/36

*T*he IBM System/36 was an easy computer to program. It didn't take a computer science degree to master RPG II and operations control language (OCL). Programmers didn't need four-year degrees, but could train for a year or two in a trade school and go to work. Like its predecessor, the System/34, the S/36 came with a set of easy-to-use application development tools. Ordinary people could learn to use source entry utility (SEU), screen design aid (SDA), and data file utility (DFU).

The S/36 was a roaring success for IBM. It was probably not the most sophisticated minicomputer on the market at the time. Nevertheless, the S/36 was popular because it was effective. Effectiveness, however, is a two-edged sword. On one hand, the computer helps people get their jobs done. On the other hand, people find it difficult to give up their applications as technology changes. If the Y2K issue taught us nothing else, it was that there is still a lot of S/36 code in production.

This chapter addresses some of the problems and challenges that face programmers who maintain S/36 applications. Even though the Y2K crisis is past, programmers still have to sort files with two-digit years. Therefore, you will find some tips for dealing with dates. The other tips, divided into several categories, deal with interoperability between S/36 applications running in the S/36 Execution Environment and OS/400. You'll find several tips here to help you integrate the two operating systems. Some of those tips can help you convert S/36 code to native, while others can save you the trouble of conversion. After all, why convert to native if you can make an application take advantage of native features?

Many of the programmers who have to keep S/36 code going have never even seen a S/36, much less worked on one. Whether you are one of them or an S/36 old-timer, these tips will help you.

—*Ted Holt*

In This Chapter

Conversion to Native

Database Files

Date and Time

Messages

Performance

Printing

Program Development

S/36 Environment

System Administration

✦ ✦ ✦ Conversion to Native

Access DDS Keywords in S/36 $SFGR Source Members

Any display file DDS desired may be embedded in $SFGR source by inserting the line(s), with correct DDS syntax, at the point you want the DDS merged with the converted $SFGR. The first seven columns must be changed to *DDSbx* where b is a space and x is normally S or D to match the statement above it. The remainder of the statement follows the DDS A-spec format for display files.

IBM added this capability to enable adding record-level keywords to specific formats. But the same technique can be used to add field-level options, hidden fields for cursor output row and column, or anything else that DDS supports.

—Douglas Handy

Active Job Checking

Q: On the S/36, it is possible to have the system check for the presence of a specific active job by using the IF ACTIVE OCL command. Is there an AS/400 command to perform this same function?

A: No, there is no way to do that.

If you want to determine if program X is running, the best thing you can do is change program X so that it allocates an existing data area X for exclusive use (*EXCL), and deallocates it when the program ends. If any other program needs to know if program X is running, it can attempt to allocate data area X; if the allocation fails, it's because program X is still running.

—Ernie Malaga

Calling Native Programs from a S/36 Program

Q: I am trying to call the Send to Data Queue (QSNDDTAQ) API from a S/36 RPG II program, but it's not working. I believe the problem is with one of my parameters, but I can't tell for sure. Can you find the problem?

A: S/36 RPG programs pass numeric parameters in zoned decimal format. Your problem is that your program is passing zoned decimal data into the third parameter of QSNDDTAQ, which should be five digits, packed decimal. S/36 programs do not have a way to pack variables.

I ran into a similar situation a few years back in my consulting practice. I wrote a program NBR011RG to handle the needed data conversion (see Figure 17.1). It's far from rocket science, but it does the job.

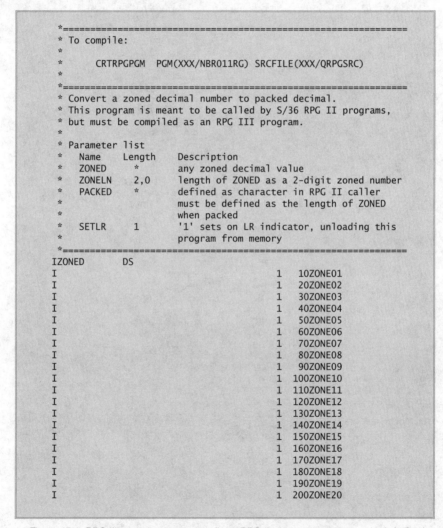

```
*========================================================
* To compile:
*
*      CRTRPGPGM  PGM(XXX/NBR011RG) SRCFILE(XXX/QRPGSRC)
*
*========================================================
* Convert a zoned decimal number to packed decimal.
* This program is meant to be called by S/36 RPG II programs,
* but must be compiled as an RPG III program.
*
* Parameter list
*    Name     Length    Description
*    ZONED    *         any zoned decimal value
*    ZONELN   2,0       length of ZONED as a 2-digit zoned number
*    PACKED   *         defined as character in RPG II caller
*                       must be defined as the length of ZONED
*                       when packed
*    SETLR    1         '1' sets on LR indicator, unloading this
*                       program from memory
*========================================================
IZONED          DS
I                                          1  10ZONE01
I                                          1  20ZONE02
I                                          1  30ZONE03
I                                          1  40ZONE04
I                                          1  50ZONE05
I                                          1  60ZONE06
I                                          1  70ZONE07
I                                          1  80ZONE08
I                                          1  90ZONE09
I                                          1 100ZONE10
I                                          1 110ZONE11
I                                          1 120ZONE12
I                                          1 130ZONE13
I                                          1 140ZONE14
I                                          1 150ZONE15
I                                          1 160ZONE16
I                                          1 170ZONE17
I                                          1 180ZONE18
I                                          1 190ZONE19
I                                          1 200ZONE20
```

Figure 17.1: RPG III program NBR011RG allows RPG II programs to pass packed-decimal parameters to other programs (part 1 of 3).

```
I                                        1   210ZONE21
I                                        1   220ZONE22
I                                        1   230ZONE23
I                                        1   240ZONE24
I                                        1   250ZONE25
I                                        1   260ZONE26
I                                        1   270ZONE27
I                                        1   280ZONE28
I                                        1   290ZONE29
I                                        1   300ZONE30
IPACKED     DS
I                                   P    1    10PACK01
I                                   P    1    20PACK03
I                                   P    1    30PACK05
I                                   P    1    40PACK07
I                                   P    1    50PACK09
I                                   P    1    60PACK11
I                                   P    1    70PACK13
I                                   P    1    80PACK15
I                                   P    1    90PACK17
I                                   P    1   100PACK19
I                                   P    1   110PACK21
I                                   P    1   120PACK23
I                                   P    1   130PACK25
I                                   P    1   140PACK27
I                                   P    1   150PACK29
I                                   P    1   160PACK31
IZONELN     DS
I                                        1    20ZL
C           *ENTRY    PLIST
C                     PARM           ZONED
C                     PARM           ZONELN
C                     PARM           PACKED
C                     PARM           SETLR    1
C*
C                     SELEC
C           ZL        WHEQ 1
C                     Z-ADDZONE01    PACK01
C           ZL        WHEQ 2
C                     Z-ADDZONE02    PACK03
C           ZL        WHEQ 3
C                     Z-ADDZONE03    PACK03
C           ZL        WHEQ 4
C                     Z-ADDZONE04    PACK05
C           ZL        WHEQ 5
C                     Z-ADDZONE05    PACK05
C           ZL        WHEQ 6
C                     Z-ADDZONE06    PACK07
C           ZL        WHEQ 7
C                     Z-ADDZONE07    PACK07
C           ZL        WHEQ 8
```

Figure 17.1: RPG III program NBR011RG allows RPG II programs to pass packed-decimal parameters to other programs (part 2 of 3).

```
C                       Z-ADDZONE08   PACK09
C           ZL          WHEQ 9
C                       Z-ADDZONE09   PACK09
C           ZL          WHEQ 10
C                       Z-ADDZONE10   PACK11
C           ZL          WHEQ 11
C                       Z-ADDZONE11   PACK11
C           ZL          WHEQ 12
C                       Z-ADDZONE12   PACK13
C           ZL          WHEQ 13
C                       Z-ADDZONE13   PACK13
C           ZL          WHEQ 14
C                       Z-ADDZONE14   PACK15
C           ZL          WHEQ 15
C                       Z-ADDZONE15   PACK15
C           ZL          WHEQ 16
C                       Z-ADDZONE16   PACK17
C           ZL          WHEQ 17
C                       Z-ADDZONE17   PACK17
C           ZL          WHEQ 18
C                       Z-ADDZONE18   PACK19
C           ZL          WHEQ 19
C                       Z-ADDZONE19   PACK19
C           ZL          WHEQ 20
C                       Z-ADDZONE20   PACK21
C           ZL          WHEQ 21
C                       Z-ADDZONE21   PACK21
C           ZL          WHEQ 22
C                       Z-ADDZONE22   PACK23
C           ZL          WHEQ 23
C                       Z-ADDZONE23   PACK23
C           ZL          WHEQ 24
C                       Z-ADDZONE24   PACK25
C           ZL          WHEQ 25
C                       Z-ADDZONE25   PACK25
C           ZL          WHEQ 26
C                       Z-ADDZONE26   PACK27
C           ZL          WHEQ 27
C                       Z-ADDZONE27   PACK27
C           ZL          WHEQ 28
C                       Z-ADDZONE28   PACK29
C           ZL          WHEQ 29
C                       Z-ADDZONE29   PACK29
C           ZL          WHEQ 30
C                       Z-ADDZONE30   PACK31
C                       ENDSL
C*
C           SETLR       IFEQ '1'
C                       SETON                         LR
C                       ENDIF
C*
```

Figure 17.1: RPG III program NBR011RG allows RPG II programs to pass packed-decimal parameters to other programs (part 3 of 3).

Call NBR011RG from your RPG II program, passing it the following parameters:

- A zoned decimal variable.

- The length (number of digits) in the zoned number.

- A character variable the same size (in bytes) as the packed variable needs to be.

- A 1 to deactivate NBR011RG, or a 0 to leave it active.

NBR011RG will return a packed value in the third parameter. Pass this as a character variable, instead of a numeric variable, to QSNDDTAQ. Because QSNDDTAQ's third parameter is five digits long, you'll need to pass a 3-byte character variable to NBR011RG and QSNDDTAQ. You'll need some way to convert that character variable to a numeric field in your RPG II program. For that, you can use NBR012RG, which converts packed decimal values to zoned decimal (see Figure 17.2).

```
*=============================================================
* To compile:
*
*        CRTRPGPGM  PGM(XXX/NBR012RG)  SRCFILE(XXX/QRPGSRC)
*
*=============================================================
* Convert a packed decimal number to zoned decimal.
* This program is meant to be called by S/36 RPG II programs,
* but must be compiled as an RPG III program.
*
* Parameter list
*    Name     Length      Description
*    PACKED   *           defined as character in RPG II caller
*                         must be defined as the length of ZONED
*                         when packed
*    ZONED    *           any zoned decimal value
*    ZONELN   2,0         length of ZONED as a 2-digit zoned number
*    SETLR    1           '1' sets on LR indicator, unloading this
*                         program from memory
*=============================================================
IZONED       DS
I                                            1   10ZONE01
I                                            1   20ZONE02
I                                            1   30ZONE03
I                                            1   40ZONE04
I                                            1   50ZONE05
I                                            1   60ZONE06
I                                            1   70ZONE07
I                                            1   80ZONE08
```

Figure 17.2: RPG III program NBR012RG converts packed data to zoned decimal format (part 1 of 4).

```
I                              1    90ZONE09
I                              1   100ZONE10
I                              1   110ZONE11
I                              1   120ZONE12
I                              1   130ZONE13
I                              1   140ZONE14
I                              1   150ZONE15
I                              1   160ZONE16
I                              1   170ZONE17
I                              1   180ZONE18
I                              1   190ZONE19
I                              1   200ZONE20
I                              1   210ZONE21
I                              1   220ZONE22
I                              1   230ZONE23
I                              1   240ZONE24
I                              1   250ZONE25
I                              1   260ZONE26
I                              1   270ZONE27
I                              1   280ZONE28
I                              1   290ZONE29
I                              1   300ZONE30
IPACKED     DS
I                         P    1    10PACK01
I                         P    1    20PACK03
I                         P    1    30PACK05
I                         P    1    40PACK07
I                         P    1    50PACK09
I                         P    1    60PACK11
I                         P    1    70PACK13
I                         P    1    80PACK15
I                         P    1    90PACK17
I                         P    1   100PACK19
I                         P    1   110PACK21
I                         P    1   120PACK23
I                         P    1   130PACK25
I                         P    1   140PACK27
I                         P    1   150PACK29
I                         P    1   160PACK31
IZONELN     DS
I                              1    20ZL
C           *ENTRY    PLIST
C                     PARM          PACKED
C                     PARM          ZONED
C                     PARM          ZONELN
C                     PARM          SETLR    1
C*
C                     SELEC
C           ZL        WHEQ 1
C                     Z-ADDPACK01   ZONE01
C           ZL        WHEQ 2
C                     Z-ADDPACK03   ZONE02
```

Figure 17.2: RPG III program NBR012RG converts packed data to zoned decimal format (part 2 of 4).

```
C              ZL        WHEQ 3
C                        Z-ADDPACK03      ZONE03
C              ZL        WHEQ 4
C                        Z-ADDPACK05      ZONE04
C              ZL        WHEQ 5
C                        Z-ADDPACK05      ZONE05
C              ZL        WHEQ 6
C                        Z-ADDPACK07      ZONE06
C              ZL        WHEQ 7
C                        Z-ADDPACK07      ZONE07
C              ZL        WHEQ 8
C                        Z-ADDPACK09      ZONE08
C              ZL        WHEQ 9
C                        Z-ADDPACK09      ZONE09
C              ZL        WHEQ 10
C                        Z-ADDPACK11      ZONE10
C              ZL        WHEQ 11
C                        Z-ADDPACK11      ZONE11
C              ZL        WHEQ 12
C                        Z-ADDPACK13      ZONE12
C              ZL        WHEQ 13
C                        Z-ADDPACK13      ZONE13
C              ZL        WHEQ 14
C                        Z-ADDPACK15      ZONE14
C              ZL        WHEQ 15
C                        Z-ADDPACK15      ZONE15
C              ZL        WHEQ 16
C                        Z-ADDPACK17      ZONE16
C              ZL        WHEQ 17
C                        Z-ADDPACK17      ZONE17
C              ZL        WHEQ 18
C                        Z-ADDPACK19      ZONE18
C              ZL        WHEQ 19
C                        Z-ADDPACK19      ZONE19
C              ZL        WHEQ 20
C                        Z-ADDPACK21      ZONE20
C              ZL        WHEQ 21
C                        Z-ADDPACK21      ZONE21
C              ZL        WHEQ 22
C                        Z-ADDPACK23      ZONE22
C              ZL        WHEQ 23
C                        Z-ADDPACK23      ZONE23
C              ZL        WHEQ 24
C                        Z-ADDPACK25      ZONE24
C              ZL        WHEQ 25
C                        Z-ADDPACK25      ZONE25
C              ZL        WHEQ 26
C                        Z-ADDPACK27      ZONE26
C              ZL        WHEQ 27
C                        Z-ADDPACK27      ZONE27
C              ZL        WHEQ 28
```

Figure 17.2: RPG III program NBR012RG converts packed data to zoned decimal format (part 3 of 4).

```
C               Z-ADDPACK29     ZONE28
C        ZL     WHEQ 29
C               Z-ADDPACK29     ZONE29
C        ZL     WHEQ 30
C               Z-ADDPACK31     ZONE30
C               ENDSL
C*
C        SETLR  IFEQ '1'
C               SETON                        LR
C               ENDIF
C*
C               RETRN
```

Figure 17.2: RPG III program NBR012RG converts packed data to zoned decimal format (part 4 of 4).

An RPG II program must pass character variables instead of packed variables to native programs. Upon return from the native program, the character variables contain packed data. To unpack the data, the RPG II program calls NBR012RG, passing it the following parameters:

- A character variable containing a packed decimal value.
- A zoned decimal variable to contain the unpacked data.
- The length (number of digits) in the zoned number.
- A 1 to deactivate NBR011RG, or a 0 to leave it active.

NBR012RG will return a zoned value in the second parameter.

—Ted Holt

Converting S/36 SFGR to DDS

Those contemplating converting S/36 SFGR formats to DDS should be aware that the Create S/36 Display File (CRTS36DSPF) command automatically converts SFGR source statements to DDS.

Use the To DDS source file (TOFILE) and the To DDS source member (TOMBR) parameters of the CRTS36DSPF command to specify the source physical file and member that you want to contain the converted DDS. The CRTS36DSPF command creates a DDS source member of source type DSPF. From that point forward, you can maintain your display files from DDS instead of SFGR. To compile display file DDS, use the Create Display File (CRTDSPF) command.

—Richard Shaler

CRT Files in S/36E

Back in the good old days when we were using a S/36, we had occasion to use some CRT files in our RPG II programs. Not often, but sometimes. At times, we would allow the program to put out a few lines on the screen and then prompt via a KEYBORD file. And sometimes we would let the data run up the screen until end-of-file condition was reached.

In migrating one of these programs to the AS/400, we encountered a strange problem: the data was appearing only on the bottom line of the screen, instead of filling up the whole screen. The two programs (one running in S/36E on the AS/400 and the other running on a S/36) were identical. I checked the IBM manual *S/36 Compatible RPG User's Guide and Reference* and found its three-page section, "Using a CRT File," was virtually identical to the chapter in the original S/36 manual. There was no clue that a change had been made.

Regarding column 18 of the O-specs (line after), both manuals say that it "can contain a number from 0 to 3" without saying what happens if you leave that column blank. A blank in that column on the S/36 is interpreted as meaning "1" and the data rolls up the screen nicely. A blank in the same column in the S/36E of the AS/400 means "0" and the data sits on the bottom of the screen, without moving.

—Eric Lee

Help Key Support and Other DDS Mysteries

The AS/400 will convert your most complicated $SFGR specifications to native DDS for you automatically! The S/36 FORMAT procedure generates intermediate DDS for creation of the display file. Put another way, the AS/400 does not know how to make a display file from S and D specifications. That is why it generates the DDS first.

The best way to control the creation of the DDS is by using the Create System/36 Display File (CRTS36DSPF) COMMAND. BY USING THE GENOPT(*CONVERT) option and specifying a DDS source file and member name on the additional parameters screen, native DDS will be generated in the place you choose.

—Steven Kontos

Editor's Note: *For more on this topic, see prior tip entitled "Converting S/36 SFGR to DDS."*

IF EVOKED in CL?

Q: Is there a way to duplicate the // IF EVOKED-YES OCL command in CL?

A: Yes, there is. Use the RTVJOBA as follows. If &SUBTYPE is '**E**', then the job is evoked.

```
DCL       VAR(&SUBTYPE) TYPE(*CHAR) LEN(1)
RTVJOBA   JOB(*) SUBTYPE(&SUBTYPE)
```

—*Ernie Malaga*

Multiformat Files

Q: Has anyone out there converted S/36 multiformat files to native AS/400 externally described files? We have our order-entry file in two different formats. The first line—line item zero—has the basic customer information. The next lines, detail lines, have what the customer ordered. Because almost 75 percent of our programs use this order file, there is no way to convert this overnight.

Can I create a line item zero file and a detail file and join them with a logical file? For example, our order file is WF.ORD. Can I make two files called ZERO and DETAIL and make a join logical file called WF.ORD without changing any of my programs? They all use the file WF.ORD with both records in it.

A: I've done this many times; it's fairly straightforward. You're on the right track. The first thing to do is to create two externally described physical files—one for each record. Copy each record type from the S/36 flat file to the appropriate externally described file.

Now, create a multiformat logical file (not a join logical file). Figure 17.3 shows a sample of the DDS required for a multiformat logical file. The record format and field names must be the same as the names in the based-on physical files unless you want to create specifications for each field.

```
A            R HEADR              PFILE(HEADP)
A            K INVNO
A*
A            R DETR               PFILE(DETP)
A            K INVNO
A            K LINENO
```

Figure 17.3: A multiformat logical file DDS includes at least two record definitions.

When you create the logical file, you specify a format selector program, or you can add the format selector later with the Change Logical File (CHGLF) command.

Each time you add a record to the database, the format selector program is automatically called and passed two parameters. The first is the entire output buffer and the second is a return parameter in which your format selector returns the name of the record format that the data is to be written to. As shown in Figure 17.4, a simple CL program can do this.

```
PGM     PARM(&BUFFER &FORMAT)
DCL     VAR(&BUFFER) TYPE(*CHAR) LEN(256)
DCL     VAR(&FORMAT) TYPE(*CHAR) LEN(10)
IF      COND(%SST(&BUFFER 3 1) *EQ 'H') +
        THEN(CHGVAR VAR(&FORMAT) VALUE(HEADR))
        ELSE CMD(CHGVAR VAR(&FORMAT) VALUE(DETR))
ENDPGM
```

Figure 17.4: Use a Format Selector Program to help the database select the appropriate record format.

In this example, &BUFFER is declared with a length of three because that's the last byte that's referenced. The program is really passed a pointer to the data buffer. The record format name is always 10 bytes long.

The only real "gotcha" is if your multiformat physical doesn't have a key. It's required. If that's the case, you have to manufacture one somehow or live with a flat file. You need to look at the OCL that manipulates the new file, too. Many things that are done with a single physical file on the S/36, such as the copy-delete-rename reorganization technique, are not appropriate with a multiformat logical. You also must replace DELETE with the Clear Physical File Member (CLRPFM) command (in this case twice) and get rid of any BLDFILES.

—*Pete Hall*

Replacing S/36E File DELETEs/CREATEs

Q: AS/400 file creation and deletion is very time-consuming and something to avoid. I assume this is also true in S/36E. Is it worth the time to change all the typical DELETEs, RENAMEs, and so on used in purging deleted records after file maintenance?

A: Look up the Reorganize Physical File Member (RGZPFM) command in the *CL Reference* manual. With this command, you can perform complete reorganization in a single step, without bothering to delete (and rebuild) your alternate index files. If what you need to do is to get rid of old records (the whole file), use Clear Physical File Member (CLRPFM) instead of deleting the file and rebuilding it.

—Ernie Malaga

S/36 to AS/400 CL Conversion Tip

RPG III programs may be executed in the S/36 Environment via CALL or // LOAD and // FILE statements. The IBM preferred method is to use LOAD/RUN because of some implicit processing that occurs. This allows a gradual move of programs from RPG 36 to RPG as modifications require additional function. This should not be attempted until file integrity has been checked for decimal data errors.

—Douglas Handy

Treating Indicators as Data in RPG II Programs

RPG III and RPG IV allow you to treat indicators as fields, but RPG II does not. A workaround technique I've been using for years has served me well on both the S/36 and the AS/400. I set a field to either 0 or 1, depending on the status of the indicator, and reference the field. See Figure 17.5 for an example.

```
*                                            HILOEQ
C          KEYF      CHAINSOMEFILE            50
C                    MOVE '0'      #IN50  1
C   50               MOVE '1'      #IN50
C          #IN50     IFEQ '0'
... calcs to do if indicator 50 is off
C                    ELSE
... calcs to do if indicator 50 is on
C                    END
```

Figure 17.5: You can test an indicator as if it were a variable in RPG II.

If you later convert this program to RPG III, you can remove the two MOVES and change field #IN50 to *IN50. (Of course, the program will still run correctly, even if you don't.)

—Ted Holt

◆ Database Files

Library List Support for S/36E Files

Files do not have to reside in QS36F. Library list support can be globally enabled via CHGS36, or temporarily enabled or disabled via // FILELIB LIBL- YES|NO or the FLIB procedure. Files will still be created in QS36F unless you also change the current file library. For example, for testing you might want to have a procedure similar to the one shown in Figure 17.6.

```
// FILELIB LIB-S36TESTF,SESSION-YES,LIBL-YES
// FILELIB LIB-S36TESTF,SESSION-NO
ADDLIBLE QS36F (*AFTER S36TESTF)
STRDGB UPDPROD(*NO)
```

Figure 17.6: This testing procedure causes the S/36 environment to find files using the library list.

This will cause new files to be created in S36TESTF, and existing files in QS36F to be used only if the program does not attempt to open the file for update (assuming S36TESTF is created as a *TEST library).

—Midrange Computing Staff

The FLIB Command

On the System/36, data files were not stored in libraries, but were global to the system. IBM mimics this by providing a library, called QS36F, in which data files are placed. However, by using the FLIB procedure, you can use some other library instead.

The FLIB procedure can be entered on the command line or you can use the // FLIB OCL statement to change the library in the procedure. For example, if you want a CATALOG listing of the files in QGPL, do as follows:

```
STRS36
FLIB QGPL
CATALOG ALL,F1
```

This can be handy when testing S/36 applications. Your test data can be in a test library and you can issue the FLIB command before you start testing. The new file library will be in effect until it is changed again or until you sign off.

—Alon Fluxman

✦ ✦ ✦ Date and Time

?DATE? with Eight Digits

If you're running SSP release 7.1 or above, you can use the ?LONGDATE? procedure control expression to return an eight-digit system date. If you're running OCL on another platform, you might need an alternative.

Of course you can't change the way ?DATE? works, but you can do the next best thing: create an OCL procedure that returns an eight-digit date. Such a procedure is DATE8 (Figure 17.7).

```
** DATE8: Return the job date with 8 digits.
**
** Parm 1: LDA position for returned date. Default = 1.
** Parm 2: Edit character. Default = (none).
** Parm 3: Current date format. Default = 'MDY'.
**
* Set omitted parameters to their default values.
// IF '?1?'= EVALUATE P1=1
// IF '?2?'= EVALUATE P2=''
// IF '?3?'= EVALUATE P3='MDY'
*
// LOCAL OFFSET-?1?,DATA-'?DATE?'
*
* Branch to appropriate segment of the procedure.
// IF ?3?='MDY' GOTO MDY_DMY
// ELSE IF ?3?='DMY' GOTO MDY_DMY
// ELSE IF ?3?='YMD' GOTO YMD
*
* Report error in date format.
// PAUSE 'Invalid date format specified in parameter 3.'
// RETURN
*
* Build 8-digit date in MDY or DMY format.
// TAG MDY_DMY
// EVALUATE P21,3=?1?
// EVALUATE P22,3=?1?+2
// EVALUATE P23,3=?1?+4
*
// IF '?L'?23?,2'?''39' EVALUATE P11='19'
// ELSE EVALUATE P11='20'
// EVALUATE P12='?L'?21?,2'??2??L'?22?,2'??2??11??L'?23?,2'?'
// GOTO CONTINUE
*
* Build 8-digit date in YMD format.
// TAG YMD
// EVALUATE P21,3=?1?
```

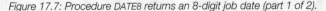

Figure 17.7: Procedure DATE8 returns an 8-digit job date (part 1 of 2).

```
// EVALUATE P22,3=?1?+4
// EVALUATE P23,3=?1?+6
*
// IF '?L'?21?,2'?''39' EVALUATE P11='19'
// ELSE EVALUATE P11='20'
// EVALUATE P12='?11??L'?21?,2'??2??L'?22?,2'??2??L'?23?,2'?'
// GOTO CONTINUE
*
* Store 8-digit date in LDA.
// TAG CONTINUE
// LOCAL OFFSET-?1?,DATA-'?12?'
// RETURN
```

Figure 17.7: Procedure DATE8 returns an 8-digit job date (part 2 of 2).

Whenever you need an eight-digit job date in your OCL procedures, just code the DATE8 procedure and then retrieve the date from the LDA, which is where DATE8 places its output. DATE8 uses three parameters:

- A numeric value that indicates in which position of the LDA to place the eight-digit date. If you don't give parameter 1 a value, it defaults to 1. Because you no doubt have other uses for the LDA, the purpose of this parameter is to provide flexibility.

- An edit character. For example, you could enter a slash for parameter 2. When you do so, the LDA would contain an edited version of the job date, using the character to separate day, month, and year; the eight-digit date, therefore, occupies 10 bytes of the LDA. If you don't give parameter 2 any value, it doesn't use any editing; the eight-digit date uses 8 bytes of the LDA.

- The current date format. The S/36 supports three-date formats—MDY, DMY, and YMD—and a job's date format can be changed on the fly with the SET procedure. Because I couldn't find any means to programmatically retrieve the current date format, I provided a way to specify it in the DATE8 procedure. If not given, it defaults to MDY.

So, let's suppose you have a procedure in which you need an eight-digit job date, and you're currently working in the DMY date format. Because your application programs already use LDA positions 1 through 200, you want DATE8 to return the date beginning at position 201 (remember, the S/36 supports 512 characters in the LDA):

```
// DATE8 201,,DMY
```

You can then retrieve the date from LDA positions 201–208, using the substitution expression **?L'201,8'?**. Notice that I gave no value to parameter 2, resulting in an unedited date.

—Ernie Malaga

True Julian Date Subroutines

In a true Julian date system, each date is assigned a relative number that is one higher than the previous date's number. It doesn't matter if these numbers are in the thousands, or millions—it is only important that each date's number is one higher than the previous. For example, our Julian routines return the number 32,082 for 12/31/87 and 32,083 for 01/01/88. The difference between these two numbers is 1, which is the correct number of days between the two dates.

The subroutines use March 1, 1900 as day number one. The date conversions are accurate through February 28, 2100. The RPG II or III subroutine GTOJ$ (Figure 17.8) will convert a Gregorian date to a 5-digit Julian date. Before invoking GTOJ$, place the month, day, and year in G$MM (2.0), GG$DD (2.0), and G$YYYY (4.0) parameters (INCLUDE CENTURY). The resulting Julian date will be in G$JD (5.0). This subroutine will even give you the day of the week for that date by checking the number in G$DW (1.0) — 0=Wednesday, 1=Thursday, 6=Tuesday.

```
 *   GTOJ$ - Convert a date between March 1, 1900 and
 *           February 28, 2100 to a sequential number
 ***********
 *   Input:
 *     G$YYYY: 4-digit year
 *     G$MM  : 2-digit month
 *     G$DD  : 2-digit day
 *   Output:
 *     G$JD  : 5-digit sequential number
 *     G$DW  : day of week (0=Wednesday, ..., 6=Tuesday)
 ***********
 C           GTOJ$     BEGSR
 C                     Z-ADD0         G$JD
 C           G$MM      SUB  3         G$MMWK  20
 C                     Z-ADDG$MMWK    GMWKSV  20
 C           G$MMWK    IFLT 0                       LVL-01
 C                     ADD  12        G$MMWK
 C                     END                          END-01
 C           GMWKSV    IFNE 0                       LVL-01
```

Figure 17.8: GTOJ$ converts a date to a serial number (part 1 of 2).

```
C              G$MMWK    MULT 30.6     G$JD       H
C                        END                              END-01
C                        ADD  G$DD     G$JD       50
C              G$YYYY    SUB  1900     G$YYWK     30
C              G$YYWK    IFNE 0                           LVL-01
C              GMWKSV    IFLT 0                           LVL-02
C                        SUB  1        G$YYWK
C                        END                              END-02
C                        END                              END-01
C              G$YYWK    MULT 365.25   G$JYD      70
C                        ADD  G$JYD    G$JD
C              G$JD      DIV  7        G$WK7      70
C                        MVR           G$DW       10
C                        ENDSR
```

Figure 17.8: GTOJ$ converts a date to a serial number (part 2 of 2).

The RPG II or III subroutine JTOG$ (Figure 17.9) will convert a Julian date that is origi-
nally generated from GTOJ$ to a Gregorian date. Before calling JTOG$, place the Julian
date in J$JD (5.0) parameter. The resulting month, day, and year will be in J$MM (2.0),
J$DD (2.0), and J$YYYY (4.0).

```
 **********
 *   JTOG$ - Convert a sequential number to a date between
 *           March 1, 1900 and February 28, 2100
 **********
 *   Input:
 *      J$JD  : 5-digit sequential number
 *   Output:
 *      J$YYYY: 4-digit year
 *      J$MM  : 2-digit month
 *      J$DD  : 2-digit day
 **********
C              JTOG$     BEGSR
C              J$JD      DIV  365.25   J$YYWK     30
C              J$JD      DIV  365.25   J$TST      99
C              J$TST     IFEQ 0                           LVL-01
C                        SUB  1        J$YYWK
C                        END                              END-01
C              J$YYWK    MULT 365.25   J$YD       70
C              J$JD      SUB  J$YD     J$YD
C              J$YD      IFGT 306                         LVL-01
C                        ADD  1        J$YYWK
C                        END                              END-01
C                        Z-ADD0        J$X        20
C              J$YD      DOULEJ$MD                        LVL-01
C                        ADD  1        J$X
C              J$X       MULT 30.6     J$MD       30H
```

Figure17.9: JTOG$ converts a serial number to a date (part 1 of 2).

```
C                          END                              END-01
C                          SUB   1         J$X
C            J$X           MULT  30.6      J$MD       H
C            J$YD          SUB   J$MD      J$DD       20
C            J$X           ADD   3         J$MM       20
C            J$MM          IFGT  12                        LVL-01
C                          SUB   12        J$MM
C                          END                              END-01
C            J$YYWK        ADD   1900      J$YYYY     40
C                          ENDSR
```

Figure17.9: JTOG$ converts a serial number to a date (part 2 of 2).

The subroutines are easy to use. For example, suppose you want to determine how many days past due an invoice is. Just convert UDATE and the invoice record's date to Julian dates using GTOJ$, and calculate the difference between them. Another example would be to use the routines in a scheduling system. If you wanted to schedule a date *x* number of days in the future, you could convert UDATE to a Julian date, add *x*, and then convert that number to a Gregorian date. The day of the week field could also be helpful in avoiding weekends.

—Midrange Computing Staff

✦ ✦ ✦ Messages

MONMSG in OCL Procedures

Use the message ID substitution parameter ?MSGID? after embedded CL commands in an OCL36 procedure. This parameter will be null if the command executed successfully. It will contain the CPF error message if it was not successfully completed.

—Midrange Computing Staff

Not Quite an S/36E MONMSG

The S/36E on the AS/400 provides a terrific way to "dabble" in native CL commands while staying within the comfortable confines of S/36E OCL. It allows you to use most native CL commands from within your OCL procedures.

The problem is that if a native command fails, the system takes the default response to the OS/400 error message and returns control to the procedure as if nothing happened! Your OCL then goes merrily on its way thinking that the native command ran successfully when actually it did not. When you try to use the MONMSG command to check for error conditions, you find that this is one of those CL commands that doesn't work in OCL.

There is a solution, albeit not very well documented. The S/36E provides a new system variable ?MSGID?. This is similar to a return code (?CD?) and can be used to check for error conditions in lieu of MONMSG.

To take advantage of the ?MSGID? substitution parameter, you must code it following the CL command you think might cause an error. If no error message is issued, ?MSGID? will be blank. If OS/400 issues an error message, ?MSGID? will have the seven-character message ID of the escape message, such as CPF1234.

For example, Figure 17.10 shows an OCL procedure in the S/36E containing the RGZPFM native command, which might result in an error if the file is not found.

```
// RGZPFM FILE(?1?) MBR(*FIRST)
// IF ?MSGID?= GOTO OK
// ** Procedure aborted - File ?1? not found
// CANCEL
// TAG OK
// LOAD PGM1
// FILE NAME-?1?,DISP-OLD
// RUN
```

Figure 17.10: Use ?MSGID? to implement S/36E error trapping.

As you can see, the procedure will take care of the problem should the file not be found. Although this particular case could have been handled by the // IF DATAF1 procedure control expression, the example clearly demonstrates the ?MSGID? technique.

—Rich Loeber

✦ ✦ ✦ Performance

Improve Response Time

It is possible that response time can be dramatically improved by a simple modification to your display file.

System/36 $SFGR members migrated to the AS/400 through IBM's Migration Aid software are converted to DDS source members. If a $SFGR screen does not use Suppress Input (most don't), the converted DDS member will have the keyword INVITE added to the screen. INVITE causes a read request at the time of the screen output operation. On the AS/400, this takes a noticeable amount of time. In cases where there is no input defined for a screen, the INVITE is not necessary. Most variable-line screens do not define input. Therefore, if you remove the INVITE keyword from the converted DDS member, you will notice quite a reduction in the time it takes to display multiple variable line screens.

—Midrange Computing Staff

Tuning Tip for S/36E

Some of the older 400s that ship to former S/36 sites come with the system value QSPCENV preset to *S36. This way, everyone who uses the system automatically starts in S/36 mode. The problem is that every job on the system runs in this mode even if it is not a S/36 job. This setup slows these non-S/36 jobs.

IBM recommends setting the system value to *NONE using the CHGSYSVAL command, and then IPL'ing. For users who want S/36 mode on all of the time, changing their User Profiles can still do this. Using the WRKUSRPRF command for each of these users, change the Special Environment parameter on the third screen to *S36.

An alternative is to have users issue a STRS36 command when they want S/36 mode and ENDS36 to get out. When you set the user profile to *S36, you're stuck in S/36 mode for the duration of every session. ENDS36 does not work with the user profile set this way.

IBM also recommends changing the QPFRADJ parameter to 0 (it comes set to 1), turning off the automatic configuration parameter, and changing the controlling subsystem from QBASE to QCTL.

—Midrange Computing Staff

✦ ✦ ✦ Printing

Change Defaults for System

Q: Is it possible to change the default for print quality (PRTQLTY) for the S/36 Environment listings from *NLQ to *STD? The Override Printer File (OVRPRTF) command does the job for individual OCL procedures or for the workstation session if you enter it from the command line.

A: There is a printer file in library #LIBRARY with the same name as each S/36 Environment printer device (P1, P2, and so on). Changing the attributes of any of these printer files

default values for all S/36 Environment jobs that print to the corre-
'RTQLTY can be changed with the Change Printer File (CHGPRTF)

Get Printer File Information in RPG II Programs

In RPG II, the only INFDS allowed is for WORKSTN files. Sometimes you need information for printer files, like the current printer line number or forms length, which is only
available in a printer INFDS. You can get the data using shared open data paths. Before
running the RPG II program, issue an OVRPRTF FILE(FILE_NAME) SHARE(*YES).

Then, whenever you need the INFDS status, CALL a short RPG III program (such as
RTVINFDS, in Figure 17.11) sharing the same printer file. It needs to perform a printer operation to update its INFDS, but a space before and after of zero lines without any output
fields does the trick. Then just pass back whichever fields you need.

```
FPRTFNAMEO  F     132    OV     PRINTER     KINFDS PRTFDS
IPRTFDS     DS
I* define INFDS subfields here
I*
C* Define parms for passing INFDS data back to caller
C          *ENTRY    PLIST
C                    PARM        X
C                    PARM        Y
C                    PARM        Z
C*
C* dummy output causes system to load the INFDS
C                    EXCPTDUMMY
C*
C* convert numeric fields to character for passing to RPG II pgm
C* move fields into parms
C                    RETRN
OPRTFNAMEE 00            DUMMY
```

Figure 17.11: RPG II programs can call RPG III program RTVINFDS to retrieve the INFDS.

Leaving a S/36 Environment Spool File Open

Q: I have several job streams that use multiple RPG II programs to produce a single spool file. I do this using the CONTINUE-YES parameter on the // PRINTER command in OCL. The problem I now face is that I have replaced one of the RPG II programs in the job stream with an RPG III program. Is there any way I can insert this report into my S/36 job stream to have it blend seamlessly with my other RPG II reports? If I convert the existing RPG II reports to RPG III, can I do the same thing with the Override Print File (OVRPRTF) command?

A: In a CL program, you can override the print file to SHARE(*YES) and then open the print file. At that point, any programs called at a lower invocation level will use the open file. When the job returns to the point where the print file was overridden and opened, you can close the file or let it close when the program ends. You will have only one spool file.

—Midrange Computing Staff

✦ ✦ ✦ Program Development

PDM Options for S/36 Programs

Here are a few ideas on customizing the AS/400 Programming Development Manager (PDM). When I work on the AS/400, I work in the native mode to take advantage of the increased speed. However, most of the programs I work with are System/36 compatible. These commands help the programmer "in and out" of the System/36 environment:

The MP command is useful when using the Work with Members screen. It allows you to modify the procedure in QS36PRC, without having to change the file name. It will use the same name as the program in QS36SRC.

```
STRSEU SRCFILE(&L/QS36PRC) SRCMBR(&N) TYPE(OCL36)
```

Command R6 will start the S/36 session, run the procedure, and return to the work with members screen when it is complete.

```
STRS36PRC CURLIB(*SAME) PRC(&N)
```

The S6 command is similar to R6, except that it will not run any procedure. It is useful when you want to run a catalog or run a DFU update program.

```
STRS36
```

Command SD will start the S/36 session and call SDA, passing the member name to SDA. This command is useful after a successful compile is generated of a $SFGR member, and you want to either view the screen formats or generate RPG II Input/Output Specs.

```
STRS36PRC CURLIB(*SAME) PRC(SDA) PARM(&N)
```

On the System/36, the cross-reference listing option defaults to NOXREF. On the AS/400, it defaults to *YES. Printing the cross-reference when not needed is a waste of paper and computer time. The CS command will compile your RPG II program without the cross-reference.

```
SBMJOB CMD(CRTS36RPG PGM(&L/&N) SRCFILE(&L/QS36SRC) +
        SRCMBR(&N) OPTION(*NOXREF))
```

You can add these commands as user-defined options to the Work with Members screen of PDM. To do so, press function key 16, and then F6 to add. Put the two-character option code to call the command in the first field and the command in the second field.

—Art Tostaine, Jr.

Prompt CL Commands in OCL Procedures

When working in SEU with OCL, CL commands cannot be prompted. To use commands in these members, you have to either find the manual or a command line and prompt the command, remember or write the keywords down, then return to SEU, and type the command. This is not only time-consuming, but also error-prone.

There is a simple way to prompt the command in SEU. While editing, press F13 to change defaults, tab down to "Source Type," change it to CL or CLP, and press Enter. When you return to SEU, you're working on a CL program. Now you can prompt the command, fill in the blanks, and let the system generate the keywords and do syntax checking for you.

When the CL command is displayed in the source member, it will be indented and line wrapping might occur.

To change back, press F13 and change the "Source Type" back to its original value. The OCL statements will generate syntax errors if edited before switching back to the original source type.

Now you have a good CL command in your OCL procedure in a lot less time and without having to worry about syntax errors.

—Brad Hooley

✦ ✦ ✦ S/36 Environment

?WS? Error in S/36E

I'm currently working in the S/36 Environment. Procedure control expressions—in this case, the substitution parameter ?WS?—is "converted" when you run a procedure or CL command. This is okay except for FNDSTRPDM. When you search for '?WS?' in QS36PRC, it looks for *xx* (where *xx*=your workstation ID); or if you submit the command to batch, it substitutes #0 because the submitted job doesn't have a workstation ID of its own.

The IBM solution is to ENDS36 and run the FNDSTRPDM. In my case, my user profile was set up with special environment *S36, so I changed it to *NONE. (Otherwise, you get the message that you have to sign off to end S/36 Environment.) As shown in Figure 17.12, I created STRS36CL. I made this my initial program. Now if I want to "go native," I can type ENDS36.

```
PGM
STRS36
ENDPGM
```

*Figure 17.12: Sometimes it's better to make an initial program start the *S36 special environment.*

—Timothy Phinney

AS/400 Workstation Substitution

Q: After going on the AS/400, I decided to take advantage of being able to use more than two characters for our workstation IDs. It has allowed me to be more descriptive of each workstation. I am using four characters for each WS. However, I have OCL that uses the SNDBRKMSG command. I substituted ?WS? for the workstation message queue parameter and it worked great until I renamed the displays. When I displayed the value being passed to the WS parameter, it showed the old two-letter ID even though it no longer existed in the system. I plan to write a CL program to get around this, but I'm still curious as to why this happens. My users are in S/36EE and my QDEVNAMING value is set to *S36.

A: When a user is signed on to the S/36 environment, he or she uses the workstation IDs from the "System/36 environment configuration." To view this, type DSPS36. It will show you the AS/400 workstation ID (i.e., DSP01), and the S/36 ID (W1). As far as I know, all S/36 environment procedures that use ?WS? will retrieve the two-letter naming convention. You can change these with the CHGS36 command.

—Midrange Computing Staff

Better Control over S/36E Shared Files

The S/36E implicit shared opens of files can cause incompatibilities in certain circumstances, especially in a mixed environment. Instead of disabling it altogether via CHGS36, only disable it in procedures where you experience errors related to the file opens.

A specific file may be excluded from implicit shared opens by adding BYPASSPRF to the // FILE statement. An entire session may be disabled by executing CALL QEXSHRO '2' and reenabled by executing CALL QEXSHRO '1'.

—Douglas Handy

Faster AS/400 #GSORT

In the AS/400 System/36 environment, #GSORT often drastically slows down all other interactive users. One of the reasons for this is that #GSORT is run at an interactive run priority of 20. Batch jobs (like #GSORT) should be submitted to batch, where they are run more efficiently without bogging down the interactive environment.

But when you must run #GSORT in an interactive job, you can improve the interactive environment's performance by lowering the priority of the #GSORT jobs. You should use a number of 80 or higher (99 max), depending on the size of the input file. The higher the number is the lower the priority. I added the following line to the beginning of each procedure:

```
CHGJOB RUNPTY(80)
```

This lets the #GSORT job run with almost no noticeable slowdown, and allows the other interactive jobs to run at normal speed. Any user running these procedures has to have *JOBCTL authority in their user profile to run CHGJOB.

—Midrange Computing Staff

Using the S/36E RUF Technique

Q: We have migrated a S/36 application to our AS/400 and are running it in S/36 Environment. The S/36 procedures that use the read-under-format (RUF) technique won't run. The RPG program that reads the data from the prompt screen bombs. Can you suggest a solution?

A: All you need to do is change the display file used in the PROMPT OCL statement to use a shared open data path. Use the Change Display File (CHGDSPF) command with a SHARE parameter value of *YES.

—Midrange Computing Staff

✦ ✦ ✦ System Administration

Log OCL Procedure Usage

Keeping a clean system and preparing for major projects is difficult if you have no idea what's good and what's garbage. OS/400 can help you with that chore. The system keeps up with the last time an object is used and how many times it has been used.

However, it doesn't keep up with OCL procedure usage. To fill this void, we wrote the LOGOCLPROC utility. It consists of four objects—physical file PROCLOG, command LOGOCLPROC, a CL program OCL001CL, and RPG III program OCL001RG—shown in Figures 17.13 through 17.16.

```
 *=================================================================
 * To compile:
 *
 *      CRTPF      FILE(XXX/PROCLOG) SRCFILE(XXX/QDDSSRC) +
 *                 TEXT('Log OCL procedure usage')
 *
 *=================================================================
 A           R RECCNT
 A             MBRNME       10A         COLHDG(' ' 'Procedure' 'name')
 A             MBRLIB       10A         COLHDG(' ' 'Library' 'name')
 A             ORGDAT        8A         COLHDG('Date' 'first' 'logged')
 A             MBRDAT        8A         COLHDG('Date' 'last' 'used')
 A             PRCACC       7S 0        COLHDG(' ' 'Times' 'accessed')
 A             USER         10A         COLHDG(' ' ' ' 'User')
 A           K MBRNME
 A           K MBRLIB
```

Figure 17.13: The procedure logging file, PROCLOG, contains data about OCL procedure usage.

```
/*==================================================================*/
/* To compile:                                                      */
/*                                                                  */
/*          CRTCMD     CMD(XXX/LOGOCLPROC) PGM(XXX/OCL001CL) +       */
/*                     SRCFILE(XXX/QCMDSRC) TEXT('Log OCL +          */
/*                     procedure usage')                            */
/*                                                                  */
/*==================================================================*/
           CMD        PROMPT('Log OCL Procedure Usage')
           PARM       KWD(PROC) TYPE(*CHAR) LEN(10) MIN(1) +
                      PROMPT('Procedure')
           PARM       KWD(LIB) TYPE(*CHAR) LEN(10) MIN(1) +
                      PROMPT('Library')
```

Figure 17.14: The LOGOCLPROC command can be added to any OCL procedure.

```
/*==================================================================*/
/* To compile:                                                      */
/*                                                                  */
/*          CRTCLPGM   PGM(XXX/OCL001CL) SRCFILE(XXX/QCLSRC) +       */
/*                     TEXT('Log OCL procedure usage')              */
/*                                                                  */
/*==================================================================*/
PGM        PARM(&PROC &LIB)

DCL        VAR(&PROC) TYPE(*CHAR) LEN(10)
DCL        VAR(&LIB)  TYPE(*CHAR) LEN(10)

OVRDBF     FILE(PROCLOG) TOFILE(MAGWORK/PROCLOG)
CALL       PGM(MAGWORK/OCL001RG) PARM(&PROC &LIB)
DLTOVR     FILE(PROCLOG)

ENDPGM
```

Figure 17.15: Program OCL001CL is the command-processing program of LOGOCLPROC.

```
*==================================================================
* To compile:
*
*          CRTRPGPGM  PGM(XXX/OCL001RG) SRCFILE(XXX/QRPGSRC) +
*                     TEXT('Log OCL procedure usage')
*
*==================================================================
FPROCLOG UF  E           K          DISK                         A
```

Figure 17.16: RPG program OCL001RG logs the procedure data to disk (part 1 of 2).

```
I          SDS
I                          254 263 S#USER
I                          276 279 S#MD
I                          280 281 S#Y
C          *ENTRY  PLIST
C                  PARM          MBRNME
C                  PARM          MBRLIB
C*
C          KEY1    KLIST
C                  KFLD          MBRNME
C                  KFLD          MBRLIB
C*
C          KEY1    CHAINRECCNT           99
C*
C                  MOVE S#USER   USER
C          S#Y     IFGE '40'
C                  MOVEL'19'     YEAR    4
C                  ELSE
C                  MOVEL'20'     YEAR
C                  ENDIF
C                  MOVE S#Y      YEAR
C                  MOVELYEAR     MBRDAT
C                  MOVE S#MD     MBRDAT
C*
C          *IN99   IFEQ *ON
C                  Z-ADD1        PRCACC
C                  MOVE MBRDAT   ORGDAT
C                  WRITERECCNT
C                  ELSE
C                  ADD  1        PRCACC
C                  UPDATRECCNT
C                  ENDIF
C*
C                  MOVE *ON      *INLR
C                  RETRN
```

Figure 17.16: RPG program OCL001RG logs the procedure data to disk (part 2 of 2).

Include the LOGOCLPROC command at the beginning of any OCL or REXX procedure you want to log. See the following example:

```
LOGOCLPROC PROC(xxx) LIB(?CLIB?)
```

We use generic reporting tools, such as Query/400, to view the file.

—*Steve Barnard*

Security

*I*t's well-known that the AS/400 has the highest level of security of any computer system ever made. Considering that the AS/400 has never been successfully hacked, you've got yourself one heck of a security giant. However, there is more to security than simply creating a user profile and setting its authority level to *USER. To take full advantage of OS/400 security, you must also understand group profiles, adopted authority, object authority, OS/400 system security values, network security and much more.

It's easy to say that you have a secure system, but how do you know that for sure? If you create a physical file and store records in it, is it automatically secure? Probably not. To provide true security to this file, you'll probably want to set its access level to *PUBLIC *NONE, and then authorize use by using individual user profiles or a security authorization list. The same holds true for program objects and other system objects. How about if you have users accessing your AS/400 via Client Access or other network connectivity tools? Do you know how to keep those users from being able to delete files in the QSYS.LIB file system?

To help you understand security ins and outs, this chapter includes some of the best tips and tricks on controlling OS/400 security. By the time you finish reading this extremely informative chapter, you'll find that you know more about OS/400 security than you ever thought possible!

—Shannon O'Donnell

◆   ◆   ◆   ◆

✦ ✦ ✦ Authority

Controlling Adopted Authority

The Use Adopted Authority (USEADPAUT) program attribute is a powerful tool for controlling the amount of authority that users of your software will adopt. If the program has the USRPRF(*OWNER) attribute, that program and all subsequently called programs that have the attribute of USEADPAUT(*YES) will use the authority of the program owner as well as the profile calling the program. This tool is very handy when a user needs authority to some object—while that user is running a program—but shouldn't have that authority otherwise.

You should be aware of some problems, however. Not only does the program with USRPRF(*OWNER) adopt authority, but also every program it calls adopts. This is bad if the program is owned by a profile with extra authority and there's a command line available. If you must provide a command line, put the command line function in another program, change it to USEADPAUT(*NO), and call it from the program that adopts. You must change the program after it is compiled, because the Create commands don't let you specify USEADPAUT(*NO) at compile time.

The QUSEADPAUT system value, new in V3R2 and V3R7, gives you better control over the USEADPAUT attribute. The default value for QUSEADPAUT is *NONE, which means all programs compiled on the system are created with USEADPAUT(*YES). If an authorization list is named in QUSEADPAUT and a user does not have at least *USE authority to that authorization list, all programs created by that user will have their USEADPAUT property set to *NO.

—Martin Pluth

✦ ✦ ✦ Commands

Security Report Commands

Considering how thorough and sophisticated (complicated) OS/400 security is, you'll be glad to know about five commands (available in V3R7 and higher) that print reports about security issues.

- Print Job Description Authority (PRTJOBDAUT): Given a library, it lists job descriptions that do not have a public authority of *EXCLUDE and do have a user profile in the USER parameter. Armed with this report, you can track down job descriptions that may allow users to run jobs while using someone else's authorities.

- Print Publicly Authorized Objects (PRTPUBAUT): Given a library and a type of object (e.g., *PGM or *FILE), it lists objects for which the public has an authority other than *EXCLUDE. Therefore, the report tells you which objects may not have protection against undesirable user access.

- Print Private Authorities (PRTPVTAUT): Given a library and a type of object, it lists the private authorities of all objects (i.e., which users have been specifically authorized to access the objects). In this way, PRTPVTAUT complements PRTPUBAUT.

- Print Queue Authority (PRTQAUT): Given a library, it lists the authorities to job queues and output queues in that library.

- Print Subsystem Description Authority (PRTSBSDAUT): This command is similar to PRTJOBDAUT, except that it lists subsystem descriptions that have a default user in one of their entries.

All these commands accept *LIBL, *USRLIBL, *CURLIB, *ALL, or *ALLUSR instead of a library name. In addition, they all print two reports: the "full" report (containing all information) and the "changes" report (which lists only whatever has changed since the last time you ran the command). With the CHGRPTONLY parameter, you can indicate whether to print the "changes" report only or both reports.

—Ernie Malaga

✦ ✦ ✦ Device Security

Security and the Unattended Workstation

The AS/400 provides a built-in global solution for unattended security through the QINACTITV system value. But, when you want to secure only individual workstations, this method cannot be used. The following technique will solve this problem by allowing an interactive program to control the timeout function. Let's say that you assign a value of 45 seconds to WAITRCD. This means the display will remain visible for 45 seconds before control is returned to the program that sent the file. To detect inactive workstations from your RPG/400 programs, do the following:

1. Code the INVITE keyword in the DDS for the display file.

2. Supply a value for the display file's WAITRCD parameter.

3. Specify the INFDS data structure in your RPG program with the *STATUS special keyword included.

4. If a workstation timeout occurs, the *STATUS field will contain a value of 1331. Code a test for this value in your program following your installation standards.

5. If a timeout is detected, you might want to have your program call an installation standard program that signs off the workstation, alerts the system operator, or takes some other corrective action.

The Figure 18.1 sample code (not a complete working program) illustrates the concept. Indicator 50, and a status of 1331, signals a workstation timeout—in which case a program is called to deal with the potential security problem.

```
A          INVITE
A R SCRN1 TEXT('MY SUBFILE RCD')

FPROMPT   CF    E WORKSTN
F                 KINFDS INFDS
F                 KNUM1
IINFDS DS
I                 *STATUS STATUS
.
.
.
C          WRITESCRN1
C          READ PROMPT              50LR
*
C   *IN50  IFEQ *ON
C   STATUS ANDEQ1331
C          MOVE *ON *INLR
C          CALL 'QCMDEXC'
C          PARM 'SIGNOFF'   CMD 7
C          PARM 7 LEN 155
C          ENDIF
```

Figure 18.1: With code, such as the fragment shown here, you could have potential security problems with workstation timeout.

—*Midrange Computing Staff*

✦ ✦ ✦ Field Security

Securing Individual Database Fields

The AS/400 database does not directly support field-level security for a file; in other words, there's no direct way to protect an individual field from unauthorized access while leaving all others unprotected. At most, you can give users *READ authority (to read records), *ADD (to add records), *UPD (to update records), or *DLT (to delete records), but this is a blanket authority that covers the entire record, not a specific field.

What you want is a way for all users to read the nonsensitive part of a record (such as employee number, name, and the department number). However, you don't want everyone to be able to read the rest of the fields (such as hourly pay rate and deductions).

There is a way to allow access to only certain fields in a physical file while protecting others: Create a logical file that contains a subset of the fields. The physical file might look like the one shown in Figure 18.2.

```
A     R  EMREC
A        EMEMPL      5P 0  TEXT('Employee number')
A        EMNAME      30A   TEXT('Employee name')
A        EMDEPT      4P 0  TEXT('Department number')
A        EMHPAY      5P 2  TEXT('Hourly pay rate')
A     K  EMEMPL
```

Figure 18.2: This is a typical employee master physical file layout.

The logical file created for selected field access would look like the examples shown in Figure 18.3.

```
A     R  EMREC       PFILE(EMPMST)
A        EMEMPL
A        EMNAME
A        EMDEPT
A     K  EMEMPL
```

Figure 18.3: You can restrict access to the employee master by using a logical file.

The logical file only "sees" the employee number, name and department number, and virtually ignores the rest of the confidential information.

Consider which users would be given access to the limited information. Give them all *OBJOPR authority to the logical file. This gives the users the authority to open the logical file and use the data authorities of the physical file on which the logical is based. Then give the users the desired data rights to the physical file. If you want them capable of reading the data, give them *READ authority to the physical file. Don't give them *OBJOPR authority to the physical file, though. If they don't have *OBJOPR authority, they cannot open the physical file itself and the confidential fields remain protected.

You can use the same technique to allow some users to change certain fields but not others. Again, create a logical file with *OBJOPR authority to the users, and give *CHANGE authority (but not *OBJOPR) to the physical file.

—Midrange Computing Staff

✦ ✦ ✦ Group Profiles

Don't Misuse Group Profiles

Group profiles can simplify authorization management, but—if not used properly—they can actually create problems and decrease system performance. Follow these guidelines for group profiles:

- To eliminate the chance that someone will sign on with a group profile, use the special password value of *NONE for all group profiles.

- For users who are members of group profiles, consider assigning object ownership to the group profiles rather than to the user profiles. When you create a user profile with the Create User Profile (CRTUSRPRF) command, set the OWNER parameter value to *GRPPRF rather than the default of *USRPRF.

- If you discover that a user has authorities that should belong to a group profile, do the following:

  1. Use the Grant User Authority (GRTUSRAUT) command to give the user's authorities to the group profile.

  2. Use the Revoke Object Authority (RVKOBJAUT) or Edit Object Authority (EDTOBJAUT) command to remove the private authorities from the users, because they are no longer needed.

—Steve Bisel

Security Loophole with Group Profiles

If the security administrator's user profile has the same group profile as the profiles the security administrator is creating, it is possible that any user in the group could use any other user's profile belonging to that same group to submit jobs. This includes unauthorized use of the system administrator's user profile for batch jobs. One does not need to know the password of the other user profiles to use them on the Submit Job (SBMJOB) command. With this type of abuse, one user could gain the rights of a more powerful user profile within the group when running a batch job.

When a system administrator who belongs to a group profile creates an object, OS/400 grants *ALL authority to the group by default. Because they are also objects, this rule applies to user profiles as well. Every user in the group is thus automatically granted access to every other user's profile within the group.

On the SBMJOB command, there is a USER parameter for overriding the user profile running the job. This option allows one user to submit a job on behalf of another user, provided that the former has authority to use the latter's user profile. In this case, everyone has *ALL authority to all profiles within the group.

How do you plug this loophole? One solution is to remove the security administrator from the group—that is, set the system administrator's group profile (GRPPRF) to *NONE or assign it to a different group not used by "ordinary" users. Another solution is to issue the Revoke Object Authority (RVKOBJAUT) command:

```
RVKOBJAUT OBJ(user profile) OBJTYPE(*USRPRF) USER(group profile)
AUT(*ALL)
```

You could use this command just after creating a new user profile assigned to the group.

—*Richard Leitch*

✦ ✦ ✦ Logging

Use Security Auditing to Log Object Usage

Although some shops use the Send Message (SNDMSG) command to log sent messages, there is a much simpler way to achieve the same results by using the built-in security auditing of the AS/400.

Here's the procedure to log SNDMSG commands:

1. Set up security auditing on the AS/400 (see the instructions in the *OS/400 Security Reference* manual SC41-4302, CD-ROM QBJALC01). This is recommended for all AS/400s.

2. Add *OBJAUD to the system value QAUDCTL.

3. Enter the following command to start object auditing on the SNDMSG command:

```
CHGOBJAUD OBJ(QSYS/SNDMSG) OBJTYPE(*CMD) OBJAUD(*ALL)
```

4. From this point on, all messages that are sent using the SNDMSG command will be logged in the audit journal (QAUDJRN) as an entry type of CD. The CD entries can be viewed by using the Display Journal (DSPJRN) command on the QAUDJRN journal:

```
DSPJRN JRN(QAUDJRN) ENTTYP(CD)
```

5. Place a 5 next to the entry you want to view. The CD entries will include the sender, receiver, time, and text. This type of auditing can be used on any object, not just commands, on the AS/400.

—*Michael Adamson*

✦ ✦ ✦ Logical Files

Logical File Security

Q: I want to fully secure my AS/400 database from PC clients using Client Access/400 tools (such as file transfer, remote command, and ODBC) while also giving them access to the data they are authorized to query. I could give them authority to logical files or SQL views (which limit what they can see), but then I must also give them authority to the based-on physical file. Is there a way around this problem?

A: To solve this problem, grant the data authorities on the physical file so the users can see the data in any logical file, but control access to the physical file through operational authority. Use the Edit Object Authorities (EDTOBJAUT) command for the physical file, and be sure you display the detailed object authorities; press F11 if not displayed. If you now remove the *X* from under the **Opr** on the detail authorities, the users can't open the physical file directly, but they will still be able to access the data through a logical view.

—Dave Shaw

✦ ✦ ✦ Network Drives

Locking Down Your Network Drive

Are you looking for a quick way to keep your Client Access/400 users from getting into your sensitive document files stored in the QDLS directory in the AS/400 Integrated File System (AS/400 IFS)? One method to do so is to create a generic user ID that does not have a directory entry on the AS/400. When the client connects to the AS/400, it cannot access QDLS because it doesn't have a directory entry. The other method is to rename the Client Access/400 network drivers executable program (CWBBS.EXE).

Renaming the executable will keep the client from being able to use the CA/400 Operations Navigator to get to your AS/400. Before you can rename the executable, you'll need to stop it. To do so, press the Ctrl+Alt+Del keys once, and you'll be presented with the Close Program window. Click on the CWBBS.EXE program to highlight it, and then click on the End Task button. This will stop the program. After it's stopped, you can then rename it.

—Gerald R. Posey

Editor's Note: *Renaming CWBBS.EXE does not work with the Client Access Express product.*

Renaming or removing CWBBS.EXE should be done only after careful consideration. Because you will no longer be able to use drives mapped to your AS/400, it could negatively impact your user's client-side connection. If you don't want to rename CWBBS.EXE, you can keep it from running by moving it from its default folder. Of course, any PC-literate user might find the program in its new folder and move it back.

Perhaps a better approach would be to remove its reference from the Windows 95/NT registry. Removing the reference will not only keep CWBBS.EXE from starting when Windows 95/NT starts, it will also keep most users from being able to restore CWBBS.EXE's use by moving the program back to its original folder or renaming it to its original name.

To remove it from the Windows 95/NT Registry, do the following:

- From the Windows 95/NT Run box, type REGEDIT and click on OK.

- Double-click the folder named HKEY_LOCAL_MACHINE.

- Double-click Software.

- Double-click Microsoft.

- Double-click Windows.

- Double-click CurrentVersion.

- Double-click RunServices.

- In the right-side panel, you'll see a key entry for Client Access Network Drive.

Double-click on this and a dialog box will appear. To remove this key value, press the Delete key. In the bottom of the REGEDIT window, the path to the key value that you are deleting is displayed. If you ever want to manually restore this key, this is useful information to know and record.

You should always back up the Registry before making any changes to it. One way to do this is to make copies of the **system.dat** and **user.dat** files. Another way is to export the file from REGEDIT before any changes are made. (The Registry can be exported in its entirety or any part of a key thereof.) That way, if you make a mistake, you can restore the Registry back to its original configuration.

—*Shannon O'Donnell*

Prevent Network Drive Users from Accessing QSYS.LIB

Client Access for Windows 95 users can access AS/400 libraries, files, and members by using the Network Drives function to view the contents of the QSYS.LIB file system. By default, this file system is available through the Network Neighborhood portion of the Windows 95 Explorer.

If you don't want users to access this file system through Network Drives, change the authority of the AS/400 authorization list QPWFSERVER. This authorization list controls whether or not a user has access to the QSYS.LIB file system through Network Drives. For example, if you want to exclude all users (except those with *ALLOBJ authority), change the *PUBLIC authority to *EXCLUDE in this authorization list.

—*Robin Klima*

✦ ✦ ✦ Objects

Potential Concerns with CRTDUPOBJ

Q: We have recently restricted all production data on our AS/400. Because the information services (IS) staff has only USE rights to production data, they cannot use the Create Duplicate Object (CRTDUPOBJ) command. When this command is used, the system returns a "not authorized" error. I know that other shops have their production data secured from the IS staff. How did you deal with this command? CRTDUPOBJ is used primarily to build work files in QTEMP.

A: I created my own CRTDUPOBJ command and compiled the CL command processing program (CPP) to adopt the authority of the program owner (which is QSECOFR). This allows anyone to use the command with the authority of the security officer. I also added code to allow only the duplicate to be created in a test library.

—Mark McCall

A: At a previous employer, we created a CRTDUPOBJ work-alike called Duplicate Production Object (DUPPRDOBJ) with the same keywords and everything. It adopted sufficient authority to perform CRTDUPOBJ, then granted the object's creator (the person who ran the command) sufficient authority to the new object.

—Michael Polutta

Security Loophole?

If you need to create a duplicate of any object, the Create Duplicate Object (CRTDUPOBJ) command requires you to have *OBJMGT authority to the object. *CHANGE isn't enough. If the object you need to duplicate is a file, however, you can use the Copy File (CPYF) command, specifying CRTFILE(*YES).

CPYF doesn't require *OBJMGT to copy because you're only reading the object. The CRTFILE(*YES) parameter, however, essentially duplicates the work of CRTDUPOBJ without actually running that command. This results in a security loophole you should know about.

Here's the interesting part. Because the user created it with the CPYF command, that unauthorized user becomes the owner of the newly created file. Being the owner, the unauthorized user has *ALL authority to it, and can therefore change records, delete them, add to it, ad nauseam. And, the unauthorized user can move the file to another library that's higher in the library list than the original file!

Suppose then that the file in question is the employee master file. This user runs CPYF, creates a copy, changes his or her own pay rate in the duplicated file, moves it higher in the library list than the original file, and lets it sit there. Next time payroll checks are printed, the program accesses the duplicate file (with the higher pay rate), and he's got a nice raise without asking anyone.

—Midrange Computing Staff

Editor's Note: There are three methods you can use to protect yourself from this undesirable scenario.

First, revoke *CHANGE *public authority to the production libraries. Make sure the public only has* *USE *authority. Grant* *CHANGE *authority (or higher) only to those users who really need it.*

Even programmers might not need *CHANGE *authority to the production libraries if they always work on their own libraries. In this case, assign one person (security administrator or equivalent) the task of moving new objects to the production libraries. Then give this person* *CHANGE *authority to the production libraries.*

*Second, you could qualify everything to a library in order to make sure you're using the objects you want to use. In the case of database files, issue an Override Database File (*OVRDBF*) command prior to running any HLL programs, using the* TOFILE *parameter to point to the appropriate qualified file name. Qualifying names should be avoided whenever possible, however.*

Third, ensure your regular users can't run standard OS/400 commands from the keyboard. You can do this by (a) not ever giving them a command line, or (b) changing their user profiles to LMTCPB(*YES).

✦ ✦ ✦ Passwords

Hands Off the Passwords!

Do you have a problem with people using either the AS/400 or Windows to make unauthorized password changes to AS/400 profiles? Here's a simple solution: Create a password validation program. Every time someone attempts to change an AS/400 password, the system will pass four parameters to your new validation program:

- The new password, which has a length of 10 alpha.

- The old password, which has a length of 10 alpha.

- A return code, which has a length of 1 alpha.

- The user profile, which has a length of 10 alpha.

In your password validation program, find the user profile you don't want changed and set the return code value to 1. When processing returns to OS/400, the system will not accept the requested password change and an appropriate message will be sent to the user. If the return code parameter shows anything other than a 1, the change will be accepted.

One final note: Don't forget to change the system value QPWDVLDPGM (Password Validation Program) to point to the new program you created. Also, be aware that the data, including the password, is passed as unencrypted text. So make sure you apply the proper security!

—Greg Leister

Invisible Passwords

Q: I have a command that contains an AS/400 password. I use Display Input (DSPINPUT) with a value of *NO for the password on the PARM statement of the command definition. However, when I wrap this command in a Submit Job (SBMJOB) command, my password is visible in the submitted job's job log. Is there a way to avoid this? By the way, I use data type *CHAR. Will this cover everyone's password?

A: The password value does not appear in the submitted job's job log if the job log runs under the QCMD routing-entry program. The password value does appear in any job log running under a custom-routing entry program, but you can remove it and other DSPINPUT(*NO) values by passing the message reference key of the request message to the Process Command (QCAPCMD) API's options control block. For example, the job log might first look like this:

```
CHGUSRPRF  USRPRF(AAA)  PASSWORD(BBB)
```

However, pass the message reference key to QCAPCMD API, and the job log will look like this:

```
CHGUSRPRF  USRPRF(AAA)  PASSWORD()
```

—Gene Gaunt

Password Management Made Easier

When it comes to password management, one of the most useful system values is the Password Validation Program (QPWDVLDPGM). By specifying a program and its library in this parameter, you can allow a program to process the information entered in the Change Password (CHGPWD) command. This can be very useful in refining your security. I have written my own password validation program. It has two functions: it checks for certain words that you do not want used as passwords (e.g., user name), and it captures the password information at the time it is being changed. By capturing password information, a security administrator could inquire into passwords (something OS/400 doesn't normally allow you to do).

Once you assign a validation program to QPWDVLDPGM system value, every time the CHGPWD command is called (explicitly or automatically at password expiration time), the validation program is executed.

You should be aware of several considerations associated with this technique. Only passwords changed through the CHGPWD command will be processed, and passwords created by CRTUSRPRF or changed by CHGUSRPRF will not be processed. In addition, you must have special authority of *SECADM to update the QPWDVLDPGM system value.

—Midrange Computing Staff

Rules for Passwords

User profiles are supposed to identify users, but such identification works only as long as passwords are kept confidential. If you disclose your password to a coworker or if someone guesses your password correctly, that coworker can impersonate you on the system by signing on using your user profile name. From that point on, anything that person does would be recorded as having been done by you.

It's important, then, to make sure that no one guesses your password. Of course, this also means that you should never give your password to anyone. If you suspect someone is impersonating you, your immediate solution would be to notify the data processing department and then change your password. You can change your password anytime with the Change Password (CHGPWD) command.

Changing passwords is sometimes a chore, however. Your system might insist that you use a password you haven't used before or one that complies with a rather strict set of guidelines (e.g., you must not repeat characters, or you must use digits). Then, you have to memorize the new one.

Rather than change the password, you can use an operating system-provided service that is controlled by the Change User Profile (CHGUSRPRF) command. With this service, every time you sign on, the system will inform you when your user profile last signed on, and whether and how many invalid passwords were entered. Armed with this information, you can determine if that last sign-on was made by you.

To activate this service, use the DSPSGNINF(*YES) parameter in CHGUSRPRF. If you want to turn it off later, use DSPSGNINF(*NO). There's also a system value (QDSPSGNINF) that can be used to control this service for more than one user. If a user profile has DSPSGNINF(*SYSVAL), the system value is used to determine whether to show the previous sign-on information.

—*Ernie Malaga*

Program Security

If you recompile a program, be aware that the system handles security differently than you might expect. If the program already exists in the object library to which you are compiling, the new object will have the same security as the old one. For example, if you use the Authority (AUT) parameter value of *USE on the Create RPG Program (CRTRPGPGM) command and the current authority of the program is *EXCLUDE, the authority will still be *EXCLUDE after the compile. As a result, if you want to change the authority of a program when you recompile it, you must first delete the program.

—*Doug Payton*

✦ ✦ ✦ QSECOFR

Resetting the QSECOFR Password

The company I work for fired the MIS director, and he was the only one who knew the password for QSECOFR. In case you ever find yourself in that situation, here's how to solve the problem:

1. Manually IPL the system.

2. Take option 3 to access the dedicated service tools (DST).

3. When prompted for the DST password, key in QSECOFR.

4. From the DST menu, take option 5 to work with the DST environment.

5. Take option 9 to change DST passwords.

6. Take option 4 to reset system default passwords.

7. QSECOFR will now have a password of QSECOFR.

—Tony Cassella

Because of the security implications of this technique, *Midrange Computing* magazine asked our security expert, Wayne O. Evans, to contribute his thoughts on the subject. The following is his response.

DST can be used to recover the password of QSECOFR if it is lost, but this can also be a potential method for a hacker to gain control of your AS/400. One of the hacker magazines described this procedure in detail as a means to get the password of the security officer. There are some important steps that should be followed to protect your AS/400:

- Ensure the physical security of the computer system. Do not allow unauthorized persons to have access to the computer. You can also restrict those authorized but curious individuals by controlling access to the system key and DST passwords.

- Remove the key from the system unit. Put it in a secure location. This does not mean hide the key somewhere on the system. Hackers know enough to look for keys in common hiding places.

- DST is protected by passwords that should be changed. The DST passwords can be changed as follows while your system is active without requiring an IPL:

    1. Put the key in the system unit and set the system to MANUAL.

    2. Change the system indicators to 21 and press Enter.

    3. The DST sign-on screen will appear on the system console. Enter the default password QSECOFR and press Enter.

    4. Select option 5 to work with DST environment.

    5. Select option 9 to change the DST passwords.

6. Select option 3 to change the DST password for the DST security officer. Enter the old and new passwords. I recommend writing the password down and putting it with the key.

7. While you are here, also change the other two passwords for DST:

    a. Option 1 Basic DST-Default password 11111111

    b. Option 2 Full DST-Default password 22222222

8. Option 4 from this screen recovers the password of the security officer. If you choose option 4, the password of the QSECOFR password will be reset to QSECOFR.

—Wayne O. Evans

✦ ✦ ✦ User Profiles

Keep Your Profile Names Secret

The less information you give someone who's trying to break into your system, the more secure it will be. One valuable piece of information is the name of your user profiles. If you can keep them secret, you'll be a step ahead.

Unless you change a couple message descriptions, you are giving anyone who can get to a sign-on display on your system a tool to find out user profile names. If you type in an invalid user profile name, you will get error CPF1120 - User *xxx* does not exist. If the profile name is correct but the password is wrong, the error message is CPF1107 - Password not correct for user profile. The way to plug this hole is to change the CPF1107 and CPF1120 messages to have the same text:

```
CHGMSGD MSGID(CPF1107)MSGF(QCPFMSG) MSG('User profile or password not
valid.')
```

```
CHGMSGD MSGID(CPF1120) MSGF(QCPFMSG) MSG('User profile or password not
valid.')
```

It will now be impossible to find out profile names from the sign-on display.

—Martin Pluth

SQL

*T*he earliest AS/400s did not support SQL. SQL was tacked on as sort of an afterthought. DDS was the only way to define data and high-level language programs were the only way to manipulate data. SQL was added as another, alternate interface to the built-in database management system.

IBM is attempting to change that by actively promoting SQL. IBM continues to enhance the iSeries database, but is not enhancing "native" interfaces (i.e., high-level language file opens and the Open Query File [OPNQRYF] command) to take advantage of new database features. This means, for example, if you want to use a file that contains a binary large object (BLOB) field, you must access it through SQL.

IBM is telling iSeries programmers to wake up and smell the coffee. SQL is an industry standard. Everybody who is anybody in the database world uses SQL. All the major relational database management systems—Oracle, DB2 UBD, Microsoft SQL Server, etc.—support SQL. The most widely used programming languages—Visual Basic, Java, and others—rely on SQL interfaces like ODBC and JDBC to connect to relational databases. SQL is where it's at, and if you want to remain marketable, you'd better learn it.

This sounds ominous, but it's not all bad. SQL is a good language. It's easy to learn and it's an effective mechanism for defining and manipulating data. Its set-at-a-time record access might seem cumbersome to someone who's accustomed to record-at-a-time access, but then again, record-at-a-time access is just set-at-a-time access over an entire file. So, let this chapter be an encouragement to you. SQL is powerful and you can master it and use it to solve problems.

—Ted Holt

✦ ✦ ✦ Administration

Convert Query to SQL

Q: How can I get Query/400 definitions into an SQL statement? I have all my pertinent files mirrored down to Microsoft SQL Server, which is where my user community can get to the data via Excel, Access, Word, etc. I would like to get the definitions into SQL format so that we don't have to rewrite every query.

A: You can easily retrieve an SQL statement from a Query/400 definition by using the Retrieve Query Management Query (RTVQMQRY) command. This command is intended to be used with a Query Management Query (QMQRY) object; however, it also can be used with a Query Definition (QRYDFN) object. The trick to making it work is to change the ALWQRYDFN parameter to *YES. When you run the command, the results are placed in a source member that you can download to a PC. Before you can run the SQL, you must clean up the extraneous information that is placed in the source member along with the SQL statements.

—Robin Klima

Running SQL/400 Statements in Batch

There is a problem with SQL/400 in that it allows you to run SQL statements only inter-actively. Fortunately there is a technique that allows you to submit SQL statements to batch. Here's how it's done. Enter the Start Query Manager (STRQM) command. At the Query Manager menu, select option 1 to work with Query Manager queries. Press F19 if necessary to be sure that the query creation mode is set to SQL. Use option 1 to create a new query. Here you can enter your SQL statement by using the F4 key to prompt just as in SQL/400. After you have completed entering your SQL statement, press F3 to save and exit. To run the SQL statement in batch, select option 9 next to the query you want to run, change the run query mode parameter to '2', and press Enter.

—Midrange Computing Staff

✦ ✦ ✦ Character Manipulation

Left and Right Justification

Sometimes, data in fields needs to be right- or left-justified (just the opposite of the way you have it stored). For example, suppose you have data in a field that is four characters in length. For your original purpose, the characters were right justified. Due to a new requirement, you need to change the field so that it is six characters in length. If you use the Copy File (CPYF) command to copy the data to a six-character field, the data in the new file appears in a left-justified format. CPYF copies the data into the first four positions of the new field, beginning with the left-most position. In order for the data to have the same meaning in the new file, the data needs to be moved to the four right-most positions of the field.

Here's another situation. Perhaps you have data that needs to be loaded to your AS/400 from a PC application such as Microsoft Access. A common method to perform this function is to export Microsoft Access data to an ASCII file and then upload the ASCII file to the AS/400. During the export process, numeric fields might be written in a left-justified character form. After the data is uploaded to the AS/400, sorting on the fields could produce an incorrect sequence. For example, *2b/b/b/* would become greater than *10b/b/,* where the original data was 2 and 10.

Here is a quick solution. Assume that there is a file named EMPMAST with a field named CODE that is four characters in length. The two SQL/400 statements that follow justify the contents of the field either to the right or to the left, as indicated.

Right justify:

```
UPDATE EMPMAST SET CODE =
   SUBSTR('      '
   CONCAT STRIP(CODE),
   LENGTH('      '
   CONCAT STRIP(CODE))-4+1,4)
```

Left justify:

```
UPDATE EMPMAST
   SET CODE = SUBSTR(STRIP(CODE)
   CONCAT '      ',1,4)
```

The number 4 in the formula is the length of the field to be justified. The number of spaces included is equal to the length of the field.

—*Vijay Yadav*

Easy Right Justification

Q: I want to right-justify a character field in SQL the same as I can with EvalR in RPG IV. Is this possible?

A: Yes, see the SQL SELECT statement shown in Figure 19.1 for how to do this. Make sure that the first argument of the substring operation has as many blanks as the length of the field.

```
select substr(' ',1,length(charfld) - length(trim(charfld))) || trim(charfld)
from filename
```

Figure 19.1: SQL can right-justify character fields.

—Bill Robins

Translate and Sort Lowercase Data

I would like to point out a very nice function in SQL that you can use to translate character fields in any file from lowercase to uppercase.

The following SQL statement translates all lowercase characters in field TEXT in file TXTFIL to uppercase through the SQL TRANSLATE function. (Characters in TEXT that are not lowercase alphabetic characters are not affected by the TRANSLATE function.)

```
UPDATE TXTFILE
    SET TEXT=TRANSLATE(TEXT)
```

Every AS/400 is capable of executing SQL statements (even those without the SQL/400 licensed program) through Query Management/400, which is part of OS/400. For those who are unfamiliar with this feature, the following briefly describes how to execute an SQL statement through Query Management.

Query Management executes SQL statements that have been keyed into a source member and compiled into an object (type *QMQRY). You create *QMQRY objects with the Create Query Management Query (CRTQMQRY) command and execute them with the Start Query Management Query (STRQMQRY) command. This process can be broken down into four basic steps:

1. Create a source physical file called QQMQRYSRC with a record length of 91.

2. Create a source member in file QQMQRYSRC (member type QMQRY) to contain the SQL statement you want to execute.

3. Create a QMQRY object from the source member with the CRTQMQRY command.

4. Execute the query with the STRQMQRY command.

—Vincent van Steen

Translate and Sort Mixed-case Data

When data in a database file is sorted on a field that contains mixed-case characters, it doesn't always sort the way you might want it to. The reason is that lowercase letters always come before uppercase letters in the EBCDIC collating sequence.

To correct this problem, the field can be translated to uppercase before being sorted. Then the original untranslated data can be presented to the user. There are several ways to accomplish this. One way is to create a logical file; another way is to use an SQL statement. I'll show you both of these methods. Assume that the mixed-case data resides in the MIXED field in the MIXEDPF file:

```
A              R MXREC
A                MIXED        30
A              K MIXED
```

The first way I'll show you is to create a logical file over the physical file and use the RENAME and TRNTBL keywords:

```
A              R MXREC                      PFILE(MIXEDPF)
A                MIXED
A                UPPER           I          RENAME(MIXED)
A                                           TRNTBL(QSYSTRNTBL)
A              K UPPER
```

In this case, the field UPPER contains a capitalized version of MIXED. Notice that the file is keyed on UPPER. When the file is read in keyed sequence and field MIXED is presented, the data appears to be more "naturally" sorted. That is, all records starting with upper- or lowercase A will be together, followed by all records starting with B, and so on.

You can also use an SQL statement to translate a field to uppercase before sorting, like this:

```
SELECT MIXED, TRANSLATE(MIXED)
   FROM MIXEDPF
   ORDER BY 2
```

This SQL statement uses the TRANSLATE function to translate the data in the MIXED field to uppercase. The statement then uses an ORDER BY clause to sort the data on the translated value.

—Robin Klima

Using SQL to Update a Portion of a Field

Q: I know that with SQL it is very easy to update a field, but is it possible to substring part of a field and update that partial field?

A: Certainly! You can use the SUBSTR operator to get a substring from a field. For example, to get bytes 3–7 of a field called MYNAME, use the expression SUBSTR(MYNAME,3,5).

You can update part of a character field by concatenating the parts you want to stay intact with the new value. Let's say you're going to replace the first character of a field called CITY with 'X' in file SOMEFILE. The following SQL statement could accomplish the task:

```
UPDATE SOMEFILE
   SET CITY = 'X'
   CONCAT SUBSTR(CITY,2)
   WHERE ...
```

—Ted Holt

✦ ✦ ✦ Embedded SQL

SQL RPG Variable Declarations

RPG programmers have gotten used to the idea of being able to define variables anywhere they like in a program. As long as you state the size and type of variable somewhere in the program, it will compile. It doesn't matter if the definition is physically after your first use of the variable. However, this concept could fail you when writing an RPG program with embedded SQL.

I was writing a report program that needed the three main SQL parts: DECLARE CURSOR, OPEN CURSOR, and FETCH. To make the mainline of the program less cluttered, I decided to put each of these three sections in separate subroutines and call them in the proper sequence.

The program would not compile. The error message in the compile listing told me that I could not OPEN a CURSOR without a DECLARE, but there was a DECLARE in the program. After a few minutes of head scratching, I found my problem. I had arranged my three subroutines in no particular order, and I did not realize that—unlike variable definitions—I had to have them in the proper physical order. After I rearranged the physical location of the subroutines in the proper DECLARE, OPEN, FETCH physical order, the program compiled.

When you compile an SQL RPG program, the compile command first runs an SQL "precompiler" that looks at the SQL part of the program. It appears that this "precompiler" is not as robust as the regular RPG compiler because it does not look ahead to verify that all the pieces are in the program.

—Kenneth Fordham

✦ ✦ ✦ Field Names

AS/400 SQL Field Name Sizes

Q: Because the AS/400 uses only 10-character field names, does this mean we have to limit our client/server application or can we set up aliases for the larger field names?

A: At V3R1, IBM added support for SQL fields larger than 10 characters. SQL now automatically creates a 10-character field name and an alias for each field name that is larger than 10 characters. So, when you use SQL to create a table with a field Reorder_Part_Number, SQL will create the field with a name like REORD00001 and an alias of Reorder_Part_Number. You can use this alias interchangeably with the generated field name in SQL. For example:

```
Select Reorder_Part_Number from ...
```

is identical to

```
Select REORD00001 from ...
```

—Brian Singleton

✦ ✦ ✦ File Processing

Nonstandard File Names and SQL

Using SQL on the AS/400 is a very fast and useful feature for finding information quickly and efficiently. However, what do you do when you want to retrieve information from a file that contains a period (.) in its name? For example, if you try to select file AP.MASTER through SQL, you will get error message SQL0104 ("Token . was not valid..."). To get around this, put the file name in quotes, (e.g., "AP.MASTER") in your SQL statement. This method still allows you to prompt the SELECT fields line. Plus it saves you time and aggravation by eliminating the need for the OVRDBF command for each file. The best thing about using the quotes is that you won't have to exit and restart SQL to do an override if you decide to search for records in different files.

— Michael J. LoPue

SQL's UNION Merges Data

Q: I need to write an SQL query that retrieves customer address information. These addresses are fields **cadd1** and **cadd2** in the customer master file. However, if the alternate address flag, **altadd**, has a value of Y, I want to retrieve fields **aadd1** and **aadd2** from the alternate address file instead. Can that be done?

A: You need to use SQL's UNION operator. UNION combines the results of two queries into one resulting set of data. See the example shown in Figure 19.2.

```
select custno, cnme, cadd1, cadd2
   from custmast
   where altadd < > 'Y'
union select custno, cnme, aadd1, aadd2
   from custmast
   join altadd on custno = acustno
   where altadd = 'Y'
```

Figure 19.2: SQL's UNION operator combines two result sets into one.

—Bill Robins

Using a Specific Member in SQL

SQL by default reads the first member of the file(s) being processed. You can get around this limitation by executing the Override with DatabBase File (OVRDBF) command before you use the Start SQL (STRSQL) command. For example, the following statement makes SQL use member **ABC123** if you process file FNAME.

```
OVRDBF FILE(FNAME) MBR(ABC123)
```

—Midrange Computing Staff

Using SQL to Merge Files

In years past, the RPG cycle and MR indicator allowed RPG programmers to merge the contents of files based on common keys. This technique was commonly known as *matching records processing*. Lately, however, the RPG cycle (and matching records processing in particular) has fallen out of favor, but the need to merge the contents of files still exists.

For those who have SQL on their AS/400s, there is an alternative to matching records processing. The trick is to use a union to merge data via a left join combined with an exception join. The left join selects all records from the primary file; the exception join picks up unmatched records from the secondary file. Using ORDER BY on the last union presents merged records in order.

You enter the SQL statement as shown in Figure 19.3. I have used this technique with IBM-supplied output files to match related information. For example, you can merge the output of the Display Object Description (DSPOBJD) command with corresponding Display File Description (DSPFD) *MBR information and use the merged information to generate reports via SQL. See Figure 19.4.

```
SELECT Table1.Column1, Table2.Column2... From Table1
       Left Join Table2 On Table1.Column1 = Table2.Column1
UNION ALL
SELECT Table1.Column1, ifnull(Table2.Column2, ' ')... From Table2
       Exception Join Table1 On Table1.Column1 = Table2.Column1
Order By Table1.Column1, Table2.Column2
```

Figure 19.3: These SQL statements perform the matching record function.

```
DSPOBJD OBJ(OBJLIB/*ALL) OBJTYPE(*ALL) OUTPUT(*OUTFILE) OUTFILE(QTEMP/OBJ)
DSPFD FILE(SRCLIB/Q*) TYPE(*MBR) OUTPUT(*OUTFILE) OUTFILE(QTEMP/MBR)
```

Figure 19.4: These commands load information about all objects in a given location to OUTFILEs*.*

After you run these two commands, you can run the SQL statement shown in Figure 19.5 to merge the object and member creation information generated by the commands.

```
SELECT odlbnm, odobnm, mblib, mbfile, mbname, ...
    From obj Left Join mbr
      On odsrcl = mblib And
         odsrcf = mbfile And
         odsrcm = mbname
    Where Substr(odobnm,1,1) = 'Q'

UNION ALL

Select odlbnm, odobnm, mblib, mbfile, mbname ...
    From mbr Exception Join obj
      On mblib = odsrcl And
         mbfile = odsrcf And
         mbname = odsrcm
    Where mbname = ' '
    Order By odlbnm, odobnm, mblib, mbfile, mbname
```

Figure 19.5: These SQL statements merge the object and member creation information generated by the previous commands.

The output of the SQL statement is a list of objects and their corresponding source members. You can run this statement interactively or run it within an SQL program. To handle null values returned for unmatched records when this statement is embedded in an SQL program, you must define a null indicator area or surround the field names with an **IFNULL** function. For character fields, use **IFNULL(FldNam, ' ')**; for numeric fields, use **IFNULL(FldNam, 0)**.

—*David Morris*

✦ ✦ ✦ Interactive SQL

Building an SQL SELECT Statement on the Fly

The Build SQL (BLDSQL) utility builds a SELECT statement containing all the fields of a file:

- It builds an SQL SELECT statement for the version of SQL I'm using.

- Prompts the statement so that I can make changes to it before execution.

- Executes the statement.

- Sends the generated SQL statement back to the caller as a request message so that I can press the F9 key to recall the generated command.

BLDSQL consists of two objects: the BLDSQL command and the command processing program SQL004CL (shown in Figures 19.6 and 19.7). BLDSQL has three parameters: the qualified name of the file to be queried, any additional clauses to be added to the command (e.g., WHERE and ORDER BY), and the device to produce the output on.

```
/*==============================================================*/
/* To compile:                                                  */
/*                                                              */
/*         CRTCMD    CMD(XXX/BLDSQL) PGM(XXX/SQL004CL) +         */
/*                   SRCFILE(XXX/QCMDSRC)                        */
/*                                                              */
/*==============================================================*/
          CMD       PROMPT('Build an SQL statement')

          PARM      KWD(FILE) TYPE(Q1) MIN(1) FILE(*IN) +
                      PROMPT('File name')
          PARM      KWD(CLAUSES) TYPE(*CHAR) LEN(256) +
                      PROMPT('Additional SQL clauses')
          PARM      KWD(OUTPUT) TYPE(*CHAR) LEN(8) RSTD(*YES) +
                      DFT(*) VALUES(* *PRINT) PROMPT('Output')

Q1:       QUAL      TYPE(*NAME) LEN(10)
          QUAL      TYPE(*NAME) LEN(10) DFT(*LIBL) +
                      SPCVAL((*LIBL)) PROMPT('Library')
```

Figure 19.6: The BLDSQL command creates a SELECT statement with field names.

795

```
/*================================================================*/
/* To compile:                                                    */
/*                                                                */
/*          CRTCLPGM   PGM(XXX/SQL004CL) SRCFILE(XXX/QCLSRC)       */
/*                                                                */
/*   This program builds an SQL Select statement containing all   */
/*   the fields in a database file. The generated statement is    */
/*   sent to the requesting program through a request message,    */
/*   so it may be retrieved with the F9 key.                      */
/*================================================================*/
             PGM       PARM(&FILE &CLAUSES &OUTPUT)

             DCL       VAR(&SQL) TYPE(*CHAR) LEN(1024)
             DCL       VAR(&CLAUSES) TYPE(*CHAR) LEN(256)
             DCL       VAR(&FILE) TYPE(*CHAR) LEN(20)
             DCL       VAR(&FILENAME) TYPE(*CHAR) LEN(10)
             DCL       VAR(&FILELIB) TYPE(*CHAR) LEN(10)
             DCL       VAR(&OUTPUT) TYPE(*CHAR) LEN(8)
             DCL       VAR(&SEPFIELD) TYPE(*CHAR) LEN(1)
             DCL       VAR(&CMDCHK) TYPE(*CHAR) LEN(1024)
             DCL       VAR(&MSG) TYPE(*CHAR) LEN(80)
             DCL       VAR(&MRK) TYPE(*CHAR) LEN(4)

             DCL       VAR(&MSGDTA) TYPE(*CHAR) LEN(132)
             DCL       VAR(&MSGF) TYPE(*CHAR) LEN(10)
             DCL       VAR(&MSGFLIB) TYPE(*CHAR) LEN(10)
             DCL       VAR(&MSGID) TYPE(*CHAR) LEN(7)

             DCLF      FILE(QADSPFFD) RCDFMT(QWHDRFFD)

             MONMSG    MSGID(CPF0000) EXEC(GOTO CMDLBL(SNDRQSMSG))

/* Split the qualified file name into separate file & library */
             CHGVAR    VAR(&FILENAME) VALUE(%SST(&FILE 1 10))
             CHGVAR    VAR(&FILELIB) VALUE(%SST(&FILE 11 10))
             IF        COND(&FILELIB *EQ ' ') THEN(CHGVAR +
                         VAR(&FILELIB) VALUE('*LIBL'))

/* Get the field names */
             DSPFFD    FILE(&FILELIB/&FILENAME) OUTPUT(*OUTFILE) +
                         OUTFILE(QTEMP/QADSPFFD)
             RCVMSG    MSGTYPE(*LAST)

/* Generate the SELECT statement */
             CHGVAR    VAR(&SQL) VALUE('Select')
             OVRDBF    FILE(QADSPFFD) TOFILE(QTEMP/QADSPFFD)

READ:        RCVF
             MONMSG    MSGID(CPF0864) EXEC(DO)
             RCVMSG
             GOTO      CMDLBL(END_READ)
             ENDDO
             CHGVAR    VAR(&SQL) VALUE(&SQL *TCAT &SEPFIELD *CAT +
                         &WHFLDI)
```

Figure 19.7: SQL004CL runs the SQL statement and enables it to be retrieved with the F9 key (part 1 of 2).

```
                CHGVAR     VAR(&SEPFIELD) VALUE(',')
                GOTO       CMDLBL(READ)

END_READ:       CHGVAR     VAR(&SQL) VALUE(&SQL *BCAT 'FROM')
                IF         COND(&FILELIB *NE ' ' *AND &FILELIB *NE +
                             *LIBL) THEN(DO)
                CHGVAR     VAR(&SQL) VALUE(&SQL *BCAT &FILELIB *TCAT +
                             '/' *CAT &FILENAME)
                ENDDO
                ELSE       CMD(DO)
                CHGVAR     VAR(&SQL) VALUE(&SQL *BCAT &FILENAME)
                ENDDO

                IF         COND(&CLAUSES *NE ' ') THEN(DO)
                CHGVAR     VAR(&SQL) VALUE(&SQL *BCAT &CLAUSES)
                ENDDO

                CHGVAR     VAR(&CMDCHK) VALUE('?EXCSQLSTM SQLSTM(''' +
                             *CAT &SQL *TCAT ''') OUTPUT(' *CAT +
                             &OUTPUT *TCAT ')')

/* Prompt the SQL command */
                CALL       PGM(QCMDCHK) PARM(&CMDCHK 1024)
                MONMSG     MSGID(CPF6801) EXEC(GOTO CMDLBL(SNDRQSMSG)) +
                             /* F3 or F12 */

/* Execute the SQL command */
                CALL       PGM(QCMDEXC) PARM(&CMDCHK 1024)

/* Send the SQL command to the calling program */
 SNDRQSMSG:     SNDPGMMSG  MSG(&CMDCHK) TOPGMQ(*PRV) MSGTYPE(*RQS) +
                             KEYVAR(&MRK)
                RCVMSG     PGMQ(*PRV) MSGKEY(&MRK) RMV(*NO)

/* Send all messages back to the calling program */
 FWDMSG:        RCVMSG     MSGDTA(&MSGDTA) MSGID(&MSGID) MSGF(&MSGF) +
                             SNDMSGFLIB(&MSGFLIB) /* FORWARD MESSAGES */
                MONMSG     MSGID(CPF0000)

                IF         COND(&MSGID *NE ' ') THEN(DO)
                SNDPGMMSG  MSGID(&MSGID) MSGF(&MSGFLIB/&MSGF)
MSGDTA(&MSGDTA)
                MONMSG     MSGID(CPF0000)
                GOTO       CMDLBL(FWDMSG)
                ENDDO

                ENDPGM
```

Figure 19.7: SQL004CL runs the SQL statement and enables it to be retrieved with the F9 key (part 2 of 2).

SQL004CL uses the Display File Field Description (DSPFFD) command to get the names of the fields. (It might run a little faster if I used APIs, but I wrote this before the APIs were introduced, and it runs plenty fast enough as it is.) Next, it puts the SELECT statement into a proper command and calls QCMDEXC to prompt it. In this example, the version of SQL used is Execute SQL Statement (EXCSQLSTM) command.

At this point, I can make changes to the generated command. I often delete unwanted fields and add additional clauses (such as ORDER BY). At this point, I can see the field names. When I press Enter, the SQL statement runs. SQL004CL sends the generated SQL statement back to the caller in a request message so I can retrieve it with the F9 key.

I use this command when I want to select many or most of the fields in a file. It's often easier to delete the fields I don't want than to key in the names of those I do want. I also use it when I'm working with a file whose field names I don't know off the top of my head. The only problem I've had with this utility is that sometimes the resulting string is too large to fit into the generated command. Fortunately, this doesn't happen often.

—Ted Holt

Store SQL Output in a File

Q: How do I save the results of an SQL query to an output file? I'm using interactive SQL to do queries, and I need to be able to save the results into a table.

A: When you are in interactive SQL, press F13. Select option 1—Change Session Attributes. Change the SELECT output parameter to 3 (which means that output goes to a file). You will be asked for a name and library for the output file. You also can choose whether or not to create the file or whether to append to an existing file.

—Brian Singleton

✦ ✦ ✦ Null Values

Replacing Null Values with Default Values

Q: How do I get rid of null values in my SQL query result set? I want to retrieve the records with null values, but I would like to put a default value in the field instead of just receiving NULL.

A: The SQL VALUE function will handle this nicely. The function will return the first value that is not null from a list of values given to it. So, to make it return a default value when a field is NULL, use the following syntax:

798

```
Select Field1, VALUE(Field2,'Default') from File
```

Now, whenever Field2 is NULL, you will get the value 'Default' in the field. You also can use this technique to avoid getting null results in SQL outer joins when there is no matching record.

—Brian Singleton

SQLRPG Gotcha Workaround

We have a network with both PCs and an AS/400 on it. Our PC users have some files, which we created with SQL statements, in a library on the AS/400. Some of the columns are defined as data type TIMESTAMP and some are defined as NULL capable.

The PC users access and maintain these tables with PC programs written in a client/server language. I also have some AS/400 programs—RPG programs that contain embedded SQL statements (source type SQLRPG)—which access and maintain these tables.

I ran into a problem on the AS/400. The Create SQL RPG (CRTSQLRPG) command used to create SQLRPG-type programs does not have the parameters for conversion options (CVTOPT) and does not allow null values (ALWNULL). Fortunately, I found a workaround.

Start by creating the SQLRPG program interactively with the CRTSQLRPG command. Besides creating a program object, the CRTSQLRPG command places a temporary source member into file QSQLTEMP in library QTEMP. This temporary source member contains the embedded SQL statements translated into standard RPG operations. The source member can be compiled with the Create RPG Program (CRTRPGPGM) command, just like any other RPG source member, and herein lies the solution to the problem.

Compile the temporary source member with the CRTRPGPGM command. Compile to the same library you used in the CRTSQLRPG command and specify the parameters CVTOPT(*DATETIME) and ALWNULL(*YES). The resulting program object will replace the program object that was created when you ran the CRTSQLRPG command.

—Brian Spiece

✦ ✦ ✦ Performance

Find Access Plan Information

Q: I've started dabbling with using embedded SQL in my RPG programs. I've heard a great deal about access plans and how they affect the performance of my applications. How can I find out the access plan information for my embedded SQL programs?

A: In a number of cases when you're developing applications that use SQL, you can use interactive SQL to help you find out the access plan information. That helps you know whether the SQL processor is, for example, using an existing index or having to build one on the fly. In some cases, however, it might not be practical to run your statements interactively to find out the access plan information.

Another option is to use the Print SQL Information (PRTSQLINF) command. For example, an SQLRPG program that I created had to build an index on the fly to return the records in the order I wanted. The evidence of that is a line that says "SQL4009 Access path created for file 1" in the PRTSQLINF output.

For this example, I created a keyed logical file. The difference is that the SQLRPG program used my new index instead of building one on the fly. The line to look for is "SQL4008 Access path *xxx* used for file 1."

—Jim Hoopes

Improving SQL Fetch Performance

When retrieving information with embedded SQL, it's common for programmers to set up a loop to execute multiple FETCH statements. For example, a DO loop iterates 100 times to retrieve 100 rows of information. Within the loop, the SQL FETCH statement executes 100 times.

You can improve the SQL program's performance in these situations. Consider replacing the DO loop with a single FETCH FOR n ROWS statement. The DO loop (previously mentioned) could be replaced with the following SQL statement:

```
FETCH cursor_name
   FOR 100 ROWS
   INTO :host_variable ...
```

The database manager needs to perform only one SQL call instead of 100.

A word of caution: For performance reasons, do not mix single- and multiple-row fetches against the same cursor.

—Richard Shaler

SQL Access Paths

Q: How do I see what indexes are being used by my SQL statements?

A: You can see the access plan of an SQL query by starting debug (STRDBG) before you issue the Start SQL (STRSQL) command. After entering interactive SQL, type in and execute your query as normal. When your query is finished, press the SYSREQ key and press Enter. Select option 3 (Display current job); the Display Job panel appears. From the Display Job panel, select option 10 (Display job log...); the Display Job Log panel appears. Press F10 to display detailed messages. You might have to scroll back a bit, but eventually you'll see the SQL statement preparation and execution job log entries.

The second level help text of these messages, accessed by putting the cursor on the message and pressing Help, is usually very specific about which access paths were used and the reasons for the optimizer's decisions. Making sure the SQL statement uses an access path instead of the arrival sequence (meaning the query optimizer reads the file one record at a time for the entire file) can make a tremendous difference in the speed of your SQL statement.

—Brian Singleton

SQL Join Improvement

Q: How can I improve the performance of AS/400 multiple-file SQL joins? I tried tuning my query to use indexes, but it still takes a while to process. Is there anything I can try to speed it up further?

A: Sometimes when you have to join several large files with a single dynamic SQL statement, you can optimize all day long and not get the desired level of performance. Another technique to improve performance would be to create an AS/400 join logical file that performs the joins at the system level (meaning the SQL optimizer doesn't have to). Then just change your SQL statement to select from the single join logical file.

Creating a join logical file allows the system to have the recordset prepared as much as possible before the SQL statement is executed, which could result in a shorter recordset retrieval time. The tradeoff is that each time one of the joined files is updated, performance of that update might suffer a little because of the required update of the join logical file. You still have to pay the performance penalty somewhere, but it might be better to pay it a little at a time than to wait and pay it all at once while your dynamic recordset is built.

—Brian Singleton

✦ ✦ ✦ Sorting

Sorting Tips

In database files, you sometimes find that a date has been stored in three separate fields: one for the year, one for the month, and one for the day. If you need to compare two such dates using SQL, you can do it by calculating a single value for each date. For example, suppose the first date occupies fields YY1, MM1, and DD1, and the second date occupies fields YY2, MM2, and DD2. In this case, you could use the following SQL statement:

```
SELECT * FROM EMPMST
WHERE (YY1*10000+MM1*100+DD1) >
      (YY2*10000+MM2*100+DD2)
```

In many situations, part of a field is used as the key for the sorting purposes. For example, suppose you have a 10-byte character field called CODE and you want to sequence the records by the first 2 bytes followed by positions 5 and 6. Here's what the SQL statement might look like:

```
SELECT SUBSTR(CODE,1,2) CONCAT SUBSTR(CODE,5,2),
       NAME, REGN
FROM SUPMST
WHERE REGN = 'NORTH'
ORDER BY 1
```

The first field in the SELECT statement is derived by extracting two portions of the CODE field and concatenating them. In the ORDER BY clause, 1 means use the first field in the SELECT list. To sort by more than one field, separate the field numbers with a comma (e.g., ORDER BY 4, 2).

If you have a database file in which a date has been defined as a six-digit numeric field in YYMMDD format, you might need to sort on just the YY portion of the date followed by another field in the file. For example, suppose you want to sort on the year portion of a field called ORDDAT followed by a field called ITEM#. In this case, the SQL statement might look like this:

```
SELECT INTEGER(ORDDAT/10000),
       ITEM#, DEPT
FROM ITMTRN
WHERE DEPT = '02'
ORDER BY 1, 2
```

In this example, the first field in the SELECT clause is derived by dividing ORDDAT by 10,000. This process moves the decimal point four places to the left, immediately following the year. The INTEGER function eliminates the fractional portion of the field containing the month and day, thereby leaving only the year. The ORDER BY clause sequences the records by the derived year and the ITEM# field.

—Vijay Yadav

TCP/IP and the Web

TCP/IP
and the Web

◆   ◆   ◆   ◆

In This Chapter

APIs

Batch FTP

Email

FTP and *SAVF

FTP and Commands

FTP and IFS

FTP Utility

FTP

HTTP

IFS

PC Commands

SNMP

TCP/IP Address

TCP/IP
    Communication

TCP/IP Maintenance

TCP/IP Services

◆   ◆   ◆   ◆

*I*n today's Internet-connected world, you need to understand more than how to simply turn on your computer and fire up your browser. You also need to understand the basics of using TCP/IP and its associated services. And once you learn the basics, you'll then need to learn how to get "behind the scenes" of the TCP/IP world. You'll also need to learn all about TCP/IP services on your iSeries 400. And that's not always an easy thing to do, because, let's face it, working with the iSeries TCP/IP services isn't easy. There's a lot of information and a lot of complexity built into these services. It's more than one person can know.

That's where this chapter on TCP/IP can help. This chapter offers the best of the combined knowledge of our technical editors and our readers so that you can gain the most complete understanding of how to use your iSeries system and its TCP/IP services in the most effective way possible. With that in mind, you'll find a whole wealth of tips on such varied topics as:

- Transferring iSeries Save Files (*SAVF) with TCP/IP.
- Working with HTTP Server.
- Finding out which port a TCP/IP service is running on.
- Learning to use the QSYS.LIB file system in ways you never thought possible.
- Using SNMP and SMTP.
- Emailing files using the Send Distribution command.
- And much, much more.

So get ready to learn the TCP/IP tips and techniques that will make you the TCP/IP star in your shop.

—*Shannon O'Donnell*

✦ ✦ ✦ APIs

API Really Means "Apply Patch Immediately"

The AS/400's HTTP server provides an excellent way to gather information from your customers and suppliers. To make this task easier, IBM provides several APIs that allow you to process data entered on a form on a Web page with the languages most familiar to AS/400 programmers, such as RPG and COBOL. Unfortunately, if you have upgraded to V4R1 or higher, you have probably discovered that the Convert to Database (**QtmhCvtDb**) API no longer processes form data correctly.

QtmhCvtDb is used in conjunction with another API, Standard Input (**QtmhStdIn**), to map data entered into a Web page form to fields in a physical file. Figure 20.1 shows the code for a simple form that allows a customer to enter name and address information in order to be added to a mailing list that is stored in a physical file. (For this example, Name and Address serve as the name and address.) Clicking on the Process Form button initiates a call to the CGI program TESTRPG001. (This is specified as the action on the form tag.)

```
<html>
<head>
<title>QtmhCvtDb API Fix</title>
</head>
<body>
<form METHOD="post" action="/cgi-bin/testrpg001.pgm"">
<div align="center">
<center>
<p><strong>QtmhCvtDb API Fix</strong></p>
</center>
<hr>
<table>
<tr>
<td>Name</td>
<td><input type="text" name="name" SIZE="30"></td>
</tr>
<tr>
<td>Address</td>
<td><input type="text" name="address" size="40"></td>
</tr>
<tr>
<td colspan="2"><input type="submit" value="Process Form"></td>
</tr>
</table>
</div><hr>
<!- The following line of code solves the problem ->
<input type="hidden" name="junk">
</form>
</body>
</html>
```

Figure 20.1: Use this HTML form to allow entry of a name and an address.

A call to QTMHSTDIN retrieves the data from the standard input buffer of the HTTP server and returns the following string to the CGI program:

```
name=Anyone&address=Anywhere
```

The QTMHCVTDB API is then called to map the data entered into the corresponding fields of a physical file. At this point, the physical file field **name** should have a value of **Anyone** and the field **address** should have a value of **Anywhere**. Unfortunately, QTMHCVTDB contains a bug that causes corruption of the data entered in the last form element. If the last form element has a size of one, the data entered is lost entirely; if the form element has a size other than one, the value of the address is returned as a string containing the data entered followed by garbage. Therefore, in this example, address is returned as **Anywhere** plus 32 indecipherable characters that do not look very nice on a mailing label!

Fortunately, there is a simple way to overcome this obstacle. Simply add the following line of code as the last element of the HTML table:

```
<input type="hidden" name="junk">
```

This code causes the corrupted data to be parsed into the hidden field, where it no longer poses a problem. Until a PTF is announced to correct the situation, using this method provides a simple fix.

—David Mayle

✦ ✦ ✦ Batch FTP

FTP Batch Transfer from AS/400 to PC

Are you looking for a way to get data from your AS/400 to your PC in batch mode? Well, if your PC is attached to your AS/400 via TCP/IP or even a shared network, you can do it. The code shown in Figure 20.2 is a batch program named MYFTP. BAT. MYFTP. BAT uses the FTP switch -s to indicate that the batch program—the PC file extension of *. BAT—uses another file (MYFTP.CMD) for FTP commands.

```
FTP -s:C:\windows\myftp.cmd
```

Figure 20.2: Use this PC batch program to download data from your AS/400.

Now, look at the code shown in Figure 20.3. This file contains the commands to connect to my AS/400. The second and third lines are my user ID and password. The FTP command get is used to download the file from the AS/400 to the PC. In this case, it downloads a file named CFM05P from the library named SCHEDULE and places that file on my PC's hard drive in a file named CFM05P.TXT. When the FTP program finishes downloading, it ends via the FTP command quit. Notice that all the commands are in lowercase. This distinction is important because FTP is an import from UNIX, and UNIX is case-sensitive.

```
open 100.59.191.50
MYUSERID
MYPASSWORD
get SCHEDULE/CFM05P C:\CFM05P.TXT
quit
```

Figure 20.3: These FTP commands connect to and download AS/400 data.

Adding this batch program to an application's macro or even to a scheduling system on your PC is now a simple matter. This method allows your users to download data without needing to run to you for help every time.

—*Shannon O'Donnell*
—*Bradley V. Stone*

✦ ✦ ✦ Email

TCP/IP and MIME

Q: Our company is new to the world of TCP/IP. Lately, in discussions with other TCP/IP folks, I've been hearing about something called MIME. Can you give me a brief explanation of MIME?

A: Multipurpose Internet Mail Extension (MIME) is a compound document messaging standard for the Internet. MIME allows users to transmit multimedia email. This email could include graphics, video, audio, and text. Rich text information, which defines the layout, fonts, and format of email documents, may also be included.

—*Kris Neely*

Emailing Messages and Files with the SNDDST Command

The Send Distribution (SNDDST) command enables you to send messages and files by email from a CL program or command line to non-AS/400 systems. You can send various types of information or objects with SNDDST. This tip explains three types of information and objects you can send: Long Message (*LMSG), File (*FILE), and Document (*DOC). The *LMSG type allows you to send a message of up to 5000 characters. The only place I've seen documentation for *LMSG is on the cover letters for the PTFs. *LMSG has only two formatting commands, :/N and :/P. The :/N command creates a new line, while :/P creates a new paragraph (which means a blank line and a new line). Here is an example of a SNDDST command using *LMSG and how the received email would look:

```
SNDDST TYPE(*LMSG) TOINTNET((murphyfa@uiuc.edu)) DSTD('Test Message') +
LONGMSG('This is a test message.:/NA new line.:/PA new paragraph.') +
SUBJECT('Tech Talk Long MessageDemo')

This is a test message.
A new line.

A new paragraph.
```

You can also send physical files, logical files, or source files as email with SNDDST. This is an example of SNDDST used to send a file:

```
SNDDST TYPE(*FILE) TOINTNET((murphyfa@uiuc.edu)) DSTD('Test Message') +
MSG(*NONE) DOCFILE(LIB/FILE) DOCMBR(*FIRST) DOCTYPE(*FFT) +
SUBJECT('Tech Talk File Demo')
```

This command places the contents of the file in the body of the email message. The trick is to specify a DOCTYPE of *FFT or 2, causing the file to be converted into ASCII text. There are limitations, however. SNDDST adds no carriage return or line feed. Line-feeds characters to the ends of records, so the beginning of the next record starts where the previous one stopped. In addition, source file records have their line numbers and date fields at the front, and packed decimal and binary fields are clobbered when SNDDST tries to convert their bytes into ASCII text.

Using the Copy to PC Document (CPYTOPCD) and Copy from PC Document (CPYFRMPCD) commands is a quick-and-dirty way to get the CR (Carriage Return) and LF (Line Feed) characters into a file (and get rid of the line numbers and date fields in source files). Translation Format (TRNFMT) (*TEXT) on CPYTOPCD adds the CR and LF, and TRNFMT (*NOTEXT) on CPYFRMPCD keeps them in the new file. The new file can have any record length, even 1 byte. SNDDST reads it as a stream of characters, and record length doesn't matter. That's what causes the formatting problem in the first place. When you send the new file with SNDDST, the text is formatted properly. Of course, if your file has a very long record length, it wraps around anyway because most email readers can't properly display something that wide. Here are some examples:

```
CPYTOPCD FROMFILE(LIB/OLDFILE) TOFLR(FOLDER) FROMMBR(MEMBER) +
TODOC(PCDOX.TXT) REPLACE(*YES) TRNTBL(*DFT) TRNFMT(*TEXT) *

CPYFRMPCD FROMFLR(FOLDER) TOFILE(LIB/NEWFILE) FROMDOC(PCDOC.TXT) +
TOMBR(MEMBER) MBROPT(*REPLACE) TRNTBL(*DFT) TRNFMT(*NOTEXT)

SNDDST TYPE(*FILE) TOINTNET((murphyfa@uiuc.edu)) +
DSTD('Test Message') MSG(*NONE) DOCFILE(LIB/NEWFILE) +
DOCMBR(*FIRST) DOCTYPE(*FFT) SUBJECT('Tech Talk File Demo')
```

An email attachment is a better way to send a file, and this is where the *DOC information type comes in. First, copy the file to a PC document just as you did previously. Then, send the PC document. SNDDST looks something like the following example:

```
SNDDST TYPE(*DOC) TOINTNET((murphy@uiuc.edu)) DSTD('PC Document') +
DOC(PCDOC.TXT) FLR(FOLDER) SUBJECT('Attached File')
```

You still have to worry about packed decimal and binary fields being mangled, but everything else comes through okay.

Before you can use SNDDST as just described, you must prepare your system. You must first have SNADS, TCP/IP, and Simple Mail Transfer Protocol (SMTP) all configured and working properly. All of that is a tad beyond the scope of this section. See the *OS/400 TCP/IP Configuration and Reference* manual if you haven't done all of that stuff already. Next, if you are not using V4R3, you need to apply one set of the following PTFs:

- SF45257 and SF48224 for V4R2.
- SF45226 and SF48223 for V4R1.
- SF45415 for V3R7.
- SF45328 for V3R2.

On all OS versions, the Change Distribution Attributes (CHGDSTA) command must be executed to make SNDDST work with the Internet, and, for CHGDSTA to work, you must make an entry for a gateway to SMTP in your system directory. Details are on the help screens for the CHGDSTA command.

—Guy Murphy

Set Up a Postmaster Account on the AS/400 with SMTP

Q: I've set up Simple Mail Transfer Protocol (SMTP) on my AS/400 so that my OfficeVision users can exchange email with users on the Internet. On most email systems, a profile is set up so that a remote user having a problem sending a message can ask a question to get the problem resolved. For example, a remote user who tries to send a message to an address that doesn't exist will often want to ask if the email address is different or if the person no longer works for the company. Usually, you'd send an email message to postmaster@yourdomainname.dom in that case. Is there a way to accomplish that with SMTP on the AS/400?

A: Yes, there is. Using the Add Directory Entry (ADDDIRE) command, you can create a postmaster account. Use a user ID of POST and an address of MASTER. Set the user ID to someone who isn't already set up in the distribution directory. That person will start getting messages for the postmaster user through SMTP.

—Jim Hoopes

✦ ✦ ✦ FTP

Trimming Blanks with FTP

Some folks have problems when FTPing a file from the AS/400 to a PC: It tends to trim blanks from the end of the record. So, if you have a record that is 100 characters long and the longest record is only 85 characters long (followed by 15 blanks), the record length on your PC will be 85. To fix this, use the following command before sending the data to tell the AS/400 not to trim ending blanks:

```
LOCSITE TRIM 0
```

You can also use the following commands:

```
LOCSITE TRIM 1
LOCSITE TRIM
```

The former of these two commands will trim blanks; the latter will display the current value for TRIM.

—Bradley V. Stone

✦ ✦ ✦ FTP and *SAVF

Can I Convert a PF to a *SAVF with FTP?

Q: I used FTP to transfer a save file from one AS/400 to another, but I forgot to create the save file on the receiving AS/400 first. Now, I have a physical file. Can I convert this physical file back to a save file?

—Dale Monti

A: You cannot take the physical file and create a save file from it, but you can re-FTP the file from your PC. Use the following commands to recreate your save file without losing the data in it. Assume, for example, that you inadvertently created a physical file named DATA1 on your AS/400. It should have been a save file, but you forgot to create the save file first. To transfer the data from DATA1 into a new save file in library QGPL, do the following:

1. From an AS/400 command line, create a save file named NEWSAVF in a library. (In this example, I'll use library QGPL):

```
CRTSAVF QGPL/NEWSAVF
```

2. Now, start the FTP on the AS/400 and use the following FTP commands to move the data from your physical file (that should have been a save file) into the new save file in QGPL:

```
ftp system name
user Your User ID
pass Your Password
binary
put DATA1 QGPL/NEWSAVF
quit
```

—Chuck Pence

Create a Save File Before You Transfer a Save File

Q: I am trying to transfer a save file (*SAVF) from one AS/400 to another using FTP. Everything seems to work fine until I try to restore the save file on the target system. I get a message CPF3782, "File {save file name} in {library name} not a save file." Can you help?

A: Before you perform the transfer, create a save file on the target system. You can create the save file on the target system in your FTP session with the FTP subcommand quote and the server command rcmd (as illustrated in Figure 20.4).

```
binary
  quote rcmd CRTSAVF TGTLIB/SAVEFILE
  put srclib/savefile tgtlib/savefile
  quote rcmd RSTOBJ OBJ(PGMX) SAVLIB(SRCLIB) DEV(*SAVF)
                    SAVF(TGTLIB/SAVEFILE) RSTLIB(TGTLIB)
```

Figure 20.4: Using FTP, this sample code allows you to transfer a save file.

When you transfer the file with the FTP put subcommand, be sure to specify the name of the save file you created on the target system as the remote file name. (The remote file name is the same as the local file name if the remote file name is not specified.) Figure 20.4 illustrates a sample FTP session that transfers a save file to a target system and restores the object contained in the save file to library TGTLIB.

—Richard Shaler

FTPing Save Files

Here's a very easy method of saving data to an AS/400 save file, and then emailing it to someone at a remote site to load and restore on their AS/400.

1. Save the object(s) or library(s) in an AS/400 save file (*SAVF) using the standard AS/400 Save Object (SAVOBJ) or Save Library (SAVLIB) commands.

2. Start an FTP session on your PC (or on your AS/400, depending on which one you are most comfortable using).

3. Here's the key to making this work correctly. Enter the FTP command binary in lowercase letters. This will cause the data to be transferred as a binary image.

4. Now use the FTP put command or get command (the command you use will depend on whether you are sending data to the PC from your AS/400 or getting data from your AS/400 and loading it onto the PC), to load the save file onto your PC.

5. Email the file to wherever you want it to go.

6. At the remote site, use the same steps as outlined above to put the save file on the remote AS/400. Make sure the remote site also uses the FTP **binary** command to ensure the file is transferred as a binary image.

7. Use the AS/400 command Restore Object (RSTOBJ) or Restore Library (RSTLIB) to restore the save file.

That's all there is to it!

—*Shannon O'Donnell*
—*Brad Stone*

Transferring AS/400 Save Files with FTP

AS/400 save files are the PKZIP of the midrange. I transfer them all the time using FTP. I can quickly transfer a save file from one AS/400 to another, or I can download a save file to my PC and send it to whomever as an email include. The process is simple, and, if you are comfortable with FTP, I can summarize it in one word: binary. The AS/400's implementation of FTP assumes, unless told otherwise, that file transfers are for text files and, as such, will require EBCDIC-to-ASCII translation. Just think what that'll do to your save file! The **binary** FTP directive says, "don't do that" to the AS/400.

In a nutshell, then, here's how to FTP a save file from an AS/400 to a PC and from an AS/400 to another AS/400.

Downloading an AS/400 Save File to Your PC

1. Start FTP on your PC (FTP.EXE).

2. Type in the **open** command, and FTP will prompt you for the TCP/IP address or Host Name of the AS/400 system from which you are transferring files. It will also prompt you for the user profile name and password to use when logging on to your AS/400. Enter the appropriate information.

3. Enter the **binary** directive (or the abbreviation, BIN).

4. Get your save file to the PC with the **get Library/SaveFileName PCFileName** command.

For instance, to download a save file called SAVESTUFF in my DENONCOURT library to the C:\work\mc\september directory on my PC, I entered the following command:

```
get DENONCOURT/SAVESTUFF c:\work\mc\september\SaveStuff.sav
```

Uploading a PC File That Contains an AS/400 Save File to an AS/400

1. Create or clear the AS/400 save file that is to be uploaded. If the save file does not already exist, FTP will create a file for you, and it will not be of type *SAVF:

```
quote rcmd CRTSAVF DENONCOURT/RESTORSTUF
```

Or

```
quote rcmd CLRSAVF DENONCOURT/RESTORSTUF
```

2. Start FTP on your PC (FTP.EXE).

3. Type in the **open** command, and FTP will prompt you for the necessary login information, including TCP/IP address or Host Name of the AS/400 system, user profile name, and password.

4. Enter the **binary** directive (or the abbreviation, BIN).

5. Transfer the file from your PC to the AS/400 with FTP's **put** command:

```
put c:\work\mc\september\SaveStuff.sav DENONCOURT/RESTORSTUF
```

Transferring an AS/400 Save File Between AS/400s

1. Start FTP:

```
STRTCPFTP RMTSYS(Other400DomainName)
```

2. Enter your user profile and password.

3. Create or clear the AS/400 save file that is to be uploaded. If the save file does not already exist, FTP will create a file for you, and it will not be of type *SAVF:

```
quote CRTSAVF DENONCOURT/RESTORSTUF
```

Or

```
quote CLRSAVF DENONCOURT/RESTORSTUF
```

4. Enter the **binary** directive (or the abbreviation, BIN).

5. Transfer the file from the local or current AS/400 to the host AS/400 with FTP's **put** command:

```
put DENONCOURT/RESTORSTUF HOSTLIB/RESTORSTUF
```

Optionally, you could transfer the file from the host AS/400 to the current or local AS/400 with FTP's **get** command:

```
get HOSTLIB/RESTORSTUF DENONCOURT/RESTORSTUF (REPLACE
```

For the **get** command only, you need to use the (REPLACE parameter to clear out the save file on your AS/400 (the **put** command clears out the save file for you). Note that there is no closing parenthesis on this parameter.

Caution: Take care when transferring a save file from one AS/400 to another or you might overlay an important save file. It's easy to get confused if the library and file names are the same. FTP is so easy to use that you can easily update the new version of a library with an old version—effectively wiping out all of your updates. Just remember that the TCP/IP address that FTP uses is considered the host site. The FTP **get** command copies the file from the host to the local machine (the one from which you entered the Start TCP/IP FTP (STRTCPFTP) command). The FTP **put** command copies the file from the local machine to the host machine.

—Don Denoncourt

◆ ◆ ◆ FTP and Commands

Execute Remote Commands with FTP

Q: Can you recommend a product on the AS/400 that will accept remote commands? I use the remsh (Remote Shell) command from our RS/6000 to execute processing on other UNIX platforms. We also have an RS/6000 communicating with our AS/400 using TCP/IP. I would like to execute CL commands on the AS/400 from the RS/6000.

A: You can execute AS/400 commands from a remote system by using FTP. After you FTP to your AS/400, use the QUOTE subcommand with the RCMD parameter followed by the command you want to execute. For example, if you want to run the Work with Active Jobs (WRKACTJOB) command, you would enter this from within an FTP session:

```
QUOTE RCMD WRKACTJOB OUTPUT(*PRINT)
```

—Robin Klima

◆ ◆ ◆ FTP and IFS

Pick the Right Name Format

If you want to take advantage of the FTP support for shared folders, which IBM added to FTP in V3R1, you have to use the new FTP subcommand NAMEFMT. It allows you to change the default naming format of Library/File.Member (NAMEFMT 0) to /QSYS.LIB/ Library.Lib/Filename.File/Member.MBR (NAMEFMT 1).

While this might seem like more work to access regular system objects, it is the only way to access shared folders with FTP. For example, the files for Client Access for DOS are in directory /QDLS/QIWSFL2. But there's a problem with the NAMEFMT command: It only works when an AS/400 is the FTP client. If you FTP from your PC to the AS/400, executing subcommand NAMEFMT produces an error. This is because the PC's FTP client doesn't know anything about name formats. You need to change the FTP server on the AS/400, which you can do with this command:

```
QUOTE SITE NAMEFMT 1
```

The FTP server on the AS/400 (not on the client) executes this command. The AS/400 will then understand the new naming format.

—Martin Pluth

FTP Files Directly to AS/400 Folders

Q: Is it possible to FTP a file from an NT workstation directly to an AS/400 folder?

A: The answer to your question is yes and—according to IBM's AS/400 manuals—you should be able to FTP to a number of different directories in the AS/400 Integrated File System (IFS) directory structure. I looked in the online *OS/400 TCP/IP Configuration and Reference V4R2* manual (*http://AS400bks.rochester.ibm.com/library.htm*) and found that OS/400 supports FTP for the following AS/400 file systems (this information is quoted from chapter 9 of the manual):

- QSYS.LIB library file system—libraries, files, members. FTP supports the transfer of save files and members in physical files, logical files, DDM files, and source physical files.

- QDLS document library services—folders and documents.

  The QDLS file system is registered with the hierarchical file system (HFS) on an AS/400 system.

  FTP transfers files that reside in registered HFS file systems that are accessed using the HFS APIs. In addition to the QDLS file system, HFS file systems include:

  - QOPT optical file system

    See "Transferring HFS Files" in topic 9.12.54.4 and "Transferring QDLS Documents" in topic 9.12.54.5 for additional information. For further information about HFS APIs, see the *System API Reference* book.

  - "root"

    The / file system. This file system is designed to take full advantage of the stream file support and hierarchical directory structure of the integrated file system. It has the characteristics of the DOS and OS/2 file systems.

  - QOpenSys

    The open systems file system. This file system is designed to be compatible with UNIX-based open system standards, such as POSIX** and XPG. Like the root file system, it takes advantage of the stream file and directory support provided by the integrated file system. It supports case-sensitive names.

- QLANSrv

  The LAN Server file system. This file system provides access to the same directories and files that are accessed through the LAN Server licensed program. It allows users of the OS/400 file server and AS/400 applications to use the same data as LAN Server clients.

- QFileSvr.400

  The OS/400 file server file system. This file system provides access to other file systems that reside on remote AS/400 systems. Access to QSYS.LIB, QDLS, and QOPT using QFileSvr.400 is not supported by FTP.

There are also some tricks with FTPing to an AS/400 regarding whether you want to FTP to the OS/400 file system (QSYS.LIB) or to other directories on the AS/400 IFS system. This manual will answer most of your questions about how to configure your AS/400 as an FTP server, the configuration settings that need to be set, and the syntax for transferring files up and down. In particular, you'll want to read over the parts that discuss the FTP server NAMEFMT parameter because that will affect the FTP file syntax.

If you're not on V4R2 and want to read the TCP/IP manual for your particular operating system, you can go to the AS/400 Online Library for all versions and look up the TCP/IP manual for your particular OS version. It's a great online reference that has all the OS/400 manuals as well as the Redbooks. In addition, if you're running a slow modem connection or want to bypass the online manual, you can download the RISC machine manuals as Portable Data Format (PDF) files and use Adobe Acrobat to read them.

—Joe Hertvik

✦ ✦ ✦ FTP Utility

FTP the Easy Way

We all like to make things easier so thatwe can perform better and accomplish more in a shorter amount of time. If you find yourself making a lot of repetitive keystrokes, you might find that you're wasting a lot of time that could be better spent doing something else.

I found myself in this situation when sending data and objects between multiple AS/400s. I was constantly typing the same commands over and over again. I finally got tired of repeating myself, so, one day, I sat back and wrote a command to eliminate almost all the keying required to send objects from one system to another. What I needed was a way to automate the save and restore processes on the source and target systems. I ended up with the AUTOFTP command (Figure 20.5). Source code is shown in Figure 20.6.

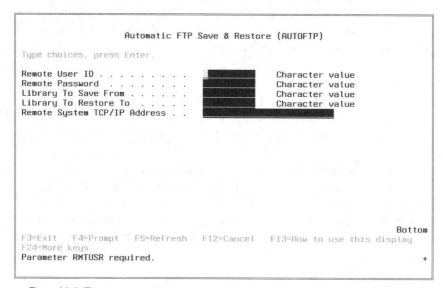

```
                  Automatic FTP Save & Restore (AUTOFTP)

Type choices, press Enter.

Remote User ID . . . . . . . . .              Character value
Remote Password  . . . . . . . .              Character value
Library To Save From . . . . . .              Character value
Library To Restore To  . . . . .              Character value
Remote System TCP/IP Address . .

                                                                  Bottom
F3=Exit    F4=Prompt   F5=Refresh   F12=Cancel   F13=How to use this display
F24=More keys
Parameter RMTUSR required.                                              +
```

Figure 20.5: The AUTOFTP utility helps you automate save/restore on remote AS/400s.

```
/****************************************************************************/
/*                                                                        */
/* CRTCMD CMD(XXX/AUTOFTP) PGM(XXX/FS001C) SRCFILE(XXX/QCMDSRC) +          */
/*        MBR(AUTOFTP)                                                     */
/*                                                                        */
/****************************************************************************/
             CMD         PROMPT('Automatic FTP Save & Restore')

             PARM        KWD(RMTUSR) TYPE(*CHAR) LEN(10) MIN(1) +
                           PROMPT('Remote User ID')

             PARM        KWD(RMTPASS) TYPE(*CHAR) LEN(10) MIN(1) +
                           PROMPT('Remote Password')

             PARM        KWD(FROMLIB) TYPE(*CHAR) LEN(10) MIN(1) +
                           PROMPT('Library To Save From')

             PARM        KWD(TOLIB) TYPE(*CHAR) LEN(10) MIN(1) +
                           PROMPT('Library To Restore To')

             PARM        KWD(SYS) TYPE(*CHAR) LEN(20) RSTD(*NO) +
                           MIN(1) PROMPT('Remote System TCP/IP Address')
```

Figure 20.6: Use this source to create the AUTOFTP command shown in Figure 20.5.

The command works like this. Enter the command name on a command line and give it the following parameters:

- A valid user ID and password on the remote system.
- The library on the source system from which objects are to be saved.
- The library on the remote system to which objects are to be restored.
- The TCP/IP address of the remote system.

When the command runs, you are prompted for the names of the objects you want to save. The objects are saved in a temporary save file created in QTEMP. CL program FS001C (Figure 20.7), which is also the command processor, builds the FTP command variables by using the information you enter on the command. You then write these variables to the temporary FTP script file QTEMP/FTPCMD by using RPG program FS001R (Figure 20.8). All that's left is for the program to run the FTP command. Your saved objects are then on their way to the remote system—where they are restored. This little utility has made my life a whole lot easier.

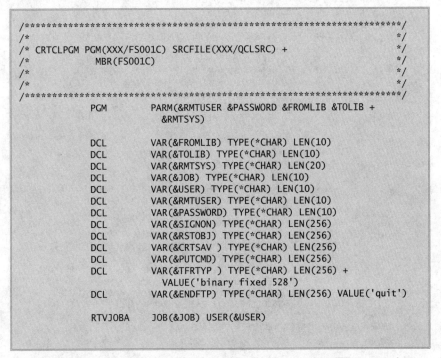

```
/****************************************************************/
/*                                                              */
/*                                                            */
/* CRTCLPGM PGM(XXX/FS001C) SRCFILE(XXX/QCLSRC) +             */
/*          MBR(FS001C)                                       */
/*                                                            */
/*                                                            */
/****************************************************************/
            PGM         PARM(&RMTUSER &PASSWORD &FROMLIB &TOLIB +
                          &RMTSYS)

            DCL         VAR(&FROMLIB) TYPE(*CHAR) LEN(10)
            DCL         VAR(&TOLIB) TYPE(*CHAR) LEN(10)
            DCL         VAR(&RMTSYS) TYPE(*CHAR) LEN(20)
            DCL         VAR(&JOB) TYPE(*CHAR) LEN(10)
            DCL         VAR(&USER) TYPE(*CHAR) LEN(10)
            DCL         VAR(&RMTUSER) TYPE(*CHAR) LEN(10)
            DCL         VAR(&PASSWORD) TYPE(*CHAR) LEN(10)
            DCL         VAR(&SIGNON) TYPE(*CHAR) LEN(256)
            DCL         VAR(&RSTOBJ) TYPE(*CHAR) LEN(256)
            DCL         VAR(&CRTSAV ) TYPE(*CHAR) LEN(256)
            DCL         VAR(&PUTCMD) TYPE(*CHAR) LEN(256)
            DCL         VAR(&TFRTYP ) TYPE(*CHAR) LEN(256) +
                          VALUE('binary fixed 528')
            DCL         VAR(&ENDFTP) TYPE(*CHAR) LEN(256) VALUE('quit')

            RTVJOBA     JOB(&JOB) USER(&USER)
```

Figure 20.7: Program FS001C assembles the FTP script and runs the FTP command (part 1 of 3).

```
          CRTSAVF    FILE(QTEMP/&USER) TEXT('temp sav file')
          MONMSG     MSGID(CPF0000)

          CLRSAVF    FILE(QTEMP/&USER)

          ?          SAVOBJ ??OBJ(*N) ?-LIB(&FROMLIB) ?-DEV(*SAVF) +
                     ??OBJTYPE(*FILE) ?-VOL(*N) ?-SEQNBR(*N) +
                     ?-LABEL(*N) ?-EXPDATE(*N) ?-ENDOPT(*N) +
                     ?-SAVF(QTEMP/&USER) ?-UPDHST(*N) +
                     ?-CLEAR(*N) ?-PRECHK(*N) ?-SAVACT(*N) +
                     ?-FILEMBR(*N) ?-ACCPTH(*N) ?-STG(*N) +
                     ?-DTACPR(*N)

       /* CPF6801 - F3 OR F12 PRESSED */
          MONMSG     MSGID(CPF6801) EXEC(GOTO CMDLBL(END))

       /* ANY OTHER ERROR MESSAGE       */
          MONMSG     MSGID(CPF0000) EXEC(DO)
          SNDBRKMSG MSG('INVALID LIBRARY OR OBJECT(S)') TOMSGQ(&JOB)
          GOTO CMDLBL(END)
          ENDDO


/* BUILD REMOTE FTP COMMAND STRINGS */

          CHGVAR     VAR(&SIGNON) VALUE(&RMTUSER *BCAT &PASSWORD)


          CHGVAR     VAR(&RSTOBJ) VALUE('quote rcmd RSTOBJ +
                     OBJ(*ALL) SAVLIB(' *TCAT &FROMLIB *TCAT +
                     ')' *TCAT ' DEV(*SAVF) SAVF(QTEMP/' *TCAT +
                     &USER *TCAT ') MBROPT(*ALL)   +
                     ALWOBJDIF(*ALL) RSTLIB(' *TCAT &TOLIB +
                     *TCAT ')')

          CHGVAR     VAR(&CRTSAV ) VALUE('quote rcmd CRTSAVF +
                     FILE(QTEMP/' || &USER || ')')

          CHGVAR     VAR(&PUTCMD) VALUE('put' *BCAT 'QTEMP' *TCAT +
                     '/' *TCAT &USER *BCAT 'QTEMP' *TCAT '/' +
                     *TCAT &USER *BCAT '          ')

/* CREATE TEMP FILES FOR STORING FTP COMMAND OUTPUT */
          CRTSRCPF   FILE(QTEMP/FTPCMD) RCDLEN(500) MBR(*FILE) +
                     AUT(*EXCLUDE)
          MONMSG     MSGID(CPF0000) EXEC(CLRPFM FILE(QTEMP/FTPCMD))

          CRTSRCPF   FILE(QTEMP/FTPLOG) MBR(*FILE) AUT(*EXCLUDE)
          MONMSG     MSGID(CPF0000) EXEC(CLRPFM FILE(QTEMP/FTPLOG))

/* WRITE FTP COMMANDS TO TEMP FTP COMMAND SCRIPT FILE */
```

Figure 20.7: Program FS001C assembles the FTP script and runs the FTP command (part 2 of 3).

```
                CALL        PGM(FS001R) PARM(&SIGNON &TFRTYP &CRTSAV  +
                            &PUTCMD &RSTOBJ &ENDFTP)


     /* EXECUTE FTP SCRIPT */
                OVRDBF      FILE(INPUT) TOFILE(QTEMP/FTPCMD) MBR(*FIRST)
                OVRDBF      FILE(OUTPUT) TOFILE(QTEMP/FTPLOG) MBR(*FIRST)

                FTP         RMTSYS(&RMTSYS)

                DLTOVR      FILE(INPUT OUTPUT)

     /* PRINT LOG OF OUTPUT FROM FTP RUN */
                CPYF        FROMFILE(QTEMP/FTPLOG) TOFILE(QSYSPRT)


     /*  DELETE FTP WORK FILE */
                DLTF        FILE(QTEMP/&USER)

     END:   ENDPGM
```

Figure 20.7: Program FS001C assembles the FTP script and runs the FTP command (part 3 of 3).

```
     **********************************************************************
     *
     *   CRTBNDRPG PGM(xxx/FS001R) SRCFILE(xxx/QRPGLESRC) +
     *             MBR(FS001R)
     *
     *
     **********************************************************************
     FFtpcmd    O  F 256       Disk
     *
     D Signon          S            256
     D Tfrtyp          S            256
     D Crtsav          S            256
     D Putcmd          S            256
     D Rstobj          S            256
     D Endftp          S            256
     D Chgdat          S              6  0
     D Nxtseq          S              6  0
     D Srcdta          S            244
     *
     C     *Entry       Plist
     C                  Parm                      Signon
     C                  Parm                      Tfrtyp
     C                  Parm                      Crtsav
     C                  Parm                      Putcmd
     C                  Parm                      Rstobj
     C                  Parm                      Endftp
     *
```

Figure 20.8: FS001R is the backbone of the AUTOFTP command (part 1 of 2).

```
C                      Move      Udate      Chgdat
C* Add ALL RECORDS TO FTPCMD FILE
C                      Movel     Signon     Srcdta
C                      Z-Add     1          Nxtseq
C                      Except    Doit
C                      Movel     Tfrtyp     Srcdta
C                      Add       1          Nxtseq
C                      Except    Doit
C                      Movel     Crtsav     Srcdta
C                      Add       1          Nxtseq
C                      Except    Doit
C                      Movel     Putcmd     Srcdta
C                      Add       1          Nxtseq
C                      Except    Doit
C                      Movel     Rstobj     Srcdta
C                      Add       1          Nxtseq
C                      Except    Doit
C                      Movel     Endftp     Srcdta
C                      Add       1          Nxtseq
C                      Except    Doit
C                      Eval      *Inlr = *On
OFTPCMD      E         Doit
O                      Nxtseq                  6
O                      Chgdat                 12
```

Figure 20.8: FS001R is the backbone of the AUTOFTP command (part 2 of 2).

—Reza Rafiee

PC Downloads Made Easy with FTP

I often have reason to download AS/400 source physical file members to my PC. And just as often, I need to upload a PC file to the AS/400. Maybe I want to put the text from a lengthy AS/400 source member into a Word document or maybe I want to use a PC editor to write the source for what will become an AS/400 program. I performed these tasks years ago with the source for C programs, and now I'm doing them with Java source. At any rate, here is my streamlined process to use FTP for upload or download of source members:

1. From a DOS window on your PC, execute FTP.EXE with the TCP/IP address of your AS/400; a DOS window will come up requesting your user profile name and password.

2. Enter your user profile name and password.

3. Change your current directory to be the library where your source member resides; for example, to set the current directory to my personal AS/400 library, I'd enter the following:

```
cd DENONCOURT
```

4. Change your local directory to be the PC directory that you are copying your source member to; for example, to set the local directory to my working PC directory for MC's September issue, I would enter the following:

```
lcd C:\Work\MC\September
```

5. To copy an AS/400 source file member to your PC, use FTP's **get** command. For example, to copy the source member called CUSTMAINT from the QRPGLESRC source file in FTP's current directory (DENONCOURT) to a file in my local PC directory called **CustMaint.rpg**, I used the following:

```
get QRPGLESRC.CUSTMAINT CustMaint.rpg
```

This command uses the current directory for the library qualifier of the source file and the local directory for the PC to copy the source member to.

```
get DENONCOURT/QRPGLESRC.CUSTMAINT +
C:\Work\MC\September\CustMaint.rpg
```

This code fully qualifies the location of the library, file, and member to copy and the location of the PC directory and file name to copy it to.

6. To copy a PC text file to an AS/400 source file member, use FTP's **put** command. For example, to copy a file from my local PC directory called **CustMaint.rpg** to a source member called CUSTMAINT from the QRPGLESRC source file in FTP's current directory (DENONCOURT), I used the following:

```
put CustMaint.rpg QRPGLESRC.CUSTMAINT
```

For a complete listing of the FTP command set, type **help** (in lowercase). For a detailed description of one of the FTP commands, type **help** followed by the command name (e.g., **help get**). Note that OS/400's FTP help is superior to the PC's FTP help.

—Don Denoncourt

✦ ✦ ✦ HTTP

End the HTTP Server Safely

When you end certain TCP/IP applications such as the HTTP server, you need to be careful not to end someone else's instance. For example, to end the HTTP application, you don't really need to use ENDTCPSVR SERVER(*HTTP) because the default value of the HTTPSVR parameter is *ALL. Instead, end your instance this way:

```
ENDTCPSVR SERVER(*HTTP) HTTPSVR(your_instance_name)
```

—Bradley V. Stone and Richard Shaler

HTTP Logs Made Easy

If you are like me and have used the IBM HTTP Server for AS/400, you no doubt have started logging activity and errors on your Web site. I found right away that storing these logs in DDS format wouldn't work for me. Therefore, I used the Common log format, which produces logs in a standard format used by other HTTP servers. When I wanted to view these logs, I would view them by using Notepad, resulting in a continuous string of text that was hard to read.

As my site received more hits, my logs reached that magic point where, "This file is too large for Notepad to open." Using WordPad instead turned out to be great. Apparently, in the logs are end-of-line characters that Notepad doesn't recognize, but that WordPad thankfully does. Now with each entry in the logs on a separate line, studying the logs is a lot easier.

—Bradley V. Stone

Managing Web Server Files

If you've been using the HTTP server on the AS/400, you might be wondering how to create and edit your Web pages and upload other objects. I've been using a couple of techniques that have been helpful when storing items in the Integrated File System (IFS).

The first technique is to use Client Access for Windows. It lets you directly access files in the IFS so that you can use your regular PC tools (Notepad, HTML editor, or word processor) to edit the pages. This is also the best way to upload objects such as sounds, graphics, and Java applications to the IFS.

If you simply edit HTML pages, you can use the other technique and do it all on the AS/400. Put the pages in a source physical file, and use SEU to edit the text. Then use the Copy to Stream File (CPYTOSTMF) command to copy the source member to the IFS. I've created a simple PDM option to help with this (see Figure 20.9). The destination, /html, is hardcoded, but you can change it by using F4 to prompt the option. The crucial part of the command is the use of the translation table QSYS/QASCII (/qsys.lib/qascii.tbl in IFS style) to convert the text from EBCDIC to ASCII.

```
CPYTOSTMF FROMMBR('/qsys.lib/&l.lib/&f.file/&n.mbr') +
          TOSTMF('/html/&n.htm') STMFOPT(*REPLACE) +
          CVTDTA(*TBL) TBL('/qsys.lib/qascii.tbl')
```

Figure 20.9: Use this PDM option to easily convert IFS data.

With either method, you might need to modify authority on the newly created IFS files. Use the Change Authority (CHGAUT) or Work with Object Links (WRKLNK) command to set the authority so that *PUBLIC has *EXCLUDE authority and QTMHHTTP (the Web server user profile) has *RX (read and execute) authority.

—Martin Pluth

Resolving Slow HTTP Server Performance on Networks

If you're finding that your HTTP server is experiencing excessive lag time when you use the WAN or the Internet, the problem might be the result of the AS/400 logging the DNS names. Why? Because, by default, the AS/400 performs a reverse-DNS query before sending the requested Web page or before returning the results from a Common Gateway Interface (CGI) or Net.Data query. Consequently, when a client accesses the AS/400's HTTP server, the server sends back a request to the DNS server to verify the client's IP address. This reverse-DNS query is used to retrieve the client's host and domain names so that they can be logged into the AS/400's access log. This query will obviously affect the performance of the HTTP server and CGI programs running on the AS/400, especially if the network bandwidth is narrow (slow connection) or the network's DNS server is overburdened with requests.

To remedy this problem, turn off the reverse-DNS query of the HTTP server by editing the HTTP Server Configuration file and adding this directive: Dnslookup Off. This prevents the reverse-DNS lookup from executing, and only the IP address of the client is logged.

—Thomas M. Stockwell

✦ ✦ ✦ IFS

Cleaning up the AS/400 IFS

I've written several RPG IV applications that create files in the AS/400 Integrated File System (AS/400 IFS) on our AS/400. Too often, during testing, I'll miskey something. As a result, the file name I've created in the AS/400 IFS will contain invalid characters. Such characters might include a file name containing slashes or quote marks: a definite no-no. You'd think that I could use the Work with Links (WRKLNK) command in that directory to delete those files, but that's not the case. The Remove (delete) function of WRKLNK needs a valid AS/400 IFS file name as a parameter to locate the file and remove it. Because the misnamed files I created contain invalid characters, the Remove function fails.

There is a way around this problem, however: using FTP to delete the misnamed files in the AS/400 IFS. To accomplish this, do the following:

1. Start an FTP session on your AS/400 by typing FTP on any command line.

2. Change the Name Format to 1 using the NAMEFMT 1 FTP command. This tells FTP that you are using a directory naming structure rather than a library naming structure.

3. Either change the directory to the AS/400 IFS directory where your misnamed files reside by using the FTP Change Directory (CD) command, or enter a fully qualified path name on the next step.

4. Enter the FTP command DEL YourFileName to delete the file. Remember that, if you didn't use the CD command to set the directory to the location of the misnamed file, you need to enter the fully qualified path name on the DEL command. Also, keep in mind that directory and file names are case-sensitive in some AS/400 filing systems. Take care when typing.

Now you know how to clean up all those misnamed files before anyone else finds them.

—Shannon O'Donnell

Unconventional Use of QSYS.LIB

One of the great things about the AS/400 IFS is that it gives you a place to store all those strange (strange to the AS/400 anyway) PC file types such as *.JPG image files and *.ZIP compression files. But what happens if you need to store a nontraditional file in the AS/400's QSYS.LIB file system? You might think you'd be out of luck. Not so. Actually, you can store nontraditional files (i.e., PC files) in the QSYS.LIB file system. Just use FTP. Here's how.

Let's say you want to store a Visual Basic project, form, and workspace on the AS/400 and you want to put it in the QSYS.LIB file system. To do this, start an FTP session on the AS/400 and retrieve the VB files from the PC. When you specify the AS/400 file name the VB files are going to, create a name with the PC file extension. For example, if you have a VB Form named FORM1.FRM and you want to put it in the QGPL library on the AS/400, use the following FTP command:

```
get C:\FORM1.FRM    QGPL/FORM1.FRM
```

You just have to make sure that you keep the name within the 10-character naming limit used by the QSYS.LIB file system.

Using FTP, you might be tempted to think that you need to use a binary transfer mode to keep the PC data from being corrupted. That's not the case for most PC files you're putting in QSYS.LIB. Actually, using bin mode will corrupt the data you're putting on the PC for most file types, including Visual Basic *.FRM files. The exception to this is if you're putting ZIP files or image files such as *.BMPs, *.TIFs and *.JPGs onto the AS/400. That's because the data formats of these files are already a binary representation of their parent data. You have to use binary mode to maintain data integrity.

For example, to put a ZIP file named MyZip.zip onto the AS/400, use the following two FTP commands:

```
bin
get C:\MyZIP.zip   QGPL/MyZIP.zip
```

Just reverse the process, replacing get with put to move the files to another PC. That's it! Now you have a method for getting and putting nontraditional PC files onto the AS/400.

—Shannon O'Donnell

✦ ✦ ✦ PC Commands

How to Run PC Commands from Your AS/400

To run a PC command from an AS/400, users can use either Start PC Command (STRPCCMD) or Run Remote Command (RUNRMTCMD). The connection type will, in general, determine which command to use. If the PC is connected to the AS/400 through a router (such as NS/Router from NetManage), STRPCCMD is the command to use. If the PC is connected through TCP/IP, RUNRMTCMD is the right choice. Each command has its own unique requirements that must be met before users can successfully use it. To use STRPCCMD (Figure 20.10), users must be enrolled in the AS/400 system directory. You can enroll them by using the Work with Directory Entries (WRKDIRE) command.

```
STRPCCMD PCCMD('C:\PROGRA~1\ACCESS~1\MSPAINT.EXE') PAUSE(*YES)
```

Figure 20.10: This is an example of using the STRPCCMD.

Before users attempt to use STRPCCMD, you need to ensure, by either of two methods, that the Start PC Organizer (STRPCO) command has been run once. The first method is to add the STRPCO command to the user's initial program so that it executes at sign-on. Unfortunately, if the user's PC is connected through TCP/IP instead of a router, the command will end abnormally with the message "PCO must be run from a programmable workstation."

The second method is to add a macro to the user's Client Access/400 session on the PC connected by a router. To use this approach, start a PC5250 session on the user's PC. Click on the ASSIST option from the menu at the top of the 5250 panel and select Macro Setup from the drop-down menu. With the Macro Name window empty, click on the Customize button. Enter the script, shown in Figure 20.11, in the Macro Statements window.

```
[wait app]
"User ID
[field exit]
inputnd Please enter your Password
[enter]
[wait app]
"strpco
[enter]
```

Figure 20.11: Use this macro code with PC5250 to start the PC Organizer automatically.

"Wait app" means wait until the 5250 session starts before continuing. "User ID" will be the User ID of the person logging into this session. "Field exit" causes the cursor to move to the next input-capable field. "Inputnd Please enter your Password" causes an input box to be displayed with the message "Please enter your Password" on it. The password will not be displayed when it is typed in. "Enter" will send the Enter key escape sequence to the session. "STRPCO" will start the PC Organizer. Save this macro under some descriptive name, and—the next time a 5250 session is started on that PC—this macro will automatically run. (The problem with this approach is that you're expecting the same user to sign on to this workstation each time.)

Now, you can run the STRPCCMD from that PC to execute PC applications. The syntax of STRPCCMD is extremely simple. All you need to pass it is the path to the PC command you want to run. For example, the following command will start the Microsoft Paint program:

```
C:\PROGRA~1\ACCESS~1\MSPAINT.EXE
```

You also can suspend the AS/400 program while the PC program is running by using the default *YES on the STRPCCMD PAUSE parameter. A value of *NO will cause the AS/400 program and the PC application to run at the same time. The Run Remote Command (RUNRMTCMD) command can be used with IP connections as well as SNA connections. For this example, I'll concentrate on using RUNRMTCMD for IP connections.

```
RUNRMTCMD CMD('C:\PROGRA~1\ACCESS~1\MSPAINT.EXE')
          RMTLOCNAME('104.122.56.19' *IP)
```

RUNRMTCMD works like STRPCCMD in that you enter the path to the PC command or program you want to execute. In addition, you specify the connection type, either *SNA or *IP. In this case, you would enter *IP. For all IP connections, you also must enter the IP address. Each PC connected via IP will have its own unique address. Sometimes the host server dynamically assigns that address. Other times, the address will be specified on the PC under the IP configuration.

You can determine the PC's IP address in a couple of ways. The first way is to run the WINIPCFG command on the PC after connecting to the AS/400 (see the subsequent tip, "Using WINIPCFG to Find Your PC's IP Address"). This command displays the network connection type as well as the PC's IP address. The other method requires a bit of programming on the AS/400, but basically it uses the Retrieve Device Description (QDCRDEVD) API to retrieve the IP address from within an RPG IV or CL program.

Running RUNRMTCMD over an IP connection also requires that the target PC is running the IBM Remote Command Daemon (the CWBRXD.EXE program that resides in the Client Access/400 directory on your PC). To run this program in for example, Windows 95, you can type CWBRXD.EXE on the Windows 95 Run command screen, or you can click the Automatically Start Remote Command box from the Remote Command panel of the Client Access/400 Properties icon. The latter method places the CWBRXD.EXE program in your Windows 95 Registry, and the program will start each time you start Windows 95.

For Windows NT, the CWBRXD.EXE program is run as a service called Client Access Remote Command Services, and the Windows NT Security Manager is used to control access.

—Shannon O'Donnell

✦ ✦ ✦ SNMP

Community Names Are Case Sensitive with SNMP

Q: I'm having a problem with Simple Network Management Protocol (SNMP). I've configured a community on my AS/400 called Plant using the Add Community for SNMP (ADDCOMSNMP) command. However, when I try to use my SNMP management software to query the AS/400, it doesn't respond to that community name. If I use the community name Public, the AS/400 does respond. Therefore, I know I've got the SNMP interface started, and I'm using the management software correctly. What am I doing wrong?

A: The most common problem that I've seen people have with community names is that they forget these names are case sensitive. The community names Plant, plant, and PLANT are three different communities. This often causes a problem on the AS/400 because, if you prompt the ADDCOMSNMP command, it might translate what you enter for the community name into uppercase. If you want to enter a mixed-case community name, just put it in quotes in the ADDCOMSNMP command. Here's an example:

```
ADDCOMSNMP COM('Plant')
```

Another solution is to use the Configure TCP/IP SNMP (CFGTCPSNMP) command. This brings up a menu, and one of the options is "Work with communities for SNMP." This option makes it easier to enter mixed-case community names because the command puts the quotes around the name automatically. If your AS/400 isn't responding to an SNMP community name, check your case.

—Jim Hoopes

✦ ✦ ✦ TCP/IP Address

TCP/IP Printer Address Problems

When you add a printer to your TCP/IP network, one of the parameters you have to add in your Domain Name System (DNS) server configuration is the IP address for that printer. If you give that printer device a new IP address at some future time, you might be in for an unexpected surprise. Your AS/400 might continue to use the old IP address instead of your new one. This is because the AS/400 caches the DNS information for a period of time, determined by the DNS server, for up to 24 hours. If you need to use this device with the new address, you have only two choices: You can wait until the DNS server cache time expires and resets itself, or you can IPL the AS/400.

—Shannon O'Donnell

Using WINIPCFG to Find Your PC's IP Address

Want a quick way to tell what your PC's IP address is? Windows provides the WINIPCFG command that will display information about your IP configuration. To run this command, first connect to your IP host. Then, click on the Windows Start button, and click RUN. Type in WINIPCFG and click the OK button. You'll see information such as your IP address, subnet mask, and connection type. For more detailed information, click on the More Info> button.

—Shannon O'Donnell

Who Hosts That Address?

Looking for a way to determine, via a program, which TCP/IP host name is assigned to which TCP/IP address? File QATOCHOST in library QUSRSYS contains host table entries added using option 10 from the Configure TCP/IP (CFGTCP) menu. QATOCHOST contains IP addresses, host names, and descriptions. You can create a query or RPG program to generate a report of this information. Such a report would be an improvement over the OS/400 TCP/IP Host Table Entries Information report, which you create via F6 from Work with TCP/IP Host Table Entries panel. You also can use the Client Access file transfer function to download this information into the HOSTS file on your PC.

—Tim Cortez

Changing the AS/400 TCP/IP Address

Q: I need to change the IP address on my AS/400, and I can't find any information about how to do this in the IBM manuals. I hope you can help.

A: The TCP/IP address on the AS/400 is stored in the TCP/IP interface. To change the address, you have to end the TCP/IP interface, delete it, recreate it, and then start it back up. You can do all of those things from the Work with TCP/IP Interfaces screen. To get to that screen, run the Configure TCP/IP (CFGTCP) command and select option 1.

—Robin Klima

Retrieving the IP Address of a TCP/IP Printer

Q: I've found that if I want to retrieve the Internet Protocol (IP) address of a display device in an RPG program, I can use the Retrieve Device Address (QDCRDEVD) API with format DEVD0600 for display devices. However, using this API to retrieve the IP address for a printer with format DEVD1100, which is a format for printer devices, does not seem to work. Is there another way? All our printers are set up in the TCP/IP host table.

A: While QDCRDEVD is enhanced via a PTF to return the IP address of display devices for OS/400 V4R1 and below, I do not believe the PTF includes support for printer devices. However, the capability to retrieve the IP address of printer devices using the QDCRDEVD API is supported in V4R2 and above at decimal offset 1404 of format DEVD1100.

—Bruce Vining

✦ ✦ ✦ TCP/IP Communication

Ping AS/400 Connections

The PING command is very helpful for checking the physical connection between two hosts in a TCP/IP network. If you are running SNA protocol, you can use the Verify APPC Connection (VFYAPPCCNN) command (APING for short) to do the same job! I have used APING to test connections to other AS/400s and to 5494 workstation controllers. The 5494's microcode must be up-to-date; the old microcode doesn't support APING.

—Diego Santini

✦ ✦ ✦ TCP/IP Maintenance

Start Host Servers at IPL

In order to sign on to an AS/400 through TCP/IP, you must start the IP Host servers. Otherwise, you will get the dreaded, "Communications error occurred while validating security information" message. To avoid this problem, add the code shown in Figure 20.12 to the bottom of your startup program (the one referred to in the QSTRUP system value). This is a small "gotcha" that had me stumped for days.

```
STRTCP (with whatever parameters you normally use)
MONMSG MSGID(CPF0000)
STRHOSTSVR SERVER(*ALL)
MONMSG MSGID(CPF0000)
```

Figure 20.12: Start host servers when you IPL.

—*Jeff Ford*

✦ ✦ ✦ TCP/IP Services

What's Running on Which Port?

Having trouble connecting your TCP/IP-based service, such as a Java Data Queue application you wrote, to your AS/400? The problem might be that the port that service has been assigned to on your AS/400 is not listening. Here's how you can find out.

From an AS/400 command line, issue the Network Status (NETSTAT) command and then select option 3, Work with TCP/IP connection status. This will display all active (listening) connections on your AS/400. If the service isn't active, use the Start Host Servers (STRHOSTSVR) command to start the service you are interested in.

On the other hand, if the service is already active and listening, then the problem is likely with the TCP/IP service or application that's trying to connect to your AS/400. It might be attempting to connect to the wrong port. In that case, use Table 20.1 to make sure that your application is attempting to connect to the right port.

Table 20.1: Guide to TCP/IP Services on the AS/400

Port Numbers for Host Servers and Server Mapper

Service Name	Description	Port Number
as-central	Central server	8470
as-database	Database server	8471
as-dtaq	Data queue server	8472
as-file	File server	8473
as-netprt	Network print server	8474
as-rmtcmd	Remote command/ Program call server	8475
as-signon	Signon server	8476
as-svrmap	Server mapper	449
drda	DDM	446
as-usf	Ultimedia facilities	8480
as-admin-http	HTTP administration	2001
as-mtgctrl	Management central	5555
telnet	Telnet server	23

Port Numbers for Host Servers and Daemons That Use Secure Sockets Layer (SSL)

Service name	Description	Port Number
as-central-s	Secure central server	9470
as-database-s	Secure database server	9471
as-dtaq-s	Secure data queue server	9472
as-file-s	Secure file server	9473
as-netprt-s	Secure network print server	9474
as-rmtcmd-s	Secure remote command/ Program call server	9475
as-signon-s	Secure signon server	9476
ddm-ssl	DDM	448
as-usf-s	Ultimedia facilities	9480
as-admin-https	HTTP administration	2010
as-mgtctrl-ss	Management central	5566
Telnet-ssl	Telnet server	992

—Shannon O'Donnell

Utilities

*O*ver the years, *Midrange Computing* magazine has been known for publishing a tremendous number of quality, and useful, AS/400 utilities. While a majority of those utilities were described in stand-alone feature articles, a vast number of them were also sent in to Tech Talk by our talented readers. So, this final chapter gathers the absolute very best of Tech Talk's utilities. Actually, within this chapter, you'll find over 45 utilities you can begin using right away to make your shop run as efficiently and as smoothly as possible. The utilities included in this chapter will:

- Automatically display job completion messages.

- Use SQL to change the column heading of any field in any file.

- Create RPG Key Lists.

- Move Spooled Files to the Web as HTML documents.

- Put break messages in a Window.

- Use QHST to verify backups.

- Display PC files stored in folders.

- And much, much more!

Even better is that the complete code for every one of these utilities is included for you right in the tip itself (and on the accompanying CD). That makes it easy to not only use the technique described, but also to learn from it by studying the code used to make it all work. This chapter on utilities will soon turn you into an AS/400 wizard!

—Shannon O'Donnell

✦ ✦ ✦ Backups

Use QHST to Verify Backups

We use the AS/400 job scheduler and the GO BACKUP scheduler to do daily and weekly backups. Initializing the tape and ending the subsystems are parts of the nightly run. Sometimes, the backup does not complete successfully, and no job log is provided for the backup scheduler, so we don't know which libraries weren't backed up completely.

I developed the Display Backup Diagnostics (DSPBUDIAG) command, shown in Figure 21.1, to print any errors that occur during the nightly save and startup. The CPP is BU001CL (shown in Figure 21.2.) To run the command, you must supply beginning and ending dates, as well as an option to tell the system what to do with the printed report. By default, DSPBUDIAG shows on the screen the diagnostics for the current date and keeps the report on hold in the output queue. I've successfully used this method for quite some time. My daily backup, *NONSYS, saves all objects in all user libraries, including QUSRSYS, in the nightly backup.

```
/*==============================================================*/
/* To compile:                                                  */
/*                                                              */
/*            CRTCMD     CMD(XXX/DSPBUDIAG) PGM(XXX/BU001CL) +   */
/*                       SRCFILE(XXX/QCMDSRC)                    */
/*                                                              */
/*==============================================================*/
             CMD        PROMPT('Display Back-Up Diagnostics')

             PARM       KWD(ENDDAT) TYPE(*DATE) DFT(*TODAY) +
                        SPCVAL((*TODAY 000000)) PROMPT('Ending +
                        date')

             PARM       KWD(BGNDAT) TYPE(*DATE) DFT(*ENDDAT) +
                        SPCVAL((*ENDDAT 000000)) PROMPT('Beginning +
                        date')

             PARM       KWD(SPLFOPTN) TYPE(*CHAR) LEN(4) RSTD(*YES) +
                        DFT(*HLD) VALUES(*HLD *RLS *DLT) +
                        PROMPT('Spooled file option')
```

Figure 21.1: Command DSPBUDIAG can be used to verify that your backups ran successfully.

```
/*======================================================================*/
/* To compile:                                                          */
/*                                                                      */
/*            CRTCLPGM    PGM(XXX/BU001CL) SRCFILE(XXX/QCLSRC)          */
/*                                                                      */
/*======================================================================*/
PGM            PARM(&ENDDAT7 &BGNDAT7 &SPLFOPTN)


  DCL          VAR(&BGNDAT6) TYPE(*CHAR) LEN(6)
  DCL          VAR(&BGNDAT7) TYPE(*CHAR) LEN(7)
  DCL          VAR(&BGNDATJOB) TYPE(*CHAR) LEN(6)
  DCL          VAR(&DATFMT) TYPE(*CHAR) LEN(4)
  DCL          VAR(&ENDDAT6) TYPE(*CHAR) LEN(6)
  DCL          VAR(&ENDDAT7) TYPE(*CHAR) LEN(7)
  DCL          VAR(&ENDDATJOB) TYPE(*CHAR) LEN(6)
  DCL          VAR(&MSGDTA) TYPE(*CHAR) LEN(256)
  DCL          VAR(&MSGF) TYPE(*CHAR) LEN(10)
  DCL          VAR(&MSGFLIB) TYPE(*CHAR) LEN(10)
  DCL          VAR(&MSGID) TYPE(*CHAR) LEN(7)
  DCL          VAR(&SPLFOPTN) TYPE(*CHAR) LEN(4)

  MONMSG       MSGID(CPF0000 MCH0000) EXEC(GOTO CMDLBL(ERROR))


  RTVJOBA      DATFMT(&DATFMT)

  /* Resolve special values for dates */
  IF           COND(&ENDDAT7 *EQ '0000000') THEN(DO)
    RTVSYSVAL  SYSVAL(QDATE) RTNVAR(&ENDDATJOB)
  ENDDO
  ELSE         CMD(DO)
    CHGVAR       VAR(&ENDDAT6) VALUE(%SST(&ENDDAT7 2 6))
    CVTDAT       DATE(&ENDDAT6) TOVAR(&ENDDATJOB) +
                   FROMFMT(*YMD) TOFMT(&DATFMT) TOSEP(*NONE)
  ENDDO

  IF           COND(&BGNDAT7 *EQ '0000000') THEN(DO)
    CHGVAR       VAR(&BGNDATJOB) VALUE(&ENDDATJOB)
  ENDDO
  ELSE         CMD(DO)
    CHGVAR       VAR(&BGNDAT6) VALUE(%SST(&BGNDAT7 2 6))
    CVTDAT       DATE(&BGNDAT6) TOVAR(&BGNDATJOB) +
                   FROMFMT(*YMD) TOFMT(&DATFMT) TOSEP(*NONE)
  ENDDO

  /* Produce desired information */
  OVRPRTF      FILE(QPDSPLOG) PRTTXT(*BLANK) HOLD(*YES) +
                 USRDTA(&ENDDATJOB) SPLFNAME(BUDIAG)
  DSPLOG       LOG(QHST) PERIOD((000000 &BGNDATJOB) (*AVAIL +
                 &ENDDATJOB)) OUTPUT(*PRINT) MSGID(CPI1E23 +
                 CPC3707 CPI1146 CPA400F CPA4086 CPI2404 +
                 CPI0C04 CPF3771 CPF3777 CPI1E62 CPF1240)
```

Figure 21.2: CL program BU001CL is the heart of the DSPBUDIAG command (part 1 of 2).

```
/* Display the report */
DSPSPLF    FILE(BUDIAG) JOB(*) SPLNBR(*LAST)

DLTOVR     FILE(QPDSPLOG)

/* Determine what to do with report */
IF         COND(&SPLFOPTN *EQ '*DLT') THEN(DO)
   DLTSPLF    FILE(BUDIAG) JOB(*) SPLNBR(*LAST)
ENDDO
ELSE       CMD(IF COND(&SPLFOPTN *EQ '*RLS') THEN(DO))
   RLSSPLF    FILE(BUDIAG) JOB(*) SPLNBR(*LAST)
ENDDO

RETURN

ERROR:
   RCVMSG     MSGTYPE(*EXCP) MSGDTA(&MSGDTA) MSGID(&MSGID) +
                 MSGF(&MSGF) SNDMSGFLIB(&MSGFLIB)
   MONMSG     MSGID(CPF0000)
   SNDPGMMSG  MSGID(&MSGID) MSGF(&MSGFLIB/&MSGF) +
                 MSGDTA(&MSGDTA) MSGTYPE(*ESCAPE)
   MONMSG     MSGID(CPF0000)

ENDPGM
```

Figure 21.2: CL program BU001CL is the heart of the DSPBUDIAG command (part 2 of 2).

—*Andre Nortje*

✦ ✦ ✦ Cool Programming Tools

Easy Random Number Generator

I know this type of thing has been written and published in every language known to man (and I know there's an API, too), but CL program NBR001CL (Figure 21.3) provides an easy way to get a random number in any range from 0 to 32,767. NBR001CL calls on REXX procedure NBR010RX (Figure 21.4) to generate a random number in the desired range. REXX returns the random number as a completion code. The STRREXPRC command generates a CPF7CFF on any nonzero completion code, and that completion code can be extracted from the message (beginning in position 31).

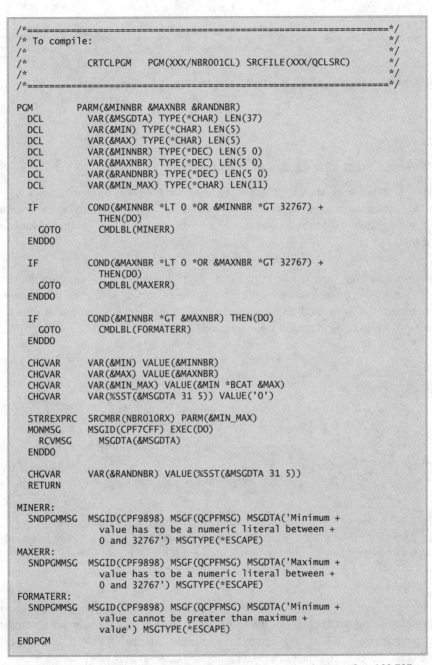

```
/*================================================================*/
/* To compile:                                                    */
/*                                                                */
/*           CRTCLPGM   PGM(XXX/NBR001CL) SRCFILE(XXX/QCLSRC)      */
/*                                                                */
/*================================================================*/

PGM        PARM(&MINNBR &MAXNBR &RANDNBR)
  DCL      VAR(&MSGDTA) TYPE(*CHAR) LEN(37)
  DCL      VAR(&MIN) TYPE(*CHAR) LEN(5)
  DCL      VAR(&MAX) TYPE(*CHAR) LEN(5)
  DCL      VAR(&MINNBR) TYPE(*DEC) LEN(5 0)
  DCL      VAR(&MAXNBR) TYPE(*DEC) LEN(5 0)
  DCL      VAR(&RANDNBR) TYPE(*DEC) LEN(5 0)
  DCL      VAR(&MIN_MAX) TYPE(*CHAR) LEN(11)

  IF       COND(&MINNBR *LT 0 *OR &MINNBR *GT 32767) +
             THEN(DO)
    GOTO      CMDLBL(MINERR)
  ENDDO

  IF       COND(&MAXNBR *LT 0 *OR &MAXNBR *GT 32767) +
             THEN(DO)
    GOTO      CMDLBL(MAXERR)
  ENDDO

  IF       COND(&MINNBR *GT &MAXNBR) THEN(DO)
    GOTO      CMDLBL(FORMATERR)
  ENDDO

  CHGVAR   VAR(&MIN) VALUE(&MINNBR)
  CHGVAR   VAR(&MAX) VALUE(&MAXNBR)
  CHGVAR   VAR(&MIN_MAX) VALUE(&MIN *BCAT &MAX)
  CHGVAR   VAR(%SST(&MSGDTA 31 5)) VALUE('0')

  STRREXPRC SRCMBR(NBR010RX) PARM(&MIN_MAX)
  MONMSG   MSGID(CPF7CFF) EXEC(DO)
    RCVMSG    MSGDTA(&MSGDTA)
  ENDDO

  CHGVAR   VAR(&RANDNBR) VALUE(%SST(&MSGDTA 31 5))
  RETURN

MINERR:
  SNDPGMMSG MSGID(CPF9898) MSGF(QCPFMSG) MSGDTA('Minimum +
             value has to be a numeric literal between +
             0 and 32767') MSGTYPE(*ESCAPE)
MAXERR:
  SNDPGMMSG MSGID(CPF9898) MSGF(QCPFMSG) MSGDTA('Maximum +
             value has to be a numeric literal between +
             0 and 32767') MSGTYPE(*ESCAPE)
FORMATERR:
  SNDPGMMSG MSGID(CPF9898) MSGF(QCPFMSG) MSGDTA('Minimum +
             value cannot be greater than maximum +
             value') MSGTYPE(*ESCAPE)

ENDPGM
```

Figure 21.3: CL program NBR001CL gives you a random number between 0 and 32,767.

```
parse arg min max
EXIT random(min,max)
```

Figure 21.4: This REXX procedure generates the random number.

—Tom Conover

Retrieving Commands Executed from a Menu

A typical technique for allowing users to retrieve commands run through a menu requires that each command processing program (CPP) send the executed command to the caller as a request message. The disadvantage to this method is that all CPPs must include this same logic.

I have written a command I call F9 (see Figure 21.5) that will run any CL command and log it so that it can be retrieved with the F9 key. The F9 command has two parameters: the command to be executed, and an option that allows you to choose whether or not the command should be prompted before execution.

```
/*================================================================*/
/* To compile:                                                    */
/*                                                                 */
/*          CRTCMD     CMD(XXX/F9) PGM(XXX/F9PGM) +                */
/*                     SRCFILE(XXX/QCMDSRC)                        */
/*                                                                 */
/*================================================================*/
             CMD        PROMPT('Execute Cmd for F9 Retrieval')

             PARM       KWD(CMD) TYPE(*CMDSTR) LEN(3000) MIN(1) +
                        PROMPT('Command')

             PARM       KWD(PROMPT) TYPE(*LGL) LEN(1) DFT(*NO) +
                        SPCVAL((*YES '1') (*NO '0')) +
                        PROMPT('Prompt command')
```

Figure 21.5: Command F9 can be used to retrieve commands.

As shown in Figure 21.6, the CPP is F9PGM. If the command being run is to be prompted before execution, F9PGM calls the QCMDCHK API, which allows the user to fill in the desired parameters. Next, F9PGM executes the command. At label ERROR, it sends the command to the caller's message queue in a request message. This is what lets the user retrieve the command with the F9 key. It retrieves the request message so that the caller will not attempt to execute the request message when it gets an opportunity. Last, it forwards any messages it has received to the caller.

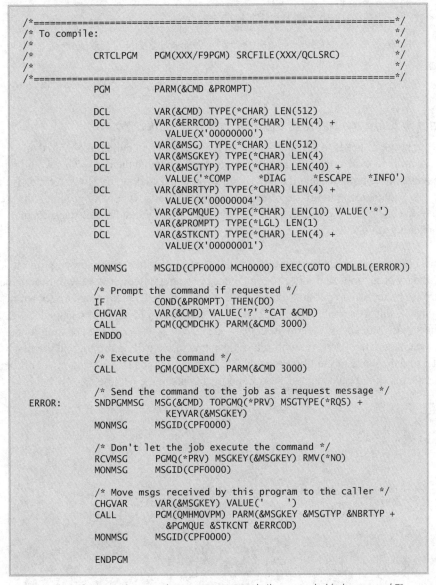

```
/*===================================================================*/
/* To compile:                                                       */
/*                                                                   */
/*          CRTCLPGM    PGM(XXX/F9PGM) SRCFILE(XXX/QCLSRC)           */
/*                                                                   */
/*===================================================================*/
          PGM         PARM(&CMD &PROMPT)

          DCL         VAR(&CMD) TYPE(*CHAR) LEN(512)
          DCL         VAR(&ERRCOD) TYPE(*CHAR) LEN(4) +
                        VALUE(X'00000000')
          DCL         VAR(&MSG) TYPE(*CHAR) LEN(512)
          DCL         VAR(&MSGKEY) TYPE(*CHAR) LEN(4)
          DCL         VAR(&MSGTYP) TYPE(*CHAR) LEN(40) +
                        VALUE('*COMP      *DIAG      *ESCAPE    *INFO')
          DCL         VAR(&NBRTYP) TYPE(*CHAR) LEN(4) +
                        VALUE(X'00000004')
          DCL         VAR(&PGMQUE) TYPE(*CHAR) LEN(10) VALUE('*')
          DCL         VAR(&PROMPT) TYPE(*LGL) LEN(1)
          DCL         VAR(&STKCNT) TYPE(*CHAR) LEN(4) +
                        VALUE(X'00000001')

          MONMSG      MSGID(CPF0000 MCH0000) EXEC(GOTO CMDLBL(ERROR))

          /* Prompt the command if requested */
          IF          COND(&PROMPT) THEN(DO)
          CHGVAR      VAR(&CMD) VALUE('?' *CAT &CMD)
          CALL        PGM(QCMDCHK) PARM(&CMD 3000)
          ENDDO

          /* Execute the command */
          CALL        PGM(QCMDEXC) PARM(&CMD 3000)

          /* Send the command to the job as a request message */
ERROR:    SNDPGMMSG   MSG(&CMD) TOPGMQ(*PRV) MSGTYPE(*RQS) +
                        KEYVAR(&MSGKEY)
          MONMSG      MSGID(CPF0000)

          /* Don't let the job execute the command */
          RCVMSG      PGMQ(*PRV) MSGKEY(&MSGKEY) RMV(*NO)
          MONMSG      MSGID(CPF0000)

          /* Move msgs received by this program to the caller */
          CHGVAR      VAR(&MSGKEY) VALUE('    ')
          CALL        PGM(QMHMOVPM) PARM(&MSGKEY &MSGTYP &NBRTYP +
                        &PGMQUE &STKCNT &ERRCOD)
          MONMSG      MSGID(CPF0000)

          ENDPGM
```

Figure 21.6: Command processing program F9PGM is the power behind command F9.

Figure 21.7 illustrates how to use the F9 command in a menu.

```
F9 CMD(WRKACTJOB)
F9 CMD(WRKOUTQ)   PROMPT(*YES)
```

Figure 21.7: Here's how you might use the F9 command to retrieve commands.

—Ricky Daugherty

Want to Know the Name of the Program That Called Yours?

If your program needs to know the name of the program that called it, one method you could use is to send a message and then immediately receive the reply. This would return the name of the program that the message was funneled back up to. However, this isn't the best way to go about this task because the method fails when your program hits the top of the call stack. You'll get error message CPF24A3: "Value for call stack counter parameter not valid."

Your program could run at the top of the call stack if it is the transfer group program in a secondary group job, or if it is a routing entry program that you invoke with routing data. Here's a better way to get the caller's name. First, run the REXX procedure shown in Figure 21.8. It will create a small MI language program in library QGPL named RTVCALL. When a program needs to know its caller's name, call QGPL/RTVCALL, passing it one 20-byte parameter. RTVCALL will return the name of the calling program in the first 10 bytes and the name of the library in which it is stored in the last 10 bytes. If your program is at the top of the call stack, RTVCALL returns blanks in the parameter.

```
/************************************************************************/
/*    LANGUAGE - REXX                                                   */
/*    FUNCTION - one-time procedure to create MI program QGPL/RTVCALL    */
/*    AUTHOR   - Gene Gaunt                                              */
/*                                                                      */
/*    use STRREXPRC to execute one time                                 */
/*    then call RTVCALL with one 20-byte parameter from HLL program     */
/*    RTVCALL returns program & library name of caller                  */
/************************************************************************/
MI =,
'DCL SPCPTR ?NAME      PARM;                                  ' ,
'DCL DD     NAME       BAS(?NAME) CHAR(20);                   ' ,
'DCL OL     MAIN       (?NAME) EXT PARM MIN(1);               ' ,
'DCL DD     MAT        AUTO CHAR(25632);                      ' ,
```

Figure 21.8: Use this REXX procedure to create MI program RTVCALL (part 1 of 2).

```
'DCL DD     SIZE       DEF(MAT) BIN(4) INIT(25632);    ' ,
'DCL DD     TOTAL      DEF(MAT) POS(9) BIN(4);         ' ,
'DCL DD     LEVEL(200) DEF(MAT) POS(17) CHAR(128);     ' ,
'DCL SYSPTR ?PGM(200)  DEF(LEVEL) POS(33) AEO(128);    ' ,
'DCL SPCPTR ?MAT       AUTO INIT(MAT);                 ' ,
'DCL DD     CALLER     AUTO BIN(4);                    ' ,
'          ENTRY   * (MAIN) EXT;                       ' ,
'          CPYBREP NAME, " ";                          ' ,
'          MATINVS ?MAT, *;                            ' ,
'          SUBN    CALLER, TOTAL, 1;                   ' ,
'LOOP: SUBN(SB)    TOTAL, 1 / NPOS(BYE);               ' ,
'          CMPPTRE(B) ?PGM(TOTAL), ?PGM(CALLER) / EQ(LOOP); ' ,
'          MATPTR  ?MAT, ?PGM(TOTAL);                  ' ,
'          CAT     NAME, MAT(12:10), MAT(44:10);       ' ,
'BYE:  PEND;'
Size = D2C(Length(MI),4)
"CALL QPRCRTPG (&MI  &Size 'RTVCALL    QGPL      ' "," +
 'Retrieve Program Name of Caller           ' '*NONE' +
 "," ' '   ' '    'QSYSPRT   *LIBL' X'00000001' '*ALL' +
 "," '*LIST   *REPLACE ' X'00000002' )    "
```

Figure 21.8: Use this REXX procedure to create MI program RTVCALL (part 2 of 2).

—Gene Gaunt

✦ ✦ ✦ Data Integrity

Modulus 10 Calculation/Validation Program

One way to ensure that account numbers are input correctly is to use a check digit. A check digit is normally a single digit calculated from an algorithm applied to the original number. One of the most widely used check digit methods is Modulus 10 (M10). The M10 algorithm works like this:

- For each position in the base number, there is a weight factor. Positions are counted from the farthest right digit (not including the check digit).

- The Modulus 10 weight factor is 2 for all odd positions (1, 3, 5, ...) and 1 for all even positions (2, 4, 6, ...).

To calculate the Modulus 10 self-check digit, do the following:

- Starting from the right-most digit of the base number, multiply every other digit by a factor of 2.

- Add the digits in the products to the digits in the base number that were not multiplied.

- Subtract the sum from the next higher number ending in zero. To create an M10 number, you append the result of step 3 to the end of the base number.

For example, to calculate the check digit for the number 256, perform the following steps:

- Multiply the first right-most digit (6) by 2 (**2 * 6 = 12**).

- Multiply the third digit from the right (2) by 2 (**2 * 2 = 4**).

- Add each digit of the products and each digit of the base number that wasn't multiplied by a factor (**1+2+5+4 = 12**).

- Subtract the result from the next highest number that ends in a zero (**20-12 = 8**).

The M10 check digit for the base number 256 is 8. The resulting M10 number would be 2568.

IBM supports the validation of an M10 number through display files with the DDS CHECK keyword with a parameter value of M10. However, there are no programs in OS/400 that will generate an M10 check digit for a number. I wrote an RPG program (M10001RG) to calculate the check digit of a number or, alternatively, to validate a number that already has a check digit. This way I have the capability to not only validate an M10 number, but I can also generate an M10 check digit; and, both can be done by calling the same program. Figure 21.9 contains the source code for RPG program M10001RG.

```
*===============================================================
* To compile:
*
*       CRTRPGPGM  PGM(XXX/M10001RG)  SRCFILE(XXX/QRPGSRC)
*
*===============================================================
*. 1 ...+... 2 ...+... 3 ...+... 4 ...+... 5 ...+... 6 ...+... 7
E                     NA        15   1
*
C           *ENTRY    PLIST
C                     PARM           NBR    15
C                     PARM           VALI    1
```

Figure 21.9: Use this program to calculate Modulus 10 (part 1 of 2).

```
C                     PARM            CKDIG   1
C                     PARM            VALID   1
C                     MOVE *BLANK     VALID
C                     MOVE *BLANK     CKDIG
 *
C                     MOVEANBR        NA
 *
C           NA,2      IFNE *BLANK
C           NA,15     ANDEQ*BLANK
C           ' '       CHEKRNBR        I       20
C           VALI      IFEQ 'Y'
C                     MOVE NA,I       CKDIG
C                     SUB  1          I
C                     ENDIF
 *
C                     MOVE *ZEROS     TOGLE   10
C                     MOVE *ZEROS     CHSUM   70
 *
C           I         DOWGE1
C                     MOVE NA,I       HOLD    10
C           TOGLE     IFEQ *ZERO
C           HOLD      MULT 2          WRK     20
C                     ELSE
C                     Z-ADDHOLD       WRK
C                     ENDIF
C                     ADD  5          TOGLE
C           WRK       IFGT 9
C                     SUB  9          WRK
C                     ENDIF
C                     ADD  WRK        CHSUM
C                     SUB  1          I
C                     ENDDO
 *
C                     MOVE CHSUM      NXTHI   20
C           100       SUB  NXTHI      CHDIG   10
C                     MOVE CHDIG      CHDIC   1
C           VALI      IFEQ 'Y'
C           CHDIC     IFEQ CKDIG
C                     MOVE '1'        VALID
C                     ELSE
C                     MOVE '0'        VALID
C                     ENDIF
C                     ENDIF
C                     MOVE CHDIC      CKDIG
C                     ENDIF
 *
C                     RETRN
```

Figure 21.9: Use this program to calculate Modulus 10 (part 2 of 2).

The program uses two input parameters and two output parameters:

- Input parameter one: 15 character number to validate or to generate a check digit for.

- Input parameter two: Validate flag (a value of 'Y' indicates that the program is to validate the number).

- Output parameter one: Contains calculated Modulus 10 check digit if input parameter two is 'Y'.

- Output parameter two: If validate flag parameter is set to 'Y', this parameter will contain a 1 if the number is a valid M10 number; otherwise, it will contain a value of 0.

—Andrew Longo

✦ ✦ ✦ Data Queues

View and Remove Data Queue Entries

Testing an application that uses a data queue can be difficult, because OS/400 does not supply a command to let a programmer view or change the contents of a data queue. I created the SHWDTAQ command (Figure 21.10) to let me view, and optionally delete, FIFO data queue entries.

```
/*==============================================================*/
/* To compile:                                                  */
/*                                                              */
/*            CRTCMD    CMD(XXX/SHWDTAQ) PGM(XXX/DTQ001CL) +     */
/*                      SRCFILE(XXX/QCMDSRC)                     */
/*                                                              */
/*==============================================================*/
            CMD       PROMPT('Show Data Queue')

            PARM      KWD(OUTQ) TYPE(QUALDTAQ) MIN(1) PROMPT('Data +
                      queue')

QUALDTAQ:   QUAL      TYPE(*NAME) LEN(10) EXPR(*YES)
            QUAL      TYPE(*NAME) LEN(10) DFT(*LIBL) SPCVAL((*LIBL) +
                      (*CURLIB)) EXPR(*YES) PROMPT('Library')

            PARM      KWD(OUTPUT) TYPE(*CHAR) LEN(8) RSTD(*YES) +
                      DFT(*) VALUES(* *PRINT *PRTWRAP) +
                      PROMPT('Output')
```

Figure 21.10: Command SHWDTAQ will display the contents of a data queue.

The command processing program DTQ001CL (Figure 21.11) first verifies that the data queue exists. Next, it allocates the data queue with an exclusive lock so that no other program can use the data queue while the program processes it.

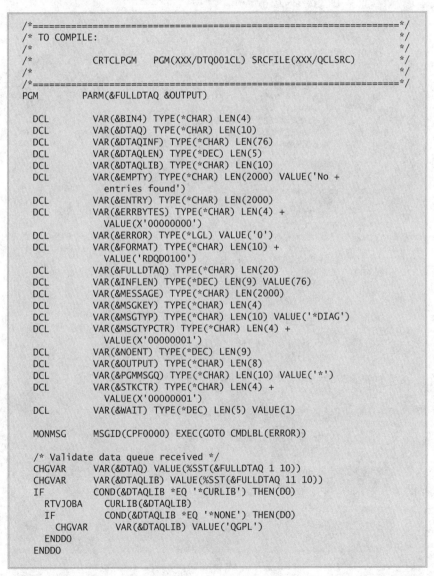

```
/*===============================================================*/
/* TO COMPILE:                                                   */
/*                                                               */
/*             CRTCLPGM   PGM(XXX/DTQ001CL) SRCFILE(XXX/QCLSRC)  */
/*                                                               */
/*===============================================================*/
PGM        PARM(&FULLDTAQ &OUTPUT)

  DCL        VAR(&BIN4) TYPE(*CHAR) LEN(4)
  DCL        VAR(&DTAQ) TYPE(*CHAR) LEN(10)
  DCL        VAR(&DTAQINF) TYPE(*CHAR) LEN(76)
  DCL        VAR(&DTAQLEN) TYPE(*DEC) LEN(5)
  DCL        VAR(&DTAQLIB) TYPE(*CHAR) LEN(10)
  DCL        VAR(&EMPTY) TYPE(*CHAR) LEN(2000) VALUE('No +
               entries found')
  DCL        VAR(&ENTRY) TYPE(*CHAR) LEN(2000)
  DCL        VAR(&ERRBYTES) TYPE(*CHAR) LEN(4) +
               VALUE(X'00000000')
  DCL        VAR(&ERROR) TYPE(*LGL) VALUE('0')
  DCL        VAR(&FORMAT) TYPE(*CHAR) LEN(10) +
               VALUE('RDQD0100')
  DCL        VAR(&FULLDTAQ) TYPE(*CHAR) LEN(20)
  DCL        VAR(&INFLEN) TYPE(*DEC) LEN(9) VALUE(76)
  DCL        VAR(&MESSAGE) TYPE(*CHAR) LEN(2000)
  DCL        VAR(&MSGKEY) TYPE(*CHAR) LEN(4)
  DCL        VAR(&MSGTYP) TYPE(*CHAR) LEN(10) VALUE('*DIAG')
  DCL        VAR(&MSGTYPCTR) TYPE(*CHAR) LEN(4) +
               VALUE(X'00000001')
  DCL        VAR(&NOENT) TYPE(*DEC) LEN(9)
  DCL        VAR(&OUTPUT) TYPE(*CHAR) LEN(8)
  DCL        VAR(&PGMMSGQ) TYPE(*CHAR) LEN(10) VALUE('*')
  DCL        VAR(&STKCTR) TYPE(*CHAR) LEN(4) +
               VALUE(X'00000001')
  DCL        VAR(&WAIT) TYPE(*DEC) LEN(5) VALUE(1)

  MONMSG     MSGID(CPF0000) EXEC(GOTO CMDLBL(ERROR))

  /* Validate data queue received */
  CHGVAR     VAR(&DTAQ) VALUE(%SST(&FULLDTAQ 1 10))
  CHGVAR     VAR(&DTAQLIB) VALUE(%SST(&FULLDTAQ 11 10))
  IF         COND(&DTAQLIB *EQ '*CURLIB') THEN(DO)
    RTVJOBA    CURLIB(&DTAQLIB)
    IF         COND(&DTAQLIB *EQ '*NONE') THEN(DO)
      CHGVAR     VAR(&DTAQLIB) VALUE('QGPL')
    ENDDO
  ENDDO
```

Figure 21.11: CL program DTQ001CL provides the power behind the SHWDTAQ command (part 1 of 3).

```
ALCOBJ      OBJ((&DTAQLIB/&DTAQ *DTAQ *EXCL)) WAIT(1)

/* Create the message queue where the entries will be */
/* displayed */
CRTMSGQ     MSGQ(QTEMP/SHOWDTAQ)
MONMSG      MSGID(CPF2112)
CLRMSGQ     MSGQ(QTEMP/SHOWDTAQ)

/* Determine the number of entries in the data queue */
CHGVAR      VAR(%BIN(&BIN4 1 4)) VALUE(&INFLEN)
CALL        PGM(QMHQRDQD) PARM(&DTAQINF &BIN4 &FORMAT +
              &FULLDTAQ)
CHGVAR      VAR(&BIN4) VALUE(%SST(&DTAQINF 73 4))
CHGVAR      VAR(&NOENT) VALUE(%BIN(&BIN4 1 4))
IF          COND(&NOENT *EQ 0) THEN(DO)
  CHGVAR      VAR(&MESSAGE) VALUE(&EMPTY)
  SNDMSG      MSG(&MESSAGE) TOMSGQ(QTEMP/SHOWDTAQ)
ENDDO

/* Receive all the data queue entries, then send the */
/* entries to the message queue we have just created */
MSGQLOOP:
  IF          COND(&NOENT *EQ 0) THEN(GOTO CMDLBL(DSPENTRY))
  CALL        PGM(QRCVDTAQ) PARM(&DTAQ &DTAQLIB &DTAQLEN +
                &ENTRY &WAIT)

  CHGVAR      VAR(&MESSAGE) VALUE(%SST(&ENTRY 1 &DTAQLEN))
  SNDMSG      MSG(&MESSAGE) TOMSGQ(QTEMP/SHOWDTAQ)
  CHGVAR      VAR(&NOENT) VALUE(&NOENT - 1)
  GOTO        CMDLBL(MSGQLOOP)

/* Display the message */
DSPENTRY:
  DSPMSG      MSGQ(QTEMP/SHOWDTAQ) OUTPUT(&OUTPUT) +
                START(*FIRST)

/* When user exits out of displaying the message, send */
/* the messages back to the data queue */
DTAQLOOP:
  RCVMSG      MSGQ(QTEMP/SHOWDTAQ) MSG(&MESSAGE) +
                MSGLEN(&DTAQLEN)
  IF          COND(&DTAQLEN *GT 0) THEN(DO)
    IF          COND(&MESSAGE *EQ &EMPTY) THEN(DO)
      GOTO        CMDLBL(RESET)
    ENDDO
    CHGVAR      VAR(&ENTRY) VALUE(%SST(&MESSAGE 1 &DTAQLEN))
    CALL        PGM(QSNDDTAQ) PARM(&DTAQ &DTAQLIB &DTAQLEN +
                  &ENTRY)
    GOTO        CMDLBL(DTAQLOOP)
  ENDDO
```

Figure 21.11: CL program DTQ001CL provides the power behind the SHWDTAQ command (part 2 of 3).

```
    /* Reset back to the previous condition */
RESET:
    DLCOBJ      OBJ((&DTAQLIB/&DTAQ *DTAQ *EXCL))
    DLTMSGQ     MSGQ(QTEMP/SHOWDTAQ)
    MONMSG      MSGID(CPF0000)

    RETURN

    /* Error routine */
ERROR:
    DLCOBJ      OBJ((&DTAQLIB/&DTAQ *DTAQ *EXCL))
    MONMSG      MSGID(CPF0000)
    DLTMSGQ     MSGQ(QTEMP/SHOWDTAQ)
    MONMSG      MSGID(CPF0000)
    IF          COND(&ERROR) THEN(GOTO CMDLBL(ERRDONE))
    ELSE        CMD(CHGVAR VAR(&ERROR) VALUE('1'))
    /* Move all *DIAG messages to previous program queue */
    CALL        PGM(QMHMOVPM) PARM(&MSGKEY &MSGTYP +
                    &MSGTYPCTR &PGMMSGQ &STKCTR &ERRBYTES)

    /* Resend last *ESCAPE message */
ERRDONE:
    CALL        PGM(QMHRSNEM) PARM(&MSGKEY &ERRBYTES)
    MONMSG      MSGID(CPF0000) EXEC(DO)
      SNDPGMMSG  MSGID(CPF3CF2) MSGF(QCPFMSG) +
                    MSGDTA('QMHRSNEM') MSGTYPE(*ESCAPE)
      MONMSG     MSGID(CPF0000)
    ENDDO

ENDPGM
```

Figure 21.11: CL program DTQ001CL provides the power behind the SHWDTAQ command (part 3 of 3).

SHWDTAQ creates a temporary message queue, called SHOWDTAQ in QTEMP, and then copies all entries in the data queue to that message queue as messages. It uses the Display Message (DSPMSG) command to display all entries in the data queue. From the DSPMSG panel, you can press F11 to delete individual messages or F13 to remove all of them.

When you're done, press Enter, F3, or F12. SHWDTAQ sends all remaining messages back into the data queue. There is no escape mechanism for this utility. If you accidentally delete a message, you cannot get it back. SHWDTAQ is helpful for testing an application, but don't use it for production work.

—*Alex Nubla*

✦ ✦ ✦ Date and Time

Delete Performance Data by Date

Q: The Delete Performance Data (DLTPFRDTA) command lets you specify performance data member names or select the members from a list. How can I clean up my old data by date without manually having to key the DLTPFRDTA command and select the performance data members?

A: The command Delete Performance Data (DLTPFRDTA2), shown in Figure 21.12, and its command processing program PFR001CL, shown in Figure 21.13, will do what you want. It works just like the IBM command, but—instead of the member parameter—there is a date parameter. Any performance data older than that date will be deleted.

```
/*==============================================================*/
/* To compile:                                                  */
/*                                                              */
/*            CRTCMD     CMD(XXX/DLTPFRDTA2) PGM(XXX/PFR001CL) + */
/*                       SRCFILE(XXX/QCMDSRC)                    */
/*                                                              */
/*==============================================================*/
            CMD        PROMPT('Delete Performance Data')

            PARM       KWD(DATE) TYPE(*DATE) MIN(1) PROMPT('Delete +
                         data older than')
            PARM       KWD(LIB) TYPE(*NAME) DFT(QPFRDATA) +
                         PROMPT('Library')
            PARM       KWD(JOBD) TYPE(JOBD) PROMPT('Job description')
JOBD:       QUAL       TYPE(*GENERIC) LEN(10) DFT(QPFRJOBD)
            QUAL       TYPE(*NAME) LEN(10) DFT(QPFR) +
                         SPCVAL((*LIBL)) PROMPT('Library')
```

Figure 21.12: Command DLTPFRDTA2 allows you to control your performance data deletions.

```
/*==============================================================*/
/* To compile:                                                  */
/*                                                              */
/*            CRTCLPGM   PGM(XXX/PFR001CL) SRCFILE(XXX/QCLSRC)   */
/*                                                              */
/*==============================================================*/
PFR001CL:   PGM        PARM(&DATE &LIB &FULLJOBD)
            DCL        VAR(&DATE) TYPE(*CHAR) LEN(7)
            DCL        VAR(&LIB) TYPE(*CHAR) LEN(10)
            DCL        VAR(&FULLJOBD) TYPE(*CHAR) LEN(20)
            DCL        VAR(&CMD) TYPE(*CHAR) LEN(1024)
```

Figure 21.13: Program PFR001CL is the heart of the DLTPFRDTA2 command (part 1 of 3).

```
          DCL        VAR(&CMDLEN) TYPE(*DEC) LEN(15 5)
          DCL        VAR(&COUNT) TYPE(*DEC) LEN(3 0)
          DCL        VAR(&MSGID) TYPE(*CHAR) LEN(7)
          DCL        VAR(&MSGDTA) TYPE(*CHAR) LEN(256)
          DCLF       FILE(QAFDMBRL)
          MONMSG     MSGID(CPF0000) EXEC(GOTO CMDLBL(ERROR))

          CHKOBJ     OBJ(%SST(&FULLJOBD 11 10)/%SST(&FULLJOBD 1 +
                       10)) OBJTYPE(*JOBD)
          CHKOBJ     OBJ(&LIB) OBJTYPE(*LIB)
          DSPFD      FILE(&LIB/QAPMJOBS) TYPE(*MBRLIST) +
                       OUTPUT(*OUTFILE) OUTFILE(QTEMP/PFR001PF)
          OVRDBF     FILE(QAFDMBRL) TOFILE(QTEMP/PFR001PF)
          CHGVAR     VAR(&CMD) VALUE('DLTPFRDTA LIB(' *CAT &LIB +
                       *TCAT ') JOBD(' *CAT %SST(&FULLJOBD 11 +
                       10) *TCAT '/' *CAT %SST(&FULLJOBD 1 10) +
                       *TCAT ') MBR(')

RCVF:     RCVF
          MONMSG     MSGID(CPF0864) EXEC(GOTO CMDLBL(FINISH))
          IF         COND(&MLCHGC *LE %SST(&DATE 1 1) *AND +
                       &MLCHGD *LT %SST(&DATE 2 6)) THEN(DO)
          CHGVAR     VAR(&CMD) VALUE(&CMD *BCAT &MLNAME)
          CHGVAR     VAR(&COUNT) VALUE(&COUNT + 1)
          IF         COND(&COUNT = 50) THEN(DO)
          CHGVAR     VAR(&CMD) VALUE(&CMD *TCAT ')')
          CHGVAR     VAR(&CMDLEN) VALUE(1025)
CALCLEN1: CHGVAR     VAR(&CMDLEN) VALUE(&CMDLEN - 1)
          IF         COND(%SST(&CMD &CMDLEN 1) *EQ ' ') THEN(GOTO +
                       CMDLBL(CALCLEN1))
          CALL       PGM(QCMDEXC) PARM(&CMD &CMDLEN)
          CHGVAR     VAR(&CMD) VALUE('DLTPFRDTA LIB(' *CAT &LIB +
                       *TCAT ') JOBD(' *CAT %SST(&FULLJOBD 11 +
                       10) *TCAT '/' *CAT %SST(&FULLJOBD 1 10) +
                       *TCAT ') MBR(')
          CHGVAR     VAR(&COUNT) VALUE(0)
          ENDDO
          ENDDO
          GOTO       CMDLBL(RCVF)

FINISH:   IF         COND(&COUNT *EQ 0 *AND &CMDLEN *EQ 0) THEN(DO)
          SNDPGMMSG  MSGID(CPF9898) MSGF(QCPFMSG) MSGDTA('No +
                       members are older than the date +
                       submitted') MSGTYPE(*ESCAPE)

          ENDDO

          IF         COND(&COUNT *NE 0) THEN(DO)
          CHGVAR     VAR(&CMD) VALUE(&CMD *TCAT ')')
          CHGVAR     VAR(&CMDLEN) VALUE(1025)
CALCLEN2: CHGVAR     VAR(&CMDLEN) VALUE(&CMDLEN - 1)
          IF         COND(%SST(&CMD &CMDLEN 1) *EQ ' ') THEN(GOTO +
                       CMDLBL(CALCLEN2))
          CALL       PGM(QCMDEXC) PARM(&CMD &CMDLEN)
          ENDDO
```

Figure 21.13: Program PFR001CL is the heart of the DLTPFRDTA2 command (part 2 of 3).

```
            GOTO        CMDLBL(ENDPGM)
ERROR:      RCVMSG      MSGTYPE(*EXCP) MSGDTA(&MSGDTA) MSGID(&MSGID)
            MONMSG      MSGID(CPF0000)
            SNDPGMMSG   MSGID(&MSGID) MSGF(QCPFMSG) MSGDTA(&MSGDTA) +
                          MSGTYPE(*ESCAPE)
            MONMSG      MSGID(CPF0000)
ENDPGM:     ENDPGM
```

Figure 21.13: Program PFR001CL is the heart of the DLTPFRDTA2 command (part 3 of 3).

Performance data is stored in multiple files in a performance tools data library, which is QPFRDATA by default. Each time a data collection is run, a new member is added to each file by default. Because the performance data collection programs can save data into existing members, all date comparisons are done with the member change date.

The program works by retrieving a member list from one of the performance data files, QAPMJOBS. It then checks each member in QAPMJOBS to see if it was changed before the date specified on the DLTPFRDTA2 command. If it was, the member name is added to a command string that will be executed by QCMDEXC. Because DLTPFRDTA can accept only 50 member names, the program will execute the delete for every 50 members that pass the date test.

—Martin Pluth

Millisecond Timer

While trying to create a unique identifier for data transfers, we needed to obtain the system time in milliseconds. Although it is possible to retrieve this time using the Retrieve System Value (QWCRSVAL) API, we found that the Convert Date and Time Format (QWCCVTDT) API is easier to use and understand. (See Figure 21.14.) When *CURRENT is passed as the input format value, the current system date and time are returned. You can control the returned date format by changing the output format value.

```
*================================================================
* To compile:
*
*              CRTBNDRPG PGM(XXX/TIMER) SRCFILE(XXX/QRPGLESRC)
*
*================================================================

* Convert date / time (QWCCVTDT) API

d InpFmt          s             10    inz('*CURRENT')
```

Figure 21.14: RPG IV program TIMER can be used to determine milliseconds.

```
   d InpTim          s              16     inz(*ZEROS)
   d OutFmt          s              10     inz('*YYMD')

    * Current date and time

   d CurDatTim       ds
   d   CurDat                        8s 0
   d   CurTim                        9s 0

    * Error code data

   d ErrData         ds
   d   BytesProv             1       4b 0 inz(272)
   d   BytesAval             5       8b 0
   d   ExcpId                9      15a
   d   Reserved             16      16a
   d   ExcpData             17     272a

   c     *entry      plist
   c                 parm                   CurDatTim

   c                 call        'QWCCVTDT'
   c                 parm                   InpFmt
   c                 parm                   InpTim
   c                 parm                   OutFmt
   c                 parm                   CurDatTim
   c                 parm                   ErrData

   c                 return
```

Figure 21.14: RPG IV program TIMER can be used to determine milliseconds.

—Terrance Ramirez

Daylight Saving Time Conversion Program

Here is a utility that automates daylight saving time changes using the OS/400 job scheduler to automate the task of changing between standard time and daylight saving time.

I wrote two CL programs that run every month. Job DST_APR runs on the first Sunday each month at 2:00 A.M. It is a simple call to program TIMEAPR (Figure 21.15). DST_OCT runs at 2:00 A.M. on the last Sunday of each month and calls TIMEOCT (Figure 21.16). I used the two Add Job Schedule Entry (ADDJOBSCDE) commands shown in Figures 21.17 and 21.18 to set the programs up to run at the correct times of the month.

```
/* SWITCH SYSTEM CLOCK WHEN DAYLIGHT SAVINGS TIME BEGINS/ENDS */
/* TO ACTIVATE, USE THE FOLLOWING COMMAND FROM A COMMAND LINE */
/*      ADDJOBSCDE JOB(DST_APR) +                            */
/*         CMD(CALL PGM(TIMEAPR)) +                          */
/*         FRQ(*MONTHLY) SCDDATE(*NONE) +                    */
/*         SCDDAY(*SUN) SCDTIME(020000) +                    */
/*         RELDAYMON(1 *LAST)                                */

  PGM   /* TIMEAPR */

  DCL VAR(&MONTH) TYPE(*CHAR) LEN(2)
  DCL VAR(&DAY) TYPE(*CHAR) LEN(2)
  DCL VAR(&HOUR) TYPE(*CHAR) LEN(2)
  DCL VAR(&HOUR#) TYPE(*DEC) LEN(2 0)
  DCL VAR(&SAVEHOUR) TYPE(*CHAR) LEN(2)

  MONMSG CPF0000

  RTVSYSVAL SYSVAL(QMONTH) RTNVAR(&MONTH)
  RTVSYSVAL SYSVAL(QDAY) RTNVAR(&DAY)
  RTVSYSVAL SYSVAL(QHOUR) RTNVAR(&HOUR)
  CHGVAR VAR(&SAVEHOUR) VALUE(&HOUR)

  CHGVAR VAR(&HOUR#) VALUE(&HOUR)
  IF COND(&MONTH = '04' *AND &DAY < '15') +
     THEN(CHGVAR VAR(&HOUR#) VALUE(&HOUR# + 1))

  CHGVAR VAR(&HOUR) VALUE(&HOUR#)

  IF (&HOUR *NE &SAVEHOUR) DO
     CHGSYSVAL SYSVAL(QHOUR) VALUE(&HOUR)
     SNDMSG      MSG('System clock was changed from' *BCAT +
                 &SAVEHOUR *BCAT 'to' *BCAT &HOUR) TOUSR(TED)
  ENDDO

ENDPGM
```

Figure 21.15: CL program TIMEAPR allows you to adjust for the time change in April.

```
/* SWITCH SYSTEM CLOCK WHEN DAYLIGHT SAVINGS TIME ENDS      */
/* TO ACTIVATE, USE THE FOLLOWING COMMAND FROM A COMMAND LINE */
/*      ADDJOBSCDE JOB(DST_OCT) +                            */
/*         CMD(CALL PGM(TIMEOCT)) +                          */
/*         FRQ(*MONTHLY) SCDDATE(*NONE) +                    */
/*         SCDDAY(*SUN) SCDTIME(020000) +                    */
/*         RELDAYMON(1 *LAST)                                */

  PGM   /* TIMEOCT */

  DCL VAR(&MONTH) TYPE(*CHAR) LEN(2)
  DCL VAR(&DAY) TYPE(*CHAR) LEN(2)
  DCL VAR(&HOUR) TYPE(*CHAR) LEN(2)
  DCL VAR(&HOUR#) TYPE(*DEC) LEN(2 0)
  DCL VAR(&SAVEHOUR) TYPE(*CHAR) LEN(2)
```

Figure 21.16: CL program TIMEOCT lets you adjust for the time change in October (part 1 of 2).

```
    MONMSG CPF0000

    RTVSYSVAL SYSVAL(QMONTH) RTNVAR(&MONTH)
    RTVSYSVAL SYSVAL(QDAY) RTNVAR(&DAY)
    RTVSYSVAL SYSVAL(QHOUR) RTNVAR(&HOUR)
    CHGVAR VAR(&SAVEHOUR) VALUE(&HOUR)

    CHGVAR VAR(&HOUR#) VALUE(&HOUR)
    IF COND(&MONTH = '10' *AND &DAY < '15') +
        THEN(CHGVAR VAR(&HOUR#) VALUE(&HOUR# + 1))

    CHGVAR VAR(&HOUR) VALUE(&HOUR#)

    IF (&HOUR *NE &SAVEHOUR) DO
        CHGSYSVAL SYSVAL(QHOUR) VALUE(&HOUR)
        SNDMSG    MSG('System clock was changed from' *BCAT +
                    &SAVEHOUR *BCAT 'to' *BCAT &HOUR) TOUSR(TED)
    ENDDO

ENDPGM
```

Figure 21.16: CL program TIMEOCT lets you adjust for the time change in October (part 2 of 2).

```
ADDJOBSCDE JOB(DST_APR) CMD(CALL PGM(TIMEAPR)) FRQ(*MONTHLY) SCDDATE(*NONE) +
    SCDDAY(*SUN) SCDTIME(020000)
```

Figure 21.17: Add this job schedule entry for program TIMEAPR.

```
ADDJOBSCDE JOB(DST_OCT) CMD(CALL PGM(TIMEOCT)) FRQ(*MONTHLY) SCDDATE(*NONE) +
    SCDDAY(*SUN) SCDTIME(020000) RELDAYMON(*LAST)
```

Figure 21.18: Add this job schedule entry for program TIMEOCT.

—Lori Nesje

✦ ✦ ✦ Display Files

Command to Send Scrolling Messages

If you want to attract a user's attention, or you simply want to add some excitement to your programs, the Send Scrolling Message (SNDSCRMSG) command is for you (see Figures 21.19 and 21.20). The command sends a scrolling message at the bottom of the screen with changing colors. Try it; it's fun!

```
/*==============================================================*/
/* To compile:                                                  */
/*                                                              */
/*          CRTCMD    CMD(XXX/SNDSCRMSG) PGM(XXX/SCR001CL) +     */
/*                    SRCFILE(XXX/QCMDSRC)                       */
/*                                                              */
/*==============================================================*/
            CMD       PROMPT('Send Scrolling Message')
            PARM      KWD(MSG) TYPE(*CHAR) LEN(78) MIN(1) +
                      PROMPT('Message')
```

Figure 21.19: Use the SNDSCRMSG command to add excitement to your display screens.

```
/*==============================================================*/
/* To compile:                                                  */
/*                                                              */
/*          CRTCLPGM   PGM(XXX/SCR001CL) SRCFILE(XXX/QCLSRC)     */
/*                                                              */
/*==============================================================*/
SCR001CL: +
   PGM PARM(&MSG)
   DCL VAR(&MSG)       TYPE(*CHAR) LEN(78)
   DCL VAR(&MSGDTA)    TYPE(*CHAR) LEN(78)
   DCL VAR(&COLOR)     TYPE(*CHAR) LEN(1)
   DCL VAR(&COLORS)    TYPE(*CHAR) LEN(5)       VALUE(X'2022283A38')
   DCL VAR(&I)         TYPE(*DEC)  LEN(2 0)
   DCL VAR(&J)         TYPE(*DEC)  LEN(2 0)
   DCL VAR(&K)         TYPE(*DEC)  LEN(2 0)
   DCL VAR(&L)         TYPE(*DEC)  LEN(2 0)

   /* Do scrolling */
LOOP: +
   CHGVAR VAR(&I) VALUE(&I + 1)
   IF COND(&I *EQ 79) THEN(GOTO CMDLBL(END))
   CHGVAR VAR(&J) VALUE(79 - &I)
   CHGVAR VAR(&K) VALUE(&I - 1)
   IF COND(&I *EQ 1) THEN(CHGVAR VAR(&MSGDTA) VALUE(%SST(&MSG &I &J)))
   ELSE CMD(CHGVAR VAR(&MSGDTA) VALUE(%SST(&MSG &I &J) *CAT +
      %SST(&MSG 1 &K)))

   /* Add some color */
   CHGVAR VAR(&L) VALUE(&L + 1)
   IF COND(&L *EQ 6) THEN(CHGVAR VAR(&L) VALUE(1))
   CHGVAR VAR(&COLOR) VALUE(%SST(&COLORS &L 1))
   CHGVAR VAR(&MSGDTA) VALUE(&COLOR *CAT &MSGDTA)

   /* Send the message */
   SNDPGMMSG MSGID(CPF9897) MSGF(QCPFMSG) MSGDTA(&MSGDTA) +
      TOPGMQ(*EXT) MSGTYPE(*STATUS)
   GOTO CMDLBL(LOOP)
END: +
   ENDPGM
```

Figure 21.20: CL program SCR001CL is the power behind the SNDSCRMSG command.

—Jean-Jacques Risch

858

Indicators Used in Display Files

One of the most irritating chores the maintenance programmer must undertake is to modify interactive programs. Such programs use display files, which (sometimes) use indicators heavily. The difficult part is finding an indicator that hasn't yet been used anywhere in the display file. Under normal circumstances, the programmer must scan the source code, jot down all conditioning indicators, and hope to catch all response indicators.

There's a better way: Run the Display File Field Description (DSPFFD) command on the display file. It lists all fields and indicators used by the display file, whether the display file uses the INDARA keyword or not. Still, DSPFFD presents the information in an inconvenient fashion. The Display Display File Indicators (DSPDSPIND) command presented here shows only the indicator information, sorted by indicator number and record format name.

To use DSPDSPIND, simply supply the name of the display file. (This utility will also work with printer files.) Notice that DSPDSPIND does not work with the source code, but rather with the compiled *FILE object itself. DSPDSPIND is shown in Figure 21.21, its CPP is shown in Figure 21.22, the display file DSP001DF is shown in Figure 21.23, and the RPG IV program DSP001RG is shown in Figure 21.24.

The technique I've used is to direct DSPFFD's output to an outfile, and then process the records with Open Query File (OPNQRYF), selecting only the indicators and sorting the information as previously mentioned.

```
/*================================================================*/
/* To compile:                                                    */
/*                                                                */
/*          CRTCMD      CMD(XXX/DSPDSPIND) PGM(XXX/DSP001CL) +     */
/*                      SRCFILE(XXX/QCMDSRC)                       */
/*                                                                */
/*================================================================*/
            CMD         PROMPT('Display Display Indicators')

            PARM        KWD(DSPFILE) TYPE(Q1) MIN(1) PROMPT('Display +
                        file')

Q1:         QUAL        TYPE(*NAME) LEN(10) MIN(1) EXPR(*YES)
            QUAL        TYPE(*NAME) LEN(10) DFT(*LIBL) +
                        SPCVAL((*LIBL) (*CURLIB)) EXPR(*YES) +
                        PROMPT('Library')
```

Figure 21.21: Command DSPDSPIND helps you to determine what indicators are used in a display file.

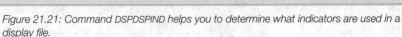

```
/*================================================================*/
/* To compile:                                                    */
/*                                                                */
/*            CRTCLPGM   PGM(XXX/DSP001CL) SRCFILE(XXX/QCLSRC)     */
/*                                                                */
/*================================================================*/
PGM        PARM(&QUAL_DSPF)

  DCL        VAR(&DSPF) TYPE(*CHAR) LEN(10)
  DCL        VAR(&DSPFLIB) TYPE(*CHAR) LEN(10)
  DCL        VAR(&OBJATR) TYPE(*CHAR) LEN(10)
  DCL        VAR(&MSGDTA) TYPE(*CHAR) LEN(256)
  DCL        VAR(&MSGF) TYPE(*CHAR) LEN(10)
  DCL        VAR(&MSGFLIB) TYPE(*CHAR) LEN(10)
  DCL        VAR(&MSGID) TYPE(*CHAR) LEN(7)
  DCL        VAR(&QUAL_DSPF) TYPE(*CHAR) LEN(20)

  MONMSG     MSGID(CPF0000 MCH0000) EXEC(GOTO CMDLBL(ERROR))

  /* Break qualified name */
  CHGVAR     VAR(&DSPF) VALUE(%SST(&QUAL_DSPF 1 10))
  CHGVAR     VAR(&DSPFLIB) VALUE(%SST(&QUAL_DSPF 11 10))

  /* Check existence of file */
  RTVOBJD    OBJ(&DSPFLIB/&DSPF) OBJTYPE(*FILE) +
               OBJATR(&OBJATR)
  IF         COND(&OBJATR *NE 'DSPF' *AND &OBJATR *NE +
             'PRTF') THEN(DO)
    SNDPGMMSG  MSGID(CPF9898) MSGF(QCPFMSG) MSGDTA('File' +
               *BCAT &DSPFLIB *TCAT '/' *CAT &DSPF *BCAT +
               'must be a display file or printer file') +
               MSGTYPE(*ESCAPE)
  ENDDO

  /* Retrieve display file definition */
  DSPFFD     FILE(&DSPFLIB/&DSPF) OUTPUT(*OUTFILE) +
               OUTFILE(QTEMP/DSPFFD)
  OVRDBF     FILE(QADSPFFD) TOFILE(QTEMP/DSPFFD) SHARE(*YES)
  OPNQRYF    FILE((QADSPFFD)) QRYSLT('%sst(whflde 1 3) = +
               "*IN"') KEYFLD((WHFLDE) (WHNAME))
  /* Display indicators */
  CALL       PGM(DSP001RG) PARM(&DSPFLIB &DSPF)
  CLOF       OPNID(QADSPFFD)
  DLTOVR     FILE(QADSPFFD)

  RCLRSC
  RETURN

  /* Forward escape message to caller */
ERROR:
  RCVMSG     MSGTYPE(*EXCP) MSGDTA(&MSGDTA) MSGID(&MSGID) +
               MSGF(&MSGF) SNDMSGFLIB(&MSGFLIB)
  MONMSG     MSGID(CPF0000)
  SNDPGMMSG  MSGID(&MSGID) MSGF(&MSGFLIB/&MSGF) +
```

Figure 21.22: CL program DSP001CL is the processing power behind displaying which indicators are being used in your display file (part 1 of 2).

```
                      MSGDTA(&MSGDTA) MSGTYPE(*ESCAPE)
          MONMSG      MSGID(CPF0000)

ENDPGM
```

Figure 21.22: CL program DSP001CL is the processing power behind displaying which indicators are being used in your display file (part 2 of 2).

```
    *=================================================================
    * To compile:
    *
    *       CRTDSPF    FILE(XXX/DSP001DF) SRCFILE(XXX/QDDSSRC)
    *
    *=================================================================
    A                                             DSPSIZ(24 80 *DS3)
    A                                             CA03
    A                                             CA12
    *-----------------------------------------------------------------
    A          R FKEYS
    A                                       24  2'F3=Exit    F12=Cancel'
    A                                             COLOR(BLU)
    *-----------------------------------------------------------------
    A          R INDSFLDTA                        SFL
    A            INDICATOR     2A  O   5 10
    A            RCDFMTNAM    10A  O   5 21
    A            OUTBUFPOS     5Y 00   5 40EDTCDE(2)
    A            INBUFPOS      5Y 00   5 59EDTCDE(2)
    *-----------------------------------------------------------------
    A          R INDSFLCTL                        SFLCTL(INDSFLDTA)
    A                                             SFLSIZ(0020)
    A                                             SFLPAG(0018)
    A                                             BLINK
    A                                             OVERLAY
    A  80                                         SFLDSP
    A                                             SFLDSPCTL
    A N80                                         SFLCLR
    A N81                                         SFLEND(*MORE)
    A                                       1 29'Display File Indicators'
    A                                             DSPATR(HI)
    A                                       2 27'File:'
    A            QUALDSPF     21A  O   2 33
    A                                       4  7'Indicator'
    A                                             DSPATR(HI)
    A                                       4 19'Record Format'
    A                                             DSPATR(HI)
    A                                       4 35'Output Buffer Pos'
    A                                             DSPATR(HI)
    A                                       4 55'Input Buffer Pos'
    A                                             DSPATR(HI)
```

Figure 21.23: Display file DSP001DF displays what indicators are used in a given display file.

```
*=================================================================
* To compile:
*
*       CRTBNDRPG  PGM(XXX/DSP001RG) SRCFILE(XXX/QRPGLESRC)
*
*=================================================================
Fqadspffd  IF   E           K DISK
Fdsp001df  CF   E             WORKSTN SFILE(indsfldta:indrrn)
 ***************************************************************
D dspf            S             10A
D dspflib         S             10A
D indrrn          S              4P 0
 ***************************************************************
C     *ENTRY        PLIST
C                   PARM                    dspflib
C                   PARM                    dspf

C                   EVAL      qualdspf = %TRIMR(dspflib) + '/' +
C                             dspf
C                   EXSR      lodsfl

C                   WRITE     fkeys
C                   EXFMT     indsflctl

C                   EVAL      *INLR = *ON
C                   RETURN
 *_____
C     lodsfl        BEGSR
C                   EVAL      indrrn = 0
C                   EVAL      *IN80 = *OFF
C                   EVAL      *IN81 = *OFF
C                   EVAL      *IN99 = *OFF

C                   DOU       *IN99 = *ON
C                   READ      qadspffd                           99
C                   IF        *IN99 = *OFF
C                   EVAL      rcdfmtnam = whname
C                   EVAL      indicator = %SUBST(whflde:4:2)
C                   EVAL      outbufpos = whfobo
C                   EVAL      inbufpos = whibo
C                   EVAL      indrrn = indrrn + 1
C                   WRITE     indsfldta
C                   ENDIF
C                   ENDDO

C                   IF        indrrn > 0
C                   EVAL      *IN80 = *ON
C                   ENDIF
C                   ENDSR
```

Figure 21.24: *RPG IV program* DSP001RG *builds the display that shows what indicators are used in a display file.*

—Ernie Malaga

✦ ✦ ✦ **Editing**

Create Special Effects in Source Code

Did you ever wish you could bring more attention to your source code comments by using a display attribute such as highlight, reverse image, or even colors such as blue, yellow, or red? Here's how you can.

The physical file ATR001PF, shown in Figure 21.25, is used to store the hexadecimal values that control these display attributes. The RPG program ATR001RG (Figure 21.26) loads the physical file. After program ATR001RG is executed, run the Copy File (CPYF) command with the FMTOPT(*CVTSRC) parameter to copy the file into a source member. The command would look similar to the following:

```
CPYF FROMFILE(MYLIB/ATR001PF) TOFILE(MYLIB/QTXTSRC) +
     TOMBR(ATTRIBUTES) MBROPT(*REPLACE) +
     FMTOPT(*CVTSRC)
```

Replace MYLIB with the library of your choice. You can also specify a source file other than QTXTSRC or a source member other than ATTRIBUTES if you want. This command copies the data in ATR001PF into a source member.

Once you've created the source member, you can browse or copy the desired effect into your source code using SEU. After you copy one of these statements into your program, you can move the first position of the statement over to where you want the comment to begin (e.g., past position 7 in an RPG program). Then, without spacing over the first or last position, blank out the sample data text. You can use the copy (C) line command to copy the statement with the attribute and the overlay (O) line command to overlay it on a comment line. The source code should now have the desired effect.

This technique can work in any source code that allows a comment line (e.g., RPG, DDS, CL) because the attribute byte is part of the comment. Keep in mind that the first position is the hexadecimal value needed for the effect, and the last position is the hexadecimal value to turn off the effect. As long as these are within the comment line, the entire line is treated as a comment line, and the effect will exist.

```
*===============================================================
* To compile:
*
*      CRTPF      FILE(XXX/ATR001PF) SRCFILE(XXX/QDDSSRC)
*
*===============================================================
A          R ATR001RC
A            BEGVAL          1H          TEXT('Beginning Attribute')
A            SMPDTA         20           TEXT('Sample Data')
A            ENDVAL          1H          TEXT('Ending Attribute')
```

Figure 21.25: Use this physical file layout for file ATR001PF.

```
*===============================================================
* To compile:
*
*      CRTRPGPGM  PGM(XXX/ATR001RG) SRCFILE(XXX/QRPGSRC)
*
*===============================================================
FATR001PFO  E                    DISK                          A
*
I          DS
I I            1                 B   1   20HEX
I I            33                B   3   40BIN
I                                    4   4 ATR
I            '<====SampleData====>'C        DTA
*
C                  MOVELX'20'    ENDVAL
*
C                  DO   31
C                  MOVELATR      BEGVAL
C                  MOVELDTA      SMPDTA
C                  WRITEATR001RC
C                  ADD   HEX     BIN
C                  END
*
C                  MOVE *ON      *INLR
```

Figure 21.26: RPG program ATR001RG will be used to set the special effects in your code.

—Darren Molitor

Don't Add Bugs When Adding a File to an RPG Program

I've done a lot of maintenance programming, and I think I've been bitten by just about every bug there is. Several years ago, I decided that never again would I let adding a file create bugs in an RPG program. This happens when a file I add to a program has a field with the same name as a field or variable already used in the program. Bugs creep in when the program uses the field from the added file instead of using the one already existing in the program.

At first, I visually checked all the field names in the file I was adding to a program and then built renamed input specs (I-specs) for the field names that were already defined to the program. That method was acceptable only when the file I was adding had just a few fields in it. So I wrote the BLDISPEC utility. It builds I-specs that rename all the fields of a file to a two-character prefix of my choosing, followed by a four-digit sequential number (e.g., XX0001, XX0002, and so forth).

BLDISPEC consists of the BLDISPEC command, CL program ISP001CL, and RPG program ISP001RG (see Figures 21.27 through 21.29). I must provide the following information:

- The name of the database file for which I need renamed I-specs.

- The qualified name and the member name of the source member to contain the I-specs.

- The two-character prefix I want the renamed fields to begin with.

```
/*================================================================*/
/* To compile:                                                    */
/*                                                                */
/*          CRTCMD   CMD(XXX/BLDISPEC) PGM(XXX/ISP001CL) +        */
/*                   SRCFILE(XXX/QCMDSRC)                         */
/*                                                                */
/*================================================================*/
 BLDISPEC:  CMD        PROMPT('Build renamed I specs')

            PARM       KWD(FILE) TYPE(Q1) MIN(1) FILE(*IN) +
                         PROMPT('Database file name')
            PARM       KWD(SRCFILE) TYPE(Q1) MIN(1) FILE(*IN) +
                         PROMPT('Source file name')
            PARM       KWD(SRCMBR) TYPE(*NAME) MIN(1) +
                         PROMPT('Source member')
            PARM       KWD(PREFIX) TYPE(*CHAR) LEN(2) MIN(1) +
                         FULL(*YES) PROMPT('Field prefix')
            PARM       KWD(RPGTYPE) TYPE(*CHAR) LEN(3) RSTD(*YES) +
                         DFT(III) VALUES(III IV) PROMPT('RPG +
                         source type')
            PARM       KWD(FLDTEXT) TYPE(*CHAR) LEN(4) RSTD(*YES) +
                         DFT(*YES) VALUES(*YES *NO) +
                         PROMPT('Include field text?')

 Q1:        QUAL       TYPE(*NAME) LEN(10)
            QUAL       TYPE(*NAME) LEN(10) DFT(*LIBL) +
                         SPCVAL((*LIBL)) PROMPT('Library')
```

Figure 21.27: Command BLDISPEC is used to add I-specs to a program.

```
/*================================================================*/
/* To compile:                                                    */
/*                                                                */
/*              CRTCLPGM   PGM(XXX/ISP001CL) SRCFILE(XXX/QCLSRC)   */
/*                                                                */
/*================================================================*/
PGM PARM(&FILE &SRCFILE &SRCMBR &PREFIX &RPGVER &FLDTEXT)

  DCL        VAR(&PREFIX) TYPE(*CHAR) LEN(2)
  DCL        VAR(&RPGVER) TYPE(*CHAR) LEN(3)
  DCL        VAR(&FILE) TYPE(*CHAR) LEN(20)
  DCL        VAR(&FILENAME) TYPE(*CHAR) LEN(10)
  DCL        VAR(&FILELIB) TYPE(*CHAR) LEN(10)
  DCL        VAR(&FLDTEXT) TYPE(*CHAR) LEN(3)
  DCL        VAR(&SRCFILE) TYPE(*CHAR) LEN(20)
  DCL        VAR(&SRCNAME) TYPE(*CHAR) LEN(10)
  DCL        VAR(&SRCLIB) TYPE(*CHAR) LEN(10)
  DCL        VAR(&SRCMBR) TYPE(*CHAR) LEN(10)

  DCL        VAR(&MSGDTA) TYPE(*CHAR) LEN(132)
  DCL        VAR(&MSGF) TYPE(*CHAR) LEN(10)
  DCL        VAR(&MSGFLIB) TYPE(*CHAR) LEN(10)
  DCL        VAR(&MSGID) TYPE(*CHAR) LEN(7)

  MONMSG     MSGID(CPF0000) EXEC(GOTO CMDLBL(FWDMSG))

  CHGVAR     VAR(&FILENAME) VALUE(%SST(&FILE 1 10))
  CHGVAR     VAR(&FILELIB) VALUE(%SST(&FILE 11 10))
  IF         COND(&FILELIB *EQ ' ') THEN(CHGVAR +
               VAR(&FILELIB) VALUE(*LIBL))

  CHGVAR     VAR(&SRCNAME) VALUE(%SST(&SRCFILE 1 10))
  CHGVAR     VAR(&SRCLIB) VALUE(%SST(&SRCFILE 11 10))
  IF         COND(&SRCLIB *EQ ' ') THEN(CHGVAR +
               VAR(&SRCLIB) VALUE(*LIBL))

  /* Make sure the member exists */
  RTVMBRD    FILE(&SRCLIB/&SRCNAME) MBR(&SRCMBR)

  /* Get the field names */
  DSPFFD     FILE(&FILELIB/&FILENAME) OUTPUT(*OUTFILE) +
               OUTFILE(QTEMP/QADSPFFD)
  RCVMSG     MSGTYPE(*LAST)

  OVRDBF     FILE(QADSPFFD) TOFILE(QTEMP/QADSPFFD)
  OVRDBF     FILE(SRCOUT) TOFILE(&SRCLIB/&SRCNAME) +
               MBR(&SRCMBR)
  CALL       PGM(ISP001RG) PARM(&PREFIX &RPGVER &FLDTEXT)
  DLTOVR     FILE(QADSPFFD SRCOUT)
  SNDPGMMSG  MSG('Input specs have been generated.') +
               MSGTYPE(*COMP)

  RETURN
```

Figure 21.28: CL program ISP001CL is the housekeeping CPP for command BLDISPEC (part 1 of 2).

```
    /* Send all messages back to the calling program */
FWDMSG:
  RCVMSG      MSGDTA(&MSGDTA) MSGID(&MSGID) MSGF(&MSGF) +
                MSGFLIB(&MSGFLIB)
   IF         COND(&MSGID *NE ' ') THEN(DO)
    SNDPGMMSG MSGID(&MSGID) MSGF(&MSGFLIB/&MSGF) +
                MSGDTA(&MSGDTA)
    GOTO      CMDLBL(FWDMSG)
   ENDDO

ENDPGM
```

Figure 21.28: CL program ISP001CL is the housekeeping CPP for command BLDISPEC (part 2 of 2).

```
*=================================================================
* To compile:
*
*       CRTRPGPGM  PGM(XXX/ISP001RG)  SRCFILE(XXX/QRPGSRC)
*
*=================================================================
FQADSPFFDIP  E                     DISK
FSRCOUT  O   F      92             DISK
IQWHDRFFD
I                                            WHNAMEL1
C          *ENTRY    PLIST
C                    PARM                    PFX    2
C                    PARM                    RPGVER 3
C                    PARM                    ADDTXT 4
C*
C          *INL1     IFEQ *ON
C                    EXCPTHDR
C                    ENDIF
C*
C                    ADD  1         CT       40
C                    EXCPTDTL
C*
C          ADDTXT    IFEQ '*YES'
C                    EXCPTTEXT
C                    ENDIF
C***********
C          *INZSR    BEGSR
C*
C          RPGVER    IFEQ 'IV '
C                    MOVE *ON        *IN42
C                    ELSE
C                    MOVE *ON        *IN41
```

Figure 21.29: RPG Program ISP001RG is the real heart of the BLDISPEC command (part 1 of 2).

```
C                    ENDIF
C*
C                    ENDSR
OSRCOUT  E           HDR
O                            32 '*        File:'
O                    WHFILE + 1
O        E           HDR
O                            32 '*        Format:'
O                    WHNAME + 1
O        E           HDR
O                            32 '* Description:'
O                    WHTEXT + 1
O        E           HDR
O                            18 'I'
O                    WHNAME + 0
O        E           DTL
O                            18 'I'
O                    WHFLDI   42
O              41    PFX      66
O              41    CT     + 0
O              42    PFX      62
O              42    CT     + 0
O        E           TEXT
O                            19 'I*'
O                    WHFTXT + 20
```

Figure 21.29: RPG Program ISP001RG is the real heart of the BLDISPEC command
(part 2 of 2).

I also can specify whether I want RPG III or RPG IV I-specs. So far, I have not used this
utility with RPG IV programs because the PREFIX keyword, used in definition specifications, provides a similar function. However, I added the capability to generate RPG IV
I-specs so I'd have that alternative. I also can choose to include the description of each
field in comments in the generated source.

When I use this utility, I first look at a compiler listing to find a two-character combination that has not been used as the first two characters of any field or variable names.
Next, I generate the I-specs. Last, I delete or modify the renamed I-specs of any fields
that I want to use in the program, leaving only the undesired fields renamed with the generated names.

The way I wrote BLDISPEC requires that the source member already exist. I specify the
name of the program I'm adding the file to. The I-specs are added to the end of the program, and I move them to their proper place.

—*Ted Holt*

♦ ♦ ♦ File Access

Who Locked the Record?

Q: An RPG application that I am working on must be able to capture a locked record and display the name of the user who has the record. The File Information Data Structure doesn't contain this information, and I would appreciate help with writing a CL routine to determine which user has the record locked.

A: You can get that information from your RPG program by using the Program Status Data Structure (PSDS). When a record lock occurs, the text for the error message is in positions 91 through 170 of the PSDS. The full job name of the user who has the record locked is embedded within the message text. You can easily substring out the user name from the message. The RPG program must have an error indicator in the "Lo" position of the input calculation. The error text will read something like, "Record 5 in use by job 047237/SOMEUSER/QPADEV0010."

—Mark McCall

A: In our shop, we integrate a utility to handle locked records into our interactive programs. Figures 21.30 and 21.31 show CL program SHWLCKCL and the source code for display file SHWLCKDF. When an I/O error occurs in an RPG program, we call SHWLCKCL. The user is presented with a display identifying who has the lock on the record and asking him to wait until the lock is released.

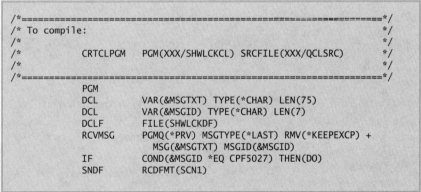

```
/*===============================================================*/
/* To compile:                                                   */
/*                                                               */
/*          CRTCLPGM   PGM(XXX/SHWLCKCL) SRCFILE(XXX/QCLSRC)      */
/*                                                               */
/*===============================================================*/
           PGM
           DCL        VAR(&MSGTXT) TYPE(*CHAR) LEN(75)
           DCL        VAR(&MSGID) TYPE(*CHAR) LEN(7)
           DCLF       FILE(SHWLCKDF)
           RCVMSG     PGMQ(*PRV) MSGTYPE(*LAST) RMV(*KEEPEXCP) +
                        MSG(&MSGTXT) MSGID(&MSGID)
           IF         COND(&MSGID *EQ CPF5027) THEN(DO)
           SNDF       RCDFMT(SCN1)
```

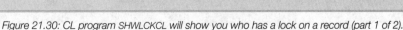

Figure 21.30: CL program SHWLCKCL will show you who has a lock on a record (part 1 of 2).

```
                DLYJOB      DLY(20)
                ENDDO
                ELSE        CMD(DO)
LOOP:           SNDRCVF     RCDFMT(SCN2)
                IF          COND(&IN24 *EQ '0') THEN(GOTO CMDLBL(LOOP))
                ENDDO
                ENDPGM
```

Figure 21.30: CL program SHWLCKCL will show you who has a lock on a record (part 2 of 2).

```
        *================================================================
        * Display the name of the job holding a record lock.
        *================================================================
        * To compile:
        *
        *     CRTDSPF    FILE(XXX/SHWLCKDF) SRCFILE(XXX/QDDSSRC)
        *
        *================================================================
        A           R SCN1                      FRCDTA LOCK
        A                                   1 25'UNABLE TO ALLOCATE RECORD'
        A                                        COLOR(WHT)
        A                                   3  2'CAUTION:  Please'
        A                                        DSPATR(BL)
        A                                     +1'do not press any keys.'
        A                                        DSPATR(BL)
        A                                     +2'Thank you.'
        A                                        DSPATR(BL)
        A                                   8  2'The patient record you'
        A                                        COLOR(YLW)
        A                                     +1'requested is currently'
        A                                        COLOR(YLW)
        A                                     +1'being used by:'
        A                                        COLOR(YLW)
        A             MSGTXT        75        9  2
        A                                        COLOR(RED)
        A                                  11  2'Please contact the above'
        A                                        COLOR(TRQ)
        A                                     +1'user asking them to'
        A                                        COLOR(TRQ)
        A                                     +1'return to their main'
        A                                        COLOR(TRQ)
        A                                     +1'menu.'
        A                                        COLOR(TRQ)
        A                                  12  2'The computer will'
        A                                        COLOR(TRQ)
        A                                     +1'automatically retry'
        A                                        COLOR(TRQ)
```

Figure 21.31: Display file SHWLCKDF is used to present the locked record information to the user (part 1 of 2).

```
A                                       +1'if you continue to'
A                                          COLOR(TRQ)
A                                       +1'receive this message'
A                                          COLOR(TRQ)
A                                    13  2'ask the above user to'
A                                          COLOR(TRQ)
A                                       +1'SIGNOFF.'
A                                          COLOR(TRQ)
A                                    18  2'CAUTION:  Please'
A                                          DSPATR(BL)
A                                       +1'do not press any keys.'
A                                          DSPATR(BL)
A                                       +2'Thank you.'
A                                          DSPATR(BL)
A                                    22  2'1'This screen will stay'
A                                          COLOR(PNK)
A                                       +1'active for 20 seconds.'
A                                          COLOR(PNK)
A             R SCN2                       FRCDTA CF24(24)
A*CF24 will not be shown to the user.  You can use CF24 to try
A*chain or read again.
A                                     1 25'DATA BASE RETRIEVAL ERROR'
A                                          COLOR(WHT)
A                                    10  7'Could not retrieve the'
A                                          DSPATR(BL)
A                                       +1'data record.'
A                                          DSPATR(BL)
A                                       +1'Please call Data'
A                                          COLOR(YLW)
A                                       +1'Processing.'
A                                          COLOR(YLW)
```

Figure 21.31: Display file SHWLCKDF is used to present the locked record information to the user (part 2 of 2).

—Richard Clark

✦ ✦ ✦ File Keys

Create RPG Key Lists with the CRTKLIST Utility

When you want to READ or CHAIN to a file by key using RPG, you often need to create a key list. If there are many key fields in the file, this can be time consuming. I wrote a utility called Create Key List (CRTKLIST) that makes this task much easier.

The CRTKLIST command will create an RPG or RPGLE source member containing a key list for a keyed physical or logical file. The source code for the utility is shown in Figures

21.32 through 21.34. The CRTKLIST command prompts you for a database file, a source file, a source member, and the member type.

After you run the command, the newly created source member contains the code for a key list that you can copy into your program and modify if necessary. The key list code contains one KLIST statement followed by one or more KFLD statements. Because the KLIST statement requires a key list name in factor 1, the utility uses the first six characters of the record format name. For the KFLD statements, it uses the database field names in the result column.

The next time you need to create an RPG key list, try using the CRTKLIST utility. It might save you some time.

```
/*================================================================*/
/* To compile:                                                    */
/*                                                                */
/*          CRTCMD     CMD(XXX/CRTKLIST) PGM(XXX/KLS001CL) +       */
/*                     SRCFILE(XXX/QCMDSRC)                        */
/*                                                                */
/*================================================================*/
            CMD        PROMPT('Create RPG Key List')
            PARM       KWD(FILE) TYPE(FILLIB) MIN(1) PROMPT('Keyed +
                         file')
            PARM       KWD(SRCFILE) TYPE(FILLIB) MIN(1) +
                         PROMPT('Source file')
            PARM       KWD(SRCMBR) TYPE(*NAME) LEN(10) MIN(1) +
                         PROMPT('Member')
            PARM       KWD(MBRTYP) TYPE(*CHAR) LEN(10) RSTD(*YES) +
                         DFT(RPG) VALUES(RPG RPGLE RPG38) +
                         PROMPT('Member type')
 FILLIB:    QUAL       TYPE(*NAME) LEN(10)
            QUAL       TYPE(*NAME) LEN(10) DFT(*LIBL) +
                         SPCVAL((*LIBL) (*CURLIB)) PROMPT('Library')
```

Figure 21.32: The CRTKLIST command is very handy for generating RPG key lists.

```
/*================================================================*/
/* To compile:                                                    */
/*                                                                */
/*          CRTCLPGM    PGM(XXX/KLS001CL) SRCFILE(XXX/QCLSRC)      */
/*                                                                */
/*================================================================*/
            PGM        PARM(&FILE &SRCF &SRCMBR &MBRTYPE)

            DCL        VAR(&FILE) TYPE(*CHAR) LEN(20)
            DCL        VAR(&SRCF) TYPE(*CHAR) LEN(20)
            DCL        VAR(&SRCMBR) TYPE(*CHAR) LEN(10)
            DCL        VAR(&MBRTYPE) TYPE(*CHAR) LEN(10)
            DCL        VAR(&MSGID) TYPE(*CHAR) LEN(7)
            DCL        VAR(&MSGF) TYPE(*CHAR) LEN(10)
            DCL        VAR(&MSGFLIB) TYPE(*CHAR) LEN(10)
            DCL        VAR(&MSGDTA) TYPE(*CHAR) LEN(80)

            MONMSG     MSGID(CPF0000) EXEC(GOTO CMDLBL(RCVERRORS))

            DSPFD      FILE(%SST(&FILE 11 10)/%SST(&FILE 1 10)) +
                         TYPE(*ACCPTH) OUTPUT(*OUTFILE) +
                         OUTFILE(QTEMP/KLS001PF) OUTMBR(*FIRST +
                         *REPLACE)

            ADDPFM     FILE(%SST(&SRCF 11 10)/%SST(&SRCF 1 10)) +
                         MBR(&SRCMBR) SRCTYPE(&MBRTYPE)

            OVRDBF     FILE(SRCMBR) TOFILE(%SST(&SRCF 11 +
                         10)/%SST(&SRCF 1 10)) MBR(&SRCMBR)
            OVRDBF     FILE(QAFDACCP) TOFILE(QTEMP/KLS001PF)

            CALL       PGM(KLS001RG) PARM(&MBRTYPE)

            IF         COND(&MBRTYPE *EQ 'ARRIVAL') THEN(DO)
            RMVM       FILE(%SST(&SRCF 11 10)/%SST(&SRCF 1 10)) +
                         MBR(&SRCMBR)
            MONMSG     MSGID(CPF0000)
            SNDPGMMSG  MSG('File' *BCAT %SST(&FILE 1 10) *BCAT +
                         'is not a keyed physical or logical +
                         file.') MSGTYPE(*INFO)
            ENDDO
            ELSE       CMD(SNDPGMMSG MSG('Key list for file' *BCAT +
                         %SST(&FILE 1 10) *BCAT 'created in file ' +
                         *CAT %SST(&SRCF 11 10) *TCAT '/' *TCAT +
                         %SST(&SRCF 1 10) *BCAT 'member ' *CAT +
                         &SRCMBR *TCAT '.') MSGTYPE(*COMP))

            GOTO       CMDLBL(ENDPGM)

RCVERRORS:  RCVMSG     MSGTYPE(*EXCP) MSGDTA(&MSGDTA) MSGID(&MSGID)
            SNDPGMMSG  MSGID(&MSGID) MSGF(QCPFMSG) MSGDTA(&MSGDTA) +
                         MSGTYPE(*ESCAPE)
ENDPGM:     ENDPGM
```

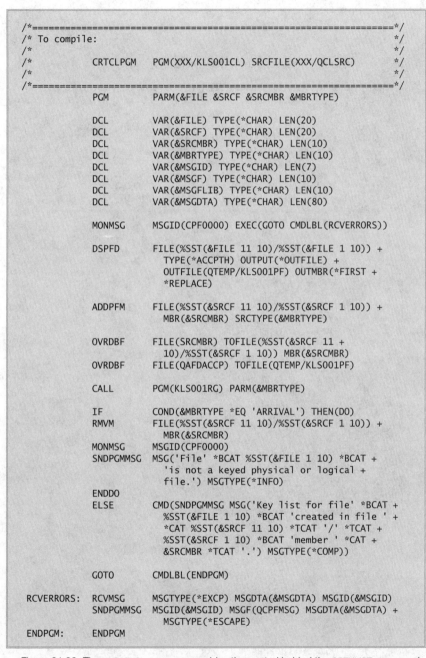

Figure 21.33: The KLS001CL program provides the control behind the CRTKLIST command.

```
*=============================================================
* To compile:
*
*        CRTRPGPGM  PGM(XXX/KLS001RG) SRCFILE(XXX/QRPGSRC)
*
*=============================================================
*. 1 ...+... 2 ...+... 3 ...+... 4 ...+... 5 ...+... 6 ...+... 7
FSRCMBR  O  F    112              DISK
*
FQAFDACCPIF E                     DISK
*
ISRCTXT     DS
I I         0                        1  60SRCSEQ
I I         0                        7 120SRCDAT
I                                   13 112 SRCDTA
*=============================================================
C         *ENTRY    PLIST
C                   PARM              MBRTYP 10
*
C                   READ QAFDACCP                    99
C         *IN99     IFEQ *OFF
C         APACCP    ANDEQ'A'
C                   MOVEL'ARRIVAL' MBRTYP     P
C                   ELSE
C         *IN99     DOWEQ*OFF
C         APBOLF    IFNE SVBOLF
C                   EXSR KLIST
C                   MOVE APBOLF    SVBOLF 10
C                   ENDIF
C                   EXSR KFLD
C                   READ QAFDACCP                    99
C                   ENDDO
C                   ENDIF
*
C                   MOVE *ON       *INLR
*=============================================================
C         KLIST     BEGSR
*
C                   ADD  100       SRCSEQ
C                   CLEARSRCDTA
C         MBRTYP    IFEQ 'RPGLE'
C                   CAT  'C':5     SRCDTA
C         APBOLF    CAT  '00001':0 FILE6   6
C                   CAT  FILE6:5   SRCDTA
C                   CAT  'KLIST':8 SRCDTA
C                   EXCPTRPGLE
C                   ELSE
C                   CAT  'C':5     SRCDTA
C         APBOLF    CAT  '00001':0 FILE6
C                   CAT  FILE6:11  SRCDTA
```

Figure 21.34: The KLS001RG program is the processing power for generating key lists for the CRTKLIST command (part 1 of 2).

```
C                       CAT   'KLIST':4 SRCDTA
C                       EXCPTRPG
C                       ENDIF
 *
C                       ENDSR
 *==========================================================
C           KFLD        BEGSR
 *
C                       ADD   100       SRCSEQ
C                       CLEARSRCDTA
C           MBRTYP      IFEQ  'RPGLE'
C                       CAT   'C':5     SRCDTA
C                       CAT   'KFLD':19 SRCDTA
C                       CAT   APKEYF:20 SRCDTA
C                       EXCPTRPGLE
C                       ELSE
C                       CAT   'C':5     SRCDTA
C                       CAT   'KFLD':21 SRCDTA
C                       CAT   APKEYF:11 SRCDTA
C                       EXCPTRPG
C                       ENDIF
 *
C                       ENDSR
 *==========================================================
OSRCMBR    E            RPG
O                       SRCSEQ
O                       SRCDAT
O                       SRCDTA
O          E            RPGLE
O                       SRCSEQ
O                       SRCDAT
O                       SRCDTA
```

Figure 21.34: The KLS001RG program is the processing power for generating key lists for the CRTKLIST command (part 2 of 2).

—*T.V.S. Murthy*

DSPKEY Utility

From time to time, I need to quickly find out what keys are available on a particular file. I can run the Display File Description (DSPFD) command with the TYPE(*ACCPTH) parameter set. It always takes me a while to sort through all of the information I don't need on that display to find the keys. So, I wrote the Display Key (DSPKEY) utility shown in Figures 21.35 and 21.36.

```
/*==============================================================*/
/* To compile:                                                  */
/*                                                              */
/*          CRTCMD     CMD(XXX/DSPKEY) PGM(XXX/KEY003CL) +       */
/*                     SRCFILE(XXX/QCMDSRC)                      */
/*                                                              */
/*==============================================================*/
           CMD        PROMPT('Display Key Information')
           PARM       KWD(FILE) TYPE(QUAL) MIN(1) PROMPT('File')
 QUAL:     QUAL       TYPE(*NAME) LEN(10)
           QUAL       TYPE(*NAME) LEN(10) DFT(*LIBL) +
                      SPCVAL((*LIBL)) PROMPT('Library')
```

Figure 21.35: *The DSPKEY command displays the keys available for a given physical file.*

```
/*==============================================================*/
/* To compile:                                                  */
/*                                                              */
/*          CRTCLPGM    PGM(XXX/KEY003CL) SRCFILE(XXX/QCLSRC)    */
/*                                                              */
/*==============================================================*/
           PGM        PARM(&FILLIB)

           DCL        VAR(&FILLIB) TYPE(*CHAR) LEN(20)
           DCL        VAR(&FIL) TYPE(*CHAR) LEN(10)
           DCL        VAR(&LIB) TYPE(*CHAR) LEN(10)
           DCL        VAR(&KEY) TYPE(*CHAR) LEN(2000)
           DCL        VAR(&FST) TYPE(*LGL) VALUE('1')
           DCL        VAR(&LOOPCNT) TYPE(*DEC) LEN(3 0)
           DCL        VAR(&MSGID) TYPE(*CHAR) LEN(7)
           DCL        VAR(&MSGDTA) TYPE(*CHAR) LEN(80)
           DCLF       FILE(QAFDACCP)

           MONMSG     MSGID(CPF0000) EXEC(GOTO CMDLBL(ERROR))

           CHGVAR     VAR(&FIL) VALUE(%SST(&FILLIB 1 10))
           CHGVAR     VAR(&LIB) VALUE(%SST(&FILLIB 11 10))

           DSPFD      FILE(&LIB/&FIL) TYPE(*ACCPTH) +
                      OUTPUT(*OUTFILE) FILEATR(*PF *LF) +
                      OUTFILE(QTEMP/KEY003PF)
           OVRDBF     FILE(QAFDACCP) TOFILE(QTEMP/KEY003PF)

 LOOP:     RCVF
           MONMSG     MSGID(CPF0864) EXEC(GOTO CMDLBL(ELOOP))
```

Figure 21.36: *The KEY003CL program provides the processing power for the DSPKEY command (part 1 of 2).*

```
               IF        COND(&FST *EQ '1') THEN(DO)
               IF        COND(&APNKYF *EQ 0) THEN(GOTO CMDLBL(ELOOP))
               CHGVAR    VAR(&FST) VALUE('0')
               CHGVAR    VAR(&LOOPCNT) VALUE(&APNKYF)
               ENDDO
               ELSE      CMD(CHGVAR VAR(&KEY) VALUE(&KEY *TCAT '+'))
               CHGVAR    VAR(&KEY) VALUE(&KEY *TCAT &APKEYF *TCAT '(' +
                           *CAT &APKSEQ *TCAT ')')
               CHGVAR    VAR(&LOOPCNT) VALUE(&LOOPCNT - 1)
               IF        COND(&LOOPCNT *NE 0) THEN(GOTO CMDLBL(LOOP))
 ELOOP:        IF        COND(&FST *EQ '1') THEN(SNDPGMMSG +
                           MSGID(CPF9898) MSGF(QCPFMSG) MSGDTA('File +
                           ' *CAT &LIB *TCAT '/' *TCAT &FIL *BCAT +
                           'is not a keyed file'))
               ELSE      CMD(SNDPGMMSG MSGID(CPF9898) MSGF(QCPFMSG) +
                           MSGDTA('File' *BCAT &LIB *TCAT '/' *TCAT +
                           &FIL *BCAT 'key' *BCAT &KEY))
               GOTO      CMDLBL(ENDPGM)
 ERROR:        RCVMSG    MSGTYPE(*EXCP) MSGDTA(&MSGDTA) MSGID(&MSGID)
               SNDPGMMSG MSGID(&MSGID) MSGF(QCPFMSG) MSGDTA(&MSGDTA) +
                           MSGTYPE(*ESCAPE)
 ENDPGM:       ENDPGM
```

Figure 21.36: The KEY003CL program provides the processing power for the DSPKEY command (part 2 of 2).

The command I wrote uses DSPFD TYPE(*ACCPTH), but the output format is different. A single message that is generated lists all of the keys for a physical or logical file. That message is then displayed so that you can easily find out what you need to know.

There are two parts you need to create: the command DSPKEY and the command processing program KEY003CL. I hope you find this utility as useful as I do.

—Avik Dey

Show File Keys Utility

When you're looking at a program, one of the things you might wonder about is what the keys for a certain file are. We've written a small utility that we use from the command line window in SEU (you can get this by pressing F21). When you run the command DSPKEY2, it shows the keys for the file on the message line. The source for the command, and the programs it uses, is shown in Figures 21.37 through 21.39.

```
/*================================================================*/
/* To compile:                                                    */
/*                                                                */
/*          CRTCMD      CMD(XXX/DSPKEY) PGM(XXX/KEY002CL)    +     */
/*                      SRCFILE(XXX/QCMDSRC)                       */
/*                                                                */
/*================================================================*/
 DSPKEY:    CMD         PROMPT('Display Keys in a File')
            PARM        KWD(FILE) TYPE(QUAL1) MIN(1) PROMPT('File')
 QUAL1:     QUAL        TYPE(*NAME) LEN(10)
            QUAL        TYPE(*NAME) LEN(10) DFT(*LIBL) +
                        SPCVAL((*LIBL)) PROMPT('Library')
```

Figure 21.37: The DSPKEY2 command source displays the keys for a file.

```
/*================================================================*/
/* To compile:                                                    */
/*                                                                */
/*          CRTCLPGM    PGM(XXX/KEY002CL) SRCFILE(XXX/QCLSRC)      */
/*                                                                */
/*================================================================*/
KEY002CL: +
   PGM PARM(&LIBFILE)

   DCL VAR(&LIBFILE)    TYPE(*CHAR) LEN(20)
   DCL VAR(&FILE)       TYPE(*CHAR) LEN(10)
   DCL VAR(&LIB)        TYPE(*CHAR) LEN(10)
   DCL VAR(&MSG)        TYPE(*CHAR) LEN(133)
   DCL VAR(&TXT)        TYPE(*CHAR) LEN(150)
   DCL VAR(&MSGID)      TYPE(*CHAR) LEN(7)
   DCL VAR(&MSGDTA)     TYPE(*CHAR) LEN(80)

   CHGVAR VAR(&LIB) VALUE(%SST(&LIBFILE 11 10))
   CHGVAR VAR(&FILE) VALUE(%SST(&LIBFILE 1 10))

   CHKOBJ OBJ(&LIB/&FILE) OBJTYPE(*FILE) AUT(*OBJOPR)
   MONMSG MSGID(CPF0000) EXEC(DO)
      RCVMSG MSGDTA(&MSGDTA) MSGID(&MSGID)
      RTVMSG MSGID(&MSGID) MSGF(QCPFMSG) MSGDTA(&MSGDTA) MSG(&TXT)
      GOTO CMDLBL(MSG)
   ENDDO

   DSPFD FILE(&LIB/&FILE) TYPE(*ACCPTH) OUTPUT(*OUTFILE) +
      OUTFILE(QTEMP/KEYF) OUTMBR(*FIRST *REPLACE)

   OVRDBF FILE(QAFDACCP) TOFILE(QTEMP/KEYF)
```

Figure 21.38: Program KEY002CL is one of the processing programs behind the DSPKEY2 command (part 1 of 2).

```
        CALL PGM(KEY002RG) PARM(&MSG)
        DLTOVR FILE(QAFDACCP)

        CHGVAR VAR(%SST(&TXT 1 10)) VALUE(&FILE)
        CHGVAR VAR(%SST(&TXT 12 4)) VALUE('KEY:')
        CHGVAR VAR(%SST(&TXT 17 133)) VALUE(&MSG)

MSG: +
        SNDPGMMSG MSGID(CPF9897) MSGF(QCPFMSG) MSGDTA(&TXT) MSGTYPE(*INFO)
        ENDPGM
```

Figure 21.38: Program KEY002CL is one of the processing programs behind the DSPKEY2 command (part 2 of 2).

```
    *===============================================================
    * To compile:
    *
    *        CRTRPGPGM  PGM(XXX/KEY002RG)  SRCFILE(XXX/QRPGSRC)
    *
    *===============================================================
    *. 1 ...+... 2 ...+... 3 ...+... 4 ...+... 5 ...+... 6 ...+... 7
    FQAFDACCPIP  E                    DISK
    C            *ENTRY   PLIST
    C                     PARM              WKMSG 133
    C                     CAT  APKEYF:1  WKMSG
```

Figure 21.39: Source member KEY002RG is the power behind the DSPKEY2 utility.

—Mike Hall

✦ ✦ ✦ File Transfer Alternative

Cut-and-Paste File Transfer

I often use the cut-and-paste features of Windows and OS/2 to copy source code between my PC and AS/400. Sometimes, I have no choice because the emulation I am using at the time does not have file-transfer capabilities. Other times, I do it because it's quicker than cranking up FTP.

Copying from an AS/400 is easy. First, I use the Display Physical File Member (DSPPFM) command, specifying the qualified file name in the first parameter and the member name in the second. Next, I type **w13** in the top line and press Enter to window past the date and sequence numbers. This enables me to copy one or more source lines to the clipboard, using the Edit menu or appropriate command of the emulation package, and paste into a file on my PC using a word processor or editor.

Copying from the PC to the AS/400 is altogether different. The AS/400 doesn't have a program that will accept more than one line of data from the clipboard and put it into a source member. (SEU lets me paste only one line at a time.) Therefore, I wrote a utility called PASTE SOURCE to let me do just that.

PASTE SOURCE consists of the PSTSRC command, the CL program PST001CL, the display file PST001DF, and the RPG program PST001RG (see Figures 21.40 through 21.43.) To use this utility, key PSTSRC on an AS/400 command line, press F4 to prompt it, and fill in the blanks with the qualified source file and member names. PASTE SOURCE will present a screen with one input field.

Move to a PC window, select one or more lines of source code to be transferred to the AS/400, and copy the code to the clipboard—using the appropriate command (e.g., Control+C). Return to the AS/400 emulation session and choose the option to paste from the clipboard (usually Control+V). You will see the data being inserted into the input field. To help you keep up with what you have pasted, the display file will also show you the last line copied to the source member.

You might have to activate the CHECK(ER) keyword in the display file. Some emulators automatically press Enter after each source statement is pasted, while others don't.

```
/*===============================================================*/
/* To compile:                                                   */
/*                                                               */
/*           CRTCMD     CMD(XXX/PSTSRC) PGM(XXX/PST001CL) +       */
/*                      SRCFILE(XXX/QCMDSRC)                      */
/*                                                               */
/*===============================================================*/

            CMD        PROMPT('Paste clipboard to source mbr')
            PARM       KWD(FILE) TYPE(QUALFILE) PROMPT('Paste to +
                       source file')
            PARM       KWD(MBR) TYPE(*NAME) DFT(*FIRST) +
                       SPCVAL((*FIRST) (*LAST)) EXPR(*YES) +
                       PROMPT('Member')
QUALFILE:   QUAL       TYPE(*NAME) MIN(1) EXPR(*YES)
            QUAL       TYPE(*NAME) DFT(*LIBL) SPCVAL((*LIBL) +
                       (*CURLIB)) EXPR(*YES) PROMPT('Library')
```

Figure 21.40: Command PSTSRC is a great tool for cutting and pasting code.

```
/*================================================================*/
/* To compile:                                                    */
/*                                                                */
/*          CRTCLPGM   PGM(XXX/PST001CL) SRCFILE(XXX/QCLSRC)       */
/*                                                                */
/*================================================================*/
PGM          PARM(&FILE &MBR)

  DCL        VAR(&FILE) TYPE(*CHAR) LEN(20)
  DCL        VAR(&MBR) TYPE(*CHAR) LEN(10)
  DCL        VAR(&FILENAME) TYPE(*CHAR) LEN(10)
  DCL        VAR(&FILELIB) TYPE(*CHAR) LEN(10)
  DCL        VAR(&ERRBYTES) TYPE(*CHAR) LEN(4) +
               VALUE(X'00000000')
  DCL        VAR(&ERROR) TYPE(*LGL) VALUE('0')
  DCL        VAR(&MSGKEY) TYPE(*CHAR) LEN(4)
  DCL        VAR(&MSGTYP) TYPE(*CHAR) LEN(10) VALUE('*DIAG')
  DCL        VAR(&MSGTYPCTR) TYPE(*CHAR) LEN(4) +
               VALUE(X'00000001')
  DCL        VAR(&PGMMSGQ) TYPE(*CHAR) LEN(10) VALUE('*')
  DCL        VAR(&STKCTR) TYPE(*CHAR) LEN(4) +
               VALUE(X'00000001')

  /* Send all errors to error handling routine */
  MONMSG     MSGID(CPF0000) EXEC(GOTO CMDLBL(ABEND))

  CHGVAR     VAR(&FILENAME) VALUE(%SST(&FILE 1 10))
  CHGVAR     VAR(&FILELIB) VALUE(%SST(&FILE 11 10))

  CHKOBJ     OBJ(&FILELIB/&FILENAME) OBJTYPE(*FILE)
  ADDPFM     FILE(&FILELIB/&FILENAME) MBR(&MBR)
  MONMSG     MSGID(CPF7306)
  OVRDBF     FILE(SOURCE) TOFILE(&FILELIB/&FILENAME) MBR(&MBR)
  CALL       PGM(PST001RG)
  DLTOVR     FILE(SOURCE)
  RETURN

ABEND:
  /* Error handling routine */
  IF         COND(&ERROR) THEN(GOTO CMDLBL(ERRDONE))
  ELSE       CMD(CHGVAR VAR(&ERROR) VALUE('1'))

  CALL       PGM(QMHMOVPM) PARM(&MSGKEY &MSGTYP +
               &MSGTYPCTR &PGMMSGQ &STKCTR &ERRBYTES)

ERRDONE:
  CALL       PGM(QMHRSNEM) PARM(&MSGKEY &ERRBYTES)
  MONMSG     MSGID(CPF0000) EXEC(DO)
    SNDPGMMSG  MSGID(CPF3CF2) MSGF(QCPFMSG) +
                 MSGDTA('QMHRSNEM') MSGTYPE(*ESCAPE)
    MONMSG     MSGID(CPF0000)
  ENDDO

ENDPGM
```

Figure 21.41: CL Program PST001CL is the CPP for the copy-and-paste utility.

```
*===============================================================
* To compile:
*
*       CRTDSPF    FILE(XXX/PST001DF) SRCFILE(XXX/QDDSSRC)
*
*===============================================================
A                                       DSPSIZ(24 80 *DS3)
A                                       CF03(03)
A          R SCREEN01
A            INPUT        80   I  4  1CHECK(LC)
A*****                                   CHECK(ER)
A                              8  2'Last line:'
A            LASTLN       80   O  9  1
A                             11  2'Lines copied:'
A            LINECT       5Y  0B 11 16EDTCDE(J)
A                             23  2'F3=Exit'
```

Figure 21.42: Display file PST001DF is used to keep the user informed of the status of the copy-and-paste utility.

```
*===============================================================
* To compile:
*
*       CRTRPGPGM  PGM(XXX/PST001RG) SRCFILE(XXX/QRPGSRC)
*
*===============================================================
FPST001DFCF E                  WORKSTN    KINFSR *PSSR
FSOURCE  O  F    92            DISK       KINFSR *PSSR
C           *ZERO    DOWEQ*ZERO
C                    EXFMTSCREEN01
C           *IN03    IFEQ *ON
C                    LEAVE
C                    ENDIF
C                    ADD  1        LINECT
C                    MOVELINPUT    LASTLN
C                    EXCPTADDREC
C                    ENDDO
C                    MOVE *ON      *INLR
C***********
C           *PSSR    BEGSR
C                    ENDSR'*CANCL'
OSOURCE  E           ADDREC
O                    INPUT    92
```

Figure 21.43: RPG program PST001RG provides the power behind the PSTSRC command.

—*Ted Holt*

✦ ✦ ✦ IFS

Display PC Files Stored in Folders

Because I sometimes like to look at the data in a PC file stored in a folder, I wrote the Display PC Document (DSPPCD) utility. It consists of the DSPPCD command (Figure 21.44) and the PCD001CL program (Figure 21.45).

```
/*===============================================================*/
/* To compile:                                                   */
/*                                                               */
/*      CRTCMD  CMD(XXX/DSPPCD) PGM(XXX/PCD001CL) +              */
/*                SRCFILE(XXX/QCMDSRC)                            */
/*                                                               */
/*===============================================================*/
   CMD        PROMPT('Display PC document')
   PARM       KWD(FOLDER) TYPE(*CHAR) LEN(80) MIN(1) +
                EXPR(*YES) PROMPT('Folder')
   PARM       KWD(DOC) TYPE(*CHAR) LEN(12) MIN(1) +
                EXPR(*YES) PROMPT('Document')
```

Figure 21.44: The DSPPCD command allows you to display which PC files are stored in folders on the AS/400.

```
/*===============================================================*/
/* To compile:                                                   */
/*                                                               */
/*      CRTCLPGM  PGM(XXX/PCD001CL) SRCFILE(XXX/QCLSRC)          */
/*                                                               */
/*===============================================================*/
   PGM        PARM(&FOLDER &DOC)

   DCL        VAR(&DOC)       TYPE(*CHAR) LEN(12)
   DCL        VAR(&FILE)      TYPE(*CHAR) LEN(10)
   DCL        VAR(&FOLDER)    TYPE(*CHAR) LEN(80)
   DCL        VAR(&MSGDTA)    TYPE(*CHAR) LEN(132)
   DCL        VAR(&MSGF)      TYPE(*CHAR) LEN(10)
   DCL        VAR(&MSGFLIB)   TYPE(*CHAR) LEN(10)
   DCL        VAR(&MSGID)     TYPE(*CHAR) LEN(7)

   MONMSG     MSGID(CPF0000) EXEC(GOTO FWDMSG)

   CHGVAR     VAR(&FILE) VALUE(%SST(&DOC 1 10))
   CRTPF      FILE(QTEMP/&FILE) RCDLEN(256)
   MONMSG     MSGID(CPF7302)
```

Figure 21.45: Program PCD001CL provides the processing power behind the DSPPCD command (part 1 of 2).

```
      MONMSG    MSGID(CPF0001) EXEC(DO)
      CHGVAR    VAR(&FILE) VALUE('PCFILE')
      CRTPF     FILE(QTEMP/&FILE) RCDLEN(256)
      MONMSG    MSGID(CPF7302)
      ENDDO


      CPYFRMPCD FROMFLR(&FOLDER) TOFILE(QTEMP/&FILE) +
                  FROMDOC(&DOC)
      DSPPFM    FILE(QTEMP/&FILE)
      RETURN

FWDMSG: /* FORWARD MESSAGES */
      RCVMSG    MSGDTA(&MSGDTA) MSGID(&MSGID) MSGF(&MSGF) +
                  SNDMSGFLIB(&MSGFLIB)
      IF        COND(&MSGID *NE ' ') THEN(DO)
      SNDPGMMSG MSGID(&MSGID) MSGF(&MSGFLIB/&MSGF) +
                  MSGDTA(&MSGDTA)
      MONMSG    MSGID(CPF2469)
      GOTO      CMDLBL(FWDMSG)
      ENDDO
      ENDPGM
```

Figure 21.45: Program PCD001CL provides the processing power behind the DSPPCD command (part 2 of 2).

The utility requires two parameters: the name of the folder in which the document (which is what a PC file is considered to be) is stored, and the name of the document. It copies the PC file into a temporary physical file, which is viewed with the DSPPFM command.

If possible, the program creates the temporary file with the same name as the PC file. This is so that the PC file's name (or at least 10 characters of it) shows on the DSPPFM display. If the PC file name is not a valid physical file name, it names the physical file PCFILE.

—Ted Holt

✦ ✦ ✦ Jobs

Job Information with Just a Job Number

Are you looking for a quick way to find job information when all you know is the job number? Figure 21.46 shows a little utility I developed called Work with Job by Number (WRKJOBNUM). To obtain job information, simply pass WRKJOBNUM the number of the job in question, and it displays the information. You can even modify this technique to retrieve information programmatically in an interactive program.

I've often wondered why IBM has never provided a command like this before, seeing as how the job number is unique, but this handy utility makes up for Big Blue's lack of foresight. The CPP is shown in Figure 21.47.

```
/*==============================================================*/
/* To compile:                                                  */
/*                                                              */
/*          CRTCMD     CMD(XXX/WORKJOBNUM) PGM(XXX/WRKJOBNUMC) + */
/*                     SRCFILE(XXX/QCMDSRC)                      */
/*                                                              */
/****************************************************************/
           CMD        PROMPT('Work with job by number')

           PARM       KWD(JOBNO) TYPE(*DEC) LEN(6) RANGE(1 999999) +
                      MIN(1) PROMPT('Job number')
```

Figure 21.46: Here's the command WRKJOBNUM that you can use to display a job by job number.

```
/****************************************************************/
/*    To Create:                                                */
/*                                                              */
/*          CRTCLPGM PGM(XXXLIB/WRKJOBNUMC) SRCFIL(XXX/QCLSRC)   */
/****************************************************************/
PGM        PARM(&JOBNO)

           DCLF       FILE(PRT132)
           DCL        VAR(&JOBNO) TYPE(*DEC) LEN(6 0)
           DCL        VAR(&JOB) TYPE(*CHAR) LEN(10)
           DCL        VAR(&USER) TYPE(*CHAR) LEN(10)
           DCL        VAR(&JOBNBR) TYPE(*CHAR) LEN(6)
           DCL        VAR(&JOBNO$) TYPE(*CHAR) LEN(6)

           CHKOBJ     OBJ(QTEMP/PRT132) OBJTYPE(*FILE)
           MONMSG     MSGID(CPF0000) EXEC(DO)
           CRTPF      FILE(QTEMP/PRT132) RCDLEN(132) SIZE(*NOMAX)
           ENDDO

           CHGVAR     VAR(&JOBNO$) VALUE(&JOBNO)
           OVRPRTF    FILE(QPDSPSBJ) OUTQ(QEZDEBUG)

           WRKUSRJOB  USER(*ALL) STATUS(*ALL) OUTPUT(*PRINT) +
                        JOBTYPE(*ALL)
           CPYSPLF    FILE(QPDSPSBJ) TOFILE(QTEMP/PRT132) +
                        SPLNBR(*LAST)
           DLTSPLF    FILE(QPDSPSBJ) SPLNBR(*LAST)
           OVRDBF     FILE(PRT132) TOFILE(QTEMP/PRT132)
```

Figure 21.47: This is the command processor for command WRKJOBNUM (part 1 of 2).

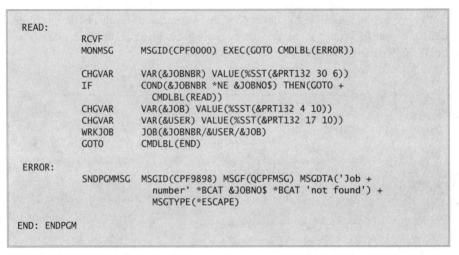

```
    READ:
                RCVF
                MONMSG    MSGID(CPF0000) EXEC(GOTO CMDLBL(ERROR))

                CHGVAR    VAR(&JOBNBR) VALUE(%SST(&PRT132 30 6))
                IF        COND(&JOBNBR *NE &JOBNO$) THEN(GOTO +
                            CMDLBL(READ))
                CHGVAR    VAR(&JOB) VALUE(%SST(&PRT132 4 10))
                CHGVAR    VAR(&USER) VALUE(%SST(&PRT132 17 10))
                WRKJOB    JOB(&JOBNBR/&USER/&JOB)
                GOTO      CMDLBL(END)

    ERROR:
                SNDPGMMSG MSGID(CPF9898) MSGF(QCPFMSG) MSGDTA('Job +
                            number' *BCAT &JOBNO$ *BCAT 'not found') +
                            MSGTYPE(*ESCAPE)

    END: ENDPGM
```

Figure 21.47: This is the command processor for command WRKJOBNUM (part 2 of 2).

—Albert York

✦ ✦ ✦ Library Lists

Save and Restore Library List

Much has been written about the library list; it's a topic that confuses enough people to deserve repeated treatment and explanations. For instance, one of the common questions is, "How can I make sure the library list returns to its original setup after I've changed it?" The ideal solution is to store the library list in some kind of object so that it can be retrieved later from the same object. Data areas come to mind as the repositories for library lists, except that you have to give them names—even if placed in QTEMP.

So far, the best solution I've found is to use not data areas, but data queues. This approach prompted me write two utility commands: Save Library List (SAVLIBL) and Restore Library List (RSTLIBL). SAVLIBL (Figure 21.48) uses a LIFO data queue named LIBLSTACK in QTEMP, which is created if nonexistent. Its processing program, LIBL007CL, takes care of everything (see Figure 21.49). It retrieves the user portion of the library list, as well as the current library name, and calls QSNDDTAQ to write that information into the data queue. The first 10 characters of the entry contain the current library name, and the next 275 characters contain the user portion of the library list—in 25 eleven-byte buckets.

```
/*================================================================*/
/* To compile:                                                    */
/*                                                                */
/*          CRTCMD     CMD(XXX/SAVLIBL) PGM(XXX/LIBL007CL) +       */
/*                     SRCFILE(XXX/SOURCE) TEXT('Save Library List*/
/*                                                                */
/*================================================================*/
           CMD        PROMPT('Save Library List')
```

Figure 21.48: The SAVLIBL command can be used to save your library list.

```
/*================================================================*/
/* To compile:                                                    */
/*                                                                */
/*          CRTCLPGM   PGM(XXX/LIBL007CL) SRCFILE(XXX/SOURCE) +    */
/*                     TEXT('CPP for SAVLIBL command')            */
/*================================================================*/
PGM

    DCL        VAR(&CURLIB) TYPE(*CHAR) LEN(10)
    DCL        VAR(&DTAQE) TYPE(*CHAR) LEN(300)
    DCL        VAR(&DTAQELEN) TYPE(*DEC) LEN(5) VALUE(300)
    DCL        VAR(&USRLIBL) TYPE(*CHAR) LEN(275)

    MONMSG     MSGID(CPF0000 MCH0000) EXEC(GOTO CMDLBL(ERROR))

    /* Create library list stack if necessary */
    CHKOBJ     OBJ(QTEMP/LIBLSTACK) OBJTYPE(*DTAQ)
    MONMSG     MSGID(CPF9801) EXEC(DO)
      RCVMSG     MSGTYPE(*LAST) RMV(*YES)
      CRTDTAQ    DTAQ(QTEMP/LIBLSTACK) TYPE(*STD) MAXLEN(300) +
                 SEQ(*LIFO) TEXT('Library list stack')
    ENDDO

    /* Save library list into stack */
    RTVJOBA    USRLIBL(&USRLIBL) CURLIB(&CURLIB)
    IF         COND(&CURLIB *EQ '*NONE') THEN(DO)
      CHGVAR     VAR(&CURLIB) VALUE('*CRTDFT')
    ENDDO

    CHGVAR     VAR(&DTAQE) VALUE(&CURLIB *CAT &USRLIBL)

    CALL       PGM(QSNDDTAQ) PARM('LIBLSTACK' 'QTEMP' +
                 &DTAQELEN &DTAQE)
    RETURN

ERROR:
  FWDPGMMSG
  MONMSG     MSGID(CPF0000)

ENDPGM
```

Figure 21.49: CL program LIBL007CL stores the old library list.

RSTLIBL (Figure 21.50) performs the opposite function: It retrieves the last entry in the data queue and changes the library list accordingly. For that, its processing program LIBL008CL (as shown in Figure 21.51) calls QRCVDTAQ, runs the Change Current Library (CHGCURLIB) command, and builds a Change Library List (CHGLIBL) command in a CL variable—which is then executed via a call to QCMDEXC. If you're going to run a program that needs to change the library list, code a SAVLIBL before any changes. Then, do whatever you need to do and code a RSTLIBL at the end. Because SAVLIBL and RSTLIBL use a LIFO data queue, your program might call another program, which, in turn, uses SAVLIBL and RSTLIBL.

```
/*================================================================*/
/* To compile:                                                    */
/*                                                                */
/*          CRTCMD     CMD(XXX/RSTLIBL) PGM(XXX/LIBL008CL) +       */
/*                     SRCFILE(XXX/SOURCE) TEXT('Restore Library +*/
/*                     List')                                     */
/*                                                                */
/*================================================================*/
           CMD         PROMPT('Restore Library List')
```

Figure 21.50: Command RSTLIBL lets you restore the saved library list.

```
/*================================================================*/
/* To compile:                                                    */
/*                                                                */
/*          CRTCLPGM    PGM(XXX/LIBL008CL) SRCFILE(XXX/SOURCE) +   */
/*                      TEXT('CPP for RSTLIBL command')            */
/*                                                                */
/*================================================================*/
PGM

    DCL        VAR(&CMD) TYPE(*CHAR) LEN(300)
    DCL        VAR(&CMDLEN) TYPE(*DEC) LEN(15 5) VALUE(300)
    DCL        VAR(&CURLIB) TYPE(*CHAR) LEN(10)
    DCL        VAR(&DTAQE) TYPE(*CHAR) LEN(300)
    DCL        VAR(&DTAQELEN) TYPE(*DEC) LEN(5) VALUE(300)
    DCL        VAR(&USRLIBL) TYPE(*CHAR) LEN(275)
    DCL        VAR(&WAIT) TYPE(*DEC) LEN(5) VALUE(0)

    MONMSG     MSGID(CPF0000 MCH0000) EXEC(GOTO CMDLBL(ERROR))
```

Figure 21.51: CL program LIBL008CL is used to restore the library list using the RSTLIBL command (part 1 of 2).

```
    /* Reject request if SAVLIBL not executed before */
    CHKOBJ      OBJ(QTEMP/LIBLSTACK) OBJTYPE(*DTAQ)
    MONMSG      MSGID(CPF9801) EXEC(DO)
      SNDPGMMSG  MSGID(CPF9898) MSGF(QCPFMSG) MSGDTA('RSTLIBL +
                  not allowed before SAVLIBL') MSGTYPE(*ESCAPE)
    ENDDO

    /* Restore library list */
    CALL        PGM(QRCVDTAQ) PARM('LIBLSTACK' 'QTEMP' +
                  &DTAQELEN &DTAQE &WAIT)

    /* Reject request if nothing to restore */
    IF          COND(&DTAQE *EQ ' ') THEN(DO)
      SNDPGMMSG  MSGID(CPF9898) MSGF(QCPFMSG) MSGDTA('Library +
                  list stack is empty') MSGTYPE(*ESCAPE)
    ENDDO

    CHGVAR      VAR(&CURLIB) VALUE(%SST(&DTAQE 1 10))
    CHGVAR      VAR(&USRLIBL) VALUE(%SST(&DTAQE 11 275))

    CHGCURLIB   CURLIB(&CURLIB)
    CHGVAR      VAR(&CMD) VALUE('CHGLIBL (' *BCAT &USRLIBL +
                  *TCAT ')')
    CALL        PGM(QCMDEXC) PARM(&CMD &CMDLEN)

    RETURN

  ERROR:
    FWDPGMMSG
    MONMSG      MSGID(CPF0000)

  ENDPGM
```

Figure 21.51: CL program LIBL008CL is used to restore the library list using the RSTLIBL command (part 2 of 2).

This means that SAVLIBL and RSTLIBL provide you with an unlimited number of "versions" of the library list. And you don't need to bother naming them! SAVLIBL is smart enough to create the necessary data queue if it doesn't find it (as would be the case the first time SAVLIBL runs in a job). RSTLIBL ends with an escape message (CPF9898) if the data queue doesn't exist (i.e., if SAVLIBL has never run in the current job) or is empty (i.e., if there is no corresponding SAVLIBL to the RSTLIBL you're running now). SAVLIBL and RSTLIBL must always go in pairs.

—Ernie Malaga

✦ ✦ ✦ Message Queues

Search Message Queue

Trying to find completion messages or an error message in a message queue can be troublesome. When scrolling through pages of messages, you not only get tired of visually scanning the messages, but you also might overlook what you're searching for. I created the Search Message Queue (SCHMSGQ) command, as shown in Figure 21.52, to search for a selected string of information. This command lets you enter a specific message queue that you want to search, along with the search string you want to search for.

```
/*================================================================*/
/* To compile:                                                    */
/*                                                                */
/*          CRTCMD    CMD(XXX/SCHMSGQ) PGM(XXX/MSG015CL) +        */
/*                    SRCFILE(XXX/QCMDSRC)                        */
/*                                                                */
/*================================================================*/
          CMD       PROMPT('Search Message Queues')

          PARM      KWD(MSGQ) TYPE(QUAL1) MIN(1) PROMPT('Message +
                    queue name')
QUAL1:    QUAL      TYPE(*NAME) LEN(10) DFT(' ')
          QUAL      TYPE(*NAME) LEN(10) DFT(*LIBL) SPCVAL((*LIBL))

          PARM      KWD(ARGUMENT) TYPE(*CHAR) LEN(50) +
                    DFT(MESSAGES) PROMPT('Search')
```

Figure 21.52: The SCHMSGQ command can be used to search a message queue for a given message.

Once you've entered the desired parameters and pressed Enter, a screen will appear as if you ran a Display Physical File Member (DSPPFM) command. The search argument will be highlighted, and you can continue to scan by pressing F16. The search argument is not case-sensitive because you're using the Find String PDM (FNDSTRPDM) command. This can be a big benefit if you do not know how the message is formatted. The CPP (MSG015CL) for the SCHMSGQ command is shown in Figure 21.53.

```
/*================================================================*/
/* To compile:                                                    */
/*                                                                */
/*              CRTCLPGM   PGM(XXX/MSG015CL) SRCFILE(XXX/QCLSRC)   */
/*                                                                */
/*================================================================*/
MSG015CL: +
   PGM PARM(&MSGQLIB &ARGU)

   DCL VAR(&MSGQLIB)    TYPE(*CHAR) LEN(20)
   DCL VAR(&MSGQ)       TYPE(*CHAR) LEN(10)
   DCL VAR(&ARGU)       TYPE(*CHAR) LEN(50)
   DCL VAR(&LIB)        TYPE(*CHAR) LEN(10)
   DCL VAR(&MSGDTA)     TYPE(*CHAR) LEN(100)

   CHGVAR VAR(&MSGQ) VALUE(&MSGQLIB)
   CHGVAR VAR(&LIB) VALUE(%SST(&MSGQLIB 11 10))

   DSPMSG MSGQ(&LIB/&MSGQ) OUTPUT(*PRINT)
   MONMSG MSGID(CPF2403) EXEC(DO)
      CHGVAR VAR(&MSGDTA) VALUE('''Message Queue'' *BCAT &MSGQ +
         *BCAT ''in'' *BCAT ''Library'' *BCAT &LIB *BCAT ''Not +
         Found'')')
      GOTO CMDLBL(ERROR)
   ENDDO

   CRTPF FILE(QTEMP/MSGQF) RCDLEN(132) SIZE(*NOMAX)
   MONMSG MSGID(CPF7302) EXEC(CLRPFM FILE(QTEMP/MSGQF))

   CPYSPLF FILE(QPDSPMSG) TOFILE(QTEMP/MSGQF) SPLNBR(*LAST)
   DLTSPLF FILE(QPDSPMSG) SPLNBR(*LAST)
   FNDSTRPDM STRING(&ARGU) FILE(QTEMP/MSGQF) MBR(*ALL) OPTION(*DSP +
      *NOPROMPT)
   DLTF FILE(QTEMP/MSGQF)
   GOTO CMDLBL(END)
ERROR: +
   SNDPGMMSG MSG(&MSGDTA) MSGTYPE(*COMP)

END: +
   ENDPGM
```

Figure 21.53 Command processing program MSG015CL is the power behind the SCHMSGQ command.

A shortcoming to this approach is that the command runs interactively. Therefore, if the message queue is large, running the command could take some time. Because most message queues are cleared periodically, this might not be an issue.

—*Jim Walker*

✦ ✦ ✦ Messages

Automatically Display Job Completion Messages

When you run the Submit Job (SBMJOB) command, the system sends you back a message
to let you know whether the job completed normally or not. Typically, you have to use
the Display Message (DSPMSG) command to view this message. Alternatively, you can
set your message queue to *BREAK mode, but having these messages interrupt your work
can be annoying.

A better way is to use a break-handling program like the one shown in Figure 21.54. A
break-handling program gets called whenever a message arrives on a specific message
queue. This technique can be used to send job completion messages to the bottom of your
screen as well as to your message queue.

```
/*================================================================*/
/* To compile:                                                    */
/*                                                                */
/*          CRTCLPGM   PGM(XXX/MONMSGCL) SRCFILE(XXX/QCLSRC)      */
/*                                                                */
/*================================================================*/
            PGM        PARM(&MSGQ &MSGQLIB &MSGK)

            DCL        VAR(&MSGQ) TYPE(*CHAR) LEN(10)
            DCL        VAR(&MSGQLIB) TYPE(*CHAR) LEN(10)
            DCL        VAR(&MSGK) TYPE(*CHAR) LEN(4)
            DCL        VAR(&MSGDTA) TYPE(*CHAR) LEN(132)
            DCL        VAR(&MSGID) TYPE(*CHAR) LEN(7)
            DCL        VAR(&RED) TYPE(*CHAR) LEN(1) VALUE(X'28')

            RCVMSG     MSGQ(&MSGQLIB/&MSGQ) MSGKEY(&MSGK) RMV(*NO) +
                         MSG(&MSGDTA) MSGID(&MSGID)
            IF         COND(&MSGID *EQ 'CPF1240') THEN(CHGVAR +
                         VAR(&MSGDTA) VALUE(&RED *CAT &MSGDTA))
            SNDPGMMSG  MSGID(CPF9897) MSGF(QCPFMSG) MSGDTA(&MSGDTA) +
                         TOPGMQ(*EXT) MSGTYPE(*STATUS)

            ENDPGM
```

*Figure 21.54: Break-handling program MONMSGCL can be used as your break-handling
program.*

To use this break-handling program, you need to change your message queue to specify
the name of the break-handling program—in this case, MONMSGCL. You can accomplish
this with the following command:

```
CHGMSGQ MSGQ(usrprf)    DLVRY(*BREAK) PGM(MONMSGCL)
```

In the MSGQ parameter, replace usrprf with the name of the message queue defined in your user profile. In most cases, it will be the same as your user profile name because that's the default when you create a user profile. If you want to assign a break-handling program to your message queue every time you sign on to the AS/400, consider putting this command into your initial program.

—Robin Klima

Don't Miss "Job Ended Abnormally" Messages

If you're a programmer, you've often seen message CPF1240, "Job ended abnormally." Abnormal ends (or abends for short) are common, particularly during compilations that were submitted to batch. Unfortunately, if your attention is elsewhere, you might miss the message and accidentally press the Enter key—which erases the message.

You can reduce the likelihood of missing an abend message by creating a suitable break-handling program, such as USRMSGMGT (shown in Figure 21.55). The program uses display file USRMSGMGTD (shown in Figure 21.56). USRMSGMGT receives the message and checks to see if it's message CPF1240. If it is, USRMSGMGT presents a panel on the screen and sounds an alarm. It's much harder to miss that!

```
/*===============================================================*/
/* To compile:                                                   */
/*                                                               */
/*            CRTCLPGM   PGM(XXX/USRMSGMGT) SRCFILE(XXX/QCLSRC)   */
/*                                                               */
/*===============================================================*/
PGM         PARM(&MSGQ &MSGQLIB &MSGKEY)

  DCL       VAR(&BLANK) TYPE(*CHAR) LEN(1) VALUE(' ')
  DCL       VAR(&ERROR) TYPE(*LGL) LEN(1)
  DCL       VAR(&JOBNAM) TYPE(*CHAR) LEN(10)
  DCL       VAR(&JOBNBR) TYPE(*CHAR) LEN(6)
  DCL       VAR(&JOBUSR) TYPE(*CHAR) LEN(10)
  DCL       VAR(&MSGDTA) TYPE(*CHAR) LEN(256)
  DCL       VAR(&MSGKEY) TYPE(*CHAR) LEN(4)
  DCL       VAR(&MSGQ) TYPE(*CHAR) LEN(10)
  DCL       VAR(&MSGQLIB) TYPE(*CHAR) LEN(10)
  DCL       VAR(&TRUE) TYPE(*LGL) LEN(1) VALUE('1')

  DCLF      FILE(USRMSGMGTD)

  RCVMSG    MSGQ(&MSGQLIB/&MSGQ) MSGKEY(&MSGKEY) +
              RMV(*NO) MSG(&MSGTXT) SECLVL(&SECLVL) +
```

Figure 21.55: CL program USRMSGMGT should be used as the break-handling program (part 1 of 2).

```
                  MSGDTA(&MSGDTA) MSGID(&MSGID) MSGF(&MSGF) +
                  SNDMSGFLIB(&MSGFLIB)
      MONMSG      MSGID(CPF0000)

      IF          COND(&MSGID *EQ 'CPF1240') THEN(DO)
        CHGVAR    VAR(&IN98) VALUE('1') /* Sound alarm */
AGAIN:
        SNDRCVF   RCDFMT(BEEP)

        CHGVAR    VAR(&IN98) VALUE('0') /* Don't sound alarm +
                  again */

        IF        COND(&IN10) THEN(DO)
          CHGVAR    VAR(&IN99) VALUE('0')
          CHGVAR    VAR(&JOBNAM) VALUE(%SST(&MSGDTA 1 10))
          CHGVAR    VAR(&JOBUSR) VALUE(%SST(&MSGDTA 11 10))
          CHGVAR    VAR(&JOBNBR) VALUE(%SST(&MSGDTA 21 6))
          DSPSPLF   FILE(QPJOBLOG) JOB(&JOBNBR/&JOBUSR/&JOBNAM) +
                    SPLNBR(*LAST)
          MONMSG    MSGID(CPF0000) EXEC(DO)
            CHGVAR    VAR(&IN99) VALUE('1')
          ENDDO
          GOTO      CMDLBL(AGAIN)
        ENDDO

        RETURN
      ENDDO

      ELSE        CMD(DO)
        SNDPGMMSG MSGID(CPF9897) MSGF(QCPFMSG) MSGDTA(&MSGTXT) +
                  TOPGMQ(*EXT) MSGTYPE(*STATUS)
        MONMSG    MSGID(CPF0000)
      ENDDO

ENDPGM
```

Figure 21.55: CL program USRMSGMGT should be used as the break-handling program (part 2 of 2).

```
     *=================================================================
     * To compile:
     *
     *      CRTDSPF    FILE(XXX/USRMSGMGTD) SRCFILE(XXX/QDDSSRC)
     *
     *=================================================================
     A                                       DSPSIZ(24 80 *DS3)
     A                                       PRINT
     A                                       CA10(10 'Display job log')
     *=================================================================
```

Figure 21.56: Display file USRMSGMGTD provides the user with the status of the command (part 1 of 2).

894

```
A               R BEEP
A                                        BLINK
A      98                                ALARM
A                               1 31'Job Ended Abnormally'
A                                        DSPATR(HI)
A                               3  2'Message'
A               MSGID      7A  O 3 10DSPATR(HI)
A                               5  2'from message file'
A               MSGF      10A  O 5 20DSPATR(HI)
A                               5 31'in'
A               MSGFLIB   10A  O 5 34DSPATR(HI)
A                               6  2'                              -
A                                                              '   -
A                                        DSPATR(UL)
A                                        COLOR(BLU)
A                               8  2'Message:'
A                                        DSPATR(UL)
A               MSGTXT    256A  O 9  2
A                              14  2'Second Level:'
A                                        DSPATR(UL)
A               SECLVL    512A  O 15 2BLKFOLD
A                              23  2'Press Enter to continue.'
A                                        COLOR(BLU)
A               DUMMY      1A  I 23 27DSPATR(PC)
A                                        DSPATR(PR)
A                              23 61'F10=Display job log'
A                                        COLOR(BLU)
A      99                      24 61'No job log exists.'
A                                        COLOR(RED)
```

Figure 21.56: Display file USRMSGMGTD provides the user with the status of the command (part 2 of 2).

The panel shows the entire first- and second-level text of the message, and you can press Enter to continue or F10 to display the job log of the job that abended. If the system cannot display the job log for some reason (it may have been printed already), the "No job log exists" message appears in red when you press F10.

To activate this program, assign it to your user profile message queue, like this:

```
CHGMSGQ MSGQ(*USRPRF)  DLVRY(*BREAK)  PGM(XXX/USRMSGMGT)
```

—*Ernie Malaga*

How to Forward Messages in CL

Surely, you have noticed that each time you run a command incorrectly, OS/400 gets back to you with an error message of some sort. For example, you might want to display the contents of library XYZ with the Display Library (DSPLIB) command, as follows:

```
DSPLIB XYZ
```

If you don't have a library named XYZ, however, OS/400 tells you "Library XYZ not found" via a program message. Actually, most OS/400 activities produce messages of some sort, and not just for error conditions. There are many types of messages, but the four types that stand out are:

- Informational (*INFO).

- Completion (*COMP).

- Diagnostic (*DIAG).

- Escape (*ESCAPE).

In many cases, these messages carry important information. The problem is that, whereas running DSPLIB from the command line makes any error message immediately visible, running the same command from a CL program hides the message. The reason is that OS/400 sends the message to the caller of the program that contains the command in error; if you run the command from the command line, the command's CPP sends the error message to its caller (the command line). If you run the command from a CL program, it's the CL program, not the command line, that gets the message.

It's easy to see, therefore, the importance of forwarding messages up the call stack. In this utility, I present a command that makes forwarding such program messages very simple and convenient. The call stack is a last-in, first-out queue (or "stack") that contains an ordered list of all the programs that a particular job is running. At the top of the call stack, you'll find program QSYS/QCMD in most jobs. Then, as programs are called, they are added at the bottom of the stack.

Figure 21.57 shows a typical call stack. Let's suppose you're running an interactive job. Call stack level 1 contains QCMD. Then, you call OPM program A directly from the command line; at that point, the call stack contains program A in level 2. Program A then calls ILE program B, which contains two procedures—procedure 1 and procedure 2—in such a way that procedure 1 calls procedure 2. Finally, procedure 2 calls OPM program C.

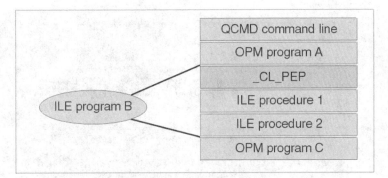

Figure 21.57: Typically, the call-stack structure allows for error messages to be forwarded up the call stack.

When any of these programs and procedures ends in error, the error message must be forwarded up the call stack so that the caller becomes aware of the error condition and can take corrective action (or merely pass the bucket further up the call stack). For example, if OPM program C ends in error, ILE procedure 2 gets the error message. The procedure can then either take corrective action or forward the error message to its caller, ILE procedure 1.

The problem, then, is what procedure 1 should do about it. If it cannot take corrective action, it should forward the message to its own caller. But its caller is OPM program A, which is two levels up the stack; OS/400 inserted a procedure of its own, called _CL_PEP, inserted by the CL compiler. The name stands for "CL Program Entry Procedure," and all ILE CL programs have one.

Over the years, I've seen dozens of variations of message-forwarding algorithms. The simplest involves a Receive Message (RCVMSG) command and a Send Program Message (SNDPGMMSG) command, which forward to the caller the escape message with which a CL program has ended in error. Although simple to code, it's a deficient technique. Often, the escape message doesn't contain enough information to find out what went wrong.

A better technique involves the use of two APIs: QMHMOVPM and QMHRSNEM. The first API moves to the caller any diagnostic messages, and the second API resends the escape message. While this technique is better, coding an API call is not something you can do with your eyes closed. These difficulties led me to develop the Forward Program Messages (FWDPGMMSG) command (Figure 21.58).

```
/*================================================================*/
/* To compile:                                                    */
/*                                                                */
/*            CRTCMD    CMD(XXX/FWDPGMMSG) PGM(XXX/PGM007CL) +     */
/*                      SRCFILE(XXX/QCMDSRC) TEXT('Forward +       */
/*                      Program Messages') ALLOW(*IPGM *IMOD +     */
/*                      *BPGM *BMOD) HLPPNLGRP(XXX/PGM007PG) +     */
/*                      HLPID(*CMD)                                */
/*                                                                */
/*================================================================*/
             CMD       PROMPT('Forward Program Messages')

             PARM      KWD(MSGTYPE) TYPE(*CHAR) LEN(9) RSTD(*YES) +
                       DFT(*DIAGESC) VALUES(*DIAGESC *INFOCOMP +
                       *ALL) PROMPT('Message types')

             PARM      KWD(CVTESCAPE) TYPE(*CHAR) LEN(4) RSTD(*YES) +
                       DFT(*NO) VALUES(*YES *NO) PROMPT('Convert +
                       *ESCAPE to *DIAG')
```

Figure 21.58: Command FWDPGMMSG lets you easily forward program messages up through a job stack.

The purpose of this command is to facilitate coding the message-forwarding algorithm as much as possible:

- You code only two lines of code.

- Because you don't need any variables, you can't forget any Declare (DCL) commands.

- You always code the same two lines, regardless of CL program type (OPM or ILE).

FWDPGMMSG has only two parameters, both of which accept default values:

- Message type (MSGTYPE). With this parameter, you tell FWDPGMMSG which messages you want to forward to the caller. There are only three valid values: *DIAGESC (default), *INFOCOMP, and *ALL. *DIAGESC forwards diagnostic and escape messages only; *INFOCOMP forwards informational and completion messages only; *ALL, forwards all four message types.

- Convert escape to diagnostic (CVTESCAPE). Sometimes, you want to forward messages to the caller in such a way that any escape messages don't interfere with the smooth operation of the caller. To do that, you must convert any escape messages to diagnostic while forwarding. FWDPGMMSG makes this easy if you specify *YES for this parameter. Or you can leave the default value *NO if you want escape messages to remain as escape messages.

FWDPGMMSG can be used in any CL program or CL procedure. In most cases, you'll want to forward error messages to the caller. Therefore, you can take the default values for both parameters and write your CL source code as shown in Figure 21.59.

```
PGM
DCL VAR(...)
...
MONMSG MSGID(CPF0000 MCH0000) EXEC(GOTO CMDLBL(ERROR))
/* Normal processing */
RETURN
ERROR:
FWDPGMMSG
MONMSG MSGID(CPF0000)
ENDPGM
```

Figure 21.59: Here's how to use the FWDPGMMSG command.

First, your CL program or procedure must contain a global Monitor Message (MONMSG) command, branching control to tag ERROR if any unexpected CPF, MCH, CEE, or other messages show up. You should at least monitor for CPF messages, but think of any others that might pop up. As usual, the global MONMSG must sit between the DCLs and the normal processing (or "body") of the program. Second, code a RETURN command at the end of the body of the program, immediately followed by label ERROR, which in turn should be followed by the message-forwarding mechanism. Finally, code a FWDPGMMSG with no parameters and a MONMSG to monitor CPF0000 (any CPF messages).

FWDPGMMSG without parameters will forward any diagnostic and escape messages to the CL program's caller, without converting the escape message to diagnostic. The caller can then monitor for error messages immediately after the CALL (or CALLPRC) command, take corrective action, or forward the messages further up the call stack. It's very important that you code a MONMSG for CPF0000 immediately after FWDPGMMSG.

If FWDPGMMSG were to fail for any reason and you had omitted this MONMSG, your CL program would enter an infinite loop. The reason is simple: If FWDPGMMSG fails and there's no MONMSG, the global MONMSG traps it and branches control to tag ERROR, where it finds FWDPGMMSG again—failing again. And repeats this process in a rather tight and CPU-intensive loop. The only way out would be to press **SysRq** and select option 2 to run the End Request (ENDRQS) command. If the job is running in batch, you'd have to run the End Job (ENDJOB) command from a display station.

FWDPGMMSG's processing program is PGM007CL (Figure 21.60). It might look complicated at first glance, but it's really not that difficult to follow.

```
/*==================================================================*/
/* To compile:                                                      */
/*                                                                  */
/*            CRTCLPGM    PGM(XXX/PGM007CL) SRCFILE(XXX/QCLSRC) +    */
/*                        TEXT('CPP for FWDPGMMSG command')         */
/*                                                                  */
/*==================================================================*/
PGM        PARM(&MSGTYPE &CVTESCAPE)

  DCL      VAR(&APIERRCDE) TYPE(*CHAR) LEN(8) +
             VALUE(X'0000000000000000')
  DCL      VAR(&CALLER2) TYPE(*CHAR) LEN(10)
  DCL      VAR(&CVTESCAPE) TYPE(*CHAR) LEN(4)
  DCL      VAR(&MSGKEY) TYPE(*CHAR) LEN(4)
  DCL      VAR(&MSGTYPE) TYPE(*CHAR) LEN(9)
  DCL      VAR(&MSGTYPEARR) TYPE(*CHAR) LEN(40)
  DCL      VAR(&NBRMSGTYPE) TYPE(*CHAR) LEN(4)
  DCL      VAR(&RCVVAR) TYPE(*CHAR) LEN(512)
  DCL      VAR(&STRUCT) TYPE(*CHAR) LEN(38)
  DCL      VAR(&TOPGMQ) TYPE(*CHAR) LEN(10) VALUE('*')
  DCL      VAR(&TOPGMQLEN) TYPE(*CHAR) LEN(4) +
             VALUE(X'0000000A') /* Dec = 10 */
  DCL      VAR(&TOPGMQCTR) TYPE(*CHAR) LEN(4)
  DCL      VAR(&TOPGMQQUAL) TYPE(*CHAR) LEN(20) +
             VALUE('*NONE      *NONE')

  /* Bridge over _CL_PEP if present */
  CALL     PGM(QMHSNDPM) PARM(' ' ' ' 'Dummy' +
             X'00000005' '*INFO' '*' X'00000002' +
             &MSGKEY &APIERRCDE)
  CALL     PGM(QMHRCVPM) PARM(&RCVVAR X'00000200' +
             'RCVM0300' '*' X'00000002' '*ANY' &MSGKEY +
             X'00000000' '*REMOVE' &APIERRCDE)
  CHGVAR   VAR(&CALLER2) VALUE(%SST(&RCVVAR 492 10))

  IF       COND(&CALLER2 *EQ '_CL_PEP') THEN(DO)
    CHGVAR   VAR(%BIN(&TOPGMQCTR)) VALUE(3)
  ENDDO
  ELSE     CMD(DO)
    CHGVAR   VAR(%BIN(&TOPGMQCTR)) VALUE(2)
  ENDDO

  /* Requested to preserve *ESCAPE messages */
  IF       COND(&CVTESCAPE *EQ '*NO') THEN(DO)
    /* Move program messages */
    IF       COND(&MSGTYPE *EQ '*DIAGESC') THEN(DO)
      CHGVAR   VAR(&MSGTYPEARR) VALUE('*DIAG')
```

Figure 21.60: CL program PGM007CL is the heart of the FWDPGMMSG command (part 1 of 2).

```
      CHGVAR     VAR(%BIN(&NBRMSGTYPE)) VALUE(1)
   ENDDO
   ELSE       CMD(IF COND(&MSGTYPE *EQ '*INFOCOMP') THEN(DO))
      CHGVAR     VAR(&MSGTYPEARR) VALUE('*INFO      *COMP')
      CHGVAR     VAR(%BIN(&NBRMSGTYPE)) VALUE(2)
   ENDDO
   ELSE       CMD(IF COND(&MSGTYPE *EQ '*ALL') THEN(DO))
      CHGVAR     VAR(&MSGTYPEARR) VALUE('*INFO      *COMP      +
                   *DIAG')
      CHGVAR     VAR(%BIN(&NBRMSGTYPE)) VALUE(3)
   ENDDO
   CALL       PGM(QMHMOVPM) PARM('    ' &MSGTYPEARR +
                &NBRMSGTYPE '*' &TOPGMQCTR &APIERRCDE +
                X'00000001' '*NONE      *NONE' '*CHAR' '*' +
                X'00000001')
   MONMSG     MSGID(CPF0000)

   /* Resend escape message */
   IF         COND(&MSGTYPE *EQ '*DIAGESC' *OR &MSGTYPE +
                *EQ '*ALL') THEN(DO)
      CHGVAR     VAR(&STRUCT) VALUE(&TOPGMQCTR *CAT +
                   &TOPGMQQUAL *CAT &TOPGMQLEN *CAT &TOPGMQ)
      CALL       PGM(QMHRSNEM) PARM('     ' &APIERRCDE &STRUCT +
                   X'00000026' 'RSNM0100' '*' X'00000001')
      MONMSG     MSGID(CPF0000)
   ENDDO
ENDDO

/* Requested to convert *ESCAPE messages */
ELSE       CMD(DO)
   IF         COND(&MSGTYPE *EQ '*DIAGESC') THEN(DO)
      CHGVAR     VAR(&MSGTYPEARR) VALUE('*DIAG      *ESCAPE')
      CHGVAR     VAR(%BIN(&NBRMSGTYPE)) VALUE(2)
   ENDDO
   ELSE       CMD(IF COND(&MSGTYPE *EQ '*INFOCOMP') THEN(DO))
      CHGVAR     VAR(&MSGTYPEARR) VALUE('*INFO      *COMP')
      CHGVAR     VAR(%BIN(&NBRMSGTYPE)) VALUE(2)
   ENDDO
   ELSE       CMD(IF COND(&MSGTYPE *EQ '*ALL') THEN(DO))
      CHGVAR     VAR(&MSGTYPEARR) VALUE('*DIAG      *ESCAPE    +
                   *INFO      *COMP')
      CHGVAR     VAR(%BIN(&NBRMSGTYPE)) VALUE(4)
   ENDDO
   CALL       PGM(QMHMOVPM) PARM('    ' &MSGTYPEARR +
                &NBRMSGTYPE '*' &TOPGMQCTR &APIERRCDE +
                X'00000001' '*NONE      *NONE' '*CHAR' '*' +
                X'00000001')
   MONMSG     MSGID(CPF0000)
ENDDO

ENDPGM
```

Figure 21.60: CL program PGM007CL is the heart of the FWDPGMMSG command (part 2 of 2).

To begin with, you must realize that the CPP of a command you run within a CL program or procedure is one level below the CL program or procedure. For example, suppose that, as in Figure 21.60, ILE procedure 1 runs the FWDPGMMSG command. The command's CPP, PGM007CL, takes up the level right below ILE procedure 1. With this in mind, it's clear that PGM007CL must consider the program immediately above it as the source and the one above that as the target. Therefore, FWDPGMMSG executed from ILE procedure 1 must forward messages from that procedure to the caller.

But, from the call stack diagram, ILE procedure 1's caller is none other than _CL_PEP. If PGM007CL were to send the ILE procedure 1's messages there, they would fall into a black hole and never emerge.

Clearly, PGM007CL must determine if _CL_PEP, at the time it is running, occupies a position two levels up the call stack. If that is the case, PGM007CL must forward the messages three levels up the stack so that it reaches OPM program A.

That's the first thing PGM007CL does. It uses the QMHSNDPM API to send a dummy informational message two levels up, obtaining the 4-byte key to the message in CL variable &MSGKEY. Then, it receives the same message by calling QMHRCVPM, retrieving the message information in variable &RCVVAR, which is 512 bytes long and structured according to data format RCVM0300. In this format, bytes 492 to 501 of &RCVVAR contain the name of the program or procedure from which the message is being received. All I have to do, then, is compare those bytes against _CL_PEP. If they are equal, I set to 3 the number of levels to move messages up. Otherwise, I set that number to 2.

Next, I determine whether PGM007CL must convert escape messages to diagnostic. If not, I need to call two APIs: QMHMOVPM to move program messages from one program to another, and then QMHRSNPM to resend the escape message as another escape message. Otherwise (if PGM007CL must convert escape messages to diagnostic), I call only QMHMOVPM. One of the capabilities of this API is that it automatically converts escape messages to diagnostic.

Let's look at the parameters I have coded for each of these API calls. When moving program messages without conversion, QMHMOVPM gets the following parameters:

1. Four blanks for the message key. I don't supply a message key, because I want QMHMOVPM to move more than one message and to do so by message type.

2. An array of message type codes, which has been set to an appropriate value beforehand. For instance, if you specified MSGTYPE(*INFOCOMP), the array will contain *INFO in the first 10 bytes and *COMP in the following 10. The remaining 20 bytes will be blank.

3. A 4-byte binary number that indicates how many message types I am providing in parameter 2.

4. An asterisk, which indicates that the target program is based on the program (PGM007CL) that called the API.

5. Another 4-byte binary number, which indicates how many levels up to go, starting from PGM007CL. Previously, I have set this number to 2 or 3, depending on _CL_PEP.

6. The API error code structure, preset to nulls.

7. A number 1 expressed in binary, indicating the length of parameter 4.

8. Two qualifiers for the target call stack level, both of which must be *NONE.

9. The string *CHAR, to indicate that parameter 4 contains a character value instead of a pointer.

10. An asterisk, to indicate that the source program is based on the program (PGM007CL) that called the API.

11. A number 1 expressed in binary, indicating that the source program is one level up from PGM007CL (i.e., PGM007CL's caller).

If the message types you selected for forwarding are either *DIAGESC or *ALL and no conversion is desired for escape messages, you need to call QMHRSNEM to resend the escape message up the call stack. There are seven parameters:

1. Four blanks for the message key (you don't know the key to the escape message).

2. The API error code structure, preset to nulls.

3. A data structure organized according to data format RSNM0100, which is 38 bytes long. This structure tells the API where to send the escape message. The components of the data structure are:

       a)   The number of levels to go up the stack, either 2 or 3.

       b)   The target call-stack entry qualifiers, both set to *NONE.

       c)   The number 10 in binary, to indicate the length of the next component.

       d)   An asterisk, to indicate that the target program is based on the program (PGM007CL) that called the API.

4. The number 38 in binary, which is the length of the data structure given in parameter 3.

5. The string RSNM0100, which identifies the organization of the structure.

6. An asterisk, to indicate that the source program is based on PGM007CL.

7. The number 1 in binary, to indicate that the source program is PGM007CL's caller.

I call QMHMOVPM again in the second part of PGM007CL in order to move program messages when escape message conversion is desired. The parameters are nearly identical, however, so I won't belabor the point.

Figure 21.61 shows the panel group that provides help for the FWDPGMMSG command.

```
.*================================================================
.* To compile:
.*
.*                CRTPNLGRP  PNLGRP(XXX/PGM007PG) SRCFILE(XXX/QPNLSRC) +
.*                           TEXT('Help text for FWDPGMMSG command')
.*
.*================================================================
:PNLGRP.

:HELP NAME=fwdpgmmsg.
Forward Program Messages (FWDPGMMSG)
:P.
FWDPGMMSG forwards up the call stack messages of type *INFO, *COMP,
*DIAG, and *ESCAPE.  Optionally, *ESCAPE messages may be converted
to *DIAG.
:EHELP.
```

Figure 21.61: Panel group PGM007PG is used to provide help for the FWDPGMMSG command (part 1 of 2).

```
.*===================================================================
:HELP NAME='fwdpgmmsg/msgtype'.
Message type (MSGTYPE) Parameter
:XH3.Message type (MSGTYPE) Parameter
:P.
Enter a special value that describes the kind of messages you want
to forward up the call stack.  The valid values are&colon.
:P.
:PARML.
:PT.:PK DEF.*DIAGESC:EPK.
:PD.
Forward *DIAG (diagnostic) and *ESCAPE (escape) messages only.
:PT.*INFOCOP
:PD.
Forward *INFO (informational) and *COMP (completion) messages only.
:PT.*ALL
:PD.
Forward *INFO, *COMP, *DIAG, and *ESCAPE.
:EPARML.
:EHELP.


.*===================================================================
:HELP NAME='fwdpgmmsg/cvtescape'.
Convert escape (CVTESCAPE) Parameter
:XH3.Convert escape (CVTESCAPE) Parameter
:P.
Enter an option that describes whether you want to convert *ESCAPE
messages to *DIAG, or leave them as *ESCAPE.  The valid values
are&colon.
:P.
:PARML.
:PT.:PK DEF.*NO:EPK.
:PD.
Do not convert *ESCAPE messages to *DIAG.
:PT.*YES
:PD.
Convert *ESCAPE messages to *DIAG.
:EPARML.
:EHELP.


.*===================================================================
:EPNLGRP.
```

Figure 21.61: Panel group PGM007PG is used to provide help for the FWDPGMMSG command (part 2 of 2).

—Ernie Malaga

How to Send Status Messages

Programs should have a user-friendly interface. In particular, it's important to give the user feedback that tells him when the program he's running is actually doing something (particularly if the program runs for a long time). In this way, the user will feel reassured that something is happening, instead of wondering if the system just went down.

CL programs typically use the Send Program Message (SNDPGMMSG) command to send status messages to the external program message queue. Such messages appear at the bottom line of the display station's screen and remain on the screen until replaced by another status message or until the program ends and control returns to the keyboard. There are two problems with status messages, however.

First, they require a somewhat complicated coding technique. The SNDPGMMSG command cannot use the MSG parameter to send impromptu status messages; it must use the MSGID parameter and, typically, the generic CPF9898 or CPF9897 message descriptions. In addition, the message type must be *STATUS, and the program message queue must be *EXT. If you miss any of these items, either your program won't compile or the message will never show up.

Second, there's a job attribute that controls whether status messages show up or not. This attribute can be set at the system value level, the user profile level, or the job level. If the attribute is set to *NONE, status messages are not meant to appear on the screen at all. So, before you send a status message that you definitely want to show, you must change the Status Message (STSMSG) attribute to *NORMAL so that the message can appear, and then you must change the attribute back to *NONE if it was set to that value. As you can imagine, these changes complicate your CL program unnecessarily.

Instead of going through so much trouble, you might want to use my Send Status Message (SNDSTSMSG) command.

Unlike SNDPGMMSG, it allows you to send impromptu messages, doesn't require any special parameter combinations, and takes care of the job STSMSG attribute. You might need to force the appearance of the status message, overriding the job's STSMSG attribute with the FORCE parameter.

Figure 21.62 shows the SNDSTSMSG command, and Figure 21.63 is its command-processing program named STS001CL. They're both simple enough not to require explanation. If you need to send status messages from a non-CL program (such as an RPG program), you can call STS001CL directly, making sure to pass a 256-byte parameter containing the message text and a 4-byte parameter that contains either *YES or *NO.

```
/*==============================================================*/
/* To compile:                                                  */
/*                                                              */
/*        CRTCMD     CMD(XXX/SNDSTSMSG) PGM(XXX/STS001CL) +      */
/*                   SRCFILE(XXX/QCMDSRC) TEXT('Send Status +    */
/*                   Message')                                   */
/*                                                              */
/*==============================================================*/
          CMD        PROMPT('Send Status Message')

          PARM       KWD(MSG) TYPE(*CHAR) LEN(256) DFT(*NONE) +
                     SPCVAL((*NONE ' ')) EXPR(*YES) +
                     PROMPT('Status message')

          PARM       KWD(FORCED) TYPE(*CHAR) LEN(4) RSTD(*YES) +
                     DFT(*YES) VALUES(*YES *NO) PROMPT('Forced +
                     display')
```

Figure 21.62: Send status messages with the SNDSTSMSG command.

```
/*==============================================================*/
/* To compile:                                                  */
/*                                                              */
/*        CRTCLPGM   PGM(XXX/STS001CL) SRCFILE(XXX/QCLSRC) +     */
/*                   TEXT('CPP for SNDSTSMSG command')           */
/*                                                              */
/*==============================================================*/
PGM          PARM(&MSG &FORCED)

  DCL        VAR(&FORCED) TYPE(*CHAR) LEN(4)
  DCL        VAR(&MSG) TYPE(*CHAR) LEN(256)
  DCL        VAR(&MSGDTA) TYPE(*CHAR) LEN(256)
  DCL        VAR(&MSGF) TYPE(*CHAR) LEN(10)
  DCL        VAR(&MSGFLIB) TYPE(*CHAR) LEN(10)
  DCL        VAR(&MSGID) TYPE(*CHAR) LEN(7)
  DCL        VAR(&STSMSG) TYPE(*CHAR) LEN(7)

  MONMSG     MSGID(CPF0000 MCH0000) EXEC(GOTO CMDLBL(ERROR))

  /* Change job's STSMSG setting to *NORMAL */
  /* if FORCED(*YES) specified */
  IF         COND(&FORCED *EQ '*YES') THEN(DO)
    RTVJOBA    STSMSG(&STSMSG)
CHGJOB       STSMSG(*NORMAL)
```

Figure 21.63: The SNDSTSMSG command's CL program, STS001CL, is responsible for actually sending the status message (part 1 of 2).

```
ENDDO

/* Send the status message */
SNDPGMMSG   MSGID(CPF9897) MSGF(QCPFMSG) MSGDTA(&MSG) +
              TOPGMQ(*EXT) MSGTYPE(*STATUS)

/* Restore job's STSMSG setting */
IF          COND(&FORCED *EQ '*YES') THEN(DO)
  CHGJOB      STSMSG(&STSMSG)
ENDDO

RETURN

/* Forward error messages to caller */
ERROR:
  RCVMSG      MSGTYPE(*EXCP) MSGDTA(&MSGDTA) MSGID(&MSGID) +
                MSGF(&MSGF) SNDMSGFLIB(&MSGFLIB)
  MONMSG      MSGID(CPF0000)
  SNDPGMMSG   MSGID(&MSGID) MSGF(&MSGFLIB/&MSGF) +
                MSGDTA(&MSGDTA) MSGTYPE(*ESCAPE)
  MONMSG      MSGID(CPF0000)

ENDPGM
```

Figure 21.63: The SNDSTSMSG command's CL program, STS001CL, is responsible for actually sending the status message (part 2 of 2).

—Ernie Malaga

Logging SNDMSG Usage

Recently, I received a letter from an AS/400 programming instructor at a technical school. His problem is that his students are a playful and irresponsible lot who abuse the Send Message (SNDMSG) command by sending offensive messages to one another, which sometimes results in disruptive behavior. Because he is in charge, he has to arbitrate these altercations. Unfortunately, he has only one student's word against another's to go on. Once the messages are deleted, there's no record of them anywhere. He therefore wanted to know whether there was a way to log all usage of the SNDMSG command.

Displaying the job log would seem to be a solution, but the offending user can easily delete it because he owns it. Besides, the job log would store a preposterous amount of useless information, and it keep jobs "alive" on the system for as long as the job log remains on a spooled file. That's why I decided to create a validity-checking program (VCP) for the SNDMSG command.

First, I created a physical file that would store the messages sent as well as the identifying information, such as user profile name and system date. The file (MSGLOG) is a simple one, and you can see its DDS as shown in Figure 21.64. Then, I wrote a simple RPG III program (MSG018RG, in Figure 21.65) that writes one record to MSGLOG. Finally, I wrote a simple CL program (MSG018CL) that works as the VCP of the SNDMSG command. You can see its code in Figure 21.66.

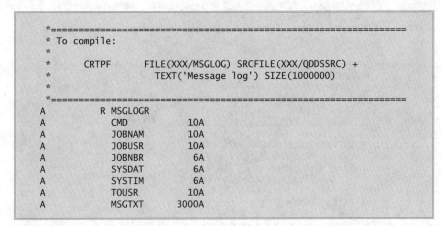

```
*================================================================
* To compile:
*
*       CRTPF       FILE(XXX/MSGLOG) SRCFILE(XXX/QDDSSRC) +
*                   TEXT('Message log') SIZE(1000000)
*
*================================================================
A           R MSGLOGR
A             CMD           10A
A             JOBNAM        10A
A             JOBUSR        10A
A             JOBNBR         6A
A             SYSDAT         6A
A             SYSTIM         6A
A             TOUSR         10A
A             MSGTXT       3000A
```

Figure 21.64: Physical file MSGLOG is used to store the job information for logging messages.

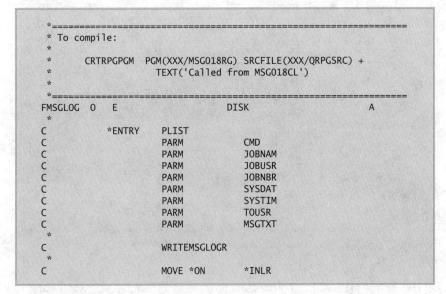

```
*================================================================
* To compile:
*
*       CRTRPGPGM   PGM(XXX/MSG018RG) SRCFILE(XXX/QRPGSRC) +
*                   TEXT('Called from MSG018CL')
*
*================================================================
FMSGLOG  O   E                      DISK                      A
*
C           *ENTRY    PLIST
C                     PARM           CMD
C                     PARM           JOBNAM
C                     PARM           JOBUSR
C                     PARM           JOBNBR
C                     PARM           SYSDAT
C                     PARM           SYSTIM
C                     PARM           TOUSR
C                     PARM           MSGTXT
*
C                     WRITEMSGLOGR
*
C                     MOVE *ON        *INLR
```

Figure 21.65: RPG III program MSG018RG is used to write to the message log.

```
/*==================================================================*/
/* To compile:                                                      */
/*                                                                  */
/*      CRTCLPGM PGM(XXX/MSG018CL) SRCFILE(XXX/QCLSRC) +            */
/*         TEXT('VCP for SNDMSG command')                          */
/*      CRTDUPOBJ  OBJ(SNDMSG) FROMLIB(QSYS) OBJTYPE(*CMD) +        */
/*         TOLIB(ALTQSYS) NEWOBJ(*OBJ)                              */
/*      CHGCMD CMD(ALTQSYS/SNDMSG) VLDCKR(XXX/MSG018CL) +           */
/*         PRDLIB(XXX)                                              */
/*                                                                  */
/*==================================================================*/
PGM          PARM(&MSG1 &Q_MSGQ_L &TOUSR1 &MSGTYPE +
               &Q_RPYMSGQ &CCSID)

   DCL       VAR(&CCSID) TYPE(*CHAR) LEN(4)
   DCL       VAR(&CMD) TYPE(*CHAR) LEN(10) VALUE('SNDMSG')
   DCL       VAR(&JOBNAM) TYPE(*CHAR) LEN(10)
   DCL       VAR(&JOBNBR) TYPE(*CHAR) LEN(6)
   DCL       VAR(&JOBUSR) TYPE(*CHAR) LEN(10)
   DCL       VAR(&MSG) TYPE(*CHAR) LEN(3000)
   DCL       VAR(&MSGTYPE) TYPE(*CHAR) LEN(5)
   DCL       VAR(&MSG1) TYPE(*CHAR) LEN(3002)
   DCL       VAR(&Q_MSGQ_L) TYPE(*CHAR) LEN(1002)
   DCL       VAR(&Q_RPYMSGQ) TYPE(*CHAR) LEN(20)
   DCL       VAR(&SYSDATE) TYPE(*CHAR) LEN(6)
   DCL       VAR(&SYSTIME) TYPE(*CHAR) LEN(6)
   DCL       VAR(&TOUSR) TYPE(*CHAR) LEN(10)
   DCL       VAR(&TOUSR1) TYPE(*CHAR) LEN(12)

   /* Ignore all errors */
   MONMSG    MSGID(CPF0000 MCH0000) EXEC(GOTO CMDLBL(ERROR))

   /* Retrieve id data for message log */
   RTVJOBA   JOB(&JOBNAM) USER(&JOBUSR) NBR(&JOBNBR)
   RTVSYSVAL SYSVAL(QDATE) RTNVAR(&SYSDATE)
   RTVSYSVAL SYSVAL(QTIME) RTNVAR(&SYSTIME)
   CHGVAR    VAR(&MSG) VALUE(%SST(&MSG1 3 3000))
   CHGVAR    VAR(&TOUSR) VALUE(%SST(&TOUSR1 3 10))

   /* Log message */
   CALL      PGM(MSG018RG) PARM(&CMD &JOBNAM &JOBUSR +
               &JOBNBR &SYSDATE &SYSTIME &TOUSR &MSG)

ERROR:
   RMVMSG    PGMQ(*SAME (*)) CLEAR(*ALL)
   MONMSG    MSGID(CPF0000)

ENDPGM
```

Figure 21.66: CL program MSG018CL is the controlling program for logging messages.

A VCP runs before the command processing program (CPP) and has the same parameter structure as both the command and the CPP. Once a user runs SNDMSG (whether from a command line or within a program), the VCP captures all parameter data, retrieves identifying information, and calls MSG018RG to write into the message log file.

This solution requires that you change the SNDMSG command. However, changing IBM-supplied objects is almost never a good idea. Therefore, it's safer to do the following:

1. Create a user library named ALTQSYS (if you don't have one already) and place it higher than QSYS in the system portion of the library list. To alter the library list, change system value QSYSLIBL using the Work with System Values (WRKSYSVAL) command.

2. Compile all three objects presented here, placing them all in ALTQSYS.

3. Create in ALTQSYS a duplicate of the SNDMSG command with the Create Duplicate Object (CRTDUPOBJ) command:

```
CRTDUPOBJ OBJ(SNDMSG) OBJTYPE(*CMD)  FROMLIB(QSYS)
          TOLIB(ALTQSYS)
```

4. Change the duplicate so that it uses MSG018CL as its VCP:

```
CHGCMD CMD(ALTQSYS/SNDMSG) VLDCKR(ALTQSYS/MSG018CL)
```

From this point on, all messages sent with SNDMSG will be recorded in MSGLOG. You can review MSGLOG at any time using a program such as SQL, Query, OPNQRYF, or any other query method of your choosing. So that it never becomes full, remember to purge old records from MSGLOG periodically.

You might want to do the same for the Send Break Message (SNDBRKMSG) command.

—Ernie Malaga

Monitoring Job Completion Messages

If you would like to access your completed job messages without having to look for them with a Display Message (DSPMSG) command and you do not want the annoyance of break messages interrupting your current work, try the Monitor Message (MONMSG) message-handling program shown in Figure 21.67.

```
/*================================================================*/
/* To compile:                                                    */
/*                                                                */
/*           CRTCLPGM    PGM(XXX/MONMSG) SRCFILE(XXX/QCLSRC) +     */
/*                       TEXT('Display completed job messages')   */
/*                                                                */
/*================================================================*/
PGM         PARM(&MSGQ &MSGQLIB &MSGK)

  DCL       VAR(&MSGDTA) TYPE(*CHAR) LEN(132)
  DCL       VAR(&MSGK) TYPE(*CHAR) LEN(4)
  DCL       VAR(&MSGQ) TYPE(*CHAR) LEN(10)
  DCL       VAR(&MSGQLIB) TYPE(*CHAR) LEN(10)

  RCVMSG    MSGQ(&MSGQLIB/&MSGQ) MSGKEY(&MSGK) RMV(*NO) +
              MSG(&MSGDTA)
  SNDPGMMSG MSGID(CPF9897) MSGF(QCPFMSG) MSGDTA(&MSGDTA) +
              TOPGMQ(*EXT) MSGTYPE(*STATUS)

ENDPGM
```

Figure 21.67: Use the MONMSG CL program to access completed job messages.

After compiling program MONMSG, execute the following command to cause your completion messages to appear unobtrusively as status messages at the bottom of your screen. You might add this command to your initial program or setup routine.

```
CHGMSGQ MSGQ(current_message_queue) DLVRY(*BREAK) PGM(MONMSG)
```

It works by changing a message queue to *BREAK delivery mode and specifying a message-handling program. This will cause OS/400 to call the MONMSG program each time a message arrives at the message queue. MONMSG will then send the message to the external program message queue.

—Bill O'Toole

Put Break Messages in a Window

Q: I have a batch job that needs to send a break message to several interactive sessions. I'd like the message to appear in a small window on the screen instead of break in and take over the entire screen. Any ideas?

A: Here's a solution. First, create a display file with the window the way you'd like to see it displayed. The design of this display file is entirely up to you. Next, create the CL program shown in Figure 21.68, but make the following changes:

1. Change the Declare File (DCLF) statement so that it specifies the actual name of the display file you created.

2. Change the Change Variable (CHGVAR) statement so that the value of &MSGTXT (which is a 512-byte character string) is copied into whatever field you use in the display file, within the window. You can change the length of variable &MSGTXT to something else if you want.

3. Change the Send/Receive File (SNDRCVF) statement so that it references the name of the window record format in the RCDFMT parameter.

4. Compile the program with a standard Create CL Program (CRTCLPGM) command.

```
PGM          PARM(&MSGQ &MSGQLIB &MSGKEY)

   DCLF      FILE(dspf_name)

   DCL       VAR(&MSGKEY) TYPE(*CHAR) LEN(4)
   DCL       VAR(&MSGQ) TYPE(*CHAR) LEN(10)
   DCL       VAR(&MSGQLIB) TYPE(*CHAR) LEN(10)
   DCL       VAR(&MSGTXT) TYPE(*CHAR) LEN(512)

   RCVMSG    MSGQ(&MSGQLIB/&MSGQ) MSGKEY(&MSGKEY) +
                           RMV(*NO) MSG(&MSGTXT)

   CHGVAR    VAR(&field_name) VALUE(&MSGTXT)

   SNDRCVF   RCDFMT(window_fmt)

ENDPGM
```

Figure 21.68: Use this break-handling program to display break messages in a window.

Your users must activate the CL program as their break-handling program. To do so, each user must run the Change Message Queue (CHGMSGQ) command:

```
CHGMSGQ MSGQ(*USRPRF) DLVRY(*BREAK) PGM(pgm_name)
```

The PGM parameter must contain the actual name of the program just compiled. To ensure that all users run this command interactively, you can insert it as a line in their initial programs (that is, the program that runs automatically whenever the user signs on).

—*Ernie Malaga*

Send Break Messages to Users

If you want to send break messages to a certain user, no matter what terminal he or she is signed on to, the Send Break Message (SNDBRKMSG) command won't help you. It lets you send break messages to a workstation message queue (not user profile message queues).

For this reason, I wrote the Send Break Message to User (SNDBRKMSGU) command. SNDBRKMSGU consists of a command definition (Figure 21.69) and CL command processing program BRK002CL (Figure 21.70).

```
/*==============================================================*/
/* To compile:                                                  */
/*                                                              */
/*          CRTCMD    CMD(XXX/SNDBRKMSGU) PGM(XXX/BRK002CL) +    */
/*                    SRCFILE(XXX/QCMDSRC)                       */
/*                                                              */
/*==============================================================*/
            CMD       PROMPT('Send Break Msg by User')
            PARM      KWD(MSGTXT) TYPE(*CHAR) LEN(120) RSTD(*NO) +
                      MIN(1) PROMPT('Message Text')
            PARM      KWD(USRPRF) TYPE(*NAME) LEN(10) +
                      SPCVAL((*ALL) (*ALLACT)) MIN(1) +
                      PROMPT('Profile name, *ALL, *ALLACT')
```

Figure 21.69: Command SNDBRKMSGU can be used to send break messages to users.

```
/*==============================================================*/
/* To compile:                                                  */
/*                                                              */
/*          CRTCLPGM   PGM(XXX/BRK002CL) SRCFILE(XXX/QCLSRC)     */
/*                                                              */
/*==============================================================*/
PGM         PARM(&MSGTXT &USRPRF)

  DCL       VAR(&DLVRY) TYPE(*CHAR) LEN(10) VALUE('*BREAK')
  DCL       VAR(&ERRCDE) TYPE(*CHAR) LEN(26) +
            VALUE(X'0000001A0000001A')
  DCL       VAR(&ERRMSGNO) TYPE(*CHAR) LEN(10)
  DCL       VAR(&ERRMSGVAL) TYPE(*CHAR) LEN(10)
  DCL       VAR(&FNRQS) TYPE(*CHAR) LEN(4)
  DCL       VAR(&MSGSENT) TYPE(*CHAR) LEN(4)
  DCL       VAR(&MSGTXT) TYPE(*CHAR) LEN(120)
  DCL       VAR(&MSGTXTLEN) TYPE(*CHAR) LEN(4) +
            VALUE(X'00000078') /* 120 */
```

Figure 21.70: Command-processing program BRK002CL is the power behind the SNDBRKMSGU command (part 1 of 2).

```
DCL         VAR(&MSGTYP) TYPE(*CHAR) LEN(10) VALUE('*INFO')
DCL         VAR(&NAMTYP) TYPE(*CHAR) LEN(4) VALUE('*USR')
DCL         VAR(&NBRELM) TYPE(*CHAR) LEN(4) +
              VALUE(X'00000001') /* 1 */
DCL         VAR(&QUAL_MSGQ) TYPE(*CHAR) LEN(20)
DCL         VAR(&SHOWDSP) TYPE(*CHAR) LEN(1) VALUE('N')
DCL         VAR(&USRPRF) TYPE(*CHAR) LEN(10)

CALL QEZSNDMG ( +
            &MSGTYP    /* IN Message Type           */ +
            &DLVRY     /* IN Delivery Mode          */ +
            &MSGTXT    /* IN Message Text           */ +
            &MSGTXTLEN /* IN Message Text Length    */ +
            &USRPRF    /* IN User Profile Array     */ +
            &NBRELM    /* IN Number of Elements     */ +
            &MSGSENT   /* OUT Message Sent Indicator */ +
            &FNRQS     /* OUT Function Requested    */ +
            &ERRCDE    /* I/O Error Code            */ +
            &SHOWDSP   /* IN Show Display           */ +
            &QUAL_MSGQ /* IN Qualified Message Queue */ +
            &NAMTYP    /* IN Name Type              */ +
            )

CHGVAR      VAR(&ERRMSGNO) VALUE(%SST(&ERRCDE 9 7))
IF          COND(&ERRMSGNO *NE '       ') THEN(DO)
  CHGVAR      VAR(&ERRMSGVAL) VALUE(%SST(&ERRCDE 17 10))
  SNDPGMMSG   MSGID(&ERRMSGNO) MSGF(QCPFMSG) +
                MSGDTA(&ERRMSGVAL)
ENDDO
ENDPGM
```

Figure 21.70: Command-processing program BRK002CL is the power behind the SNDBRKMSGU command (part 2 of 2).

It uses the QEZSNDMG API to send break messages to a user profile. If a user is signed on to multiple sessions, all sessions get the break message. This command also permits two special values. You can specify *ALL to send the message to all user profiles. Or you can specify *ALLACT to send a message to the users who are currently signed on.

—Tim Johnston

Send Message to Group

If you want to send a message to every active user profile belonging to a group profile or a list of group profiles, you can use the Send Message to Group (SNDMSGGRP) command.

The command displays all user profiles with the Display User Profile (DSPUSRPRF) command and outputs to an outfile. It then uses the Open Query File (OPNQRYF) command to select from the outfile the user profiles that belong to the group specified to receive the message. The command source is shown in Figure 21.71 and the CPP for the command, MSG016CL, is shown in Figure 21.72.

```
/*==============================================================*/
/* To compile:                                                  */
/*                                                              */
/*           CRTCMD    CMD(XXX/SNDGRPMSG) PGM(XXX/MSG016CL) +    */
/*                     SRCFILE(XXX/QCMDSRC)                      */
/*                                                              */
/*==============================================================*/
            CMD       PROMPT('Send Message to Group')

            PARM      KWD(MSG) TYPE(*CHAR) LEN(512) MIN(1) +
                      PROMPT('Message')

            PARM      KWD(GROUP) TYPE(*NAME) MIN(1) PROMPT('Group +
                      profile')
```

Figure 21.71: The SNDMSGGRP command can be used to send a single message to a group of users.

```
/*==============================================================*/
/* To compile:                                                  */
/*                                                              */
/*           CRTCLPGM   PGM(XXX/MSG016CL) SRCFILE(XXX/QCLSRC)    */
/*                                                              */
/*==============================================================*/
            PGM        PARM(&MSG &GROUP)
            DCL        VAR(&GROUP) TYPE(*CHAR) LEN(10)
            DCL        VAR(&MSG) TYPE(*CHAR) LEN(512)
            DCL        VAR(&CNT) TYPE(*DEC) LEN(3)
            DCL        VAR(&ACNT) TYPE(*CHAR) LEN(3)
            DCL        VAR(&QRYSLT) TYPE(*CHAR) LEN(50)
            DCL        VAR(&MSGID) TYPE(*CHAR) LEN(7)
            DCL        VAR(&MSGDTA) TYPE(*CHAR) LEN(80)
            DCLF       FILE(QADSPUPB)
            MONMSG     MSGID(CPF0000) EXEC(GOTO CMDLBL(ERROR))
            DSPUSRPRF  USRPRF(*ALL) OUTPUT(*OUTFILE) +
                       OUTFILE(QTEMP/QADSPUPB)
            OVRDBF     FILE(QADSPUPB) TOFILE(QTEMP/QADSPUPB) +
                       MBR(*FIRST) SHARE(*YES)
```

Figure 21.72: CPP CL program MSG016CL is responsible for sending messages to a group of people (part 1 of 2).

```
            CHGVAR     VAR(&QRYSLT) VALUE('UPGRPF *EQ ''' +
                         *TCAT &GROUP *TCAT '''')
            OPNQRYF    FILE((QADSPUPB)) QRYSLT(&QRYSLT)
LOOP:       RCVF
            MONMSG     MSGID(CPF0864) EXEC(GOTO CMDLBL(DONE))
            SNDMSG     MSG(&MSG) TOUSR(&UPUPRF)
            CHGVAR     VAR(&CNT) VALUE(&CNT + 1)
            GOTO       CMDLBL(LOOP)
DONE:       CHGVAR     VAR(&ACNT) VALUE(&CNT)
            SNDPGMMSG  MSG('Message sent to' *BCAT &ACNT *BCAT +
                         'users.')
            CLOF       OPNID(QADSPUPB)
            DLTF       FILE(QTEMP/QADSPUPB)
            GOTO       CMDLBL(ENDPGM)
ERROR:      RCVMSG     MSGTYPE(*EXCP) MSGDTA(&MSGDTA) MSGID(&MSGID)
            SNDPGMMSG  MSGID(&MSGID) MSGF(QCPFMSG) MSGDTA(&MSGDTA) +
                         MSGTYPE(*ESCAPE)
ENDPGM:     ENDPGM
```

Figure 21.72: CPP CL program MSG016CL is responsible for sending messages to a group of people (part 2 of 2).

Before you run the SNDMSGGRP command, you might want to determine who will receive the message based on the group profile you specify. One way to do this is to run the following command:

```
DSPAUTUSR SEQ(*GRPPRF)
```

When you run the Display Authorized Users (DSPAUTUSR) command with the SEQ(*GRPPRF) parameter, you will be presented with a list of user profiles sorted by group profile. This display makes it easy to tell which user profiles belong to a specific group profile.

—Sorin Caraiani

Send Message to Group (Another Technique)

Option 3 of OfficeVision/400's main menu lets you send a message to a distribution group. If you don't have OV/400, or if you need to send messages to groups from CL programs, you might want to use the Send Group Message (SNDGRPMSG) utility. This utility consists of two objects: command SNDGRPMSG and CL program GRP005CL. Source code for the two objects is shown in Figures 21.73 and 21.74.

First, you must set up a way to define groups of users. SNDGRPMSG uses members of a source physical file called MSGGROUPS. Each member is a group, and each record in a member contains a user profile name. To create the MSGGROUPS file, see the compilation instructions for program GRP005CL. Notice that the record length is 22 bytes, which allows for the fields SRCDAT (length 6), SRCSEQ (length 6), and SRCDTA (length 10). User IDs are stored in the SRCDTA field. Use PDM or SEU to maintain the source members. I have found this command very useful. For instance, I include it in month-end programs to let all users in a certain department know when month-end is running.

```
/*================================================================*/
/* To compile:                                                    */
/*                                                                */
/*          CRTCMD     CMD(XXX/SNDGRPMSG) PGM(XXX/GRP005CL) +      */
/*                     SRCFILE(XXX/QCMDSRC)                        */
/*                                                                */
/*================================================================*/

CMD  PROMPT('Send Group Message')
PARM KWD(MSG) TYPE(*CHAR) LEN(512) PROMPT('Message text')

PARM KWD(GRP) TYPE(*NAME) LEN(10) PROMPT('Group') CHOICE('Name')

PARM KWD(MSGTYP) TYPE(*NAME) LEN(5) PROMPT('Message type') +
     CHOICE('*INFO, *INQ') DFT(*INFO) SPCVAL((*INFO) (*INQ))
```

Figure 21.73: SNDGRPMSG sends messages to a group of users.

```
/*================================================================*/
/* To compile:                                                    */
/*                                                                */
/*          CRTSRCPF   FILE(XXX/MSGGROUPS) RCDLEN(22) +           */
/*                     TEXT('Groups for SndGrpMsg command')       */
/*          CRTCLPGM   PGM(XXX/XXX001CL) SRCFILE(XXX/QCLSRC)       */
/*                                                                */
/*================================================================*/
Pgm (&Msg &Group &MsgType)
   DclF MsgGroups
   Dcl &Msg      *Char 512    /* Group Message text     */
   Dcl &Group    *Char 10     /* Group Message group    */
   Dcl &MsgType  *Char 5      /* Group Message type     */
   Dcl &MsgDta   *Char 256    /* Error message text     */
   Dcl &MsgF     *Char 10     /* Error message file     */
```

Figure 21.74: The command processing program for SNDGRPMSG is another way to send messages to a group of users (part 1 of 2).

```
    Dcl  &MsgFLib *Char  10    /* Error message file library      */
    Dcl  &MsgID   *Char  7     /* Error message ID                */

    MonMsg MsgID(Cpf0000 Mch0000) Exec(Goto CmdErr)

    /* Validate group/set up file override                        */
    ChkObj DpPMsgG *File Mbr(&Group)
    OvrDbF DpPMsgG Mbr(&Group)
    /* Send message to all users in the group                     */
Loop:
    RcvF
    MonMsg MsgID(Cpf0864) Exec(GoTo Exit)
    SndUsrMsg  Msg(&Msg) MsgType(&MsgType) ToUsr(&SrcDta)
    MonMsg Cpf0000 Exec(GoTo Loop)
    GoTo Loop

    /* Handle any error message, exit program                     */
CmdErr:
    RcvMsg MsgType(*Excp) MsgDta(&MsgDta) MsgID(&MsgID) +
          MsgF(&MsgF) SndMsgFLib(&MsgFLib)
    MonMsg Cpf0000
    SndPgmMsg MsgID(&MsgID) MsgF(&MsgFLib/&MsgF) MsgDta(&MsgDta) +
           MsgType(*Escape)
    MonMsg Cpf0000
    GoTo Exit

/* Exit program                                                   */
Exit:
EndPgm
```

Figure 21.74: The command processing program for SNDGRPMSG is another way to send messages to a group of users (part 2 of 2).

—Dan Wilson

Sending Break Messages to a User (Yet Another Approach)

Sometimes, users sign on to multiple display stations. For instance, programmers might have several Client Access/400 sessions going simultaneously. Or a middle manager in the plant might use a dumb terminal capable of displaying two or three sessions at a time. Whatever the case, a problem occurs when a user is signed on to multiple display stations: You can never tell where the user is physically. And if you need to send that user a break message, there's no way of making sure he or she sees the message immediately.

The solution is to send the break message to all display stations to which the user is signed on. The Send Break Message (SNDBRKMSG) command doesn't make this easy;

you have to determine the names of the display stations first and then enter them into the TOMSGQ parameter. A better approach is to use a system API named QEZSNDMG, which is part of Operational Assistant (OA). The Send Break Message to User (SNDBRKUSR) command, shown in Figure 21.75, is a convenient front-end for the API. It accepts a user profile name in its USER parameter and a message text in its MSG parameter, which can have a maximum length of 494 characters. If that maximum length strikes you as odd, that's not our fault; it's imposed by QEZSNDMG.

```
/*================================================================*/
/* To compile:                                                    */
/*                                                                */
/* CRTCMD CMD(XXX/SNDBRKUSR) PGM(XXX/BRK003CL) +                  */
/* SRCFILE(XXX/QCMDSRC) TEXT('Send Break +                       */
/* Message to User')                                              */
/*                                                                */
/*================================================================*/
CMD PROMPT('Send Break Message to User')
PARM KWD(USER) TYPE(*NAME) LEN(10) MIN(1) +
EXPR(*YES) PROMPT('User profile')
PARM KWD(MSG) TYPE(*CHAR) LEN(494) MIN(1) +
EXPR(*YES) PROMPT('Message text')
```

Figure 21.75: The SNDBRKUSR command sends break messages to every display station a user is signed on to.

The CPP for the command, BRK003CL (Figure 21.76), does little besides checking that the user profile exists and then calling the API with some assumed parameter values. For example, it assumes you want to send an informational, rather than an inquiry, message. We've found that using SNDBRKUSR is far more convenient than going through OA to access the API directly. BRK003CL uses utility command Forward Program Messages (FWDPGMMSG). See this chapter's section entitled "How to Forward Messages in CL."

```
/*================================================================*/
/* To compile:                                                    */
/*                                                                */
/* CRTCLPGM PGM(XXX/BRK003CL) SRCFILE(XXX/QCLSRC) +              */
/* TEXT('CPP for SNDBRKUSR command')                             */
/*                                                                */
/*================================================================*/
```

Figure 21.76: CL program BRK003CL checks that the user profile exists and calls the API with parameter values (part 1 of 2).

```
PGM PARM(&USER &MSG)
DCL VAR(&APIERRCDE) TYPE(*CHAR) LEN(8) +
VALUE(X'0000000000000000')
DCL VAR(&FNRQS) TYPE(*CHAR) LEN(4)
DCL VAR(&MSG) TYPE(*CHAR) LEN(494)
DCL VAR(&MSGLEN) TYPE(*CHAR) LEN(4)
DCL VAR(&MSGSENT) TYPE(*CHAR) LEN(4)
DCL VAR(&USER) TYPE(*CHAR) LEN(10)
MONMSG MSGID(CPF0000 MCH0000) EXEC(GOTO CMDLBL(ERROR))
CHGVAR VAR(%BIN(&MSGLEN)) VALUE(494)
/* Verify existence of user profile */
CHKOBJ OBJ(&USER) OBJTYPE(*USRPRF)
/* Send message */
CALL PGM(QEZSNDMG) PARM('*INFO' '*BREAK' &MSG +
&MSGLEN &USER X'00000001' &MSGSENT &FNRQS +
&APIERRCDE'N' ' ' '*USR')
RETURN
ERROR:
FWDPGMMSG
MONMSG MSGID(CPF0000)
ENDPGM
```

Figure 21.76: CL program BRK003CL checks that the user profile exists and calls the API with parameter values (part 2 of 2).

—*Bill Williams*
—*Ernie Malaga*

✦ ✦ ✦ Object Creation

List Required Objects

There's nothing I dislike more than running a program only to discover that some of the files I need for that program aren't on my library list. This is especially annoying when the missing files are found in a program buried within another job stream. I might have files that are only partially updated or I might have a nearly irrecoverable situation because my procedure abends because of missing files.

To avoid this problem, I have developed the Check Program References (CHKPGMREF) command to ensure that all the files I need for a given program are on the library list before I begin. See Figure 21.77.

```
/*=================================================================*/
/* TO COMPILE:                                                     */
/*                                                                 */
/*          CRTCMD     CMD(XXX/CHKPGMREF) PGM(XXX/CHKPGMREFC)       */
/*                     SRCFILE(XXX/QCMDSRC)                         */
/*                     TEXT('CHECK PGM REFERENCE ')                 */
/*                     PRDLIB(XXX)                                  */
/*=================================================================*/
           CMD        PROMPT('Check PGM References in *LIBL')

           PARM       KWD(PGMNAME) TYPE(QUALPGM) PROMPT('Program +
                      Name')


QUALPGM:   QUAL       TYPE(*NAME) LEN(10)
           QUAL       TYPE(*NAME) LEN(10) DFT(*LIBL ) +
                      SPCVAL((*LIBL )) PROMPT('Library')
```

Figure 21.77: CHKPGMREF finds missing files before you run your program.

This command uses CL program CHKPGMREFC to check for the existence of the program's files by running Display Program Reference (DSPPGMREF) to get a list of files used by the program and sending that list to an outfile (Figure 21.78).

```
/*=================================================================*/
/* TO COMPILE:                                                     */
/*                                                                 */
/*  CRTCLPGM PGM(XXX/CHKPGMREFC) SRCFILE(XXX/QCLSRC)               */
/*                                                                 */
/*=================================================================*/
           PGM        PARM(&PGMPATH )


/***********************************************************/
/* declare parameters        */
/***********************************************************/
           DCL        VAR(&PGMPATH) TYPE(*CHAR) LEN(20)


/***********************************************************/
/* Working Fields            */
/***********************************************************/
           DCL        VAR(&PLIB) TYPE(*CHAR) LEN(10)
           DCL        VAR(&PGM ) TYPE(*CHAR) LEN(10)
           DCL        VAR(&BLANKS10) TYPE(*CHAR) LEN(10) VALUE(' ')
           DCL        VAR(&MSG) TYPE(*CHAR) LEN(128)
```

Figure 21.78: CHKPGMREFC uses DSPPGMREF and CHKOBJ to ensure that your program files are not missing (part 1 of 3).

```
              DCL        VAR(&SVWHFNAM) TYPE(*CHAR) LEN(11)
              DCL        VAR(&SVWHOTYP) TYPE(*CHAR) LEN(10)
              DCL        VAR(&ALLOBJFND) TYPE(*CHAR) LEN(1) VALUE('Y')

/********************************************************/
/* Global Message  Monitor Declares */
/********************************************************/
              DCL        VAR(&##MSGFLIB) TYPE(*CHAR) LEN(10)
              DCL        VAR(&##MSGF) TYPE(*CHAR) LEN(10)
              DCL        VAR(&##MSGID) TYPE(*CHAR) LEN(7)
              DCL        VAR(&##MSGDTA) TYPE(*CHAR) LEN(128)


/********************************************************/
/* declare File              */
/********************************************************/
              DCLF       FILE(QSYS/QADSPPGM) /* Outfile used by +
                         DSPPGMREF */

/********************************************************/
/* Global Message  Monitor            */
/********************************************************/
              MONMSG     MSGID(CPF0000 MCH0000) EXEC(GOTO +
                         CMDLBL(##ERROR))


START:

/* Get  Program/library                            */
              CHGVAR     VAR(&PLIB) VALUE(%SST(&PGMPATH 11 10))
              CHGVAR     VAR(&PGM) VALUE(%SST(&PGMPATH 1 10))

/* Retreive LIBRARY If *LIBL was defaulted from command */
              IF         COND(&PLIB *EQ *LIBL) THEN(RTVOBJD +
                         OBJ(&PGM) OBJTYPE(*PGM ) RTNLIB(&PLIB))

/* get all Referenced objects */
              DSPPGMREF  PGM(&PLIB/&PGM) OUTPUT(*OUTFILE) +
                         OUTFILE(QTEMP/WRKPGM)

/* override System outfile definition to work file */
              OVRDBF     FILE(QADSPPGM) TOFILE(QTEMP/WRKPGM)


/* Read each object referenced in the program and loop for next read */
  READ:       RCVF       RCDFMT(QWHDRPPR) /* Read a record */
              MONMSG     MSGID(CPF0864) EXEC(GOTO EOF)
                         /*                            */

/* Check mult-format files once */
              IF         COND(&SVWHFNAM *EQ &WHFNAM *AND &SVWHOTYP +
```

Figure 21.78: CHKPGMREFC uses DSPPGMREF and CHKOBJ to ensure that your program files are not missing (part 2 of 3).

```
                              *EQ &WHOTYP) THEN(DO)
              GOTO            CMDLBL(READ)
              ENDDO


/* Does object exist   */
              IF              COND(%SST(&WHFNAM 1 1) *NE '*' *AND &WHFNAM +
                                *NE &BLANKS10) THEN(DO)
              CHKOBJ          OBJ(*LIBL/&WHFNAM) OBJTYPE(&WHOTYP)
              MONMSG          MSGID(CPF0000) EXEC(DO)
              CHGVAR          VAR(&MSG) VALUE('Object' *BCAT &WHFNAM +
                                *BCAT 'Object Type' *BCAT &WHOTYP *BCAT +
                                'Not Found' )
              SNDPGMMSG       MSG(&MSG)
              CHGVAR          VAR(&ALLOBJFND) VALUE('N')
              ENDDO
              CHGVAR          VAR(&SVWHFNAM) VALUE(&WHFNAM)
              CHGVAR          VAR(&SVWHOTYP) VALUE(&WHOTYP)
ENDDO

              GOTO            READ /* Loop back for next record */


  EOF:                        /* All records have been read */
              IF              COND(&ALLOBJFND *EQ 'Y') THEN(DO)
              SNDPGMMSG       MSG('OK, All objects found') MSGTYPE(*COMP)
              ENDDO

GOTO ENDPGM

/* if error occured, send to program message queue   */
  ##ERROR:    RCVMSG          MSGTYPE(*EXCP) MSGDTA(&##MSGDTA) +
                                MSGID(&##MSGID) MSGF(&##MSGF) +
                                MSGFLIB(&##MSGFLIB)
              MONMSG          MSGID(CPF0000 MCH0000)
              SNDPGMMSG       MSGID(&##MSGID) MSGF(&##MSGFLIB/&##MSGF) +
                                MSGDTA(&##MSGDTA) MSGTYPE(*ESCAPE)
              MONMSG          MSGID(CPF0000 MCH0000)
              RETURN

ENDPGM:
      ENDPGM
```

Figure 21.78: CHKPGMREFC uses DSPPGMREF and CHKOBJ to ensure that your program files are not missing (part 3 of 3).

CHKPGMREF then reads the outfile and uses Check Objects (CHKOBJ) to ensure the file can be found on the library list. If the file is not found, a message containing the name of the file is sent to the external message queue, where the user can view it. Thanks to this little utility, running a program with missing files has become a thing of the past!

—*Paul Ladouceur*

✦ ✦ ✦ **Operations**

Jobs Are Easy to Sort Using This Command

Programmers and operators need to review the status of interactive and batch jobs daily. The commands often used for this are Work with Active Jobs (WRKACTJOB) for interactive jobs and a combination of Work with Job Queues (WRKJOBQ) and either Work with Subsystem Jobs (WRKSBSJOB) or Work with Submitted Jobs (WRKSBMJOB) for batch jobs.

WRKACTJOB uses a great deal of resources, gives me more information and power than I usually need, and is not sequenced in a way that is useful for me. In addition, although WRKJOBQ, WRKSBSJOB, and WRKSBMJOB do give useful information, it would be more convenient just to combine the information into a single display so that I could see for each subsystem which jobs are waiting to run with the jobs already activated.

Using the Work with User Jobs (WRKUSRJOB) command solves both of these problems by allowing me to display interactive jobs in a more meaningful way and, for batch jobs, combining waiting and active jobs into a single display. However, the command parameters for WRKUSRJOB can be confusing.

For that reason, I have created a new command that uses WRKUSRJOB but simplifies the parameter options. I call this command Work with Users (WRKUSERS); see Figure 21.79. The command processing program for this command is WRKUSERC (Figure 21.80).

```
/*===============================================================*/
/* To compile:                                                   */
/*                                                               */
/*          CRTCMD     CMD(XXX/WRKUSERS) PGM(XXX/WRKUSERC)       */
/*                                                               */
/*===============================================================*/
          CMD        PROMPT('Work with Users')

          PARM       KWD(USER) TYPE(*NAME) LEN(10) DFT(*ALL) +
                       SPCVAL((*) (*ALL)) PROMPT('User')

          PARM       KWD(TYPE) TYPE(*CHAR) LEN(6) RSTD(*YES) +
                       DFT(*BATCH) SPCVAL((*BATCH) (*INTER)) +
                       PROMPT('Type')
```

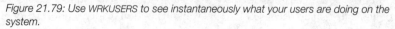

Figure 21.79: Use WRKUSERS to see instantaneously what your users are doing on the system.

```
/*******************************************************************************/
/* To Create:                                                                 */
/* Crtclpgm Pgm(xxx/WrkUserc) Srcfil(xxx/Qclsrc)                              */
/*******************************************************************************/
PGM PARM(&USER &TYPE)
DCL VAR(&USER) TYPE(*CHAR) LEN(10)
DCL VAR(&TYPE) TYPE(*CHAR) LEN(6)
/*******************************************************************************/
/* When "Batch", display Batch Jobs for User Specified. */
/*******************************************************************************/
IF COND(&TYPE = '*BATCH') THEN(DO)
WRKUSRJOB USER(&USER) JOBTYPE(*BATCH) ASTLVL(*BASIC)
GOTO CMDLBL(ENDPGM)
ENDDO
/*******************************************************************************/
/* When "Inter", display Interactive Jobs for User Specified.      */
/*******************************************************************************/
IF COND(&TYPE = '*INTER') THEN(DO)
WRKUSRJOB USER(&USER) STATUS(*ACTIVE) +
JOBTYPE(*INTERACT) ASTLVL(*BASIC)
GOTO CMDLBL(ENDPGM)
ENDDO
ENDPGM: ENDPGM
```

Figure 21.80: Here's the WRKUSERC command processing program.

WRKUSERS has just two parameters: USER and TYPE. For USER, you can specify *ALL
(the default) for all users, * for the current user, or a user name. In this way, you can indicate whose jobs you want to see. The TYPE parameter has only two options: *BATCH (the
default) for batch jobs or *INTER for interactive users. When executed, the command runs
WRKUSERC, which examines the value specified for TYPE and fills in the appropriate parameters to execute WRKUSRJOB.

When *BATCH is specified, you can see all the batch jobs waiting or running for all users,
the current user, or the user indicated. These jobs are grouped by subsystem. Therefore,
you can see the sequence in which jobs are processed. If *INTER is keyed in, for example,
you get a list of users (sorted initially by user ID) currently logged on.

Once a list is displayed, look at the command keys available, and you will see options for
changing the sort sequence, the information being displayed, or even the user value from
what was initially requested. Be aware that, as written, I have selected the *BASIC level of
information to be displayed because I like the way this option displays information. Because *BASIC is the most restrictive as far as user options are concerned, you might not

have the same level of job manipulation as you are accustomed to having. Consequently, you might want to try experimenting with WRKUSRJOB parameters and choose values different from those I have provided if you want a higher level of job control and are less concerned with the actual sort sequence.

I use this command many times each day to find out why one of my batch jobs hasn't started, to see if a remote user is currently logged on, and to gather many other pieces of useful information about batch and interactive jobs. In addition, operations doesn't complain about system response time slowing down because I no longer need to use WRKACTJOB. Try it. I think you'll find it as useful as I have.

—Bruce Guetzkow

Move Objects by Generic Name

The Move Object (MOVOBJ) command allows you to move an object from one library to another. One limitation, however, is that it cannot process multiple objects with a single command, as it does not accept generic object names. I've found a way to circumvent the generic name exclusion by running the Move (MOV) command.

However, MOV is somewhat clumsy for everyday use because you have to enter an object path name, instead of a qualified object name, in its OBJ parameter. (I'll explain paths in a bit.) I created the Move Generic Object (MOVGENOBJ) command, which has CL program GEN001CL as its CPP. See Figure 21.81.

```
/*===============================================================*/
/* To compile:                                                   */
/*                                                               */
/*          CRTCMD      CMD(XXX/MOVGENOBJ) PGM(XXX/GEN001CL) +    */
/*                        SRCFILE(XXX/QCMDSRC)                    */
/*                                                               */
/*===============================================================*/
            CMD         PROMPT('Move Generic Object')

            PARM        KWD(OBJ) TYPE(Q1) MIN(1) PROMPT('Object')
Q1:         QUAL        TYPE(*GENERIC) LEN(10) MIN(1) EXPR(*YES)
            QUAL        TYPE(*NAME) LEN(10) DFT(*LIBL) +
                          SPCVAL((*LIBL) (*CURLIB)) EXPR(*YES) +
                          PROMPT('Library')
```

Figure 21.81: Use command MOVGENOBJ to move a group of objects (part 1 of 2).

```
       PARM      KWD(OBJTYPE) TYPE(*CHAR) LEN(7) RSTD(*YES) +
                   VALUES(*ALRTBL *BNDDIR *CHTFMT *CLD *CLS +
                   *CMD *CRQD *CSI *CSPMAP *CSPTBL *DTAARA +
                   *DTAQ *FCT *FILE *FNTRSC *FNTTBL *FORMDF +
                   *FTR *GSS *JOBD *JOBQ *JRN *JRNRCV +
                   *LOCALE *MENU *MODULE *MSGF *MSGQ *M36 +
                   *M36CFG *NODGRP *NODL *OUTQ *OVL *PAGDFN +
                   *PAGSEG *PDG *PGM *PNLGRP *PRDAVL *PRDDFN +
                   *PRDLOD *PSFCFG *QMFORM *QMQRY *QRYDFN +
                   *RCT *SBSD *SCHIDX *SPADCT *SRVPGM *SSND +
                   *SVRSTG *TBL *USRIDX *USRQ *USRSPC +
                   *WSCST) MIN(1) EXPR(*YES) PROMPT('Object +
                   type')
       PARM      KWD(TOLIB) TYPE(*NAME) LEN(10) +
                   SPCVAL((*CURLIB)) MIN(1) EXPR(*YES) +
                   PROMPT('To library')
```

Figure 21.81: Use command MOVGENOBJ to move a group of objects (part 2 of 2).

Let's say you have 10 files you want to move from library PGMR to library ACCTNG, and all files have names beginning with CUST. Instead of running MOVOBJ 10 times, you can move all objects with a single execution of MOVGENOBJ, as follows:

```
MOVGENOBJ   OBJ(PGMR/CUST*)   OBJTYPE(*FILE)   TOLIB(ACCTNG)
```

In GEN001CL (Figure 21.82), Label A shows the code that builds the OBJ path name (in variable &IFSOBJ) and the TODIR path name (variable &IFSTODIR).

```
MOV OBJ('/QSYS.LIB/PGMR.LIB/CUST*.FILE') TODIR('/QSYS.LIB/ACCTNG.LIB')
```

Figure 21.82: Using MOV directly is easy using this format.

Let's go back to object path names. Even without MOVGENOBJ, you can move objects with generic names by invoking the MOV command directly. To move the same 10 files, you'd run the command shown in Figure 21.83.

```
/*===================================================================*/
/* To compile:                                                       */
/*                                                                   */
/*            CRTCLPGM   PGM(XXX/GEN001CL) SRCFILE(XXX/QCLSRC)        */
/*                                                                   */
/*===================================================================*/
PGM          PARM(&Q_OBJ &OBJTYPE &TOLIB)

  DCL        VAR(&CURLIB) TYPE(*CHAR) LEN(10)
  DCL        VAR(&IFSOBJ) TYPE(*CHAR) LEN(512)
  DCL        VAR(&IFSTODIR) TYPE(*CHAR) LEN(512)
  DCL        VAR(&MSGDTA) TYPE(*CHAR) LEN(256)
  DCL        VAR(&MSGF) TYPE(*CHAR) LEN(10)
  DCL        VAR(&MSGFLIB) TYPE(*CHAR) LEN(10)
  DCL        VAR(&MSGID) TYPE(*CHAR) LEN(7)
  DCL        VAR(&OBJ) TYPE(*CHAR) LEN(10)
  DCL        VAR(&OBJLIB) TYPE(*CHAR) LEN(10)
  DCL        VAR(&OBJTYPE) TYPE(*CHAR) LEN(7)
  DCL        VAR(&Q_OBJ) TYPE(*CHAR) LEN(20)
  DCL        VAR(&TOLIB) TYPE(*CHAR) LEN(10)

  MONMSG     MSGID(CPF0000 MCH0000) EXEC(GOTO CMDLBL(ERROR))

  /* Break qualified object name */
  CHGVAR     VAR(&OBJ) VALUE(%SST(&Q_OBJ 1 10))
  CHGVAR     VAR(&OBJLIB) VALUE(%SST(&Q_OBJ 11 10))

  /* Retrieve name of current library */
  RTVJOBA    CURLIB(&CURLIB)
  IF         COND(&CURLIB *EQ '*NONE') THEN(DO)
    CHGVAR     VAR(&CURLIB) VALUE('QGPL')
  ENDDO

  /* Resolve special values */
  IF         COND(&OBJLIB *EQ '*CURLIB') THEN(DO)
    CHGVAR     VAR(&OBJLIB) VALUE(&CURLIB)
  ENDDO
  ELSE       CMD(IF COND(&OBJLIB *EQ '*LIBL') THEN(DO))
    RTVOBJD    OBJ(&OBJLIB/&OBJ) OBJTYPE(&OBJTYPE) +
                 RTNLIB(&OBJLIB)
  ENDDO

  IF         COND(&TOLIB *EQ '*CURLIB') THEN(DO)
    CHGVAR     VAR(&TOLIB) VALUE(&CURLIB)
  ENDDO

  /* Source and target libraries must not be same */
  IF         COND(&OBJLIB *EQ &TOLIB) THEN(DO)
    SNDPGMMSG  MSGID(CPF9898) MSGF(QCPFMSG) MSGDTA('Source +
                 and target libraries cannot be the same') +
                 MSGTYPE(*ESCAPE)
```

Figure 21.83: CL program GEN001CL is the heart behind the MOVGENOBJ command (part 1 of 2).

```
    ENDDO


/* Move objects */
    CHGVAR     VAR(&IFSOBJ) VALUE('/QSYS.LIB/' *CAT &OBJLIB +
                 *TCAT '.LIB/' *CAT &OBJ *TCAT '.' *CAT +
                 %SST(&OBJTYPE 2 6))
    CHGVAR     VAR(&IFSTODIR) VALUE('/QSYS.LIB/' *CAT +
                 &TOLIB *TCAT '.LIB')
    MOV        OBJ(&IFSOBJ) TODIR(&IFSTODIR)

    RCVMSG     MSGTYPE(*LAST) MSGDTA(&MSGDTA) MSGID(&MSGID) +
                 MSGF(&MSGF) SNDMSGFLIB(&MSGFLIB)
    MONMSG     MSGID(CPF0000)
    SNDPGMMSG  MSGID(&MSGID) MSGF(&MSGFLIB/&MSGF) +
                 MSGDTA(&MSGDTA) MSGTYPE(*COMP)
    MONMSG     MSGID(CPF0000)

    RETURN

ERROR:
    RCVMSG     MSGTYPE(*EXCP) MSGDTA(&MSGDTA) MSGID(&MSGID) +
                 MSGF(&MSGF) SNDMSGFLIB(&MSGFLIB)
    MONMSG     MSGID(CPF0000)
    SNDPGMMSG  MSGID(&MSGID) MSGF(&MSGFLIB/&MSGF) +
                 MSGDTA(&MSGDTA) MSGTYPE(*ESCAPE)
    MONMSG     MSGID(CPF0000)

ENDPGM
```

Figure 21.83: CL program GEN001CL is the heart behind the MOVGENOBJ command (part 2 of 2).

Both parameters, OBJ and TODIR, require an object path name. All object path names must be enclosed in single quotes (if given as literals) and must begin with a slash (/), followed by subdirectories, separated by other slashes, until you reach the object itself. If you have ever worked with DOS or UNIX, you'll feel right at home.

When referring to the "standard" AS/400 objects (i.e., libraries and their contents), use object names of up to 10 characters followed by a dot and a name extension of up to six characters (the extension is the object type minus the asterisk). So, in Figure 21.82, I begin the OBJ parameter with /QSYS.LIB, which refers to library QSYS as the first item in the path. Then, there's /PGMR.LIB, which is contained within QSYS. And, finally, there's /CUST*.FILE, which refers to all files with a generic name CUST*.

—Ernie Malaga

One-step Access to a Second Session

To get a second interactive session on a terminal, you can use the Transfer to Secondary Job (TFRSECJOB) command or option 1 of the System Request menu. The first session is suspended, and the user sees a sign-on screen into which he must enter a user ID and password. We needed an easy way for a user to temporarily sign on under a different user ID, do a task, and return to his original session. Therefore, I developed the SIGNON command. SIGNON allows me to specify the user ID and password to be used to sign on with, allowing a user to start a second session and sign on with one step. I use this command in CL programs and behind menu options. When SIGNON is used in a CL program, the password does not appear in the job log.

The SIGNON utility consists of the SIGNON command (Figure 21.84) and the SIGNONCL program (Figure 21.85). It works by allowing the user to pass through to the same AS/400. The first time it is used, it creates the controller and devices needed to accomplish this. It then uses the Start Pass-Through (STRPASTHR) command to start a new session and sign on as the desired user.

```
/*================================================================*/
/* To compile:                                                    */
/*                                                                */
/*         CRTCMD    CMD(SIGNON) PGM(XXX/SIGNONCL) +              */
/*                   SRCFILE(XXX/QCMDSRC)                         */
/*                                                                */
/*================================================================*/
         CMD       PROMPT('Sign on as other user')
         PARM      KWD(USERID) TYPE(*NAME) LEN(10) MIN(1) +

                   PROMPT('User profile')
         PARM      KWD(PASSWORD) TYPE(*NAME) LEN(10) MIN(1) +
                   DSPINPUT(*NO) PROMPT('Password')
```

Figure 21.84: The SIGNON command source code shown here can be used to log on to a second session.

```
/*================================================================*/
/* To compile:                                                    */
/*                                                                */
/*         CRTCLPGM   PGM(XXX/SIGNONCL) SRCFILE(XXX/QCLSRC) +     */
/*                    TEXT('CPP for SIGNON command') LOG(*NO)     */
/*                                                                */
/*================================================================*/
```

Figure 21.85: The SIGNONCL program uses pass-through to start another interactive session (part 1 of 3).

```
PGM         PARM(&USERID &PASSWORD)

  DCL       VAR(&ERRBYTES) TYPE(*CHAR) LEN(4) +
              VALUE(X'00000000')
  DCL       VAR(&ERROR) TYPE(*LGL) LEN(1) VALUE('0')
  DCL       VAR(&MSGKEY) TYPE(*CHAR) LEN(4)
  DCL       VAR(&MSGTYP) TYPE(*CHAR) LEN(10) VALUE('*DIAG')
  DCL       VAR(&MSGTYPCTR) TYPE(*CHAR) LEN(4) +
              VALUE(X'00000001')
  DCL       VAR(&PASSWORD) TYPE(*CHAR) LEN(10)
  DCL       VAR(&PGMMSGQ) TYPE(*CHAR) LEN(10) VALUE('*')
  DCL       VAR(&STKCTR) TYPE(*CHAR) LEN(4) +
              VALUE(X'00000001')
  DCL       VAR(&USERID) TYPE(*CHAR) LEN(10)

  MONMSG    MSGID(CPF0000) EXEC(GOTO CMDLBL(ERRPROC))

  /* Validate the user profile name */
  CHKOBJ    OBJ(QSYS/&USERID) OBJTYPE(*USRPRF)
  MONMSG    MSGID(CPF9801 CPF0001) EXEC(DO)
    SNDPGMMSG  MSGID(CPF1120) MSGF(QCPFMSG) MSGDTA(&USERID) +
                 MSGTYPE(*ESCAPE)
  ENDDO

  /* Create the controller and devices for local */
  /* passthrough the first time this program runs */
  CHKOBJ    OBJ(LOCALCTL) OBJTYPE(*CTLD)
  MONMSG    MSGID(CPF9801) EXEC(DO)
    CRTCTLAPPC CTLD(LOCALCTL) LINKTYPE(*LOCAL) ONLINE(*NO) +
                 TEXT('Controller for local passthrough') +
                 CMNRCYLMT(2 5) AUT(*ALL)
    CRTDEVAPPC DEVD(LOCAL1) RMTLOCNAME(LOCAL2) ONLINE(*NO) +
                 LCLLOCNAME(LOCAL1) RMTNETID(*NETATR) +
                 CTL(LOCALCTL) MODE(*NETATR) +
                 MSGQ(*LIBL/QSYSOPR) APPN(*NO) SNGSSN(*NO) +
                 SECURELOC(*NO) TEXT('For local +
                 passthrough') LOCADR(00) AUT(*ALL)
    CRTDEVAPPC DEVD(LOCAL2) RMTLOCNAME(LOCAL1) ONLINE(*NO) +
                 LCLLOCNAME(LOCAL2) RMTNETID(*NETATR) +
                 CTL(LOCALCTL) MODE(*NETATR) +
                 MSGQ(*LIBL/QSYSOPR) APPN(*NO) SNGSSN(*NO) +
                 SECURELOC(*NO) TEXT('For local +
                 passthrough') LOCADR(00) AUT(*ALL)
    /* Make sure system values are correct for function */
    CHGSYSVAL  SYSVAL(QAUTOVRT) VALUE(10)
    CHGSYSVAL  SYSVAL(QRMTSIGN) VALUE(*VERIFY)
  ENDDO
```

Figure 21.85: The SIGNONCL program uses pass-through to start another interactive session (part 2 of 3).

```
/* Make sure the controller is varied on */
VRYCFG      CFGOBJ(LOCALCTL) CFGTYPE(*CTL) STATUS(*ON) +
              RANGE(*NET)
MONMSG      MSGID(CPF0000)

/* Display status message that we're signing on */
SNDPGMMSG   MSGID(CPF9898) MSGF(QSYS/QCPFMSG) +
              MSGDTA('Signing on as' *BCAT &USERID) +
              TOPGMQ(*EXT) MSGTYPE(*STATUS)

/* Pass through and sign on */
STRPASTHR   RMTLOCNAME(*CNNDEV) CNNDEV(LOCAL1) +
              RMTUSER(&USERID) RMTPWD(&PASSWORD) +
              PASTHRSCN(*NO)

/* Invalid password */
MONMSG      MSGID(CPF8936) EXEC(DO)
  SNDPGMMSG  MSGID(CPF1107) MSGF(QCPFMSG) MSGDTA(&USERID) +
              MSGTYPE(*ESCAPE)
ENDDO

RETURN

ERRPROC:
  IF        COND(&ERROR) THEN(GOTO CMDLBL(ERRDONE))
  ELSE      CMD(CHGVAR VAR(&ERROR) VALUE('1'))

/* Move all *DIAG messages to previous program queue */
CALL        PGM(QMHMOVPM) PARM(&MSGKEY &MSGTYP +
              &MSGTYPCTR &PGMMSGQ &STKCTR &ERRBYTES)

/* Resend last *ESCAPE message */
ERRDONE:
  CALL      PGM(QMHRSNEM) PARM(&MSGKEY &ERRBYTES)
  MONMSG    MSGID(CPF0000) EXEC(DO)
    SNDPGMMSG  MSGID(CPF3CF2) MSGF(QCPFMSG) +
              MSGDTA('QMHRSNEM') MSGTYPE(*ESCAPE)
    MONMSG    MSGID(CPF0000)
  ENDDO

END:
ENDPGM
```

Figure 21.85: The SIGNONCL program uses pass-through to start another interactive session (part 3 of 3).

—*Albert York*

933

✦ ✦ ✦ PDM

Copy Member Descriptions Easily

Here's a handy way to copy member text descriptions from one member to another in PDM. First, you must define two PDM options, S1 and S2, as in Figure 21.86. For option S2 to work, you'll need program CHGTXT, shown in Figure 21.87. Enter **S1** in front of a member's name to save its member text to positions 951 through 1000 of the local data area (LDA), and press Enter. Enter **S2** in front of all members to receive text, and press Enter. To see the updated text, press F5 to refresh the WRKMBRPDM screen. If you work in one source file, you can enter S1 on the first member and S2 for subsequent members, and press Enter.

```
S1:
CHGDTAARA DTAARA(*LDA (951 50)) VALUE(&X) /*save member text to LDA */
S2:
CALL PGM(XXX/CHGTXT) PARM(&F &L &N) /*get member text from LDA (951 50) */
```

Figure 21.86: This code demonstrates how to define PDM options for copying files.

```
/*===============================================================*/
/* TO COMPILE:                                                   */
/*                                                               */
/* CRTCLPGM PGM(XXX/CHGTXT) SRCFILE(XXX/QCLSRC)                  */
/*                                                               */
/*===============================================================*/
PGM PARM(&FILENAME &LIBRARY &MEMBER)
DCL VAR(&FILENAME) TYPE(*CHAR) LEN(10)
DCL VAR(&LIBRARY) TYPE(*CHAR) LEN(10)
DCL VAR(&MEMBER) TYPE(*CHAR) LEN(10)
DCL VAR(&TEXT) TYPE(*CHAR) LEN(50)
MONMSG MSGID(CPF0000)
CHGVAR VAR(&TEXT) VALUE(%SST(*LDA 951 50))
CHGPFM FILE(&LIBRARY/&FILENAME) MBR(&MEMBER) + TEXT(&TEXT)
ENDPGM
```

Figure 21.87: Use this CL Program, CHGTXT, for PDM Option S2.

—Andre Nortje

Merge PDM Option Files

I work in an environment where development standards require me to use a standard PDM option file that I am not allowed to customize.

I considered copying the standard option file and adding my own options to it. The disadvantage of this approach is that I would have to monitor changes to the standard option file and make the same changes to my copy.

Instead, I wrote a simple CL program, MRGPDMF, as shown in Figure 21.88. This program allows me to merge the options from a custom option file with the options of the standard option file. I invoke MRGPDMF from my initial program. This ensures that I pick up the latest version of the standard option file each time I sign on.

```
/*==================================================================*/
/* To compile:                                                      */
/*                                                                  */
/*            CRTCLPGM   PGM(XXX/MRGPDMF) SRCFILE(XXX/QCLSRC)        */
/*                                                                  */
/*==================================================================*/
/* Program name:    MRGPDMF                                         */
/* Description:     Merge PDM Option Files                          */
/*==================================================================*/
/* Parameter definitions                                           */
/*     &LIBRARY1 - Primary PDM option file library                 */
/*     &LIBRARY2 - Secondary PDM option file library               */
/*     &LIBRARY3 - Merged PDM option file library                  */
/*==================================================================*/

PGM          PARM(&LIBRARY1 &LIBRARY2 &LIBRARY3)


  DCL        VAR(&LIBRARY1) TYPE(*CHAR) LEN(10)
  DCL        VAR(&LIBRARY2) TYPE(*CHAR) LEN(10)
  DCL        VAR(&LIBRARY3) TYPE(*CHAR) LEN(10)
  DCL        VAR(&MSGDTA) TYPE(*CHAR) LEN(512)
  DCL        VAR(&MSGF) TYPE(*CHAR) LEN(10)
  DCL        VAR(&MSGFLIB) TYPE(*CHAR) LEN(10)
  DCL        VAR(&MSGID) TYPE(*CHAR) LEN(7)

  MONMSG     MSGID(CPF0000) EXEC(GOTO CMDLBL(ERROR))

  IF         COND(&LIBRARY3 *EQ ' ') THEN(DO)
    CHGVAR     VAR(&LIBRARY3) VALUE(QTEMP)
  ENDDO

  CRTDUPOBJ  OBJ(QAUOOPT) FROMLIB(&LIBRARY1) +
```

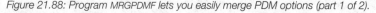

Figure 21.88: Program MRGPDMF lets you easily merge PDM options (part 1 of 2).

```
                 OBJTYPE(*FILE) TOLIB(&LIBRARY3) +
                 NEWOBJ(QAUOOPT) DATA(*YES)
    CPYF         FROMFILE(&LIBRARY2/QAUOOPT) +
                 TOFILE(&LIBRARY3/QAUOOPT) MBROPT(*ADD) +
                 CRTFILE(*NO) FMTOPT(*NOCHK) ERRLVL(*NOMAX)
    GOTO         CMDLBL(EXIT)

ERROR:
    RCVMSG       MSGTYPE(*EXCP) MSGDTA(&MSGDTA) MSGID(&MSGID) +
                 MSGF(&MSGF) MSGFLIB(&MSGFLIB)
    MONMSG       MSGID(CPF0000)
    SNDPGMMSG    MSGID(&MSGID) MSGF(&MSGFLIB/&MSGF) +
                 MSGDTA(&MSGDTA)
    MONMSG       MSGID(CPF0000)

EXIT:
    RCLRSC
ENDPGM
```

Figure 21.88: Program MRGPDMF lets you easily merge PDM options (part 2 of 2).

My program requires three parameters (all library names). The first two parameters are the libraries containing the standard and custom option files. If any options are found in both files, the option from the library named in the first parameter will take precedence.

If you let the standard options file take precedence over your custom options file, be aware that someone could cause problems for you by modifying the standard options file. For example, you might add option DF, display a file member, to your custom options file. If someone later added option DF, delete a file, to the standard options file, you could be in for an unpleasant surprise.

The third parameter is the name of the library that will contain the file of merged options. I store the file of merged options in library QTEMP. To use this utility, create a blank copy of file QGPL/QAUOOPT in a library of your choosing.

```
CRTDUPOBJ OBJ(QAUOOPT) FROMLIB(QGPL)  OBJTYPE(*FILE)  TOLIB(xxx)
```

Then, use option 9 of the PDM menu to maintain your options file. To activate the merged options file, press the F18 key from any of the PDM "Work with" displays. Specify the library of merged options in the library parameter of the option file.

Finally, add a call to MRGPDMF to your initial program.

—Jeffrey Haddix

✦✦✦ RLU

Convert RLU-generated PRTF Source to Readable Source

RLU generates printer file DDS that's difficult to read. The main problem is that RLU writes to either the left side (everything except the functions area) or the right side (the functions area) of a DDS spec, not to both sides at once. This means that the generated source code is much longer than it needs to be. I wrote the Convert RLU Printer File (CVTRLUPRTF) utility to make the DDS more readable. My utility (Figure 21.89) merges the entries from both sides into one readable record. The CPP is shown in Figure 21.90; it calls an RPG program (Figure 21.91) to reformat the source code.

```
/*================================================================*/
/* To compile:                                                    */
/*                                                                */
/*          CRTCMD      CMD(XXX/CVTRLUPRTF) PGM(XXX/PRT006CL) +    */
/*                      SRCFILE(XXX/QCMDSRC)                       */
/*                                                                */
/*================================================================*/
           CMD         PROMPT('Convert RLU-generated prtf')

           PARM        KWD(SRCF) TYPE(QUALNAME) PROMPT('Source file')

           PARM        KWD(MBR) TYPE(*NAME) LEN(10) MIN(1) +
                       EXPR(*YES) PROMPT('Source member')

QUALNAME:  QUAL        TYPE(*NAME) LEN(10) MIN(1) EXPR(*YES)
           QUAL        TYPE(*NAME) LEN(10) DFT(*LIBL) +
                       SPCVAL((*CURLIB) (*LIBL)) EXPR(*YES) +
                       PROMPT('Library')
```

Figure 21.89: The CVTRLUPRTF command is used to convert RLU to readable source.

```
/*================================================================*/
/* To compile:                                                    */
/*                                                                */
/*          CRTCLPGM    PGM(XXX/PRT006CL)   SRCFILE(XXX/QCLSRC)    */
/*                                                                */
/*================================================================*/
           PGM         PARM(&QUALFILE &MEMBER)

           DCL         VAR(&CMD) TYPE(*CHAR) LEN(100)
           DCL         VAR(&FILE) TYPE(*CHAR) LEN(10)
           DCL         VAR(&LIBRARY) TYPE(*CHAR) LEN(10)
           DCL         VAR(&MEMBER) TYPE(*CHAR) LEN(10)
```

Figure 21.90: Command-processing program PRT006CL is the real heart of the CVTRLUPRTF command (part 1 of 3).

```
          DCL       VAR(&MSGDTA) TYPE(*CHAR) LEN(256)
          DCL       VAR(&MSGF) TYPE(*CHAR) LEN(10)
          DCL       VAR(&MSGFLIB) TYPE(*CHAR) LEN(10)
          DCL       VAR(&MSGID) TYPE(*CHAR) LEN(7)
          DCL       VAR(&NEWNAME) TYPE(*CHAR) LEN(10)
          DCL       VAR(&NUMREC) TYPE(*DEC ) LEN(10 0)
          DCL       VAR(&QUALFILE) TYPE(*CHAR) LEN(20)
          DCL       VAR(&SRCTYPE) TYPE(*CHAR) LEN(10)
          DCL       VAR(&TEXT) TYPE(*CHAR) LEN(50)

          MONMSG    MSGID(CPF0000) EXEC(GOTO CMDLBL(ABEND))

          CHGVAR    VAR(&LIBRARY) VALUE(%SST(&QUALFILE 11 10))
          CHGVAR    VAR(&FILE) VALUE(%SST(&QUALFILE  1 10))
          RTVMBRD   FILE(&LIBRARY/&FILE) MBR(&MEMBER) +
                      SRCTYPE(&SRCTYPE) NBRCURRCD(&NUMREC)
          CHGVAR    VAR(&CMD) VALUE(&LIBRARY *TCAT '/' *TCAT +
                      &FILE *BCAT &MEMBER *BCAT &SRCTYPE)

          IF        COND(&NUMREC *EQ 0) THEN(DO)
          SNDPGMMSG MSGID(CPF9897) MSGF(QCPFMSG) MSGDTA('Empty +
                      member' *BCAT &CMD *BCAT 'cannot be +
                      converted.') MSGTYPE(*ESCAPE)

          ENDDO

          IF        COND(&SRCTYPE *NE 'PRTF') THEN(DO)
          SNDPGMMSG MSGID(CPF9897) MSGF(QCPFMSG) MSGDTA(&CMD +
                      *BCAT 'is not a printer file.') +
                      MSGTYPE(*ESCAPE)

          ENDDO

          SNDPGMMSG MSGID(CPF9897) MSGF(QCPFMSG) MSGDTA(&CMD +
                      *BCAT 'converting...') TOPGMQ(*EXT) +
                      MSGTYPE(*STATUS)

          DLTF      FILE(QTEMP/DDSOUT)
          MONMSG    MSGID(CPF0000)

          CRTPF     FILE(QTEMP/DDSOUT) RCDLEN(80)

          OVRDBF    FILE(DDSINP) TOFILE(&LIBRARY/&FILE) +
                      MBR(&MEMBER)
          OVRDBF    FILE(DDSOUT) TOFILE(QTEMP/DDSOUT)

          CALL      PGM(PRT006RG)

          DLTOVR    FILE(*ALL)
/* Copy back to lib */
          CHGVAR    VAR(&NEWNAME) VALUE(&MEMBER *TCAT '#')
```

Figure 21.90: Command-processing program PRT006CL is the real heart of the CVTRLUPRTF command (part 2 of 3).

```
              CPYF       FROMFILE(QTEMP/DDSOUT) +
                           TOFILE(&LIBRARY/&FILE) TOMBR(&NEWNAME) +
                           MBROPT(*REPLACE) FMTOPT(*CVTSRC)
              MONMSG     MSGID(CPF0000)

/* Transfer type and text */
              RTVMBRD    FILE(&LIBRARY/&FILE) MBR(&MEMBER) TEXT(&TEXT)
              CHGPFM     FILE(&LIBRARY/&FILE) MBR(&NEWNAME) +
                           SRCTYPE(PRTF) TEXT(&TEXT)

              RETURN

/* Forward escape message to caller */
ABEND:        RCVMSG     MSGTYPE(*EXCP) MSGDTA(&MSGDTA) MSGID(&MSGID) +
                           MSGF(&MSGF) SNDMSGFLIB(&MSGFLIB)
              MONMSG     MSGID(CPF0000)
              SNDPGMMSG  MSGID(&MSGID) MSGF(&MSGFLIB/&MSGF) +
                           MSGDTA(&MSGDTA) MSGTYPE(*ESCAPE)
              MONMSG     MSGID(CPF0000)

              ENDPGM
```

Figure 21.90: Command-processing program PRT006CL is the real heart of the CVTRLUPRTF command (part 3 of 3).

```
   *================================================================
   * To compile:
   *
   *      CRTRPGPGM  PGM(XXX/PRT006RG) SRCFILE(XXX/QRPGSRC)
   *
   *================================================================
FDDSINP  IF  F    92          DISK
FDDSOUT  O   F    80          DISK                              A
   ****************************************************************
IDDSINP  NS  01
I                                    13  92 SRCDTA
 *
I            DS
I                                     1  80 SRCDTA
I                                     7   7 SRC7
I                                     7   9 SRCPCT
I                                    17  17 SRC17
I                                     1  44 SRC144
I                                     7  44 SRC744
I                                    45  80 SRC45
I                                    45  50 SRCSPA
   ****************************************************************
C            *LIKE      DEFN SRC144    PRV144
C            *LIKE      DEFN SRC744    PRV744
C            *LIKE      DEFN SRCDTA    PRVDTA
 *
```

Figure 21.91: RPG program PRT006RG is used to build the output file from the CVTRLUPRTF command (part 1 of 4).

```
C                       EXSR  PRCDDS
 *
C                       MOVE  *ON        *INLR
C                       RETRN
 ******************************************************************
 * PRCDDS - Process DDS input.                                    *
 *                                                              ***
C           PRCDDS      BEGSR
 *
C                       MOVE  *BLANKS    RFMT     1
 *
C           *IN41       DOUEQ*ON
C                       READ  DDSINP                          41
C           *IN41       IFEQ  *ON
 * Output previous record.
C           PRV744      IFNE  *BLANKS
C                       EXCPTOUTPRV
C                       ENDIF
C*
C                       LEAVE
C                       ENDIF                                *IN41 EQ
 *
 * Not record format.
 *
C           SRC7        IFEQ  *BLANKS
C           SRC17       ANDEQ*BLANKS
C           SRC744      ANDNE*BLANKS
C                       MOVE  *BLANKS    RFMT
C                       ENDIF
 *
 * Output current record as-is.
 *
 * Comment.
C           SRC7        IFEQ  '*'
 * Record format.
C           SRC17       OREQ  'R'
 * No merge/save.
C           PRV744      OREQ  *BLANKS
C           SRC744      ANDEQ*BLANKS
 * Output previous record.
C           PRV744      IFNE  *BLANKS
C                       EXCPTOUTPRV
C                       MOVE  *BLANKS    PRV744
C                       ENDIF
 * Output comment before record format.
C           SRC17       IFEQ  'R'
C                       EXCPTOUTCMT
C                       MOVE  'Y'        RFMT
C                       ENDIF
 * Output current record.
C           SRCPCT      IFNE  '*%%'
C                       EXCPTOUTDTA
C                       ENDIF
 * Output current after SPACEA.
```

Figure 21.91: *RPG program PRT006RG is used to build the output file from the CVTRLUPRTF command (part 2 of 4).*

```
C              SRCSPA    IFEQ 'SPACEA'
C              RFMT      ANDNE'Y'
C                        EXCPTOUTCMT
C                        ENDIF
 * Next record.
C                        ITER
C                        ENDIF                           SRC7 EQ
 *
 * No merge/save.
 *
C              PRV744    IFNE *BLANKS
C              SRC744    ANDNE*BLANKS
 * Output previous record.
C                        EXCPTOUTPRV
C                        MOVE *BLANKS    PRV744
 * Output current record, if columns 45-80 are not blank.
C              SRC45     IFNE *BLANKS
C                        EXCPTOUTDTA
C                        ELSE
 * Columns 45-80 are blank: save.
C                        MOVELSRC144     PRV144
C                        MOVELSRC744     PRV744
C                        MOVELSRCDTA     PRVDTA
C                        ENDIF
 *
C                        ITER
C                        ENDIF                           PRV177 NE
 *
 * Save left-hand side.
 *
C              PRV744    IFEQ *BLANKS
C              SRC744    ANDNE*BLANKS
C              SRC45     ANDEQ*BLANKS
 * Save.
C                        MOVELSRC144     PRV144
C                        MOVELSRC744     PRV744
C                        MOVELSRCDTA     PRVDTA
 * Next record.
C                        ITER
C                        ENDIF
 *
 * Match left-hand and right-hand side.
 *
C                        MOVE *BLANKS    RFMT
 *
C              PRV744    IFNE *BLANKS
C                        MOVELPRV144     SRCDTA
C                        ENDIF
 *
C                        EXCPTOUTDTA
C                        MOVE *BLANKS    PRV744
 * Output comment after SPACEA.
C              SRCSPA    IFEQ 'SPACEA'
C                        EXCPTOUTCMT
C                        ENDIF
```

Figure 21.91: RPG program PRT006RG is used to build the output file from the CVTRLUPRTF command (part 3 of 4).

```
     * Next record.
     C                        ITER
     *
     * Next DDSINP record.
     *
     C                        ENDDO                        *IN41 DOUEQ*ON
     *
     C                        ENDSR
     ***************************************************************
ODDSOUT  EADD                 OUTPRV
O                             PRVDTA
     *
O        EADD                 OUTCMT
O                                        7 'A*'
     *
O        EADD                 OUTDTA
O                             SRCDTA
```

Figure 21.91: RPG program PRT006RG is used to build the output file from the CVTRLUPRTF command (part 4 of 4).

RLU also generates too many comment lines. Therefore, CVTRLUPRTF drops all comment lines. You might want to modify your RPG program to keep certain comment lines, such as the parameters for the Create Printer File (CRTPRTF) command, at the bottom of the source member.

The CVTRLUPRTF command requires two parameters: the qualified file name and the member containing the RLU-generated DDS. This utility generates another member in the same file. The name of the new member is the name of the old member with a pound sign (#) appended to it. (The pound sign behaves differently under the support of different national languages, so you may want to append some other character instead.)

If the name of the RLU-generated member is 10 characters long, CVTRLUPRTF replaces the member with the converted source. I've never changed this, because I never use 10-character printer file names, but you might want to use a different solution if overlaying the input file presents a problem for you.

I added option A1 to PDM to allow me to run this utility more easily. To add this option to PDM, do the following:

1. From the PDM Work with Members panel, press F16 for user options.

2. Press F6 to add a new option.

3. In the Option blank, enter A1 (or whatever you prefer to call the option).

4. In the Command blank, enter the following string:

```
CVTRLUPRTF SRCF(&L/&F) MBR(&N).
```

If CVTRLUPRTF is not in a library in the library list, you'll have to qualify it.

5. Press Enter.

—Andre Nortje

✦ ✦ ✦ SEU

Easy Access to SEU

When I work at a client's location, I am often restricted to only one display device. If I am editing a source member and realize I forgot to create a printer file, for example, my choices for creating the new member are limited. I can:

- Exit the source member I am currently working on and start a new edit session for the new member.

- Press the F21 key to get a command line and start SEU or PDM.

- Use the System Request menu to start a second display session and start SEU from there.

No matter which way I go, it's easy to get distracted and forget where I was in the first edit session while I'm taking care of the problem in the second. When I am exceptionally busy, I sometimes forget I even had a previous SEU edit session going and attempt to start SEU on the same member I am already editing.

To avoid this problem, I created the Edit Source (EDTSRC) utility. It allows me to run multiple SEU sessions from a command line. As I am editing one member, I can press the F21 key to get a command line, run this utility, and start editing a second member. When I exit the second member, my session resumes at the command line activated in the first member.

The EDTSRC command (Figure 21.92) prompts for the name of a source file, the library, the source member, the member type, and an SEU option. This utility lets me edit, browse, or print a source member. EDTSRC's command processing program, EDT01C, is shown in Figure 21.93. If the member name I enter does not exist in the source file, a new member is added to the source file, and SEU starts with a blank member. If the member name I enter is already in use, SEU starts in BROWSE mode. When I exit the SEU session, the Create Object (CRTOBJ) command is called.

Source code for CRTOBJ and its CPP, CRT01C, is shown in Figures 21.93 and 21.94. The relevant source file, library, and member name are passed to CRTOBJ, and I am prompted to create the object. If I specify *NO on the create parameter, control returns to EDTSRC and then back to the original edit session. If I specify *YES on the create parameter, the appropriate CRTOBJ command, based on the source member type, is executed and sent to batch.

I added only the most commonly used CRTOBJ commands to this utility. You can easily expand this utility if you need to create other object types, such as panel groups. Both CL programs use the Forward Program Message (FWDPGMMSG) utility (see Figure 21.58).

```
/*================================================================*/
/*   To compile:                                                  */
/*                                                                */
/*         CRTCMD      CMD(XXX/EDTSRC) PGM(XXX/EDT01C) +           */
/*                     SRCFILE(XXX/QCMDSRC)                        */
/*                                                                */
/*================================================================*/

          CMD         PROMPT('Edit Source Member')

          PARM        KWD(SRCFIL) TYPE(QUAL1) MIN(1) +
                        PROMPT('Source File')
          PARM        KWD(MEMBER) TYPE(*CHAR) LEN(10) MIN(1) +
                        PROMPT('Source Member')
          PARM        KWD(TYPE) TYPE(*CHAR) LEN(10) RSTD(*YES) +
                        VALUES('CMD' 'CLP' 'RPG' 'RPGLE' 'CBL' +
                        'CBLLE' 'DSPF' 'PF' 'LF') MIN(1) +
                        EXPR(*YES) CHOICE('Member Type') +
                        PROMPT('Source Member Type')
          PARM        KWD(OPTION) TYPE(*CHAR) LEN(1) RSTD(*YES) +
                        VALUES('2' '5' '6') MIN(1) EXPR(*YES) +
                        PROMPT('Edit Option')

QUAL1:    QUAL        TYPE(*NAME) LEN(10) RSTD(*NO)
          QUAL        TYPE(*NAME) LEN(10) DFT(*LIBL) +
                        SPCVAL((*LIBL)) CHOICE('Name, *LIBL, +
                        *CURLIB') PROMPT('Library name')
```

Figure 21.92: The Edit Source (EDTSRC) command lets you edit multiple source files from a single session.

```
/*===============================================================*/
/* To Compile:                                                   */
/*                                                               */
/*              CRTCLPGM PGM(XXX/EDT01C) SRCFILE(XXX/QCLSRC)      */
/*                                                               */
/*===============================================================*/
PGM  PARM(&SRC_LIB &MEMBER &TYPE &OPTN)

    DCL       VAR(&CREATE) TYPE(*CHAR) LEN(4)
    DCL       VAR(&SRC_LIB) TYPE(*CHAR) LEN(20)
    DCL       VAR(&OBJ_LIB) TYPE(*CHAR) LEN(20)
    DCL       VAR(&OBJNAM) TYPE(*CHAR) LEN(10)
    DCL       VAR(&OBJLIB) TYPE(*CHAR) LEN(10)
    DCL       VAR(&SRCFIL) TYPE(*CHAR) LEN(10)
    DCL       VAR(&SRCLIB) TYPE(*CHAR) LEN(10)
    DCL       VAR(&MEMBER) TYPE(*CHAR) LEN(10)
    DCL       VAR(&TYPE) TYPE(*CHAR) LEN(10)
    DCL       VAR(&OPTION) TYPE(*CHAR) LEN(6)
    DCL       VAR(&OPTN) TYPE(*CHAR) LEN(1)

    MONMSG    MSGID(CPF0000 MCH0000) EXEC(GOTO CMDLBL(ERROR))

    /*===============================================================*/
    /* EXTRACT SOURCE FILE AND LIBRARY NAME FROM COMMAND PARMS.       */
    /*===============================================================*/
    CHGVAR    VAR(&SRCFIL) VALUE(%SST(&SRC_LIB 1 10))
    CHGVAR    VAR(&SRCLIB) VALUE(%SST(&SRC_LIB 11 10))

    /*===============================================================*/
    /*  VERIFY EXISTENCE OF SOURCE LIBRARY/SOURCE FILE               */
    /*===============================================================*/
    CHKOBJ    OBJ(&SRCLIB/&SRCFIL) OBJTYPE(*FILE)

    /*===============================================================*/
    /*  VERIFY EXISTENCE OF SOURCE LIBRARY/SOURCE FILE/MEMBER        */
    /*===============================================================*/
    CHKOBJ    OBJ(&SRCLIB/&SRCFIL) OBJTYPE(*FILE) +
                MBR(&MEMBER)
    MONMSG    MSGID(CPF9815) EXEC(DO)
        ADDPFM    FILE(&SRCLIB/&SRCFIL) MBR(&MEMBER)
    ENDDO

    /*===============================================================*/
    /*  EDIT SOURCE MEMBER                                           */
    /*===============================================================*/
    CHGVAR VAR(&OPTION) VALUE(&OPTN)

STRSEU:
    STRSEU    SRCFILE(&SRCLIB/&SRCFIL) SRCMBR(&MEMBER) +
                TYPE(&TYPE) OPTION(&OPTION)
    MONMSG    MSGID(EDT9007) EXEC(DO) /* +
                    Source Member In Use. Use Browse Mode. */
        CHGVAR    VAR(&OPTION) VALUE('5')
        GOTO      CMDLBL(STRSEU)
    ENDDO
```

Figure 21.93: The Edit Source (EDTSRC) command processor, EDT01C, is used to create the required source member if it doesn't already exist (part 1 of 2).

```
/*===============================================================*/
/*  PROMPT FOR CREATE OBJECT                                     */
/*===============================================================*/
IF          COND(&OPTION *EQ '2') THEN(DO)
    CRTOBJ     ??OBJECT(&SRCLIB/&MEMBER) +
               ??SRCFIL(&SRCLIB/&SRCFIL) +
               ??MEMBER(&MEMBER) ??TYPE(&TYPE) +
               ??CREATE(*YES) /* Only Prompt For +
               Create Object If Source Member Was In +
               Edit Mode.' */
    ENDDO
    RETURN

ERROR:
    FWDPGMMSG
    MONMSG     MSGID(CPF0000 MCH0000)
EXIT:
    ENDPGM
```

Figure 21.93: The Edit Source (EDTSRC) command processor, EDT01C, is used to create the required source member if it doesn't already exist (part 2 of 2).

```
/*===============================================================*/
/*  To Compile:                                                  */
/*                                                               */
/*          CRTCMD     CMD(XXX/CRTOBJ) PGM(XXX/CRT01C) +         */
/*                     SRCFILE(XXX/QCLSRC)                        */
/*                                                               */
/*===============================================================*/

            CMD        PROMPT('Create Object')

            PARM       KWD(OBJECT) TYPE(QUAL1) MIN(1) +
                       PROMPT('Object Lib/Name')
            PARM       KWD(SRCFIL) TYPE(QUAL1) MIN(1) +
                       PROMPT('Source File')
            PARM       KWD(MEMBER) TYPE(*NAME) MIN(1) +
                       PROMPT('Source Member')
            PARM       KWD(TYPE) TYPE(QUAL2) MIN(1) PROMPT('Object +
                       Type')
            PARM       KWD(CREATE) TYPE(*CHAR) LEN(4) RSTD(*YES) +
                       VALUES(*YES *NO) MIN(1) PROMPT('Create +
                       Object')

QUAL1:      QUAL       TYPE(*NAME)
            QUAL       TYPE(*NAME) LEN(10) DFT(*LIBL) +
                       SPCVAL((*LIBL)) CHOICE('Name, *LIBL, +
                       *CURLIB') PROMPT('Library name')

QUAL2:      QUAL       TYPE(*NAME) RSTD(*YES) SPCVAL((RPG) (CLP) +
                       (CBL) (RPGLE) (CBLLE) (PF) (LF) (CMD) (DSPF))
```

Figure 21.94: The Create Object (CRTOBJ) command is called by the EDTSRC utility.

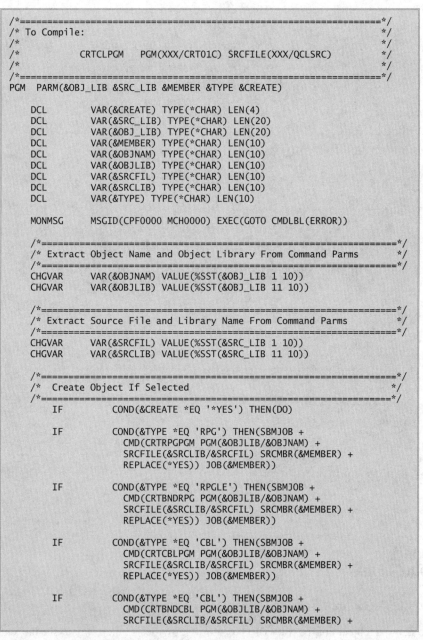

```
/*================================================================*/
/* To Compile:                                                    */
/*                                                                */
/*           CRTCLPGM   PGM(XXX/CRT01C) SRCFILE(XXX/QCLSRC)        */
/*                                                                */
/*================================================================*/
PGM  PARM(&OBJ_LIB &SRC_LIB &MEMBER &TYPE &CREATE)

    DCL       VAR(&CREATE) TYPE(*CHAR) LEN(4)
    DCL       VAR(&SRC_LIB) TYPE(*CHAR) LEN(20)
    DCL       VAR(&OBJ_LIB) TYPE(*CHAR) LEN(20)
    DCL       VAR(&MEMBER) TYPE(*CHAR) LEN(10)
    DCL       VAR(&OBJNAM) TYPE(*CHAR) LEN(10)
    DCL       VAR(&OBJLIB) TYPE(*CHAR) LEN(10)
    DCL       VAR(&SRCFIL) TYPE(*CHAR) LEN(10)
    DCL       VAR(&SRCLIB) TYPE(*CHAR) LEN(10)
    DCL       VAR(&TYPE) TYPE(*CHAR) LEN(10)

    MONMSG    MSGID(CPF0000 MCH0000) EXEC(GOTO CMDLBL(ERROR))


    /*================================================================*/
    /* Extract Object Name and Object Library From Command Parms      */
    /*================================================================*/
    CHGVAR    VAR(&OBJNAM) VALUE(%SST(&OBJ_LIB 1 10))
    CHGVAR    VAR(&OBJLIB) VALUE(%SST(&OBJ_LIB 11 10))


    /*================================================================*/
    /* Extract Source File and Library Name From Command Parms        */
    /*================================================================*/
    CHGVAR    VAR(&SRCFIL) VALUE(%SST(&SRC_LIB 1 10))
    CHGVAR    VAR(&SRCLIB) VALUE(%SST(&SRC_LIB 11 10))


    /*================================================================*/
    /*  Create Object If Selected                                     */
    /*================================================================*/
        IF        COND(&CREATE *EQ '*YES') THEN(DO)

        IF        COND(&TYPE *EQ 'RPG') THEN(SBMJOB +
                    CMD(CRTRPGPGM PGM(&OBJLIB/&OBJNAM) +
                    SRCFILE(&SRCLIB/&SRCFIL) SRCMBR(&MEMBER) +
                    REPLACE(*YES)) JOB(&MEMBER))

        IF        COND(&TYPE *EQ 'RPGLE') THEN(SBMJOB +
                    CMD(CRTBNDRPG PGM(&OBJLIB/&OBJNAM) +
                    SRCFILE(&SRCLIB/&SRCFIL) SRCMBR(&MEMBER) +
                    REPLACE(*YES)) JOB(&MEMBER))

        IF        COND(&TYPE *EQ 'CBL') THEN(SBMJOB +
                    CMD(CRTCBLPGM PGM(&OBJLIB/&OBJNAM) +
                    SRCFILE(&SRCLIB/&SRCFIL) SRCMBR(&MEMBER) +
                    REPLACE(*YES)) JOB(&MEMBER))

        IF        COND(&TYPE *EQ 'CBL') THEN(SBMJOB +
                    CMD(CRTBNDCBL PGM(&OBJLIB/&OBJNAM) +
                    SRCFILE(&SRCLIB/&SRCFIL) SRCMBR(&MEMBER) +
```

Figure 21.95: The Create Object (CRTOBJ) command processor, CRT01C, is used to create the source member (based on its object type) (part 1 of 2).

```
                        REPLACE(*YES)) JOB(&MEMBER))
          IF            COND(&TYPE *EQ 'CLP') THEN(SBMJOB +
                        CMD(CRTCLPGM PGM(&OBJLIB/&OBJNAM) +
                        SRCFILE(&SRCLIB/&SRCFIL) SRCMBR(&MEMBER) +
                        REPLACE(*YES)) JOB(&MEMBER))

          IF            COND(&TYPE *EQ 'PF') THEN(SBMJOB CMD(CRTPF +
                        FILE(&OBJLIB/&OBJNAM) +
                        SRCFILE(&SRCLIB/&SRCFIL) SRCMBR(&MEMBER)) +
                        JOB(&MEMBER))

          IF            COND(&TYPE *EQ 'LF') THEN(SBMJOB CMD(CRTLF +
                        FILE(&OBJLIB/&OBJNAM) +
                        SRCFILE(&SRCLIB/&SRCFIL) SRCMBR(&MEMBER)) +
                        JOB(&MEMBER))

          IF            COND(&TYPE *EQ 'DSPF') THEN(SBMJOB +
                        CMD(CRTDSPF FILE(&OBJLIB/&OBJNAM) +
                        SRCFILE(&SRCLIB/&SRCFIL) SRCMBR(&MEMBER) +
                        REPLACE(*YES)) JOB(&MEMBER))

          IF            COND(&TYPE *EQ 'PRTF') THEN(SBMJOB +
                        CMD(CRTPRTF FILE(&OBJLIB/&OBJNAM) +
                        SRCFILE(&SRCLIB/&SRCFIL) SRCMBR(&MEMBER) +
                        REPLACE(*YES)) JOB(&MEMBER))

      ENDDO

      RETURN     /* Normal end of program */

      /*===========================================================*/
ERROR:
      FWDPGMMSG
      MONMSG     MSGID(CPF0000 MCH0000)

EXIT:
      ENDPGM
```

Figure 21.95: The Create Object (CRTOBJ) command processor, CRT01C, is used to create the source member (based on its object type) (part 2 of 2).

—Shannon O'Donnell

✦ ✦ ✦ Source Files

Browse the Source Code for an Object

The Browse Object Source (BRWOBJSRC) utility provides a quick way to see the source code used to create an object. This utility consists of the BRWOBJSRC command (Figure 21.96) and CL command-processing program OBJ021CL (Figure 21.97).

```
/*===============================================================*/
/* To compile:                                                  */
/*                                                              */
/*          CRTCMD      CMD(XXX/BRWOBJSRC) PGM(XXX/OBJ021CL) +   */
/*                       SRCFILE(XXX/QCMDSRC)                    */
/*                                                              */
/*===============================================================*/
            CMD        PROMPT('Browse object source')
            PARM       KWD(OBJ) TYPE(QUALNAME) PROMPT('Object name')
            PARM       KWD(OBJTYPE) TYPE(*CHAR) LEN(10) MIN(1) +
                        EXPR(*YES) PROMPT('Object type')
QUALNAME:   QUAL       TYPE(*NAME) MIN(1) EXPR(*YES)
            QUAL       TYPE(*NAME) DFT(*LIBL) SPCVAL((*LIBL) +
                        (*CURLIB)) EXPR(*YES) PROMPT('Library')
```

Figure 21.96: The BRWOBJSRC utility can be used to quickly browse a source member.

```
/*===============================================================*/
/* To compile:                                                  */
/*                                                              */
/*          CRTCLPGM    PGM(XXX/OBJ021CL) SRCFILE(XXX/QCLSRC)    */
/*                                                              */
/*===============================================================*/
PGM           PARM(&QUALOBJ &OBJTYPE)

  DCL         VAR(&LIB) TYPE(*CHAR) LEN(10)
  DCL         VAR(&MSGDTA) TYPE(*CHAR) LEN(256)
  DCL         VAR(&MSGID) TYPE(*CHAR) LEN(10)
  DCL         VAR(&MSGF) TYPE(*CHAR) LEN(10)
  DCL         VAR(&MSGFLIB) TYPE(*CHAR) LEN(10)
  DCL         VAR(&OBJ) TYPE(*CHAR) LEN(10)
  DCL         VAR(&OBJTYPE) TYPE(*CHAR) LEN(10)
  DCL         VAR(&QUALOBJ) TYPE(*CHAR) LEN(20)
  DCL         VAR(&SRCF) TYPE(*CHAR) LEN(10)
  DCL         VAR(&SRCFLIB) TYPE(*CHAR) LEN(10)
  DCL         VAR(&SRCMBR) TYPE(*CHAR) LEN(10)

  MONMSG      MSGID(CPF0000) EXEC(GOTO CMDLBL(ABEND))

  CHGVAR      VAR(&OBJ) VALUE(%SST(&QUALOBJ 1 10))
  CHGVAR      VAR(&LIB) VALUE(%SST(&QUALOBJ 11 10))
  RTVOBJD     OBJ(&LIB/&OBJ) OBJTYPE(&OBJTYPE) SRCF(&SRCF) +
                SRCFLIB(&SRCFLIB) SRCMBR(&SRCMBR)
  IF          COND(&SRCMBR *NE ' ') THEN(STRSEU +
                SRCFILE(&SRCFLIB/&SRCF) SRCMBR(&SRCMBR) +
                OPTION(5))
  ELSE        CMD(SNDPGMMSG MSGID(CPF9898) +
                MSGF(QSYS/QCPFMSG) MSGDTA('Source member +
```

Figure 21.97: Command-processing program OBJ021CL is the heart of the BRWOBJSRC command (part 1 of 2).

```
                    cannot be determined from object') +
                    MSGTYPE(*ESCAPE))
        RETURN
      ABEND:
        RCVMSG    MSGTYPE(*EXCP) MSGDTA(&MSGDTA) MSGID(&MSGID) +
                    MSGF(&MSGF) SNDMSGFLIB(&MSGFLIB)
      SNDPGMMSG   MSGID(&MSGID) MSGF(&MSGFLIB/&MSGF) +
                    MSGDTA(&MSGDTA) MSGTYPE(*ESCAPE)

      ENDPGM
```

Figure 21.97: Command-processing program OBJ021CL is the heart of the BRWOBJSRC command (part 2 of 2).

To see the source code for program X in library Z, for example, I can key in the following command at a command line and then press Enter:

```
BRWOBJSRC Z/X *PGM
```

BRWOBJSRC will find the source member used to create the file and invoke SEU in browse mode so that I can view the source.

To make this utility easier to use from the Work with Objects Using PDM (WRKOBJPDM) display, I defined PDM option BR to execute the following command:

```
BRWOBJSRC OBJ(&L/&N) OBJTYPE(&T)
```

—Dave Shaw

Comparing Objects Against Source

This utility produces a report about the objects in a library. It checks all commands, programs, and files. It looks at the date/time of the source used to create the object, and then checks if the source member has been changed since then. A report is printed showing the results. This helps to identify which objects do not have source or have source with a different date/time. Both situations are a problem. The utility (Figure 21.98) consists of command Compare Objects and Source (CMPOBJSRC), two CL programs (OBJ006CL and OBJ006CLA, as shown in Figures 21.99 and 21.100), and an RPG program (OBJ006RG, as shown in Figure 21.101).

```
CMPOBJSRC: CMD PROMPT('Compare Object and Source')
PARM KWD(OBJ) TYPE(NAME1) MIN(1) PROMPT('Objects')
PARM KWD(ERRONLY) TYPE(*CHAR) LEN(4) RSTD(*YES) +
DFT(*YES) VALUES(*YES *NO) PROMPT('Print +
errors only')
NAME1: QUAL TYPE(*GENERIC) LEN(10) SPCVAL((*ALL)) MIN(1)
QUAL TYPE(*NAME) LEN(10) SPCVAL((*LIBL) +
(*USRLIBL) (*CURLIB) (*ALL) (*ALLUSR)) +
MIN(1) PROMPT('Library')
```

Figure 21.98: Use command CMPOBJSRC to compare object source.

```
OBJ006CL: +
PGM PARM(&OBJ &ERRONLY)
DCL VAR(&OBJ) TYPE(*CHAR) LEN(20)
DCL VAR(&LIBRARY) TYPE(*CHAR) LEN(10)
DCL VAR(&SCANOBJ) TYPE(*CHAR) LEN(10)
DCL VAR(&ERRONLY) TYPE(*CHAR) LEN(4)
/* Split qualified name */
CHGVAR VAR(&SCANOBJ) VALUE(%SST(&OBJ 1 10))
CHGVAR VAR(&LIBRARY) VALUE(%SST(&OBJ 11 10))
/* Run DSPOBJD for requested objects */
DSPOBJD OBJ(&LIBRARY/&SCANOBJ) OBJTYPE(*PGM *FILE *CMD) +
OUTPUT(*OUTFILE) OUTFILE(QTEMP/DSPOBJD)
MONMSG MSGID(CPF2123) EXEC(DO)
SNDPGMMSG MSG('No objects were selected. Report not +
executed.') MSGTYPE(*DIAG)
SNDPGMMSG MSGID(CPF0002) MSGF(QCPFMSG) MSGTYPE(*ESCAPE)
GOTO CMDLBL(ENDPGM)
ENDDO
/* Read object description and produce report */
OVRDBF FILE(QADSPOBJ) TOFILE(QTEMP/DSPOBJD)
CALL PGM(OBJ006RG) PARM(&ERRONLY)
DLTOVR FILE(*ALL)
/* Delete work file */
DLTF FILE(QTEMP/DSPOBJD)
/* End program */
ENDPGM: +
ENDPGM
```

Figure 21.99: CL program OBJ006CL is the CPP for the CMPOBJSRC command.

```
OBJ006CLA: +
PGM PARM(&LIBRARY &FILE &MEMBER &SRCCHGDATE)
DCL VAR(&LIBRARY) TYPE(*CHAR) LEN(10)
DCL VAR(&FILE) TYPE(*CHAR) LEN(10)
DCL VAR(&MEMBER) TYPE(*CHAR) LEN(10)
DCL VAR(&SRCCHGDATE) TYPE(*CHAR) LEN(13)
RTVMBRD FILE(&LIBRARY/&FILE) MBR(&MEMBER) SRCCHGDATE(&SRCCHGDATE)
MONMSG MSGID(CPF9810 CPF9812 CPF9815) EXEC(CHGVAR +
VAR(&SRCCHGDATE) VALUE(' '))
ENDPGM
```

Figure 21.100: CL program OBJ006CLA is used to retrieve a member description when comparing source.

```
     FQADSPOBJIP E                    DISK
     FQPRINT  O  F    132     OA      PRINTER
     *
     I               'OBJ006CLA'         C       PGM1
     I               'Missing source'    C       MSG1
     I               'Different date/time' C     MSG2
     *
     I          DS
     I                                  1 13 MBRCHG
     I                                  2  7 MBRDAT
     I                                  8 13 MBRTIM
     I          DS
     I                                  1 13 OBJCHG
     I                                  1  1 ODSRCC
     I                                  2  7 ODSRCD
     I                                  8 13 ODSRCT
     *
     * Parameter is whether to print errors only (*YES, *NO)
     C        *ENTRY    PLIST
     C                  PARM           OPTION  4
     *
     C        ODSRCM    IFNE *BLANK
     * Format object name for printing
     C                  CLEAROBJECT
     C        ODLBNM    CAT  '/':0    OBJECT 21
     C        OBJECT    CAT  ODOBNM:0 OBJECT
     * Format source member name for printing
     C                  CLEARSRCMBR
     C        ODSRCL    CAT  '/':0    SRCMBR 32
     C        SRCMBR    CAT  ODSRCF:0 SRCMBR
     C        SRCMBR    CAT  '/':0    SRCMBR
     C        SRCMBR    CAT  ODSRCM:0 SRCMBR
     * Get last date/time changed for source used to create object
     C                  CALL PGM1
     C                  PARM           ODSRCL
```

Figure 21.101: The RPG program OBJ006RG produces the output when comparing object source using the CMPOBJSRC command (part 1 of 2).

```
C                       PARM          ODSRCF
C                       PARM          ODSRCM
C                       PARM          MBRCHG
 * Check for errors
C                       CLEARMESSAG
C           MBRCHG      IFEQ *BLANK
C                       MOVELMSG1     MESSAG 24
C                       ELSE
C           MBRCHG      IFNE OBJCHG
C                       MOVELMSG2     MESSAG
C                       END
C                       END
 * Print
C           OPTION      IFEQ '*NO'
C           MESSAG      ORNE *BLANK
C                       EXCPTPRINT
C                       END
C                       END
 * Before first cycle:  get system date and time
C           *INZSR      BEGSR
C                       TIME          SYS    120
C                       MOVELSYS      SYSTIM  60
C                       MOVE SYS      SYSDAT  60
C                       ENDSR
 *
OQPRINT  H  202   OA
O           OR          1P
O                             SYSDATY    8
O                             SYSTIM    18 'O :  :  '
O                                       69 'INTEGRITY OF SOURCE USED'
O                                       87 'TO CREATE OBJECTS'
O                                      127 'CMPOBJSRC - Page'
O                             PAGE  3  132
O           H  0    OA
O           OR          1P
O                                        6 'Object'
O                                       55 'Source Member'
O                                       84 'Comments'
O           H  2    OA
O           OR          1P
O                                        6 '_____'
O                                       55 '_____'
O                                       84 '_____'
O           EF 1        PRINT
O                             OBJECT    21
O                             ODOBTP    30
O                             ODOBAT    41
O                             SRCMBR    74
O                             MESSAG   100
O           TF1    LR
O                                     + 10 '** END OF REPORT **'
```

Figure 21.101: The RPG program OBJ006RG produces the output when comparing object source using the CMPOBJSRC command (part 2 of 2).

—*Rex M. Oliva*

✦ ✦ ✦ Spool Files

Automatically Move Spool Files from One OUTQ to Another

One morning, you arrive at the office and realize that one of your printers is broken. You need a quick way to redirect spooled files from the output queue of the broken printer to the output queue of a working printer. Sound familiar? I've got an easy way to handle this situation.

I've written a command called Redirect Output Queue (RDTOUTQ) and an associated CL program called RDT001CL. You can see the command and the CL program in Figures 21.102 and 21.103. (Note that the CL program uses the %BIN command from QURSTOOL, so you'll need to create that also.) The command associates a data queue with an output queue and monitors the data queue for new entries.

```
/*===============================================================*/
/* To compile:                                                   */
/*                                                               */
/*            CRTCMD    CMD(XXX/RDTOUTQ) PGM(XXX/RDT001CL) +      */
/*                      SRCFILE(XXX/QCMDSRC)                      */
/*                                                               */
/*===============================================================*/
             CMD       PROMPT('Redirect an Output Queue')

             PARM      KWD(FRMOUTQ) TYPE(QUAL) MIN(1) PROMPT('From +
                       Output Queue')

             PARM      KWD(TOOUTQ) TYPE(QUAL) MIN(1) PROMPT('To +
                       Output Queue')

QUAL:        QUAL      TYPE(*NAME) LEN(10)
             QUAL      TYPE(*NAME) LEN(10) DFT(*LIBL) +
                       SPCVAL((*LIBL)) PROMPT('Library')
```

Figure 21.102: Command RDTOUTQ can be used to redirect output.

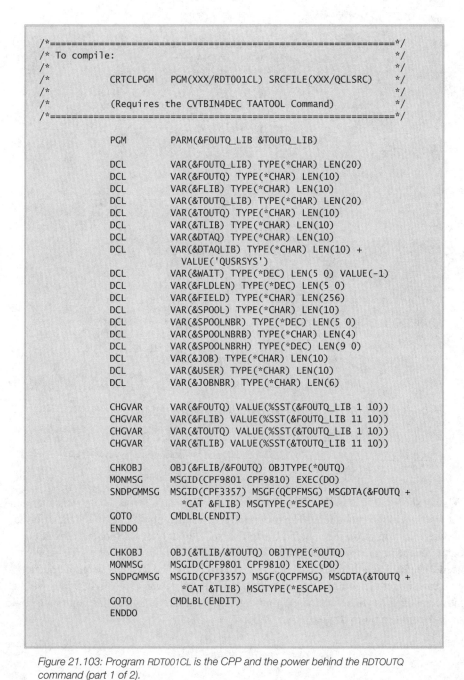

```
/*================================================================*/
/* To compile:                                                    */
/*                                                                */
/*          CRTCLPGM   PGM(XXX/RDT001CL) SRCFILE(XXX/QCLSRC)      */
/*                                                                */
/*          (Requires the CVTBIN4DEC TAATOOL Command)             */
/*================================================================*/

           PGM        PARM(&FOUTQ_LIB &TOUTQ_LIB)

           DCL        VAR(&FOUTQ_LIB) TYPE(*CHAR) LEN(20)
           DCL        VAR(&FOUTQ) TYPE(*CHAR) LEN(10)
           DCL        VAR(&FLIB) TYPE(*CHAR) LEN(10)
           DCL        VAR(&TOUTQ_LIB) TYPE(*CHAR) LEN(20)
           DCL        VAR(&TOUTQ) TYPE(*CHAR) LEN(10)
           DCL        VAR(&TLIB) TYPE(*CHAR) LEN(10)
           DCL        VAR(&DTAQ) TYPE(*CHAR) LEN(10)
           DCL        VAR(&DTAQLIB) TYPE(*CHAR) LEN(10) +
                        VALUE('QUSRSYS')
           DCL        VAR(&WAIT) TYPE(*DEC) LEN(5 0) VALUE(-1)
           DCL        VAR(&FLDLEN) TYPE(*DEC) LEN(5 0)
           DCL        VAR(&FIELD) TYPE(*CHAR) LEN(256)
           DCL        VAR(&SPOOL) TYPE(*CHAR) LEN(10)
           DCL        VAR(&SPOOLNBR) TYPE(*DEC) LEN(5 0)
           DCL        VAR(&SPOOLNBRB) TYPE(*CHAR) LEN(4)
           DCL        VAR(&SPOOLNBRH) TYPE(*DEC) LEN(9 0)
           DCL        VAR(&JOB) TYPE(*CHAR) LEN(10)
           DCL        VAR(&USER) TYPE(*CHAR) LEN(10)
           DCL        VAR(&JOBNBR) TYPE(*CHAR) LEN(6)

           CHGVAR     VAR(&FOUTQ) VALUE(%SST(&FOUTQ_LIB 1 10))
           CHGVAR     VAR(&FLIB) VALUE(%SST(&FOUTQ_LIB 11 10))
           CHGVAR     VAR(&TOUTQ) VALUE(%SST(&TOUTQ_LIB 1 10))
           CHGVAR     VAR(&TLIB) VALUE(%SST(&TOUTQ_LIB 11 10))

           CHKOBJ     OBJ(&FLIB/&FOUTQ) OBJTYPE(*OUTQ)
           MONMSG     MSGID(CPF9801 CPF9810) EXEC(DO)
           SNDPGMMSG  MSGID(CPF3357) MSGF(QCPFMSG) MSGDTA(&FOUTQ +
                        *CAT &FLIB) MSGTYPE(*ESCAPE)
           GOTO       CMDLBL(ENDIT)
           ENDDO

           CHKOBJ     OBJ(&TLIB/&TOUTQ) OBJTYPE(*OUTQ)
           MONMSG     MSGID(CPF9801 CPF9810) EXEC(DO)
           SNDPGMMSG  MSGID(CPF3357) MSGF(QCPFMSG) MSGDTA(&TOUTQ +
                        *CAT &TLIB) MSGTYPE(*ESCAPE)
           GOTO       CMDLBL(ENDIT)
           ENDDO
```

Figure 21.103: Program RDT001CL is the CPP and the power behind the RDTOUTQ command (part 1 of 2).

```
          CHGVAR      VAR(&DTAQ) VALUE(&FOUTQ)
          DLTDTAQ     DTAQ(&DTAQLIB/&DTAQ)
          MONMSG      MSGID(CPF0000)
          CRTDTAQ     DTAQ(&DTAQLIB/&DTAQ) MAXLEN(256)

          ALCOBJ      OBJ((&DTAQLIB/&DTAQ *DTAQ *EXCL)) WAIT(0)

          CHGOUTQ     OUTQ(&FLIB/&FOUTQ) DTAQ(&DTAQLIB/&DTAQ)

GET_NEXT: CALL        PGM(QRCVDTAQ) PARM(&DTAQ &DTAQLIB &FLDLEN +
                        &FIELD &WAIT)

          CHGVAR      VAR(&SPOOL) VALUE(%SST(&FIELD 39 10))
          CHGVAR      VAR(&SPOOLNBRB) VALUE(%SST(&FIELD 49 4))
          CVTBIN4DEC  FROMBIN(&SPOOLNBRB) TODEC(&SPOOLNBRH) +
                        SETLR(*ON)
          CHGVAR      VAR(&SPOOLNBR) VALUE(&SPOOLNBRH)
          CHGVAR      VAR(&JOB) VALUE(%SST(&FIELD 13 10))
          CHGVAR      VAR(&USER) VALUE(%SST(&FIELD 23 10))
          CHGVAR      VAR(&JOBNBR) VALUE(%SST(&FIELD 33 6))

/* The next statement moves the spooled file to the "to" output  */
/* queue, but you could also either copy the spooled file or use */
/* the SNDNETSPLF to send it to another system.                  */

          CHGSPLFA    FILE(&SPOOL) JOB(&JOBNBR/&USER/&JOB) +
                        SPLNBR(&SPOOLNBR) DEV(*OUTQ) +
                        OUTQ(&TLIB/&TOUTQ)
          MONMSG      MSGID(CPF0000)

          GOTO        CMDLBL(GET_NEXT)
```

Figure 21.103: Program RDT001CL is the CPP and the power behind the RDTOUTQ command (part 2 of 2).

When a spooled file is in the "from" output queue in a ready status, an entry is automatically placed in the data queue. The program receives the entry and extracts the information necessary to move the spooled file to the "to" output queue. (Spooled files in the output queue in a ready status when the program starts will not be moved. Those files need to be held and then released before they will be moved to the new output queue.) You can submit the command to a multithreaded batch subsystem; spooled files will be moved as long as you leave the job running. As you might imagine, this command could save you quite a bit of time.

—Jean-Jacques Risch

Looking to Move Your AS/400 Spool Files to the Web?

Here's a handy little utility to move spool files to the Web. It transforms your AS/400 spool files into HTML documents so that they can be displayed in almost any Web browser. The utility consists of four objects:

- CRTHTM (Figure 21.104) converts your spool files to HTML documents. Give this command your spool file information, such as your name and job information and (optionally) the name and email address of the person to contact if questions about the document arise.

```
/*================================================================*/
/* TO COMPILE:                                                    */
/*                                                                */
/*      CRTCMD     CMD(XXX/CRTHTM) PGM(XXX/CTLHTMCL) +            */
/*      SRCFILE(XXX/QCMDSRC) TEXT('Create HTML from spool files') */
/*================================================================*/
             CMD         PROMPT('Create HTML from Spool File')
             PARM        KWD(SPOOL) TYPE(*CHAR) LEN(10) MIN(1) +
                            CHOICE('Name') PROMPT('Spool File')
             PARM        KWD(JOBNAM) TYPE(NAME1) KEYPARM(*NO) +
                            PROMPT('Job Name')
             PARM        KWD(SPOOLN) TYPE(*CHAR) LEN(6) DFT(*LAST) +
                            CHOICE('1-9999, *ONLY, *LAST') +
                            PROMPT('Spool Number')
             PARM        KWD(USERN) TYPE(*CHAR) LEN(30) +
                            CHOICE('Name') PROMPT('Users Name')
             PARM        KWD(EMAIL) TYPE(*CHAR) LEN(30) +
                            CHOICE('Name') PROMPT('Email Name')

NAME1:       QUAL        TYPE(*NAME) LEN(10)
             QUAL        TYPE(*CHAR) LEN(10) choice('Name') +
                            PROMPT('User')
             QUAL        TYPE(*CHAR) LEN(6) PROMPT('Job Number') +
                            choice('000000-999999')
```

Figure 21.104: The CRTHTM command is used to convert spool files to HTML.

- CTLHTMCL (Figure 21.105) is the command-processing program for command CRTHTM. It ensures that the spool file exists and copies its contents to a temporary file named REPORT in library QTEMP. It then calls RPG program CRTHTMRG, which reads the REPORT file and generates HTML code from the document. The resulting HTML code is written to a temporary file named REPORTH in library QTEMP. When the RPG program is finished, the CPP FTPs QTEMP/REPORTH to the client's hard drive using the FTP instructions stored in text file FTPSCRIPT.

```
/****************************************************************/
/*                                                            */
/*    To Compile:                                             */
/*                                                            */
/*      CRTCLPGM   PGM(XXX/CRTHTMCL)  SRCFILE(XXX/QCLSRC) +    */
/*                 TEXT('CPP for CRTHTM')                      */
/*                                                            */
/****************************************************************/
            PGM        PARM(&FILE_NAME &JOB +
                       &SPOOLN &RNAME &ENAME)

/* Input parameters: */
            DCL        VAR(&FILE_NAME) TYPE(*CHAR) LEN(10)
            DCL        VAR(&JOB) TYPE(*CHAR) LEN(26)
            DCL        VAR(&SPOOLN) TYPE(*CHAR) LEN(6)
            DCL        VAR(&RNAME) TYPE(*CHAR) LEN(30)
            DCL        VAR(&ENAME) TYPE(*CHAR) LEN(30)

/* Parms for Job information */
            DCL        VAR(&JOB_NAME) TYPE(*CHAR) LEN(10)
            DCL        VAR(&USER) TYPE(*CHAR) LEN(10)
            DCL        VAR(&JOB_NUM) TYPE(*CHAR) LEN(6)

/* Delete work files */
            DLTF       FILE(QTEMP/REPORT)
            MONMSG     MSGID(CPF2105)
            DLTF       FILE(QTEMP/REPORTH)
            MONMSG     MSGID(CPF2105)

/* Delete work files */
            CRTPF      FILE(QTEMP/REPORT) RCDLEN(140)
            CRTPF      FILE(QTEMP/REPORTH) RCDLEN(150)

/* Extract specific job information from single parmater */
            CHGVAR     VAR(&JOB_NAME) VALUE(%SST(&JOB 1 10))
            CHGVAR     VAR(&USER)     VALUE(%SST(&JOB 11 10))
            CHGVAR     VAR(&JOB_NUM)  VALUE(%SST(&JOB 21 6))

/* If Job info is left blank, no need to include it on CPYSPLF */
            IF         COND(&JOB_NAME *NE '          ') THEN(DO)
               CPYSPLF    FILE(&FILE_NAME) TOFILE(QTEMP/REPORT) +
                          JOB(&JOB_NUM/&USER/&JOB_NAME) +
                          SPLNBR(&SPOOLN) MBROPT(*REPLACE) +
                          CTLCHAR(*PRTCTL)
            MONMSG     MSGID(CPF3303) EXEC(GOTO CMDLBL(ERROR))
            ENDDO

            OVRDBF     FILE(REPORT) TOFILE(QTEMP/REPORT)
            OVRDBF     FILE(REPORTH) TOFILE(QTEMP/REPORTH)

/* Call RPG program to convert into HTML.  Parms are real name +
```

Figure 21.105: This CL program gathers the spool file into a database and prepares it for processing (part 1 of 2).

```
          and email name */
          CALL        PGM(CRTHTMRG) PARM(&RNAME &ENAME)

          DLTOVR      FILE(*ALL)

/* Enter your Batch FTP process here to automatically transfer +
   to server */

          OVRDBF      FILE(OUTPUT) TOFILE(XXX/FTPSRC) +
                        MBR(FTPOUTPUT)

          OVRDBF      FILE(INPUT) TOFILE(XXX/FTPSRC) +
                        MBR(FTPSCRIPT)

          FTP         RMTSYS('100.100.100.100')

          GOTO        CMDLBL(GOOD)
ERROR:
          SNDPGMMSG   MSG('An error occured.  Please check +
                        parameters and try again.') TOPGMQ(*PRV)

GOOD:     ENDPGM
```

Figure 21.105: This CL program gathers the spool file into a database and prepares it for processing (part 1 of 2).

- CRTHTMRG (Figure 21.106) reads temporary file REPORT and converts its records to HTML code. The resulting records are written to file REPORTH in library QTEMP. The HTML commands <PRE> and </PRE> preserve the formatting of the report. If a user name and email address are entered on the command, they're added to the bottom of the HTML document using the mailto: tag so the user's default email program is displayed when this link is clicked.

```
     /title crthtmrg     create html from a spool file
     ****************************************************************
     *  To Compile:
     *              CRTBNDRPG(xxx/CRTHTMRG) SRCFILE(xxx/QRPGLESRC) +
     *                SRCMBR(xxx/QRPGLESRC)
     ****************************************************************
     fReport     if  f  140      disk
     fReporth    o   f  150      disk
     d Lit           s       65      dim(2) ctdata perrcd(1)
     d A             s        1      dim(150)
     d Ename         s       30
     d Fout          s      150
     d F65           s       65
```

Figure 21.106: Here's the RPG IV source for the CRTHTM command, which converts a spool file to an HTML file (part 1 of 3).

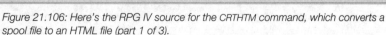

959

```
d Rname            s              30
ireport    ns
i                               1    3 Oskip
i                               4    4 Ospcb
i                               5  136  data
 *
c                  read    Report                            90
c                  dow     *in90 = *off
c                  if      Spcb > 1
c                  exsr    Space
c                  endif
c                  exsr    Html
c                  read    Report                            90
c                  enddo
 *
c                  if      Rname <> *blanks
c                  exsr    Blank
c                  exsr    Blank
c                  exsr    Email
c                  endif
 *
c                  movel   *blanks       Fout
c                  movel   '</BODY>'     Fout
c                  except  $out
c                  movel   *blanks       Fout
c                  movel   '</HEAD>'     Fout
c                  except  $out
c                  move    *on           *inlr
c                  return
 **************************************************************
 * initial subroutine
 **************************************************************
c     *inzsr       begsr
c     *entry       plist
c                  parm                  Rname
c                  parm                  Ename
c                  movel   *blanks       Fout
c                  movel   '<HEAD>'      Fout
c                  except  $out
c                  movel   *blanks       Fout
c                  movel   '<BODY>'      Fout
c                  except  $out
c                  movel   *blanks       Fout
c                  movea   Lit(1)        F65
c                  movel   F65           Fout
c                  except  $out
c                  endsr
 **************************************************************
 * blank - this will write out a blank line to conform with spcb
 **************************************************************
c     Blank        begsr
```

Figure 21.106: Here's the RPG IV source for the CRTHTM command, which converts a spool file to an HTML file (part 2 of 3).

```
 c                  movel     *blanks        Fout
 c                  movel     '<PRE>'        Fout
 c                  move      '</PRE>'       Fout
 c                  except    $out
 c                  endsr
 *
 ********************************************************************
 * space - this will calculate how many blank lines to print
 ********************************************************************
 c     Space        begsr
 c                  sub       1              Spcb
 c                  do        Spcb
 c                  exsr      Blank
 c                  enddo
 c                  endsr
 ********************************************************************
 * html - this will create the line for html with the <pre> tag
 *        the <pre> keeps the white space for columns allignment
 ********************************************************************
 c     Html         begsr
 c                  movel     *blanks        Fout
 c                  movea     *blanks        A
 c                  movea     '<PRE>'        A(1)
 c                  movea     Data           A(6)
 c                  movea     '</PRE>'       A(138)
 c                  movea     A(1)           Fout
 c                  except    $out
 c                  movel     *blanks        Fout
 c                  endsr
 ********************************************************************
 * email -  this will create an line on the bottom of the report
 *          with a email link for questions about the report
 ********************************************************************
 c     Email        begsr
 c                  movel     *blanks        Fout
 c                  movea     *blanks        A
 c                  movea     Lit(2)         A(1)
 c                  movea     Ename          A(60)
 c                  movea     '">'           A(90)
 c                  movea     Rname          A(92)
 c                  movea     '</a>'         A(122)
 c                  movea     '</PRE>'       A(126)
 c                  movea     A(1)           Fout
 c                  except    $out
 c                  movel     *blanks        Fout
 c                  endsr
 oReporth    e            $out
 o                        Fout              150
** Messages
<! --- Report Generated by Ray Welgosh
<PRE>For questions about this report email <a href="mailto:
```

Figure 21.106: Here's the RPG IV source for the CRTHTM command, which converts a spool file to an HTML file (part 3 of 3).

- FTPSCRIPT is a source file member that tells the FTP where to send the document. You can modify this member as needed. For example, you might want to pass on to it the actual name of the spool file to be created.

The new HTML document is generated onto a white background. You can dress up the document using HTML keywords. Here are some possibilities:

- **Bgcolor** changes background colors.

- **Font-1** changes default fonts.

- **Meta Tag** allows searching inside or outside the document.

—Ray Welgosh

✦ ✦ ✦ SQL

Change Any Field in a File Using SQL

Has your accounting manager ever changed the general ledger codes for a department without telling MIS until the general ledger was out of balance? Has your interface with third-party software ever stopped working correctly because of data changes in the vendor's application upgrade? Worse yet (and I'm sure no one in the AS/400 world has ever done this), have you ever released a bug into production that corrupted data? What do you do? Should you correct the data or modify your programs? Well, it depends.

For those times when you choose to correct the data, you could go about it the old-fashioned way: writing an RPG program with an F-spec for the particular file involved and adding logic to change the field to its intended value. But if you need to change multiple files and fields, you must either clone the program or add F-specs and more logic. Then, all you would need to do is compile and run the programs and hope you don't forget something.

If you have SQL on your AS/400, there is a better way to solve the problem. In these situations, I use a utility command (Figure 21.107) I wrote called Change Any Field (CHGANYFLD).

CHGANYFLD updates any field in any file in any library at any time. You supply the library and file names in the first two parameters of the command interface. The power and dynamics of the utility lie in the use of the third parameter. In the third parameter, you can simply enter a field name and its new value to make unconditional and global changes, or you can enter SQL clauses, such as WHERE, and sub-SELECTS to condition and scope the update of the field in question. Additionally, you can run the command immediately, in batch mode, or schedule it for a later date and time.

```
/******************************************************************/
/*   CRTCMD PGM(XXX/CHGANYFLDC) PGM(XXX/C00001R) +                */
/*               HLPPNLGRP(XXX/C00001H)                           */
/******************************************************************/
Cmd                     PROMPT('Chg ANY Field in ANY Lib/File')
            Parm        Kwd( Lib )    +
                        Type( *Char ) +
                        Len( 10 )     +
                        Prompt( 'Library' )
            Parm        Kwd( File )   +
                        Type( *Char ) +
                        Len( 10 )     +
                        Prompt( 'File' )
            Parm        Kwd( NewValue ) +
                        Type( *Char )   +
                        Len( 236 )      +
                        Prompt( 'field = new value' )
```

Figure 21.107: Use *CHGANYFLD* to dynamically change the contents of your file data.

Here's how the utility works. The command interface, with its context-sensitive help, accepts parameters to identify exactly which file in the DB2/400 database needs to be changed along with which conditions affect the update. The ILE program consists of an ILE CL module (Figure 21.108) and an SQLRPGLE module (Figure 21.109).

```
/******************************************************************/
/*                                                                */
/* CRTCLMOD MODULE(XXX/C00001C) SRCFILE(XXX/QCLSRC) +             */
/* MBR(C00001C)                                                   */
/*                                                                */
/* CRTPGM PGM(XXX/C000001CP) MODULE(C00001C C00001R) +           */
/* ACTGRP(*CALLER)                                                */
/******************************************************************/
Pgm ( &Lib &File &NewValue )
Dcl &Lib *Char 10
Dcl &File *Char 10
Dcl &NewValue *Char 226
Dcl &Type *Char 1
/* Submit the job */
RtvJobA Type( &Type )
If ( &Type = '1' ) +
Then( Do )
?SbmJob Cmd( CHGANYFLD Lib( &Lib ) +
File( &File ) +
NewValue( &NewValue )) +
Job( ChgAnyFld )
MonMsg CPF6801
GoTo End
EndDo
Callprc C00001R ( &Lib &File &NewValue )
End: Return
EndPgm
```

Figure 21.108: This is the command-processing program for *CHGANYFLD*.

```
***********************************************************************
*       Change CrtPgm defaults to      ...BndDir(ChgAnyFld)
*                                       ...ActGrp(*Caller)
*       CRTSQLRPGI OBJ(XXX/C00001R) SRCMBR(XXX/QRPGLESRC) +
*           MBR(C00001R) COMMIT(*NONE)
*
***********************************************************************
D Lib             S              10
D File            S              10
D NewValue        S             236
D SQLstring       S             256
D SQLcode         S               4 0

C      *Entry      Plist
C                  Parm                        Lib
C                  Parm                        File
C                  Parm                        NewValue

 * Construct the SQL statement dynamically from the parms
 * "UPDATE &lib/&file SET &newvalue"
C                  Eval      SQLstring =
C                            'Update ' + %Trim( Lib )    + '/'   +
C                                        %Trim( File )  + ' '   +
C                            'Set '    + %Trim( NewValue )

 * Process the SQL statement at execution time
C/Exec SQL Execute Immediate :SQLstring
C/End-Exec
C                  Eval      SQLcode = SQLcod

 * Create a log file in yourlib
C/Exec SQL Create Table QGPL/ChgFldStat
C+  (Lib      Char( 10 )  Not Null,
C+   File     Char( 10 )  Not Null,
C+   SQLcode  Dec(   4 )  Not Null,
C+   NewValue Char( 236 )  Not Null)
C/End-Exec

 * Add a record to log the update
C/Exec SQL Insert Into QGPL/ChgFldStat
C+   Values( :lib, :File, :SQLcode, :NewValue )
C/End-Exec

 * end
C                  Eval      *InLR = *On
C                  Return
```

Figure 21.109: This SQL RPG IV module updates file fields based on the values entered into CHGANYFLD.

I've also supplied a Help panel (Figure 21.110), which you can attach to the CHGANYFLD command. The command is self-submitting in that it interrogates the job attributes. If the job is running as an interactive job, the CL prompts the Submit Job (SBMJOB) command to submit the program and then ends. When the CL determines that the job is running in batch, the SQLRPGLE module is called. This module is very short but very powerful. Using dynamic SQL, the module builds the SQL UPDATE statement and appends the new value parameter you supply through the command interface. It then executes the SQL UP-DATE statement. When the command is finished, it creates a log file and writes the results of the command to it. If the log file already exists, it overlays the log file.

```
:PnlGrp.

:Help Name=ChgAnyFldH.
Change ANY field in ANY file in ANY lib Any time!
:p.
This command allows you to change ANY field in ANY file in ANY library
at ANY time using dynamically created and bound SQL statements.
:p.
:p.
The &newvalue parameter fits into the following SQL statement:
:p.
UPDATE &lib/&file SET &field = &newvalue
:p.
:p.
Use with extreme caution! SQL is absolutely non-forgiving!
:EHelp.

:Help Name='ChgAnyFldH/Lib'.
Library
:xh1.Library
:p.
Specify the DB2/400 library in which the file intended for update is.
:EHelp.

:Help Name='ChgAnyFldH/File'.
File
:xh1.File
:p.
Specify the DB2/400 file in which the field intended for update is.
:EHelp.

:Help Name='ChgAnyFldH/NewValue'.
New Value
:xh1.New Value
:p.
Enter the field and its new value.
:p.
:p.
- &newvalue may consist of a field followed by an equal sign followed
by a single value or an expression to unconditionally and globally
change.
```

Figure 21.110: Attach this panel to CHGANYFLD so that you can add helpful text on how to use the command (part 1 of 2).

```
:p.
I.e. "afield = 19" would change all occurrences of a new century
field to '19'
:p.
"afield = (19000000 + afield)" would add the century to a field
containing a date in the *YMD format.
:p.
- &newvalue may consist of the above followed by an SQL expression
:p.
I.e. "afield = 'N' WHERE afield <> 'Y' AND afield <> ' '"
:p.
:p.
Remember, &newvalue is programmatically embedded into the SQL as:
:p.
"UPDATE &lib/&file SET &newvalue"
:p.
Punctuation in this text is for example and readability.  The actual
contents of &newvalue, as keyed by you, must comply to SQL rules.
Note: "afield" would be a literal field name.
:EHelp.

:EPnlGrp.
```

Figure 21.110: Attach this panel to CHGANYFLD so that you can add helpful text on how to use the command (part 2 of 2).

Now, bear in mind that this is not an all-purpose, generic SQL statement generator. You cannot delete or add records to a file; you cannot create a new file (except for the audit log file); and you're limited to just 226 bytes for your SQL clause. However, it should be a simple matter to modify this little utility to handle all of the aforementioned conditions, should you decide that it would be useful.

—Claude Osgood

Easy Display of SQL Information

If you use embedded SQL statements in your applications, you have no doubt used the Print SQL Information (PRTSQLINF) command to view the SQL statements and optimization settings stored in the program. To do this usually involves three separate steps:

1. Execute the PRTSQLINF command.

2. Use the Work with Spooled Files (WRKSPLF) command to display the spooled file.

3. Delete the spooled file.

As shown in Figures 21.111 and 21.112, I have created a simple command, Display SQL Information (DSPSQLINF), to perform these three steps in a single command. While the command accepts the same parameters as the print command, instead of just creating a spooled file, it then displays the spooled file and deletes it when the user has finished viewing it.

```
/*===============================================================*/
/* To compile:                                                   */
/*                                                               */
/*          CRTCMD    CMD(XXX/DSPSQLINF) PGM(XXX/SQL004CL) +      */
/*                    SRCFILE(XXX/QCMDSRC)                        */
/*                                                               */
/*===============================================================*/
           CMD       PROMPT('Display SQL Information')
           PARM      KWD(OBJ) TYPE(OBJ) MIN(1) PROMPT('Object')
OBJ:       QUAL      TYPE(*NAME) MIN(1) EXPR(*YES)
           QUAL      TYPE(*NAME) DFT(*LIBL) SPCVAL((*LIBL +
                     (*CURLIB)) EXPR(*YES) PROMPT('Library')
           PARM      KWD(OBJTYPE) TYPE(*CHAR) LEN(7) RSTD(*YES) +
                     DFT(*PGM) VALUES(*PGM *SQLPKG *SRVPGM) +
                     PROMPT('Object type')
```

Figure 21.111: The Display SQL Information (DSPSQLINF) command is used to provide an easily displayable interface to SQL.

```
/*===============================================================*/
/* To compile:                                                   */
/*                                                               */
/*          CRTCLPGM   PGM(XXX/SQL004CL) SRCFILE(XXX/QCLSRC)      */
/*                                                               */
/*===============================================================*/
SQL004CL:  PGM       PARM(&OBJQUAL &OBJTYPE)
           DCL       VAR(&OBJQUAL) TYPE(*CHAR) LEN(20)
           DCL       VAR(&OBJTYPE) TYPE(*CHAR) LEN(7)
           DCL       VAR(&MSGID) TYPE(*CHAR) LEN(7)
           DCL       VAR(&MSGDTA) TYPE(*CHAR) LEN(256)
           MONMSG    MSGID(CPF0000) EXEC(GOTO CMDLBL(ERROR))

           OVRPRTF   FILE(QSYSPRT) HOLD(*YES) SECURE(*YES)
           PRTSQLINF OBJ(%SST(&OBJQUAL 11 10)/%SST(&OBJQUAL 1 +
                     10)) OBJTYPE(&OBJTYPE)
           DSPSPLF   FILE(%SST(&OBJQUAL 1 10)) SPLNBR(*LAST)
           DLTSPLF   FILE(%SST(&OBJQUAL 1 10)) SPLNBR(*LAST)
           DLTOVR    FILE(QSYSPRT)

           RETURN
ERROR:     RCVMSG    MSGTYPE(*EXCP) MSGDTA(&MSGDTA) MSGID(&MSGID)
           MONMSG    MSGID(CPF0000)
           SNDPGMMSG MSGID(&MSGID) MSGF(QCPFMSG) MSGDTA(&MSGDTA) +
                     MSGTYPE(*ESCAPE)
           MONMSG    MSGID(CPF0000)
ENDPGM:    ENDPGM
```

Figure 21.112: Here's the power behind the command DSPSQLINF.

This technique can also be used to give display capabilities to programs that only print. For example, IBM uses this technique with the Display File Description (DSPFD) command; both the display and print output use spooled files.

— Paul Jackson

✦ ✦ ✦ String Handling

Parsing Strings

Parsing a string to break it into individual items (or "tokens") is not something you might normally think about, or, if you do, you might cringe at the thought of having to code a very complicated string-manipulation routine. Fortunately, once the code is written, you can use it again and again in any application that needs parsing.

The PARSE command I have invented (Figure 21.113) performs that horrendous chore. I wrote its CPP in RPG III (Figure 21.114), and have included a sample of its use in Figure 21.115.

```
/*===============================================================*/
/* To compile:                                                   */
/*                                                               */
/*          CRTCMD    CMD(XXX/PARSE) PGM(XXX/PRS001RG) +          */
/*                    SRCFILE(XXX/QCMDSRC) ALLOW(*IPGM *BPGM +    */
/*                    *IMOD *BMOD)                               */
/*===============================================================*/
           CMD        PROMPT('Parse Character String')

           PARM       KWD(STRING) TYPE(*CHAR) LEN(9900) MIN(1) +
                      EXPR(*YES) PROMPT('String')

           PARM       KWD(SEPARATOR) TYPE(*CHAR) LEN(1) +
                      DFT(*SPACE) SPCVAL((*SPACE ' ')) +
                      PROMPT('Token separator')

           PARM       KWD(NBRTOKENS) TYPE(*DEC) LEN(3) +
                      RTNVAL(*YES) PROMPT('Number of tokens P(3 +
                      0)')

           PARM       KWD(TOKENS) TYPE(*CHAR) LEN(9900) +
                      RTNVAL(*YES) PROMPT('Tokens A(9900), +
                      A(100) each')

           PARM       KWD(UNLOAD) TYPE(*CHAR) LEN(4) RSTD(*YES) +
                      DFT(*NO) VALUES(*YES *NO) PROMPT('Unload +
                      CPP from memory')
```

Figure 21.113: Use the PARSE command to parse strings.

```
*=================================-================================
* To compile:
*
*        CRTRPGPGM  PGM(XXX/PRS001RG) SRCFILE(XXX/QRPGSRC)
*
*=================================================================
E                    TKN         99100
**********************************************************************
ISTRING     DS                      9900
ITOKENS     DS                      9900
**********************************************************************
* Mainline.
*
C           *ENTRY   PLIST
C                    PARM                    STRING
C                    PARM                    SEP
C                    PARM                    NBRTKN
C                    PARM                    TOKENS
C                    PARM                    UNLOAD
 *
* Check trivial case:  If STRING is blank, there are no tokens.
C           STRING   IFEQ *BLANK
C                    Z-ADD0          NBRTKN
C                    MOVE *BLANK     TOKENS
C                    ELSE
* Otherwise, get tokens.
C                    EXSR GETTKN
C                    MOVEATKN        TOKENS     P
C                    ENDIF
 *
C           UNLOAD   IFEQ '*YES'
C                    MOVE *ON        *INLR
C                    ENDIF
 *
C                    RETRN
*=================================================================
* DCLVAR:  Declare program variables.
*
C           DCLVAR   BEGSR
C                    Z-ADD0          INT        90
 *
C           *LIKE    DEFN INT        END
C           *LIKE    DEFN INT        J
C           *LIKE    DEFN INT        L
C           *LIKE    DEFN INT        LEN
C                    Z-ADD0          NBRTKN     30
C           *LIKE    DEFN INT        POS
C                    MOVE *BLANK     SEP        1
C           *LIKE    DEFN INT        STR
C                    MOVE *BLANK     UNLOAD     4
C                    ENDSR
*=================================================================
* GETTKN:  Get tokens.
*
C           GETTKN   BEGSR
```

Figure 21.114: RPG III program PRS001RG is the power behind the PARSE command (part 1 of 2).

```
     * Initialize loop.
C                         Z-ADD1          STR
C              ' '        CHEKRSTRING     LEN
C                         Z-ADD1          J
     * Add separator to end of string.
C                         CAT  SEP:0      STRING
C                         ADD  1          LEN
     * Loop forever.
C              *ON        DOWEQ*ON
     *    Find next separator.
C              SEP        SCAN STRING:STRPOS
     *    If separator not found, or beyond length of string,
     *    end loop immediately.
C              POS        IFEQ 0
C              POS        ORGT LEN
C                         LEAVE
C                         ELSE
     *    Otherwise, extract token and place it into TKN array.
C              POS        SUB  1          END
C              END        SUB  STR        L
C                         ADD  1          L
C              L          IFGT 0
C              L          SUBSTSTRING:STRTKN,J
     *    Prepare for next iteration of loop.
C                         ADD  1          NBRTKN
C                         ADD  1          J
C                         ENDIF
C              END        ADD  2          STR
C              STR        IFGT LEN
C                         LEAVE
C                         ENDIF
C                         ENDIF
C                         ENDDO
     * Array TKN contains tokens, and NBRTKN the number of tokens.
C                         ENDSR
```

Figure 21.114: RPG III program PRS001RG is the power behind the PARSE command (part 2 of 2).

```
PGM        PARM(&WORDS)

  DCL        VAR(&WORDS) TYPE(*CHAR) LEN(100)
  DCL        VAR(&TOKENS) TYPE(*CHAR) LEN(9900)
  DCL        VAR(&NBRTOKENS) TYPE(*DEC) LEN(3)

  PARSE      STRING(&WORDS) NBRTOKENS(&NBRTOKENS) +
               TOKENS(&TOKENS)
  SNDPGMMSG  MSG('First word:' *BCAT %SST(&TOKENS 1 100)) +
               MSGTYPE(*INFO)
  SNDPGMMSG  MSG('Second word:' *BCAT %SST(&TOKENS 101 100)) +
               MSGTYPE(*INFO)
ENDPGM
```

Figure 21.115: Here's an example of how to using the PARSE command in a CL program.

PARSE can examine a character string of up to 9,900 bytes and return another string of equal length in which all tokens begin at known positions, every 100 bytes. For instance, if I give PARSE the string *Midrange Computing*, PARSE returns a 9,900-byte string that contains *Midrange* in bytes 1 to 100 and *Computing* in bytes 101 to 200. The rest (9,700 bytes) is filled with blanks.

PARSE can accept any character as the delimiter, or separator, between tokens. Normally, you'll want to break strings into words. Therefore, it only seems natural to use the blank space as the separator. The default value for the SEPARATOR parameter is, therefore, the space. When PARSE finishes, it returns two pieces of information through return-value parameters: the number of tokens it found (in a three-digit packed decimal variable) and the 9,900-byte string containing the tokens in 100-byte buckets.

If you're going to do lots of parsing, you can keep the RPG III program active by specifying UNLOAD(*NO), which is the default value for that parameter. When you're done, you'll probably want to change UNLOAD to *YES so that the program is deactivated.

As you can see, the CPP (PRS001RG) is surprisingly short and simple. You can call it directly from another program, thereby using PRS001RG as an API, but you must take care of providing the parameters that the program expects, matching both type and length. If you have RPG IV on your system, you might want to convert the code to the new format, using the Convert RPG Source (CVTRPGSRC) command. Then, compile it as a program module for use in a service program. In that case, you should remove the UNLOAD parameter from the parameter list (PLIST) and remove all references to it in the C-specs.

—Midrange Computing Staff

Uploadable Code Instructions

Uploadable Code Instructions

◆ ◆ ◆ ◆

In This Appendix

Zip Files

FTP Upload Utility

◆ ◆ ◆ ◆

*I*ncluded with this book, on the accompanying CD, are zip files containing all the uploadable code. Also included is a Java FTP Upload utility you can use to very easily move the source code to your TCP/IP connected iSeries or AS/400. The following instructions will step you through how to move the source code to your system, using a variety of methods.

Zip Files

The root directory of the accompanying CD contains zip files of uploadable source code. The zip files are named for each chapter. For example, the uploadable source code for chapter 1 will be named Chapter1.zip. You may notice that there is not a zip file for every chapter. This is because not every chapter contains uploadable code. Only those chapters containing uploadable code will have a corresponding zip file.

To open a zip file, you will need a zip utility such as WinZip or PKZip. You can download an evaluation copy of each utility from many places on the Internet. For example, you might download an evaluation copy of the zip utility software from either vendor's Web site as shown:

PKZIP: *http://www.pkware.com*

WinZip: *http://www.winzip.com*

You can also download these utilities from many shareware sites on the Internet.

Unzipping the Uploadable Code

Once you've downloaded and installed the zip utility, you can then open any of the zip files on the accompanying CD. When you do, you'll notice that there are what looks like a wide variety of file types stored in each zip file. In reality all files in each zip file are nothing more than text (*.txt) files. The file name extension (i.e., *.RPG, *.RPGIV, *.DSPF, etc.) merely indicates the type of source file contained in that text file. You have the option of unzipping these text files to a folder on your local hard drive or to your network.

Once you've unzipped these files, you can then use FTP or Client Access Data Transfer, or any one of a number of other data transfer methods available to you, to move the source members to a library on your AS/400 or iSeries.

FTP Upload Utility

Included on the accompanying CD is an FTP Upload utility designed just for this book. Using it, you can very easily, and quickly, upload the source code for this book. All you need is a TCP/IP connection to your iSeries or AS/400! To use this utility, you will first need to install it. Here's how:

1. Ensure that the book's CD is loaded into the CD-ROM drive of the PC connected via TCP/IP to your AS/400 or iSeries.

2. Using Windows Explorer, open the drive your CD-ROM is assigned to.

3. Double click the INSTALL folder.

4. Look for a program named **Setup.exe** and double click that. You will then be guided through the rest of the setup process.

   Note: The FTP Upload utility is a Java-based application. As such, it requires a Java Runtime Environment (JRE) on your PC. The Setup process will install the Sun Java 2 Runtime Environment on your system for you, and then continue on with the rest of the Setup process as normal. If you receive a message after installing the JRE and before the rest of the setup process finishes, that asks if you want to "reboot your PC," select "No." You will be prompted to reboot later on. Not every PC will receive this message. During the installation process, the AS/400 Java Toolbox JAR files will be copied to your PC. These JAR files are required for running the FTP Upload utility. You can also use these JAR files for your own Java development if you like. Program shortcuts will be added to your Windows Programs menu so that you can have easy access to the utility once it is installed. Once the installation process finishes, you must reboot your PC before you can use the utility.

5. When the Setup program is finished, you can access the FTP Upload utility by clicking on the Windows Start button. Click on the Programs Menu item, then click on the Midrange Computing Software menu item, then click on the Desktop Encyclopedia Upload Utility menu item, and finally, click on the FTP Upload utility menu item.

6. When the utility starts, you will see a screen similar to the one shown in Figure A.1.

7. The book's uploadable code has been grouped into related panels on the upload screen. To get to the chapter you want to upload, move your mouse pointer to the tab that chapter is defined on and click the tab. A panel will be displayed showing you which chapters in that group are available for upload. Remember that you may not see an entry for every chapter of the book because not every chapter has uploadable source code.

8. You also have the option to upload all the code at once, rather than upload individual chapters. To do so, select the ALL CODE tab.

9. Once you've chosen a chapter (or ALL CODE) to upload, select that item's radio button and click on the Upload button. You will be prompted for the drive letter of your CD-ROM (where the book's CD is stored). Select the drive letter. The FTP Upload Utility will open the appropriate zip file on the CD-ROM for the selected chapter, and unzip the

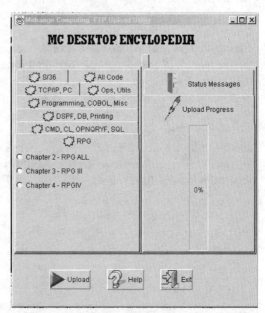

Figure A.1: Use the FTP Upload utility to easily upload the book's source code to your AS/400 or iSeries.

files to a temporary directory on your PC. When the upload process is finished, the temporary files, and temporary directory, will be deleted from your PC.

10. Next, you will be prompted for the AS/400 System Name (or TCP/IP address) and a valid user ID and password. Make sure you use a user profile that has enough authority to create a library, and a source file(s) and which can also add members to the source file(s). The rest of the upload process happens automatically.

The FTP Upload utility will connect to your AS/400 or iSeries via TCP/IP and start an FTP session. A library named MCDESKTOP will be created on your AS/400 or iSeries. For each chapter selected, a source file named after that chapter (e.g., CHAPTER12) will be created in the MCDESKTOP library. After that, uploadable source code members in each chapter will be FTP'd to your system. The source member type (i.e., RPG, CLP, DDS, etc.) will automatically be set for you. All you'll have to do is compile them!

On the right side of the upload utility, a progress meter will show you the current progress of the upload process. You can also choose to display the status messages of the upload progress by clicking on the Status Messages tab. The status of the library and source file creation process will be listed here, as well as a list of each source member uploaded to your system. You can alternate back and forth between the Status Messages panel and the Upload Progress panel as often as you like. You may also click on the HELP button at any time to display a very short help description of what the utility does.

When the FTP process is completed, a message will appear. Click OK on this message and the upload utility will exit. You can choose to leave the FTP Upload utility on your PC, or you may remove it. To remove the utility, use the Add/Remove Programs tool in your PC's Control Panel menu.

Index

retrieving number of elements using %ELEM in, 657, **657**
in RPG III, 600, 645-646
in RPG IV, 655-660
size vs. performance in, 646
stack operations using F9-Retrieve in, 554-555, **555**, **556-557**
AS/400, 109, 127, 345
attention keys and System Request menu, System/36 vs., functioning of, 355-356
changing TCP/IP address of, 834
code page of IFS files, changing, 385-386
copying files between, 489, 815-816
model type using QMODEL, 414
PC commands run from (RUNRMTCMD or STRPCCMD), 830-832, **831**
RS/6000-to-AS/400 connectivity, 144
Save Restore (SAVRST) to transfer objects between, 430
screen capture in, 501-502
self-cleaning, using DASD, 360-361
shorthand commands in, 137-138
sign-on display for, changing, 252-253
space saving tips for, 379-380
uploading files from PC to, 815
AS/400 Query, 535
ASCII
comma-delimited files and, 544, 545t, 615-617, **615**, **616-617**
converting SNA character stream (SCS) to, 514-515
Copy to Import File (CPYTOIMPF) in, 617
Copy to PC Document (CPYTOPCD) in, 617
decimal to hex conversion of, in RPG III, 602-603, **602-603**
EBCDIC conversion to, 59-61, **60**
file transfer of, via CA, 493-494
ASIN COBOL built-in function, 120
ASSUME keyword, 268
ATAN COBOL built-in function, 120
ATNPGM parameter to set Attention keys, 353-354, **353-354**
Attention Indicator (AID) byte for function keys, 634-636, **635-636**, 716
attention keys (*See also* System Request menu), 349-356
activation of, 294-295, **294**, 349
AS/400 vs. System 36, functioning of, 355-356
ATNPGM parameter to set, 353-354, **353-354**
Change User Profile (CHGUSRPRF) settings and, 349

in CL programming, 10
CMDLINE to keep keys active in, 350-351, **351**
hidden link to command line in, 709-710, **709**, **710**
keeping keys active in, 350-351, **351**
mistakenly pressing SysReq 1, recovery from, 355
quick return from interrupted session using, 355
returning to alternate job using, 350
Set Attention Program (SETATNPGM) in, 294, 353-354, **353-354**, 356
System Request (SysRq) menu modifications, 352-353
System Request (SysRq) menu, End Request (ENDRQS) and, 349
attributes of entry fields, 228
auditing
command logging in CL, 129-130
Send Message (SNDMSG) in, 773-774
authorities (*See* security)
autoconfiguration warning, device management, 376
AUTOEXEC.BAT, startup program customization, 387-388
automatic answer and dial modems, 150
automatic current library, 295
Automatic FTP (AUTOFTP) utility, 819-824, **820**, **821-824**
automatic reply to inquiry messages, 67
autorefresh screens, 48, **48**, 637-639, **637**, **638**, **639**
Auxiliary Storage Pool (ASP)
access paths and, 346
space requirements for, 369-370
utilization displayed in, 169-170

B

BACKGROUND processing, 325
backup and recovery, 428-430
for communications configurations, 144-145
Copy File (CPYF) in, 27
Display Backup Diagnostics (DSPBUDIAG) utility in, 838-840, 838-840
Integrated File System (IFS) and, 428
monthly backup procedures for, 428-429
Reclaim Storage (RCLSTG) and, 428-429
reloading system and, 429
restoring file to new name in, 429-430, **430**
Retrieve Configuration Source (RTVCFGSRC) in, 144
Save Restore (SAVRST) to transfer objects in, 430
SAVSTG in, 429
banner pages to identify printouts, 516, **516**
base 36 algorithm in REXX, 340-341, **340**, **341**

Note: boldface numbers indicate illustrations, italic t indicates a table.

987

Note: boldface numbers indicate illustrations, italic t indicates a table.

G

Note: boldface numbers indicate illustrations, italic t indicates a table.

Note: boldface numbers indicate illustrations, italic t indicates a table.